U.S.S.R.
D1093484
PLE'S REPUBLIC
MONGOLIAN AUTONOMOUS REGION
Paotow
Chengteh
Mutanchiang
Chang-chun
KIRIN
Tunghus
LIAONING
Mukden (Shenyang)
Chin-chou
Fushun
Anshan
Penshi
Lienshankuan
Luta (Dairen)
NORTH KOREA
SEA OF JAPAN
Peking
Ta-t'ung
Shihchingshan
Mukuawei
Taiyuan
Yang-chüan
Pingting
HOPEH
Tientsin
Tangshan
SHANSI
Hantan
Yangchan
Tzupo
T'aian
Yentai (Chefoo)
SOUTH KOREA
SHENSI
Linfen
SHANTUNG
Tsingtao
YELLOW SEA
Chin-ch'eng
Anyang
Loyang
Chiaotso
Kaifeng
Sian
Cheng-Chow
Ping-ting-shan
HONAN
KIANGSU
JAPAN
Huainan
Huaiyuan
Sinyang
Nanking
Nant'ung
Maanshan
Chung-hsiang
HUPEH
ANHWEI
Wushi
Soochow
Shanghai
Kungshan
Wuhan
Ta-ye
Hangchow
Shaohing
Hupei
Kiukiang
CHEKIANG
EAST CHINA SEA
Nanchang
HUNAN
Hsiang-t'an
Liu-yang
KIANGSI
Chu-chou
Sinyu
Yungsin
Lei-yang
FUKIEN
I-chang
Liuchou
Sanming
WANGSI
HUANG
Leip'eng
NOMOUS
EGION
Ying-te
KWANGTUNG
Kwangchou
(Canton)
TAIWAN
PACIFIC OCEAN
HONG KONG
Mao-ming
INAN
SOUTH CHINA SEA
THE PHILIPPINES

OTHER BOOKS BY BARRY M. RICHMAN

Soviet Management: With Significant American Comparisons

Comparative Management and Economic Progress
(with R. Farmer)

Incidents for Applying Management Theory
(with R. Farmer and W. Ryan)

International Business: An Operational Theory
(with R. Farmer)

Management Development and Education in the Soviet Union

Industrial Society *in* Communist CHINA

A Firsthand Study

of Chinese Economic Development

and Management

—with Significant Comparisons

with Industry in India,

the U.S.S.R., Japan, and

the United States

Industrial Society *in* Communist CHINA

BARRY M. RICHMAN

RANDOM HOUSE / *New York*

FIRST PRINTING

 Published in the United States by Random House, Inc., New York, and simultaneously in Canada by Random House of Canada, Limited, Toronto. Manufactured in the United States of America by H. Wolff Book Manufacturing Co.

Library of Congress catalog card number: 67–22660

Designed by Janet Gasson

For the many Chinese Communist, Canadian, American and British citizens who made the writing of this book possible—I hope that they, as well as other readers, will view this book as an honest study of a fascinating and unique country

CONTENTS

PREFACE

THIS BOOK WAS written on the basis of studies made during a two-month visit to Communist China in 1966. It is the result in large part of the findings, observations, and impressions derived from my first hand study of management, industry, society, and economic development in China. Numerous secondary sources, not only in English, but also in Chinese, Russian, and various other languages, have also contributed to the preparation of this book.

Because I was a Canadian citizen, the Chinese were willing to issue me a visa that enabled me to undertake my research project. Personal letters of introduction to influential Communist Chinese officials from a number of leading Canadian educators, professional people, and businessmen who have been to Red China in recent years were no doubt a critical factor with regard to the cooperation extended to me in China.

In China I visited eleven major cities and surveyed thirty-eight industrial enterprises in a wide range of industries. At enterprises I met with and interviewed managers at all levels, Communist Party and trade union officials, staff specialists, engineers, technicians, and workers. I also interviewed key personnel at various central, provincial and municipal level planning, administrative, industrial, labor, trade and commercial organizations, retail stores, major educational institutions, communes, hospitals, and other types of organizations. In total, I had formal interviews directly related to my research project with more than two hundred Chinese citizens, and informal discussions with many more.

My main credentials for writing this book are not as a China expert or Sinologist; in fact, I am a newcomer to this field per se. My chief credentials are as a scholar, practitioner, and consultant in the fields of management and economic development. I have undertaken extensive firsthand studies, similar to the one in China, in the Soviet Union several years ago, in India for a period of nearly one year during 1965 and 1966, and briefly in 1968, as well as in various other countries for shorter periods. I have also worked as a manager, consultant, and/or professor not only in the United States and Canada but also in a number of other countries. Hence, my background is such that I have been able to gain some insights and make some hopefully meaningful comparisons regarding industrial management and economic development in Communist China.

The book has been written with both the specialist—in Chinese affairs, communist economic systems, management, and economic development —and nonspecialist in mind. Hopefully it will prove valuable to persons interested in a variety of fields, in addition to those indicated above, because of the comparative and interdisciplinary nature of the study. Scholars, students, and practitioners in the fields of sociology, psychology, anthropology, education, political science, law, international business, various branches of business administration, and perhaps other fields, as well as intelligent laymen may find the book, or at least substantial parts of it, both useful and enlightening.

Many nonspecialists may find certain parts of the book difficult to understand and possibly not of much interest. On the other hand, various specialists are likely to find some sections to be too elementary and unsophisticated. This is the price one must pay in aiming a book at a broad market comprised of nonspecialists, intelligent laymen, and specialists in a wide variety of fields. I hope this effort will prove worthwhile since there are few studies on Red China based on firsthand research and objective analysis.

The presentation will hopefully provide the nonspecialist with significant insights into how the Chinese economy and various aspects of society function, and in particular into the roles of ideology, the environment, and management in China's industrial development. For the specialist, this study provides some presumably original and pertinent information obtained from my firsthand research. Perhaps some specialists will find value unknown to me in some of the raw data to be presented. For this reason I shall present all of the data obtained which I think may be of significant interest to various kinds of specialists. The study is broad, eclectic, and integrative in nature, and is based on a multidisciplinary approach to industrial management and economic development. Hopefully it will provide specialists in various fields with some original worthwhile concepts and some new ways of looking at well-known basic problems. All types of readers may find interesting the comparisons made between China, India, the Soviet Union, the United States, Japan and, at certain points, various other countries.

A central thesis in this study is that effective and efficient enterprise management is the key to industrial progress and general economic development in any country. The expectations revolution now raging in the world has led citizens of virtually every country—whether capitalist, socialist, communist, or any other type—to expect a better material life in the foreseeable future than they now enjoy. The key factor in such material gains will be the manner in which the management of productive enterprise is handled. If a country has a stated or implied goal of income expansion and economic progress, it can best be achieved by concentrating on those external and internal environmental factors which bear most heavily on the management, operations, and performance of productive enterprises.

Communist China, with its own rather unusual type of Communist ideology, has a unique environment for productive firms and their managements different from that of most other countries. Some aspects of this ideology and environment are fairly well known—for example, the usual Communist objective of state ownership of most productive resources and factories. Other factors are so subtle and little known that even highly qualified Sinologists may be unable to agree on the correct facts.

An even more complex problem is created by the inability of outside observers to determine what in fact is actually going on at the operating level, since travel in China has been closely restricted for some time, not only by the Chinese but also by the United States government. Thus Chairman Mao may pronounce on some issue—say, that the struggle for a classless society should be further intensified or that monetary incentives be eliminated. Such statements are duly publicized within and outside China. Sinologists may debate the impact of such proclamations, but it is virtually impossible to determine what actually results at lower levels as a result of the pronouncement. Actually, very little might have happened, and productive enterprises are operating as before. Or, as has happened more than once in recent Chinese history, such a statement may lead to far-reaching changes in lower-level activities, including the management and operation of factories and retail stores. Thus the author actually observed enterprise managers spending one or two days a week in physical labor, such as sweeping floors, apparently in response to various pronouncements made at the top about the moral virtue of manual labor and the obliteration of class distinctions. Such direct impacts on firm operations and the grass-roots level of Chinese society may or may not take place in response to high-level statements, and the outsider has difficulty in determining if, how, or when they do.

The relevance of this problem is seen when it is realized that many environmental conditions in any country can be modified and/or controlled at the top. Such changes are often particularly easy in a very tightly organized, relatively centralized government, such as Communist China has had, and the Chinese regime has not hesitated to use its considerable power in this regard. Such changes may be for the better or worse in regard to how well productive firms can function. The utilization of high-talent executives to sweep floors may not appear to enhance efficiency, but effective appeals to workers to work harder, to develop their skills, and attempt to be virtuous in regard to petty thefts of state goods in the plant may prove extremely useful. But as before, there is little concrete knowledge in the West about how effective such appeals may be.

Thus, one major thrust of this book is to attempt to provide linkages between the macro-factors, or environmental changes, in the Chinese society, and how these affect the management, operations, and performance at the enterprise or factory level. Clearly, given the complexity of the Chinese society, any exploration of this sort will be merely tentative and suggestive—any thorough effort along these lines will have to await detailed and extensive studies of the total Chinese economy which, at present, cannot be done. It is hoped that this study will at least prove provocative and suggestive.

The environment in this study has four major dimensions—educational, sociological-cultural, political-legal, and economic. A basic hypothesis here is that the first two are the most crucial for managerial effectiveness and economic progress in an underdeveloped or newly developing country—particularly the sociological-cultural dimension—and that the latter two dimensions become of primary importance only as the economy becomes fairly sophisticated and relatively advanced, such as that of present-day Russia. It is contended that the basic economic system —whether Marxist, capitalist or a type combining the two—is not as important for economic progress as the sociological-cultural or educational environment in a country such as present-day China or India. In fact the economic system can be rather sloppy and inefficient without hindering substantial progress in a relatively backward economy. While it is virtually impossible to empirically validate this hypothesis in a quantified way, the experiences of such countries as China, as well as India, Japan, Russia, and the United States, suggest that this proposition may have considerable merit.

Another important aspect of this study which will be explored is that in some crucial dimensions a purely—in terms of pure ideology—Communist state is economically and managerially unworkable over time. This is not to say that existing Communist countries do not function; rather, it suggests that they do not function—at least for long—as purely Communist states. Many kinds of compromises between the true faith or ideology and actual practices occur in every Communist country, and Red China is no exception. However, the Red Chinese style of Communism does have its own unique features, including some highly theological points of the gospel of Marx and Lenin as interpreted and added to by Mao.

The argument here is that some points of the Chinese Maoist doctrine, if actually applied in practice over time, would lead to economic chaos and probably the total collapse of production. The "Great Leap Forward" of the 1958–61 period suggested the kinds of problems which might be expected if and when certain aspects of theology are used as operational economic policy. But the orthodox Chinese leaders really believe their doctrine and theology, and there is a constant struggle between ideology and managerial, technical, and economic reality. It is important to point out, however, that several aspects of this ideology that may seem very strange and unrealistic to the typical Western mind have proved effective for economic development when implemented in Communist China.

In general, China, like nearly every other country, is interested in greater production and gains in income and living standards. Failures here are intolerable. Yet much (though by no means all) of the doctrine results in economic futility. It appears that one major factor in the tortuous twists and turns of practical Chinese policy stems from this conflict. Communism is a rare religion in that it purports to be economically operational. Hence decisions which in most countries are essentially secular tend to become objects of theological debate in Marxist countries. Since China's brand of Communism, as interpreted by Mao, is particularly intense, the struggle is most vivid and emotional here.

China is one of the world's poor countries in per capita terms, and along with India is the largest and most important of these. In a world which is highly conscious of development, and where smaller poor countries are anxiously looking for a successful example of development strategy, any significant activities in the industrial or managerial sphere which the Red Chinese do are carefully pondered by capitalist, socialist, and Communist countries alike. China also would like to be (or remain) a great power, and military power and political prestige are closely dependent on economic power. Rapid industrial progress and economic growth thus would serve two major functions in China: first, to demonstrate to the rest of the world the essential rightness of China's type of Communist development strategy; and second, to meet the tremendous internal material needs and aspirations of the nation. In the former case, failure to grow, relative to countries like India, or even failure to grow more rapidly, could lead to loss of prestige all over the world.

But if Communism in the Chinese Maoist mold is unworkable over time, we have a conflict between growth and development goals and official doctrine. This problem will be decided in the end largely at the industrial enterprise level. This is why this book focuses on this sphere.

The number of people and organizations in Communist China, Canada, the United States, Great Britain, India, Russia, Japan, Hong Kong, and elsewhere who have contributed in various but significant ways to this study is so large that I cannot thank them all individually here.

I am particularly indebted to the China International Travel Service, China's Commission for Cultural Relations with Foreign Countries, and China's Council for the Promotion of International Trade for arranging most of my interviews and visits to organizations, and for providing me with such competent interpreters—not to mention so much hospitality and cooperation.

Dr. Claude Bissell, President of the University of Toronto, and Professor K. A. C. Elliott, Chairman of McGill University's Biochemistry Department, warrant a special word of thanks for their letters on my behalf to Chinese officials, and for their encouragement. Mr. Daniel Molgat of Canada's Department of External Affairs also gave me valuable help, advice, encouragement, and suggestions. Senator D. Cameron of the Canadian government, whom I met in Peking, took the time to put me in touch with some prominent and very helpful Chinese officials. I also want to thank the Canadian businessmen and industrialists who helped me on my China research project.

I am immensely grateful to Franz Schurmann, director of the Center for Chinese Studies at the University of California at Berkeley for several reasons. He was the first person to really encourage me to undertake my firsthand research project in China. He provided me with crucial background materials in preparation for my trip, and since my return he has provided me with a great deal of source materials, information, sound advice, and constructive criticism. In fact, he has reviewed the entire manuscript, which reflects many of his valuable ideas and suggestions. It must be said, however, that I am at odds with him on some pertinent issues.

I want to thank Audrey Donnithorne, a veteran Sinologist at London's University College, for providing me with the manuscript of her new book before it was published, and for her help in other ways. I have drawn quite a bit on her important and comprehensive book in this study, as can be seen from the footnotes. I am indebted to Evsey Domar of the Massachusetts Institute of Technology (he was raised in North China [Manchuria] and worked as a factory accountant there in his youth) for his review of much of this study and for his valuable insights and suggestions. There is no room here to thank all of the other Sinologists or Soviet experts who have reviewed some of my work on China and provided me with valuable comments, information, and suggestions. Nevertheless, their help is greatly appreciated.

Dean Neil Jacoby of The Graduate School of Business Administration of the University of California, at Los Angeles, deserves a special word of thanks for his encouragement, close cooperation, and advice, from the time that I originally made plans to go to China until the present. Several of my other colleagues at U.C.L.A., especially George Steiner, Fred Weston, and Samuel Nerlove, have read parts of my manuscript and have offered much in the way of sound advice and constructive criticism. I wish also to thank Professors Jack Gurley of Stanford and Dwight Perkins of Harvard for their encouragement, comments, and advice in connection with various portions of this book. Vice President John Wynne of M.I.T. deserves a special word of thanks for his support during the planning stages of my project.

My good friend and intimate colleague Richard Farmer of Indiana University has read the entire manuscript and given numerous valuable suggestions and much pertinent advice. I have been working closely with him for several years, and in fact we have jointly written three books and several articles. Many of the ideas and concepts in this book have evolved from my close and stimulating association with him.

This book has benefited much and was completed in a substantially shorter time because of the very conscientious and invaluable efforts of my four major research assistants. Akira Arakawa, a visiting Fulbright Scholar and a major executive of one of Japan's largest corporations, Nippon Telegraph and Telephone, did an outstanding job in searching out, translating, and interpreting pertinent Chinese, Japanese, and English source materials used in this book. Surendra Mansinghka competently compiled many of the Indian and United States figures and related information used in this study; he also made valuable comments and suggestions. Tien-liang Liu did an excellent job in searching out and translating Chinese-language sources. Armin Schafler, who has worked with me on several of my previous books, obtained, translated, and interpreted many of the Russian and other foreign-language materials used in compiling this book—his Russian is much better than mine—and he also rendered useful advice and constructive criticism.

My exceptionally able and dedicated administrative assistant and personal secretary, Mrs. Edith Weiss, managed to coordinate miraculously the typing and collating of this book and to interpret my highly illegible handwriting. I also want to thank Mrs. Helen Schwartz, my area secretary, for the long and undoubtedly frustrating hours she spent typing much of the manuscript.

I want to express sincerely my gratitude to the University of California and the Massachusetts Institute of Technology for their roles in making my research project possible. I also want to thank the indispensable contribution of my financial benefactors: The Ford Foundation; the Chancellor's Committee for Comparative and International Studies at the University of California, Los Angeles; and the Division of Research at U.C.L.A.'s Graduate School of Business Administration.

Finally, I want to thank my family for bearing with me so patiently and affectionately in my most arduous, challenging, and frustrating—but most satisfying—project to date.

Barry M. Richman
Malibu, California

Industrial Society *in* Communist CHINA

INTRODUCTION

IDEOLOGY HAS PLAYED a vital role in bringing Communist China into the modern industrial—and military—world in a remarkably short period of time. But ideology, when pushed to extremes, has also caused and may again lead to the virtual collapse of Red China's industrial management system and to severe economic crisis.

This book is essentially a study of economic development and particularly of the impact of ideology on the environment and performance of management and industry in China. Industrial progress, as well as economic and military power, in any nation depends directly on how well industrial enterprises are managed at the grass-roots level of the economy, and how well they perform. Not a great deal is known in the West—or outside China, in general—about the management or performance of Communist Chinese industry or the individual enterprises which comprise the overall industrial sector. I was fortunate to be extended an opportunity to undertake a two-month firsthand study of Chinese industrial management during April and June of 1966.

It has been through a unique combination of rational pragmatism and the implementation of possibly the most unusual ideology in the world that China has achieved impressive, if erratic, industrial and general economic progress since 1949. The Red Chinese nation has done better with regard to industrial development than the Soviet Union did during its first two decades under communism. It has so far done substantially better than India. However, ideological extremism was a chief cause of China's temporary but severe economic crisis during the Great Leap Forward and its aftermath (1958–62); and ideological extremism could lead to a similar crisis again under conditions prevailing in 1968 or in the future.

The Red Chinese regime seems to follow an oscillation theory of industrial and general economic management, with ideology implemented most intensively when economic conditions are relatively good, and relaxed when the reverse is true. For the regime has seen from the Soviet experience in particular that economic progress and relative affluence can lead to revisionism and softness with regard to pure Communist ideology. This may explain much about the current Chinese political and civil crisis; the regime's growing fanatical emphasis on ideology at all levels of society follows several years of substantial economic progress—or economic recovery. Hence, a type of vicious circle is in operation where economic progress results in extreme stress on ideology, which in turn leads to economic crisis, and then to a relaxation of ideology.

How long this cycle can or will go on is anyone's guess. However, Mao and his dwindling body of fanatical and loyal supporters have met with great opposition during the Great Proletarian Cultural Revolution, the current phase or cycle of ideological extremism, not only from the intelligentsia, professionals, experts, scientists, and artistic members of society, but also from the workers, peasants, and part of the military, and particularly from Communist Party functionaries including national leaders. Mao's opponents have apparently learned from the disastrous Great Leap experience that China cannot have ideological fanaticism and sustained economic development at the same time. Various aspects of the pure theology, if pushed too far, are sharply in conflict with managerial, technical, and economic rationality. Hence, Mao's opponents prefer economic development and the building of a strong and powerful China—economically, industrially, technologically, and militarily—even if ideology has to be significantly compromised, as has been the case in the Soviet Union.

The Communists came to power in China largely because they appealed to the people's dominant interests and aspirations, notably nationalism, freedom from foreign domination, economic development, and a better life. But these aims and aspirations can no longer be achieved when the implementation of ideology is in serious conflict with managerial, technical, and economic rationality in industry. It was possible for the Communist leaders to implement a high degree of pure ideology, gain popular support, and achieve their limited objectives during the period from 1937 to 1949. But during that time conditions were vastly different. The country was being attacked and occupied by the Japanese. After Japan's defeat there were clear indications that China was still not free from foreign domination. Moreover, the period from 1946 to 1949 was one of bitter civil war in China—between the Communists and Chiang Kai-shek's Kuomintang or Nationalist regime—of economic chaos, and fantastic inflation. During both the Japanese period and the civil war the Chinese Communists relied on guerrilla war tactics and strategies, with their main support coming from the peasantry in rural areas. They gained a growing number of followers by promising a strong and independent China free from foreign domination, land reform, economic development, and a better life. The objective that had overwhelming priority at the time was the first one, although modest land reforms in some areas were achieved by the Chinese Communists before 1949. The supporters of the Chinese Communists were quite willing to go along with the ideology of the Communist leaders during the period from 1937 to 1949 because such ideology was not in conflict with their most pressing objectives and aspirations relating to survival, national independence, and hopes for a better life in the future. Their ideology called for selflessness, altruism, complete dedication to the cause, no class distinctions, and close comradeship. In an environment of struggle for survival, guerrilla warfare, and subsistence-level living through improvisation in rural areas, such an ideology could and did work effectively in practice.

The early successes of the Chinese Communist leaders were made possible by a system of ideology and related practices which contained within itself the seeds of policy failure and economic crisis of the 1958–62 period and the profound political crisis of the 1966–68 period. For the Maoist-Marxist-Leninist ideology in its pure form was no longer congruent with the social conditions in a developing nation that was becoming industrialized and modernized, and it no longer reflected the genuine interests and desires of the population. In fact, policies and practices based on ideology in various critical ways have been in conflict with the prevailing interests and objectives of the population and have produced disastrous results.

At the same time, however, Mao and his dwindling body of orthodox supporters have persistently retained faith in the ideology and have sought to reassert it in order to preserve the general orientation of the regime and to strengthen its foundations. Thus two basic opinion groups have emerged in opposition to each other in Red China. Their conflicts can no longer be reconciled, harmonized, or resolved on the basis of the ideology because the applicability of basic features of the ideology is itself the central issue in the dispute. There is no longer any fundamental standard to judge "right" and "wrong," for the standards embodied in the ideology have been and are the subject of the debate. The ideology which had performed an integrative function at an earlier stage has become itself a basic disintegrative force. In the struggle for power it has been used as a weapon by one group to attack the other, and party unity has virtually disappeared in the process. There certainly is a power struggle for leadership in Communist China, but ideological differences are the central theme around which this struggle revolves.

Let us draw a few oversimplified analogies to drive home this point. Let us assume that a given zealous Christian group or sect has historically maintained basic internal unity on theological and philosophical matters by using the Bible for resolving basic issues of right and wrong. To be sure, problems of interpretation have risen, but some workable solution has been achieved since all of the group members agree in principle with the major tenets set forth in the Bible. Then, one day, part of the total group decides that the Bible itself is defective and can no longer provide correct value or behavioral standards. Great emotionalism, disunity, and possibly much worse can be expected in such a situation.

Or let us assume that the management and the trade union in a given enterprise or industry of a given capitalistic country have both long agreed that private enterprise and the profit motive are basic to economic progress and that they lead to better living standards for both managers and workers. Disputes between management and the union leaders have involved issues concerning wages, welfare, and working conditions, but the feasibility of private enterprise or the profit motive has never been questioned. In fact, the amount of profits earned has served as an important standard in many instances for coming to an agreement on the other issues dealt with in the bargaining process. Then one day a new union leadership, having the support of most of its members, emerges. But this new leadership firmly takes the position that private enterprise and the profit motive are ethically bad and must be eliminated. Management, of course, is in complete opposition. How can compromises be reached in such a situation? In the real world such a basic ideological difference between management and trade unions in various countries has greatly hindered productive efficiency and industrial progress.

From the above analogies I do not mean to imply that Red China's ideological controversy is as drastic as communism versus free enterprise or capitalism. This is far from the case. Even the large majority of Mao's most ardent opponents no doubt consider themselves to be communists and believe in a communist economic system. But they disagree with the orthodox Maoists on how best to run the economy and on the form that society in general should take. For there are clearly different basic alternatives and different brands of communism. Mao's opponents do not want to discard all of Marxism, Leninism, or even Maoism. But they do want to abandon—at least for a long time to come—some basic aspects of the Thought of Mao Tse-tung. In addition, there also is heated and very emotional opposition with regard to the interpretation of various other ideological tenets.

In general, ideology or theology probably plays an important role in regard to many areas of human experience for most people in most societies. Ideology in its various forms has the grand advantage of offering—or appearing to offer—total and absolute truths and aims to resolve many of life's most vexing problems. On the other hand, effective management, technology, productivity, and economic progress all lie in the rational, scientific realm. No one ever built or ran a railroad, a steel mill, or a textile factory with even a modicum of efficiency on the strength of ideological zeal alone. For that matter, no enterprise ever solved a planning, budgetary, production, or engineering problem solely through ideology.

But even in the United States, ideology at times hinders managerial effectiveness, productive efficiency, and general economic progress. There is much heated debate on ideological grounds over minimum wage laws, welfare benefits, price controls, price subsidies, government regulations, hiring practices and job discrimination, taxes, and various other matters. At times ideology prevails at the considerable expense of managerial, technical, and economic rationality, and hence general economic progress. But in general, ideology does not interfere severely, extensively, or constantly with economic, managerial, or technical performance in the United States —or for that matter in Sweden, Japan, and many other countries of the world.

When I was in China in 1966, the Great Proletarian Cultural Revolution was already underway, but the Red Guards were not formed until shortly after I left. However, there were already some emerging forms of ideological extremism at the industrial enterprise level which have been central to the political crisis and civil unrest in Red China in late 1966 and during 1967. These forms of ideological extremism resembled those that became pervasive during the Great Leap Forward. Their chief aim was the rapid creation of a nation of selfless, altruistic, classless, equal, and completely dedicated pure Communist citizens, as defined by Mao.

Ideological extremism in China's industrial management system can be viewed as having four key prongs: (1) "class struggle" and the elimination of class distinctions; (2) nonmaterial incentives, self-sacrifice and altruism versus material incentives and self-interest; (3) the Reds versus experts pendulum; (4) the amount of time spent in political education and ideological indoctrination.

With regard to the first, during periods of ideological extremism, policies and practices are implemented with the aim of eliminating significant differences in the roles, status, privileges, and material benefits of managers, workers, superiors, subordinates, leaders, followers, generalists, specialists, party cadres, the well-educated and the poorly educated, and so forth. As for the second, material incentives and self-interest as motivating forces are replaced by moral stimuli and appeals to altruism and self-sacrifice for the sake of the collective and the state. The third prong of ideological extremism is crucial for implementing the first two because it involves the Reds or party cadres who take over operational management from the experts and career managers. Politics and ideology tend to take precedence over managerial, technical, and economic rationality when a choice must be made—which is typically frequently. With the breakdown of party unity in late 1966 and during 1967, Super-Reds—in the form of Red Guards, followed by the military purists, the people's militia, and newly created revolutionary groups and committees—took over the functions of the regular party cadres in numerous cases. Political education, the fourth prong, becomes intensified in an effort to support the effective and sustained implementation of the other ideological aspects. Indoctrination sessions are increased greatly, stressing Mao's Thought and written works and focusing on "class struggle," selflessness, and other traits of the pure Communist. At an early stage such sessions are held for the most part after working hours, but they eventually occupy an increasing amount of time during working hours.

This study is particularly concerned with the impact of ideology on the management, operations, and performance of Chinese industrial enterprises. In order to assess this impact comprehensively it is necessary not only to examine what goes on internally at the individual enterprise but also to note the relationships between critical external environmental factors, or constraints, which bear significantly on the enterprise and its management. How and how well enterprises are managed and perform depend largely on externally imposed conditions. The four prongs of ideological extremism noted above are by no means restricted to Chinese industry. They pervade virtually all of society from top to bottom, affecting the educational, legal, political, and economic systems, as well as sociological-cultural and psychological attitudes (and resulting behavior patterns) and the regime's basic economic, political, and military policies. The environmental factors, or constraints, under study in this book have been divided into four broad categories: (1) educational; (2) sociological-cultural; (3) political-legal, and (4) economic.

There is another very important reason for focusing on the environmental factors external to the enterprise. By identifying and analyzing the critical environmental factors that impinge significantly on enterprise management, operations, and performance it is possible to understand and explain a great deal about China's industrial development and overall economic performance to date. The analysis also provides considerable insight into China's industrial and economic potential. Moreover, the examination of critical environmental conditions is likely to shed much light on many facets of life in China which are of secondary interest to the focus of this study, but which may be of particular interest to many readers. For example, information and impressions regarding living standards and conditions, health and welfare, housing, agriculture and the communes, food, birth control, education, morality, entertainment, transportation and travel, retail stores, and various other subjects could, in many instances, have been left out but they have been kept because of possible reader interest.

The book is divided into three major parts: (1) conceptual framework; (2) environment and ideology; (3) structure and performance.

The first part contains Chapters 1 and 2. Chapter 1 deals with universal economic goals, the nature of management in general, a comparison of basic features of the management and economic systems of the United States and Communist China, and the nature and role of ideology in Communist China's economy. Chapter 2 attempts to answer the question: "Why is an underdeveloped country underdeveloped?" This chapter presents a brief analysis of critical environmental constraints common to underdeveloped countries. It provides the basic conceptual framework and definitions that are used in analyzing, explaining, and predicting managerial patterns, industrial development, and economic performance in China in later chapters. Chapter 2 makes it possible to gauge in a more meaningful and accurate manner the effectiveness of Red China's response to environmental constraints and her industrial progress to date.

These two conceptual chapters are probably essential for the typical nonspecialist to fully comprehend and appreciate later chapters. In fact, some readers who know little or virtually nothing about how a communist economy or enterprise functions may find that the conceptual and background information provided in Part I is not adequate for him to fully understand Chapters 3 through 6 in Part II. If this is the case, I suggest that before delving into Part II he look at Chapters 8 and 9, since they contain much more extensive and detailed information on the nature, structure, and operations of Chinese industry as a whole, as well as on the individual Chinese enterprise. On the other hand, specialists on China, communist economies, management, and/or economic development may not want to spend too much time on various sections in Chapter 1 and/or Chapter 2 because they are likely to be familiar with the topics covered.

Part II is the heart of the book. It contains four major chapters, 3 through 6, each dealing with a category of environmental constraints. For analytical purposes each constraint is analyzed separately, although in reality these factors, in many cases, tend to be intimately related. Because of this close interrelationship some repetition in the discussion and analysis of various environmental factors has been unavoidable. However, I feel that such repetition is more than justified by the gain in understanding of the role and significance of each constraint in China's industrial progress.

Part III contains Chapters 7 through 12. Chapter 7 deals with quantitative measures of China's industrial and general economic performance. China's performance in key areas is compared with that in India, the Soviet Union, Japan, and the United States. Some projections regarding China's performance in the future are also presented.

Chapter 8 deals with the nature and structure of industrial organization and planning in Communist China, drawing heavily on information obtained from my firsthand research. Chapters 9 and 10 deal in depth with the Chinese industrial enterprise, again drawing heavily on firsthand data and observations. In Chapter 9 major topics include, in part, enterprise objectives, the enterprise plan, success indicators, organization structure,

Significant American Comparisons, along with some of my other published works. I filled out a visa application form requesting a one-month visa for the July-August period of 1966. I would be finished with my work in India by then. I also indicated briefly on the form why I wanted to go to China and what cities I desired to visit. One of the embassy officials suggested that I write a more detailed letter to him, as well as to the officials in China who had been contacted by my Canadian acquaintances, about my intended research project.

By January 1966 I still had not received approval from the United States government to go to China. My dean at U.C.L.A., Neil Jacoby, contacted certain high-level United States government officials, whom he knows, to expedite this approval, and as it turned out, this action probably did help. I received approval in February and immediately contacted the Chinese embassy in New Delhi to find out about my visa. Within a matter of days I received a telegram saying that a visa had been granted by Peking and that I was to pick it up at Delhi.

I went to the Chinese embassy in Delhi in March 1966. To my delight I was told that a three-month visa, instead of the one-month visa requested, had been granted, because it was felt that this amount of time might be required to carry out my research. It was also suggested that I go to China as soon as possible so that my wife and I could be there for the festive May Day celebrations. Besides, they said, the weather is more pleasant in the spring than in July, and it may be more difficult for me to see people in the summer. As it turned out, it was lucky that I did not wait until July to go to China, since by then the Cultural Revolution was greatly intensified, the Red Guards had been formed, and it would have undoubtedly been very difficult, if not impossible, for me to carry out my project. It is even possible that my visa would have been canceled.

Since I decided to go to China for a bit longer than two months during the April-June period, rather than in the summer, when my commitments in India would be ended, I requested and speedily obtained approval from M.I.T. that it was all right for me to go to China earlier than originally scheduled. I would return to India in late June and stay through part of July to finish my work there.

Only a few days before my departure for China I found that I needed approval from the Indian government if I was to return to India from China. The Ford Foundation's representative in India, Dr. Douglas Ensminger, immediately contacted India's Foreign Minister, Swarayan Singh, who gave the necessary approval, and I was on my way.

In China I visited eleven major cities—most of them important industrial centers—several communes and towns, and when there was time, I traveled through much of the rural countryside by train rather than by airplane. (The map presented on the end paper indicates the cities that I visited.) I was permitted to go to all of the cities requested on my visa except those in north China (Manchuria). Not being allowed to go to Manchuria was not too important because other Westerners have visited industrial enterprises there and have published their findings and impressions, some of which will be cited at appropriate points in this book. I cannot explain why the Chinese authorities would not let me go to north China. An Australian geographer, a Swiss scientist, a group of Scandinavian athletes, Western diplomats, and delegations of Japanese, British, French, and West German visitors were all permitted to go there around the time I was in China. On the other hand, I was permitted to go to certain cities that some of these other foreigners were not allowed to visit. I was even told that I could go to Chungking, a city rarely visited by foreigners, and one which I did not request in my visa application; but this was conveyed to me only toward the end of my stay and I had no time to go.

Most of my time was spent at thirty-eight industrial enterprises in a wide range of industries. In most cases I spent one to two days at each enterprise. In many cases a fairly detailed list of standard questions that I had prepared was given to enterprise officials shortly before I came to see them. This greatly conserved my time and made my stay much more productive because information relating to many of my more clear-cut questions was ready by the time I arrived. For example, such information pertained to salaries and wages, breakdowns of employment, incentive systems, plan targets requiring higher approval, organization structure, educational backgrounds of personnel, and various other topics that are not too sensitive to be asked or answered accurately without personal contact.

I asked to visit at least two enterprises in most of the branches of industry surveyed for comparative purposes. In many cases I specified the approximate sizes of the firms I would like to visit. I honestly do not think that I was "managed" very strictly with regard to the enterprises I was permitted to survey. I did visit what I perceived as examples of good, average, and poor firms in terms of technology, managerial know-how, productivity, and general operating efficiency. I was permitted to visit all of the types of factories requested, except those producing automobiles, electronic computers, and ball bearings. In the case of ball-bearings factories, in those cities where I asked to see this kind of plant I was told that there weren't any, and this may well have been true. They probably did not let me see the automobile plant in Shanghai because car production is negligible and erratic. As for the computer plants, strategic or security reasons may have been involved.

At the industrial enterprises I met with managers, party officials, and trade union leaders at all levels, as well as engineers, technicians, and workers. I interviewed a total of about one hundred forty or one hundred fifty industrial-enterprise personnel.

In addition to industrial enterprises, I visited organizations at all levels of China's governmental, economic, and industrial hierarchy. At the center in Peking I met with officials of the State Planning Commission, the Council for the Promotion of International Trade, the Ministry of Labor, the Ministry of Commerce, and the Commission for Cultural Relations with Foreign Countries. The only type of central organization that I was eager to visit but could not were the industrial ministries. The excuse usually given was that they were "very busy."

I also met with officials of a few provincial industrial and business bureaus, but at this level it was very difficult to get appointments or much pertinent information. It was easier and more productive to visit municipal organizations, and at this level I met with personnel of several industrial, planning, commercial, and labor bureaus, as well as municipal-level corporations.

In addition to the above, I also interviewed key personnel at China's largest retail department stores, wholesale organizations, research institutes, the leading engineering and social science universities and other educational institutions, hospitals, communes, and various other kinds of organizations.

For almost all of my interviews I was provided with very competent interpreters. Some of the people interviewed spoke English or Russian—they typically seemed much more eager and willing to speak English than Russian. A few spoke some French. I found my Russian particularly useful in a number of instances where sticky statistical, accounting, measurement, and/or technical terms were referred to, since such concepts are often similar in the Soviet Union.

How accurate are the statistics and other information given to me by the Chinese citizens whom I interviewed? I do not believe that intentionally distorted information, with very few exceptions, was given to me, although there may have been some unintentional errors due to faulty recording, analysis, or estimates. Most of the data that I sought was clearly not strategic or confidential in terms of national security. In addition, the Red Chinese have not been inclined to make significantly exaggerated industrial or economic claims since the Great Leap period, when statistics were inflated and highly inaccurate. Furthermore, when persons interviewed at any level in China did not want to give me a certain figure or piece of information, they usually said so, often in a subtle or indirect way at first, but if pushed, quite directly. For example, I was able to obtain very few statistics of a macro nature, few capital investment figures from individual enterprises, and on a number of occasions I could not get figures for physical production, value of output, cost, profit, labor productivity, and other data.

Of course, I am fully aware that even with my firsthand research I have barely scratched the surface of facts concerning Chinese industry, management or society at large, and levels of productivity and efficiency. So the story I have to tell is far from clear-cut; it is necessarily oversimplified and for the most part suggestive, rather than conclusive. However, I hope that it will still shed meaningful, important, and interesting light on the world's largest country—a country that is truly unique.

PART I

CONCEPTUAL FRAMEWORK

CHAPTER 1

Maoism, Marxism, Management, and Economic Progress

Universal Economic Goals and the Case of Communist China

Like virtually every other country in the contemporary world, Communist China is basically interested in economic growth, and economic growth depends directly on industrial development. Like many countries, economic growth per se is not the only ultimate end or objective in China, but the attainment of other important political, social, and ideological goals depends on how well the economy and industry in particular manages to progress.

Thus one major aim of Red China is to show the world that its version of communist ideology is superior to every other form of political and social organization, and also to have its political and social ideology eventually pervade the globe. But in this economic-growth-conscious world, any country which failed to develop and industrialize rapidly and impressively over time would be viewed as inferior, or at best second-rate. Another aim of China is to maintain its independence from foreign domination and to become a first-rate military power. But the bigger guns (and atomic weapons) are on the side of the countries that are relatively advanced industrially and have relatively large gross national products. Not to be overlooked, particularly in a country like China, is the necessity to have the economy grow at least as fast as the population, in order to avert mass famine and starvation. Moreover, industrialization and mechanization are essential if agricultural yields are to be significantly increased.

Hence, the paramount economic goal in China, as elsewhere, is to obtain more useful goods and services and to achieve a higher level of per capita real income. In economic terms, what is wanted is steady and, if possible, rapid economic growth in the nation's GNP, or gross national product. (GNP is defined as value added in productive activity, and the key organization which produces value added is, conceptually and practically, the industrial enterprise.)

Regardless of what type of output is wanted by a society, be it atomic bombs, consumer goods, farm produce, roads, steel mills, or even art objects, the goal can be reached more easily if productivity growth is sustained and an increasing level of managerial and economic efficiency is achieved. To be really effective, such growth should be in terms of increases in productivity per employee, although growth caused by expansion of the labor force is also accepted. To date, no modern country has expressed a serious desire to reduce the total flow of goods or services, no matter what the precise goals may be.

One important limitation on this economic-growth process is that the goods and services be in usable form. It is not enough to produce things generally—production must be desired or needed by some person or organization. If output does not adequately fulfill the intended end of functional use, but rather, rots in warehouses or stores, it represents no real gain, even though such output may enter into economic-growth statistics.

A second possible limitation might be that unemployment be kept down. Hence inputs should be used in a way that does not lead to extensive unemployment (for example, through automation), since many societies—including China with its vast population—would probably opt for a slower rate of growth (but not an absolute decline in income) in order to keep most of the population gainfully employed.

There may also be other restraints placed on the rate of economic growth because of various noneconomic goals. However, the evidence is overwhelming that economic progress through industrial development and increased productive efficiency is desired by virtually all countries, China not excluded. The way to such increase lies in the direction of making the individual productive enterprises and their managements in each country more efficient and, if necessary, creating new productive enterprises.

If we grant that China, like other nations, desires industrial progress, the next question is how this might be achieved. Let us now turn to the role and significance of business and industrial management in any nation's industrial progress. For, as I have indicated earlier in previous works, the train of economic activity leads directly to the study of the enterprise and its management as the key link in industrial progress, and hence, economic growth.

Management and Industrial Progress

Management of industrial enterprise involves the coordination of human effort and material resources toward the achievement of organizational objectives. The economic objectives of industrial or business organizations in any country ultimately reflect the desires of societies for useful goods and services. This is true whether the enterprise is a private corporation attempting to achieve a desired level of profitability or a public entity attempting to fulfill a production plan established by state authorities. In the final analysis, all enterprises are social organizations, and their survival is directly linked to their ability to provide useful goods and services, regardless of whether these goods and services are consumed by other organizations, the government, or the public at large.

A basic problem of management, from society's point of view, is to become steadily more efficient over time. Increasing productive efficiency may be regarded as a basic inherent social desideratum of virtually every managerial job: In capitalistic countries, improved efficiency typically means higher profits and greater rewards for firm owners, and ideally for managers and workers as well; at the same time the public benefits from more useful goods and services. In communist states, the planners stress managerial and enterprise efficiency so that the country can produce more useful outputs with the same inputs. Since a country's total production will be the sum of the output of component productive enterprises, the more efficient each enterprise is, the more efficient the country will be. The Chinese industrial enterprise is almost unique inasmuch as it pursues certain important noneconomic objectives (discussed in a later chapter).

In order to analyze business and industrial management in China, or in any other country, one must have some useful description of the things that organizations and their managements do.[1] Attention will first be given to the types of basic economic decisions that must be made and executed and to the types of production or enterprise functions that must be organized and performed in any society if it is to survive through time. Closely related are the common types of policy decisions pertaining to the productive functions which managers formulate and implement. The emphasis here will be on the role of management in the economic and policy decision-making process and in the organization and performance of the basic productive functions. Attention will then be given to common basic managerial functions performed by the managements of enterprises throughout the world.

In this study, management is thought of as the hierarchy of individuals who play a direct and major role in the performance of the basic managerial functions, the making of economic and policy decisions, and/or the organization and performance of the productive functions. In many cases a manager is a person having subordinates, but this need not be the case. A so-called staff man, or a Communist Party official, may also fit into our conception of the managerial hierarchy.

Basic Economic Decisions and the Critical Productive Functions

In all societies human beings make the necessary economic decisions, and human beings carry them out. Human beings also organize and perform the critical productive functions essential to survival. Since human beings do not react solely according to biological instincts, they must somehow be induced to do the right thing at the right time if the basic economic decisions and critical productive functions are to be carried out in a manner consistent with industrial progress. Economic decision making and the effective and efficient organization and performance of the productive functions are the task of management in all of its forms.

The first problem is production. Land (including natural resources), labor, and capital must be combined to produce usable goods and services. Production can range from combining factors in the most automated factories to handicraft production in peasant huts; but whatever the process, a society must produce a certain minimum amount of goods to house, feed, and clothe its population if it is to survive. A modern industrial state must produce far more than the minimum in order to maintain its advanced status and to achieve its various national (and international) objectives.

In all cases it must somehow be decided what is going to be produced and how much of each item is needed. It must also be decided how to produce the commodities in the production plan. Since production can be combined in unending variations—more so as the economy develops—our choice, over time, is great. For any given period, however, production of a given commodity is limited. Increased production of one commodity means decreased production of another; directly related to the critical function of production is the problem of procurement and the allocation of scarce resources among competing ends for the achievement of maximum desired output. The proper quantity and quality of resources must be directed to those productive sectors which can deliver the needed goods and services.

The second critical productive function is distribution, or marketing. While the production function is concerned with the problems of what to produce and how much of each item to produce, these problems are intimately linked with the distribution problem: for whom to produce. An economy must somehow distribute the commodities it produces to their intended destinations, regardless of whether the goods in question are processed or raw materials, medicines, components, or consumer goods. Distribution, or marketing, is concerned with both the organization of distribution channels, involving the interrelationships between buyers and sellers, and the physical distribution of goods, requiring warehousing, transportation, and inventory planning. Such distributive organization and facilities can range from the most primitive barter systems to elaborate world-wide networks of trade.

Third, an economy must finance its production and distribution activities and, here too, resource allocation in the form of capital is essential. This goes deeper than mere money financing, although such activity is extremely important. Real savings must somehow be accumulated in the form of stocks and capital if there is to be economic growth in the future.

Fourth, a progressive society must do research and development to obtain improved and new products and processes. This can range from activities in elaborate laboratories of the most advanced type to mere observation and adoption of simple innovations emerging in the next village. But no society can make substantial industrial advances without innovation in the nature of products made and the processes used.

In addition to the above critical functions, any economy, as well as each enterprise, must keep track of its economic activities in order to plan effectively and make sound decisions for tomorrow. Statistics of every type perform this function, as do various systems of accounting. Without knowledge of what is going on at present, no meaningful or efficient pattern can be planned for the future.

In most societies there are many integrated enterprises performing all of the above productive functions, and there are also numerous organizations performing only one or a few. In capitalist nations the productive functions are typically diffused in all sorts of complex ways throughout the economy. The American businessman who sets about establishing a new enterprise is generally limited only by his imagination in taking advantage of the different types of organizations open to him. By contrast, in China and other Marxist states, the various types of productive enterprises are usually assigned one or more of the productive functions, and the state consciously fashions their basic forms of organization.

In most economies, including China's, the bulk of the nation's industrial wealth is the result of the work of integrated enterprises engaged in varying degrees in all of the critical productive functions. It is this integrated type of enterprise that is of major interest in this study.

Common-Policy Decisions

Business and industrial enterprises and their managements virtually everywhere operate consciously, unconsciously, or by default in accordance with a common framework of policy decisions pertaining to the different productive functions they perform. The common-policy decisions are the operational basis upon which the functions of production and procurement, marketing, finance, research, and development are organized and concretely performed.

For example, regarding production and procurement, enterprises must decide whether they will make or buy various components, and if they buy them, from whom, when, and in what quantities. In the marketing or distribution sphere, the nature of products to be produced and their prices must be determined. In finance, there are policies pertaining to such questions as types of financing to use, sources of funds, and use of funds.

The common-policy decisions of enterprises are indicated under B6 through B10 in Table 1–1 of this chapter. I have chosen to categorize personnel policies under the managerial function of staffing. I have also chosen not to present a separate classification of policies pertaining to accounting, statistics, or data processing since they are inherent in the managerial functions of planning and control. I have, however, included policies pertaining to the relationships between enterprise managements and external parties and organizations.

The Functions of Management

While the tangible economic results of a given enterprise are achieved through the various productive functions and implementation of policy decisions, the coordination and execution of such activities is only part of the managerial job. In business and industrial organizations, management coordinates the productive functions and integrates policy decisions by engaging in certain basic managerial functions. In reality, the productive functions, policy decisions, and managerial functions are closely and intricately interwoven, with the conscious or unconscious aim of coordinating human effort and material resources toward the achievement of organizational objectives. The precise manner in which this is done has a direct and crucial bearing on the productive efficiency of the enterprise.

If a productive enterprise is to continue operating, certain common functions of management must be performed, regardless of whether the enterprise is owned privately or by the state, and regardless of whether resources are allocated through state planning or a competitive market-

TABLE 1–1

Critical Elements of the Management Process

B1: *Planning and innovation*

1.1 Basic organizational objectives pursued and the form of their operational expression.
1.2 Types of plans utilized.
1.3 Time horizon of plans and planning.
1.4 Degree and extent to which enterprise operations are spelled out in plans (i.e., preprogrammed).
1.5 Flexibility of plans.
1.6 Methodologies, techniques, and tools used in planning and decision making.
*1.7 Extent and effectiveness of employee participation in planning.
*1.8 Managerial behavior in the planning process.
*1.9 Degree and extent of information distortion in planning.
*1.10 Degree and extent to which scientific method is effectively applied by enterprise personnel—both managers and nonmanagers—in dealing with causation and futurity problems.
*1.11 Nature, extent, and rate of innovation and risk taking in enterprise operations over a given period of time.
*1.12 Ease or difficulty of introducing changes and innovations in enterprise operations.

B2: *Control*

2.1 Types of strategic performance and control standards used in different areas; e.g., production, marketing, finance, personnel.
2.2 Types of control techniques used.
2.3 Nature and structure of information-feedback systems used for control purposes.
2.4 Timing and procedures for corrective action.
2.5 Degree of looseness or tightness of control over personnel.
*2.6 Extent and nature of unintended effects resulting from the overall control system employed.
*2.7 Effectiveness of the control system in compelling events to conform to plans.

B3: *Organization*

3.1 Size of representative enterprise and its major subunits.
3.2 Degree of centralization or decentralization of authority.
3.3 Degree of work specialization (division of labor).
3.4 Spans of control.
3.5 Basic departmentalization and grouping of activities. Extent and uses of service departments.
3.6 Extent and uses of staff generalists and specialists.
3.7 Extent and uses of functional authority.

TABLE 1–1 (*continued*)

- *3.8 Extent and degree of organizational confusion and friction regarding authority and responsibility relationships.
- 3.9 Extent and uses of committee and group decision making.
- 3.10 Nature, extent, and uses of the informal organization.
- *3.11 Degree and extent to which the organization structure (i.e., the formal organization) is mechanical or flexible with regard to causing and/or adapting to changing conditions.

B4: *Staffing*

- 4.1 Methods used in recruiting personnel.
- 4.2 Criteria used in selecting and promoting personnel.
- 4.3 Techniques and criteria used in appraising personnel.
- 4.4 Nature and uses of job descriptions.
- 4.5 Levels of compensation.
- 4.6 Nature, extent, and time absorbed in enterprise training programs and activities.
- 4.7 Extent of informal individual development.
- 4.8 Policies and procedures regarding the layoff and dismissal of personnel.
- *4.9 Ease or difficulty in dismissing personnel no longer required or desired.
- *4.10 Ease or difficulty of obtaining and maintaining personnel of all types with desired skills and abilities.

B5: *Direction, leadership, and motivation*

- 5.1 Degree and extent of authoritarian vs. participative management. (This relates to autocrats vs. consultative direction.)
- 5.2 Techniques and methods used for motivating managerial personnel.
- 5.3 Techniques and methods used for motivating nonmanagerial personnel.
- 5.4 Supervisory techniques used.
- 5.5 Communication structure and techniques.
- *5.6 Degree and extent to which communication is ineffective among personnel of all types.
- *5.7 Ease or difficulty of motivating personnel to perform efficiently and to improve their performance and abilities over time (irrespective of the types of incentives that may be utilized for this purpose).
- *5.8 Degree and extent of identification that exists between the interests and objectives of individuals, work groups, departments, and the enterprise as a whole.
- *5.9 Degree and extent of trust and cooperation or conflict and distrust among personnel of all types.
- *5.10 Degree and extent of frustration, absenteeism, and turnover among personnel.
- *5.11 Degree and extent of wasteful time and effort resulting from restrictive work practices, unproductive bargaining, conflicts, etc.

B6: *Marketing (policies pursued)*

6.1 Product line (degree of diversification as specialization, rate of change, product quality).

6.2 Channels of distribution and types and location of customers.

6.3 Pricing (for key items—in relation to costs, profit margins, quantity and trade discount structure).

6.4 Sales promotion and key sales appeals (types used and degree of aggressiveness in sales promotion).

B7: *Production and procurement*

7.1 Make or buy (components, supplies, facilities, services, extent to which subcontractors are used, etc.).

7.2 Number, types, and locations of major suppliers.

7.3 Timing of procurement of major supplies.

7.4 Average inventory levels (major supplies, goods in process, completed output).

7.5 Minimum, maximum, and average size of production runs.

7.6 Degree to which production operations are stabilized.

7.7 Combination of factor inputs used in major products produced.

7.8 Basic production processes used.

7.9 Extent of automation and mechanization in enterprise operations.

B8: *Research and development*

8.1 Nature and extent of research and development (e.g., product development and improvement, new material usages, new production processes, and technology, etc.).

B9: *Finance*

9.1 Types and costs of financing (e.g., equity, debt, short-term, long-term, etc.).

9.2 Sources of capital.

9.3 Major uses of capital.

9.4 Protection of capital.

9.5 Distribution of earnings.

B10: *Public and external relations*

(The relationships, attitudes, and policies of enterprise management regarding major types of external agents and organizations)

10.1 Customers and consumer relations (e.g., whether firm management regards consumer loyalty and satisfaction as being important, or whether it is chiefly interested in short-run results, quick profits, etc.).

10.2 Supplier relations.

10.3 Investor and creditor relations.

10.4 Union relations.

10.5 Government relations.

10.6 Community relations (e.g., educational institutions, chamber of commerce, business and professional associations, community welfare activities, etc.).

price system. In this regard, at least some objectives and plans must be formulated, operations must be controlled and organization structures must be established; at least some authority must be delegated and responsibility exacted; and personnel must be recruited, selected, trained, appraised, motivated, directed, supervised, and led. Moreover, managers are generally expected to improve operations and results through innovation where feasible. In addition, at least some administrators of each enterprise engage in negotiations of various sorts with external parties and organizations.

In this study the basic functions of management are classified as planning (including decision making and innovation), control, organization, staffing, and direction (including motivation, supervision, and leadership). The critical elements of these managerial functions are presented under B1 through B5 in Table 1–1. The functions are defined briefly below.

The planning function determines organizational objectives and the plans, policies, programs, schedules, methods, and procedures for achieving them. Planning is essentially decision making because it involves choosing among alternatives, and it also encompasses innovation. This planning is the process of making decisions on any phase of organized activity.

The control function includes those activities which are designed to compel events to conform to plans. It is thus the measurement and, if necessary, the correction of human activities to assure the accomplishment of plans and objectives. It involves the establishment of control standards and the gathering and analyses of information required for evaluating performance, and it forms the basis for subsequent planning.

The organization function of management involves the determination and enumeration of activities necessary to carry out the plan, the grouping of these activities, the assignment of such groups of activities to units headed by managers, and the delegation of authority to carry them out. Sometimes all these factors are included in the single term "organization structure"; sometimes they are referred to as authority relationships. In any case, it is the totality of such activities and relationships that make up the function of organization.

The staffing function comprises those activities that are essential in manning, and keeping manned, the positions provided by the organization structure. It thus encompasses the activities of defining the human requirements for the jobs to be done and includes the activities of inventorying, recruiting, selecting, and appraising candidates for positions and of training and developing both candidates and incumbents to accomplish their tasks as effectively and efficiently as possible. It also includes the provision of adequate basic inducements to attract and maintain needed personnel.

The managerial function of direction embraces those activities which are related to leading, motivating, guiding, and supervising personnel so that they will perform their tasks effectively and efficiently. This function entails personal communication, man-to-man relationships, and the use of incentives and/or penalties to motivate personnel in desired directions. It is at the heart of getting things done with and through people. While clear plans, sound organization, and proper staffing set the stage for coordinated efforts, a manager must also provide direction, motivation, and leadership if the people in his organization are to work together in such a way as to achieve the organization's objectives. It is the job of effective management to maintain a suitable balance between individual motivation and cooperative efficiency.

We could add to our list of functions that of assembling the nonhuman resources which are required to keep the enterprise functioning; however, such activity is implicit in the productive functions of procurement and finance as well as the managerial function of planning.

Even in poorly managed firms in underdeveloped countries, such as Communist China, capitalistic Saudi Arabia, or nominally socialist India, managements engage in the above basic managerial functions—at least to some extent—although this activity may not be very evident to an outsider. However, the ways in which these and the productive functions tend to be performed in different countries vary strikingly in many cases. Such variations are due to the different environments in which the enterprises and their managements must function, and in the case of China in particular they are the result of implementing a unique ideology as well.

Critical Elements of the Management Process

Table 1–1 presents a categorization of the key elements of the management process, broken down according to the functions of management and the key policy decisions pertaining to the basic productive functions. The list is far from exhaustive or conclusive, but it may provide a meaningful classification scheme for discussing and analyzing business and industrial management in China, or any other country. (It is, of course, not possible to deal in depth in this study with each of the elements listed in Table 1–1. However, consideration will be given to many of the strategic ones throughout this book.)

Each element presented in the table is a variable corresponding to a specific type or pattern of managerial or organizational behavior and is coded as a *B* with appropriate subscripts. The majority of the *B*'s are basically structural elements of the management process; in many cases they represent techniques or methods employed. The others are essentially dynamic, problem-oriented variables, which are present in varying degrees in different enterprises and countries. The latter are indicated by an asterisk.

From my research, observations, and experiences in various countries so far, it appears that there are dominant patterns of managerial and enterprise behavior in different countries, which can be depicted by analyzing the critical elements of the management process as I have defined them. In this study the primary interest is in such dominant patterns and trends, rather than the exceptions, in Communist China. An attempt will be made to explain important patterns and trends in the Chinese system of management in terms of the environment and ideology of that country.

Micromanagement and Macromanagement

In discussing management in any country it is useful to distinguish between micromanagement and macromanagement.[2] We define micromanagement as the management of individual productive enterprises on the lower operating levels of the economy, whence production and wealth actually come. In any relatively large country there are typically thousands of productive units which contribute to and largely determine overall national economic performance. Managements at this level engage in the basic managerial and productive functions within their respective enterprises.

On the micromanagement level are found the production managers, sales directors, financial executives, and all other persons concerned with the management of individual enterprises, large or small. Such managers may be working in public or private organizations. A plant superintendent and a company sales manager are clearly micromanagers, as is a steel-company president, unless, as is common in some smaller countries, it is the only firm in the industry.

In China and other Marxist states, micromanagement and macromanagement clearly represent a continuum of control. It is difficult to determine at times where one stops, and the other begins.

Macromanagement deals with the management of an entire economy. Here the problem of interpretation can be quite vexing. In China, and other communist countries, this type of management is pervasive and detailed. All important phases of economic activity are regulated through comprehensive state plans, and virtually all industrial organizations and assets are owned by the state. In other countries, most typically those considered capitalistic, such as the United States, such management is often by law, tradition, or custom rather than by comprehensive or detailed design. In this type of system the key economic regulators are competitive market prices and the profit motive; another distinguishing feature is widespread private property ownership of productive assets.

In either case, however, macromanagerial activity imposes various restraints on micromanagers and determines various rules of the game for them to operate under. The United States Federal Reserve Board is exercising macromanagement when it alters interest rates; so is the United States government when it approves changes in corporate tax rates or antitrust laws. So, for that matter, is a Chinese central planner who makes investment or resource-allocation decisions for the steel industry, or a Chinese municipal administrator who makes such decisions for local clothing enterprises within his area of jurisdiction.

Macromanagement may not be considered by many to be management, in the sense that the word is used in business or industrial administration. But in fact it is because it involves economic decision making, policy formulation, and execution of basic managerial functions. Macromanagerial organizations include the entire governmental economic, regulatory, and administrative apparatus, apart from productive enterprises per se—for example, economic regulatory and planning agencies, central and banking and budgetary organizations, and various other governmental departments at various levels. In China and in many other countries, numerous macroagencies play a significant and direct role in planning, controlling, organizing, staffing and directing the activities of the productive enterprises in the system. They also play a major role in organizing the productive functions which are performed by micro-level enterprises. This is far from the case in privately owned American firms.

This study is primarily concerned with micromanagement in China. But macromanagement will also be given due consideration, because the manner in which various macroagencies are managed and perform their activities has a direct bearing on micromanagerial performance and on the productive efficiency of enterprises.

In general, societies have endless ways of organizing and performing the productive and managerial functions. In theoretical political terms, the possible range is from laissez-faire capitalism, with very little macromanagement, through monolithic totalitarian communism, with a great amount of macromanagement. But regardless of how a particular economy is organized, the ultimate economic objective is generally to create more useful goods and services, resulting in increased absolute and per capita Gross National Product, and a basic desideratum of the managerial job is to increase productive efficiency.

Because the Chinese macromanagerial structure differs significantly from the capitalistic macrostructure, it is useful to examine briefly the distinguishing features of both. At the risk of some oversimplification, I have made the following brief comparative analysis of economic organization and the interaction of macromanagement and micromanagement in the United States and China.

Economic Organization and the Interaction of Macromanagement and Micromanagement in the United States

In a basically capitalistic country, such as the United States, it is common to find that there are few or no national economic goals that are precisely stated. That is, the managers of individual productive organizations are generally quite free to produce whatever they wish, for whomever they wish, and however they wish. However, the American economy by no means resembles a pure laissez-faire capitalistic system. It is rather a mixed capitalistic enterprise system since it contains many public enterprises, considerable governmental regulation and control, and various other elements that hinder the perfect functioning of objective market forces. Nevertheless, the key automatic regulator of the system is market price competition in conjunction with the pursuit of profits. In contemporary times this twofold regulator tends to solve quite effectively the major economic problems common to all societies.

In general, wanted items in short supply tend to be expensive, thus creating profitable opportunities for businessmen to supply the demand. No one seriously asks (in the economic sense) whether or not the desired items are useful, aesthetic, or trivial—the critical feature of such a system is consumer sovereignty. Consumers, backing their wants with purchasing power, effectively determine the course of economic production, although government spending has become an increasingly significant determinant. However, much of the government spending is done through contracts awarded to private firms on a competitive basis, and this factor tends to keep economic efficiency within reasonable bounds.

The rules in such a system tend to be constraints rather than positively stated national economic plans or goals. Hence a manager is not allowed to defraud anyone, nor can he sell poison to consumers for food, or float highly watered securities in financing his enterprise. He may be required to negotiate with unions, pay certain kinds of taxes and subject his books to annual audits by suspicious tax collectors. Such rules basically tell a manager what he cannot do or what persons he must have precisely defined relationships with, but no law tells him what he must do or how to perform his managerial functions. General Motors, for instance, has a large legal staff to advise management on what is legal and what is not. But the idea of such a staff or anyone else telling management what it must do in the productive sense is alien to American thought. As pointed out above, management is generally quite free to produce what it chooses in accordance with the law, in the way it chooses; if it is wrong, the market tends to correct quite quickly significant errors in judgment.[3]

It is true, however, that macromanagement in a capitalistic system can be active. Hence the central banking authorities' activities in a capitalistic economy influence supplies of money, interest rates, and foreign exchange rates. Such activities are designed to achieve vaguely defined national goals, such as the reduction of price inflation, the flows of foreign trade, and the rate of growth in the economy. To the individual manager, however, these activities appear as changes in prices, and he is free to select whatever options he chooses in planning his own operations. If interest rates rise, for example, no businessman is prevented from borrowing; nevertheless, the central authorities can be sure that such a price increase will in fact prevent some businessmen from borrowing.

Such government policies as tax law can also be used in a capitalistic system to channel productive efforts into desirable roles. The high tax on the printing of national bank notes has effectively prevented private national banks from taking part in such activities, and the large depletion allowances available to mineral producers have encouraged such production. Again, to the individual manager such macrocontrols are not necessarily absolute—if in his judgment the price or tax is right, he can take part in any type of activity as long as legal requirements are met.

Management of productive enterprises in such an economy tends to be complex, full of risk, and quite rewarding to those far-sighted enough to produce useful goods and services in demand. Much of the management's task is the problem of seeing an opportunity and taking advantage of it by organizing to meet the expected need.

National economic performance and economic well-being in America are chiefly dependent on the activities of tens of thousands of productive organizations, each one devising its own plan of action and shaping its own destiny. Any person or group can establish any type of business unit as long as it meets prescribed legal requirements. There are approximately four and three-quarter million business units in the United States, and most of them are small-scale units owned by a single person. In terms of asset value, sales, payroll, employment, and economic power, a few hundred giant corporations occupy a strategically dominant position in the modern American economy. However, the myriad small-scale, privately owned, productive organizations play a crucial role in the American competitive system since they are often in a position to provide many goods and services in a more efficient manner than the giant corporations.

In such a society, the productive functions become diffused in all sorts of complex ways throughout the economy. There are many integrated firms that perform all the critical economic functions, and there are also numerous organizations performing only one or a few. For example, there are enterprises whose only basic function is to perform marketing activities for others on a commission basis; there are subcontracting firms concerned primarily with production; there are research and design organizations providing a service for manufacturing enterprises; and in the area of finance there are not only traditional banks but also many other different kinds of financial institutions that provide capital to productive enterprises. No one can be sure what the activities, policies, and goals of the Little Nifty Company may be until after careful investigation. The name reveals nothing—the firm may in fact be involved in the distribution of export merchandise for another company, financing the activities of stockbrokers, or performing research and development in the hope of obtaining salable patents.

Although every productive enterprise formulates its own plans and policies and pursues its own objectives, no enterprise operates in a vacuum. If the enterprise is to survive it must fulfill some need in the economy; having initial capital is not enough. In the case of private enterprise the earning of profits is essential for survival. Various companies may not strive to maximize short-run profits, or even long-run profits.[4] This type of managerial behavior has become quite common as ownership and control have become divorced in large corporations.[5] Nevertheless, every company tends to pursue as a minimum the earning of adequate profits. Moreover, the importance of private property inherent in the American culture tends to instill in corporate management a sense of obligation to conserve corporate assets, even if management does not have an ownership interest.

The precise operational objectives an individual company establishes for itself, and the results actually achieved, are dependent on the expected and actual contributions of various parties both within and outside the company. These parties provide a flow of goods, services, and money crucial to the company's survival. For example, a large manufacturing company is usually dependent on suppliers, institutional customers, and/or the consuming public, transportation firms, investors, bankers, and often distributors. In addition, it may have to deal with labor unions, and it must also gain the cooperation and desired contributions from its own personnel.

The insiders and outsiders who contribute to the survival of the company have a direct interest in the company as long as they can be induced to cooperate and participate.[6] They may be thought of as interest participants. Each necessary participant, be it an individual or another organization, must find it advantageous to deal with the company, and the inducements offered must be feasible. That is, the goods, money, and satisfactions generated by the company must be at least equal to the combined demands of all participants. It is the task of management to strive for maximum contributions from participants with the inducements at its disposal and in the face of complex competitive forces. How well this task is done will determine the size of company profits. If some key participants place too high a price on their contributions, there may not be enough inducements in the company kitty to go around, and the company fails. Management thus has the dual role of trying to increase the size of the company's surplus by devising ingenious ways of running the business and of maintaining alliances with participants that will permit the company's survival and growth.

In such an environment a manager soon learns the meaning of economic efficiency, tolerance, flexibility, and cooperation. Since survival depends on one's customers, it would be disastrous not to carefully consider and satisfy their demands. A manager must worry not only about what his customers want but also about what his competitors are doing. Stark disaster faces any firm that fails to adjust over time to the changing whims and needs of its customers. Concerning personnel, firms cannot easily exploit labor, even if there is no union with which to contend. If the labor in question is skilled or in short supply, the payment of wages that are ten percent under the going rates quickly results in inferior performance as the more competent employees drift away to better-paying opportunities. Considering another aspect, if the company tries to squeeze the last discount out of suppliers, it finds itself at the end of the line when special service is wanted or if a temporary shortage appears. In many instances, a given company is highly dependent on its suppliers, and the costs entailed in developing new dependable sources of supply are great. The company also cannot long ignore the wishes of investors and creditors, or the commitments to them, if it is to remain financially sound. The exploited, be they workers, investors, suppliers, or customers, also have the option of appealing, through the ballot box, to politicians who are quite sensitive to the grievances of large groups of downtrodden citizens.

The essence of the capitalistic enterprise system is mutual self-interest, cooperation, and interdependence through mutual consent and free choice. These mutual relationships are entered into in a competitive environment and are therefore subject to discontinuation if more favorable opportunities arise for either party. It is through this free but interdependent enterprise system, rather than a comprehensive national plan, that the critical productive functions are performed, coordinated, and integrated on a national scale. The interaction between the competitive price system and the pursuit of profits tends automatically to keep economic mistakes within reasonable limits. This joint economic regulator rather effectively solves the key economic problems of what and how to produce, how much of each item to produce, and for whom to produce. It tends to insure that needed and desired goods are produced at the right time and distributed to the right place and that production is carried on in a reasonably efficient manner. Moreover, it tends to encourage innovation in products and processes because such activity often results in a competitive advantage for the innovating organization.

Effectively functioning enterprises require extensive feedback of knowledge about current operations so that management can plan for the future. In a capitalistic society, much pertinent information is obtained almost automatically through inventory levels and from other organizations and parties that have a vested interest in the company in question. The company also can obtain various types of information from such organizations as chambers of commerce, trade journals, private publishing firms, trade unions, and various governmental agencies charged with accumulating relevant data for specific types of industries. Hence an American firm wanting to know about the market for nursery products in El Salvador can obtain needed market information from the Department of Commerce. A chemical company needing vital statistics can similarly get them from local and federal agencies. The individual enterprise may also have its own comprehensive statistical and accounting systems which enable it to keep track of current operations in order to plan and make decisions for the future.

There is no need for any one enterprise or the numerous governmental agencies to have at their disposal information about everything that is going on in the economy as a whole, or even in a particular region or industry. Governmental departments obtain and compile masses of statistical data, and the government also maintains a fairly comprehensive system of national accounting. However, these data are not used comprehensively to plan, coordinate, or control national economic activity. Rather, they are used to assess national economic performance for a given period and to formulate broad economic policy.

Hence, in a capitalistic enterprise system one finds chaos oriented to precise organizational goals and economic efficiency. Literally billions of independent managerial decisions contribute to desirable economic performance on a national scale. Nothing seems logical at first glance, but the system works surprisingly well because the market is a regulator, capable of penalizing the lax and short-sighted and of rewarding those who can take advantage of existing opportunities.

Because of various imperfections, however, there are negative features inherent in such an economic system. For example, there can be disequilibrium, strikes, unemployment, monopoly, discrepancies between intended savings and investment, and distribution of income so unequal that the wants of many are not properly satisfied. In order to contain such problems within reasonable limits, governmental regulations, policies, and controls which often interfere with objective market forces are adopted. It is notable that the most serious economic problems and the biggest economic failures of capitalist countries arise when, for reasons of social welfare, national security, or venal self-interest, the law of supply and demand is violated. American agriculture, shipbuilding, and ocean shipping are cases in point.[7]

Capitalist economic systems in their pure form have no ethical content whatsoever beyond the general belief that ownership of private property is desirable and that if enterprises and individuals seek to maximize their individual monetary advantage, resource allocation and economic efficiency will be ideal. Efforts to inject ethics into the system—to aid underprivileged farmers, workers, or even capitalists—have generally resulted in substantial deviations from the efficient production of needed and desired goods and services.[8]

Capitalist systems also have the problem that they are typically democratic states, and the voters do inject substantial ethical content into the system, often at the expense of economic efficiency. Hence, the support of inept small businessmen by government loans, minimum wage bills, fair-trade pricing laws, and protection from destructive competition by entry control laws may have the effect of putting too many resources into a given industry, causing redundant capacity, higher-than-necessary prices, and general economic inefficiency. One is likely to find high taxes on whiskey and tobacco—reflecting the popular opinion that such commodities should be expensive—and this too distorts ideal resource allocation in accordance with consumer sovereignty. Moreover, some commodities, such as habit-forming narcotics, are not freely sold at all. Probably most of the macromanagerial rules that managers of a given productive enterprise must abide by are ethical rather than economic in nature.

Economic Organization and the Interaction of Macromanagement and Micromanagement in Communist China

The Chinese Communists, like their Soviet brothers, came to power through action based on the doctrines of Marx. Marx said little about the future communist economic system, and what he did say was rather vague. He did point to state ownership of productive resources and some sort of planned economy as being distinctive features of the future communist society, but he left no blueprint or operational theory describing how a communist economic system was to function. The Soviets had to develop an operational system from scratch, and their system provided China with a basic blueprint, which has been modified by China over time.

By 1956 virtually all private industrial enterprises were nationalized in China, although many of the former capitalist owners stayed on to manage them. (More will be said about the Chinese capitalists in a later chapter.) Since the Communist takeover of China in 1949, tens of thousands of new state-owned enterprises have been built and organized. The virtually complete state ownership of productive enterprises, as in Russia, had the effect of destroying the market price system, since without competition among rival firms there could be no meaningful price competition. This in turn rendered the profit motive rather impotent as an automatic economic regulator.

With the collapse of the competitive market price system, another means had to be developed for solving basic economic problems and performing the critical productive functions common to all societies. The automatic regulators of economic and managerial activity, however imprecise they may be, were now gone. To date, there has been only one known, logically consistent economic system: that of general equilibrium developed by Walrus and amplified by Leontief in his input-output analysis. This system forms the basis for all capitalist and most mixed economies.[9]

The method of deciding key economic questions in China—that is, what should be produced, how much, how, for whom, when, where, and the allocation of resources necessary to achieve the desired production—is through comprehensive national economic planning. (As we shall see later, however, the Chinese planning system is somewhat more decentralized and flexible than the Soviet system has been.) Hence, what is done primarily by market forces in the United States must be done largely through conscious bureaucratic action in China. In such a system there is a fusion of political, economic, and social leadership, and all economic activity tends to be subordinate to the politically and socially motivated decisions of the state. By "the state" is meant the highest party and governmental bodies in the land, with the party playing the dominant role. Macro-planners decide all major economic questions in the light of goals and values set forth by the leaders.

In a capitalist, market-price-system economy, it is implicitly assumed that individual consumers and organizations will themselves determine whatever goals they desire, and their expressions, indicated by effective demand, will determine the course of economic activity. On the other hand, a country with fixed ideas about the goals of the economy and the society—be they rapid industrialization, growth in military power, or higher living standards—must plan in detail how economic-resource allocations are to be made. The leaders must determine their important objectives and plan the economy to meet them.

In such a system, long-range economic planning—when there is any—is essentially investment planning, and annual planning is primarily production planning. The annual plan and, in many cases, the quarterly or monthly plan are the operational documents for Chinese productive enterprises. The macro-planners must decide how to divide production between consumer and producer goods, and they must also determine the rate of accumulation (savings) necessary for desired future economic expansion. Each production target must be limited so that the total of all targets does not exceed the productive power of the nation or a given sector. The plan must provide for allocations of economic factors into the necessary sectors in the light of national objectives. In other words, the plan must be essentially all-inclusive.

Although Marx never clearly indicated whether he was for or against consumer sovereignty, in the Chinese or Soviet kind of economy it is not possible to have consumers determine the course of production to any significant degree. Such interference would tend to deflect scarce productive resources from other planned uses, thus upsetting the entire plan. Prices in such a system also have had little guiding function; rather they are subservient to the plan. Commodity prices are used chiefly for aggregation, control, and evaluation, although retail prices for consumer goods are used as a rather crude device for equating demand with supply (rather than vice versa). Commodity prices in some sectors do, however, seem to play a somewhat greater role in resource allocation in China as compared with the Soviet Union, and this will be discussed later in the book. On the other hand, China makes less use than Russia of wage differentials for channeling manpower resources among different sectors, labor mobility is much more restricted, and income distribution substantially more equal.

The Chinese or Soviet type of planned system requires that central planners make a vast number of ethical decisions which in a free-market economy are left to individuals. The stipulated national objectives are in themselves value objectives, as are many policies. The volume of domestic-consumer-goods production is typically dependent on available resources after the resources required to achieve the other aims of the plan are accounted for. National production has been influenced by consumer demand only to a limited degree, and free consumer choice is limited to the goods the regime decides to produce for the consuming public. Although the planners, particularly in China, are not entirely sensitive to the desires and needs of the population the planners' preferences do essentially take the place of the consumers' preferences—which implies that the planners know better than the public what is good for it. It was noted in the previous section that in a market economy, similar decisions about the propriety of certain commodities are made, but these decisions are regarded as aberrations from the ideal rather than a necessary and critical part of the economic system.

In the planned state, it may be decided that consumers should have more books and fewer shoes than they would desire if they had free choice. Or certain highly desired commodities, such as cosmetics, jazz records, and automobiles, may be produced in negligible quantities or not at all. The setting of wage rates for different occupations also involves value judgments. Hence, if the national—or provincial or municipal—economic plan is really comprehensive, as it must be to function properly, a very high degree of centralized ethical-decision making is built into the system.

Instead of the apparent chaos of the capitalist economic system, all is in order in the Chinese system—at least on paper. The macrorules for micromanagers, rather than being of the "thou shalt not" variety, are chiefly of the "thou shalt" type. In reality, the complexities and problems involved in planning the economic activities of an entire country, such as China, are beyond human imagination. The literally billions of planning decisions that must be made to achieve consistency result in a complex and virtually complete interlocking of macromanagement and micromanagement. Predetermined tasks and resource allocations, rather than competitive buying and selling, regulate the activities of the myriad interdependent enterprises on the basis of one comprehensive national plan. The necessary number of planned interconnections increases much more rapidly than the size of the economy, and since China started comprehensive national planning in 1952 the economy has expanded several fold in terms of national production. The job of planning, controlling, and coordinating national economic activity may be roughly compared mathematically to the square of the number of different commodities produced, plus the number of productive units.

An industrial society, such as China, will produce perhaps fifteen thousand or twenty thousand basic classes of output (that is, steel, bolts, shoes, radios, pants, and so forth). Each class of output may have dozens, if not hundreds, of subcategories of products (that is, bolts of various sizes, made of various steels and other metals, different varieties of shoes and pants, and so on). Even with the most sophisticated mathematical techniques and electronic computers, the task of interrelating demands and factor inputs for every possible item for every possible subcategory becomes impossible for the central planners alone. A giant intermediate bureaucratic apparatus is needed—even though the Chinese tend to be antibureaucratic—and the micromanagers themselves are called on to participate substantially in the planning process and to make many operating decisions.

The various types of productive enterprises in the system are assigned one or more of the basic productive functions, and their duties are spelled out in considerable detail. The state carefully guides the emergence and development of all productive units and consciously fashions their forms of organization. The result is a degree of homogeneity which may not please those who live in the society but which nevertheless serves to greatly facilitate central planning and control and information reporting.

In China certain types of enterprises are charged with the function of production, others with distribution or finance, and still others with research and development. In addition, certain organizations are charged with collecting and analyzing detailed statistical and accounting data from all the productive enterprises. Such data are crucial for macrodecision making and control. The macromanagerial apparatus must have at its disposal detailed information on all phases of economic activity if the economy is to function properly.

Productive enterprises in China do not deal with each other, except in relatively few cases, through mutual consent or free choice, but rather by higher decree. Since virtually all economic activities are assigned somewhere in the system, competition is rarely allowed. The organization which bears the responsibility need not worry about aggressive competition from outsiders. The system is orderly and neat on paper, but highly complex for the micromanagers charged with carrying out directives from above.

Of major concern in this study are the more than a hundred thousand Chinese industrial enterprises engaged in the production of goods.[10] It is here that the key economic questions—what to produce, how much of each item, how and when to produce each, and for whom—are translated into detailed operating plans in a manner which should be consistent with the national economic plan. Higher-level plans must allocate to each enterprise adequate resources and funds if the desired production is to be forthcoming. It is from the industrial enterprise that goods are distributed to their intended destinations; and it is at the enterprise that new technical processes are introduced and new products are developed and produced. Moreover, it is from the enterprise that the state obtains a major portion of statistical and accounting information necessary for planning and controlling overall economic activity.

The Chinese manager is not concerned with the survival of his enterprise because, as long as the state wants the organization in question to continue functioning, its future is provided for in the state plan. The earning of profits is not a requisite to survival, although the state generally prefers enterprises to earn more profits—or smaller losses—than less, since enterprise profits are the major source of state investment and future expansion.

The state prescribes the ultimate objectives to be pursued by all industrial enterprises. Some of them are noneconomic objectives, and they will be discussed in later parts of the book. With regard to economic objectives, each enterprise is supposed to achieve, with given resources, as great a quantity of production as possible; or, given certain production targets, they should be achieved with minimum practical resources and costs. The production program is supposed to be carried out in accordance with a predetermined time schedule. Within the overall output targets and resource limits prescribed by the plan, the detailed product mix, including product quality, is supposed to conform to the requirements of customers. A balance between short-run and long-run considerations is also called for so that current decisions and activities do not endanger future operations —for example, through suppression of product or process innovation—but rather, will enhance them and further the future needs of society. In addition to these ultimate economic objectives or basic desiderata of enterprise performance, the state prescribes various policies to be followed for their achievement—for example, the use of the most progressive factor-input-utilization norms (standards) in planning, and the constant improvement of technical processes and products.

Since the ultimate objectives to be pursued by the Chinese enterprise represent a high level of abstraction—in the same way that a profit-maximization goal does in an American firm—they must be translated into concrete operating terms. A system of interconnected-plan indices which constitutes the annual, quarterly and/or monthly enterprise-operating plan, and which is directly linked to higher-level plans, is the device utilized for this purpose. The great majority of Chinese industrial enterprises receive an annual plan having quarterly subdivisions. If the plan is sound, and if the managers do their jobs properly, the result should be the production of the right amount of goods and services, of the right assortment and quality, delivered to the right place at the right time. In theory, the proper decision and execution of the plan means that resources available are efficiently utilized and that nothing is wasted, since no unneeded excesses or shortages of goods would appear at any point; it is also hoped that enterprise managers would carry out innovations or improvements in both products and processes.

Although the micromanagers are narrowly confined by the targets and resource limits prescribed in the plan, their expert knowledge and participation are indispensable to its formulation and execution. It is physically impossible for superior authorities to plan in detail without close consultation with enterprise executives, or to exert instantaneous effective control over the execution of plans at the vast number of industrial and business establishments. The men on the spot are in the best position to determine the capabilities and resource needs of their enterprises and to adjust their plans to unforeseeable changing conditions. In addition, product and process innovation depends greatly on what the enterprise and its leaders choose to do or not do. Those who imagine the Chinese economy to be a pure "totalitarian command economy" in which enterprise managers merely carry out orders have no conception of the reality.

Hence, in the absence of a market-price system, detailed direction and rules of behavior (based in large part on Chinese Communist ideology) from above must guide managerial decision making in Chinese enterprises. In China, unlike Russia, nonmaterial rather than material or monetary incentives play the chief role in an attempt to achieve an identity in managerial or individual interest and the interests of the state.

Management within the Chinese enterprise is in many respects quite similar to management within an American firm, particularly an American factory. The same managerial and productive functions are performed in many similar ways. However, the nature of Chinese ideology, as well as external environmental conditions, also results in many significant basic differences. For example, the external relations that Chinese micromanagers engage in differ rather dramatically from those of their American counterparts. The capitalist enterprise is related to other organizations primarily through the market; it buys and sells according to price-cost relationships and to fulfill predetermined quotas; it expands and contracts as profit expectations dictate. In all these relations there is little, if any, of the red tape of the kind which a Chinese manager must cope with. The bureaucratic impediment lies primarily in the external relations of the Chinese enterprise rather than in its internal structure or environment. If anything, the Chinese enterprise tends to be less internally bureaucratic than its American counterpart.

The administrator of a Chinese enterprise is not charged in any substantial way with the major task of achieving desired contributions from other organizations by generating enough inducements to insure their participation. This delicate balancing job is, in the main, done for him. With few exceptions, the plan prescribes the relationships among productive enterprises, the contributions forthcoming from each, and the payments to be made for contributions rendered. For example, a Shanghai machine-tool enterprise had the following external relationships prescribed from above in 1966: It was to receive supplies from several dozen other producers; it was to produce goods for nearly a hundred different assigned customers; it was to deal with several research and design organizations and two higher educational institutions on a continual basis; it was to maintain an account at a prescribed branch of the state bank; it was to deal with a member of transportation organizations; and its management was to have continuous contact with various higher governmental and party authorities.

It will become evident during the course of this study that a system of prescribed relationships among productive enterprises, rather than a system based primarily on free choice and mutual consent, does not necessarily provide for mutual self-interest, cooperation, or interdependence.

In general, how efficiently the productive and managerial functions are performed in any country depends on both macromanagement and micromanagement. Macromanagement forms an important part—much more so in communist as compared with capitalist countries—of the external environment of productive enterprises. But managerial and enterprise performance in any country also depends greatly on a broad range of other external environmental dimensions as well.

Dimensions of the External Environment of the Enterprise: An Introduction

A productive enterprise necessarily forms part of a complex educational-sociological-cultural-political-legal-economic whole.[11] This is particularly significant in Communist China where the state plays a conscious, pervasive, and intensive role in shaping this environment, often on the basis of ideological considerations. Environmental changes are often relatively easy to introduce in a very tightly organized and centralized government, such as China has, and the regime has not hesitated to use its vast power in this regard. Such changes may be for better or for worse in regard to how well enterprises and their managements can and do function.

The following chapter deals in greater depth with the impact of the external environment on business and industrial firms and their managements, but a brief word of introduction seems in order here. Throughout this study I use the terms environmental or external factors, characteristics, forces, conditions, variables, and constraints synonymously unless otherwise noted; however, I prefer the term "constraint" and use it with a twofold meaning. When constraint is used in relation to managerial effectiveness the connotation is typically negative. Managerial effectiveness is defined as the degree or level of efficiency, from society's point of view, with which the overall management process is performed in a given enterprise or on a national scale. This is a relative rather than an absolute concept of efficiency. A given environmental factor may limit or serve as a constraint upon managerial effectiveness in varying degrees over time. In some cases a given external constraint may have an extremely negative impact on managerial effectiveness; in others the impact may be negligible.

The term environmental constraint is also used when I deal with specific elements in the overall management process, but here the term does not necessarily have a negative connotation. In this context we are interested in how environmental conditions tend to produce dominant patterns of managerial and enterprise behavior in China, or other countries; these relationships are depicted by analyzing elements of the management process. It does not necessarily follow that a given dominant behavior pattern, which is largely the product of a particular environmental constraint or set of constraints, is negative in terms of managerial effectiveness. In many instances, dominant behavior patterns may have a positive effect on managerial effectiveness. In any event, the word "constraint" is used in this connection since environmental factors frequently tend to confine behavior in certain directions, at least in a majority of cases in a given country.

One intuitively expects that the external environments, in which business and industrial enterprises and their managements must function, vary greatly among different countries—particularly between capitalist and communist nations and between underdeveloped and advanced countries. Since most discussion of how enterprises and their managements operate has historically taken place in the framework of capitalist, private-enterprise societies, the very notion of productive enterprises and management in the environment of communist states is considered somewhat odd, and relatively few studies of how they operate have appeared even for more advanced communist countries such as the Soviet Union. Firms in the West are typically associated with private enterprise, but of course in communist countries such firms are rare or nonexistent. Hence, the most obvious environmental factor, which affects communist firms and their managers, is that in their economic system most or all of them are state-owned enterprises.

There are many other kinds of environmental factors which directly affect the performance of productive enterprises in China, as well as in other countries. In this study these environmental factors are grouped into four broad categories: educational, sociological-cultural, political-legal, and economic.

The educational environment determines in large part the types and levels of skills, knowledge, and abilities possessed by personnel, including managers, working in business and industry. The performance of productive enterprises depends largely on the types and overall quality of the persons in the organization. Hence, the nature and quality of the educational process within a country is a critical factor in determining the level of managerial effectiveness and the nature of enterprise and managerial activity. Also important is the dominant attitude toward education because this bears significantly on the types of education that are viewed as most desirable, as well as the motivation of individuals to improve their talents and skills through self-education, part-time education and, even on-the-job training.

The overall sociological-cultural environment of a given country has a significant impact in shaping the values, attitudes, philosophies, and motivations of business and industrial personnel, as well as the population at large. This tends to have a direct and quite uniform effect on behavior, particularly in China. For operational purposes, sociological-cultural factors or constraints in this study correspond to the dominant human attitudes, values, beliefs, and motivations in China—or elsewhere—and the way they tend to influence the behavior and performance of individuals working in productive enterprises.

Productive enterprises, like all other types of social organizations, must also operate in some type of legal and political environment. Laws must generally (but not always) be obeyed and political factors taken into account in formulating and implementing business and industrial decisions. In general, legal and political constraints directly affect the operations and performance of enterprises through their impact on the critical elements of the management process. It is particularly difficult to isolate and analyze various political and legal constraints in this way in China, since these types of constraints tend to be intimately interrelated with economic, sociological-cultural (including ideological), and educational factors. Moreover, not much is known about Chinese law insofar as it actually affects productive firms. However, an attempt will be made to deal with some of the more important political and legal factors in this study.

The types of critical economic constraints that have an impact on enterprise and managerial performance in China, and elsewhere, are not clear-cut single variables, but complex sets of interrelated economic phenomena. One of our problems is to generalize for industry as a whole, in terms of how the various economic constraints affect the performance of management and the firm. More previous work has been done in the field of economic analysis than in the other environmental-constraint areas under study here.

Ideology[12] versus Managerial, Technical, and Economic Rationality

The conceptual framework or categorization of environmental constraints, which is presented in more detail in the following chapter, can be utilized for analyzing managerial and enterprise performance in any country. However, Red China offers a peculiar problem in this environmental sense. For most countries—particularly noncommunist states—this study's classification of environmental factors enables a comprehensive explanation and analysis of managerial and enterprise performance without the need to consider the problem of ideology per se.

With regard to China, there are certain unique aspects of Chinese ideology which have a significant bearing on such performance, but which cannot be handled entirely by our categorization of environmental factors. Contemporary Chinese ideology does help shape many of the external environmental conditions which directly affect managerial and enterprise performance; here the chain of analysis would be from ideology to environmental conditions to managerial and enterprise performance. But in some significant cases certain aspects of the total ideology have a direct impact on various critical elements of the management process and cannot be analyzed solely with reference to the environmental constraints. In general, in order to understand more fully how Chinese management and Chinese organizations function, it is essential to have an understanding of Chinese ideology.

Perhaps the strongest way to describe the uniqueness of the Chinese situation is to indicate that in the past several decades, Communist China has discovered a new religion, which basically is Marxism-Leninism as interpreted by Mao Tse-tung. It also draws on some portions of Chinese historical culture. The Chinese have evolved a unique philosophy which tends to be more of a religion than economic philosophy, and it also contains much political and social ideology. This theology has probably been believed in quite passionately by literally tens of millions of individuals, and it has been stronger and more widely accepted and implemented than the basic communist ideology in the Soviet Union.

The problem which this new religion presents to the Chinese economic, industrial, and managerial system is basically that, like any other religion, theology if pushed far enough tends to take precedence over economics, technology, good management, productive results, or any other materialistic factors. If, in a given situation, one must decide between rational practical solutions and theology, the theology will tend to dominate if it is strong enough. The Great Leap Forward, introduced by Mao and other party leaders, toward the end of the 1950's was the product of a theological vision rather than a rationally thought-out operational plan. This vision encompassed political, social, as well as economic aspects of ideology, and it led to severe economic crisis. China's First Five-Year Plan (1952–57) was a relatively rationally thought-out technical plan for economic development, and quite impressive economic progress emerged during that period.

Before we go deeper into a discussion of ideology, a few more examples may further clarify the nature of the problem. One tenet of Chinese Communist faith is that a classless society is really desirable and achievable. Industrial managers would behave basically like anyone else, and autocratic behavior, special privileges, large pay differentials and similar factors would be reduced to a minimum and eventually eliminated. But no other country has yet discovered how to run complex business and industrial organizations effectively or efficiently over time without giving skilled managers, engineers, and key technicians special pay, privileges, powers, or special activities to perform. Indeed, even the Soviet Union is one of the relatively more stratified societies in this sense.

Now, given the problem of getting more production or productivity, the Chinese may be faced with a choice—either to abandon important aspects of the true faith or to continue with the religion and sacrifice production and productivity. To date, the Chinese have wavered on this sort of decision between demanding allegiance to the faith and being considerably more pragmatic in situations where production is deemed essential. This sort of cyclical wavering between ideology and rational pragmatism has characterized much Chinese behavior since the 1949 revolution.

Another example may be found in education. Everyone must be indoctrinated in the faith, and much time is spent on the study of the works of Chairman Mao and other great Communist thinkers. Such thinking is not operational in the technical sense, but one often hears or reads serious statements that managers, technicians, or workers have been inspired operationally by Chairman Mao's works. If this is actually true—and it seems to be in many cases—such indoctrination in the educational system may clearly do more good than harm, up to a point. However, if mathematics is dropped or greatly reduced in engineering programs in order to have even more Maoism, the eventual result can only be industrial deterioration and slower economic growth. Note that this sort of problem is subject to the conscious decision making of Chinese leaders, who, if they choose, can abolish all technical training and substitute pure ideology, or turn in the direction of the reverse educational philosophy. Such decisions in a centralized communist state can have far-reaching effects on managerial effectiveness and industrial progress. The manner in which these decisions between ideology versus managerial, technical, and economic rationalism are resolved will determine in large part how well Communist China performs economically.

Now let us examine more closely ideology in Communist China. It is in part the pure ideology of Marxism-Leninism and in part practical ideology based on the "Thought" of Mao Tse-tung. Pure ideology is viewed as theory based on universal truths dealing with values and ethics, and the core of such ideology is Marx's thesis of the class struggle. Pure ideology is essentially a set of ideas designed to give the individual a unified and conscious world view. Practical ideology states norms and rules which prescribe behavior and have action consequences, but such ideology must be interpreted concretely to be operational. Hence, practical ideology is a set of ideas designed to give the individual rational instruments for action.

Marx envisaged a pure communist state where there would be a classless altruistic society and a good life for all based on the principle "from each according to his ability, to each according to his needs," which would be made possible through economic abundance. Class struggle, he felt, was at the root of all significant social, political, and economic conflicts in the world and was based primarily on the antagonistic relationship between capital (the haves or exploiters) and labor (the have-nots and exploited). An essential initial step in eliminating class struggle was to have the workers revolt—achieving a great proletarian revolution—and to take over the productive assets of the owners. They would form a dictatorship of the proletariat, and the economy would be operated under some system of state planning, direction, and control for the good of the masses. Eventually class distinctions would disappear, and a utopian society would evolve throughout the world. Individual antagonisms based on class conflicts within a given nation would disappear, and eventually antagonisms between nations would also disappear as international Communism triumphed.

Marx believed in dialectical materialism—which relates to the law of the unity of opposites—whereby every being or concept (thesis) had by its very nature and essence to give rise to its opposite (antithesis). But the contradictions between these two were inevitably overcome in a newly emergent synthesis in which some elements of the original contradiction might be conserved, others annulled, and the entire process elevated to a new, higher level. The synthesis in turn would become a new thesis, giving rise in a new triadic relationship to a new antithesis and thence to the "negation of the negation" in another synthesis. Eventually this process would stabilize as the utopian Communist society evolved and the state withered away.

After the Soviet Revolution of 1917, Lenin found that Marx did not give operational guidelines on how to run an economy once the proletarian revolution actually took place. He was concerned with the problem of combining central leadership and direction with "democracy" which would involve the participation and initiative of the masses. There had to be leaders and followers, he found, and some operational balance of "democratic centralism" had to be developed.

It was not until 1928, under Stalin's leadership, that the nationalization of industry was virtually completed, and operational, comprehensive national economic planning began. Under Stalin's rule various forms of mass or worker participation in the management of industry did emerge in varying degrees over time, but the dominant pattern of economic administration was one of a high degree of centralization. Stalin found that it was very difficult, if not impossible, to run an economy and apply pure ideology at the same time. Hence, material incentives and self-interest became dominant motivating forces, large occupational pay differentials evolved, and various intellectual elites—including a type of managerial class—also emerged.

These bourgeois trends continued under Khrushchev and have persisted under the leadership of Brezhnev and Kosygin. In fact, various other bourgeois and revisionist tendencies, which have been well publicized in the West, have emerged under Khrushchev, Brezhnev, and Kosygin. At the same time, however, these Soviet leaders have also been concerned with the problem of "democratic centralism" and much emphasis has been placed on mass participation in industrial management. Under Khrushchev's rule an attempt was made to reduce distinctions between mental and manual labor, and to combine theory and practice, through the introduction of a system of part-work, part-study educational programs throughout the nation. In general, however, the Soviet economy is viewed by the Chinese regime as being revisionistic and in large part untrue to pure Communist theology.[13]

Mao Tse-tung and his loyal supporters seem more persistent than the Soviets ever were—even perhaps during their most fanatical, but brief, ideological periods—about the implementation of ideology in practice. Mao's contributions to the total contemporary Chinese ideology is contained in the four selected volumes of his major works and in scores of articles, essays, and speeches. His ideological contributions are essentially practical rather than pure in nature and are referred to as the "Thought of Mao Tse-tung." Other Chinese leaders, such as Chou En-lai, Liu Shao-chi, and Marshal Lin Piao, have helped interpret and shape the total Chinese ideology.

The Thought of Mao Tse-tung is a process of combining pure theory or universal truths with concrete practice—practical ideology cannot be used until one has worked out correct thought, which does not simply mean a certain manner of thinking developed through intensive study, but also a manner of behaving. The basic values of pure ideology—such as the class struggle—are designed to bring about a moral and psychological transformation of the individual through both thought reform and practice.

The total Chinese ideology involves a fusion of universal class ideology and a particular individual ideology. The Chinese leaders strongly believe that the class struggle cannot take place abstractly within the class as a whole but must be fought out within each individual human being. Hence even a capitalist can be transformed into a good proletarian citizen through thought reform which involves both "correct" thought and "correct" behavior acquired through practice. (One might note that none of the major Red Chinese leaders is of proletarian—or even poor peasant—origin.)

Thought reform is the method by which ideology is implanted in the individual. Since it is very intensive and time-consuming, it is usually only key personnel, such as party members and higher-level managers, who fully undergo it. For the others, ideology is fed through mass movements, education and training, and study and discussion groups.

A quite extraordinary characteristic of Maoist thinking is its simplicity. Having borrowed a few basic philosophical premises from Marxism-Leninism—that is, pure ideology—it then proceeds to combine ideas into a never-ending series of dualities. The chief criterion for incorporating an idea into ideological thinking is the possibility of ferreting out its dialectical opposite; if the duality turns out to be a contradiction, then ideological thinking will proceed further to envisage the way in which resolution is possible.

Whereas the pure ideology of the Chinese Communists consists of a fixed set of universal principles or ideas, their practical ideology is made up of a changing and expanding set of particular ideas derived from the dialectical combination of ideological thinking and concrete problems. If some combinations turn out to be wrong or useless, this makes little difference, since the products of such thinking will always be particular ideas rather than universal ones. The manner of thinking, and not necessarily its particular products, will always be true and universal. Hence, thought can change in a never-ending struggle for perfection, and the Thought of Mao is used in a never-ending process of combining theory (pure ideology) with practice and practical ideology.

According to the Marxian dialectic, which was influenced by the thinking and writings of Hegel, and Mao's interpretation of it, all conflicts or contradictions in society can be dealt with effectively through correct thought and analysis and by applying the "law of the unity of opposites," where opposites change and new opposites arise, but the laws that govern their interrelationships remain constant. If the law of the unity of opposites works in practice, it creates the possibility of dynamic politics and management within a framework of general agreement on ultimate ends and values—such as the law of planned and proportional development of the economy and class struggle.

In discussions the dialectic principle would make possible debate through a sharp juxtaposition of views, and in the process, all relevant facts and opinions would come to the surface. As long as the minority—if it is not won over—follows the majority, the basic unity of the group remains intact. The Chinese Communists would argue that indeed it becomes stronger, for final agreement reached through a process of discussions is more effective than agreement reached through unquestioning assent. Hence countervailing forces can play a useful and constructive role.

At times the Chinese regime has intentionally preserved certain contradictions if they could serve useful purposes when it has not been necessary to do so. For example, the capitalist class, or bourgeoisie, has been preserved as an official class even after virtually all private businesses were nationalized by 1956. More will be said about this paradox in a later chapter.

Mao's two major works are "On Contradictions" and "On Practice," with the former relating to the law of the unity of opposites. Many contradictions are viewed as particular in nature, and their concrete forms as well as their solutions differ in time and place.

Mao views contradictions among the Chinese people as nonantagonistic and amenable to peaceful solutions, while contradictions between China and its external enemies are seen as antagonistic.[14] Many of the nonantagonistic contradictions in contemporary Chinese society pertain directly to Mao's conception of the class struggle, where class has never been clearly defined. For example, there are contradictions regarding intellectuals and workers, mental versus physical labor, leaders versus the led, bureaucrats versus the masses, bureaucrats versus party cadres, and party cadres versus the masses. Some other important social contradictions perceived in Chinese society include the Reds or party cadres versus Experts, who are typically professional managers, engineers and technicians; specialists versus generalists; individuals versus collectives; self-interest versus collective interest; material incentives versus nonmaterial incentives or ideology; and individual rewards versus collective rewards.

The Chinese regime also perceives political contradictions such as centralism versus democracy (from "democratic centralism"), from "the top down" versus from "the bottom up"; and contradictions of administration, such as center versus region, centralization versus decentralization, branch principle (vertical) versus territorial or committee principle (horizontal), and worker versus inspector or controller. In addition, Mao and other leaders perceive various economic contradictions such as select development versus simultaneous development; long term versus short term, heavy versus light industry, industry versus agriculture, large-scale versus medium- and small-scale industry, capital intensive versus labor intensive, production versus consumption, seller or producer versus customer, quality versus quantity, cost versus quality, and so forth.

It is evident that the above contradictions are closely related to the problems of management and industrial development, and many of them will be discussed in later chapters.

Mao feels that contradictions are essential to the struggle for unity and transformation of individuals and organizations. He regards his theory of contradictions, and the related law of the unity of opposites, as having a number of practical uses. It can be used as a way of perceiving, stating, and analyzing problems. His theory, used in this way, can be consistent with managerial, technical, or economic rationality if contrary political, social or purely ideological elements are not involved. Articulation and analysis are characteristics of everyday life in modern China, and Mao's Thought creates a way of thinking and problem solving. It has been found that refugees who leave mainland China usually leave pure ideology behind but bring with them the practical ideology which continues to express itself in their articulation and methods of analysis.

The theory of contradictions serves as a basis for behavioral norms, particularly in group settings such as thought reform—the juxtaposition of individual and group through struggle, which sharpens contradictions to a point of polarization leading to a dialectical solution. This theory can also be used as an approach to create and use organizations. Organizations are typically marked by contradictory elements, and through this approach, contradictions are brought out into the open. Organizational contradictions may be basically nonantagonistic or antagonistic, but this cannot be known until they are brought to a level of consciousness. Analysis, using the theory of contradictions, reveals what and where they are. Analysis leads to discussion through which contradictions can be revealed and resolved, either through individual or group processes.

I ran into the practical use of the theory of contradictions at many Chinese enterprises (this topic will be discussed and illustrated in more detail in later chapters). At this time, however, let us glimpse at how it works by using as a concrete example an article published in a recent issue of the *Peking People's Daily.*[15] The article is entitled "The Practice of Economy in Bicycle and Enamel Factories," and it involves contradictions between "cost and quality," or "durability for the customer and economy."

The Second Bicycle Factory in Tientsin received many complaints from customers that its product was too slow and heavy. The plant decided to replace scattered steel balls in the middle shaft by ball brackets to make the bike easier to ride, but it seemed that this would increase the cost by 3.5 cents in Chinese currency (Chinese 2.5 cents = U.S. 1 cent). Could this quality improvement be accomplished without increasing the cost? There appeared to be a contradiction between cost and quality. But through an analytic struggle the plant aimed to carry out the "general line" of "greater, faster, better and cheaper."

The enterprise party committee made this problem a subject of mass discussion and analysis. All personnel attended various meetings and many formed problem-solving teams consisting of managers, technicians, and workers. Employees submitted more than three hundred "innovation" measures for practicing economy, with the aim of saving 3.6 cents instead of increasing the cost of the bike by 3.5 cents. Many innovations were introduced, the quality was improved, and in a few months unit cost decreased by 50 cents. Hence, the problem of quality versus cost was solved by relying on the Thought of Chairman Mao and applying in practice his theory of contradictions.

On the basis of practical ideology and pure theory, various policies and programs are implemented in Chinese industry. Practical ideology is made operational and concrete through the theory of contradictions and the law of the unity of opposites.

At Chinese enterprises one hears much reference to, and can observe, the "three taking-part-ins," whereby managers and party cadres take part in physical labor, workers take part in management, and customers play a role in shaping the product-variety plans of producers and sellers in terms of their needs and requirements. One also hears much about and observes the "three-in-one method," through which managers and leaders, technicians, and workers form teams in order to solve various problems. And much emphasis is placed on "democratic centralism" in practice by drawing the masses or workers into the formulation and implementation of plans and decisions through committees, conferences, meetings, elections, and other means. Many enterprises refer to the "two-ups and two-downs" when discussing democratic centralism in the planning process. Such activities are ways in which the elimination of class distinctions and various other contradictions are dealt with. An attempt is made to have leaders become workers, workers to become decision makers, intellectuals to do physical labor, physical laborers to do menial work, Reds to become Experts, Experts to become Reds, and so forth.

One also hears many other ideological slogans and phrases at Chinese plants which seem, on the surface, to be abstract jargon or propaganda but which, in fact, often have significant but subtle motivational and operational consequences. An underlying contradiction in many cases is man versus a variety of obstacles which can be overcome. For example, in factory after factory I heard about "socialist or mass emulation," which involves learning from, imitating, catching up with, overtaking, and surpassing advanced individuals, groups, or enterprises. Other slogans were: "dare to think, dare to create, dare to do," "technical innovation and technical revolution," "Bring science to the masses," "quality first," "economy and durability," "Put politics in command," "balanced development," and "Strive for self-sufficiency." I was also told much about and met "five-good workers," who are elected by their peers on the basis of social and political as well as productive criteria.

It is difficult, if not impossible, for the foreigner—even if he understands Chinese—to make much sense out of, or take seriously, what seems to be rather childish gibberish and slogans, unless he knows something about Communist Chinese ideology. One of the most important manifestations of Chinese ideology in action is the communication system used in organizations and throughout society. Ideology is an integral part of the communication system in China, and it takes concrete expressive form through systematic sets of categories and language.

All organizations need information to function, and ideology, as a systematic set of ideas, provides the basic elements of the Chinese communication system. Individuals are constantly taught the standardized terminology and its interpretation in practice through formal and informal education and training, study and discussion groups, and the mass media, such as newspapers, radio, television, and films. Through mass media the correct ideological interpretation of policy decisions and terminology is defined and explained. Examples of correct interpretation and use in practice—such as the article on the bicycle factory—receive much attention, and criticisms and examples of incorrect behavior, such as excessive authoritarianism or arrogance on the part of intellectuals and Experts, are also published.

This systematized ideological language is used for transmitting policy commands, instructions, and information feedback throughout the Chinese economy. Communication based on ideology deals with social, political, and economic issues, although economic matters are often also expressed in the nonideological language of standardized statistical categories.

Categories and language derived from Chinese ideology must be precise enough to be applied practically, but also general enough to cover a wide range of different conditions if they are to be effective. Policy orders are put in general terms, but they must be carried out under particular conditions. The local party cadres and managers must understand the intent of the higher-level policy decisions. If all key terms were exactly defined as to their implementation, they would be made too precise and so would tie down the policy makers and executors. On the other hand, these terms are used with enough precision to prevent them from being so vague and abstract that no one can apply them.

It is the combination of precision of use, despite the lack of a clear-cut operational definition, and reliance on oral transmission of meaning in study and discussion sessions that assures the leadership of being able to communicate the intent of its decision to a given sector or throughout society at large. The major and most rapid channel of communication is through the pervasive Communist Party organization which has committees, branches, and cadres at all levels of society. When choices involving unclear priorities must be made with regard to the formulation or fulfillment of enterprise plans, the enterprise party cadres often define these priorities in accordance with their interpretation of policy. At times they can and do go overboard in implementing a specific policy.

In general, the various ideological slogans cited above have important and operational meanings throughout the Chinese economy, and they serve to set off various behavior patterns or responses. They are a means through which theory is merged with practice, and through which the socialist transformation of the individual progresses.

The ideal Chinese—and American—organization man is fully committed to the organization's cause (or objectives) but also knows how to act "correctly" on the basis of his commitments. When an organization consists of individuals with the same commitments and the same action ideas, it has a basis for solidarity. Probably relatively few, if any, Chinese organizations have reached a pure state of solidarity, but many, if not most, are attempting to move in this direction.

Hence, the values and norms of the total Chinese ideology are tools through which two key organizational functions are accomplished: they serve to motivate individuals to give full commitment to the organization; and they give individuals a set of ideas with which to carry out the actions demanded by theory and rules of correct behavior. When an organization consists of individuals with the same commitments and the same action ideas, it not only has a basis for solidarity but probably also for effective performance in terms of common objectives. The Chinese conviction that social mobilization and ideology could motivate men through organization arose from a belief that men in a truly solid group can work better than in a team which is only an aggregate of individuals. This belief is similar to what American sociologists call "group dynamics."

While certain major aspects of Chinese ideology are apparently in conflict with managerial, technical, and economic rationality—and hence economic progress—some aspects appear to have a favorable impact on economic progress and industrial development. In fact, some aspect of Chinese ideology could possibly provide part of an effective development model for other underdeveloped and newly developing countries.

Before concluding this chapter, some comments about those portions of Mao's works that seemed to be most commonly read, studied, and discussed by enterprise personnel in particular when I was in China may be of some general interest. Although Mao's writings run to four fat volumes, in addition to numerous other shorter publications, the essays that were most extensively and intensively studied were relatively few and quite short. "On Contradictions" was, of course, one of them. A major reason for having enterprise employees study this work is apparently to provide them with a "correct" and "scientific" view of reality and to help them in solving problems and overcoming obstacles. They are encouraged to persist in working out solutions to problems, even where seemingly conflicting or incompatible factors are involved.

Much time was also being spent on "On Practice." One aim here seemed to be to get people to behave according to correct ideological standards through constant practice, experience, and evaluation and in a manner based on correct thought. Another aim was to merge theory in general—including nonideological theories ranging from physics and engineering to bookkeeping and operating machines—with practice or application. Here, too, overcoming obstacles, problem solving, and persistence were stressed, as well as self-improvement and better performance.

Mao's "In Memory of Norman Bethune" was also receiving much attention. Bethune served with the Chinese Communist Army in the field in the 1930's and gave his life doing so. He was a Canadian surgeon and a graduate of McGill University, one of my alma maters. When Chinese citizens were told that, like Norman Bethune, I was a Canadian and a McGill graduate, they became more friendly, interested, and even excited. Mao's eulogy to Bethune extols the virtues of selflessness, moral stimuli, purely altruistic and compassionate dedication to one's fellow man, classlessness, and humility. This work is probably used with the aim of eliminating self-interest and material gain as key motivating forces and of illustrating the value and correctness of a classless society.

"The Foolish Old Man Who Removed the Mountains" was being widely read to encourage people to overcome their difficulties and obstacles in general, however great they may seem. It was often tied in with phrases such as "learn from," "catch up to," "overtake," and "surpass" the advanced worker, collective, enterprise, or foreign country. It stresses such virtues as persistence, self-confidence, and effort.

Considerable use is also made of articles, not written by Mao, in the popular media dealing with "model" workers, "model" soldiers, "model" farmers, and the like. The characteristics and behavior of such model citizens are closely woven into the ideological standards and values emphasized in Mao's works.

In general, the study of Mao's works and other ideological writings is in some basic respect like the intensive study in Christian societies of portions of the Bible and the consideration and discussion of their application in daily life.

CHAPTER 2

The Environment of Management and Industry

PERHAPS THE BEST WAY to assess China's actual and potential industrial progress is to examine the external environment within which enterprises and their management function. It may be easier in the political sense to alter various environmental conditions rather than the detailed internal affairs of a vast number of individual firms in order to increase managerial effectiveness and industrial development on a national scale over time. Hence, it seems extremely important to try to determine what environmental factors tend to have a significant impact on managerial effectiveness and economic progress generally and in specific situations, and to understand the nature of such impacts.

One intuitively expects that the external environments of management and industry would vary greatly among underdeveloped or developing and advanced nations. This situation is clearly reflected in the following quotation which appears in a recent United Nations report based on data provided by teams of experts in different fields.

> The manager of an enterprise in a developing country generally has a more difficult task than his counterpart in a developed country. As a rule, the operation of industry in the more advanced countries takes for granted the existence of the so-called external economics; that is, of a complex of economic overheads, including transportation, power and water supply, repair facilities, and availability of spare parts and of a variety of skills ranging from highly complex managerial skills to a labor force brought up in an industrial tradition and possessing at least a minimum of general and professional education. The entire institu-

tional framework, which has gradually evolved throughout the course of economic development, provides a favorable climate for the operation and growth of the industrial sector, or at least does not interfere with it. In the developing countries, economic and social changes brought about by industrialization are relatively recent phenomena and are accompanied by a number of frictions and maladjustments; many and varied obstacles have still to be overcome. The manager cannot always recruit workers with the necessary understanding of the functions of the enterprise and of such matters as administrative discipline. Moreover, there is no body of managerial colleagues who can help him solve his problems and correct his mistakes when necessary. He has to be highly self-reliant and must constantly help other members of the staff to do their work properly.[1]

There do seem to be a number of common and critically negative environmental factors operating in varying degrees on firms and their managements in most, if not all, underdeveloped and newly developing countries. However, some of the developing countries deal with various environmental constraints more effectively than others, and as a result they progress more rapidly and impressively. Later on we shall make some comparisons between China and India. But first we must identify the environmental factors that appear to be significant in any country.

Identification and Classification of Critical Environmental Constraints

In one of my earlier studies coauthored with Professor Richard Farmer—which was based on extensive field research, the experiences of many scholars and experts, and hundreds of secondary sources—we tentatively identified, defined, and classified what seem to be the most critical external constraints bearing on industrial and business management.[2] We have hypothesized that these constraints or factors tend to have direct and significant influence on managerial and enterprise performance in general.

Table 2–1 presents the environmental constraints identified as being most critical. They have been classified into four broad categories: education, sociological-cultural, political-legal, and economic. The variables presented are obviously very complex, and detailed study of even a few could take a lifetime; however, if only the portion of each constraint directly bearing on industrial management is considered, the task becomes much simpler and more manageable. Hence, we are interested not in all laws or political theory but only in the portions of law and politics which bear directly and significantly on the management process and productive effi-

TABLE 2–1

Environmental Constraints

C1: *Education*

1.1 LITERACY LEVEL: The percentage of the total population and those presently employed in industry who can read, write, and do simple arithmetic calculations, and the average years of schooling of adults.

1.2 SPECIALIZED VOCATIONAL AND TECHNICAL TRAINING AND GENERAL SECONDARY EDUCATION: Extent, types, and quality of education and training of this type not directly under the control or direction of industrial enterprises. The type, quantity, and quality of persons obtaining such education or training and the proportion of those employed in industry with such education and training.

1.3 HIGHER EDUCATION: The percentage of the total population and those employed in industry with post high school education, plus the types and quality of such education. The types of persons obtaining higher education.

1.4 SPECIAL MANAGEMENT-DEVELOPMENT PROGRAMS: The extent and quality of management-development programs which are not run internally by productive enterprises, and which are aimed at improving the skills and abilities of managers and for potential managers. The quantity and quality of managers and potential managers of different types and levels attending or having completed such programs.

1.5 ATTITUDE TOWARD EDUCATION: The general or dominant cultural attitudes toward education and the acquisition of knowledge in terms of its presumed desirability. The general attitude toward different types of education.

1.6 MATCHING OF EDUCATION WITH THE REQUIREMENTS OF INDUSTRY AND MANPOWER UTILIZATION: The extent and degree to which the types of formal education and training in a given country fit the needs of productive enterprises and all levels of skill and achievement, and the degree to which manpower utilization is effective. This is essentially a summary category: depending on the type of job involved, different educational constraints indicated above would be more important.

C2: *Sociological-Cultural*

2.1 VIEW TOWARD INDUSTRIAL MANAGERS AND MANAGEMENT: The general or dominant social attitude toward industrial and business managers of all sorts, and the way that such managers tend to view their managerial jobs.

2.2 VIEW OF AUTHORITY, RESPONSIBILITY, AND SUBORDINATES: The general or dominant cultural attitude toward authority, responsibility, and persons in subordinate positions and the way that industrial managers tend to view their authority, responsibility, and their subordinates.

2.3 INTERORGANIZATIONAL AND INDIVIDUAL COOPERATION: Extent and degree to which business enterprises, government agencies, labor unions, educational institutions, and other relevant organizations cooperate with each other in ways conducive to industrial efficiency and general economic progress. The degree to which individuals employed in productive enterprises cooperate with each other toward this end.

2.4 VIEW TOWARD ACHIEVEMENT AND WORK: The general or dominant cultural attitude toward individual or collective achievement and productive work in industry.

2.5 CLASS STRUCTURE AND INDIVIDUAL MOBILITY: The extent of opportunities for social class and individual mobility, both vertical and horizontal, in a given country, and the means by which it can be achieved.

2.6 VIEW TOWARD WEALTH, MATERIAL GAIN, AND SELF-INTEREST: Whether or not the acquisition of wealth from different sources is generally considered socially desirable, and the way that persons employed in industry tend to view material gain.

2.7 VIEW TOWARD SCIENTIFIC METHOD: The general social and dominant individual attitude toward the use of rational, predictive techniques in solving various types of business, technical, economic, and social problems.

2.8 VIEW TOWARD RISK TAKING: Whether or not the taking of various types of personal collective or rational risks is generally considered acceptable, as well as the dominant view toward specific types of risk taking in business and industry. The degree and extent to which risk taking tends to be a rational process in a particular country.

2.9 VIEW TOWARD CHANGE: The general cultural attitude toward a social change of any type which bears directly on industrial performance in a given country, and the dominant attitude among persons employed in industry toward all types of significant changes in enterprises operations.

C3: *Political-Legal*

3.1 RELEVANT LEGAL RULES OF THE GAME: Quality, efficiency, and effectiveness of the legal structure in terms of general business law, labor law, tax law, and general law relevant to business. Degree of enforcement, reliability, etc.

3.2 DEFENSE AND MILITARY POLICY: Impact of defense policy in industrial enterprise in terms of trading with potential enemies, purchasing policies, strategic industry development, labor resources competition, and similar factors.

3.3 FOREIGN POLICY: Impact of policy on industrial enterprise in terms of trading restrictions, quotas, tariffs, customs, unions, foreign exchange, etc.

3.4 POLITICAL STABILITY: Influence on industrial enterprises of revolutions, changes in regime, stability, or instability over protracted periods, etc.

3.5 POLITICAL ORGANIZATION: Type of organization in constitutional terms; degrees of centralization or decentralization; degree and extent of red tape, delays, uncertainty, and confusion in industry-government dealings; pressure groups and their effectiveness; political parties and their philosophies, etc.

3.6 FLEXIBILITY OF LAW AND LEGAL CHANGES: Degree to which relevant barriers to the efficient management of industrial enterprises can be changed and the timeliness of such changes; predictability and certainty of legal actions, etc.

C4: *Economic*

4.1 BASIC ECONOMIC SYSTEM: Including such factors as the overall economic organization of the country (i.e., capitalistic, Marxist, mixed), property rights, and similar factors.

4.2 CENTRAL BANKING SYSTEM AND MONETARY POLICY: The organization and operations of the central banking system, including the controls over

TABLE 2–1 (*continued*)

commercial banks, the ability and willingness to control the money supply, the effectiveness of government, policies regarding price stability, commercial bank reserves, discounting credit controls, and similar factors.

4.3 FISCAL POLICY AND THE STATE BUDGET: General policies concerning government expenditures, their timing, and their impact; the general level of deficit, surplus, or balance; total share of government expenditures in gross national product.

4.4 ECONOMIC STABILITY: The vulnerability of the economy to economic fluctuations of depression and boom, price stability, and overall economic growth stability.

4.5 ORGANIZATION OF CAPITAL MARKETS: The existence of such markets as stock and bond exchanges, their honesty, effectiveness, and total impact; the size and role of commercial banking, including loan policies and availability of credit to businessmen; the existence of other capital sources, such as savings and loan associations, government-sponsored credit agencies, insurance-company loan activities, etc.

4.6 FACTOR ENDOWMENT: Relative supply of real capital and land (agricultural, minerals, and other raw materials) per capita; size and general health of the work force.

4.7 MARKET SIZE: Total effective purchasing power within the country plus relevant export markets for different branches of industry making up the total industrial sector.

4.8 SOCIAL-OVERHEAD CAPITAL: Availability and quality of power supplies, water, communications systems, transportation, public warehousing, physical transfer facilities, housing, etc.

ciency in industrial enterprises. Similarly, our concern with education includes not all pedagogy but only the portion which directly concerns industrial management. By focusing our attention in this way, it may be possible to gain meaningful insights into how these constraints actually do affect managerial performance in China, or elsewhere.

It is evident from Table 2–1 that many of the constraints are closely interrelated, and this makes any analysis of them even more difficult. Attitude toward education may be closely connected with the view toward achievement and work, attitude toward scientific method, attitude toward change, and class structure and individual mobility; attitude toward achievement may be closely connected with class structure, attitudes toward risk taking and change, and various educational and political factors. Basic literacy may have a significant bearing on many of the economic, political-legal, and sociological-cultural constraints; nature and effectiveness of central banking on monetary policy may be ultimately linked with economic stability and may depend in part on various legal-political factors, and so forth. The result is an extremely complex set of interrelationships, which determine in lage part how efficiently individual firms and an entire country perform economically.

Key Relationships

Even more complex than the above interrelationship problem is the problem of analyzing significant relationships that tend to exist between environmental constants, critical elements of the management process, and managerial effectiveness. The nature of the impact of environmental constraints on the enterprise and its management is illustrated in Figures 2–1 and 2–2. The industrial enterprise is taking available inputs of various types and creating usable outputs.

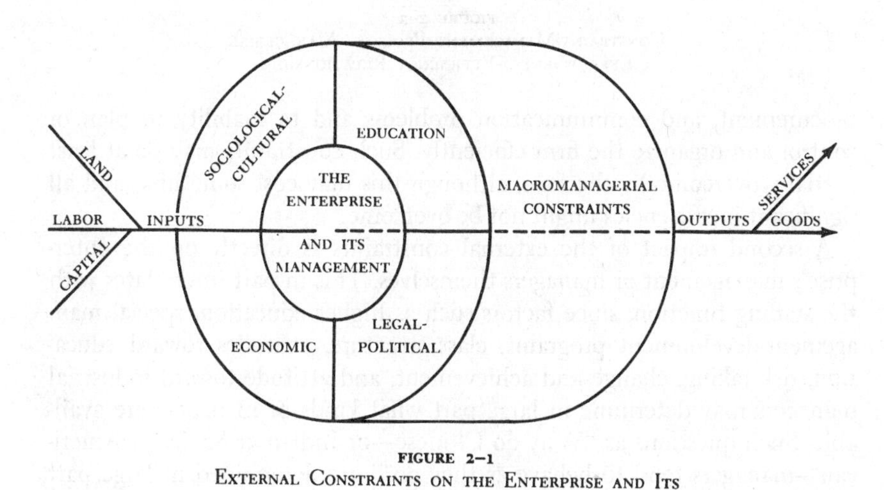

FIGURE 2–1
External Constraints on the Enterprise and Its Management

Analysis of the environmental constraints reveals a number of closely interrelated phases, as shown in Figure 2–2 below.

The first relationship is that between the external constraints and elements of the management process. Some constraints in effect give the management of the enterprise little or no choice in the way the various critical elements of the management process are performed or manifest themselves. Hence, if most of the population has an unfavorable attitude toward scientific method, it may prove difficult to staff the firm with adequate numbers and types of persons who do have a favorable attitude in this important area. The result can be serious inefficiencies within various departments or shops of the firm. A lack of social overhead capital, such as an adequate transportation or telephone network, can lead to distribution,

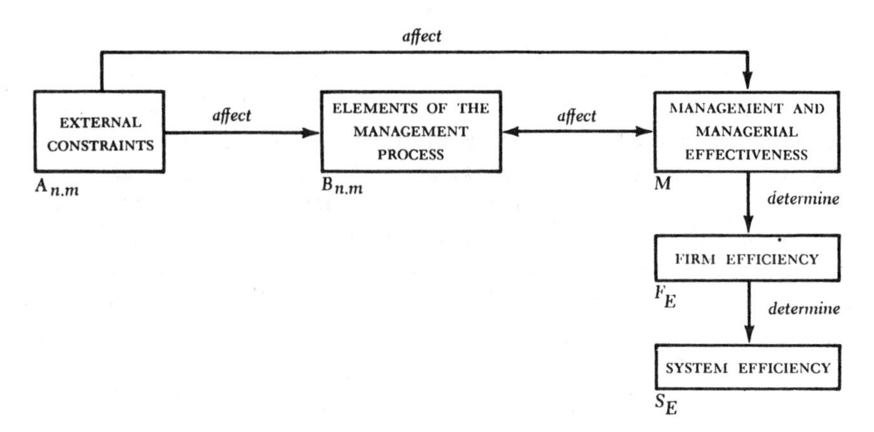

FIGURE 2–2
CONSTRAINT-MANAGEMENT PROCESS—MANAGERIAL EFFECTIVENESS–EFFICIENCY RELATIONSHIPS

procurement, and communication problems and to inability to plan or control and organize the firm efficiently. Such constraints may be at least partially overcome by the firm, although this may cost something and all significant inefficiencies might not be overcome.

A second impact of the external constraints is directly on the enterprise's management or managers themselves. This in part interrelates with the staffing function, since factors such as higher education, special management-development programs, class structure, attitudes toward education, risk taking, change and achievement, and attitude toward industrial managers may determine in large part what kinds of managers are available. Such questions as "Why do Chinese—or Indian or Soviet or American—managers tend to behave as they do?" are determined in large part by external constraints.

Also important is the impact of environmental constraints on managerial effectiveness, which has been defined earlier as the degree or level of efficiency from society's point of view, with which the overall management process is performed in a given enterprise or on a national scale. By exploring the impact of the constraints on the management process, we may gain considerable insight into their impact on managerial effectiveness; however, it appears that the total impact of the external constraints on managerial effectiveness cannot be determined by studying only their impact on the critical elements of the management process, since in many instances they may influence managerial effectiveness directly through their impact on managers themselves. For example, managers may want to improve firm efficiency, but they don't know how; here various educational constraints are relevant. If managers do not care about improving performance and enterprise efficiency, various sociological-cultural constraints may be important.

These two types of relationships between constraints and the productive enterprise are both relevant in determining how well the enterprise operates, although specific interactions may be different. In Figure 2–2, these two relationships are indicated by the lines drawn from the $Ac_{n.m}$ box to the $B_{n.m}$ box and from the $Ac_{n.m}$ box to the M box.

In the case of China another dimension—that of ideology—should be added to Figure 2–2. Ideology in China has an impact on managerial effectiveness and firm efficiency through its impacts on the environmental constraints, as well as directly on the critical elements of the management process and the managers themselves.

The Constraint Management-Process Matrix

Table 2–2 presents a constraint-behavior matrix which indicates suggestive relationships between the environmental constraints and the critical elements of the management process for any country. The environmental factors, following the notation on Table 2–1, are placed horizontally across the page, while the elements of the management process, following the notation of Table 1–1, are listed vertically. The X's in Table 2–2 indicate which constraints and managerial elements might be related.

These hypothesized relationships can be presented in the form of equations. For example, following Table 2–1 we have:

$B\ 3.3 = f(C\ 1.1, C\ 1.2, C\ 1.3, C\ 1.4, C\ 1.6, C\ 2.1, C\ 2.2, C\ 2.3, C\ 2.4, C\ 2.5, C\ 2.6, C\ 2.7, C\ 3.1, C\ 4.1, C\ 4.6, C\ 4.7, C\ 4.8)$

The most significant variables might be C 1.1, C 1.2, C 1.3, C 1.4, C 1.6, C 2.4, C 2.5, C 3.1, and C 4.1.

$B\ 7.4 = f(C\ 2.3, C\ 2.7, C\ 2.8, C\ 3.2, C\ 3.3, C\ 4.1, C\ 4.4, C\ 4.5, C\ 4.6, C\ 4.7, C\ 4.8)$

The most significant variables might be C 2.3, C 2.7, C 4.1, C 4.4, C 4.7, and C 4.8.

In words, the first equation says that degree of work specialization (division of labor) depends significantly on all but one of the educational constraints; on attitudes toward industrial managers and management, authority and subordinates, achievement and work, scientific method, wealth and material gain; and on interorganizational cooperation, class structure and individual mobility, legal rules, general economic framework, factor endowment, market size, and social overhead capital. Of these, the educational constraints, attitude toward achievement and work, class structure and individual mobility, legal rules, and economic framework might be the most important.

The second equation states that average inventory levels (major supplies, goods in process, completed output) depend on interorganizational cooperation, attitudes toward scientific method and risk taking, defense

TABLE 2–2

RELATIONSHIPS BETWEEN CRITICAL MANAGERIAL ELEMENTS AND EXTERNAL CONSTRAINTS

	C1 *Educational*						C2 *Sociological*									C3 *Political-Legal*						C4 *Economic*							
	1	2	3	4	5	6	1	2	3	4	5	6	7	8	9	1	2	3	4	5	6	1	2	3	4	5	6	7	8
B1: 1				X			X		X	X	X	X	X	X	X	X	X	X	X	X	X	X	X	X	X	X	X	X	X
2	X	X	X	X		X		X	X	X			X	X	X	X	X	X	X	X	X	X	X	X	X	X	X	X	X
3		X	X	X					X	X			X	X	X	X	X	X	X	X	X		X	X	X	X	X		
4		X	X	X		X		X	X	X		X	X	X	X	X	X	X	X	X	X	X			X	X			
5		X	X	X					X				X	X	X	X	X	X	X		X	X	X	X	X	X			
6		X	X	X				X	X			X	X	X	X	X	X	X			X	X				X			
7	X	X	X	X	X	X	X	X	X	X	X	X	X	X	X	X						X					X		
8		X	X	X	X	X	X	X		X	X	X	X	X	X														
9	X	X	X	X	X	X	X	X	X	X	X	X	X	X	X					X	X								
10	X	X	X	X	X	X		X		X	X		X	X	X														
11	X	X	X	X	X	X	X	X		X	X	X	X	X	X	X	X	X	X	X	X	X	X	X	X	X	X	X	X
12	X	X	X	X	X	X	X	X	X	X	X	X	X	X	X	X	X	X	X	X	X	X	X	X	X	X	X	X	X
B2: 1	X	X	X	X	X	X	X	X		X	X	X	X	X	X	X	X	X				X			X	X			
2	X	X	X	X		X	X	X		X			X	X	X	X	X	X				X			X	X			
3	X	X	X	X		X	X	X		X			X	X	X	X						X				X			
4	X	X	X	X		X		X		X			X	X	X	X						X				X			
5	X	X	X	X	X	X	X	X	X	X	X	X	X		X	X			X	X		X					X		
6	X	X	X	X	X	X	X	X		X	X	X	X	X	X	X			X	X	X	X							
7	X	X	X	X		X	X	X	X	X	X	X	X		X	X	X	X	X	X	X	X	X	X	X	X			
B3: 1	X	X	X	X		X	X	X	X	X	X	X	X	X	X	X	X	X	X	X	X	X	X	X	X	X	X	X	X
2	X	X	X	X	X	X	X	X		X	X	X	X			X						X					X		X
3	X	X	X	X		X	X	X	X	X	X	X	X			X						X					X	X	X
4	X	X	X	X		X	X	X		X	X		X														X		
5	X	X	X	X		X	X	X	X	X	X		X																X
6		X	X	X		X	X	X	X	X	X		X			X						X				X		X	X
7	X	X	X	X		X	X	X		X	X		X			X													
8	X	X	X	X	X	X	X	X		X	X		X			X				X		X							X
9		X	X	X		X	X	X		X	X		X		X														
10	X	X	X	X		X	X	X		X	X																		
11		X	X	X	X	X	X	X		X	X		X	X	X	X						X							
B4: 1	X	X	X	X	X	X	X	X		X	X	X	X			X	X										X		X
2		X		X	X	X	X	X		X	X	X	X			X											X		X
3		X	X	X	X	X	X	X		X	X	X	X			X													
4		X	X	X		X	X	X		X	X		X			X													
5							X	X		X	X	X	X			X						X			X	X	X		
6	X	X	X	X	X	X	X	X		X	X	X	X		X	X											X		
7	X	X	X	X	X	X	X	X		X	X	X		X													X		

	C1 *Educational*						C2 *Sociological*									C3 *Political-Legal*						C4 *Economic*							
	1	2	3	4	5	6	1	2	3	4	5	6	7	8	9	1	2	3	4	5	6	1	2	3	4	5	6	7	8
8					x			x		x	x		x			x											x		x
9							x	x		x	x					x				x	x								
10	x	x	x	x	x	x	x	x		x	x	x	x			x	x					x	x	x	x		x		x
B5: 1	x	x	x	x			x	x		x	x																		
2		x	x	x		x	x	x		x	x	x	x			x													
3	x	x			x	x	x	x		x	x	x	x			x													
4	x	x	x	x	x	x	x	x		x	x	x	x																
5	x	x	x	x		x	x	x		x		x	x			x													
6	x	x	x	x	x	x	x	x		x	x	x															x		
7	x	x	x	x	x	x	x	x		x	x	x	x														x		
8	x				x		x	x		x	x	x		x	x	x											x		
9							x	x	x	x	x	x										x							
10	x	x	x	x	x	x	x	x	x	x	x	x		x	x	x									x		x		
11							x	x	x	x	x	x				x				x	x	x			x		x		
B6: 1									x				x	x	x	x	x	x				x	x	x	x	x	x	x	x
2									x				x	x	x	x	x	x				x	x	x	x	x	x	x	x
3									x				x			x	x	x				x	x	x	x	x	x	x	x
4	x										x	x	x	x		x						x			x			x	x
B7: 1									x				x			x	x	x				x			x	x	x	x	x
2									x				x			x	x	x				x			x	x	x	x	x
3									x				x				x					x			x	x		x	x
4									x				x	x			x	x				x			x	x	x	x	x
5									x				x	x			x	x				x			x	x	x	x	x
6									x				x	x		x	x	x	x	x		x	x	x	x	x	x	x	x
7	x	x	x	x		x	x	x		x	x	x	x			x	x	x				x	x	x	x	x	x	x	x
8	x	x	x			x	x			x						x	x	x	x			x			x	x	x	x	x
9	x	x	x			x							x			x	x	x	x			x			x	x	x	x	x
B8: 1	x	x	x	x	x	x							x	x	x		x	x	x			x			x	x	x	x	x
B9: 1												x	x	x		x			x	x		x	x	x	x	x	x	x	
2							x					x	x	x		x		x	x			x	x	x	x	x	x		
3							x					x	x	x	x	x	x	x				x	x	x	x	x	x	x	x
4												x	x	x	x	x	x	x	x			x	x	x	x	x			
5							x			x	x	x	x	x	x	x						x			x	x			
B10: 1											x	x	x	x	x	x		x	x			x				x		x	
2								x	x	x	x	x	x	x		x	x	x	x			x			x	x	x		x
3								x	x	x	x	x	x	x	x	x		x	x			x	x	x	x	x	x		
4	x	x	x			x	x	x	x	x	x	x	x			x		x	x	x	x	x	x	x	x		x		
5							x	x	x	x	x	x	x	x	x	x	x	x	x	x	x	x							
6	x	x	x	x	x		x	x	x	x	x	x	x	x	x	x			x	x	x	x							

policy, foreign policy, general economic framework, economic stability, organization of capital markets, factor endowment, market size and social overhead capital. Of these, interorganizational cooperation, attitude toward scientific method, general economic framework, economic stability, market size, and social overhead capital might be the most important.

Table 2–2 permits, if nothing else, the statement of a large number of suggestive interrelationships in a very small space. What it does not indicate, however, is what quantitative relationships are indicated by the *C* to *B* relationships. It is, of course, not possible to undertake such a quantitative analysis in our study of China, nor is it possible to consider more than a limited number of the relationships suggested in Table 2–2. We have presented this table only to indicate the types of relationships that seem to be significant in analyzing management and industrial progress. Hopefully, the matrix will provide a worthwhile conceptual framework—or at least a check list—for those who wish to do research on or work out an analysis of managerial and industrial problems in China, or for that matter in any other country.

In general, the total interrelationships of the variables presented in Table 2–2 are extremely complex. Only intensive empirical research can help us to verify these hypotheses with a high degree of confidence, and only extensive research can enable us to determine the relative significance of different constraints in terms of their impact on a given element of the management process in a given type of situation.

The problem of measuring managerial effectiveness and productive efficiency is very complex. The interested reader is referred to other sources for a rigorous analysis of this problem.[3] It will suffice to indicate here that at the enterprise level improvements in managerial effectiveness, productive efficiency, and general industrial progress show up in such ways as increases in labor productivity, better utilization of physical, financial, and human resources which leads to greater output and/or sales with the same amount of inputs, reductions in unit costs and other expenses, improved and new products and technology, greater profits or profitability, and so on. At the national level, significant gains in the real total and per capita gross national product, national income, or industrial output generally reflect improvements in industrial managerial effectiveness and productive efficiency on a widespread scale.

The Environment of an Underdeveloped Country: Why Is an Underdeveloped Country Underdeveloped?

At this point it might prove fruitful to consider the nature of the environment of management and industry in a roughly typical, but hypothetical, truly backward country.[4] Let us call the country Stagnatia. This might shed much light on the crucial question: Why is an underdeveloped country underdeveloped? or Why is a poor country poor? With this general background it might be easier to gauge how effective China has been in coping with its environmental constraints to date. China was an underdeveloped, backward, and extremely poor country before she began to organize conscientiously and vigorously for industrial progress at the beginning of the 1950's. Most of the environmental constraints discussed below were evident to a relatively high degree in pre-1949 China.[5]

Our aim in the balance of this chapter is not to analyze in depth the impact of each environmental factor considered—a more thorough and concrete analysis of this type will be undertaken for China in Chapters 3 through 6—but rather to illustrate with a few examples why each constraint is important in terms of management, productive efficiency, and industrial progress, and more important, to provide the necessary concepts and definitions for a fuller understanding and appreciation of the following chapters.

Educational Constraints

The overall educational system in any country affects virtually every aspect of managerial and industrial life. In particular it has a great bearing on the entire staffing function, the size of industrial enterprises and their overall organization structures, degrees of work specialization, types of processes, techniques and technology used, costs of production, and the overall productivity of firms and their managements.

Education, as it relates to managerial performance and industrial progress, has both quantitative and qualitative dimensions. It is true that any kind of education imparts some knowledge; but it is the type of depth of knowledge that is crucial in this connection. Knowledge about music, Latin, or even literature is not very important in running an industrial enterprise, while knowledge about engineering, technology, mathematics, economics, human behavior, the techniques and functions of management, and the various productive functions, is of great importance. The types of education and knowledge possessed by those persons employed by other organizations such as governmental economic, legal, and regulatory agencies and banking institutions, which have a significant bearing on the activities of industrial firms, are also important to industrial management.

Literacy Level

Of primary importance in a truly backward country, such as Stagnatia, is the problem of basic literacy and primary education, where the term literacy implies the ability to read, write, and do simple arithmetic computations with reasonable accuracy. Unless the literacy level in such a country improves very substantially it is unlikely that much industrial progress will be possible. It is true that in countries with a high rate of illiteracy—such as Saudi Arabia, Nigeria, or Sudan—the proportion of literate persons employed in industry tends to be above the national average; however, most enterprises in such a country find that they must employ a substantial number of illiterate or barely literate personnel. Moreover, management must deal with many illiterate or barely literate people outside the firm.

The organization of a literate firm would tend to be very different from one using a large proportion of illiterates, mainly because the possibilities open to an enterprise with literate personnel are so much greater than one operating with many illiterates. It is common for management theorists to advocate that in devising an organization structure, one should begin with the ideal structure, then try to get the men with the necessary qualifications to fill this structure. In fitting the men to the job it is realized that at times modifications must be made in the structure because of the unavailability of suitable personnel. In countries having a severe shortage of skilled manpower and many barely literate persons, it is frequently necessary to build the organization division of work around available people rather than to fit people to an ideal structure. This tends to limit greatly the amount of specialization that is possible.

It is difficult to effectively organize and operate many large industrial enterprises in an illiterate society, and industry in underdeveloped countries is typically characterized by small firms. The cement which holds a relatively big enterprise together is usually the tremendous amount of horizontal, upward, and downward communication in the organization. Much of this communication must necessarily be written; who, then, performs this communication function if few can read or write? If the workers, foremen, and supervisors are illiterate, they must always be instructed orally—a difficult and very time-consuming job for senior men. While illiterates may have more keenly developed memories than literates, few instructions, particularly complex ones, can be remembered completely, which means that errors and inefficiencies crop up all over the enterprise.

The usual consequence is that firms tend to be quite small, often restricting themselves to sizes which can be managed by one or two people. With small firms, many of the potential advantages derived from economies of scale are not obtained. The possibilities of a high degree of decentralization in industry is virtually impossible for an illiterate society. The few educated managers and technicians must be carefully husbanded in industrial organizations if a reasonable level of productive efficiency is to be achieved. The demands placed on such scarce educated personnel frequently overburden their spans of control, and the formal chain of command is often circumvented by top-level managers and experts who find it necessary to delve into the detailed affairs of the lowest levels because of incompetent lower-level supervisors. Such incompetence of the lower levels also tends to breed distrust and lack of competence on the part of higher-level managers.

One senses a pervasive feeling of apathy in an enterprise where a substantial portion of employees are illiterate or barely literate. Employees tend to lack self-confidence and seem resigned to the fact that they cannot get ahead regardless of how hard they work—they are trapped in their jobs because literacy may be essential to get a better job in the organization. Introducing changes and innovations, even quite simple ones, in such an organization tends to be difficult because of the amount of training, direction, and control that is usually needed to implement them effectively.

Illiteracy also creates striking planning and control problems for industrial firms. It is extremely difficult to make much use of written policies, procedures, or methods. The typical modern business control system has at its very heart a series of interrelated reporting documents. But who will fill out and analyze such documents when few can write? A firm may have a warehouse full of inventory, and practically no one—certainly not a low-paid worker—can go through the warehouse and even count the materials or write down a list of items in long or short supply; or a firm may have a job-order report form which is not made out because the foreman cannot write. Such examples could be multiplied endlessly, but the result is typically the same—the relatively large firm trying to operate in such an environment runs out of control most of the time. Even when the work force is diligent and cooperative, the inability to handle even simple control devices, such as oil pressure gauges, air pressure readings, and rulers leads to serious control problems.

The staffing problem is virtually overwhelming in a highly illiterate society. Even where there are a few educated persons, the difficulty of filling even routine positions, to say nothing of important managerial and technical jobs, is extremely difficult. A literate clerk becomes valuable; and if he can type and do routine filing, he becomes very valuable. In such a society much time must be spent in training at the enterprise if it is to continue functioning. Such training often has to start from the very beginning, since the typical worker will have had no experience to speak of in modern industry. Even where the management and experts are very well educated and competent, this training problem is complex, very time-consuming, and tends to absorb tremendous amounts of critically scarce and relatively expensive talented manpower.

One cannot simply pass on an instruction book to even a barely literate worker or give him a set of rules to follow—he must be taught orally and visually every possible step of his job, including all necessary exception routines. Driving a truck or operating a lathe seems simple enough, until one tries to train illiterates to do the job. It is incredible how many supposedly simple, relatively unskilled industrial jobs require large amounts of reading, calculating, rechecking, and evaluating before they are done properly. Training in many such cases starts with a basic literacy program, since this skill is so essential to rapid progress later on.

The importance of basic functional literacy, at least among a substantial part of the working population, cannot be underestimated. It is one of the most critical of all environmental constraints. It seems to be more important for industrial development at earlier stages than most, if not all, economic or political-legal constraints. That is, substantial industrial progress can often be made in an underdeveloped country by substantially raising the literacy level of the work force, regardless of the economic or political-legal environment. The greater the rate of illiteracy, the more serious will be the management problems discussed in this section. In the same vein, greater illiteracy means greater waste and spoilage in production and distribution, less innovation and progress, and lower overall human productivity.

One of the major tasks of a country faced with a large literacy problem is to improve the quality of future—and present—workers and managers by instituting large-scale educational programs. Unfortunately, even the management of a major educational effort is quite complex, and many underdeveloped countries tend to have great difficulties in planning, organizing, and carrying out such an effort—assuming that they want to do so.

Specialized Vocational and Technical Training and General Secondary Education

The extent, quality, and diversity of vocational and technical training and general secondary education in a given country have a significant bearing on the types and quality of personnel available, organization of activities, degrees of work specialization, managerial performance, and overall productivity of industrial enterprises. In a relatively advanced country these types of educational programs provide firms with the bulk of their semiskilled and skilled labor, foremen, mechanics, technicians, and lower-level technical supervisors. General secondary education provides business and industry with clerical staff, white-collar supervisory personnel, and salesmen.

In many underdeveloped countries training of the above types of jobs must typically be done by the enterprises themselves, or the jobs cannot be carried out properly, if at all. In the more underdeveloped countries—such as the Sudan, Saudi Arabia, Niger, Ethiopia, Haiti, and China a few decades ago—citizens having the equivalent of a secondary education constitute between .1 percent and 1.0 percent of the entire population. Such persons fill the key positions in the country, and in most cases these tend to be governmental, educational, and/or religious rather than industrial jobs. Hence, industrial firms are faced with very severe shortages of formally educated and trained personnel. In the majority of cases, skilled workers, technicians, foremen, and often even higher-level managers are illiterate or barely literate. In many cases, the precious few managers or engineers who have had higher education cannot make full use of their education or skill since they must spend much of their time doing the type of work that persons with a vocational, intermediate, technical, or secondary education do in a more advanced country.

Higher Education

Modern industries are voracious consumers of high-grade manpower. Even a cursory examination of the types of managerial and technical tasks to be done in a relatively modern industrial enterprise suggests that this type of high-skill manpower is critical to the production and distribution of the firms' products. Many of the tasks, if they are to be performed quite efficiently, call for people with advanced education beyond the secondary or intermediate technical level.

Take, for example, the productive functions of production, procurement, and research and development. Here some of the essential skills include: engineering and possibly scientific and mathematical skills of all sorts, including the ability for product design; ability to purchase materials and equipment logically and to efficiently integrate new equipment into older processes; quality-control analytical ability; ability to conduct statistical analyses of existing outputs in terms of factor inputs and production norms; knowledge of plant and layout planning; value engineering, including analyses of present utilization of materials and operations to obtain greater efficiencies; ability to manage maintenance and repair of machinery and plant; costing and preparation of cost-effectiveness studies; knowledge of inventory control; and so on. Complex skills are also needed for marketing, finance, accounting, planning, as well as the other enterprise and managerial functions.

In advanced countries, such as the United States, most of the skills noted above are typically taught in a systematic fashion at higher educational institutions, and some of the more advanced techniques of production management and control are not encountered by students until they are in graduate schools of business or engineering. Some persons might be able to teach themselves such skills, but only at considerable cost and effort; and firms would suffer if the proper trained personnel are not available. In underdeveloped countries, there are severe shortages of high-talent manpower of this type.

Hence, the overall system of higher education in a given country has a crucial and direct bearing on the activities and effectiveness of industrial enterprises and their managements. Some underdeveloped countries, such as Nyasaland, Niger, and until very recently Saudi Arabia, do not even have any local higher educational institutions. Where there are higher educational institutions in underdeveloped countries, they tend to overemphasize the humanities, arts, law, and possibly medicine, at the expense of training in engineering, science, technology, and business administration and management. This is because of various social and cultural reasons, as well as the costs involved, particularly in connection with engineering and the physical sciences. Only relatively few countries of any type throughout the world place much emphasis on professional management and business administration education.

Management-Development Programs

We are interested here in special management-training programs which are not part of the regular higher educational system and which are not undertaken internally by industrial enterprises. They include part-time or live-in programs offered by educational institutions, associations, or government organizations with the aim of developing and improving the performance of managers or potential managers who are sent by their enterprises.

In many underdeveloped countries there are no special management-training programs of this type. In such countries it is extremely difficult, if not impossible, for local managers to acquire information or knowledge which can improve their performance. In some newly developing countries where such programs do exist it seems that the participants might not put to use what they do learn in these programs because of their attitudes toward achievement and change, or because they are not given the opportunity by their superiors when they return to their enterprises.

Attitudes toward Education

The prevailing attitude toward education in a given country is a product of various cultural, sociological, and political factors. The problem is further complicated by historic and institutional views of what constitutes an educated man. Many societies—especially less developed ones—still see law, the liberal arts, political science, religion, or medicine as being the only suitable fields of study for a "gentleman." If and as the society attempts to shift to a mass educational system in the pursuit of economic progress, such attitudes can be very costly. Status seekers and the better students tend to pursue the traditionally elite fields and to ignore engineering, science, administration, and perhaps economics; and the result—in spite of expanded educational opportunities—is a critical shortage of such important skills for industrial development.

Attitude toward education is one of the most critical of all of the environmental constraints for a number of reasons. First, it has a direct bearing on whether or not people are inclined to want to improve their skills and abilities through education, training, and self-development. Attitude toward education tends to be an important determinant of how much effort and sacrifice people are willing to undertake in educational and training pursuits. Secondly, it has a great bearing on the extent, quality, and content of the overall educational system within a given country, and this determines in large part the types of persons found in industrial enterprises and in other organizations which influence the operations of industrial firms. Thirdly, it has a significant bearing on the fields that attract the better students.

In many newly developing countries where an educational revolution is taking place, much of the population fails to recognize or identify with the kind of social and economic revolution their country is undergoing and also fails to stress to their children the need for literacy, education, and functional skills. Parents, not being literate, do not realize the advantages of education, particularly in the more traditional rural cultures.

It is important to point out that the dominant attitude of individuals in a given society toward education, training, and self-improvement depends largely on the opportunities for career advancement and/or greater status, prestige, and material gain, as well as on their own attitude toward achievement and work. If, for example, there is a rigid class structure which prevents much of the population from getting ahead because of race, religion, sex, wrong family background, and the like, there will be little or no incentive for those actively and acutely discriminated against and blocked from improving their skills or abilities. This type of situation would tend to be a serious obstacle to managerial effectiveness and productive efficiency.

Matching Education with Industrial Requirements and Manpower Utilization

Underdeveloped countries are generally typified by educational systems that do not match the manpower requirements of industrial progress and by a frequent misutilization of the scarce talented manpower available. Even in newly developing countries that expand their educational systems substantially in the pursuit of rapid industrial development, the mismatch and misutilization problem is frequently critical.

People with specialized skills are needed by business, industry, and society in general. A productive enterprise typically requires or desires an electrical engineer, a financial specialist, an accountant, or a manager with a background in particular fields, and not a college graduate with a general background. Or a firm may want to obtain potential machinists who already have learned some basic algebra, or even some geometry or trigonometry, since such knowledge would be important in their future work. The usual desire—and the more efficient course of action—is to train a basically qualified candidate to fill his role and future roles in the firm, rather than to take a completely unsuited individual and make him work as well as possible. In an underdeveloped country the latter course of action tends to be the dominant one, primarily because of the educational constraints. In addition, ideally all of the business and industrial skills of a given person will be used in performing his job—that is, there would be a perfect fit between the man's qualifications and the requirements of his job. If he is substantially overqualified there is much waste of talent, and if he is underqualified the job won't get done efficiently or effectively. Both types of problems tend to be pervasive and critical in underdeveloped countries, with the latter type generally much more so.

In reality, a person who has received a secondary or higher education in almost any field may be better suited to the needs of industry than one who has had no education at these levels. For substitutability of nonspecialists and nonprofessionals in specialist and professional jobs would tend to be greater where persons have a good education in almost any field, rather than an inadequate general education. In the former case at least some trade-offs of knowledge or skill are likely to be possible.

There is also the problem of static versus dynamic match. There tend to be time lags between education and application. A person who graduates this year will probably be working, say, thirty more years, and it is impossible to predict accurately the changes which may occur in personnel requirements in that time. Skills and knowledge which now seem important may become obsolete, while still newer requirements cannot be forseen with certainty. This is as true for an underdeveloped country striving to develop as for an advanced country, in today's rapidly changing world. It is easier to cope with this problem over time if industrial personnel have fairly broad, high-quality education in their particular fields than if they have highly specialized, narrow training. The problem of statics versus dynamics can also be dealt with by refresher courses, part-time education, management-development programs, and various other retraining programs for all types of industrial personnel. Relatively few underdeveloped countries have much, if anything, in the way of such programs.

Further complications regarding the matching of education with manpower utilization are added when, as often happens in underdeveloped countries, a country lacks an adequate job-announcement system. Vacancies may exist and persist, but few potential applicants may know about them, and firms may not know about the existence of suitable recruits. This communication problem is further compounded if much of the population is illiterate. There is also often little, if any, exchanges of information in many countries between industry and educational institutions regarding human resource development and requirements.

As a result of the above problems, countries fail to match the requirements of productive enterprises in varying degrees, and the degree tends to be the most pronounced in backward countries. The larger the discrepancies in this regard, the greater the constraint on managerial effectiveness and productive efficiency. The types of problems discussed in the previous sections on education become serious realities in many countries because of the problem of coordinating education and manpower utilization.

Concluding Remarks on Education

A country is no better, in economic terms, than the skills, education, and training of its inhabitants. The educational constraints discussed are closely interrelated with other types of constraints in the sense that if a country suffers from poor educational standards and performance the entire productive organization of the country will be sadly deficient. Not only will productive enterprises suffer because of internal deficiencies, but quite probably the overall economic, political, and legal systems will also be far from adequate. In the general absence of qualified persons, nothing works well. In this connection, a top-priority task of any country interested in making real economic gains is to consider what must be done to improve the quality of the persons who will be directly responsible for such gains at the operational level.

Without a basically literate, skilled, education-oriented population, all other reforms and development strategies are doomed at best to less than mediocre results. At worst, literally nothing much in the productive sense can be done, since there are so few people capable of doing anything. Productive firms tend to remain small, static, and inefficient; and if relatively large ones are organized—typically by the government—they tend to be static, conservative, and even more inefficient, since large-scale production of almost anything requires sizable numbers of capable persons who can keep the organization going.

A familiar picture in the less developed countries in the past two decades has been that of a poor country trying to make major gains by establishing industrial enterprises of relatively large size, typically owned by the state. The hope is that such firms will be able to skip a generation of effort in reaching higher production levels. More commonly, the result is near chaos—the plant remains unfinished, much plant capacity is unused, the organization runs out of control, much waste and spoilage result, and costs are often so high and quality so low as to make products unsalable even on the domestic market. The difficulty here is in the implicit assumption that well-educated and trained persons possessing specific types of skills are really unnecessary for sound and effective management and for industrial programs. Until such qualified people emerge in sizable numbers, the outlook for such a society is dim indeed.

Sociological-Cultural Constraints

For operational purposes, sociological-cultural factors or constraints in this study correspond to the dominant human attitudes, values, and beliefs in a given society or country, and the way they tend to influence the motivation, behavior, and performance of individuals working in productive enterprises. Since there may be various subcultures in a particular country, research in this area can be very complex, and overgeneralization can lead to a false view of industrial reality.

There do, however, seem to be a number of sociological-cultural conditions prevalent in most underdeveloped countries which act as significant constraints on managerial effectiveness and industrial development. In fact, it seems that in many cases sociological-cultural constraints are the most significant limiting factors of all in this connection.

If a substantial portion of a country's population does not have sociological-cultural attitudes and values that are conducive to industrial progress, it is unlikely that economic, political, legal, or even educational reforms will prove very effective for industrial progress. It is true that such reforms can do much to change the sociological-cultural environment, but their effectiveness depends on the existence of a significant number of people in the society who have latent or untapped attitudes and values of the proper sort; otherwise, the industrial development process will probably take much longer. For it is generally easier and less time-consuming to make economic, political, legal, and educational changes—even big changes—in a given society than to change the basic attitudes, beliefs, and values of a large number of its citizens. In other words, people per se, on a massive scale, may be the most difficult of all things to change. Of course, some countries have handled social change more effectively, quickly, and dramatically than others.

In general, the prevailing or dominant culture in a given society interacts constantly with that society's industrial enterprises, and no enterprise operates in a vacuum. The activities of work-centered institutions in turn have their impact on the culture as well. For any point in time, the sociological environment produces various constraints—factors taken as given—for the large majority of enterprises operating in a given country.

A major problem here is that sociological-cultural constraints which apparently have a significant bearing on managerial performance are difficult to measure and quantify. While the variables to be discussed below are clearly relevant, it is difficult at times to determine how they affect the operations of industrial enterprises.

More accurate measures of cause-and-effect relationships can generally be determined by studying what people do and why they do it, rather than what they say; but this typically entails costly and time-consuming research if accurate results are to be gained. There has not been a large number of scientific studies of this type, and many more are needed before we can explain or predict with a high degree of accuracy managerial and enterprise performance in terms of sociological-cultural constraints. However, there do seem to be a number of significant sociological-cultural constraints common to underdeveloped countries in general.

View of Managers and Management

Every society has its high-prestige careers and heroes. Some professions and occupations are always considered better than others and are held up to the young as examples of what they might be able to practice if they try hard enough to succeed. Usually, though not always, such occupations are economically better rewarded than other less-esteemed jobs; as a minimum, there would typically be in such occupations some substantial nonmaterial rewards, such as prestige, status, power, or self-gratification.

The place of industrial and business managers in the prestige hierarchy of a particular country is quite relevant in determining managerial effectiveness and the efficiency of productive enterprises. Closely connected to this point is the way in which alternative elite groups are viewed in the culture. If, as is common in underdeveloped countries, traditional elite occupations of the government bureaucracy, the military, the clergy, law, and perhaps medicine are regarded so highly and rewarded so well as to drain off the great majority of the talented and well-educated persons from management, it is obvious that productive enterprise will suffer. The impact of such status ranking will be reflected not only in the recruiting of competent people for management and industrial firms, but also in the way in which managers see themselves and in their influence in society.

Unfortunately, in many underdeveloped countries the personal goals and material gain of managers are not conducive to, but in conflict with, industrial progress, social responsibility, fair treatment, and national achievement. The managers themselves do not view management as a profession; in fact, the dominant view of society at large and of the managers is that management requires no special training, qualifications, or skills—only authority and power—and that managerial jobs need not be filled on the basis of personal ability or objective criteria. Distrust of managers and skepticism about management, as a worthy profession, often linger on in such societies, even long after a more positive managerial philosophy emerges on a fairly widespread basis.

View of Authority, Responsibility, and Subordinates

In underdeveloped countries authority is commonly viewed as an absolute natural right of enterprise managers and other types of formal leaders.

Top-level managers in particular feel that they are born to manage and rule others and that their authority is based on some type of natural law and/or charismatic endowment, rather than a clearly defined role in the organization or the possession of specific skills and knowledge. The effect of this view of authority, in terms of managerial behavior, is typically a high degree of centralization and little delegation of authority within industrial enterprises. Middle- and lower-level managers, as well as workers, are prevented from exerting initiative, and few dare to assume individual responsibility for anything. Hence, there is much buck-passing and blaming of others when something goes wrong, and top-level managers are consulted and asked to approve even minor routine decisions.

Such dominant notions of authority, responsibility, and the role of the subordinate in a given country could perhaps be compatible with a favorable level of managerial effectiveness and productive efficiency only where higher-level enterprise managers are competent, well-motivated, and well-trained men, and where subordinates respect and perform best under a strong, domineering type of leader. The latter condition seems to exist in varying degrees in underdeveloped countries, but few such countries have very many properly qualified managers. A higher degree of participative management, as opposed to a high degree of authoritarianism, might also serve to motivate many of the personnel, particularly the better educated and/or more ambitious, to perform more efficiently even in an underdeveloped country.

Another common view in many underdeveloped countries is that it is natural, proper and/or desirable for enterprise management to independently assume responsibility for the overall welfare of employees. This is often referred to as paternalistic management. In many cases this attitude is not altruistic, but rather necessary for the survival of the firm since there are no other welfare services, facilities, or benefits available to employees. This is related to the social-overhead-capital constraint to be discussed later. Such an arrangement is also particularly common when the transition to industrialization in a particular society does not involve a major break from feudalistic tradition.

Interorganizational and Individual Cooperation

The extent to which various enterprises, organizations, groups, and individuals in any country cooperate voluntarily with one another determines in large part how efficiently the productive system of the nation functions. A society marked by pervasive labor-management conflicts, suspicion between government and firms and among the people employed by firms, and mistrust of motives between intellectuals or educators and businessmen will not normally be as productive in a country as one in which such frictions are minimal.

Every human society needs some cooperation between its members in order to survive. Man is a gregarious animal, and few hermits are able to survive and prosper entirely alone; however, the range and degree of cooperation can vary enormously. All members of the culture are subject to varying pressures, economic, legal, and sociological, to conform and cooperate.

In most countries there appear to be dominant patterns of cooperation with regard to the different categories of organizations involved. Such interorganizational cooperation—or lack of it—is the result of tradition, plus a variety of historical, cultural, and sociological factors, including society's view of industrial managers, management's view of itself, and views toward authority and subordinates.

Interorganizational and individual relationships of the type under study here can have a significant impact on managerial performance, productive efficiency, and hence industrial progress. In underdeveloped countries the impact, more often than not, tends to be negative.

Let us consider union-management relationships as one example. In many of the underdeveloped countries which do have labor unions, there seems to be a basic, deep-seated conflict between management and labor organizations. In many cases such conflict is based to a high degree on ideology, political identification, and class struggle. The unions want to change society—not merely to get more for the worker; and it is generally much more difficult to reach a compromise on ideological as compared to economic issues. Management, as well as labor leaders, is often extremely stubborn, and it often holds to moral principles at the expense of work stoppages, inefficiency, and even profits.

In numerous underdeveloped and newly developing nations, particularly those characterized by political, economic and/or social instability and growing union power, management-union conflicts are pervasive and serious. Labor union unrest and bargaining are frequently based on noneconomic grounds, and sympathy strikes based on remote events or even political moves in other countries tend to be frequent. In many cases there is constant pressure to raise wages without any concern for the economics of the situation, and seniority and political favoritism lead to the creation of unneeded jobs. One is likely to find rather frequent strikes, both official and unofficial; extensive informal restrictive work practices and featherbedding; and probably a great amount of unproductive time, effort, and expense absorbed in politicking and bargaining. The nature of union-management relations is also likely to have a significant bearing on the rate and extent to which more productive technology is developed and introduced by industrial firms, with poor relations acting as a very significant constraint.

Other important dimensions of interorganizational cooperation that will be taken up in Chapter 4 include cooperation between industry and government, educational and research institutions and industry, cooperation among productive firms and within them. It is common for the degree of cooperation in most or all of these spheres to be relatively low in underdeveloped nations.

View of Achievement and Work

Cultures vary widely in their views of productive achievement and work. Work for the sake of work and the will to succeed rank highly in some cultures, of which the American Society is one example—our behavior is based on our Horatio Alger legends, the Calvinist ethic, and several centuries of achievement-oriented tradition.

Few underdeveloped countries show this ambitious attitude toward productive achievement and work. In many such countries, achievement and work not directly associated with economic progress are regarded as the ultimate status symbols. Leisure is a particularly desired status position in many cultures because of its association with wealth: a rich man is an idle man. In other countries, the wealthy engage in work that is artistic, cultural, religious, educational, military, or governmental; they are rarely involved in business and industry. A wealthy man's sons are typically instilled with many of their father's values—which is unfortunate for many underdeveloped countries where it is only the wealthy who can substantially spur industrial progress under the existing political and social order.

Our concern here is achievement only in the economic sense. It is clear that other types of achievement and work in areas such as the arts are important in the formulation of the total culture; but however important such noneconomic activities may be, they are not relevant to our analysis.

In general, the dominant attitude toward achievement and work in underdeveloped countries typically places a highly negative constraint on managerial effectiveness and industrial development, and it is likely to prove vital in raising achievement aspirations in the society and thus quickening the pace of industrial progress and economic growth. The importance of a country's view of achievement and productive work cannot be understated. Indeed, it may be the most critical determinant of all in terms of managerial effectiveness and industrial progress. One outstanding scientific study, based on substantial empirical and experimental evidence, of achievement motivation and economic development has this to say about the subject:

> A concern for achievement as expressed in imaginative literature—folk tales and stories for children—is associated in modern times with a more rapid rate of economic development. The generalization is confirmed not only for Western free-enterprise democracies like England

> and the United States, but also for Communist countries like Russia, Bulgaria or Hungary, or primitive tribes that are just beginning to make contact with modern technological society. . . . In other words, there is a strong suggestion here that men with high achievement motives will find a way to economic achievement given fairly wide variations in opportunity and social structure. What people want, they somehow manage to get, in the main and on the average, though other factors can modify the speed with which they get it.[6]

This pioneer study, unlike most behavioral, cultural, social, and economic studies, emphasized the importance of management and entrepreneurship in economic progress. It is clearly not enough merely to have a population with a high achievement drive—which it typically not the case in underdeveloped countries; such human resources must be effectively combined and coordinated through able management if there is to be substantial industrial progress. In particular, both industrial managers and those they manage must, in sizable numbers, have a favorable view of achievement and work.

It should be stressed that it is not essential that an individual be solely concerned with self-interest and his own personal achievement for him to work hard, although in extensively Calvinistic countries, individual achievement is highly valued and may be the chief reason for diligence. In various countries, the individual's identification with a commitment to some notion of collective or even national achievement may result in hard work. For example, in the United States the primary emphasis is generally on individual achievement; in Japan it is on group or enterprise achievement and on national achievement, which may also play a more critical role there than in the United States. In various Communist countries emphasis on hard work to gain either individual, collective, or national achievement has contributed substantially to industrial progress, but there are differences in this regard among Communist countries, largely because of ideological reasons. For example, the Soviet Union has stressed all three levels of achievement, with greater emphasis on individual achievement evolving in recent times. Red China has oscillated between emphasizing and de-emphasizing individual achievement during different periods since 1949.

Industrial managers with a high achievement drive would be inclined to desire and strive to accomplish fairly challenging, but realistic, enterprise plans and objectives. Such objectives would typically pertain to some notion of greater output, sales, productivity, efficiency, and/or profitability. Such managers would also be more likely to take calculated rational risks, to innovate, and to be quite favorably disposed to change in the direction of greater economic progress, so long as innovation and change are not in substantial conflict with their other operational goals.[7] It appears that there are typically relatively few managers of this type in underdeveloped countries.

In a society that is oriented toward achievement and productive work it is generally easier for industry to recruit personnel who are willing to work reasonably hard and efficiently. Where the culture is not achievement-oriented in the economically productive sense, even highly competent managers and effective leaders may well have greater difficulty in motivating personnel to work hard and efficiently than would less able managers and leaders in an achievement-oriented country. Moreover, in a culture where achievement is highly valued, both managers and workers would tend to put considerable effort into self-development and improvement of their qualifications, so that their performance will be better in the future.

A country's system of formal education undoubtedly has an impact on the achievement level of the population. Education usually corresponds quite closely to the cultural, religious, and ideological values prevailing in the culture. If there is a generally negative attitude toward achievement and productive work, the educational system would tend to reinforce this attitude, and here again many underdeveloped countries are caught in a vicious circle.

Class Structure and Individual Mobility

If a country deliberately or unconsciously prevents a substantial majority of citizens from entering the ranks of management or other responsible industrial jobs, there is likely to be a negative impact on managerial effectiveness—in many if not most industrial enterprises—and on industrial progress. Where certain large religious groups, races, or castes are excluded from various business and industrial careers, including management, the constraint on the staffing function is clear. The same is true where people are either extensively favored or discriminated against for various jobs, not on the basis of personal ability but solely because of family connections, nepotism, social background, educational institution attended, political affiliation, age, or sex.

Clearly no country is without some such prejudices, but it does appear that generally such prejudices tend to be most pervasive and significant in less developed countries. In such situations it may be possible to bend local custom and attitudes to some extent, but gross violations may, in the short run, be very risky and costly; they may lead to considerable instability, insecurity, friction, and general unrest among enterprise personnel accustomed to certain staffing procedures and to a certain status or class hierarchy linked to various occupations. This would tend to be even more true in a poor country where there is considerable unemployment and relatively few opportunities for advancement. In such an environment, disregard for the traditional class structure in staffing various positions and selecting persons for promotion—or even in connection with wage and salary scales—could also result in a destructively informal organization.

Individual mobility of the horizontal kind may also have a significant bearing on economic development. If cultural values and tradition prevent most individuals in a given country from relocating to other enterprises or communities which offer opportunities for them to use their talents more fully and effectively in other jobs, this barrier can hamper industrial progress over a period of time. In traditional rural cultures in particular, such as those found in Africa, there tends to be virtually no individual mobility. Here, urbanization in the economy does tend to increase class and individual mobility, but this typically takes considerable time.

View of Wealth and Material Gain

Throughout most of the world today, wealth—individual and particularly national wealth—tends to be considered a desirable thing, and those who have it are envied. But in most countries some, and frequently much, weight is given to the means through which an individual obtains his wealth, income, and assets—some methods of acquiring wealth are socially unacceptable. In a given society if the rich or relatively prosperous are highly regarded and if industrial management and entrepreneurship are considered a respectable path to riches, the profession in industry is likely to benefit by the participation of an elite group.

Traditionally, however, a man who has earned his money as a merchant or manufacturer has been less highly regarded in most societies than one who has earned his income from the land in farming and/or various traditional high-prestige professions. In some societies there were, and in some cases still are, religious or ideological taboos placed on income derived from interest on capital and/or business profits. Most enviable of all, throughout much of the world historically—including many European countries in earlier times—has been the man who had an unearned income through land rents or inheritance or because of his aristocratic or noble position. This set of values grew in the period when wealth was mostly in land and acquired through inheritance or birthright, but it has persisted well into the modern era in many societies, particularly underdeveloped countries. Such attitudes serve as significant constraints upon efficient industrial staffing and hence industrial progress. The traditional prestige occupations continue to drain off most of the capable, educated persons in the society, and industrial enterprise is left in large part with the dregs.

The dominant attitude toward wealth and material gain among members of the business managerial class in a given country also has a significant bearing on economic progress. Incomes and profits may be desired by managers only for what they can buy outside of the business, or they may be viewed in part as a symbol of achievement and success to be largely reinvested in order to expand the business. The former attitude tends to be dominant in many underdeveloped countries; industry-created wealth would tend to be expended primarily on conspicuous-consumption items, material status symbols, and/or pursuits of a social status higher than that associated with business activity. Managers of this type would tend to have a fairly low achievement drive and would be inclined to pursue an egocentric, conservative, and essentially noninnovating course in operating their enterprises, typically stressing immediate profits through rapid turnover of capital. Instead of using their incomes and profits to expand their firms, such managers typically prefer to speculate and invest in land, goods, and, at times, foreign stocks in more advanced and stable countries.

This type of attitude among the managerial class is common in many African, Asian, and Latin American countries. The situation is vividly described as follows by one authoritative source:

> The prevalent orientation toward money making is different in a typical Asian or African or Latin American nation from our own. The psychology of most businessmen is not that of the Western entrepreneur. It is more that of the bazaar merchant. Not large-scale production and long-term return, but fast trading and quick profit are the usual objectives. Nor is this surprising in an economic environment where much business tends to be petty and transient, and in which even big business depends for its profits more on the vagaries of international commodity fluctuations than on the slow improvement of the domestic market.[8]

Both the societal and managerial attitude toward wealth and material gain are more conducive to industrial progress in substantially Calvinistic societies than in typical underdeveloped countries. Calvinism or the Protestant ethic stresses as supreme virtues not only hard work and achievement but also thriftiness. It discourages expenditures of income on luxury items of conspicuous consumption and insists that funds saved should be invested, either in productive ventures or charitable works; children are taught these virtues at the earliest possible age. On the economic level, this ethic has traditionally come to mean that an individual should be motivated largely by monetary stimuli.

In Marxist countries, including China, the state rather than the individual follows the "Calvinist" ethic by replacing private thrift and accumulation with state investment in order to expand production and industry. However, China in particular has oscillated in its use of monetary stimuli as a motivating force for managers and other industrial personnel because of ideological reasons. (More of this in the next chapter.)

In many newly developing countries that are not basically Marxist, the state is also playing the major role in capital accumulation and investment for industrial expansion. A major problem remains, in most cases, at the industrial enterprise level where the managers and other personnel still often lack the achievement drive and attitude toward wealth and material gain which are essential to a high level of managerial effectiveness and industrial progress.

The way that the typical nonmanagerial industrial employee or worker tends to view money and material gain in a given culture can have a significant bearing on productive efficiency. Here Maslow's famous hypothesis of human motivation and the hierarchy of human needs is relevant.[9] Modern psychology suggests that new human needs take priority when former or higher-level basic needs are reasonably satisfied. Human needs are generally recognized to be placed in some order, with economic-security needs preceding social needs and needs for satisfying the ego (psyche or self-expression). Wealth and material gain relate most directly to physiological needs; money serves to satisfy such basic needs as hunger, shelter, and clothing.

In probably the large majority of the less-developed and even semi-advanced nations, regardless of the stated goals of their elites, much if not most of the working population, having entered the material-acquisition stage, are likely to be highly money-conscious and materialistic. In such countries, material rewards linked to productivity performance in industrial firms can prove very effective in terms of industrial progress. A major obstacle here is that enterprise managements, in numerous cases, are ignorant of this fact and/or do not have the proper training or motivation to design and implement potentially effective employee incentive and compensation programs.

As we shall discuss in the following chapters, Communist China is a peculiar country, indeed, in terms of the hierarchy of human needs and individual material gain. Its ideology is not compatible with Maslow's theory, and at times neither is its behavior. The regime seems to follow an oscillation theory in connection with monetary incentives.

View of Scientific Method

Scientific method here refers to the methodology developed for the analysis of various problems in the physical and social sciences. Critical to this notion is the idea that events can be described, explained, predicted, and controlled. The thinking runs, If we do A, then *B* will occur, with the idea that the hypothesis can be verified by trying A to see if *B* in fact occurs. If it does not, a new hypothesis might be proposed and tried. Another way of looking at this problem is to suggest that Event X depends on factors *y* and *z*, and then to relate, mathematically if possible, the relationship between the variables. Once hypothesized, the prediction is verified by observation, experience, and/or experimentation. This kind of thinking is not ancient. It dates back essentially to seventeenth-century England, mainly to the writings of Sir Francis Bacon, although limited effective use was made of scientific method in earlier periods, most notably by the Greeks, Romans, Chinese, and Arabs. All of the major technical and scientific gains in the past few centuries have been made by application of this type of scientific method. More recently, the same methodology has been applied to the social and behavioral sciences, with considerably less meaningful results. Even here, however, considerable progress has been made, particularly in the Western world. The major difficulty here is in trying to experiment, predict, or control events in a situation where extraneous variables cannot be eliminated from the system, as in economics, management, sociology, or psychology. But in any case, the notion of observing a system, proposing various hypotheses about the behavior within the system, and checking results is central to scientific methodology. This type of thinking tends to be so common in advanced countries today that it is taken for granted in literally millions of relatively simple situations. Managers, technicians, machinists, electricians, salesmen, in addition to persons working in hundreds of other types of occupations, apply this technique or way of thinking without even considering what methodology they are using.

Hence a typical American skilled worker will plan his work, thinking intuitively: if *A* then *B*. In fact, even relatively routine types of skilled work involves such thinking on a fairly complex level which becomes apparent if one looks closely at the type of work such a person does. An American electrician does not use, as a matter of course, Number 14 wire for 220-volt circuits because to do so would be a failure to predict burnouts, short circuits, and fire hazards. Similarly an American machinist is inclined to make sure that his equipment is oiled at regular intervals, lest it function improperly and eventually break down. Only when one has lived in a culture where such apparently trivial rules are frequently violated does he realize and appreciate the nature of such an attitude and preconditioning in workmen and other personnel in advanced countries.

In management, in advanced countries, the use of scientific methodology is even more pronounced. Managers spend much time in predicting what will happen, given certain conditions, and in trying to prevent undesirable results by adapting to or changing the conditions. If we change x dollars per unit, how will this relate to sales, profits, and costs? If we introduce Project A, how much financing will be required, and what will the net effect over time be? If we introduce new equipment p, how much will costs go down? If we introduce this incentive system, will productivity increase x units? To fill job opening q effectively we need a man with qualifications *x*, *y*, and *z*. The whole area of planning and decision making is basically this sort of activity, as is much of control, staffing, organization, and direction. In the functional business area—i.e., production, marketing, research and development, finance, and so on—a prime consideration is that the manager will be able to predict events and eventually control them as far as possible through his adaptation to and manipulation of his environment.

In general, underdeveloped countries typically do not have a very scientific view of the world because of various religious, ideological, cultural, and educational factors. Scientific method is basically a future-oriented, revolutionary way of looking at one's environment—it implies that somehow one can alter his environment through conscious action. In many cultures, such an attitude would tend to be considered heretical, unsound, and even dangerous. Because of the view that God or His equivalent, and not puny man, is responsible for the future, managerial competence, as well as science and engineering, comes close to interference with established religious order. Few young persons in such a culture are trained to think scientifically, and this deficiency is revealed in the way in which firms operate and are managed and in the way the economy functions. Things run out of control much of the time, and it is difficult to plan effectively for the future. There is a vicious circle operating here: Since relatively few persons or organizations make much use of scientific method in planning, plans tend not to work out, pessimism becomes prevalent, and people become even more reluctant to plan for the future.

To be mystical and/or emotional in regard to many areas of human experience is probably a powerful force in most people in the world. However productivity, managerial effectiveness, and economic progress all lie in the rational, scientific realm. No one ever built or ran a railroad, a steel mill, or a shoe factory with even a modicum of efficiency with prayers or emotions alone. For that matter, no enterprise ever solved a budgetary, production, engineering, or marketing problem with prayers or emotion. This type of problem is solved effectively and efficiently only with consistent, sound applications of scientific methodology and thinking. One of the more critical problems throughout the underdeveloped world at this point is the inexorable conflict between the widespread use of scientific method elsewhere in the world and the reluctance of many members, if not the vast majority, of underdeveloped countries to recognize and accept this methodology with all its implications in all phases of human endeavor.

View of Risk Taking

Risk is an inherent part of economic activity. Since productive operations are necessarily forward-oriented in time and involve at least some degree of uncertainty, any economy and any industrial firm must assume some risks. The dominant view of risk taking and resulting risk-taking behavior at the national, enterprise, and individual levels in underdeveloped countries seems to serve typically as a significant constraint on managerial effectiveness and industrial progress.

There are two dimensions of risk taking of interest here: (a) rationality and its boundaries and (b) degree of aggressiveness or conservatism. Let us deal with the former first. Rational risk taking in the truly optimum sense defies precise definition. Human beings and organizations are typically at least somewhat limited in knowledge, information, foresight, skill, and time in arriving at decisions involving uncertainty and estimates of the future. It is essentially a matter of semantics whether the process of rational risk taking and decision making is a "satisisficing" or maximizing process. In spite of these conceptual problems it still makes sense to talk in terms of the degree and boundaries of rationality in risk taking and decision making. The degree to which risk taking is rational in a given situation would be dependent on the degree and extent to which the following conditions are present:

(1) The decision is based on the realities of the situation, including a well-reasoned evaluation of the relevant facts which are available. (At times the evaluation may be the result of basically unconscious thought processes.)

(2) The decision is based on logical assumptions and carefully calculated courses of action with weighted estimates of the potential risks and probabilities of success involved. Such weighting may be essentially unconscious or conscious, depending on the significance and uniqueness of the decision and the related risks involved.

Hence, rational risk taking and the effectiveness of risk taking depend largely on the level of skill in applying scientific method, knowledge, and the availability and uses of pertinent information. The boundaries of rational risk taking may be enlarged through better education and through the generation and provision of more relevant information that the decision maker can draw upon, and by creating a more favorable attitude toward the scientific method.

Many basically rational persons in various countries may, for example, expose themselves to typhoid fever by drinking impure water because they are not aware there is a potential connection between disease and water. Here the boundaries of rationality are clearly defined by lack of knowledge. On the other hand an individual, because of mystical, religious, or other purely emotional forces, may behave irrationally and drink impure water even if he is aware that he may become ill. In a similar manner, managers and politicians in various countries—particularly underdeveloped ones—take risks that seem highly irrational and strange to Americans. They may take such risks either because they are in fact irrational in their decisions, which depend on mysticism, faith, or ideology, or because they lack the knowledge, information, motivation, and/or skill necessary for adequate evaluation of the risks entailed. In the latter situation, it is also possible that relevant information may be available but is not utilized because of lack of knowledge of its existence.

A major problem in many underdeveloped countries is that risk taking —both macro and micro—bearing on industrial enterprise performance often tends to be quite irrational, and probably even more frequently the boundaries of rationality are very narrow. In such an environment, managerial effectiveness and productive efficiency would be significantly hampered, and one can expect to find much in the way of idle and underemployed resources, wasteful production, and considerable unproductive time and effort in a relatively large proportion of productive enterprises. Many of the elements of the management process would probably be performed in a relatively inefficient manner. The planning function in particular is directly related to the degree to which risk taking is rational and effective.

The second dimension of risk taking pertains to the degree of conservatism or aggressiveness. Here individual preferences toward risk taking under similar conditions can be measured in order to determine general attitude and degree of conservatism or aggressiveness. Available evidence to date suggests that in terms of managerial effectiveness and industrial progress, managers (and other persons) possessing a relatively high achievement drive tend to be the best risk takers. They tend to be neither highly conservative nor overly aggressive and speculative. As was pointed out earlier, they are inclined to undertake moderate, calculated risks— given their boundaries of rationality—which entail some challenge but at the same time a relatively good chance of payoff and success. Such persons also tend to prefer moderately ambitious operational objectives and plans and would be inclined to innovate—assuming that other constraints do not substantially act against innovation—in order to improve performance and results.

The highly conservative or ultraconservative risk taker is likely to have a low achievement drive, although in some cases such conservatism may be due to nonsociological-cultural factors, such as various economic, political, or legal constraints operating on him or his firm. The highly conservative risk taker would also tend to oppose innovation, change, and expansion of courses of action, and enterprises under this type of management would be likely to remain quite static.

If a substantial portion of the managers or political leaders in a given country are explicitly or implicitly willing to frequently take long chances, it is likely that through a period of time losses will outweigh gains and their firms as well as the country will be poorer and less efficient as a result. Conversely, if managers and politicians tend to be overly cautious and conservative and hence are unwilling to take virtually any kind of meaningful risk, the individual firm and ultimately the country will be unable to make productive gains. The former situation will be revealed by excessive and widespread business losses and possibly failures, resulting in considerable waste and inefficiency, while the latter will emerge as a situation where firms and the country fall behind their foreign rivals and fail to substantially expand useful outputs and increase productive efficiency. A reasonable balance between conservative and aggressive risk taking throughout the economy is essential for a relatively high level of managerial effectiveness and industrial progress, although such a balance is not subject to precise measurement. Underdeveloped countries are typically characterized in this regard by serious imbalances of one or both extremes.

In general, the ideal environment in terms of risk taking, as it relates to managerial effectiveness and economic progress, would be one in which there is a favorable view toward scientific method, achievement, and change; an extensive and diverse system of high-quality education at all levels; and a high degree of interorganizational and individual cooperation which permits the extensive generation, dissemination, and utilization of information and knowledge relevant to individual, industrial enterprise, and national decision making. Underdeveloped countries typically are faced with very significant negative constraints in all of the above areas which bear on effective rational risk taking.

View of Change

The initiation and implementation of change—be it technical, economic, social, educational, political, legal, or managerial in nature—is of course essentially a human process. Changes, however large, that are desired by the people involved can usually be implemented quite effectively and assimilated with little social disruption. Changes, even quite small ones, that are not acceptable or desired can be put into effect only at considerable social, personal, and often economic cost.[10] As a prominent anthropologist has pointed out:

> We have learned the pleasing truth, that society talks back. Even the small-scale, technologically inferior peoples of the world have tremendous powers to resist changes they do not want, and to adhere, often at great cost, to their valued and distinct way of life. At the same time, we have learned that changes which people desire, radical or not, can be made swiftly, without great cost, and that a society may nearly redo itself—in a generation—if it wants to.[11]

Japan, and Russia after 1917 (and as we shall see in the following chapters, China after 1949), are examples of the latter type of society; numerous countries throughout the underdeveloped and newly developing world correspond to the former type.

While those holding political power, intellectuals, business entrepreneurs, managers of all types, and/or external forces may be the key potential initiators of change in a given society, the effective implementation of change does, in the final analysis, generally depend on its acceptance by the people involved and affected. Hence, the rate and extent of actual change in the direction of greater managerial effectiveness and industrial progress in a particular country depend not only on the presence of initiators of change who desire such progress, but also on the acceptance of such change by the persons involved.

In general, resistance to change by enterprise managers, as well as workers, in underdeveloped and perhaps most newly developing countries is pervasive and strong. In many such countries conformity is considered a virtue while nonconformity is viewed with considerable suspicion. In the private sector highly inefficient firms frequently survive and reap easy profits with little or no change or improvement in operations over a period of time, because of the sellers' markets and generally protective environments in which they function. Subsistence-level worker wages—and also labor legislation regarding dismissals in some countries—serve as a deterrent to the introduction of modern equipment and technical processes. Businessmen in such environments typically become psychologically and culturally adjusted to poverty, apathy, economic stagnation, and backwardness, and the status quo. In larger firms and in the public sector, authority and responsibility tend to be highly centralized; consequently there is little or no flexibility or authority at lower levels which would permit the introduction of minor changes in operations.

In some underdeveloped and frustrated developing nations a major revolution by the discontented may be seen as the only path by which substantial social change and economic progress can be brought about. A Communist revolution and takeover in a given country typically leads to quite rapid and extensive social change, often at the expense of great human sacrifice and suffering. Individual desires tend to be subordinated to the interests of the states and its rulers, and personal freedom is greatly restricted. At the same time, however, a conscious and vigorous effort is typically made to shape an environment conducive to greater managerial effectiveness and industrial progress. If a substantial portion of the population desires such progress and is willing to accept drastic reforms, considerable gains are likely to be made. However, where ideology takes extreme precedence over rationality in environmental changes—as has periodically been the case in Red China in particular—managerial effectiveness and industrial progress are likely to suffer considerably.

Legal-Political Constraints

Productive enterprises must operate in some type of legal and political environment, like other types of social organizations. Laws must generally (but far from always) be obeyed and political factors taken into account in business decision making and operations. Our argument is that political and legal constraints directly affect the internal operations of productive enterprises, and hence managerial effectiveness and industrial progress. A given law, or political event, can cause firms to shift the way the critical elements of the management process are performed and hence directly affect the firms' efficiency.

Our purpose here is to consider briefly some of the critical types of legal and political constraints that tend to be common in underdeveloped countries.

Relevant Legal Rules of the Game

Any society has a legal code, written or traditional, which bears directly on the operations of productive enterprises. Included in relevant legal structures are such codes as general business law, tax law, labor law, and general law which may have some relevance to business.

General and business law includes such items as rules governing property rights, the law of contract, and similar matters. Depending on the country, this law can range from simple traditional religious or tribal law, generally defining the rights of parties, to elaborate and complex legal codes, covering all phases of these subjects exhaustively. The degree of codification generally follows other developments in a country, in the sense that as literacy, incomes, and living standards rise, law tends to become more organized and complex. The judicial process itself, in terms of organization of courts, systems of judicial appeal, qualifications of judges, and similar matters, tends to become equally complex—and probably more predictable—as a society finds need for such organization.

It is common to find in underdeveloped countries that much or most of the law has not yet been formally codified, and this tends to make business activity subject to considerable uncertainty. Unclear laws, difficulties in interpretation, and erratic or ununiform enforcement make the planning process difficult for firms and their managers. Law enforcement is often dishonest and corrupt and inefficient firms frequently gain, while more efficient ones suffer in such an environment. For example, black-marketing activities that are inefficient and unproductive for the economy may be tolerated. Many laws are unsound for managerial effectiveness and industrial progress. In general, the legal environments of many underdeveloped countries lead to considerable uncertainty and to less overall efficiency in productive enterprises.

Labor law in countries of all types is now complex, and its provisions have a direct impact on firm and managerial functions. Among other important restraints, labor legislation applies to hours and conditions of work, unemployment compensation schemes, tenure and job security requirements, employer responsibility for the health and welfare of employees, and other similar provisions. In poorer countries where labor laws provide industrial personnel with better wages, working conditions, and welfare benefits, these laws can have a positive effect on industrial progress by producing a more energetic, better-motivated work force. In the more stagnant underdeveloped countries which do little or nothing in the way of enacting and enforcing such legislation, the working population is likely to remain straitjacketed by apathy.

In many poorer countries, the supply of ill-trained and unskilled labor far exceeds demand, and many such countries have tried to protect workers through such devices as indemnity pay, tenure requirements, and minimum wages. The laws frequently tend to be self-defeating, however, since they provide an incentive for firms to avoid long-term employees as much as possible. Getting in an economic downturn with such labor can wreck the firm. Since few firms in such countries have ever calculated the cost of labor turnover, this method of circumventing legal requirements is not seen as expensive—which in fact it is.

Minimum-wage legislation in poor countries is not without its problems. A typical result of such legislation is to cause firms, particularly private enterprises, to shift their combination of factor inputs by using less labor and more capital. By placing a higher price on less-skilled manpower, this tends to make more highly skilled labor even more scarce since this type of employee is required in more heavily capitalized plants, while it makes the less-skilled type of worker even more abundant.

In underdeveloped and developing countries, which are not basically Marxist in nature, the absence of effective laws regulating competition and formation of business combinations in restraint of trade tends to serve as a significant constraint on productive efficiency and economic progress. Many inefficient firms tend to engage in monopolistic behavior in an environment of sellers' markets and government protection. In such an environment, costs tend to be higher than necessary, product quality and efficiency low, and the needs and requirements of customers frequently ignored. This type of environment is common in poorer countries, and effective antitrust and cartel legislation could in many cases reduce inefficiencies.

Flexibility of Law and Legal Changes

Law tends to be conservative, seeking precedents for action; and this tendency conflicts with the necessity of being able to keep pace with the rapid changes demanded in an emerging modern industrial state. Ultraconservatism, and in fact stagnation, regarding laws in many underdeveloped countries hinders them from substantially increasing managerial effectiveness and industrial progress. Here social change is required in order to bring about legal changes more conducive to better management and industrialization. The law books of virtually any country are full of anachronistic rules which presently serve no purpose and in fact often retard desirable action. The problem is particularly acute in poor countries ruled by dynastic elites or basically malevolent military dictatorships.

Ultimately, resistance to necessary legal change prevents change of all kinds. Consider a situation, which is not unknown in various countries, in which railroads or roads are being built and the right of eminent domain is not part of the law. Unless the law is modified, it will probably be impossible to build the roads or railroads, since the problems of negotiating purchases of land rights of way from thousands of individual landholders will be virtually insurmountable. Unless legal strictures can be removed, no development will take place, the railroad or construction firm will not even be able to commence operations, and productive firms in the area will suffer greatly in their roles as suppliers and customers. In fact, new firms would be discouraged from starting operations. Similarly, it may turn out that a country badly needs a modern corporation law (with limited liability and immortality for firms) in order to allow the framework necessary to the creation of fairly large companies. In the absence of changes in law, the large enterprises may never come into being, and the development process may well be aborted at the outset.

Another important problem in many poorer countries is the question of certainty of law enforcement. Any prosecutor has options about how the law will be interpreted and enforced. If it is too nebulous and flexible it is likely to cause considerable uncertainty for business enterprise; if it is too rigid and stagnant it will not be able to cope properly with changing business conditions. Only if the enforcement process is reasonably consistent, fair, and equal can productive efficiency lean in the direction of maximization.

Unduly frequent and unpredictable changes in law enforcement activity or focus can also have extensive impacts on productive enterprises in the direction of lower managerial effectiveness. The planning process is directly affected by such problems because, in laying out fairly long-term policies and programs on such key issues as firm expansion and the ways in which this is to be accomplished, knowledge of legality of the plans for a given contemplated period is crucial. In many countries, prosecution of law violations may depend more on who is influential than on the law, and productive efficiency suffers accordingly. In general, a major problem in numerous underdeveloped and developing countries in particular, is one of balanced flexibility of law and timely legal changes.

Defense and Military Policy

All countries have some defense posture, ranging from such massive military establishments as are found in the United States and Russia to the small ceremonial guard forming the major defense force in such countries as Monaco. Advanced nations obviously can much better afford large defense and military expenditures than poorer countries, but numerous underdeveloped and developing nations also spend a large portion of their incomes and resources on this sector, often for childish, illogical, or purely emotional reasons. The result is a great drain of critically scarce managerial, technical, and skilled worker talent, materials, equipment, and financial resources from civilian production. This of course greatly constrains managerial effectiveness and productive efficiency in nondefense areas. It is true that military expenditures do show up in GNP and national income accounts, but they do little, if anything, to improve living standards in poorer countries.

Another potential impact of defense policy is linked closely to sociological views about the desirability of the various professions and class mobility. Relevant here is the notion that in some countries only a military career is desirable for sons of the elite class. Relatively poor Latin American countries, as well as many poor countries in Asia and Africa, have been noted for maintaining large defense forces far in excess of any reasonable need for them. Often this is due to the insecurity of the ruling elites. It is not uncommon to find that half of the budgets of such countries go to the military, although the nation may have not had a war for fifty years. Here the pressures of military men to build up their prestige, particularly in comparison with their counterparts in nearby countries, is evident. If country X obtains an aircraft carrier or new jet fighter planes, country Y must also have one, for prestige reasons which are quite obscure to outsiders. The usual result is a relatively low level of managerial effectiveness and industrial progress throughout most of the economy. The major impact of big military expenditures in poor countries at the enterprise level is usually on production, research and development procurement and finance, as well as staffing and organization.

Foreign Policy

In its relationships with other countries, a nation will be faced with various political, economic, and social decisions affecting the lives of virtually all its citizens. Such decisions also have direct impact on the internal activities and performance of business enterprises. In underdeveloped or developing countries interested in industrial progress, trade with foreign countries is particularly crucial because they are usually not nearly as self-sufficient as advanced nations. They may have a few commodities in more than abundant supply—such as oil, sugar, coffee, tea, cotton, copper, and gold—because of benevolent factor endowment; these must be exported in order to earn the foreign exchange required to import various types of industrial materials, equipment, consumer goods, and so forth. The less diverse the industrial base of a given country, the more crucial the import problem becomes for industrial progress.

Some countries refuse to engage in potentially productive trade, both import and export, with various other countries because of real or imagined defense and security reasons, or ideology, or other emotional rather than rational factors. This means that critically scarce items are often imported elsewhere at greater cost or not at all, and the efficiency of the firms which are the users or potential users of such items suffer. For similar reasons a number of countries do not engage in educational, technical, or other types of exchange programs with various foreign countries, and in the case of less developed countries in particular great potential gains in productive efficiency and industrial progress are lost.

In underdeveloped and developing countries it may make good sense to protect new industries through tariffs and import quotas so that they can develop and eventually become relatively efficient producers. A real difficulty here is that the protection of local firms need not necessarily lead to a more efficient productive system or greater managerial effectiveness, especially if managers lack the drive or capability to improve performance substantially over a period of time. It is common that, in such cases, protected managements, not having to fear what external competition will do if they make mistakes, tend to become more sloppy in their internal operations. This is even more likely if there are inadequate pressures—economic, social, cultural, legal, or political—within the country which make them strive for greater efficiency and progress.

In many less developed countries enterprises in monopolistic or tight oligopolistic positions, and which are highly protected from foreign competition through tariffs and import controls, are more noted for high costs and prices, inept management, and inferior workmanship than they are for their contributions to national welfare. Here a real conflict often arises, as individuals and governments are torn between their desire to obtain the best at the lowest prices and their desire to protect jobs, prestige, and welfare at home.

Numerous countries, especially those striving to develop rapidly, have exchange controls in effect which require firms to obtain licenses for imports. The usual pattern in such cases is that the firm has to apply for licenses for a wide range of items needed by the firm. After review of the application, the exchange authority issues permits or rejects the application.

The complexities of the industrial process frequently lead to serious difficulty, including a great deal of uncertainty for enterprise managers which makes it difficult for them to plan and control efficiently, and to staff and organize operations. Production managers generally know exactly why they may need a Carborundum cutting wheel of a certain size or grade, but this need is not immediately obvious to the nontechnician in the exchange-control governmental bureaucracy. Any manufacturing plant needs an incredible variety of bits and pieces of specialized items, the absence of any one of which may cause the factory to curtail operations. While these items are not typically expensive individually, in aggregate they may represent a fairly large foreign exchange drain; and government planners are likely to take a very dim view of unrestricted imports. The result is frequently likely to be a great deal of supply uncertainty on critical items which leads to costly plant-down time, changes in plans, use of high-cost local substitutes, and often inefficient vertical integration of production.

Numerous countries that have been under colonial or semicolonial rule failed to develop industrially in large part because the dominant foreign power or powers insisted on importing most machinery, equipment, components, and other manufactured goods from their own countries. The dominated poorer country typically engaged primarily in agro-industry, involving simple processing, mining, and traditional textile industries and much handicraft production; secondary manufacturing, modern heavy industry in general, and diverse industrial production were generally suppressed in order to provide a market for the dominant foreign powers. Any relatively large-scale industrial frame that did exist locally was typically under foreign ownership and control. At times a favored subcultural group of local entrepreneurs was fostered by the foreign officials and the local ruling elite, and they were permitted to organize and run fairly large-scale manufacturing plants, typically as monopolies or tight oligopolies.

China before 1949 was in effect a semicolonial power of the type described above.

Political Stability

This constraint usually affects planning more than any other managerial function. The complex and often tenuous interconnections between government and business are difficult enough to maintain in a stable environment, where firms have a pretty clear picture of the government's policies, personalities, and actions. Even slow and evolutionary developments, such as routine changes in policies toward corporate registrations, can have an unsettling effect on firms. The most stable governments are rarely completely static, as close examination of any modern stable state will demonstrate. Change is necessary, but it creates a variety of problems for productive enterprises.

Where political change is frequent, abrupt, descriptive, and/or violent, however—as is common throughout much of Africa, Asia, and Latin America—enterprises are often placed at a serious disadvantage in terms of productivity. Where the new political party that overthrows the previous one has a substantially different ideology or philosophy, the impact on business and industrial enterprise is likely to be even more disruptive.

A revolution of the Indonesian, Cuban, Syrian, or Algerian type has such a dramatic effect on planning, staffing, control, and organization of productive enterprises that they almost invariably show declines in productivity in such a situation. Countries racked by frequent and violent revolutions, rapid changes of government and policy, and similarly disruptive forces seldom are noted for efficient productive enterprises or for industrial progress. The proper organization and functioning of any firm involves, among other things, fairly long-term arrangements with suppliers, customers, labor, and government; and any factors which tend to disrupt such arrangements typically lead to low efficiency. Any effective planning very far ahead is difficult or impossible in such circumstances.

Political Organization

The nature and organization of political parties can have considerable impact on the operation of business and industrial enterprises. One- or two- or even three-party systems are typically more stable than multiparty governments based on ever-shifting coalitions, and they tend to lead to better planning possibilities for firms. The existence of a large number of parties usually means that at least one of them will be violently antibusiness—which may lead to considerable uncertainty about the course of action to take because it may be subject to public debate. Plant closures, reductions of staffs, new factory sites, key price changes, and similar business decisions might not be questioned seriously in a one- or two-party state, but such decisions may become the focal point of disapproval when made by a minority party.

However, in many underdeveloped and developing countries having a basically one-party system, such as Egypt, Ghana, Burma, and Haiti, if the party—which may essentially be the tool of a dictatorship—is significantly antibusiness, managerial effectiveness and industrial progress would tend to suffer because of governmental legislation and pressures. Moreover, if the government is not interested in or committed to industrial progress, little will be done to create an overall environment conducive to greater progress. This is typical of traditional dynastic societies and many military dictatorships that may operate under some political party banner. Communist states are basically one-party systems, but here the generalization on efficiency would not apply because the regime is usually very interested in rapid industrial progress.

In developing countries and communist states in particular, one commonly finds an extremely bureaucratic and/or highly centralized system of political organization which serves as a significant constraint on managerial effectiveness in various ways. The inability to get reasonably fast or predictable decisions from the government bureaucracy on crucial matters, such as resource allocations, import and export allowances, foreign exchange, prices, expansion approvals, and government contracts, make planning, control, organization, staffing, direction, and the various productive functions much more difficult for firms and their managements to perform effectively and efficiently. In some countries the net effect, in terms of the total economy, of having a bureaucratic and/or centralized system of political organization may be positive, given the great shortages of all kinds of resources that exist. But probably more often than not, the net effect is negative because bureaucratic centralization gets out of control; many of the bureaucrats are incompetent in their jobs; priorities are unclear; and corruption, favoritism, emotionalism and/or ideology rather than objective criteria dominate.

Economic Constraints

Basic Economic System

Every society has to develop some type of basic economic organization to answer the fundamental economic questions: What kinds of goods and services are to be produced? How much of each kind? By whom? For whom? This is essentially the problem of resource allocation discussed briefly in Chapter 1, which dealt with economic organization in the United States and Red China. No society is wealthy enough to give all citizens all of the goods or services they may want. Given this fundamental constraint, some form of rationing of scarce resources must be developed at both the producer and consumer levels.

There are two basic types of economic systems available for handling this resource-allocation problem: capitalist (involving free enterprise) and communist, or Marxist. The former allocates resources primarily through a competitive market-price system where firms pursue profits as a major objective and individuals pursue self-interest. The latter allocates resources primarily through some type of state planning where enterprise profits have not typically provided a very meaningful measure of economic efficiency, and where the interests of the state and its planners frequently take precedence over individual self-interest. Virtually all economies have at least some elements of both capitalist and communist economic systems, although in most countries one or the other forms a distinctly dominant pattern.

However, in contemporary times a growing number of "mixed" economies have emerged, particularly in developing countries, where substantial elements of both competitive market prices and state planning exist. For example, India, Pakistan, Ghana, and Yugoslavia may be placed in this category. Often such countries refer to themselves as socialist states, even though there may be a considerable amount of private property ownership.

It is common to associate private property ownership with capitalism and hence with a competitive market-price system and the pursuit of profits. Communism is generally associated with public property and resource allocation through state planning, but there is no inherent reason why a basically communist country in which industrial enterprises are state-owned cannot make extensive or even dominant use of competitive market prices and the pursuit of profits as key economic regulators in allocating resources. In fact, Yugoslavia is just such a country.[12] It would appear then that one chief reason that other communist states have not, until very recently, followed the path of Yugoslavia is ideological and/or political.

It is our thesis that in a relatively backward country the basic economic system is not as important, in terms of managerial effectiveness and industrial progress, as educational and sociological factors. The economic system tends to become more important as the economy of a particular country becomes increasingly complex and more developed. Substantial progress can be made in a relatively poor country regardless of its type of economic systems as long as the educational and sociological environment is substantially improved. If the country also improves its political-legal environment, progress would tend to be that much greater. For in such a country almost anything produced will be useful, and therefore resource-allocation errors—whether through market competition or state planning—would not generally be as significant as in complex, advanced nations.

Starting from relatively low levels of industrialization, a number of diverse types of economies have made impressive progress over various fairly prolonged periods in recent decades. These include in part Mexico, Puerto Rico, and Pakistan, which are predominantly capitalistic, although significant elements of socialism and state planning (particularly in Pakistan) have been present; Yugoslavia with its mixed economy involving "market socialism"; and Rumania, North Korea, and China which are Communist states. At the same time numerous capitalistic and economies of the mixed type have done rather poorly. Some communist countries, such as Albania and Cuba (at least until very recently) have also done quite poorly. However, communism does tend to yield relatively good industrial results, up to a certain point, not primarily because of the type of economic system that communist states typically adopt but because of the types of improvements in the educational and sociological environment which typically follows from a Communist takeover. As of the late 1960's countries such as Albania and Cuba have not yet introduced very effective environmental changes of this type. United States foreign policy involving Cuba has also undoubtedly done much to hinder that country's progress, but local environmental constraints are just as or more important, since Cuba has been getting much help from sister communist nations.

In the last few decades, a number of diverse countries starting from partially developed economic levels have achieved impressive economic results and have evolved into semiadvanced or advanced economies. These include basically capitalistic Japan, Italy, and Venezuela, Israel with her mixed economy, and communist Russia, Hungary, and Poland. However, it is unlikely that the communist countries can evolve into truly advanced or affluent economies unless they adopt fairly extensive uses of such capitalistic features as market or scarcity prices, a meaningful profit motive, and even competition. For evidence strongly indicates that a complex, relatively advanced communist state can no longer handle the crucial resource-allocation problem effectively or efficiently through pervasive and detailed state planning. The more advanced European communist nations, including Russia, have run head-on into this problem, and most of them are now revising their economic systems in the direction of greater reliance on capitalistic techniques.

Czechoslovakia, which was a relatively advanced country before the Communist takeover in 1948, undoubtedly would have done much better economically if it had followed a more capitalistic course since 1948. Realizing its past mistakes in this regard, it vigorously began to follow a capitalistic course in the 1960's which, however, was probably affected adversely by the Russian invasion of 1968.

It is significant to note that all of the fifteen most advanced (in per capita terms) nations of the world are predominantly capitalistic, and not communistic, economic systems. Most of them cannot even be labeled as true mixed economies, even though several of them, such as the Scandinavian countries, have a high degree of socialism in terms of welfare programs. The present list of most advanced nations includes several Western European nations that suffered great damage during the Second World War and were reduced for a time to having only partially developed economies, if that. But they were able to recover because they still had educational and sociological-cultural environments that were conducive to industrial progress.

The structure of typical Marxist or communist economies has traditionally been that of a centrally planned state where the great bulk of resources are government-owned and where enterprise managers receive their key instructions from planners above them. As long as the product mix of these societies is relatively simple, this sort of direct planned economy can work reasonably well, provided that planners and managers are fairly well educated and motivated to do their jobs properly. The Soviet Union also was in a good position to try such an experiment several decades ago because of its vast size, possession of natural resources, and resulting minimal economic interaction with the rest of the world. If the local Marxist economy is closely interlocked with events beyond the country's borders, planning is made much more difficult.

In recent years, as the more developed Marxist countries have grown and become more complex, the problem of detailed planning for the entire economy has become so complicated as to threaten to swamp the planners. A main problem here has been that of designing an information-feedback mechanism that can show errors and discrepancies in efficient operations and thus make possible timely corrective action, as well as the design of consistent, well-balanced plans. Several consecutive plans in the Soviet Union and various other communist countries have had to be canceled because the economy could not meet the demands placed on it. When there are only a few grades of steel to produce, the planners can possibly lay out intelligible and practical plans; but when the product types, extending over a wide range, expand to thousands, and then to millions, planning control and informational errors become so huge as to make the plan unworkable. Rapid information feedback and timely corrective action are greatly hindered without a market-price system and a meaningful profit motive which could be used as a measure of economic success. Hence, in order to achieve further industrial progress, there comes a point when growing reliance must be placed on a system of scarcity or of market prices, a meaningful profit motive, and even competition.

In poor or less developed communist countries state planning and resource allocation can work fairly adequately without much use of the kinds of capitalistic practices mentioned above. But even here, if there is no substantial improvement in the educational and sociological-cultural environment, and/or if various political-legal and other economic constraints are extremely negative, such an economic system can do little, if anything, by itself to improve managerial effectiveness and to achieve economic progress. However, a comprehensively planned communist type of economic system, with rigid controls on managerial behavior and enterprise performance and which has a relatively well-educated, well-motivated working population seeking relatively simple and straightforward industrial results, would undoubtedly be more efficient than a capitalistic country populated by poorly educated, poorly motivated workers and managers. The question of which economic system a country has—particularly a relatively advanced nation—is important, but it is far from being the only relevant question.

Many developing countries have experimented widely with various kinds of mixed economies. Thus, in India, for example, the state is directly responsible for many sectors, such as public utilities and most transportation facilities while private firms have various industrial sectors staked out for them. In intensive capital industries, such as those producing steel, chemical fertilizers, and certain types of machinery, there is a combination of mixed and private ownership of enterprises. To date, such systems in poorer countries have, more often than not, worked very well. In part, this is because it is not yet clear how the public firms are to be controlled, in the major sense of rationing to them only necessary factor inputs. A firm which can turn to government to cover almost any deficit is in an enviable position from the firm's point of view, but such a practice may prove wasteful and inefficient from society's point of view. So far, Indian public industry has not performed even as well as similar private firms, and it remains to be proved whether the experiment can create the best of all possible worlds.

In poorer countries having mixed economies their overall industrial performance, in most cases, has not been very impressive because there are also many other environmental constraints of the types discussed in this chapter which operate against managerial effectiveness and productive efficiency.

It would appear that enterprise management is in a position to be more efficient economically in the long run as the economy advances and the more capitalistic (at least in terms of the profit motive, market prices, and competition) the economic system becomes. This favorable result stems from the basic nature of resource allocation. If a country is interested in productive efficiency, it wants its resources placed in the most valuable places, and the price system can potentially do this more efficiently than any planner conceivably could. The usual attacks on capitalism are not really focused on the allocation problem in this sense, but rather on the ethical aspects of the system. In a country where prices and incomes are free to go as high or as low as the market might take them, it is typically true that there will be great extremes of concentrated wealth and grinding poverty—millionaires may throw ten-thousand-dollar parties, while masses of unfortunates starve outside. Volatile shifts in demand may destroy both wealthy and poor alike. The numerous historic efforts to modify the rigors of a truly capitalist system typically revolve around such social considerations.

A second kind of modification which businessmen hesitate to discuss is that involving the protection of business firms and managers. Price supports, subsidies, price controls, import controls, entry controls, and similar measures are often intended to control competition to benefit the firms now in business. It is often easier, particularly in poorer countries, to get one's government to hold up prices than to become more efficient because of competitive forces, and incompetent businessmen and managers seek protection from the rigors of the market as avidly as do other "unfortunate" groups in the society. A key point in restricting competition is that it tends to render information feedback from the market regarding errors much less effective. It is possible to ignore an irate letter from a captive customer of a monopolistic firm producing machinery, shoes, steel, and other commodities or providing a public utility because the customer may have no alternatives. The world, and particularly the less developed world, is full of incompetent managers and firms who have been able to hide their incompetence from society because society lacks the information on what really is going on in the economic sphere.

In general, in capitalistic and mixed economies there are a number of features which serve as significant restraints on the market-price system and competition. They include input controls, output and price controls, and business entry controls, as well as legal-political constraints. Such controls tend to be more pervasive in less developed countries, as compared to those that are more advanced, since the former are confronted with great shortages of many types of economic resources.

The more distorted the pattern of outputs and related prices in a given country, the less likely it is that the economy will be efficient. In this case, such controls as overpricing of goods, along with production quotas, make such items either more or less expensive and more or less scarce than they otherwise might be, and tend to distort the output patterns of the firms, thus making them relatively less efficient. Here again, standards of values are important: a country may well decide that it wants lots of drugs and machinery and very few or even no television sets or other luxury items. Resource-allocation distortions of this type tend to be most acute in poorer countries where there are enough resources to produce abundant amounts of only a small number of products.

The constraint of the nature of the basic economic system is interrelated to a substantial extent with various other constraints discussed in this chapter. In the illustrations noted above, it is easy to see how other constraints in part determine the kind of economic system a country may have; but the system itself tends to influence directly all of the managerial and enterprise functions, making them more or less efficient than they otherwise might be. Countries all over the world are perpetually tinkering with their economic systems to try to make them work more efficiently. Underlying this experimentation is the notion that if the economic system can be set up more effectively, managers of productive enterprises will be able to function more effectively, industrial progress will be more rapid, and real income per capita will be higher. Of course, there are still many stagnant underdeveloped countries which have as yet done little or nothing to improve their economic systems in this direction.

In general, there is a tendency to impute too much to any economic system. Implicit assumptions about a system—such as the rights of private property—lead to often violent condemnation or support, without much reasoned analysis of what it is. Thus, it is common in the United States to find criticism of communist states on rather irrational grounds that no communist country can possibly produce anything efficiently. Similarly, Communists often cannot see anything useful about any capitalist country, simply because it is a capitalist country. Persons in countries like Egypt, India, Syria, Burma, Albania, Ghana, Cuba, and Indonesia—and numerous other underdeveloped and developing nations—expect economic miracles to occur through economic reorganization because they originally set up economic reorganization as being the panacea the country needed. They have felt somehow that once key industries were brought under local government control, better management would emerge automatically, industrial progress would be rapid, and incomes would soar dramatically.

In reality, major economic reorganizations *alone* rarely improve productive efficiency very much in the short run, particularly in less developed countries, and not very often in the long run. The reason is that income streams are generated not from abstract economic systems but from actual production and distribution of goods and services at the enterprise level. A sound economic system can help a manager to become more efficient over a period of time; but mere economic organization cannot substitute for good management. Other factors, including all of the environmental constraints discussed in this book, are also very important. Thus, the result of rapid or extensive economic reorganization is often disillusionment, because relatively little will change immediately, in terms of productivity, because of it.

The century-long dialogue between Marxist and capitalistic supporters has often assumed that the ideal basic economic system would somehow give ideal results, but this assumption ignores all of the other factors which help create either maximum or grossly minimal managerial effectiveness and industrial progress.

Central Banking System and Monetary Policy

One of the more important problems in efficient macromanagement, as well as micromanagement, is that of providing credit (that is, liquid capital) to industrial enterprises. To achieve a high degree of efficiency the capital must be provided in the correct amounts to the right firms and people. Everyone—or every firm—is typically sure that he could use more money; the problem is rationing out scarce resources, expressed in money terms, to the people who will use this asset most efficiently. A second related problem is to control the supply of money in an economy so that there is neither too little nor too much on hand at any time. Too much money will lead to price inflation, as excess money chases scarce goods and services; too little may well lead to deflation and depression, with correspondingly poor overall results.

The basic organizer of the money stream in most economies is the central banking system. A few countries manage without central banks, but they still have some institution in the economy that performs traditionally accepted central banking functions. A major central-banking task is to control the supply of money in the economy. The central bank has various tools to accomplish this task, typically including the right to discount commercial bank papers to set interest rates. In communist countries, the central banks are not usually concerned with the first two functions.

The manner in which the central bank (or similar institution) performs its duties has a direct bearing on the way in which management is performed in industrial enterprises. Poor planning about the available supply of money can lead to unnecessary crises and depressions, causing firms literally to be destroyed or to operate vastly below potential capacity. A sharp decrease of money in circulation will mean that less is available for loans to business and thus will have a very direct effect on business, planning, organization, and staffing. It may also lead to less demand for consumer and/or capital goods, with direct effects on marketing, production, and financial policies at the enterprise level. As aggregate demand shrinks in recessions, such functions as sale strategies, product lines, production needs, and inventory policies must change in order to reflect these external changes beyond the control of micromanagement. Too much money frequently results in artificial booms, excessive industrial expansion for the longer term, imbalances among different sectors, and eventually recession. In a country where significant changes in monetary policy are frequent, planning ahead for firms tends to be made much more difficult, and the result is inefficient use of productive resources over a period of time.

In many underdeveloped countries central banking and monetary policy tend to be passive and ineffective in terms of maintaining economic stability; even though such a bank or similar institution exists, it seldom takes appropriate action. The quality of central bank personnel in numerous underdeveloped and developing countries is perhaps a greater constraint affecting productive efficiency and industrial progress than are legislative details. The goals of central banking are typically agreed on and clear-cut, but such goals must be accomplished within a given institutional framework by men who must keenly appreciate and can forecast often subtle economic events well in advance of their occurrence. Poor timing, moves in the wrong direction, or simple incompetence of the macromanagers can cause an economy to fluctuate wildly, bring on heavy depressions or severe inflations, produce foreign exchange crises, and generally create an atmosphere of considerable uncertainty for enterprise managers. Questions of timing here can be critical, and the central bank may do many of the right things at the wrong times. In the long and sometimes tumultuous history of central banking, virtually every country has had the misfortune to have key monetary decisions made erroneously. However, the quality and effectiveness of central banking and monetary policy tend to be lower in poorer countries, as compared with those that are advanced.

Central banking in communist countries typically has a somewhat lesser role to play than in capitalistic or mixed economies. The latter typically use a system which will allow economic control by means of aggregate monetary decisions, leaving many or most other business decisions to micromanagers; in contrast, communist countries typically are involved in extensive state planning on resource allocation to enterprises, thus excluding micromanagers from major policy decisions.

In this situation the state banks also play a relatively passive role by merely providing what funds are necessary to meet the requirements. Hence, some of the major powers of central banks in a capitalist or mixed economy become relatively unimportant in similar banks in a Marxist country.

Even communist nations, however, use money and bank accounts extensively, and central banking systems are required to control this function. The national plan could be well conceived and the country's resource allocation sound, but too much or too little currency available at the proper time to handle the necessary purchase of goods, services, and labor or improper remittances of profits and taxes to the state could result in confusion, waste, and delay in the system—with a corresponding impact on managerial effectiveness and productive efficiency at the enterprise level. A well-conceived banking system in such an economy acts as an effective control system on firms, which may be piling up cash or losing it in excessive amounts, Too much cash may prove tempting, as can the misuse of cash, since desired goods or services not allocated to the firm in the plan might be purchased with it.

A major part of the activities of the central banking systems in such a society involves the careful control and audit of the activities of bank branches and industrial enterprises in the country. The banks must also plan, control, and organize their own activities efficiently if monetary control is to be effective. Poorly audited firm accounts, or incompetent bank planning and control can lead to serious monetary problems, including inflation. If excess cash gets into individuals' hands through income payments, excess demand is generated and can cause serious price problems in the economy. Most communist states at one time or another have had significant problems of balancing consumption and investment, supply and demand, and so forth, partly because of ineffective monetary policy. The plan provides for too few consumer goods (at going prices) for the money put in circulation by the enterprises hiring labor. With fixed prices, the result is that people queue up at stores, waiting to get their share of the scarce goods. The direction and motivational function of management can be influenced here because if personnel feel that it is useless to work hard, because much of the money they earn cannot be used as they wish, it may prove difficult to raise productive efficiency.

In general, it can be inferred that the central banking system and monetary policy are effective if a particular country has experienced relatively little price-level fluctuation, if the currency holds its value on international markets, if business recessions and booms are relatively mild, if economic growth and industrial progress continue steadily, if productive enterprises that deserve capital can use it efficiently and can get it. Not all of these factors are entirely under the control of central banking and monetary policy, as we shall see later; but if such economic stability is to occur, it is necessary that central banking and monetary policy be effective. This is typically not the case in numerous underdeveloped and developed countries.

Fiscal Policy

The cost of government accounts for anywhere from about 5 percent to over 80 percent of all expenditures in an economy. In stagnant underdeveloped countries, with poorly developed systems of public administration and macromanagement, government expenditures typically are from 5 percent to 15 percent of all expenditures. Here little or no use is made of potential governmental fiscal powers to maintain economic stability and to provide various incentives or disincentives for productive enterprises at appropriate times. In developing and more advanced capitalist and mixed economies the government's share typically ranges from 20 percent to 35 percent. Here fiscal policy is usually used by governments, but generally less effectively in the poorer countries for many of the same reasons discussed in the previous section on monetary policy. In communist countries, where most or all of productive effort is under direct state control, the percentage of government expenditures typically runs higher than in other types of economies.

The form that government expenditures take has a greater bearing on the different sectors of the economy affected. Where large sums, in terms of total expenditures and national income, are spent for religious purposes, as is common in various poor countries, the practice does nothing to spur industrial progress or to facilitate economic stability. Where large amounts go to the military and defense sector in poorer countries that can ill afford it, overall industrial progress and higher living standards would tend to suffer accordingly. The problem is even more acute if the country in question must use scarce foreign exchange reserves to import large portions of its military and defense hardware.

Stability in expenditures is also relevant for managerial effectiveness and enterprise efficiency. In countries whose public budget is stable and consists largely of standard items which vary little from year to year it is easier for business enterprises to plan, organize, control, and staff their activities efficiently than in countries where the budget fluctuates widely and is spent on different items from year to year or in shorter periods. While various advanced nations, such as the United States, do have significant instability regarding the amounts and nature of government expenditures from time to time, this problem is generally more serious in poorer countries striving for rapid development. Moreover, advanced nations typically have more flexibility and devices that can be used to meet changing government fiscal requirements without leading to serious instability, as compared with less developed countries that are critically short of strategic economic resources.

Governments have the power to create money through their central banking systems and monetary policies. They also have the option of raising money through fiscal policies pertaining to taxation and selling government bonds to the public. The manner in which they obtain the funds they spend has a direct impact on the economy and on business firms. Tax policy will have the effect of altering resource allocation with corresponding impact on various firms. Through its tax policy a government can encourage or discourage the production of different goods through the impact on prices.

In general, the very complexity of fiscal policy makes evaluation—in terms of business and industrial efficiency—difficult, and even skilled economists differ sharply in their views about the impact of given policies. However, if the net result of a country's fiscal policy is to create a situation which is quite stable, which does not distort resource allocation unduly, and which helps to create an economic environment in which enterprises can plan with reasonable accuracy, the policy can be judged relatively successful. If, on the other hand, the country is characterized by extreme resource-allocation problems caused by government spending, if prices rise or fall erratically, if government spending enhances booms unduly and deepens depressions, this factor may prove to have a large negative effect on efficient firm management. It seems that ineffective and unsound fiscal policies tend to be a serious constraint on managerial effectiveness and industrial progress in numerous underdeveloped and developing countries.

As with monetary policy, communist countries have a somewhat different kind of problem with fiscal policy. The state makes, by plan, virtually all of the investment expenditures, and private spending is only in the sphere of consumer goods and services. Hence, much of the complicated fiscal incentives and disincentives necessary to get desired levels of investment and consumption in a capitalist country are unnecessary. But the problem is far from easy, since the state must somehow extract from consumers and producers of all types revenues equal to the amount invested for each period. (More will be said about this problem when we explore Red China in a later chapter.) It will suffice to say here that Marxist countries have had inflations quite similar to those in capitalist countries, and a major contributing factor has often been ineffective fiscal policies.

Economic Stability

We are interested here in the stability of both prices and the general economy. An economic system may be said to have price stability when various indices of price changes (such as the prices of consumer and capital goods, wholesale prices, and agricultural prices) tend to remain stable over fairly long periods of time. Perfect stability is rarely possible, and small positive movements of a few percentage points per year—typically upward—are regarded as reasonably normal even in stable economies, given the complexity of the pricing problem.

In the contemporary world, where government deficits and printing-press money are common, the general trend of prices tends to be up; and considerable concern is expressed in most economies most of the time about such inflationary pressures. Proper monetary and fiscal policies can go far to minimize this impact. However, prices and price indices can change for a variety of reasons only loosely connected with monetary and fiscal policies. Crop failures, strikes, political instability, natural catastrophes—such as fires, floods, and earthquakes—and wars often caused severe supply shortages and sharp price increases, at times followed by serious recessions. Extraordinarily good weather conditions have led to bumper crops and price collapses as well. This type of price change normally affects only a few prices directly, but the effects percolate over to other prices as well. In an agricultural country whose major crop is largely exported—and this is characteristic of numerous underdeveloped and developing countries—a key crop failure reduces income for growers, causing declining demand for imports and domestic production of both producer and consumer goods. Poorer countries with economies based on one or two crops or on an export commodity are particularly vulnerable to such changes. For example, in 1960, the economy of Colombia suffered seriously because the price of coffee was low, but in 1964 it boomed because the price was high. Such external fluctuations in key prices have significant effects on local incomes, changing demand drastically and causing other prices to shift. In a similar manner, changes in prices of key imports can cause price indices to change sharply.

The problem of price stability tends to be more acute in smaller and poorer countries than in more developed, larger, and relatively self-sufficient nations not hit as hard by import-export price conditions. In the poorer countries where many items must be imported, as domestic inflation proceeds, the value of the country's currency in relation to other currencies declines, raising the prices of imports even more rapidly. Speculators, seeing the decline, often force the currency still lower, while flight of capital and extensive black-market operations may also begin to present a problem.

A most disturbing impact on business and industrial enterprises stems from serious price inflation or deflation in the economy. When prices rise sharply—say, ten percent or more per year—the firm is faced with the problem that inputs at any future date will cost more than they do now. Moreover, inventories of finished goods will be more valuable than they are now. Hence, in such a position, the inventory policies of firms tend to undergo a sharp change, which directly influences the planning function. Enterprises will buy large inventories of inputs when this is possible, and they will produce for finished-goods inventory as well. In effect, they will try to stay away from cash (the depreciating asset) in order to hold things (the appreciating assets). Where capital-goods prices are also rising rapidly, enterprises will tend to overinvest in fixed assets as well, since failure to do so will raise the cost of investment later. Such scrambling for things, instead of money—so common in less developed countries confronted with serious price inflation—by many firms will cause still more pressure on prices, encourage speculation and black marketing, and increase uncertainty and risks for the firm. The impact of such a situation on enterprise management and productive efficiency can be profound.

Sharp deflation, while rarer in today's world, can be equally disastrous. Here, the reverse of price inflation occurs; enterprises scramble to get out of things and into cash. Excess firm liquidity, bare minimum inventories, and increased speculation about the further decline in prices occurs, with serious negative impacts on managerial effectiveness and economic progress.

Communist countries tend to have stability problems different from those of capitalist nations. They are more inclined to keep productive factors employed, even though the need for the good product is small or nonexistent. The basic economic problem is not only to keep human and nonhuman resources at work but also to keep them engaged in the production of *useful* goods and services. Whereas capitalist states typically allow unemployment of resources rather than production of useless items, Marxist countries often do the reverse.

A serious problem facing many Marxist countries is that past plans have focused too many resources in sectors which are overexpanded in relation to demand, while putting too few resources in others. In an attempt to correct imbalances in the economy which are eventually recognized as being seriously out of hand, major shifts in resource-allocation patterns among different sectors are made, and this typically leads to considerable economic instability. Much in the way of idle resources results with such shifts in economic policy, even though the outward manifestations of such instability might not be the same as in capitalist countries when similar shifts occur.

In general, as with prices, the best situation of general economic stability for enterprise managers is as much stability coupled with reasonably attainable growth as possible. No country is perfect in this regard, since even in the best-run economies some anomalies persist; however, countries do differ widely in stability, and the most stable are those most conducive to the effective internal management of enterprises. The stability problem tends to be greatest in poorer and/or smaller nations that have low degrees of industrial self-sufficiency.

Organization of Capital Markets

Liquid capital is the lifeblood of any business enterprise operating in the contemporary world. Lack of access to needed money capital can force a firm out of existence, or at least cause it considerable harm. A key problem for productive enterprises thus becomes one of obtaining supplies of capital, at costs they can afford to pay, in the economy in which they function.

Industrial and business enterprises in an advanced, essentially capitalistic country such as the United States have many sources of capital they might turn to. Capital markets are well organized and tend to behave quite rationally and efficiently; for example, there are commercial and investment banks, mutual savings banks, savings and loan companies, life insurance firms, pension funds, credit cooperative, installment finance companies, and a variety of government investment, credit and loan organizations.

In underdeveloped, and also most newly developing countries, capital available to productive enterprise is usually critically scarce and often very costly. There are some types of banking institutions in all such countries, and many have some type of government agency willing to lend money to firms under certain conditions; but, in general, the demand for capital by business enterprises greatly outstrips the supply. In such an environment numerous firms that might become more efficient if they had more capital, cannot obtain it—often at any cost. The possibilities of growth for economies of some scale and industrial progress through expansion, diversification, entry into new markets, and many similar opportunities are greatly constrained by capital shortages. The government of a poor country that may wish to invest in new industries is typically constrained in the same way, although it may be able to generate capital through foreign and other external financial sources, domestic monetary and fiscal policy, and various other means. But there are limits as to how far any government can go in obtaining additional capital. Such limitations on governments are influenced by domestic economic and political policies and political stability, as well as by foreign policy. Generally, the government in a relatively affluent society is much less constrained with regard to availability of capital than it is in a poor country.

It is also common to find in numerous poorer countries that the only firms or individuals usually able to obtain funds of any magnitude from capital markets are those favored by family, political, or close personal relations with the banks or other lending institutions. Managerial effectiveness and industrial progress in these countries would tend to be far lower than they would be if scarce funds were typically allocated, after careful analyses, to enterprises and individuals most able to use them efficiently and effectively.

Communist countries also have capital and monetary problems, though of a somewhat different sort from those mentioned above. As was pointed out earlier, money is used in such countries as elsewhere, and firms must have credits to meet their obligations. However, capital requirements are spelled out for the most part in the state plan, and state banks play a relatively passive role by merely providing funds to meet plan requirements. Nevertheless, capital constraints are very important for industrial enterprises as well as for the state, and the state banks do play a major role in monetary control.

Factor Endowment

In economics the term "factor" means an item of production necessary to create useful goods and services. The usual basic division of factors is in the form of land (including natural resources), labor, capital, and management (or entrepreneurship). The last is the most dynamic and is the key factor in our analysis, since we are arguing that the effectiveness of management in fact determines how well a country does industrially and economically. The relative supply of the other factors of production is of course very relevant, however, since it is clearly easier to manage in a system where they are present in overall abundance, than where severe shortages of many specific factors exist.

The land factor can be defined as all that nature supplies—with the exception of man. Thus, land in a given country would include all agricultural land, all mineral resources, all resources found in the rivers, lakes, and oceans, inhabitable plots, and so on. Climate would be important in connection with the potential productivity of agricultural land.

A critical problem for any country is the amount of available natural resources per capita. Indonesia is known to have excellent resources; but it also has a very large population, and the exploited resource base is not large enough to yield more than a very low level of living to Indonesians in general. A common problem of poorer countries is that they do not have enough closely extractable resources per capita to allow for more than a poverty-stricken standard of living for most of their people. Favored countries which do have more resources per capita tend to have fewer complex industrial-management problems for some levels of managerial competence.

Firms in the better-endowed countries will tend to have, other things being equal, superior managerial effectiveness and greater industrial progress. However, some poorly endowed countries have achieved relatively high levels of managerial effectiveness and industrial progress in spite of severe disadvantages. Japan and Israel are outstanding examples. In such cases, favorable educational and sociological-cultural environments compensate for factor-endowment constraints regarding natural resources. In contrast, many poor countries, which are favorably endowed, remain poor because of other environmental constraints.

While the supply of land (and natural resources) is relatively fixed, changes can be made, both for the better and for the worse. Farm lands can be exhausted by poor farming practices, and range lands can be overgrazed into deserts. Conversely reclamation and irrigation projects can expend the supply of arable land, and dredging and filling can create land in shore areas. Knowledge, education, and proper motivation are also key factors in finding and obtaining potential industrial supplies, particularly in the area of mineral deposits. Moreover, minerals considered valueless at a certain point of time may later prove very useful if technological changes make their use feasible in industry or agriculture.

In the rapid development of technology since 1800, resources once considered critical (for example, indigo, and natural rubber) have lost much of their importance or have faded completely from the scene, while other resources, such as uranium and petroleum, have become extremely important. Relatively affluent countries with diversified natural resources are in a potentially better position to adjust to the shifting importance of different kinds of basic materials. But also of great importance is the ability to make poor or limited resources more useful through human skill and management.

The supplies of land and natural resources definitely influence the managerial effectiveness and productive efficiency of enterprises. Thus, if one country has very large supplies of low-cost, easy-to-mine coal or petroleum, one result will usually be relatively low fuel costs for industries using these minerals. Many production costs will tend to be lower in a well-endowed country than in a poorly endowed one, and production planning gains increasing flexibility when natural resources are in abundant supply. In general, the more accessible and cheaper the natural resources are, the easier enterprise management becomes. On the other hand, hard-to-get or costly resources imply that considerable ingenuity must be used by management to obtain consistently efficient production where such resources are important. The factor-endowment problem regarding natural resources is very often a critical constraint on managerial effectiveness and industrial progress in poor countries, but it is never the only serious constraint.

The labor factor consists of the potential available man-hours per period of time in a country. Clearly, few if any countries ever use all potential man-hours, since many persons do not work up to the physiological maximum, and still others prefer not to work or do not work in the formal sense at all. A country may also have involuntary unemployment in the sense that people want to work but cannot get jobs.

An important dimension of the labor factor is the general health and well-being of the employed labor force. In poorer countries, it is typical that most workers are at least a little sick most of the time, and the general energy level tends to be quite low. Parasitic infections, venereal diseases, and other debilitating maladies affect a major portion of the work force in numerous countries. The usual result is low levels of worker productivity; extensive absenteeism; high labor turnover; and, if the firm is required to pay some of the necessary medical expenses, higher operating expenses and the need in many cases to provide clinics, doctors, and nurses. The general level of health in the labor force depends in part on the educational and income levels of the workers. It also depends in part on the very important basic social-overhead-capital facilities, such as hospitals, public health programs, sewer systems, clean water supplies, and similar investments which directly affect the health of the population. Housing conditions are also important, since very poor housing can lead to rapid spread of many diseases and illnesses.

One entire constraint section, that on education, dealt with a major problem in all labor forces. The types and quality of education which the work force has determine in large part the general level of managerial effectiveness and industrial progress in the country.

The meaning of capital as a factor here is not money capital but goods —such as equipment—used in future production. Real capital of this type must be manufactured laboriously by using previously existing capital, management, labor, and land. With modern technology, it is often true that the most efficient processes use capital intensively—that is, the more capital applied in production, the lower unit costs will be. The notion here is that capital goods can be used to produce either more capital or more consumption goods efficiently. Labor and land are required, but in lesser amounts than before. Some types of production are, however, almost impossible without considerable capital investment. This includes such things as electric-power generation, petroleum processing, the manufacture of various chemicals and drugs, and so forth. There is almost no second best alternative in such a situation, and an economy critically short of capital becomes less efficient and productive for this reason alone.

Capital-equipment supply is also related to capital-market organization and efficiency in an economy. A firm may be competent and willing to obtain new equipment; but if it is unable to obtain money capital, it cannot finance the desired real capital. This type of problem is quite common in less developed countries.

It is true that the countries with the highest amount of capital per worker are the wealthiest, and one result of this observation has been a scramble among less developed countries to obtain capital in any way possible. However, implicit in the concept of having large relative amounts of capital is the notion that the country also has the necessary human resources and management to use it intelligently and efficiently. An all too familiar and depressing sight in the underdeveloped world is the new or expanded plant standing unused or used very inadequately because of lack of technical know-how, lack of demand, or because management failed to see the need for spare parts to maintain expensive machinery.

In general, ample supply and good quality of each type of basic factor tend to reinforce development of another. Poorer countries and their enterprises faced with serious deficiencies in all basic factors are confronted with significant constraints over managerial effectiveness and industrial progress; but it is not impossible to reduce substantially the impact of such constraints over time. Thus, more development of skilled labor tends to make possible the efficient use of larger amounts of more complicated capital equipment, while extensive and more efficient development of natural resources may well depend on more development of certain types of skilled labor, plus perhaps more capital. Attempts to force the question by overrapid development of one factor—as is common in less developed countries—may well prove less effective than an integrated approach which takes into account the simultaneous development of all basic factors.

Market Size

It has long been noted in economics, and in practical business as well, that in many lines of business a firm's costs will decline, at least up to a certain point, as production increases. In cases such as automobile manufacture, the minimum efficient size of plant may be huge, requiring the production of tens of thousands of vehicles per year; chemical fertilizer or steel production typically has to be tens of thousands of tons annually in order to make reasonably efficient use of plant. In other industries, such as those producing various types of machinery, construction equipment, or motor trucking, the minimum-sized plant may be much smaller, where a firm with a very limited output might prove as efficient as a larger one. Even in this situation, however, the market must be large enough to utilize for a substantial portion of the time the fixed capital of the firm.

Also relevant are marketing economies; the minimum size for an efficient plant may be too small for effective marketing organization. Here, it is difficult to organize a sales force to cover very small markets; or warehouses are too small in a given market to be efficient; or advertising cannot be placed in rural media. Too many small and inefficient middlemen may be required to serve a scattered population or one with relatively low purchasing power. However, joint production or marketing ventures involving interorganizational cooperation may help overcome to some extent the constraint of market size. Even an advanced country may be too small, from the technical or marketing point of view, to support a plant of fairly optimum size in various industries. Here foreign policy may be important since potential export markets, as well as the domestic, should be considered, and if the country's foreign policy is such as to enable substantial exports of a certain item, it still might be desirable to set up an efficient-sized plant in the country.

Poorer countries very often have several strikes against them regarding market size and the economies of scale of operations. There is the problem of effective purchasing power and number of potential users of a given product within the country. If it is a small, less developed country, the constraint becomes that much more serious. Because only a very minute portion of the population, even in a relatively large poor country, may be able to afford a certain product, such as a car or a TV set, it would not be possible to set up even one efficient-sized plant. The income distribution of the population is also relevant here. If the item in question is producer goods rather than consumer goods, the size of the consuming industrial sector is critical, and unless industry is quite diversified, there will not be an adequate market for numerous producer goods. Finally, regardless of the foreign policies that an underdeveloped or developing country may pursue, in numerous cases the quality of output is not adequate to enable substantial export volume, or costs are too high to enable the products to compete in foreign markets.

It is particularly common in developing nations with mixed economies for the government to set up certain key manufacturing industries—such as steel, heavy machinery, and chemicals—where market size is grossly inadequate, for reasons of prestige, pride, or perhaps a desire to promote long-run self-sufficiency. Hence, a new steel factory may be built, even though the internal market is too small to allow its managers to become efficient. A plant or a whole industry enjoys protection from imports in the form of high duties or tariffs. The small market means high-cost production, which in turn usually means that the manufacturers cannot export. Many poorer countries have deliberately created this sort of problem, and the management of their enterprises is consequently inefficient. No amount of internal management improvement, however, can offset entirely the initial disadvantage. In such cases the organization structure of the firm will be directly influenced. The absence of scale economies (for example, in a Chilean steel firm as compared with an American or Soviet firm) causes great organizational differences. The production function is equally affected, particularly in terms of less work specialization, since the way in which underutilized plants are organized may differ considerably from that in a more efficiently utilized plant.

Because of limited market size, both private and public monopolies and/or duopolies with colluding firms are the rule rather than the exception in many sectors in numerous underdeveloped and developing countries. (Monopolies may also be created for reasons other than market size, as in communist states where, for political reasons, virtually every branch of industry is organized in this way.) The monopolist or colluding duopolists typically need not fear competition in any type of economy. Customers who are dissatisfied usually have no alternative sources of supply, nor can they effectively play one firm against another. Inefficiencies within the enterprise can be glossed over, since prices can be raised as costs increase. A seller's market exists, and the firm is likely to be much less concerned about the marketing function and much more concerned about procurement than in a competitive environment.

Social-Overhead Capital

Social-overhead capital is defined as the supply and quality of services for public utility and welfare which are available to enterprises and consumers. Such services include all types of transportation systems, all types of communications systems, electric and gas transmission systems, postal facilities, housing, public warehousing, hospitals, and so forth.

Industrial and business enterprises in countries which have poorly developed social-overhead capital facilities are usually more difficult to manage than those in countries with good facilities. Affluent countries typically have much better facilities than poorer nations. Numerous firms in India, Saudi Arabia, Sudan, Egypt, and Brazil, which is even more developed—as well as scores of other less developed countries—have problems of erratic power supply, poor telephone service, and inadequate sewers around the plant. If the enterprise is a major user of electricity, stoppages of power mean unexpected shutdowns, which will raise costs as personnel, capital, and other resources wait idly for power to be restored. Production planning is difficult in this case because the firm cannot be sure that schedules can be met. Failure to meet production and delivery schedules also has an impact on marketing and finance. An alternative open to the firm here might be to build its own power plant, but this also would raise costs considerably.

Lack of good telephone communications means that much time is wasted, and money must also be spent sending messages in other ways. In such a situation it is difficult to communicate with customers, suppliers, and other organizations and individuals having business with the enterprise. Moreover, when outsiders must visit officials rather than telephone them, there is a needlessly great consumption of time. Sewer defects can create health problems, even if the enterprise is not a heavy user of such facilities. If the enterprise has large amounts of industrial waste to dispose of, lack of good sewer systems can result in production delays because production must stop periodically to manually clear the plant of noxious waste. Such social-overhead capital constraints tend to restrict the locational possibilities of firms within the country—they can locate only where these facilities are available, or face expensive problems of building their own.

The absence of key transportation facilities may force the firm to set up its own rail or handcart trucking and services providing other types of transport. Inadequate and erratic transportation typically causes firms to carry larger inventories than they otherwise might, in order to cover likely shortages of key items. Poor housing, hospital, warehousing, and other types of facilities also tend to have quite obvious negative impacts on managerial effectiveness and industrial progress. Here again, industrial enterprises may have the option of establishing their own such facilities, with the effect of raising costs substantially.

Of equal importance as the quantity of social-overhead capital are the management of the social-overhead capital facilities themselves and the question of whether they are publicly or privately owned. Bad management of these facilities is particularly common in poor countries, and this means poor service to users—which in turn directly affects and hinders the internal operations of industrial enterprises. Numerous countries probably suffer as much from inept management of social-overhead capital as they do from absolute lack of such capital.

PART II

ENVIRONMENT

CHAPTER 3

China's Response to Environmental Constraints: Education

Now we turn to Communist China's response to environmental constraints which greatly hindered managerial effectiveness and industrial progress prior to 1949. Before 1949 China was a truly underdeveloped country. Most if not all of the environmental constraints on managerial effectiveness and industrial progress discussed in the previous chapter were potent negative forces in the old China. It is true that there were a number of large-scale heavy industry enterprises—mostly under foreign control, and primarily in north China (Manchuria)—and that Shanghai and Tientsin were fairly large industrial centers primarily involved in light industry such as textiles and food processing. But both in absolute and per capita terms, China's level and diversity of industrialization were low—considerably lower than in India, for example.

I would classify China of the period between 1966 and 1967 as a semi-advanced industrial nation on the basis of absolute levels and diversity of industrial production. Even in per capita terms, China is clearly a developing country rather than an underdeveloped one, and in this connection I would classify it as being partially developed. Quantitative measures of Red China's economic performance will be presented in a later chapter.

In this and the following three chapters, we shall attempt to explain the key reasons for Communist China's substantial, but erratic, gains to date in managerial effectiveness and industrial progress.

Chinese Education: General Background[1]

The overall system of Chinese formal education is patterned quite closely after the Soviet system. The Chinese educational system, like that in typical communist countries, is designed to serve not the individual but the state and its goals. While all Chinese education is free for those who gain admittance into schools, it is only within the confines of choice determined by the state that the individual may develop his abilities. This substitution of the utilitarian concept of service of the state for the concept of individual benefit and interests constitutes the basic distinguishing characteristic of Chinese—and traditional communist—educational philosophy and practice. The Chinese concept of education also includes indoctrination propaganda and anything else that produces an impact on human minds and brings about changes in thought and behavior. Chinese education has the twofold purpose of importing skills that are useful to the state and of molding the pure communist man as interpreted by Mao.

It is a major thesis of communism that all significant phases of economic activity, including all aspects of manpower requirements, should and can be planned. Since it is the educational system of China that largely serves to fulfill manpower requirements, it is subject to rigid state planning and control. Education and manpower policies and plans are much more integrated with the state's economic, political, and social objectives than in any capitalist or mixed economy. The Chinese overall educational plans are closely linked to their national economic plans. The central planners under party leadership determine enrollment quotas by considering field of specialization, programs and methods of instruction, text materials, and all other important educational problems. The educational system is adjusted in the light of the goals and needs of society as determined by the Chinese leaders. It is a highly standardized system imbued with a considerable amount of ideology and indoctrination at all levels. Higher and specialized secondary education programs are the most important for providing high-talent industrial manpower, and such programs are quite narrow, highly functional, and applied in content. There is nothing comparable to general liberal education in Western countries. China's scientific research has also been mostly highly functional and applied rather than basic.

The overall structure of the Chinese educational system is depicted in Figure 3–1 below.[2]

From nursery school on, students are indoctrinated not only in political ideology, but also in communist values as interpreted by the regime. Some of these values are essentially Calvinistic in nature and, in general, much of the value indoctrination probably has had and still has a positive effect on industrial progress. Values which appear to be stressed throughout the Chinese educational system include, in part, hard work and dedication to one's job, regardless of what it is, the importance of subordinating one's own ambitions to the service and interests of the state, of accepting sacrifice and austerity uncomplainingly, of cooperating with and aiding each

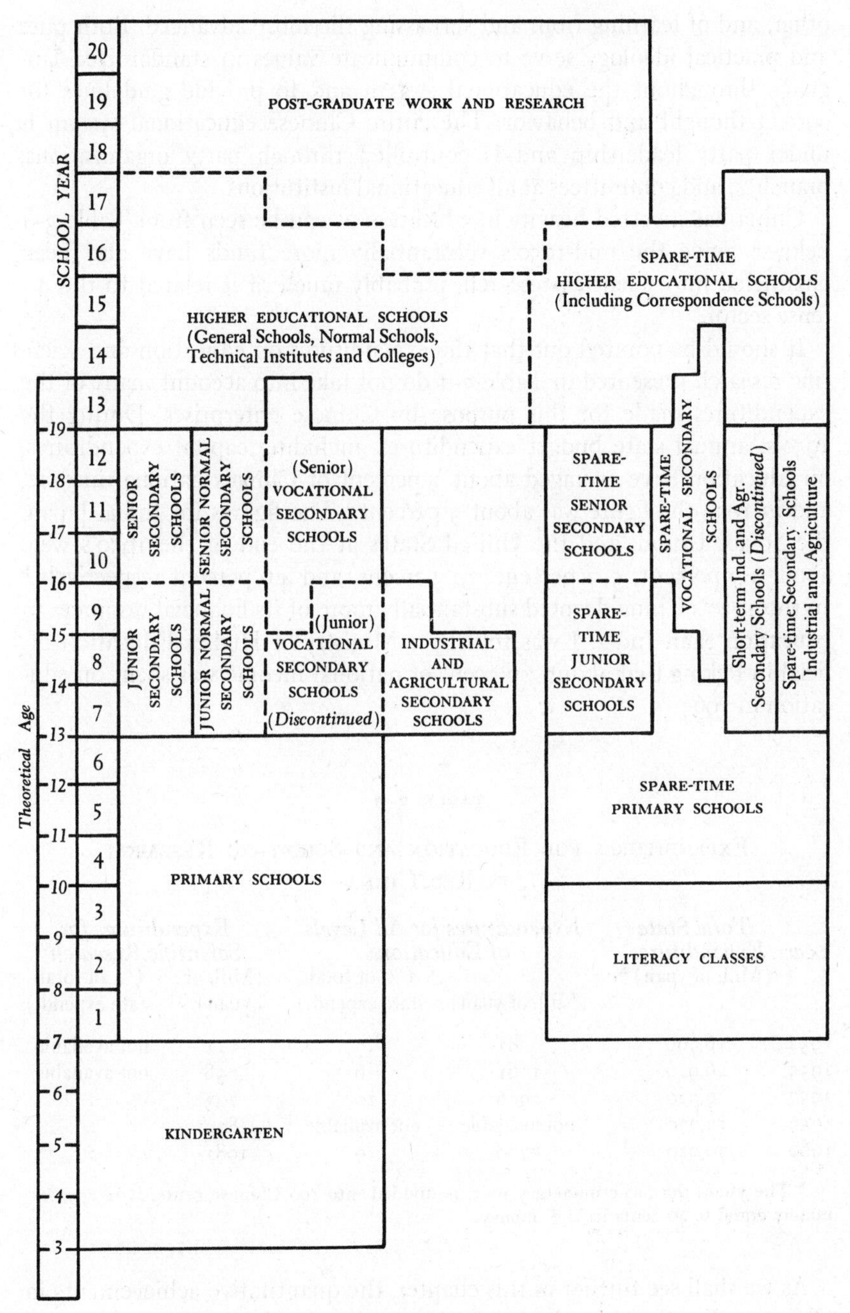

FIGURE 3–1

STRUCTURE OF EDUCATIONAL SYSTEM (CIRCA 1960)

other, and of learning from and surpassing the more advanced. Both pure and practical ideology serve to communicate values in standardized language throughout the educational system and to provide guidelines for correct thought and behavior. The entire Chinese educational system is under party leadership and is controlled through party organizations, branches, and committees at all educational institutions.

China has invested heavily in education as can be seen from Table 3–1 below.[3] Since the mid-1950's substantially more funds have also been channeled into scientific research, probably much of it related to the defense sector.

It should be pointed out that the expenditures on education and scientific research presented in Table 3–1 do not take into account many of the expenditures made for this purpose by Chinese enterprises. During the 1950's, annual state budget expenditures, including capital expenditures, on education have averaged about 3 percent of China's national income, and in 1959 the figure was about 5 percent.[4] The figures for India, Japan, the Soviet Union, and the United States at the end of the 1950's were about 1.7 percent, 5–7 percent, 7.1 percent, and 4.6 percent respectively.[5] In the 1950's China devoted substantially more of its financial resources to education than India. I was told by a Ministry of Higher Education official in Peking that about 5 percent of national income was spent on education in 1965.

TABLE 3–1

EXPENDITURES FOR EDUCATION AND SCIENTIFIC RESEARCH IN RED CHINA

Year	*Total State Expenditures* (Mill. of yuan)*	*Expenditures for All Levels of Education* (Mill. of yuan)	(% of total state expend.)	*Expenditures for Scientific Research* (Mill. of yuan)	(% of total state expend.)
1952	16,790	81	7	11	not available
1955	26,920	1761	6	38	not available
1957	29,020	2906	10	293	1
1959	53,770	not available	not available	820	2
1960	70,020	6400	9	1081	2

* The yuan, the basic monetary unit, is divided into 100 Chinese cents; it is approximately equal to 40 cents in U.S. money.

As we shall see further in this chapter, the quantitative achievements in Chinese education have been very impressive since 1949. The content of educational programs and the general attitude toward education—as compared with that in the past—have also undoubtedly done much to increase managerial effectiveness and industrial progress on a national scale. However, the quality of Chinese education in general still lags significantly behind advanced industrial nations, and the effectiveness of Red China's educational system has been erratic, with negative results emerging during periods when the regime has gone overboard with the implementation of ideology in the system.

When the principles and policies of the Great Leap Forward were extended to the fields of education and culture in 1958, the system for training professional and semiprofessional manpower for industry and business was particularly gravely affected.[6] Quantity in education became the watchword, and quality suffered immensely. Hundreds of new educational institutions of all types were rashly established at all levels and enrollments exploded. Numerous new students were admitted purely because of their political loyalty and ideological correctness, and they were grossly deficient in the pretraining nationally required at a given level of education.

Early in 1958, the Ministry of Education decreed that all types of students must combine with their formal education physical work in factories or on farms. Educational institutions were required to set up miniature, and at times full-scale, shops and farms, while factories and communes were required to set up schools. Larger factories and communes set up schools of all levels, while most smaller ones set up at least literacy classes and, in many cases, primary and junior high schools. Enrollments in spare-time educational programs mushroomed greatly at all levels, bursting available facilities at the seams. By 1960 there were about twenty-five million workers and employees attending spare-time programs at all levels. This strategy was seen as a strong march toward a classless society. Distinctions between brain and brawn workers would disappear as everybody evolved into a mentally, physically, and ideologically balanced worker, and hence into a pure communist proletarian. Another chief aim here was universal education for all who qualified within fifteen years.

Embarking so rashly on such a widespread educational reform turned out to have quite chaotic results. Much time was also taken up by student-faculty ideological and political meetings and discussions at educational institutions, and ideological indoctrination became extremely intensive. This became a period of anti-intellectualism, and faculty members educated in non-Marxist countries—and a substantial number of professors were—were particularly suspect.

By late 1960 it was evident to the Chinese leaders that a crisis had emerged in the educational system, as well as in the economy, and the regime made a sharp retreat from its earlier educational reforms. The period between 1961 and 1962 was one of readjustment and consolidation in the overall educational system. Many educational institutions were merged or closed down, and enrollments dropped. Better-quality education was to be stressed; less time was to be spent on meetings and ideological discussion; and a more balanced and thought-out program of physical labor was to be introduced. By late 1962 or early 1963 the worst was probably over. Enrollments started to rise again, and the educational system became more effective in terms of providing required manpower for industry.

This seems to have been the situation until about 1965. At that time economic conditions and performance were again relatively favorable, and the regime once again became concerned that revolutionary fervor was endangered because of relative affluence and that revisionism was a real potential threat. Soviet revisionism, including deviationism in education, was being assailed in the Chinese press. Foreign visitors were told that the Chinese society would not allow Soviet-style revisionism which enables intellectuals to become detached from the masses. They were also told that the Soviets don't emphasize politics, ideology, and physical labor sufficiently in their educational system and that they place too much stress on technical aspects—thus causing a separation of intellectuals and workers.[7]

In 1966 I was told the same thing by almost every education official, teacher, and professor I met in China. Since 1965 there seems to have been an emerging trend of more emphasis on physical labor—for faculty as well as for students—and student employment in regular educational programs. The current goal seems to be to transform the educational system into one of half work and half study, particularly in specialized secondary and higher programs. There were all types of such experiments going on in 1966. For example, in some programs students were spending half days working, in others alternate days, alternate weeks, or alternate months, and I was told in some cases that, in the future, students will spend as much as half the year working and the other half studying. It seems that, in the future, secondary and higher-level students will probably devote forty to fifty percent of their time working and the rest in their formal studies.

There have been a few experiments involving half-work and half-study educational programs in China for several years. For example, in 1961 a higher educational program of this type was established at the Yang-pu Cotton Textile Machinery Enterprise. There have been a variety of problems regarding the effectiveness of this experimental program.[8] It was not until 1965 that official party policy advocated an extensive system of such half-work and half-study programs; and in 1966 there was much evidence that such a transformation was underway. If too much stress is placed on the work aspect of educational programs, this would tend to slow down greatly the training of vitally needed skilled manpower for industry.

During my visit to China in April through June of 1966, the Chinese educational system did not yet seem to be seriously affected by overemphasis on ideologically motivated reforms. There was somewhat more stress on ideology and politics than in the Soviet educational system but, given the heavy instructional load, this did not yet seem to be diluting other subjects severely. While some schools at various levels had recently introduced added compulsory physical labor, none of them had yet switched to a half-work, half-study program, although some of them expected to do so in the future. Many of the industrial enterprises surveyed—and all of the larger ones—ran regular primary and junior middle schools. Some of them operated regular schools at all levels, including higher educational programs. In these enterprise-operated schools there did appear to be somewhat more time devoted to physical labor than at schools not attached to factories, but employment did not generally constitute more than about one-third of the students' time.

The large majority of the enterprises surveyed ran their own literacy classes as well as spare-time primary and junior middle school programs for employees. A number also ran spare-time senior middle schools and specialized secondary programs as well as those of an even higher level. At all of the enterprises surveyed at least ten percent of their employees were enrolled in some type of spare-time educational program at the enterprise or elsewhere. At several enterprises more than half of the employees were attending such programs. In most major Chinese cities radio and television are utilized to supplement lower-level spare-time—including correspondence—educational programs.

In general, during my stay in China I came across no concrete evidence that the educational system had, at any point, actually embarked on extreme or irrational courses of action similar to those that emerged during the Great Leap Forward. However, there was much in the air, and in the press, indicating that such action was on the threshold of taking place. By May 1966 the Great Proletarian Socialist Cultural Revolution was well underway. The regime was calling for much more time in the overall educational system to be devoted to physical labor and employment, ideological indoctrination, meetings, self-criticism therapy, and the like. Clear elements of anti-intellectualism again began to emerge, and some prominent educators were purged. Professors and teachers were called on to spend more of their time in physical labor.

Toward the end of June 1966, very shortly after I had left China, it was announced that most schools would not reopen for the fall term because facilities, programs, and educational materials were to be studied and revised under the direction of reliable party cadres, teachers, and students—including Red Guard members—who had displayed ideologically correct thought and behavior. During the following months the Chinese press frequently proclaimed that "the whole country should become a great school for the teaching of Mao Tse-tung's Thought" [9] and that through correct education everyone should be molded into a worker-peasant-soldier-intellectual. This gives us a preview of what might be in store for the Chinese educational system. As of mid-1968 many schools that had been shut down had apparently been reopened, but many were not functioning very effectively, if at all.

It seems reasonable to predict that the longer the educational institutions remain closed the greater will be the negative impact on future managerial effectiveness and industrial progress. If the reopening of the schools is accompanied by substantially more time devoted to political meetings, ideological indoctrination, excessive and rashly introduced physical labor or work-study programs, along with the creation of a general atmosphere of anti-intellectualism, such restrictions would also tend to have a negative impact on industrial progress. It may take a few years for serious educational deficiencies to be revealed in China's aggregate economic and industrial results, but they will no doubt show up again if ideology does go too far in the educational system.

One should not conclude, however, that work and study programs, or physical labor in education, and spare-time education in China are necessarily ineffective or irrational. It is only when they have been introduced very rashly and too extensively that serious problems have emerged in China. Where such programs are utilized in a reasonably balanced manner they probably have a positive impact on managerial effectiveness and industrial progress. Given China's huge population and limited financial and high-talent human resources, a full-time educational system where all eligible students are admitted is impossible. It would be irrational to sacrifice massive labor power to a wholly food-dependent educational system that is by its very nature nonproductive in the economic sense. Yet China does believe strongly in mass education or education for all those who qualify. A substantially large portion of the population can become educated at different levels if there are many spare-time and work and study programs. Such a system would enable greater use of facilities and teaching staffs and make it possible for many students to support themselves entirely with the incomes they earn from employment, thus relieving the state, and in some cases their families, of the financial burden of paying for such expenses as their room and board. It also provides a larger pool of manpower resources for industry and agriculture.

The stress on physical labor in educational programs also tends to bring about greater respect for the dignity of labor—an attitude that is drastically needed in numerous countries, including India, desiring economic development. In China before 1949 even primary school graduates were considered intellectuals, since there were relatively few of them. Now there are so many primary and even middle school graduates that many of them must work as laborers in factories or on farms, and the only way they can continue their formal education is through part-time programs. Moreover, if they were not imbued with a respect for physical labor in primary and middle school, they would tend to be much more resentful and frustrated in their work after graduation.

For those students who eventually become managers, participation in physical labor in the educational system may well make them more sensitive to the problems and needs of workers and hence make them more effective managers. This may in fact be the best way to break down the old dominant attitude of disdain for physical labor that was held in the past by the Chinese intelligentsia and those in positions of authority. Where the aim in Red China has been not to reduce intellectuals to the level of laborers but to teach them the meaning and problems of labor, this system has probably had a positive impact on managerial effectiveness and industrial progress. The same would be true where the aim of spare-time education for workers has been to enable them to better comprehend the work of intellectuals and its practical applications in order to improve results. However, during the Great Leap Forward, numerous intellectuals, including faculty members, as well as educated managers, technicians, and engineers, were in fact disparaged, misutilized greatly, and often reduced to the level of students or workers, while students and industrial personnel without adequate education or training were often permitted to make and implement irrational and inefficient decisions. If such a situation emerges again on an extensive scale for a prolonged period, economic crisis seems to be inevitable.

Literacy and Primary Education

It is substantially more difficult in China to acquire basic literacy, in terms of reading and writing, than in America because the Chinese written language contains some four thousand complex characters that are currently in use. The Chinese have recently made a major effort to simplify and even to romanize many of the characters. They appear to have made quite impressive progress, and in the larger cities one can observe that numerous names of stores, factories, streets, signs, and the like are written in a transliterated romanized form, as well as in Chinese characters.

A Chinese urban citizen is considered basically literate if he comprehends about fifteen hundred to two thousand characters—about half the number required for completion of primary education. This is adequate for reading newspapers and magazines of the mass media type. Peasants are considered literate if they comprehend about fifteen hundred characters.

Fortunately for China the written language is quite standardized throughout most of the country. However, there are a number of major spoken languages, notably Mandarin and Cantonese, and a variety of dialects. This can pose somewhat of a problem when industrial personnel are transferred from one part of the country to another. For example, a key technical manager and a foreman whom I met at the Wuhan Iron and Steel Works were shifted there recently from their native Anshan in north China (Manchuria), where a different language is spoken. Since they had not acquired the local language, at times they had to make use of interpreters when communicating with other members of the personnel.

However, the language problem in China is not nearly as serious as in India, where there are about twelve different written scripts, sixteen official languages, and some two hundred different dialects. This situation serves as a significant constraint on communication at numerous enterprises and requires much expenditure of time for translations. A typical case that I observed was at a Calcutta factory where managers had to communicate with substantial portions of the labor force in Bengali, Tamil, Urdu, standard Hindi, a Bihar dialect of Hindi, Assamese, and Oria. At a Madras enterprise large numbers of workers could clearly understand only one of the following languages: Tamil, Telugu, Hindi, Malalayam, or Kannada.

China has been more successful than India in raising the literacy level of its population. Prior to 1949 over 90 percent of the Chinese population was illiterate, and among industrial personnel it was about eighty percent. In 1957 Chou En-lai estimated that the illiteracy rate had fallen to 70 percent. In the mid 1950's nearly 50 percent of the industrial work force was still illiterate. By 1960 it was about 66 percent for the rural population and 24 percent in urban areas.[10] In 1966 I was told by various Chinese officials that national illiteracy was under 60 percent, urban illiteracy was under 20 percent, and among industrial personnel it was probably no more than about 10 percent, in spite of the vast increase in industrial employment in the last decade.

At the enterprises I surveyed, only three claimed that they had illiteracy rates of 10 percent or more: these were the Wusih Silk Factory No. 2 with a rate of 15 percent to 20 percent; the Fu Chong Clothing Factory in Hankchow, 10 percent–15 percent; and the Lan Yang Electrical Appliance Enterprise in Canton, 10 percent–15 percent. These three enterprises said that their relatively high rates of illiteracy were due to the fact that they had many old workers who lacked the ability, desire and/or energy to become literate through spare-time education. All of the illiterates were engaged in very simple routine manual jobs.

But even these enterprises have reduced the illiteracy rate among personnel from well over 50 percent about a decade ago. Likewise, many of the other enterprises surveyed have done the same through spare-time basic literacy programs. For example, the Tientsin Shoe Factory had an illiteracy rate of 80 percent in 1949 and by the mid-1960's this had been reduced to about 6 percent; the Sung Sing Cotton Mill No. 9 in Shanghai reduced illiteracy from 80 percent to 3 percent during the same period. I was told of similar achievements at many of the other firms surveyed. Many of the enterprises surveyed claimed to have less than 1 percent or no illiteracy.

In India in 1951 about 83.5 percent of the population was illiterate, and by 1961 this was reduced to 76 percent.[11] The standard of literacy in India involves basic reading and writing in any one of the major languages and scripts. In 1966 I was told by Indian education officials that the illiteracy rate was still around 70 percent. There are no official statistics available regarding the literacy level in Indian industry. Estimates given to me by various officials indicate that about 20 percent to 30 percent of the industrial work force is illiterate. At about fifteen of the Indian factories and firms where I inquired about literacy levels of employees, none had a rate of less than 10 percent, most fell between 20 percent and 30 percent, and some—in jute, textiles, and railway-wagon production—had illiteracy rates of 35 percent–40 percent and more.

China's success in wiping out illiteracy in industry can be attributed in large part to the pervasive system of spare-time adult literacy programs. During the period from 1958 to 1962 about nine million workers learned to read and write through spare-time education.[12] Most of the enterprises surveyed ran their own literacy classes, while some small ones either ran such classes jointly with other enterprises or made provision for sending personnel to programs run by educational institutions or other organizations. In many cases better-educated enterprise personnel conduct these classes for their co-workers—apparently with nominal extra pay in some cases and as a voluntary service in others. Schoolteachers also participate in many of these programs. In some of the enterprise literacy programs, employees were also exposed to elementary arithmetic. Television is also used in China for literacy education. There is no television in India as of 1968, except for very limited experiments with closed circuit TV in Delhi.

On a national scale, enrollments in spare-time adult-literacy programs in China for the years for which statistics are available are presented in Table 3–2.[13]

TABLE 3–2

ADULT LITERACY PROGRAM DATA

Year	Enrollment
1952	656,000
1955	3,678,000
1957	7,208,000
1958	40,000,000

With the inception of the Great Leap Forward in 1958, there was nearly a sixfold increase in enrollment as compared with 1957. No doubt many people were coerced into attending these classes, and probably numerous citizens did not successfully complete the program. However, the programs were probably generally quite successful among industrial personnel, who may be more eager to become literate since they tend to have more opportunities to get ahead than do typical peasants in rural areas.

A number of large, progressive Indian firms have had literacy classes for many years, and recently the Indian government has offered incentives for all types of enterprises to offer part-time literacy programs for their employees. However, such programs are not apparently meeting with much enthusiasm by most enterprises, and where enterprises do set up literacy classes, there does not generally seem to be much interest on the part of illiterate employees. In many cases, management does not have a serious interest in raising the literacy level of employees, and the employees themselves tend to be apathetic because they feel that even if they become literate there is little opportunity for advancement. The general feeling of apathy, pessimism, insecurity, and uncertainty, which seems to pervade Indian industry, as compared with a general sense of optimism, opportunity, security, and certainty about industrial progress in China, probably explains much about the difference in the extent and effectiveness of literacy education in the two countries. In China, the social structure is such that numerous illiterate workers who become literate can obtain better jobs and/or proceed further with their education. This is generally not the case in India.

In China one does get the feeling that by acquiring basic literacy the worker substantially raises his aspiration level, self-image, and confidence, that he gets a thirst for even more knowledge and education, and that he is motivated to improve his performance and his position in life. At the Chinese enterprises surveyed, I observed many workers, alone and in small groups, studying their characters during breaks. In many cases other personnel were helping them in their studies. In India, there seems to be a low ceiling on the aspiration levels of poorly educated workers, and their self-images seem to be straitjacketed at low levels.

The Chinese regime desires universal literacy among industrial personnel for ideological and political as well as economic reasons. At all factories there are many ideological posters, slogans, and reports all over the walls and grounds, and personnel are expected to read the works of Mao and the newspapers as part of their ideological indoctrination. Hence, literacy facilitates the molding of the pure communist man.

At the same time, however, literacy also enables employees to improve their performances by reading articles in newspapers and magazines which pertain to their jobs. Frequently there are articles dealing with a wide variety of occupations, such as welding, machine operation, maintenance and repair work, care of equipment, quality control, handling and storage of materials, and heat equipment. Often these articles are written in simple language and are aimed at workers with only a modicum of education. What may seem childish or very unsophisticated to a well-educated person can often provide the motivation to improve the performance of barely literate workers.

There are other apparent significant differences in Chinese enterprises as compared with those in India which are probably due in part to higher literacy levels and—as will be discussed later—to more extensive primary education in China.[14] One sees many more workers reading, writing, and even compiling data in Chinese enterprises than in Indian firms. One also sees Chinese workers perusing drawings, designs, charts, and various other types of reports and instructions. In general, there seem to be more written communication and greater worker participation in reporting, planning, and control at the lower operating levels of Chinese firms than in Indian ones. Moreover, supervision, direction, and control over workers do not seem to be nearly as tight in China as in India. One also senses less frustration among Chinese workers, and self-education is clearly much more in evidence in Chinese industry.

In Chinese factories, individual, work-group, and shop statistical performances are displayed for all to see, as a means for creating "socialist competition" whereby lagging performers try to "learn from, catch up with, and overtake the advanced ones." One rarely sees this type of thing on the work floors of Indian enterprises, and an important reason may often be that many workers cannot understand such statistical compilations, even simple ones.

One other dimension of literacy in a country such as China is worth mentioning here, and that is literacy in foreign languages. Since China is still a newly developing country, much of the technical, scientific, managerial, and economic literature significant for industrial progress is written in foreign languages, particularly English, Russian, German, and French. This in itself is somewhat of a constraint on potential managerial effectiveness and industrial progress. If Chinese industrial enterprises are to make use of the writings and experiences of the advanced nations, scarce educated manpower must be used to translate such data. There do seem to be sizable numbers of people, employed full or part time in industrial ministries, the Academy of Sciences, research organizations, educational institutions, and even factories, who translate Russian sources; there is an increasing number translating English, Japanese and, to a lesser extent, other foreign language sources.

No doubt the defense sector absorbs many and perhaps the largest number of such translators. At some of the enterprises I visited, there were full-time translators employed. For example, at the Wuhan Iron and Steel Corporation there are seven translators who work with sources in about nine foreign languages. I met some of them, and also observed that they were translating several American technical journals. Even the Peking Clothing Factory had a few people translating American and other foreign fashion magazines and clothing publications with the aim of designing new styles and products for export.

India may have a potential advantage over China regarding dissemination of foreign sources and experiences because most significant information is available in English language sources and a fairly substantial proportion of the educated population understands English. However, the typical indigenous Indian firm does not seem to capitalize very much on available foreign experiences, and this is probably due in part to the relatively low achievement drive of many Indian managers. (More will be said about this in the next chapter.)

China has also done substantially better than India in primary or elementary education. During the period from 1959 to 1960, 36 percent of the population aged five to fourteen were enrolled in elementary schools in China as compared with 24 percent in India.[15] In 1955–56 there were about 53 million students enrolled in Chinese primary schools as compared with about 25 million in India.[16] The 1962–63 figure for India was about 42 million as compared with over 90 million in China during 1959–60, 126 million in 1964–65 and, I was told, over 130 million in 1965–66.

Table 3–3 below contains statistics on Chinese regular and spare-time adult primary education for selected years where data are available. During the period from 1958 to 1962 over one million workers finished spare-time primary school programs.[17] (There is relatively little spare-time adult primary education in India.)

Again we can see the great increase in enrollment, particularly in adult

TABLE 3–3

STATISTICS ON PRIMARY EDUCATION

Year	*Regular Programs* (In Thousands)		*Adult Spare-Time Programs* (In Thousands)	
	ENROLLMENT	GRADUATES	YEAR	ENROLLMENT
1949–50	24,391	2,829	1949	657
1952–53	51,100	9,945	1952	1,375
1955–56	53,126	12,287	1955	4,538
1957–58	64,279	16,225	1957	6,267
1959–60	over 90,000	not available	1958	26,000
1964–65	126,000	" "	1960	13,000
1965–66	over 130,000	" "		

programs, during the Great Leap Forward. The success rate in the adult programs was probably quite low during that period. Enrollment dropped sharply in these programs to 13 million in 1960.

Regular primary education in China involves a six-year program of study, while the spare-time adult programs are from two to four years in length, depending on the student's ability and progress. Industrial personnel attending part-time elementary schools are supposed to be guaranteed by their enterprises at least two hundred and forty hours a year with pay for their studies.

About half of the enterprises I surveyed had their own primary schools, most of them had spare-time adult elementary programs, and those that did not provided for their personnel to attend such programs elsewhere. At all of the enterprises I visited, at least a majority of employees had completed either regular or spare-time elementary educations. At the majority of these enterprises, 75 percent or more of their personnel had had elementary education. At some enterprises 20 percent to 30 percent were currently enrolled in spare-time elementary education programs. Even at factories where many employees were not yet primary school graduates, considerable progress has been made. For example, in 1949 at the Tientsin Shoe Factory only 10 percent of the employees had had primary education, but by 1966 the large majority did, and those who didn't were old workers, mostly former private shoemakers.

Elementary education in China includes courses in politics and ideology (Marxism-Leninism and Maoism), history, mathematics, literature, natural science, and geography. Of course, there is great stress on ideology and politics, and this I observed in a number of classrooms. In regular programs students begin taking a foreign language around the fourth year. I was told at the schools I visited that English is now the most popular foreign language, which was what Russian used to be until a few years ago. From what I observed, efforts are made to familiarize students in regular elementary schools with industrial life. In the classroom some time is spent on reading and discussing various types of tools, machinery, equipment, and simple industrial processes. Some of the books are illustrated with industrial objects. Apparently primary school children usually have the opportunity also to visit factories, and in some cases even work briefly in plants as part of the requirement for physical labor. They all must engage periodically in some type of physical labor, and I observed school children working in parks and on streets and communes, as well as in factories.

Exposure to industrial concepts and industry itself in primary schools probably does much to create an interest in and awareness of industrial life and to imbue a respect for the dignity of labor. When Chinese primary school graduates enter industry, they probably tend to feel more at home than the typical Indian who has gone through primary school because there does not seem to be much, if any, stress on industrial life in primary schools in India.

Specialized Vocational and Technical Training and General Secondary Education

This section is concerned with Chinese junior and senior middle school education and particularly with specialized secondary education. Regular junior middle schools in China are roughly analogous to American junior high schools. Students are typically in the thirteen-to-sixteen-age category, and the programs are three years in length. Chinese regular senior secondary or middle school students are typically in the sixteen-to-nineteen-age bracket, and these programs also last three years. The vast majority of entrants into higher educational programs in normal times are graduates of senior secondary schools.

There has been a very substantial increase in enrollments and the number of graduates in Chinese junior and senior general secondary schools since 1949, as can be seen from Table 3–4.[18]

TABLE 3–4

Statistics on General Secondary Education

Year	*Enrollment* (In Thousands)			*Number of Graduates* (In Thousands)		
	JUNIOR	SENIOR	TOTAL	JUNIOR	SENIOR	TOTAL
1949–50	831.8	207.2	1,039	250	46	296
1957–58	4,340	780.0	5,120	1,091	221.7	1,313
1958–59	7,340	1,180	8,520	not available	242	not available
1959–60	7,740	5,160	12,900	" "	not available	" "
1964–65	21,000	2,100	23,100	" "	" "	" "

We see from the above table that there was a great increase in enrollments at the outset of the Great Leap period in 1958. The 1959–60 and 1964 enrollment figures are questionable. The American author Edgar Snow was given the 1959–60 figures by a Chinese vice-minister of education in 1960. The senior middle school enrollment figure seems very high, and it is possible that this figure includes specialized secondary school enrollment for that period. The 1964–65 junior middle school figure also seems to be very high, and it might include spare-time program enrollments, although this does not seem likely. The 1964–65 figures were given to Charles Lynch, a Canadian journalist, by the director of industrial education of the Chinese Ministry of Higher Education in 1965.

If the 1964–65 Chinese figures are correct, China now has a substantially larger number of students enrolled in junior high school programs than India, but it still lags significantly behind India in senior high school enrollment. In India in 1962–63 there were 8.3 million students enrolled in junior high school programs and 3.9 million in programs equivalent to Chinese general senior middle schools. During the 1958–61 period about 24.2 percent of the estimated Indian population aged fifteen to nineteen inclusive—adjusted for the duration of school years at this level—was enrolled in secondary schools; the figure for China was only about 14.2 percent.[19] There is much more individual freedom in India and virtually any primary school graduate who wishes to proceed with his formal education and can get the necessary financial support, either from family or other sources, can do so. While China may or may not currently lead India in junior secondary school enrollment—depending on the accuracy of the 1964–65 enrollment figure—the rate of growth in Chinese secondary education has been much greater than that of India. Total enrollment in Indian secondary-level education in 1949–50 was about 4.4 million; in 1955–56, 6.2 million; and in 1962–63, 12.2 million.[20]

I am in no position to assess confidently the quality of general secondary education in China as compared with that of India. However, it does seem that the Chinese system might give somewhat better preparation to those graduates who embark on industrial careers because of its apparently more applied and practical emphasis. The Indians themselves admit that their system of secondary education has many serious deficiencies, and this widespread sentiment is summed up in the words of a prominent Indian education official thus:

> It is rightly pointed out that secondary education in India suffers from aimlessness, its primary aim being to prepare children for entrance into the universities or for clerical jobs. Colleges are being clogged with undeserving students, and unemployed matriculates are running amuck for getting a job on a couple of rupees a day. Unfortunately secondary education is a victim of its own traditions.[21]

It is true that India is more openly critical of its educational—and other—problems than China, and this often tends to place India in a less favorable light to the outside world. Yet, although India may produce more secondary-level graduates, the nature of training might not be as effective in terms of industrial progress as in China. In Chinese general secondary education there seems to be somewhat more emphasis on mathematical, scientific, technical, and industrial subjects than in India, where there seems to be more stress on the classics, literature, and the humanities.

There is, of course, much more stress on ideology and politics in China, and this does significantly reduce the time spent on functional training. In both countries there is some emphasis on bookkeeping and accounting—more so at the senior high school level, but here too the Chinese emphasis seems to be somewhat more strictly applied. While both systems may be about equally effective—or ineffective—in turning out white-collar clerks, the Chinese system is probably significantly better in turning out industrial workers and graduates who eventually will become technical personnel. The Chinese system also exposes students to physical labor and industrial life even at the junior middle school level, while this practice seems to be a rarity in India's general secondary education system.

The great majority of Chinese junior middle school graduates do not go on to senior middle schools upon graduation. Most of them go to work, although many of them do continue their educations through spare-time programs. A sizable proportion of graduates from senior middle schools do go on to higher education, as can be seen in Table 3–5 below.[22]

TABLE 3–5

SENIOR HIGH SCHOOL GRADUATES AND NUMBER ENTERING HIGHER EDUCATION

Year	*Total Number of Graduates*	*Entrants into Higher Education*
1950–51	44,300	35,000
1955–56	156,000	165,600
1957–58	221,700	152,000
1958–59	242,000	270,000

We see from the above table that in 1958–59, during the height of the Great Leap Forward, there were more entrants into higher education than high school graduates. Thousands of inadequately prepared soldiers, workers, party officials, and peasants entered Chinese universities and colleges during this period, and the quality of higher education obviously suffered a serious setback. Many of the hastily established "Red and Expert" universities were subsequently closed down. It seems that by 1962 or 1963 a more rational policy of admissions to higher education programs had evolved in China.

A leading Canadian industrialist was told by the National Director of Higher Education in Peking that in 1964 only about 25 percent of the graduates of senior middle schools were admitted to higher educational programs. At the Number 3 Middle School in Chungking, he was told that 60 percent of their 1964 graduates entered higher programs, that a small number were sent to a school for training primary schoolteachers, and the rest were sent to factories, communes, and commercial organizations.[23] I was told by the head of a senior middle school in Nanking that about 40 percent of the graduates went on to higher studies, while about one third went into industry. An English teacher at a junior middle school in Shanghai told me that about 15 to 20 percent of their graduates went on to general senior middle schools and a slightly larger percentage to specialized secondary schools; nearly 40 percent were sent to factories, and the rest to communes and other organizations.

Unlike India, numerous junior and senior middle school graduates in China receive their education through spare-time adult programs. Such education may generally be inferior in breadth and quality to regular programs, but they should be taken into account when comparing Indian and Chinese educational performance. Table 3–6 presents some enrollment statistics on spare-time secondary education in China; junior and senior middle school figures are lumped together. During the 1958–62 period, about 600,000 workers finished spare-time secondary education programs of all types.[24]

TABLE 3–6

SPARE-TIME ADULT GENERAL SECONDARY EDUCATION ENROLLMENT FIGURES

Year	*Enrollment* (In Thousands)
1952	249
1955	1167
1957	2714
1958	5000

Again we can see the sharp increase in enrollment with the onslaught of the Great Leap Forward. Edgar Snow was told by a top-level Chinese trade union official that in 1960 enrollment in spare-time senior middle school programs was 1.5 million, and the combined figure for junior middle schools and specialized secondary programs was 4 million.[25] Industrial personnel have constituted a large proportion of the students enrolled in secondary-level spare-time programs. Both junior and senior middle-level spare-time programs run from about eighteen to twenty-four months.

At twenty-six Chinese industrial enterprises surveyed, where statistics were obtained regarding the proportion of employees who had graduated from at least junior middle school programs, a majority of employees were not such graduates at seven enterprises. These were Wusih Silk, 18 percent; Hangchow Clothing, 30 percent; Peking Clothing, 40 percent; Canton Electrical Appliance, 30 percent; and Wuhan Diesel Engine, 30 percent; Hangchow Machine Tool, 40 percent; Wusih Machinery, 40 percent; and Tientsin Instrument, about 40 percent. The Wuhan Diesel and Hangchow Machine Tool factories were engaged in fairly complex operations, and they seemed to be operating rather inefficiently. Of the seven, only the Hangchow Clothing, Peking Clothing, and Wusih Silk factories seemed to be relatively efficient enterprises; they were engaged in fairly simple operations, and both had many employees with more than twenty years of experience. Table 9–3 in Chapter 9 presents a grading of the enterprises surveyed in terms of their general productive and managerial efficiency. At most of the enterprises surveyed, a greater proportion of white-collar workers were junior middle school graduates than were blue-collar workers. (I use the terms "white-collar" and "blue-collar" in the Western context; most Chinese industrial personnel of all types seem to dress the same, in blue clothing.) For example, at the Wuhan Paper Mill 50 percent of the workers were graduates, while the figure for all employees was about 70 percent.

In general, the proportion of junior middle school graduates at the enterprises surveyed has risen sharply in the last ten to fifteen years. For example, the proportion at the Tientsin Instrument Plant was only about 10 percent in 1958, and in 1966 it increased to about 45 percent; at Tientsin Shoe the proportion increased from about 6 percent in 1950 to 50 percent in 1966. At a number of enterprises 70 percent or more of their employees were junior middle school graduates. These included Tientsin Watch, Peking Coke, Shanghai and Peking Pharmaceutical, Wusih Diesel, Wuhan Heavy Machinery, Wuhan Iron and Steel, Wuhan Paper, Shanghai Heavy Machine Tool, and Shanghai Machine Tool No. 3. All but two of these firms operate their own regular junior middle schools, and all of them have spare-time junior middle school programs for their employees. All of them had some employees enrolled in such spare-time programs, and some had more than 10 percent of their employees so enrolled.

A sizable proportion of employees at other enterprises surveyed were also enrolled in spare-time junior middle school programs at the plant or elsewhere. Examples of such enrollment are: Tientsin Instrument, 40 percent; Shanghai's Joint Sung Sin Cotton Mill, 20 percent; and Shanghai Cotton Textile Number 19, 10 percent. The last two firms run their own regular and part-time junior middle schools. A substantial proportion of junior middle school graduates at all of the enterprises surveyed received their educations through spare-time programs. From what I observed, it seems that enterprise-operated junior middle school programs and particularly the spare-time programs stress functional and applied training even more than other types of regular programs. There also seems to be somewhat less emphasis on ideology and politics; the reason for this may be because the employee is already exposed to much of this subject matter in his working life.

Junior middle school graduates can be found in all types of industrial jobs, both blue-collar and white-collar, managerial and nonmanagerial. However, the average length of formal schooling of the directors at the enterprises surveyed was around nine to eleven years, or about the equivalent of junior middle school or one or two years of senior high school. For party secretaries it was only about eight or nine years. In many cases, even this relatively low level of schooling of directors and party secretaries was achieved through spare-time programs. It is typically the vice directors, department heads, workshop chiefs, engineers, and key technicians at industrial firms who often have had more than a junior middle school education. These are the Experts in most cases, while the director is typically more Red than Expert.

At only one of nineteen industrial firms where statistics were obtained a near majority of employees were senior middle school graduates. This was the Shanghai Heavy Machine Tool Plant, where over 40 percent of the employees had completed this level of education, and many of them had done so through spare-time programs. At only four other firms there were 20 percent or more of their employees who were such graduates; these were Shanghai and Peking Pharmaceuticals, Tientsin Watch, and Wuhan Heavy Machinery. On the average, only about 10 to 12 percent of the employees at the nineteen enterprises were graduates of this type, and at some of them there were less than 5 percent and even none. While several of these enterprises did have 5 to 10 percent—and in a few cases more—of their employees enrolled in spare-time senior high school programs, the figures were not nearly so substantial as those for junior middle school.

It seems that there may be a higher proportion of senior high school graduates in terms of total employment in Indian industrial firms than in Chinese firms. At seven Indian enterprises where I obtained such statistics, the proportions of high school graduates (matriculates) ranged from about 15 to 30 percent. At both Indian and Chinese enterprises most graduates of this type seem to be employed in white-collar rather than in blue-collar jobs. Clerical jobs are often done by such graduates in Chinese industry, and it is fairly common to find them in accounting work and white-collar managerial jobs at the middle and lower rungs of the administrative organization.

A major source of skilled manpower in the Chinese economy is the system of specialized secondary education. The aim of instruction here is to train students in skill and knowledge that will qualify them for employment at the intermediate levels of professional competence and become "technicians," as their counterparts are called in the Soviet Union. The specialized system provides diversity of training not found in the standard-curriculum, essentially one-track general secondary schools.[26]

There are two basic types of specialized secondary schools in China:

normal and vocational, or technical. The normal schools are engaged in training teachers and are not of interest for this study. The vocational-technical schools, however, are of major interest because they offer specialized training in many fields, such as economics, accounting, forestry, and agriculture, directly linked to the requirements of industry, business, and economic development in general. These schools offer several hundred specialties or fields of concentration.

In the 1950's there were both junior and senior specialized secondary schools, but the former were apparently terminated around the end of the period of the Great Leap Forward. Currently, programs range in duration from two and a half to four years, and new entrants usually are junior general middle school graduates. Students in Chinese specialized secondary schools are typically in the fifteen-to-twenty-age bracket, although one does find some in their late twenties and even early thirties. Technical-industrial programs—sometimes referred to as engineering—last at least three years, and probably in most cases four years. Economics, planning, statistics, accounting, trade, and other programs of the business administration type are typically two and a half to three years in length; this area of semiprofessional education is much smaller than the technical area.

There is no directly comparable equivalent to Chinese—or Soviet—semiprofessional training of this type in the American educational system. Many of the Chinese graduates of these specialized schools are roughly comparable to the graduates from the vocational and technical high schools and technical institutes in America. Perhaps Chinese graduates from the best semiprofessional programs are roughly comparable to American graduates of various junior and community colleges and better technical institutes, such as Wentworth in Boston. However, Chinese programs are typically narrower and provide for more intensive specialized training than is offered in most comparable American programs. American schools typically combine under the same auspices several types of specialized training that would be offered separately in individual Chinese schools.

There has been a substantial increase in the enrollments and number of graduates in regular Chinese specialized vocational secondary schools, as can be seen in Table 3–7.[27]

The quality of vocational training apparently fell drastically with the great increase in enrollment during the Great Leap Forward. Many of the hastily established and expanded specialized secondary schools were poorly equipped, and the quality of graduates was often too low to meet the requirements of their jobs. The problems and deficiencies of this type of education may well be imagined from the following quotation which appeared in the May, 1958, issue of the Chinese journal *People's Education:*

In 7-days' time, beginning March 18, 1958, without using a penny from state funds, Nanking Municipality set up 263 vocational middle schools, enrolling a total of 17,000 students. This was accomplished in a few days what otherwise might take 5 to 10 years. . . . Of the 263 schools, 117 were set up within the city area to train personnel for work in machine, motors, and chemical industries, as well as the production of food, woodwork, needlework, printing, and hygiene.[28]

TABLE 3–7
STATISTICS ON SPECIALIZED SECONDARY EDUCATION

Year	*Enrollment* (In Thousands)			*Graduates* (In Thousands)		
	VOCATIONAL-TECHNICAL	NORMAL	TOTAL	VOCATIONAL-TECHNICAL	NORMAL	TOTAL
1949–50	77.1	151.7	228.8	25	50	75
1952–53	290.4	345.2	635.6	54	64	118
1955–56	318.1	219.0	537.1	103	71	174
1956–57	337.0	273.4	610.4	81	65	146
1957–58	458.0	320.0	778.0	112	79	191
1958–59	850.0	620.0	1470.0	113	90	213

The increase in enrollments of spare-time secondary vocational schools during the 1950's was even more substantial than in the regular schools, as can be seen from Table 3–8.[29] The spare-time programs are typically about two years in length.

TABLE 3–8

ENROLLMENT IN SPARE-TIME VOCATIONAL SECONDARY SCHOOLS

Year	*Enrollment* (In Thousands)
1950	.1
1952	.7
1955	195.0
1956	563.0
1957	588.0

I did not obtain any concrete current figures on the enrollment and number of graduates of Chinese specialized secondary vocational schools. The vice-head of the part-work, part-study specialized secondary vocational school operated by the Wuhan Heavy Machinery Plant speculated that overall enrollments and number of graduates in the country at this level of education were probably once again as high or higher than the peak figures of the Great Leap period. He also said that there was probably a cutback in the early 1960's, but in that period quality of training was improved, programs consolidated, and enrollments and graduates once again started to increase. In his own school in 1966, there were 1,100 students, as compared with 800 in 1960. The majority of graduates from this school stay at the enterprise; the others usually go to similar types of firms elsewhere.

A number of the firms surveyed ran their own semiprofessional schools. Some were considered to be regular schools, where mostly teenagers were enrolled; while the majority were referred to as spare-time specialized secondary programs where students were primarily adults who were working on a permanent basis for the enterprise. At about a dozen of the enterprises questioned about semiprofessional spare-time education, 5 percent or more of their personnel were enrolled in such programs. Most of the enterprises surveyed had at least some employees enrolled in such programs at the plant or elsewhere.

In general, there are three types of specialized vocational schools: (a) those set up at and operated by one or more enterprises; (b) an existing school attached to an enterprise to provide it with required manpower; (c) more or less independent schools, but still having a relationship with one or more firms because their students are required to engage in labor. In reality there does seem to be a considerable amount of overlapping between regular and spare-time programs, on-the-job training, and work and study programs. The Wuhan Heavy Machinery school seems to be a cross between a regular and part-time program. Experiments have been made over the years with various combinations of work and study programs. At the Wuhan school there has been increasing emphasis in the last few years on specialized training, applied subjects, and ideology.

Table 3–9 presents a rough breakdown of time spent on various activities and subjects at the Wuhan school in 1966 as compared with the breakdown for the period around 1963.

The vice-head of the above school indicated that there might be even more time devoted to employment in the future. Some of the specialties offered at Wuhan's school deal with (1) metal-processing machines, (2) metal cutting, (3) forging and pressing, (4) maintenance and repair of machinery, and (5) measuring instruments and techniques. According to Edgar Snow, who visited this school and factory in 1960, students prior to graduation received room and board and a monthly allowance of three yuan; after graduation monthly wages began at 33 yuan, with a top of 107, plus the usual welfare benefits.

In spite of problems of quality and program content, Chinese specialized secondary schools do provide industry with an important source of

TABLE 3–9

ROUGH BREAKDOWN OF TIME SPENT ON SUBJECTS IN SPECIALIZED SECONDARY VOCATIONAL PROGRAM AT WUHAN HEAVY MACHINERY ENTERPRISE

	Around 1963 (%)	*1966 (%)*
Politics, Marxism-Leninism, ideology	10–15	15–20
General academic (including science and mathematics)	15	10–15
General engineering (technical subjects)	20	10–15
Specialized engineering (technical subjects)	20	20–25
Applied projects and physical work	30–35	40

middle-level technical and managerial manpower. Upper-level managerial and engineering jobs are also filled by semiprofessionals in many cases. To give some idea of what type of jobs is filled by semiprofessional graduates, Table 3–10 indicates the specialties for which a number of semiprofessional graduates were trained at some of the Chinese enterprises surveyed.

TABLE 3–10

OCCUPATIONS OF VARIOUS TYPES OF SEMIPROFESSIONAL GRADUATES IN CHINESE INDUSTRY

Enterprise	*Position*	*Semiprofessional Specialty*
WUHAN HEAVY MACHINERY	Maintenance and repair supervisor	Maintenance and repair of equipment
	Technician in design department (also set material standards)	Metal cutting
	Shop chief	Forging and pressing
	Machine operator	Metal-processing machines
SHANGHAI STEEL NO. 3	Deputy chief accountant	Accounting
	Foreman (group leader)	Blast furnace production
	Mechanic	Blast furnace production
	Metalworker (recent graduate)	Steel production
PEKING STEEL WIRE	Vice-head, technical department	Wire and cable production
	2 apprentice-students operating machines	Metal-rolling production
	Shop chief	Heat treatment

TABLE 3–10 (*continued*)

Enterprise	*Position*	*Semiprofessional Specialty*
WUSIH DIESEL ENGINE	Workshop chief	Diesel engine construction
	Workers	Internal combustion engines
SHANGHAI FORGING AND PRESSING	Vice-director	Forging and pressing
SHANGHAI HEAVY MACHINE TOOL	Vice-chief technologist	Metallurgical machine building
	Head material and supply section	Material and technical supply
	Vice-head, planning department	Planning and organization in machine building
	Employee in finance department	Finance
WUHAN PAPER	Technician	Paper manufacturing
PEKING COTTON	Technician	Technology of fibers
	Vice-director and chief engineer	Technology of fibers
PEKING WOOL FABRICS	Head of production	Processing and sorting of wool
TIENTSIN SHOE	Vice-head, technical department	Technology of leather products
PEKING CLOTHING	Head of design department	Trade and merchandising
	Stylist and designer	Trade and merchandising
SHANGHAI PHARMACEUTICAL	Planning analyst in production-planning department	Planning in the chemical industry
SHANGHAI TRUCK	Several workers and technicians	Motor vehicle construction

In general, it seems that a greater proportion of semiprofessional graduates are employed as skilled workers in Russian industry than in Chinese industry. Since there is a much greater shortage of high-talent manpower in China, it is necessary to utilize most semiprofessionals as technicians, supervisors, and even middle- and upper-level managers and engineers in many cases. Skilled workers are frequently developed through on-the-job training in Chinese factories rather than through specialized secondary schools. Notable exceptions to this employment practice in Chinese factories were observed at the Wuhan Diesel and Shanghai Truck factories where a substantial number of the skilled workers were semiprofessional graduates. These factories belong to fairly new and complex industries in

China and apparently have not found it feasible to staff various skilled-worker jobs with personnel who are not semiprofessional graduates—or perhaps they cannot develop an adequate supply of skilled workers through on-the-job training. At most of the enterprises surveyed, however, the vast majority of semiprofessional graduates were employed as technicians, engineers, and as administrative officials (often referred to as cadres).

By 1955 the majority of students in Chinese secondary specialized vocational schools were majoring in technical and industrial fields. This is shown in Table 3–11 below.[30]

TABLE 3–11

ESTIMATED ENROLLMENT IN TECHNICAL AND INDUSTRIAL FIELDS IN SECONDARY VOCATIONAL EDUCATION

Year	*Enrollment in Technical and Industrial Specialties as a percentage of total enrollment*
1949–50	27.8
1950–51	29.7
1954–55	50.6
1955–56	55.8
1956–57	61.7
1957–58	61.7

It is likely that the majority of specialized secondary vocational students in China are still enrolled in and are graduates of technical and industrial fields. Table 3–12, below, presents the estimated number of employed Chinese technicians who have graduated from specialized secondary vocational schools for selected years during the 1952–63 period.[31]

TABLE 3–12

ESTIMATED NUMBER OF TECHNICIANS WHO HAVE GRADUATED FROM SPECIALIZED SECONDARY EDUCATION PROGRAMS

Year	*Number* (In Thousands)
1952	132
1955	271
1958	487
1959	851
1960	928
1961	1053
1962	1129
1963	1200

In spite of substantial quantitative gains, China currently lags behind the Soviet Union in specialized secondary education.[32] On the average, the quality of this type of training is probably also significantly poorer in China. In the 1958–59 period there were 213,000 graduates from regular Chinese specialized secondary programs, of whom 113,000 were vocational graduates, and about 75,000 were in technical and industrial fields. The corresponding Soviet figures for 1959 were approximately 527,900, 460,-000, and 260,000 respectively. Even in 1952 the Soviets did better than China in 1958–59, and the approximate corresponding 1952 Soviet figures were 280,600, 250,000, and 120,000. The Chinese figures apparently do not take into account graduates from spare-time adult programs, and such figures are not available. Even if this type of graduate is included the Soviets would probably still be ahead in terms of semiprofessional graduates. In 1964 the Soviets graduated a total of about 600,000 semiprofessionals, of whom roughly 540,000 were from vocational fields, and approximately 325,000 were from technical and industrial programs. It is unlikely that the Chinese have approached this level of performance in specialized secondary education as of 1967; although the gap between China and Russia has probably been narrowing.

The Soviet Union is clearly well ahead of China in total employment of technical and industrial graduates from secondary specialized education programs. However, the gap here also has narrowed significantly in the past fifteen years. By 1957 there were about 357,000 semiprofessional graduates—often called technicians—of this type in China (as compared with 1,278,000 in the Soviet Union); or a ratio of about three and a half to one. In 1959 the figure for China was about 851,000 as compared with 1,685,000 in Russia, as of January 1960; and in 1963 the Chinese figure was approximately 1,200,000 and for Russia, 2,446,400. The current ratio in favor of the Soviets is probably in the area of two to one—still a wide lead—but much less proportionally than it was ten years ago. As of 1963 there was a total of 6.2 million semiprofessional graduates of all types employed in the Soviet Union. It is doubtful whether the Chinese figure in 1967 exceeds 2.5 or, at most, 3 million.

While China lags behind Russia in specialized secondary education, it is well ahead of India, where there is not very much in the way of semiprofessional training. There are a number of industrial training institutions in India offering programs lasting about one to two years. Entrants must usually have a junior or senior high school education, depending on the program of study. Some programs of the technical and engineering type provide for in-plant training. In 1966 total enrollment in these programs was less than 100,000, and the large majority of the students were studying for technical and engineering trades. In 1958 some junior technical schools were established, offering three-year programs corresponding to grades nine through eleven. However, total enrollment in 1965 was less than 15,000. During the last fifteen years in India only about 10 to 12 percent of students at the overall secondary education level were in vocational or technical programs, but there has been a significant increase in recent years.

India's overall system of specialized, technical, and vocational education, below the university and college level, lags significantly behind that of China. A number of leading Indian education officials are calling for reforms in this type of education similar to those introduced in China since 1949. Such reforms include work and study programs, more specialization, greater emphasis on application, apprenticeship schemes, and so forth.

From my own research, and that of others, in Indian industry, it seems that there is a greater shortage of skilled workers and craftsmen, such as machinists, mechanics, toolmakers, welders, and especially of technicians and middle- and lower-level technical managers than in China. There is an obvious tendency for many Indian firms to use higher-education graduates and other overqualified persons for many jobs filled by semiprofessional graduates in China. (The same is also true in the United States, but to a much more limited extent.) In China, rather than underutilizing high-talent manpower in various jobs, they often tend to overutilize persons who do not have adequate training or education.

In the American educational system the weakest link is probably in the area of secondary level vocational and technical training.[33] In recent years there has been an acute shortage of skilled toolmakers and various types of technicians. This has forced many manufacturers into expensive overtime operations and has also extended by several months the delivery dates of shipments to customers. It is true that this and similar manpower shortage situations in the United States may be due in part to general economic conditions, but they are often due largely to inadequacies in the system of vocational and semiprofessional technical training. Shortages of various types of technicians show up on very low ratios of semiprofessionals to professionals in many firms in such departments as production, design, and research and development.

Table 3–13, presented in the next section, indicates the proportions of specialized secondary school graduates in relation to total employment at thirty-seven industrial enterprises and three higher-level organizations surveyed in China in 1966. It is evident that large- and medium-sized heavy industry firms are the largest users of this type of manpower. This is to be expected because of the relatively complex nature of technology and operations in this sector.

In the Soviet heavy industry sector, in the late 1950's and early 1960's approximately 8.5 percent of all employees were semiprofessional gradu-

TABLE 3–13

EDUCATIONAL DATA ON THIRTY-SEVEN INDUSTRIAL ENTERPRISES AND THREE HIGHER-LEVEL ORGANIZATIONS SURVEYED IN 1966

Enterprise and Industry	*Total Employment*	*Higher Education*		*Specialized Secondary Education* (Semiprofessional)	
	Number	Percent	Number	Percent	Number
HEAVY INDUSTRY					
Large- and medium-sized machinery and equipment, steel, motor vehicles, engines					
Wuhan Iron and Steel Corporation	35,000	5.5	1,925	11	3,850
Loyang Tractor	20,500	3.0	615	6	1,230
Shanghai Steel No. 3	13,000	1.6	208	5.5	715
Wuhan Heavy Machinery	7,000	5.5	385	20	1,400
Peking Machine Tool	4,000	5.0	200	12.5	500
Shanghai Machine Tool	6,000	3.3	198	5	300
Canton Machine Tool	3,100	3.5	119	5	165
Wusih Diesel Engine	2,700	9.0	243	15	405
Nanking Machinery	1,300	5.0	65	10	130
Shanghai Truck	1,050	9.0	95	22	231
Hangchow Machine Tool	1,000	6.0	60	5	50
Shanghai No. 3 Machine Tool	1,000	5.0	50	2	20
Wuhan Diesel Engine	992	2.0	20	1	10
Peking Steel Wire	800	4.0	32	6	48
Totals	97,442	4.3	4,215	9.3	9,054

Small-scale machinery, small tools, instruments, components					
Wusih Machinery	300	1.0	3.0	1.0	3.0
Shanghai Forging & Pressing Machine Tool	405	.5	2	1.5	6
Tientsin Instrument	165	0	0	0	0
Totals	870	.6	5	1.0	9
Other					
Wuhan Paper	2,000	1.0	20	4	80
Soochow Cement Products	680	.6	4	1.5	10
Totals	2,680	1.0	24	3.3	90
ALL HEAVY INDUSTRY TOTALS	100,992	4.2	4,244	9.1	9,143
CHEMICALS AND DRUGS					
Nanking Chemical Fertilizer	10,000	5.5	550	1.4	140
Peking Pharmaceutical	3,000	6.0	180	4.0	120
Canton Chemical Fertilizer	2,400	4.0	96	7.0	168
Peking Chemical Coke	2,100	5.0	105	6.0	126
Shanghai Pharmaceutical	1,200	7.0	84	3.5	42
Totals	18,700	5.4	1,015	3.2	596
LIGHT INDUSTRY					
Light engineering					
Tientsin Watch	1,400	7.0	98	3.0	42
Canton Electrical Appliance	840	.25	2	1.5	13
Shanghai Battery	563	1.0	6	2.5	15
Totals	2,803	3.8	106	2.5	70

TABLE 3–13 (*continued*)

Enterprise and Industry	*Total Employment*	*Higher Education*		*Specialized Secondary Education* (Semiprofessional)	
	Number	Percent	Number	Percent	Number
Textiles					
Shanghai Joint State & Private Cotton Textile No. 9	6,000	.7	42	.5	30
Peking Cotton Textile No. 3	5,000	1.0	50	2.0	100
Shanghai Cotton Textile No. 19	4,800	2.0	96	2.0	96
Peking Woolen Carpet	2,700	1.5	41	2.0	54
Peking Wool	1,800	1.5	27	2.5	45
Tientsin Joint State and Private Wool	1,800	1.0	18	1.4	25
Wusih Silk Reeling No. 2	1,500	.7	10	.7	10
Totals	23,600	1.2	294	1.5	360
Clothing					
Peking Clothing	1,700	.6	10	.9	15
Hangchow Clothing	400	0	0	0	0
Totals	2,100	.5	10	.75	15
Shoes					
Tientsin Shoe	1,000	3.0	30	1.0	10
All Light Industry Totals	29,503	1.5	440	1.5	455
GRAND TOTALS	149,195	3.7%	5,569	6.8%	10,194
HIGHER-LEVEL ORGANIZATIONS					
Tientsin Daily Usage Corporation	55	14.5	8	9	5
Tientsin First Light Industry Bureau	102	20.0	20	8	8
Wusih Municipal Planning Commission	15	26.7	4	20	3

ates. This figure is slightly less than the 9.1 percent figure for my sample of Chinese enterprises, which undoubtedly reflects a significant upward bias because of disproportionate representation of relatively large and complex factories.

In the Soviet chemical industry—which includes drugs— approximately 10 percent of all employees during the same period were semiprofessional graduates, as compared with only 3.2 percent at the Chinese firms surveyed in this sector. Since this is a relatively new sector in China, it is likely that a fairly extensive network of specialized secondary schools offering specialties of this type has not yet been established. In Soviet light industry the proportion of semiprofessional graduates has been about 3.5 percent, as compared with 1.5 percent for my sample of Chinese enterprises in this sector. Here too, the Chinese may not have yet developed an extensive network of semiprofessional schools. However, as will be discussed in a later chapter, several of the Chinese light-industry firms seem to be relatively well managed and efficient. This is probably due in large part to the fact that they employ many older workers and managers who have much experience, and in a number of cases original capitalist-owners are still employed as managers.

At all Soviet industrial enterprises in 1963 about 6 percent of all employees were semiprofessional graduates, as compared with 6.8 percent for our sample of thirty-seven Chinese firms. Here again, there is undoubtedly a substantial upward bias in the Chinese figure because of the type of sample studied; nevertheless, the figure does indicate that Red China has made impressive progress in specialized secondary education in its relatively short history.

Our sample of three higher-level industrial organizations, ranking above the ordinary enterprises, is, of course, too small for us to draw from it any concrete conclusions. It does suggest, however, that such organizations do tend to employ a larger proportion of semiprofessional graduates than do lower-level industrial firms. The higher the place occupied by organizations in the industrial hierarchy the more they seem to employ a greater variety of such graduates because the higher-ranking enterprises typically deal with an increasingly broad range of products, activities, and enterprises. It also appears that such organizations employ a significantly larger proportion of nontechnical semiprofessionals than do industrial enterprises. For example, about half of the semiprofessional graduates employed by the Wusih Municipal Planning Commission majored in such nonengineering technical fields as planning, economics, finance, accounting and costing, material and technical supply, and statistics. The other two organizations also employed a number of similar nontechnical semiprofessionals.

Table 3–14, below, indicates the proportion of specialized secondary education graduates in relation to the total number of administrative and technical personnel at thirty-one Chinese industrial enterprises surveyed. It should be pointed out that the education statistics for some enterprises in this table are estimates, and may involve small margins of error. While most enterprises did give me precise education figures from their records, some gave me ranges such as five to six percent or 120 to 140 semiprofessional graduates. Where ranges were given I have arbitrarily selected the midpoints of such estimates. Technical personnel consists of all engineers and technicians employed as such. Administrative personnel includes all managers, supervisors, party and trade union officials holding executive posts, and white-collar specialists (such as accountants, bookkeepers, economists, planners, and statisticians), specialists in finance, labor and wages, distribution, material and technical supply (procurement), and so forth. Such administrative personnel are often referred to as administra-

TABLE 3–14

PERCENTAGE* OF ADMINISTRATIVE AND TECHNICAL PERSONNEL HAVING HIGHER AND SPECIALIZED SECONDARY EDUCATIONS AT THIRTY-ONE ENTERPRISES SURVEYED

	Total No. of Admin. and Tech. Personnel	*Percent Having a Higher Education*	*Percent Having a Specialized Secondary Education*
HEAVY INDUSTRY			
Large- and medium-sized			
Wuhan Iron and Steel	9,300	20%	41%
Shanghai Steel	2,730	13	24
Wuhan Heavy Machinery	2,550	15	54
Peking Machine Tool	1,100	18	45
Shanghai Machine Tool	1,200	16	25
Hangchow Machine Tool	200	30	25
Shanghai No. 3 Machine Tool	200	25	10
Wuhan Diesel Engine	138	15	7
Peking Steel Wire	235	14	20
Totals	17,653	(3,078) 17%	(6,893) 38%
Small-scale machinery, instruments, tools and components			
Wusih Machinery	40	8	8
Shanghai Forging and Pressing	49	4	12
Tientsin Instrument	10	0	0
Totals	99	(5) 5%	(9) 9%

	Total No. of Admin. and Tech. Personnel	*Percent Having a Higher Education*	*Percent Having a Specialized Secondary Education*
Other			
Wuhan Paper	420	5	19
Soochow Cement Products	60	7	17
Totals	480	(24) 5%	(90) 19%
ALL HEAVY INDUSTRY TOTALS	18,232	(3,107) 17%	(6,992) 33%
CHEMICALS AND DRUGS			
Nanking Chemical Fertilizer	2,700	20%	5%
Canton Chemical Fertilizer	552	17	29
Peking Pharmaceutical	540	33	22
Shanghai Pharmaceutical	306	27	14
Peking Chemical Coke	420	20	24
Totals	4,518	(1,015) 22%	(596) 13%
LIGHT INDUSTRY			
Light Engineering			
Tientsin Watch	218	45	19
Canton Electrical Appliance	134	1	9
Shanghai Battery	73	8	20
Totals	425	(106) 25%	(70) 17%
Textiles			
Shanghai Joint Cotton Textile No. 9	450	9	7
Shanghai Cotton Textile No. 19	374	20	20
Peking Cotton Textile No. 3	500	10	20
Peking Wool	234	12	21
Tientsin Joint Wool	187	10	13
Wusih Silk Reeling No. 2	188	5	5
Totals	1,933	(253) 13%	(306) 15%
Clothing			
Peking Clothing	85	12	18
Hangchow Clothing	16	0	0
Totals	101	(10) 10%	(15) 15%
Shoes			
Tientsin Shoe	225	(30) 14%	(10) 4%
ALL LIGHT INDUSTRY TOTALS	2,694	(399) 15%	(401) 15%
OVERALL TOTALS	25,444	(4,521) 18%	(7,988) 31%

*** Numbers and percentages have been rounded; figures in parentheses represent absolute numbers.**

tive cadres by the Chinese. I could not obtain a precise definition of exactly who falls within this category.

It should be noted that Table 3–14 assumes that all semiprofessional graduates are employed in either technical or administrative jobs, and as a result there is a small margin of error in some cases. At most of the enterprises surveyed the great majority, probably over 95 percent, of their semiprofessionals were employed in administrative and technical jobs. Those employed as skilled workers were usually recent graduates serving their required one- or two-year terms as apprentices in physical labor.

However, the two notable exceptions mentioned earlier, the Wusih Diesel and Shanghai Truck enterprises are not included in Table 3–14. At these two firms a large proportion of semiprofessional graduates were employed as workers. At Wusih Diesel there were 540 employees classified as technical and administrative, while there were 405 semiprofessional graduates and 243 higher education graduates employed here. The director estimated that between 150 and 200 semiprofessional graduates were employed as workers. At Shanghai Truck there were about 105 technical and administrative employees, while the firm's personnel included 231 semiprofessional graduates and 95 higher graduates. The trade union chairman here pointed out that more than half of the semiprofessional graduates were employed as workers. Reasons given for employing so many semiprofessional graduates as workers at these two enterprises were that many of the graduates were recent ones; that many skilled-worker jobs cannot be efficiently filled through on-the-job training because of their complexity; that they were having some difficulties with their operations in recent years because of the lack of adequately trained manpower; and that many of the younger semiprofessional graduates would be sent to other new and/or expanding diesel engine and truck factories in the future —and these two factories were being used as a kind of training ground.

Table 3–14 indicates that the proportion of administrative and technical personnel who are semiprofessional graduates at enterprises in the heavy industry sector is about double that of the light industry sector. The proportion at the five chemical and drug firms surveyed is slightly lower than that for the light industry sector, and this may be due in large part to a still very limited number of specialized secondary programs relating to the chemical and drug industry. However, this sector does apparently have a fairly well-developed network of related higher educational programs.

Our grouping of administrative and technical personnel for Chinese enterprises in Table 3–14 corresponds roughly to the Soviet category of "leading enterprise personnel." In 1957, 34.4 percent of all leading or administrative-technical personnel at Soviet industrial enterprises were semiprofessional graduates, as compared with about 31 percent for our sample of thirty-one Chinese enterprises. The 1966 Soviet figure is most likely significantly higher, and may be as high as 40 percent or even more. As mentioned above, the Chinese and Soviet figures are not directly comparable. There seem to be some types of white-collar jobs of the clerical type included in the Chinese category which are not included in the Soviet definition. While full-time teachers, medical technicians, nurses, doctors, and school and hospital administrators employed by Chinese enterprises are apparently included, I am not sure whether they are in the Soviet case. Moreover, there are not as many of these types of employees in Soviet industry as in China because of better external social-overhead capital facilities in the Soviet Union. Taking the limitations of comparability into account, it appears that while a substantial proportion of administrative and technical personnel at Chinese enterprises are semiprofessional graduates, China still lags significantly behind the Soviet Union quantitatively and probably qualitatively.

The Soviets also have an employment category referred to as Engineering-Technical-Managerial-Personnel, or ETMP.[34] The ETMP group constitutes the key enterprise employees and includes only those who play a direct and major role in the management and technical operations of the enterprise. Of the 25,444 administrative and technical employees in our sample of thirty-one Chinese enterprises, probably in the range of 17,000 to 21,000 of them correspond to the Soviet ETMP category. This is based on estimates given to me by several Chinese firms regarding the proportion of administrative cadres who play a major role in the management process. Using such estimates, roughly 40 to 47 percent of the Chinese ETMP are semiprofessional graduates as compared with 65.8 percent in all Soviet industrial enterprises in 1963. Even in 1956 about 38.5 percent of the Soviet ETMP were semiprofessional graduates. Therefore, at this point in time Chinese industry as a whole is undoubtedly at least ten or possibly even fifteen years behind Soviet industry in terms of the proportion of ETMP who are semiprofessional graduates. However, in this area the Chinese have probably accomplished, at least quantitatively, in seventeen years what it took the Soviets about thirty-five years to do—since the revolution in 1917. Of course, the Chinese have had the advantage of learning much from the Soviet educational system.

Higher Education

General Background

A graduate of a Chinese higher educational institution receives a diploma rather than a degree. This diploma is granted to a graduate of a two-year normal (teachers) college as well as to an individual successfully completing a 5- or 6-year course at a technical, scientific, or medical institute. Despite the substantial difference in the length of study and content of curriculum, published Chinese sources seldom differentiate between two-, three-, four-, five-, or six-year graduates.

The large majority of graduates are from four- to six-year programs that are more directly equivalent to those in Soviet higher education. For example, in 1960 there were 814,000 higher education graduates in China, of which 660,000 or 81 percent were from four- to six-year programs. Most programs are actually four or five years in length, while there are a few five-and-a-half- and 6-year programs in certain fields of medicine, science, technology, and architecture.

There are three basic types of higher educational institutions in Communist China: (1) comprehensive universities, (2) polytechnic universities, (3) specialized professional and technical colleges, often referred to as institutes. The total number of higher educational institutions in China in the peak year before 1949 was 207. By 1957, many institutions were reorganized, many specialized technological and industrial institutes were set up, and the total number of all higher schools was 227. During the height of the Great Leap Forward in 1959, the total number mushroomed to 839, as hundreds of new ones, including many "Red and Expert" universities, were set up. (Our higher education statistics in this chapter exclude most of these Red and Expert universities, and many of them were either merged or abolished after the Great Leap.) As of the mid 1960's, there are about 400 regular higher educational institutions. These include about 20 comprehensive universities, 15 polytechnic universities, and the rest are specialized professional and technical (engineering) institutes, the largest number being of the latter type.

Comprehensive universities, such as Peking, China People's, Fu-ton, Chi-nan, Nanking, and Hunan, are the closest to interdisciplinary American universities offering a general education. These universities are not as important a source of higher graduates for employment in industrial and business enterprises as the other two types of higher schools. Their main function is to train educators, researchers, and scientists of high quality in many different fields. While such universities are roughly comparable to American universities, training in the former tends to be distinctly narrower and more specialized, and there is generally more emphasis on applied rather than basic education.

Polytechnic universities, such as Tsinghua, Tientsin, Harbin, Teng'chi, and Kirin, offer programs in engineering, technical, and applied scientific fields. They offer a number of fields—typically five to ten—of specialization or specialties and a fairly wide variety of courses. They are somewhat similar to American engineering schools, although Chinese training is more specialized, narrower, and more applied. At the polytechnic institutions most of the specialties offered relate to different branches of industry such as machine building, metallurgy, chemical technology, and so forth, while American engineering programs typically train mechanical, chemical, electrical, civil, and various other types of engineers who obtain employment in any one of many branches of industry. The Chinese polytechnic universities are an important source of high-talent industrial manpower as well as a key source of researchers, educators, and scientists. It seems that some of the leading schools of this type, such as Tsinghua, have an "Ivy League" type of image, and their graduates who are employed in industry seem generally to advance quite far up the ladder.

The specialized professional institutes, particularly engineering schools, are the major source of higher education graduates for industry. The engineering institutes, such as the Peking Mining and Iron and Steel institutes, Wuhan and Anshan Iron and Steel institutes, Sian Institute of Aeronautics, East China Institute of Textile Industry, offer only a limited number of technical specialties and applied science courses related to a specific branch of industry. Training here is typically even more specialized and applied than at polytechnic universities and substantially more so than in engineering programs in the United States.

There are also about five or six finance and economic institutes in China which offer applied programs which come closest—but not very close—to those found in American schools of business administration and management and in some economics departments at American universities. These institutes are an important but limited source of high-talent managerial and white-collar specialized manpower for Chinese industry and business.

The quality of education varies within all three types of Chinese higher educational institutions. Polytechnic universities, as a whole, probably offer better training than specialized institutes, but the best technical institutes probably compare quite favorably with good Soviet or American programs, as do the best comprehensive Chinese universities, although both are more specialized than comparable American programs. As a whole, higher technical training in China is probably substantially more effective for industrial development than in India. We shall return later to the discussion of the content of Chinese higher education.

Aggregate Quantitative Trends

Let us turn to the quantitative aspects. During the period from 1948 to 1963 the Chinese higher educational system produced 1,176,000 graduates, a number more than five times greater than the period from 1912 to 1947, when there were only 210,827 graduates. Over 90 percent of Red China's higher-educated engineers and scientists have been trained since 1949. In 1949, there was only one college student for every 10,000 persons in the Chinese population; by the end of 1962 the number had increased to 12 for every 10,000.

Table 3–15 presents aggregate statistics on entrants (admissions), enrollment, and graduates in Chinese higher education during the 1949–66 period.[35] These figures do not include spare-time programs, which are discussed later.

TABLE 3–15

AGGREGATE STATISTICS* ON CHINESE HIGHER EDUCATION
(In Thousands)

Year	*Entrants*	*Enrollment*	*Graduates*
Pre–1949 peak year	—	155	21
1949–50	—	117	18
1950–51	35	137	19
1951–52	35	153	32
1952–53	65.9	191	48
1953–54	71.4	212	47
1954–55	94	253	55
1955–56	96.2	288	63
1956–57	165.6	403	56
1957–58	107	441	72
1958–59	152	660	70
1959–60	270	814	135
1960–61	—	955	162
1961–62	—	819	178
1962–63	—	820	200
1963–64	—	—	—
1964–65	—	700	150
1965–66	—	900	—

* Blanks indicate figures not available.

Table 3–15[36] shows that there was a steady and probably reasonable increase in all aggregate aspects of higher education from 1949 to 1956. In 1956 and 1957 there was a large increase in the number of entrants and in enrollment, and the regime may have felt that the higher educational system was overstrained in 1957 and 1958 when there was a sizable cutback in the number of admissions. However, by 1958 the Great Leap was underway, and admissions and enrollments once again mushroomed. The number of graduates hit an all-time high in 1964. By 1961 there was probably a significant reversal in the number of entrants, and enrollment soon declined sharply as the system was reorganized and consolidated. Quality of training became increasingly emphasized.

In late 1964 the director of Chinese higher education told a prominent Canadian industrialist in Peking that the total number of higher graduates planned for employment in the early 1960's was greater than the need for educated personnel because of the sharp decline in industrial activity caused by the Great Leap Forward, the defection of the Soviets, and natural calamities. He said this was also true of secondary school graduates. It was also found that many higher programs and courses were not sufficiently comprehensive to give the students the broader training required in several fields to carry on without the assistance of the Soviet Union. As a result, new courses and specialties were added, and many existing programs were broadened in content as quality of training improved.

According to one expert Western firsthand observer of the China scene, by 1966 there were approximately 900,000 students enrolled in Chinese higher education. He does not indicate his source, but if his figure is correct it would suggest that the regime may once again be interested in quantity, perhaps at the expense of quality. However, the 1965–66 enrollment figure is still not as high as in the peak year of 1960–61, and the educational system is probably in a better position now than it was six or seven years ago to handle an enrollment of around 900,000.

One cannot help being impressed by China's quantitative performance in higher education. In terms of growth and expansion it has done much better than India since 1949, although India still leads in aggregate and per capita terms.[37] While there were 12 college students for every 10,000 persons of China's population by 1963, the figure for India was 22. During the 1958–60 period, a peak period for Chinese education, enrollment in Chinese higher education as a percent of the estimated population aged twenty to twenty-four inclusive was 1 percent as against 2.2 percent for India. The comparable figures for some other countries were 11.8 percent for the Soviet Union, 33.2 percent for the United States, 8.4 percent for Japan, .1 percent for Saudi Arabia, and .01 percent for Tanganyika.[38] The latter two countries did not even have higher educational institutions, and their students were enrolled in foreign countries. During 1962–63 there were about 1,270,000 million students enrolled in higher schools in India, a figure one-third higher than that in China's peak period of 1960–61. Indian enrollment in 1949–50 was about 383,000. Hence, enrollment in India increased by about 350 percent during 1949–63 as compared with about 700 percent in China. While India still leads China in aggregate quantitative measures of higher education, it probably lags significantly behind in terms of contribution to industrial progress.

China still falls substantially behind the Soviet Union in higher education, both quantitatively and qualitatively, in spite of its impressive performance to date.[39] Enrollment in Soviet higher education in 1964–65 was about 3.5 million, or approximately five times greater than China's, and nearly four times greater than that in China's peak period of 1961–62. The Soviet figure for 1962–63 was about 2.9 million, as compared with 820,000 in China, or more than 350 percent greater. In 1965 there were about 400,000 higher graduates in the Soviet Union, or about double the number in China's peak year of 1963.

China lags even further behind the United States.[40] Total enrollment in the United States in 1964–65 was nearly 4.8 million, and 4.5 million in 1962–63. Hence United States enrollment has been more than five times that of China's in recent years. In 1962–63 there were about 450,000 higher graduates in the United States, or about 250 percent more than in China in 1962–63, the peak period.

If the enrollment figures for China's spare-time higher education programs are taken into account, the gap between the figures for China and those for India, the Soviet Union, and the United States would be reduced. Table 3–16 presents available enrollment figures for Chinese spare-time higher education.[41] During the 1958–62 period, 15,000 students graduated from spare-time higher programs.[42] In recent years the enrollment in such programs has probably dropped substantially below the 1960 figure of 400,000.

TABLE 3–16

ENROLLMENT IN SPARE-TIME HIGHER EDUCATION SCHOOLS

Year	*Enrollment* (In Thousands)
1949	0.1
1950	0.4
1951	1.6
1952	4.1
1953	9.7
1954	13.2
1955	15.9
1956	63.8
1957	75.9
1958	150.0
1960	400.0

In general, spare-time higher education tends to be inferior in quality to regular programs—nonetheless it undoubtedly serves a useful purpose. Most spare-time programs are five to six years in length with roughly thirty-five to forty weeks of study each year for an average of nine hours per week and about eighteen hours of homework per week. From such programs come many managers, engineers, technicians, economists, planners, and full-fledged Red and Expert Communist Party officials.

Graduate education—corresponding roughly to American master's and doctoral degree programs—is still in its embryonic form in China and is almost a negligible source of high-talent personnel for industrial and business enterprise.[43] I came across only four graduate-degree holders at all of the Chinese enterprises surveyed, and two of them were apparently on temporary assignment. What graduate education there is in China is conducted through the leading higher educational institutions and the research institutes of the Chinese Academy of Sciences. While graduate enrollment increased more than tenfold from 1949 to 1956, it only totaled 4,800 students in 1956. In 1963 there were 10,000 applicants for 800 graduate places, and the number of places was to have doubled in 1964.

In the Soviet Union in 1962, graduate enrollment was about 62,000, and in 1961 about 6,900 graduate degrees were awarded. In the United States, graduate enrollment has been in the hundreds of thousands annually in recent years, and in 1961 alone about 89,000 graduate degrees were awarded. The figure today in the United States is well over 100,000 graduate degrees annually. A substantial number of managers, engineers, and natural and social scientists employed in American industry are graduate-degree holders. While Russia lags greatly behind the United States in this regard, it is still much ahead of China; I observed that there were more graduate-degree holders in Soviet industry than in Chinese industry.

I came across substantially more graduate-degree holders in Indian industry—many of them trained in the West—than I did in either China or the Soviet Union. I have no figures on Indian graduate education, but I am sure that it is substantially more developed and extensive than in China; China, however, may lead in the quality of training in engineering and the natural sciences, where most of the emphasis is placed.

Employment of Higher Graduates

By 1957 there were over 500,000 higher education graduates working in China, and by January 1960 there were about 625,000.[44] As of the end of 1966, there were probably between 1.5 and 2 million. While no figures are readily available, India undoubtedly has more higher graduates in employment. However, it is possible that not as great a proportion of Indian graduates are employed in industry and business as in China because of the type of training, dominant attitudes toward education, and quite pervasive negative attitudes on the part of many well-educated Indians toward business and industrial careers, as opposed to other more favored careers, such as work in government, law, medicine, journalism, and education.

The Soviet Union is still substantially ahead of China in the total number of higher graduates employed. In 1963, the Soviet figure was about 4.3 million, or more than double and possibly nearly triple the 1966 Chinese figure. Even in 1957, there were more Soviet graduates employed, about 2.8 million, than there were in China as of 1967. China is even further behind the United States, which had over 5.8 million employed graduates in 1957 and over 8.3 million living graduates in 1959.

During the 1940–60 period, 27 percent of all Soviet graduates and 28 percent of American graduates were employed in industrial and related activities. The proportion of Chinese graduates employed in this sphere has probably been even greater during the last decade, although no precise figures are available. In 1963, 36.4 percent of all Soviet higher graduates were employed in industrial and related activities, and the current proportion in China may well be at least this high. In 1957 in China, 35 percent of all engineering and technical personnel were employed by industrial enterprises, while the majority of the others were employed in construction work, communications, and transportation.[45] In 1958, of 32,800 Chinese scientific research personnel employed in China 14,700 or 45 percent, were employed in industry and communications.[46]

Quantitative Trends in Engineering Education and Employment

The most spectacular growth in Chinese education has been in engineering fields. From 1928 to 1947—a period of about twenty years—China produced only 31,700 engineering graduates; from 1948 to 1963—a period of fifteen years—the country produced 387,840 graduates, or almost thirteen times more than it did during the earlier period (1928–47). In the last several years China has been the third largest producer and consumer of engineers in the world, after the Soviet Union and the United States, and it is possible that China has now surpassed the United States. Table 3–17 presents statistics on enrollments and number of graduates in China's higher engineering programs.[47]

We see from Table 3–17 that the absolute enrollment figures and number of graduates, as well as their proportions in the overall Chinese higher educational system, have increased substantially since 1949. In recent years one third or more of all higher education graduates have been in engineering fields. It appears that the number of engineering graduates has not been significantly affected even with the cutbacks in higher education following the Great Leap period, thus suggesting the great importance attached to this type of training by the regime. In fact there has been greater emphasis on engineering, technological, and applied scientific training in Red China's system of higher education than in almost any other country.

At the end of the 1950's, about 55.7 percent of all students in Chinese higher education were studying in technological and scientific fields, as compared with 27.3 percent in India, 45.3 percent in the Soviet Union, and 22.7 percent in the United States.[48] Chinese sources refer to their higher educational system as a system of industrial education, and it is evident why. At the end of the 1950's, China had 3.1 engineers and scientists for every 10,000 people in its population, as compared with 2.4 for India. The figures for the Soviet Union and the United States were 48.1 and 61.7 respectively.[49]

TABLE 3–17

STATISTICS ON ENROLLMENT AND NUMBER OF GRADUATES IN HIGHER ENGINEERING PROGRAMS
(In Thousands)

Year	*Enrollment*		*Graduates*	
	NUMBER	PERCENT OF TOTAL	NUMBER	PERCENT OF TOTAL
1947–48 (pre–1949 peak period)	27.6	28	4.8	23
1949–50	30.0	26	4.7	26
1950–51	38.5	29	4.4	23
1951–52	48.5	31	10.2	32
1952–53	66.6	35	14.6	30
1953–54	80.0	38	15.6	33
1954–55	95.0	38	18.6	34
1955–56	109.6	38	22.0	35
1956–57	150.0	37	17.2	31
1957–58	177.6	41	17.5	24
1958–59	—	—	23.3	33
1959–60	283.0	35	45.0	33
1960–61	—	—	54.0	33
1961–62	—	—	59.0	33
1962–63	—	—	77.0	33
1963–64	—	—	—	—
1964–65	—	—	80.0	53
1948–63 TOTALS	—	—	388.0	33

During the 1948–63 period 33 percent of all higher graduates in China were in engineering fields, and 6 percent were in scientific fields, for a combined total of 39 percent. Other Chinese figures for graduates during this period are: education, 27 percent; medicine, 10 percent; agriculture, 6 percent; economics (including business administration fields) and all other specialties, 10 percent.[50] During the 1926–60 period in the Soviet Union, 57 percent of all graduates were in engineering and scientific fields, while the figure for the United States was 24 percent. The Soviet figure for engineering graduates only during the 1926–60 period was 27 percent, and for the United States 9 percent.

In the Soviet Union during 1962 and 1963 there were nearly 1.4 million students enrolled in higher engineering programs, or 48 percent of the total enrollment. Soviet engineering enrollment at that time was about five times greater than in China's peak period of 1959–60. There were 115,600 Russian graduates in engineering in 1962, and this figure constituted 36.3 percent of all higher graduates. This figure was about 50 percent greater than the number of graduates in China's peak year to date. In

1962 the United States graduated about 35,000 engineers—about 8.3 percent of all bachelor's degree graduates—or slightly less than half as many as China has graduated in each of the last few years.

China has done strikingly better than India in training engineers. In the period 1962–63 enrollment in Indian higher engineering programs had only reached 69,000 or 4.5 percent of total enrollment in higher education. Although India's 1962–63 enrollment represented more than a 300 percent increase from 1956–57, it was only about equal to China's engineering enrollment in 1952–53, only about one-third of China's enrollment in 1957–58, and less than one-quarter of China's in 1959–60. In 1963 only 8,400 engineering degrees were awarded in India. If we add the 12,100 engineering diplomas earned from junior technical colleges—which are roughly equivalent to or perhaps a bit better than China's specialized secondary technical schools—the total number of engineering-technical graduates was about 21,500 in India for 1963. This total figure for India is only about 25 to 30 percent of the number of Chinese engineering graduates in recent years.

In 1952 there were only about 32,000 graduate engineers employed in the Chinese economy. By 1961 the number had reached 217,000, and by 1964 about 207,000.[51] In India in 1961, there were only 65,000 engineering degree holders, and 7,000 of them were unemployed. There were also 85,000 technical diploma holders, of whom 75,000 were employed. Hence, if we take the total of all holders of engineering degrees and technical diplomas in India for 1961, we get a figure of 150,000, still about 45 percent less than the Chinese figure for 1961. If we added the million or so semiprofessional technical graduates working in China in 1961 to the Chinese higher engineering graduates, the difference between Indian and Chinese figures would be tremendous.

While China is substantially ahead of India in the employment of engineering graduates, it still lags far behind the Soviet Union. The Soviet Union employs roughly twice as many engineering graduates as the United States. In 1957 there were about 832,000 engineering graduates employed in the Soviet economy, and by 1963 over 1.4 million. The Chinese figure for 1957 was only 114,000, and for 1963, 330,000. While China has narrowed the gap from about seven to one to about four to one in the last decade, it still has a long way to go if it is to catch up with the Soviet Union in the employment of engineering graduates.

Table 3–18 indicates the number and percent distribution of Chinese engineering graduates by field for the 1953–62 period.[52] We see from this table that a great effort was made to build up a strong base of high-talent manpower for heavy industry, with 24 percent of all engineering graduates majoring in machine building and toolmaking. In order to expand social-overhead capital greatly in order to industrialize rapidly, it was necessary to undertake numerous large-scale building projects and to improve and develop important urban centers. Hence, 20 percent of the engineering graduates were from programs specializing in construction and city planning. Graduates in power, transportation, post, and telecommunication—all important social-overhead-capital items—constituted 12 percent. China has always been relatively rich in natural resources, but it was not until after 1949 that a vigorous and extensive effort was made to exploit such resources. Hence, 17 percent of all engineering graduates during the period 1953 to 1962 majored in mining or geology and prospecting.

There are some trends which are not indicated in Table 3–18 which pertain to changes in the pattern of engineering graduates during 1958–62 as compared with 1952–57. During the 1952–57 period 26 percent of all graduates were in construction and city planning, and this dropped to 17 percent during 1958–62, probably because of the great gains made in construction and urbanization during the former period. On the other hand, graduates in machine and tool making increased from 20 to 25 percent, and metallurgy from 3 to 5 percent in 1958–62 as compared with 1952–57. Graduates in the other category jumped from 5 percent during 1952–57 to 12 percent during 1958–62 as new programs were added in such fields as electronics, aeronautics, petroleum, radar, and atomic energy.

TABLE 3–18

CHINESE ENGINEERING GRADUATES, BY FIELD: 1953–62

Field	*Number*	*Percent Distribution**
Machine and tool making	64,226	24
Construction and city planning	55,542	20
Geology and prospecting	24,228	9
Mining	20,687	8
Power	20,234	7
Chemical technology	13,973	5
Transport, post and telecommunications	12,703	5
Metallurgy	11,610	4
Manufacture of electric motors and supplies	9,613	4
Light industry	6,716	2
Surveying, drafting, meteorology, and hydrology	6,079	2
Papermaking	1,090	less than 5
Other	25,482	9
Total	272,183	100

* Percent detail does not add to totals because of rounding.

It is interesting to make some comparisons between the above pattern of Chinese engineering graduates with the Soviet pattern in 1960. In the Soviet Union in 1960, the largest proportion, 20 percent, of engineering graduates also specialized in machine building. The proportion in Soviet construction was only 15 percent, as compared with 20 percent for China during the period 1953–62, and this reflects the greater need that China has in this area. The Soviet proportion for mining and geology (and prospecting) was 8.5 percent as compared with 17 percent for China, suggesting that the Soviet Union had gone much further in exploiting its natural resources than China. The Soviet proportion for light industry—which includes most types of consumer goods—was 6 percent as against 2 percent for China, and this might reflect in part the relative consumer affluence of the two countries. As for the other fields, the Soviets had a greater proportion of graduates in papermaking, transportation, and production of electrical items; China was higher in surveying, drafting, meteorology, and hydrology; in the other fields the differences between the two countries were small.

It is more difficult to compare the pattern of engineering graduates in China and India, since somewhat different categories are used. In 1961 about 30 percent of all engineering graduates in India were in civil engineering. This also reflects the effort to build up social-overhead capital in India. But this large proportion may also be due to a higher preference for this branch of engineering—possibly a holdover from the time of British rule. Numerous civil engineers are employed by the government, a status and prestige sector in India. However, the proportion of unemployed civil engineering graduates, as compared with other types of engineering graduates, is apparently quite high in India. India, like China, graduated a large proportion of engineers in basically heavy industry fields, 27 percent in mechanical engineering and 18 percent in electrical engineering. However, only 1 percent of India's graduates were in mining as compared with 8 percent in China during 1953–62. While India is substantially poorer in natural mineral resources than China, perhaps a greater effort in this area would prove effective for India's industrial progress. Other Indian figures for 1961 were: chemical engineering, 4 percent; metallurgy, 4 percent; and telecommunications, 3 percent. As mentioned earlier, the total number of engineering graduates in India has been substantially lower than in China.

Let us now turn our attention to the nature and content of Chinese higher engineering programs.

The Nature of Chinese Engineering Programs

The best and broader Chinese higher engineering programs seem to be fairly similar to better American undergraduate programs, such as those at

M.I.T. and the Caifornia Institute of Technology, in terms of general scientific and certain general engineering subjects.[53] In some respects, such as the amount of knowledge transmitted and the requirement of a diploma project or thesis, Chinese programs rank with portions of master's degree programs found at American engineering schools. However, there are certain basic differences between Chinese and American types of engineering education, and the former corresponds quite closely to that in the Soviet Union.

Even the better Chinese engineering programs are more specialized and limited in scope than American programs; and the programs offered by specialized Chinese institutes are particularly narrow. A Chinese student majoring in railway bridge construction, for example, may learn practically everything about the railway bridge, but probably little about the railway itself or about a highway bridge. Many of the courses in Chinese engineering education are based on text materials that are no more than detailed technical manuals. There is typically less training offered in the social sciences—including courses in economics, management, and business administration—and humanities than in most American programs; and what little training of this type that there is in Chinese engineering education is fertilized with much ideology. In general, Chinese engineering schools typically emphasize memorization of facts and descriptive presentations more than independent thought, creativity, problem solving, and analytical training.

Most Chinese engineering schools prepare students for employment in a specific branch of industry and, in some cases, for only a limited number of enterprises. Many of the things the Chinese student learns while still in school the American student, after graduating, learns on the job in a specific firm. Since most Chinese engineering education is closely linked with a specific type of technology, its graduates, unlike their American counterparts, need little on-the-job training.

The concentration on the development of narrowly trained engineering specialists has been providing a fast payback for investment in Chinese higher education. Large numbers of such specialists have been essential to, and adequate for, rapid growth and industrial development in the relatively simple Chinese economy. However, it would seem that China will have to broaden engineering education in many programs in the foreseeable future if its engineers are to cope effectively with future changes in technology and to play major roles in the management of increasingly complex enterprises. In addition, broader training is essential for a more effective interchange of specialists and of information between specialists.

The Soviets have found during the last decade or so that their engineers had to obtain a broader theoretical base in technical and scientific fields and that many of them had to acquire a broader background in economics, management, and business administration because engineers have been the key source of high-talent manpower. As a result, a number of reforms have been introduced in Soviet engineering education in recent years, mostly in the direction of providing greater breadth of training. While some of the better Chinese engineering schools, such as Tsinghua, currently offer training broader than that offered in Russia a few years ago, and possibly as broad as Russia does today in technical and scientific fields, it seems that more comprehensive training on a much more extensive scale will be required for continued and substantial industrial progress. Moreover, it appears that more emphasis on courses in economics, management, and business administration in engineering programs will also become essential as long as engineers constitute a key source of high-talent managerial manpower.

Indian engineering education suffers from serious deficiencies for reasons that are almost the exact opposite of those in China. With the exception of a small number of first-rate engineering schools—most notably the few recently established Indian Institutes of Technology—engineering education in India seems to be too abstract, theoretical, and general—rather than too functional, applied, or specialized. It also suffers, like its Chinese counterpart, from lack of emphasis on creativity, problem solving, and analytical training. Many American—and British—managers who are employed in India, and whom I have interviewed and observed, point out with frustration that it typically takes about five years to train an Indian engineering graduate to do a job effectively, as compared with about two years for an American graduate to be similarly trained. It may take only a year or less to train a Chinese engineering graduate to perform a similar job effectively, but he may well have to be retrained within a few years if technology and operations change significantly.

Tsinghua Polytechnic University

It might be of interest to examine in detail the type of engineering education offered by Tsinghua Polytechnic University in Peking, where I spent a productive day, meeting with faculty members and students. This university is reputed to be China's best and biggest engineering school, and its program is broader in technical and scientific fields than at most Chinese engineering institutes.[54] I was told that only about five other polytechnic universities were comparable to Tsinghua. My main host for the day was Professor Jing, who did his graduate work in engineering at the University of Michigan, and who is still fluent in English. He is a full professor and also the head of the department of machine building and precision instruments, probably the best department of its type in China.

Tsinghua University was founded in 1911 as a preparatory college for students intending to go to the United States. It was raised to university status in 1925 and, prior to Communist control, was a fairly important center for Sino-American scientific cooperation. In 1952, the Red Chinese government took over the university, which still was a general university with major emphasis placed on nonengineering fields. After 1952, Tsinghua underwent profound changes and was reorganized as a polytechnic university drawing on the best technical and scientific talent available. Currently the technical and scientific aspects of training are similar to those in Soviet engineering programs, and many of the texts used are translations of Soviet sources.

During the period 1949–65, Tsinghua graduated about 17,000 students, nearly four times the total number during the entire 1911–49 period. During its initial thirty-eight years of existence, only 700 engineers were graduated, and very few of them were women. Since 1949 about 20 percent of the graduates have been women, and more than 50 percent of all graduates have been from worker and poor families and from relatively well-off peasant families. About 70 percent of the students since 1952 have received government financial aid to pay for their board, lodging, books, and other out-of-pocket expenses.

By 1960, Tsinghua was graduating over 1,000 students annually, and in 1963 there were over 2,000 graduates as a result of the large enrollment during the Great Leap period. In 1965 the number of graduates was 2,000, and I was told that the same number was to graduate in 1966. I learned also that 2,000 would be about the maximum number of graduates in the foreseeable future and that enrollment would probably remain around 11,000, the 1966 figure. Enrollment has declined somewhat from the peak of over 12,000 in the late 1950's and early 1960's. However, enrollment in 1966 was still about five times the enrollment in 1947, the peak year before 1949. In 1966, there were some 2,000 women enrolled. Only about one in twenty applicants are admitted to Tsinghua, where the failure rate is less than 10 percent.

The regular or undergraduate type of programs offered by Tsinghua are five to five and a half years in length. Almost all entering students are senior high school graduates, and very few are from specialized high schools. There are also three-year programs for graduate students, of whom there were 300 in 1966.

The total membership of the faculty in 1966 numbered 2,000, about 200 more than in 1963. Of the 2,000, 200 were professors and associate professors, while the rest were lecturers and assistants (there is no rank of assistant professor). About half of the 200 professors and associate professors had been educated abroad. Of the former, many had gone to universities in the United States and the United Kingdom, while some had been trained in the Soviet Union. Many of the associate professors and lecturers had also been educated in Russia. I met a number of professors who had been trained in the United States, Hong Kong, the Philippines, and Western Europe and who had returned since 1949.

The pay scale for professors ranged from a minimum of 200 yuan monthly to a maximum of 300 yuan. Professor Jing's salary was 300 yuan, an amount greater than that paid anyone I came across in industry. In fact, his pay was equivalent to the salary of many national ministers and deputy ministers. Chairman Mao, Liu Shao-chi, the President, and Chou En-lai, the Prime Minister, get a monthly salary of only about 400 yuan, plus, of course, many perquisites such as good housing, the use of a car, and so on. However, professors and even associate professors at Tsinghua and other leading higher schools seemed to get housing that was well above the average type, and many of them apparently had either their own cars or the use of a car. Rent paid by university faculty members for their housing was usually about 5 percent, maximum, of their salaries.

The monthly pay range for associate professors at Tsinghua was 150 to 200 yuan, or as much as the salaries for most of the highest paid personnel in industry. For lecturers and assistants the range was 80 to 150 yuan, amounts substantially greater than the pay range for industrial enterprise workers.

Most of the professors fell within the forty-to-fifty-age bracket, and almost all of the associate professors were between thirty and forty.

Professor Jing and the university's president, Chiang Lan, stated that faculty promotions were based primarily on merit. Apparently political and ideological factors were not particularly stressed in early May 1966, when I visited Tsinghua, and many of the professors and associate professors were not party members. However, the situation may have changed with the Great Proletarian Cultural Revolution which became intensified by June and mushroomed in August with the formation of the Red Guards. Even in June, before I had left Red China, I read some hostile statements in translations of the Chinese press about Chiang Lan, Tsinghua's president, and various Tsinghua faculty members. If faculty members and top administrators of Tsinghua and other leading higher educational institutions have in fact been purged and removed, this will surely have a very serious negative effect on higher education, and hence on industrial progress.

In 1966, Tsinghua had twelve departments which offered more than forty specialties or fields of specialization. The departments were: (1) machine building and precision instruments, (2) metallurgical engineering, (3) mechanical engineering, (4) chemical engineering, (5) power engineering, (6) engineering physics, (7) electrical engineering, (8) radio engineering (which includes television), (9) civil engineering and architecture, (10) hydraulics, (11) agricultural machinery, (12) automatic control (which deals with electronic computers).

In 1957, there were only eight departments offering a total of twenty-two fields of specialization. Since that time new departments have been added in the specialties of metallurgical, chemical and power engineering, automatic control, and agricultural machinery, while civil engineering and architecture have been combined into one department. The machine-building department in 1957 did not include precision instruments, and hydraulics was called water conservation engineering.

Tsinghua and a few other leading Chinese polytechnic universities are unlike most specialized engineering institutes in that they offer broader training in electrical, chemical, and other branches of engineering, rather than training in only one type of technology or branch of industry. Professor Jing felt that the leading polytechnic universities offer more effective training and better research opportunities than the specialized engineering institutes because they provide for a better exchange of information, a more interdisciplinary approach, and a wider range of concepts and experiences. He pointed out that specialized engineering institutes are under different ministries with their own specific interests, while polytechnic universities are under the Ministry of Higher Education and tend to have broader interests. As an example, he said that the mechanical and electrical engineering, automatic control, and machine-building departments were working together on projects involving numerically controlled machine tools with the use of computers. Collaborations of this type are not possible within most specialized institutes. However, he felt that the trend seemed to be in the direction of expanding specialized institutes rather than polytechnic universities.[55]

Tsinghua has played a pioneering role in many important technological innovations in China. The automatic-control department—including some students and with the help of several other departments—developed an electronic analogue computer for scientific work at the university. The computer, which is now in use at various other organizations, was started in 1959 and completed in 1964. It can do an average per second of 10,000 calculations, 40,000 additions, and 4,000 multiplications. Tsinghua has also done much pioneer work in Chinese television and was doing some work on the development of color TV.

Faculty and students of the machine-building department had collaborated with the First Peking Machine Tool Factory in the production of China's first numerically controlled machine tool-operated computers. Faculty and students in the hydraulics department played a major role in the design and construction of the huge Ming Reservoir near Peking. In general, Tsinghua has relationships with many industrial and other types of organizations involving applied research projects and the employment of its students while they are still in school.

Tsinghua seems to be a very well-equipped technical university. During the Great Leap period, many workshops and laboratories were set up at the university in order to implement the "physical labor and combine theory with practice" policies of the regime. By the early 1960's, there were eleven workshops and pilot plants and ninety-eight laboratories, and the university had set up a full-scale engineering and design factory, a multiple machinery plant, and 2,000-kilowatt experimental power station. By 1963, the number of laboratories had been reduced to about eighty-one and a few of the workshops were eliminated. As of 1966, there were, I was told, eight laboratories—I saw several briefly—about eight or nine workshops and pilot plants, and at least one full-scale type of factory. The total floor space of the university in 1966 was 400,000 square meters, and two large new buildings were under construction. As is typical of Chinese educational institutions, Tsinghua offers a wide range of cultural and recreational facilities and activities for its students. In all programs, students have two hours a week of compulsory physical education, if they have no physical disability.

For the university as a whole, 60 to 70 percent of the students are employed by industrial enterprises upon graduation, about 20 percent go to scientific research organizations, and the rest become assistants or lecturers at Tsinghua or other schools or enter Tsinghua's three-year graduate program. For the machine-building and precision instruments department, about 80 to 90 percent of its graduates are employed by industrial enterprises; this is the highest proportion of any department and about the same as that at many specialized engineering institutes. I met a few Tsinghua graduates from this department who were employed in key positions as higher-level technical managers and engineers at large machine-tool factories. They impressed me favorably and seemed to know more than the average Chinese manager did, not only about technical matters but also about management and managing, even though they received very little management or business training at school.

All graduates of Tsinghua are employed as workers for one year following graduation, and their monthly pay during this period is about 46 yuan (it varies by a few yuan for different regions). In the second year of employment, they get about 56 yuan, and subsequently they can earn increasingly more as technicians, engineers, and eventually as managers.

The electrical engineering department has the largest enrollment—over 1,000 students. In the machine-building department, there were 800 undergraduate and 30 graduate students in 1966. This department graduates about 150 to 160 students annually. In 1966 the department had four professors, one of whom was a party member, five associate professors, three of whom were party members, and over one hundred lecturers and assistants.

The program breakdown (which was roughly the same in all of Tsinghua's departments) for the machine-building and precision instruments department was as follows in 1966. About 10 percent of instruction time was devoted to political education, which included Marxism-Leninism and the works and Thought of Mao. This was undertaken during the first three years. In addition, as part of political education, students beyond the fifth-year level sometimes went to work briefly in villages or in militia work so that they gained some rapport with the proletariat and the masses. However, this type of activity struck me as being more ad hoc and voluntary—perhaps under pressure—than compulsory. There were also a few hours each week of political meetings and ideological discussion groups for students as well as for faculty.

In general, it did not seem that an excessive amount of time was being spent on political education and ideology at Tsinghua, and it seemed to be much more of an Expert rather than a Red university. Less time was being spent on such activities than at Chungking Polytechnic University in 1964, when a Canadian industrialist was told that 15 percent of instruction time was spent on political and ideological subjects, and six compulsory hours was spent by students in meetings of this type. However, I was told by Professor Jing and various other Tsinghua officials that there were discussions regarding political and ideological education and that it was likely that such education would be increased in the future to 15 or 20 percent of the students' study time. If this is actually carried out, it will certainly significantly dilute the university's expert type of training.

Courses in fundamental science and engineering in the machine-building department constituted about 50 percent of the student's course work—significantly more than at most specialized engineering institutes. Fundamental-science courses include chemistry, physics, and mathematics, while the fundamental technical or engineering courses consist of such subjects as engineering drawings, strength of materials, engineering and theoretical mechanics, metal technology, machine design and drawings, and electrical engineering; these are generally taken during the first three years. Foreign language is included in the 50 percent figure, and English rather than Russian is now the most popular foreign language.

About 30 percent of the student's time is spent in his field of specialization and related laboratory, practical work, and employment. The proportion of time spent on specialized training at engineering institutes is usually greater. There were six fields of specialization in the machine-building department in 1966: (1) machine-tool design and construction; (2) metal-cutting tools; (3) theory of metal cutting; (4) mechanical technology of manufacturing; (5) technology of heat treatment (which deals with foundries and forging); and (6) plant design. The plant-design specialty had been added quite recently, and in 1957 there were only five specialties, some of them with titles different from those in 1966.

Specialized training begins in either the first or second year, depending on the department, and continues until graduation, with greatest emphasis on it in the last two years. The pattern of practical work and employment in physical labor is as follows: During the first two years, students in the machine-building department spend about twelve to thirteen weeks in practical work and physical employment, as compared with only six to eight weeks in most other departments. I was told that there was greater emphasis on practical work in this department because a substantially larger proportion of its graduates go to work at industrial enterprises. In the last three years at the university, about eleven to twelve weeks are spent on practical work and employment by students in all departments.

Practical work and employment are undertaken by Tsinghua's students in both its own shops and factory as well as at regular industrial enterprises. Professor Jing candidly said that there were a number of problems entailed in combining formal study and theory with practice and employment. It is not always possible for the student to work at a job related to his field of study, and there are also problems of effectively timing formal study with employment activities and practical training.

On the average, Tsinghua students were spending about two and a half months annually in practical work and physical labor, and in the machine-building department about three months or slightly more. I was told that there had been about a one-month increase in such activities in the last few years—in line with the regime's policy of part-work, part-study. At Chungking Polytechnic University in 1964, students were spending only about one month annually working in factories and two months in communes. In 1965 a Canadian journalist was told by a top-level Ministry of Higher Education official in Peking that up to two months' physical labor was required of higher students. Hence, it does seem that there has been a trend in the direction of more time spent on physical labor and employment in the Chinese higher education system. I was told at Tsinghua University in May 1966 that they were contemplating an extension of physical labor activity and that some experiments might be conducted in the use of half-work, half-study programs in the future.

About 10 percent of the student's time is spent on his diploma project. This is undertaken for a period of about five months during his last term, when he has no other courses. The diploma project, which is also referred to as a thesis, typically involves some design work relating to processes, products, or projects. While in some cases projects are undertaken by students individually, usually they are done by groups of students, and even by the entire graduating class, under faculty guidance, of a particular department. The same general procedure exists for graduate students. I was told that the trend has been away from individual projects in order to simulate conditions in the real industrial world, where cooperation and teamwork rather than self-interest and individual pursuits are more important.

In the machine-building department in recent years, diploma projects have dealt with the numerical design of different types of machine tools, such as milling, drilling, boring, and pressing machines. In the department of automatic control, emphasis has been on computers, and in radio engineering on television. In the past, students in hydraulics, civil engineering, and various other departments undertake diploma projects involving survey work, blueprints, design, and construction of the huge Ming Reservoir.

For all programs, there are two terms each year and nine weeks for vacation. About two half-days are spent each week in laboratory and related applied study. In any one term, maximum class hours per week amount to twenty-five, and the minimum is fifteen hours, with more class hours in the lower grades. On the average, students are expected to spend from two to three hours studying for every class hour. This represents a heavier overall workload than in most American engineering programs; it is roughly equivalent to that in the Soviet Union.

There was little or no choice for Tsinghua students regarding the courses or electives they could take in their fields of specialization. There was also very little emphasis on economics, management, or business administration, and in 1966 there was apparently less emphasis on these fields than there was in the 1950's.[56] There was only one course in the machine-building department and in some of the other departments which dealt directly with economics and industrial management; this was a one-term course on "economics and organization" in various branches of industry, such as machine building and metallurgy. This type of course deals briefly with the organization structure of a particular branch of industry and of enterprises within the industry, descriptive aspects of industrial planning, economic calculations relating to technical norm setting and various technical operations and processes, the calculation of production costs, and so forth. The emphasis here seems to be on description, the memorization of facts, and standardized procedures and regulations rather than on problem solving, analytical skill development, creativity, or independent thought. Cases or case problems like those used in American programs are not utilized. However, lectures and discussion groups, arranged at enterprises from time to time, expose students to managerial and economic problems.

I was told that a number of specialized engineering institutes offer courses in the special area of economics and organization of the branch of industry in which they specialize. There are apparently specialties of this type at institutes which deal with machine building and metallurgy, mining, shipbuilding, construction, transportation, communications, petroleum, and perhaps other sectors as well. At some institutes, there are some courses in the field of specialization centered on economics and organization that deal with accounting, finance, labor law and wages, and various other aspects of management and business administration. But here, too, there is apparently little emphasis on problem solving, analysis, or creativity, and the stress is primarily on technical, engineering, and scientific subjects.

Quantitative Trends in Nonengineering Education

Table 3–19 presents data on Chinese graduates in selected nonengineering fields.[57] This table indicates a fairly steady increase in the number of graduates in the natural sciences, while the proportion of such graduates has remained quite constant during the last decade. The table also indicates the great effort in the field of education to produce an adequate number of teachers to staff its extensive overall educational system. The

TABLE 3–19

GRADUATES IN SELECTED NONENGINEERING FIELDS
(In Thousands)

Year	*Finance and Economics* (Includes business administration)		*Natural Sciences*		*Education*	
	NUMBER	% OF ALL GRADUATES	NUMBFR	% OF TOTAL	NUMBER	% OF TOTAL
1948–49	3.1	15%	1.6	8%	1.9	9%
1949–50	3.3	18	1.5	8	.6	4
1950–51	3.6	19	1.5	8	1.2	6
1951–52	7.3	23	2.2	7	3.1	10
1952–53	10.5	22	1.8	4	9.7	20
1953–54	6.0	13	.8	2	10.6	22
1954–55	4.7	8	2.0	4	12.1	22
1955–56	4.5	7	4.0	6	17.2	27
1956–57	3.7	6	3.5	6	15.9	28
1957–58	2.3	3	4.6	6	32.0	44
1958–59	2.5	4	4.4	6	21.0	30
1959–60	4.7	4	8.5	6	40.5	30
1960–61	5.7	4	10.0	6	49.0	30
1961–62	6.2	4	11.0	6	56.0	32
1962–63	3.0	2	10.0	5	46.0	23
1964–65	not available	not available	not available	not available	50.0*	33*
Totals (1948–63)	71.1	6%	67.4	6%	316.8	27%

* For 1948–63 only.

large increase in education graduates in 1964–65 may be a reflection of Chinese policy in the early 1960's aimed at providing an adequate number of teachers to staff its substantially overextended educational system.

For the fields of finance and economics—which include programs most similar to those found in American schools of business administration and management—we see that in the early 1950's there was a sizable proportion of graduates. This was probably in anticipation of the substantial need for such specialists under a system of state economic planning and rapid industrialization. However, by the end of the First Five-Year Plan there was a sharp drop in the number and proportion of graduates in this sphere. While the absolute number of such graduates rose during the 1959–62 period, the proportion remained quite constant. There is no apparent explanation for the sharp decline in the number of graduates in finance and economics in 1962–63. Perhaps this was an outgrowth of the sharp decline in enrollment in these fields during the Great Leap period, and the decline may have been due to the regime's view that graduates of this type were no longer of much importance. During the Great Leap period much of the state-planning apparatus was dismantled as much greater decentralized control over industry—primarily by local party cadres—emerged, and local party cadres came to play the major role in the financial, economic, and overall management affairs of numerous enterprises throughout the country. The role and effective utilization of graduates in the fields of finance and economics were greatly reduced during this period, and eventually financial, economic, business, industrial, and managerial chaos and inefficiency became widespread.

Although the Soviets also have not placed much emphasis on the fields of finance, economics, business administration, and management, the number of graduates in this sphere has been substantially greater than in China. In 1962 the Soviet Union graduated about 20,000 in this general area, and this constituted about 6.5 percent of all graduates that year. The Soviet figure is about double the number for China's peak period of 1952–53, and several times greater than the figures for China during more recent years. The proportion of all higher graduates employed in the Soviet Union who graduated from programs like economics and business administration increased from 5.4 percent in 1957 to 6.6 percent in 1963. In absolute numbers the increase was from about 157,500 to 278,000. It is likely that in both absolute and proportionate terms China currently lags substantially behind the Soviet Union in this area.

As the Soviet economy has expanded and grown more complex and as greater decentralization of authority in industry and business has emerged, the Soviets have found that inadequate education in applied economics, business administration and management, the behavioral sciences, and the social sciences, in general, has proved to be a significant bottleneck in terms of economic progress. They are now taking steps to rectify this serious educational gap by reorganizing, expanding, and establishing new educational training and research programs in these fields. The Chinese will undoubtedly come to the same impasse, as their economy expands and grows more complex, unless appropriate steps are taken in time.

The United States is the world's front-runner in business administration, management, applied economics, and social science education as a whole. In 1962 there were nearly 70,000 graduates in business administration, management, and economics in the United States, and this represented over 15 percent of all first-degree graduates. The figure for business administration and management only was about 60,000. These figures do not include the master's and doctoral degrees, of which there are many thousands, awarded in these fields in the United States. In recent years there have been about as many graduate degrees awarded in these fields in the United States as the total number of all graduate degrees awarded in the Soviet Union. The annual number of graduate degrees in this area in the Soviet Union has been small, less than 2,000 per year, and mostly in economics. The number in China has been negligible.

India is substantially ahead of China quantitatively, and probably ahead qualitatively, in business administration, management, economics, and general social science education, although the content and quality of training in many programs leave much to be desired in terms of the requirements of industry and business. Most of the Indian universities offer programs in all of the social sciences, including economics, and in commerce, and a growing number of higher schools are offering courses and programs in business administration and management. The quality of the latter is generally much better than that of commerce programs, and unemployment among commerce graduates has become a serious problem in India because most of them are trained to be glorified clerks. In 1962 there were about 130,000 students enrolled in commerce programs in India, and this represented 10.2 percent of the total enrollment in higher education.

In general, managers of Indian industrial and business firms complain that graduates in economics, business administration, commerce, and management are inadequately trained in terms of the firms' requirements and that there is not enough stress on practical application, analytical thought, or problem solving in such programs. Notable exceptions are the graduates of the two recently established Indian institutes of management. M.I.T. collaborates with the Calcutta Institute, where I worked during 1965 and 1966, and Harvard with the Ahmedabad Institute. These institutes offer graduate training in management and business administration. The quality of training, as well as the quality of students, at these two institutes compares favorably with leading American programs. Most of the graduates from the first graduating classes in 1966 obtained very good positions in industry and business. These institutes, if properly operated in the future, can become a very important source of high-talent managerial manpower in India.

Hence, even though there are clearly serious limitations and deficiencies in Indian education in the fields of business administration, commerce, management, economics and the social sciences, India seems to have a distinct edge over China in these areas.

The Nature of Economic, Business Administration, and Management Education in China

In China the whole area of business administration is considered part of economics—sometimes referred to as the economic sciences. In the mid-1960's there were five finance and economics institutes and about a dozen universities offering economics programs. They offered a total of about eight or nine fields of specialization in such areas as industrial, agricultural, and trade economics, political economy, accounting, industrial statistics, finance and credit (banking), planning of the national economy, and foreign trade and international finance. Each field of specialization usually corresponds to a particular department at an institute or university. The field of industrial economics seems to come closest to American business administration and industrial management, and I was told that there were only about six departments of this type in China in 1966. With the exception of the Peking Institute of Foreign Trade, which has only one department, the other economics institutes offer several, and in some cases most, fields of specialization. The majority of the graduates of the institutes are employed in either macromanagerial organizations or in financial, commercial, and industrial enterprises. All of the universities having economics departments have a department of political economy, which deals primarily with Marxist theory and economic philosophy and history rather than with applied economics. At most of the universities there are only a few other fields of specialization offered in economics. China People's University is one of the exceptions, and it has five economics departments. A substantially smaller proportion of graduates of most university economics programs are employed by macrobusiness or microbusiness and industrial organizations, while many more become researchers and teachers.

Most programs in economics and related higher fields are four years in length, although some run for five years. All programs are patterned quite closely after the traditional Soviet economic and business administration type of programs—the greatest differences seem to be in political and ideological subjects—and much use is made of translated Soviet textbooks and other published materials.

While I do not have any detailed breakdown of program content or courses offered in each field of specialization, I do have some idea of the general content of various programs and of the types of courses offered. In general, it seems that more time is spent on political and ideological education in economics programs than on engineering programs. This is also true in the Soviet Union, although the emphasis seems to be even greater in China. About 20 to 30 percent of course work is in this area, and in some departments, such as political economy, the percentage may even be greater. About 20 to 25 percent of the student's time is devoted to basic subjects, such as Chinese and foreign languages, literature, mathematics, geography, and physical education. And approximately 50 to 60 percent is taken up with the student's field of specialization. The amount of time spent in practical work, physical labor, and employment seemed to be in an experimental state in economics programs in 1966, and it apparently varied greatly among different schools and departments. The minimum time spent on such activity generally averaged about two months annually.

Both theoretical and applied economics courses in China seem to suffer from many of the same deficiencies found in the Soviet Union. Even applied courses seem to be extremely descriptive, quite historical, and not particularly operational. Such courses typically dwell on the economic laws of socialism, history, goals, tasks, and performance of the Chinese economy—with less statistical data than in the Soviet Union because many Chinese statistics are not for public consumption—on descriptions of national plans and the planning process, price formation, organization of the economy, rules, regulations, paper flows, standard economic calculations and reports, and so forth. Little attention seems to be given to objective criteria or guidelines for implementing economic laws or theory in practice. In fact, economics is not basically treated as an empirical or a predictive science.

Macroeconomics in particular is viewed as a philosophy of politics and state action. Facts seem to be memorized to form value judgments, not to reach analytical conclusions or to solve problems. The "what ought to be" or normative aspects of the Chinese economy are studied in depth in various courses, while there is little explanation of the "whys"; and predictive theory, even in crude form, seems to be virtually nonexistent. There is apparently little in the way of conceptual framework or scientific body of knowledge that can indicate the best way to pursue ideal economic conditions or to obtain desired results. The most operational aspects of courses in macroeconomics seem to deal with balance sheets for sectors, raw material and other resources and with simple input-output techniques. Training of this type seems to be highly technical and narrow, without much of a theoretical basis. There is not even as much emphasis on mathematical techniques, computers, econometrics, or operations research as there is currently in the Soviet Union.

In microeconomics courses marginal and equilibrium economics apparently receive little, if any, attention. Only a few courses dealing with economic analysis and cost accounting seem to contain rather sparse subject matter somewhat similar to certain aspects—mostly production—found in Western courses in managerial economics, economics of the firm, or cost accounting. It is true that marginal and equilibrium economics are probably not as crucial in a planned economy, where a system of fixed prices is used, as in a basically capitalistic economy, where much use is made of competitive market prices. Nevertheless, such concepts are still important for sound economic decision making—both macro and micro—in a Marxist economy. Also apparently not adequately covered in Chinese economics are such significant concepts as the opportunity cost principle, law of diminishing returns, theory of capital investment and depreciation, and cash flow analysis.

It is of course possible for a fairly backward developing country, such as China has been, to achieve considerable economic progress with relatively inefficient resource-allocation decisions. Almost anything produced can be used, and there are many possible trade-offs in the use of factor inputs to produce a given type of output when production processes and product specification are relatively simple. Hence, sophisticated education in economics is not that crucial. However, as the Chinese economy grows more complex—and its intricacy approaches that of the Soviet economy—the selection of alternatives based on economic calculation and predictive ability will become increasingly important for managerial efficiency and real industrial progress. Hence, the need for training in marginal and equilibrium economics and in other aspects of operational economic theory will grow more acute.

As has been the case in the Soviet Union until very recently, the major reason for the rather backward state of Chinese education in economics and in the social sciences, in general, has been the conflict between dialectical materialism, which is essentially ideological, and scientific methods. Economic theory is accepted as a matter of dogma and faith, and there is little or no need to test and validate theory through empirical or experimental studies.

The same is true for business administration courses where inadequate attention is paid to the development of predictive or analytical ability. Such ability is extremely important in coping with uncertainty, but the Chinese seem to assume—at least in their educational system—that there is no uncertainty in a planned economy because plans will all go according to schedule. But there often is in fact considerable uncertainty regarding supplies, production, financial planning, and delivery schedules. If more emphasis were to be placed on predictive, analytical, and problem-solving skills in business administration courses, managers trained in the various productive enterprise functions would be in a much better position to plan, organize, and control operations more effectively and efficiently under conditions of uncertainty.

Students who major in accounting, finance and banking, and statistics acquire a great deal of information in their chosen field. They are evidently quite well trained to perform highly standardized tasks that correspond to the prescribed planning, control, and informational requirements of the economic system. They learn the official rules, regulations, and types of reports relating to their discipline; standard methods and procedures for compiling and submitting data; the nature and content of forms to prepare, and so on. Such specialists are trained to analyze data primarily in historical rather than predictive terms. They do not seem to be well equipped with any theory concerning the solution of complex problems and which could be used in the application of standard methods or norms for future-oriented decision making and control. Statistics courses in Chinese economic programs, for example, are merely descriptive courses dealing with industrial and economic statistics, and there is no training in probability or decision theory, correlations analysis, or other analytical and predictive techniques found in American programs.

Courses dealing with supply planning, distribution and trade, labor and wages, and other business fields also provide much detailed descriptive data. Here students also learn in detail the rules, regulations, standard methods and procedures, and types of data and reports required. The student is apparently not provided with a scientific approach or conceptual framework for analyzing data for future decision making, and the emphasis is on memorization.

In the area of management per se, the only Chinese course that can even be compared with American courses in general management is called "management of industrial enterprises," and is apparently offered only by departments in industrial economics. In this course the student learns something about the enterprise's formal organization structure and authority relationships, various productive functions, components of the enterprise plan, prescribed methods and procedures for preparing plans, establishing targets, and controlling and analyzing results, as well as about various other topics spelling out in detail who should do what, when, and how. There is also much stress on "democratic centralism" (worker participation in enterprise management) and on some aspects of Chairman Mao's works and thought. There appears to be somewhat more ideology in Chinese courses than in similar Soviet management courses.

Little attention is given to operational theory, explanation, prediction, or problem solving in the Chinese management course, and there is virtually no study of underlying principles or concepts. Little emphasis is placed on the managerial functions of staffing, control, or direction—apart from ideological factors—and virtually no attention is given to empirical aspects of organizational or human behavior, organization theory, the behavioral sciences, and various other courses covered in American management courses. In fact, behavioral science education of the Western type is completely absent in Chinese economic programs. The Chinese management course may serve to develop mechanical managerial skills of various types and to introduce the student to some of the managerial functions in a largely descriptive way, but it does little to develop a basic theoretical underpinning or a creative and analytical approach to management problems.

Management as a system of techniques and processes is viewed as being part of economics in China; but as a philosophy involving human motivation and behavior, and in its personnel management aspects, it is viewed primarily as part of politics and ideology. This dichotomy regarding management education is also found in the real management world. Party cadres tend to play the major role in personnel management, particularly in the leadership and motivation of industrial employees, and they also play an important role in the staffing function, particularly political training, selection, and appraisal of character. The Chinese professional manager's role typically involves technical decision making, performing the managerial functions of planning, organization, and control, handling certain aspects of staffing and direction, and seeing that the productive functions of the enterprise are arranged, coordinated, and carried out properly.

In the long run the Red Chinese regime hopes to develop a nation of pure uniform Communist men, as the ideal is interpreted by Mao, through "correct" ideological indoctrination of the population as a whole. The prediction and control of human behavior and human motivation become quite simple tasks if virtually everyone has the same ideas and resulting behavioral responses because of a common basic and practical ideology and related values (which involve standardized language and communication). In such a situation the function of direction (which includes leadership and motivation) which is part of the managerial job would also become quite simple.

To the degree that political and ideological education has been effective in the effort to mold the Chinese mind—and it has apparently been surprisingly effective to date—to that extent managerial direction has been facilitated. Hence, political and ideological education, when not too excessive, in all types of educational programs, including engineering, may play a functional or beneficial role in terms of managerial effectiveness and industrial progress. However, this type of education and indoctrination has long lost its motivational potency in the Soviet Union, and the direction function of management has become increasingly difficult and complex as human needs and motivation have grown more complicated and as human behavior has become more difficult to predict and control. As a result, in Soviet research, theory building, and higher education, increasing attention is now being given to the behavioral sciences—sociology, psychology, and sociopsychology. One important aim here is to make more effective the direction, leadership, and motivation of personnel of all types.

In the Chinese higher educational system there are no separate departments of sociology, psychology, or behavioral sciences in general. What limited training in sociology there is is highly philosophical and ideological rather than empirical or experimental, and it is tied in with political and ideological courses, such as those dealing with Marxism-Leninism and Mao's works and thought. Psychology also forms part of ideological training, and its more scientific aspects are studied in some medical programs. I would speculate with some confidence—in view of the Soviet experience and the contemporary history of mankind—that the Red Chinese will eventually have to follow the Soviet path in dealing with the behavioral sciences if managerial effectiveness and industrial progress are not to suffer seriously in the long run. In this connection, it might also be said that it is unlikely that the dichotomy of managerial functions between party cadres and professional managers will continue to be nearly as distinct as it is today.

It also seems inevitable that the Chinese will have to follow the Soviet path—and hence a more American path—in general management education, as a whole, and in business administration and economics. Even today, there are serious and widespread inefficiencies in Chinese industry which are due in large part to both quantitative and qualitative deficiencies in these fields of education. At most of the enterprises surveyed I observed clear-cut inefficiencies of various types in the performance of managerial and productive functions, and at some firms such inefficiencies were very acute. (More about this in a later chapter.)

Let us now examine the programs for economics, business administration, and management at China People's University in Peking.

China People's University[58]

China People's University was established in Peking to provide a major center for the training of Marxist-oriented social scientists, and it was patterned after Soviet universities having this type of education. Even though the aim has been to develop Marxist social scientists, many Western-trained social scientists were on the faculty in the 1950's. But currently, I was told, there are not very many. There was a significant purge at this university in late 1957 and early 1958 following the "hundred-flowers" period when free speech was allowed. During the hundred-flowers period numerous faculty members, including many Chinese-educated ones, and students of China People's University spoke out vigorously against the regime and the party about the educational and other policies that were being pursued. There was much criticism of the neglect and deterioration of social science education in China while theology and dogma were being favored. When the short-lived free speech period was suppressed by the regime, large numbers of faculty members and students of this and other universities were reprimanded and punished—many were sent to villages to work and to be reindoctrinated, and many were permanently suspended.

China People's University is currently reputed to be Red China's best higher educational institution in the social sciences. It is under the Ministry of Higher Education and provides many of the teachers for other universities and institutes. I spent a productive one and a half days at this university. My major hosts, whose names I cannot recall, were two professors of economics, one of whom was a woman who was the head of the industrial economics department, and the other an associate professor of industrial management.

In 1966 the university's student enrollment was 3,000, and in recent years there have been slightly over 500 graduates annually. I was told that the university has a capacity for 4,000 students, and enrollment around the time of the Great Leap was about 4,000. In the early 1960's there were about 600 graduates annually. The faculty in 1966 numbered 900, including lecturers and assistants as well as scholars of professorial rank.

There were twelve departments, and all offer five-year programs of study leading to a diploma, except the department of library science and archives, which gives a four-year program. There were five economics departments: (1) political economy; (2) industrial economics; (3) finance and trade; (4) national economic planning and economic statistics; and (5) agricultural economics. Until a few years ago there were six economics departments, but since then finance and trade economics (marketing and procurement in the wholesale and retail sector) have been combined into one department.

The other university departments in 1966 were international politics, philosophy, history, law, journalism, and foreign language and literature. The program in international politics was established after 1960. There are no departments—and apparently no courses—in psychology, sociology, anthropology, or the behavioral sciences in general.

In addition to the 3,000 regular students, there were about 8,000 spare-time correspondence students scattered throughout the country who can earn diplomas or certificates by successfully completing a five- or six-year program of study. Both regular and correspondence students must be senior secondary school graduates to gain admission. Most of the departments also ran special advanced classes primarily for teachers and researchers who came to study for one to three years. After completing the advanced program they usually went back to their original places of employment. There were several hundred students of this type at the university in 1966. No degrees are awarded for advanced students, and in fact the university apparently awards only diplomas and certificates, and no degrees of any type.

At least 20 percent of the students' course work in all departments was in politics and ideology. It seems that in 1966 at least an average of two months per year, in most if not all departments, were spent on physical labor and employment, and this was nearly twice as much time spent on such activity a few years ago. In some departments, including industrial economics, experiments were started in 1965 entailing much more student time spent in physical labor and employment.

There was no diploma project or laboratory work of the type found at Tsinghua University in any of the five economics departments at China People's University. There were two terms per year, and the academic year ran for forty-six weeks. About twenty hours per week were spent in classes in the first three years and approximately ten hours in the last two years. Students were expected to spend from one to two hours on homework and self-study for every class hour. In the lower grades students took five or six courses per term, and in the higher grades four or five. A course ran from one to three terms.

There were both oral and written examinations for most courses every term. At the end of the final year there was a comprehensive written and oral examination involving the students' entire program of study. From what I could learn about examinations in the economics departments, they appeared to stress very heavily the memorization of facts, even though essay-type questions were sometimes asked. Students received forty-six yuan per month—with slight differences in some regions—during their first year of employment following graduation. I was told that future pay depended on merit, ability, and of course on correct behavior.

About 75 percent of the students received state subsidies for all of their basic requirements. When students worked in various organizations to fulfill their labor requirements, they were given subsistence allowance but received no regular pay.

Let us look more closely at the university's department of industrial economics, where I spent most of my time. In this department there were about a hundred and fifty regular students in 1966, and in recent years it turned out about thirty graduates annually. It graduated over forty graduates annually in the early 1960's. There were also nearly a hundred students taking advanced courses, and over a hundred taking correspondence courses in this department in 1966.

On the average, one-third of the graduates of this department were employed by industrial enterprises where they worked in planning, labor and wages, procurement, finance, and various other types of administrative activities. A larger proportion of graduates from this department went into industry than most, if not all, of the graduates from other departments at the university; but the proportion was somewhat lower than at some of the finance and economics institutes.

About one-third of the graduates also went to organizations of the macromanagerial type, such as central, provincial, and municipal planning organizations as well as economic and industrial organizations. The remainder became teachers—primarily of specialized economics middle schools and, in some cases, of higher educational institutions—party functionaries, and researchers at social science research institutes, such as the Coal Economics Institute and institutes belonging to other branches of industry (these institutes are under industrial ministries and central scientific organizations).

Graduates were assigned by the Ministry of Higher Education to jobs all over the country. In this regard the ministry, the university, and the department of industrial economics operated according to a five-year plan and an annual state plan. There was apparently a high degree of central control at all times regarding the job assignments of higher graduates.

The department had a total of forty-five faculty members, including five full professors, and six associate professors. The head of the department was an energetic middle-aged woman who was a long-time party member with a distinguished military career in the war against Japan. She knew many of the top Chinese leaders personally. She was a very warm and friendly person, who did not seem to know very much about operational economics, business administration, or management. It was likely that her appointment as department head and full professor was a type of reward based primarily on political loyalty and past services rendered to the party and her country, rather than a recognition of her skill, ability, or contributions in the field of economics. Her monthly salary was 230 yuan, and she also received the usual perquisites given to educators of her rank.

The monthly pay range for the four other professors in this department was 170 yuan to 330 yuan. For associate professors it was 150 to 230 yuan, for lecturers 70 to 150 yuan, and for assistants 46 to 76 yuan. There was one American-trained and one Soviet-trained economist in the department. Nobody had a doctoral degree. About half of the faculty—all of the full professors and five of the associate professors—were party members.

About 20 percent of the instruction time in the industrial economics field was devoted to politics and ideology, 20 percent to basic courses, and 60 percent to specialized courses. There was a limited choice of elective courses—less than 10 percent of instruction time—the students could take within the department. Electives here included such courses as "history of the national economy," and "planning of the national economy." While students were allowed to attend optional courses in any other department, they had to do it on their own time, and not for credit.

Among the compulsory courses in this department were the "thinking of Mao," "industrial economics," "management of industrial enterprises," "industrial statistics," "industrial accounting," and "foreign industrial economics." This last course, I was informed, dealt with economic conditions, probably only unfavorable ones, in advanced capitalist nations such as the United States, West Germany, and Japan; it also included criticisms of incorrect revisionistic economic and managerial thoughts and ideas in the Soviet Union and Yugoslavia and the lessons China could learn from its socialist brother countries of Albania, Korea, and North Vietnam.

The subjects covered in the courses offered by the industrial economics department included: history of the development of Chinese industry, direction of industrial development, fundamental construction of industry, location of industries, scales (sizes) of enterprises, direction and policy of technical development, material and technical supply, labor and wages, specialized production, coordination of enterprises, and management of enterprises.

The course "management of industrial enterprises" was two terms in length. It covered general management topics similar to those discussed earlier, as well as cost accounting, finance, production planning and organization, supply of materials, technical aspects, and labor and wages. This is a general course dealing with industrial firms in general, rather than with a specific branch of industry. There were no cases or problem-solving exercises of the type found in American programs.

Since 1965 this and other economics departments had been experimenting with various study-and-work programs, all requiring three years of study and two years of work. A typical student's study-and-work program involved half days for study and half days for work during the first year; alternate weeks of study and work during the second and third year; and an average of five to six consecutive months of work and then of study during the fourth and fifth years, with somewhat more work in the fourth year.

Prior to 1965, students averaged less than one year of work during the five-year program—they worked about four or five weeks and two to three months in higher grades. With the introduction of the extended work program, some courses, such as "the history of the national economy," were reduced in length or were eliminated. The number of electives was also reduced.

In the first year, students usually worked in the university's own large machinery workshop. During the next two academic years employment was generally arranged for them in the Peking area (I met some students from this department working at the First Peking Machine Tool Plant). In their last two years many students were sent to other cities to work, and in 1966 a number were working in factories in Dairen and other industrial cities of north China (Manchuria).

In general, most students were being sent to industrial enterprises to work, although some were assigned to various macromanagerial organizations. During their first three years students worked as manual laborers and apprentices, and during their last two years they worked in offices, doing routine types of white-collar jobs, but they still had to spend about two days a week in physical labor in the plant. After graduation they were rarely assigned to the same enterprises where they had worked, but quite often they were sent to similar types of firms—but this depended on job openings and on the state plan.

Students could state their preferences for the type of enterprise, job, or city where they would be placed after graduation, and I was told that if their wishes could be accommodated by the state plan, they were fulfilled. However, the better students—and "better" may have meant political loyalty and activity in school—generally received first priority.

Analysis of Higher Education and Related Employment Data from 1966 Survey of Chinese Industry

Table 3–20, below, indicates the type of jobs held by some of the higher graduates at a number of the Chinese industrial enterprises surveyed in 1966. There is much similarity between the titles of many specialties or fields of specialization offered in higher and secondary specialized pro-

TABLE 3–20

TYPES OF JOBS HELD BY HIGHER EDUCATION GRADUATES AT CHINESE INDUSTRIAL ENTERPRISES SURVEYED

Enterprise	*Job*	*Field of Specialization in Higher Education*
PEKING MACHINE TOOL	Chief engineer & vice director	Machine building & precision instruments
	Head of the director's staff	Machinery manufacture
	Head of Planning Dept.	Economic and organizational aspects of machine building
PEKING STEEL WIRE	Chief engineer	Pressure processing of metals
SHANGHAI MACHINE TOOL NO. 3	Vice chief engineer	Machine building and precision instruments
	Deputy Head of Production Planning	Industrial economics

TABLE 3–20 (*continued*)

Enterprise	*Job*	*Field of Specialization in Higher Education*
SHANGHAI HEAVY MACHINE TOOL	Director	Education
	Head of the director's staff	Metal pressure processing
	Chief designer	Machine building
	Chief engineer & vice director	Electrical engineering
	Technician	Mechanics
	Vice Director & Head of Production Planning	Industrial economics
	Shop accountant	Accounting
	Engineer	Plant design
SHANGHAI STEEL	Workshop director	Metallurgical engineering
	Engineer	Power engineering
	Deputy Head of Planning Dept.	Economic & organizational aspects of metallurgy
SHANGHAI TRUCK	Head of director's staff	Literature
	Workshop chief & worker	Water-vehicle manufacturing
	Technician	Welding industry and equipment
WUHAN HEAVY MACHINERY	Vice chief engineer	Machine building
	Head of Technical Dept.	Metal processing
	Head of director's staff	Metal rolling
	Shop planner	Industrial economics
WUHAN IRON & STEEL	Party secretary	Civil engineering
	Engineers	Metallurgical, power, electrical, chemical
	Workshop director	Heat treatment of steel & iron
	Technician & head of technical Dept. of Steel Mill	Foundry technology
	Vice chief of Corp. Mine	Mining equipment
	Section head	Material-handling equipment
	Chief of Scientific Research Lab.	Physical-chemical analysis of metallurgical processes (USSR)
	Translators of foreign publications	Foreign languages
WUSIH DIESEL ENGINE	Director	Law (did not graduate)
	Vice director, Technical	Agricultural machinery
	Technician	Instrument manufacturing
	Plant worker	Internal combustion engines
	Cadre in Planning Dept.	Economic planning
	Accountant	Accounting
	Head of Research Dept.	Internal combustion engines (USSR)

Enterprise	*Job*	*Field of Specialization in Higher Education*
PEKING PHARMACEUTICAL	Head of scientific research	Pharmacology
	Research worker	Chemistry
SHANGHAI PHARMACEUTICAL	Chief engineer	Biochemistry (Japan)
	Vice chief engineer	Biochemistry (U.S.)
	Deputy head of Technical Dept.	Pharmacy technology
	Head of Finance Dept.	Accounting
NANKING CHEMICAL FERTILIZER	Director	Chemical machinery and equipment
	Engineer	Chemical engineering
	Technician	Precision-measuring instruments
CANTON CHEMICAL FERTILIZER	Vice director	Chemistry
	Shop chief	Petroleum and natural gas engineering
	Technician	Electrochemical processing
	Cadre in Finance Dept.	Accounting
PEKING CHEMICAL COKE	Vice head of Research Section	Chemical engineering
TIENTSIN WATCH	Head of Technical Dept.	Light industry machinery & equipment
SHANGHAI BATTERY	Head of Production Planning	Industrial economics
PEKING COTTON	Vice chief engineer	Fiber technology
	Head of Finance Dept.	Finance and credit
SHANGHAI SUNG SING COTTON MILL	Head of Finance Dept.	Accounting
PEKING CLOTHING	Vice director, Commercial Affairs	Trade economics
	Vice director, Welfare	Literature
	Chief accountant	Mathematics
TIENTSIN SHOE	Head of General Office	Philosophy
	Director	Political economy

grams, although the depth and breadth of training are, of course, much greater in higher programs.

Let us now turn our attention to the employment of higher education graduates at thirty-seven of the Chinese industrial enterprises that I surveyed in 1966. Table 3–13, presented earlier, indicates the number and percent of higher graduates in relation to these enterprises and at three higher-level organizations.

We see that firms in the chemical and drug sector have, on the average, the largest proportion (5.4 percent) of higher graduates. Unlike other sectors, this sector relies more heavily on higher graduates than on semiprofessional graduates for its high-talent manpower. Higher educational programs related to this industry are probably more extensive and developed than secondary specialized programs. The two pharmaceutical firms employed a number of medical doctors, chemists, biologists, pharmacologists, and engineers in chemical technology and other engineering fields and a limited number of graduates of finance and economic programs. They also employed several foreign-trained graduates. For example, a vice director, who is also chief engineer at the Shanghai pharmaceutical firm, was a graduate biochemist educated in Japan, and the vice chief engineer obtained his degree in biochemistry in the United States. Of the four holders of Chinese graduate degrees that I met at Chinese enterprises, two of them were employed in the research and development departments of these drug enterprises. (The other two were doing research and development work at Wuhan Iron and Steel and Wusih Diesel Engine, respectively.)

Most of the graduates at the two chemical-fertilizer firms were in technical fields. This was also the case at the Peking Chemical Coke Plant, where several dozen graduates were employed in the scientific research department. In general, there has been a tremendous increase in the volume and diversity of chemical and drug production in China since 1949, and an even greater expansion of this sector was being undertaken in the mid-1960's. Part of this expansion was taking place through collaboration with a number of West European and Japanese companies, which were setting up new chemical plants, particularly fertilizer plants. During the 1949–63 period there was a forty-fold increase in the employment of chemical engineers and technicians in the Chinese economy. In 1949 there were only 100 types of chemicals produced in China, by 1957 there were 2,000, and by 1960 more than 8,000. Today there are probably well over 10,000, an amount substantially greater than in India.

The heavy-industry sector in our sample has the next highest proportion (4.2 percent) of higher graduates in relation to total employment. However, small-scale firms in this sector lag greatly behind the larger enterprises. The vast majority of graduates, probably over 90 percent, in the heavy-industry sector were trained in engineering and technical fields. Shanghai Truck and Wusih Diesel Engine employed relatively large proportions of graduates (9 percent). These were relatively new and complex industries in China, and both firms were allocated a fairly large number of graduates in recent years in order to improve the efficiency of operations. Many of these graduates were employed as workers in 1966, since all new higher graduates had to spend from one to two years in physical labor following their graduation.

The proportion of graduates (1.5 percent) in the light-industry sector lags greatly behind that of heavy-industry firms. A noticeable exception is the Tientsin Watch Enterprise (7 percent), which was experiencing many difficulties when I visited there. Perhaps the planners had allocated a relatively large number of graduates to this firm in an effort to make it more efficient. The watch industry is a relatively new one for China, and also relatively complex, compared with most consumer-goods industries. A majority of the graduates at Tientsin Watch were from spare-time higher technical programs. Tientsin Shoe had a surprisingly high proportion of graduates (3 percent), most of whom were from spare-time programs of different types. One reason for the relatively high proportion of graduates at Tientsin Shoe seemed to be that this enterprise made much of its own shoe machinery and equipment, and there was a number of higher technical graduates engaged in this type of activity. It is possible that there was a concerted drive, under Tientsin party leadership, to get all those industrial personnel who were eligible to get a spare-time higher education. A majority of the graduates at the Tientsin Wool Factory also received their higher education through spare-time programs, and most of the eligible non-higher graduates of the Tientsin Light Industry Bureau and the Daily Usage Corporation were enrolled in spare-time higher programs related to their jobs.

The overall proportion of graduates at the textile (1.2 percent) and clothing (.5 percent) enterprises surveyed was relatively small. They are part of the traditional consumer goods sector in China and rely heavily on personnel with long experience for their high-talent manpower. Most of the pre-1949 managers and technical personnel who were still working were employed in this sector, and most of the capitalists who still help manage their former industrial enterprises were also employed in the textile sector.

In general, light-industry firms seemed to employ a greater variety of graduates than heavy industry. I came across more graduates in such fields as literature, philosophy, mathematics, the humanities and the social sciences in general in the former sector. However, in all sectors a large majority of the higher graduates were from engineering and technical programs.

More than half of the enterprises surveyed employed at least one graduate in finance and economics, and a number of them employed several such graduates. All of the firms employing over 2,000 people had graduates of this type, while many of the small-scale enterprises did not have any. The Shanghai Truck factory did not employ any, but (as will be discussed in a later chapter) the degree of authority delegated to the management of this firm in nontechnical areas was very low. In a later chapter there will be a discussion of the serious deficiencies in the performance of the managerial and enterprise productive functions at most of the enterprises surveyed. At many enterprises the deficiencies were very much in evidence and very acute. Such deficiencies are probably due in large part to the critical shortage of high-talent personnel who have effective training in business administration, general management, and economics.

While the majority of higher graduates at the Tientsin enterprises and at several other firms surveyed are products of spare-time programs, at most of the enterprises the majority were graduates of regular programs. In general, there were more spare-time graduates than regular ones at most light-industry enterprises, rather than at most heavy-industry enterprises or chemical and drug firms. However, sizable numbers of employees at all types of enterprises were enrolled in spare-time higher programs in 1966. At several, five percent or more of all personnel were studying in spare-time higher schools. Several of the larger enterprises operate their own spare-time higher schools, and a few run regular higher educational programs—for example, Wuhan Iron and Steel operates the Wuhan Iron and Steel Institute in collaboration with the Ministry of Metallurgy and under the general direction of the Ministry of Higher Education. At the Shanghai Steel Mill, 300 of its employees were enrolled in its own part-time higher school; at Shanghai Heavy Machine Tool, 400 were enrolled in its school; Nanking Chemical had 250 employees in its program; and Shanghai Sung Sing Joint Textile No. 3 had about 50 in its school. Peking Chemical Coke had about 100 of its employees enrolled in various spare-time higher schools.

The very sparse data, presented in Table 3–13, for three of the higher-level industrial organizations surveyed do suggest that as one goes up the industrial hierarchy the proportion of higher graduates in relation to total employment tends to increase. At the Tientsin Daily Usage Corporation, which is the direct superior of the Tientsin Watch Enterprise, nearly 15 percent of its employees had had higher education. At the Tientsin First Light Industry Bureau, the direct superior of the above corporation, the proportion was 20 percent. At the Wusih Planning Commission, which is directly above Wusih's municipal industrial bureaus, the proportion of graduates was nearly 27 percent. Higher-level organizations of this type may rely more heavily on higher graduates than on semiprofessional graduates for their high-talent manpower.

The proportion of technical graduates among all higher graduates at these three organizations was not as great as at industrial enterprises. They employed a substantially greater proportion of graduates from finance and economics programs because they are involved in nontechnical functions to a higher degree than are most industrial enterprises. Three of the eight graduates at the Tientsin Corporation were of this type, while eight of twenty graduates at the Tientsin Bureau specialized in such nontechnical fields as economic planning, trade and industrial economics, finance, accounting, labor and wages, and procurement, supply, and distribution.

At the Wusih Planning Commission only one of its four higher graduates was from an engineering school. There were graduates in economic planning, statistics, and finance and credit.

In our sample of thirty-seven Chinese industrial enterprises, the proportion of higher graduates in relation to total employment for all these enterprises was 3.7 percent. For all industrial and related activities in the Soviet Union in 1963, the proportion of higher graduates was 3.9 percent, and only 2.5 percent for industrial enterprises. Obviously the figure from our Chinese sample is not representative for Chinese industry as a whole. The large majority of Chinese enterprises are still small in size and utilize relatively simple technology. It is unlikely that the proportion of higher graduates in relation to total employment in all Chinese industrial enterprises currently exceeds 1.5 percent.

The United States is substantially ahead of the Soviet Union in the proportion of higher graduates employed in industrial enterprises. The proportion in 1950 was 4.7 percent, and from my own observations of and experiences in United States industry, I would guess that today the figure is probably not very far from 9 or 10 percent.

From my research in Indian industry, I would estimate that the proportion of higher graduates as a percent of the total industrial enterprise employment is significantly higher than in China, and may even be as high as in the Soviet Union. The proportion of graduates in Indian firms involving American-Indian collaborations tends to be higher than in purely indigenous Indian firms; however, I came across only one industrial firm in India where the proportion of higher graduates was less than 5 percent. In the majority of the Indian firms surveyed, the proportion exceeded 10 percent, and in a few cases it was as high as 15 to 20 percent. In fact, the proportion of graduate-degree holders—master's and doctoral—in several of the American collaborations in India was over 1 percent of total employment, and in a few cases over 2 percent. In a few of these firms, the proportion of graduate-degree holders was substantially higher than in their American-based counterparts. Even in indigenous Indian firms, graduate-degree holders are quite common and plentiful in many cases.

In all types of firms in India, the majority of the clerical staff are commonly higher education graduates, and in one indigenous firm that I surveyed about 80 percent of all clerical personnel were higher graduates—mostly with Bachelor of Commerce and Bachelor of Arts degrees. In spite of the surprisingly high proportion of higher graduates in Indian industry, China seems to be doing better in the coordination of education with industrial requirements and in the utilization of higher graduates. (More about this subject in a later section.)

Of interest may be some brief comments on the proportions of higher graduates for enterprises in different branches of industry in our Chinese sample as compared with the proportions for the same branches of industry as a whole in the Soviet Union—even though the two sets of data are clearly not comparable because of the nature of the Chinese sample. The proportion for Soviet heavy industry—taking metallurgy, machine building, equipment manufacturing, and metal processing as a combined whole—at the end of the 1950's and early 1960's was approximately 4 percent, as compared with our Chinese figure of 4.2 percent for heavy industry. The Soviet proportion for metallurgy only was about 4.5 percent, and for the other types of heavy industry firms 4 percent. The Soviet figure for the chemical industry was 5.5 percent, very close to our Chinese figure of 5.4 percent. In both cases, of all the sectors this particular one has the highest proportion of higher graduates in relation to total employment. The Soviet approximate proportions for light industry (1.5 percent), and the paper industry (1 percent), are identical to our corresponding Chinese figures.

In general, the ranking order of Soviet industries is the same as that in our Chinese sample, with the exception of metallurgy which ranks higher in Russia. However, the Soviet figure for metallurgy is based on both ferrous and nonferrous metallurgical enterprises, while both of the Chinese firms in this sector are in ferrous metallurgy. Nonferrous metallurgy firms typically require more high-talent manpower than do ferrous firms.

Table 3–14, presented earlier, indicates the proportion of administrative and technical personnel having a higher education at thirty-one Chinese industrial enterprises surveyed. As was done with secondary semiprofessional graduates, we have assumed in this table that all higher graduates are employed within the ranks of administrative or technical (technicians and engineers) personnel. It is not likely that the resulting margin of error is more than five percent, if that, for any of the thirty-one enterprises. At these enterprises, the only higher graduates not employed as administrative cadres, engineers, or technicians were almost entirely recent graduates who were required to spend from one to two years after graduation as workers engaged in physical labor. At the Wusih Diesel Engine and Shanghai enterprises, which are not included in Table 3–14, there seemed to be an abnormally high number of graduates employed as workers, and I was told that most of them were recent graduates. Wusih Diesel had 540 administrative and technical personnel and about 250 higher graduates, while Shanghai Truck had about 147 of such personnel and 105 graduates.

At Wusih Diesel Engine, there were a few professors, writers, and a philosopher—all higher graduates—on leave from their regular occupations and employed as workers at this plant. They were, I was told, learning more about the lives and tasks of workers so that they could carry out their regular professions more effectively. I am not sure whether this was a voluntary or a penalty type of assignment, but a professor and philosopher whom I met at the Wusih factory seemed to be reasonably content and enthusiastic in their physical labor pursuits.

We see from Table 3–14 that for our entire sample about 18 percent of all administrative and technical personnel are higher graduates. The largest proportion (22 percent) of graduates is in the chemical and drug sector, and this may be due in part to the relatively large amount of research and development work being conducted. The firms in this sector are quite large, and relatively large numbers of high-talent personnel may be required to manage them and keep them operating with reasonable efficiency. Skilled technicians and engineers are required to keep the costly machinery and equipment functioning properly.

The proportion of graduates for the large- and medium-scale heavy industry firms is also higher (17 percent) than the average for all of the enterprises. Here, too, sizable numbers of competent engineers, technicians, and managers are required to keep them operating with tolerable efficiency because of their size and the complexity and diversity of operations. At some enterprises in this sector, there are also fairly large research and development staffs. The proportion of graduates for heavy industry as a whole in our sample is only about 13 percent, or less than that for light industry as a whole which is 15 percent. The light-industry figure is pulled up significantly by the Tientsin Watch enterprise, which was employing an atypically high proportion of higher graduates as administrators and technical personnel.

In general, the light-industry firms were not as managerially intensive as the heavy-industry firms, nor did they employ as great a proportion of technicians and engineers because their operations were not as complex, diverse, or capital intensive. Yet many of the light-industry enterprises were quite large—in textiles, for instance, they were larger than is typical in most countries, including the United States—therefore they required at least a hard core of well-educated administrative and technical personnel if they were to operate with tolerable efficiency. So given the relatively small number and proportion of administrative and technical personnel in this sector and the need for at least some well-educated persons of this type, the proportion of higher graduates in relation to the number of administrative-technical personnel was slightly higher than that for the heavy-industry firms as a total group.

Most of the higher graduates at the Chinese firms surveyed were employed as department and section heads, vice directors, workshop chiefs and their deputies in research, design, and development work and as engineers. A number of heads of director's staffs—whose title is director of the director's office—who are like executive assistants in American firms, were also higher graduates generally where the director was not a graduate. They were typically relatively young, and perhaps they served as a buttress for the directors on various managerial and technical matters because of their superior education.

It was also common to find technicians of various types who were higher graduates; but the majority of them who were such graduates apparently had not been employed at the enterprises for more than about four or five years, and many of them probably will eventually become engineers or managers. A majority of the technicians in many firms seemed to be either semiprofessional graduates or skilled employees who had been promoted from the ranks of workers. A substantial majority of persons employed as and called engineers were apparently higher graduates at the enterprises surveyed, although there were also some who were not, and even a few who had been promoted from the workers' ranks. In general, a somewhat greater proportion of the engineers and technicians were graduates than the administrative cadres at most of the enterprises surveyed.

Chinese written sources do not distinguish clearly between engineering and technical personnel and engineers and technicians. It seems that the latter group actually has the title of engineer or technician, while the former category includes other technical personnel who do not have such a title. To the best of my knowledge, all of the technical personnel included in Table 3–14 are either engineers or technicians. Technicians generally engage in relatively routine drafting, design, laboratory, and other technical activities, while engineers, even if they are not managers, seem to be more directly involved in managerial functions, such as the planning and organizing of activities of other personnel.

Several of the enterprises surveyed did not have any engineers. These were mostly smaller enterprises, and more of them were in light industry than in heavy industry. However, a large majority of the firms did employ engineers, and in some firms more than 20 percent of the technical personnel were engineers. For example, at Wuhan Iron and Steel there were 800 engineers out of a total of about 2,300 engineers and technicians, and at Shanghai Pharmaceutical there were 35 engineers out of about 150.

About two-thirds of the enterprises surveyed had a chief engineer, and about half of them had a vice chief engineer as well. In all cases where information was obtained, either the chief engineer or vice chief engineer was a higher graduate. At several enterprises both were, and in about 75 percent of the cases the chief engineer was a higher graduate. I came across only one chief engineer who was not at least a semiprofessional graduate; he was a worker who became a technician, an engineer, and eventually a chief engineer.

A 1955 survey indicated that only 6 percent of the industrial leaders in China at that time were higher graduates.[59] The term "industrial leader" was not clearly defined, but it apparently related to enterprise directors and vice directors. In my sample roughly 25 to 50 percent of the vice directors were higher graduates at a majority of the enterprises surveyed. However, among thirty-six enterprise directors, the top managers, only three were graduates, and one had had some college education. The director of Shanghai Heavy Machine Tool was a graduate in education, at Nanking Chemical he was a graduate engineer, at Tientsin Shoe he was a graduate in political economy from a spare-time university, and the director of Wusih Diesel Engine had been a law student before 1949, when he was expelled for his revolutionary activities. It should be pointed out that some of the capitalists still managing their former firms were also graduates, and this subject will be discussed in a later chapter. At thirty-four enterprises where I obtained information on the educational background of Communist party secretaries, only one had had higher education. He was the party secretary of the Wuhan Iron and Steel Corporation and a graduate in civil engineering.

As was mentioned earlier, the category of administrative and technical personnel in our sample of Chinese enterprises corresponds very crudely to the Soviet category of "leading personnel," which includes managerial, administrative, and specialized personnel. For all Soviet industrial enterprises, in January 1957, 17.3 percent of all leading personnel were higher graduates. The proportion was undoubtedly significantly higher as of 1966, and may have well been as high as 25 percent or even more. For our 1966 sample of thirty-one Chinese industrial enterprises which undoubtedly has a significant upward bias as compared with the figure for all Chinese enterprises, the proportion of higher graduates in relation to the total number of administrative and technical personnel was about 18 percent. Hence, in spite of substantial progress in this sphere to date, the Chinese lag some ten years behind the Russians and on a national scale may lag as much as fifteen years behind them.

Earlier we made a rough comparison between China and the Soviet Union regarding the proportion of Engineering-Technical-Managerial Personnel, or ETMP, who are higher graduates. We estimated that roughly 17,000 to 21,000 of the administrative-technical personnel in our sample of thirty-one Chinese industrial enterprises corresponded to the Soviet ETMP definition. Using this range, roughly 22 to 26 percent of the ETMP at the Chinese firms were higher graduates. The Soviet proportion in 1963 was 26.7 percent; and in 1956, 19.5 percent. Hence, as of the mid-sixties even the proportion of the sample of Chinese firms was clearly behind the Soviet proportion on a national scale, and for all Chinese industrial enterprises the gap is probably substantially more—perhaps as much as fifteen years. However, Red China has accomplished in about seventeen years what it took the Soviets about thirty-five years to do, regarding the proportion of ETMP having higher education. The Chinese can do much to narrow this existing gap quite rapidly—through both regular and spare-time higher education—but if they move too fast, the quality of training will tend to suffer substantially.

There are no available comparable figures for the proportions of leading or ETMP types of personnel in American industry who have had higher education. I would guess that the United States is substantially ahead of the Soviets on both counts and probably several decades ahead of the Chinese. There are some suggestive figures available which support this position.[60] In 1960, 35.4 percent of all managers, officials, and proprietors (excluding farm owners) employed in the United States civilian labor force had attended one or more years of college or university. Even in 1940, the percentage was 23.5. The 1960 figure for professional, technical, and kindred workers was 74.5 percent, and in 1940, 72.7 percent. Various surveys conducted in the 1960's indicate that about 75 percent of top-level managers, 60 to 70 percent of major executives, and roughly 25 percent of lower-level managers are higher graduates. While these samples typically involve relatively large enterprises, they do suggest that American industry is ahead of Soviet industry and way ahead of Chinese industry in the proportion of managers who have a higher education. Probably the vast majority of engineers and a substantial number of technicians employed in American industrial firms are college graduates. Numerous graduates of junior colleges in particular are employed as technicians.

Although there are no figures available on Indian industry, India is also probably ahead of China in the proportion of managers, engineers, technicians, and other leading administrative personnel who are graduates of higher educational institutes. It is common to find that over half of the managerial and administrative personnel in Indian firms are college graduates. As was pointed out earlier, the proportion of clerks who were graduates in some of the enterprises I surveyed in India was surprisingly large. Probably a large majority of engineers are higher graduates—at times not in engineering fields—and a substantial proportion of technicians are also either degree or diploma holders in various fields. However, as was indicated earlier, the coordination of education with manpower utilization problems seems to serve as significantly greater constraints on managerial effectiveness and industrial progress in India than in China.

Management-Development Programs

There do not seem to be any special management-development programs in China of the types found in the United States which focus on the functions of management or organizational behavior. From time to time short-term courses or educational meetings are conducted for managers and other key personnel of various industrial enterprises. Such educational programs may be run by industrial ministries, provincial industrial departments, or municipal bureaus, and are anywhere from a few days to a few months in length. From what I could learn from my survey of Chinese industry, programs of this type are keyed to the needs of particular branches of industry, last only a few days or at most a few weeks, and are often tied in with national supply and sales conferences or meetings. They are somewhat informal in nature; various firms send a few of their personnel; and the emphasis tends to be on technical subjects, rather than on business administration or general management. Sometimes leading enterprises in a particular industry hold short-term informal and formal educational programs—primarily technical or ideological but sometimes managerial—for personnel sent by other firms in the industry. Interorganizational cooperation of this type probably does serve to increase managerial effectiveness in many cases. However, the main source of functional or skill education for enterprise personnel are the spare-time schools at all levels, and they have already been discussed as part of the regular education system.

There are special educational programs for party members, including those who may be industrial managers.[61] Here, the vast majority of programs stress ideological and political subjects in order to prevent party members from backsliding and also to keep them up-to-date with party policies and their rights and duties. In a broad sense, various programs of this type can be said to deal with some aspects of management, since the motivation and mobilization of personnel is often an important topic. Party education is conducted by party organizations and committees at all levels of the economy. Often they are run by the political departments of central organizations—including industrial ministries—provincial organizations, and municipal bureaus, or in some cases at enterprises. There are also special party schools at various levels, such as the Higher Party School and Central Research Institute of the Central Party Committee, which hold study sessions and give one- to three-month courses. At times the facilities of regular educational institutions are taken over for these courses.

All types of organizations, at all levels, also hold a few regular sessions of study and discussion—during or after work—for party cadres on a weekly basis. Managers and technical personnel who are party members often attend these sessions, as well as party secretaries and other party cadres. This was the case at many of the enterprises surveyed. Sometimes party educational programs do devote some attention to technical and managerial subjects, but for the most part party members obtain their "expertness" training through the regular spare-time educational system.

In general, there are many more special types of expertness educational programs for managers, leading technical personnel, and party cadres in Soviet industry than in China.[62] Such Soviet programs provide refresher courses for participants, serve to disseminate relevant information on recent developments, and generally serve to keep them up-to-date in their fields of specialization. The emphasis in Soviet programs of this type has been primarily on technical and engineering courses. However, in recent years, there has been somewhat greater emphasis in some programs on economics and business administration.

In the last few years, a few Soviet programs have been set up for managers which deal with managerial functions and important managerial problems. A number of prominent Soviet authorities have been advocating management development programs similar to those found in America—for example, the programs of this type run by the Harvard Business School has been investigated and praised by some Soviet experts.[63] The Soviet government has recently had negotiations with M.I.T. about the possibility of having M.I.T. collaborate in the establishment of new management-development programs as well as a graduate school of management. I was invited by the Soviet government to give some lectures and to hold seminars on American management education with various Soviet experts, including managers, during the summer of 1966. Unfortunately, prior commitments forced me to postpone this trip.

The lack of management-development programs in Chinese industry—for party cadres who play a direct and significant role in the management process, as well as for managers per se—no doubt serves as a constraint on managerial effectiveness and industrial progress. For it is just as important, if not more important, to improve the quality of existing managers in a developing country, such as China, as it is to increase the number of managers. Perhaps not much progress has yet been made with management-development programs in China because of significant limitations of facilities, instructors, knowledge, financial resources, and time. It is unlikely that much progress will be made until the regime recognizes and tries to rectify the deficiencies in management education, business administration, economics, and the social sciences in general, as well as in its system of higher education. In general, there is a close correlation in most countries between the extent and content of management-development programs and the content and extent of management training in the system of higher education.

A Canadian senator named Cameron, whom I met in Peking, and who is one of the organizers of an important management-development program conducted every summer at Banff, Alberta, offered scholarships to Red Chinese citizens to attend this program. He made this offer to various top-ranking Chinese officials, including Nan Han-chen, who is president of the China Council of International Trade, as well as governor of the Bank of China. His offer was apparently received with interest, but I do not know whether any Chinese people are going to be sent to the Banff Program. If and when there is enough awareness by top-ranking Chinese officials of the need for management-development programs and management education, in general, steps will probably be taken in this direction. If appropriate steps are not taken before Chinese industry develops much further, this would probably serve as a significant constraint on future industrial progress. An industrial nation can go only so far relying almost solely on practical experience and trial and error for the development of managerial skill and ability.

It is important to point out, however, that the existence of management-development programs cannot by itself do much to significantly improve managerial effectiveness and industrial progress. Managers who attend such programs must have the proper motivation to apply effectively in practice what they learn. Here achievement drive seems to be very important. There is some evidence which suggests that where managers who attend management-training programs have a low achievement drive, their attitudes, behavior, and performance do not change significantly in the direction desired or anticipated.

In India there are a substantial number and wide variety of management-development programs available to practicing managers. Some of these programs—particularly those run by the All India Management Association and the two Indian institutes of Management—are of high quality in content. However, it does seem that, more often than not, there is little, if any, difference in the performance, behavior, or attitudes of managers after they return to their enterprises. When this is the case, it is probably due to a relatively low achievement drive and/or the lack of opportunity to put into practice what they have learned because of the limitations placed on their authority by their superiors. While both these factors are pervasive and significant constraints in Indian industry, I would guess that low achievement drive is the more important one.

While India clearly has the edge in number and types of management-development programs available, China seems to have a significant potential advantage in making more effective use of such programs if they were established. This would probably be the case because of what appears to be the generally higher achievement drive of Chinese managers, and because there would probably be fewer restraints on managers on a national scale from putting into practice what they would learn.

Attitude toward Education

The strategies of human-resource development and closely related dominant attitudes toward education are greatly influenced by the dominant elites of a given country.[64] In old China the ruling elites desired to preserve the traditional class structure and existing power structure and little was done to eliminate mass illiteracy, develop an extensive educational system, or to change traditional values through education. Education was primarily reserved for the select members of the privileged classes. Education emphasized the Confucian classics, humanities, law, religion, and some of the social sciences, and training in these and military fields, and not technical or engineering education, were typically the avenues to real prestige, wealth, and power.

Moreover, in pre-1949 China an educated person typically viewed manual labor with considerable disdain and revulsion. This attitude undoubtedly retarded the growth and development of technical and engineering education, since employment in these fields was associated directly with "dirty-hands" work and manual labor. A dominant attitude held by the educated elite and the intelligentsia was that no educated person should soil his hands, or even associate closely with people who did; rather, he should become an official and/or engage in purely mental pursuits in order to glorify his family.

While undoubtedly there are still people—mostly older persons—in China who still cling to such earlier traditional attitudes, the dominant attitude toward education in contemporary Chinese society from top to bottom has undergone a tremendous transformation.[65] Formal education today in Red China in generally viewed as a privilege not for a small privileged elite but for the masses. The tens of millions of citizens who do obtain a formal education, regardless of level of termination, are expected and generally seem eager to use their education in productive pursuits for the benefit of the state. An unprecedented thirst for functional education has been generated throughout China.

In China, like Russia, it is generally accepted that man is developed through education primarily for his service to the state and not for his own sake. A conscious attempt is made to achieve a close match between the overall educational system and the requirements of productive organizations. Since the Chinese regime is striving to develop a pure proletarian industrial society, education that is most proletarian and industrial in content tends to receive the greatest attention. Hence, there has been a tremendous expansion in functionally oriented vocational, technical, and engineering education at the expense of general or liberal education. Knowledge for the sake of knowledge is greatly limited in the Chinese educational system in favor of a practical and applied emphasis—at times, to the point of ridiculing, as bookish, fundamental science and theory, basic research, and frontier knowledge.

Technical engineering and applied scientific education has top priority and prestige in Red China, and probably attracts and accepts the best students. Ideology and politics dominate education that is basically nontechnical or nonscientific in the applied sense, and broad education in the social sciences and humanities receives relatively little attention. These latter fields probably attract and accept the most politically dedicated and zealous students because of their ideological orientation, but it is doubtful whether a substantial number of the best students are enrolled in nontechnical, nonscientific programs. Hence, even in the Chinese educational system there is probably somewhat of a dichotomy between Reds and Experts, with students in technical fields tending to be somewhat more Expert than Red, and with the reverse situation in various other fields. However, given China's vast population, and the highly selective admission system in senior secondary and higher education, in particular, it seems safe to say that students in China's secondary and higher schools compare favorably in quality and intelligence with those found in more advanced countries. In dedication and motivation they may compare more favorably.

On the whole, the strategy of human-resource development pursued and the dominant attitude toward education which has evolved in China have undoubtedly done a great deal to improve managerial effectiveness and accelerate the pace of industrial development. In the foreseeable future a somewhat modified strategy and attitude toward different types of education, involving more emphasis on broader education and improvement and expansion of the social sciences, will undoubtedly become more crucial for continued industrial progress.

Because Chinese students typically view education, in general, very favorably and as a privilege, they tend to undertake their studies with a great deal of dedication. This is reflected by the apparent enthusiasm with which they undertake heavy—by almost any other country's standards—programs of study and work, not to mention various time-consuming extracurricular activities. This highly favorable attitude toward education also is reflected by the fact that literally millions of people who are fully employed enroll in spare-time education programs. This usually entails anywhere from twenty to forty or more hours per week of study, on top of a regular work week of over forty-eight hours, although some time off from work may be granted for study purposes. While some persons may undertake such spare-time education because of social pressures exerted on them, a large majority who work in industry and business probably do so in order to improve their performance, and perhaps to get ahead, in their jobs.

Given this generally favorable attitude toward education in China, industrial personnel are inclined to want to improve their skills and abilities through on-the-job training, self-education, and self-development, as well as through formal education. On-the-job training programs, as well as informal education and self-development, are pervasive throughout Chinese industry and, in fact, throughout China's urban society. Hotel employees study foreign languages on their own and in informal groups so that they can give better service to foreign visitors; interpreters try to master additional foreign languages and constantly try to perfect the ones they know; drivers on their own time study about the repair and maintenance of motor vehicles; and so forth. Practically every Chinese citizen one encounters in a Chinese city is studying and reading something related to his job. Almost everybody seems to carry around books, magazines, and/or journals, as well as writing pads and pens or pencils. And one sees people reading and writing in buses, in parks, in factories, stores and offices, and even on the streets. They are not only studying the works of Chairman Mao; they are frequently trying to improve their occupational skills and job performance.

With such a generally favorable attitude toward education and self-development, it becomes much easier to train industrial personnel and to improve their performance. They are inclined to want to learn new things and to learn them quickly; they are less likely to resist or fumble at new changes or innovations introduced at the enterprise—whether they be technical, procedural, or managerial in nature. With enterprise personnel motivated in the direction of self-improvement through education, participation in planning and communication tend to be more effective, and authority can be decentralized more readily, with the result that supervision and control need not be as tight if the reverse were true. In fact, worker participation in enterprise planning in China is viewed as an important part of the educational process.

A favorable attitude toward education of the applied type is also spurred in China by the existence of many opportunities to get ahead in industry and business. Career advancement is frequently possible through the improvement of one's qualifications and skills. In general, this pervasive overall favorable attitude toward functional education in China is related to the relatively high achievement drive of much of its population, and probably most of its urban industrial population. (More about this in the next chapter.)

In India, and many other newly developing countries, where an attempt is made to expand and overhaul the educational system, much of the population fails to recognize or identify with the kind of educational and social revolution their country is trying to undergo. Parents fail to stress to their children the need for education or the acquisition of functional skills. Parents who are poor and/or illiterate, typically do not realize the advantages of education. Sizable expenditures are made by the government on education, international agencies are consulted, teams of education experts are invited to the country; but the policy choices between quantitative expansion and more selective qualitative improvements in education, particularly at the secondary and higher levels, are not adequately thought out or effectively implemented by Indian government or educational leaders.

While there has been some expansion in technical and engineering education in India, and a somewhat more favorable view toward such education has evolved in some segments of Indian society, the traditionally elite educational fields and occupations—for example, law, political science, political economy, the humanities, arts and classics, religion, medicine, and some of the natural sciences, such as physics—continue to be favored by most educators and the more able students alike. As a result, the educational system does not turn out adequate numbers of basically qualified people for productive enterprises. There still seems to be a widespread tendency on the part of well-educated Indians to look down on manual labor or "dirty-hands" work. Even engineering graduates frequently prefer office work or other white-collar jobs ill suited to their training, rather than working, even at higher pay, in a factory. Strong vested interests prevent the contents of most educational programs from changing effectively in response to the manpower requirements of industry. Education and manpower planning, and particularly the implementation of such plans, are not very effective in terms of economic development.

India may well be more democratic than Red China inasmuch as individuals are freer to pursue their own educational interests and careers, and education is viewed primarily as a means of developing the individual rather than the servant of the state. At the same time, however, secondary and particularly higher education in India is still available primarily only to the privileged classes, even though somewhat more financial aid is being provided for the underprivileged. Moreover, large numbers of graduates either cannot find any job, much less a suitable one, or they are unhappy and frustrated in the jobs they obtain.

Indian students do not generally seem nearly as dedicated or enthusiastic in their studies as their Chinese counterparts. (The students of the Indian Institute of Management in Calcutta have clearly been an exception to this general statement.) Study loads are also generally much lighter in India.

It is rare to find someone working in Indian industry—as a manager, administrator, engineer, technician, clerk, worker, or in any other position—who is undertaking a spare-time educational program in order to improve his qualifications or performance. As was noted earlier, there is even relatively little enthusiasm for literacy courses where they are offered. On-the-job training does not generally seem to be as effective in Indian industry as it is in Chinese industry, and Indian personnel do not seem to be nearly as interested in self-development through self-education. Apathy, a perceived lack of opportunities for advancement, and relatively low-achievement motivation, are probably major reasons for such apparently pervasive negative attitudes toward spare-time self-education and self-training among Indian industrial personnel.

Matching Education with Industrial Requirements and Manpower Utilization

While Red China has made impressive, if not remarkable, progress in its overall educational system, it still falls far short of satisfying the high-talent and skilled manpower requirements of its expanding industries. Tens of thousands of engineers, technicians, and key industrial managers have been and still are being promoted, because of their practical experience and, at times, political standing, from the ranks of workers and have very limited formal education or training other than that gained on the job. A sizable proportion of China's higher-level industrial managers also consists of ex-military officers and improperly trained party cadres. Literally millions of skilled workers have achieved all of their occupational training on the job rather than through formal educational programs. For example, one Chinese source states that during the 1949–60 period some 5.6 million skilled workers were trained directly on the spot at industrial, transportation, mining, and communication enterprises.[66]

Not only has it been necessary to devote much more time to on-the-job training of all types in Chinese industry as compared with such activity in more advanced nations, but thousands of Chinese enterprises also run their own spare-time and, in many cases, full-time formal schools. The operation of schools of various types and levels undoubtedly absorbs considerable time, energy, and effort on the part of the enterprise management which would be devoted to more directly productive and industrial managerial pursuits if the regular educational system was adequate. Hence, industrial enterprises and their managements are themselves called on to play very major roles in overcoming significant problems concerning the coordination of education and industrial requirements that are solved to a much greater extent by the regular external educational system in a country like the United States.

The educational-match problem by no means has only a quantitative dimension in China; it also has a qualitative dimension. There have been, from time to time, complaints published in Chinese sources that the quality, content, and narrowness of specialized training received by semiprofessional and higher graduates have not served to fulfill adequately the job requirements at industrial enterprises.[67] There have also been complaints that industrial managers are often hastily trained for their jobs, and are strong on ideological and political qualifications but weak on managerial, economic, technical, and productive-function types of skills.[68] However, such complaints were much more common several years ago than they are today, and the quality problem with regard to education and training was most pronounced during the Great Leap Forward period.

While the overall quality of Chinese education certainly lags significantly behind that of the United States, and probably also behind that of the Soviet Union, it should not be underestimated or disparaged, considering what has been done in only seventeen years. The facts seem to be that by reason of their rigorous and intensive schedules, their highly selective admission system, and the quality, intelligence, application, and concentration of their students, graduates of Chinese educational institutions in general, although perhaps less broadly educated, compare quite favorably in their specialized knowledge with those of many advanced countries, and more favorably than those in most developing nations. However, if the Chinese educational system continues once again to move substantially in the direction of the Great Leap period, the educational-match problem will again become very serious.

There does currently seem to be a lack of balance in Chinese higher education in particular, which could also cause serious problems for managerial effectiveness and industrial progress. This lack of balance relates primarily to the lack of emphasis—both quantitative and qualitative in terms of an objectively scientific and operational approach—on economics, business administration, management, and the social sciences in general. As Chinese industry expands and grows more complex, such factors as the lack of emphasis in the fields, intensive educational specialization in all fields, and the inability of the educational system to develop adequate numbers of well-rounded, creative generalists would serve as very significant handicaps in achieving the flexibility and adaptability in management, technology, and science which are required for sustained industrial progress.

On the whole, China seems to be doing significantly better than India in the matter of educational match and particularly in the utilization of high-talent and skilled manpower. China has the lead in literacy and primary education and lags behind somewhat quantitatively but not probably qualitatively in secondary education. In higher education, India has the quantitative lead, but China's strategy involving great emphasis on technical and engineering fields has apparently been substantially more effective to date, even though India has a big edge in the social sciences. India has a clear-cut edge in management-development education.

There is much more unemployment among high school graduates and higher graduates in India than in China. This situation is due in large part to the failure of India's educational system to produce the types of people required by industry. It is also due to the sociological-cultural factors touched upon in the previous section. Too many graduates in the arts, general science, and commerce are produced and not enough engineers and technicians of the right types. India is also handicapped by a job-announcement and employment-agency system that has great deficiencies, as well as by a lack of close ties and exchanges of information between educational institutions and productive enterprises. Another problem here may be that Indian industry has not been expanding fast enough to absorb certain types of graduates. And finally, India's educational system does not seem to adjust to changing industrial-manpower requirements as fast as China's.

Since educational and manpower planning is closely tied in with economic planning in China, and since there is a high degree of central control over the assignment, employment, and transfers of specialized high school graduates and particularly higher graduates, unemployment of high-talent manpower in China is probably negligible. (Underemployment or misutilization is a problem of a different type to be discussed shortly.) Governmental attempts at educational and manpower planning in India have been seriously handicapped by the ultraconservative vested interests—and at times insecurities—of faculty members of educational institutions, as well as by dominant attitudes toward different types of education and occupations on the part of educators, students, and other influential segments of society. While in India there is greater free choice than in China for individuals regarding educational fields they may pursue as well as jobs they can accept, such a democratic procedure may not be particularly meaningful to Indian graduates who cannot find jobs at all, or the kind of jobs they want.

In 1955 in India there were about 379,000 senior high school graduates (matriculates) and 93,000 university graduates who were unemployed and who desired employment.[69] An upward trend in unemployment of educated persons has continued in India—by 1964 there were over one million matriculates unemployed who were seeking work and still as many as 83,000 higher graduates, for a combined total of about 1.09 million. In 1955, when there were 3.2 million matriculates and higher graduates employed in the Indian labor force, the proportion of unemployed graduates of these types was about 15 percent. By 1961, when there were about 6.2 million such graduates in the employed labor force, the proportion of unemployed was about 16.2 percent.

The vast majority of unemployed higher graduates in India have been, and are, those who specialized in the liberal arts, general science, and commerce. In the ranks of the unemployed have been, and are, thousands of advanced-degree holders—of the master's and Ph.D.—in these fields and in law. Many of the unemployed graduates have been from India's leading universities, and not only from schools of inferior quality. For example, in 1959, 3.3 percent of all graduates of Delhi University (one of India's most prestigious and best) since 1950, and 7.2 percent since 1954 were involuntarily unemployed. Many honor graduates, including many with M.A. degrees, in the arts, science, and law, were working as clerks even eight years after graduating. In fact, about 25 percent of all 1950 graduates and 40 percent of the 1954 graduates were working as clerks.[70] At the same time numerous enterprises were—and are—faced with critical shortages of qualified engineers, technicians, and administrators of all types. A great deal of time, energy, and resources are spent by Indian firms on recruiting and training such personnel because of the serious educational-match problem.

Even among India's limited number of engineering and technical graduates there has been a high degree of unemployment. For example, at the end of 1961 there were 65,000 graduate engineers available for employment, of whom 7,000 were unemployed. There were also 85,000 engineering technicians—holders of diplomas from junior colleges—available, of whom 10,000 were unemployed. However, the vast majority of these unemployed holders of degrees and diplomas were in civil engineering, a field which has been overproducing graduates, while other engineering and technical fields fall short of meeting demand. One major reason why civil engineering probably attracts so many students in India is that graduates hope to find managerial and other white-collar jobs in offices—particularly in government offices—rather than with "dirty-hands" work crews in the field and in factories.

There is a great deal of misutilization of high-talent manpower in Indian industry. It is very common to find persons with master's degrees and Ph.D.'s—often trained at leading Western universities—in engineering fields and the physical sciences who are working in sales, finance, accounting, personnel, and general administration; many of those graduates in commerce, law, economics, and various other social science fields are employed in engineering and technical jobs—both managerial and nonmanagerial. One reason for such misutilization is the attitude toward different types of occupations. For example, high-caste Indians trained in engineering or the physical sciences often greatly prefer to work in offices, particularly the head office, rather than in a factory, while those who are not Brahmins, for instance, regardless of their fields of formal training, are much more willing to take positions that involve work in factories or direct association with personnel working in factories. Class structure, nepotism, discrimination, limited individual mobility, and the lack of suitable opportunities all tend to be significant constraints on the effective utilization of high-talent manpower in Indian industry.

When ideology is not pushed too far in Red China, it seems that there is a much higher degree of effective utilization of high-talent manpower in

Chinese industry than in Indian industry. In general, the degree to which the utilization of high-talent and skilled manpower has been effective in Red China has oscillated with the degree to which ideology has taken priority over managerial, technical, and economic rationality.[71] This has been true not only in the utilization of high-talent industrial manpower, but also in the utilization of natural and social scientists, engineers, and educators who play an important role in national-policy formulation and decision making, and in shaping the overall macroenvironment in which industrial firms must function.

During the 1949–55 period the great majority of the well-educated people remaining in Red China were mobilized in the regime's effort to industrialize and achieve rapid economic development. Although much thought remolding and indoctrination were conducted, especially among the pre-1949 and Western-trained higher graduates, the knowledge and skills of the well-educated and higher intellectuals were utilized quite effectively. During the Hundred Flowers period of free speech in 1956 and 1957, the higher intellectuals attained the acme of their status and respect in Red China. A vigorous effort was made to use their talents to the "fullest possible extent," and they were encouraged to put forth their candid opinions and criticisms. At that time the social scientists who had been trained prior to 1949 and particularly the Western-educated social scientists were the most outspoken critics of the regime and the party.

The Great Leap period of the next three years led to a nationwide, vigorous anti-intellectual campaign, with a chief aim being the obliteration of class distinctions based on formal educational qualifications. Contradictions involving intellectuals—which involved the well-educated of all types, including natural and social scientists, educators, managers, engineers, technicians, artists, writers, and so on—became polarized in the extreme. Intellectuals were accused of being Expert at the expense of Red, of favoring individualism rather than collectivism, self-interest rather than collective interest, of being specialists rather than generalists, of placing technical economic and other nonpolitical issues above politics and ideology. There was also a clear-cut contradiction between objective scientific truth in many areas and dogma, and a "bourgeois outlook" and mentality were associated with Expertness. The knowledge of illiterate and barely literate workers and peasants was termed "science," while the knowledge of experts and professionals, even those with international reputations—and these included hundreds of Western-trained Ph.D.'s in economics, business administration, engineering, the natural sciences, and various other fields[72]—was termed "bookishness" and "superstition."

During this period hundreds of thousands of grossly unsuited and relatively ignorant workers were placed in responsible managerial, technical, and scientific jobs at enterprises, scientific research institutes, and government organizations. Where the educated experts still maintained their positions, it frequently happened that their status, authority, and decisions were undermined and reversed by improperly trained workers and zealous party cadres. Thousands of experts of all types underwent intensive brainwashing, many were purged, demoted, and removed from their jobs. Even top scientists, and particularly "old school" social scientists were dismissed during this "antirightist" campaign, and many were possibly even imprisoned. The government and the party made very little use of the knowledge or skill of intellectuals and scientists, particularly social scientists, in the formulation of national policies or decisions, and many very serious avoidable errors were made. At the industrial-enterprise level serious errors resulting in great inefficiencies also arose from the gross misutilization of the limited number of well-educated experts and professionals.

In 1961 it became clear to the Red Chinese leaders that they were faced with a severe economic crisis and by the end of that year the regime reversed its anti-intellectual policies and campaigns. By 1962 a nationwide effort was underway to give back the scientists, educators, managers, engineers, technicians, and other intellectuals their former positions, status, respect, influence, and authority. However, because of the very sharp cutback in industrial activity many of them could not be effectively utilized immediately in spite of such efforts.

With the end of the Great Leap Forward, the party organ, *Peking People's Daily*, reversed its former policy denouncing individualism to advocate that "in science, personal research will forever remain important." [73]

High-talent managerial and technical personnel in industrial enterprises also regained their former authority, influence, and respect, and an effort was once again made to utilize their talents effectively. In this regard, the highly influential party organ, *Red Flag*, proclaimed in 1962: "Technical and managerial staff on nontechnical work must, as far as possible, be allowed to return to technical work . . . the top jobs on the technical side should generally be held by technical men, and technical problems must be solved primarily by them." [74]

In Peking, the Central Committee of the Communist Party and the State Council gave a banquet for leading scientists and engineers to celebrate the 1962 New Year. By the end of 1962 about one-third of all persons labeled as higher intellectuals by the regime had become party members, whereas in the past relatively few had been admitted to membership. In the 1964 general election of deputies to the third National People's Congress—the highest elected government body in China—hundreds of prominent engineers, scientists, and other higher intellectuals were elected.

With the end of the Great Leap the regime also sought to utilize the talents of the social scientists more effectively, and to give them greater status, respect, and influence. However, the response on the part of the "old school" social scientists was generally not very enthusiastic. Even in relatively good times China's older social scientists have been under varying degrees of suspicion, and during purge periods they have been humiliated, abused, and harassed more than anyone.[75] The official liberal attitude toward these social scientists which was adopted at the end of 1961 did not last very long. By the end of 1963 relatively minor but new attacks began to appear against social scientists and philosophers, accusing them of revisionism. In the 1964 general election of the National People's Congress only a small number of social scientists were elected, and most of those trained before 1949 or educated abroad lost their seats. In recent years it seems that there has been a further downward trend in the prestige, influence, or participation of Red China's older social scientists in policy making. This has meant ineffective utilization of most of China's best minds in the fields of social science.

There is, of course, still a very limited number of "old school" social scientists who are probably fully trusted and utilized—and frequently even overutilized—by the regime. Since there are so few of them, those who fall within this group typically maintain several important jobs at the same time. A typical example is Yung Sung-kuei, with whom I spent a very productive afternoon in Peking. He is a close friend of Chou En-lai, and a leading Red Chinese economist who did his graduate work in London. In 1966 he was vice president of the China Council for the Promotion of International Trade, a senior official of the State Planning Commission, an active professor of economics, a Permanent Council member of the Institute of Foreign Affairs, and an important official of three other organizations.

In general, China's trustworthy and leading brains in all fields typically hold several important jobs at the same time so that their critically scarce knowledge and talents can be put to full use.[76] In 1966, Po I-po, for instance, was chairman of the State Economic Commission, director of the powerful coordinating Staff Office for Industry and Communication, a member of the party's Central Committee and Secretariat, and, I was told, he also held a number of other important posts.

By the end of 1965, symptoms of general anti-intellectualism again appeared on the horizon in Red China. The attack on higher intellectuals became more pronounced with the emergence of the Great Proletarian Cultural Revolution in the spring of 1966, and even more so with the formation of the Red Guards and the closing down of the schools announced in the summer of 1966.

When I was in China during the April–June period of 1966 a number of leading educators, writers, artists, and social scientists were attacked by name in the press and some were dismissed, but the anti-intellectual campaign had not yet apparently led to serious misutilization problems involving high-talent, well-educated managers, engineers, or technicians in industry. At many enterprises I did observe manpower-misutilization problems which seemed to be primarily due to the lack of managerial know-how regarding the planning and organization of activities, the appraisal and training of personnel and so forth. It also appeared that in many cases too much stress was placed on practical experience—and, at times, on political loyalty—and personnel members who did not have adequate training were promoted, while it seemed that many higher and semiprofessional graduates were not promoted fast enough, given their critically scarce knowledge and qualifications. In general, manpower-utilization problems at the enterprise level seemed to be primarily the result of internal inefficiencies at enterprises rather than the result of the external environment of the enterprise as shaped and influenced by the regime.

Even the attacks in the Red Chinese press against higher intellectuals and the well-educated in the first half of 1966 were aimed primarily at educators, artists, writers, and other types of personnel not employed in industry. There were some general statements about everyone being a scientist, innovator, and expert, but there were few, if any, direct attacks involving industrial managers or technical experts. There were also general proclamations about politics being placed in command of scientific work.[77] During the second half of 1966 a growing number of attacks appeared in the Chinese press against industrial managers, engineers, and technicians. The *People's Daily* and the *Red Flag* advocated ideological reform for leading industrial cadres, urged them to learn from the masses, and attacked managers and technical experts as being too scholastic and arrogant.[78]

However, even with such proclamations in the Chinese press the Red Guards were instructed not to disrupt production, management, labor, or operations in factories or on farms. Then, rather surprisingly, when it seemed that the Red Guards were losing their influence and perhaps even being dismantled, the *Peking People's Daily* advocated at the end of December 1966 that the Red Guards should go and revolutionize the management of factories and mines—but not farms.[79] Industrial enterprises would henceforth organize their own "revolutionary groups, committees, and conferences." "Revolutionary workers" would be chosen to manage industry "by a system of general elections in accordance with the principles of the Paris Commune" (a nineteenth-century social experiment which failed on all counts).

At the time of this writing there were no other accounts available indicating whether the Red Guards were actually going ahead on a widespread scale with the revolutionization of management and industry.[80] The Chinese mass media declared 1967 a year of "universal class struggle" on all fronts, with the Red Guards playing a major role. If this policy was carried out, extremely serious misutilization of high-talent, well-educated industrial manpower was probably inevitable, along with another national industrial and economic crisis.

CHAPTER 4

China's Response: Sociological-Cultural Factors

IT IS MY OPINION that sociological-cultural factors are the most important of all broad types of environmental forces that influence managerial effectiveness and industrial progress in an underdeveloped or newly developing country. While some specific sociological-cultural factors or constraints may be more important than others in the development process, I feel that, taken as a category of environmental constraints, they have generally been more responsible for Red China's progress to date than any of the other categories of environmental conditions examined in this book.

This thesis is of course very difficult, if not impossible, to prove, given the tremendous complexity of the processes of industrial development and management. With the data available it is impossible to achieve an accurate relative weighting of the various environmental constraints explored in this study in terms of their impact on managerial performance and industrial progress. It is also not possible to gauge with quantitative precision the impact of each of the sociological-cultural variables discussed in this chapter.

However, a few years ago there was an excellent detailed study of economic development in two Asian countries, Japan and Thailand.[1] Japan's rate and extent of economic, and particularly industrial, development has been substantially higher than Thailand's. Both countries have had relatively stable political systems, considerable foreign aid, roughly comparable basic economic systems, and both were exposed to Western economic and technological changes at about the same time; yet Japan leapfrogged into the modern industrial era, whereas Thailand's economy remained relatively stationary. Why? What are the major reasons for this phenomenon? An obvious inference, since external and many critical domestic environmental conditions remained more or less constant, is that the Japanese had certain values, motivations, and interests that led them to industrialize rapidly, whereas the Thais had basic values that led them not to take significant advantage of the opportunities offered. The study referred to describes in convincing detail the differences in the value systems of the two countries that ought certainly to have led to the marked differences in their rates of economic growth. Critical human values serve to shape the sociological-cultural as well as the educational environment in which industry and management must function in different countries.

Convincing studies of the above type are quite rare. Even in the United States there have been only a limited number of important empirical studies which focus on the relationships between dominant sociological-cultural factors in society and managerial effectiveness, which would influence industrial progress. This type of research is generally very complex, costly, and time-consuming if accurate description, significant explanation, and/or reliable prediction are to result from such research.

It is difficult, to say the least, for qualified social scientists anywhere in the world to accurately describe, explain, and predict human behavior in terms of an understanding of human values gained through interviews, observation, and firsthand experience.

In the case of Red China, to the best of my knowledge, there has never been an intensive scientifically experimental study of human values and resulting behavior, as shaped by the sociological-cultural environment, and of their impact on managerial effectiveness and industrial progress. My own research in Communist China certainly does not fall into this category. Therefore, what I have to say in this chapter is, in substantial part, speculative, suggestive, and subjective rather than definitive or conclusive.

There is, however, a surprisingly high degree of consensus among people who have visited China in recent years, as well as those who are considered Sinologists or China experts, that since 1949 Red China's urban population in particular has undergone a significant psychological transformation, and that dominant sociological-cultural values have been and are conducive to industrial progress and general economic development. This general consensus includes people with varying degrees of sympathy and hostility toward Red China. Even relatively cynical American "China-watcher" journalists peering from Hong Kong share this general opinion.[2]

Visitors to Red China and Sinologists, in describing the Chinese people, typically use such terms as hard-working, dedicated, self-sacrificing, nationalistic, proud, pragmatic, flexible, well-disciplined, clean, resourceful, energetic, entrepreneurial, inventive, productive, well-motivated, honest, puritanical, sincere, cooperative with each other, thrifty, frugal, respectful of the virtues and dignity of labor, and so forth.[3] Our classification of sociological-cultural factors serves to encompass those human values and resulting behavior patterns that appear to have the most critical bearing on managerial effectiveness and economic progress.

Chinese society prior to 1949 had an image throughout much of the world as having such dominant characteristics as suspicion, nepotism, despotism, favoritism, corruption, the dominance of conservative ruling elites, avoidance of responsibility, venality, face-saving at any cost, sloth, a lust for money, emphasis on family loyalty, and so forth. The present-day sociological-cultural environment in Red China can perhaps best be described as a unique and rather strange mixture of Maoism, Marxism-Leninism, certain elements of Calvinism, as well as some elements of Confucianism, and other historical values.

It is true that much of the contemporary Red Chinese dominant personality has evolved through an eradication of various aspects of the feudalistic mind, traditional religious values, superstitions, and fatalism. In this sense the social transformation has involved some sharp breaks from history and tradition. However, this break from the past is probably not as broad or all-encompassing as many people may think; in fact, there seems to be some continuity with the past in the retention of various human values and behavior patterns. Contrary to popular opinion, it seems that much, and perhaps most, of Chinese society desired social change by 1949. There was apparently much discontent with the existing social structure, the great stress on family loyalty and solidarity, the dominant authoritarian role of the father, the submissive role of other members of the family, the role of women, and so forth. A majority of the Chinese Communists' most ardent followers prior to 1949 were women and youths. Hence, it was not really very difficult to bring about a shift from identification with and loyalty and dedication to the family to a similar attitude toward the party and the state.

What the Communist Party has done in large part was to capitalize on various latent values inherent in much of the population that are conducive to industrial progress—such as nationalism and the desire for achievement, motivation, pride, dedication, loyalty, willingness to work hard, self-sacrifice, resourcefulness, and so forth. The party has been able to put these human forces into productive operation on a national scale through effective and persuasive organization, mobilization, and motivation. Without such organization, mobilization, and motivation, which are functional in terms of industrial progress, the more positive human values would have remained latent rather than operational on a widespread scale. The Japanese have also capitalized on various similar functional human values through effective organization and mobilization of a different type. In Japan, nationalism has also played a crucial role, but microorganization and mobilization at the level of the enterprise have played a greater role than the influence of a political organization like that of the party in China. In India, the shaping of a sociological-cultural environment conducive to substantially greater managerial effectiveness and industrial progress has been a slow and rather ineffective process because of the absence of effective organization, mobilization, and motivation that are necessary for social change on a widespread scale.

In general, then, the contemporary sociological-cultural environment in Communist China is the product of some traditional and historical human values that the regime has capitalized on and put into widespread application, a reshaping or modification of various other earlier values, and a molding of some entirely new values. In shaping this environment the regime has relied on and utilized effectively the country's overall educational system, mass media and entertainment of all types, and at the microlevel of the organization—group and individual—intensive indoctrination, study, discussion, self-criticism, and appraisal, typically under party leadership, direction, and control. Hero workers and, at times, managers and technicians, are praised and idolized in the Chinese press with the aim of getting the population to emulate these pure and dedicated communist men. There can be little doubt that human values, motivation, and related dominant patterns of behavior are substantially more conducive to managerial effectiveness and industrial progress in contemporary China than they were in old China. However, when the Communist regime has gone overboard with the implementation of ideology during certain periods since 1949, potentially functional values and behavior, in terms of managerial effectiveness and industrial progress, have been substantially sacrificed. This was the case during the Great Leap Forward. It may well again have been the case in 1967 and 1968 as Red China seemed to be on the brink of civil war, and as the Red Guards and other Super-Red fanatics attempted to revolutionize factory management and operations and as industrial personnel engaged in strikes.

Attitude toward Industrial Managers and Management

The place of industrial and business managers in the occupational-prestige hierarchy of a particular country is quite relevant in determining managerial effectiveness and the efficiency of productive enterprises. Closely connected to this point is the way in which alternate occupations or elite groups are viewed in the culture. The impact of such status ranking will be reflected not only in the recruiting of competent people for management and industrial firms but also in the way in which managers see themselves, and in the leadership effectiveness and influence they have within their enterprises and in society at large. As was discussed in Chapter 2, various elements of the management process would tend to be carried out more efficiently if the dominant view toward managers in a particular country is relatively favorable rather than unfavorable.

The general attitude toward managers and management in communist nations is just as important as in other nations. In China, Russia, and various other communist countries the party and the state play the key role in determining the attitude, preferability, and prestige ranking regarding various occupations through their control over education, ideology, human values, remuneration, other rewards, and penalties. In the Soviet Union, managerial and other important industrial jobs tend to be viewed favorably and have been filled by much of that nation's high-talent, well-motivated manpower.

In Red China much of its high-talent manpower has also been allocated by the state to fill managerial and leading technical and specialized jobs in industry and business. It is China's educational system, particularly at the specialized secondary and higher levels, that has been reshaped to provide considerable manpower of this type, and among the fields of study with the greatest prestige and selectivity are those that a growing number of managers and technical experts have majored in. However, the effective utilization of competent managers and other high-talent industrial specialists, as well as the dominant attitude toward industrial managers and experts, has oscillated with the degree to which ideology has taken precedence over managerial, technical, and economic rationality.

Pre-1949 China

In old China prior to 1949 businessmen and industrial managers, as a total group or class, generally may have been regarded more favorably than in some other underdeveloped countries, but the dominant social appraisal of this group was far from favorable. It is difficult to conceive of a country where a Communist takeover, and the resulting nationalization of private business and industry, can achieve widespread popular support where private managers, owners, and businessmen are very highly regarded by society at large. Even in a democratic capitalist country the nationalization of a particular branch of industry is frequently related to and made possible by a generally negative feeling toward owners and managers in that sector. This has been the case with the nationalization of the steel industry in England, the railways in Canada, and in numerous other cases.

In old China the Kuomintang government under Chiang Kai-shek's leadership allied itself with the business and industrial class, but was obsessed with political control and was largely indifferent to economic development.[4] The wealthy and powerful capitalists served as the link between government and business. Many of them held key government posts while government officials served on their boards of directors. The result was much backscratching, favoritism, corruption, and inefficiency, with the wealthy, prestigious capitalists exerting considerable monopoly power in business and industry. They are now referred to as "bureaucratic capitalists" and "higher bourgeoisie" in Red China.

While the government supported and favored the big capitalists, the population, in general, apparently looked upon them with fear, contempt, suspicion, and distrust, even though they had—at least on the surface—considerable status, prestige, and respect. The major capitalists in old China were typically not interested in managing or running their businesses and factories, and failed to exert effective industrial leadership or entrepreneurship in the direction of substantial economic progress. They often preferred government work and, in general, much of their time was typically devoted to nonindustrial pursuits. Their children were frequently educated in fields that would enable them to pursue the top-prestige careers in the country, such as politics, science, education, and the military.

Where the owner of a business or factory was rich enough, and where his enterprise was big enough, he typically hired a trusted general manager to run it. Such a manager was usually a relative or close friend of the family. The fairly big capitalist in old China was typically not interested in managing his business, and frequently had little adequate knowledge to do so competently. There were frequently very big communication gaps between the different levels of business and industrial firms in old China. The owners and board of directors were usually only interested in financial control and broad policy, with little interest in concrete management and operations which they associated with undignified work and physical labor. This lack of operational concern led to a serious deterioration of enterprise conditions and much grass-roots hostility in many cases, and gave rise to severe criticism during the 1930's and 1940's.

The hired managers frequently lacked management ability and technical knowledge, and tended to disdain physical labor and close association with the workers. They worked through "gang bosses," but they generally did not know or care much about local operating conditions or how production was going. Their main concern was the fulfillment of key financial targets, such as profit. Staff men and specialists, who were part of management, typically viewed themselves as an educated elite and they, too, rarely went down to the plant. No doubt, the general attitude of the workers regarding managers and their key aides was not a very favorable one, although this may not have always come to the surface because of fear and insecurity.

In general, industry in old China was characterized by sharp cleavages between managers and workers, educated intellectuals and workers who were illiterate and barely literate, white-collar and blue-collar employees, and mental and physical labor. Class distinctions, including income differentials and living standards, were strong, large, and very real. The sporadic ideological revolutions in Red China since 1949 have been attempts by the regime to obliterate such cleavages and class distinctions.

Prior to 1949 even in smaller businesses and factories in China owned and managed by small capitalists or the "lower bourgeoisie," cleavages and distinctions of this type tended to be quite sharp. In this pre-1949 environment, friction, distrust, suspicion, frustration, apathy, serious information gaps, ineffective communication, conflict of objectives, confusion, considerable absenteeism, low productivity, and general inefficiency were common in business and industry. Problems of this type were frequently due in large part to the general view of managers, and the attitude of owners and managers toward management or managing.

Communist China

When the Communists came to power in 1949, Mao and the regime promised the capitalists—with the exception of the large "bureaucratic capitalists"—managers, and other business and industrial experts a positive role in the new China. (The role of Red China's capitalists since 1949 will be discussed in a later chapter.) The new Red regime apparently realized the importance of people with business, industrial, and managerial know-how in the effort to reach the goal of rapid industrialization and economic development. However, the importance of managerial and technical skill was made clearly subservient to ideology during the Great Leap Forward, and apparently the regime has again been moving in this direction in the mid-1960's.

In examining the role and attitude toward managers and management in Communist China, we must break down these terms into several categories. The managers, technicians, and specialists who play major roles in the management process because of their professionalism, which is usually derived in large part from formal education and training, are referred to as Experts in China. They are primarily concerned with the management and transformation of things. The Experts are commonly employed as chief engineers and their deputies, regular engineers and technicians in key jobs, vice directors of various types, department heads and their deputies and key aides, workshop and section chiefs and their deputies and key aides, accountants, planners, economists, and statisticians.

It seems that, in the large majority of cases, the enterprise director is substantially more Red than Expert. It is common for workers to be promoted to the above types of important positions because of qualifications and skills they have learned through experience and/or training, and/or because they are good Reds. If they are promoted because of their expertness, they would, of course, be viewed as Experts, but if they have achieved this status even though they do not have a good formal education, they would probably not be subject to the same degree of criticism or abuse during periods of acute anti-intellectualism. In a typical Chinese industrial firm, then, one finds Experts holding some higher-level line management jobs, and more commonly middle-level line and staff positions.

The Reds also play major roles in enterprise management, with the extent of their roles varying during different periods of time. When the enterprise is placed under the collective leadership of the Communist Party committee, the Reds tend to play a greater part in management. The enterprise party secretary is the key Red and is usually not also an Expert. The enterprise director, as mentioned above, various vice directors, and at times middle- and lower-level line managers, as well as shop party secretaries, other party cadres, and trade-union officials, make up the rest of the Reds who are involved in the management of the enterprise.

The Reds in Chinese firms are primarily interested in policies and ends rather than plans and means, which are the chief concerns of the Experts.[5] Plans involve managerial, technical, and economic criteria and analysis, while policy in Chinese industry tends to be intimately linked with ideology, both pure and practical, as well as the sometimes rather abstract goals of the regime—for example, "democratic centralism." The Reds have considerable leeway in interpreting and implementing policies and "ends," and when they are in control of enterprise management, policies frequently take precedence over plans and disrupt them. Where the Reds are too fanatical ideologically and go overboard in implementing various policies, much inefficiency often results. In normal times the Reds are primarily interested in the motivation and transformation of people rather than of things.

In the Soviet Union, the Experts (the professional managers, technicians, and specialists), and not the Reds, have long played the major role in industrial management.[6] Such professional careers and those employed in them have, for some time, generally been viewed favorably in Soviet society, and probably even more so in recent times. It is true that the party or the Reds in the Soviet Union formulate national goals, policies, and programs, but their operational expressions, and particularly their implementation, are placed quite firmly in the hands of the Experts. In many cases, key Soviet industrial positions are staffed by persons who are both quite solidly Red and Expert, but Communist China has relatively few people employed in industry who are both. At the Soviet enterprise the director is usually an Expert and is typically involved primarily in managerial problems.

Since 1949 the Chinese have oscillated between Expert and Red control of industrial enterprises.[7] When the Experts have been in command, they and their occupations have tended, in general, to be highly regarded, and they have been encouraged to devote most of their energies to managerial, technical, and economic problems. When the Reds have taken over, the status of the Experts and their jobs have tended to deteriorate, and ideology and politics have tended to be the priority focal point of the management process.

With the Communist takeover of China in 1949, industrial management was in a state of rehabilitation and flux for a few years. Industrial enterprises were placed under the leadership of committees composed of party, union and military officials, managers, owners (in many cases), and worker representatives. There was, however, individual responsibility for operations, and the regime mobilized managers, technicians, and other experts to play an important roll in Red China's economic development. By 1952, with the formulation of the First Five-Year Plan, the Soviet system of industrial management was introduced. This entailed a system of one-man authority under unified party and Expert leadership, with the qualified managers and Experts playing the major role in the operational management of enterprises. The party committee still played an important ideological and political role, and the status of the party versus the Experts and managers was essentially separate but equal.

During this period the regime's attitude toward industrial managers and Experts, including the intellectuals, was favorable and they were accorded considerable status, prestige, influence, and authority. While many industrial personnel, particularly workers, still no doubt vividly remembered sharp cleavages and class distinctions of the past, the general attitude toward managers and management was undoubtedly substantially more favorable than it was, prior to 1949. By the mid-1950's a national wage reform showed open favoritism to higher elements of society, including well-educated and qualified managers, technicians, and other industrial specialists, indicating that the regime was committed to a new class society, but one that was not based on private ownership of productive resources.[8] Income differentials between different occupations have always been relatively low in Red China as compared with those in most other countries, including Russia, the United States, and particularly India. However, with this wage reform the leading industrial experts were among the highest-paid groups in Chinese society. The average wage for a worker was about 65 yuan per month, and around 280 for a top-paid chief engineer. Directors and vice directors could earn as much as 263 yuan, with a minimum of about 132. Middle-level managers and key specialists frequently earned two to three times more than workers. In the early and mid-1950's people in high leadership positions in industry were also often provided with substantially above-average housing, the use of a car, vacations at the best resorts, and at times even servants.[9]

By 1957, partly for ideological reasons, partly because the regime felt that there were not enough Experts and professional managers for sustained rapid industrial development, the regime turned to the relatively large pool of party cadres to play a somewhat bigger and more direct role in enterprise management. Enterprises were officially placed under the collective leadership of the party committee, but the attitude and status of the Experts remained more or less intact in a system of individual managerial responsibility. In November 1957 there was a major industrial reform which entailed a substantial territorial decentralization of authority, and at the same time significantly increased the independence, powers, and initiative of industrial enterprises. This decentralization enhanced the powers of local party cadres because they were placed in charge of assuring that the goals, policies, interests, and instructions of the state were carried out properly.

With the onslaught of the Great Leap Forward in 1958, the party committee or Reds gradually assumed virtually complete operational authority in the running of probably the vast majority of enterprises. They played the major role in both the design and implementation of plans, as well as the formulation and interpretation of policy, and ideology and politics tended to take precedence over managerial, technical, and economic rationality. In many cases, even in huge enterprises such as Wuhan Iron and Steel, the jobs of party secretary and top manager were held by the same person.

During this period the professional managers and Experts were humiliated, disparaged, and maligned by both Reds and workers, and their status, prestige, influence, authority, and power deteriorated severely. More often than not, their decisions and advice were ignored and even scoffed at. The well-educated managers and experts undoubtedly were viewed upon even less favorably than those who had been given such positions for reasons other than formal education. Those workers who undertook spare-time educational programs and got promoted were probably viewed somewhat more favorably than those who attended a regular school.

Many experts were even removed from their jobs, while income differentials were narrowed and extra perquisites and special privileges were eliminated. Under party leadership and direction, unqualified workers with little or no education or expertness were told that they were the real managers, experts, technicians, innovators and scientists. It is man's will, zeal, and dedication only that count, not his formal knowledge, skill, education, or qualifications. Managers and experts were accused of being "bookish," "blindly scholastic," "individualistic," concerned only with "self-interest," superstitious, authoritarian, and arrogant. They were portrayed in many dramas, films, operas, radio, television shows, books, newspapers, and magazines as being villains, who were ultraconservative and opposed to progress and the revolution.

In this environment, incompetent workers took over major managerial, accounting, economic, technical, and quality-control functions, engaged blindly in all types of "innovation" and experimentation activities, and frequently ignored the advice or pleas of the Experts. The mass media made numerous heroes out of workers who behaved in this way. The party cadres issued detailed instructions and assignments on all aspects of management and technology, and frequently undertook detailed management, technical, and economic activities for which they were grossly unsuited. Top-level Reds constantly went right down to the shop floor to manage production and motivate workers, thus ignoring intermediate levels of managers and Experts. In some enterprises the term "management personnel" was even changed to "service personnel," and the party secretary became service personnel Number 1. Much time was taken up by service personnel in making beds for the workers, making and serving them tea, while their professional and expertise duties were relegated to a minor role.

In 1958 the participation by managers in physical labor became compulsory throughout China. All enterprise managers were required to spend at least one or two days in physical labor each week, and they often spent considerably more time on such activity as a form of punishment or ideology remolding. Even higher-level managers and Experts with status above the enterprise level—in ministries, and provincial and municipal departments—were required to spend at least one month each year in manual labor at factories or on farms, unless exempted because of health or age. They were also often "sent down" to work in production in excess of the compulsory one-month period.

The practice of requiring managers and experts to spend some time in physical labor has probably had some significant benefits in terms of managerial effectiveness and industrial progress in Red China. It has undoubtedly served to break down the traditional negative attitude toward labor on the part of intellectuals, managers, and Experts. It probably has provided for a better insight into grass-roots operating conditions and problems, including the needs, behavior, attitudes, and problems of workers. It probably has often contributed to greater organizational solidarity and identification, more effective communication, and a reduction in the information gap at different levels of the enterprise. However, when critically scarce professional managers and Experts must spend a considerable amount of their time and energies in physical labor, the disadvantages may well outweigh the advantages. Moreover, when a major purpose is to punish or humiliate them, and to vigorously remold them through intensive indoctrination, amounting to abuse, in the name of "class struggle," this tends to greatly hinder their leadership ability, status, influence, and authority. This, in turn, leads to severe misutilization or nonutilization of their knowledge, talents, skills, drive, and productive energies.

By 1961, under the pressure of a severe economic crisis in China the regime asked the professional managers and Experts to help pull the country out of the crisis. They were once again officially accorded considerable status, prestige, respect, influence, and authority. A system of independent, operational managerial authority was reinstated, the party committee was officially to act essentially like a board of directors, concerned with basic policy and the most important issues, and the regime advocated a strict responsibility system with a clear division of work at all levels.

By 1962 the mass media of the country were trying to reverse the negative attitude toward industrial managers, technicians, other Experts, and intellectuals through an intensive campaign. For example, the key party magazine, *Red Flag*, in discussing technical personnel, which usually includes managers in Red Chinese terminology, urged the following:

> As to problems of concrete technological measures and management which occur in the execution of technological policies, they should be solved by the responsible technological personnel concerned in accordance with the assignment of duties. No one else should interfere.[10]

The influential party paper, *Daily Worker*, intensively sought to change the image of technical experts, including managers, to a favorable one. One typical article in this campaign strongly condemned the existing negative image and pointed out:

> The odds are one to a million against technical personnel being portrayed as good men in novels, films, plays, or operas. In almost every instance they are cast in the role of a villain. Over the past three or four years this tendency has been more or less universal. The worker-peasant masses are depicted as courageously pioneering innovations, while authors always create a conservative, backward, passive and selfish image for technical personnel.[11]

Numerous other articles appeared in the Chinese press under such titles as "Be Friendly to Engineers, Managers, and Technologists," "We Must Humbly Listen to the Opinions of Technologists," and "They are Working-Class Intellectuals."[12] The accepted view of managers, engineers, technicians, accountants, and planners, economists, and other experts gradually became increasingly more favorable, and this undoubtedly contributed substantially to greater managerial effectiveness and industrial progress. The policy of management participation in labor, however, was not rescinded, although it has apparently been carried out in a more limited and systematic manner.

With a new major overhaul in wage and salary scales in 1963, managers and key technical staffs benefited significantly more than workers—another sign of a more favorable attitude toward the experts.[13] The monthly wage of leading experts employed by major industrial enterprises ranged around 200 to 250 yuan, while the average worker wage was in the range of 60 to 70 yuan.

A substantial industrial and economic recovery was underway after 1962. By the end of 1964, with the emergence of relatively favorable conditions and greater affluence, the regime once again began turning more of its attention to ideology. This was probably also stimulated by the clear trends of further revisions in the Soviet Union, and by this time the Sino-Soviet split had burst wide open and had become acute.

Since the year 1965, pronouncements advocating control of enterprises by the Reds and the masses, and laying greater stress on ideology and politics in the industrial and economic life of the country, have become increasingly strong and widespread. Once again, the attitude toward professional managers and experts became increasingly less favorable. It appears that since around that time the term "cadres" has been used instead of managerial and administrative personnel. New "political work organs" were established under party leadership at all levels of the economy to provide for more political and ideological leadership, and to focus on the "class struggle" in business and industry.

In early 1965, articles appearing in the mass media stated that although the director assumes full operational authority and responsibility for the management of the enterprise, this was to be under the close collective leadership of the party committee. Party control at the industrial enterprise level has undoubtedly increased since 1965. However, until the Great Proletarian Cultural Revolution, which began around mid-1966, there was apparently some hesitancy on the part of China's top leaders as to how much authority and power the Reds should be given in enterprise and general industrial management. For example, in April 1966, a *People's Daily* editorial, translated in *Peking Review,* proclaimed that party leadership and control should be absolute in order to manage enterprises in line with Mao's thinking.[14] In the same month the *People's Daily* warned party secretaries not to take over too much managerial and administrative responsibility in their enterprises, and not to neglect their political duties.[15]

During 1965 and early 1966 much stress in official party publications was placed on the participation of cadres (managers, administrators, and officials) in physical labor, and it has been reasserted as a basic compulsory national practice. There were reports that managers, engineers, and other experts at enterprises were being required to spend one day each week in manual labor. Cadres of higher-level organizations were being required to spend at least one month annually as laborers in factories or on farms, or they were to take annual leave on a rotation basis to engage in physical labor. Chinese sources admitted that compulsory physical labor has been unpopular among cadres, and often such labor requirements are disregarded, or complied with, in letter but not in spirit.[16] The party has been called on to fight such antisocialist attitudes on the part of cadres. There were also some reports in 1965 that the salaries of some highly paid industrial experts had been cut to provide for greater equality in income.[17]

By the end of 1965 the Chinese press was calling for thorough ideological reform for leading cadres in industry and business. Politics should be placed in command in the management of enterprises, and primary attention should be on ideology and class struggle.[18] The *People's Daily* proclaimed that a new revolution in socialist management was underway in response to Mao's call to "sweep away bureaucratic, metaphysical, and scholastic ways of management; discard bourgeois ideas, and establish a new and scientific system in line with socialist principles and China's specific conditions." [19] The article went on to condemn the tendency to copy foreign management practices and methods. This was aimed chiefly at Russian revisionism. It also advocated that enterprise regulations should not be regarded as fixed or as a fetish, and that managerial control should not be allowed to stifle initiative.

More concrete reports began appearing, describing in detail how the party committee played the major and detailed operational role at various enterprises in solving managerial and technical problems. In Chapter 2 we discussed the article "The Practice of Economy in Bicycle and Enamel Factories," which described in some detail how the Reds at a Tientsin bicycle firm mobilized the workers to solve the contradiction of cost versus quality; no mention was made of the role of management or experts.

Many articles appeared in the Red Chinese press in late 1965 and early 1966 praising the Reds and the workers for their initiative, inventiveness, and their opposition to conservatism, bureaucratic mentality, and general lack of socialist spirit on the part of managers, technical personnel, and other experts. Contradictions, such as professional and individualist versus mass management, cadres versus masses, proletarian politics versus business, and centralism versus democracy, would be resolved through ideologically correct thought and behavior.

Firsthand Observations and Impressions

At the time of my visit to Red China in mid-1966 the Cultural Revolution was just getting underway. At all of the enterprises surveyed I was told that enterprise management was under the leadership of the party committee. However, it did appear that at a majority of the enterprises the management still had considerable leeway and authority in running the firm. In most cases, the role of the Reds seemed to pertain mainly to basic policy, formal approval of the major targets and tasks of the enterprise plan, defining unclear priorities, major personnel matters, welfare, and, of course, ideological, educational, and political work. There seemed to be a fairly reasonable balance between Reds and Experts, with the Experts generally making the types of managerial and technical decisions that they were best suited to make at the majority of firms.

In most instances, managers seemed to be treated with respect and often with considerable spontaneous warmth and friendliness by other enterprise personnel, including workers. I got the general feeling during my visits to Chinese enterprises that higher-level managers and key experts still had quite a bit of status and prestige. At larger enterprises, there was typically a surprisingly large number of vice directors, as many as a dozen at some. Even at enterprises having only a few hundred employees, or even fewer, there were usually three or four vice directors. Why appoint so many vice directors if this high-level management title doesn't mean much in terms of status, prestige, influence, or authority?

In general, most of the managers I interviewed seemed quite proud to be executives. The title of engineer or even technician also seemed to be generally highly regarded. However, I did often get the feeling that managers, engineers, technicians, and other Experts who achieved their positions primarily because of their formal education seemed to be somewhat self-conscious and apologetic about being part of the "intelligentsia." When people without much formal education or those who were products of spare-time educational programs attained such key positions, they seemed to be more openly proud of their positions and titles. Their colleagues frequently told me how they had worked their way up to key jobs from the bottom worker ranks of the organization.

I did come across a number of factories where incompetent party cadres seemed to be running the show, and as a result there typically seemed to be considerable confusion and inefficiency. I was told, for example, at the Wuhan Diesel plant that under party leadership many "bureaucratic" regulations, restrictions, and procedures established by management had been abolished because they were stifling mass initiative and innovation. As a result, the party secretary claimed, the workers have developed much interest in innovation and greater initiative. He cited the case of Tao-An, a veteran worker who had designed a new special machine tool for working on axles. The technical department asked him to submit a blueprint—this was too much for an uneducated old worker who learned to write only after 1949. The bureaucratic procedure of requiring employees to submit blueprints, reports, or paperwork with their innovation proposals was abolished by the party committee. Tao-An, I was told, had recently been written up as a hero-worker in various papers, magazines, and periodicals because of his struggle against "old ways of doing things." [20]

A major theme in all kinds of mass media and entertainment, while I was in China, was the hero-worker, hero-cadre, and only rarely the hero-manager or technician. For instance, I was told on a number of occasions by Chinese officials in Shanghai of Pan Ah-yao, a barely educated veteran worker with thirty years' experience at the Yungshin Rolling Mill, who was written up in the April 1966 issue of *China Reconstructs.* This worker, as well as other hero-workers, were referred to in operas, plays, and television shows that I saw. Pan was a hero because of his "struggle" against bureaucratic and unsocialistic management. The sales department of his enterprise had been turning down many orders for special steel tubes on the excuse that they were too difficult for the firm to make. Pan went to higher management but to no avail. He then turned to the party committee which reversed the most recent decision to refuse a particular order, and advocated a policy of not turning down special orders. This was in line with the general policy "Serve the customer at all costs." Pan became head of a new product-development group which was concentrating on product innovation. This was in line with the general party policy of "innovation," and "Dare to do, dare to create."

While most theatrical productions involving managers, technicians, and experts did not portray them in a favorable light, during my stay in China, they were apparently not being cast as villains to the same degree as during the Great Leap. In fact, in some operas and dramas, in translations of various Chinese publications, and in another 1966 issue of *China Reconstructs*, I learned about a hero who was actually a manager or cadre. I don't recall his name, but he was the chief organizer of the major drilling team at the Taching oil fields in north China.[21] He was from a poor peasant family who suffered severely prior to 1949. He served in the Red Army and received a partial technical education in his spare time, while holding down a full-time job as a worker. At Toching he overcame major obstacles and dangers—in fact, some people were killed because of inadequate safety precautions—in the drilling project. He worked around the clock for months as a self-sacrificing worker, on a basis of equality with his work crew. They used the "three-in-one method" of combining cadres, technicians, and workers into a harmonious team with full cooperation and equality. He eagerly sought the advice, decisions, initiative, and inventiveness of his co-workers. Hence, he was a pure proletarian manager-worker-peasant-soldier, who engaged in both mental and physical labor with much self-sacrifice, humility, and whole-hearted team spirit.

In my survey of Chinese enterprises, I was given many diverse concrete examples of Reds "persuading" managers to revise and/or reverse their decisions, policies, and procedures, even at many firms that seemed to be relatively efficient and well managed. I was also given many examples indicating that managers had revised and often reversed their positions because of worker initiative and opposition. I will discuss more concretely some of these examples at later points in this book. In many cases, managers had apparently reversed or revised their positions without conflict because they were sincerely convinced that the Reds and workers had presented good countersuggestions and arguments. However, in many other cases the managers' and experts' authority and status were undoubtedly undermined. Worker or party participation in management is one thing—and often a good thing in terms of effective management. However, when workers and incompetent Reds take over management, and when the undermining of the roles of managers and experts is carried out as a general and rather blind policy in the name of ideology and class struggle, managerial effectiveness and industrial progress undoubtedly tend to suffer substantially.

During my stay in China the trend certainly seemed to be in the direction of a less favorable attitude toward managers and experts in Chinese industry, and of less emphasis on rational management as we understand it in the West; but this trend was apparently leading to severe inefficiency and confusion at only a limited number of the enterprises surveyed. However, the trend has undoubtedly intensified since my departure, with the great intensification of the Cultural Revolution.

During my visit to China I also came across some indications that a trend in the direction of reducing the incomes of highly paid industrial managers and technicians might be underway. At some of the enterprises surveyed I was told that key managers and engineers had recently "voluntarily" accepted cuts in their pay to put them more in line with the workers. For example, this was the case at Wuhan Iron and Steel, Wuhan Heavy Machinery, Loyang Tractor, and Canton Chemical Fertilizer. The director of Nanking Chemical Fertilizer claimed that he had recently refused a salary increase.

James Duncan, a Canadian industrialist, visited the same Canton Chemical firm in 1964 and was told that the chief engineer's monthly salary was 240 yuan.[22] I talked with the same chief engineer in 1966 and his monthly salary was only 200 yuan. Charles Lynch, a Canadian journalist, was told that the chief engineer at the Peking First Machine Tool (Lathe) enterprise received a monthly salary of about 200 yuan.[23] I was told by the same chief engineer in 1966 that his monthly pay was 180 yuan. The top-paid engineer at Wuhan Iron and Steel received 230 yuan in 1960, according to the American author Edgar Snow who visited this firm.[24] I was told that the top-paid employee in 1966 was the vice chief engineer who was receiving 180 yuan per month, and that he had taken a pay cut recently. In general, top-paid personnel at enterprises visited by Snow seemed to be getting significantly more than at the firms I surveyed.[25]

It is also significant to note that, as I was told, bonuses for all enterprise directors, vice directors and party secretaries had been abolished by law a few years ago. None of these types of officials were receiving bonuses at the firms surveyed, although other enterprise personnel in a majority of firms were still entitled to bonuses. (We shall discuss wages and bonuses in Chinese industry in more detail in a later chapter.) It will suffice to point out here that occupational-income differentials are probably lower in China than in any other country, and that further narrowing of income differentials between the group comprising managers and Experts and the workers is usually accompanied by a generally more negative attitude toward managers and Experts as well as toward rational industrial management.

The participation by managers in physical labor was evidently being enforced, in varying ways, at all of the enterprises I surveyed. During my first visit to a Chinese enterprise, the Peking Woolen Mill, I thought it was a joke or strange aberration when, during lunch in the cafeteria, I was introduced to the director who was cooking dumplings in the kitchen. He was doing one of his two days a week of labor. I soon learned that all enterprise directors, vice directors, party secretaries, and trade-union leaders, spend from one to two days—and in some cases more—each week in some form of manual labor. So, when I later saw the director of the Tientsin Watch firm cleaning up a workshop, and a vice director of the Shanghai Steel Mill working on a machine, I was no longer shocked. In fact, managers, Experts, and Reds of organizations above the enterprise also go to plants each week to engage in physical labor. For example, when I visited the Shanghai Truck factory, there were three cadres from the Shanghai Bureau of Transportation and Communication working in the shops.

It seemed, however, that some of the better managers—experts who may not be pure Red—typically at relatively well-managed factories, were not taking "participation in physical labor" very literally. For instance, some of them were spending their one or two physical labor days working out managerial or technical problems through the "physical" process of writing. But at most of the enterprises the upper-level managers were partaking in some kind of actual physical labor.

As was mentioned earlier, managerial participation in labor at Chinese plants can, and frequently does, have some favorable effects in terms of improving managerial effectiveness and productive efficiency. But where competent managers—in a country that has a critical shortage of truly qualified and knowledgeable managers—are forced to spend as much as two days or more each week in physical labor, the disadvantages may well outweigh the advantages.

Intensification of the Cultural Revolution

In the second half of 1966, after I had left China, extremely strong anti-management articles began appearing with increasing frequency in the most influential Red Chinese publications. One typical article praised a young electrical engineer at the Anshan Steel Works for "defying established authorities and specialists." [26] Chao Cheng-shun invented and introduced a new steel-plate cutting machine against management's will, with the cooperation of the workers and under Chairman Mao's inspiration.

Numerous translations of Chinese articles have recently flooded the West, claiming that the workers and the Reds can do practically anything under Mao's Thought and leadership, while bureaucratic managers and Experts frequently interfere with their revolutionary spirit and progress. The implication has typically been that the role of professional managers and technicians is not really that important in China's emerging brand of socialist industrial and business management. In an attempt to glorify Mao and make a saint of him, Mao's Thought and works have been credited with all types of technical, scientific, economic, and managerial achievements, including, for example, the design of new machines and lamps, production of bigger watermelons, increase in machine capacity, greater economy in the use of materials, increased productivity of cement kilns, improved precision of production plans, and reduction of spoilage and costs.[27]

Until the end of 1966, the Red Guards had been instructed by the regime not to go into factories or to interfere with production and management. But in late December they were told by those in power—most notably Lin Piao, probably with Mao's consent—to go into the factories and revolutionize the system of management.[28] This could only mean greater hostility toward managers and experts and less emphasis on managerial, technical, and economic rationality. This would probably be accompanied by even greater emphasis on physical labor for managers and a lowering of their status, authority, and influence, and perhaps even their incomes. However, there were reports in 1967 and 1968 that China was on the brink of civil war. Apparently regular Reds, cadres, and workers in major cities, such as Shanghai, Wuhan, and Nanking, resisted the takeover by Red Guards and other types of Super Reds. In many cases factories were temporarily closed down and protest strikes took place.[29]

It is impossible to predict at this time what the outcome of this struggle will be, in terms of the dominant attitude toward managers and management in Red China. In any event, in my opinion, it seems unlikely that industrial managers and experts could fully regain favorable public opinion after another period of the Great-Leap-Forward type of industrial environment.

A Comment on India

In normal times in Red China—when there is no ideological extremism —the general attitude toward industrial and business managers and management is probably more favorable for management effectiveness and industrial progress than in India. While managers in India are probably viewed somewhat more favorably than in the past, only the managers of a limited number of well-run public enterprises and privately owned progressive firms—often foreign subsidiaries—seem to be highly respected in Indian society. The managements of most of the privately owned and family-controlled firms still tend to be regarded with varying degrees of fear, suspicion, and hostility by most segments of society, often including their own personnel. The traditional prestige occupations still probably attract the large majority of the well-educated, energetic, ambitious, and well-motivated citizens in India.[30]

In many developing and underdeveloped countries, including India, only higher-level executives are regarded as managers in many firms. Lower-level supervisors, and particularly foremen, are not viewed as part of the managerial hierarchy, and are given little, if any, status. Thus even where higher-level executives are regarded favorably in an Indian firm, the lower-level managerial and supervisory positions often tend to rate low on the occupational preference scale. It appears that front-line supervisors and foremen and their positions may be more highly regarded in Soviet industry than in most other countries.[31] The same situation seems to be true in Red China. Even during intensive ideological campaigns, managers of this type are probably viewed more favorably in China than higher-level managers and experts, because most of them are promoted from the workers' ranks.

The attitude toward managers in India is generally not very favorable in large part because of the way they perceive their managerial jobs. Many of them tend to pursue a highly egocentric, short-run managerial philosophy which often breeds considerable antagonism, frustration, and distrust. They frequently emphasize quick turnover on capital and high profit margins on limited output. They may operate and even grow rich in a sellers' market, often under government patronage and protection, and in an environment of relatively cheap surplus labor—in terms of direct unit cost, not necessarily total labor cost—while their firms remain static and inefficient. Such managers tend to have little sincere interest in economic progress and little or no conception of social responsibility.

They also tend to look down on physical labor. In such an environment, relatively few managers view management as a profession requiring special knowledge, skills, or qualifications; to them, only authority and power are important, and they feel that managerial positions need not be filled on the basis of personal ability or objective criteria.

Attitude toward Authority, Responsibility, and Subordination

The prevailing sociological-cultural-institutional environment of a particular country tends to form dominant views of authority, responsibility, and subordination. In turn, such dominant views tend to result in dominant behavior patterns involving managerial authority, responsibility, and superior-subordinate relationships at industrial and business enterprises.

David McClelland, a leading American psychologist at Harvard University who knows a good deal about economic development, management, and entrepreneurship, has developed some objective criteria for measuring roughly in a standardized way the values, interests, and concerns of the people in different countries. Some of these that he has measured for both the old and the new China relate to attitudes toward authority, responsibility, and subordination, as well as to the need for achievement, which will be discussed in a later section.[32] Briefly, his scientific method of investigation involves the selection of a random standardized sample of popular literature used to teach children to read in elementary public schools during different time periods. The messages that such stories relay have typically proven, through behavior patterns, to reflect the inner values, interests, and concerns of the people who write, approve, and read them. For such literature usually reveals what comes most readily to mind among significant elites in the countries studied, and reflect the values of key influential groups and value shapers.

A study of children's readers used in old China during the 1920's and in Red China in the 1950's provides some significant insights into values associated with authority, responsibility, and subordination during these periods. These insights serve to explain much about human behavior involving authority, power (superior-subordinate) relationships, and responsibility in Chinese industry and business. They certainly have given me a deeper understanding of my observations, experiences, and impressions derived from my research project in China in 1966.

Old China

In old China the dominant attitudes toward authority, responsibility, and subordination were shaped largely by Confucianism and other traditional historical values which defined interpersonal relationships and obligations almost wholly in terms of the family system. One's duties to others typically derived from one's status, rather than from the contractual type of relationships, and also from one's relationship to others as represented normally in the ties of kinship. Filial piety became the ideal that governed one's relations to others, and hence there is almost no mention in the Chinese children's stories of the 1920's of individuals who are concerned with establishing, maintaining, or repairing an affiliative relationship with another individual. They simply existed and were taken for granted. There was no need for a motive to establish friendly relations with others as there is in societies which had shifted from status to contract relationships. When one operates in terms of a limited or contractual relationship to another person for a specific purpose, then the question of initiating and consummating relationships with others becomes salient. This was not the case in old China; hence, the need for affiliation —as expressed in children's readers—was negligible.

Business and industrial enterprise in old China typically functioned as an extension of the family system, placing high value on family-type obligations and personal relationships.[33] What held the organization together were personal relationships rather than a contractual Weberian type of legal national system. The managers were not simply overseers; they were personal representatives of the board of directors and usually had considerable financial interests themselves in the firm. Although personal ties linked the directors and the managers, the managers and the staff, and, in many instances, employers and employees, personal relationships did not foster harmony. Working conditions were generally very poor in Chinese industry; wages were low. Within organizations, conflict and competition were rife. Under the mantle of family-type personal relationships all kinds of economic and technological irrationalities and, hence, much inefficiency flourished, so that they impeded the national development of Chinese industry. These were the "feudal" vestiges so bitterly criticized by the Chinese Communists.

Chinese children's readers of the 1920's also stress that authority is something to be feared and responsibility something to be avoided. Authority is typically represented as a large force that gobbles up the little people. It is dangerous to try to put oneself in a position of authority, or to try and take responsibility even for the welfare of others. One may only get punished or even be killed for his pains.

Hence, it is not surprising that the common man or industrial worker in old China did not typically question higher authority or strive for much authority himself, thus reinforcing the subordinate's subservience and dependence on superiors. Moreover, workers in old China were subservient to a system of industrial and business management concerned almost wholly with short-term financial gain for those in control rather than economic development or social responsibility. Authority in industry and business was typically viewed as an absolute right of owners and the managers in control. Higher-level managers tended to feel that their authority and power were based on some type of natural law, rather than on a clearly defined contractual type of role in the organization, or on specific skills and knowledge. Superior-subordinate relationships were typically personal, subjective, and viewed as father-son or master-servant (regarding managers and workers) relationships (a holdover from the feudal period). Subordinates were generally expected to be unquestioningly loyal, obedient, and subservient in executing the orders and instructions issued by their superiors. Under this system of authoritarian management and autocratic direction—similar to that found in the father-dominated family—there was very little worker participation in managerial decision making. Since individual responsibility was also something to be avoided, individual initiative or inventiveness involving risk and the possibility of failure was probably significantly constrained. This resulted in firms that had rather static and conservative production. Where enterprises did grow and expand significantly, this usually occurred through mergers and acquisitions rather than through internal innovation, development, or efficiency. While subordinates and workers may have applied themselves to their jobs out of a sense of duty, obligation, and perhaps fear, there tended to be little desire or opportunity for them to put forth their worthwhile ideas or suggestions to higher management.

Because of relationships based on the family and on feudalism—and also given the great lack of social-overhead-capital facilities, such as housing, medical care, and other welfare benefits—there was a relatively high degree of paternalism in Chinese industry. However, the welfare benefits provided to workers under this system were typically barely adequate for subsistence.

In countries characterized by relatively high degrees of authoritative management, autocratic direction, and paternalism, it is also common to find a very high degree of centralization of authority in productive enterprises. However, in old China there was generally a somewhat higher degree of decentralization of authority than is common in such a sociological-cultural setting. Because of the family-type system of human organization based on personal relationships, lower-level managers and workers tended to be trusted by their superiors to a greater degree than in most underdeveloped countries. This was because they tended to be loyal, dedicated, and relatively hard-working, with a strong sense of duty and obligation to the organization.

The policy-operations dichotomy that existed between the owners and/or board of directors and the managers in charge of operations required considerable delegating of authority—apart from broad policy and financial matters—to the salaried managers. Since higher-level managers seldom went to the plant, plant managers were given considerable latitude in fulfilling the major targets and responsibilities given to them by their superiors. Within the plant, gang bosses or foremen, who were usually from the workers' ranks and not considered part of management, had considerable leeway in determining how the work was to be done, as long as the group fulfilled its allotted tasks and responsibilities. Within the relatively decentralized work group there was typically not much emphasis placed on division of work or individual responsibility. Although there may have been some scope for initiative and inventiveness within the work team, there was little if any such scope in relationships with higher authorities.

Chinese society traditionally had a considerable capacity to link human groups and organizational levels by intermediary devices. Gang foremen acted as intermediaries between managers and workers; managers functioned as the link between the head office and the plant. Much of the insufficient industrial development prior to 1949 was not caused by this system of human organization per se, but by the failure of those in control to make full use of the potential organizational opportunities. The system of human organization itself probably had greater potential in terms of industrial progress than in many other poor countries. Nevertheless, there were factors not very conducive to a modern rational system of management, such as subjectivism, authoritarian management, the absence of employee participation in higher-level decision making, superior-subordinate relationships based on personal and status factors rather than on impersonal contractual-type relations, fear of authority and individual responsibility, and subservience. Far too little stress was placed on technical organization based on a clear impersonal system of authority relationship, division of work, and individual responsibility. This led to policy decisions made at all managerial levels in ignorance of the means that would be used to carry them out, ineffective coordination of activities, ineffective communication, and large information gaps at all organizational levels which greatly impeded managerial effectiveness and productive efficiency.

In many countries subordinates and workers tend to perform best under a system of authoritarian management, autocratic direction, general subservience to the will of owners and superiors, and paternalism. However, it is highly questionable whether the majority of Chinese industrial personnel, particularly workers—who typically had considerable latent pride, dignity, initiative, intelligence, and resourcefulness, in spite of their low level of formal education—did, in fact, prefer and work most productively under the existing order, including bare-subsistence paternalism, up until 1949. If they did, why did so many of them support the Communist revolution? Moreover, the way they have responded to a new view of authority, responsibility, and superior-subordinate relationships also strongly suggests that probably a majority of them were not content or as productive under the traditional order.

Red China: Historical Perspective

Red Chinese children's readers in the 1950's show a sharp increase in the expression of the need for affiliation, although it is still below the international average. This increase is most easily interpreted in terms of the hypothesis that need for affiliation is most likely to develop in a modern "atomized" society in which traditional ties no longer function. It is interesting to note that emphasis on this need still remains low in the children's readers of Nationalist China (Taiwan). A case can be made for the fact that a contractual type of society is necessary for a modern economic order and for the fact that need for affiliation tends to rise in such contractual societies. Hence, the significant increase in need for affiliation in the Chinese Communist stories suggests that they are moving in a more "modern" direction than the leaders of Nationalist China. If, however, an individual or a society places too much stress on this need, this emphasis can be in conflict with economic efficiency. But the Red Chinese are not near this high a level of the need for affiliation.

It is particularly interesting to note how the Chinese Communists have adapted the traditional high value put on family obligations and relationships to the needs of a modern state. This is best illustrated by a story dealt with by McClelland entitled "Chairman Mao's Visit to a Play." While some workers are putting on a play in a crowded auditorium, someone discovers that Chairman Mao is already there but seated inconspicuously in the back. All the people in the front row stand up to offer him their seats, but he refuses a place of honor. Finally, "after seeing that no one wanted to sit down, Chairman Mao walked to the front and sat down on a chair occupied by a young boy. Chairman Mao held the young boy and let him sit in his lap. The curtain went up and Chairman Mao and the young boy saw the play together."

Here Chairman Mao appears explicitly as a father figure benignly concerned and responsible for the welfare of his people. What seems clearly intended is that the typical Chinese schoolchild, on reading such stories, will transfer his normal filial feeling from his own father to the father of his country. This obviously requires more explicit treatment of affiliative concerns than traditional stories of family life. Hence, the affiliation score increases. The Communists also succeed in this way in transferring loyalties from particular fathers to the "generalized other" or the country as a whole—another psychological and social shift which has occurred more often in rapidly modernizing countries. The story also suggests that while Mao is a highly respected person with great authority and power, he is, at the same time, a humble, kind, and considerate leader who desires no special "class" privileges.

His followers or subordinates, who are loyal and devoted to him, exert initiative in persuading him to take a seat of honor by not sitting down. Therefore, they are major participants in his decision to take a place of honor. This is directly compatible with "democratic centralism."

Under the Chinese Communist regime, stories dealing with authority or power relationships are even more common than in the China of the 1920's, and this raises the need-for-power score. However, they are now of a different sort. Most of the contemporary stories deal with the repression and cruelty of the landlords, and, to a lesser extent, the bureaucratic capitalists under the former regime. Power or authority in this context is clearly shown to be bad. Then the Communist Party is described as a good source of power and authority which overthrows the evil established order and gives the poor people what they need and want. But over and over again an attempt is made to show how this new authority derives from the people themselves.

Chairman Mao is pictured as sharing his blanket with poor soldiers, or distributing gifts he receives among the wounded, and so on. What extra privileges he may derive from his position of authority he shares with the poor and needy, unlike the wicked villains of the past, as pictured in these stories. Furthermore, other people should emulate him by assuming individual and collective responsibility for others. Or, on a somewhat different plane, a long detailed story describes how an elderly blind woman who goes to work in a factory every day is one day met by a small schoolchild who leads her there. Furthermore, he shows up every morning thereafter to help her on her way. She is touched and a little puzzled because he is no relation of hers. But he explains that they have been discussing the matter in school, and he has decided to volunteer to take on this responsibility at his own initiative. In contrast to the Chinese stories of the 1920's, the emphasis here is clearly on everyone's assuming responsibility, insofar as he can, for the welfare and problems of others. The authority or power to help, guide, and control others is not way off somewhere else, as a kind of dangerous impersonal force, but resides in every person, at least to some degree. Whether this ideological shift will eventually move the Red Chinese political system in a truly more democratic direction remains to be seen. Political control, in general, still remains quite dictatorial and at times ruthless in Red China. However, it has already had major impacts on the system of industrial management, including dominant attitudes toward authority, responsibility, and subordination. This shift represents a more "modern" conception of the state or organization as an institution which derives its authority from the people or masses and exercises it for their benefit.

Let us briefly examine dominant behavior patterns involving authority, responsibility, and subordination at the industrial-enterprise level in China, following the Communist takeover in 1949.[34] Then I shall present the findings based on my research in China in 1966. It is important to point out that the party is the ultimate and dominant authority in Red China. The party can and does determine dominant attitudes toward authority, responsibility, and subordination in industry and business; and enterprise personnel tend to adopt the prescribed party attitudes quite quickly when there are official changes in the party's position.

Of central theoretical and ideological importance in industrial management in Communist countries, including China, is the concept or principle of "democratic centralism," a term coined by Lenin. The degree to which this principle is implemented in practice has varied among different communist countries, and also within particular communist states, including China, during different periods of time. Democratic centralism basically involves participation of the masses in management and the harnessing of local initiative under a general system of centralized party and state direction and control. It is similar in many respects to the philosophy of "consultative direction," "participative management," "bottom-up management," or "grass-roots budgeting," under a balanced system of centralization and decentralization of authority, found in a growing number of American companies. While it is essentially a micromanagerial concept in the United States, it typically involves both macromanagement and micromanagement as a continuum in communist countries.

Liu Shao-chi has defined democratic centralism in Chinese management thus:

> The system adopted in managing our enterprises is a system which combines a high degree of centralization with a high degree of democracy. All enterprises must abide by the unified leadership of the Communist Party and the state, and by observing strict labor discipline, ensure unity of will and action among the masses. At the same time, they should bring into full play the initiative and creativeness of the workers, develop the supervising role of the masses, and get them to take part in the management of their enterprises.[35]

In reality the Red Chinese regime has oscillated in its implementation of democratic centralism in industrial management since 1949. It has also oscillated in its dominant view regarding various other aspects of authority, responsibility, and subordination.

In the early 1950's workers' representative conferences or committees were established at virtually all industrial enterprises and were given real consultative functions in the management of enterprises. In that period, with the introduction of the First Five-Year Plan, the then Soviet model of industrial management and organization was introduced. This involved a highly technical system of organization under the relatively highly centralized direction and control of a branch of industry ministries headquartered in Peking. At the enterprise level, wherever possible, men were placed in work positions according to their skills; and one-man authority, clear division of labor, and individual responsibility were stressed. While participative management and worker consultation still existed in theory, in reality the "democratic" or "bottom-up" facet of democratic centralism declined in practice and importance during the 1952–57 period. This system of management seemed to be well suited to Chinese conditions of the time, and very impressive industrial progress was achieved. Industry as a whole was not yet so extensive or complex as to require greater decentralization of authority. Workers and others in subordinate positions undoubtedly had a greater consultative role in higher management than they did before 1949, but this role was quite limited, and this made good sense, considering their relatively low educational level and the need for clear and expedient direction and leadership at this earlier stage of industrialization.

By the mid-1950's, however, the Chinese leaders became increasingly concerned about the extremes and contradictions of the Soviet-type system. They began to emphasize the importance of human solidarity. It was soon believed that the party could bring about the enterprise-wide human solidarity and real democratic centralism which technical organization and management was unable to do. At the end of 1957, shortly before the Great Leap Forward, a major decentralization of authority was implemented by giving local party committees greater powers. During the Great Leap Forward this turned out to be much closer to anarchy than effective decentralization of authority and control. This decentralization was territorial in nature, with chain of command extending from the center down through provincial industrial departments, municipal industrial bureaus, and finally the industrial enterprises. While a small number of enterprises were still directly under central industrial ministries, many ministries were dismantled and most firms were placed directly under local regional authorities. During the Great Leap period, party committees at all levels of the economy, including the level of the firm, gained increasingly greater authority and control in industrial management. This, of course, was accompanied by a great decline in the authority and status of the experts and professional managers.

The Great Leap Forward

With the Great Leap, there emerged an air of boundless trust in the ability of workers under party leadership to achieve economic wonders. A Rousseau-like belief in the virtue of unsophistication prevailed. No responsibility was considered too great, no task too complicated for ordinary workers to undertake. Rather than resolving the inherent contradiction between centralism and democracy through the unity of opposites at the enterprise level, worker participation in management typically resulted in a takeover of managerial decision making and functions by workers under the leadership and control of the Reds. A great amount of time, much of it on ideology and politics, was spent on the job in worker-and-party meetings, committees, and conferences. Authority based on Expertness or formal position was constantly undermined, while authority based on Redness was the basis of management. To give a typical example of the nonfunctional consequences of the dominant prevailing attitude toward managerial authority and judgments made by subordinates, I can cite the case of the Shenyang Transformer Factory, where the quality of products fell so sharply as to make them unusable in many cases. The workers at the factory proposed that in order to economize silicone steel sheets should be dipped in varnish only once. "Although it was evident that it would affect the quality of the products, nobody would venture to say it would not"—objection on the part of managers or technicians would have been held tantamount to unsocialistic bureaucratic conservatism; they did not want to take such responsibility.[36]

Given such an environment, the professional managers and experts tended to fear and avoid responsibility. On numerous occasions managers not wishing to assume any responsibility preferred, and often asked, to be sent down to work on the production line rather than be responsible for assigning tasks, making decisions, or fulfilling plans.

Under this system, division of labor and individual responsibility were largely replaced by the informal human organization and collective responsibility. Since expertness, specialization, and individualism were suspect, the emphasis was on generalists, and personnel of all types were encouraged to become jacks-of-all-trades. This, it was felt, would make it easier to integrate people into interchangeable cohesive work teams. Considerable authority and decision-making powers were transferred down to the work teams. Furthermore, the "three-in-one method" (also called the "three-unification movement") was introduced. This movement was aimed at uniting cadres, technicians, and workers into single work teams. Cadres are leaders, either Red or Expert, party or managerial; technicians are Experts and typically intellectuals; and workers are the masses. According to Mao and other party leaders at the time, each was seen as being in a contradictory relationship to the others. The three-in-one method launched by the party was aimed at resolving these contradictions and thereby creating a unity of opposites. Resolution was not just the product of putting the three together. Rather, each was expected to become the other—workers becoming technicians, technicians becoming workers, both showing leadership with the cadres, and cadres becoming both workers and technicians. In reality, Reds and workers, rather than qualified managers or technicians, tended to dominate these project work teams, and much wasted time and inefficiency resulted throughout industry.

At the time of the Great Leap the regime undoubtedly believed that party-led solidarity—with its disregard for formal managerial authority, individual responsibility, clear divison of work, and balanced, well-defined superior-subordinate relationships—would not imperil technical and economic development. We can overlook the question of whether that solidarity was generally real or not. The point is that, during the Great Leap, people—particularly Reds and workers—worked very hard. But their work was technically barren and frequently not compatible with managerial, technical, and economic rationality.

The 1960's

With the economic crisis of 1960–61, the regime's attitude toward authority, responsibility, and the role of subordinates changed. Much greater emphasis again came to be placed on technical organization. Some major activities—particularly financial—that had been decentralized down to the enterprise level were recentralized, but considerable territorial and local decentralization remained in effect. Formal authority based on position and Expertness was reinstated, more emphasis was placed on clearly defined individual responsibility without fear, as well as on the division of work, and the "master of one technique" was now hailed as the ideal worker. While both theoretical and practical emphasis continued to be placed on democratic centralism and worker participation in management, this was to be carried out in a more balanced and rational way, with qualified managers and experts making the final decisons. The amount of time that workers and other personnel spent in meetings, conferences, and committees during working hours was greatly reduced.

By the mid-1960's, however, there were signs that the pendulum was again beginning to swing in the direction of greater stress on ideology in industrial management. There apparently has been somewhat of a shift to greater centralization of authority in the overall industrial hierarchy. Some of the formerly abolished central industrial ministries have reappeared, and they, as well as the other central planners, seem to have obtained somewhat greater powers. The authority and independence of industrial enterprises have also apparently become somewhat more restricted, although in 1966 they were within the limits of constraints placed on the firm by higher authorities. In the workshops and larger sections there are also party committees on the spot who can make sure that party and state interests and policies are not violated. Party committees at all levels have come to play a somewhat greater direct role in industrial management.

There has evidently also been more intensive emphasis on employee participation in management, collective responsibility, and in human, as opposed to technical, organization. As indicated in the previous section, articles have appeared since 1965 which indicate that managerial authority has been undermined at various enterprises by worker and Red opposition to their decisions.[37] These trends are in line with the impressions and information that I derived during my stay in China in 1966 and appear to have been intensified after my departure from China.[38]

Survey of Industrial Enterprise in 1966

My survey of Chinese enterprises seemed to indicate that while authority based on Expertness and formal positions was generally viewed quite favorably and with respect, there were forces at work in opposition to this view. At several firms I was given examples of managerial decisions being reversed because of the opposition of subordinates and workers who had the support of party cadres. For example, at the Canton Electrical Appliance Factory some of the upper-level managers decided to buy a new machine, and funds were provided for this in the plan, but the workers and some of the supervisors complained, the party committee intervened, and the plant rebuilt an old machine at a fraction of the cost of a new one. This, I was told, was in line with the general party and state policy of "self-reliance" and "technical innovation." At the Hangchow Machine Tool enterprise, the heads of the production-planning and technical departments refused to accept an unplanned order for a special machine needed by a customer because they claimed that they did not have the productive capacity or the capability to fulfill this order. Here, too, the "collective will of the workers" was "victorious"—with party support in making management accept the order.

While actual reversals in managerial decisions because of the opposition of subordinates and Reds appeared to be the exception rather than the rule at the thirty-eight enterprises surveyed, I was showered at most enterprises with glowing examples of workers' innovations and worthwhile suggestions by workers that had been introduced because of their initiative through the process of employee participation in management, which was an element of democratic centralism. In many cases the implication was that the workers had achieved impressive feats without the help of managers, engineers, or technicians. I was even given as examples cases where complex and costly machines and instruments had been designed, developed, and produced by the workers—at times under party leadership—with no mention of the role of managers or experts. Upon more intensive and detailed questioning on my part, however, it usually became clear that the managers and experts did play an important role in these innovations and accomplishments, particularly in the more complex ones.

Nevertheless, there did generally seem to be considerable opportunities for subordinates, and particularly workers, to participate in managerial decisions, to put forth suggestions, to innovate, and to exert initiative in various other ways. In most cases workers' suggestions and innovations seemed to be rather simple; nonetheless, they were often worthwhile and admirable, given their sparse formal educations in many cases. For example, at the Peking Chemical Coke factory some lower-level supervisors and workers initiated some ideas relating to a more effective utilization of various waste products which were implemented. At Shanghai Steel a work group developed a way to economize on materials, and this was introduced in other work groups and shops as well. At Wusih Machinery a team of leading workers increased the speed of some old lathes, thus increasing their productivity. At Shanghai Machine Tool No. 3 a worker proposed that two additional drills be added to a boring machine, and this slightly increased the efficiency of some of the machine processes. At Tientsin Shoe several new styles were developed as a result of employee suggestions. I was told by a manager at the Wuhan Iron and Steel Corporation that the workers at one of the corporation's mines doubled the capacity of two lifts by adding another deck to them. In cases such as the above the suggestions and innovations were introduced after formal managerial approval. For the most part, employee participation in management seemed to take place rather informally. Special informal meetings were called at times, but not much use was made of formal meetings, conferences, or committees in order to implement employee participation, consultative direction, or democratic centralism in general. In fact, considerably less use seemed to be made of such formal platforms and procedures than in Soviet industry. The major formal on-the-job worker meeting (conference) at Chinese enterprises was usually held monthly and/or quarterly to discuss the enterprise plan and current performance. But even here, at most of the factories surveyed, all of the workers did not join in; attending were only a committee (or conference) of worker representatives elected by the different shops, sections, and departments. White-collar employees also had similar meetings or conferences. Such conferences were officially organized and presided over by the Enterprise Trade Union Committee which operated directly under the leadership and control of the party committee. The party clearly played the dominant role here. In fact, the trade union in Soviet enterprises, although not very powerful or influential, seems to be significantly more important than in China.

Officially the white-collar staff and worker representative conferences have broad powers. They can consider any proposals within the limits of higher directives and policies. They are even nominally empowered to demand the dismissal of the enterprise director and other managers. However, I never heard of any such case during my investigation. If a manager's dismissal is the subject of such a conference, the party committee would have undoubtedly determined the action to be taken before the meeting. In general, staff and worker conferences are viewed as a good way for handling and resolving contradictions through a discussion and analysis of all views and information set forth. The party committee's role is seen as a similar one, regarding the resolving of contradictions and problems.

Some Chinese managers whom I interviewed admitted that in the past—presumably during the Great Leap Forward—workers, and all personnel for that matter, spent too much on-the-job-time in meetings, and now most worker meetings are held "voluntarily" after hours. As of 1966 much time was being spent in after-work meetings. In fact, I did unexpectedly drop in on some when I stayed late at various enterprises. Such meetings are held in unused offices and shops, in the dormitories, in the yard, in the recreation rooms, on the factories' sports fields, and just about anywhere around the plant. Here employees discuss how to improve their own skills and performance, their planned tasks, and, of course, much ideology and politics. The workers also vote on who should get what size bonus, as well as who should be elected as leading workers (five-good workers) for the period because of their job performance, cooperation with others, self-development, ideologically correct behavior, and helping others to study and understand Chairman Mao and politics. Even though management and the party committee formally approve the distribution of bonuses and election of leading workers, it does seem that the workers' proposals generally are accepted.

However, there is one type of worker and staff election that seemed to be rather superficially conducted. This was the "election" of managers by the employees. This trend in electing managers, I was told, had started quite recently, and such elections take place annually or every few years at about 40 percent of the enterprises surveyed. Several others were contemplating elections of this type in the future. Most of the firms already having elections were in Peking and Shanghai. The workers, and other personnel, supposedly elect the directors, vice directors, and group leaders (who are like front-line supervisors or floor foremen). They may play the major role in the selection of group leaders, but it is doubtful that they do so, regarding the higher-level managers. The elections, not surprisingly, are under the direct leadership of the enterprise party committee, and appropriate higher-level administrators and party committees above the enterprise also formally approve the election of directors and vice directors. I was told that such formal higher approval is almost always given.

There seemed to be a general reluctance on the part of managers and Reds interviewed to discuss the mechanics of these elections. When I pushed for more details, some of them seemed to get embarrassed or upset. It seems that there are several after-hours meetings and screening sessions involved in coming up with a slate of managerial candidates. By the time the list of candidates is processed through the formal worker and staff representative conferences of workers and staff and party committee meetings, and then is presented to the electorate, there is typically only one candidate for each position. But, I was told, "employees can still vote 'yes' or 'no' for each candidate." What if the majority vote in a specific case is "no?" I asked. This has never happened, I was told, and if it ever did, a new candidate would be proposed for the job, and a new election would take place. A British diplomat who had been stationed in Red China for several years told me that employees wishing to vote "no" for a candidate in an election of this type would probably have to ask for a special pencil to mark his ballot and would become very conspicuous. It was implied that all candidates at the enterprises surveyed which had elections are elected with a 99 or 100 percent majority.

It seemed clear during my visit to China that the regime was not willing at that time to have the workers actually play dominant roles in the management of their enterprises, particularly in the election of higher-level managers. The Chinese system of management was still a long way from the Yugoslav system where worker councils evidently play a much more significant role in the selection of managers. In Yugoslavia the education level and work-skill level of members of worker councils are undoubtedly, on the average, substantially higher than in China. If the Chinese go too far or too fast in the Yugoslav direction, or in the direction that they did during the Great Leap, chaos and extreme inefficiency would surely result once again on a widespread scale. It is interesting to note that at a majority of the Chinese industrial firms that I visited,[38] there were no workers on the enterprise party committee, and at the others, workers did not make up more than about 10 percent of the committee membership.

Yet, employee participation in management, including the elections, did appear to have some favorable effects at Chinese enterprises. It seemed to give the workers and lower-level managers a direct sense of identification with, loyalty, a sense of belonging and commitment to their enterprises, and this probably has a favorable motivating effect. It appeared to serve as a good educational device, since workers are called on to analyze problems, plans, and results, to extend their initiative, and to make suggestions for improvements in performance and operations. It also tends to provide far more effective communication, greater dissemination of information regarding attitudes, opinions, and capabilities, and to generally narrow the information gap at different levels of the organization. Furthermore, it seems to be a good way to keep the managers on their toes, since their subordinates and the workers must at least be listened to. They can and do evaluate the managers and point out what they perceive as deficiencies in managerial performance. The workers, white-collar staff, and lower-level managers still were entitled to bonuses as of 1966. Such bonuses were based largely on favorable economic results, and if their bonuses are lost because of the decisions or incompetence of higher-level managers, their voices would probably not remain silent or uncritical. More important perhaps to the regime, is that employee participation in management provides for a type of bottom-up control not only over economic and technical performance but also over the proper interpretation of party and state policy and ideologically correct behavior.

It is not possible to measure the effectiveness of employee participation in Chinese industry in terms of economic or technical results, although I would guess that in 1966 it was rather effective. In Soviet industry there are some quantitative indicators of how effective employee participation in management really is, an important one being the effectiveness of formal suggestion systems found at all enterprises. Fairly careful tabulations are generally made of the number of suggestions put forth by employees for a particular period, the number implemented, costs entailed, and the economic, technical, and other improvements resulting from the implemented proposals. At many Soviet enterprises, and on a national scale, the results are quite impressive. The same is true for many American companies that have formal employee-suggestion systems. In China apparently very few industrial enterprises have formal suggestion systems for which records are kept.

While there was undoubtedly greater stress on hierarchical authority, division of work, and technical organization in general in 1966 than there was during the Great Leap Forward period, I was nevertheless surprised to find how much emphasis was given to human organization at the enterprises surveyed. In virtually any industrial firm, having at least several members, in any country one finds both a formal and informal organization. In its pure form, the formal organization is a technical, Weberian type of organization with clear-cut hierarchical authority-responsibility relationships, clearly defined division of labor based on specialization and technology, and many routinized activities and procedures. An informal or strictly interpersonal organization is built around natural human-behavior patterns, personalities, and interpersonal relations often largely independent of formal hierarchical positions.

In perhaps no other country does the interpersonal and informal organization play such a pervasive and significant role in the functioning of enterprises as in Communist China. This ties in with the regime's negative attitude toward bureaucracy—to be discussed in later chapters—its view of organizational solidarity, and its concept of "bottom-up" and horizontal control.

At the Chinese enterprises surveyed, I frequently observed workers and managers disregarding the formal chain of command by bypassing their subordinates and going directly to higher-level managers or Red officials for advice and instructions. On the other hand, higher-level managers and party cadres often went directly to workers. Personnel from different departments and shops also frequently were communicating and interacting directly with one another and undertook joint decisions and tasks on a horizontal plane without higher or vertical approval. While formal authority relationships tended to be maintained for major decisions, they were frequently disregarded for minor decisions, communication purposes, and the exchange of information, knowledge, and skills.

In general, authority within the enterprise seemed to be fairly decentralized and dispersed both vertically and horizontally at all levels. Self-coordination and self-control were evident in many cases. In many instances there was no clear-cut division of work. It seemed common for managers, Reds, technicians, other Experts, and "leading skilled workers" to drift around doing all types of jobs, from working on different technical problems and machines, innovating, giving advice or instructions; and/or training other personnel. Even workers trained other workers. At many enterprises I was told much about, and observed in practice the "three-in-one" method which combines cadres, technicians, and workers in project-type work teams. However, unlike the situation during the Great Leap Forward period, it appeared in the majority of cases observed that the cadres were reasonably well-qualified managers who extended general leadership over the team, the technicians were employing their expertise, and the workers were performing tasks suited to their skills and often were also being trained in new skills. But this was clearly not always the case.

In general, disregard for formal authority relationships, division of labor and work specialization, and clearly defined individual responsibility did, in many instances, seem to be resulting in varying degrees of confusion, unproductive time, and general inefficiency at the enterprises surveyed. If such trends were pushed much further at many of these enterprises rather serious problems and inefficiencies would surely result. However, this considerable stress on informal organization based on personal relationships in Chinese industry makes more sense than meets the eye when applied in a country that does not have nearly enough experts or skilled people to operate tens of thousands of fairly complex—and in many cases very complex—Weberian-type technical organizations. When only a relatively small proportion of personnel are highly skilled or knowledgeable about managerial, technical, and economic problems, the pooling of know-how, the sharing of information, mutual aid, and cooperation can, and does frequently, lead to net gains in productivity and efficiency over time. Moreover, it often appears to promote trust, cohesiveness, harmony, and unity of purpose, and probably better information for decision making at all levels than would otherwise be the case in Chinese enterprises. However, if Chinese industry and individual industrial firms are to expand substantially and become even more complex, it appears that unless more stress is placed on formal organization, serious problems and even stagnation are likely to emerge. The stress on informal organization seemed to be resulting in serious inefficiencies particularly in some of the larger and more complex firms surveyed.

While there was undoubtedly more emphasis on individual responsibility and apparently less fear on the part of managers for assuming responsibility in 1966 than in the Great Leap period, individual responsibility is not generally stressed as much in Chinese industry as it is in the United States or, for that matter, the Soviet Union. Responsibility for overall enterprise performance seems to fall on the enterprise party committee and the top-level management group which consists of the director and vice directors. These top-level managers no longer get bonuses based on enterprise-plan fulfillment, and there does not seem to be very much weight placed on individual responsibility at this level regarding overall economic or technical results. This view of top-management collective responsibility is also quite common in Japanese industry; however, in China, there is considerable stress placed on individual blame and self-criticism at all levels when it comes to ideological deficiencies.

In 1966, there seemed to be quite a bit of emphasis on individual responsibility at the middle- and lower-management levels. These managers can still get monthly or quarterly bonuses, and the awarding of such bonuses is generally based largely on an analysis of their job performance and contributions. While they often function within the informal organization, their formal rolls generally seem to be reasonably well defined. If trends continue in the direction taken during the Great Leap Forward period, however, stress will probably tend to be placed on collective responsibility at all managerial levels, and managers will probably become increasingly reluctant to assume individual responsibility.

At the worker level in 1966 there typically seemed to be a balance between individual and collective responsibility. Workers, in most cases, are also entitled to bonuses—not piece-rate incentives, however—which are based in part on how well they carry out their assignments. But the performance of their work group is also taken into account in many cases, and this is done to promote cooperation, as well as a sense of collective responsibility. Although many workers—typically the "leading" or skilled workers—spend much of their time operating in the informal organization, the majority of workers do seem to have reasonably well-defined formal jobs and tasks upon which they can be evaluated.

As was mentioned earlier, even before 1949, there was a relatively high degree of paternalism, in terms of various welfare benefits and facilities, in Chinese industry. Since 1949 the degree of paternalism as measured by employee welfare has increased substantially, and the welfare benefits and facilities provided at enterprises are probably significantly better and more extensive, in general, than they were in the past. In 1966 such benefits and facilities typically included subsidized meals, very low-cost family housing at larger enterprises and at least dormitories for single workers at most smaller factories, medical care, recreational facilities, opera, choral, and literary groups, social security and pension benefits, educational programs, nurseries, and so forth. Given Chinese conditions, paternalism of this type undoubtedly makes for a more energetic, better motivated, and generally more productive work force. However, such paternalism is not managerial paternalism since major welfare services, benefits, and facilities are provided chiefly by the state by law and by plan.

While enterprise management must devote some of its time and energies to the administration of welfare programs, such programs, as well as personal and social problems in general, are primarily the local concern of the party cadres and enterprise trade union officials. Hence, the dependency and loyalty and gratitude of enterprise personnel for welfare programs have shifted from the enterprise owners and managers to the party and the state. There does not seem to be much of a paternalistic relationship between managers and workers or supervisors and subordinates. It is certainly nowhere comparable with the dominant pattern in Japan where subordinates often get the personal advice and even the help of their superiors on a wide range of personal problems, including marriage.

In general, there can be little doubt that as of the spring of 1966 the dominant attitudes toward authority, responsibility, and subordination in Chinese industry were much more conducive to greater managerial effectiveness and industrial progress than they were, prior to 1949. Enterprise employees are probably, for the most part, healthier, less frustrated, more secure, more grateful and loyal, and identify more closely with organizational objectives, have a greater sense of purpose, commitment, and purpose, and are better motivated and more productive than they were in old China. I was told by both older managers and workers at some of the enterprises that were originally established prior to 1949 that absenteeism before 1949 typically averaged in the range of 10 to 20 percent annually. This is quite possible since the absenteeism rate of most enterprises in India that I surveyed in 1965 and 1966 was in this range—and in some cases even higher—with the lowest rate at a firm in India being about 8 or 9 percent. Absenteeism is one likely indication of the compatibility of dominant views of authority, responsibility, and subordination and resulting behavior patterns with employee needs, motivation, and productivity. All of the Chinese enterprises questioned on absenteeism in 1966 claimed that their annual average absenteeism rates were not more than about 3 percent, with some seasonal variations. In most cases, the annual average rate was about 1 to 2 percent. In several cases, enterprise officials looked at the personnel records in response to my question about absenteeism, and I am inclined to believe that the figures given to me were not intentionally distorted. Of course, there are probably much social control and, at times, significant penalties, which place considerable pressure on Chinese personnel from being absent without good cause. Nevertheless, I am inclined to believe that absenteeism is substantially less than it was, prior to 1949, and that this is due, in significant part, to a better overall work environment rather than to mere coercion. Contemporary authority relationships, responsibility patterns, and the contemporary role of subordinates and workers have undoubtedly contributed to this better work environment.

Current Trends and the Future

However, given the trends in the 1966–68 period which bear on attitudes toward authority and subordination, managerial effectiveness and industrial progress are likely to suffer greatly if such trends continue and become intensified. With a takeover of factories by Red Guards or other Super-Reds, the work environment would undoubtedly become even more chaotic, and operations even more inefficient than during the Great Leap period. There were apparently a significant number of strikes and plant shutdowns during 1967. Factory workers and other industrial personnel are, in many cases, in a dilemma regarding whose authority to respond to. They have been accustomed to accepting as paramount the authority and leadership of the party as exerted by local party cadres and committees. However, the Red Guards followed by the military, people's militia, and new "revolutionary" groups, have been given considerable powers in Mao's name. But such powers, in many instances, are being opposed by local party officials who have commanded the loyalty and following of industrial personnel under their jurisdiction for quite some time. Hence it is difficult to determine or predict how the personnel of different enterprises are responding, or will respond, to the "Great Cultural Revolution."

If the Super-Reds and the extremist leadership group in China have their way, workers would not only probably really elect managers, but would run enterprises under the leadership of zealous cadres, who are even less expert than many, and probably most of the regular enterprise party cadres and Reds. Authority based on formal position or expertise would probably be virtually eliminated, and most managers and experts would tend to avoid responsibility like the plague. The technical organization would tend to evaporate, as the human organization and the transformation of people rather than things become the dominant form of industrial life. A great deal of working time would be spent in ideological sessions and political meetings. Since the Super-Reds may generally be trusted by the extremist leadership group, there could be a fairly high degree of decentralization of authority under their surveillance and control. However, such a decentralization would clearly not be based on managerial, technical, or economic rationality.

In general, the formation and activities of the Red Guards and other grass-roots Super-Red groups seem to be in line with the conception of Mao and the other extremist leaders of grass-roots or bottom-up authority and control by and of the masses. The extremist group probably views the Red Guards as an army of zealous, well-indoctrinated youths who can be counted on to stir mass opposition in the event that a "revisionistic" leadership group obtains ultimate power in Red China after Mao leaves the scene. Hence, the Red Guard is seen as a potent force against revisionism and an easy line regarding the "class struggle."

If a compromise is reached in the power struggle but with the Mao-Lin Piao group claiming victory, this could lead to greater centralization of authority in industry, since many of the local and grass-roots party committees may not be considered trustworthy enough to maintain the existing pattern of industrial management under local control. However, the Red Guards and other Super-Reds would be called off, and dominant attitudes toward authority, responsibility, and subordination might revert basically to the early 1966 position within industrial enterprises. If Mao's opponents are victorious, Mao would undoubtedly remain as the key figurehead, but dominant views of authority, responsibility, and subordination, and the general system of management at the enterprise level are likely at the outset to be basically similar to that which existed just prior to the great Proletarian Cultural Revolution. However, the trend would probably be in the direction of greater emphasis on authority based on expertise and formal position, individual responsibility, clear-cut division of work, and technical organization in general. Democratic centralism and employee participation would probably continue to be emphasized, but would be carried out through a relatively national and balanced pattern of superior-subordinate relationships. Regardless of the outcome of the leadership struggle there is not likely to be a significant change in state and party paternalism at the enterprise level.

India versus China

In general, when ideology is not pushed too far in China, dominant attitudes toward authority, responsibility and subordination, and resulting behavior patterns, seem to be more conducive to managerial effectiveness and industrial progress than they are in Indian industry.[39] In India, paternalistic management and autocratic direction are entrenched in the private sector, even in most of the large firms operated through the managing agency (holding company) system. Authority tends to be highly centralized, and even when there is delegation of authority to intermediate and lower-level managers there tends to be a reluctance on their part to exert it independently or to accept responsibility. Subordinates tend to prefer a dependent and rather submissive role vis-à-vis their superiors. Even low-level supervisors or workers are often summoned to the highest seats of power for a command or reprimand, thus circumventing the chain of command, and undermining the authority and status of intermediate managers. This type of behavior frequently leads to unfavorable consequences in terms of control, supervision, and leadership at the lower levels of the firm.

Even in the larger privately owned Indian firms—except for a relatively small number of progressive ones—there is a strong tendency for the head of the family to maintain virtually complete authority and responsibility on all major issues even where there are other well-educated and potentially effective family or nonfamily members in the managerial hierarchy. There is also typically a high degree of centralization, accompanied by autocratic direction in the larger public firms, since they are commonly staffed largely by managers with a civil service background who are accustomed to this style of administration.

The system of management which allows worker participation is still quite rare in Indian industry and can be found only in a relatively small number of progressive firms. The dominant attitude toward subordinates, particularly workers, seems to be that they have little to offer in the way of initiative, ideas, or suggestions, and that they must be supervised and controlled closely. Since democratic values have been increasingly stressed in India, direction over subordinates may become, over a period of time, less autocratic and more willing to allow worker participation, particularly as the educational level of the population rises. Great pressures exerted by labor legislation and trade unions, as well as by growing labor expectations, are restricting managerial authority over various personnel matters. In this connection, voluntary managerial paternalism is being replaced in some areas by compulsory state paternalism backed by laws. In general, the welfare programs and benefits available to enterprise employees in India do not seem to be as substantial or as extensive as in China. Chinese industrial enterprise employees appear to be more willing than Indian employees to identify with their firm, to subordinate individual objectives to group and organizational objectives and interest, and also generally seem to be much more inclined to view their work lives as being at least equal in importance to their personal lives.

Interorganizational and Individual Cooperation

We are interested here in the sociological-cultural dimension of interorganizational and individual cooperation; various economic and legal aspects of cooperation are dealt with in other chapters. While the extent of voluntary cooperation that exists between a specific productive enterprise and other organizations, and among individuals within a given enterprise, may be partly under the enterprise's control and an expression of its policies, in most countries, including China, there appear to be dominant patterns in interorganizational and individual cooperation. Such dominant patterns—whether positive or negative in nature—are shaped substantially by historical, sociological, and cultural factors.

In general, voluntary cooperation involving organizations, groups, and individuals would tend to be greater where there is a relatively high degree of trust, psychological security, and altruism; where the values and basic ideology of the parties involved are similar; where there is no class conflict; and where the objectives, aims, and/or interests involved are perceived as mutually compatible or shared. Conversely, where these conditions are virtually absent or exist in highly negative degrees, conflict rather than cooperation is likely to be the dominant pattern of interacting behavior. Interorganizational and individual cooperation of the types under study here tend to have a significant bearing on managerial performance and industrial progress.

Old China

In old China the extended family type of cooperation was regarded as the norm, but even in family-type systems there was often considerable conflict. If the owners and key managers of a Chinese firm trusted anyone, it was typically a member of the family, a relative, or a close personal friend—"outsiders" tended to be viewed with varying degrees of suspicion. Because such "outsiders"—particularly those not employed within the firm—were commonly distrusted, there tended to be a lack of cooperation in business and industry unless the parties involved were next of kin, relatives, or good friends, and hence, financial dealings, supply relationships, prices, and other business transactions were frequently inefficient. For in such cases the economics of the situation was not usually considered of major importance.

Moreover, business and industrial firms typically functioned in an environment where immediate self-interest and personal gain took precedence over more altruistic cooperative behavior that could lead to greater managerial effectiveness and economic development. For increased managerial effectiveness and industrial progress on a broad scale were not commonly viewed as mutually shared objectives, aims, or interests by or among productive enterprises, or in their relationships with other organizations or individuals that they dealt with, such as the government, trade unions, banks, and educational institutions where firms had relationships with them.

The trade unions were largely controlled by the Kuomintang-dominated government, and until the Communists gained considerable influence among the labor force, the unions were not very strong or disruptive. As the Communists gained more influence, ideological conflict was, of course, promoted and greater labor unrest, including more strikes, emerged.

Ties between industry and educational institutions were probably not very close, and were, in fact, largely nonexistent. Hence, there was relatively little cooperation in this sphere. As there were very few research and development organizations in old China, there could be little cooperation between industry and this type of organization. The absence of research and development organizations that could aid in industrial development was probably due in large part to the lack of emphasis on technical, engineering, and applied-scientific education.

We have already discussed hierarchical relationships—between managers and workers, and between superiors and subordinates—in the preceding sections. While relationships of this type within enterprises in old China probably tended to be better than those in many other underdeveloped and developing countries, mutual hierarchical cooperation in this area was probably not present to a very high degree, given the large gaps in education and values between managers and the foremen and workers, the attitude on the part of owners and managers toward physical labor, and various other sociological-cultural factors. Although there was typically not very much mutual cooperation of a hierarchical type involving mutually shared goals or interests, there was also probably not a great deal of conflict, at least until ideological conflict was brought into play by growing Communist influence. For until the Communist influence made itself sharply felt, the existing class structure was generally accepted by the working population. It is not likely that there was much horizontal cooperation between work groups and departments within productive firms in old China. Each group or department tended to operate relatively autonomously in pursuit of its own assigned tasks, objectives, and interests, rather than in accordance with well-integrated mutually shared interests or objectives of a higher order. Hence the coordination of interdependent activities was frequently carried out inefficiently.

Let us now examine some of the important aspects of interorganizational and individual cooperation in industry in Communist China. Primary attention is given here to the impressions and findings derived from my visit to China in 1966. However, consideration is also given to apparently significant oscillations in pertinent cooperative-relationship patterns since 1949.

The Role of the Party in Maintaining Cooperative Relationships

Before going into specifics, it is important to note the role of the Communist Party in maintaining integral cooperative relationships in Chinese industry and business.[40] The enterprise party committee is supposed to identify, at all times, with the larger interests, objectives, and policies of the party and the state, rather than with the relatively narrow or vested interests of the enterprise. In fact, the party committee is the key local-control agent responsible for making sure that managerial decisions, plans, operations, and results at the enterprise are formulated and achieved in accordance with the best interests of the regime. This function of control and interpretation extends to the firm's cooperative relations with higher state industrial authorities, suppliers, customers, educational institutions, research and development organizations, the state bank, the trade union, and so forth, as well as to interpersonal relationships within the firm.

Apart from the political crisis that evolved in Red China in 1967 and 1968, it seems that the enterprise party committee has generally been more effective in making sure that the enterprise maintain effective external cooperative relationships with other organizations than have the Russians in Soviet industry during recent decades.[41] It should be pointed out that such cooperation is not always conducive to greater economic efficiency or industrial progress. The party in Chinese industry was not as generally effective in this regard, however, during the Great Leap period as it seemed to be during my 1966 visit. The effectiveness of the party committee in helping to maintain a high degree of individual hierarchical cooperation within the enterprise has tended to oscillate somewhat with the degree to which ideology has taken priority over managerial, technical, and economic rationality. For example, as was discussed in the two preceding sections, cooperation between managers and workers, superiors and subordinates, and Reds and Experts deteriorated sharply during the Great Leap Forward, and may again be on the threshold of serious deterioration, given the current political and ideological crisis in China.

Where the enterprise party committee has been more effective in promoting interorganizational and individual cooperation in Chinese than comparable efforts in Soviet industry, this has been due substantially to the system of incentives utilized, economic pressures, and legal rules of the game (these are topics discussed elsewhere in this book). However, local party officials in China also appear to identify more strongly with the objectives, interests, and policies of the regime than in Russia because of sociological-cultural factors. In this regard they generally seem to be somewhat more altruistic and dedicated to the interests of the state. Perhaps this is due, in large part, to the fact that the revolution is still relatively young in China, as compared with that of the Soviet Union. It may also have something to do with traditional cultural attitudes involving obligation, loyalty, and duty to the family which have now been transferred to the party and the regime. The fact that enterprise directors in China are typically significantly more Red than Expert also facilitates interorganizational and individual cooperation since they are less inclined to allow cooperative relationships involving their firm to deteriorate because of reasons of self-interest or localism. The basic thinking and behavior of these Red directors probably tend to be quite similar in many ways to those of the party secretary.

Union-Management Cooperation and Labor Unrest

To explore the more important concrete dimensions of interorganizational and individual cooperation in Communist Chinese industry, let us first consider union-management relationships. We shall consider the activities of the enterprise trade union in greater detail in a later chapter, but some background data on Chinese trade unions are warranted here.

Chinese trade unions, like those in the Soviet Union, are organized by a branch of industry, and their membership includes both workers and managers in a given branch of the economy.[42] At the Chinese enterprises surveyed, the vast majority of personnel were union members, and most of those who were not were either new employees or apprentices. All of the trade unions are under the central leadership of the All China Federation of Trade Unions which was established in Harbin in 1948. This was a revival of an organization of the same name which existed in the 1920's, but which later had to go underground. Until 1954 the Minister of Labor was also chairman of this federation.

In 1948 there were about 2.83 million industrial trade-union members (including urban handicraft workers) in China. By 1953 there were over 10 million; in 1957, over 16 million; and as of 1965, 20.8 million. By the Trade Union Law of 1950 all employed persons whose wages or salaries constitute their sole or main means of livelihood are eligible to join. Those engaged in, for example, collective agricultural or handicraft cooperatives are ineligible; but employees in state trade, commerce, and financial organizations are eligible for membership. In 1947 there were about 5 million union members of all types, and by 1960 there were about 40 million, according to a national Red Chinese union leader interviewed by Edgar Snow. In 1965 the federation was listed as having sixteen constituent sectoral unions, including unions in finance, trade, and education, as well as in sectors concerned directly with industrial production. These industrial unions operate at national and provincial levels. In addition, trade-union councils, embracing activities of all unions within a given area, exist at provincial, municipal, and, in most cases, county levels. Union organizations at the primary or basic level at industrial enterprises and other places of work numbered 160,000 in 1965.

At every enterprise surveyed in 1966 there was a trade-union committee headed by a chairman who is subordinate in reality to both the enterprise party committee and the union agency directly superior to the enterprise. Union committees with their own chairmen were also common in the larger enterprise workshops. The structure of Soviet trade unions, which are comparable to Chinese unions, is nominally democratic, with elected committees at each level, and with the central organization elected at national conferences. However, trade unions in Red China seem to be even less influential and play a more limited role than they do in the Soviet Union.[42]

The Chinese Communist Party is in virtually complete control of all important aspects of union activity, and usually selects the candidates for election. In most, if not all, instances, elected union officials are party members. The three enterprise trade-union chairmen whom I interviewed were elected annually, and all were party members of long standing. Two of them were shop party secretaries before they became union committee chairmen. I was told that enterprise trade-union committee chairmen are almost always on the enterprise party committee. The union officials whom I interviewed, as well as national union leaders interviewed by other foreigners, seemed eager to emphasize that the trade unions function under the direct control and guidance of the party. Hence, the unions have little formal independence or authority to express their members' interests if they are not compatible with the wishes or policies of the party or state.

From what I learned about trade unions in China, and from available published sources, it is evident that trade-union organizations and committees serve as transmission belts between the party and the masses or workers. The enterprise-union committee is primarily concerned with social welfare activities, including the organization, administration, and utilization of clinics, mess halls, dormitories and housing, educational programs, clubs, recreational and cultural facilities, and so on. It also administers employee insurance and other welfare funds on behalf of the state. Union officials are involved in matters pertaining to safety programs and working conditions. They also play a role in mobilizing and motivating employees to strive for greater productivity and efficiency in their work, and much of this is done through publicity campaigns and political and ideological work. In this connection, they organize socialist emulation (actually competition) campaigns so that lagging individuals and work groups can learn from, catch up with, overtake, and surpass the advanced.

The union committees at the firms that I surveyed seemed to spend quite a lot of time on disseminating worthwhile worker ideas, proposals, and information about experiences and achievements throughout appropriate parts of the enterprise—this is often referred to as "spreading good deeds, good thoughts, and good things"—and at times revealing, investigating, and criticizing bad methods, thoughts, and deeds. However, they are primarily concerned with promoting cooperation, enthusiasm, and high morale rather than conflict among enterprise personnel.

In general, it did seem that cooperation rather than conflict was the dominant pattern in the relationship between trade-union officials and managers in Chinese industry in 1966. The enterprise union committee, as well as management and the party cadres, are all supposed to be interested in increasing productivity, improving operations and working conditions, and raising the cultural, educational, ideological levels and living conditions of employees. However, when conflicts between Reds and Experts evolve, as was the case during the Great Leap, this also tends to lead to a deterioration in cooperation between union cadres and Expert-type managers.

In China—unlike the Soviet Union—the right to strike is officially guaranteed by law. I was, of course, told by union and party officials, as well as by managers, that since the enterprise is owned by the population as a whole, it makes no sense for a worker to strike against himself. When strikes have occurred in Chinese industry—and this is currently quite common under the Great Cultural Revolution—the workers often strike in spite of, rather than with the help of, the trade-union officials. The current strikes are undoubtedly under the direction of local party cadres who oppose the Red Guards and extremist leadership of Mao and Lin Piao, and who support a more moderate and rational leadership. They are not strikes aimed against management.

Before the current cultural revolution there were occasional strikes on a local scale, primarily before the period of the Great Leap Forward. Labor disputes and strikes in Red China are perceived as contradictions among the people, not as class struggles. When unsettled grievances at the enterprise level have led to slowdowns or strikes, they have usually been settled at the next level of the party, union, and/or industrial administrative hierarchy. There have been some strikes in the past resulting from workers' demands for greater material benefits, and they have typically been blamed on inadequate ideological education. This is reflected in the following statement made by the vice chairman of the All China Trade Union Federation to Edgar Snow a few years ago.

> Strikes for higher wages cannot occur if workers have been properly educated to understand that their wages are based on fair standards of values of production set by the state, which makes no profit for itself

but merely acts for the whole people to reinvest rational savings for the future enrichment of all.[43]

The vice chairman went on to say that if workers want higher wages they can make proposals when general adjustments are made by the state. However, they may need more political education, or they can work harder for bonuses, or learn higher skills through functional education. In the 1950's there were occasions where limited strikes led to the acceptance of some of the demands of the workers involved. Higher "bureaucratic" authorities were blamed for not "understanding the conditions, needs, and demands of the real situation."

In general, when ideology—which often involves emotional rather than rational motivations—has not been pushed too far in the Chinese economy, strikes, slowdowns, and labor unrest have been quite rare, and relationships between the union and management and between the workers and management have tended to be basically cooperative in nature. Apart from the situation in 1967 and perhaps during the Great Leap period, there has undoubtedly been substantially less conflict in union-management and worker-management relationships in China than in India during the last fifteen years. Much of the conflict in union-management relations in India is based on ideological and political rather than on purely economic issues, and it is generally more difficult to achieve cooperation or compromises where the former type of issues persists.

Cooperation between Industry and Government

As was discussed in Chapter 3, the extent of voluntary cooperation between government and industry in a particular country tends to have a significant impact on managerial performance and productive efficiency. Some of the major reasons for this have already been described in that chapter.

One may be inclined to assume that in countries, such as China and Russia, where industrial enterprises are state-owned, lack of cooperation between industrial managers and the government or state apparatus would not be a significant problem, since the state owns and controls the enterprises and would be fighting, so to speak, against itself. Yet even in a Marxist economy there is, in fact, often considerable conflict of interest and ineffective cooperation between enterprise management and higher state authorities. In the Soviet Union, for example, there has long been a basic conflict of objective between higher state planners and the managers (macromanagers and industrial enterprise managers), which has significantly hindered effective cooperation.[44] The former attempt to establish tight enterprise-operating plans calling for maximum production with allocated and available resources, while the latter strive for modest or easy plans because of deficiencies in the supply- and resource-allocation system, in conjunction with the system of incentives within which they must operate. While this type of environment may pressure many managers into maximum effort and performance, it also has had serious consequences affecting their function. It has led to ineffective cooperation, poor communication, information distortion, and a variety of other undesirable practices involving a wide range of economic, technical, and managerial matters. This situation is due, in large part, to various economic and political constraints, which will be discussed later; but the problem also has a sociological-cultural dimension.

Chinese industry has been subject to the same kinds of resource allocation and supply deficiencies that are found in Soviet industry. Where industrial firms in China have also been confronted with tight plans in conjunction with a managerial-incentive system similar to that found in the Soviet economy, some of the same problems involving ineffective cooperation between management and government have emerged. Where the enterprise party secretary in China, as in Russia, has also been entitled to bonuses along with the industrial managers for the fulfillment and overfulfillment of key targets of the enterprise plan, this has tended to further aggravate the situation. This was the case during certain periods of the 1950's and early 1960's; but in recent years neither the top-level enterprise managers nor the party secretaries in Chinese industry have been entitled to such bonuses. During the Great Leap Forward period in China, when the Reds were in control of most enterprises under a fairly decentralized arrangement, even the party secretary often allowed or engaged in the distortion of statistics and other information channeled up the industrial hierarchy for purposes of planning, decision making, and control. Apart from the crisis in early 1967, this in fact may have been the worst period in Red China regarding effective cooperation and communication between industrial enterprises and the regime as a whole.

However, in spite of some periodic, and quite serious, lapses in cooperation and communication between enterprise officials and higher government agencies in Communist China, there has probably been a somewhat higher degree of voluntary cooperation between these parties in China than between similar groups in the Soviet Union. The Red directors and party cadres of Chinese firms have probably been more inclined to place the interests and objectives of the state above their own interests, where necessary, than have Soviet enterprise managers and party cadres. In comparing Russia and China, it appears that personal gain and local vested interests have been more potent motivating forces in Soviet industry, while altruism, self-sacrifice, obligation and a spirit of candidness resulting in the possibility of compromise, have been somewhat more dominant in

Chinese industry. This may be largely due to the fact that the Soviet revolution is much older than the Chinese; and it may also be due to various historical or traditional cultural values which still exist in China.

I got the fairly strong impression that in China, when enterprise officials were faced with the possibility of unrealistic plans or resource-allocation deficiencies, they were more inclined than their Soviet counterparts to put all of their cards and problems on the table in an open manner, and thus reach an acceptable cooperative compromise or solution based on an objective analysis of the facts and the entire situation. Such interaction seems typically to be conducted in an environment of trust and sincerity, with mutually shared objectives in the state's interests playing a significant role in the solution of problems. This often entails a lengthy process of committee meetings and discussions, which can and probably does lead to significant delays in decision making, and results in inefficiencies in enterprise operations. Whether such inefficiencies generally outweigh inefficiencies that would arise from less effective cooperation and communication and from greater distortion of information, is open to speculation. I should guess that on the whole they do not.

I am not trying to suggest that there are no conflicts between enterprise officials and higher-level state agencies in China—there is probably considerable conflict and ineffective cooperation in many instances. However, it seems likely that there is, in general, a relatively higher degree of voluntary cooperation than in the Soviet Union. In enterprise-government relationships in the Soviet Union, the parties directly involved are probably more inclined to engage in less than candid gamesmanship, to put forth misleading data of various shades and degrees, and to pursue self-interest or narrow vested interests at the expense of the aims, objectives, and interests of the regime.

While cooperation based on corruption (including bribery) in enterprise-government dealings is far from rampant in the Soviet Union, there is probably even substantially less corruption in China. Western diplomats, journalists, and businessmen whom I have met, and who have lived for some time in China or visit there quite often, are unanimously amazed at how little corruption there is in the Red Chinese economy, especially when compared with that of old China.

There certainly is substantially more corruption in industry-government dealings in India than in Red China. Probably more often than not, cooperation derived through corruption is not conducive to greater managerial effectiveness or industrial progress. There might, of course, be many exceptions; but a corrupt environment in the sphere of industry-government cooperation probably has many subtle and intangible, but nevertheless substantial, negative effects on managerial effectiveness and industrial progress on a national scale over a period of time.

In general, cooperation between industry and government seems to be significantly more effective in China than in India—and this includes the Indian public sector, as well as private industry. However, relationships between the government and industry in India are probably not quite as bad as many people who have not researched the problem may think. A major constraint on effective cooperation in India pertains to political organization and the fantastic government bureaucracy that has evolved, and which seems to get increasingly out of hand. Given such a large and complex bureaucratic structure, it is difficult even for well-intentioned government officials to cooperate effectively, and to make timely and correct decisions affecting industrial firms. However, Red China also has a very sizable state bureaucratic apparatus—though probably not as rigid or suffocating as India's. The basic economic systems of India and China require relatively large macromanagerial bureaucracies to function. Hence, it seems that certain sociological-cultural factors also contribute substantially to cooperation problems involving government and industry in India. Numerous Indian government officials tend to have a rather negative, suspicious—and often outright hostile—attitude toward industrial managers and businessmen. This attitude is often justified because of the way managers behave and the attitude they take toward their function. Managers, on the other hand, frequently resent and are frustrated by the huge government bureaucracy with which they must deal, and often are antagonistic toward, and suspicious of, the government.

In general, in China there does seem to be greater cooperation, consultation, and communication between industry and government on economic, technical, and managerial problems of common concern than in India. As a result, the collection and dissemination of statistics and other information for both micromanagerial and macromanagerial decision making are facilitated in China. A greater attempt is also made in China to obtain the advice, knowledge, and opinions of all parties involved in preparing both public and private economic plans, and there also tends to be greater voluntary cooperation in the achievement of such plans.

Cooperation among Educational Institutions, Research Organizations, and Industry

Under normal conditions in China, as in Russia, there is a relatively high degree of cooperation between educational institutions and industry. From what I learned and observed in Red China—before the higher and secondary schools were closed down—such cooperation takes the form of joint consultation and collaboration on problems and research projects of common concern, exchange and dissemination of ideas and information, and so on. At times, educational institutions hold special courses and training programs for industrial personnel, and also send faculty members to work as consultants in industry. Industrial experts also give lectures and discuss problems at educational organizations. Much of this cooperation is essentially voluntary rather than prescribed by laws, regulations, or plans. Such cooperation is most common with technical, engineering, and scientific schools, although it did exist, to a limited extent, with schools dealing with economics and business administration. Such cooperation between the educational and industrial sectors in China has undoubtedly made for a much better educational match with the requirements of industry, as well as a more effective placement of graduates. Moreover, educational institutions have generally been inclined to cooperate with industrial firms in part-study, part-work programs.

This seemed to be the situation during April and May of 1966. However, in June the schools were closed, and as of the spring of 1967 they had apparently not been reopened. Significant potential gains in managerial effectiveness and industrial progress have undoubtedly been lost, with the elimination of most possibilities of cooperation between industrial and educational organizations. During the Great Leap Forward period, when a serious anti-intellectual environment evolved, it is also unlikely that cooperation between educational institutions and industry was very effective in many cases. The zealous and sparsely educated Reds who controlled industrial firms tended to greatly underestimate the benefits that could be derived through greater cooperation with faculty members of educational organizations. When the schools reopen, if another period of pervasive anti-intellectualism emerges, cooperation between well-educated faculty members and industrial enterprises will, in numerous instances, undoubtedly deteriorate again. For the most part, since 1949, there has probably been a much greater degree of effective cooperation between the educational and industrial sectors in China than in India. In fact, the limited cooperation of this type that does exist in India is largely a recent development. The two recently established Indian institutes of technology seem to be way ahead of most, if not all, other educational organizations in cooperative ventures with industrial firms.

In China, in addition to the mutually beneficial exchange between ordinary schools and industry, there is also considerable cooperation between research, design, and development organizations and industrial enterprises. This cooperation usually pertains to technical collaboration and problem solving, involving new technical processes or products. In the mid-1960's there were about a hundred research institutes under the Chiness Academy of Sciences, many of which collaborated on problems with industrial firms.[45] In addition, industrial ministries, other central agencies, as well as industrial, planning, and economic organizations of various types on the provincial and municipal level, have their own research and development units which collaborate with industrial enterprises on technical and, at times, other problems of mutual concern.

While collaboration on specific problems between such research organizations and industrial enterprises is frequently prescribed by higher authorities and spelled out in the operating plans of the organizations involved, there also seems to be quite a bit of voluntary cooperation of this type resulting from the initiative and interests of the enterprises and/or research organizations themselves. Most of the enterprises surveyed had relationships with research organizations of various types.

For example, in 1966 the Wuhan Iron and Steel Corporation was collaborating on a wide range of technical problems with more than a dozen research, development, and design organizations. These included both central and local (provincial and municipal) research organizations. While the corporation's relationships with the central institutes were for the most part prescribed in their plans, there was considerable voluntary cooperation with some of the local research organizations. Wuhan Steel also had fairly extensive research and development facilities and staffs of its own, which were utilized by other industrial enterprises. Moreover, leading scientific and technical personnel of this enterprise also attended meetings and exchanged ideas and information through their membership in the Hupeh Province Metal Association.

Wuhan Heavy Machinery has its own research institute which is under the joint jurisdiction of this firm and the First Machine Building Ministry. Other industrial enterprises collaborate with this institute on both an obligatory and voluntary basis. The Wuhan firm also deals with about seven other research institutes, including the Scientific Research Institute of Heat Treatment and the Surveying and Measuring Institute. Most of these institutes are assigned to the firm by its ministry.

Nanking Chemical collaborates on technical problems, primarily on a prescribed basis with a research unit of the Chemical Ministry, but it also has some voluntary cooperative relationships with several Shanghai and Peking research institutes, as well as with certain universities. The two pharmaceutical enterprises that I surveyed have both assigned and voluntary relationships with various medical-research and chemical institutes.

Even consumer-goods producers frequently collaborate with research organizations on various problems and innovations. The Soochow Embroidery Research Institute, which I visited, had over a hundred employees. This institute gives designs and technical aid to a number of embroidery and textile factories in Soochow. The Tientsin Wool Enterprise exchanges information and ideas through a municipal scientific association concerned with the technical problems of light industry.

In general, there appears to be somewhat more cooperation of a voluntary nature between industrial enterprises in China than in the Soviet Union. The system of incentives and other environmental conditions that Soviet enterprise managers have operated under has created considerable resistance on their part to major technical-process and product innovations.[46] This in turn has, in numerous instances, significantly retarded the effectiveness of cooperation and collaboration between Soviet industrial enterprises and research institutes. In Chinese industry, for various reasons to be explored in later chapters, enterprises and their managements seem to be generally more enthusiastic and interested in innovation, and hence in cooperating with research organizations where this is feasible. However, there is a superior—in terms of quality of personnel—and a much more extensive network of research, design, and development organizations in the Soviet economy. And through various pressures, penalties, rewards, and clear-cut plan assignments, prescribed cooperation and collaboration between Soviet industrial enterprises and research organizations still probably result in greater and more effective technological and product innovations and improvements than in China. Nevertheless, if Soviet enterprise managers had the same enthusiasm for innovation and desire for voluntary cooperation with research organizations as their Chinese counterparts tend to have, industrial progress would probably be even greater in the Soviet Union.

In India, there are very few research organizations—either private or public—with which industrial enterprises can collaborate on technical or other types of problems, assuming that they wanted to do so. There are some scientific and professional associations which deal in a limited exchange of information and ideas. Many of the more progressive and larger Indian firms have their own fairly sizable research and development staffs and facilities. However, the possibilities for, and effectiveness of, collaboration and cooperation between industry and organizations for research, design, and development are much greater in China than in India.

With the intensification of the Great Proletarian Cultural Revolution in Red China in late 1966 and early 1967, there is no available information as to whether cooperation and collaboration between industrial enterprises and research organizations still exist on the same scale as they did during my visit to China. Even at some of the enterprises that I surveyed, I sensed some antagonism about the usefulness of cooperating or collaborating with research organizations. Some of the party cadres and managers interviewed seem to feel that, under Mao's inspiration and the three-in-one method, the enterprise had little or no need for the help of the intellectuals employed by research organizations. I firmly believe that during the Great Leap period, with its pervasive environment of anti-intellectualism and anti-expertise, relationships between industrial enterprises and research organizations deteriorated significantly. If, for ideological reasons, this type of environment has already evolved, or evolves again in the future, substantial losses in managerial effectiveness and industrial progress are to be expected.

Cooperation within Industry

It appears that there is a considerable amount of voluntary cooperation among Chinese industrial enterprises, particularly in connection with the training of personnel. At many of the enterprises surveyed in 1966, they were either sending employees of various types to other firms for training purposes, or were training visiting personnel on their own premises. In many cases this was being done on the initiative of the enterprises themselves, rather than because of assignments prescribed in the plan or by higher authorities. There seemed to be much more cooperation of this type than in Soviet industry, but this is understandable, given Russia's much better-educated and better-trained industrial manpower.

In Chinese industry, workers are often sent to other enterprises to perfect their skills and develop new ones, managers are sent to learn more about how to manage better, and even technicians and engineers go to improve their qualifications and skills. When a new plant is set up, there is frequently a great deal of cooperative training activity of this type. At times employees are also sent to other firms for ideological training.

To cite a few concrete examples: A group of managers and technicians of the Shanghai Truck Plant were sent to the Changchun Motor Vehicle Enterprise in 1966 for on-the-job training, while a group of workers came to the Shanghai factory from Nanking to be trained in certain new techniques. Shanghai Steel Mill No. 3 sent over a hundred employees of many types to the steel firms in Wuhan and Anshan for training in the first half of 1966. A number of engineers and technicians from other enterprises were undergoing training at the Canton Chemical Fertilizer Enterprise when I visited there in June of 1966. A group of leading workers from Chengchow were learning a new combing process at Shanghai Cotton Textile Mill No. 19.

The party secretary of the Wuhan Diesel Engine Factory was taking a group of "leading" managers, technicians, and workers to the Loyang Tractor firm the day I visited the Wuhan plant. The Wuhan group was going on tour, so to speak, for the main purpose of rendering ideological training, first, to the Loyang personnel, and then to employees at other plants in Shanghai, Wusih, and elsewhere. They were going to bring their "revolutionary spirit and dedication" to these other factories. This was to include training in the creative spirit—"dare to think, dare to create, dare to do"—as well as in "individual cooperation, self-sacrifice, and technical innovation." Wuhan Diesel Engine, which seemed to be operating very inefficiently, also was planning to send some of its managers, technicians, and workers to other plants to improve their own work skills and qualifications.

At many of the enterprises surveyed, there was also considerable cooperation with other firms in connection with research and development activities. As was mentioned earlier, enterprises and some of their key personnel often belong to various associations through which they exchange information and ideas, usually of a technical nature. When their plans permit, there is also often much in the way of cooperative subcontracting relationships among Chinese factories.

It seems that there is more voluntary cooperation among enterprises in their roles as suppliers and customers in China than in the Soviet Union. In both countries, firms are frequently faced with critical supply shortages —of materials, components, equipment, and so forth—since state planning and resource allocation are far from perfect. And in both countries sellers' markets clearly exist throughout the economy. It is likely that sellers' markets and supply problems exist to a significantly higher degree in China than in Russia because the Soviets have a much more substantial and diversified industrial base. However, Chinese industrial enterprises may generally be more concerned about fulfilling the supply requirements of their customers. It is quite common for them to invite their customers to meetings called for the purpose of overcoming production, supply, and delivery problems that relate to their demands, and to send their own personnel to the customers' enterprises to get a better picture of their requirements.

In general, I sensed a deeper and more serious concern among Chinese enterprise managers about their customers' needs than among their counterparts in the Soviet Union. There seems to be a greater sense of cooperation in this regard in China. This is undoubtedly due, in substantial part, to the system of managerial incentives utilized in Soviet industry, whereby Soviet managers have been able to earn lucrative bonuses for fulfilling aggregate production and other targets or success indicators of the enterprise plan. Frequently, it has been possible to fulfill these success indicators only by producing items not according to plan and/or of substandard quality, without showing much concern about customer requirements.[47] Such behavior further aggravates the supply situation in Soviet industry.

When the managements of Chinese enterprises operated under a similar incentive system in the past, they often responded in similar ways as their Soviet counterparts, but perhaps not to the same degree intentionally. While distortions in product mixes and substandard-quality products —resulting in critical problems for customers—have been problems of concern in Chinese industry, it is likely that a greater spirit of cooperation has nonetheless existed there than in Soviet industry. In recent years, with the elimination of the Soviet type of managerial incentives, cooperation has probably been facilitated to an even substantially higher degree.

Supplier-customer relationships in both Chinese and Soviet industry are formally based on a system of legal contractual agreements, which will be discussed in more detail in later chapters. In both countries contractual violations can result in penalties, in the form of fines and damages, imposed on the delinquent party. This system of contracts and penalties has been rather ineffective in the Soviet economy, although attempts are frequently made to make use of it to pressure firms to respond to the requirements of their customers.[48] It appears that much less use is made of contractual enforcement and penalties to pressure suppliers in Chinese industry, while greater stress is placed on voluntary cooperation and other pressures.

One type of pressure in China that seems to be definitely effective is the use of the *dazeba,* which is merely a letter of criticism or praise. It is common for an irate or abused customer enterprise to send a dazeba to its supplier, who is frequently required to post it in a convenient place for all to see. The supplier firm's superior authorities may also get a copy of the dazeba if the customer is upset enough. I am convinced that management undergoes considerable loss of face and embarrassment, which is taken very seriously if its enterprise is prone to receiving dazeba complaints. There were some dazebas posted near the general manager's office at the Wuhan Steel Corporation and in various places at a few other enterprises that I visited. In some cases, the dazeba contained words of praise from customers and various other parties, and here the managers seemed, understandably, to be quite proud. I am sure that numerous Soviet enterprises often receive letters of complaint from customers, but I doubt whether this generally does much to increase their concern or voluntary cooperation in their roles as suppliers.

There also seems to be more effective cooperation of a voluntary nature between consumer-goods producers and their retail-store customers in China than in the Soviet Union. This type of cooperation often goes as far as industrial-enterprise personnel spending time working as sales personnel in retail stores so that they can learn more about consumer demands, needs, and wishes. For example, both of the Chinese clothing factories surveyed send designers, workers, managers, and other employees quite frequently to the major stores that sell their products. They also organize consumer-opinion panels and exhibitions several times a year. (More about this in a later chapter.) It will suffice to say here that cooperative relationships between industrial enterprises in the consumer-goods sector and retail customers appeared in 1966 to be significantly more extensive and pervasive in China than in Russia.

In general, there seems to be considerably more effective cooperation among enterprises in China than in India. Indian firms also typically function in relatively strong sellers' markets, but there is a rather pervasive attitude of "The customer be damned." There is also a general reluctance among Indian firms to exchange information or ideas on common problems or to undertake potential mutually beneficial cooperative ventures of virtually any type. This relatively uncooperative environment is probably due, in large part, to lack of trust, as well as ignorance about the mutual benefits that may be derived through cooperation, and at times sheer lack of interest in improving operations.

Individual Cooperation within Industrial Enterprises

As was pointed out earlier, the degree of individual cooperation of a hierarchical nature in Chinese enterprises has tended to oscillate with the degree to which ideology has taken priority over managerial, technical, and economic rationality. During my visit to China, there seemed to be a relatively high degree of individual cooperation of this type at most of the enterprises surveyed. There also seemed to be generally a high degree of individual cooperation of a horizontal nature—among members of work groups, and among members of different groups, shops, and departments. This was reflected in the nature of the informal organization discussed in an earlier section. However, individual cooperation, particularly of the hierarchical type, deteriorated sharply during the Great Leap period, and may again be in the throes of serious deterioration if ideology continues to be pushed to extremes.

In general, it is possible that individual employees within Chinese enterprises tend to have a somewhat greater sense of cooperation, altruism, and team spirit in the collective and national interest than in the Soviet industry. This situation, if true, is probably due to the relative youth of the Chinese revolution, as well as to more intensive and effective ideological indoctrination, greater identification with the aims and policies of the regime, and a greater sense of familial togetherness.

There certainly seems to be a considerably higher degree of cooperation among individuals in Chinese industry than in Indian industry. Communication among Indian enterprise personnel frequently seems to be rather ineffective, and one senses considerable reluctance to exchange information freely. There also does not generally seem to be much interest in helping one's co-workers to solve problems or to improve their skills and performance. Indian industrial personnel frequently seem to function as islands unto themselves.[49] Greater insecurity—both psychological and economic—distrust, suspicion, apathy, lack of interest, little altruistic spirit, and fear of being proven wrong or embarrassed are all probably common reasons for less individual cooperation in India than in China. In addition, the class structure, including the caste system, in India is still probably a significant constraint on the effectiveness of both interorganizational and individual cooperation in many instances.

ATTITUDE TOWARD ACHIEVEMENT AND WORK

The importance of the dominant attitude toward achievement and productive work in industry and business in a particular country as a vital determinant of managerial performance and industrial progress should not be underestimated. Indeed, it may well be one of the most critical determinants of all. On the basis of scientific studies, there is a fairly close correlation between the achievement drive—also referred to as need for achievement—of different peoples and their respective countries' rate of economic growth. There is also evidence, although derived from a more limited sample, indicating a significant correlation between the average achievement drive of samples of managers in different countries and the relative rates of economic development of those countries.[50]

If a given country succeeds in significantly raising the achievement of its population, it is likely to improve managerial effectiveness and industrial progress on a national scale. For people having a relatively high need for achievement tend to be significantly more favorably disposed toward hard work and doing a job well—particularly nonroutine jobs—than people having a low need for achievement. Moreover, people with a relatively high achievement drive tend to have a greater desire to overcome obstacles, are generally more concerned about, and happy over, their successes, and tend to worry more over their failures.

Equally important for substantial industrial progress is the allocation and/or distribution of high-achievement human resources in different jobs and occupations throughout the society. In a society that is oriented toward achievement and productive work, it would generally be much easier to recruit people for industry who are willing to work reasonably hard and efficiently. It is critical for substantial industrial progress that there be sizable numbers of industrial managers, specialists, and workers who have a relatively high achievement drive, as well as substantial entrepreneurial forces at work.

Industrial managers with a relatively high achievement drive would be inclined to desire and strive to accomplish fairly challenging—but realistic—enterprise plans and objectives. Such plans and objectives would typically pertain to some notion of greater productivity, production, efficiency, growth, and/or profitability. Such managers would also be more likely to take calculated rational risks, to innovate, and to be quite favorably disposed to change in the direction of greater economic and technical progress, as long as the attainment of their priority operational goals is not threatened. In a substantially planned economy, in particular, it is also important for key political leaders to have a relatively high achievement drive and a strong priority commitment to industrial progress, if such progress is to be achieved in significant measure. Evidence strongly suggests that able persons who have a relatively high achievement drive are likely to make the best managers—micro as well as macro—and probably the best political leaders of the entrepreneurial type. High achievers of such types are crucial if productive enterprises are to grow, and particularly if new ones are to be created. . .

David McClelland's study of Chinese children's readers (referred to in an earlier section), which were used in Republican China in the 1920's and in Red China in the 1950's, reveals a much higher score of the achievement drive for those of the latter period. Few objective persons who know anything about both the old China and Communist China are likely to dispute that the population, as a whole, in contemporary China has a significantly higher achievement drive than in the China of the past. McClelland's research serves to give more weight to this conviction because of its objective and scientific nature. The achievement-drive score for China in the 1920's was sharply below the world average, and in the 1950's it had surpassed it. The Red China score for the 1950's is also greater than the score for the Nationalists on Taiwan which had also risen significantly in the 1950's from that of Republican China in the 1920's.[51] Apparently the Republican revolution in mainland China in the early 1900's had not been strong enough to change the motivational patterns of the population to a more distinctively modern one, at least by about 1930. Perhaps it was, in substantial part, for this reason that an even stronger revolution and wave of reform developed later during the Communist period.

The Chinese children's readers of the 1920's placed very little stress on task-oriented achievement or on positive concern for achievement connected with knowledge or self-improvement. The importance of knowledge is stressed quite often, but usually in a negative sense, through the ridiculing of stupidity. In general, references to individual, collective, or national achievement, self-improvement, or productive work associated with industry or business receive little attention in Chinese stories of this period.

It is generally agreed that the population as a whole in old China was low in achievement drive, but what about the managers, businessmen, and firm owners in China before 1949? A commonly held image of Chinese businessmen and managers has long been that even before 1949 they were, as a group, good entrepreneurs, and hence probably had a relatively high achievement drive. In reality, this was probably more true for the Chinese businessmen and managers who left China prior to 1949 to set up successful, and often dynamic, enterprises in other countries throughout many parts of the world. It is common for high achievers of this type in a stagnant or underdeveloped country to leave their homelands, if they are able to, and seek their opportunities and fortunes elsewhere.

Exposure to Chinese entrepreneurs and managers with a relatively high achievement drive in Western and other foreign countries led to an exaggerated image of the entrepreneurial effectiveness and achievement drive of the businessmen and managers who remained in China. Undoubtedly many relatively high achievers of this type did remain in China before 1949. However, from what is generally known about the behavior and performance of industrial managers, firm owners, and businessmen in old China, it does not appear that, as a total group or class, they had a very high achievement drive. Moreover, their entrepreneurial talents were typically not strongly directed toward increasing productive efficiency or industrial progress. They frequently became rich and powerful and their firms expanded as a result of protected markets, mergers, and acquisitions, and not through any increase in managerial effectiveness or improvement in productive efficiency.

The key political leaders in old China who may have had a high achievement drive were typically much more concerned about political control and power than about economic development. It was not until the 1930's that the central government in China began to show any serious concern about economic modernization. In general, the major entrepreneurial forces that effected economic change, innovation, and industrial progress in old China were (a) foreign enterprises and their native personnel based in the treaty ports, (b) foreign governments and their chosen instruments, particularly in Manchuria, (c) a few outstanding Chinese statesmen of the late nineteenth century with a preponderantly provincial power base.

The predominantly American influence on Taiwan has increased the amount of concern over achievement in children's stories used there, but not as decisively as among the Communists on the mainland. The quantitative achievement-drive scores are supported even more strongly by qualitative analysis of the stories themselves. For instance, the emphasis on achievement in the Taiwanese stories is largely concentrated in the tales of Western heroes—for example, Magellan, Washington, Alexander Graham Bell—whereas in Red China the stories deal with local and other indigenous Chinese heroes. In general, a strong concern for achievement that the local population can identify with is missing in the Taiwanese stories.

Yet it cannot be disputed that Taiwan has made considerable economic progress since 1950. The rise in achievement drive as compared with the situation in mainland China in the 1920's has probably contributed to this progress, but this rise has not been as sharp as in Red China. Therefore, it must be assumed that other environmental conditions have contributed more to Taiwan's economic development than greater drive alone. Some of these other important factors are the great amount of American aid, investments, and assistance, the fact that Taiwan is not faced with anything like the tremendous overpopulation problem that exists on the mainland, and the flight of sizable numbers of the better entrepreneurs, skilled managers, and other professionals from the mainland to Taiwan because of the Communist takeover.

In general, then, available evidence indicates that the motivational concerns, including the achievement drive, which favor economic and social modernization are more prominent in the stories used in Communist China than those in Taiwan. The inference clearly seems to be that Communist China has been more successful in moving its nation toward the psychology and sociological-cultural preconditions for a "modern" economic, technical, and social order than Taiwan. Communist ideology has played a crucial role in this movement. But paradoxically, if ideology continues to be pushed to extremes in Red China, that country will probably place second to Taiwan in industrial progress and general economic development over a period of time. However, if a reasonable balance between ideology and managerial, technical, and economic rationality is followed in Communist China it will probably, at a certain point, move substantially ahead of Taiwan in industrial progress, given its significant lead in the psychological and sociological-cultural sphere, including, in particular, the achievement drive.

The nature of the qualitative emphasis on achievement in Communist Chinese readers published in the 1950's has probably done considerably more to raise the level of the drive in China than the quantitative score indicates. Let us examine some excerpts from a representative Chinese story dealing with learning. The story is entitled "How I Do Like to Learn," and is found in a second-grade reader, published in Peking in the late 1950's.

> After we were freed by the party, I was sent to an accelerated technical high school by the party. I was so happy I cried.
>
> Learning is not very easy. In the beginning I couldn't understand what the teacher taught us. I always got a red cross mark on my papers.
>
> Once they had a party meeting and I met our secretary. He asked me, "How are your studies? Any difficulties? Are you scared?" I firmly answered that I was not scared. I promised the party that I would complete my studies very well.
>
> The boy sitting next to me was very enthusiastic and also an outstanding student. He found that I couldn't do the problems so he volunteered to explain them to me. Sometimes he was so anxious that he gave his paper to me and said, "Look what I did!"
>
> I could not copy his work. I must learn through my own reasoning, so I can grasp the work. I gave his paper back and explained in a low tone, "Thank you, but I can't see your work. I have to do it myself."

> Sometimes I worked on a problem until midnight. If I could not finish it by midnight, I started in the morning. I conquered all my difficulties this way. The red cross marks on my work were getting less common.
>
> My marks rose. I spent only four and a half years there; then I went to college . . . but still I felt I did not study enough. I want to study harder to accomplish this duty assigned to me by the party—to complete my education and serve my country!

In the above story the emotional involvement with learning and the concern for achievement are very explicit throughout. The boy wants to learn, likes to learn, works long hours, overcomes difficulties, is concerned about whether he does well or not, is helped by others to do well, and all of it is phrased in terms of completing his education to serve his country better. The story reflects values associated with the Calvinist ethic and individual achievement, as well as strong identification with national achievement, and a collective type of cooperative spirit. The story also has a kind of local Horatio Alger quality that is completely missing from the Chinese stories of the 1920's, and from those of Taiwan of the 1950's. One can scarcely doubt after reading it and others like it that the achievement concern injected by the Communists in their stories is very much higher than that which is characteristic of the stories of the other two samples.

If anything, the quantitative scores underestimate the difference. Another study dealing with Communist China by J. Lewis strongly supports this conclusion. He cites evidence of the vigor with which the Red Chinese have whipped up enthusiasm for education and achievement.[52] The achievement drive has been inculcated in students through the use of competitive, individualistic games—which are compatible with Western values and the Calvinist ethic—balanced with the emphasis on helping one another to do better, which is basically both a Communist and Christian value.

Thus far in our analysis of achievement motivation, we have equated the results of a quantitative and qualitative analysis of the content of children's readers with the *actual* achievement drive of the population at large in a particular country. I believe it can be said that a study of children's readers gives some indication of the direction being taken by the population's actual achievement drive, and whether it is very high or low relative to the same drive in various other countries. However, for some countries there may be a fairly significant margin of error between the achievement-drive score derived from children's stories and the actual existence of the drive among the population. A careful qualitative analysis of the stories may reduce this margin of error significantly, but it still may not eliminate it. In the final analysis, one must also study the behavior of people or groups of people to get a more accurate assessment of the achievement drive of the population at large or of certain sections of society.

What factors can explain a significant margin of error that might exist between the score derived from children's stories in a particular country and the actual achievement drive of that country's population or certain portions of the population? A major factor here is the number of people in the society who have read and comprehend this type of children's stories. If a substantial portion of the population is illiterate, and/or if much of the older population has not been exposed to stories of this type, it is likely that there might be a significant margin of error. Even where children are exposed to such stories in school, it is possible that traditional child-rearing practices and parental-behavior patterns, which are not conducive to instilling relatively high-achievement motivation in children, may significantly reduce the motivational impact of such stories. Furthermore, prevailing orthodox religious beliefs and customs also reduce the behavioral impact of achievement-oriented stories.

How accurately, then, does the available analysis of Communist Chinese stories reflect the actual achievement drive of the Chinese population, and particularly of industrial personnel? Does the industrial work force tend to work hard primarily because of coercion, forced labor, and other ruthless tactics which we know the regime has resorted to on some occasions? Has the glorified image of achievement introduced by the Chinese Communist Party in published services and other popular media of all types really had an impact on the rank and file and made them work harder voluntarily? Or has the high aspiration level set by the ruling elite merely been a "front," or sheer ideological jargon, without significant motivational and behavior consequences?

It would seem that the vigorous and intensive campaign to raise the achievement drive of the population in Red China has paid off, especially in the urban areas and among industrial personnel. The literacy rate is much higher in urban areas, particularly among the industrial work force, than in the rural areas among the peasants. Traditional child-rearing practices, parental-behavior patterns, and religious values also seem to have given way to the new order substantially more in the cities than in the countryside. Moreover, the majority of people employed in industry are relatively young and have been educated largely under the Communist system. In fact, about 40 per cent of Red China's population is under the age of fifteen, and this suggests that the achievement drive of the newly emerging generation of industrial personnel is likely to be even substantially higher than that of the present generation.

Case studies involving Soviet citizens strongly suggest that the achievement drive may be higher in individuals brought up wholly under the

Soviet Communist system since the 1917 Revolution than in an earlier generation.[53] Typically the rigid attempt of the older Soviet citizen to reach the high levels of aspiration set by the party actually hides, and is a reaction against, a basic feeling of weakness and a need for dependence derived from earlier upbringing. The younger Soviet citizen, on the other hand, brought up under the high ideals and strong achievement orientation of the Young Communist League and the party, may have experiences much like the young Chinese with high achievement drive, and, in fact, he acts and thinks in ways that strongly indicate that he has a greater drive. Furthermore, a content analysis of Soviet children's readers in 1925 and 1950 reveals that the score increased significantly between 1925 and 1950.[54]

It is likely that, as regards the achievement drive of its population, Communist China is moving in a direction similar to that of the Soviet Union. The great stress on achievement in all types of mass media in China has probably also had some positive effect on many—but certainly far from all—of the older industrial personnel who were born and raised before 1949. The extensive system of literacy training and spare-time education has also probably had some effect on raising the achievement drive among the older urban population.

The Communist takeover has brought to the Red Chinese population a much stronger sense of national pride, prestige, and power, as well as greater self-respect, dignity, and self-confidence at the individual level. Apathy, illiteracy, filth, disease, and squalor, which resulted in a pervasive atmosphere of pessimism, has given way to a general atmosphere of optimism, cleanliness, self-development, and progress. Where there used to be a low ceiling on the aspiration level and a low self-image among probably a large majority of industrial workers—not to mention other types of Chinese citizens—both the aspiration level and self-image of industrial employees have probably risen significantly since 1949. In the past, people tended to be quite fatalistic and were inclined to feel that little could be done to control one's environment. In contemporary times, industrial personnel have much greater self-confidence and are more inclined to feel that they can overcome obstacles and problems through their own efforts. All of these changes have undoubtedly had a significant positive impact on the achievement drive of the industrial work force in general, including many of the older people. A great increase in the possibilities and opportunities for career advance, promotions, and higher pay in industry, as compared with past conditions, has also probably done much to raise the achievement drive of the industrial workers and motivated them to work more efficiently and to improve their performance.

Communist-Maoist ideology—particularly practical ideology—has played a major role in raising the drive for achievement. Ideology has provided a standardized system of communication and language regarding rules on action, ideas, and behavior which emphasize achievement and productive proletarian work. This goes far beyond the printed word; it is utilized in discussion groups, political study sessions, and on a day-to-day basis in the working lives of virtually all industrial personnel. Mao's treatise "On Practice" is important in this connection as it stresses the philosophy and behavior pattern of "If you don't succeed, try and try again." One learns best through practice and experience, and one can overcome virtually any obstacles or problems, and can improve his performance if he is persistent, hard-working, and dedicated. Mao's essay "On Contradictions" focuses on the solution of problems and the overcoming of obstacles through the law of the unity of opposites.

The achievement stress in Communist China has been on a combination of individual, collective, and national achievement. However, during periods when ideology has been pushed to extremes, individual achievement associated with self-interest has been played down, and its relation to service of the national interest has been forcefully emphasized. During such extremist periods, the top political leaders become obsessed with achievement pertaining to ideological purification and human transformation at the expense of economic and technical achievement. While the achievement drive of workers and Reds was clearly misdirected but probably not adversely affected during the Great Leap Forward period, it probably was both misdirected and adversely affected for numerous managers and experts because of the misuse of their talents and the undermining of their status, authority, and influence. If the current political crisis continues for long in China it could have an adverse impact on the achievement drive of a very substantial portion of the industrial work force, including not only professional managers and experts, but Reds and workers as well.

Under normal conditions, a substantial number of professional managers and experts in Red China probably have a relatively high achievement drive. Most of them are relatively young and have gone through an educational system which vigorously stresses achievement at all levels. In the case of higher technical graduates, in particular, they have had to carry heavy study and course loads which are rather difficult and which tend to require considerable energy, hard work, and drive. It is also likely that many of the Red managers and party cadres also have a relatively high achievement drive. This includes many of the older ones who have undergone very intensive ideological and character training, even where their formal education has been sparse. Moreover, many of the older managers are long-time party members or ex-army officers who probably had a high achievement drive before 1949.

From my very limited and rather superficial observations of human behavior in Chinese industry, I am inclined to conclude that, if anything, the actual achievement drive of industrial personnel, in general, is higher than that suggested by the available achievement-drive score derived from Red Chinese readers of the 1950's. I would also speculate that the average achievement drive of Chinese managerial personnel—including Reds and Experts—under normal conditions, is somewhat higher than that for workers. However, it is quite possible that the gap between the achievement drive for workers, as a total group, and that of managers is not as great as in many other countries. This is because Chinese workers seem to have a fairly high achievement drive, as well as many opportunities to allow this drive to express itself.

I am by no means implying that the achievement drive among Chinese industrial personnel in general, or among Chinese managers, is the highest in the world. The Communist Revolution in China is still a relatively recent phenomenon; traditional values, attitudes, and motivational patterns that are not compatible with high achievement drive have certainly not been completely eliminated, even among the urban industrial population. There are still a number of countries which rank higher than China in actual achievement drive among the working population, although this number has declined very sharply since 1949 and may well continue to decline in the future. The achievement drive among Chinese industrial personnel is, however, probably significantly higher than in most other underdeveloped and developing countries. And there is also probably a significantly more favorable attitude toward productive work associated with industry and business in China.

Some interesting and suggestive comparisons can be made between Red China and India regarding the achievement drive. The difference between the scores derived from McClelland's study of children's readers used in these two countries during the 1950's is not significant. However, the Indian score, rather surprisingly to me, is slightly higher than the Chinese score.[55] There can be little doubt that the achievement drive of the Indian population in general, and of Indian industrial personnel in particular, has risen quite substantially in recent decades. However, from my own findings, impressions, and observations in Indian and Chinese industries, I feel strongly that the actual achievement drive is significantly higher among Chinese personnel in general, and at least somewhat higher among Chinese managers.

McClelland's study of Indian children's readers does not include a qualitative analysis of the stories. From what I know—which is not very much—about Indian elementary schoolbooks and other Indian literature I doubt if the concern with task-oriented achievement is as strong as in Chinese stories, or that it is likely that the Indians can identify with such stories as strongly as the Chinese. In many Indian children's books there is still considerable stress on non-Indian heroes, who are often famous people of the Western world. There is also a substantially higher illiteracy rate in general and among industrial personnel in India, and there is not much in the way of spare-time adult education. Traditional child-rearing practices and parental-behavior patterns also seem to persist on a more extensive and intensive scale in India than in China. Furthermore, it appears that traditional religious and cultural values still play a more pervasive and important—although declining—role in the behavior and working lives of Indians, including industrial personnel. Elements of orthodox Hinduism, which explicitly teaches that concern with earthly achievements is a snare and a delusion, still affect numerous Indians, as do various Gandhian-type values which are not very compatible with a positive view of task-oriented achievement or productive work associated with industry.

India lacks a practical ideology of the Chinese type which transmits, in standardized language, concern with achievement on a continual basis to the working population; and there is also no monolithic and effective political organization like the Chinese Communist Party which constantly stresses achievement and productive work at the grass-roots level of society. Moreover, nationalism as a force in increasing the achievement drive has not been nearly as strong in India as in China, and not as much progress has been made in overcoming apathy, pessimism, low ceilings on aspiration levels, low self-images, insecurity, lack of confidence, squalor, or mass poverty in India. Opportunities for upward mobility and career advancement seem to be substantially more limited in Indian industry than in Chinese industry, and this is due in part to the class structure and the rate of industrial expansion. Such a lack of opportunities tends to constrain the achievement drive on a widespread scale.

Finally, it seems to me that, judging them on the basis of their behavior patterns, India's political leaders since 1947 have not been as genuinely interested in or concerned about economic achievement as Red China's leaders, apart from the intervals when ideology has been carried to extremes in China. Red China's leaders, as a group, seem to have a significantly higher achievement drive and entrepreneurial spirit than India's leaders.

On the microbehavioral level, Chinese industrial enterprises seem to hum with more activity aimed at greater accomplishment than Indian firms. This shows itself in a number of ways. One typically finds considerably more concern with self-development, education, and training and in generally improving skills and performance among personnel of all types in Chinese industry. There also appears to be more persistence in overcoming obstacles and solving problems, as well as more extensive innovational activities of many diverse types, and a greater acceptance of and interest in change beneficial to productive efficiency. Chinese managers typically seem to desire fairly challenging—but realistic—enterprise plans, targets, and tasks, and several of them told me that they often ask for, or commit their firms to, higher targets than those assigned by superior authorities. It is possible, of course, that some of them lied to me or exaggerated in this connection, but I am inclined to believe that they often respond well to challenging plans and gain considerable satisfaction in trying to fulfill them.

Under the Soviet system of tight plans, pressure, and bonuses, the level of aspiration and the achievement drive of managers—and workers—have undoubtedly been raised and spurred on rather effectively, perhaps even more so than under the more relaxed Chinese system. I was generally more impressed with how the Chinese, as compared with the Indian managers whom I interviewed, went about searching out alternatives in order to overcome obstacles, such as supply bottlenecks, technical problems, the development of new products, reorganization of activities, quality control, material wastage maintenance, and so forth. Even though the Chinese managers typically had less education or knowledge about management than their Indian counterparts, they seemed to be generally more action-oriented, pragmatic, and persistent in tackling problems and improving operations. This is not to say that I did not come across Indian managers —or workers—who appeared to have a relatively high achievement drive. I did encounter several of this type, although most of them were from subcultural groups, such as the Marwaris and Parsees, who have a greater flair for entrepreneurship and are more achievement-oriented. A number of Indian Christian, Hindu, and Moslem managers also seemed to be relatively high in need for achievement, although most of those of this type that I met were Western-trained and employed by American and British subsidiary companies in India.

On the average, and in general, Chinese managers do seem to reflect a higher achievement drive in their observable behavior patterns than do their Indian counterparts. On the other hand, I would subjectively rate Soviet and American managers somewhat higher in the possession of this drive than Chinese industrial managers. I would rate Chinese workers, however, about as high in the positive attitude toward work as the workers in Russia and the United States.[56]

Class Structure and Individual Mobility

The class or social structure and the degree of individual mobility in a particular country bear most heavily and directly on the staffing function of management. The ideal staffing situation, in terms of managerial effectiveness and industrial progress, would be one in which industrial jobs are filled by individuals who, on the basis of objective evaluation, seem to have the knowledge, skill, abilities, and motivation necessary to do the job well. Each individual would be selected or promoted on the basis of merit, with little or no weight given to his general class standing, age, religion, sex, and so on. For such a staffing philosophy to be adhered to extensively in industry—leaving aside the difficult problems involved in accurately appraising the abilities of job candidates in terms of job requirements, which is basically a knowledge or educational problem—it would be necessary for society at large to generally support or at least to accept it. There is obviously no society in the real world where this ideal situation exists to a truly high degree; however, the degree and extent of social discrimination in staffing that does exist in industry has varied historically and still varies enormously among countries.

Old China

Compared with most other underdeveloped or newly developing countries, China, even before 1949, had a stronger tradition of social mobility and personal freedom.[57] Nevertheless class structure and limited individual mobility still served as a significant constraint on managerial effectiveness and industrial progress. It is probably true that practically anyone able enough, and who could acquire enough capital, could set up a business or factory. Many Chinese citizens did possess enough basic ability and could scrape up enough capital to open up small retail shops, and, to a much lesser extent, small backyard or garage-type industrial establishments which typically employed no more than one or two dozen people. Few could afford to acquire enough education, or could obtain enough capital to establish or operate with even a modicum of efficiency a fairly complex industrial enterprise. The dominant attitude toward business and industrial managers also significantly constrained the flow of capital as well as the flow of well-educated and highly motivated persons into industrial pursuits.

The key positions in foreign-owned firms operating in old China were typically filled by foreigners, and this further restrained the development of a sizable pool of effective high-level Chinese industrial managers and first-rate technical personnel. Within indigenous Chinese firms, nepotism, family, and close personal ties, and amount of education—in a country where the vast majority of the population could afford little, if any, education—were typically the key factors in the staffing of the more responsible jobs. However, the social structure was probably generally not a very significant constraint over staffing at the worker level and low-ranking supervisory or foreman levels. But for the great majority of the working population the ceiling on upward career advancement—regardless of ability—

was a front-line supervisory job. This situation undoubtedly tended to restrict the aspiration level and dampen the achievement drive of much of the industrial work force. Yet, the fact that China has been a relatively homogeneous country in terms of race and religion—with the exception of its indigenous Moslem and converted Christian populations which were not acutely discriminated against—has probably resulted in a more flexible class structure than in many countries having more heterogeneous populations.

In old China there was probably a somewhat higher degree of individual mobility of the geographical type than in many other underdeveloped countries, although language problems were a constraint in China in numerous cases. Many people did, however, leave their native communities to seek out places with better opportunities, where they could earn more money, use their talents more fully, and/or learn new skills. However, there was a relatively low degree of horizontal mobility involving relocations from one enterprise to another. There was a pervasive philosophy of lifetime employment at one enterprise similar to that found in Japanese industry today. However, there was less job security in Chinese industry because of unstable economic conditions.

While it was not too uncommon for women to be employed as workers in industry, it was very rare for a woman to obtain a managerial or an important technical position. Because of the traditional role of women in family life, and the fact that few women went to school, it is not surprising that few women held responsible jobs. Moreover, the idea of having a woman in charge of a group of male industrial employees must have seemed extremely radical in old China.

Red China

When the Chinese Communists came to power in 1949, their ultimate social aim was to abolish all classes and significant class distinctions so that a utopian society based on virtually complete equality would eventually evolve. The way they have pursued this ideology since 1949, and the manner in which this ideology when carried too far too fast conflicts with managerial, technical, and economic rationality, is a major theme of this book. Our primary concern in this section is with the impact of class structure and individual mobility on industrial staffing in contemporary China.

With the establishment of a Communist regime in China the traditional patterns of nepotism, family, and close personal friendships as the central factors in staffing decisions were, of course, essentially abolished. The major authority in industrial staffing became the party committees at the various levels of the economy. As a Chinese citizen moves up the managerial hierarchy, party approval becomes increasingly important, and at the top organizational levels party membership is almost always a requirement for promotion. To become a party member requires much more than mere loyalty to the regime. It requires zealous activist work on party-sponsored activities and participation in intensive indoctrination and political sessions. In Communist China there are two basic paths up the industrial hierarchy: the path of Redness and the path of Expertness. Under normal conditions, unless a Chinese enterprise employee is judged to be either one or the other or both, he generally has little chance of obtaining an important managerial or technical post. He must be at least very Red to become the top director of an industrial enterprise; if he is also relatively Expert, so much the better. And it is generally much easier and much more common to be judged very Red in Red China if one is of worker or peasant, but not rich peasant, origin. This is somewhat paradoxical because most of China's top leaders since 1949 have not been from these humble classes.

This policy of having Reds as directors of Chinese enterprises has proved rather effective for industrial progress, except during the periods when the Experts have been grossly misutilized. It has been the Communist Party or the Reds who have played the key role in organizing and motivating industrial personnel on a national scale and within industrial firms to identify with the need for, and to strive for, greater productive efficiency and industrial progress. Hence, enterprise management, including the Experts, has much of its job already done at the outset, in terms of motivating personnel to work hard and more efficiently. The fact that the great majority of the Reds are from humble families—as are most workers—has probably increased their leadership effectiveness with the masses or workers. It has undoubtedly made for a large core of well-motivated and dedicated Reds who identify closely with the revolution and, indeed, truly feel it is their revolution. However, Red directors are likely to lack some of the expertise required for effectively coordinating the work of the Expert-type managers under them.

Moreover, the great emphasis on Redness has undoubtedly eliminated many able and well-motivated individuals from obtaining key managerial posts. However, the resulting negative impact on managerial effectiveness and industrial progress—with the exception of the Great Leap period and perhaps again in late 1966 to 1968—has probably not been very substantial on a national scale. In fact, as long as the Experts have been utilized effectively, this staffing policy has probably been, on the whole, rather effective. Considerable use has even been made of the talents and knowledge of the Chinese capitalists who have stayed on as managers of their nationalized enterprises. However, the need for greater Expertness in top management will inevitably become more crucial in the future. Moreover, inefficient staffing decisions are probably made because the party committees or Reds do not always possess adequate knowledge for selecting candidates for Expert-type managerial jobs.

For a Chinese citizen to follow the "Expert" path up the industrial hierarchy, an important requirement is education and training. It is true that during periods when ideology, anti-intellectualism, and downgrading of Experts have been carried to extremes the Experts have been grossly misutilized, and large numbers of poorly educated and ill-suited workers have been hastily promoted to important managerial and technical jobs. However, in more normal periods there has been considerable emphasis on the link between education plus training and Expertness. Moreover, education, training, and consequent career advancement at all levels in industry have been open to probably the large majority of qualified candidates, regardless of their social backgrounds. Where there have been social prejudices in admissions to educational institutions and in promotions, the victims have typically been persons from bourgeois and wealthy families—landlord, capitalist, rich peasant, and, to a lesser degree, white-collar.

If, for instance, the choice for an important managerial job is between a person from a peasant or worker family and an individual from a bourgeois or wealthy family, and there is not a really sharp difference in their abilities, the job would surely go to the former. Such discrimination has certainly constrained managerial effectiveness and industrial progress in many instances; but it should be remembered that the vast majority of Chinese citizens are from families of the working class or from either poor or moderately prosperous peasant class. By providing them with free access to education and training, and with numerous opportunities for career advancement, this has undoubtedly done much to raise the aspiration level and achievement drive of much of the Chinese population. At the same time, the proportion of Chinese citizens from families of the former "privileged" classes is not very large, and given the critical shortage of high-talent manpower, the regime has sought to utilize such citizens in important managerial posts of the Expert type.

Class Origin of Key Enterprise Personnel

It may be both interesting and suggestive to examine the data on the social backgrounds of key enterprise personnel which I obtained during my survey of Chinese industry in 1966. Table 4–1 contains data on the class origin of thirty enterprise directors and twenty-nine party secretaries. By class origin, we mean the social standing of the respondent's father. Capitalists who are still managing their nationalized enterprises are not included in this table or in the other tables presented in this chapter.

We see from Table 4–1 that the large majority of directors and party secretaries are from nonbourgeois worker families and poor- and middle-peasant families. The party secretaries as a group have even "purer" backgrounds than the directors. Among all of the party secretaries, only one of them comes from a somewhat bourgeois family—his father was an office manager for a business firm. All of the five directors

TABLE 4–1

CLASS ORIGINS OF ENTERPRISE DIRECTORS AND PARTY SECRETARIES

	Total	*Worker*	*Poor Peasant*	*Middle Peasant*	*Rich Peasant*	*Hired Manager, Admin. Staff or Technical Personnel*	*Capitalist*	*Land-lord*
Number of directors	30	12	10	3	0	2	2	1
Percent of total	100%	40%	33%	10%	0%	7%	7%	3%
Number of party secretaries	29	9	13	6	0	1	0	0
Percent of total	100%	31%	45%	21%	0%	3%	0%	0%

from bourgeois families were party members of long standing. One is the son of a salaried manager, one of a technician, one of a landlord, and two are the sons of capitalists who have been dead for many years.

The thirty-eight-year-old director of the Wusih Silk Factory No. 2 is the son of an antique dealer who died in 1937. Before becoming director of the enterprise three years ago, he was a party worker elsewhere. He is a senior high school graduate who joined the party before 1949. The thirty-nine-year-old director of the Wusih Diesel Engine Firm is the son of a landlord, whose property was confiscated when the Communists came to power. When he was a university law student he was expelled for revolutionary activities. He joined the party in 1946, and has been director of the enterprise for nine years. Previously he had been a vice director of another firm.

It is interesting to note that of the three directors in the sample who are sons of capitalists or landlords, two of them work in Wusih. One of the enterprise vice directors whose father was a capitalist works for the Wusih Red Flag Machinery Plant. The only female enterprise party secretary whom I met in China also works in Wusih for the No. 2 Silk Factory. Perhaps the city of Wusih would be a very interesting place for a sociologist to study in depth.

Table 4–2 contains data on the class origins of other key enterprise managers, including vice directors, chief engineers, department heads, and workshop directors. Chief engineers, in most cases, are also vice directors, but not, of course, vice versa.

Table 4–2 indicates that a significantly higher proportion of this managerial group has bourgeois or "impure" types of family backgrounds, as compared with our sample of directors and party secretaries. While some

TABLE 4–2

CLASS ORIGINS OF OTHER KEY ENTERPRISE MANAGERIAL PERSONNEL

	Total	Worker	Poor Peasant	Middle Peasant	Rich Peasant	Hired Manager, Admin. Staff or Technical Personnel	Capitalist	Landlord
Vice-directors and chief engineers	26	13	2	3	1	5	2	0
Dept. heads	11	5	0	1	0	3	1	1
Workshop directors	8	3	2	1	1	1	0	0
Total number	45	21	4	5	2	9	3	1
Percent of total	100%	47%	9%	11%	4%	20%	7%	2%

of the managers in Table 4–2 were probably given their positions primarily because of their Redness, it is likely that the majority of them attained their jobs because of their Expertness, which is based substantially on their education, training, and/or experience. Middle and particularly poor peasant families in old China were the least likely to have been in a position to afford their sons a good education. And even after 1949 the value, backgrounds, and motivations among such families in numerous cases have continued to constrain their children from getting much formal education. It was somewhat more common for urban workers than the poorer peasants in old China to send their sons to school, and a larger proportion of the managers in Table 4–2 are from worker families than is the case with the directors and party secretaries in Table 4–1.

The data in Table 4–2 suggest that, regardless of class origin, Chinese industrial personnel have been able to move far up the industrial-enterprise hierarchy on the strength of ability, but in order to become an enterprise director or party secretary, Redness becomes crucial and more weight tends to be placed on "pure" proletarian and peasant background. The fact that the Red Chinese regime has made many concessions—ideological as well as economic—in order to utilize the talents of Chinese capitalists lends further weight to this tentative conclusion.

Class Origin of Students

Since formal education is frequently an important criterion in promoting personnel to positions requiring greater expertness in Chinese industry, it would be useful to examine some available educational statistics. Table 4–3 indicates the proportions of students of worker and peasant origin enrolled in higher, technical secondary, and regular high schools for selected years since 1951.[58]

TABLE 4–3

STUDENTS OF WORKER AND PEASANT ORIGIN AS A PERCENT OF TOTAL ENROLLMENT

	Higher Education	*Technical Secondary Schools*	*Regular Senior High Schools*
1951–52	19%	57%	51%
1955–56	29	62	62
1958–59	48	77	75
1962–63	67	not available	not available

From this table we see a steady upward trend in the proportion of students of worker and peasant origin enrolled in all three types of education. There are no pre-1949 figures of this type available, but students of this origin no doubt constituted a much smaller proportion of total enrollment than they did by 1951 and 1952. I was told at Tsinghua Polytechnical University that a majority of its graduates have been from worker and peasant families in recent years, while prior to 1949 the proportion of such graduates was negligible. Seventy percent of the students of this university and 75 percent at China People's University received financial aid. I was told that a large majority of its students were of worker and peasant origin. In general, when ideology has been pushed to extremes, however, thousands of ill-suited and unqualified students from worker and peasant families have been enrolled in higher and secondary schools. For example, in 1958–59 there were only 242,000 senior high school graduates, but 270,000 new students entered higher educational institutions.[59] While there has been some discrimination involving the admission of "bourgeois elements" in higher education, as well as a misutilization of resources resulting from the admission of unqualified students on ideological grounds, formal education at all levels in Red China has probably been accessible, and will remain so, to the large majority of those persons who have the required intellectual ability.

Age as a Factor in Upward Mobility

There is some evidence that a Chinese citizen can move quite rapidly up the enterprise managerial hierarchy through either the Expert or Red path. Many enterprise personnel are promoted to important positions at a fairly young age, and seniority does not seem to be a significant constraint on managerial effectiveness in Chinese industry. Table 4–4 contains data on the ages of key personnel which I obtained from the enterprises surveyed in 1966. Table 4–5 indicates the length of time that a sample of key enterprise managerial personnel had been in their jobs, as of 1966.

TABLE 4–4

AGES OF KEY ENTERPRISE MANAGERIAL PERSONNEL

	Total	*Under 30*	*30–34*	*35–39*	*40–44*	*45–49*	*50–54*	*50 and over*
Directors	24	0	2	4	12	4	2	0
Party secretaries	22	0	1	3	9	7	1	1
Vice-directors, chief engineers	31	3	2	4	11	6	2	3
Department heads	14	2	3	3	3	2	0	1
Workshop directors	7	2	1	2	1	1	0	0

TABLE 4–5

LENGTH OF TIME KEY ENTERPRISE MANAGERIAL PERSONNEL HAD BEEN IN PRESENT JOB AS OF 1966

	Total	*Less than 1 year*	*Under 4 years*	*4–7 years*	*8–10 years*	*Over 10 years*
Directors	22	0	3	12	6	1
Party secretaries	21	1	3	11	4	2
Vice-directors, chief engineers	18	2	3	5	4	4
Department heads	10	1	2	2	3	2
Workshop directors	5		1	2	0	0

The data in Tables 4–4 and 4–5 indicate that the typical director in my limited sample was in his early forties in 1966, and obtained his post as director when he was in his mid- or late thirties. The typical party secretary was a few years older—in his mid-forties—than the typical director in 1966, but he also obtained his job as party secretary when he was in his mid- or late thirties. Most of the directors and party secretaries had been party members for at least ten years. Hence it seems that dedicated Reds in Chinese industry can obtain top-level enterprise positions at a relatively young age, as compared with the ages of people appointed to top enterprise-management jobs in many other countries. However, it should be noted that the average life expectancy is still somewhere around forty-four to fifty years in China, as compared with over sixty or sixty-five years in advanced countries. Moreover, the official retirement age for male industrial personnel in China is sixty years, for female white-collar staff fifty-five, and female physical workers fifty. In spite of these qualifications, it still seems that seniority or age is not a significant constraint in staffing decisions in Chinese industry.

The data also suggest that many relatively young people were appointed to top management posts at enterprises particularly during the Great Leap period. The youngest director whom I met was at the Shanghai No. 3 Machine Tool Factory. He was thirty-three years old, and had become director when he had just turned twenty-seven in 1959. Previously he had been director of a smaller enterprise since the age of twenty-four. At twenty-one he became shop chief at this other enterprise. He joined that firm immediately after he was graduated from primary school, but while working he was graduated from a spare-time junior middle school. He became a party member when he was only twenty. His father, who was a factory worker, died when he was very young, but his mother was a party member of long standing and an ardent and active supporter of the revolution. As a worker, this director was constantly chosen as a leading or "five-good" worker.

Among the vice directors and chief engineers there are somewhat higher proportions of young ones under thirty-five and older ones over fifty than is the case with the directors and party secretaries. It seems that those over fifty are typically Experts who have acquired their expertness primarily through long experience at their enterprises. Most of them in this category are employed by relatively old consumer-goods firms. For example, the vice director and chief engineer of the Shanghai No. 19 Cotton Textile Mill was fifty-seven in 1966. He had been in his job for eight years, but had been employed by the factory for twenty years. He joined the enterprise as a worker after he finished junior middle school. After 1949 he graduated from a spare-time senior high school and was promoted to workshop director. He was not, however, a party member as of 1966. Another vice director of the same cotton textile firm, who has the labor and wages, supply, and sales departments under his authority, was thirty-nine years old in 1966. He had held his present job since 1960, but had been employed by the enterprise for twenty-one years. He joined as a worker and graduated from a spare-time junior middle school in the 1950's. By 1959 he had become head of the production planning department, and shortly thereafter vice director. He became a party member around 1958. One of the vice directors—in charge of technical operations—at the Shanghai Battery plant had held this job for ten years, and had been employed by the plant for over twenty years.

Many of the vice directors in the thirty-five-to-fifty age bracket seem to have been given their high-level jobs primarily because of their Redness rather than because of their expertness, experience, or formal education. However, few of them were directly involved very much with technical operations. Typical departments under the authority of this type of vice director included welfare, labor and wages, and commercial affairs.

Most of the young group—under thirty-five—of vice directors and chief engineers were Experts largely through their formal education, and a few of them were also party members. For example, the vice director who is also in charge of the technical department at the Shanghai No. 3 Machine-Tool Enterprise was only twenty-seven in 1966. He obtained his job in 1965, after serving first as a technician and then as head of the technical department since 1963. He came to the enterprise about one year after he graduated from a higher technical school. He was employed for one year as a worker at another factory after his graduation. He is from a worker family, and he became a party member in 1964.

It is more difficult to generalize about middle-level enterprise managers—department heads and workshop directors—since our sample here is even more limited than that for our higher-level managers. The middle-level managers as a group—and particularly the workshop directors—are younger than the higher-level executives, and this is to be expected since higher-level managers are frequently promoted from the levels of department head and workshop director. Among the middle-level managers there is a higher proportion of Experts than among the higher executives. Several of those over forty who are employed in light industry—particularly textile and clothing firms—have been with their enterprises since before the revolution, and have acquired their expertness through long experience. Of the under-thirty-five group, the majority of them have acquired much of their expertness through formal education.

A few of the middle-level managers whom I met are both Red and Expert. For example, the head of the design department of the Shanghai Heavy Machine Tool Enterprise is such a person. He represents the ideal Red Chinese Horatio Alger type, which is not too uncommon in Chinese industry. He became head of the design department at this large and important enterprise in 1964, at the age of thirty-six. He may well become a vice director in the near future. The son of quite poor, illiterate peasants, he joined the firm in 1946 at the age of eighteen as a cleaner, with only about five years of formal schooling. At that time the firm was producing small agricultural implements under Kuomintang and American ownership. Over a seventeen-year period he managed to improve himself through the spare-time educational system and to graduate from a higher technical school. He joined the party in 1955. As he progressed with his spare-time education, he was promoted first to semiskilled, then to skilled jobs, and then in succession he became a technician, designer, chief designer, engineer, and finally head of the design department.

Last Job Held by Key Enterprise Executives

There are some interesting data which indicate the jobs held by enterprise directors and party secretaries immediately before they obtained their top executive posts, as shown in Tables 4–6 and 4–7.

TABLE 4–6

LAST JOB HELD BY ENTERPRISE DIRECTORS BEFORE OBTAINING PRESENT POSITION

	Total	*Dir. Else-where*	*Party Sec.*	*Vice Dir.*	*Dept. Head*	*Work-shop Dir.*	*Worker*	*Mili-tary*	*Other**
Directors	21	2	4	5	1	2	1	4	2

* One was a vice party secretary and the other a department head of a municipal industrial bureau.

Of those two enterprise directors who were previously directors of other firms, they claimed that the other firms were smaller. None of them who were previously party secretaries held this job at the same enterprise. All but one who was a vice director held this position at the same enterprise. The one who was promoted directly from the workers' ranks was a director of a small plant. However, about half of the directors in this sample had started their industrial careers as production workers. Three of the four directors who came directly from the military were employed by relatively large heavy-industry enterprises. Several of the other directors interviewed mentioned that they had been army officers sometime in the past, and some of the older ones held such posts prior to 1949.

A majority of the enterprise party secretaries were party cadres immediately before they obtained their present jobs. Only two held enterprise-director or vice-director positions, and none were middle-level managers. The two who were previously workers were employed at smaller enterprises. About 35 or 40 percent of them, somewhat less than the proportion of directors, had been employed as full-time production workers in the past. Like the directors, all but one party secretary who came directly from the army were employed by relatively large heavy-industry firms. Even more of them mentioned that they had been military officers sometime in the past.

TABLE 4-7

LAST JOB HELD BY ENTERPRISE PARTY SECRETARIES BEFORE OBTAINING PRESENT POSITION

	Total	*Enterprise Party Sec. Elsewhere*	*Enterprise Vice- or Shop-Party Sec.*	*Vice Dir.*	*Dept. Head or Workshop Dir.*	*Dir.*	*Worker*	*Military*	*Other**
Party secretaries	22	1	8	1	0	4	2	4	4

* Two were party cadres at higher-level government organizations, one was an enterprise trade union committee chairman, and one was a party cadre on a commune.

Women in Industry and Management

There has been a very sharp rise in the employment of women in industry, and of female enrollment—absolute and proportionate—in education at all levels in China since 1949. However, China still lags significantly behind the Soviet Union in both spheres, and may still lag behind the United States in the proportion of female enrollment in higher education.[60]

Before 1949 there were relatively few women enrolled in Chinese higher education, and even a small proportion of high school graduates were women. During the 1951–59 period female enrollment in higher education increased steadily from 35,000 to 180,000. In 1946 there were only 28,000 female students in Chinese higher education, and only 81,000 in secondary vocational schools of all types. By the 1956–57 academic year female students comprised 25 percent of the total higher educational enrollment. Since 1949 a growing number and proportion of students and graduates in engineering and scientific fields have been women. During the 1949–65 period about 20 percent of all graduates from China's leading polytechnical university, Tsinghua, were women.

However, the Soviet Union still leads substantially in the educational achievement of its female population. In the U.S.S.R. in the 1960–61 period, 43 percent of all students, numbering over one million, enrolled in higher education were women. In 1960 in the Soviet Union there were over 129,000 women engaged in scientific research, 30,000 of them having the equivalent of doctoral or master's degrees, and 700 the title of professor. In Communist China in 1963 there were fewer than 200 females having the equivalent of a Ph.D. and not many more having the equivalent of a master's degree.

Nevertheless, the emancipation of Chinese women under the Communist regime has led to a very sharp rise in the educational level of the female population. This has also been accompanied by a sharp increase in female industrial and urban employment, as well as in the number of women filling important jobs. During the 1949–60 period, women workers and employees in the Chinese economy—excluding most rural agricultural workers—increased from 600,000 to 8,000,000. In 1949 females constituted only 7.5 percent of workers and employees, and by 1959 their proportion had increased to 15.4 percent. By 1963, when 48 percent of China's total population was female, about 25 percent of all personnel working in industry, commerce, education, and culture in China's major cities were women.

In 1962 Shanghai industry employed nearly 1,000 female engineers and technicians, and more than 500 important managerial posts were reported to be held by women. Prior to 1949 there were virtually no women managers or technicians in Anshan, China's leading steel and heavy-industry center. In 1962 there were more than 600 female managers, engineers, technicians, and designers employed in Anshan's heavy industry, all of them post-1949 graduates.

However, China still lags significantly behind the Soviet Union in female industrial employment and in the employment of women in managerial and technical jobs. This gap is due, in part, to the fact that women have outnumbered men in Russia for several decades because of the great loss of male lives in World War II. It is also due to cultural and time factors which have prevented Chinese women from becoming emancipated as extensively as Russian women. In 1958, in the Soviet Union nearly half of all industrial enterprise personnel were women. In 1963, 31 percent of all professional engineers, and 61 percent of all professional economists, including business administration specialists, with higher education in the U.S.S.R. were women. The 1963 proportions for female semiprofessional technicians and economists were even greater. Women constituted 45 percent of all managers and staff specialists at Soviet industrial enterprises in the late 1950's, but only 12 percent of the top management positions at Soviet enterprises of all types were held by women. This suggests that there may be some discrimination against women regarding top-level management jobs in Russia, but the 12 percent figure can be attributed, at least in part, to a desire among many married women for less responsible positions which are more convenient and compatible with family obligations.

Table 4–8 indicates the proportion of female personnel in relation to total employment at thirty-five Chinese industrial enterprises that I surveyed in 1966.

This table indicates that for about half the enterprises the proportion of female personnel falls in the 10 to 39 percent range, with the largest num-

TABLE 4–8

PROPORTION OF FEMALE PERSONNEL AT 35 CHINESE INDUSTRIAL ENTERPRISES

Female Employees as a Percent of Total Employment

	TOTAL	UNDER 10%	10–19%	20–29%	30–39%	40–49%	50–59%	60% AND OVER
Number of Enterprises	35	1	4	10	4	4	4	8

ber of firms falling in the 20 to 29 percent range. These thirty-five enterprises employed a total of approximately 145,000 in 1966, and I would estimate that female employment was about 25 to 30 percent of this total. However, there are some distinct branches of industry variations and patterns. All of the firms where the proportion of female personnel exceeded 59 percent were either cotton, wool, silk, or clothing factories. In fact, of all such enterprises surveyed, only the Peking Clothing Firm had women as less than 60 percent of its employees, and even here the proportion was 50 percent. Only one firm surveyed had more than 70 percent female employees; this was Wusih Silk with 90 percent. Those enterprises where women constituted less than 20 percent of their total employment were three machinery plants, and Shanghai Steel (with only 8 percent).

In general, the heavy-industry enterprises typically employ a smaller proportion of women than do the light-industry firms. One is also more likely to come across female managers and technicians in light-industry firms. However, I did not encounter many high-level female managers. This might suggest that sociological-cultural values pertaining to the roles of the sexes still serve as significant constraints in the promotion of women to high-level posts, which are accompanied by considerable authority over male subordinates. While I noted two female directors and two women chief engineers at sixteen industrial enterprises—three of them in light industry—in the Soviet Union, I did not come across any in Chinese industry. I did, however, observe that there were two enterprise party secretaries in Chinese industry; one worked for Wusih Silk and the other for another textile enterprise. The party secretary at Wusih Silk was thirty-eight years old, and had just obtained this position in 1966. She was previously the party secretary at a local cotton-textile plant. She is the daughter of poor peasants, a primary school graduate, and she was attending a part-time junior middle school.

I was introduced to six or seven female vice directors—out of a total of about eighty or ninety—in Chinese industry, and only one of them was employed by a heavy-industry plant. Three or four of them were employed at textile and clothing enterprises, and two of them at the pharmaceutical firms. About half of these women seemed to be primarily Red, and the other half primarily Experts. For example, the female vice director at Peking Pharmaceutical was a medical school graduate who was in charge of the technical and production-planning departments. The female vice director in charge of the welfare and general-administration departments at Shanghai Pharmaceuticals seemed to be a Red who had just enrolled in a spare-time senior-middle school.

Roughly 15 percent of the department heads and 10 percent of the workshop directors whom I encountered in Chinese industry were female. And again most of these women managers were employed by consumer-goods producers. In general, the proportion of female lower-level managers, particularly floor foremen or group leaders, was substantially higher than higher-level female managers. In some light-industry firms 50 percent or more of the lower-level managers were female, and in a few cases the vast majority of the group leaders were women.

In general, there seem to be ample opportunities for female employees to become lower-level managers in Chinese industry, and fairly numerous opportunities to make it to the middle-management level. As a female approaches the top ranges of the executive hierarchy, however, there seem to be substantially fewer opportunities for promotion.

Horizontal Mobility

There is very little freedom to change jobs in Red China. If a manager, technician, or worker at a particular Chinese enterprise wants to obtain a job at another firm he must not only obtain permission from the top manager and party committee of his enterprise but also from an appropriate superior authority above his enterprise. In this connection there is much less personal freedom for lower-level supervisors and workers than in Soviet industry where they are free to relocate after giving fairly short advance notice.

However, this does not mean that there is little horizontal mobility involving the transfer of personnel among different organizations in Chinese industry. In fact, there is a fairly high degree of mobility, primarily at the lower-managerial and worker levels. But the shifting is done through state plans and administrative allocation of personnel, rather than through free choice. The aim of transferring personnel in Red Chinese industry is usually basically similar to that in a market economy: to get a good fit between the talents and skills of a specific employee and the requirements of the job he is selected for. In a less developed country, where there is a crucial shortage of skilled and high talent manpower, state planning and administrative allocation may often be more effective in terms of industrial progress than a market-price system of manpower allocation. However, the former is likely to place much greater restrictions on personal freedom—particularly for skilled persons who can easily get several jobs if they are free to do so.

No doubt, many Chinese citizens have not been happy in their assignment to particular jobs, firms, cities, or regions of the country. Coercion and at times extreme pressure, or even penalties, have been resorted to in order to make people relocate. This has undoubtedly caused considerable resentment, frustration, and low-productive efficiency in many cases. In the large majority of cases, however, the people have no doubt been willing to accept without ill-will the jobs assigned to them in industry in order to serve their country. The segment of the population—and this is a very large segment—which has probably been the most unhappy because of the strongest restrictions on its mobility is the group comprising the rural unskilled people, who are eager to come to the urban areas to find more prestigious work in industry at higher wages. However, the lack of such restrictions would surely result in a great deal of urban unemployment. Probably most of the people permitted to work in industry are happy about the opportunity, and do not mind being subservient to higher authorities in their job assignments.

It is common to find a fairly large cross section of people from other Chinese provinces and regions working at all levels in industrial enterprises in major Chinese cities. Although this is a very superficial judgment on my part, I did not sense any acute hostility among employees from different parts of the country. With the great stress that the regime has placed on nationalism and the integration of people from all parts of China—including national minority groups—into cohesive work groups, discrimination of this type is probably not a serious problem at most organizations. For example, some of the Shanghai factories that I visited had many Chinese Moslem employees. Some of them held important positions. Special eating facilities are provided for Moslem employees because of their dietary traditions (they do not eat pork or ham).

India versus China

It seems that class structure and individual mobility are substantially more of a constraint on managerial effectiveness and industrial progress in India than in China.[61] Empirical studies, including my own research, indicate that the unique caste system in India still tends to play a significant, albeit gradually declining, role in shaping the occupational structure and hierarchy in the Indian economy, but apparently this role is less important in the cities than in the rural areas. One recent source sums up the nature and consequences of this situation thus:

> The recruitment policy pursued within the private sector of the economy is said to follow caste lines especially as far as the higher and middle administrative positions are concerned. Thus personnel belonging to the

> same caste or region as the founder of the concern may be "imported" from places hundreds of miles away from the seat of the company. Employment policies may thus degenerate into a form of caste and kinship charity which is liable to cause serious undercurrents of resentment among those aspirants who do not belong to the "right caste," quite apart from the fact that positions are not filled by the most competent persons available.[62]

Because a high degree of regional or provincial chauvinism exists in many parts of India, this also leads to inefficient staffing decisions in many cases, since people from the same area are often selected primarily because of their place of origin. Language differences contribute to regional chauvinism, however, and, in some cases, choosing a person for a key job because he speaks the same language may not be a decision that would cause inefficiency. I also found more color discrimination—between relatively light- and dark-skinned Indians—in India than I had expected, although this type of prejudice seems to be more subtle and significantly less acute than in the United States.

Nepotism is, of course, still a very important element in the staffing of managerial posts and often other positions in private firms, and this often constrains managerial effectiveness and industrial progress, particularly where kinship members have a relatively low achievement drive and/or inadequate education and training to carry out their jobs efficiently. Friendship ties, favoritism, business or government connections, and religion often tend to be important criteria used in staffing important positions in industry. As one prominent Indian management specialist points out: "Heredity, status, nepotism, and favoritism play an uncomfortably large part in the selection and employment of management personnel, and the system of recruitment on the basis of potential ability, competence, and skill has not yet taken firm root." [63] The proportion of women employed in Indian industry is substantially less than in China, and one seldom comes across an Indian woman in an executive or important technical position.

I found that the class structure was not as significant a negative constraint on efficient staffing in some of the public firms and large progressive private firms—particularly American and British subsidiary companies—as in typical private indigenous Indian enterprises. However, even in such public and progressive private firms, class structure and social discrimination in individual upward mobility seemed to constrain efficient staffing more than in typical enterprises in China, Russia, or the United States. Subtle prejudices were particularly noticeable in connection with high-level executive positions, and in the Indian public sector political connections and regional considerations seemed to be important factors in staffing.

Education is frequently an important factor in promotions up the managerial hierarchy in Indian industry, but type of education is generally not given nearly as much weight as amount of education. Nor are education and ability alone generally enough to help an aspirant make it to the upper echelons of the great majority of indigenous Indian firms—social background and connections tend to become very important at that level. While it is fairly common to find relatively young men in high-level managerial jobs in Indian industry, more often than not they seem to have obtained their positions largely because of "the right social background" and/or "proper connections"; if they also happen to have a background of "good" formal education, this is certainly an added plus factor.

It is true that the lack of job opportunities and large-scale unemployment in the Indian economy are major reasons why social factors of the types noted above tend to play a dominant role in staffing decisions, especially for important managerial jobs. Nevertheless, inefficient staffing practices on a widespread scale in India greatly hinder managerial effectiveness and industrial progress.

I had an interesting discussion with a senior official at the Red Chinese Embassy in New Delhi, when I went there to apply for my Chinese visa. The gist of his remarks regarding the Indian economy was that the class structure greatly hindered India's economic development. This was not really a surprising statement from a dedicated Chinese Communist who has been taught to think in terms of "class struggle." However, he supported his position with many perceptive comments, and on this subject I was inclined to concur with much that he had to say.

Attitude toward Wealth, Material Gain, and Self-Interest

Old China

In traditional China, until around the turn of the twentieth century, economic welfare was conceived not in terms of economic growth, spurred by savings, capital investment, and industrially created wealth, but in terms of bare subsistence, of satisfying the basic physiological needs of the masses. The principal function of the state was the maintenance of social peace and harmony. In this view, a commitment to the pursuit of wealth and power by the state would in no way differ from the behavior of an official who pursued his own selfish interest. Such values were embodied in the orthodox line of Confucianism.[64]

Hence, from about the fourteenth to twentieth century the state—that is, the emperors and ruling elites who were the embodiment of the state—emphasized maintenance rather than development through accumulated and reinvested productive wealth. Maintenance of a minimum subsistence for the peasantry, of a standard of living for the gentry that was comfortable but was characterized by frugality, maintenance of law and order and public works, and protection from barbarian incursions. The accent was on stability—political, social, economic—rather than on progress or growth.

During the Chinese Republican period of 1911–49 the government was obsessed by the problem of political control, and had insufficient appreciation of basic industrial development through the help of state saving and investment. In the 1930's the state became somewhat more concerned about economic development, but could do little since this was a decade of war and political crisis. Moreover, where the government did officially or unofficially provide capital to businessmen and industrialists, it was largely ignorant of its use. There was no effective government support during this period that would have made it possible for the business and industrial class to provide economic leadership.[65]

In old China, landed and inherited wealth was typically significantly more highly regarded than industrially created riches. Given this dominant attitude toward different types of wealth, the need for the state to finance costly military operations, and the economic and political instability that existed in the twentieth century, there was a general reluctance to invest in industrial ventures. Moreover, large-scale industrial ventures required capital outlays of a magnitude that often only foreign interests were able to provide. Such foreign interests were typically much more interested in reaping large profits than in increasing managerial effectiveness or spurring economic progress in China.

Traditionally, the typical indigenous Chinese businessman or industrialist preferred quick turnover on limited capital and quick profits in the short run. This dominant attitude toward wealth was due primarily to the great uncertainty of market conditions, political instability, and probably also to the fact that many, if not most, businessmen and industrialists had a relatively low achievement drive. Because of such prevalent environmental conditions, wealth was frequently viewed as something that is here today and may well be gone tomorrow. To invest rather heavily in industry was seen as a very perilous risk. Most entrepreneurially minded Chinese businessmen preferred small-scale operations. There was a general reluctance on the part of Chinese investors to capitalize industrial undertakings on a large scale. The inevitable result was that even most modern indigenous industries that existed were undercapitalized, with insufficient margins to meet competition and to weather periodic unfavorable market conditions.[66]

The large-scale indigenous industrial firms that did exist usually grew through mergers, amalgamations, and acquisitions, rather than through major internal expansions resulting from large plowbacks of profits.

In general, there was little individual saving and investment in old China, and, in fact, there was a strong tendency to dissolve and use up accumulated capital stocks.[67]

Material gain in conjunction with self-interest was probably a significant motivating force for the large majority of industrial personnel. However, money was typically viewed as something to spend while you had it; and, in the case of business owners and managers, to spend on luxury items, or if they were wealthy enough, to invest in land, property, and/or in relatively stable foreign countries. Incomes and profits from business and industry tended to be desired primarily for what they could buy outside of the firm and to raise one's social status, rather than as the fruits of productive achievement or success to be reinvested in order to substantially expand the enterprise. The traditional Confucian emphasis on frugality was not adhered to very ardently by the emerging, but still small, class of relatively wealthy Chinese businessmen, industrialists, and managers during the Republican period of the twentieth century.

There are many signs that the traditional dominant attitudes and behavior patterns regarding wealth, material gain, and self-interest found in Chinese industry prior to 1949 still exist on a fairly extensive scale in the Indian industrial sector. Red China seems to have gone further than India in developing attitudes toward wealth, material gain, and self-interest that are more conducive to industrial progress. However, when China has pushed ideology to extremes in connection with material gain and self-interest, serious economic problems have resulted.

Red China

Since the Communist takeover of China in 1949 there has been no new elite of wealth in that country because the basis of sustained wealth, namely private property, in effect no longer exists. It is true that there are still capitalists possessing varying degrees of wealth in Red China, but they cannot really be considered as an elite since they have very little real power, and not a great deal of prestige. Moreover, they are a transitory aberration in the Red Chinese social structure. The real elites in Communist China have been the Reds, and, except during short ideological intervals, the Experts. Their eliteness has been based on prestige and power rather than wealth.

In Communist China, industrially created wealth, which can be used to further expand industry and economic development, is most highly valued by the regime. The state is an ardent practitioner of the "Calvinist ethic" on a large scale because it stresses savings—much of it forced savings—and capital accumulation so that it can invest heavily in order to expand production substantially. At the same time, thrift and frugality have been extensively and intensively stressed at the individual level in Red China, through education, indoctrination, the press, entertainment, and other media.[68] The regime has also largely discouraged conspicuous consumption. Such policies have been utilized rather successfully to get the worker population to accept low wages and still work hard so that the state can accumulate large sums of capital for productive investment.

In general, the Chinese regime seems to have been more effective than the Indian government in pursuing a Calvinistic ethic with regard to saving, investment, and the creation and use of productive wealth for industrial progress. China also appears to have been more successful than India in instilling this type of ethic regarding wealth and material gain in its population at large.

The urban working population in particular has been, and is, constantly urged, and at times pressured, to deposit whatever savings they have managed to accumulate in the state-owned People's Bank so that they can be used for economic-development purposes.[69] It is estimated that around 1957 about 5 percent of urban wages were being deposited in savings accounts. In 1959 over 100,000 establishments, in addition to numerous rural credit cooperatives, were reported to be handling individual savings deposits. At times street committees, under party leadership, have acted as bank agents in savings matters.[70] In 1966, during my visit to China, slightly more than 3 percent interest was paid on one-year individual savings accounts. This was a bit less than the 1959 interest rate paid on such deposits.[71]

At the individual level the Communist Chinese regime has followed a kind of oscillation theory with regard to the use of material gain, particularly monetary incentive, as a motivating force.[72] Orthodox Communist theology points to altruism and other spiritual-type incentives, rather than self-interest and material gain, as being the only pure motivating forces in society; of course, the basic material necessities must be provided to the working population and their families, but nonmaterial incentives should be emphasized.

The Soviet regime has, however, accepted material gain and self-interest as key motivating forces for both managers and workers—not to mention party cadres—for several decades.[73] Indeed, the contemporary Soviet philosophy of monetary incentives is basically similar to the philosophy which has long prevailed in American industry. In both cases the basic aim of a given material-incentive scheme in use at a particular time is to harness the satisfaction of individual self-interest and goals to the attainment of formal organizational objectives. The Soviets claim that they still believe in the evolution of a utopian altruistic society where "to each according to his needs," rather than "from each according to his ability," is the basis for human motivation and behavior. They rationalize that although this utopian society is still a vision of the distant future, material incentives in conjunction with self-interest are an important means of contributing to its attainment, because such incentives can help bring about the society of great affluence and abundance that is seen as necessary if the rule "for each according to his needs" is to become a reality.

The Communist Chinese regime has apparently not yet given up their ideological aim of transforming the population into pure communist men —as interpreted by Mao and his apparently dwindling number of followers—simultaneously with the achievement of rapid and sustained industrial progress. They have not, however, been very successful in eliminating self-interest in the form of material gain as a key motivating force among the population, both urban and rural. They have had to make major compromises in their ideological stand on material incentives and self-interest because of unfavorable industrial performance and poor general economic results verging on extreme crises.

This does not mean, however, that nonmaterial incentives linked to social and psychic needs have not played a very important role in motivating industrial personnel of all types. On the contrary, nonmaterial incentives stressing the satisfaction of social and psychic needs have been used more effectively in China to motivate industrial personnel to work hard and more efficiently than in perhaps any other underdeveloped or developing country. Indeed, they have probably been as effective as material incentives in motivating the industrial work force. A developing country like India could perhaps learn quite a bit from China about the effective use of nonmaterial incentives for motivating its people. The various forms that social and psychic satisfaction take in China have already been discussed in the chapter on education and in the preceding sections of this chapter.

In spite of the effective use that has been made of nonmaterial incentives and appeals to altruism in Red China, the state has also had to rely quite heavily on material gain linked to self-interest as motivating forces for industrial progress and general economic development. The reliance on material incentives has been even more heavy in agriculture than in industry. The regime has not yet been able to solve the contradiction between material and nonmaterial incentives. The Maoists seem to feel that revisionism and softness toward true Communist ideology are likely to evolve on a substantial scale under conditions of economic progress and relative affluence. When unfavorable economic conditions emerge, pressing on the vulnerably low subsistence level of the masses, too great a dependence on nonmaterial incentives compounds the difficulties, and material incentives and self-interest must soon be reinstated. With the official restoration of material incentives, economic progress and relative affluence again evolve, and the regime again worries about "contradictions" between material and nonmaterial incentives, individual versus collective interests, and wages versus distribution according to need.

At a certain point on the oscillation pendulum, the orthodox Red Chinese leaders perceive an extreme polarization in their ideological revisionism and begin to panic. They may solve some of the perceived contradictions through various compromises by applying the "law of the unity of opposites," but if they panic enough, they are likely to try to eliminate the thorny contradiction almost in its entirety for the sake of ideology.

It is significant that substantial shifts in emphasis regarding material incentives involving self-interest versus nonmaterial incentives involving social mobilization, have coincided with major shifts in the authority of Reds versus Experts in industrial management. Only the Reds have been viewed as being able to organize, motivate, and lead mass movements that make nonmaterial incentives effective.

The 1950–57 Period

Not long after the Communists came to power in China, considerable emphasis began to be placed on material gain and self-interest as a key motivating force. No doubt the Chinese were influenced by prevailing Soviet practices involving material incentives in their economy. By the end of 1952 some 35 percent of all industrial workers were on piece-rate systems, which, of course, involved wage payments based on ability, skill, and productivity.[74] During the First Five-Year Plan period of 1952–57, the use of material incentives increased further. By 1956 about 42 percent of all industrial workers were paid according to piece rates, and bonus payments to industrial personnel of virtually all types, including managers, technicians, and party cadres became common throughout industry.[75] In fact, bonuses for managerial and technical personnel were apparently greater than for workers at that time. The major wage reform of 1956 provided even greater reward than before for skill and productivity.

By 1957 sizable wage differentials evolved among the workers, and between the different levels of the industrial hierarchy. Piece rates and other forms of material incentives were acknowledged as helping to increase productivity and reduce absenteeism during this period. However, by their very nature, and particularly in the case of piece-rate payments, the system led to substantial income differentials, especially unfavorable for those workers not on piece rates because of the nature of their work. While a serious and generally successful effort was made to provide for the basic minimum material needs of the industrial work force, the wage policy was based largely on the principle of ability and individual material rewards.

The Great Leap Forward

Then in 1957 the Great Leap Forward was conceived by Mao and other Chinese leaders. The emphasis on material incentives and self-interest had probably been polarized to such an extreme point in the minds of China's leaders that they felt only a fantastic ideological revolution could bring the working population back on the correct ideological track. Hence the Great Leap was based largely on a conviction that social mobilization could motivate men through organization much better than material incentives or self-interest. Men must be appealed to, not through material rewards, but through spiritual values linked to social and psychic satisfaction which can be transmitted through ideology.

By the end of 1957 the regime moved in the direction of a "rational low-wage" policy stressing social mobilization. Piece work was attacked as ideologically repugnant since it provoked in workers "mercenary and unsocialistic attitudes of mind." By 1958 there were many complaints that those on piece-rate wages were earning too much, and workers were reported to be "spontaneously and unanimously" urging an end to piece rates.[76] In 1958 bonuses for managers, party cadres, and other types of industrial personnel were abolished at numerous enterprises.

Widespread stress was placed on need rather than ability in wage payments. The orthodox leaders viewed wages as a whole as out-of-date, and numerous workers were paid by "distribution," particularly in construction and the new commune industries where large numbers of unskilled workers, mostly peasants, were employed. Distribution meant that each worker was supplied with a basic amount of goods and money necessary for maintaining himself and his family, with cash wages reduced to the function of pocket money.[77] The regime no doubt intended at that time to introduce this type of distribution payment policy throughout industry in the near future.

Where material incentives were still used in industry during the Great Leap, they usually took the form of collective rather than individual rewards. The dominant form of basic income payment in industry was wages based on time worked, and piece-rate wages were largely eliminated. Mass campaigns, emulation drives, worker participation in management, and more lavish awarding of titles such as "labor head" and "model worker" were some of the major forms that nonmaterial incentives took.

It cannot be concluded that social mobilization involving nonmaterial incentives was ineffective during the Great Leap period. Numerous, and perhaps even a majority, of the workers and Reds in particular still worked relatively hard during most of this period. However, it seems clear that the effectiveness of nonmaterial incentives did wear off during this period, and productivity would probably have been significantly greater if material gain and self-interest had not been de-emphasized to such a high degree. Red Chinese sources have admitted that toward the end of the Great Leap period there was a decline in productivity, enthusiasm, work discipline, and attendance at many firms. It was reported, for example, that a number of mine workers felt that no matter how much they worked it made no real difference, and so they gradually relaxed their efforts.[78]

It became evident to the regime by 1960 that nonmaterial incentives—and disincentives such as public criticism—had been pushed to a point where they produced diminishing returns; boredom and indifference had clearly set in with regard to social mobilization.

After the Great Leap: The Early 1960's

In the early 1960's a much more rational analysis of wages, labor norms and grades, bonuses, and other incentives appeared in the Chinese press and leading journals. The effective use made of material incentives before the Great Leap was referred to as a key factor in explaining the favorable economic performance during the First Five-Year Plan. In general, material incentives, better living standards—and by implication, self-interest—were seen as major factors in raising work enthusiasm, productivity, and in decreasing absenteeism and sluggishness.[79] Influential party authorities and publications emphasized the dictum "from each according to his ability," and proclaimed that "pay, according to work, skill, and productivity" cannot possibly be altered basically before a fundamental change in the social nature of socialism takes place.[80]

By 1961 renewed emphasis on piece rates became quite widespread, and by the end of 1961 the use of material incentives in industry was in full swing. The overwhelming majority of enterprises were under a system of some type of piece rate or hourly wage, plus reward, for paying workers; the straight hourly wage without possibility of an added bonus was seldom used. Refinements were made, however, so that, in many cases where feasible, wages were based on team rather than individual piece rates—a felicitous ideological combination of collective and individual interests. Where this was not technically feasible, the individual piece-rate system was still quite often used.

A more comprehensive wage-grading system with bigger differentials based on skill and performance was also soon introduced, as well as bonuses for managerial personnel. The 1963 wage reform involved wage increases for 40 percent of the labor force, as well as bigger bonuses for numerous industrial personnel.[81] A Western visitor to Anshan in 1964 reported that workers were receiving bonuses up to 14 percent of their basic wages.[82] Around that time bonuses were also being used at many Chinese industrial enterprises, apparently with success, to keep absenteeism to a minimum. While absenteeism has not been as serious a problem in Red Chinese industry as in many other underdeveloped and developing countries, there still has been a tendency for many workers—particularly those from the textile mills in the major cities—to visit with their families in the rural areas during the summer.[83]

Material rewards given for inventions and technical improvements (innovations) became an important type of incentive payment with the adoption of specific regulations concerning such achievements which were promulgated by the State Council in 1963.[84] Provisional regulations were issued in 1954, but the definitive regulations were not adopted until 1963. Inventions and improvements are divided into several categories, carrying both graded monetary and nonmonetary rewards. From time to time special campaigns, usually under party direction, to encourage innovations have also been launched with an emphasis on both material and nonmaterial incentives. The existence of material rewards, along with campaigns, probably helps to explain the large number of technical innovations reported from time to time in the Chinese press—more than 90,000, for example, in Shanghai industry alone in the first five months of 1965.[85] In Red China no patent rights are given to any enterprise or individual industrial inventor. Technical innovations seen and analyzed by European technicians working in Red China were of uneven merit. Some they considered "pretty old hat by European standards," while others "were worthy of introduction" even in industrial Czechoslavakia.[86] My own impressions were pretty much the same, although I would judge the large majority of "innovations" in Chinese industry to be "old hat" or relatively simple by American standards. Nevertheless, most of them seem to be worthwhile, and due credit should be given to the numerous Chinese industrial personnel who propose and introduce innovations, especially considering the relatively low level of technical skills, education, and industrialization in China. No doubt, material rewards have motivated numerous personnel in Chinese industry to innovate and invent.

During the 1960's—at least until the Cultural Revolution became sharply intensified—there was more emphasis placed on the production and acquisition of consumer goods than before. In fact, a certain amount of conspicuous consumption appears to have been viewed favorably by the regime. For example, it was considered quite desirable to have people earn more money by being more productive and/or by improving their skills so that they could buy the "four-good things": watches, bicycles, radios, and sewing machines. Cameras, a somewhat greater variety in clothing, cosmetics, and various other consumer goods also gradually became more plentiful in the 1960's, and their purchase was not discouraged by the state.

The Mid-1960's and Findings from My 1966 Survey of Chinese Enterprises

Even as early as late 1965 and early 1966—before my trip to Communist China—attacks against material incentives and self-interest began to appear in leading Chinese publications.[87] For economic conditions had again become quite favorable, relative affluence had again evolved, and the regime once again was becoming very concerned about ideological revisionism. The Soviet Union was attacked for relying too much on material incentives and self-interest. Emphasis on material gain, it was claimed, leads to falsification and fraud, and is in conflict with quality. Those who advocated money, profit, and self-interest as goals rather than the "politics and the Thought of Mao Tse-tung" were being branded as "anti-social," "anti-state," and "anti-party" bourgeois elements. There are indications that as early as 1965, and perhaps even by late 1964, piece-rate wages had already been eliminated at numerous enterprises, worker bonus payments had been reduced, bonuses for top managers and party secretaries had been virtually eliminated entirely, some relatively high-paid industrial personnel had reductions in their salaries, and material incentives and self-interest in general had been de-emphasized at many firms.

To turn briefly to what I learned about material gain and incentives in Chinese industry during the April–June period of 1966, I shall deal with this subject only in general terms here, reserving a more detailed examination of monetary incentive schemes, wages and salaries for a later chapter.

From my visits to thirty-eight Chinese industrial enterprises I found that individual piece-rate payments for workers had been completely eliminated, and there was apparently very little use made of collective piece-rate wages. There was, however, an occupational wage-grading system in effect for virtually all types of jobs which provided for fairly sizable basic wage and salary differentials based primarily on skill and ability, and to a lesser degree on length of service and various other factors. At about 80 percent of the enterprises, workers could still earn monthly or quarterly bonuses, varying from a minimum of about 3 percent of basic wages to a maximum of around 15 percent, but such bonuses were not usually based solely on productivity or efficiency. Politics and aid to co-workers were also important criteria. There was no particular branch of industry or type of firm where workers did not receive any bonuses, but it seems that some type of experiment was going on at the Wuhan factories under party leadership because three out of the four enterprises surveyed there had recently ended their worker-bonus schemes. All of the factories surveyed in Shanghai still had worker-bonus schemes in effect. In retrospect, this might be significant in view of the strikes and labor unrest reported in Shanghai in 1967. Perhaps municipal and enterprise committees in Shanghai favored less ideological emphasis than those in other parts of the country, and hence vigorously opposed the Red Guards. Shanghai industrial personnel were offered more pay and better living conditions by local leaders who opposed the Maoists.

It was, of course, too early to assess the impact of eliminating worker monetary incentives for productivity in Chinese firms, and I also did not get adequate data from the factories to make such an assessment. However, the Great Leap experience might indicate what the future may hold in store.

Middle-level managers, such as department heads and workshop directors, and most technical personnel and lower-level supervisors could still earn bonuses at about 80 percent of the enterprises surveyed. In many cases, bonuses as a percent of basic pay were slightly less for these personnel than for the workers. For the middle-level managers to earn bonuses, the fulfillment of certain enterprise targets—for example, quantity of production, sales, profit, production costs, product quality, labor productivity, and so on—was a required condition at only about 20 percent of the firms. In other cases they were evaluated for their own contributions and performance rather than for overall enterprise performance.

The directors, party secretaries, and vice directors were not entitled to any bonuses at any of the enterprises surveyed. I was told that a state regulation prohibiting the payment of bonuses to such leading personnel had been introduced a few years earlier. Several of the top-level managers and party secretaries said that they had received bonuses prior to this regulation, and others claimed that they had not been entitled to bonuses for about ten years. It seems, therefore, that bonus payments to top-level personnel may have not been reinstated at some enterprises after the Great Leap.

As was mentioned in an earlier section, some of the relatively highly paid key personnel at some of the enterprises visited had recently taken cuts in their salary. It is possible that a trend in this direction has emerged since 1966.

A number of the enterprises surveyed claimed that monetary rewards were no longer made to individuals for their inventions, technical improvements, or innovations. They indicated that the practice of making such rewards had been stopped quite recently, and that the main incentives for innovators were honor, recognition, and at times special trips to other cities for the purpose of introducing their innovations to other firms. Sometimes the innovators received small gifts, such as books. Apparently these enterprises were still entitled to material rewards for innovations and inventions, under certain conditions, but these rewards went to the firm as a whole, rather than to individuals. The money received was used for such purposes as acquiring scientific literature, sending people on special trips, improvement of operations, and welfare. At enterprises where individuals could still receive cash rewards for their inventions and innovations, in most cases the awards were of a joint or collective nature given to the team or group of individuals involved in proposing and successfully implementing the inventions or innovation.

During my stay in China the retail stores in all of the cities that I visited were better stocked with a wider variety of consumer goods than I had expected. A campaign against the buying of consumer goods had not yet emerged, and there were even signs of conspicuous consumption. Numerous people seemed to have watches and bicycles. In most homes, even in the communes, there were radios, and in many homes there was a sewing machine. Cameras were also in evidence on a fairly widespread scale. People seemed to take considerable pride in their consumer goods. On many occasions I was told by individuals that they had bought their prized items by working hard and saving enough money. Several people were in the process of saving enough money to buy these luxury (by Chinese standards) goods. I came away with the rather strong impression that material gain, the acquisition of material things, and self-interest were still potent motivating forces in the Chinese economy.

1967 and the Future

After I left China in June 1966, the campaign against material gain (also called economism) and self-interest was sharply intensified.[88] There has also been a campaign against the purchase of "bourgeois"-type consumer goods, such as cosmetics, perfume, and Western-style clothing. I do not know whether the proscribed items include such things as cameras, sewing machines, and watches. The orthodox Chinese leaders probably perceived that a highly polarized position, involving material gain, self-interest, and hence ideological revisionism, had evolved, particularly in view of the growing opposition to the regime's policies. This polarization was seen as being so extreme that it was probably viewed as an antagonistic contradiction that could be resolved only through a virtual elimination of material incentives and self-interest, rather than through compromise. Hence, the super-Reds have been called upon by the Maoists to take over industrial enterprises and revolutionize their management and operations. No doubt, one chief aim here is to replace material incentives and self-interest with nonmaterial incentives and altruistic motivation. This campaign is probably a major reason for the strikes and labor unrest. Some of these leaders and cadres in opposition to the Maoists have offered better pay and living standards to industrial personnel in Shanghai and elsewhere in order to gain their support.[89]

It is questionable whether Chinese top-level enterprise managers or middle-level managers and technical personnel can be adequately motivated over time to perform efficiently, with no material incentives, such as bonuses, and in a situation where material gain is, in general, de-emphasized. The same goes for the workers. During my stay in China there did seem to be considerable zeal, dedication, patriotism, and other nonmaterial stimuli motivating many of the industrial personnel, particularly the Reds, to work hard and do the best job they could. Yet centuries of world history strongly suggest that the Red Chinese regime will not be able to eliminate material gain and self-interest as important motivating forces—for managers, technicians, or workers—and at the same time achieve sustained and impressive industrial progress in the long run.

The Soviets, who tried briefly in the past to place extreme emphasis on nonmaterial incentives at the expense of material gain and self-interest, long ago abandoned such an ideological policy because they found it to be managerially, economically, and technically unfeasible. In fact, during the past several decades, few if any other countries have made as much use of material incentives for motivating industrial personnel of all types as has the Soviet Union. Hence, the Chinese charge that the Soviets are revisionists is indeed well grounded if one interprets it in terms of orthodox communist theology as interpreted by Mao. One wonders, however, if the Red Chinese will not also have to become revisionists in the not-too-distant future.

Attitude toward Scientific Method

It is true that China has a rich and very old tradition of scientific and technological development. But modern science did not develop in China until this century, and no attempt was made to bring the notion of scientific methodology to the population at large until the Communists came to power in 1949.

The notion of observing a system, either human or nonhuman, by proposing various hypotheses about the behavior within the system and checking and verifying results is central to scientific methodology. Critical to this notion is the idea that events can be described, explained, predicted, prescribed, and/or controlled. The thinking runs: "If we do A, then B will occur," and the hypothesis is either verified or proved invalid by trying A to see if B, in fact, occurs. Another way of looking at this problem is to suggest that "Event X depends on factors Y and Z," and then to determine the relationships among the variables, quantitatively if possible. Once hypothesized, the prediction is verified by observation, experience, and/or experimentation.

Old China

Prior to the Communist takeover of China, cultural values, religion, traditional superstitions, and the lack of education prevented the typical Chinese citizen from having a scientific view of the world or any real notion of scientific method.[90] While old China did have a number of educated people, including some outstanding scientists and other professionals in various fields, who thought in modern terms, the proportion of people who had a favorable view of scientific methodology and who were inclined to make use of such methodology as a matter of course was negligible.

The idea that somehow one can alter his environment through conscious action never occurred to the typical Chinese citizen. He tended to be highly fatalistic and felt that natural calamities, or even problems and obstacles of a much lesser nature, were essentially uncontrollable because they were fixed by heaven or the wrath of the gods. There was widespread mysticism, belief in ghosts, and many other superstitions. I was told by officials of several communes that before 1949 the peasants believed that mythical overlords and gods controlled the weather and determined how good or bad their crops would be.

While the dominant attitude toward scientific methods was no doubt more negative in rural areas than in cities, it was far from positive in urban areas, even among industrial personnel. I was told by managers and workers at several of the older factories about the superstitions and lack of scientific attitude that prevailed among factory personnel in the past. While workers were taught mechanically to operate machines and to work on various production processes, it rarely occurred to them that the machines or processes could be improved, much less that they themselves might be able to do it.

Among the owners, managers, and technicians of industrial firms in old China, probably only relatively few of them had much of a notion of the complex problems inherent in effectively managing a productive organization by identifying casual and dependent variables and working out predictive relationships. Since one of the major factors bearing on industrial managerial effectiveness is the successful application of scientific methodology to technical, economic, business, and human problems, its lack of application in old China undoubtedly contributed significantly to considerable confusion and inefficiency in industry. Without scientific methodology, industry and society at large will run out of control most of the time —in the economically productive sense—and industrial enterprise has no way of effectively planning for its future. It is true that periods of great instability and economic uncertainty in old China greatly constrained firms and people from effectively planning for the future, but the generally negative attitude toward scientific method substantially aggravated the problems of economic and political instability. In a very real sense a vicious circle was functioning. Since few enterprises or individuals made significant use of scientific method, plans were even less likely to work out, pessimism became even more prevalent, and firms and people became even more reluctant to try to plan for the future, even where they had a keen interest in, and awareness of, the importance of managerial planning and control.

Emergence of Scientific Method in Red China

Since the Communists came to power in China the regime has placed great stress on the popularization of science and technology, and on bringing scientific methodology and experimentation to the masses, in its effort to achieve industrial progress by transforming an old tradition-based society into a modern one.[91] This strategy has proven to be an important catalyst for technical, economic, and social change in Red China. The regime has gone far in "smashing" old superstitions and in replacing traditional cultural and religious values with a more scientific and rational view of the world—it has been more successful in cities than in rural areas.

The introduction of comprehensive economic planning in China has forced industrial personnel at all levels to make greater use of scientific method and analysis in planning for the future. A planned economy of the Chinese type requires that not only the government and macromanagerial agencies but also micromanagers and other enterprise personnel spend considerable time in preparing detailed plans and looking ahead, much more than in old China, and more than in present-day Indian industry as a whole. Emphasis on employee (including worker) participation in planning, decision making, and innovation at the enterprise level in China serves as a significant catalyst for bringing scientific method and experimentation down to the grass-roots level of the economy.

However, the Red Chinese regime has been only partially and erratically successful in popularizing scientific method and its uses, even in the new urban industrial society. It has been only erratically successful because scientific methodology in general has been sacrificed during periods when ideology has been pushed to extremes, such as during the Great Leap of the late 1950's and the Cultural Revolution of the mid-1960's. The regime has been only partially successful even during periods of relative ideological moderation because, even then, only limited use has been made of scientific methodology in the social and behavioral sciences. We shall return to these points later. First let us examine the popularization of scientific method in essentially nonhuman and nonideological technical fields.

Scientific Methods in Technical Fields

Science, which, of course, emphasizes scientific methodology in the physical and natural sciences and technical fields, is one of the five areas of study taught in both regular and spare-time school in Red China. (The other four areas of study are people, labor, country, and care of public property.) The student is taught not only the laws of nature, but also the ways to use his knowledge to control his environment and to solve and overcome problems primarily of a technical nature. He is now confronted with a rational, logical approach to what was formerly commonly regarded as fate and the wrath of the gods. He is taught scientific explanations of technology, floods, weather, disease, and the like.

Formal education is by no means the only method utilized for bringing scientific explanations, scientific method, and an attitude that man can control his physical environment to the masses. Scientific and industrial exhibitions, both on a grand scale and on a small scale in factories and in communes, are found throughout the country. Here charts, diagrams, and models are frequently used to give scientific explanations for old superstitions about such things as machinery and famines. Mass media and entertainment of all types also serve to extensively and intensively popularize science, technology, and the scientific method. But ideology—primarily practical ideology—has probably been the most significant force in creating a favorable attitude toward scientific method on the part of the masses in Communist China.

Ideology and political indoctrination with regard to instilling a more favorable view of science and scientific method throughout Chinese society should not be summarily dismissed as nonsense, as I had been prone to do before I visited China. Ideological indoctrination seems to have been a faster way to achieve the purpose than by relying primarily on lengthy formal-education programs. In a very real sense the works of Mao have done much to liberate "the thoughts and spirits of the masses" and have given them confidence to improve their performance and knowledge through analyses, experimentation, and trial and error. Politics and ideology in China help to generate enthusiasm for experimentation, innovation, and scientific conquest. If this enthusiasm is directed into productive channels, much useful experimentation, innovation, and rational solving of problems can evolve. Once industrial personnel are taught to believe it is possible to innovate and improve performance through the application of scientific methodology and experimentation, they are inclined to find many areas in the enterprise where even relatively simple innovations can improve productivity and results. Successful utilization of even relatively unsophisticated scientific methodology and experimentation, which lead to innovations and improvements, breeds confidence and further innovation, and hence reinforces the desirability of using the scientific method. Opportunities for employee (including worker) participation in enterprise management and decision making also tend to have a positive effect in this regard.

Mao's essay "On Practice" advocates "dare to think, dare to do, dare to experiment, dare to create"—if you don't succeed, try and try again, for man can overcome many obstacles through persistence and practice. Slogans urging people to combine theory and knowledge with practice and experiment are omnipresent in Red China. While this combination is as old as Bacon and Newton in the West, it is a new concept in China, and Mao's "On Contradictions" provides relatively unsophisticated or sparsely educated Chinese industrial employees with a useful methodology for analyzing and solving problems. It stimulates them to think in causal terms. It helps them to identify and analyze the key obstacles (contradictions) in a given situation, and to solve the problem by combining the various points of the problem—through the "law of the unity of opposites"—into a workable solution.

The Chinese press contains many real-life examples of how ideology—particularly the works of Mao—helps industrial personnel to solve problems through scientific method and experimentation. In Chapter 2, we discussed how "On Contradictions" was reported to have stimulated the employees of the Tientsin Bicycle Factory to improve product quality without increasing costs. In a cement plant a worker was reported to have sharply increased the productivity of the cement kilns as a result of studying the works of Chairman Mao. Studying Mao gave him both "revolutionary fervor and a scientific attitude" which in turn gave him the confidence and desire necessary to "fight the kiln" through practice and experimentation.[92] Other examples of this nature presented in the Chinese press have been discussed at various points in this book.

I came across many such examples during my visits to Chinese enterprises.[93] Frankly, I was surprised to find that industrial personnel in many kinds of jobs explained in causal terms problems they were confronted with and innovations they had introduced—which indicated a keen, though often unsophisticated, awareness of scientific method. Workers explained in considerable detail their appraisal, analysis, and solution of problems dealing with the increase in the operating speeds and productivity of machinery. Managers and technicians gave me scientific explanations regarding preventative maintenance and its rationale, the reasons why the various parts of the enterprise plan should be consistent, the gains in productivity derived from reorganizing activities and reorganizing plant layouts, the interdependence of firms regarding failures in supply and delivery schedules, and various other problems. The chief constraint among managers and technicians in connection with technical problem solving seemed to be educational, and not their attitude toward scientific method.

It is quite true that the application of scientific methodology and experimentation and the introduction of innovations in Chinese industry is, for the most part, unsophisticated and simple-minded by Western standards. But given the limited education of Chinese industrial personnel, and the relatively backward nature of the Chinese economy, considerable industrial progress has been made possible even with the use of relatively unsophisticated scientific methods. Indian industry would undoubtedly be significantly more productive if more extensive and intensive utilization of scientific methodology and implementation of innovations, even of the simple-minded type, could be stimulated among industrial personnel, including the workers.

As Chinese industry develops and grows more complex, however, there will be decreasing marginal gains from the application of unsophisticated scientific methodology and experimentation which leads to simple innovations and to the introduction of relatively simple technology copied from more advanced nations. It seems likely that the windfall of worthwhile "scientific discoveries" and innovations initiated by laymen and workers in Chinese industry will reach a saturation point in the not-too-distant future. When that happens, Chinese industry will have to place substantially greater emphasis on more sophisticated science-based innovations for continued growth, and it must also encourage an increase in the number of well-trained experts.

Such statements about future requirements regarding scientific needs should not be taken as a detraction from the effective job that the Chinese regime has done to date in popularizing scientific method, experimentation, innovation, and a more rational approach to problem solving.

Ideology versus Scientific Method

Serious problems have emerged during periods of ideological extremism when the spirit of "scientific method" and "research," and the craze for technical change through worker and Red initiative, have gone too far without the proper education and training to back them up. This was clearly the case during the Great Leap, when there suddenly appeared thousands of "worker engineers" and "peasant scientists" in factories and research organizations and in the communes. Students and young instructors took over the leadership of many educational institutions. Foreign science was automatically disdained as "bookish" and "superstition," and Experts and intellectuals who understood sophisticated scientific methodology were grossly misutilized. The Great Leap was a disastrous experience in nonscientific method and irrational decision making. The Leap, in essence, was a product of the fanatical ideological illusion of the party leadership that through "thought reform" and by "men's subjective determination anything can be done"; Mao was convinced that his "On Contradictions" was flawlessly and omnisciently scientific, that all contradictions and dualities present in the Chinese economy and society could be merged through the "law of the unity of opposites" and ideological will power alone. As it turned out, severe economic crisis was the result.

Vast amounts of resources were wasted on irrational projects, including the hundreds of thousands of steel furnaces that were so hastily erected throughout the land—in backyards, sheds, small shops, and on the farms. Most of the steel-making and smelting units were built without proper technical design or proper facilities, and those built in the open air were often made inoperative by rain and snow. More than sixty million people were assigned to building and operating the blast furnaces and other commune industries. The public was required to contribute scrap iron and steel, iron ore and coal to feed these crudely constructed clay and brick furnaces. Frequently they were fueled with coal of such poor quality that the pig-iron output contained too much sulfur to be usable. While iron and steel production showed sharp, though substantially exaggerated, gains, the output was achieved largely at the expense of producing metal of unusable quality, and involved great waste of resources and manpower.

Moreover, agricultural workers were transferred by the tens of millions to industrial work, and the result was a sharp drop in agricultural production. In addition, the irrational campaign for deep plowing and close planting introduced in the countryside further contributed to the agricultural crisis.

The fanaticism of the Great Leap also severely undermined the statistical system and made rationally planned development of the economy virtually impossible. Many of the "old-school" and less well-indoctrinated Chinese economists and social scientists had predicted—but to no avail—the various serious problems and crises that emerged because of irrational decision making and failure to apply scientific methodology.

Prior to the Great Leap period, science—even the social sciences to some degree—had been regarded as systematic knowledge which required lengthy education and considerable specialization. A much more rational view of scientific method and experimentation prevailed, even in the social sciences, to some extent. Considerable use was made of scientific method in analyzing and preparing the First Five-Year Plan. Many of the prominent "old" social scientists were employed as consultants, advisers, and staff specialists in various macromanagerial planning and economic agencies. The regime's leaders often made use of their advice and recommendations, which were based largely on scientific method. For example, in 1956 the government increased its capital investment outlays by 62 percent over 1955. This caused a great strain on the commodity market, and led to serious inflationary pressures. Many older economists—many of them foreign-trained—openly criticized this overinvestment. The government responded by ordering a considerable reduction in investment and production targets for 1957 and 1958.[94] Similarly, leading "old-school" sociologists and economists played a major role in the initiation, design, and implementation of the national birth-control program in 1956. They convinced the regime that birth control was essential for increasing the rate of capital formation and for speed-up industrialization.[95]

A more rational view of science, scientific method, and experimentation again emerged after the Great Leap in the early 1960's, although less effective use has been made of older social scientists than before the Leap. By the mid-1960's, however, with the onslaught of the Great Cultural Revolution, there seems to be a serious regression of attitudes towards science, scientific method, and rationality. Nevertheless, significant damage has probably already been done to the Red Chinese economy under the Cultural Revolution. However, if we can use Soviet history to predict the future in Red China, one would be inclined to bet that significant compromises in the direction of scientific method and rationality at the expense of ideology, will evolve and will persist in the future.

India versus China

While there have been serious lapses in the application of scientific method in decision making on the national and macro level in the Indian economy to date, India has clearly had a more consistent and stable record in this regard than Red China. Moreover, ideology has not apparently hindered the effective use of scientific method in the social and behavioral sciences (including economics) at both the macro- and micro-levels to the same degree in Indian industry as in China. This is not to say that widespread use is made of scientific method in these areas in the Indian economy—India still lags way behind the United States in this regard largely because of educational constraints and various motivational constraints of a sociological-cultural nature, such as deficiencies in the achievement drive and in attitudes toward risk taking, change, and the scientific method. There is also frequently great difficulty in implementing carefully designed plans in Indian industry. Nevertheless, somewhat more use is probably made of scientific method in the social and behavioral sciences by macromanagers and micromanagers in Indian industry than in Chinese industry. At the same time, India probably lags significantly behind China in the application of scientific method and experimentation of a technical nature at all levels, and even more so among lower-level industrial personnel, including the workers.

Scientific Method in the Social and Behavioral Sciences

It is, of course, generally more difficult to apply scientific methodology to the solution of problems in the social and behavioral sciences, including economics and management, than in the fields of the natural, physical or technical sciences. The major difficulty here is in trying to experiment in, or deal with, a situation where extraneous variables cannot be eliminated from the system. Complex difficulties arise because of the human element, the lack of adequate numbers of comparable situations, problems of measurement of the importance to be assigned to pertinent and, at times, contradictory factors, and the problem of reproducible controlled experiments.

In spite of such problems, considerable progress has been made in the Western world, particularly in the United States, in the application of scientific methodology in the social and behavioral sciences. This does not mean, however, that ideology, theology, and politics are never in conflict with scientific method even in the United States. To be sure, decisions dealing with such problems as government spending, income distribution, taxation, welfare benefits, price controls, and so forth, are, at times, made primarily on the basis of ideology, theology, and/or politics rather than on the basis of the criteria of scientific method or economic efficiency. However, in Red China, as well as in Russia and various other communist countries, much less use has been made of scientific methodology in social and behavioral fields than in the United States.

There is a basic conflict in communist states between scientific method and ideology, particularly where it deals with dialectical materialism.[96] The Soviet Union and some of its sister Marxist countries have recently come to realize that this conflict has been having a significantly negative impact on managerial effectiveness and economic progress. As a result, they are embarking on a new educational and research revolution in the social and behavioral sciences.[97]

The Communist Chinese have not yet faced up squarely to this problem, although at times the pendulum has swung toward somewhat greater emphasis on scientific method in the social and behavioral sciences.[98] In Red China these areas of study are still perceived to be, for the most part, ideological fields belonging to the study of Marxism-Leninism-Maoism. They tend to be treated as pure black and white, pure right and wrong, and it is extremely difficult, if not impossible, for a Chinese citizen educated, trained, and brought up under such a system to look rationally and objectively at the social sciences or at human motivation and behavior and arrive at independent conclusions. There is little, if any, attempt to describe, explain, predict, or control events in the social and behavioral sciences in an objective or scientific manner. In arriving at decisions involving human motivation and behavior, the regime and its well-indoctrinated decision makers tend to assume that "what ought to be," as prescribed by ideology, is really "what is" in the real world. This is at the heart of Red China's dilemma regarding the effective use of scientific methodology in the social and behavioral sciences.

For example, if workers "ought to" respond best to nonmaterial incentives and "ought not" to be motivated by self-interest, the ideologically oriented decision makers are inclined to assume that this is the real situation. Facts, objective analysis, and statistics are superseded by ideology, higher directives, and/or ideological slogans. Even if a particular Chinese manager, technician, or worker has applied the scientific method and rationally worked out on his own a solution to a specific problem relating to the social or behavioral sciences, he would typically not be able to implement his solution if it is not consistent with prevailing ideology and "correct political thinking."

I had the strong impression during my survey of Chinese industry that there was little tendency to utilize scientific methodology or objective analysis in the sphere of human motivation and behavior. If one were to ask the following questions, he is likely to get the following answers:

Q. What makes personnel work hard?
A. They work hard because they want to serve their country and the party.
Q. Can anything be done to motivate personnel more effectively?
A. Political education is the best solution.
Q. Is Mr. Wong content with his job?
A. Yes, because the state has assigned him to it, and he wants to serve the state in any way possible.
Q. Why do you have so many problems with Mrs. Chen who often comes in late and usually works so slowly?
A. Mrs. Chen requires more ideological indoctrination, should study Chairman Mao more conscientiously, and should learn from the leading workers in her group.

Such answers to such questions may in some cases, of course, be a façade. It is usually not possible to tell what is really on the minds of the Red Chinese respondents. But it is likely that the well-indoctrinated citizens of the younger generations in particular actually tend to believe many of the answers that they give. If enough people believe in ideological solutions to problems, such solutions may well work in many cases. Where the respondents are not convinced of their answers, and where they have a more objective solution in mind—derived through scientific methodology—little can usually be done to implement their solution.

The application of scientific methodology in the solution of economic, business, and managerial problems of a technical nature is encouraged under normal conditions in Chinese industry, but when such problems have a significant ideological content, scientific method tends to be sacrificed. When ideology is not pushed to the extreme in China's system of state economic planning, considerable use is made of scientific method in preparing industrial plans at the different levels of the economy. However, many alternative policies and courses of action are perceived to be ideologically incorrect and hence labeled as taboo automatically, even though they might help to raise managerial effectiveness and spur industrial progress. Hence, such things as interest charges on capital, the use of commodity market prices based on degree of scarcity and/or competition, a meaningful profit motive in business and industry, and various resource-allocation strategies are not even analyzed as possible policy alternatives because they are in conflict with ideology and politics. There are far more constraints on scientific method and objective analysis in the economic, business, and managerial spheres in a "thou shalt" type of economy like that of the Red Chinese than in an economy of the American type.

Attitude toward Risk Taking

Risk, which is defined as taking a chance on the degree of probability of loss, is an inherent part of economic activity. It was pointed out in Chapter 2 that productive operations are necessarily at least somewhat forward-oriented in time and involve at least some degree of uncertainty, and therefore any economy or industrial firm must assume some risks. The two major dimensions of risk taking that are of interest here are degree of rationality and its boundaries, and degree of aggressiveness or conservatism.

Old China

In pre-1949 China, political and economic instability, the lack of knowledge and adequate education, and the great dearth of statistics and other information required for sound decision making—both macro and micro—greatly constrained the boundaries of rationality with regard to risk taking and decision making. In such an environment even a rational, potentially aggressive risk taker in industry or government tended to be seriously constrained in his risk-taking activities, and this tended to pressure him in the direction of conservatism. Such a risk taker typically had a relatively high achievement drive which frequently could not realize its potential in industrial development activities. It is probably in large part for this reason that many Chinese with a high entrepreneurial achievement drive went to other countries to seek better opportunities.

At the same time, it is likely that there were a substantial number of irrational risk takers in industry and particularly in government in old China, and many of the irrational risk-taking decisions they undertook contributed significantly to economic inefficiency and waste in Chinese industry. They may have been irrational risk takers because they did not adequately apply scientific method in their decision making, lacked adequate knowledge, education, or skill in arriving at their decisions, and/or failed to recognize the narrow boundaries of rationality in which they were constrained in reality.

While there were overly aggressive and overly speculative risk takers of the irrational type in old China, and more so in the government, the dominant pattern of risk taking in Chinese industry was cautious and conservative.[99] In addition to narrow boundaries of rationality and low achievement motivation acting as potent forces for conservatism in industrial risk taking, the dominant attitude toward wealth and material gain, as discussed earlier, also contributed significantly to this conservatism.

Because of the generally unfavorable environment and lack of positive leadership for large-scale industrial undertakings in pre-1949 China, the entrepreneurs and managers tended to prefer relatively small-scale or conservative operations. The traditional Chinese businessman or industrialist typically preferred quick profits and quick turnover of capital. There was a general aversion to sizable capital investment in industrial pursuits. While speculative profits were attractive to many entrepreneurs and managers, such profits lacked the elements of regularity and continuity that characterized the idea of income—income which can be used for further industrial expansion.[100]

The government in old China played a rather ineffective and passive role with regard to entrepreneurship and risk taking in the industrial sector. The state gave relatively little direct attention to the creation of new industrial enterprises or the aggressive expansion of existing ones.

Industry and business were not perceived or treated as the same thing in old China. Business involved commercial, financial, trade, and retailing activities and did not usually require nearly as much capital as substantial industrial ventures. Modern industry, in particular, requires the careful management of money, because it generally receives a sizable amount of the capital. Moreover, the development of industry, particularly in its formative stages, requires a radical, innovative, risk-taking mentality.

A major reason for Japan's relatively early and impressive industrialization in Asia was the result of cooperation between her industrial leadership and business conservatism in the private sector in the creation of a modern nation. In Japan the technology- and innovation-minded samurai —members of the military caste in feudal Japan—allied themselves with the more money-minded merchants or business class to lay the basis for modern industry.[101]

In old China there was no equivalent of samurai leadership or industrial entrepreneurship to impress businessmen with the need for technological innovation and industrial development; nor was the government very interested in such matters. While industry did develop somewhat, despite the absence of positive indigenous leadership, it was the conservative business group that had to take the initiative; and they built their firms on the basis of the only principles they knew—namely, the networks of personal linkage and personal financial control. The result was that technological development and integration failed to match the integration derived from the human organization.

Risk Taking in Communist China

When the Communists came to power in China, one of their chief goals was rapid and extensive industrialization. The state became the omnipotent entrepreneurial and risk-taking force in industrial development. The major risk-taking and entrepreneurial functions required in setting up new firms and industries, and in sharply expanding existing ones, were transferred from the micro or individual level to the macro-level of the state, as represented by the governmental and party leaders. And China's leaders have certainly displayed a high achievement drive with regard to industrial progress. This has not meant that the degree of probability of loss in entrepreneurial decision making has been eliminated, or even reduced in many cases. Faulty decisions made by the regime's leaders or its state agencies can, and do, result in losses, waste, and inefficiencies—at times very large—for the economy and society. Poor decisions can, and do, result in considerable idle resources, waste, and other types of serious inefficiencies within individual productive enterprises. At the same time, however, the state has been in a position to undertake massive capital-investment projects and other major risk-type decisions which could not, and in numerous cases would not, have been undertaken by individuals or groups of individuals in China.

It is true that transferring personal losses and individual responsibility in risk taking to state losses and collective responsibility is not always conducive to managerial effectiveness or industrial progress. But given the overall environment of risk taking in China historically, this may well have been the best general course of action for Red China to follow in promoting industrial progress. However, as will be discussed shortly, when the regime has failed to apply scientific methodology in its major risk decisions, and when it has made and implemented highly irrational decisions, the damage to managerial effectiveness, industrial progress, and society in general has, at times, been enormous.

Under Communist China's planned economy the boundaries of rationality for both macro- and micro-industrial decision making have been greatly broadened and the degree of uncertainty sharply reduced. This is due in large part to the system of statistical information reporting and control that has been developed and introduced along with economic planning. It is true that Chinese economic statistics and other data have been so inaccurate in some areas as to be completely inadequate as guides to action; and during the Great Leap period in particular there was a vast amount of falsification of statistics and other information, even much more so in agriculture than in industry. While the problems of data collection for economic planning and decision making have been similar in nature to those facing other developing economies, such as India, they have been less serious in degree than in probably most other underdeveloped and developing countries. On the whole—but leaving the Great Leap period aside—Red China's statistical and data collection system has been better and more effective than India's.[102] Macro-level risk taking in the economic system has probably been somewhat more effective in Red China than in India, except during periods when ideology has been pushed to extremes in China. In a mixed economy of the Indian type it has proved extremely difficult to design and implement an effective statistical and information reporting system for macro- and micro-industrial decision making that takes into account the nature, problems, requirements, and interests of both the public and private sector.

National or Macro Risk Taking

The major problem in risk taking at the macro- or national-level in Red China has not been nearly so much that of narrow boundaries of rationality per se as it has been one of ideology which has taken precedence over scientific method and economic, technical, and managerial rationality and efficiency. Until the Great Leap Forward period, the Red Chinese regime and its macro policy makers and planners proved to be relatively rational risk takers and decision makers. Considerable emphasis was placed on available knowledge and information, educational skill, objective analysis, and scientific methodology, as well on as effective motivation in the design and implementation of major decisions involving risk and uncertainty.

Then came the Great Leap, a great experience in irrational risk taking. Mao and most of his loyal supporters and followers probably did not realize at the time that this great revolutionary experiment was based, in large part, on a series of irrational risks and decisions. The regime was blinded by ideology, faith, and emotion, and it failed to base its assumptions and predictions of the outcome of this tremendous social, economic, and political experiment on available information, facts, and careful analysis or logical reasoning. The achievement drive of Mao and other Chinese leaders with regard to the overall transformation of society was excessively high, and their resulting policy decisions were, for the most part, overly aggressive and irrational.

Many of the serious negative impacts of ill-conceived and irrational Great Leap policies on managerial effectiveness and industrial progress have already been discussed in previous sections and chapters, and further discussions will be presented in future sections. In fact, most of the educational, sociological-cultural, political, legal, and economic environmental constraints or variables discussed in this book were adversely affected by irrational risk taking during the Great Leap period. Irrational and overly aggressive risk taking at the macro-level led to a vast amount of waste and inefficiency at the industrial enterprise or micro-level.

For example, of the hundreds of thousands of steel-making and smelting units which sprouted up throughout China during the Leap, only a few hundred were in operation as of the mid-1960's.[103] Idle capacity and great underutilization and misutilization of other productive resources became widespread throughout industry; high-talent and skilled manpower was greatly misutilized; quality of production dropped sharply; financial control deteriorated greatly, and, in general, firms ran out of control. In fact, the entire system of economic planning and reasonably rational resource allocation was greatly undermined, serious bottlenecks in the economy became more intensive and extensive, and eventually a severe economic depression resulted in plant shutdowns and huge cutbacks in industrial production. Because of the irrational nature of the Great Leap, it was not possible for most firms or macro-organizations to plan effectively for the future, or to control, organize, staff, or direct operations efficiently.

With the end of the Great Leap a more rational view of risk taking evolved at both the macro- and micro-levels of the Chinese economy. (Evidence of this development was presented earlier.) However, with the onslaught of the Great Cultural Revolution in the mid-1960's, a great deal of irrational risk taking on ideological grounds again emerged, particularly at the macro-level under the direction of Mao and Lin Piao. Much evidence to this effect was reported in the press and other popular media. But this time Mao and his loyal supporters were being opposed by other top leaders and party officials, not to mention the "masses," many of whom have a substantially more rational view of reality and risk taking, and who have apparently learned from the Great Leap experience a lesson in the consequences of irrational risk taking. Unlike the period of the Great Leap, when political stability was not very seriously affected, great political instability has evolved because of irrational risk taking based on theology during the current Cultural Revolution.

Irrational risk taking in Red China has taken place primarily in the sphere of domestic policy and activity. In foreign affairs China's irrational bark has tended to be much greater than its more rational bite. The only direct and significant external military confrontation that China has engaged in since Korea has been with India in 1962. The precise reasons for this confrontation still seem to be rather unclear; and, in any event, it was brief and did not cause serious problems for the Chinese economy or industrial management. Red China has quite rationally taken great pains to avoid direct military engagement in Vietnam or with Taiwan on any significant scale.

In China's foreign policy regarding the Soviet Union the regime has probably not acted as rationally in its policies and decisions. The Sino-Soviet conflict has cost China a great deal in economic aid and technical assistance associated with industrial progress. To the extent that this conflict has been, and is, the result of pure ideological stubbornness and emotional hostility on the part of China, we can classify the Chinese regime's behavior in this conflict as irrational risk taking and decision making. But, as will be discussed in the section on foreign policy, China's role in the Sino-Soviet rift has certainly not been entirely irrational. However, if China's leaders go as far as creating a real border conflict of serious magnitude with the Russians in order to unify opposing internal factions in response to an external threat, this would indeed be a form of irrational risk taking which could do great damage to China's industry.

Ever since the Sino-Soviet rift became serious, Red China has pursued a rather rational and aggressive foreign policy in the area of trade with other countries. It has sharply increased its trade with Western and capitalistic nations in recent years. In fact, during the current Cultural Revolution even the Maoists have taken pains—not always successfully—to ensure that foreign-trade commitments are not upset, and a number of foreigners interested in trading with Red China are apparently still being granted visas to go to China on business trips. The traditional large trade fairs held in Canton in the spring and fall were held in 1966, though the fall fair was apparently somewhat limited, and there were no indications that the 1967 Canton trade fairs were to be canceled.

Risk Taking at the Enterprise and Individual Levels

Let us now turn to risk-taking attitudes and behavior at the enterprise level in Chinese industry. At Chinese industrial enterprises there is substantially less potential opportunity for independent entrepreneurship and risk-taking initiative of a major nature than in private enterprise in other countries. Higher authorities make the more important decisions on resource allocation, finance, production, and various other matters. Even in India's private sector a rational, fairly aggressive entrepreneur or manager with a relatively high achievement drive would typically have considerably more leeway or freedom than a Chinese manager to utilize his energies in initiating, as well as implementing, major risk-taking decisions, such as decisions on the establishment of a new venture, a major expansion of existing operations, and major innovations in product and in technology. It is true that the relatively aggressive and rational Indian manager is often stifled from undertaking major and potentially productive risks by the cumbersome government bureaucracy—not to mention various other environmental constraints—but he still is substantially less constrained from undertaking and particularly in initiating major risk projects than his Red Chinese counterpart. Regarding this type of risk taking India probably has an advantage over China in the matter of flexibility, opportunity, freedom, and incentive, which may often be conducive to industrial progress and managerial effectiveness. A major problem in India, however, is the limited supply of owners and managers who have a high achievement drive and who are rational, relatively aggressive, and effective risk takers. There are, of course, a variety of other constraints on risk taking in Indian industry, several of which are mentioned at different points in this book.[104]

While much of the risk function is shifted from the individual micro-level to a more impersonal macro-level in Chinese industry, rational and balanced risk taking in the face of uncertainty at the enterprise level still has a significant bearing on managerial effectiveness and industrial progress. It is very evident from my survey of Chinese industry that enterprises and their staffs do make many independent decisions, typically of a relatively minor nature, involving risk and uncertainty. They are also called on to successfully implement major innovational risk-type decisions initiated by superior authorities, but which nevertheless entail risk and uncertainty in their implementation at the enterprise level. Taken as a whole, independent risk decisions initiated at the enterprise also can, and do, have major impacts—negative or positive—on productive efficiency at numerous enterprises. If they tend to be rational risk decisions, managerial effectiveness and productive efficiency tend to benefit substantially.

Much use has been made of practical ideology to instill a risk-taking spirit in Chinese industrial personnel. Mao's essay "On Practice," with its emphasis on "do to create, do to do, and do to experiment," is a particularly important work in this regard.

Risk-type decisions and activities at Chinese enterprises typically involve product and technical innovation, changes in processes, procedures, practices and operations, and various other types of experimentation. Lack of education, skill, and knowledge tend to be the major constraints on this type of risk taking, and when ideology is pushed to extremes, the absence of scientific methodology becomes a very serious constraint. During periods of relative ideological moderation it seems that Chinese enterprise managers and technicians are relatively rational and aggressive risk takers. Workers also frequently play significant roles in innovational risk taking and pragmatic experimentation, usually of a minor nature, in Chinese industry. This "mass" emphasis on innovational activity can, and often does, serve a very useful training and motivational purpose, and helps to build up self-confidence.

Serious problems arise, however, when workers or other enterprise personnel who do not have the proper education, knowledge, and/or skill in applying appropriate scientific methodology are, as a matter of policy, permitted to play a central or dominant role in risk-type decisions and activities. This is precisely what happened throughout industry during the Great Leap; and I ran into emerging trends of this nature at a number of the enterprises that I visited in 1966. To me there seemed to be too much irrational risk taking at various enterprises, which went far beyond serving a useful training or motivational purpose. Because of ideological reasons and/or the Reds' interpretation of party and state policies, some firms seemed to be carrying "mass" innovation and experimentation to extremes. All types of apparently ill-suited and improperly trained personnel at a number of plants were involved in activities concerning technical innovation and product development.

Groups of workers, party cadres, and inadequately trained managers were trying to design new production processes, develop new products, modify existing equipment and products, and reorganize activities in ways that clearly seemed to be wasteful, unproductive, and, at times, very inefficient. In response to the state policy calling for "self-sufficiency," several enterprises had decided on their own initiative to make or rebuild equipment, components, and parts required for current production rather than procure them from suppliers. This, it was felt, would save money for the state. However, in a number of cases the firms did not realize the risks and uncertainties entailed in pursuing such a policy. They found that production and deliveries to customers suffered because they could not make or rebuild the equipment or components nearly as fast or as effectively as they had anticipated.

A number of enterprises surveyed had requested higher targets in their plans than those which had been formally approved by higher authority, because they were convinced that through sheer hard work, will power, zeal, and dedication they could meet these higher targets. Officials at some of these enterprises admitted that they found they were "too optimistic" in having the targets revised upward, and that they should have undertaken a more careful analysis of the "concrete situation." They subsequently had to have their plans reduced, and presumably the plans of other interdependent firms were either upset or revised.

On the whole, I do not feel that the typical Chinese enterprise manager —or technician or worker—lacks aggressiveness as a risk taker; in fact, the degree of aggressiveness appears to be substantially higher in China than in India, particularly among workers. The major problem in Chinese industry seems to be that of not recognizing the boundaries of rationality in many cases.

Chinese industrial enterprises and their staffs seem to be more inclined toward innovational risks involving product and process development and the introduction of new technology than their Soviet counterparts.[105] There are a number of reasons for this difference in attitude and behavior regarding innovation, including major innovations.

In Soviet industry there is substantially more emphasis on individual responsibility, the fulfillment of priority success indicators (targets), and bonuses for managers and workers for fulfilling and/or overfulfilling their assigned success indicators. The priority success indicators at Soviet enterprises usually pertain to quantity of production, cost reduction, and labor productivity; in current times profitability is becoming a more important success target. While some rewards may be earned by various types of personnel for innovational activities, bonuses and praise for favorable performance in connection with the priority success indicators are generally much more substantial, often involve less risk and uncertainty in their realization, and frequently tend to be in conflict with innovational activity. In effect, a Soviet firm or manager is likely to be penalized if it or he undertakes risk-type innovational activities which hinder the fulfillment of priority success indicators. Furthermore, because of the Soviet system, only relatively small profit margins have generally been officially allowed on new products—typically 3 to 5 percent—and this tends to hinder product-development activity. By contrast, the Chinese industrial enterprise is typically allowed roughly a 20 percent profit on its new products in order to encourage new product development.

At Chinese industrial enterprises, innovation activities—including those of a major kind—do not tend to entail as much potential risk, penalties, or losses for individuals as they do in the Soviet Union. The stress seems to be more on collective risk taking in China. If a risk-type decision or activity does not work out as anticipated, as long as it is not judged ideologically incorrect, there does not generally seem to be very significant stress placed on individual responsibility, blame, or penalties. This lack of emphasis on individual responsibility or blame for failure in Chinese industry can, and does at times, hinder managerial effectiveness and industrial progress because irrational, unwarranted, and/or unproductive risks are more likely to, and do probably, occur. On the other hand, it does undoubtedly serve to promote a considerable amount of risk-type activity that would not otherwise occur, and as was mentioned earlier, such activity, even if it does not work out as intended, can frequently serve a useful training, motivational, and confidence-building purpose in Chinese industry. Moreover, top-level Chinese enterprise executives are not awarded bonuses, priority success indicators are not emphasized as much or defined as clearly as in Soviet industry, and plans tend to be more flexible. These factors tend to encourage more risk taking of the innovational type in Chinese industry, although the innovations introduced are typically not very sophisticated or productive, even by Soviet standards.

The Soviet enterprise manager, technician, or worker should not be underestimated as a rational, relatively aggressive, and effective risk taker. There are various negative environmental constraints on innovational-type risk taking which tend to be more potent in Russia than in China. At the same time, however, because of better education, knowledge, information, application of scientific methodology, and various other environmental conditions, the boundaries of rationality for both macro- and micro-decision making and risk taking tend to be broader in Soviet industry. For similar reasons, and in spite of substantial resistance to major technological and product innovations in Soviet industry, the level and sophistication of technology employed and the complexity of products produced—particularly producer goods, as opposed to consumer goods—still are substantially higher in the Soviet Union than in China.

Nevertheless, Red China has come a long way in creating a more favorable attitude toward risk taking and in bringing about more productive risk-taking behavior and activity on a very substantial scale. In time, because of certain basic features of the Chinese personality, the dominant view of risk taking and actual risk-taking behavior could become more conducive to managerial effectiveness and industrial progress in China than in the Soviet Union.

Attitude toward Change

Society at Large and Social Change

A major theme running throughout this book is that of social change at the general societal level in China. We are focusing on changes in environmental constraints or conditions which tend to have a significant impact on managerial effectiveness and industrial progress. In the national or macro sense, such changes can be classified as social change. It is clear from our chapters dealing with Red China's response to environmental constraints that the Communist regime has vigorously achieved very substantial changes in educational, sociological-cultural, political, legal, and economic environmental conditions since it came to power in China.

Where ideology has not been pushed too far, to the detriment of economic, technical, and managerial rationality, the environmental changes have tended to have a beneficial effect on management and development.

Much of the explanation of the dichotomous results of environmental changes can apparently be discovered by analyzing the regime's and the people's attitudes toward, and responses to, change during different critical periods. This will lead to a better understanding of why major environmental changes introduced by the Red Chinese leaders have proved effective in terms of better management and greater industrial progress at certain times, and why environmental changes desired by the regime have proved ineffective during the Great Leap Forward and again during the current Great Proletarian Cultural Revolution.

The Yenan Period of Communism[106]

To undertake a meaningful analysis of the economy and society of Red China, it is necessary to go back briefly into Chinese history and look at certain key features of the communist movement during the Yenan period of Communism in the 1930's and 1940's, and to examine briefly how the Communists achieved victory in China.

In the mid-1930's the caves of Yenan, in the northern part of Shensi Province, became the central headquarters, or base, from which Mao and the Communist Party carried out guerrilla warfare behind the Japanese lines, and determined the strategies and tactics to be pursued in achieving political control in mainland China. As Chalmers Johnson points out: "Yenan is a time, a place, and a symbol; it is also, and above all, the name of a revolutionary strategy which uses the mass line to serve a revolutionary purpose. Yenan Communism is to a large extent synonymous with the strategy of people's war, and it is this aspect of the Yenan experience that has had the most tenacious hold over a segment of the Chinese Communist leadership."

By "mass line" the Chinese Communists mean that in order to effectively organize people or the masses for any purpose, and bring about desired major changes effectively, the party must perform two key functions. First, it must discover what social issues or problems are of deepest concern to the mass of the population, what the best rallying cry is for the party's use in organizing the masses and in bringing about desired changes. Second, having discovered what program has the greatest potential for eliciting a favorable response from the masses, the party must organize, motivate, and lead the people on the basis of this program.

The masses are much more likely to view such a program and such changes as their own, and hence would tend to have a strong commitment to their successful implementation. Mao's famous principle of the "mass line" proved very effective during the Yenan period of Communism in defeating the Japanese, in enabling the party to take over China, and in bringing about major environmental changes conducive to greater managerial effectiveness and industrial progress. Without the mass line, there could be no "people's war," or revolution, as the Communist Party conceives it. According to the mass line, the party must meet the people and gain their support on the basis of equality, and it must engineer an "ad hoc" community of interests with them.

The mass line, as conceived during the Yenan period, is, in essence, the ultimate and purest form of "democratic centralism" because it links the masses at the grass-roots level directly with the top-level party leadership in the formulation of basic programs, changes, and policies to be pursued. As we shall discuss shortly, democratic centralism has rarely taken this pure form since the Communists came to power in 1949. It has been used in the design and particularly the implementation of derivative operational plans and programs. Such derivative plans and programs are based on general priorities, policies, objectives, programs, and social changes determined by the top party leaders of the nation, and usually formulated without much if any mass participation, and, during some periods, with little or no genuine consultation even with intermediate-level administrators or party cadres in the industrial hierarchy.

During the Yenan period, Mao showed considerable flexibility, sound intuition, and pragmatism in implementing the mass line, and this is apparent from his analysis of the various "contradictions" that existed within Chinese society. As early as 1930, he identified the following issues as potentially exploitable bases for the mass line: (1) the contradictions between imperialism, foreign control, and the Chinese nation, and among the imperialists themselves; (2) contradictions within the counterrevolutionary ruling cliques; (3) contradictions between the rulers and the broad masses of the ruled; (4) contradictions between the landlords and the peasantry; (5) contradictions between the bourgeois and capitalists and the working class; (6) contradictions between the warlords and their troops; and (7) contradictions between the counterrevolutionary regime and the intellectuals and students.[107]

At the outset of his guerrilla revolution, Mao chose to focus on the fourth contradiction inherent in the agrarian situation as the most promising immediate basis for the mass line, and he experimented with several different types of Red Army land policy in trying to exploit this issue which affected most of the population. But he never forgot the other contradictions and always stood ready to shift his priority efforts to one of them and adjust to changing realities to achieve the changes and goals he desired.

As the Japanese gained greater control over China in the 1930's and eventually launched a full-scale invasion in 1937, Mao shifted his mass line to a nationalistic, anti-Japanese united front. The logic of Mao's shift in mass-line tactics was pure "people's war." From the point of view of Mao's theory, the earlier attempts to exploit the contradictions between the landlords and the peasantry had not been ill advised; it was, rather, that new events opened up much more promising opportunities. Moreover, the agrarian strategy had not worked well enough. Hence there was a drastic modification in the party's earlier land policy which involved direct and wholesale confiscation, expropriation, and redistribution, although the contradictions inherent in the agrarian situation were by no means abandoned entirely.

Mao's wartime mass line, as of the second half of the 1930's, consisted of two key complementary policies. The first was the reorganizing of the rear-guard and basically rural population, which had been mobilized largely by the brutality of the Japanese occupation and invasion, through an appeal to its nationalistic and patriotic interests. Mao had much intelligence information—gained directly from the "masses" and through his experiment involving the anti-Japanese line during the Red Army's 1936 invasion of Shensi Province—which indicated that nationalism and victory over the Japanese invaders was of great interest to the Chinese masses. Because of great nationalistic feeling and because of the enthusiasm and dedication of Mao's political cadres, not only peasants of all strata but also landlords who had not fled, students, and middle-class refugees from the cities all responded to the party's call for armed resistance against the Japanese.

The second policy involved reductions in rent and interest payments for the peasantry, who were the backbone of the war effort and the civil revolution to follow. This policy appealed to the economic interests of the peasants. The reduced-rent program helped to solidify a good deal of the party's rear-guard peasant support, which was won initially primarily on the basis of resistance to invaders. The number of middle-class peasants during the 1940–45 period increased considerably, and the proportion of both poor and rich peasants declined. There was a marked growth in the number of middle-class peasant households, a change brought about chiefly by raising the level of land ownership among former poor peasants. The land made available to the poor peasants came primarily from the sale of surpluses formerly held by absentee landlords. The average farm sizes for landlords and rich peasants declined substantially.[108]

Hence agrarian reform, although not really drastic, helped to win mass peasant support for the Communist Party and encouraged peasants to trust the Communists and to work harder for the resistance and for the revolution. The two critical facets of Mao's mass line—appeals to nationalism and modest reform of agriculture compatible with economic improvement—reinforced each other. The peasants supported an agrarian policy designed to further the war effort and the revolution and, with the exception of landlords and rich peasants, profited from it.

During the Yenan period of communism many social changes were introduced in areas where there was substantial Communist support, and much preparatory groundwork for extensive environmental changes on a national scale were effectively laid. The war against Japan was won, and Mao and his party turned their attention to a takeover of China as a whole. In addition to the peasants who joined his armies, the Communists gained the support of the urban population, and in 1949 the party and its armies won their revolutionary victory over the Nationalists. Mao and his party had succeeded in developing a genuine mass line—one based on policies, programs, and changes that most of the people wanted to support. For the peasants it was nationalism and agrarian reform leading to economic improvement. For the urban population the appeal was to nationalism—the end of foreign aggression, exploitation, and control—as well as to hopes for economic development and a better life.

Because the Communists met with mass support, following their takeover in China, the party could effectively introduce major environmental changes that were conducive to greater managerial effectiveness and industrial progress. The party, with its pervasive and dedicated organization of cadres, has played the crucial role in seeing that environmental changes desired by the regime have been effectively implemented by mobilizing, organizing, and motivating the masses at the grass-roots level to respond effectively to those changes.

Although the leaders of the Chinese Republican Revolution in the early part of the twentieth century may have been interested in various kinds of social change, the regimes of the Republican era generally failed to effectively pursue policies or programs that appealed very strongly to the interests and aspirations of the masses, and they failed to gain mass enthusiasm and support. Moreover, they did not have an organization of cadres extending right down to the masses throughout the nation which could mobilize the people to respond effectively to environmental changes desired by the leaders. The leaders during this era were much more concerned with political control than with environmental changes that could yield substantial economic development or substantial improvement in living standards for the masses. Moreover, they were not effective in dealing with foreign invasion or in getting rid of foreign exploitation and control in China. The Chinese Nationalist Army could not have defeated the Japanese without the Chinese Communists and their supporters and much foreign help—and the masses knew this by the mid-1940's.

Communist China: 1949–57

When the Communists came to power in 1949, they had the confidence, enthusiasm, and loyalty of the population at large. This gave the Communist regime great latitude in undertaking major and rapid environmental changes, some of which were compatible with traditional dominant values and interests in Chinese society, some of which served to capitalize on latent values and interests, and some of which led to a modification of existing values and interests and the inculcation of new ones. Since 1949 the Red Chinese regime has viewed change and "struggle," rather than stagnation, stability, and harmony for the sake of harmony, as the natural condition of life.[109] This is the reverse view of the ruling elites in old China who were influenced strongly by Confucianism.

Until the Great Leap Forward Period, environmental changes in Red China tended to be consistent with the interests of the population at large. Efforts were aimed at building a strong, powerful (economically, politically, technologically, militarily), richer, better-educated and modern China, and this goal was compatible with the population's interest in nationalism, economic development, and a better life in general. Both the regime and its citizens desired greater managerial effectiveness, industrial progress, and general economic development, and many substantial environmental changes were introduced in an effort to bring this about. The regime's policies and environmental changes were still being based largely on the "mass line," or at least were compatible with the interests and aspirations of the masses.

The Chinese Communist leaders did not abandon their great concern about ideology during the 1949–57 period, but they kept the implementation of ideology largely within the boundaries of economic, technical, and managerial rationality. Probably only a small proportion of the Chinese population really understood much about Marxist-Leninist ideology and the Thought of Mao, apart from the more general, basic, and well-publicized tenets involving class struggle, equality, distribution of wealth, national and state control of productive resources, party political control of the state until it withered away, nationalism, and so forth. However, they were quite willing to go along with the regime's ideology in general because it seemed to be compatible with their interests and aspirations regarding economic improvement and nationalism.

The Great Leap Forward

Then came the Great Leap Forward in 1958. Mao saw this as the greatest experiment in social change in history. There were changes affecting virtually all of the environmental conditions of interest that are discussed in this study—most of them introduced with the aim of "building socialism" and rapidly attaining the pure communist utopian state. At this point in Chinese Communist history Mao began to noticeably move away from the effective use of the "mass line" which proved so successful in the past. He became obsessed with the notion that virtually any program, policy, or change could be carried out effectively through the "spirit" of the masses and their "will power" alone.

Will power and spirit certainly had played a key role in the Chinese Communists' revolutionary past, particularly during the Yenan period, when the party was continually aware that the sources of the spirit that led the people into guerrilla battles or risky productive undertakings (such as agricultural improvement projects and relatively small-scale industrial and military production ventures) were nationalism and hatred of the invader, and a belief in the possibility of economic improvement. The people's will power and spirit were, in effect, stimulated by the conditions of the time in conjunction with their own interests and aspirations. The party's main achievement was to recognize the existence and nature of this spirit and to make genuine use of the mass line, its chief task was to convince the people, through its programs and actions, that the party could harness this spirit to the common good.[110]

With the Great Leap Forward, Mao and his chief party associates seemed to forget where the heightened spirit of the population had come from in the past. They began instead to think and speak of will power and spirit in isolation, as independent variables affecting the outcome of any kind of change, program, or activity that the party chose to define as a revolution or struggle. This renewed party interest in the "miracles" achieved during the Yenan period by will power and spirit alone—divorced from environmental factors, and concrete earthly interests and aspirations of the masses—gave rise to a highly idealistic and irrational tendency in the thinking and behavior of Mao and his close associates. They felt that spirit influences the environment and not vice versa, and that spiritual force can turn directly into material force.[111] (There are still many Chinese references to "spiritual atomic bombs," "spiritual machine tools," and so on.) Hence politics and ideology were made to take command of economics, technology, and management.

During the Great Leap the party tried to translate the Yenan military and political experience into economic, technical, and managerial strategy and policy. The party leadership failed to recognize that natural, or environmental, constraints should not necessarily be conceived as being analogous to an enemy in a guerrilla struggle, and that methods, strategies, and tactics that work well in a war—especially guerrilla warfare—do not necessarily work well in building and running complex industries or in industrial management.

The Great Production Movement, during the Yenan period of Communism, probably provided more economic, technical, and managerial precedences for the Great Leap Forward than any other campaign or program in the party's revolutionary past.[112] During the war against Japan the Chinese Communists and their troops were up against a tight blockade by both the Japanese and Chiang Kai-shek's troops. Mao's answer to this blockade was the Great Production Movement that would enable them to survive and fight on.

The aim was to achieve self-sufficiency by producing everything—food, housing, weapons, supplies, implements, equipment, components, materials, and so on—through makeshift methods. Since there were very few skilled engineers, technicians, craftsmen, or production managers among them, the people had to pool their knowledge and train each other. Everyone was encouraged to become a jack-of-all-trades. To motivate the population to undertake experiments and try new techniques the party used many devices and methods. It set up work and study schools, used masses of manpower in place of machinery, selected labor heroes for praise and emulation, established true equality, democracy, and encouraged grass-roots initiative, criticism, and self-criticism. Because the masses supported the basic aims, programs, and policies of the party, and because of the environmental conditions of the time, people tended to be very altruistic, accepted a great deal of self-sacrifice, and generally worked extremely hard.

What Mao did at the time of the Great Leap was to define in general ideological terms the interests and aspirations of the people as the "building of socialism" rather than following the mass line and investigating or analyzing their concrete interests and aspirations. Hence the environmental changes introduced were based on an idealistic conviction that the spirit, will power, and ideological zeal of the people alone would lead to their effective implementation. Not utilizing the mass line in the way that the party had done in the past narrowed the boundaries of rationality in national-level risk taking and decision making.

The Great Leap Forward apparently failed for two main basic reasons. One reason has already been indicated—that is, a number of the social changes introduced turned out to be incompatible with the interests or aspirations of the people affected. At the outset, probably most people did accept Mao's generally stated paramount goal of the "building of socialism." There was no reason to firmly believe that this goal was incompatible with their more concrete and materialistic interests and aspirations, which no doubt involved nationalism symbolized by a strong and independent China, economic development, and a better life. There were, of course, many skeptics—particularly among the intelligentsia and professionals—who felt that the Great Leap was an ill-conceived and irrational program from the outset, but the population at large probably were confident that Mao knew what he was doing, although they did not understand many of the implications at the outset. They were probably even willing to dedicate themselves to the cause and undertake personal sacrifices, at least in the short run.

As the Great Leap program progressed, there was evidently growing resistance to some of the environmental changes associated with it—such as the de-emphasis of monetary incentives and self-interest, the intense ideological and political-education campaigns, extreme stress on class struggle and the elimination of class distinctions, the constant slogans and calls for even harder work and greater sacrifice. The general state of chaos and inefficiency that emerged throughout industry and the economy at large undoubtedly led to considerable frustration, demoralization, and apathy among the masses. The anti-intellectual campaign and the humiliating tactics and abuses aimed at the experts and professionals certainly tended to have an extremely adverse impact on their motivation and effectiveness. Growing use was made of coercion, punishment, and other ruthless tactics where people showed resistance to the changes, programs, and policies desired by the regime.

The means used and changes introduced by the regime during the Great Leap in an attempt to achieve desired goals led to economic crisis. Moreover, it humiliated China—and made it appear weak in the eyes of much of the world. Hence, the Leap actually reaped results that were no doubt in direct conflict with the real interests and aspirations of the population at large.

The second main reason why the Great Leap failed was probably more important than the first. Many of the ideologically motivated and ill-conceived environmental changes introduced were in conflict with economic, technical, and managerial rationality, and we have already dealt at some length with this topic in previous sections. Even if virtually all industrial personnel had accepted whole-heartedly all of the environmental changes introduced during the Great Leap period, it still would undoubtedly have been a failure because many of the changes were in sharp conflict with managerial effectiveness and industrial progress.

Even though the Leap was a failure, probably a large majority of Red China's citizens nevertheless remained loyal and dedicated to Mao. They had not forgotten what Mao and the party had done for them and their country in the past, and they also accepted the regime's explanation of the causes of the economic crisis. The regime pointed to natural calamities—particularly poor weather resulting in poor agricultural results—and the Soviet pullout as chief reasons for the failure. There was considerable truth in this, although ideological fanaticism, irrational risk taking, lack of scientific method, and, in particular, the regime's attitude and behavior with regard to change were, I feel, substantially more important reasons—reasons which, I may add, contributed significantly to the poor harvest and probably also to the Soviet pullout.

Mao also blamed the Great Leap failure, including the resulting economic crisis, on "enemies of the people" within Red China itself. Shortly before the Great Leap, Mao discovered the brand new Marxist-Leninist-Maoist concept of the "people" and "enemies of the people." [113] He stated and wrote in 1957: "At this stage of building socialism, all classes, strata, and social groups which approve, support, and work for the cause of socialist construction belong to the category of the people, while those social forces and groups which resist the socialist revolution and are hostile to, and try to wreck, socialist construction, are enemies of the people." [114]

Hence, according to Mao's thinking, something had gone wrong with "the people" during the Great Leap Forward. There were far too many "enemies of the people" who had resisted or responded inappropriately to the environmental changes of the Great Leap. Because of his idealism and ideological fanaticism he refused to acknowledge that many of the environmental changes introduced could not work to produce desired results, and that he had based his notions of spirit and will power of the masses on blind faith, rather than on a genuine utilization of the "mass line"—a mass line that would harness the people's interests and aspirations to the policies and programs which the regime formulated and pursued.

Mao's isolation of the categories "people" and "enemies of the people" had already moved him some distance away from the basic sociological validity of his mass-line concept and into the communist quagmire of ideological definition—that is, into the realm of dogmatism which he had so often warned against in the past. And Mao's position in 1957 and during the Great Leap was only the beginning of his own transformation; he moved further and further away from the original spirit and effective use of the mass line—the Socialist Education Campaign began at the end of 1962, and about mid-1966 evolved into the Great Proletarian Cultural Revolution.[115] In this regard, at least, Mao has proved himself to be a revisionist.

Since the Great Leap

In order to bring the country out of economic crisis the regime was forced to retreat from its extreme ideological position. As has been discussed in previous sections, by 1962 major environmental changes in the direction of economic, managerial, and technical rationality were being introduced and implemented quite effectively. Further environmental changes aimed at increasing managerial effectiveness and industrial progress were implemented until around 1965, when the pendulum began to swing in the direction of ideological extremism. This swing became very sharp as the Cultural Revolution evolved and expanded from mid-1966 on.

In spite of the environmental shift from ideological extremism to productive rationality and efficiency during the 1962–65 period, Mao had evidently not really abandoned his ideological fanaticism; he merely postponed his grandiose ideological program to a more auspicious time. Mao and his orthodox associates felt that before a new and successful Great Leap Forward could be launched, the "enemies of the people"—and they must have felt that there were plenty of them, given the results of the original Great Leap—would have to be reeducated and remolded to think and behave as Mao's people should. When the people were revolutionized and transformed, then "spirit," "will power," and the mass line would once again produce their miracles, just as they did during the Yenan period.

Unlike the Yenan period, however, Mao and his party would be shaping the interests and aspirations of the people, rather than responding effectively to their interests and goals by harnessing them to the programs, changes, and goals desired by the party. It is quite possible that Mao did not, and has yet to, recognize his basic difference in strategy from that used in Yenan. In 1965 the Chinese Communist Party still regarded the mass line as "the party's fundamental political and organizational line." [116] Toward the end of the Socialist Education Campaign, Soong Ching-ling (the wife of the late Dr. Sun Yat-sen, the leading figure of China's revolution of 1911 who is still a revered hero among all factions of Red Chinese society, including the Maoists), a top-level associate and supporter of Mao, described the mass line as follows:

> From the masses; back to the masses. Herein lies the role of the Communist Party and its members: to go among the people so as to learn from them; to analyze in Marxist-Leninist terms their demands and insights; crystallizing and systematizing these ideas and elevating them to a theoretical level. On the basis of this, to project the right policies and methods of work; to take these back to the masses, explain and popularize them, and arouse the masses to support these policies so they will act on them as their own.[117]

Contained within the Socialist Education Campaign and Movement were many concrete sub-campaigns, such as those dealing with part-work, part-study programs, compulsory physical labor for cadres and managers, and those to counter the growth of "modern revisionism" through ideological indoctrination, and to train revolutionary heirs. Special new political education departments were established at various levels of the economy.[118] The Socialist Education Campaign urged the following: learn from the People's Liberation Army, the Ta'ching Oil Fields and Refinery, and the Ta'chai Commune; conceive of socialist construction as a new revolution; revolutionize all thinking; and, above all, learn from the Thought of Mao Tse-tung.

Until around late 1965 or early 1966 the concrete sub-campaigns, themes, and slogans of the Socialist Education Campaign did not interfere significantly with managerial effectiveness and industrial progress. Industrial results improved sharply, foreign trade expanded, agriculture reached approximately peak pre-Great-Leap levels, certain specially favored endeavors—such as projects for nuclear weapons, the petroleum and chemical industries, and the production of agricultural equipment and supplies—made especially notable progress. These successes were due to the rationally calculated environmental changes that had been introduced, and to which the masses—not to mention the managers, cadres, and experts—responded effectively. Little, if anything, was accomplished through the use of mass-line methods that was commensurate with the rhetoric of the period of the Socialist Education Campaign.

The Socialist Education Movement evolved into the greatly stepped-up ideologically grounded Cultural Revolution, and eventually led to serious civil strife and conflict bordering on widespread civil war. Mao and his orthodox top-level supporters apparently panicked at the course that the environment had taken, at the expense of major ideological compromises. Hence the end result of the Socialist Education Campaign was not a second Yenan-type victory or an effective launching pad for a successful new Great Leap of social change, but the most serious inner-party struggle since the establishment of the Chinese Communist state. Clearly, not only Experts, professionals, local party cadres, and intellectuals but also the masses and powerful party leadership groups within Red China had grown disenchanted with the latest manifestation of the mass line and the types of environmental changes that Mao and Lin Piao wanted to introduce. The policies of the Cultural Revolution indicate that there are many "enemies of the people" who resist Mao's desired social changes. They include, in part, "antiparty," "antistate," "counterrevolutionary," and other "bad elements," "bourgeois survivals," "modern revisionists," and, of course, "freaks" and "monsters," and "treacherous traitors."

In the Socialist Education Campaign and the subsequent Cultural Revolution, as with the Great Leap, Mao did not investigate the interests and aspirations of the people; he defined them again as the "building of socialism." Furthermore, he sought to impose his own will and the social changes and programs associated in his own mind with the building of socialism, on society at large. In doing so, he has apparently violated the main working principle of his own mass line. If such an investigation had been made, it is likely that it would not have sustained the general policy of building socialism or various social changes related to this policy as a proper or effective platform for mass-line organizational efforts. It appears that contemporary mass interests and aspirations may well be similar to those of the Yenan period—namely, Chinese nationalism, economic development, and a better life now in the short run.[119]

Many of the environmental changes desired by Mao and his dwindling staunch supporters during the current Cultural Revolution and civil strife period have met with strong resistance by all classes making up the masses, including numerous cadres at all levels within the party. These "enemies of the people"—possibly a substantial majority of the population by now—have evidently learned a lesson from the Great Leap experience and feel that various ideologically conceived social changes and programs would again weaken China substantially, lead to economic crisis, and result in many hardships and sacrifices that they no longer want to undergo. Among the changes and programs desired by the extremist leaders which seem to be meeting with strong resistance are further deemphasis of material incentives and self-interest, rapid elimination of class distinctions, assignment of numerous unqualified Reds and Red Guards to posts that put them in virtually complete charge of industrial management, anti-intellectualism, a serious deterioration in the quality of scientific, technical, and applied education for the sake of more political education, and extremely intensive ideological indoctrination.

The regime has responded to mass resistance to its program with extreme coercion, purges, severe penalties, and violence. It has even apparently toyed with the idea of achieving national unity and acceptance of its desired changes and policies by claiming that the Russians are on China's borders, ready to invade the nation at any moment.

It is clear that Mao and his loyal supporters can no longer rely on persuasion, intensive thought reform, or even moderate coercion to gain acceptance for some of their most desired environmental changes, programs, or policies. It appears that Mao's attempts to achieve a utopian "communist" China, as he visualizes it, via a genuine mass line are doomed to failure because a number of his most cherished aims, interests, and aspirations evidently do not correspond with those of the masses. Hence there are strong indications that Mao must either replace the mass line with strong coercion, penalties, force, purges, and perhaps even ruthless tactics that may well outdo anything that Stalin did in the Soviet Union or abandon major social changes relating to his ideological vision of communism in favor of some form of "modern revisionism." [120] In the long run, the second course of action would seem to be the only workable one.

Social Change: India versus China

India has certainly achieved significant social changes in the direction of greater managerial effectiveness and industrial progress since she gained independence in 1947. However, it does not appear that India's response to environmental constraints in general has been as effective as Red China's, with the exception, of course, of periods of ideological extremism in China.

India's efforts to improve the environment of industry and management have been less erratic than those of the Chinese Communist regime; but the Indian government has not succeeded in arousing the enthusiasm or in gaining the cooperation of the masses in its desired environmental changes or programs to the same degree or extent as has been done in China. Nationalism has not had the same universal appeal in India as it has had in China because of India's very strong provincial and regional chauvinism. In fact, lack of cooperation and, at times, serious conflict among India's states—not to mention different classes and social groups—have tended to hinder effective social change on a national scale. Moreover, increasing managerial effectiveness, industrial progress, and general economic development have not apparently served as highly desired operational goals for the Indian population at large to the same degree or extent as they have in China. This difference is probably due, in large part, to cultural, religious, sociological, and psychological factors.

India's leaders, even within the ruling Congress Party, have often been constrained from introducing potentially effective environmental changes because of conflict (including ideological conflict) within the government. Such conflict often leads to inaction, mistakes, and/or compromises in adopted environmental changes and programs. The results of India's 1967 elections suggest that even more conflict may be in store within the governmental bodies. But this is the price—and it is often a large one in terms of economic development—that a poor or developing nation often must pay if it tries to follow a genuine democratic road instead of setting up a one-party dictatorship. India also lacks anything comparable to a Chinese Communist Party type of organization which could mobilize, organize, motivate, persuade, and, if necessary, coerce the people or masses at the grass-roots level of the economy to respond in desired ways in connection with the implementation of environmental changes.

During most of Red China's history to date, ideological conflict within the ruling party has not tended to seriously hinder effective social change. This of course is not true during China's current inner-party struggle which has reached very serious proportions.

India's leaders, like China's, have at times attempted to introduce various major changes and programs too rapidly, without careful thought or analysis. In both countries the attitudes toward risk taking, the boundaries of rationality in macro risk taking, and ineffective utilization of scientific method have, in a number of instances, been major obstacles to the design and implementation of effective environmental changes. It seems, however, procrastination, inaction, and resistance, rather than extreme haste or irrationality, have been the more potent negative constraints regarding effective social change in India.

In general, cultural, sociological, and religious values that are incompatible with change seem to persist more strongly in the Indian economy and among industrial personnel than in Red China. As one prominent Indian industrialist points out:

> An inhibiting factor in the adaptation of technological changes is the spirit of other-worldliness that prevails in many countries of Asia. Almost all religions have glorified the simple life, but this feeling has had a greater impetus in Asia than in Europe, particularly in India: The world is an illusion; what matters is not this life but the life hereafter. While this feeling has been a consolation in periods of stagnation and degeneration, it is certainly not conducive to the adaptation of technological changes.[121]

The same Indian industrialist goes on to state that what is lacking in Indian industry and in other poor countries is a spirit of inquiry, a desire to find a better way, particularly with regard to technical change. He vividly describes this situation as follows:

> One of the necessary attitudes for bringing about technological changes and implementing them is a spirit of inquiry. To ask oneself, "What?" "Why?" and "Why not?" is a necessary condition of bringing about change. The entire industrial structure of Europe and America is based on the spirit of logical reasoning. Methodology of science, observation,

> experiment, and deduction has been the basis of the Industrial Revolution and it has permeated Western thinking until technological innovations which were a mere trickle in the eighteenth century has now become a flood. In developing nations, societies have been used to doing things in a particular manner, and they got used to doing it in that manner. They never question as to whether there is no better method. In a few cases this habit has been glorified as something sacred. Until such time as the habit of tradition and belief is replaced by a spirit of logical reasoning, a number of technological innovations cannot be expected from developing nations and implementations of such innovations will meet with considerably more resistance.[122]

Red China, it appears, has gone considerably further than India in creating a spirit of inquiry, a thirst and desire for change—particularly regarding technical change and managerial improvement—among industrial personnel at all levels. There also seem to be substantially more opportunities for lower-level enterprise personnel to participate in the process of change in China than in India.

In my opinion Red China so far has been significantly more effective than India in developing a potential overall environment for the creation of an industrial and advanced nation. This seems to be particularly noticeable in the sociological-cultural dimension of the environment. However, China may well stagnate or even retrogress significantly if ideology continues to be pushed at the great expense of economic, technical, and managerial rationality.

Change within Industry and at the Enterprise Level

In Chapter 2 we discussed a number of factors that tend to significantly retard technical, managerial, and economic change at industrial enterprises in underdeveloped and newly developing countries. Change conducive to greater managerial effectiveness and industrial progress in pre-1949 China was sharply constrained by many of the conditions dealt with in Chapter 2. In the present chapter we have also already indicated that a number of underlying environmental constraints acted against effective industrial change in old China.

Some of the more important barriers to effective change at the level of the enterprise in pre-1949 China were: adverse economic and political conditions, often resulting in considerable uncertainty; lack of education, knowledge, and skill; ineffective application of scientific methodology; negative attitudes toward risk taking and narrow boundaries of rationality in risk taking and decision making; relatively low achievement drive; ineffective interorganizational cooperation; great capital scarcity and a pervasive desire for wealth and material gain; rigid attitudes of authority, responsibility, and subordination; psychological and economic insecurity; and the tendency of business owners and managers to become psychologically adjusted to stagnation, the status quo, and backwardness in industry.

It is true that industrial personnel in old China did frequently display more resourcefulness and ingenuity in discovering makeshift methods and in introducing minor changes and innovations in operations than their counterparts in many other backward countries. The relatively decentralized and flexible nature of enterprise operations often encouraged the development of productive traits at the lower levels. However, managerial, technical, and economic changes introduced at industrial enterprises in old China did not nearly approach the diversity, extensiveness, magnitude, or effectiveness of those introduced by the Communists since they came to power in 1949.

The Chinese Communist regime has done a great deal to create a substantially better overall environment for the initiation and effective implementation of changes, both major and minor, of virtually all kinds in industry and at the enterprise level. While most major changes bearing on managerial effectiveness and industrial progress are initiated by superior authorities, including the top-level planners, they still must be implemented effectively at the enterprise level if desired results are to be obtained; and enterprise personnel have tended to respond rather effectively in this connection. The initiation and implementation of relatively minor innovations and changes in operations, methods, practices, procedures and techniques have become a way of life in modern Chinese industry.

In general, industrial personnel at all levels within Chinese Communist enterprises have tended to be quite receptive to technical, economic, and managerial changes, as long as such changes have been compatible with their interests and aspirations for the building of a powerful, strong, and modern China, economic development, and opportunities for a better life. They have come to realize that given the relatively backward nature of their economy, technical change and improvement are essential for industrial progress. Even relatively minor technical changes can lead to substantial improvements in productivity and, in many instances, for society at large. Economic changes that lead to lower costs, less waste in the utilization of resources, better economic decisions, greater output, productivity, and efficiency are also generally desired. Technical and economic progress depends directly on the quality of management employed in productive enterprise; and changes in managerial processes, practices, techniques, and methods which lead to better economic and technical results also tend to meet with popular approval and support.

This is not to say that obstacles to effective change or innovation in Chinese industry have been virtually eliminated. This is far from the case. China's economic system and political-legal framework often retard technical, economic, and managerial change. For example, if an enterprise wants to introduce a new cost-saving device—or institute some other kind of potentially beneficial change—but the resources required are not provided for in the enterprise plan, it may be very difficult, if not impossible, to obtain these resources once the plan is put into effect. Indian firms may often have a potential advantage—because of their flexibility with regard to change, especially major ones—over Chinese industrial organizations operating according to a more restrictive plan. While economic planning in China may be somewhat more flexible than in Russia, there are still a great many lost opportunities involving changes and innovations because of the very nature of the pervasive state planning and resource allocation.

It is also true that the systems of incentives, success indicators, prices, and pressures from the top down may not act against changes and innovations—particularly major ones—to the same degree in Chinese industry as in Soviet industry. However, Russia still has a big advantage in the effective introduction of major changes and innovations because of greater knowledge, education, skill, general know-how, and experience. What a Chinese firm might view as a substantial change or innovation might well be viewed as relatively minor or simple in Soviet industry. Moreover, it is likely that in many more instances in China than in Russia the effort, time, and resources expended on the introduction of changes and innovations will turn out to be unproductive and wasteful. Here again, greater know-how and experience are on the side of the Russians.

In spite of many problems and obstacles that still exist, the Red Chinese regime seems to have been surprisingly successful in creating a much more favorable general attitude toward change within industry. It has effectively utilized a number of organizational devices—such as employee and worker participation in management at all levels, widespread educational and training programs, and various incentive schemes, both material and nonmaterial—to bring about desired changes. The regime has also apparently been quite successful in integrating peasants recruited for industrial employment into an industrial way of life. These are some of the general impressions regarding change I gained from my interviews, observations, and findings in Chinese industry during the spring of 1966. Also, I am convinced that some of Mao's works, especially "On Practice" and "On Contradictions," have played an important role in creating a more favorable view of, and response to, change in Red Chinese industry.

However, as we have already seen, when changes have been forced upon industrial personnel against their will or have been introduced in extreme haste—and this has typically been the case because of ideological reasons—the process of change has not been effective, and managerial effectiveness and industrial progress have tended to suffer as a result.

In order to gain a better understanding of the attitudes toward change and the process and effectiveness of change in Chinese industry during different periods, it may prove worthwhile to examine briefly certain basic types of leaders, managers, and administrators that have a significant bearing on industrial change. We shall look at the traditional bureaucrat, the modern bureaucrat, the party cadre, and the modern manager, as seen by Communist China's leaders, as well as by various Western sociologists.[123]

A dominant type of manager, administrator, or formal leader—both in business and in government—in pre-1949 China was the traditional bureaucrat. This type of bureaucrat typically functioned through a creation of webs of personal relationships and mutual involvement. He was preoccupied with human solidarity and informal organization rather than technical solidarity or formal organization. He sought to achieve harmony by maintaining the status quo; and he tended to view change as a threat, as a passing challenge to stability. Hence, changes that were potentially conducive to greater managerial effectiveness or industrial progress were not generally of much interest to him, especially if they were likely to upset the existing pattern of personal relationships.

The Chinese view the modern bureaucrat in conventional Weberian terms. He is preoccupied with objective and rational legal rules, regulations, and procedures. He tends to stress technical and formal organization at the expense of human organization and solidarity. Like the traditional bureaucrat, he tends to resist change, to strive for routinization, institutionalization, continuity, and the creation of stable predictable environments, but unlike the traditional bureaucrat his frame of reference is technical rationality and formal organization rather than human solidarity and personal relationships. There were modern bureaucrats in old China, but they were more likely to have been found in the government than in industrial organizations.

The cadre—in Communist China a "Red" or party cadre—is a formal leader of the personal rather than institutional type. He is more concerned about human relationships and values than with technical or formal organization. He tends to be in favor of change and sees constant "struggle" as the means to change the status quo and create a new order. Both the party cadre and the traditional bureaucrat stress human organization, but the former desires change while the latter desires stability. The Red cadre evolved as a combat-style, activist leader with the evolution of the Communist Party in China. In some ways the Chinese Communist cadre is similar to the Japanese samurai of the early Meiji period. Both had the capacity to lead men, were committed to higher ideals, and regarded the development of industry and technology as basic goals for themselves and their countries.

The modern manager—typically an expert or professional—is concerned with rational techniques, methods, and practices. Like the modern bureaucrat he tends to stress formal organization and technical integration, and both are concerned with expertness. However, in his attitude toward change he is more like the party cadre or a military commander. For the modern Chinese manager, change, rather than harmony or stability, is the natural order of things, and both he and the party cadre live in a world of change, challenge, uncertainty, and, at times, insecurity. However, they tend to employ different means in achieving organizational objectives and solidarity. The modern manager tends to employ the system of formal organization and objective, more impersonal techniques and criteria, while the cadre is more inclined to focus on the informal organization and on personalities, and to use ideology, political education, persuasion, manipulation, and combat-team tactics. There were, of course, modern-type managers in China before 1949, but their number has grown greatly since the Communists came to power.

The dichotomy between cadre and managerial leadership styles is sharper in Chinese Communist industry than in American industry. In American industry there is really nothing equivalent to the groups of party cadres found in China. An effective, dynamic American manager must be concerned with both the formal and informal (interpersonal) organization, and he must undertake various motivational, directional, and staffing functions that tend to be handled by party cadres in China. In other words, there is not the distinct split in managerial functions between professional managers and cadre-type personal leaders in American industry. However, many American industrial managers and formal leaders do correspond quite closely to the Chinese modern manager—they are what some scholars might call Theory X managers[124]—while some, particularly among personnel managers, correspond roughly to the Chinese party cadres.

During the 1949–57 period there was a pretty good balance of party-cadre, modern-manager, and modern-bureaucrat leadership styles in Chinese Communist industry. The party cadres played the key role in mobilizing, organizing, and motivating personnel to respond effectively to the environmental changes and programs introduced with the aim of achieving greater managerial effectiveness and rapid industrial progress. They succeeded in creating a substantially more favorable attitude toward technical, managerial, and economic change at the enterprise level than that which had existed in the past.

The growing corps of modern managers and experts gave balance to this revolution of change by focusing on operational feasibility, technical integration, and formal organization. They also contributed directly to the initiation, design, and implementation of productive and other beneficial changes and innovations throughout industry.

Modern bureaucrats also have an important role to play in the improvement of managerial effectiveness and industrial progress. This is particularly true in a planned economy, where at least a fair amount of routinization, rules, regulations, and prescribed methods and procedures are essential for achieving reasonably coordinated and consistent interdependent plans and decisions, as well as timely information feedback for central purposes. During the 1949–57 period the Chinese regime did develop a workable industrial structure—patterned largely after the Soviet structure, and staffed with modern bureaucrats—which gave essential stability and continuity to the industrial and economic system. The modern bureaucrats typically filled intermediate positions, between the top-level policy makers and the industrial enterprises, in the industrial hierarchy. Resistance to change, excessive routinization, "vested interestism," and "localism" on the part of modern bureaucrats were not actually problems of truly serious magnitude during the 1949–57 period. Any resistance that did exist on the part of the modern bureaucrats was no doubt more than compensated for by the interests, motivations, and activities of the top-level leaders, planners, and policy makers, the party cadres at all levels, the modern managers and experts, and the masses.

Yet by 1957 the top party leaders had become increasingly concerned about the conservatism, vested interestism, localism, excessive stress on routinization, rules and regulations, and general resistance to change by the rapidly growing class of the modern bureaucrats. They felt, with some justification, that the bureaucrats often did not correctly interpret or implement their policies, programs, or priorities. They were also concerned that the modern bureaucrats might become a powerful new elite with attitudes, interests, and aspirations different from those cherished by the party leadership, particularly in the areas of human values and change. Hence, with the decentralization of 1957, in preparation for the Great Leap, the macromanagerial industrial bureaucracy was for the most part dismantled. In fact, the regime came close to destroying this bureaucracy altogether.[125]

Mao was convinced that only the party cadres were capable of effectively implementing his grand vision of the Great Leap, for only they were capable of transforming people, of mobilizing, organizing, and motivating the masses through nonmaterial incentives and of releasing the great "spiritual forces" and will power that were seen as essential for the success of the Leap. Mao was undoubtably influenced by the Great Production Movement of the Yenan period. He wanted to create a similar environment regarding mass enthusiasm for grass-roots improvisation and change. This, he was convinced, was the best way to transform people into good Communists and to achieve the desired output of things at the same time.

Hence the industrial Red cadre was to become once again a true combat soldier. The qualities of the cadre which the Chinese Communist leaders felt were essential in the struggle for economic development and social transformation are similar to those that the prominent American sociologist Morris Janowitz attributes to the combat soldier. His description of the combat soldier bears a remarkable resemblance to many Chinese statements made about cadres during the Great Leap Forward. Janowitz says:

> The combat soldier, regardless of military arm, when committed to battle, is hardly the model of Max Weber's ideal bureaucrat following rigid rules and regulations. In certain aspects he is the antithesis. The combat fighter is not routinized and self-contained. Rather, his role is one of constant improvisation, regardless of his service or weapon. Improvisation is the keynote of the individual fighter or combat group. The impact of battle destroys men, equipment, and organization that need constantly to be brought back into some form of unity through on-the-spot improvisation. In battle, the planned division of labor breaks down.[126]

The regime felt that the modern manager or expert did not possess the proper attitudes or interests regarding change, mass innovation, and improvisation during the Great Leap. Moreover, his preoccupation with formal organization and technical rationality made him suspect as a potential modern bureaucrat. Even though the modern manager still tended to be receptive to change and innovation, he was seen as too cautious, as compared with the Red cadre. Moreover, as far as the regime was concerned, he did not utilize the human organization or rely enough on the spirit and will power of the masses.

With the Reds placed in charge of industrial organizations policies tended to take priority over, and often superseded, plans. Some of the priority policies of the time were mass innovation, grass-roots improvisation, and self-sufficiency. Enterprises were run like combat teams operating under policy directives issued by the party committees. These directives were carried out under a system of decentralization of authority and improvisation.

In the United States the word "policy" has several definitions, a common one being a course of action—often repetitive—to be pursued with the aim of achieving a given objective. In Red China practically very policy command demands that something new be done; hence, policy is both a response to change and a cause of change.[127] Moreover, in Chinese terms, policy usually refers to the objectives to be attained. Plans, on the other hand, represent predetermined courses of action, targets, and objectives to be pursued, and are viewed as essentially routine in China. Hence, policy in a sense is seen as the opposite of plans or routine. It was felt that since managers and experts tended to be preoccupied with the design and fulfillment of plans, they were inclined to ignore or resist policy directives that upset plans, and they were also not likely to respond correctly to grass-roots impulses from the masses involving change, innovation, and improvisation.

Under the system of industrial management that emerged with the Great Leap, mass improvisation and innovation were greatly stressed at industrial enterprises. However, much, if not most, of it turned out to be technically barren. A great deal of unproductive time, effort, and great waste of resources was expended on the introduction of ill-conceived changes and innovations which were initiated and implemented by poorly qualified personnel. It also proved impossible to run a "planned" economy with plans that were constantly and pervasively being disregarded in favor of policies interpreted by local party cadres.

By 1961 China's leaders came to realize that modern managers and experts are indispensable if the process of change, innovation, and general industrial development is to be effective. They also accepted the fact that some type of modern macrobureaucratic structure was also necessary, and that no complex productive enterprise can function efficiently without at least some bureaucracy. No matter how innovative in character a specific organization or an industrial hierarchy as a whole may be, consolidation is necessary after change has taken place, and continuity must follow any leap forward. During the early 1960's the modern managers and experts were returned to the good graces of the regime. A substantial portion of the macromanagerial bureaucracy was restored, although it has never become as large as it was before the Great Leap. There has been more decentralization of authority to date than that which existed under the former highly centralized system under large industrial ministries. The regime's deep commitment to change, struggle, and innovation has created an endemic suspicion that bureaucracy, if uncontrolled, can deprive society of its élan, and this suspicion still strongly persists today.

In any event, a reasonably good balance of leadership styles combining those of party cadre, modern manager, and modern bureaucrat once again emerged in Chinese industry in the 1960's, and this lasted until around the onslaught of the Cultural Revolution. The most recent attacks on bureaucracy and bureaucratic managers actually began in the Chinese press as early as 1965 toward the end of the Socialist Education Campaign. Party publications urged the "sweeping away of bureaucratic, metaphysical, and scholastic ways of management." They condemned the practice of having regulations as a fetish, and proclaimed that control should not stifle initiative and change. Managers should encourage mass initiative, creativeness, and innovation.[128]

Some sources even praised enterprises for discarding plans and regulations in favor of creativity, change, initiative, flexibility, and inventiveness.

They urged firms to spend money wisely, not to follow working capital and investment plans entirely if good opportunities for change and innovation arise. For example, one firm received plaudits for using funds allocated for the purchase of machinery to buy white jade paste which was used to polish equipment as a substitute for regular polish paste that was in short supply and high-priced. Another plant was commended for spending unauthorized working capital funds to install heating and ventilation equipment in its warehouse. "After concrete analysis it was realized that savings from waste reduction would be more than the cost of investment over time." [129]

No doubt these individual enterprises increased their efficiency by such innovative behavior; but what about subsystem optimization and the upsetting of the plans of other organizations in China's planned economy? Flexibility and unplanned changes may be good for an individual firm, but in a planned economy of even the Chinese type the net effect of independent changes in enterprise plans and excessive flexibility for the economy at large is frequently likely to be negative. In other words, Red China cannot have her cake and eat it at the same time: it is not feasible to have firms in a planned economy act like dynamic relatively independent enterprises in a capitalist economy with regard to change, innovation, or flexibility in planning. This is a price—and it may often be a substantial price—that goes along with having a system of comprehensive state economic planning.

During my survey of Chinese industry in 1966 party cadres, modern managers, and modern bureaucrats were still all playing important roles in industrial management. Severe imbalances resulting from an acute dominance of one leadership style in connection with change and innovation over the other two styles did not seem generally to exist on a really intensive or extensive scale. However, at a number of enterprises it did seem that the pendulum was clearly swinging in the direction of the party cadres; and among these enterprises in particular there seemed to be a preoccupation with changes, innovations, and policies that were hindering productivity and efficiency. I also did get the general impression that Chinese industrial enterprises—as well as higher-level industrial agencies, from what I saw of them—are not bureaucratic enough. Somewhat greater routinization, more use of formal or written reports, procedures, and methods, and less flexibility would probably improve efficiency in numerous cases.

After my departure from China, there was the intensification of the Cultural Revolution, and the pendulum no doubt swung further in the direction of the party cadre's leadership style. However, this pendulum seems to have been cut far short of the situation which existed during the Great Leap period. The industrial managers, experts, and workers were not the only ones resisting the policies and changes in the system of industrial management desired by the regime; many party cadres were also in opposition. Hence Mao could no longer depend on the party as he had done in the past. He may have even developed fears, with some justification, that party cadres would degenerate into traditional bureaucrats who favor the status quo and stability—traditional bureaucrats, with no revolutionary zeal, who acquire permanent status and get fat.

So Mao and his loyal and zealous associates saw the newly and hastily formed Red Guards as the best way to revolutionize the system of industrial management. The Red Guards would run factories like the combat troops of the Yenan period. They would carry out the policies, changes, and programs desired by the regime, and they would encourage mass innovation, change, and improvisation. However, the regime's Red Guard and the new Yenan, or Great Leap, vision was very short-lived because of strong opposition by virtually all elements of society, by tens of millions of "enemies of the people."

Change within Industry: India versus China

During periods of ideological moderation in Red China the dominant attitude toward change and the actual process of change at industrial enterprises have probably been more conducive to managerial effectiveness and industrial progress than in Indian industry. Human values that are incompatible with change at the enterprise level still seem to persist more strongly in Indian industry, particularly among indigenous Indian enterprises. Numerous firms in various sectors of the Indian economy function in relatively protected markets and they can survive, and even reap substantial profits, without having to introduce changes or innovations that significantly improve managerial effectiveness or spur industrial progress. Neither effective competition nor adequate pressures exerted through state planning exist to compel them to change or innovate in any substantial way.

Where Indian managers desire to introduce changes in operations they often do so without adequate rational analysis and/or they meet with strong resistance from other enterprise employees and workers. Furthermore, there is typically neither the enthusiasm nor the opportunities that exist in Chinese enterprises for initiative and direct participation in the process of change at the lower and grass-roots levels of indigenous Indian firms.

It seems that there are far too many traditional bureaucrats and rigid modern bureaucrats in the Indian economy—the latter seem to constitute a particularly acute problem in the government bureaucracy and in the public sector—too few modern-type industrial managers, and a negligible number of cadres who act as effective agents of change like the Red cadres in Chinese industry. Moreover, relatively few Indian managers, as compared with American or even Soviet managers, are at the same time both real professionals or experts and cadre-type personal leaders. Some form or system of management which adequately combines both leadership styles is essential for sustained initiation and implementation of changes and innovations which result in substantially greater managerial effectiveness and industrial progress. This is as true for India as it is for Communist China—or for any other country, for that matter. When the Chinese regime becomes blinded by ideology and forgets this fact of industrial life, managerial effectiveness and industrial progress invariably tend to suffer greatly.

CHAPTER 5

China's Response: The Political-Legal Dimension

OUR CONCERN IN THIS chapter is to examine, in a general way, how important political and legal processes, structures, actions, events, and rules tend to affect critical elements of the management process at Chinese enterprises which lead to either significant positive or negative effects on managerial effectiveness and industrial progress. The political-legal dimension of the environment has a great bearing on how and how well industrial firms are managed and perform. Unfortunately, we can do little more than scratch the surface in our analysis of a number of the Chinese political-legal constraints because of informational and observational limitations.

It is difficult to discern how a specific law tends to actually affect the management, operations, and results of Chinese enterprises, or, for that matter, to identify precisely all of the Chinese laws and regulations which actually have a generally important bearing on productive enterprise. In the sphere of Chinese defense policy not a great deal is known, and little concrete data have been published. Hence, deductive reasoning and sparse, fragmented pieces of information must be relied upon to reach suggestive explanations and conclusions. The same is true for political organization and its impact on managerial effectiveness and industrial progress, though in this area I did manage to obtain somewhat more relevant information—there are more published sources, and in drawing tentative conclusions considerable use can be made of the Soviet experience regarding political organization. In the spheres of foreign policy and political stability we are on somewhat firmer and more empirical ground, but there are still large gaps in our knowledge.

In spite of serious limitations in our information, and the need for many speculative judgments, I am hopeful that this chapter will throw some additional and meaningful light on Communist China's managerial and industrial progress.

Relevant Legal Rules of the Game

Some of the important questions regarding the impact of a given legal system on managerial effectiveness and industrial progress are: Does the legal system tend to reduce uncertainty in enterprise-level planning and decision making, or does it have the reverse effect? Does the legal system generally act as a positive force in insuring that legal agreements essential to the fulfillment of a rationally conceived plan, a plan which is conducive to industrial progress, is properly enforced and fulfilled? Do various legal rules tend to deter or encourage enterprise managers to pursue more efficient courses of action conducive to industrial progress? Does the law lead to a better-motivated and more effective labor force, does it tend to have an opposite effect, or is it neutral in this regard?

A particular legal rule of the game may benefit a specific firm or group of firms at the expense of industry, the economy, or society at large. We are interested here in the impact of law on managerial effectiveness and industrial progress from the standpoint of society at large.

Pre-1949 China

In pre-1949 China the legal system was underdeveloped, like the country, and there was not very much formal codification of laws affecting business and industry. Legal rules of the game did little to improve managerial effectiveness or spur industrial progress. Rather, the absence of laws in critical areas, unclear laws, erratic, unsound, and often dishonest enforcement of laws, all tended to lead to considerably more uncertainty, greater risks, and less efficiency for firms than would have been the case with a better legal system.

Under the prevailing legal rules and conditions of their enforcement, inefficient firms in political favor and with proper connections frequently benefited in obtaining capital, loans, government contracts, protected markets, and in reaping inefficiently high prices for their products. Potentially more efficient firms that were not in favor often suffered greatly. Tax laws were erratic and in a state of flux; and tax evasion, as well as bribery and corruption, was rampant. Black marketeering was also widespread and tolerated in business and industry, even when such activity had an extremely negative impact on productive efficiency and industrial progress. A wide variety of other inefficient and illegal managerial and business practices also went unchecked.

Law was highly ineffective or nonexistent in connection with trust, cartel, and collusion arrangements and with destructive competition in general. Hence, there was little if any legal recourse or effective protection from abuse for the potentially efficient and dynamic firm struggling to survive in the face of destructive competition from companies in government favor, powerful monopolies and oligopolies, cartels, collusive practices, or foreign interests.

In the sphere of contract law, the legal system was also ineffective. An industrial enterprise could not depend on the law to uphold or defend his contractual-type agreements with suppliers, customers, employees, and other interested participants with whom the firm did business. It is true that businessmen and industrial managers in old China—like those today—had a deep sense of obligation to do their best to fulfill the agreements and conditions that they entered into voluntarily with other parties in the course of doing business. Not to do so would have meant "loss of face" and could even have ruined a man's reputation. But the absence of effective contract law nevertheless resulted in greater uncertainty and risks, which seriously hindered managerial planning and control.

Virtually the whole field of labor law was underdeveloped and ineffective. Labor legislation did practically nothing to produce a better-trained and motivated labor force or a more energetic and secure one. Moreover, it did very little in providing for minimum wages, welfare and social benefits, better working conditions and safety or in reducing mass unemployment. This led to an atmosphere of pessimism, apathy, and unrest throughout the nation. Paternalistic management and managerial prerogatives, rather than the law, determined practically all important personnel matters, and the results were typically damaging to managerial effectiveness and industrial progress. The legal system also did not serve to deal effectively with grievances, labor unrest, or strikes, which were very violent at times. Arbitrary political and managerial power rather than objective or national law was typically resorted to in order to solve serious labor problems.

Much of what I know—which is not very much—about the legal system and its impact on industrial enterprise in old China I have learned from interviews with former and present Chinese citizens, including a few of the Red capitalists whom I met during my recent trip to Communist China. These Red capitalists are of course inclined to exaggerate, for purposes of propaganda, some of the negative points that they so vividly make. I have also learned something about law in old China from a number of British businessmen and other Westerners who spent a good deal of time in China before 1949. I became convinced that the legal rules of the game in old China were far from conducive to efficient management and industrial progress and that, in fact, the effect of the legal system on these areas was undoubtedly substantially more negative than positive. The nature of the legal system in pre-1949 China was probably one additional negative factor that led to the Communist takeover.

Communist China: The Law and the Plan

Little has been written about the Chinese Communist legal system, in general, or about the way it affects the management of productive enterprise.[1] But there is not really a great deal that can be learned about this subject without considering at the same time the nature of Red China's economic system, political structure, and various other economic and political factors.

In the industrial sphere, and for the individual enterprise, the formally approved plan is considered in its entirety to be *law*. In effect, the "law" in this connection is subservient to the plan. What this really means is that the laws, policies, objectives, targets, tasks, regulations, rules, and agreements—which, as a whole, make up the formal state plan and its myriad derivative and intertwining sub-plans—are officially binding on the parties and organizations concerned, unless and until formal revisions in plans are adopted by appropriate authorities.

In a very real sense, then, law viewed in this way can be no better or no worse—in terms of managerial effectiveness and industrial progress—than the design and implementation of the plan. Moreover, the numerous policies, targets, regulations, and so on which make up China's economic plan cannot, for the most part, be viewed as laws in the same way that laws are thought of in other countries having a pretty well-defined, comprehensive, and largely enforced system of law and legal codes, such as the Anglo-Saxon and Napoleonic codes of Western nations. In Red China, violations pertaining to most aspects of enterprise plans or higher-level operating plans are not linked to any clear or formal legal process involving prosecutions, trials, penalties, sanctions, punishment, damages, or the like. Little attention has been paid in China to an official compilation or codification of violations, cases, judgments, disciplinary action, or precedents in connection with breaches of the plan. In general, legal-type precedents provide little in the way of meaningful predictive guidelines for industrial managers or, for that matter, for almost anyone else.

As was mentioned in Chapter 2, the macro or legal type of rules for the Chinese enterprise manager are basically of the "thou shalt" kind rather than the "thou shalt not" variety common to capitalistic countries. Hence, the plan in Red China is filled with a myriad of "thou shalts." Chinese managers have relatively little legal freedom, as compared, for example, with their American counterparts, in designing and especially in fulfilling the enterprise plan.

No person or organization in China is legally allowed to set up a new enterprise, significantly expand an existing one, buy new equipment, develop or market a new product of much importance, or do practically anything of a major nature in the industrial sphere unless such action is officially sanctioned by the plan. Because of the nature of comprehensive state planning in China, a great many opportunities and potentially beneficial activities are foregone because they are not provided for in the plan. There is very little room for individual entrepreneurship on any substantial scale in such a politico-legal system. In spite of numerous legal restrictions—and various other environmental constraints—India has an entrepreneurial advantage over China at the micro-organizational and individual levels, and independent entrepreneurial activity of a major nature often contributes to greater managerial effectiveness and industrial progress in India.

Red China's Formal Legal System

Communist China does have its system of formal law and justice, modeled essentially along the lines of Soviet legal institutions. Its apex is the People's Supreme Court and the People's Supreme Procuracy. However, formal law has played, and still plays, a much smaller role in Chinese life than in the Soviet Union. As of 1956 there were only 2,100 practicing state lawyers for a population of some 600 million citizens, and there were only 670 legal counseling officers to serve a nation consisting of 1,972 counties and 171 cities.[2] It is unlikely that this situation differs substantially at present.

In 1957, nonjudicial institutions were given broad powers to judge and impose sanctions on individuals and organizations, including corrective labor for long periods of time. The courts became less and less of a force in the exercise of justice as the party came to play a growing role in meting out sanctions and rendering judgments. The party has in large part displaced the legal system. Party justice has tended to be informal, swift, and, at times, very harsh. By the spring of 1959 the Ministry of Justice was formally abolished, and since then no real institutional foundation has existed for an independent judiciary.[3] Justice, for about the last decade, has been administered for the most part without formal court trials.

No concrete codes of trial procedure have yet been enacted by the Chinese Communist regime, and work on the compilation of a legal code has been halted for some time. However, formal law has not disappeared entirely; it still exists in the economic sphere in connection with contract law, which will be discussed shortly. However, the courts continue to function primarily in major criminal cases, such as those involving "counterrevolutionary" crimes, murder and rape, major thefts, and gross misuse of state property—crimes which are likely to bring stiff penalties, including death, or which are seen to have important propaganda value. The party, rather than the courts, is more likely to handle social disorders where the punishment is not harsher than corrective labor and the charge is not serious enough to incur formal criminal liability.

India, with its formal legal system patterned largely along the lines of Anglo-Saxon law, seems to have an edge over China with regard to relevant legal rules of the game bearing on managerial effectiveness and industrial progress. It is true that there are many serious shortcomings in Indian law and its enforcement which contribute to considerable economic inefficiency and poor managerial performance. However, the Indian legal system does seem to generally provide for somewhat greater clarity, certainty, consistency, protection from breaches in the law, and less unproductive time for industrial enterprises, their managers, and their employees, as compared with that of Communist China.

A Shanghai Court Trial

Although it is rather peripheral to the focus of this study, it may prove interesting to devote a moment to an actual Chinese Communist criminal court trial. Edgar Snow, the American author and veteran Sinologist, attended a formal trial of a rather minor nature in Shanghai in 1960.[4]

The defendant, Yang Kuan-fu, thirty-nine years old, was charged with embezzlement of 1,527 yuan (about $610, the equivalent of the annual wage of an unskilled worker) during his employment with the Shanghai Light and Power Company as a bill collector for maintenance and repair work. The state provided the defendant with a defense lawyer. The judge was a Mr. Mo, a machinist and local labor-union leader who had been given special training in a school operated by the state judicial department to teach the relatively simple legal codes of the people's courts.

Early in the trial it was made clear that Yang had worked as a special policeman under the Kuomintang regime before 1949. In that job he "intrigued with gangsters to blackmail, intimidate, rob and even beat citizens." After liberation in 1949 he remained in Shanghai, but failed to report and confess his past misdeeds. He donned civilian clothes and took a civilian job. He had been employed with the light and power firm since 1957.

Employees of defrauded factories and other organizations and the head accountant of his own company uncovered and reported his embezzlement activities. Several of them came to testify against him in court. Yang embezzled by writing one figure on the top receipt given to the customer and another figure on the lower carbon copy. He was first suspected of fraudulent activities when he was seen in expensive restaurants where the capitalists go. Then he got hold of some "bad women" whom he paid to sleep with. (The Chinese citizen, a co-worker of Yang, who made this point about bad women claimed that they were not prostitutes. But he admitted that "there are still some women around who will make love for money." I frankly never came across or heard of any prostitutes during my stay in China, and the number of prostitutes and part-time playgirls is negligible, compared to the pre-Communist period. However, the Chinese Communist regime has still not been 100 percent successful in wiping out the oldest profession in the world!)

Yang pleaded guilty to the embezzlement charge and his past misdeeds. The only thing his lawyer did to defend him was to ask for leniency. The law under which he was tried provided either for criminal-type punishment or reform through education. The maximum sentence was ten years; he received a three-year sentence. The judge indicated that the reasons for the leniency were Yang's full confession of his sins and the possibility that after some reeducation he could still do something useful in society. The prisoner was notified that he had a right to file an appeal within ten days, and the court adjourned.

One of Yang's co-workers in the courtroom told Snow that if Yang had confessed when they first got the evidence on him, he might have been given only one year. I think it is quite possible that if Yang had confessed his crime at the outset and/or didn't have the pre-1949 history that he did he may indeed have been treated more leniently. He might not have even been brought to a formal court trial. Instead he might have been judged and punished by his own company or by a local party committee—Chinese business firms and other organizations often establish their own "comrade-trial committees" which have quasi-judicial disciplinary powers. Given his past history, however, his formal criminal trial did have propaganda value—it gave the judge the opportunity to compare life in the corrupt Shanghai of the past with the wholesome present.

Uncertainty Caused by the Informal and Quasi-Legal System

Violators of social or work discipline, as well as individual civil disputes, are commonly dealt with by social organizations and economic enterprises under the guidance and direction of appropriate Communist Party committees. Committees formed for trying and judging comrades frequently act as quasi-judicial disciplinary agencies within industry. They deal with such matters as labor and work discipline; "antisocial" managerial or worker behavior, which can range from tardiness and absenteeism to fraud and theft; incompetence bordering on negligence; and so forth. Criticism and self-criticism meetings are also employed to deal with people who display undersirable, or antisocial, tendencies or behavior patterns involving violations of the plan. All of these quasi-legal and disciplinary activities tend to take up considerable time at numerous enterprises. If a formal legal system dealt with more of the activities, there would be less uncertainty for managers, less time lost at enterprises, and probably greater industrial progress.

Comrade-trial committees at Chinese organizations seem to roughly resemble the "comrade courts" that I came across in Soviet industry in the early 1960's, and which were becoming very common at that time. Both types of comrade courts function under local party guidance and act as quasi-judicial disciplinary powers. However, in China they do not seem to be as formalized in their procedures, composition, or rendering of punishments as in the Soviet Union.

Unless a particular Chinese manager or other industrial employee has worked out reasonably clear behavioral guidelines and established a modus vivendi with the party cadres or higher authorities who are likely to initiate disciplinary action for violations in the enterprise plan—or other activities he may engage in—he is likely to be confronted with considerable uncertainty and insecurity in his day-to-day life. This is perhaps one reason why the regime seems to be so concerned about the blending of personalities in staffing major executive jobs and why the regime is reluctant to shift around key industrial personnel to the same extent as in Soviet industry.

During the Great Leap Forward when the Reds controlled industry, they tended to view rules, procedures, regulations, and plans as bureaucratic impediments to progress. At that time, numerous industrial managers and other personnel must have been very uncertain and insecure about what behavior or activity would lead to what type of disciplinary action by local party cadres and superior authorities. If a manager was abused and/or subjected to the arbitrary disciplinary powers of party organizations, he typically had no formal legal recourse; nor does he have it today. As a result, managers were inclined to avoid responsibility and risks, and often preferred to work on the production line rather than make decisions, even where their decisions would have improved efficiency significantly if implemented.

When the status, powers, and authority of the industrial experts and managers were restored in the 1960's, much greater emphasis was again placed on formal regulations, rules, and procedures in the management and operations of enterprises. This decreased substantially the arbitrary, unpredictable, erratic, and, at times, whimsical nature of party-enforced discipline and punishment.

With the intensification of the Cultural Revolution and widespread civil strife in late 1966 and 1967, the nature of the legal system and the quasi-legal process has contributed to much of the confusion and uncertainty. Legal rules, procedures, and regulations are very unclear about what should be done by whom if Red Guards or other Super-Reds try to take over a factory, if management resists them, if personnel stage a work slowdown or strike. And in 1967 they were also not clear on the status of military personnel assigned to industrial firms.[5] Who is the proper authority, and what is the proper agency for dispensing justice and rendering judgments in such cases? Who should be charged and prosecuted, by whom, on what grounds, and for what act? Should a given manager take orders from the Red Guards, his industrial superiors, party cadres, military officials, people's militia, and/or other new revolutionary committees assigned to the plant? Should he encourage or try to prevent a strike in his enterprise? Whose policies, directives, and priorities should he follow in trying to fulfill a disrupted plan? Local party cadres might promise more material incentives to the workers in return for their cooperation, but this is contrary to existing regulations and the plan. What should management do? I should certainly hate to be a Chinese manager under present conditions.

In general key terms such as "counterrevolutionary" activities, "antisocial," "antistate," "antiparty," and even "criminal" behavior are typically not clearly defined in Red Chinese legal or quasi-legal codes. This provides far too much flexibility, arbitrariness, and uncertainty in the administration of justice and discipline. One party committee—a "comrade court" or a formal court of law—may view a certain managerial activity as counterrevolutionary or antisocial, while another may not, because of differences in interpretation or for other reasons. The same legal or quasi-legal body may view a particular action as criminal or antiparty at one point in time, but not at another because the emphasis or interpretation of a particular policy of the regime has changed. When the regime is having an antibureaucracy or anti-intellectual campaign, various managerial attitudes and practices may be viewed in a very negative way, while under other conditions they are not viewed as negative. If managers strive to fulfill the aggregate output or sales targets of the enterprise plan and must sacrifice "innovation," quality, and/or "self-reliance" to do so, they may be subject to disciplinary action at one point in time—perhaps even be charged with serious misuse of state property—and may face no rebuke or sanctions, and possibly even be encouraged, at another time. If a manager is caught falsifying results of the plan, he may be faced with stiff punishment, whereas he may well have been condoned or even supported by party cadres had he committed the offense during the Great Leap.

Laws and Regulations Involving Strikes and Labor Discipline

The right to strike is apparently still guaranteed by law in Communist China.[6] Strikes have not been very common until recently, but the law does not help the manager to decide what to do in the event of strikes, petitions of grievances, and other types of breaches in labor discipline. The uncertainty resulting from unclear laws pertaining to strikes and labor discipline is reflected in Mao's 1957 essay "On the Correct Handling of Contradictions among the People." (This is a different essay from the famous "On Contradictions," which was written in 1937.) In his 1957 essay Mao states:

> In 1956, small numbers of workers and students in certain places went on strike. The immediate cause of these disturbances was the failure to satisfy certain of their demands for material benefits, of which some should and could be met. . . . But a more important cause was bureaucracy on the part of those in positions of leadership. In some cases, responsibility for such bureaucratic mistakes should be placed on the higher authorities, and those at the lower level should not be made to bear all of the blame. . . .
>
> The guiding spirits in disturbances (including strikes) should not be removed from their jobs or expelled without good reason, except for those who have committed criminal offenses or active counterrevolutionaries who should be dealt with according to law. In a big country like ours it is nothing to get alarmed about if small numbers of people should create disturbances; rather, we should turn such things to advantage to help us get rid of bureaucracy.[7]

Laws, Regulations, Rules, and Policies Regarding General Personnel Matters

Regulations, rules, policies, plans, and administrative control, rather than Western-style labor legislation, are primarily used in Chinese industry to lay down and enforce rules involving personnel matters such as wages, welfare, educational and other social benefits, working conditions, hiring, transfers, dismissals, discipline, and so forth. In general, the labor policies, regulations, and controls of the Chinese Communist regime have proved far more effective in developing an energetic, relatively healthy, well-motivated, more secure, and better-educated and better-trained industrial labor force than ever existed in pre-Communist China. In theory, this has been accomplished by greatly restricting individual mobility and freedom of choice because the state now has the omniscient voice in important personnel matters. In reality, there is little doubt that the large majority of the industrial population favor the current state of affairs—at least as of mid-1966—to the conditions that existed in the past, when freedom of choice regarding wages, working conditions, better opportunities, and so on meant little, if anything, to the typical industrial employee.

In Communist China basic wage and salary scales are determined by state authorities, with the Ministry of Labor playing the central role. Each type of job or occupation has a grading point system, with maxima and minima that vary slightly among different regions. Local, industrial, and party organizations, do however, play the major role in determining what grade should be assigned to a given employee, with the exception of key executives and technologists in centrally controlled firms. They also have some independence in determining the specifics of monetary-incentive and bonus schemes to be employed. High-level enterprise managers and party cadres, however, are no longer entitled to bonuses.

Wage and salary scales in Chinese industry certainly appear to provide virtually all personnel with a better-than-bare subsistence income, although their living standards, on the average, still lag far behind those of their counterparts in the Soviet Union. The standard of living for the typical Chinese worker seems to be better than that of the Indian worker, while upper-level Indian enterprise managers typically live extremely well, compared with their Chinese counterparts.

If market forces were allowed to determine wages in Chinese Communist industry and freedom of mobility were to be allowed, the majority of workers would probably receive substantially less pay than they do now, given the vast surplus of unskilled and semiskilled labor.[8] Keeping wages substantially above the level that would exist if supply and demand were allowed to take their course is a policy basically motivated by ethical and/or political reasons rather than being an economic one. This type of policy is particularly common and far-reaching in socially conscious, over-populated countries which have large surpluses of poorly educated and unskilled manpower. It typically means that total labor costs are higher than need be, at least in the short run. It is impossible to determine whether higher labor costs are more than offset in time by a healthier, more energetic, better-motivated, and more secure labor force. If a great effort is made to educate, train, and generally improve the skills and productivity of the labor force, as has been the case in Red China, such a wage policy is likely to benefit managerial effectiveness and industrial progress in the long run.

In Communist China there are also stringent restrictions on rural migration into the cities.[9] This is done in order to check urban unemployment, and to keep people working on the farms—a matter of importance because of China's huge population and the subsistence level of its agricultural output. India does not have this type of stringent control on rural migration largely because of the value it places on individual freedom and mobility, and as a result she is faced with a very serious urban-unemployment problem.

Within Chinese industry there are great restrictions on labor mobility and freedom of choice in selecting jobs. In effect, labor mobility is almost totally subservient to the plan. The appropriate higher-level authority must formally approve all transfers and new hirings of personnel at the enterprise level. The firm's department of labor and wages, with the sanction of the director and the party committee, indicates personnel changes of this type. But the appropriate territorial labor bureau, as well as the appropriate superior industrial organization, must approve the transfer or new hiring. Where important managerial, technical, or party positions are involved, central authorities frequently must approve the decision.

In Soviet industry today there is much greater individual freedom in obtaining jobs than in China. On April 1956 a "liberalization" edict repealed an earlier Soviet law tying people to their jobs at the will of the state, and also gave enterprise managers more authority over the recruitment and selection of personnel. In Soviet industry in 1958, direct hiring by enterprises constituted about 84 percent of all those selected for employment in industrial establishments subordinate to regional economic councils. The process of direct hiring by individual enterprises from among the available labor supply includes outbidding other organizations by offering personnel substantially more money and other inducements.[10] The fact that Soviet industrial personnel have significantly more freedom in the job market than their Chinese counterparts is not necessarily due to a more humane attitude on the part of the Soviet regime; it is probably due, in large part, to the fact that there is a labor shortage, rather than a surplus of labor, in Soviet industry. Furthermore, the Soviet labor force is substantially better educated and more skilled than China's labor force.

Because of severe overpopulation and the resulting large surplus of unskilled and semiskilled labor, numerous Chinese enterprises are overstaffed and have much disguised unemployment which results in low productivity. This was clearly the case at many of the firms that I surveyed; at some, the law of diminishing returns seemed to have been brought into play with regard to productive efficiency because of excess manpower. In Chinese industry much use is made of grossly inefficient—by American standards—intensive-production techniques in order to utilize excess labor.

The official state plan determines whether cutbacks are to be made in excess manpower in Chinese industry. It seems that the regime does not want disguised unemployment and excess manpower to go too far in hindering productive efficiency, and there are reports of retrenchments of manpower at industrial enterprises. For example, in 1965 the Kansu Metallurgical Corporation reorganized its own departments and factories and reduced the total number of employees from 9,280 to 5,980. Some thirteen offices and forty-one departments, shops, and sections were involved in this reorganization and retrenchment. On the whole, production increased, and in some areas it increased by as much as 100 percent. The old, feeble, and sick personnel were retired on pensions, while the others, the large majority, were assigned to other plants, construction jobs, and to regular and part-time schools.[11] I was also told of less spectacular cutbacks in employment at a number of firms that I surveyed.

Retrenchment on a scale as large as in the Kansu Corporation case is probably not very common in Chinese industry, and restrictions on the retrenchment of personnel no doubt serve as significant constraints on managerial effectiveness and industrial progress at thousands of enterprises. But this is also true of many non-communist underdeveloped and developing countries which adopt and enforce restrictive labor legislation for ethical and political reasons. It is true, for example, of India where it is often difficult to dismiss excess manpower and to introduce more productive technology because of labor laws and regulations. However, Indian firms have somewhat more flexibility and independence in laying off and dismissing excess manpower under certain conditions. They do not have to operate according to a comprehensive state plan with regard to many personnel matters, and they can, and often do, convince the union and/or government authorities that retrenchment is necessary. They also have the right to take their case to the courts if they feel strongly enough about it.

Much of India's labor legislation adopted for ethical and political reasons serves to penalize the industrial enterprise economically and to make it, rather than the state, responsible for employee welfare. Firms are typically prevented from laying off unneeded personnel because of the critical shortage of jobs and the poor system of state unemployment insurance. When enterprises are allowed to dismiss people, the workers who have been released must then find other jobs on their own, and this is frequently difficult to do if they do not possess any specific skills that are in demand. In China the state assumes responsibility for finding work, training, and providing unemployment benefits for people laid off from enterprises according to the plan. India's system provides, at least in theory, for more individual freedom in the labor market, and in reality it creates more unemployment; China's system, which is more rigid, provides for more individual security and less outright unemployment. It is virtually impossible to determine with any precision which system is better in terms of managerial effectiveness and industrial progress. Perhaps the greater flexibility permitted in the Indian system gives it a slight edge in terms of purely ethical criteria. But is the system superior to China's in economic terms?

In Chinese industry there are a great many state regulations and policies pertaining to working conditions, safety, accidents, hours and days of work, holidays, spare-time education and on-the-job training, and welfare benefits. Local party and trade union committees, as well as the enterprise's vice director in charge of welfare and the enterprise's Welfare Department and Labor and Wages Department, are charged with seeing that these regulations and policies are properly interpreted and enforced on a day-to-day basis. In virtually all of these areas, with the possible exception of time off for holidays, industrial personnel are undoubtedly better off and hence tend to work better and more productively under the Communist regime than in pre-1949 China. They are provided with a wide range of welfare benefits and facilities under the Communist state, many of which have been mentioned in previous chapters. They are, on the average, better than those provided in Indian industry. Working conditions and safety have, on the average, also improved substantially, according to Westerners whom I know, who have spent time in both the old and the new China. However, particularly until the mid-1950's ruthless tactics were utilized to enforce labor discipline and to coerce personnel to conform to the will and wishes of the regime. Official state policies and regulations regarding personnel matters were frequently disregarded in the earlier years of the Red regime. For example, in 1955 the Chinese Communist *Workers Daily* revealed that alleged gains made in "speed-up" drives by shocking overuse of labor were more than offset by heavily increased losses in manpower output due to sickness, accidents, and absenteeism.[12] Here is a report from that period.

> There has been no limit to the prolongation of working hours; individual workers have worked continuously for seventy-two hours through additional shifts and working hours. As a result of exhaustion, sickness and casualties have been serious. There are quite a few cases in which, owing to exhaustion, workers have fainted, vomited, or even died.[13]

Here is another example of that era. A safety drive was demanded in 1955 by Lai Jo-yin, the then Chairman of the All China Trade Union Federation, who asserted that many accidents due to bad management were blamed on "carelessness of the workers." The *Workers Daily* accused "some units" where cadres had penalized workers "already injured" and cited an instance of a worker who had lost both fingers being "fined one one month's wages and made to criticize himself in public." Others had been sent to jail for allegedly causing "serious losses" in production while "nothing was done" to management.[14]

Since about 1956 the state has adopted and implemented a much more humane approach toward industrial employees. My general impression—and the impression of most other Westerners who have visited China in recent years—is that working and safety conditions in Chinese industry, while still appalling in many instances when compared with modern Western standards, are reasonably humane and adequate.

I did, however, encounter what appeared to be violations, in some cases rather serious, of official state policies and regulations regarding the working lives of personnel. Officially, industrial personnel are not generally supposed to work more than forty-eight hours per week or eight hours per day. In addition to spending long hours in spare-time schools and after-work meetings, employees at some enterprises surveyed spent considerable time in overtime and extra work without extra pay. Many of them worked part of an extra shift on their days off and even during vacations to which they were entitled. Typically I was told by enterprise officials that employees work overtime "voluntarily" and because they are "eager to serve the state," but I somehow doubt that this is true in many instances. Some of the more candid managers did admit that it was necessary for employees to put in extra time in order to fulfill the plan and to get urgently needed products out to restless customers. No doubt coercion and intensive social control are utilized quite often to make Chinese employees work against their true wishes. Unlike their Indian counterparts, they have no legal recourse in such instances. When oppressive tactics are commonly utilized in this way at various industrial enterprises, productive efficiency is likely to suffer eventually.

Although Chinese factories tend to be quite clean, I did encounter rather unsafe and unhealthy working conditions at some plants, which I am sure were in violation of official safety regulations. For example, at the Hangchow Machine Tool Plant workers were welding without any eye protection; some laborers were holding huge slabs of steel without any support while other workers were drilling and hammering away on the steel with big drills and hammers. At the Shanghai Drug Firm one shop was full of unpleasant fumes, and in another shop people were working in water on the floor above their ankles. At the Canton Electrical Appliance Factory a few people doing wire work seemed to keep getting electrical shocks. At the Wuhan Iron and Steel and Peking Wire enterprises it was surprising that nobody got seriously injured even while I was there, considering the lack of safety precautions utilized for materials handling internal transportation activities and storage facilities. Perhaps Chinese workers tend to be less accident-prone than their American counterparts because they are much more accustomed to working under hazardous conditions. But a number of Chinese enterprise officials did admit that accidents, sometimes quite serious ones, do occur, and I did observe a number of accident cases in enterprise medical clinics. Ineffective enforcement of safety regulations undoubtedly hinders managerial effectiveness and productive efficiency at many Chinese factories.

Safety regulations are also violated quite often at many Indian enterprises, and accidents are quite common. However, the law in India seems to provide somewhat clearer standards and more certain protection, as well as injury compensation for Indian industrial personnel—especially where there are gross safety violations and where more serious accidents occur—than are provided in Chinese industry.

China has a distinct advantage over India in the existence and enforcements of laws and regulations involving formal education and on-the-job training for industrial personnel. China also has the economic advantage over India with regard to legal holidays and sanctioned time-off for special events. In India there are many more legal and religious holidays than in China. It is also common in India for special holidays and shutdowns of offices and plants to be declared when a prominent national or local government official, active or retired, dies or when certain unusual events occur, such as food riots, hortals (strikes), protest demonstrations against such things as tram fare increases, other forms of civil and political protest or unrest, and urban floods. During the one-year period which I recently spent in India, industrial firms in Calcutta were closed on several dozen occasions—in addition to the regular weekly Sabbath closing, summer shutdowns, and company strikes, if any—because of scheduled holidays and "special" events. If Indian firms desire to stay open and have all required personnel report to work on such occasions, they are likely to run into union and/or legal problems. All this results in a substantial loss of productivity and tends to hinder industrial progress. China's problem may be the reverse—that regulations do not permit an adequate number of holidays and vacations, or enough time off, thus reducing productive efficiency somewhat because of a tired labor force.

Antitrust and Anticartel Legislation

There is of course no legislation in China of the type that is directed against trusts and cartels because the state owns industry and the state plan determines and controls all major aspects of industrial activity. Since there are also no market forces or competition which can effectively restrain undesirable monopolistic behavior and force firms to strive for greater efficiency and better overall performance, the plan must attempt to include restraining forces to perform this function. But the plan in Red China is substantially less effective in this regard than the combination of laws, competition, market prices, and the profit motive in most relatively advanced capitalistic nations because of the nature of China's basic economic system, as well as the existence of various economic and political constraints.

In India there are laws pertaining to industrial monopolies, cartels, and collusion. However, their nature and enforcement are generally not very effective in restraining undesirable monopolistic behavior, collusive agreements, or in pressuring firms to be more efficient. Moreover, competition, prices, and the profit motive do not serve as very effective devices in this regard in a number of industrial sectors—for example, in the production of steel, aluminum, and various types of machinery and equipment. Nevertheless, India's legal rules of the game in this sphere may, on the whole, do slightly more to promote managerial effectiveness and industrial progress than China's virtually total reliance on comprehensive state economic planning and control.

Price Controls

There are no price laws as such in Chinese industry, although most commodity prices are determined and/or approved by the state and its appropriate macro-agencies.[15] Commodity prices are an integral part of the plan and subservient to it. When the demand for a certain commodity exceeds its supply, the Chinese regime generally resorts to outright rationing or quotas rather than adjusting fixed prices. When supply exceeds demand, the plan is adjusted, often not soon enough, accordingly. Prices do not play the resource-allocation or automatic regulatory role that they do in market-price, capitalistic-type economies. However, even in a Marxist economy when prices do not accurately reflect scarcity values or true prevailing conditions of supply and demand, many resource-allocation errors, often major, are made. A considerable amount of undesirable and unintended managerial decision making and behavior also results because fixed prices frequently do not provide very meaningful criteria for efficient decision making or control, or for evaluating economic performance. Planning and control, to be reasonably efficient in such an economy, must be done primarily in physical rather than monetary terms; but this is impossible to do very well or comprehensively in a planned economy such as China's. It becomes even more difficult in a more advanced planned economy such as the Soviet Union's.[16]

There are laws, regulations, and controls involving commodity prices in India's mixed economy. This leads to a great deal of inefficiency, illegal practices, and black-marketing activity. (According to some Indian government reports, as much as an estimated 40 percent of all business and monetary transactions involve black-market activity.) However, in a number of sectors there still are market prices for a great many products, and this often does serve to spur managerial effectiveness and industrial progress in these industries, particularly where laws pertaining to collusion and monopolistic behavior are enforced.

Tax and Financial Regulations

Taxes paid by enterprises in China are also subservient to the plan.[17] (There has been no personal income tax for several years in Communist China.) The chief aim of tax policies and regulations in China is to provide the state with a planned and desired amount of revenue and investment funds. Taxes are not used in any significant way to influence managerial or enterprise decisions or behavior, as they are in non-communist countries. They are, in effect, a derivative or residual arising from the fulfillment of the plan. Enterprise profits are a substantially bigger source of state revenue and investment than taxes paid by industrial firms. In fact, taxes were levied on only a few of the Chinese industrial enterprises that I surveyed. In the Soviet Union enterprise taxes are a substantially more important source of state funds than in China, and profit margins at the industrial-enterprise level are, on the average, significantly smaller.

During the Great Leap Forward, tax evasion at the enterprise level became quite pervasive and a serious problem in Chinese industry. In fact, financial regulations, rules, and policies of all types were frequently violated and not effectively enforced.[18] This situation emerged with the economic decentralization which placed most enterprises and business and industrial activities under local party control. In numerous cases party cadres either could not effectively enforce rules against violations of financial and tax regulations, or they sanctioned and even participated in those violations. Moreover, as a result of the decentralization, there were large reductions in the supervisory auditing and control staffs of governmental financial and revenue departments and agencies.

Bank-agency controls also became less effective as enterprise and local party cadres and managers persuaded and, at times, coerced bank officials to disregard financial and monetary regulations regarding loans and sources and uses of funds.[19] The banking authorities were often charged with being too "bureaucratic" and even antiparty and antistate. In general there was considerable overspending and illicit use of funds during this period by enterprises. Funds earmarked for capital investment were spent for working capital purposes, and vice versa. There was much overspending of wage funds. Profit plans were not fulfilled and the amounts of profits that were supposed to be remitted to the state were often less than regulations called for.

The result of such pervasive violations of tax, financial, monetary, and profit regulations was that the plan, what there was of it, and the economy ran out of control most of the time. Hence, managerial effectiveness and industrial progress suffered greatly. By 1961 all capital-investment projects in progress and all plans for such projects, apart from some special top-priority cases, were ordered discontinued by the state. This ban was probably lifted on a piecemeal basis over the next several years.

Overall financial discipline was, for the most part, restored in the 1960's as regulations, rules, policies, and controls became more clearly defined and effectively enforced. The staffs of the state financial, revenue, auditing and banking agencies were strengthened, and the experts were restored to their positions of authority and influence in industry and throughout the economy.

There have been, and still are, violations in tax and financial regulations and plans in Chinese industry in the 1960's, but nothing in this area approaches the situation that existed during the Great Leap. There are some indications, however, that with the new antibureaucracy and general ideological campaign the regime has been encouraging violations in financial regulations, policies, and plans. For example, as mentioned in the previous chapter, there were some actual recent cases of enterprises spending earmarked capital-investment funds for working-capital uses, and vice versa. The firms were commended for their behavior by the Chinese Communist Party's leading newspaper, the *People's Daily*.[20] If financial and tax regulations are once again ignored and ineffectively enforced on a widespread scale in China's planned economy, the plan and the economy will inevitably once again run seriously out of control.

It is true that in many instances the only way that a Chinese enterprise can keep production operations and marketing activities going may be to use capital-investment funds for current supplies or working capital to buy an urgently required machine. This would be the case because of errors in the plan and/or unforeseen bottlenecks in the fulfillment of the plan. However, if a substantial number of firms violate financial regulations, the state plan is likely to be seriously undermined. A given Chinese industrial manager may of course violate financial regulations to the benefit of the state as well as his enterprise and himself. In general, the manager would be inclined to consider the risks and tradeoffs involved; should he risk violating regulations or should he underfulfill the enterprise plan? Given the rather nebulous nature of China's legal rules of the game in this regard, and the rather arbitrary system of discipline, penalties, and praise in Chinese industry, the Chinese manager is often likely to be confronted with a great deal of uncertainty in making such a decision.

The Indian industrial manager is also likely to be subject to a considerable amount of uncertainty because of the extremely complex maze of tax and financial laws and regulations and their uneven enforcement which confronts him. These rules are more complex than in the United States, and Indian company taxes are also significantly higher in most cases. Tax evasion, as well as illegal and semi-illegal financial manipulation, are probably substantially more pervasive in India than in the United States, China, or Russia. In India, tax laws and financial regulations are not only used to generate revenues and investment funds for the state but also to encourage and discourage various types of managerial and enterprise behavior. The best that can be said in a nutshell about the impact of Indian tax laws and financial regulations on managerial effectiveness and industrial progress is that the net results are uncertain, mixed, and often conflicting. It would take volumes to analyze this problem in any depth and, even then, the conclusion might still not be definitive.

Regulations Pertaining to Inventions, Innovations, and Ideas

As was mentioned in an earlier chapter, there are no patent laws in China, and officially there is supposed to be no commercial secrecy among firms. Firms are, however, permitted to have their own board names and trademarks. Instead of patent laws the regime relies on plans and incentives, both material and nonmaterial, to encourage inventions, innovations, and technical improvements in industry.[21] My findings show that in recent years monetary rewards paid to individuals for such activity have been de-emphasized for ideological reasons.

At this stage of China's development the absence of patent laws does not seem to have had a significantly negative impact on managerial effectiveness or industrial progress. Considerable progress has been made by copying and applying the technology, techniques, and products developed in more advanced countries, without paying out any royalties, and by introducing indigenous innovations and inventions of a mostly minor nature.

Unlike a private firm in a country like the United States, the Chinese enterprise worries little, if at all, about industrial sabotage or intelligence, infringements on its ideas and discoveries, or commercial secrecy in general. There is therefore no need for an enterprise legal staff, let alone the big legal department which is so common in larger American firms. This type of environment has probably done much to foster considerable dissemination of information and promote widespread implementation of inventions, innovations, and improvements in Chinese industry, particularly of a relatively minor nature. There is nevertheless a great deal of unproductive duplication in innovative activities because of the complex nature of national economic planning, information reporting, and control.

As Chinese industry develops and grows more complex, more sophisticated indigenous innovation and invention will be required for sustained progress. While this may not require patent laws similar to those found in the West, it may well require greater emphasis on monetary incentives for both individuals and organizations. It is also possible that, in an advanced economy, competition, and perhaps patent laws as well, are integral conditions for encouraging truly complex and risky innovational activity. But the Soviet Union rather than China will undoubtedly be the first communist country that will provide us with the necessary evidence to substantiate this speculative hypothesis.

While there are patent laws in India, that country also relies primarily on technology and products developed in more advanced nations—for which it often pays the royalties due. Indian patent laws have served to stimulate some indigenous inventions and innovations, in most, but not all, cases of a relatively minor nature. It is possible, however, that managerial effectiveness and industrial progress would benefit from greater dissemination of knowledge, cooperation, and less secrecy among firms with regard to discoveries, ideas, innovations, and improvements. In many instances "free enterprise" would probably not be undermined, one firm would not profit at the expense of another, and, in fact, many firms might benefit from a reciprocal and cooperative exchange of ideas and information.

Contract Law

One area in which formal Chinese law somewhat resembles business law in the West is that of contractual agreements among industrial firms and other types of economic organizations in their roles as suppliers of goods and services and customers.[22] Such contracts stipulate the quantities, prices, qualities, and other detailed specifications of products to be supplied; delivery dates, and often method of delivery as well; and the date on which payment is to be made. Contracts are also signed for capital-investment projects and various types of subcontracted work. There are legal rules and regulations regarding fines, damages, and other penalties that can be imposed for contractual violations. However, the existence of contract law in Chinese industry does not do a great deal to reduce uncertainty or to insure that contractual agreements will be met. This point has already been dealt with in the previous chapter in the section on "Interorganizational Cooperation," but a further discussion seems in order here.

Industrial contracts are actually a device used for implementing the state plan, and must conform to the plan. Such contracts are, in a very real sense, subservient to the plan. Hence, the fulfillment of contracts depends much more on how well the plan is designed and carried out than on any legal sanctions or regulations. The plan substantially limits the freedom that enterprise officials have in arriving at mutual agreements with other parties. It is common for superior authorities above the enterprise to enter into general contractual agreements based on higher-level resource-allocation decisions, and then the firms involved conclude specific contractual agreements, which spell out in detail product mix, delivery dates, exact amount to be paid, and so forth, with suppliers and customers. It is also common for two enterprises to enter into direct contracts without any general contracts negotiated between their superiors. In many cases the enterprise's superior organization handles all supply and sales contracts affecting the firm; this practice is most common where the enterprise is under a municipal corporation and produces a relatively standardized, homogeneous, and/or stable product line, particularly of consumer goods. In general, who signs what kind of contracts with whom is determined by the enterprise's position in the industrial hierarchy, the types of commodities involved in the contract, and the locations of the parties involved. Regulations pertaining to fines, damages, and other penalties, if any, that can be invoked for breaches of contracts and the determination of the liable party are also based on the above conditions.

Officials interviewed at many of the Chinese firms that I visited claimed to know little or nothing about regulations involving fines or damages which apply to their enterprises. These firms were primarily consumer-goods producers which did not enter into direct contractual agreements.

Managers of Peking Cotton Textile Mill No. 3 knew vaguely about regulations involving fines and damages, but its direct superior, the Peking Textile Corporation, handled all contractual matters for the mill. The vice director of the firm claimed that penalties for contractual violations involving his enterprise are rarely invoked, and in the few cases where they have been that he knew of, expert orders were involved. The Peking Clothing Factory, which signs many direct contracts with other parties, claimed that fines and damages had never been invoked against it because of the unpredictability of demand which results in frequent changes in its product-mix plan.

A larger number of the heavy-industry firms surveyed knew about regulations regarding fines and damages for contractual violations. These were primarily the larger machinery enterprises, as well as the two steel firms, Peking Wire, Peking Chemical Coke, and Wusih Diesel. The corporate office of the Wuhan Iron and Steel Corporation handles all contractual matters for its eighteen factories. Some of these firms (Wuhan Heavy Machinery, Shanghai Heavy Machine Tool, Peking Wire, and Wusih Diesel Engine) admitted that they had collected and/or paid fines and damages at one time or another during the last year. However, as was pointed out in the previous chapter, the Chinese seem to rely less than the Russians on fines and damages for enforcing contractual agreements and seeing that the plan is properly implemented substantially. The Chinese are more inclined to allow formal revisions in plans and to rely on social-control techniques such as the *dazeba* (a letter of criticism or praise), voluntary cooperation, and compromise. The Soviets have developed a formal and extensive system of arbitration tribunals and commissions to deal with contractual violations and the awarding of fines and damages. This arbitration system has not proved to be very effective in limiting contractual violations in the Soviet Union because of the nature of state planning, resource allocation, success indicators, and incentives.[23]

No formal or official system of arbitration tribunals has been established in Red China. Where necessary, appropriate higher authorities above the enterprise level resolve contractual disputes in Chinese industry. If they are not successful, the courts may be called on to solve the dispute, but the role of the courts in this regard is an enigma—I never met anyone in China who admitted knowing of an industrial contractual dispute being taken to court for adjudication. To the best of my knowledge there are no available reports in the Chinese press of court action in this area. When there are reports of contractual settlements involving fines or damages they are imposed by the administrative agencies concerned and not by the courts. However, even when such a contractual settlement is reached, the delinquent firm is not released from its obligation unless the plan is officially revised.

In China, as in Russia, abused customer organizations probably tend to be reluctant to file claims for breaches in contracts against their suppliers for fear of alienating them, thus upsetting or imperiling future relations. Such behavior is referred to by the Soviets as "the rotten practice of mutual amnesties," and it tends to exist in any country, including basically capitalistic ones, where strong sellers' markets exist.

When contractual suits are filed and brought before the appropriate authorities in Chinese industry, it is typically time-consuming and difficult to clearly pinpoint responsibility or blame for violations because of the nature of China's economic system. The supplier charged with a violation may not have been allocated adequate resources to carry out his plan; he may not have received adequate supplies according to the contract with his own supplier; his plan may have been disrupted by revisions of various types; or the supplier firm may have actually been negligent, incompetent, and/or inefficient, and has no one to really blame but itself.

In both Chinese and Soviet industry, the effective enforcement of contracts is also hindered in certain sectors because of the time period involved. Contracts are negotiated and signed on an annual or quarterly basis—and in some cases monthly. However, for many types of complex heavy machinery two- or three-year production cycles are required in their manufacture. Since the Chinese enterprise does not have an operational long-term plan and does not enter into contracts for longer than one year, it is not possible to enter into a really binding contract for such a product. The contractual process, in effect, starts from scratch each year. The executive in charge of supply and sales at the Wuhan Heavy Machinery Firm described some of the problems that arise under the existing system and candidly stressed the need for longer-range planning and contractual agreements.

In theory, a new type of contractual relationship, referred to as "fixed-point supply," was supposed to have been introduced around 1965 to deal more effectively with this type of problem.[24] This system would have suppliers and customers enter into a more permanent type of contractual agreements which would extend beyond one year when beneficial. According to managers of Wuhan Heavy Machinery, Wusih Diesel Engine, Shanghai Steel Mill No. 3, and a few of the other firms surveyed which are theoretically operating on this new system, "fixed-point supply" thus far had only meant that certain firms are assigned by the state to specific suppliers for an indefinite period. However, contracts were still negotiated and signed annually or quarterly chiefly on the basis of resource allocations made by higher authorities. The only thing that had really changed was that a given firm knew that it would be receiving certain types of commodities from the same supplier or selling certain products to the same customer from year to year. For example, Wusih Diesel Engine now knows that its primary steel supplier will be Shanghai Mill No. 3 in the years ahead, unless a reassignment is made by the state. This may lead to more effective supplier-customer relations since they now will work together on a more permanent and perhaps more intimate basis; but it does little to solve concretely the pervasive contractual problems discussed above.

I was informed by several Chinese industrial executives that the enterprise's customer may also be subject to fines and penalties if he does not pick up his ordered products at the time stipulated in the plan. Wuhan Heavy Machinery, for example, had collected fines from customers on a number of occasions for this reason. This regulation and its enforcement probably came about because of the great shortage of adequate warehousing facilities in the Chinese economy, and at the enterprise level. Social-overhead capital is a very significant constraint in this regard. I came across all kinds of damaged and spoiled commodities lying around in factory yards and even in the public streets near the plants, waiting to be picked up by customers. They ranged from expensive equipment components and industrial materials to clothing, textiles, and soft-drink bottles. If the customer organization also lacks adequate storage facilities, the commodities may still get damaged even if they are picked up on time.

A Chinese central-planning official whom I interviewed said that fines and damages may be stiffer and may be enforced somewhat more often—but still not very often—when firms handling heavy industry rather than light industry are involved. The reason is that more serious damage is likely to be done to the economy if, say, a producer of large and expensive machinery violates its contract with a customer than when a factory producing men's suits or cameras commits the same violation. He could have added that the state is more willing to sacrifice the consumer, particularly where a nonessential item is involved, than an industrial producer. The same official also said that it is possible that fines and damages are invoked more often when the violated organization is situated in a province other than that of the delinquent firm in order to counteract regional "localism" and other undesirable "autarkic" tendencies. (If true, this would be somewhat inconsistent with the greatly emphasized state policy of "self-sufficiency" and "self-reliance" in all areas and at all levels of the economy.)

The central-planning official, as well as a number of industrial executives whom I interviewed, stated that until around the time of the Great Leap the Chinese system of business contract law and its enforcement was patterned closely after the Soviet System. This system met with little success, they said. Since the late 1950's the emphasis has been on the conscientiousness, efforts, motivation, and cooperation of industrial managers and workers to ensure that contractual agreements are fulfilled as well as possible, rather than on fines, damages, or other penalties. This system, they claim, has worked significantly better. There may be truth in this, in view of what we know about human motivation and behavior in Chinese industry. However, contractual violations still constitute a serious problem in China's planned economy because of the very nature of state planning which is always far from perfect. For this reason, even a more formalized legal process involving breaches in contracts might not do very much to overcome this inherent problem. However, it could perhaps somewhat reduce managerial uncertainty and unproductive time.

India has a system of contract law quite similar to that found in Western countries. Because of the existence of strong sellers' markets and critical shortages of products in many spheres of Indian industry, there are numerous breakdowns in supply, serious production and marketing bottlenecks, and a good deal of uncertainty in enterprise operations. In spite of such serious problems, Indian contract law and its enforcement are probably somewhat more effective than Chinese regulations in assuring the proper and timely receipt of commodities among enterprises and in reducing managerial uncertainty. At least the laws, the processes of adjudication, and the penalties involved seem to be more clearly defined and consistently enforced in India than in China. Moreover, legal protection for Indian firms tends to be quite effective and certain in connection with the many items which are not part of the strong sellers' markets. However, this does not necessarily mean that the procurement and supply system is generally more efficient in India than in China. China seems to have a significant edge in other environmental conditions, particularly "interorganizational cooperation," affecting procurement and supply.

Illegal Procurement and Marketing Activities

There is evidence that because of breakdowns in the supply system Chinese managers sometimes engage in illegal and quasi-legal activities, mostly involving procurement, in an effort to fulfill the key targets of the enterprise plan.[25] Such activities are similar to those found in Soviet industry.[26]

In Chinese industry there are purchasing expeditors or "pushers" (called *tolkachi* in Russia) who actively try to obtain supplies through informal or unofficial channels, such as persuasion, reciprocity arrangements, personal influence, "special favors," and, at times, outright bribery. They are commonly employed by the supply department of the industrial enterprise. The use of expeditors became very pervasive during the Great Leap Forward because of major, extensive, and constant breakdowns in the supply system. Unofficial supply and trading centers spring up in various places from time to time. For example, a few years ago a teahouse in Shanghai grew into an active center for transactions and deals involving certain types of equipment. Illegal, semiofficial, and official barter deals among industrial organizations are quite common. Firms trade chemicals for equipment, trucks for steel, and textiles for dyes and small tools. Black marketing of certain critically scarce commodities have been known to exist from time to time, as have "underground" factories producing scarce items. There have also been some reports that unauthorized invoices and purchase orders have been used in an attempt to fulfill the enterprise plan and, at times, to reap personal profits. Commercial organizations receive allocations of various centrally controlled raw materials (for example, cotton, cotton textiles, and grain) because they are the most convenient channels for supplying them to small customers, including small industrial firms. Large enterprises are not supposed to buy such materials on this market, but this rule is difficult to enforce.

How pervasive are such illicit activities in Chinese industry? Of course, it is impossible to say. It is likely that they are not as widespread as in Soviet industry. There are far more reports in the Soviet press about such behavior, but this, in itself, does not necessarily mean much. However, Soviet enterprise plans tend to be more difficult to change; there are more bureaucratic impediments; the system of managerial incentives, success indicators, and tight plans has probably placed greater pressures on firms to undertake such activities; and there does not seem to be as great a sense of voluntary cooperation or candid compromise. The Chinese regime has apparently been more willing to sanction as official expeditors such informal procurement practices as barter deals and trading centers, when they prove to be beneficial for the economy at large. Many of the expeditors, barter arrangements, and the like are, in fact, not illicit in China, whereas in the Soviet Union there is a tendency to officially brand virtually all such activities as illegal, thus causing greater uncertainty for managers who may have to face disciplinary action imposed by superior authorities.

In both China and Russia there are not many reports of prosecutions or penalties imposed for illegal and semi-illegal activities of the kinds noted above. This suggests that such behavior tends to be tolerated because it aids the overall system of planning, supply, and resource allocation. This would be the result if idle or reserve resources were brought into use, and/or if supplies were deflected from low priority—in the eyes of the state—to higher priority plants.

In those relatively few cases where a buyers' market has existed for certain products in China, producers at times have resorted to illegal practices in selling their goods. For example, in 1966 some factories in southern China were denounced for giving presents to retailers to win their goodwill.[27]

The "Five-Anti" Campaigns and Business Morality

From time to time the Chinese regime has tried to crack down on illegal and unofficial industrial and business activities, perhaps for ideological reasons and/or perhaps because it has been felt that such activities were doing real damage to the economy. The last major crackdown occurred in the spring of 1963, when many illegal and unauthorized activities were reported in the press. This campaign, though apparently short-lived, resembled the "five-anti" campaign of the early 1950's.[28] The original five-anti campaign focused on five economic crimes which were common at the time: (1) bribery of public officials; (2) fraud in connection with state contracts; (3) tax evasion; (4) theft of state-owned assets; (5) betrayal and misuse of state economic secrets. However, the major purpose of the first five-anti campaign was probably to bring a large number of still private firms under Communist control. Many firms, particularly in the private sector, were investigated, and offenders were prosecuted. Punishment meted out by special tribunals ranged from fines and imprisonment to confiscation of enterprises.

Although business and managerial morality is much greater and illegal activity much less in Communist China than they were in pre-1949 China, illicit and unethical behavior has certainly not been eliminated entirely. No laws or regulations can wipe out such behavior completely, and various illegal managerial practices seem to be an inherent part of a communist-type economic system. In many instances they are conducive to managerial effectiveness and industrial progress, given the constraints under which the managers must operate. In many other cases, however, they undoubtedly have a negative impact on productive efficiency and economic development.

An American manager operating under similar conditions would be inclined to act in much the same way as his counterpart in China or in the Soviet Union. In fact, business morality may well be higher in China than in the United States. It certainly seems to be higher in China than in India or Russia. In the American economy, market prices, competition, and a meaningful profit motive which tend to spur managerial efficiency and economic progress all serve as a check on undesirable managerial behavior. They also often serve as automatic regulatory devices and to enforce laws much more effectively than a formal legal system or a system of comprehensive state planning could do on their own. But in a substantially less developed or underdeveloped capitalistic or mixed economy, market prices, competition, and the profit motive typically do not perform effectively in this regard because of the presence of other negative environmental constraints. Neither does the law in many cases.

Concluding Remarks

From what we know about relevant legal rules of the game in Chinese industry, the nature and enforcement of laws and regulations seem to be deficient in several serious aspects. The end result is considerable managerial uncertainty, much unproductive time, and a good deal of economic inefficiency, all of which substantially hinder managerial effectiveness and industrial progress.

As Chinese industry develops and grows more complex, the need for a more formalized, codified, clearly defined, and comprehensive system of laws and regulations will become increasingly great. So will the need for a more formalized, predictable, and consistent process of enforcement involving disciplinary sanctions for violators. A more effective and workable balance between the requirements of the state plan and adequate flexibility essential for carrying out the plan with a reasonable degree of efficiency will have to be supported by a more effective system of laws and regulations. Of course, this is much easier said than done in any planned economy. Nevertheless, a growing planned economy, such as Red China's, cannot depend on rather nebulous laws, regulations, and policies to effectively support its system of state planning and control. Nor can it depend on a system of enforcement and related disciplinary measures which tend to be informal, inconsistent, and rather arbitrary. A legal and regulatory system based in large part on the subjective interpretations of laws, policies, and regulations by party cadres and state administrators cannot be counted on to bring about the design and implementation of consistent and well-coordinated industrial plans and decisions.

Flexibility of Law and Legal Changes

Our conception of "flexibility of law and legal changes" as an environmental constraint is different from, although intimately related to, the constraint of "relevant legal rules of the game." That is why we deal with them separately. In analyzing the impact of legal rules of the game on management and industrial progress we focused primarily on the legal process, specific laws, and regulations and on their enforcement at particular points in time. In this section we take a more dynamic approach—as we did with social change—because we are chiefly concerned with changes in laws, and flexibility in their interpretation and enforcement over time. We are interested in the degree to which relevant legal barriers to the efficient management of industrial enterprises can be changed, and in the timeliness of such changes and the predictability and certainty of legal actions over a period of time—say, for instance, over a three-, five-, or ten-year period.

As countries shift, or try to shift, from agrarian subsistence-level economies to urban-oriented factory-based systems, the necessity for fairly rapid, timely, and pervasive change in legal system, law enforcement, and political institutions is essential to greater managerial effectiveness and industrial progress. But law and politics tend to be conservative—particularly in an underdeveloped or stagnant society—seeking precedents for action; and this tendency conflicts with the necessity of being able to keep pace with the timely and extensive legal changes demanded in a nation trying to become a modern industrial state. The law books of virtually any country are full of anachronistic and antiquated rules, laws, regulations, and possible penalties which presently serve no useful purpose and/or even retard fruitful economic and managerial trends. This problem tends to be especially acute in underdeveloped and newly developing nations which enforce relatively ancient or outdated laws from time to time in unpredictable ways, thus causing considerable managerial uncertainty. Failure to come to grips effectively with rapid changes, balanced with a reasonable degree of certainty and predictability in the legal sphere, can only mean more productive inefficiency and less industrial progress than otherwise might be possible. As pressures build to change the law, various undesirable forms of pressure and behavior arise in society which may do more harm than good.

In pre-1949 China legal institutions and laws never really began to undergo the drastic transformation essential to sustained industrial progress and major improvements in managerial effectiveness. The country's leaders were preoccupied with problems of political control and never got around to effectively introducing major legal reforms that were conducive to substantial industrial progress. Social changes of great magnitude would have been required in order to do this, and in old China the overall process of social change was disappointing, in terms of economic development, even during China's Republican era from 1911 to 1949.

It was not until the Communists came to power in China that drastic social change led to legal changes in the direction of greater managerial effectiveness and industrial progress. But even then, as has already been discussed, the plan and party control have played a much more important role in Red China's industrial development than legal changes of the kind commonly seen in the West. Nevertheless, since the population at large generally desired and accepted drastic social change when the Communists took over China, the regime was, in effect, given a mandate and a relatively free hand to introduce major changes in legal institutions and rules of the game for industrial enterprises.

The major problem in the legal sphere in Communist China has not been one primarily of lack of legal change, ultraconservatism regarding laws, and insufficient flexibility in the legal process. Rather, it has been one of hastily introduced and ineffective major changes in the rules of the game for firms—frequently for ideological reasons—and too much flexibility, uncertainty, and lack of clarity in the legal process.

New laws, reforms, regulations, rules, resolutions, campaigns, decrees, and policies which have a bearing on industrial firms and their managers have been, and are, frequently introduced by the regime.[29] Often they are in conflict or, at least, inconsistent with existing laws, regulations, policies, resolutions, and the like, which still remain on the books. Every time a new plan, campaign, or reform is formally approved, many new rules of the game are introduced. The same is typically true when a national or local Communist Party or People's Congress is held. It is even true at times when a major leader or important party publication makes official statements having policy or regulatory implication.

From my interviews with various Chinese Communist officials I gained the impression that the current policy (or regulation) requiring that managers and party cadres engage in compulsory physical labor at regular intervals came about through a rather informal process. At the dedication ceremonies for the Ming Tombs Reservoir on the outskirts of Peking in the late 1950's, Mao and other party leaders performed some minor ceremonial acts of physical labor, such as digging some dirt with a shovel. Apparently Mao declared at that time that it would be a good idea if all administrative and party cadres throughout the economy spent some time at regular intervals in physical labor. Shortly thereafter some local party committees in different parts of the country took Mao seriously and implemented a compulsory physical labor-policy for administrators and party officials under their jurisdiction. In time such a policy became widespread, and eventually it was introduced on a national scale. I am not sure whether this policy currently still takes the form of a mere policy or whether it has become a resolution, rule, regulation, or actual law. Nor could I find out whether any formalized disciplinary measures or penalties are utilized for noncompliance. The way this policy was interpreted still varied somewhat among cities and firms during my visit in 1966. For example, the type of work that qualified as physical labor varied among firms; and at some enterprises managers and party cadres were spending one day per week in physical-labor activities, while at others they were spending a day and a half, two and, in a few cases, even three days each week.

There seemed to be quite a bit of confusion in Chinese industry as to whether and when a particular new policy, resolution, or rule really becomes a law which is clearly understood, consistently interpreted, uniformly enforced, and associated with reasonably predictable sanctions and disciplinary measures. It seems that the typical Chinese manager is likely to be rather uncertain about such questions as the following: Which laws, regulations, rules, and/or policies take priority when there is inconsistency among them? Which of the existing ones are still applicable, and which have been superseded by new ones? Which are likely to be enforced, what penalties are likely to be applied for violations, and under what conditions?

In general, the relevant rules of the legal type in Chinese industry often appear to change too frequently, the changes are not clearly spelled out, and there tends to be too much flexibility in their interpretation and enforcement. This clearly has been the case in such matters as the authority, responsibilities, rights, and status of managers, party cadres, Red Guards, military personnel, and people's militia cadres assigned to factories; democratic centralism; worker elections; violations of various aspects of the plan; working and safety conditions; hours of work; breaches of contracts and the enforcement of penalties; illegal procurement practices; and various other activities, decisions, and events discussed in the previous section.

During a period when the ideological pendulum has swung sharply in the direction of extremism, far-reaching changes of the legal type affecting enterprises and their managements have been implemented, thereby causing a great amount of disruption, confusion, uncertainty, and inefficiency throughout the Chinese economy. Eventually, but usually only after severe damage has been done to management and industrial progress, more rational rules of the game are reinstated. But many of the ideologically inspired rules, regulations, decrees, and policies remain on the books to be called into play on short notice if and when the regime desires to do so—or when local party cadres have felt that it was a good idea to do so. If those rules on the books are not felt to be adequate for achieving the objectives desired by the regime's leaders or the local party committees—and currently the military and people's militia—new rules of the game, often major ones, are likely to be suddenly introduced in arbitrary and informal ways. When such changes in rules are met by strong opposition from Chinese industrial personnel and local party cadres, the inevitable result is, as we have seen, civil strife and, of course, much inefficiency.

The major problem in Indian industry regarding flexibility of law and legal changes seems to be one of conservatism rather than of too rapid and hastily introduced changes. Laws are typically not kept up to date with substantially changing economic conditions, and there is often too much rigidity in the interpretation and enforcement of various laws. In some areas of the Indian legal sphere, however, there also tend to be too much flexibility, arbitrariness, and uncertainty. To illustrate, during my stay in India the Minister of Finance made a casual remark that the practice of managers charging off depreciation on their home furnishings and luxury-type furniture, appliances, and gadgets in their offices to the company was an undesirable one, particularly when managers abused their (legally sanctioned) right to do so. Because of this criticism a number of firms that I know of were shortly thereafter investigated by zealous tax officials from various government agencies and bureaus. They were actually seeking to interpret the minister's statement as a new policy or regulation which should be enforced. I do not know the outcome of these investigations, but they did have a familiar ring when I went to Red China and looked into legal changes and flexibility of law there. Of course similar types of incidents do sometimes occur even in the United States. But, on the whole, flexibility of law and legal changes tend to be significantly less of a negative constraint on managerial effectiveness and industrial progress in the United States than in either China or India.

Defense and Military Policy

China's Republican Era

While no precise figures are available, it is clear that much of China's very limited income and productive wealth was expended on military and defense items during her Republican period, which lasted from 1911 to 1949. For during this period China was preoccupied with national and localized civil wars, fighting among war lords, and, of course, the extremely costly war against Japan. Defense and military spending did relatively little to develop the economy; and, in fact, China's leaders during this period were concerned with political control and wars and not with economic development per se.

Even if the regime had been interested in industrial progress, little could have been accomplished with the great drain of critically scarce high-talent human resources, materials, equipment, and funds into the military sector. A large proportion of China's best-educated, trained, and well-motivated citizens, including several of Communist China's present-day leaders, pursued military careers at the great expense of the civilian economy. At the same time there was not much mobility from military to business or industrial careers. The domestic economy by itself could not support China's wars—civil or external—and a vast amount of its armaments, military supplies, and technical assistance had to be imported from, and provided by, foreign countries. Although economic development was sacrificed under Republican China's military and defense policies, the country did not succeed in becoming more than a third- or fourth-rate military power even by allocating much of its resources to military needs.

It is true that military and defense expenditures do show up in a country's national income and GNP accounts; but they did very little, if anything, to improve living standards or spur industrial progress in Republican China. In fact they probably had the reverse effect on the whole.

Communist China

When the Communists came to power in 1949, they realized that effective military power and economic development must go hand in hand. In order to pursue Red China's ultimate national and international objectives pertaining to economic progress and military power, the development of heavy industry received top priority in the 1950's. This strategy, it was felt, would provide the foundation for both sustained economic development and the buildup of a strong defense sector and military machine.

During the 1950's an average of roughly 6 to 7 percent of Red China's rapidly expanding gross national product was spent annually on defense.[30] Even though the Soviet Union paid much more of the bill for the Korean War than China, investment expenditures were relatively substantially more important in China in the 1950's than in Russia at a comparable stage.[31] The only other external military confrontation of any significance that Communist China has "directly" engaged in has been with India in 1962. This confrontation was brief and did not cause very serious problems for China's economy or industrial management. However, it came at a rather strange time for China because her economy was just starting to pull out of a serious economic depression and defense spending, as well as military imports, were probably cut back at least somewhat during the 1960–62 period. The Sino-Indian conflict did significantly disrupt Indian industry because India has raised its defense spending sharply since 1962 to a current figure of around 5 percent of GNP. India has, however, obtained more foreign assistance in its defense sector than China in recent years. During the Vietnam conflict, in spite of China's "anti-imperialist" outbursts, the Soviet Union is once again bearing a much greater share of the burden for North Vietnam's military effort.

During the 1955–60 period it is probable that imports made up roughly 20 to 40 percent of Red China's total defense and military expenditures (exclusive of outlays for subsistence of its armed forces).[32] Soviet aid to China reached its peak around 1955 and has declined since then. One of the many reasons behind the Sino-Soviet rift has been Russia's refusal to help the Chinese develop a modern and advanced military establishment including nuclear weapons, rocketry, and missiles. With the Soviet pull-out in mid-1960, the Red Chinese had to rely primarily on their own know-how and resources in developing a modern defense sector. Until about 1960 China could obtain most of her defense needs and much military assistance from other communist nations, chiefly Russia. The change in foreign policy has probably cost China much in wasted resources and efficiency in both the defense and civilian sectors.

While China has sharply expanded trade with non-communist nations in the 1960's, she still must pursue a policy of self-sufficiency in the defense sector because she cannot depend very substantially on external sources for strategic imports of a military nature. China would no doubt be better off industrially and militarily if it were not for the United States' hostile foreign policy toward her. American foreign policy has hurt China primarily with regard to defense—and, even here, not very much until the 1960's—rather than in civilian industrial development. No other major trading nation has followed the U.S. policy of total embargo on trade with China.

No doubt China was forced to cut back its military expenditures, as well as its defense-related imports, in the serious economic depression of the early 1960's which was due in large part to the Great Leap Forward and ideological extremism,[33] because severe economic depression and sustained defense spending on a substantial scale tend to be in conflict—particularly in a relatively poor country. Hence, in the first six months of 1961 China's defense factories completed only 15.9 percent of planned targets for the production of military weapons, equipment, accessories and parts.[33a]

It is possible that ideological extremism was not carried as far in China's defense sector as in in its civilian sectors during the Great Leap. The authority, status, and influence of the experts in the defense sector were perhaps not quite as seriously undermined, material incentives may not have been de-emphasized to the same degree, and "class struggle" and the elimination of class distinctions may not have exceeded the boundaries of managerial, technical, and economic rationality to the same extent. Nevertheless, ideological extremism did, no doubt, enter into the defense sector, and more important was the damage done to the civilian economy which in turn hampered China's goal of becoming a first-rate military power.

With China's economic recovery and the achievement of substantial industrial progress after 1962, its defense and military budget—both in absolute terms and as a proportion of GNP—has probably increased substantially as she has striven to become a major nuclear power through her own efforts. Her sizable investments in the chemical and agricultural machinery industries in recent years are compatible with her defense and military aims inasmuch as plants in these sectors can often be converted into defense producers quite rapidly if desired, and at not very great costs. It is possible that roughly 10 percent of China's annual GNP in the last few years has been devoted directly to military and defense spending.[34] This compares with around 10 percent of the American GNP, which is some ten times greater than China's, and with roughly the same percentage for the Soviet Union. Japan, which is also much more developed industrially than China, spends less than 1.5 percent of its annual GNP on defense and the military—one of the lowest proportions in the world. Even India's sizable (for her) expenditure of roughly 5 percent of her GNP on defense has probably not been as big a drain on the civilian-industry sector as in China.[35] Moreover, India has received considerable foreign assistance in its military and defense activities in recent years and has not embarked on the build-up of a substantial nuclear striking force.

According to one estimate, the Chinese basic nuclear program may have entailed an annual investment, in U.S. dollars, of about $100 million and an annual allowance of $30 million for operating costs and fuel.[36] China's recent success in delivering a nuclear warhead has undoubtedly raised this ante considerably. The development of a modest but relatively effective nuclear-strike capability will naturally be very expensive but not necessarily beyond China's capabilities even at her present stage of development, as long as ideological extremism is not carried too far too long. One might speculate that the development of a French-type nuclear *force de frappe* may cost China $1 billion annually or more. Such outlays could well absorb at least half of her defense budget. The development of such a nuclear program may even require an allocation of as much as 2 to 3 percent of China's annual GNP.[37]

Such an allocation would represent a sizable diversion of resources for a developing country with scarce high-talent manpower and a modest industrial base. A diversion of this magnitude could not help interfering with the growth, development, and modernization of conventional military capabilities and probably with investments in civilian industry and agriculture. Therefore, the development of a modest strike capability is really a problem of planning priorities and of planner's choices.

As of 1959 about 1.5 million employees, or about half of the total employment of the firms under central machine-building ministries, were engaged in Red China's defense production, and the defense-production sector employed about 20 percent of all the engineers and technicians in the nation.[38] One source estimates that roughly 3.4 percent of China's available scientists (probably a majority of them were the country's leading scientists) have been working on her nuclear program.[39] However, this source points out that the figure greatly underrates the opportunity and manpower costs with regard to China's civilian industry. On the other hand, probably a number of China's top scientists, engineers, and technicians in the defense sector devote at least some of their time and talents to the civilian industrial sector, typically in advisory or staff roles.

It is significant that the industrial enterprises under five of China's eight central machine-building ministries are engaged primarily or exclusively in military and defense production. Below are listed these five defense-sector ministries and their major types of production.

Second	Machine Building Ministry	Nuclear weapons
Third	Machine Building Ministry	Conventional armaments
Fifth	Machine Building Ministry	Artillery equipment
Sixth	Machine Building Ministry	Naval shipbuilding
Seventh	Machine Building Ministry	Military aircraft

The fourth machine-building ministry deals with both civilian and military communications. Factories under the first and eighth machine-building ministries, as well as many industrial enterprises in other sectors (for example, metallurgy, chemicals, petroleum, and coal), also undertake some defense-related production.

From observations, impressions, and information derived from my visit to China in 1966, I gathered that the longer enterprises of all types which produce a large proportion of their output for defense and military use tend to be under central control, the more they receive relatively high-priority attention in planning and resource allocation. I did not visit any enterprise subordinate to defense-production ministries. However, I did visit a few that produce some commodities for the defense sector. I was told by officials of the Wuhan Heavy Machinery Factory and Shanghai (Heavy) Machine Tool Plant—both under central ministries—that an unspecified but fairly significant portion of their production is for national defense. Both of the Wuhan firms were also supplying North Vietnam.

All three of these enterprises have relatively large staffs for research and development, for which—and also for storage—they have relatively good facilities; they also have some personnel who translate foreign sources full time. Apparently, scientists, engineers, and technicians are also sent to these firms by central agencies to work on special defense projects. The two Wuhan firms, in particular, employ relatively large proportions and numbers of higher and semiprofessional graduates. Particularly the two machinery enterprises have modern, well-equipped plants, and Wuhan Steel's technology seems better than that of the Shanghai No. 3 Steel Mill. The Wuhan steel plant, which was producing mainly I-beams, has a separate shop for defense production where it produces special sizes and shapes of steel. When I was at this plant, a team of quality-control inspectors from unspecified central organizations was inspecting the production in this shop. I was told by officials of all three of these firms that this type of quality-control procedure for important defense commodities is quite common.

A Qualitative Appraisal of the Impact of Communist China's Defense and Military Activity on Industrial Progress and Management

Some qualitative judgments could be made about the impact of Communist China's defense and military activity on managerial effectiveness and industrial progress. On the plus side it cannot be doubted that China's achievements in the military and defense sphere, particularly its nuclear program, have greatly appealed to, and gone far in satisfying, the population's aspirations and interests regarding nationalism and the creation of a strong China. This, in turn, has probably done much to motivate industrial and other personnel to work harder and improve their skills and performance so that China can become even more powerful and self-sufficient.

I was in China at the time of her successful nuclear explosion in May 1966. Reacting to the achievement, the Chinese were uncharacteristically openly excited, enthusiastic, and proud. In fact, I never saw such a spontaneous display of jubilation again during my entire stay in China, and this includes the May Day celebrations. Factory workers, managers, high-level planners, my interpreters and guides, professors, waiters, drivers, teachers, schoolchildren, barbers, peasants—in fact persons from every walk of life—whom I encountered in China elatedly brought this accomplishment to my attention. At the theaters references to this military achievement evoked thundering applause.

In general, industrial-enterprise personnel are often spurred on to be more productive by linking their contributions to the realization of China's military and defense aims. For instance, employees at the Canton Chemical Fertilizer are told, and generally seem to believe, that more fertilizer production means more food, which in turn leads to greater national self-sufficiency and more funds for the military and defense sector, which will keep China strong and free from foreign invasion and "blackmail." The Chinese, including many overseas Chinese, really do believe that without a considerable amount of military and defense spending Red China would probably still be faced with foreign invasions, much foreign exploitation, and considerable political and economic instability. Whether or not this is really true is a matter of speculation. But the fact remains that since the Communists came to power in 1949 there has been no foreign invasion of Red China's soil; no real civil war of any type, at least until 1967; foreign exploitation has been virtually eliminated; and when ideological extremism has not been carried too far, there has also been a relatively high degree of political and economic stability. The Chinese also seem to feel that by becoming a major world military power they will not only gain much international prestige but will also be in a position to gain more favorable economic terms in foreign trade (perhaps, in some cases, through her own brand of nuclear blackmail!).

While Communist China's armed forces may employ more people than the military establishments in any other country—roughly 2.7 to 3 million personnel—China's military forces have done much work in economic development. Rather than being highly parasitical as is the case in many other underdeveloped and developing countries, they have played major roles in building roads, bridges, dams, railroads, irrigation and water-conservation projects, and in producing various other social-overhead capital and intrastructure facilities essential for industrial progress and general economic development. On a number of occasions, primarily in nonurban areas, I saw military personnel engaged in productive activity from my car or train window, or from the decks of boats. Chinese military personnel also play a major part in local education and training programs, particularly in rural areas. Because of its own educational and training programs the military is also an important source of managerial, technical, and skilled manpower for industrial enterprises. Since wages are low even in China's armed forces, the financial burden on the economy resulting from outlays for maintenance of her multimillion-man military forces have not been conspicuously great. It has been estimated to cost roughly $1 billion to 1.5 billion annually for providing such subsistence. Moreover, the size of China's armed forces is also not enormous, considering the size of her total population.

Finally on the plus side, there has probably been a considerable amount of "spin-offs" of innovations and technical improvements from the defense and military sector to civilian industries. To the extent that this has occurred it has benefited managerial effectiveness and industrial progress.

On the negative side, China's defense and military policies have unquestionably interfered with managerial effectiveness, productive efficiency, and general progress in civilian industrial sectors. Even in Communist China the military and defense business is quite sophisticated and complex in the technical sense. It will become even more complex and costly as China pushes ahead to become a major nuclear power. Given her relatively small pool of high-talent manpower, a substantial portion of China's best scientists, engineers, managers, technicians, and craftsmen are drained away from the civilian sector to create new and better defense items. Recruitment of key personnel required in lower-priority industries is greatly limited and at times impossible, and this substantially hinders managerial effectiveness and productive efficiency. Less capital-investment funds are provided to civilian industries and the technology utilized is much less productive than would be the case if the defense budgets were substantially less. Product quality suffers in numerous instances. The types of fuels, minerals, alloys, and other raw materials used in production are also significantly less efficient or effective, and waste, costs, and prices are substantially higher at numerous civilian-sector factories than would be the case with substantially smaller defense spending. All of these constraints resulting from sizable defense budgets tend to be magnified greatly in a relatively poor country like China, as compared with an advanced industrial nation like the United States or even the Soviet Union.

I came across a considerable amount of evidence to this effect during my visits to Chinese factories in 1966. On several occasions when I asked enterprise officials why they don't use more suitable technology or more efficient, economical, or durable materials and inputs—for example, steel or aluminum instead of concrete, stone, or wood; copper or zinc instead of lead or tin; petroleum, oil, or electricity instead of coal or wood—I was told that they were required for defense production.

Many of Red China's defense plants and installations are located in remote regions, primarily in northern and western areas, for security reasons. This frequently is a very costly—but perhaps sound—strategy because much in the way of investment funds and other resources is required for social-overhead-capital facilities, local feeder industries, transportation, and so forth.

Finally on the negative side, China's defense and military policies have contributed significantly to the relatively low standard of living of its population at large. With her large defense budgets the opportunity costs, in terms of greater purchasing power and more consumer goods for the masses, as well as greater investment and better resources for growth-generating industries, are undoubtedly also large.

However, under conditions of relative ideological moderation Communist China is probably capable of becoming a leading world military power, and at the same time of achieving substantial progress in civilian industries and raising the standard of living of its citizens. On the other hand, if ideological extremism persists, and if the regime continues to use the military to revolutionize and control industrial management on a widespread scale, Red China's defense programs, industrial progress, and the standard of living of its masses will surely all be the chief losers.

Foreign Policy

It is not our aim in this study to examine in depth China's foreign policy, per se. There are a number of comprehensive works on the subject available to the interested reader.[40] Our chief interest here is on the impact of China's foreign policy on industrial enterprises and their management.

A given nation's foreign policy at any point in time typically affects the activities and performance of many of its industrial enterprises. As its foreign policy undergoes change, this typically leads to changes at the enterprise level. The most direct and common impacts involve the nature and extent of imported commodities used in the production process and the types and amounts of products manufactured by the enterprises for export. The country's foreign exchange position—which is typically influenced substantially by its fiscal, and at times its monetary, policies—tends to have a great bearing on its imports and exports. Also of major relevance at the enterprise level, particularly in underdeveloped and developing countries, is the nature and extent of foreign economic aid, including educational and technical assistance.

Historical Perspective

Historically foreign trade has been a marginal activity in the Chinese economy, and not until the Communists came to power in 1949 did China's foreign policies become aimed directly at economic development and industrialization.[41] Prior to the Opium War of the 1840's China's economy had been very isolated and largely inward-oriented. The little foreign trade that existed was confined mainly to simple agricultural products and consumer goods and had a minimal effect on the character of domestic economic activity. Under the impact of Western pressure and initiative around the time of the Opium War and later, the volume of foreign trade grew, its character changed somewhat, and its effect on domestic economic trends became more significant. For example, in the twentieth century a sizable cotton-textile industry developed in China. However, in quantitative terms, foreign trade remained a minor sector of the economy. In qualitative terms it assumed greater importance as a highway for introducing innovating influences in consumption and production and as a factor which widened the market. But Republican China's foreign trade and foreign policies in general were not very conducive to substantial or sustained industrial progress.

In the century or so following the Opium War, China evolved into a nation which was more or less under quasi-colonial rule. Various European nations, Japan, and the United States gained treaty ports and other special concessions in China. These world powers exploited China's economy and did not do very much to develop it industrially. There were exceptions, of course; a number of large-scale relatively modern plants were erected primarily in Manchuria, Shanghai, and Tientsin. However, the controlling foreign powers utilized China as a market for their home products and imported rather than produced locally most of the machinery, equipment, components, and other relatively complex manufactured goods from their own countries. Hence, modern heavy industry, secondary manufacturing, and diverse industrial production, in general, were largely suppressed in order to provide markets for the dominant foreign powers. Chinese industry and exports consisted primarily of food and agro-industry products involving simple processing, traditional textile goods, some mining, and much handicraft production.

While many Chinese students went abroad to study, and foreign educators, specialists, and technicians came to China on various programs and projects, there was no real systematic or substantial attempt to build up a pool of high-talent manpower essential to industrial development. In fact, China suffered a serious "brain drain" because many of its best-educated, motivated, and most experienced citizens chose to live and work abroad. There were no stringent governmental restrictions—as there have been, and are, in Red China—on going abroad, and there were too few opportunities or inducements to keep them at home. Apart from military aid, China received very little foreign aid or assistance aimed directly at economic development prior to 1950.

Sino-Soviet Relations and Soviet Assistance

By far the most important dimension of Communist China's foreign policy with regard to managerial effectiveness and industrial progress has been its relationship with the Soviet Union. There is a wide range of opinion as to just how crucial Soviet aid and cooperation in the 1950's and the Sino-Soviet rift of the 1960's have been to China's economic development. At one end of the opinion spectrum are some authors, including some who have visited Red China, who contend that Soviet aid has been either the first or second most important factor in China's industrialization and development.[42] At the other end of the spectrum are those who contend, or at least imply, that Soviet aid has not really been of great importance and has, in fact, been overrated.[43]

Most Sinologists and commentators on China take a middle-of-the-road position.[44] They seem to feel that Soviet aid and cooperation in the 1950's were of major importance but were not the most important factor for China's economic growth, and that the Soviet pullout and emerging Sino-Soviet conflict has had a significantly negative, but not totally disastrous, impact on industrial progress in Red China.

I stand with the middle-of-the-roaders. If I were to assign relative ranks to different environmental factors bearing on managerial effectiveness and industrial progress, I would tend to rank higher several of the sociological-cultural and educational variables discussed earlier than I would Sino-Soviet relations or China's foreign policy in general.

Since 1949 the total Soviet commitment of aid for China's economic development—excluding the large amount of military aid and loans for the Korean War—has included 291 major industrial plants valued at about $3.3 billion. These commitments were to have been fulfilled by 1967 if the Sino-Soviet rift had not occurred.[45] The Soviets pulled out most of their technicians, advisers, blueprints, and drawings in mid-1960. At that time some 257 major and minor industrial and scientific projects were stopped or canceled, about 343 contracts of various types were torn up, numerous equipment and raw material orders were canceled, and an embargo was placed on the supply of many critical commodities to China.[46] As of July 1960, 130 Soviet-sponsored industrial projects, primarily heavy-industry plants in the metallurgical, machinery, and equipment categories and valued at about $1.5 billion were fully or partly completed and in operation. There were also 27 industrial installations completed with the aid of various East European countries.[47] Some of these countries continued to render modest assistance to China in completing some of the Soviet projects after the Soviet withdrawal in 1960.

During the 1950's more than 10,000 Soviet experts, technicians, and industrial advisers worked in China in the construction and implementation of plants, mines, and other economic projects.[48] They also played a major role in training Chinese industrial personnel. Some unofficial estimates imply that perhaps more than 20,000 Russians worked in China during the 1950's.[49] In addition to the Russians, about 1,500 experts and technicians from other East European countries also worked in China during this period. Immediately following the major Soviet pullout in mid-1960 it is estimated that only from 50 to 1,500 Russians remained in China. By 1962 very few, if any, senior Soviet experts or advisers remained in China, although some of them had been replaced by Czechs and other East Europeans.[50]

During the 1950's Red China sent a sizable number of its citizens to the Soviet Union for education and training, primarily in engineering, technical, and scientific fields. At least 80,000 engineers, technicians, and advanced researchers were trained in Russia.[51] One source places this figure at 38,000, but this could be a misprint or error.[52] In addition, some 7,500 Chinese students, including 2,500 graduate students went to Russia for their higher studies.[53] A few Chinese students also went to various other countries, mainly communist ones, for their higher and advanced education and training during the 1950's. Some 700 Soviet professors, lecturers, and specialists—and 10 Czechs, 17 Germans, and 5 Indians—taught in Red China in the 1950's.[54]

Soviet experts working and training people in China and Chinese citizens studying and being trained in Russia did a great deal to build up China's stock of high-talent manpower for industry. By 1960 fewer than 100 foreign professors and teachers, chiefly in engineering and advanced physics, remained in China.[55] The number of Chinese going to the Soviet Union for education and training was reduced to a trickle during the 1960's. In October 1966 all remaining Chinese students in the U.S.S.R. were sent home.

It is important to point out that China has received very little in the way of outright gifts from Russia.[56] It is true that China received free blueprints, designs, use of patents, and some free technical and educational assistance. In the 1950's the Soviets also gave up their shares in various Chinese joint-stock companies and pulled out of Dairen, Manchuria, and Sinkiang, leaving all naval, shipbuilding, and industrial facilities to China free of charge. However, the great bulk of Soviet assistance was paid for by exports, barter and credit arrangements, and the repayment of loans. Soviet loans to China have borne very small interest payments, typically 1 or 2 percent. After 1955 Soviet loans were very small, and beyond 1957 no new ones were negotiated. By 1956 China started loan repayments to Russia and, at the same time, began its own modest Southeast Asia foreign-aid program for political reasons. By the end of 1965 China had paid off in full its $1.547 billion debt with interest to the Soviet Union and now has no external debts outstanding.[57]

After examining the quantitative data one cannot dispute the fact that Soviet aid was a significant factor in China's industrial development. The Soviet Union never received anything like such substantial help from outside in her industrial development. In fact, she was pretty much isolated by the rest of the world until the 1930's, when the United States recognized her and a modest amount of foreign assistance and cooperation was extended.

On the other hand, Soviet assistance and generosity in Red China's development should not be overestimated. The total of Soviet loans was no more than enough to pay for about 31 percent of necessary equipment, supplies, and assistance for the original 156 major industrial projects which Russia agreed to help China construct in the 1950's. These were the 156 key industrial installations on which China based her whole heavy-industry development. Soviet loans covered only 11 percent of China's total imports during the 1950–57 period. And from 1952 to 1957 Soviet credit available for new investment constituted only 3 percent of the total state investment in China.[58] All Soviet loans were not really much more than the approximately $1 billion that Communist China received in the way of gifts and contributions from overseas Chinese.[59] (Red China has also been quite successful in getting Chinese managers, capitalists, professionals, and experts living in foreign countries to return home after 1949 to serve the motherland. Favored living conditions, relatively high pay, good jobs, and other privileges have been utilized for attracting these returnees.)

It is also interesting to note that in the late 1950's and early 1960's U.S. economic aid to India was more than four times Soviet economic aid to China, and U.S. economic aid to Yugoslavia was somewhat more than Soviet aid to China. During the 1960's India continued to receive much economic and technical assistance not only from the United States but also from various other countries and international organizations, such as the United Nations and the World Bank. The Chinese economy in the 1960's was able to recover from the Soviet pullout and with very little outright aid or assistance. It has evolved an industrial economy that is relatively self-sufficient, at least for a poor developing nation. China is unlike India, where sizable cutbacks in foreign aid and loans might well make her economy collapse.

There can be no doubt that the massive Soviet pullout from Red China in 1960 and the deepening Sino-Soviet conflict have had a significantly damaging impact on managerial effectiveness and industrial progress. The Soviets chose an extremely critical time to withdraw—a severe economic crisis was already emerging because of the ideological fanaticism of the Great Leap and also because of poor agricultural crops. There are still clear and rather depressing signs of the effects on Chinese industry of the sudden Soviet pullout. A number of Western observers, including myself, who have visited Chinese factories set up with Soviet assistance in the 1950's have found that many of them had not yet recovered from the abrupt Soviet withdrawal even seven or eight years later.[60] Among the most inefficient and worst-functioning Chinese industrial firms that I surveyed were some of those that had been constructed or greatly expanded with Soviet assistance in the 1950's. These included Peking Steel Wire, Tientsin Watch, and Tientsin Shoe. Wuhan Iron and Steel and Loyang Tractor seemed to be functioning a bit better than the three enterprises mentioned, but their productivity had not increased significantly since the Soviet pullout of 1960.[61] The Wuhan Heavy Machinery Plant was the only exception; in spite of the termination of Soviet assistance it seemed to be managed quite well and functioning relatively efficiently in 1966.

Why did the Soviets pull out so abruptly in 1960? What factors are at the root of the current and deepening Sino-Soviet conflict? This topic is beyond the scope of this study. As has been said before, for the interested reader there are a number of comprehensive works which address themselves to these questions.[62] We shall only very briefly touch upon a few of the key factors here.

China's ideological fanaticism during the Great Leap period was clearly a major contributing cause; in fact, it could have even been the straw that broke the camel's back. I have spoken to a number of Russians, some of whom have worked in China, about China's ideological extremism during the Greap Leap. Apparently many of the Soviet experts and technicians were exposed to the same types of hostility and abuses as the Chinese managers and experts were. Moreover, because of China's extreme emphasis on self-sufficiency and disdain of foreign methods during this period, the advice, opinions, suggestions, and decisions of the Soviet industrial experts were typically ignored and scorned.

Other major reasons behind the Sino-Soviet rift were Khrushchev's anti-Stalin speech in 1956, which the Chinese viewed as seriously weakening the international Communist movement, and which started a chain of events; Chinese disapproval of Soviet strategy, tactics, and policies against the West and its foreign policies in general, including her positions regarding Taiwan, the Cuban missile crisis, and India; Russia's reluctance to aid China in the development of advanced military weapons because of fear that China might become a powerful nation on its borders; and the Soviets' domestic policies, such as "modern revisionism" and "Libermanism." Furthermore, prior to 1949, when the Communists won control over China, the Soviet Union had not been a particularly good friend of the Chinese Communist Party. In the 1920's and 1930's Stalin did little to help the Chinese Communists, and there were serious disputes between them and the Soviet representatives that Stalin sent to China. In fact, Stalin had even recognized and supported the Chiang Kai-shek regime throughout all of World War II. After the war the Russians dismantled many of China's plants, primarily in north China, sent the equipment home, and never gave compensation for much of it even after 1949.

China Turns to the Capitalist World

During the 1960's Red China turned sharply to the West and Japan in its foreign trade (as we shall discuss shortly). Moreover, a substantial number of complete factories were being constructed in China by companies and consortiums from several West European countries and Japan. In spite of the phase of ideological extremism that began in the mid-1960's, the regime has tried to prevent the Cultural Revolution from interfering with its foreign trade.

In the 1960's there has also been a growing Western and Japanese influence in the cultural area; there have been student and faculty exchanges, borrowing of educational and technical books and materials, and the teaching of foreign languages. There is even tourism in China. In fact, during my trip, I was surprised by the substantial number of foreign visitors from capitalist countries. Chinese students and a limited number of Chinese professors and specialists have been sent to England, France, Japan, and other non-communist countries for education, training, and the exchange of ideas and information. (It is true, however, that virtually all Chinese students abroad were called home toward the end of 1966 because of the Cultural Revolution.) McGill University in Canada now has a limited faculty-exchange program in medicine and related fields with the Chinese, and the University of Toronto has been involved in negotiations for a student-exchange program. As was mentioned in Chapter 3, a Canadian senator, who was in Peking at the time I was there, extended an invitation to the Chinese authorities to send participants to a management-development program held in Banff, Alberta, each summer. The Chinese seemed interested in the offer, but I do not know if anything concrete resulted.

The Chinese have also been willing to extend visas to foreigners, such as myself, who are interested in undertaking research projects in China. They even let one Britisher—Rosemary Stewart of the Center for Management Studies at Oxford University—undertake a limited survey of factories in the fall of 1966 when the Cultural Revolution had become very intensified.[63]

Aims and Quantitative Trends of China's Foreign Trade

Communist China's trade is based on the regime's and its planners' priorities. Import and export decisions are subservient to the state plan, and foreign trade is aimed at balancing the requirements of the overall plan. For the individual enterprise its imports and exports are provided for in the plan, and its management is not directly concerned with making choices regarding the types and amounts of imports to be utilized or the amounts or kinds of products to manufacture for export. No doubt, efficiency suffers in varying degrees at many enterprises by not allowing the local managers, who have the best knowledge of the resource requirements and productive capabilities of their firms, to play a bigger or more direct role in import and export decisions. However, to allow them to do so would tend to lead to serious sub-system optimization in terms of the regime's priorities and disrupt the state plan substantially in numerous cases.

Import and export decisions in China are primarily the concern of the higher-level planners. Red China's national import and export corporations also play a major role in the details of such important decisions and in their implementation. Hence, unlike a firm in a capitalist country, the Chinese industrial enterprise is not directly concerned or involved with tariffs, import quotas, or foreign exchange even if it utilizes substantial quantities of imports and/or exports much of its output.

The principal aim of Red China's trade policy has been to facilitate and accelerate industrial development by increasing imports of required and desired equipment and raw materials. Some materials are either not available domestically or available only in small quantities in scattered locations. Factor endowment, to be discussed in the next chapter, is a key constraint in this regard. Moreover, in the early 1950's in particular, China had no manufacturing facilities for many types of machinery and equipment, and technical know-how for their design and production was inadequate. To pay for imports the Chinese consumer and living standards are kept down, at least in the short run, because China's main exports are agricultural products, processed and semiprocessed foods, textiles, clothing, handicrafts, and various other light-industry consumer goods.

While it would no doubt be erroneous to say that Chinese industry would not have developed or progressed without imports, it can be said that without them industrial growth would undoubtedly have been much slower, less diversified, and of a different character. Up to 1960, imports were chiefly producer goods, and their cessation or substantial reduction would have forced cutbacks in industrial investment and a drastic scaling down of the expansion program in heavy industry, which is the crux of China's economic and military power and potential power in the future. The economy, of course, might have gradually adjusted to such a cessation through a channeling of domestically available resources into the expansion of sectors not as dependent on imported technology and materials, but such a reorientation would have run strongly counter to the regime's scale of preferences.

Table 5–1 reflects the volume of Communist China's foreign trade during the 1950–66 period.

We see that the value of China's foreign trade grew rapidly and steadily between 1950 and 1959. The fast pace of expansion in the overall industrial sector as a whole was reflected in its foreign trade. This rise in trade was particularly sharp during the height of the Great Leap period when industrial investment increased greatly. Similarly, the severe downturn in economic activity resulting from the Great Leap, the Soviet pullout, and poor agricultural harvests led to a sharp reduction in both imports and exports after 1960.

TABLE 5–1

COMMUNIST CHINA'S FOREIGN TRADE, 1950–66
(In Billions of U.S. Dollars)

	Total	*Imports*	*Exports*
1950	1.2	not available	not available
1952	1.76	.89	.87
1953	2.15	1.11	1.04
1954	2.38	1.26	1.12
1955	2.67	1.32	1.35
1956	3.08	1.47	1.61
1957	3.02	1.40	1.62
1958	3.78	1.87	1.91
1959	4.23	2.01	2.22
1960	3.92	1.91	2.01
1961	2.98	1.41	1.57
1962	2.74	1.14	1.60
1963	2.75	1.20	1.55
1964	3.26	1.48	1.78
1965	3.86	1.77	2.09
1966 (estimate)	4.16–4.30	not available	not available
1970 (prediction)	6.00	" "	" "

SOURCES: The 1950–62 figures are from A. Eckstein, *Communist China's Economic Growth and Foreign Trade* (New York: McGraw-Hill, 1966), pp. 94–95, Table 4–1. Eckstein's adjusted figures have been used, and I have rounded them. His adjusted figures differ slightly from his unadjusted ones; in most cases they are a bit lower. The 1963 to 1965 figures, the 1966 estimate of $4.3 billion, and the 1970 prediction of $6 billion are from "China in World Trade," *Current Scene*, Parts I and II, February 1 and 15, 1966. Japanese newspapers place total Chinese trade in 1966 at $4.16 billion, according to a statement made by E. O. Reischauer to the Joint Economic Committee of the U.S. Congress on April 5, 1967. Reischauer's statement appears in *Hearings on the Economy of Mainland China* (Washington: U.S. Government Printing Office, 1967). For other Chinese foreign-trade statistics, see R. L. Price, "International Trade of Communist China," and the appendix in *An Economic Profile of Mainland China* (Washington: U.S. Government Printing Office, 1967).

The pace of China's trade expansion during the 1950's may best be gauged by comparing it with movements in total world trade, underdeveloped countries, Asian countries as a group, and India and Japan. This is reflected in Table 5–2. Through 1959, China's trade grew much more rapidly than total world trade, trade of all underdeveloped countries, or trade of all Asian countries as a group. Japan's exports, on the other hand, forged ahead at an even faster rate than China's did, but its imports lagged somewhat behind that rate. China's imports grew more rapidly than India's during this period, and the rate of growth of China's exports greatly outstripped that of India.

China's foreign trade performance in the 1950's, while very impressive and beneficial in terms of industrial progress, is somewhat less impressive, at least quantitatively, when viewed from the vantage point of long-run historical perspective. Mainland Chinese trade attained its pre-Communist peak levels in 1928 and 1929.[64] These earlier levels were not surpassed on the import side until 1954 and on the export side until 1955 or 1956. However, trade in the 1950's was aimed much more directly and vigorously at industrial development than in pre-Communist times. China's foreign trade continued to rise by about 60 percent between 1955 and 1959. In per capita terms, Red China's foreign trade has ranged roughly between $4 and $6 since 1949, somewhat less than India's per capita performance. Using a conversion figure of about 1 yuan =40 American cents, China's total trade in the 1950's averaged roughly 7.5–8 percent of its annual GNP.[65]

Just as China's growth in foreign trade was unusually rapid in the fifties, so was its decline precipitous after 1959. By 1962, imports had diminished by almost 50 percent and had fallen below the 1928–29 level. Exports decreased somewhat less drastically. They dropped to just around the pre-1949 peak. We see from Table 5–2 that while China suffered a sharp drop in both exports and imports in 1961, all of the areas and countries indicated on the table had increases of varying magnitudes.

In the early 1960's there was a vast amount of idle productive capacity in most industrial sectors, the need and desire for new imported producers goods and materials dropped sharply, and China had to cut substantially its exports of many commodities, particularly those based on agricultural inputs. With China's economic recovery, by 1964 her foreign trade—both exports and imports—began to increase substantially. It increased by about 40 percent from 1963 to 1964, another 18 percent in 1965, as compared with 1964, and about 10 percent to 12 percent in 1966, as compared with 1965. In 1965 China had run up a $320 million trade surplus.[66] The Soviet Union's foreign trade amounted to over $16 billion (converted at 1 ruble = $1.10) in 1966, but her GNP total industrial production is several times greater than China's.[67]

Since 1949 Communist China has become remarkably self-sufficient in a wide range of products, such as raw materials, alloys, minerals and petroleum, machine tools, equipment, metallurgical products, instrumentation, and radar. Nevertheless, she still has substantial deficiencies in many

TABLE 5–2

COMPARATIVE TRENDS IN CHINA'S FOREIGN TRADE, OTHER SELECTED COUNTRIES AND THE WORLD, 1952–61
(In Millions of U.S. Dollars)

Area	*Imports (c.i.f.)*			*Exports (f.o.b.)*		
	1952	*1959*	*1961*	*1952*	*1959*	*1961*
World	86,500	120,700	140,200	80,000	115,200	133,400
Communist China* (adjusted)	890	2,011	1,414	871	2,221	1,571
Communist China* (unadjusted)	979	2,029	1,430	929	2,253	1,598
India	1,696	1,986	2,246	1,299	1,304	1,386
Japan	2,028	3,599	5,810	1,273	3,456	4,236
Sterling Asia †	5,380	5,820	6,690	4,860	4,970	5,220
Other Asia †	2,720	2,600	3,320	1,940	2,250	2,280
Underdeveloped countries	24,300	27,300	30,700	20,900	25,800	27,600

* All imports f.o.b.
† Excluding Japan and Communist China.

SOURCE: Eckstein (cited in Table 5–1), Table 4–2, p. 96.

commodities, such as chemicals, various types of food and most types of machine tools, and agricultural machinery and transportation equipment. Long-term intergovernmental agreements and trade treaties have played a much larger role in Soviet, as compared with Chinese, foreign trade.

By being conservative in financial management and fiscal and monetary policies Red China has managed to avoid a serious crisis in foreign exchange or balance of payments, which is so common to many developing countries throughout the world and which adversely affects the performance of numerous industrial enterprises. Starting with almost no financial resources in 1950, China built up foreign exchange reserves to about $645 million by 1957. The Great Leap, the Soviet pullout, and poor crops led to short-term indebtedness and a decline in China's international reserves in the late fifties and early sixties. Since 1963 China has once again maintained a favorable balance of payments. By the end of 1964 her currency and gold reserves amounted to about $400 million.[68]

In general, Red China has been quite rational and pragmatic in its foreign trade policies. This has been the case in spite of ideological lip service paid to self-sufficiency, anti-Western propaganda, and campaigns to wipe out foreign influences and elements in her society.[69] It should also be pointed out that Red China has thus far had an excellent reputation for honoring its trade agreements and commitments among virtually all countries that have done business with her.

Composition of China's Foreign Trade[70]

As we mentioned earlier, China's major imports until about 1960 were producer goods aimed at the development of heavy industry. For example, during the 1955–60 period machinery and equipment imports ranged from about 23 to over 40 percent of total imports each year; the range for complete plants was approximately 12 to 25 percent, for chemicals 8 to 14 percent, and for metals, metal ores, and concentrates 8 to 24 percent. The peak period for these imports was 1958–60. In the early 1960's the volume of imports of these commodities declined drastically. For instance, machinery and equipment dropped to about 5.2 percent of total imports by 1962, and complete plants to 1.1 percent. Imports of the above items began to increase substantially after 1963 but still may not have reached their earlier peaks, even though a sizable number of complete plants are being erected in China by organizations from capitalist countries.

Since 1961 Red China has been purchasing about six million metric tons of wheat from the free world. During the 1961–63 period foodstuffs constituted about 32 to 39 percent of China's imports, as compared with a peak figure of roughly 3 percent before 1961. There have also been substantial increases in China's imports of chemicals and textile fibers in recent years.

In 1965 China's main imports were various agricultural products (including $400 million in grain), chemical fertilizers, machinery, equipment, and complete plant, motor vehicles, and transportation equipment. I was told by Chinese officials in the chemical industry that China still imports about 30 percent of her fertilizer chiefly from the Netherlands, Canada, Italy, and Japan. China's main exports in 1965 were agricultural products and foodstuffs in which she is relatively self-sufficient or for which she can get a relatively high price on world markets, textiles, clothing, various raw materials, and a limited amount of light-industry goods and handicraft products. In the long run, Communist China is likely to run into limited markets for her foodstuffs and textile products, and may have to pay more attention to the export of light durables, such as plastics, radios, batteries, and fans.

China's Trading Partners[71]

Prior to 1949 China's chief trading partners were Great Britain, the United States, Japan, Hong Kong, France, and Germany. Her trade with the Soviet Union was relatively small. When the Chinese Communists came to power, the regime's politics and ideology favored trade with communist countries. Red China's sharp growth in trade with other communist nations in the 1950's was further reinforced by the Western trade embargo initiated by the United States against China in 1950.

This trade embargo has not proved to be particularly effective because the United States has been practically the only major country that has continued to adhere strictly to its policy of not trading with Red China. However, externally imposed trade embargoes and controls adhered to by various nations in varying degrees have undoubtedly served as a constraint on China's industrial progress and general economic development. China has had to transport much of her imports in relatively uneconomical ways, such as by rail over great land distances across the U.S.S.R. and her own vast country. The free access to many sources of supply has necessarily circumscribed her choice as to varieties, types, qualities, and prices of products substantially more than would otherwise have been the case. Moreover, the foreign embargoes and controls have significantly increased China's dependence on a limited number of suppliers and foreign markets, thus weakening her economic bargaining power.

For the above reasons, it seems likely that the Chinese have had to obtain many of their imports at relatively unfavorable prices and that they may have been forced further into sub-optimal factor combinations and resource-allocation patterns at the enterprise level. These combinations and patterns have been in part a function of the types of goods available rather than the kinds best suited to China's factor endowments. It is also likely that China's export revenues have suffered because of the foreign policies of other nations concerning trade with Red China which have limited her export markets. But in the 1960's Western embargoes and trade controls against China have been lifted rapidly and on a pervasive scale, with the major exception of the United States.

During the 1950's more than two-thirds of China's foreign trade was with communist nations. In the mid-1950's it was as high as 75 to 80 percent. In 1959 trade with European communist countries, apart from Russia, made up 15 percent of China's trade. By 1965 the situation was totally reversed, with only 30 percent of China's trade being with communist countries. In 1963 China's trade with the non-communist world surpassed her trade with communist countries for the first time since 1950. During the 1962–65 period China's trade with Japan and the industrial West doubled from $700 million to $1.4 billion annually. With the great slash in imports from communist countries by 1962 there was a new infusion of foreign credit from the West and Japan. China's capitalistic trading partners in the West have provided her with substantial short-term and medium-term (up to 5 years) credits, and Japan, in particular, has entered into large-scale barter agreements. China has received such credits for such items as chemicals, equipment and complete plants. China's trade in the past with Russia was based largely on long-term credits, and she may well find it beneficial and necessary to seek larger-term credits from the advanced Western nations and Japan. Given her good record in meeting foreign trade commitments, she will probably be able to obtain such credits in the future.

During the 1963–65 period Red China's exports to Hong Kong alone totaled $1 billion; trade surplus with Hong Kong now runs over $400 million annually, enough to pay for all her grain imports. China owns and operates several dozen businesses in Hong Kong, including large department stores, a big bank, and an effective travel service. Hong Kong has been China's number-one export customer in recent years, and Japan its number-one supplier of imports.

Of China's thirteen biggest trading partners in 1965, six do not even recognize China, and ten are essentially allied to the United States and opposed to communism. In order of amount of trade, these thirteen countries were: the U.S.S.R., Japan, Hong Kong, Cuba, Australia, the United Kingdom, West Germany, Malaya-Singapore, Canada, Jordan, Italy, France, and Pakistan. By the end of 1966 Japan had probably replaced the Soviet Union as China's number-one trading partner.

A major and interesting feature of Red China's foreign economic relations since mid-1963 has been the purchase of complete industrial installations from Western European countries and Japan.[72] These installations have been financed in part by medium-term credits and include, in some cases, the services of Western and Japanese technicians, a few of whom I met in China. Contracts for some thirty to forty complete plants, valued at more than $170 million, have been negotiated with these capitalist nations since 1963. These plants will play a very important role in China's future economic development. Over half the value of these contracts have been chemical plants, including plants for the production of fertilizers, fibers, plastics, and petrochemicals. These plants, most of which could not be in operation at least until 1967–68, will either supply vital products for the Chinese economy or will advance technical competence and self-sufficiency in strategic branches of industry.

The Western nations that have entered into contracts to erect complete plants in Communist China include Great Britain, France, West Germany, Italy, Sweden, the Netherlands, Finland, and Austria. The types of plants involved include vinylon fiber, urea, petroleum refinery, ammonium nitrate, synthetic ammonia, industrial alcohol, palm-oil processing, crude-oil cracking and olefin separation, nylon, polyethylene, polypropylene, porous silica material, acetylene, air liquification, acrylonitrile, glass, polyester resin, acrylic fiber, L-D and cold strip steel, bleaching, straw cellulose, tube-expanding pipe, wire drawing, condenser manufacturing, various types of instruments, and oil hydraulic equipment.

China was negotiating in 1967 with a West German consortium for a steel-mill complex valued at between $125 and $175 million. In the mid-1960's she also placed several large orders in the West and Japan for other machinery, particularly transportation and heavy-duty construction equipment.

Red China's Trade Promotion

Communist China is not nearly as aggressive as, say, Japan in promoting foreign trade and sending trade missions abroad. As was noted above, several of China's largest trading partners do not even officially recognize her; hence, there are no Chinese embassies or trade missions in these countries, and in turn these countries have no formal representation in Red China. However a fair amount of informal trade negotiation still goes on, and I saw firsthand evidence of this, particularly with regard to Sino-Canadian trade. There are a number of helpful sources available for those readers—even from countries which do not recognize Communist China—who are contemplating doing business with China in the future.[73]

China's top trade agency is the Ministry of Foreign Trade. This organization enters into trade agreements with foreign countries, controls China's national export and import corporations, and sends trade missions abroad.

The China Council for the Promotion of International Trade, which was very hospitable and helpful to me, is the key central organization involved in the promotion of foreign trade with non-communist countries, particularly those not having diplomatic relations with China. Officially this council is classified as a permanent nongovernmental organization; in reality it is under government control, which is exercised primarily through the Ministry of Foreign Trade. There are also some sixteen national import and export corporations under this ministry which play key roles in planning, distribution, negotiations, issuance of visas, and general promotional activities with regard to China's foreign trade. These corporations have branches in major Chinese cities as well as representation (through the China Resources Company) in Hong Kong and Macao. There are national import and export corporations of the following types:

1. Machinery and equipment
2. Chemicals
3. Metals and minerals
4. Light-industrial products (e.g., sewing machines, clocks, fans, pens, cameras, films, sporting goods)
5. Cereals
6. Oils and foodstuffs
7. Tea and native products
8. Apparel
9. Textiles
10. Arts and crafts

11. Animal by-products
12. Complete plants (industrial)
13. Technical imports
14. Foreign trade transport
15. Freighter chartering and shop brokering
16. International bookstore

The Canton International Trade Fair—known officially as the Chinese Export Commodities Fair—held for one month in the spring and again in the fall every year, is by far the most important Chinese foreign-trade promotional effort. The first Canton Trade Fair was held in 1957. At that time there were 12,000 exhibits, and it attracted 1,200 visitors from twenty-six countries. About 3,800 business transactions were concluded at this first fair. Since the early 1960's China has made major efforts to expand the scope and importance of the Canton Trade Fair and has been very successful. The eighteenth fair, held in the fall of 1965, had nearly 30,000 exhibits in an exhibition hall that was five times bigger than the one in 1957. It attracted 5,900 visitors from fifty-six countries, and about 29,000 business transactions were concluded. These transactions amounted to twenty times more in monetary value than those at the first fair in 1957.[74]

I attended the Canton Fair for one full day in April 1966. It was evident that foreign businessmen going to the fair could easily get visas on very short notice; they were expedited through customs at the border and generally received excellent hospitality. A new, large hotel was built in Canton to accommodate the growing influx of foreign businessmen who attend the Canton Fair. In 1966 hotel accommodations in Canton were good, the food excellent, and the cultural entertainment quite plentiful but filled with ideology and politics. I was greatly impressed—as are most foreigners—with the way the exhibits were arranged and the goods merchandised at the fair. I was also impressed with the wide variety.

In addition to the Canton Fair, the Red Chinese distribute promotional magazines and other literature on foreign trade in many countries and in many languages. The most popular magazine of this type is *China's Foreign Trade,* which is published quarterly. The national import-export corporations also have large billboard-advertising displays in major Chinese cities.

China's Trade Specialists and Techniques of Analysis

I did not learn much about the economic criteria or techniques of analysis utilized by China's trade specialists, planners, and economists in arriving at foreign-trade decisions or commitments. I am not sure how much use is made of an analysis of opportunity costs (with regard to foreign exchange, commodity prices, production costs, alternatives, and so on) or whether much, if any, attention is paid to the law of comparative advantage.

I do know that there are a number of Western-trained economists employed by key Red Chinese foreign-trade agencies who are well grounded in such economic concepts. One whom I met is a Mr. Yung, a British-trained economist who is vice chairman of the China Council for the Promotion of International Trade. It is quite possible that the ideological Red versus Expert pendulum also greatly affects the degree of influence that China's trade specialists and economists, particularly Western-trained ones, have in foreign-trade decisions at a particular point in time.

Impact of 1966–67 Cultural Revolution on China's Trade

Even though the regime has apparently tried to keep the Cultural Revolution and political crises from hindering China's foreign trade and balance of payments, trade performance may nevertheless suffer because of these conditions. As of the spring of 1966 there was as yet no clear-cut evidence that the Cultural Revolution had significantly affected the imports allocated to the planned export production at the Chinese industrial enterprises which I visited. In fact, China's total trade increased by about 5 to 10 percent in 1966 over 1965.

Since I left China, however, a growing number of foreign businessmen and trade officials have become reluctant to go to Red China to negotiate new trade agreements because of the political situation there, during 1967 in particular. I have received several letters to this effect, and have also spoken to a number of fellow-Canadians who have expressed such concern. There are also indications that trade officials in China are reluctant to make trade decisions, particularly where new trade patterns or multi-order agreements are involved.[75] In early 1967 there were fairly widely reported delays in ship loadings and unloadings in Shanghai and this must certainly have had some negative effect on China's foreign trade and the distribution of imported goods to factories.[76] It also appears that China's sterling foreign-exchange earnings from Hong Kong, Malaya, and Singapore dropped slightly in 1966 because of a slowing of business during the Cultural Revolution. However, by late 1966, Hong Kong merchants saw the trade return to normal. There has been no general policy decision made by the Red Chinese regime to curtail or restrict trade intentionally in any way. In 1968 I had the opportunity to talk with a number of Canadians who do business with Red China. The consensus was that since late 1966 they have experienced greater confusion and inefficiency in their dealings with the Chinese. There are indications that the total volume of China's foreign trade declined by about 5 to 10 percent or so in 1967. It is not unlikely that it deteriorated further in 1968.[77]

Impact of China's Foreign Trade on Industrial Enterprises Surveyed in 1966

Table 5–3 contains data from a number of Chinese factories I visited in 1966 on their imported equipment, materials, and other supplies. There did not seem to be any clear-cut correlation between the amount of imports and the general efficiency or productivity of these enterprises. There appeared to be relatively efficient and poorly operating plants utilizing substantial amounts of imported commodities and others of the same type using few or no imports. In later chapters I subjectively rate and analyze the Chinese enterprises surveyed in terms of technology, general operating efficiency, productivity, and managerial know-how.

TABLE 5–3

DATA ON IMPORTED EQUIPMENT AND MATERIALS UTILIZED AT CHINESE ENTERPRISES SURVEYED IN 1966

Enterprise	*Brief Description of Imported Equipment and/or Materials in Use*
Peking Woolen Mill	Mostly Japanese equipment (perhaps 80–90% of total)
Peking Wool Carpet	Mostly Japanese equipment (perhaps 80–90% of total)
Peking First Machine Tool	About 20% of its equipment imported from the Soviet Union and East Europe during 1956–58 period
Peking Cotton Textile No. 3	About 10% of raw cotton from Pakistan and Tanzania; all equipment Chinese
Peking Clothing	About 20% of its sewing machines imported—mostly from Japan, a few from Italy, at least one old model from India
Peking Steel Wire	A few pieces of Soviet equipment
Peking Pharmaceutical	Some Japanese equipment; no raw material imports in recent years; formerly imported as much as half of its raw materials chiefly from communist countries, some also from Japan and West Europe
Tientsin Shoe	A few old Soviet and Czech machines
Tientsin (Joint) Jen Yi Wool	Large German dyeing machine; some Italian sewing machines; British and Swiss weaving, trimming, and dyeing machines; some of the imported equipment of pre–1949 vintage
Tientsin Watch	Primarily Swiss machinery and equipment; some British, a few Russian pieces
Shanghai Cotton Textile No. 19	Much Japanese and some British equipment, mostly pre–1949; all newer equipment Chinese; small amount of raw cottonseed from Australia

Enterprise	*Brief Description of Imported Equipment and/or Materials in Use*
Shanghai Mei Ming Battery	Imports small amounts of nickel and copper for development work from unspecified countries; has a few very old pieces of British and U.S. equipment
Shanghai Truck	East German milling machine and Czech boring machine
Shanghai (Joint) Sung Sing Cotton No. 9	Much pre-1949 British equipment, some more than 60 years old; only new Chinese equipment are combing machines
Shanghai Heavy-Machine Tool	A few pieces of material-handling equipment from Russia and West Europe
Hangchow Machine Tool	About 10% of equipment imported from the Soviet Union and East Europe
Wusih Diesel Engine	Some Swiss and Japanese equipment and instruments for quality control and research and development work
Nanking Chemical Fertilizer	Much equipment from the U.S., Britain, Japan, Germany, Canada, but mostly pre-1949
Wuhan Heavy Machinery	About 20% of equipment imported from U.S.S.R., Czechoslovakia, Britain, East and West Germany
Wuhan Steel	Much Soviet equipment; some also from various East European countries

At the enterprises visited, there seemed to be very little new equipment and not very much raw material imported from the Soviet Union, and only a small amount from East European countries such as Czechoslovakia and East Germany.

Most of the imported equipment and machinery that was less than five years old apparently came from Japan and Western Europe. Much of the pre-1949 equipment in use also came from these areas.

At a number of the plants surveyed, the lack of imported commodities—particularly equipment, machinery, components, and spare parts—seemed to be resulting in fairly substantial idle capacity, equipment breakdowns, and production bottlenecks. This was particularly noticeable with regard to Soviet equipment for which various plants had to make their own spare parts and components, typically at considerable cost and quite inefficiently, possibly because of a Soviet embargo on these items in some cases. Even for equipment imported from other countries, there seemed to be an acute spare-parts problem in many instances. This might have been due to a variety of reasons such as poor state planning and distribution of imported spares and components, the failure or reluctance of foreign suppliers to provide adequate spares, and/or a desire on the part of Chinese policy makers to strive for self-sufficiency in the manufacture of various parts and components, regardless of the short-term costs and inefficiencies. The spare-parts problem involving imported machinery and equipment was most evident at Hangchow Machine Tool, Peking Steel Wire, Tientsin Shoe, Shanghai Truck, and Wuhan Steel.

It is also clear that imported equipment and materials, rather than reliance on indigenous sources of supply, would increase productivity substantially at many of the firms surveyed. But this is primarily a problem of the regime's and its planners' priorities, given the fact that there is a limit on the total volume of imports. The Tientsin Shoe Factory was making much of its own equipment—quite inefficiently—as well as machinery for other shoe producers. Wuhan Diesel Engine, Peking Steel Wire, Canton Electrical Appliance, Shanghai Truck, and Loyang Tractor were also among firms surveyed which were making much of their own equipment, components, and parts—typically in costly and inefficient ways. The Shanghai Pharmaceutical firm made most of its own packaging machinery, which was rather primitive, because no indigenous source of supply was available, and the higher planners did not see fit to import such machinery. The Wuhan Paper Mill used local dragon-beard grass and wood reeds to manufacture paper rather than utilize imported materials of any type. The director admitted that production efficiency and the quality of output suffered somewhat by following this policy of reliance on domestic materials.

Some of China's material imports seem to be based primarily on political, rather than economic, considerations. For example, the Peking Cotton Textile Mill used to import some high-quality raw cotton from Egypt. But because of a rift in Sino-Egyptian relations in the mid-1960's the plant now uses cotton imported from Pakistan and Tanzania.

China is far from self-sufficient in the manufacture of material-handling equipment, but there is little in the way of imports of this type. As a result, productivity seems to suffer substantially, particularly at heavy-industry and chemical fertilizer plants. The regime may be purposely following this policy because material-handling equipment would eliminate many jobs or else lead to excessive and much idle manpower. Given the relatively low level of wages, labor-intensive material handling and other techniques may be more feasible from the regime's point of view than the importation of expensive equipment.

In India, the severe foreign-exchange crisis that developed in the mid-1960's has greatly restricted imports of equipment, spares, and materials. Because of import constraints one typically finds at least as much, and often much more, idle capacity, equipment breakdowns, serious production bottlenecks, high costs, and general inefficiency at Indian factories as in Chinese industry. In fact, numerous Indian heavy engineering, machinery, component, and instrument firms were operating with 40 percent, or more, idle capacity, on a one-shift basis during the 1965–66 period. Indian firms in a fairly wide range of other industries which are also dependent substantially on imported equipment, spares, components, and materials have been faced with similar problems.

In general, the managers of Chinese enterprises seem to be faced with less uncertainty than their Indian counterparts in planning and in their operations because of import constraints. State planning is much more comprehensive and all-inclusive in Chinese industry, and imports are provided for in the enterprise plan during the planning period. While there are, of course, breakdowns in the plan, it seems that allocated imports do generally arrive at the Chinese plant more or less according to plan since adequate lead time is provided for, and a reasonably adequate balancing job is done by the planners.

The Indian firm that desires to use imported commodities is typically faced with a great deal of uncertainty, which has grown increasingly acute. Officially, requests for imports and foreign-exchange licenses are compiled and processed during a specified period each year. An overwhelming manual containing a myriad of complex and detailed import regulations is issued by the Indian government each period. This huge manual is far from clear. In reality there are relatively few clear-cut guidelines for firms desiring to obtain imported goods, Furthermore, the actual timing and processes regarding import entitlements involve much uncertainty, great delays in decisions, hard bargaining, gamesmanship, pressures, arbitrariness, and ad hoc decisions. A vast amount of black-marketing activities involving imported goods has evolved in the Indian economy, and corruption, such as bribery, is fairly pervasive. The cumbersome nature of the political organizations dealing with imports also contributes substantially to these problems.

The net result is that the managers of Indian firms relying on imports probably tend to have greater planning, organizational, control, and staffing problems and more constraints on carrying out the enterprise functions efficiently because of uncertainty involving imports than their Red Chinese counterparts. At the same time, however, India does import many highly beneficial commodities from the United States and also obtains a great deal more foreign aid and assistance than China from foreign countries and international organizations, such as the World Bank, the International Monetary Fund, and the United Nations. Nevertheless, the problems faced by Indian managers and their enterprises because of import restrictions and the foreign-exchange crisis are very real and probably more frustrating than for their Chinese counterparts.

Table 5–4 presents data on the exports of a number of Chinese enterprises surveyed in 1966. Several of the textile, clothing, and light-consumer-durable-goods firms export substantial amounts of their products to non-communist countries. Where heavy-industry firms (and the paper mill) I visited export commodities, the exports are generally to Southeast Asia and to other underdeveloped countries, and to support the Vietnamese war. Such exports are probably based chiefly on political and ideological factors rather than economic considerations. It is interesting to note that the Tientsin Shoe Plant, which was struggling with serious internal technical and managerial problems in 1966, has exported some shoe machinery to newly emerging African states in recent years.

In general, it seems that the Chinese are willing to sell in unprofitable ways and markets if there appears to be adequate market potential in the long run. There are some indications that an effort is being made to sell light consumer durables and engineering products to underdeveloped and newly emerging countries in Asia, Africa, the mid-East, and, to a lesser extent, Latin America, apart from Cuba, which is a major trading partner.

I made a few scattered comparisons of the enterprise costs and factory and domestic-retail prices of some of the products produced by Chinese firms surveyed and their retail prices in Hong Kong stores in 1966. (These products were identifiable either through brand names or actual enterprise name in both the Chinese and Hong Kong stores.)

It should be noted that in all cases I am basing my comparisons of official exchange conversion rates for Chinese yuan and Hong Kong dollars, using the U.S. dollar as the underlying basis of comparison.

Shirts, suits, and other garments produced by the Peking Clothing Firm sold in Hong Kong at retail prices in the range of roughly 10 to 100 percent higher than factory selling prices. In some cases they were higher, and in other cases lower than retail prices for similar items in major Chinese cities. Retail prices of various woolen goods in Hong Kong were roughly 10 to 20 percent above retail prices in China, and substantially higher than factory selling prices. There was not much difference in the retail prices in Hong Kong and Red China for similar types of shoes produced by the Tientsin Shoe Firm.

On the other hand, batteries produced by Shanghai's Wei Ming Plant were retailing in Hong Kong at prices significantly below factory costs. This firm's major standard flashlight and radio battery costs 2.4 yuan a dozen to produce, or roughly 8 U.S. cents each. The firm's unit sales price is .267 yuan or about 11 U.S. cents. The retail sales price of this item varied in different Chinese cities from .32 to .37 yuan or about 13 to 15 U.S. cents. It was selling in Hong Kong for 30 Hong Kong cents, which is roughly equivalent to 5 U.S. cents at the official exchange rate.

A similar situation existed with Diamond-brand table fans produced by the Canton Electrical Appliance Enterprise. I was told that it costs this enterprise about 70 to 75 yuan, or 28 to 30 U.S. dollars, to produce one such fan. I do not know the retail sales price in China, but this product

TABLE 5–4

DATA ON EXPORTS OF CHINESE ENTERPRISES SURVEYED IN 1966

Enterprise	*Nature and Amount of Exports in Recent Years**
Peking Woolen Mill	12%–30% of production exported to over 20 countries.
Peking Wool Carpet	20%–40% of production exported.
Peking Clothing	10%–50% of output exported to over 30 countries. (In 1965, 50% of production exported—primarily shirts with Ice Mountain brand name. Much of its output is sold in Hong Kong.)
Tientsin Shoe	30% of shoe production exported in 1965 to 13 countries, including Britain, Sweden, and Australia. (Expected to export nearly 40% of output in 1966.) This enterprise also exports the small amount of shoe machinery which it makes to Somaliland and one other African country.
Tientsin (Joint) Jen Yi Wool	5%–20% of output exported in last 5 years (about 20% in 1965).
Shanghai Wei Ming Battery	5%–40% of output exported annually since mid–1950's. In recent years exports have been in range of 25%–40% of output. Much of its exports go to other Asian, African, and mid-Eastern countries.
Shanghai Forging and Pressing	Exports about 10% to 30% of its output which consists of Diamond brand small tools, such as pliers, tongs, wrenches, and cutting instruments. Exports go to several dozen countries, both capitalistic and communist. Much of its exports go to Asian and African countries and a small amount to Cuba and a few other Latin American nations.
Hangchow Clothing	25%–35% exported to many countries—primarily shirts and ties
Wuhan Paper	5%–10% of output exported to Southeast Asia
Wuhan Heavy Machinery	Exports some equipment to North Vietnam and North Korea; has on occasion exported some items to Africa.
Wuhan Steel	Some of its production goes to North Vietnam and at times to unspecified other Asian and African countries.
Canton Electrical Appliance	In recent years has exported 30%–60% of its fans (Diamond brand) to more than a dozen countries. Much of its fan output is sold in Hong Kong, and some is sold to Southeast Asian and African nations. It exports primarily table fans with 14- to 16-inch specifications in 5 colors.

*** In most cases the ranges reflect a five-year period.**

was selling in different Hong Kong stores for 110 to 130 Hong Kong dollars, or about 18 to 22 U.S. dollars. Price differentials in Hong Kong were due in some cases to differences in colors and other minor specifications, while in other cases different stores were apparently charging somewhat different prices for the same product.

The managers of Chinese industrial enterprises do not have much to say about the types or quantities of goods to be produced for export. This is determined for them through the state plan. Hence, no use is made of, nor is there really a need for, export incentive or promotion schemes at the industrial-enterprise level in China in order to encourage the micromanagers to increase export production. In Indian industry, especially in the private sector, considerable use has been made of a variety of export-incentive schemes to encourage enterprise managers to produce more goods for export.[78] These schemes have met with varying degrees of success, but with India's severe foreign-exchange crisis in the mid-1960's, export incentives have been in a state of flux and have resulted in considerable uncertainty and confusion for managers of firms who must assess the advantages and disadvantages of producing various items for export.

The Red Chinese regime's export policies and decisions also lead to varying degrees of uncertainty and inefficiency for Chinese industrial firms which produce export items. This seemed to be the case at some of the Chinese enterprises surveyed where the amounts and varieties of goods produced for export vary substantially in the short run, and particularly where there are significant differences between the specifications and processes entailed in the manufacture of export items and those for goods produced for the home market.

Changes in export orders requiring adjustments in product-mix plans at several firms visited are frequent, even within a given planned year, and appear to be quite disruptive in some instances. Such changes typically result from special and unplanned export orders and from changing demand, opportunities, and/or other conditions in foreign countries which buy Red China's products. Product-mix changes resulting from foreign-trade requirements appeared to be quite common at the clothing, shoe, cotton-textile, woolen-fabric, wool-carpet, and electrical-appliance factories. A fairly significant amount of the export production of these enterprises involves specifications, quality standards, and production processes that differ in varying degrees from those pertaining to output for the home market. In some cases, enterprise product-mix changes are made without giving adequate lead time to adjust resources or production in a relatively efficient manner. With the exception of the electrical-appliance and shoe firms, however, these other factories seemed to adjust to export-production changes quite efficiently, perhaps because of their superior technical and managerial know-how.

The Shanghai battery and forging and pressing plants, as well as the heavy-machinery, steel, and paper enterprises in Wuhan, are not apparently confronted with frequent changes in their operating plans because of export decisions. The battery, forging and pressing plants and paper mills produce relatively standardized commodities for export which can readily be used for the home market as well. The commodities produced for export by Wuhan Steel and Wuhan Heavy Machinery are, for the most part, based on political and military agreements with foreign countries, and economics or market conditions are of minor or no importance.

Where there are major shifts in the amounts and varieties of products produced for export from year to year at the enterprises surveyed, these probably also tend to have a disruptive influence on operating efficiency in some cases. However, the constraints on managerial effectiveness and productive efficiency caused by year-to-year changes are probably generally not as serious as frequent changes within a given operating year because there is more lead time. Moreover, appropriate provisions can often be made for such shifts when the annual enterprise plan is being prepared.

A considerable amount of attention was being paid to quality control at several of the Chinese enterprises surveyed which produce a substantial amount of products for export. For example, the Peking Cotton Textile Mill No. 3 had about 500 employees, or 10 percent of its total work force, engaged directly in quality-control inspection. Tientsin Shoe, which employs 1,000 people, had about 50 regular quality-control inspectors. In addition, a number of the shoe plant's production workers in each work group were also responsible for making in-process quality-control checks, a practice which seems to be quite common in Chinese industry, particularly light industry. About 60 (7.5 percent) of Canton Electrical Appliances' 840 employees were engaged directly in quality-control work. A majority of them were involved with checking the quality of electric fans, the only type of product this firm normally produces for export. And fans make up only about 25 to 35 percent of this plant's output in terms of sales revenues.

At some of those enterprises visited which produce nonstandardized items for export—especially clothing and shoes—there are sizable staffs of designers, stylists, and product-development personnel working on products for export. Some even study foreign (and Western) literature, magazines, and products for ideas. Several of the firms surveyed also send representatives to the Canton trade fairs.

Let us briefly examine further some of the procedures and policies pertaining to exports at Peking Clothing, one of the Chinese enterprises surveyed. This firm exported about half of its output in 1965 and expected to export a similar proportion in 1966. Its export items are sent to the China National Garment Import-Export Corporation. The head office of this corporation is in Peking, but it also has branches in other major Chinese cities, such as Canton and Shanghai. For export orders negotiated with the Peking head office of this import-export corporation, the Peking Clothing Enterprise signs annual contracts directly with the corporation. Where export items are ordered by branches of this corporation in other cities, the clothing firm's direct superiors, the Peking Handicrafts Industrial Bureau, signs annual contracts with the corporation and its branches on behalf of Peking Clothing. Product-mix changes within the aggregate limits of these contracts are common.

The factory prices of goods produced for export by Peking Clothing are set by the import-export corporation and indicated in the sales contracts. Such prices are generally influenced by competitive and/or prevailing price levels in the foreign countries buying the products. The import-export corporation always receives a higher price from its foreign customers than the price it pays to Peking Clothing. The prices that Peking Clothing receives for its export items are often less, and only in a very few cases more, than the factory selling prices of its domestic products. However—and this was apparently unique to Peking Clothing among the enterprises surveyed—profit margins on similar items produced for export and for the home market are usually the same, even though the factory sales prices may differ. This is the case since the import-export corporation also fixes the prices of major materials allocated to Peking Clothing for the fulfillment of its export orders. That is, certain materials provided by the enterprise's suppliers are earmarked for export production. The corporation not only fixes the prices of these materials, but also plays a major role in determining the quantities and qualities to be allocated, and in some cases even designates the suppliers. These procedures and policies may be followed to insure that export products are produced in desired quantities and qualities by giving special attention to the allocation of materials for export production.

If the factory price of a given product for export is lower than the domestic factory price, the prices of raw materials earmarked for export production are also usually set lower than the prices of the same materials used in domestic production. In a sense, the import-export corporation provides Peking Clothing with a price subsidy so that it can maintain the same profit margin on its export production. While the profit margin is generally the same on similar items produced for export and the home market, actual total profit differs because of differentials in the factory sales prices. I did not find out whether Peking Clothing's suppliers which provide raw materials at lower prices for export production also receive any special "subsidies" or consideration. The import-export corporation does not deal with the allocation of any capital equipment or machinery to the Peking Clothing firm. This is handled by the Peking Handicrafts Bureau.

I was told by the head of the planning department at Peking Clothing that export order contracts are revised more often than contracts involving domestic production. Export contracts can be changed with one month's notice. At times entirely new contracts involving amounts and varieties of goods substantially different from those in the original contracts are drawn up. Special unplanned export orders are also initiated by the import-export corporation from time to time. Contractual changes and special orders involving exports often require changes in the firm's contracts with its suppliers.

On occasion Peking Clothing places and pays for advertisements of its export—and domestic—products in the newspapers and other media in major Chinese cities and even abroad. But the import-export corporation handles most of the advertising involving the firm's exports, and often uses the factory's brand name. Newspapers, magazines, trade journals, billboards, and, to a lesser extent, radio are the major media used for this purpose.

Political Stability

Even the most stable governments in the most stable countries are not completely static. Some degree of political change, but within a general framework of relative political stability, is, in fact, essential for improvements in managerial effectiveness and industrial progress over time because of various social and economic changes which emerge in society. But even in a relatively stable environment, political change frequently creates a variety of problems, adjustments, and changes at industrial enterprises; but these often have the net result of being favorable in terms of productive efficiency and progress.

Political instability is closely interrelated with several of the other environmental constraints discussed in this study. Hence, serious political instability in a given country not only tends to have a direct negative impact on industrial management and progress, but it also typically has an indirect impact through its effect on other environmental factors such as political organization, legal rules of the game, economic stability, military and defense policy, foreign trade, risk taking, education, attitude toward business and industrial managers, and so forth. Evidence to this effect is presented in our analysis of various other environmental constraints.

Where political instability exists in a given country to a significant degree, the impact on managerial effectiveness and industrial progress at the level of the enterprise tends to be significantly negative. Political instability can manifest itself in a variety of ways and have a variety of impacts on industrial enterprises and their management. At the extreme it sharply deters the establishment of new enterprises and the expansion of existing ones. Where the process of political change is violent, abrupt, and/or disruptive, enterprises are at a serious disadvantage in terms of productivity, and management tends to have great difficulty in carrying out its functions efficiently. This is typically the case where political instability is accompanied by revolution, war—particularly civil war—and extensive purges, as well as strikes, riots, and other types of work stoppages or slowdowns incited and organized by opposing political factions.

Serious political instability can also arise—and negatively affect industrial management—with changes in the government leadership or ruling political parties, and even with major and/or sudden shifts in policy or ideology within a single ruling party or faction. Even where only a few key governmental or political figures are replaced, there can be a major impact on industrial firms if the political jobs entailed involve macromanagerial decision making bearing substantially on micromanagement.

Drastic political shifts might result in the nationalization—or, much less commonly, the denationalization—of whole industries or specific firms, sharp swings in attitudes toward business and industrial managers which in turn lead to dramatic changes, positive or negative, in legal rules of the game and/or economic and social policies. With sharp negative shifts in governmental policies, attitudes, or behavior, numerous managers, professionals, and technicians might be replaced or purged, and many might even flee the country.

In many cases, political change may also mean changes in governmental relationships with specific firms. For example, some firms may gain while others suffer as a result of political shifts in patronage, favoritism, the awarding of contracts or orders for goods, the allocation of scarce resources, and so forth.

In the process, much uncertainty is created at numerous interdependent enterprises. Serious political conflict or instability among provincial, state, and/or local governments or rulers in a given country can also be disruptive for industrial enterprises and their managers. For example, this may result in serious disruptions in domestic trade and the flow of commodities—or people—from one area of the country to another.

Political instability over time can make it very difficult for enterprise managers to predict important trends or directions in government fiscal and monetary policies, laws and their enforcement, product and factor prices, economic stability, potential markets, availability of resources, arrangements with labor, customers, and suppliers, and various other environmental factors which bear directly on their planning and operations. Such uncertainty can also negatively affect other managerial functions such as organization, control, staffing, and direction, as well as the performance of all the enterprise's productive functions.

The Republican Era in China

The Republican period in China (1911–1949) was one of severe political instability which manifested itself in many forms. Although there were some brief periods of relative political stability during this era it was predominantly one of political crisis, chaos, and war. Chiang Kai-shek and the other leaders could not achieve national political unity, and there were conflicts within the central government from time to time. Conflicts among political factors and war lords at the provincial and local levels were even more serious, pervasive, and frequent.

Strikes, riots, and plant shutdowns were also common during various periods. Revolutionary terror and internal civil strife reached their peak in the late 1940's after the war with Japan, as the Chinese Communists gained considerable strength and made their all-out successful bid for power.

During China's Republican period various firms at various times benefited greatly from government patronage, favoritism, and collusion, while many others suffered. In general, political instability severely affected many of the other environmental factors in negative ways. This, in turn, created a great deal of uncertainty for industrial managers and sharply constrained productive efficiency and industrial development.

Since 1949, when the Communists came to power, there has been a much higher degree of sustained political harmony and stability in China, at least until late 1966 and early 1967. Political instability bordering on extreme overt conflict and disruption or civil strife have been avoided until the most recent times. However, various forms of political instability of a more subtle nature have had a negative impact on managerial effectiveness and industrial progress at various times during the 1949–66 period.

Party and State in Communist China

In order to properly analyze political stability in Red China it is necessary to consider conflicts, problems, and changes not only within the ruling Communist Party but also within the state or governmental system. Therefore, a brief word about the conception and nature of party and state in Red China is in order.[79]

The "state" in China is represented by the formal governmental organizations which dominate society. The state is a conscious contrivance and encompasses all of the macromanagerial organizations within the industrial hierarchy above the enterprise level—for example, the central ministries, state planning commission, provincial and municipal industrial and planning organizations, and so forth. It is the most important element of the superstructure of society, the instrument or tool of its ruling class; in the dictatorship of the proletariat, it is the instrument of the proletariat, which in reality is represented by the party. As an instrument the state has "structure." It is bureaucracy, as well as army and law, and the body of formal instruments from which commands and formal plans flow.

The Communist Party, on the other hand, is viewed by the Chinese regime as being the organized expression of the will of society. In theory, at least, it is supposed to represent the "interests of the people." The core of society, for the Chinese Communists, is the masses, and the "mass line" has been a continuing feature of their organizational philosophy since Yenan times in the thirties.[80] The mass line demands that the party be physically close to the masses. Underlying the elaborate governmental structure at all levels is the party, the engine really driving the Red Chinese state.

While the party actualizes the control of society over the state, theoretically it does not command, for formal command must flow from some instrument of the state. The Communist Party may, and does, propound policy, but technically, and in theory, it cannot issue operational orders in industry. These are supposed to come from an organ of the state. However, the party determines major objectives to be pursued, as well as the broad policy directives upon which concrete commands issued by governmental organs are based. The party also guides and controls governmental or state activity. As long as this fine distinction is maintained, the party cannot be regarded as an instrument of the structure of state power or bureaucracy.

In China the actual commands and plans flowing to enterprises come from organs of the state, although they may follow long after the related policy or objectives have been announced, and wheels have begun to turn at lower levels without waiting for formal communication from the governmental macromanagerial authorities. Even during the Great Leap Forward, when the regime believed that policy could be directly translated into action and deprecated the technical command functions of governmental (state) administration, formal commands and enterprise plans, such as they were, still came from, and were approved by, the state organs.

There are powerful ideological reasons for maintaining the principle that the party is not a state or governmental organ, but there are also practical reasons. The more an organization turns into a command-issuing body, the more it has to grapple with the concrete technicalities of command. This inevitability begins to limit the freedom needed for a wide range of innovative and creative decisions. The Chinese Communists have sharply fought any tendencies toward bureaucratization of the party, and have had a strong basic interest in maintaining the ideological principle that the party is not part of the state apparatus.

Since the Communist Party is the ultimate, dominant, and pervasive political power in China, it is evident that serious instability within the party can hinder managerial effectiveness and productive efficiency at the enterprise level. However, conflicts, abrupt changes, purges, and other forms of instability within the governmental or state apparatus can also have similar effects. Instability within the state bureaucracy is essentially a form of political instability which usually results from party decisions and actions, but it is not necessarily accompanied by instability within the party itself. In fact, much of what we would label as political instability in Red China during various periods since 1949 has involved the state apparatus, although there has also been instability within the party, most notably in the present period.

The 1950's until the Great Leap Forward

There was surprisingly little serious political instability in the years following the Communist takeover of China. As is generally the case with national revolutions, the successful Communist revolution in China was accompanied by a much higher degree of political centralization in government than had previously existed. China became much more unified and its government stronger than at any other point in its history. Of course, all of this did not take place without any conflict. There was bloodshed, purges, terror, and the flight of high-talent manpower, but to a lesser degree than has been the case in other countries—such as the Soviet Union, Cuba, Algeria, and Spain to name a few—which have had civil wars.

While many capitalists, managers, technicians, professional people, academicians, and other types of skilled manpower left China because of the Communist revolution, probably a substantial majority did not. Those who did not leave before or shortly after the Communist takeover, and later desired to leave, were prevented from doing so by the regime—except, of course, those who left illegally. Through appeals to nationalism, persuasion, effective propaganda, inducements, and promises of favorable treatment, the Chinese Communist regime has been successful in attracting back many of those who did leave. No doubt many, if not most, of those who returned have serious doubts today about the wisdom of their decision to return to their homeland. But the point is that Red China's economy retained its basis for growth because the flight of high-talent manpower was not greater than it was and because many talented, motivated people, including many capitalists, managers, and technicians, chose to return after the Communists came to power. Although virtually all private industrial enterprises in Red China had been nationalized by 1956, many of their former owners and managers stayed on in important executive jobs. In a later chapter we shall discuss in greater detail Red China's capitalists and their nationalized firms which are called "joint state and private enterprises." [81]

In the early and mid-1950's there were a number of political purges, but political stability in the party and in the government was not, in general, a truly serious problem.[82] For example, in 1951 there was the *sanfan* or "three-anti" campaign which involved an attack on individuals within the party, and particularly within the state bureaucracy, but this was not an attack against bureaucracy per se—this came later.

The *wufan* or "five-anti" campaign evolved in 1962. It was primarily directed against the bourgeoisie. The bourgeoisie, including capitalists and managers of private firms, was accused of bribery, tax evasion, fraud, theft of government property, and theft of economic secrets. Many of them were investigated, purged, and punished, and this undoubtedly had a negative impact on productive efficiency in many cases. But this was a fairly short-lived campaign and did not result in serious political instability. This was an onslaught against an entire class, but, in contrast to what happened to the landlord class, the bourgeoisie was not obliterated as a class. The sanfan and wufan movements were the last time that Peking used terrorist methods extensively to exercise control until the advent of the Cultural Revolution.

The *sanfan* movement or "purge of counterrevolutionaries" evolved in the mid-1950's. This was the first major attack against bureaucracy and bureaucrats in general. This campaign was tied in with the Chinese Communist regime's first serious inner-party struggle and state conflict at the top leadership level. Mao's most powerful opponents were Kao Kong and Jao Shu-shi. Kao Kong was the first head of China's State Planning Commision in 1952, and when he was openly purged and committed suicide in 1955 he was party boss of Manchuria, China's center of heavy industry. He was a strong advocate of the existing Soviet system of industrial management with its great emphasis on bureaucracy, expertise, centralization, one-man authority, heavy industry, and monetary incentives. He was more concerned with economic development than ideology. Jao Shu-shi, labeled as Kong's accomplice and co-conspirator in the antiparty plot, was party boss of east China, which included industrial Shanghai.

This top-level purge did not by itself lead to serious political instability within the party or government apparatus. It did, however, probably have a significant effect on the direction that China's system of industrial management would take during the Great Leap Forward—a system which had inherent elements of political instability and which led to economic crisis. For if the Kao-Jao clique had won out and had their way, or at least forced the Maoists to compromise with ideology, the Great Leap would probably not have emerged in the same form, if at all.

The Great Leap Period

In the latter half of 1957, as preparations were being finalized to launch the Great Leap, the "anti-rightist" movement broke out. This campaign entailed an all-out attack against bureaucracy, though the methods utilized were less brutal and ruthless than those used by Stalin in Russia's purges of the 1930's. During the first phase of this movement, intellectuals and nonparty governmental figures, many of whom were in the macromanagerial bureaucracy, were attacked. Then it spread to the rural areas, and by the end of 1957 there was an all-out attack on state bureaucracy as well as "rightist" (revisionistic) elements in the party itself. Hence, this campaign in essence turned into a Red versus Expert struggle, with the Reds coming out on top throughout the entire structure and system of industrial management.

A great deal of the intermediate tiers of the governmental economic and industrial bureaucracy was dismantled with the onslaught of the Great Leap Forward. This was accompanied by a high degree of decentralization of authority under local party cadres. Purges within the party continued until late 1958. Key provincial, municipal, and local party cadres whose orientation, commitment, and loyalty to Peking and the central party apparatus were in question were replaced by more reliable functionaries. In a few cases, such as in Liaoning Province, the entire party-leadership groups at provincial and local levels were changed. The final major act of this antirightist, antibureaucracy campaign came in April 1959, when the Ministry of State Control, a pervasive state organization, and the Ministry of Justice were abolished. The Ministry of State Control had actually already lost much of its power by 1958. With the end of this ministry, reliance on party control over industry and management reached its peak.

China's reorganization of the governmental macromanagerial structure and the drastic change in the party's role in industrial management toward the end of the 1950's does not, on the surface, seem to be as drastic or as unstabilizing as the reorganization and reforms that occurred in the Soviet Union around the same time.[83] At least, one would get this impression by examining only changes reflected on formal organization charts. But below the surface, looking at human factors and what really happened rather than examining a bunch of boxes linked together on a chart, China's changes were much more radical, unstabilizing, and disruptive.

The Soviet industrial reorganization along territorial lines involved a modest degree of decentralization of authority, but with the experts maintaining a major role in industrial management, particularly in its operational, detailed, technical, and day-to-day aspects. Moreover, the system of state planning and control was not seriously undermined or disrupted in the Soviet Union. The Chinese reorganization and reforms involved a great deal more decentralization, with the Reds at all levels of the industrial hierarchy coming to play the major operational, as well as policy, role in management. Policies as interpreted by party cadres superseded plans on a pervasive scale; the Experts and professional managers were attacked, abused, ignored, and greatly misutilized. China's system of state planning and control was greatly undermined and disrupted.

Not only did Chinese enterprise managers suddenly have to deal with an entirely different structure of state administration, they also had to deal with many new people and personalities, and their relationships with party cadres changed abruptly and drastically. No doubt, only relatively few enterprise managers had a reasonably clear picture of meaningful guidelines for predicting policies, actions, or changes in human relationships on the government or party side. To the typical industrial manager such uncertainty with regard to his relationships with government organizations and party committees and their roles in the management process was, in essence, largely the result of political change and instability.

Political instability in this form in China has been of a cyclical nature evolving with extreme shifts in the ideological pendulum—from moderation to extremism and vice versa. But even cyclical political instability—as compared with more frequent or constant instability and uncertainty—can, if drastic enough, have a very damaging psychological as well as operational effect on industrial managers, government bureaucrats, and even party cadres.

The 1960's and the Cultural Revolution

As has been discussed earlier, a more rational, predictable, and stable system of industrial management evolved again in China during the first half of the 1960's. As the Experts were restored to their major roles in management, party cadres at the provincial and local levels were attacked and lost many of their operational powers during the economic crisis of the early 1960's. This was followed by a reasonable balance between Reds and Experts in industrial management. But then came the Great Proletarian Cultural Revolution with its ideological extremism, accompanied again by cyclical political instability. Just as China's economic program seemed to be settling into a predictable and reasonably successful pattern of growth, politics and political instability in the form of the Cultural Revolution again reared its head to cloud the future.

During my stay in Red China political instability had not yet become acute or pervasive. There were already some purges of intellectuals, key party officials, and state bureaucrats, and the schools were closed down shortly before I left. Most of the attacks were aimed at party functionaries in relatively important jobs. However, there was not, nor has there yet been, any official major reorganization of the state industrial hierarchy, although there are frequently relatively minor organizational changes. Relationships between Reds and Experts and between party cadres and regular managers in industrial management were probably shifting in favor of the Reds and the party in many cases. As has been discussed earlier, at a number of enterprises visited, the Reds seemed to have the upper hand in operational management, and in some cases considerable inefficiency was resulting from irrational stress on such policies as "Put politics in command," "innovation," and "self-sufficiency." But I got the impression, that unlike the Great Leap period where political pressures and instability led to frenzied economic effort and floods of irrational decisions at enterprises, the Cultural Revolution seemed to be having more of a paralyzing effect on decision making.

Because of the uncertainty resulting from this revolution, managers and party cadres at many enterprises seemed unsure about what action to take in such matters as the elimination of bonuses and other monetary incentives, the election of managers, the precise amount of time managers should spend in physical labor and the type of labor they should do, and so forth. For example, a number of firms claimed to be "seriously considering" an end to monetary incentives but gave no indication when a final decision would be made; others were "experimenting" with the abolishment of such incentives but were not sure that they would not be reinstated. Similarly, various enterprises did not seem to know what to do about having employees "elect" managers, or which managers should be "elected." Toward the end of my stay in China, meetings to decide on these and other policies and issues in the light of the intensification of the Cultural Revolution were becoming more common.

There also seemed to be quite a bit of uncertainty and confusion involving the direction of the roles of party cadres and managers in management at a number of firms visited. Should politics clearly take command? Should economics remain as a high-priority desideratum of enterprise performance? Or should some workable balance be the norm? I got different impressions on this score at different enterprises.

Even in times of relative ideological moderation and political stability, the Chinese regime has been reluctant to spell out very clearly or precisely the roles of party cadres and regular managers in enterprise management or macromanagement. Officially, enterprise management is under dual state and party control, and this alone means that some confusion is probably inevitable. The regime's reluctance to spell out the functions of Reds and Experts or party cadres and managers stems from its antibureaucratic mentality. By keeping the party's role flexible, it is felt that this will enhance their initiative, creativity, and innovativeness and that party cadres will be in a better position to interpret state policies and aims in the light of local conditions, and to effectively control managerial activities and enterprise operations. Hence, there are elements of political instability built into the party-manager and Red-Expert relationship, but these need not hinder managerial effectiveness and industrial progress as long as the relationship is maintained in a reasonably stable and predictive manner. On the other hand, where the relationship is suddenly disrupted and/or changed drastically because of political instability within the party or state apparatus, or because of major personnel changes, productive efficiency is likely to suffer.

In general, Red-Expert and party-manager relationships in Soviet industry, although somewhat enigmatic, have tended to be spelled out more clearly at both the micro- and macro-levels and have been more stable over time than has been the case in China.[84] This seems to be so, even though key executives as well as other personnel at Soviet enterprises must still work out the specifics of their modus vivendi. Because the relationships between party cadres and managers tend to be less clearly defined and more precarious at Chinese firms than at Soviet enterprises, the meshing of interacting personalities probably tends to be a more critical consideration in Chinese industry. Even if people in key executive jobs are shifted at Soviet enterprises, there is a somewhat greater degree of stability and clearer definition of roles built into those jobs than at Chinese firms.

This may explain, at least in part, why the Chinese regime seems to be more concerned about how key enterprise party and managerial executives interact as a team, rather than about their individual capabilities or achieving a good fit between a given person and a given job alone. An attempt frequently seems to be made to design the organization of the Chinese enterprise, particularly at the top level, around personalities more than individual skills or abilities. This may explain in large part why there seems to be much less transferring of key people among enterprises in China than in Soviet industry.

Of twenty-two Chinese enterprise directors questioned on this subject, only three of them held their present jobs for less than four years. In the Soviet Union, nine out of sixteen directors of enterprises I visited were in their positions for less than four years. Furthermore, of the twenty-one cases reported in China, the enterprise director and party secretary were appointed at the same time in ten cases, and in most of these ten cases they had previously worked together. In nine other cases they were appointed within one year of each other, and here too, in several cases, they had worked together before. This suggests a desire by higher party and state authorities to achieve an effective relationship between these two types of key enterprise executives—a relationship that can withstand the political instability, changing conditions, and uncertainties which are inherent or evolve in the system of industrial management. It was much more common at the Soviet enterprises that I visited for party secretaries and directors to be appointed at different times and to appoint a party official and directors to the same firm, even though they had not worked together previously.

Political uncertainty evolving with the Cultural Revolution has overshadowed China's Third Five-Year Plan which was supposed to begin in 1966 but which may not yet have actually gotten underway. None of the enterprises surveyed in 1966 had played a role in the drafting of this new five-year plan; all of them were operating according to an annual or shorter-term plan. Officials of planning organizations on the provincial and municipal level and industrial organizations whom I interviewed were reluctant to discuss the new five-year plan, but some of them implied that it had not yet been implemented in any operational way. I was told by officials of the State Planning Commission, the Ministry of Commerce, and the Ministry of Labor, that the Third Five-Year Plan was still being worked out.

It is likely that old and existing industrial programs and operations have tended to go along without interruption, while there may well be a general reluctance to make decisions necessary to launch new programs, projects, or substantially different operations because of prevailing political instability.[85] In this regard in particular, both macromanagerial and micromanagerial decision making has probably been paralyzed in many instances, thus hindering managerial effectiveness and industrial progress.

I encountered a number of serious delays and interruptions in projects, programs, and operations at some of the enterprises surveyed which may have been due, at least in part, to the uncertain political situation. For instance, at the Wuhan Steel Plant there was a large uncompleted shop with a planned annual capacity of 600,000 to 700,000 tons of special rolled steel. This shop was supposed to be in operation in 1966, but work on its completion had been halted. Management apparently did not have any definite idea as to when the shop would be completed and put into operation.

The Tientsin North Lake Instrument Factory began producing two new and expensive types of scientific instruments in mid-1965. Higher authorities were also considering exporting some of these new instruments. As of May 1966, the enterprise's 1966 plan was still not approved, and the plant continued producing the new products as fast as suppliers came up with the necessary components. By May the factory had produced thirty pieces of equipment, which accounted for about half of its total production. Yet, the instruments were lying in the warehouse because no customer had yet been assigned; in fact, a sales price for the new products had not yet been formally set.

Of course, the above two problems may have been due to planning inefficiency or errors of a macromanagerial nature, but it is quite possible that political instability and uncertainty were also contributing factors leading to delays in decisions and inefficiency. In the previous section, it was pointed out that the Chinese have been reluctant to make decisions or commitments involving new directions and products in foreign trade. It is quite likely that reluctance also exists with regard to managerial and technical decisions concerning the domestic economy and that such reluctance has become more pronounced and pervasive as the Cultural Revolution and political instability have becomes intensified, particularly in 1967.

China's current cycle of political instability has taken some different and much more overt forms than it did during the Great Leap. During the Leap, political instability manifested itself in drastic and abrupt changes in organizational structures, relationships, personalities, and policies. But unlike the current cycle, it did not result in extensive opposition to the regime or its policies, and it did not involve strikes, intentional work stoppages, power struggles, and inner-party conflicts at the top, or violence bordering on widespread civil war. Mao's opponents apparently place top priority on economic development and realize that careful planning and rational management are essential. The Maoists undoubtedly desire economic development, but give an even higher priority to ideological goals—particularly the rapid transformation of people into pure communist men, as interpreted by Mao.

The highly valued "mass line" of Chinese Communist organizational philosophy has in reality been abandoned during the current phase of political instability, and the regime has been confronted with mass opposition. Moreover, the regime has become increasingly reluctant to rely on regular party cadres to interpret policies or control activities in the industrial sphere. Instabilities inherent in relationships between party cadres and managers in industry have been greatly overshadowed by overt political instability resulting from the onslaught into factories by the Red Guards, followed by the military, the people's militia, and hastily formed new "revolutionary" and "counterrevolutionary" committees and organizations of various types.

As has been mentioned earlier, the regime ordered Red Guards into plants to revolutionize management in late 1966 and early January 1967. The ensuing instability and economic disruption were apparently so great that the effort was called off after only a few weeks of activity. Red Guard activities have led to strikes, work stoppages, the piling up of materials on railroad sidings, delays in the loading and unloading of ships, and worse. By late January the regime began ordering the People's Liberation Army to take charge of factories and "maintain production," and to control various macromanagerial organizations in the state bureaucracy. Soon the people's militia—reported to be some twenty million strong—was directed to back up the army in its efforts. Numerous other impromptu and variously titled committees and organizations, both in support of and in opposition to the Maoists, also got into the act. Enterprise managers and macromanagers, as well as party cadres, are probably greatly confused in numerous instances about whose authority or orders to accept.

In 1967 and 1968 there were reports from the south—Kwangtung Province and Canton—that "rebel revolutionary directorates" and "Provisional General Headquarters" were in control of certain areas and various organizations rather than the army.[87] In Nanchang, the capital of Kiangsi Province, a group established to mobilize the area's industrial and communications systems was given its orders by a military officer speaking for the provincial military commander. The group called on to implement this order was called the "Provisional Group to Promote Production." [88] In Shansi Province a number of newly formed organizations participated in efforts to take over industrial management and state administration from "authoritarian, antirevolutionary and capitalist forces." These organizations included the "Shansi Revolutionary Manufacturers' Employees Suicide Forces," the "Red Revolt People's Association," and the "Revolution Revolt Army." In Harbin the "Proletarian Revolutionary School," a newly formed party group, also sought to gain control over various industrial and state organizations.[89]

The total negative impact of overt political instability on managerial effectiveness and industrial progress in 1966 may not have been as great as one might assume. According to official Red Chinese claims, the gross value of industrial production rose 20 percent in 1966, and good gains in agricultural output over 1965 were also reported.[90] These claims might have been exaggerated for propaganda purposes, but even if this is so, 1966 was probably still a relatively good year in terms of economic progress.

The same was probably not true for 1967 and 1968 as well. Political instability and civil strife became very serious and widespread and got out of control especially during the January-April period of 1967, and again in the spring and early summer of 1968. China's industrial and general economic performance for 1967 and 1968 no doubt declined, perhaps quite significantly, although hard facts are not yet available. Continued division, conflict, and instability at the top of the party and government would probably further encourage indecision and lead to considerable inefficiency at all levels of industrial management. If the ideological extremists gain an uncompromising victory at the top, this would undoubtedly have even more serious and far-reaching negative impacts on managerial effectiveness and industrial progress.

A Comment on Political Stability and Problems in India

Unlike many, and probably most, other underdeveloped and developing nations, India has been a relatively stable country in the political and governmental sphere. However, political instability and conflict in India's government has had, and still has, negative impacts on managerial effectiveness and industrial progress.

Since India's system of government is basically democratic, real opposition parties with a wide range of different philosophies and aims exist. While the Congress Party has been in power at the national level since India gained her independence in 1947, this party has been internally split by opposing political philosophies and factions composed of left-wing, right-wing, and moderate elements. Because of the composition of India's government, it has been very difficult for the central government to gain a workable consensus on many major issues involving changes in negative environmental constraints of all types—economic, political-legal, educational, and sociological-cultural. As a result, central decision making and effective change have been seriously constrained and even paralyzed in numerous instances. Hence, at the national level the problem has not been so much one of overt political instability per se, but much more one of ineffective political action and inaction. This situation may grow even worse in the future since various minority parties—both left and right wing—made substantial gains in India's 1967 elections at the national, state, and local levels. Enterprise managers may find it even more difficult to predict the course of various governmental decisions or political actions which bear on their own plans, decisions, and operations.

While governmental inaction has tended to be a major constraint on India's industrial progress, central political decisions, and particularly state and local political conditions, have contributed substantially to many riots, strikes, plant shutdowns and slowdowns, and various other politically inspired events which have a negative impact on productive efficiency and managerial effectiveness. Civil unrest, interfering with efficient enterprise management and operations, has been, and still is stirred up by opposing political parties and activist groups—most commonly the left, including the Communists—in various parts of the country, especially shortly after independence and again in the last few years. West Bengal and its capital, Calcutta—one of India's main industrial centers and my 1965–66 home base in India—has a relatively high degree of political instability and unrest, as do Kerala, where the Communists recently won in the state elections, and Bihar.

In general, political instability has been more serious at the state and local levels than at the center. Political conflict, instability, and lack of governmental cooperation among India's states has hindered industrial development on a widespread scale. The national government has not been very effective in its control over the states or in bringing about a substantially greater spirit of cooperation among them. In view of the results of India's 1967 elections the outlook in this sphere does not look very bright.

While political instability, conflicts, and governmental inaction tend to become more frequent problems in India than in China, the negative impacts on managerial effectiveness and industrial progress during a period of a few years tend to be relatively minor when compared with those arising from China's sharp cyclical political shifts, as represented by the Great Leap and the Cultural Revolution. It is difficult to determine with precision whether India's more frequent political disruptions and problems or China's much more serious but less frequent political disruptions have a more damaging effect over a protracted period. The fact that it took Red China several years to recover from its economic crisis resulting from the Great Leap suggests that China's drastic cyclical political upheavals have a more damaging effect. Perhaps the singular "upheaval" should be used here rather than the plural, since we do not yet know the extent of damage that is being done to management, industry, and the economy during China's current "revolutionary" period. It is, however, likely to be quite substantial, or probably even severe, if China's widespread political instability and civil crisis persist.

Political Organization

Republican China

The Kuomintang-led Nationalist Government, during China's Republican period, was not particularly antibusiness. In fact, it generally favored private enterprise. Nationalization of existing indigenous companies was not one of its aims, although the Nationalist government did show some interest in developing a public heavy-industry sector, particularly for defense and military purposes. Where business and industrial pressure groups influenced government officials in Republican China the outcome was frequently not conducive to greater managerial effectiveness or productive efficiency. The nature and outcome of such pressure and influence commonly involved greater monopoly power, protection for relatively inefficient enterprises, favoritism, patronage, collusion, and corruption.

The Kuomintang undoubtedly desired industrial development and the creation of a strong and self-sufficient China economically, politically, and militarily. In fact during the 1934–37 period, a period of relative stability in Republican China, the national government attempted to introduce and expand modern industry, to attract foreign investment, and generally to encourage economic development in modern terms in as wide a part of the country as the influence of the central government could reach.[91] During this brief period there was significant economic progress.

However, as has been pointed out earlier, throughout most of its rule the Kuomintang was preoccupied with the problems of political control, civil strife, revolution, and foreign invasion. It never did develop a very clear-cut philosophy of, or a comprehensive program for, industrialization and economic development.[92] Furthermore the Nationalist government exerted little or no effective influence or control over many parts of the country. It never succeeded in achieving a very high degree of political unity. The degree of centralization in the nation's government was inadequate in terms of promoting substantial, widespread, or sustained industrial progress.

A major problem of political organization in Republican China was not that the macromanagerial government bureaucracy was too large or too centralized; rather it was that there was not enough political centralization, and the macromanagerial apparatus was too small and ineffective. Where the national government did establish macromanagerial agencies with the purpose of promoting industrial development and self-sufficiency, this was typically done for military or defense reasons, rather than as part of a plan or program of general economic development or industrial progress. For example, the Kuomintang set up a special agency, the National Resources Commission, under the Supreme National Defense Council to supervise the establishment of a nucleus of heavy industry able to meet, at least partially, the country's needs for armaments, as well as specific defense-oriented capital goods, in the event of a national emergency.[93] But little was done to create governmental macromanagerial agencies that would or could deal with industrial development on a diverse or widespread scale.

The General Significance of Governmental Macromanagerial Organizations

In any country, governmental agencies of the macromanagerial type are essential for substantial and sustained economic progress. This is true for capitalistic as well as communistic and mixed economies, although a much smaller governmental or political bureaucracy is typically required in the former. For even in capitalist countries various types of macromanagerial government organizations can, and do, play key roles in maintaining and creating an environment conducive to greater managerial effectiveness and industrial progress. They do this in part by collecting, analyzing, and disseminating information, resolving conflicts, formulating policies and rules of the game, rendering aid and assistance, and regulating and controlling activities, particularly in the economic, legal, and political spheres but also in the educational and sociological-cultural spheres.

In the United States there is a wide variety of macromanagerial governmental organizations at both the national and local levels. For example, macromanagerial functions are performed by the Federal Reserve Board, the Small Business Administration, the President's Council of Economic Advisers, various fiscal, financial, budgeting, labor, antitrust, price, and educational and training departments, bureaus, and offices, as well as many other types of federal and governmental organizations and agencies. Many American citizens may complain about the size and extent of the government bureaucracy, and in many instances the cumbersome structure no doubt hinders managerial effectiveness and productive efficiency in industry. But in spite of many shortcomings, the government bureaucracy, as long as it does not get too much out of control, has played, and at present still plays, a very important positive role in the United States' economic progress. It clearly still does more good than harm on a national scale in terms of industrial progress and general economic well-being, although there is certainly much room for improvement. Look at what happened during the Great Depression of the 1930's when there were only a few, typically ineffective, governmental macromanagerial organizations. The creation of new and rather effective macromanagerial agencies has played a crucial role in preventing similar depressions.

Communist China

As with political stability, an examination of political organization in Red China should deal with both the Communist Party and the government bureaucracy. We are particularly interested in that portion of the macromanagerial bureaucracy that bears significantly on enterprise management. Although the party and the state bureaucracy are distinct organizational entities, in reality they are closely intertwined at every level, with the party being a superstructure of direction and control. In this section we shall present only a general and brief discussion of Red China's political organization as a constraint on managerial effectiveness and productive efficiency in industry. Chapter 8 deals more specifically and in greater depth with the structure and role of the party and particularly of the macromanagerial state bureaucracy in Communist China's industrial organization and planning.[94]

While there have been philosophical and ideological differences and even serious conflicts within China's Communist Party, there has been virtually unanimous agreement that industry should be state-owned and that the economic system should be based on comprehensive state planning rather than market forces or competition. In state planning of the communist type a large central bureaucracy is needed. A very big intermediate state bureaucracy between the central policy makers and planners and the industrial enterprises is also required, and macromanagement and micromanagement are interlocked in a continuum of control. This huge bureaucracy is needed to collect, process, and analyze information for purposes of decision making, planning, and control; to allocate resources; to distribute commodities; to provide for a workable degree of consistency and balance in the myriad interconnected sections of the overall state plan and the plans of individual enterprises; to provide for timely corrective action arising from imperfections and errors in the plans; and for numerous other critical administrative reasons.

It is impossible to determine what an optimum governmental bureaucratic structure would be in an economy such as Red China's. It is clear that a very large one is needed, but it can be either too large or not large enough at any given point in time. There is actually a wide range of choices open to the regime with regard to the structure of the state bureaucracy, the specific types, functions, locations, and relationships among the numerous macromanagerial organizations which make up this bureaucracy, degrees of centralization and decentralization of authority, and so forth. Since 1949 the state bureaucracy has been in a state of constant flux and reorganization, more often of a relatively minor nature, but at times involving major and even drastic overhauls.

While the regime is committed to a system of pervasive party control superimposed on, and parallel to, all of the levels of state administration, it also has a range of choices with regard to the actual role that the party should play in governmental administration, including industrial management. Here the Red versus Expert and the policy versus plan pendulums are the most important indications of the regime's choices with regard to the party's role in industrial management during different time periods.

Throughout China's Communist era there have been various constraints on enterprise-level managerial effectiveness and productive efficiency inherent in the country's political organization. These constraints have varied in degree and extensiveness, sometimes dramatically, during different periods. But they nevertheless seem to be built into the macromanagerial state bureaucracy, as well as the structure of party control, regardless of their specific forms at a given point in time, because of their basic nature and size.[95]

Even in periods of relative ideological moderation it is impossible to prevent politics and ideology from interfering at least somewhat with managerial, technical, and economic rationality in an economy and system of governmental administration run and controlled by political cadres. In such a system political preferences, ethical values, and economic considerations tend to be closely intertwined in macro-decision making in particular. When the ideological pendulum swings in the direction of extremism and the Reds take over more of the functions and operational decisions of the state's macromanagerial organizations, interference with managerial, technical, and economic rationality tends to grow accordingly. For ideological extremism not only manifests itself and has direct negative effects within industrial enterprises; it also has very substantial noninternalized effects on enterprises through its impact throughout the higher-level governmental bureaucracy and macromanagerial decision making.

Even in relatively stable periods the roles, functions, powers, procedures, relationships, and responsibilities of the numerous macromanagerial organizations of the state bureaucracy and the party are in a state of flux, never being precisely defined. There are frequently mergers and internal reorganizations involving existing organizations, additions of new ones, and deletions of old ones. As a result, confusion, red tape, delays in decisions, inconsistent decisions, planning errors, duplication of effort, informational deficiencies, and control problems always exist to a fairly substantial degree. The need for, and the use made of, committees in decision making at all levels also lead to delay and inefficiency. Problems and inefficiencies in macro-administration lead to inconsistent plans, supply failures, production and distribution bottlenecks, waste, and idle and mismatched resources of various kinds at the enterprise level. Such problems tend to be intensified, at least in the short run, by periodic major reorganizations and disruptions in the state administration and the party. Where major organizational changes have been accompanied by ideological extremism the effect is even more damaging and lasting.

In general, different components of the enterprise plan—for example, targets, tasks, allocations of various kinds of commodities and other resources—emanate from a variety of higher-level organizations of the state bureaucracy. It is quite common for the macro-organizations and agencies to be ill informed about each other's doings, and for them to adopt different and, at times, conflicting criteria in their decisions involving a particular firm, group of firms, industry, or geographic area. The overall state economic planning and industrial bureaucracy consists of thousands upon thousands of people working in hundreds of different ministries, commissions, departments, sub-departments, agencies, offices, sections, and divisions. At each level of this bureaucracy there are separate organizations and organizational sub-units dealing with such things as the allocation of certain commodities, the sale distribution and/or delivery of certain items, the planning of certain types of production, setting prices for specific products, allocation of various types of manpower, capital-investment decisions and projects, allocations of working capital and financial planning, product development, technological innovation and improvement, monetary control, accounting data and procedures, statistical reporting, and so forth.

Although each enterprise is officially under the direct jurisdiction and control of a specific higher-governmental organization, many, often dozens, of macro-organizations play roles in shaping a given enterprise's plan and in the execution of the plan. In numerous cases, enterprises are under dual control, and, in effect, they have two direct superior organizations. For example, this is the case where a firm is directly under a provincial or local industrial department, bureau, or corporation, but also receives certain targets, tasks, and/or instructions from a central industrial ministry. Dual control is also common at higher levels of the industrial hierarchy. By its very nature, dual control (or subordination) undoubtedly leads to confusion, conflict, and inefficiency in numerous instances.

In several of my interviews with both Chinese macro-officials and micromanagers, there seemed to be considerable confusion as to which macro-organizations play what roles or make what kinds of decisions. For example, who sets the prices of the items produced or allocated by your organization? Who is responsible for the allocations or distribution of commodity X? Who has the final say in new product decisions? If you want to get a component or spare part quickly from the state-reserve stockpiles maintained at different levels of the economy because your supplier has failed you, to whom do you apply for this unplanned allocation decision? Who must give final approval if you wish to make a change in part of the enterprise plan?

Frequently, macromanagerial decisions are made without adequate knowledge of, or concern for, local operating conditions or problems. Not being allocated a specific spare part may be of great concern to the enterprise production manager who is directly affected, but to a higher-level planner who allocates this item it is one infinitesimally small element buried in a mass of aggregate data and decisions. Time pressures on macromanagerial decision makers lead to many planning errors, and it is common for enterprise-operating plans to be formally approved several months—even six months—late. Control and balancing problems also frequently arise as various enterprises underfulfill and overfulfill their plans. Informational deficiencies and inadequate statistics also hinder macromanagerial decision making and control in numerous instances, as does the critical shortage of competent and properly trained personnel. Because of the state bureaucracy, enterprise managers are often likely to find themselves in a precarious position. They may be held responsible for not fulfilling their plan, while macromanagers who, through their powers, have made inefficient decisions contributing to the underfulfillment of the plan are not held responsible because they or their errors cannot be pinpointed or traced through the bureaucratic maze.

By its very nature, Red China's overall political organization contributes to, and encourages, various kinds of undesirable, illicit, and semilegal managerial behavior at the enterprise level. Such behavior patterns have already been discussed in the section on relevant legal rules of the game.[96] Within the macromanagerial apparatus there is probably also a fair amount of undesirable behavior such as the biasing, distortion and withholding of critical information, "passing the buck," collusion, and favoritism resulting in inefficient decisions, and so on. The Chinese are reluctant to publish or provide much information about how the state bureaucracy or party really functions. But from what is known about behavior in the Soviet Union in these spheres, it is highly probably that some similar undesirable practices exist in China.[97] However, the amount of outright corruption and bribery may well be less in macromanagement in the party in China than in Russia.

There are no formally organized or officially sanctioned business, industrial, managerial, labor, or consumer pressure groups in Red China. The party has the major and final say in all important policy matters. However, there are undoubtedly numerous informal pressure groups, consisting of industrial managers, government officials, and party cadres formed for specific purposes such as obtaining more resources or getting lower production targets for their enterprise, industry, province, city, or district. Such informal pressure groups no doubt engage in considerable hard bargaining, politicking, and gamesmanship with higher authorities, and they are permitted to function within the framework and constraints of the state plan. While such pressure groups probably influence many decisions made by superior authorities and help to effect compromises, the planners' preferences and the aims of the party leadership are not likely to be sacrificed substantially.

One chief reason why the Chinese party leadership tends to be basically antibureaucratic is because it feels that bureaucracy breeds powerful pressure groups with strong vested interests and a "localistic" point of view. If powerful pressure groups do evolve, persist, and become pervasive, there is a real danger that the planners' preferences and the party's objectives and policies would be seriously undermined. The Soviet Union has experienced considerable vested interestism, localistic behavior, and autarkic tendencies because of the nature of pressures and pressure groups arising from its political organization. In Russia, the experts and the government bureaucrats, rather than the party, play the major role in the operational and technical aspects of industrial management. But the party itself in the Soviet Union is also more bureaucratic than in China.

The 1952–57 Period

Let us examine very briefly the general nature of Red China's political organization during various periods.[98] During the 1952–57 period, the state's planning and industrial bureaucracy grew rapidly and steadily as industry and the economy developed. Many new macromanagerial organizations evolved, particularly at the national level with the creation of new industrial ministries and planning organizations. This period was characterized by a high degree of industrial centralization, with the experts in control of operational management. A high degree of administration centralization was feasible during this period because the industrial base of the country was not highly developed; in fact, a major proportion of China's relatively large-scale plants were built during this period. The relatively primitive nature of China's statistical, accounting, and information-reporting systems, the great shortage of trained personnel, general lack of experience, and various other problems led to considerable inefficiency in both macromanagement and micromanagement. In spite of such problems and constraints, China's overall political organization during this period was conducive to substantial industrial progress and managerial effectiveness.

The Great Leap

With the onslaught of the Great Leap in 1957 and 1958, the industrial ministerial system and, in fact, much of the existing governmental bureaucracy, were dismantled in favor of a much more decentralized geographical system of management under party control. Greater decentralization of authority was a feasible path to follow because many new and diverse factories had been built throughout much of the country. However, the actual form that this decentralization took proved to be highly ineffective and inefficient. During the Great Leap period, there was actually not enough state bureaucracy to cope effectively with an economic system based on state planning. With the Reds in control and with policies superseding plans, state planning became so flexible that it was virtually meaningless on a pervasive scale. In fact, the system of state planning and control was greatly undermined and enterprises ran out of control in numerous instances as managerial effectiveness and productive efficiency declined steadily and dramatically.

The 1960's

During the 1960's, much of the previously dismantled state bureaucracy again emerged, and new organizations at the provincial and municipal levels, as well as at the center, were created. Various important functions and activities were recentralized, the Experts once again came to play a major role in industrial management at all levels, and the state bureaucracy became much more effective and reasonably stable. Even with the emergence of a large number of central industrial ministries and the recentralization of many decision-making powers, there has still been more decentralization of authority—particularly at the provincial and municipal levels, but also at the firm level in general—than there was in China's 1952–57 period. This has been a feasible course to follow since the number, diversity, and geographical dispersion of industrial enterprises are substantially greater than in the earlier period. It is likely, however, that some of the powers and independence extended to industrial enterprises in the early 1960's have been taken away from them in the last few years. (Managerial authority and independence at the enterprise level in Chinese industry are dealt with in Chapter 9.)

During my 1966 visit to Red China, there seemed to be greater decentralization in the form of more authority granted to territorial bodies—at the provincial and municipal levels—than ever existed under the regional economic council (*sovnarkhoz*) system in the Soviet Union. Red China has a much greater number of small enterprises than Russia, and this alone makes a high degree of centralized and comprehensive planning and control very difficult. Major deficiencies in the Chinese statistical and accounting system, and the still critical shortages of adequately trained personnel for macro-organizations as well as micro-organizations, also makes a high degree of centralization unfeasible under existing conditions.

Territorial decentralization of authority in industrial management has never really worked very well in the Soviet Union because of strong tendencies toward economically irrational self-sufficiency—also referred to as "localism" and "autarky"—and deep-rooted vested interests on the part of regional and local administrators. There are, of course, localistic tendencies and vested interests in China's structure of political organization which hinder economic efficiency; but this has evidently not been as acute a problem as in Russia.

Apart from periods of ideological extremism, party control at the provincial and local levels has probably been more effective in China. The Chinese party cadres and committees have evidently been more inclined to identify with national, as opposed to local, interests than their Soviet counterparts; this has enabled the regime to decentralize authority quite effectively, but under close party surveillance. To achieve a workable balance between national and legitimate local interests, China's provincial governors and municipal mayors—both supervised by the government rather than by the party—are usually local persons, and key party officials at these levels are typically from other parts of the country.

To provide for greater party control consistent with national interests, six new regional party bureaus were established in China a few years ago.[99] Each of these regional committees has under it the party committees of a number of provinces, autonomous regions, and/or special municipalities. There are no parallel governmental organizations at the level of the regional party bureaus, and this is the only level of the overall political-governmental structure where this is the case.

In general, China's political organization has been less monolithic than that of the Soviet Union. Because of greater decentralization of authority and flexibility in the Chinese system of government administration and party control, one finds greater differences in the policies, practices, methods, and techniques pursued and utilized in Chinese industrial enterprises than in Soviet enterprises. For example, there are significant differences, even among Chinese firms in the same industry or geographical area, in monetary-incentive schemes, the stress on various success indicators utilized for evaluating and/or rewarding performance, time spans of operating plans, dates when plans are formally approved, the forms that worker participation in management take, and even in the roles of party cadres and regular managers. As has been indicated earlier, there are also substantial differences in activity because of differences in stress and interpretation of various policies by the party cadres. To be sure, one does find differences in these and other spheres among Soviet enterprises as well, but not generally to the same degree or extent as in China.[100]

Some of the Chinese officials whom I interviewed—particularly executives of macro-organizations—were quite candid about the problems (the types of problems discussed above) inherent in China's state bureaucracy and party structure. They admitted, for example, that delays, difficulties, planning and resource-allocation errors, and control problems frequently result from the cumbersome nature of China's overall political organization and macromanagerial structure. There was also much evidence of inefficiency, manifested in the forms noted above at various enterprises surveyed, which was due in large part to inefficiencies in macromanagement and political organization.

In the spring of 1966, the macromanagerial-apparatus structure was as usual in a state of flux and reorganization, although the organizational changes that had recently or were then taking place did not seem to be excessively disruptive. In fact, some of the changes were probably conducive to greater managerial effectiveness and productive efficiency at the enterprise level.

Here are a few of the macro-organizational changes that I was informed about by Chinese officials. The State Planning Commission had taken over the task of annual economic planning from the State Economic Commission. Also at the national level, the Ministry for the Allocation of Materials had been reorganized, and its name was changed to the Ministry of Supply of Materials. The Eighth Machine-Building Ministry was undergoing an internal reorganization involving some of its departments, offices, and corporations. In Hopei, Chekiang, and Kiangsu provinces some of the provincial industrial departments were being reorganized internally, recombined, and merged. In the industrial city of Wuhan there had just been internal reorganizations, regroupings, and some mergers involving municipal industrial bureaus and municipal corporations. The city of Wusih was experimenting with the abolishment of municipal industrial bureaus. The vast majority of enterprises previously under the jurisdiction of these bureaus had very recently been placed under the direct control of municipal corporations. Some new corporations had just been established, and some of the previous ones had been recombined and reorganized internally.

One Chinese central planner whom I interviewed was quick to point out that the government bureaucracy in China is not nearly as cumbersome or overstaffed as the Soviet state bureaucracy. He also noted that the Soviets have more coordinating, control, and inspection agencies than China. It is likely that this is true. The Soviets have long had a gargantuan macromanagerial bureaucracy with many checks and balances. New supercoordinating agencies are established to coordinate other agencies which are coordinating still other agencies. Similarly, supercontrol organizations are created to check on and control organizations which are already checking on and inspecting other organizations.

It is also likely that in Russia an even larger number of macro-organizations than in China are typically involved in the formulation and implementation of the overall operating plan of a given type of enterprise. On the other hand, the Soviets have much more experience than the Chinese in managing an economy, a much bigger and better supply of trained personnel, and substantially better informational, statistical, accounting, and data-processing systems. As a result, it is possible that the Soviets' overall political organization, while clearly inefficient in many serious respects, is no more inefficient than that of China. Moreover, the Soviet Union is in the throes of streamlining and nationalizing its macromanagerial bureaucracy with the introduction of greater decentralization of authority at the enterprise level, a "profit motive" of a sort, more flexible planning, an overhauling of the pricing system, and various other reforms known to the Chinese as "Libermanism" and "modern revisionism." [101]

In general, I got the impression that in spite of many inherent problems and inefficiencies, China's industrial bureaucracy and party structure were functioning reasonably well, well enough at least to enable considerable industrial progress. However, as Chinese industry expands, grows more complex, and approaches the Soviet level, political organization might well become a more serious constraint on industrial progress. In order to reduce the seriousness of this constraint, reforms in China's economic system along Soviet or Yugoslavian lines are likely to be required.

The macromanagerial state structure and the role of the party in Chinese industrial management may have changed substantially with the widespread political crisis and civil strife in Red China during 1967 and early 1968. Even during my stay in China the pendulum appeared to be swinging from less Expertness to greater Redness at some of the central, provincial, and municipal macro-organizations that I visited. Since I left China, party control in the macro-industrial hierarchy, indeed in the economy at large, has probably broken down in numerous cases. Whether and when it will become effective again remains to be seen. Hastily formed Super-Red cadres—in the army, peoples' militia, and new "revolutionary" groups—have taken over much of the work formerly done by party cadres, and, quite possibly, government administrators as well. If this continues for long, a national economic crisis seems inevitable. The constraints on enterprise and managerial efficiency are sure to be overwhelming. It is not possible to have effective state planning and/or decentralization of authority in the industrial sphere with poorly qualified and ill-suited Super-Reds in charge—Super-Reds who are, in most cases, probably even less qualified than the regular party cadres, and much less competent than the state "bureaucrats" and macromanagers.

A Brief Comment on Political Organization in India[102]

India has a huge governmental bureaucracy at the national, state, and local levels. The most important macro-organizations that deal with industry are central ones located in New Delhi, the capital. There are tens of thousands of people working in the governmental ministries, development wings, commissions, offices, departments, sections, and divisions which are concerned with the activities of business and industrial enterprises. Several dozen pages in the Delhi telephone book are required just to list the chief executive and advisory personnel of these macro-organizations. While that portion of the overall Indian governmental bureaucracy dealing with industry and business is probably not as big as in Red China, it may well be more inefficient.

A typical governmental organization or office in India appears to be substantially more overstaffed, has much more idle manpower and significantly more administrative levels, and is cluttered with a great deal more papers and files than any central, provincial, or local macro-managerial organization that I visited in Red China. In other words, the Indian macro-managerial apparatus seems to be much more bureaucratic and unwieldy than that of China. Given India's critical shortages of many resources, her foreign-exchange crisis, her economic development and social aims, and her growing public industrial sector, it is necessary for her to have a sizable governmental bureaucracy. However, the existing bureaucracy is, without doubt, much larger and vastly more inefficient than it need be to carry out its functions and pursue its stated aims.

Industrial enterprises must deal with the government bureaucracy, particularly at the national level, in a variety of critical spheres. For instance, they need governmental permission, allocations, and/or licenses for various domestic commodities in short supply (for example, steel, iron, coal, coke, certain chemicals, and, until quite recently, cement); virtually all imports and other foreign-exchange transactions, including even short business trips abroad; export decisions; setting up new firms or plants or expanding existing ones; issuing more capital; launching new products of various types; and setting prices for many items. Morever, as the government is a large consumer in India, it awards many contracts and places many orders with a wide range of firms.

There are some Indian industrial sectors and many individual firms, such as producers of furniture, various types of clothing, textile, and processed food, which do not need to obtain governmental approval on many important matters. These are typically firms or industries that require little, if any, imports or indigenous commodities in scarce supply, do not export much, only infrequently launch new products or expand operations, produce items not subject to price controls, and do not do much business with the national or local governments. Hence, constraints on their productive efficiency and progress emanating from the political bureaucracy do not tend to be as severe as they are at Chinese enterprises in general. However, probably the large majority of India's bigger and more important industrial enterprises must deal with the government bureaucracy at least quite frequently on matters of major importance. These firms include virtually all public-sector enterprises, as well as private companies in modern sectors such as those producing steel, aluminum, equipment, machinery, components, chemicals, and drugs. These are the very sectors upon which India's overall economic development so largely depends. And firms in these sectors typically find their negotiations with the government very frustrating and filled with considerable uncertainty.

In many instances, enterprise managers in India cannot predict within the time of one year, or two, and even three years or more, when a government decision of major concern to their companies will be made. This frequently tends to be worse, in terms of efficient enterprise planning, decision making, operations, and performance, than having a negative decision made by the government but at a pre-stated and adhered-to time. For example, if a given company knew with certainty that the government would decide within four to six months on its application for an expansion program, the launching of a new product, price changes, and/or import and foreign exchange, it could draw up alternative plans and often adjust to the government's decision—whether positive or negative—reasonably well. But if the company has no idea whether the decision is likely to be made next week, next month, next year, in three years, or perhaps never, so that the firm finally gives up its idea or application, this frequently tends to hinder managerial effectiveness and productive efficiency even more severely than a negative decision per se. In many respects, the Chinese enterprise manager is confronted with less uncertainty, and certainly less frustration caused by the government bureaucracy than his Indian counterpart. At least for most macromanagerial decisions affecting his firm the Chinese manager typically can predict roughly when they will be made within a matter of months, if not weeks or days. Moreover, there is likely to be somewhat more information feedback to enterprises involved in Chinese industry as to the status of a particular macromanagerial decision or if there is to be a further unanticipated delay in reaching the decision. Therefore, even though the higher-level decisions may not be the one desired by a particular Chinese enterprise, the firm can often adjust its plans and operations without a great deal of disruption or inefficiency.

In India, macrobureaucracy decisions seem generally to be delayed in committees more often and for longer periods of time than in China. There also appear to be more conflicting interests, poorer communication among members, and less of a spirit of cooperation toward a common purpose—for example, industrial progress or productive efficiency—in committees in India's system of political organization than in China. It is likely that many more Indian politicians, macromanagers, and governmental bureaucrats are antibusiness (antiprivate management in particular), and are not as concerned about industrial progress or economic efficiency as their Chinese counterparts.

Because Indian governmental agencies and offices tend to be greatly overstaffed and have excessive numbers of administrative levels, documents pertaining to enterprise applications calling for governmental decisions get bogged down for long periods, and even lost, in the bureaucratic maze. Lower-level supervisors and clerks, having nothing much to really do, act busy by tying up such documents and pondering over them for extended periods, making all types of notations on them. Because of the way the Indian government bureaucracy works, when the documents reach the higher levels the notations made at the lower levels must usually be taken into account, and the documents sent back down for appropriate signatures at each level before a final decision can be made. The decision-making process in China's governmental bureaucracy is probably not nearly so rigid or cumbersome.

India's lower-level governmental bureaucrats actually wield a considerable amount of influence and can delay decisions almost endlessly in many cases. As a result, there is quite a bit of petty corruption, because firms must give bribes, gifts, and special favors to junior bureaucrats and clerks in order to get their applications pushed through the bureaucracy. There is also evidently a fair amount of corruption, on a larger scale, among the politicians at the upper-political and policy-making levels. Many of the professional administrators who hold the key civil service jobs of the macromanagerial type in the development wings, ministries, and so on, are capable, well-motivated individuals with a great deal of integrity. They tend to bear the brunt of the blame for the politicians and the lower-level bureaucrats. They tend to be less corrupt than either of these other groups, they are more overworked and are substantially misutilized since the nature of India's political organization tends to prevent them from peforming very effectively and efficiently.

Given India's political organization, pressure groups representing whole industries and specific firms are rampant. There is also a considerable amount of political patronage and corruption in the awarding of government contracts and in governmental purchases from industry in general. More often than not, this is undoubtedly damaging in terms of economic development and the efficient utilization of resources. The merits of tenders submitted to the government by company firms often take a back-seat to noneconomic considerations. It seems that such political patronage, corruption, and tender-awarding practices are more common at the state and local levels—particularly in poorer parts of the country—than in the central government. All in all, there seems to be a good deal more corruption in the Indian government than in China. Probably more often than not, such corruption hinders, rather than facilitates, productive efficiency and industrial progress.

CHAPTER 6

China's Response: Economic Constraints

IN REALITY THE ECONOMIC constraints to be dealt with in this chapter are not single variables but complex sets of interrelated economic phenomena. For analytical purposes, however, it is feasible to examine each of the constraints separately. Our problem here is to generalize for Chinese industry as a whole, in terms of how the various economic constraints that the management of an enterprise faces influence its performance and effectiveness.

General economic analysis, including the type of examination of the constraints considered in this chapter, is a procedure that is quite old and honored. In fact, economics is commonly regarded as the father and king of the social sciences. As early as 1750, economists were concerned with how economic structures, conditions, and constraints affected production. A vast amount of literature now exists which discusses practically every aspect of such basic economic issues.[1] However, only in recent decades has there been a substantial empirical effort to link macro-economic analysis directly with the internal management and operations of industrial firms.

There appear to be relatively few comprehensive economic studies dealing with China prior to the Communist takeover in 1949. The majority of major works on pre-1949 China seem to deal chiefly with politics, war, revolution, philosophy, religion, social conditions, literary books of various types, and a few works on inflation (most of which have been written recently). But things have changed since the Communist regime was established; among the chief aims of the new regime has been the building of a strong economy through the creation of an overall economic environment dramatically different from the one that had previously existed in China. For this and other reasons, there appear to be substantially more Western studies—and foreign studies in general—dealing with the economic portion of Communist China's environment than with any of the other groups of environmental constraints of concern in this book.

In spite of the fact that Red China has published little concrete information on her economy since 1960, a number of comprehensive, significant, and useful works dealing with Communist China's economic conditions, problems, and performance have been published recently in the United States, Europe, Hong Kong, Taiwan, Japan, and elsewhere.[2] However, very few of these studies are based on firsthand information, analysis, or observation. And relatively few of them are directly concerned with linking economic environmental conditions or constraints to the internal management and performance of industrial enterprises.

I had the opportunity to derive some firsthand fragmentary information, observations, and impressions pertaining to the impact of various economic constraints on industrial enterprises and their managements in Communist China. This chapter is based, in substantial part, on my firsthand findings and impressions and is therefore limited in its scope. The reader will be referred to various important published sources for more general and comprehensive treatments of various economic constraints dealt with in this chapter.

Basic Economic System

Pre-1949 China and a Comment on India's Present-Day Economic System

China's economic system before 1949 was basically capitalistic, although a number of public-sector state enterprises were established and operated by the government during the Republican era. It is my belief that China could have achieved substantial economic development under a substantially capitalistic economic system buttressed by a fairly sizable public industrial sector and state planning—perhaps this would have been called a "mixed" economy—if so many of the other critical environmental constraints had not been so adverse. For example, China might have prospered under this type of system if:

(1) political and economic instability had not been so severe over protracted periods.
(2) China had not been so intensively engaged in wars and revolutions.
(3) sounder and more effective monetary and fiscal policies and legal rules of the game had been pursued.

(4) governmental macromanagement in general had created a better environment for industry and micromanagement.
(5) China's foreign trade had been aimed more directly and vigorously at economic progress.
(6) there had been substantially more capital investment channeled into the establishment of a more diverse and economically rational overall industrial base. Such capital might have been obtained from abroad in the form of aid and/or direct foreign investment and also through government accumulation; but a sound long-term industrial development program would have had to accompany such capital investment for it to have been effective in terms of sustained economic growth.
(7) much more substantial effort had been made to exploit indigenous natural resources and build up social-overhead capital.
(8) the overall educational system had been aimed more directly at industrial and general economic development.
(9) enterprise managers had more and better critical information to work with and less uncertainty to cope with.
(10) a development and achievement "ethic" had evolved on a widespread scale.

A better sociological-cultural environment would have done much to facilitate China's economic development under a capitalistic or mixed economic system. Even the positive features of China's sociological-cultural environment were not effectively capitalized on in terms of development.

Even if many of the above environmental constraints had been significantly less adverse, and if a basically capitalistic or mixed economy had survived or evolved, there still would have been many serious constraints on managerial effectiveness and productive efficiency emanating from the economic system itself. For instance, because of critical shortages of many commodities and the existence of strong sellers' markets, it may not have been possible for competition, market prices, and the pursuit of profits to provide for an efficient allocation or utilization of resources in various sectors and at numerous individual firms. This is the case in India's present-day mixed economy. On the other hand, without effective government protection from foreign as well as domestic competition, many Chinese firms would have undoubtedly gone bankrupt had the capitalistic system prevailed, while powerful—and probably quite inefficient—monopolies would have gained control of various sectors. If the Chinese government decided to fix the prices of many commodities and to allocate many types of scarce resources through state planning, many of the constraints on productive efficiency and effective enterprise management common to both planned and mixed economies would have existed and persisted. This is also true of India's contemporary economic system.

In general, India's economic system contains many of the constraints and efficiency problems common to underdeveloped, developing, and mixed economies, as discussed in our general treatment of "basic economic systems" in Chapter 2. It is true that many Indian private firms, particularly essentially noncontrolled private sectors, do perform quite efficiently because of reasonably effective competition, market prices, and the profit motive. There are also private Indian enterprises in partially and even largely controlled individual sectors, as well as public firms, which perform quite efficiently because of superior management and/or because they are provided with adequate resources, typically as a result of their high priority and/or good connections. However, probably the large majority of India's industrial enterprises perform rather poorly, and in many cases very inefficiently, at least in part because of constraints emanating from India's basic economic system. It is my impression that India's economic system is neither significantly better nor worse than Communist China's in terms of its constraints on enterprise-level managerial effectiveness, operating efficiency, and general industrial progress.

Nevertheless, it is conceivable that China could have achieved considerable and sustained industrial progress and general economic development with a basically capitalistic or mixed economy. It is likely, however, that industrial development would not have been as rapid as it has been under the Communist economic system. It is also likely that China would not have been as self-sufficient as she is today. And finally, it is likely that her military capabilities and potential would not have been what they are today. On the other hand, it is quite possible that the standard of living of the population would have been at least as good, if not significantly better than it is today. And it is likely that the typical Chinese citizen would have had more personal freedom, and also would have been at least as happy as he is today.

But the fact remains that there were so many other extremely adverse environmental constraints in pre-1949 China that a capitalistic or mixed economy, by itself, could not have led to significant industrial progress. China's Communist regime, with its pervasive organization of well-motivated party cadres, its rather coercive tactics, and its ability to dramatically overhaul much of the overall environment of industry and management in a relatively short period of time, has done enormously more for China's industrial progress than could have ever been accomplished under a freer, more democratic, less totalitarian, or less coercive economic system alone.

Communist China

The direct impact of Communist China's economic system on industrial firms and their managements comes basically from the need for an apparatus for extensive state planning and control to allocate scarce resources and control the implementation of plans. Enterprise managers cannot be allowed to decide independently what they need—they must receive approval from the higher-level planners. But the planners cannot possibly know in detail all of the needs, capabilities, and problems of each enterprise, so the firm managers must present plans for higher approval. Here begins a very complex, time-consuming, and lengthy hard-bargaining negotiation process affecting virtually every managerial and enterprise function. Production plans, policies, progress, and schedules depend largely on the decisions made by higher authorities. Marketing channels of distribution and most, if not all, of the firm's customers will be those laid down by the planners from above. Finance takes a secondary role in such a system, as the necessary financing of payroll, materials, investment, and so on will follow from production plans. The process of management becomes considerably different in many respects in this type of economic system from that in capitalist systems.

Those readers who have managed American companies during World War II may have had a "taste" of the resource problems, planning constraints, and controls that confront the Chinese manager daily. But the American experience was merely a taste, unlike the parallel situation in Red Chinese industry. In China, resource allocation is very pervasive and inclusive, whereas in the U.S. wartime economy, governmental planning, physical allocation, and stringent controls focused chiefly on a relatively limited number of strategic commodities—for example, steel, copper, aluminum. The major resource problem confronting most U.S. firms was the labor shortage that grew more severe toward the war's end.

Given the nature of Red China's economic system, industrial enterprises are frequently confronted with externally imposed constraints on their managerial effectiveness and productive efficiency.[3] These constraints are similar to those common in Soviet industry, even though state planning seems to be more flexible—probably too flexible—and there is greater decentralization of authority, particularly at the provincial and municipal levels, in China than in Russia.[4]

In numerous instances the formally approved enterprise plan does not provide for enough of the various factors of production, and at times too much of some factors, required to fulfill output and sales targets—according to plan and in an efficient manner. In carrying out the plan, frequent unforeseen breakdowns in the supply and distribution systems and serious bottlenecks in production arise, resulting in idle resources of various types, misutilization of resources, waste, considerable output of improper specifications and substandard quality, and various other undesirable managerial practices and forms of inefficiency. Moreover, in both China and the Soviet Union it has proved extremely difficult to devise a system of success indicators which can provide effective decision guidelines and/or serve as a relatively accurate and balanced measure of economic efficiency at either the macro or enterprise levels. There was much evidence of these problems at Chinese firms that I visited. Several Red Chinese officials, including a few from central organizations, whom I interviewed were quite candid in their discussions about such problems.

An unimaginable amount of information and knowledge is needed for state economic planning and control of the Chinese type. In such a system it has proved extremely difficult to design an informational system required for the design of consistent, realistic, and balanced comprehensive state plans, and one that can also show discrepancies in plans and operations, thus enabling timely corrective action.

Product and factor input prices fixed by the state, rather than being determined through competition and market forces, tend to be artificial and economically illogical in numerous instances. As a result, much of the planning and control at all levels in Chinese industry must be done in physical rather than monetary terms, thus making things even more difficult.

In a capitalistic economy, like that of the United States, diverse outputs and inputs can be converted to a standard unit like money for planning, control, measurement, and evaluation purposes. But where prices are fixed administratively by the planners, as in China, the conversion of diverse inputs and outputs into monetary values frequently tells you little, if anything, about economic performance, resource needs, or productive capabilities. How can five-millimeter bolts be added to size 40 suits, a certain type of lathe, or a certain grade of steel? Unless this can be done in a meaningful way through a standard conversion unit such as money, great reliance must be placed on physical units of measure in planning, resource allocation, control, and the evaluation of economic performance. And highly disaggregate physical units are frequently required for such purposes.

China's state planners are also hindered from making efficient and economically rational capital-investment decisions in many instances because there are no interest charges or rent on capital. This also leads to serious misuses of capital stock at the enterprise level.

In the Chinese economic system a state planner or enterprise manager frequently makes a critical error, such as failing to include enough production of steel of a given shape or grade to cover all requirements in the plan. The error need not be so blatant—the steel production may be planned—but far back in the planning process a clerk may have failed to include, say, the needed brick to make the new coke ovens to make the steel. As production for the planned period gets underway, this shortage of steel begins to appear. Managers, unable to get needed inputs, fail to make necessary deliveries to other enterprises, who in turn fail to produce up to plan. A chain reaction involving supply failures and production bottlenecks at several interdependent factories evolves because most supplier-customer relationships are prescribed in the plan, and a given firm typically has no alternative source of supply to turn to if one of his assigned suppliers fails him. The information needed to make necessary corrections in the above type of situation may take months or longer to accumulate, given the complexities of both the total interdependent productive process and of the planning and control system. In the meantime, many enterprises are performing inefficiently, and no timely feedback and corrective-action system exists to prevent them from doing so.

More dramatic errors are likely to arise when capital resources are put in the wrong place. This is less likely in a capitalist system than in a planned economy where rational investment criteria are lacking because of the absence of market prices, and interest and rent charges, and where a meaningful analysis of opportunity costs is often extremely difficult. However, plenty of mistakes are made in capital investment in any economic system, given the usual uncertainties and lack of necessary knowledge; but in a planned economy, such as China's, errors are perpetuated through lack of any mechanism to call a halt at the proper time. State industrial installations may be constructed at a cost of hundreds of thousands of dollars, and operated inefficiently at large losses, but they are rarely abandoned, while similar private ventures, perhaps erroneously conceived and planned, tend to be closed quite quickly.

When China's regime embarked on state economic planning in earnest in the early 1950's, it had to develop a nationwide statistical, accounting, and general-information-reporting system practically from scratch.[5] Red China learned much from the Soviets in these spheres, and in state planning and control in general. The Chinese have had a distinct advantage over the Russians, who had to develop pragmatically a workable overall system of state planning, control and informational network entirely on their own, because the Soviet Union's was the first such comprehensive system in history.

The Red Chinese regime has struggled constantly to build up effective nationwide statistical and informational systems. While China has been substantially more successful in developing informational systems and networks in the urban-industrial sphere than in the rural-agricultural sector, planners and administrators at all levels of industry must still frequently base their decisions on incomplete, inadequate, and/or inaccurate statistics and other data. Critical shortages of properly trained personnel who collect, classify, process, analyze, and interpret data for planning and control purposes also contribute substantially to informational deficiencies.

There are both unintentional errors and intentional distortions and biases in the information available for macro-level planning, decision making, and control. Distortions of data, falsification of results, and biases in information frequently arise from the system of success indicators used to evaluate managerial and enterprise performance. They also arise because managers, faced with considerable uncertainty about whether resources will be allocated to them and whether they will actually receive the resources required to fulfill the enterprise plan, try to hedge against such uncertainty and risk by overstating resource needs, understating productive capacity, and engaging in various other practices leading to informational inadequacies and biases. The higher-level planners and decision makers frequently do not possess adequate detailed knowledge—qualitative as well as quantitative—of concrete conditions at lower levels of the industrial hierarchy, including the enterprise level. And they are often not in a position to respond effectively to new information received or to novel conditions.

Annual planning involves a very lengthy and time-consuming process. Plans pass through many levels for approval, and there is much bargaining and extensive detailed negotiations at each level and during each phase of the process. Since the planning process must necessarily start around the middle of the current operating year, much of the planning for the next year must be done before results for the current year are known. This means that numerous estimates, rather than verified results, must be used in preparing the plan.

Moreover, because of the complexities inherent in the planning process, the overall annual state plan, as well as the plans of myriad individual enterprises, are typically approved late. The state plan is supposed to be formally approved by the first of the year. In 1953 and 1959 it was approved in February, in 1954 and 1957 in mid-year, and in 1956 and 1960 around April.[6] Few of the Chinese enterprises that I surveyed had their 1966 plans approved before March, and some of them did not have their 1966 plans approved as of May or June. This, in effect, means that enterprises must operate unofficially and "by ear," so to speak, for several months, because they are without approved plans.

None of the Chinese firms surveyed in 1966 had even general five-year plans, or any concrete plans beyond one year. Apparently, they have never had any operational plans beyond one year, even when there has been a national five-year plan. This undoubtedly tends to hinder efficient decision making and performance, particularly at enterprises which are involved in major capital-investment and expansion programs and/or manufacture products such as complex heavy machinery, which requires two- or three-year production cycles.

Difficulties and efficiency problems, of the kinds mentioned earlier, arise at industrial enterprises once the plan is implemented because of errors, inconsistencies, and imbalances in the plan. The situation is aggravated by bottlenecks and problems unforeseen when the plan is initially designed and approved. Because of planning and supply deficiencies many enterprises either underfulfill or overfulfill their plans, and timely corrective action necessary to bring the overall interdependent productive system back into balance is frequently not forthcoming. Where changes are made in the plan of a given enterprise during the operating period, it is likely that required adjustments are often not made in the plans of other firms affected by these changes. Hence, chain reactions and considerable sub-system optimization result in numerous instances. When high-priority firms—for example, producers of defense armaments, steel, coal, oil, important machine tools—run into resource shortages in fulfilling their plans, the regime is inclined to shift resources to them from relatively low-priority sectors, particularly firms producing nonessential consumer goods, such as furniture, cameras, radios, TV sets, watches, and perhaps automobiles, as well as many of such firms' suppliers. This contributes substantially to sub-system optimization and imbalances among various industrial sectors over time. If pushed too far too long this seriously hinders proportionate growth and development of the economy as a whole—which is a highly proclaimed aim of communist economies.

Where the managers of a particular enterprise feel that it is not possible to fulfill the enterprise plan in its entirety, high-priority success indicators are likely to be stressed at the expense of other planned targets and tasks. For example, the product-mix plan is violated, items of substandard quality are produced, equipment is overutilized, labor is misutilized and/or overworked, various portions of the cost plan exceeded, time-consuming and complex product-development tasks and major "innovative" changes in the production process are postponed as management strives to fulfill top-priority aggregate output, sales, profit, and/or labor-productivity targets. This, in turn, leads to serious sub-system-optimization problems with the firm.

In Chapter 9 we shall deal at some length with the types of success indicators in use at the Chinese enterprises surveyed in 1966. However, a brief word seems in order here about the dilemma of measuring economic performance and devising an effective system of success indicators at the enterprise level in a Chinese-type economic system.

In spite of many limitations and problems, profits earned or profitability computed in relation to invested capital or sales generally serves as a meaningful and typically the best, all-inclusive measure of economic and managerial efficiency for firms in American industry. In Chinese industry this is generally not so, since most commodity prices are fixed by state authorities at infrequent intervals, rather than determined by market or competitive forces, and such prices typically do not reflect true scarcity values.

Profit or profitability can serve as a meaningful success indicator for the Red Chinese firm to the degree that it accurately reflects reductions in unit costs achieved through a more efficient utilization of factor inputs and/or greater volumes of output and sales achieved without proportionate increases in real costs. However, because of the price system, profit or profitability loses its meaningfulness or accuracy as a success indicator to the degree and extent that there are significant changes in the enterprise's product mix and/or factor inputs utilized from one period to the next. Similarly, profit or profitability would not be a particularly useful measure for comparing the relative degrees of efficiency for two or more Chinese enterprises if there are substantial differences in their product lines and factor inputs.

In the 1950's, gross aggregate output was the top-priority success indicator in Chinese industry. Under this system there were widespread violations in product-mix plans, much substandard output, considerable resistance to major innovations, and cost plans were frequently exceeded. However, gross output as the key success indicator worked reasonably well at that stage of China's development—as it did in the past in Russia—since almost any type of production could adequately serve the functional use intended. Some measure of profit was used as a success indicator at various Chinese firms during the 1950's, particularly the late fifties, but it was typically not the key success indicator.

In the 1960's profit and profitability typically computed in relation to total enterprise costs and expenses emerged as the key success indicator throughout much of Chinese industry. Economic recovery and further industrial progress have occurred under this system; but the regime soon found that profitability alone was not a very good success indicator in numerous instances. Moreover, by the mid-1960's, with the pendulum swinging in the direction of ideological extremism, profit as a top-priority success indicator has been increasingly attacked as a "revisionistic," capitalistic practice.

In reality, a combination of success indicators is generally required for meaningful evaluation of economic efficiency and overall performance at Chinese enterprises. But the Chinese—as well as the Russians—have found it extremely difficult to design combinations of enterprise success indicators that do not contain at least some significant inherent elements of inconsistency and conflict in terms of managerial behavior and enterprise performance. It has also proved a vexing problem to design a system which is expressed in broad-enough quantitative terms to enable timely information feedback, control, and corrective action, and at the same time detailed enough to enable an accurate, not-too-time-consuming evaluation of economic performance and to provide operational guidelines for both macro- and micro-decision making.

In 1966 various combinations of success indicators were in use at the enterprises I visited. The combinations of key success indicators varied somewhat among enterprises in different industries and in different parts of the country. The most common success indicators were profit, quantity of production in value and physical terms, product quality, reduction in unit and total costs, labor productivity, sales, and, to a lesser extent, the development and introduction of important new technological processes and products. The number of key success indicators utilized for evaluating overall performance varied in most cases from three to six at the enterprises surveyed.

Red China's Economic System in Historical Perspective and in the Future

Let us look very briefly at China's economic system since the early 1950's and also project into the foreseeable future. During China's First Five-Year Plan the system of state planning and control was actually rather crude. Informational systems and networks were in an embryonic state, and there were few well-trained statistical, accounting, data-processing, or planning personnel. Some concrete evidence of statistical deficiencies during this period was presented in a 1958 report by a deputy director of Red China's State Statistical Bureau.[7] This report revealed that in a 1954 investigation of statistics from Liaoning Province—where the organization of statistical work began at an earlier date than in the country as a whole—14,321 cases of erroneous reporting were revealed at the 232 state industrial enterprises whose statistics were examined. Of these, 708 presented major problems, while cases of deliberate falsification numbered 476, or 3 percent of the total reports. The situation in other areas was probably worse.

In spite of serious informational and knowledge deficiencies during the 1952–57 period, the state planners could still lay out crude but adequately intelligible practical and workable plans because industry was not yet very complex. The priority principle in resource allocation and in the event of breakdowns in the plan proved quite effective because the regime and its planners could concentrate on a few relatively easily defined tasks —notably the development and expansion of basic heavy industry. The planners had considerable leeway in shifting resources between industrial sectors since the production processes and commodity specifications were relatively simple in numerous instances. Centralized planning and control in connection with heavy industry were not unmanageable tasks because the bulk of output and related inputs was of a fairly homogeneous nature—for example, coal, coke, pig iron, electricity, petroleum, cement, and, to a lesser degree, steel, machinery, equipment, and components. Even in the indigenous production of steel, equipment, and components, the varieties in most cases were not yet very diverse or complex. At this stage of economic development, aggregate output was a meaningful top-priority enterprise success indicator. Pressure for forced industrialization meant shortages of virtually every type of product; hence, almost anything produced could be used somewhere or by someone in the nation.

During the Great Leap Forward, industrial activity expanded sharply, but the system of state economic planning was grossly undermined and ran out of control. Statistical reports were typically used primarily for fanning enthusiasm and exhorting the population to greater productive effort, rather than for purposes of planning, decision making, and control. While big aggregate gains in production were reported in many industrial sectors during this period, much of the output was actually unusable, unused, and unneeded. Great imbalances, dislocations, and bottlenecks evolved throughout industry, and a severe economic crisis emerged.

Along with China's economic recovery and new industrial progress in the 1960's there have been substantial improvements in her statistical, accounting, and general information-reporting systems, as well as a substantial increase and better utilization of competent personnel working in these fields. However, during the mid-1960's in particular, industry has expanded substantially and become considerably more complex with the production of sophisticated new products—notably in the chemical, machinery, electronics, nuclear, metallurgical, radar, and related component sectors. As a result, the volume, diversity, and quality of statistics and other information required for industrial planning and control have also grown sharply. As specific product types have expanded to hundreds of thousands, and now to millions, the task of planning and controlling economic activity on a national scale has increased greatly. Therefore, in spite of major improvements in information systems and personnel, deficiencies and errors in state planning and control are probably still at least as serious and extensive as they were ten and fifteen years ago.

The Chinese regime now seems to be pursuing a general policy of more balanced industrial development than in the past. While heavy-industry production is stressed, greater attention is being given to the production of agricultural machinery and supplies, chemicals (particularly chemical fertilizers, new fibers and synthetics), and various new and improved types of consumer products (largely for export), and also to production to serve the domestic market and raise living standards. Much greater stress is also being placed on self-sufficiency in defense production. More will be said about China's apparent desire for balanced industrial growth in a later chapter.[8]

Hence, in the present-day Chinese economy, as compared with the economy of ten or fifteen years ago, there are a growing number of more diverse, pressing commitments for scarce resources; there is less flexibility in maneuvering resources among different industries because of technological and product-specification constraints; and the economic objectives and programs deemed of high priority by the state have become more and more difficult to define clearly or enforce. It is no longer possible to make as fast or desirable headway by concentrating on a few relatively easily defined programs, tasks, or priorities. At the same time, aggregate-output indicators of enterprise and managerial success have become less meaningful, and new combinations of success indicators are now used in evaluating enterprise efficiency and managerial performance.

In spite of the above trends and problems, as of 1966, Red China seemed to have a workable and quite effective—though not very efficient—basic economic system. However, the types of inefficiencies that arose from errors in state planning, resource allocation, and control seemed to be very much in evidence at industrial enterprises surveyed.

For example, the Han Yang Paper Mill in Wuhan has had an annual production capacity of 40,000 tons since 1957, but has been producing only at the rate of 25,000 tons. Yet, this firm has long maintained enough manpower to produce at the rate of 40,000 tons per year. I was told that this capacity had not been put into use because of planning and coordination problems involving a number of customer publishing plants as well as plant-equipment suppliers. Moreover, Han Yang could not utilize much of the 15,000 tons of additional capacity because it had never received an integral piece of equipment that is required to put this total additional production process into operation. The director said that he expected the unused capacity to be put into operation around August 1966. At that time, the enterprise's superior, the Hupeh Provincial First Light-Industry Bureau, would raise the plant's production targets, provide additional materials, and assign customers for the additional output. The new integral piece of equipment required to put the 15,000 tons of capacity into operation had been ordered from a Shanghai supplier and was expected "momentarily."

The large Wuhan Steel Plant has had a giant steel roller for several years which is capable of rolling three million tons of steel annually. But it has been operating at only about 30 to 40 percent of capacity since it was installed. The plant manager said this has been due primarily to bottlenecks at customer enterprises. In the section on political stability I gave examples of other serious problems and inefficiencies at Wuhan Steel, as well as Tientsin Instrument. It is possible that planning deficiencies, along with political instability, have contributed to these inefficiencies and problems. The Shanghai Forging and Pressing Plant had a ten-ton press which was not in use when I visited there. The director told me that only "experimental" use has been made of this press since the factory received it some years ago.

In general, managers of several other Chinese enterprises admitted that planning and resource allocation and failures in the supply system do significantly upset their own plans and operations quite often. For instance, Peking First Machine Tool was often faced with production and delivery bottlenecks arising from shortages of certain shapes and sizes of steel. Wusih Red Flag Machinery experienced frequent difficulties in obtaining critical spare parts, and Shanghai Pharmaceutical No. 3 with various types of chemicals; and Peking Clothing had quite a bit of idle capacity at one time because of textile fabric and chemical dye shortages.

Some of the enterprises surveyed, such as Tientsin Shoe, Wusih Machinery, and Wuhan Diesel Engine, had to make or rebuild much of their own machinery, tools, and components in very inefficient, time-consuming, and relatively expensive ways because their allocations of such items were not adequate. Wuhan Diesel Engine, which had 992 employees, designed and developed a "small-armed tractor" over a period of two years in 1958 and 1959 with practically no outside help. A Shanghai plant developed essentially the same type of tractor around the same time—which meant about two years of duplicated effort. Apparently the higher-level planners and coordinators who could have cut down on, or avoided, this duplication of effort did not know it was taking place. Wuhan Diesel Engine produced the tractor in 1964 and switched over to small diesel engines. It took the firm several years to develop the diesel engine that it was producing in small and erratic quantities in 1966. The plant has met with numerous serious development delays, supply failures, production bottlenecks, and equipment breakdowns. The state has not allocated it much in the way of equipment or components. This enterprise also seems to be run by rather incompetent party cadres and managers. In 1966 the factory was still engaged in "experimental production," and it had no "fixed" production plan or targets for 1966.

During my 1966 trip to China it was evident that the highly complex and cumbersome nature of the Chinese written language—which has roughly four thousand characters—is a serious constraint with regard to information reporting and processing, and state planning and control in general. Much of the written work that is normally done by typewriters in other countries, including many underdeveloped countries, is done by hand with pens and pencils in China. Handwritten reports tend to be more cumbersome, less tidy, and more illegible than typewritten ones.

This seemed to be the case at organizations and offices which I visited at all levels of the Chinese economy. The Indian economy seems to have an advantage over China's in this regard, as English is the common written language in business and industry, and noticeably greater use is made of the typewriter.

The Soviets still make only rather limited use of automatic-data-processing equipment and electronic computers in their economy, primarily at the national level, and only very limited experimental use is made of computers at the level of the enterprise, but they use such technology for economic planning and control much more than the Chinese.[9] There also seems to be significantly more use made of computers and other data-processing equipment at many levels of the Indian economy—including the enterprise level—than in China. The Chinese still rely very heavily on the abacus at all levels. It is true that the abacus is very fast for simple arithmetic calculations involving addition, subtraction, multiplication, and division. In fact, the abacus has proved faster than computers in these types of calculations in some competitions. However, an abacus cannot be programmed like a computer; nor can it handle a complex multivariable problem that even a relatively simple computer can deal with.

I was told by some Chinese central officials and professors in the computer field that only very limited experimental use is being made of electronic computers in state planning (and control). This is confined almost exclusively to the national level, although there may also be a few computers in use at lower geographic levels of the industrial hierarchy. I never saw or heard of an electronic computer being used at a Chinese enterprise. There is also little in the way of simple data-processing equipment at industrial or business firms. Electronic computers are used primarily in Red China for solving specific scientific, technological and, to a much lesser degree, economic and commercial problems. In the sphere of economic and commercial use, they are employed particularly in relatively static programming problems, such as those dealing with transportation and location. Statistics and other aspects of information, planning, control, and retrieval apparently still do not receive much attention in the development of computer uses.

The Red Chinese are likely to follow the Soviets and make greater use of electronic computers—and more simple types of data-processing equipment—for economic planning, information processing, and control purposes in the future. However, there are serious constraints on the effective and extensive use of computers in a basic economic system of the Chinese or traditional Soviet type.

In the U.S. economy, computers along with various statistical mathematical techniques—referred to in such terms as econometrics, operations research, and management science—are now used extensively for macromanagerial decision making by individual firms. Much use is also made of them by macromanagerial governmental agencies. A variety of problems, both static and dynamic in nature, are solved with the aid of computers and related techniques. Among these are inventory levels, flow of goods, devising optimum combinations of inputs and outputs, plant locations, sales and cost analysis, delivery schedules, optimum pricing, financial and cash planning, investment decisions, and so forth. Within the framework of existing technology an unimaginable number of calculations can be undertaken, and an enormous amount of data can be processed in a short period of time. The market-price system and marginal analysis serve as ingenious and indispensable computing aids, as calculations can readily be made in the standard convertible unit of money.

In Red China, marginal analysis has received little attention, and in Russia it has only recently been receiving more attention. Neither of these two countries has an operational scarcity-price system to work with, and this greatly constrains the effective use of computers, as well as marginal analysis. (A chief aim of the Soviets is to develop a more economically meaningful price system with the help of computers and sophisticated mathematical techniques.) Moreover, the aim in Russia, and apparently in China, is to use such technology primarily for macro-economic decision making, rather than for micro decision making at the enterprise level. This means that the amount of data and calculations required is infinitely greater than is the case for decision making in a single firm, particularly a firm in a capitalistic economy which can readily use money as a converting rod.

If electronic computers do eventually come into use on a substantial scale in the Chinese economy, the actual computing stage would be only a minute part of the whole programming and planning process in such a system. Sufficient and accurate data must be collected and communicated to the planners rapidly—something that China's statistical and information system will probably not be able to do effectively for some years to come. There are also problems of information biases and undesirable managerial behavior that must be dealt with. The pertinent information must be recorded and translated into modern language, the computational jobs must be scheduled and set up. Once the data are processed, they must be broken down and retranslated into usable form before they are forwarded to the appropriate decision makers.

In a growing and increasingly dynamic and complex economy, such as China's, if such a computer system is to prove truly effective, modifications in computer programs would be required each period to take into account technical progress, changing input-output relationships, investment decisions, changing product mixes, and so forth. Assuming and utilizing fixed technical coefficients sharply limits the potential of dynamic programming even within one sector, let alone on a national scale. Undoubtedly, the planners would still be confronted with much imprecision and unpredictable changes in parameters. It would be hardly possible to define with the necessary clarity the aims of the overall computer program on a national or even provincial scale, or in very disaggregate terms, or what it is that should be optimized. Finally, many of the essential elements of the plan would in fact be dependent on the calculations for which they are to serve as a base.

In general, it appears that the Chinese system of state planning is more flexible than that of the Soviet Union, at least until now. The Soviets have long had a highly monolithic and fairly clear-cut system of planning. The vast majority of Soviet enterprises have their annual plans—reflecting quarterly subdivisions—including resource allocations approved around the same time each year. In some years the national economic plan and hence enterprise-level plans are approved after the first of the year; but this is not as frequent, nor are the plans approved as late, as in China. Formal revisions in the aggregate targets of enterprise plans in Soviet industry are probably not very common.

The Chinese system of planning, resource allocation, and control seems to be substantially more flexible, to the point of being very sloppy in many instances. Most Chinese firms do go through the motions of getting some type of annual plan approved—through a down-up-down process of negotiations with higher authorities. However, as was mentioned above, enterprises often have their annual plans approved well after the operating year has begun. For some Chinese firms the annual plan is the key operating document, and for many it is the quarterly, monthly, and, in some cases, the weekly plan. For example, the large Shanghai Heavy Machine-Tool Factory works primarily according to an annual plan, which is revised quarterly; for the Peking Pharmaceutical Factory the quarterly plan is the key one; for Tientsin Shoe it is the monthly one; and for Hangchow Clothing its monthly plans are often revised weekly. Regardless of the time perspective of planning, formal revisions even in the aggregate targets of enterprise plans appear to be more common than in Soviet industry.

At many of the Chinese enterprises surveyed, the quantities and varieties of products planned and approved by higher authorities do not add up to the approved aggregate-production targets. The firms' managements can determine independently from about 5 percent to as much as 30 percent (in a few cases, particularly small plants producing job orders, such as Wusih Machinery) of their planned outputs. Some flexibility of this type is also provided in the plans of various types of Soviet industrial enterprises but generally not to the same degree as exists at comparable Chinese firms.

Flexibility in state planning and control in Red China's economic system, as well as changes in plans, frequently leads to important interrelated decisions being overlooked and serious coordination problems at the enterprise level. I came across many symptoms of this, and a number of the examples of inefficiencies and problems at Chinese firms cited earlier were also probably due, in large part, to too much flexibility in China's planned economy. However, as has been mentioned in the section on political organization, flexibility in planning does not normally get excessively out of hand in Chinese industry because there is a higher degree of decentralization of authority than in the Soviet Union. This means that administrators closer to the operating level have the authority to take more timely action in the light of changing local conditions.

In general, the types of inefficiency problems in industry arising from China's economic system do not tend to be as serious in terms of industrial progress as compared with those in the substantially more advanced and complex Soviet economy. The opportunity, costs, and constraints on industrial progress which arise from errors in resource allocation, planning, information feedback, and control tend to be greater in an economy of the advanced Marxist type because there tend to be higher tolerances in product quality, specifications, and lead times and also less leeway to combine factor inputs in different ways because of the complexity of technology and production processes utilized.

In Chinese industry the chances are probably better that a consumer product, raw material, machine, or component that does not fulfill specifications stipulated in the plan can still be adapted to serve the functional or end use intended. Factor inputs can also typically be juggled more easily to achieve desired outputs because the production process, particularly in heavy industry, is typically not as complex as in Soviet industry. Similarly, if a given Chinese firm overproduces Product A and/or underproduces Product B in terms of the plan, or if the state commits an error in allocating capital-investment funds to Project X rather than Project Y, the resulting waste or inefficiency is not likely to be as great as in Russia since there are greater shortages of products and productive facilities of many more types in China.

It is important to point out that as long as ideology has not been pushed to extremes in industrial management—as it was during the Great Leap Forward and possibly in the later crisis—Communist China has achieved impressive industrial progress in spite of the constraints and efficiency problems inherent in her basic economic system. China's basic economic system seems to be adequate for sustained industrial progress at her present stage of development, and probably for several years to come.

However, as Chinese industry expands, grows more complex, and approaches the Soviet level, the interrelationships among factors of production will become much more delicate and crucial problems. The problem of supplying enterprises through state planning with proper materials, machinery, components, manpower, and financial resources to achieve desired and usable outputs will become increasingly difficult to do with a tolerable level of effectiveness and efficiency.

It is likely that in the next decade or two, the absence of market prices and a meaningful profit motive as effective and relatively automatic regulators of managerial and economic activity in China will become just as serious a constraint on industrial progress and managerial performance as it has already become in Soviet industry. When that time comes, the Chinese, like the Soviets today, will undoubtedly have to undergo the same vexing and agonizing process of considering and introducing major economic and managerial reforms, some that are ideologically very distasteful but which are essential for sustained economic progress. To date, the Soviets have still not been very successful in devising an economic system which effectively combines state planning and adequate flexibility with enterprise-level decision making, freedom, and initiative.

Central Banking System and Monetary Policy

A nation's central banking system and monetary policies tend to have a substantial bearing on economic progress and price stability. In general, it usually can be inferred that the central banking system and monetary policies are effective if a particular country experiences relatively little price-level fluctuation, if economic growth and industrial progress continue in a relatively steady and stable manner, if the currency maintains its value on international markets, and if productive enterprises that can make the most efficient use of funds can get them. Of course, these economic conditions are not entirely under the control of central banking and monetary policy. However, if such economic growth and stability are to occur, it is generally necessary that central banking and monetary policies be quite effective.

In the real world there tends to be an intimate relationship between monetary and fiscal policies. For analytical purposes we have chosen to deal with these two sets of policies separately, but their interdependence should be kept in mind.

Communist countries have a somewhat different type of problem in the overall sphere of monetary and fiscal policy from the kind in basically capitalistic nations. In the former, the government or state makes, by plan, virtually all of the investment expenditures, and the private sector involves only consumer goods bought and consumed by individuals. Hence, much of the complicated monetary and fiscal incentives and disincentives necessary to get desired investment in a capitalistic state are unnecessary. But the problem is far from easy because the state must somehow extract from consumers the sum approximately equal to the amount invested each year if significant inflation or recession is to be avoided. Moreover, the physical plans and allocation of resources must be supported by a system of financial controls, including monetary and fiscal resources.

Since transactions are effected through the use of money even in a communist society, it is essential for the planners to maintain a pretty high degree of financial equilibrium. Consider the following simplified model of the Chinese Communist economy. Suppose that the state plans to produce 50 billion yuan's worth of output. Furthermore, suppose that 30 billion of this is going to be consumer goods for private consumption, while 20 billion will be goods for state investment. The reason that the total planned output is worth 100 billion yuan is that it will cost (in labor) 100 billion yuan to produce it, which means that if each worker were to be paid what he is worth, the total wage bill would be 50 billion yuan. But only 30 billion yuan is intended for consumption, and the other 20 billion for state investment. Hence, unless something is done to extract 20 billion from the people's incomes, the state will have nothing with which to pay for the 20 billion's worth of investment goods. Moreover, only 30 billion yuan's worth of consumer goods is planned and if the population's real purchasing power equals 50 instead of 30 billion yuan, the result will be price inflation and/or critical shortages of consumer goods. The state could, of course, create enough new money through its central bank to buy its share of investment goods, but to create an additional 20 billion yuan of money again would mean price inflation. Clearly then, what must be done is to take away from the people 20 billion yuan of their incomes and give the money to the state to pay productive enterprises for the 20 billion yuan's worth of investment goods.

The usual way that a communist state, including China, drains off this excess purchasing power is through turnover (sales) taxes and enterprise profits derived through the difference between the selling prices and total costs of goods produced. Income taxes have been used sparsely because it is felt that this would interfere with the people's incentives and also because of ideological reasons. But the Chinese citizen is still confronted with a wide variety of turnover and sales taxes, which are considerable on many items that he buys.

Before examining monetary policy and central banking in Communist China in greater detail, a brief discussion of these topics with regard to Republican China prior to 1949 is in order, because Republican China's grossly deficient banking system and monetary policies contributed greatly to the Communist victory.

Republican China[10]

China's rampant inflation, one of the worst in world history, which began around 1937 and reached its fantastic peak and climax at the end of the 1940's, was undoubtedly a major factor in the Communist victory and takeover in 1949. As with most rampant inflations, China's led to severe economic crisis and eventually a great depression. The grossly inept banking system, in conjunction with highly ineffective monetary policies and, of course, extremely adverse fiscal policies (which will be discussed in the next section), contributed greatly to China's skyrocketing inflation and severe economic crisis. The Nationalist regime completely lost control over the country's fiscal and monetary situation.

China's four major government banks, including the Central Bank of China, set up in 1928, were not effective in handling the country's extremely critical monetary problems. In fact, the central bank never attained real central-banking status. The country did not have a unified currency system; instead, many different currencies were used in different areas of the nation. The other three government banks—Bank of China, Farmers' Bank of China, Bank of Communications—also proved ineffective in dealing with the nation's economic crisis. During this era China's private banking was concentrated very heavily in Shanghai, and available private funds for industrial financing were frequently granted chiefly on the basis of personal relationships rather than economic efficiency criteria.

Civil war, the war with Japan, political instability, and various costly government domestic programs—many of them ill-conceived and ineffectively implemented—led to vast increases in government spending during the 1937–49 period. Republican China's ever-increasing budget deficits were almost entirely financed by the creation of money. With the constant and largely inappropriate generation of money from the central bank's printing press, nominal money rose sharply after 1937 but failed to keep up with sharp price rises. Hence real money balances fell by more than 80 percent during the 1937–49 period, reflecting a massive flight from money.

In 1938, prices rose an average of 3 percent per month, by 1940 they were rising 7 percent per month, from mid-1940 to the end of 1944 10 percent per month, and 20 percent until the end of the Japanese war in 1945. From August 1945 until the late summer of 1948 prices rose some twenty-five hundred times, an increase equal to the climb during the previous eight years.[11] In the final months before total collapse and the Communist victory the price index took off and disappeared into the great beyond. From about September 1947 to the fall of 1948 the value of the yuan in relation to the U.S. dollar dropped from 60 thousand yuan to the dollar to 20 million yuan to the dollar. I remember cartoons in the Western press around that time showing truckloads and trainfuls of Chinese currency being exchanged for an American dollar or a pack of American cigarettes. I have also spoken with some Westerners who were in China in the late 1940's and remember spending 100 million and even 200 million yuan for dinner in the better restaurants in Shanghai, Peking, and Canton.

China's fantastic runaway price inflation and general economic crisis would have probably been substantially less severe if sounder and more timely monetary policies had been pursued, and if the central banking system had been more effective. It is true that the government tried bond sales to the public, gold sales, price controls, control of interest rates, and various foreign-exchange measures; but the timing and actual methods utilized were grossly inept and inadequate in most instances. The Nationalist regime also received lend-lease, gifts, guarantees, and currency backing, but to practically no avail because of the ineffective and inappropriate use typically made of such aid.

More often than not, the government failed to listen to the advice and recommendations of competent economists, monetary specialists, and bankers. As a result the monetary policies pursued by the regime and banking authorities were far too often tragically mistaken. For example, old-school, non-Keynesian bankers in top policy-making positions felt that interest rates should be kept low, rather than high, in order to fight inflation. They reasoned that the interest rate was an important element of production costs. Since prices were determined by costs, to fight rampant inflation, they argued, interest should be kept low so that prices would be kept down.[12] With this policy the banks could not absorb voluntary savings or attract funds for business-lending operations.

Political interference with rational monetary policies was very common during this era. Corruption and bribery within the government and among bankers, as well as the great extravagances of many officials, became pervasive with the inflation, further aggravating the economic situation and hindering productive efficiency and economic progress.

For the typical Chinese industrial firm during the 1937–49 period, it became increasingly difficult to function properly. A great many went out of business as the profit squeeze became too overwhelming. The dizzily spiraling inflation made it virtually impossible for industrial managers to plan ahead or to organize, staff, or control activities efficiently. A vast amount of idle productive capacity accompanied by mass unemployment emerged, as prices skyrocketed, and available funds for both working capital and investment became fantastically costly and eventually disappeared. Those firms that managed to remain in business typically operated with much idle capacity and rarely tried to expand operations. Many of them made their money by hoarding commodities and through inventory speculation rather than by increasing output. Numerous links of middlemen evolved in the distribution channels between producers and end users, and each took their profit margin from the decreasing amount of products that changed hands. Black-marketing activities were very pervasive, thus rendering most price controls ineffective. Few new domestic industrial enterprises were created during the 1940's. Product lines were cut back drastically as a growing number of factor inputs became impossible to get. Imported items required by industrial firms became impossible to obtain as China's currency approached zero value in international markets.

Communist China[13]

One of the first problems that the Chinese Communist regime turned its attention to when it gained power in late 1949 was the extremely serious inflation and the monetary and banking situation. The late 1949–51 period was one of transitional stabilization and consolidation. The regime unified and consolidated the many currencies outstanding, began nationalizing the private banks in Shanghai and elsewhere, established clearing houses, and generally checked the inflation and brought about a relatively high degree of economic stability—as compared with the situation in the past—through effective monetary and fiscal policies. Ironically, Western-trained economists influenced monetary policy to a substantially greater degree during this transitional period under Communist rule than they were able to do under the Kuomintang regime. The various Western and capitalistic types of monetary measures utilized proved effective in combating inflation, the accompanying depression, and in bringing about general economic stability.

In 1950 the Central Bank of China was replaced by the People's Bank of China, which has turned out to be a much more effective central bank. By mid-1952 the People's Bank had taken over and merged all of the country's private commercial banks. The People's Bank is directly under the State Council. It issues all currency, conducts ordinary banking business, and since comprehensive state planing began in 1952, it has been extending credits and short-term loans through deposits and liabilities to industrial enterprises and other nonfinancial organizations. Monetary policies and controls have been highly centralized in the People's Bank. In addition to performing central banking functions, the People's Bank serves as the nation's commercial banking system. In fact it is Red China's largest economic institution, with more branches throughout the land than the Post Office. I came across offices and branches of the People's Bank everywhere I went in Red China. Local branches of the bank have the duty of scrutinizing and controlling enterprise payments, checks, and receipts to see that they conform to the plan, as well as various state financial and monetary regulations. All of the enterprises surveyed, with the exception of the Shanghai Truck Factory, had their own bank accounts. This firm's monetary and financial dealings are handled almost entirely by its direct superior organization, the Shanghai Bureau of Communications and Transportation.

Under the Communist regime the old Bank of China became a joint state and private institution specializing in foreign exchange and overseas Chinese remittances, and it operates under the People's Bank. The Bank of Communications initially maintained the same name and status, specializing in loans for capital construction until October 1954, when it was taken over by the new People's Construction Bank. This bank operates under the Ministry of Finance, which is directly under the State Council, and has close liaison with the People's Bank on many matters. The Construction Bank began providing loans to small and medium-sized firms around 1964, and it also handles various types of investment funds and supervises extra-budgetary (unplanned) funds. Most of the functions of the Farmers' Bank of China were assumed by the new Agricultural Bank of China which underwent a reorganization in late 1963. Some of the Farmers' Bank's activities have also been taken over by the People's Bank itself, as well as rural credit cooperatives. The Agricultural Bank is directly under the State Council. Other new financial institutions, such as insurance companies under the Ministry of Finance, have also been created.

The Communist regime has sent mobile banks to rural areas, introduced patriotic-savings drives, individual-savings campaigns, new types of savings deposits, and issued bonds (victory bonds in the 1950's during the Korean War). (Individual savings and related campaigns were briefly discussed in Chapter 4 in the section on wealth and material gain.) In general, Communist China has rejected inflation and the excessive creation of money as methods of financing government expenditures.

When Red China embarked on comprehensive state economic planning in 1952 and 1953, the banking system and basic monetary policies were patterned closely along Soviet lines.[14] The banking system, as well as monetary and fiscal policies, are subservient to comprehensive state financial planning under this type of economic system. The basic aim of such financial planning is to balance sources and uses of funds for the whole economy. In broadest form, consumption in monetary terms is supposed to be balanced with savings and investments, consumer goods and services with total purchasing power, supply with demand in value as well as real terms. Comprehensive state financial plans are based on physical plans in real terms. This is necessary because the prices of the vast majority of goods and services are fixed by state authorities rather than determined freely through the forces of supply and demand.

The planners' priorities determine how much in the way of financial resources each sector or each individual enterprise is to receive in the light of the physical or real requirements—that is, production, factor inputs, capital projects, research and development tasks—of the enterprise plan which are also approved by higher planning authorities. While the great bulk of their financial resources are allocated by plan to enterprises, many firms apparently have the right to independently negotiate and obtain modest bank loans for exceptional seasonal needs, the introduction of new techniques, improvement in operations, and various other unplanned uses usually of a relatively minor nature. I was not informed of any loans made by the Construction Bank to the Chinese industrial firms surveyed in 1966. Some enterprises visited do, however, obtain independently negotiated short-term and medium-term loans for investment and other purposes from the People's Bank from time to time. These were larger enterprises, such as Shanghai Steel, which had loans of this type totaling "more than 100,000 yuan." These funds, I was told, bear an interest rate of "not more than 6 percent" and were being used for a variety of purposes, including modest capital-investment projects which were expected to have payback periods of "not more than three years."

Within the limits of their financial plans, enterprise managers also typically have at least a bit of officially sanctioned leeway to shuffle funds among various detailed accounts in order to carry out the overall plan. The directors of the enterprises surveyed also had discretionary funds, ranging from 250 to 1,000 yuan, which they could usually use as they saw fit, and which were generally replenished if necessary from other sources quarterly, and in some cases more frequently. Furthermore, at most of the enterprises visited they could retain in the range of 2.5 to 10 percent of total profits earned—5 percent in the majority of cases—if the key success-indicator targets of the enterprise plan were fulfilled. (A detailed discussion of enterprise-success indicators is presented in Chapter 9.) Within rather broadly defined limits, enterprise management typically has quite a bit of discretion in the spending of retained profits.

In spite of the limited amount of financial freedom that exists at the enterprise level, the key feature of Red China's overall financial and monetary system is the vast number of specifically planned and earmarked funds for industrial enterprises and other organizations. The chief component of the national financial plan is the state budget. About 80 percent of the nation's financial resources, including the bulk of industrial capital investment, is allocated through the state budget. The state budget is more closely related to fiscal policy than monetary policy or central banking, which are the major topics of concern in this section.

Working-capital allotments, credits, loans, and cash are the types of funds that are managed by the banking system. Banking control over industrial enterprises is called "control by the yuan." The enforcement of monetary policies, regulations, and controls is greatly facilitated because the vast majority of enterprise transactions involving money are made by check rather than through cash payments. They are handled through the bank by merely debiting and crediting enterprise bank accounts. Most enterprise funds are kept in the bank, and the bank is usually the only source of short-term credit. The amount of actual cash maintained by enterprises is generally very limited, and their bank accounts are generally subject to rather tight controls. However, as will be discussed shortly, bank controls over enterprise accounts and cash holdings are not as effective or detailed in many instances as the regime would like them to be.

As compared with capitalistic countries and even most mixed economies, central banking and monetary policies in Red China play a relatively passive role as far as influencing or directing economic activity is concerned. Little direct use is made of monetary policies or banking practices in China's economy to influence desired types or patterns of enterprise or managerial behavior. In such an economic system, interest rates do not play a significant role in rationing funds, allocating resources, or in channeling micromanagerial decisions in desired directions. In fact, there are no interest (or rent) charges on capital-investment funds allocated to enterprises. It also seems, from my survey of Chinese firms, that there is also no interest charge on allotments of regular working capital provided for in the plan. There are, however, interest charges—apparently rarely exceeding 6 percent and usually less than 4 percent on special credits and industrial loans, generally repayable within two or three years and negotiated by enterprise executives directly with the bank. But even here the interest rate does not serve as a particularly effective or operational resource-allocation mechanism or criterion, although interest charges may encourage firms to earn larger profits and strive for economies in order to pay off the loan and the related interest charges.

The Chinese banking system's role regarding foreign-exchange balances and reserve requirements, increases, and contractions of the money supply is defined, for the most part, by the overall state plan. Moreover, China's banking system does not engage in open-market operations or rediscount commercial paper.

A critical task of China's banking system and overall monetary policy is to provide enough money and credit at the right time so that industrial enterprises and other organizations can fulfill their plans in real terms. If the physical plans are realistic and consistent, an expansion of money and credit to meet the plans' requirements is not likely to generate significant inflation (or recession). Monetary and financial plans and policies can be no better than physical plans in real terms in such an economic system; if there are errors in physical planning, there are likely to be related errors in financial and monetary planning. Similarly, if physical plans run into unforeseen bottlenecks in their implementation, financial and monetary plans are likely to run into difficulties as well, through no fault of the banking authorities.

Where there are serious errors in physical plans and/or unforeseen bottlenecks in their execution, it is likely that either too much or too little in the way of funds would be available to industrial enterprises at the right time to handle the necessary purchases, production, and distribution of goods, services, and wage payments. This, in turn, can lead to too little improper, and/or poorly timed remittances of profits and taxes to the government budget, thus upsetting the state's fiscal programs and policies. Monetary and fiscal disruptions tend to lead to confusion, inefficiency, waste, and delay in the productive system at the enterprise level.

The two main components of the national financial plan that are directly related to monetary policy and central banking (as well as the balancing of supply and demand) are the Credit Plan and the Cash Plan. The Credit Plan determines the amount of short- and medium-term credit, including working capital, to be made available to industrial enterprises and other organizations by the People's Bank and its numerous branches. This plan is based on sources and uses of funds projections which are supposed to balance each period. The chief sources of bank loans and credits are state budgetary grants and surpluses, profits derived from banking operations, increases in deposit balances of enterprise and individual savings accounts, and expansion of the money supply.

The working-capital requirements of industrial firms are divided into (a) fixed quota, which is determined by the basic requirements of their operating plans and (b) above-quota for seasonal, temporary, and other special unplanned needs. About 80 percent of the fixed-quota funds are channeled to the People's Bank by the Ministry of Finance and industrial higher authorities who approve the enterprise plans. The other 20 percent of the fixed-quota funds, and most, if not all, of the above-quota funds are from the bank's own financial resources.

If the physical plans of enterprises are overambitious or significantly miscalculated, the Credit Plan of the banking system almost certainly would reflect these defects. Firms are likely to be provided with too little—and less commonly too much—money from the bank to procure required physical and human resources to fulfill their plans in real terms. For if the firms are not allocated various required resources in real terms, no regular or planned banking credit will be available for their purchase. The firm may be able to get approval to procure the additional required resources and it may eventually obtain enough bank financing, but in the meantime production bottlenecks continue through no fault of the banking authorities. The enterprise is officially not allowed to negotiate with the bank for special non-planned funds or credits unless it has the sanction of appropriate higher authorities to procure the specific goods or services that the finances will be used for. Where the enterprise has the right to procure unplanned goods or services of various types—typically because they are relatively minor non-allocated items, or where the firm is in a position to overfulfill its production plan—the bank's own credit plan restrictions or limitations may not enable it to extend the financing required.

The Credit Plan is essentially a plan for cash circulation with the People's Bank, the starting and finishing points of the circuit. As was noted earlier, most enterprise financial transactions involving the Credit Plan do not involve cash because they are handled by debiting and crediting enterprise bank accounts. If there are no serious leaks or loopholes in the cash circuit pertaining to the Credit Plan, this plan does not contribute to inflationary pressures. But this is not true of the bank's Cash Plan which involves actual cash circulation, where cash is used for the payment of wages and salaries and the purchase of consumer goods and services.

The basic aim of the Cash Plan is to balance total consumer-purchasing power in the country with available consumer goods and services. If this plan is significantly unsound, inflationary pressures are likely to emerge. Unpegged prices are likely to be bid up—for example, prices of various "free market" agricultural commodities—excess demand is created, black-marketing activities tend to become more widespread, and intensive and/or long queues for various items emerge. The latter two phenomena are actually symptoms of hidden or suppressed inflation.

When serious imbalances between supply and demand arise in Red China's economy, they are handled in a variety of ways.[15] For example, there may be adjustments made in the retail prices of various items. Industrial firms would generally not be affected by such a measure. An adjustment may also be made in the turnover or sales taxes of various commodities in order to bring about price changes. This is actually a fiscal measure which does not directly affect industrial enterprises unless the tax adjustment affects the enterprises' wholesale prices of various products. (Only two of the Chinese enterprises surveyed paid sales taxes on any of their products.) Supply and demand may be brought back into aggregate balance by increasing or decreasing the production of various consumer goods. This is likely to require cutbacks or increases in the production of other types of commodities and, hence, changes in enterprise plans. Increases or decreases in production are also undertaken where specifically identified items are either in excess demand or supply.

The regime may choose to cut back or expand purchasing power by increasing or decreasing wage and salary payments (including bonuses), withholding wage payments, and the like, when significant imbalances in supply and demand arise. Judging from my survey of Chinese firms it seems that bonus payments are provided for in the plan in an aggregate way so that significant errors will not be made in projecting total purchasing power.

When demand exceeds supply, the regime seems to favor rationing rather than pay cuts in coping with inflationary pressures. Many basic necessities and other consumer products were rationed during the depression of the early 1960's. During my 1966 stay in China only a small number of basic consumer items, such as rice, certain kinds of meat, and cotton cloth were rationed. However, for several other items there were long queues and waiting lists, and there were some products, such as automobiles, that consumers with enough money could not get at all. Rationing and the maintenance of critical shortages of various products show up only indirectly in enterprise plans, inasmuch as the output of such items is restricted by the plan.

In general, there has been a high degree of price stability and relatively little overt inflation in Red China. Even during the Great Leap Forward and subsequent economic crises a fairly high degree of price stability was maintained, chiefly through rationing, forced saving, and critical shortages of goods resulting in long queues. Black-marketing activity was also pervasive during this period, and it still probably exists to some degree. Nevertheless, China's banking system and monetary policies, in spite of many shortcomings, have contributed substantially to price stability, as well as the country's relatively sound foreign-exchange position. They have also contributed to general economic stability, with the notable exception of the Great Leap period when ideological extremism substantially reduced the effectiveness of the banking system and official monetary policy.

The Great Leap Period

During the Great Leap the People's Bank did not suffer from ineffective decentralization of authority, lax control over enterprise financial operations, or cutbacks in, and misuse of, competent personnel to the same degree as the Ministry of Finance. (The Ministry of Finance will be dealt with in the section on fiscal policy.) However, China's banking system and monetary policies were far from effective during this period. Party committees and local Reds whittled away at the bank's supervisory powers, regulations, and controls while condemning banking experts and monetary authorities as being too bureaucratic and mechanical if they adhered very strictly to plans, policies, or regulations.

The People's Bank and its numerous branches had to expand credit to keep pace with the overambitious, self-deluding, and abused physical plans of the 1958–60 era. During 1958, total deposits in the People's Bank increased by an amount equal to the increase during the entire 1953–57 period. In 1959, deposits rose by another 39 percent over 1958.[16] Hence, the supply of funds was not really an effective or inflexible restraint on the bank's credit operations. This demonstrated that, after all, even in China's planned economy above-plan bank deposits can be created, even though Red China's monetary and banking authorities do not recognize this, at least officially.

In reality, then, the bank actually created new deposits, and its credit and loan limits were disregarded on an extensive scale during the Great Leap. Even bans on bank loans for investment purposes were modified and abused. Moreover, working-capital loans and short-term credits were frequently diverted to investment purposes and capital projects by firms, thus causing serious bottlenecks and imbalances in the productive system. On the other hand, many firms used earmarked investment funds for current operating uses, with similar adverse effects. The bank was frequently enjoined to supply as much credit as the industrial enterprises themselves felt they needed. In numerous cases unplanned credits granted to firms led to the deflection of critically needed resources from other enterprises. Particularly heavy losses to the economy resulted from the 2 billion yuan —much of it unplanned—that the People's Bank provided to finance the nationwide iron and steel campaign.

In the nationwide drive for aggregate output, thousands of firms overfulfilled their production plans by producing large quantities of unusable, substandard, and unneeded products, as well as items that needed much reworking to serve the functional uses intended. Bank financing was liberally provided for such overfulfillment of production plans. Moreover, enterprises could then retain a substantially greater portion of their profits than they can today, and many showed large profits even when much of their output was grossly deficient. With their planned and above-plan retained profits, and various other extra-budgetary funds at their disposal, firms often used them to deflect resources from other planned uses and to finance unneeded and wasteful expansion programs and projects. At the same time, numerous firms failed to fulfill their profit targets, and profit remittances to the state were less than anticipated. Overspending of enterprise wage funds was also quite common during this period, and this contributed to inflationary pressures.

A high-level Red Chinese official whom I interviewed in Peking readily admitted that monetary policies and the banking system were far from effective during the 1958–60 period. He said that the major underlying problem was that the country overextended its resources and tried to accomplish too much, too quickly during the Great Leap.

The 1960's

With the pendulum swinging in the direction of ideological moderation, monetary policies and the banking system became significantly more effective in the 1960's. Shortly after the Great Leap, experts were again put in charge of money and banking operations, the quality of banking personnel was strengthened, banking operations became more centralized, and supervision and control much tighter. Apparently bank representatives were even posted at many enterprises to make detailed on-the-spot inspections of records, hoarded resources, and excess cash, to search warehouses, and to check on the quality and specifications of output.[17]

From what I learned about the banking system and monetary policy during my stay in Red China, it did not seem that bank officials were commonly being stationed at industrial enterprises for the above or other purposes in 1966. Executives at some of the firms surveyed said that the bank sent auditors to their enterprises to make periodic routine examinations of their financial records, but none of them indicated that banking inspectors went significantly beyond such routine checks. It seems that higher industrial authorities—not the People's Bank or the Ministry of Finance—play the major role in checking on and controlling overall enterprise operations and results.

It also seems that control over the monetary and financial activities of firms by the bank tends to be carried out in a fairly aggregate manner by focusing on major components of the enterprise's financial plan and accounts rather than the details. It would be very difficult and time-consuming for the bank to control or check in detail to see whether a given enterprise's product mix and/or factor inputs conform precisely to the plan, whether all funds and credits are expended on the exact uses and at the exact times earmarked in the detailed operating plan, to check on hoarded and above-plan resources, and so forth. Because most firms function in sellers' markets they are not usually likely to complain to the bank to stop payment to their suppliers when they receive products from them that are not in accordance with the plan. For such products are typically better than no products, and enterprises would frequently find themselves without any alternative supplies if they returned the goods to their delinquent suppliers.

It is also virtually impossible for the bank to totally prevent earmarked working-capital funds from being used for investment purposes and, similarly, funds allocated for investment from being used for operating expenses in many instances. Some of the enterprises surveyed admitted that they at times shuffle their financial resources around in ways not strictly in accordance with the plan. For example, funds for current expenses are sometimes "borrowed" or deflected from the firm's earmarked capital-repair funds; second-hand equipment is at times purchased with profits or with working-capital funds. Such monetary and financial flexibility may be beneficial for managerial effectiveness and productive efficiency at a given enterprise, but it can also lead to sub-system optimization at other firms if critical resources are deflected from them. A relatively minor amount of deflected resources or misuse of funds can do a considerable amount of harm to productive efficiency in a basically planned economy.

There are some indications that violations of monetary policies, financial plans, and in the banking system are being encouraged in many instances with the antibureaucracy emphasis that has evolved again with the Cultural Revolution. In the section "Attitude toward Change" in Chapter 4 we presented actual examples of firms being publicly praised for using earmarked capital-investment funds for working-capital uses, and vice versa.[18] Leading party publications are calling for a merger of Redness and Expertness in banking and finance. How this is to be accomplished is not clearly spelled out. However, greater emphasis is typically given to Redness—which means antibureaucracy and a struggle against inflexible monetary and financial policies, plans, and controls.[19] It is possible that the Reds and particularly the Super-Reds, in the form of the army and the People's Militia, have taken over important banking functions in some areas of the country, although there is no available concrete evidence to this effect. If this is true, however, it is quite likely that state planning and the industrial sector are heading for serious problems.

Even when experts and other relatively competent personnel are placed in charge of banking operations, bank control over industrial enterprise operations is far from perfect in the Red Chinese economy. There are undoubtedly various problems in China concerning money and banking that are common to the Soviet Union and East Europe.[20] In addition to the kinds of problems already discussed, and the fact that there is a much greater shortage of well-trained banking, monetary, and financial personnel in China than in Russia, there are a variety of other shortcomings. For example, the bank's reports are no doubt frequently too late for effective corrective action, and there are inaccuracies in the reports; because of lack of interest in enterprise affairs that do not impinge directly on the bank's performance, often no action is taken; and so forth. Pressures may, at times, be exerted on banking authorities by enterprises or higher industrial authorities which lead to undesirable action for the economy as a whole, and favoritism and personal relationships probably interfere with effective decision making and control by banking officials in some instances.

Moreover, a major part of the central bank's operations and control functions involve the audit of its own branches as well as external organizations. The People's Bank must be properly organized and managed for truly effective monetary and financial control. However, there are probably serious internal organizational and managerial problems and inefficiencies within the huge and pervasive People's Bank. But the types of problems pertaining to money, banking, and finance that exist in China's economy when the experts are allowed to play major roles tend to be small when compared with the kinds of problems and inefficiencies that emerge during periods of ideological extremism.

A Brief Note on India

It is difficult and not entirely meaningful to directly compare in depth the monetary policies and central-banking systems of Red China and India. While some of the functions and basic aims of central banking and monetary policy are similar in the two countries, they play a more direct, active, and independent role in influencing and directing general economic activity and decison making at industrial enterprises in India. In fact monetary policies and particularly central banking in India have been substantially influenced by the British and are therefore more comparable with those found in capitalistic, rather than communist, countries.

In general, central banking and monetary policies tend to be more effective in terms of industrial progress in India than in many other underdeveloped and developing nations. This is not one of India's most serious negative constraints on managerial effectiveness and productive efficiency. Nevertheless, monetary policy and central banking in India are far from perfect or highly effective. There are serious problems involving inept policies, improper timing, political interference, lack of integrity, favoritism, dysfunctional pressures, organization and management, and so on. In spite of such problems, India's central-banking system and monetary policies have contributed to price stability and general economic stability. In fact, inflation averaged less than 3 percent annually from around 1952 to 1962.

In the mid-1960's, however, inflation exceeded 10 percent, grew rapidly, and has now become a problem of major concern. The country has also been experiencing considerable economic instability, industrial stagnation in various sectors, and in 1966 India devalued her currency with little in the way of positive gains to date. However, central banking and monetary policies cannot bear the brunt of the blame for India's economic dilemmas. Many of the other environmental constraints dealt with in this book probably deserve a larger share of the blame. A major underlying cause of India's serious inflation is great overpopulation, in conjunction with her bare-subsistence agricultural sector, which has been beset by monsoons and other unfavorable weather conditions that have caused famine, great commodity shortages, pervasive black-marketing activities, and sharply rising prices. Red China has a substantially more effective distribution system involving agricultural commodities—including rationing where necessary—than India. This is a plus factor for China in checking inflation.

Fiscal Policy and the State Budget

The state budget is the basic instrument of fiscal policy in all countries. The role of the state budget in any nation is to transfer resources in accordance with government decisions from one part of the national economy to another. Governments or their closely controlled central banks have the power to create money simply by printing bank notes, expanding bank deposits, and through various other monetary policies. They also have the option of raising money by fiscal measures, the most common being taxation of various types. Taxes typically provide a major source of revenue in the state budget, particularly if the government does not follow a course of excessive deficit financing. The manner in which governments obtain the funds they spend has a direct and immediate impact on the economy and on industrial enterprises.

In general, fiscal policy tends to be closely connected with monetary policy and central-banking activity. The interwoven complex of monetary policy, banking, and the government's fiscal policy, as reflected in its revenue-raising and spending activities, forms a critical part of the general control of price levels, recessions, and loans in the economy. The way in which fiscal and monetary policy is controlled or ignored by the government and the central bank tends to have tremendous effects on industrial enterprises and their managements.

Because of its very complexity and its intimate relationship with monetary policy, it is often difficult to evaluate fiscal policy very precisely in terms of managerial effectiveness and industrial progress. In general, however, a country's overall fiscal policy can be judged quite successful over time if the net result is that it helps to create a relatively stable and growing economy in which firms can plan and operate with reasonable efficiency, in which many existing firms expand and new ones are created, where resource allocations are not grossly distorted, where unemployment (including disguised unemployment) does not increase substantially, and where real incomes tend to increase. On the other hand, when fiscal policy is grossly ineffective over time, extreme depressions and/or booms, irrational sharp price changes, critical resource-allocation problems caused by government spending patterns, foreign-exchange crises, highly inefficient firms, and industrial stagnation or even retrogression are much more likely to occur.

Republican China

In Republican China ineffective fiscal policy may well have been an even greater contributor to inflation, economic instability, and lack of economic development than inept monetary policy and the deficient central banking.[21] Even before the war-torn, extremely inflationary, and economically disastrous period of 1937–49, the fiscal policies pursued by the Kuomintang were not significantly conducive to industrial progress. Government spending on economic-development projects was very limited, and the fiscal policy did little to encourage private domestic investment in the industrial sector. For example, in 1933—one of Republican China's best years in terms of economic and political stability and relative prosperity—gross fixed investment in the national economy totaled only about 5 percent of GNP.[22] By comparison, during the 1950–57 period under Communist rule, gross fixed investment in mainland China averaged about 15.9 percent of GNP. (More about this period later.) Taxation under the Kuomintang regime did little to bring about more equitable income distribution and more effective widespread purchasing power.

Probably the main cause of Republican China's skyrocketing inflation —which began around 1937 and lasted until the Communist takeover— was the vast increase in government expenditures in conjunction with the highly antiquated and grossly deficient tax system. The ever-expanding state-budget deficits were financed for the most part by the creation of money—mainly new issues of currency from the printing press. The regime's fiscal policies contributed greatly to the severe foreign-exchange crises which greatly restricted the importation of goods. Tax evasion was rampant. Corruption, graft, unproductive patronage, conflict of class interests, and the extreme extravagances of many Kuomintang officials and politicians also helped to drain the state treasury. A major portion of state revenue came from agricultural taxes, but this source of revenue fell sharply as peasants became bogged down in war and as the countryside was lost to insurgents.

State-budget receipts in real terms fell roughly 75 percent behind expenditures during the 1937–45 period and even more sharply during 1946–49. Government spending in current prices about doubled each year during 1937–41, then tripled annually to 1944, and then jumped five-fold by 1945. In real terms these expenditures actually declined by 30 to 40 percent over this period. The tax and revenue system simply could not respond adequately to the huge increases in nominal incomes and spendings. In current prices, budget receipts lagged farther and farther behind expenditures. In real terms they fell by perhaps 75 percent from 1937 to 1945, and probably by an even greater amount during the second half of the 1940's.[23]

The government spending that trickled into the industrial sector benefited only a small proportion of enterprises, mainly those engaged in military production and a limited number of firms that supplied other items to the government. Politics, favoritism, venal self-interest, and patronage, rather than economic or efficiency criteria, were frequently the chief reasons for government orders given to particular firms in the civilian sector.

For most Chinese industrial enterprises the Kuomintang regime's fiscal policy contributed greatly to the types of severe problems and inefficiencies discussed in the previous section on monetary policy and central banking. For example, grossly inept fiscal policies contributed sharply to extreme profit squeezes, bankruptcies, idle capacity, layoffs and disguised unemployment, hoarding and inventory speculation, cutbacks in production, lack of research, development, and innovation, severe shortages of capital and critical factor inputs, particularly imported items, extreme uncertainty in planning ahead, stagnation and eventually regression on a pervasive scale at industrial enterprises. The possibilities for tax evasion had a considerable impact on the financial policies of numerous firms. Key personnel were often selected because they were relatives or close friends, with competence playing a minor, if any, role, since outsiders could not be as readily trusted where illegal financial activities were involved.

Fiscal Policy and the State Budget in Communist China

As was mentioned earlier, the role of fiscal policy and its basic instrument, the state budget, in all countries is to transfer resources in accordance with government decisions from one part of the economy to another. Communist China is no different in this respect. However, the relative importance of fiscal policy and the budget in Red China—and other communist states—as compared with those of essentially capitalistic economies is very great because of the direct responsibility of the Communist government for the bulk of economic life.[23a] In recent years roughly 80 percent of Red China's available financial resources, including the great bulk of capital investment, allocated through the comprehensive financial plan, are collected and distributed through the national budget.[24]

China's fiscal policy and state budget are distinguished from those in capitalist nations by their intimate interrelationship with the process of comprehensive economic planning. Expenditures on investment and other aspects of the economy are the financial reflections of conscious state decisions on economic growth and priorities. As with monetary policy, fiscal policy and the budget are based on physical economic plans stated in real terms. The anual state budget and the national economic plan are drafted and submitted to the top central organs—the State Council, National People's Congress, and at times the Central Committee of the Communist Party—at the same time for formal approval. The state budget is broken down into projected revenues indicating sources of funds and capital and operating expenditures subdivided by sectors and geographic areas. The central and local government budgets are the main source of both long-term and short-term capital for the economy, with the central budget providing the bulk of capital-investment funds. Most investment funds provided to industrial firms are financed by nonreturnable, interest-free grants from the state budget.

The enterprise's financial plan, which is a major subsection of its overall annual plan, is the firm's direct link with the state budget.[25] The financial plan translates the overall plan into monetary terms indicating sources and uses of funds. It indicates funds provided by the state budget (both the central and local governments' budgets), profits, depreciation changes, and taxes (if any) to be remitted to the state budgets, sales revenues, expenses, and so on.

The State Council's Office for Finance and Trade is the highest government organ in the financial sphere. The Ministry of Finance, with its budget and tax bureaus and other offices throughout the country, is directly under this office of the State Council. The major functions of this ministry include the compilation of annual state budgets, collection of revenues (taxes and enterprise profits), and the supervision and control of the financial work of other ministries and organizations.

Much of the complicated fiscal incentives and disincentives utilized to get deserved investment, to balance consumption, savings and investment, and supply and demand in a capitalist economy, where there is much greater individual and enterprise free choice, is unnecessary in Communist China's economic system. But the problem is far from easy, since the communist state must still strive to extract from individual consumers and organizations funds—in the form of savings, taxes, and profits—equal to the amount invested each year, and accomplish the overall fiscal balancing task by comprehensive planning. The financial constraints on industrial enterprises and the amount of financial leeway extended to their managements under China's monetary and fiscal system have already been discussed briefly in the previous section on central banking and monetary policy.

In addition to performing the type of aggregate financial-balancing job noted above, fiscal policy and the state budget in Red China also play the chief role in determining the types of new industries and firms to be created and the existing ones to be significantly expanded through capital allocations. Ideally, state spending, capital investment in particular, should provide for balanced and integrated growth among interrelated industrial sectors over a period of time—this is in line with the Marxist law of planned and proportionate development of the economy. Substantial overinvestment or underinvestment among closely interdependent sectors tends to lead to serious bottlenecks; idleness, mismatching, and misutilization of resources; under- and over-utilization of plant capacity; production of items that are unneeded and remain unused for much longer periods of time than desired; excess and deficient inventories of various goods; and other serious forms of waste and inefficiency. The fiscal policy followed during the Great Leap period contributed greatly to this type of situation.

In general, under China's Communist-led fiscal policy and its operational expression the state budget has been aimed directly at industrial development. The very impressive economic progress of the 1950's was based in large part on an ambitious investment program, especially in the industrial sector. The high rate of investment in the 1950's with its emphasis on heavy industry and the rapid expansion of producers' goods, combined with the lack of large quantities of foreign aid, meant that the tax burden on the consumer had to be very heavy. The heavy investment program required restraint of demand for consumption or, what amounts to the same thing, sufficient saving to match investment. The Red regime was determined not to gain the required saving through an inflationary process. The state has rejected, generally with considerable success, deficit budgets to finance expenditures, and strives to achieve small surpluses of roughly 3 to 5 percent of revenues accruing in the course of implementation of budgets. The national debt, initiated in 1950, was a form of long-term national savings. But even this debt was apparently liquidated in 1966, and the savings returned to depositors.

Instead of deficit financing, the regime has greatly increased tax receipts and held down government consumption, thereby generating large saving in the government sector. It has also used direct controls, set wages, and manipulated relative prices to achieve large profits at state enterprises, most of which have been reverted to the state budget, thus swelling government savings. In 1950 only 60 percent of the state's revenues came from profits and sales taxes earned and paid by all types of state economic enterprises—industrial, wholesale, and retail, excluding the agricultural sector. Since the late 1950's about 90 percent of the state budget's funds have come from enterprise profits and taxes.[26] Depreciation funds are remitted by firms to the state and from part of the states' revenues, but only a minor part. However, funds for major capital repairs are retained by enterprises in their bank accounts. The state has also encouraged individual saving through a variety of devices, although this source of government funds is very small compared with enterprise profits and sales (turnover) taxes. Finally the regime was able to tap some foreign savings for its investment program. Although the domestic supply of consumer goods has not expanded very vigorously since around 1954, demand has been restrained sufficiently to prevent any significant increase in prices.

Patterns of State Spending and Investment

Approximately 50 to 60 percent of Red China's annual state budgets have been spent on "economic construction" projects, which include industrial capital investment, education, public health services, and scientific research and development activities. (A geological survey's expenses, for example, falls into the economic construction category in China.) In some years this proportion has been as high as 70 percent.[27] The remainder of the state budget covers the costs of state administration, defense, foreign aid, debts, the nation's reserve fund, and so on.

The portion of the state budget devoted to direct capital investment was about 36.5 percent during the 1953–57 period, reaching 41 percent in 1957, 51.5 percent in 1958, and dropping slightly to about 49 percent in 1959 and 46 percent in 1960. During the 1958–60 period, sources outside of the state budget provided about another 20 percent of capital-investment funds.[28] It is likely that the share of the state budget used for capital investment in the last few years is in the range of the proportion at the outset of the Great Leap period—that is, between 40 and 50 percent.

The great bulk of China's state investment is centrally planned. Since 1950 more than 80 percent of the investment has been planned and allocated by the center each year, with the portion exceeding 90 percent and reaching nearly 95 percent in some years. During the course of the First Five-Year Plan the portion of centrally planned investment increased from 86 percent in 1952 to a peak of 94.5 percent in 1956, as industrial centralization under the ministerial system became tighter. With greater decentralization of authority at the provincial and municipal levels during the Great Leap, centrally planned investment dropped to around 84 percent of total state investment.[29] It is likely that the portion of centrally planned investment is currently higher than during the Great Leap, but probably not as high as in the peak year 1956. It might be in the range of 88 to 90 percent.

Gross domestic investment averaged roughly 25 percent of GNP in Red China during the 1950's, and it was probably over 30 percent if investment in human capital is included. Approximately half of this figure, or more, represented capital formation in heavy and light industry, chiefly the former.[30] For one of the world's poorest countries, in terms of income per capita, when the Communists came to power, this was a remarkable achievement.

In 1950 gross domestic investment in relation to GNP was only about 13 percent, but by 1952 it had exceeded 20 percent. During the 1958–60 period gross investment ranged from roughly 30 to 45 percent of national income, depending on the GNP used. However, much of the investment was unproductive and wasteful during this period. In 1961–62, gross domestic investment dropped greatly both in relative and absolute terms. GNP also dropped by at least 15 percent and possibly by more than 30 percent from the 1958 or 1959 peak year under Communist rule. Per capita income, of course, dropped even more than GNP because of population growth. In 1962 gross investment is estimated to have been about 21.3 percent of GNP, about the same as in 1953.[31]

According to Chinese and Western sources, my interview with a high-level Red Chinese official, and an interview with the same official conducted by Han Suyin, the famous Chinese writer who now lives in Hong Kong,[32] the regime currently allots about 20 percent of the national income to investment and intends to continue this policy in the future. This is a very considerable proportion to maintain, as, or if, the Chinese economy continues to grow. If it is maintained and the investment is put to productive use, China's aggregate industrial development and economic progress are likely to be very substantial during the next decade. Such an ambitious investment program, along with a steadily rising GNP, is unlikely to be maintained, however, if ideological extremism persists.

The gross domestic-investment figures we have been discussing include increases—or decreases—in inventories in the national economy. Available gross fixed investment figures for China exclude net charges in inventories, military expenditures, and household purchases of consumer durables other than housing.[33] Red China's record with regard to gross fixed investment in relation to GNP was also impressive during the 1950's. In 1950, gross fixed investment totaled only about 7 percent of GNP, but by 1954 it had reached 15 percent. In 1956 it was 19 percent and in 1958 and 1959 during the height of the Leap it was about 24.6 percent and 26.2 percent respectively. However, a substantial portion of fixed investment during the Great Leap was wasteful and unproductive. If we take the 1958 and 1959 figures at face value, gross fixed investment averaged roughly 20 percent of GNP during the 1950's in Red China. During the 1950–57 period the average rate of gross fixed capital formation was about 16 percent, and for 1952–57 approximately 17.5 percent.

China's rate of fixed investment during 1952–57 was higher than that of all other Asian countries during the 1950–59 period with the exception of Japan which achieved a fantastic rate of 21.6 percent (which includes private investment).[34] If we use China's 1950–57 average rate, it was higher than all other Asian countries during 1950–59 except Japan and Burma, which achieved a rate of 17.1 percent during the 1951–59 period. India's rate (including private investment) during the 1950–59 period was 14.9 percent. However, the gross fixed-investment rates for these other Asian nations probably include various military expenditures. Moreover, several Asian countries, including India and Burma, received substantially more foreign aid used for domestic investment during the 1950's than did Red China.

In the early 1960's there was a sharp decline in Communist China's gross fixed investment. It is likely that by 1964 the rate of fixed investment again approached the 1957 level of nearly 17 percent and in 1965 or 1966 the 1957 rate was surpassed.

The Industrial Sector

In 1950, only about 21 percent of China's gross fixed investment went to the overall industrial sector—heavy and light industry, public utilities, and industrial construction. By 1953 about one-third was being channeled to the industrial sector, and on the eve of the Great Leap in 1957 more than 40 percent. In 1958 and 1959 the industrial sector absorbed about half of China's gross fixed investment. Heavy industry absorbed an increasingly greater portion of fixed investment, rising from about 50 to 60 percent of the industrial total in the early 1950's, to roughly 70 percent in the mid-fifties, and over 80 percent during the Great Leap Period.[35]

In the 1950's, prior to the Great Leap, industrial investment was chiefly used for putting existing capacity back into operation and building new relatively large-scale heavy-industry plants and utilities. The Chinese may have followed the Soviet bent of viewing heavy industry as an end in itself during the First Five-Year Plan; nevertheless, considerable industrial progress was realized because serious imbalances, bottlenecks, and waste had not yet evolved in the economy. During the Great Leap, heavy industry, including small-scale heavy-industry operations such as backyard-type iron and steel operations, was fanatically pushed as an end in itself. The bulk of industrial investment was used for putting all of the large-scale plants built since 1949 into full use and creating thousands of new small-scale industrial installations throughout the nation, including commune industries in the countryside.

Overinvestment in heavy industry during the Leap resulted in capital goods being added to the economy much more rapidly than they could be absorbed in the overall productive sector. And of course much of the industrial output was of such poor quality and improper specifications that it could not serve the uses intended. Grossly inadequate attention was given to the development of feeder industries and the industrial infrastructure required to make productive use of much of the investment poured into heavy industry or the resulting output. As a result, severe imbalances and bottlenecks evolved throughout the economy which, in turn, led to idle, mismatched, and misutilized resources, waste, and general inefficiency on a grand scale. The gross misallocation and misuse of investment funds led to a very large decline in the marginal efficiency of capital during the 1958–60 period.

The proportion of gross fixed investment that went to transportation and communications during the Great Leap did not increase. This resulted in serious social-overhead-capital deficiencies which further aggravated inefficiency in the industrial sector. During the 1950's roughly 12 to 12.5 percent of gross fixed investment was allocated to the transportation and communications sector. In the peak years of 1955 and 1956 the figure was 13.8 percent, and in the low year of 1953 it was 9.4 percent. In 1958 the portion of gross fixed investment allotted to this sector was about 10 percent and in 1959 12.2 percent.

In the early 1960's a vast amount of idle capacity evolved throughout the industrial sector. Total industrial output probably declined by as much as 40 or 45 percent in 1961–62, as compared with the annual peak reached during the Great Leap Period of 1958–60.[36] By 1961 all industrial capital-investment projects in progress and all plans for such projects were, apart from a very limited number of special top-priority cases, ordered discontinued by the state.[37] This ban was probably lifted on a piecemeal basis over the next several years.

During the 1961–63 period much of the capital investment made was directed toward major plant maintenance and repair, general consolidation, industrial research and development to build up the missing industrial infrastructure, and a few strategic industries, such as petroleum, chemicals, and defense. Since about 1962 the regime has been following what it calls a "demand-oriented policy" toward heavy industry. This means that new investment is channeled chiefly into linking industries and creating an overall infrastructure required to support the intended uses and final sales of heavy-industry products.

The Chinese Communists have claimed a big upsurge in capital investment since 1964, with virtually all plants being put back into use. This is probably more or less true, and most of the plants I visited in 1966 seemed to be operating at at least 70 to 80 percent of capacity on at least one shift. Many claimed to be operating, at least in some workshops, on a two- or three-shift basis. (More will be said in a later chapter about the number of shifts worked at plants surveyed.) There was, however, considerable excess and uninstalled capacity at some of the firms surveyed. Evidence of this at the Wuhan Steel and Wuhan Paper plants and various other enterprises has been cited in earlier sections and chapters.

Although China's total capital investment in relation to GNP probably reached the 1957 rate by 1967, and may have even exceeded it since then, this may not be the case with capital investment in the overall industrial sector. In 1957, industrial plant construction amounted to about 10 percent of the total value of industrial output. In 1965 this rate was probably only around 5 percent.[38] However, even though industrial investment, particularly in heavy industry, may still be significantly below the levels achieved during the Great Leap, it is probably substantially more productive, with resulting increases in sales, as well as more timely and efficient uses of heavy-industry output in other sectors.

An Apparent Desire for More Balanced Economic Growth and Industrial Development

Communist China claims to be following a course of more balanced industrial development and economic growth in the 1960's.[39] From what I saw and was told by some high-level Red Chinese planners and economists, it does seem that the regime is allocating considerable capital investment to a fairly wide cross section of industries. One sign of this was that I found both relatively modern, well-equipped factories and old, technologically backward plants in various types of industries that I observed. (I will go into more detail in a later chapter on the equipment and technology utilized at various firms visited.) In the Soviet Union a few years ago I found the larger heavy-industry firms—such as Moscow's Red Proletariat plant, the Sverdlovsk Heavy-Machinery Plant in Leningrad, and Kharkov's Ball-Bearing Factory—to be generally modern and quite well equipped. On the other hand, consumer-goods producers, such as Leningrad's Skorokhod Shoe Firm and Kharkov's Tinakov Clothing Factory, were typically old, rather poorly equipped, and highly labor-intensive. This dichotomy between heavy and light industry, or consumer goods versus producer goods, did not seem to be as sharp in Red China—at least from what I saw.

The Chinese regime feels that it is imperative to raise agricultural productivity substantially because of the country's huge population. Moreover, the regime views the Chinese revolution as basically a peasants' revolution rather than a workers' revolution (as was the case in Russia), and therefore, may feel more strongly about improving the lives and working conditions of the peasants in the short run. A sizable proportion of the relatively new and well-equipped factories that I visited were producing chemicals, machinery, and other supplies for the agricultural sector.

A familiar charge against the fiscal and investment policies followed by the Chinese regime during the 1950's is that priority for heavy industry starved agriculture of investment funds that could have yielded much larger increases in agricultural output. The facts do not seem to bear out this charge to the degree of significance that many critics attach to it. During the 1950's the agricultural sector actually received roughly 22 percent of gross fixed-investment funds. During the 1953–57 period, fixed investment for agriculture approximately doubled in magnitude, and doubled in magnitude again during the 1958–59 period.[40] However, in China's vastly overpopulated subsistence-level rural economy sizable gains in agricultural productivity were realized during the First Five-Year Plan through labor-intensive improvement projects, such as irrigation.

The heavy-industry bias in China stressed imports of industrial equipment and other commodities for heavy industry when greater imports would probably more wisely have been in the form of chemical fertilizer and other supporting inputs for agriculture. In the 1950's too low a priority was given to increasing chemical-fertilizer production; and this is a defect that applies not to the allocations of investment to agriculture but to the allocations of investment within the overall industrial sector itself. The chemical industry was relatively weak in China, and the greater priority needed for chemical fertilizer would have meant somewhat slower growth for heavy industry. A basic problem of increasing agriculture in China is one of modernization—of improving farm technology. Another basic problem is that of ideology and incentives. Given the traditional system of production, the common deficiencies in Communist methods of socializing agriculture, and Red China's pendulum of ideological extremism, definite limits are set on potential increases in agricultural production as a result of agricultural investment.

Hence, the investment pattern within industry, ideological problems, and various other factors have probably contributed much more greatly to China's agricultural dilemmas than lack of agricultural investment per se. China's agricultural problems have, in turn, had a negative impact on those industrial sectors (such as textiles, clothing, foodstuffs) which are substantially dependent on inputs from the agricultural sector. The regime is now trying to deal with the agricultural problem by devoting much of its financial resources to the expansion of the chemical-fertilizer, agricultural-machinery, and other industries which supply critical commodities to the agricultural sector. As was noted in the section on foreign policy in Chapter 5, the regime is also importing many more commodities, including complete plants, in an effort to rapidly develop these agricultural-supply sectors.

A central defect in China's allocation of investment for light industry in the 1950's was failure of the regime to increase significantly the potential for production of raw materials, such as synthetic fibers, that could substitute for raw materials dependent on agriculture. Such a change in investment policy for light industry depends on other industrial sectors to produce the necessary raw materials and therefore involves the allocations of investment within these other sectors—particularly the chemical industry and those equipment industries which can produce the new technology required for manufacturing the new materials. In the 1960's, there has been a shift in fiscal and investment policies in this direction—an effort which should have started about a decade sooner.

In general, Red China seems to be making sizable investments in various consumer-goods industries. In order to earn foreign exchange, which is used largely for importing grain, advanced machinery, chemicals, and various other commodities that they are still far from self-sufficient in, the regime is pushing very vigorously the exports of some of their older industries such as textiles, clothing, and processed foodstuffs. But in order to compete effectively in world markets, more capital-intensive production in certain consumer-goods sectors, such as textiles and clothing, is required. As a result, one finds some surprisingly well-equipped factories in these sectors. The regime also seems sincerely concerned about providing its huge population with more and better consumer goods in the short run, and this is probably another major reason why it is willing to make sizable capital outlays in various consumer-goods industries. There is a surprisingly wide variety of consumer goods of relatively good quality available in the stores even in areas such as Wusih and Loyang, which are seldom frequented by foreigners.

The largest Soviet department store, GUM, in Moscow does not come close to the large department stores in Peking, Shanghai, or Tientsin in terms of variety or quality of consumer goods available. For example, Shanghai's General Department Store No. 1 carries over fifty thousand different types of products. Although living standards are substantially better in Russia than in China, the Soviet regime has not, until very recently, paid much attention to the variety or quality of consumer-goods production. Nor have the Soviets traditionally followed nearly as vigorous or extensive a foreign-trade policy as the Chinese.

China is by no means neglecting heavy industry or the defense sector, which still receives substantial shares of capital investment because of the technology required. In fact, the defense sector has probably been receiving an increasing portion of investment funds under China's nuclear programs. However, there does seem to be a much more balanced capital-investment policy now than in the 1950's.

The Chinese regime still earns considerable foreign exchange through highly labor-intensive and poorly equipped industries such as those producing leather shoes, batteries, and electrical appliances, such as fans. They apparently feel that sizable capital investment in these industries will not have as great a payoff as in heavy industry, agricultural processing, or some of the older or larger consumer-goods industries such as textile milling. Moreover, it would cost more to equip with modern technology a shoe or battery plant than to equip a clothing factory.

Sources of State Revenues

Thus far we have been focusing on the spending side, particularly investment, of Communist China's fiscal policies and budget. A discussion about the revenue side is in order now.

State-budget revenues rose from around 10 percent of GNP in 1950 to over 30 percent in 1958, and even higher in the following year. Government saving probably financed about half of aggregate investment in the early 1950's and more than 75 percent later on.[41] However, the extreme stresses, strains, irrational policies, and programs of the Great Leap led to a drastic fall in state revenues—and hence in investment—in the early 1960's.

Actual revenues collected in 1960 fell roughly 50 percent below those planned for in the state budget, but GNP was also falling sharply by then. The level of budget revenues probably was in the range of 30 billion to 40 billion yuan during the 1960–62 period. This was roughly 25 to 35 percent of GNP—depending on what estimates are used, but GNP was in the area of 15 to 40 percent lower than in the 1958–59 period. In 1963, state-budget revenues are estimated to have been roughly 43 billion yuan, and a small surplus was actually achieved in the budget. Revenues were somewhat greater in 1964 than originally estimated in the budget for that year. In 1965 the budget called for both revenues and expenditures to increase by over 10 percent as compared with 1964, and the budget was planned to be balanced.[42]

It is probable that the state budget in most recent times has not yet surpassed the peak levels of revenues or expenditures achieved in the 1950's, but the peak levels are no doubt being approached. Of course, if ideological extremism persists, a substantial fall in revenues is likely, followed by a substantial cutback in spending and investment.

It was noted earlier that over 90 percent of state-budget revenues come from profits and taxes paid by economic enterprises of all types—industrial, wholesale, and retail—excluding the agricultural sector. The other 10 percent or so of state revenues come from other sources such as taxes or agricultural production, house rents, and motor vehicles.[43] The personal income tax was abolished in 1959, and the state relies on a comprehensive system of prescribed wage and salary scales to achieve desired levels of income distribution. In 1950 agricultural tax revenues were about one-third of budget revenues, but by 1960 they had fallen to about 5 percent. In the mid-1960's they were about 7 percent of total state-budget revenues. Large revenues until 1958 were provided by taxes on the gross receipts and net income of business enterprises of all types and by commodity taxes. These taxes were replaced in 1958 by the turnover tax. The turnover tax is essentially a sales tax levied on commodities as they change hands through the industrial and retail sectors and eventually reach the individual consumer. They form part of the price of these commodities.

Industrial enterprises, wholesaling organizations, and retail stores all remit most of their profits to the state, but the great bulk of the profits come from industrial firms.[44] Profit remittances to the state budget are really similar to a profit tax. Until 1958 industrial firms retained 40 percent and more of their above-plan profits. In 1958 or 1959 this regulation was changed, and firms were allowed to keep about 10 percent of total profits earned on the average. The average amount of profits that the industrial enterprises I surveyed in 1966 were allowed to retain was about 5 percent of total earned profits, although some of them could keep a greater share. It is likely that the rate of retained profits has been officially reduced somewhat at the enterprise level in recent years.

Most of the turnover taxes that form part of the total state revenues are levied at the retail level as goods are passed on to ultimate consumers. Wholesaling organizations apparently do not generally pay turnover taxes, although they do remit the bulk of their profits to the state. Of the industrial enterprises surveyed in 1966 I know of only two which paid sales taxes. The Peking Clothing Firm paid taxes amounting to about 5 percent of total sales. I cannot remember with certainty which of the other firms paid turnover taxes, and I cannot find any entry on this point in my notes. But I am quite sure that it was a consumer-goods producer. In general, Chinese ideology and policy seem to favor higher profits in industry than in commerce (that is, wholesaling and retailing), which is viewed as a much less productive sector. Therefore, turnover taxes are probably substantially higher and provide for greater state revenues in the retail sector than in the industrial sector.

The total amount of enterprise profit remittances to the state provides for a substantially larger share than do turnover taxes in Red China. The reverse is true in the Soviet Union where a substantially greater, but declining, share of state revenues comes from turnover taxes. One reason for this difference is the much greater number of inefficient small firms and marginal producers in China. If relatively high taxes were levied on these inefficient enterprises many of them would incur losses, and hence require state subsidies to operate. The Chinese regime prefers to keep turnover taxes low or not to levy them at all in the industrial sector, rather than to pay out large amounts in subsidies and much related paperwork. Some firms in Soviet industry have been provided with state subsidies, but their number has been relatively small, and much smaller than would be the case if China were to follow the Soviet fiscal practices.

In 1952 the profits of state enterprises in China yielded only 13 percent of total state revenues. Profit remittances surpassed turnover and sales taxes in importance by 1954, and by 1959 had grown to twice the level of these taxes. By 1957 or 1958 enterprise profits were providing more than half of the total state revenues from all sources, and the proportion of profits has probably increased substantially since then. Enterprise-depreciation funds—often referred to as amortization charges—are also remitted to the state, but this is a relatively minor source of state revenues. Depreciation rates, with the likely exception of rates on imported equipment, tend to be significantly lower in China than in the United States. The absence of competitive forces and the relatively low planned rate of technological obsolescence are probably the chief reasons for this difference.

For accounting purposes, enterprise profits have traditionally been returned to the state as a percentage of total enterprise costs in Chinese industry. Profit as a percent of costs is higher in aggregate in heavy industry than in light industry, but profit as a percent of fixed capital is higher in light industry.[45] As there are no interest charges on enterprise fixed capital, costs tend to be underestimated particularly in capital-intensive sectors, including heavy industry. In fact there is actually a sizable hidden state subsidy for capital-intensive firms.

Table 6–1 presents some major product groups indicating the total taxes and profits as a percent of the average cost of each. The data are for 1957, but they probably roughly approximate current conditions in most cases, particularly the producers' goods.[46]

TABLE 6–1

TAXES PLUS PROFITS AS PERCENT OF AVERAGE COST FOR SELECTED COMMODITIES

Commodity	*Percent*
All Commodities	50
Average of heavy industry	43
State iron and steel enterprises	25
Electric power (1956)	101
Average of light industry (including commerce)	47
Cotton cloth	107
Rate on yarn	43
Rate on cloth	52
Cigarettes	160–335
Sugar	40
Grain	15–20

It may be interesting to look at profits in relation to value of output and costs at a number of Chinese industrial enterprises surveyed in 1966 and to make some suggestive comparisons with selected branches of Soviet industry. Table 6–2 presents 1965 data on Chinese firms, and Table 6–3 shows figures for 1960 for certain branches of Soviet industry.

Our very limited and fragmented sample of Chinese industrial enterprises does not clearly reflect the fact that profits as a percentage of costs are higher in heavy industry than in light industry. Profits in relation to costs are higher at the cotton textile and woolen firms visited than at a majority of the heavy-industry enterprises in the sample than at light-industry firms not producing cotton or woolen textiles. More will be said about profitability comparisons between firms in Chinese industry in a later chapter.

From the data presented in Tables 6–2 and 6–3 some interesting and suggestive comparisons can be made between the Chinese sample of enterprises and the selected branches of industry in the Soviet Union. In no case is profit as a percent of costs or total value of output lower at the Chinese firms in my sample than the aggregate rates for corresponding branches of Soviet industry. Even the rates for Tientsin Shoe and Soo-

TABLE 6–2

PROFITS EARNED IN RELATION TO TOTAL SALES VALUE OF OUTPUT AND COSTS FOR TWENTY CHINESE INDUSTRIAL ENTERPRISES
(All data are for 1965)*

Enterprise	*Profit as a Percent of Sales Value of Output*	*Profit as a Percent of Total Cost*
Peking Cotton Textile No. 3	26	35
Shanghai Cotton Textile No. 19	25	33
Shanghai (Joint) Sung Sing Cotton Textile No. 9	25	34
Peking Woolen	25	33
Tientsin (Joint) Jen Yi Woolen	29	41
Wusih Silk Reeling No. 2	15	not available
Peking Clothing	10	12
Hangchow Fu Chong Clothing	6	not available
Tientsin Shoe	5	(actually 5.3) 5
Shanghai Battery	22	29
Tientsin Watch	13	14
Wuhan Paper	27	37
Canton Chemical Fertilizer	18	22
Peking Coke and Chemical	21	26
Soochow Cement Products (Boats and Telephone Poles)	14	15
Wusih Diesel Engine	14	17
Shanghai Steel	23	29
Wuhan Heavy Machinery	25	33
Shanghai Forging and Pressing Machine Tool No. 3	15	17
Wusih Red Flag Machinery	30	43
Tientsin North Lake Instrument	28	38

* Total sales value of output is equal to marketable output in current sales prices. Total sales are typically somewhat less than total value of output because of inventories, goods in process, etc. Where applicable, sales taxes are included in sales value of output. Some of the figures represent estimates made from data or ranges provided by the enterprises. Where ranges were given, they rarely had more than a 5% variation, and in such cases I have arbitrarily used the mid-point of the range. All figures have been rounded.

chow Cement Products, shown in Table 6–2 to be identical with the rates of corresponding branches of Soviet industry, are actually slightly higher if the figures had not been rounded. The Hangchow Clothing Factory derived its profits from a cost-plus processing fee—averaging about 6 percent of total sales—and customers provide the firm with the materials to be

TABLE 6–3

PROFITS IN RELATION TO WHOLESALE VALUE OF OUTPUT AND COSTS FOR SELECTED BRANCHES OF SOVIET INDUSTRY (1960 Data)*

Sector	*Profit as a Percentage of Wholesale Value of Output at Enterprise Prices*	*Profit as a Percentage of Total Cost*
All industry	9	10
Ferrous metallurgy	8.3	9
Machine-building and metal-working	11.5	13
Chemical	13.4	15
Paper	7.5	8
Cement	13	15
All light industry	6.5	7
Textiles	6.5	7
Sewing (includes clothing)	4.8	5.1
Leather products (includes shoes)	4.7	5

* Wholesale value of output at enterprise prices is apparently gross value of output (including taxes and net charges in inventories), which is expressed in terms of constant base-period commodity prices. Such prices may differ somewhat from current factory sales prices which are used for the Chinese enterprises. However, the differences are not usually so great as to make comparisons meaningless.

SOURCE: J. Thornton, "Estimation of Value Added and Average Returns to Capital in Soviet Industry from Cross-Section Data," *Journal of Political Economy*, Vol. LXXIII, No. 6 (December 1965), p. 626, Table 3.

processed. I was told by Hangchow Clothing's director that his firm is rather unusual in the way it does business and in the way in which its profits are calculated. He said that the profit margin of the firm is lower than that of most clothing factories. However, even Hangchow Clothing's profit margin is greater than that of the corresponding branch of industry (sewing) in Russia. Even from this very small sample of Chinese firms the data are clearly consistent with the fact that profit margins, in relation to both costs and prices, and the rate of profit remittances to the state budget are substantially higher in China's overall industrial sector than in Russia's.

Profit-margin data which I obtained from Soviet industrial enterprises surveyed in the early 1960's are also generally consistent with this fact. For example, profits as a percentage of total sales value of output in current prices at Moscow's Sverdlov Textile Enterprise was about 10 percent, at the Tinakov Clothing Firm in Kharkov it was 9.7 percent, at Leningrad and Moscow Machinery firms about 5 percent and 10 percent respectively, at a Kharkov ball-bearing factory about 20 percent.

Managerial Problems and Fiscal Policy

The breakdown of financial control at the enterprise level, accompanied by widespread abuses of the regime's fiscal policies during the 1958–61 period, contributed greatly to the sharp fall in state revenues, misallocation and misspending of funds, and the severe bottlenecks, imbalances, waste, and general inefficiency in the industrial sector.[47] The types of fiscal abuses and financial violations which became pervasive during this period at industrial enterprises have already been discussed in the sections on monetary policy and relevant legal rules of the game. They include, in part, using investment funds for working capital purposes and vice versa, inefficient and illicit use of extra-budgetary funds which grew sharply in magnitude during the Great Leap, overspending of wage funds and exceeding cost targets, tax evasion, improper and inadequate profit remittances to the state and so forth.

A sharp reduction in the powers and effectiveness of the Ministry of Finance during the Great Leap contributed considerably to the deterioration and eventual breakdown of China's fiscal system. The ministry experienced an even greater degree of decentralization of authority and functions without effective control, as well as a substantially greater reduction of personnel and decline in overall effectiveness than did the central banking system during this period. Financial control by local tax and revenue offices of the Ministry of Finance became very lax during the Great Leap as inexperienced Reds came to usurp the influence and powers of fiscal experts. The Ministry of State Control, which had performed some fiscal control and auditing functions, also became powerless and was finally formally abolished in 1959. There were sizable cutbacks in the staffs of the Ministry of Finance. Tax collectors, controllers, auditors, and accountants were diverted to other jobs. Many of the best-trained and most experienced Ministry of Finance personnel were of bourgeois origin. They, in particular, came under heavy attack and were grossly misutilized and abused by zealous party ideologists. There was a tendency to disparage professional accounting techniques and rational financial policies.

By 1960 actual enterprise-profit remittances to the state had fallen sharply below the budgeted figure, and this was also the case in 1961. Sales tax revenues also dropped sharply as production was cut back sharply and the country entered a period of depression.

During the Great Leap Period profit was officially supposed to be a top-priority enterprise success indicator along with gross output. However, party cadres tended to favor aggregate production as the key success indicator for ideological reasons. As a result, profit, costs, and general financial results suffered on a widespread scale.

Another factor which probably hindered—and may still do so to some extent—the efficient collection of enterprise turnover taxes and proper remittances of profits to the state has been that many state revenue personnel have thought that because profits of firms are, in any case, going to the State Treasury, it is of little importance to make a clear distinction between taxes and profits. The same Ministry of Finance revenue offices are responsible for supervising and controlling the transmission of profits, as well as the collection of taxes. Enterprises are likely to prefer to pay less tax and to earn larger profits since they can retain some of their profits. Furthermore, the time lag before payment must be made appears to be somewhat longer in the case of profit remittances than tax payments, especially in connection with above-plan profits, thus giving management greater financial leeway with larger enterprise profits. Planned profits are typically deducted automatically by the bank from the firm's account when they fall due, but there are lags in the final settlement of actual and total profit payments.

Prior to 1958 when enterprises kept 40 percent or more of their above-plan profits, they had strong motives for striving for an easy or low profit target in their negotiations with higher authorities during the planning process. For an easy profit target facilitated a large degree of overfulfillment, and hence greater retained profits. The tendency to strive for a low profit target may have been reduced with the 1958 reform which allowed enterprises to retain, on the average, 10 percent of actual profits earned. Apparently around 1961 the state reduced the percentage of earned profits that could be retained by firms. This formal reduction in financial independence, derived from retained profits, at the enterprise level may have given managers stronger motives for underreporting profits in order to increase unofficially their financial independence.

However, in 1962 a higher degree of centralized authority, supervision, and control began to evolve in the Ministry of Finance. This tightening of control within and by the Ministry of Finance in the 1960's has probably made it more difficult for enterprise managements to violate regulations and policies involving profit remittances and tax payment. Moreover, the staffs of the ministry have been enlarged and strengthened, with the Experts again coming to play a major role. Profits and costs apparently became important enterprise success indicators around mid-1962 or 1963 in an effort to stress economy and better financial results, which, in turn, provide for greater state revenues that can be used for investment purposes.

In general, and in spite of many problems which have persisted, fiscal policies and financial control have become much more effective in terms of industrial progress and managerial efficiency during the 1960's than in the 1958–61 period. However, the pendulum may well be swinging in a negative direction because of the antibureaucracy campaign and ideological extremism of the Cultural Revolution. As has been discussed in previous sections, profit is apparently being de-emphasized as a key success indicator, some official encouragement is being given to firms to violate "bureaucratic" financial policies, regulations, and controls, and inexperienced Reds or Super-Reds may be taking over important fiscal and financial functions.[48] How serious the consequences will be in terms of productive efficiency is anyone's guess, although they are likely to be quite serious if the situation persists or becomes significantly intensified.

A Brief Word about Fiscal Policy in India

As with monetary policy, the role of fiscal policy in India's economy is not directly comparable with that in Communist China in certain important respects.[49] In India, as in many developing mixed economies and all communist states, fiscal policy is aimed vigorously at generating state revenues which are used, in large part, for investment to build up and expand the public sector of the economy. During the 1950–59 period India's rate of gross fixed investment in relation to GNP was 14.9 percent, not much less than China's 1950–57 and 1952–59 rates of 15.9 percent and 17.5 percent, respectively. Much of India's industrial investment has been derived through private sources and foreign aid, although government investment has also played a major role. As has been the case in Red China, a substantial portion of state industrial investment in India has been wasteful and unproductive. (More about this later.)

The Indian government uses taxation in part to provide for more equable income distribution among the population at large, rather than making extensive use of fixed wage scales and comprehensive payroll planning as is done in China. However, equable income distribution does not seem to be an aim as vigorously pursued through Indian fiscal policy as the creation of large state revenues for government spending and investment. In fact, India's taxation policies have not apparently really done very much to bring about equable income distribution to the degree one would expect in a "socialistic" economy. On this score Red China is way ahead; probably no other country has as high a degree of equable income distribution or "classlessness."

In India, unlike China, fiscal policies—particularly tax measures—are also used quite extensively to encourage and discourage various types of managerial and enterprise behavior. The best that can be said in a nutshell about the impact of Indian taxation schemes on managerial effectiveness, productive efficiency, and industrial progress is that the net results are mixed, uncertain, and often conflicting. Individual income taxes and productive enterprise tax rates, particularly in the private sector, in India are generally higher than in most other countries. Industrial enterprises are subject to relatively high profit taxes and super-profit taxes, dividend and capital-gains taxes, and a variety of other special taxes and surtaxes. Individuals who have relatively large incomes are also subject to very high taxes of various types.

Indian tax regulations are also extremely complex, often incomprehensible, and frequently in a state of flux, thus causing considerable uncertainty for firms and their managements. Where fiscal incentives have been used—for example, tax exemptions, rebates, and reliefs, liberal depreciation allowances—too often the results desired by the government have not been forthcoming, and various unintended effects have emerged.

There seems to be considerable truth in the almost unanimous criticism among Indian businessmen—and many other groups—that excessive taxation and unclear regulations substantially hinder investment and the plow-back of profits in the private productive sector. This in turn tends to constrain significantly the creation of new private firms and the expansion or diversification of existing enterprises—often even where potential product markets exist. The Indian tax structure also encourages tax evasion, keeping several sets of books, bribery, and other forms of corruption that reinforce nepotism in staffing. A vast amount of potentially productive energy and ability is expended on the slippery slope of tax avoidance. Many enterprise owners and managers apparently feel strongly that larger profits and greater personal gain can be derived much more easily through tax evasion, abuses of state financial regulations and fiscal policies, and various other corruptive practices, rather than through hard work, increasing productivity and efficiency, or personal integrity. As a result, they behave accordingly.

In the realm of government spending and investment, India has made many of the same serious mistakes as Red China. However, the consequences in India have not been as disastrous as they were in China during the 1958–62 period. Nevertheless, the obsessive interest in heavy industry on the part of many of India's politicians and the resulting overinvestment in the public sector of heavy industry have contributed significantly to India's price inflation, economic instability, and the foreign-exchange crisis. The key roots of these economic problems can be traced, in large part, to India's Second Five-Year Plan, particularly the later years of the plan, and her Third Five-Year Plan of 1961–66. Overinvestment and grossly inefficient spending in the public sector—without adequately building up the required infrastructure, social-overhead capital, or feeder industries—have led to the same types of critical bottlenecks, imbalances, waste, idle capacity, and general inefficiency common to the Chinese economy in the 1950's and early 1960's.

Excessive and irrational government spending, particularly in India's public sector, without available resources to finance this spending have resulted in large budget deficits and huge public and foreign debts. This, in turn, has fostered price inflation, economic instability, and a depletion of foreign-exchange reserves. Fortunately for India, foreign aid has prevented the situation from becoming even much worse than it has been in recent years. Fiscal experts predicted that actual foreign-exchange requirements would be at least 25 percent greater than those provided for in India's Third Five-Year Plan. The government did not take heed of these predictions, which actually underestimated foreign-exchange requirements —in part because of the Pakistani-Indian War which evolved in 1965— and this has contributed substantially to India's current economic woes. The actual gap between planned expenditures and available resources during India's Third Five-Year Plan was even more than the $7 billion (U.S.)—nearly 20 percent of GNP—anticipated by prominent fiscal experts and economists.

In numerous cases there have been very sizable errors in cost estimates, lead times, and projected completion dates involving public-sector industries and projects. As is common in the public sector in many countries, enterprise managers and project administrators take no time in appealing to the state for more funds when cost estimates are overrun, or when operating expenses exceed the plan. Such funds have typically been granted in India, since state authorities have tended to feel that to deny them might hinder pet or prestige projects and critical production. This has contributed to the state's excessive deficit financing and price inflation.

There are some current signs, however, that the Indian government is taking a somewhat more hard-nosed and economical approach toward the public sector. For example, in 1966 there were some sizable cutbacks in excess manpower—with government approval—at some large public-sector steel and heavy engineering firms in Bihar and elsewhere. The usually very liberal foreign-exchange and import allowances have also been sharply reduced in the public sector.

The Indian government, like the Chinese regime, now appears to be moving its fiscal policies at least somewhat in the direction of more balanced economic growth and industrial development. However, Communist China seems to have a lead of several years in this change of emphasis, and China also is apparently pursuing her balanced-growth policy more vigorously than India.

Economic Stability

We are interested here in both price and general economic stability. A country may be said to have a relatively high degree of price stability when various major indexes of price change remain relatively stable over a protracted period of time. Price stability involves wages, interest rates, and foreign exchange rates, as well as factory, wholesale, and retail commodity prices.

General economic stability involves a condition of relatively full utilization of productive factors; or, at least as a minimum, the avoidance of abrupt and major disruptions in the employment of the country's available productive resources. Such stability is a relative matter because no economy can fully utilize all factors of production all of the time. If, however, a country suffers periods of substantial unemployment of resources, followed by periods of overutilization of the same types of resources, it is unstable.

General economic stability also usually implies some fairly consistent growth rate as well. Production and national and per capita incomes grow, as do population and work forces, real capital is added, and reclamation projects add to land stocks. A country which has the same per capita income year after year may be stable but not very desirably so, given the existence of possibilities for improvements in production and incomes through progressively improving management, labor quality and productivity, additional capital, and technological developments.

The degree of general economic stability over time in a given country not only influences the degree of managerial effectiveness, productive efficiency, and industrial progress achieved at the enterprise level, but is itself also influenced by what goes on at industrial enterprises. There is actually a circular relationship here, which becomes a vicious circle further aggravating instability during periods of excessive boom or recession. Measurement of general economic stability is really one of the key end-point quantitative aspects of the whole analysis of environmental constraint on industrial management contained in this book. Aggregate quantitative analysis of Red China's economy is the subject of Chapter 8. Our chief interest here is in treating economic instability as an independent external constraint on firms and their managements, particularly those dimensions of instability which are substantially or entirely beyond the control of numerous individual enterprises which together make up a major portion of the total industrial sector.

Political actions and public opinion following major economic crises in many countries often focus rightly or wrongly on the firm as the major culprit. However, enterprises and their owners and/or managements typically also pay a high price for such instability. But frequently firms and their owners and/or managers are held responsible for adverse economic conditions over which they have relatively little or no control.

Price Stability[50]

Extreme price inflation in Republican China and some of its major impact on industrial enterprises have already been discussed in our sections on monetary and fiscal policy, and there is no need to belabor the point here. In these earlier sections the point was made that more effective monetary and fiscal policies and central banking could have done much to check and reduce rampant price inflation in pre-1949 China. However, they could not have eliminated price instability because there were various other forces at work that could not be dealt with in substantial part through even sound monetary and fiscal policies. Crop failures in China's primitive, subsistence-level agricultural sector were often aggravated greatly by floods and poor weather conditions; wars and strikes would have caused major shifts in prices and considerable price instability during many years. Major shifts in external commodity prices involving China's imports and exports—the latter being based largely on the output of her precarious agricultural sector—would have had an unstabilizing effect on the country's export earnings and purchasing power in world markets, thus contributing to price instability (usually inflation) at home.

Major price changes in China's agricultural sector and abrupt shifts in prices paid for imports and received for exports contributed greatly to price instability and serious inflation in the industrial sector. The bulk of Republican China's industrial sector—chiefly textiles, food processing, and light-industry consumer goods—was highly dependent on raw materials from the agricultural sector, and also on imported producer goods, components, and spare parts in numerous cases.

China's economy was essentially a market economy during this era, and price inflation, which proceeded at unpredictable rates, led firms to stay away from cash and to hold things (inventories, materials, equipment). The resulting inventory speculation, hoarding, and overinvestment caused still more pressure on commodity prices and further increased the risks of business enterprises. Long delays in paying bills, as well as credit and profit squeezes, had percolating effects throughout the industrial sector.

Under China's Communist regime a relatively high degree of price stability has been maintained through comprehensive state planning, in conjunction with various devices, which have been discussed briefly in the section on monetary policy. With the exception of the prices of certain agricultural commodities, usually produced on small private plots, most prices are determined by state authorities in Red China. This includes product and factor prices, services, wages, and interest rates. Market forces play only a relatively independent and major role in connection with the above-mentioned agricultural goods, and price changes and inflation have been most pronounced—though quite isolated and generally not too serious—in the uncontrolled portion of the agricultural sector.

Official retail price indexes record an annual increase of only barely 1 percent from 1951 to mid-1959, with the largest rises being only 3 percent and 2 percent in 1953 and 1957, respectively. There are no indications of prolonged serious inflation since 1959. These indexes probably have a downward bias because they are based chiefly on controlled prices which were at times below real equilibrium levels. Black-market prices apparently exceeded official prices for relatively short periods in 1953, 1956, and 1960–62. However, these qualifications do not negate the basic contention that price increases in Red China have been quite modest. Potential excess demand has been eliminated by other means, which have been discussed in the section on monetary policy. Some of these have included formal and de facto rationing, changing production plans, queues, wage controls, and at times bond sales to the public and savings-deposit drives. During the immediate aftermath of the Great Leap, when industrial production fell very sharply, there was a large cutback in industrial employment which cut the wage bill accordingly, reduced purchasing power, and hence kept inflation in check.

A prominent Canadian industrialist checked the prices of many products in the stores of some of Red China's larger cities in 1964.[51] I checked the prices of many of the same items in 1966 and found no significant differences. A number of Western diplomats who had been in Red China for some time told me that China has had a relatively high degree of price stability in all sectors—industrial, wholesale, agricultural, as well as retail—and even in foreign markets prices paid for imports and received for exports have not generally fluctuated very widely in recent years.

The prices paid to industrial enterprises for their outputs have probably, on the average, been even more stable than retail prices, as have been the wholesale prices paid to middlemen because they usually do not include turnover taxes. Retail prices are not necessarily related to factory costs or sales prices, wholesale prices, or prices paid for imports. Large deviations in retail prices, as compared with these other prices are common, because of variable sales taxes levied at the retail level, and to a much lesser extent retail profit margins. At the industrial-enterprise level there are price changes and new prices created where significant modifications are made in existing products and where custom-built or new products are involved. However, this does not generally lead to overt inflationary pressures or serious uncertainty. Such price changes and new product prices are approved in the enterprise plan.

Price stability in the industrial sector tends to make financial planning relatively easy, since prices can be predicted with considerable certainty in the enterprise plan. However, as has been noted elsewhere, financial planning is based on, and largely subservient to, physical planning in real terms. Hence, mere price controls and the comprehensive system of fixed prices and state planning used to maintain stability do not lead to an optimum situation in numerous instances because the result of such a system is frequently shortages of items for which prices are artificially maintained. Such situations may be as disruptive to firms as actual price changes, since they typically lead to supply breakdowns; production bottlenecks; resources that are mismatched, overutilized, and idle; waste; and inefficiency which often snowballs through the industrial sector.

By preventing prices from responding to conditions of real supply and demand a form of concealed inflation actually evolves. In turn, this leads to relatively large supply departments including sizable staffs of expeditors at many enterprises. It also leads to pressures, hard bargaining, and gamesmanship with higher-level planners in an attempt to obtain more resources, deflection of supplies from other firms and, at times, black-marketing and other illicit procurement activities. Where serious price inflation and the resulting uncertainty lead to hoarding and inventory speculation with the aim of reaping speculative profits and staying in business in a market economy, concealed inflation tends to encourage hoarding and the understating of productive capacity—with the primary purpose of insuring plan fulfillment in the face of uncertainty involving critical resource shortages.

India's economy also experienced a relatively high degree of price stability—especially for a poor, newly developing nation—during the 1952–62 period.[52] During this period India's standard monetary unit, the rupee, depreciated only at an annual average rate of 2.3 percent. Most of the major official price indexes showed annual average increases of no more than about 3 percent, with none higher than around 4 percent. The price increases that did occur from year to year were, for the most part, neither abrupt nor very sharp. However, many commodities were still subject to price controls. This has led to concealed inflation, which results in the types of managerial and enterprise problems common to Red China, though not to the same degree, at least until recent times.

Since 1963 price inflation has been rising quite sharply, and it has become an acute problem since about 1965. In 1963 there was also a relatively sharp rise of 7 percent in the wholesale price index, and sizable increases in various other price indexes. Since 1964 major price indexes have been rising by more than 10 percent in an erratic and largely unpredictable manner, while price increases in a wide range of individual commodities have been even sharper and more erratic. For example, during the month of June 1966 alone many prices rose by 15 percent and more. Price inflation has also severely hindered India's foreign exchange position, and even her devaluation of the rupee—from about 4.75 to 7.50 to the U.S. dollar—has not increased exports as much as had been hoped for. Some of the major reasons for India's current serious price inflation have been noted earlier, a major one being poor agricultural performance further aggravated by monsoons, floods, and droughts.

With this serious price inflation many more items have become subject to price controls. This has resulted in considerable concealed inflation.

The various enterprise and managerial practices that typically accompany and aggravate both concealed and overt inflation have become intensified. The negative impacts that such practices and serious price inflation tend to have on managerial effectiveness, productive efficiency, and general industrial progress have been mentioned elsewhere and need not be repeated here.

General Economic Stability

The same factors that contributed greatly to extreme price inflation and price instability also contributed to general economic stability in Republican China, particularly during the period 1937–49.

However, unlike Communist China, ideological extremism on the part of the Kuomintang regime was not a major cause of economic instability in Republican China. If one looks only at China's GNP, per capita income, industrial production, and agricultural performance in current prices during the 1937–49 period, the magnitude of general economic instability that actually existed would be grossly deceptive and understated because of rampant price inflation. If one takes fully into account the rampant price inflation and looks at performance in real or physical terms, one would find that real GNP, per capita incomes, industrial and agricultural output, employment, and per capita consumption all fell sharply and erratically, on the downside, during the decade or so of Kuomintang rule, with the nadir and grand finale reached at the end of the 1940's.

In the industrial sector during this era, severe economic instability meant growing idle capacity and underemployment of productive resources including mass urban unemployment and plant shutdowns, growing shortages of all types of materials, equipment, components, and other supplies, including, of course, critical imports, the collapse of product markets, and so forth. Those few firms that could obtain abundant supplies often tended to greatly overutilize resources and productive capacity in the short run. This typically led to serious breakdowns in operations as equipment and labor could not endure the exhausting pace for long. But usually supply failures and underemployment of productive factors occurred before extreme overutilization of resources emerged.

When the Communists came to power in China, they had economic stability coupled with growth as a major objective. This is implied in the Marxist-Leninist's principle of proportionate development of the economy. The regime was also convinced that a communist-type planned economy means, by implication, relative economic stability which would be consistent with rapid and sustained progress. In order to achieve this the regime was committed to reasonably full employment of available productive factors with the aim of maximizing the production of useful goods and services.

In practice, Red China has been faced with a stability problem common to the Soviet Union—that is, one where past plans have focused too many resources in industries, most notably the heavy-industry sector, which became overexpanded in relation to demand, while putting too few resources into others. When sectoral imbalances have become critical, and are recognized as such by the regime, to increase resources substantially in deficient sectors involves major shifts of resources out of other sectors. Where complex technology is involved, such transfers cannot be made easily or in a very stable way. Similarly, if much skilled manpower is required, major changes may be needed in educational and manpower plans. If the various types of resource transfers and related plan changes are to be made, there are difficult problems involved in maintaining production and planned rates of growth elsewhere while rapidly building up the deficient or new sector.

A considerable amount of idle resources and economic instability is likely to occur as the major transfers and changes take place, even though some of the outward manifestations of such shifts are not seen in the same way as in capitalist countries when similar shifts occur. In general, resource shifts have frequently caused stability problems in the Chinese economy, and such problems are continuing today. However, dramatic resource shifts leading to truly severe economic instability have only evolved from intensive and prolonged periods of ideological extremism.

A brief quantitative examination of economic stability in Red China since 1949 is in order here, even though some of the data will be repeated in our more comprehensive analysis of China's economic performance presented in Chapter 7.

Some Quantitative Indicators of Economic Stability for Red China

If we look at some key indicators of Communist China's aggregate performance for the 1949–66 period as a whole, it is evident that China has achieved substantial economic growth, industrial progress, and, by implication, greater managerial effectiveness, in spite of the Great Leap Forward and its disastrous aftermath. For example, aggregate GNP grew at an average annual (compound) rate of about 6 percent during the period, per capita income by roughly 4 percent,[53] industrial production by approximately 11 percent,[54] industrial employment by roughly 10 percent, and total nonagricultural employment by nearly 4 percent.[55] These growth figures compare favorably with the rates achieved by the vast majority of developing countries—not to mention advanced and stagnant underdeveloped economies—during the same period.

The Soviet Union achieved the annual average rate of growth in industrial production of 9.6 percent during the 1949–65 period, somewhat lower than China's rate. However, Russia's industrial growth has been much steadier and sustained than China's, although it has been declining somewhat in the 1960's.[56]

China's growth record has been achieved with, and in spite of, erratic performance and very sharp periods of economic instability, most notably during the superficial boom of the Great Leap and the severe economic depression of the early 1960's. If it had not been for these periods of severe instability, Red China's economic and industrial performance record would have been substantially even more impressive. The Great Leap and subsequent depression have cost Red China at least several years—perhaps as many as six or seven—in total industrial output, aggregate agricultural production, and overall economic growth. It might possibly take a decade from the height of the Great Leap before China achieves the previous peak level of per capita income, and even longer for per capita agricultural output and caloric intake.[57]

During the 1949–57 period Communist China did maintain a favorable degree of general economic stability coupled with impressive growth and development along a broad front. In the initial years of economic rehabilitation, 1949–52, GNP increased by 70 percent, with gains of about 20 percent being achieved in 1951 and 1952. Real per capita income also rose sharply. Industrial production—excluding handicrafts—grew at an annual average rate of 27 percent during the period 1950–52 as existing idle capacity and resources were quickly put into use. The annual average industrial growth rate including handicrafts was about 35 percent. Industrial employment increased at an average annual rate of 20 percent, and total nonagricultural (urban) employment by roughly 12 percent during 1950–52.

During China's First Five-Year Plan, rates of growth were not as impressive because the large backlogs or windfalls derived from putting into use idle productive resources were pretty much absorbed, and new investment was required for sustained progress. However, this was nevertheless a period of impressive economic progress and general stability. From 1952 through 1957 GNP grew steadily by an annual average rate of approximately 7.5 to 8.5 percent, and per capita income by probably at least 4 percent and possibly by as much as 6 percent. Industrial production grew at an average annual rate of 14 percent—16 percent if handicrafts are included—during 1953–57. Industrial performance was more erratic than aggregate GNP growth, but this did not result in very serious economic instability. For example, industrial output grew by 25 percent in 1953, but this was due largely to the existing plant capacity not put into use previously and the utilization of new capacity created during the 1950–52 period. Industrial production took a breathing spell during 1955 when it increased by less than 1 percent over 1954.

In spite of such erratic industrial growth during China's First Five-Year

Plan, probably most firms in operation made reasonably full use of available factors of production. At times the planners may have chosen to keep productive resources at work rather than call an immediate halt to unneeded or useless production; they probably rationalized—often rationally—that the procedure was useful for stockpiling, to maintain existing levels of employment, to keep production going—even useless production—in order to educate and train the work force, and/or for various psychological reasons. However, most output did adequately serve the functional or end use intended. In general, real improvements in managerial effectiveness and productive efficiency resulting in substantial industrial progress were achieved during the 1953–57 period. On the employment side, industrial employment grew by an average annual rate of roughly 8.5 percent during this era, but nonagricultural employment as a whole grew only at the modest annual rate of 1.5 percent. Agricultural production increased quite steadily and significantly during this period.[58]

During the 1958–60 Great Leap period aggregate economic and industrial indicators showed a very sharp rise, followed by a sharp decline by 1960–61. However, various sources and expert estimates disagree with the magnitudes and precise timing of these extreme upward fluctuations which represent great general economic instability.

Available sources and estimates all agree that total GNP and per capita income both increased sharply during 1957–58. Reconstructed Chinese Communist estimates place the increase in GNP at more than 30 percent, and in per capita terms at more than 25 percent. The lowest available Western estimates place both aggregate and per capita growth for 1957–58 at about 10 percent. Most available sources show a continued increase in both aggregate and per capita GNP in 1959 as compared with 1958, with total GNP growing in the range of 7 to 22 percent, and per capita income by as much as 16.5 percent. Only one Western estimate—that of T. C. Liu—shows decreases in GNP (of about 3 percent) and per capita income (roughly 5 percent) for 1959, claiming that agricultural output had already fallen sharply before the end of 1959. Few experts agree with him, and I am in the camp that feels strongly that GNP and per capita income did not drop until 1960. However, a substantial but indeterminable proportion of the statistical growth was unreal because it reflected unusable and unneeded output.

For 1958–60 the annual average rate of industrial growth was probably about 20 percent to 25 percent. This average growth was actually achieved at a declining rate with the figures for 1958, 1959, and 1960 being approximately 31 percent, 26 percent, and 4 percent respectively. Statistics reflect a 100 percent increase in total industrial growth from 1957 to the end of 1960, but only about 72 percent until mid-1960. By the end of 1960 it was no doubt clear to the regime that a severe economic depression was setting in. The regime declared that Red China's Second Five-Year Plan, which began with the introduction of the Great Leap in 1958, was fulfilled two years ahead of schedule; but actually the plan was abandoned because of the severe economic crisis that was emerging.

Industrial employment trebled from about 8 million in 1957 to nearly 24 million in 1958 with the large expansion of existing plants and the establishment of 300,000 new factories and workshops, mostly small-scale and many in rural areas. Nearly two-thirds of the increase consisted of newly hired personnel, the bulk coming from the agricultural sector. Handicraftsmen, reclassified as industrial personnel, accounted for another 4.5 million, and 1.3 million other nonagricultural personnel were transferred to industry, mostly from trade and government administration. Roughly 7 million of the new industrial personnel were added to the old industrial firms and more than 8 million to new industrial establishments. Total nonagricultural employment increased by 43 percent from 1957 to 1958. Most of this increase came from hiring by industrial plants that were attempting to fulfill Great Leap production targets typically without regard for costs. In 1959 industrial, urban, and nonagricultural employment all began to decline.

The seeds for the severe agricultural crisis were actually laid in 1958 with the introduction of ideologically motivated and irrational agricultural policies, programs, and techniques, as well as the transfer of millions of farm workers to nonagricultural employment. Droughts, floods, and typhoons of unusual severity during the 1959–61 period caused tremendous losses in arable land, crops, and farm draft animals. Even without the Great Leap programs Red China would have undoubtedly faced an agricultural crisis in the early 1960's, but it would not have been nearly as severe.

The experts all agree that the low point in China's economic depression following the Great Leap was reached during the 1960–62 period, but there is some disagreement as to the precise year or quarter. GNP probably fell by at least 25 percent and possibly more than 30 percent from the peak reached toward the end of the 1950's; per capita income fell even more sharply. The nation was on the brink of severe famine during this period. Industrial production fell in the range of 40 to 45 percent from the Great Leap peak, and the industrial sector was probably operating at less than 50 percent capacity.

In 1960–61 at least 10 million people returned to the farms from nonagricultural employment. Many others lost their jobs but remained in the cities. By the end of 1962 the drop in nonagricultural employment was well over 10 million, and most of this drop occurred in the industrial sector.

Even without the Soviet pullout in mid-1960 and critical shortages of raw materials from the agricultural sector required by light industry, severe overutilization and misutilization of productive capacity, the exhaustion of the labor force, and the crisis in the food supply caused chiefly by the irrational policies and programs of the Great Leap Forward, would have still been severe enough to bring an abortive end to the Leap and economic collapse. If Red China's economy had been a market economy during the Great Leap, thousands of firms would have closed down much sooner, and thousands more would have cut back production much faster.

It took Communist China some three years to officially call a halt to the Great Leap, while in a market economy the large cutbacks, retrenchment, and economic downturn would have revealed themselves in a matter of months. In both cases an excessive boom would have still led to an economic depression, but if China had been a market economy, the damage, waste, and magnitude of the depression might not have been nearly as great. But Red China's was not a market economy, and she experienced the worst depression ever in a communist country.

Red China's economic recovery began around 1962 or early 1963. During the 1962–66 period GNP probably grew at an average annual rate of at least 5 percent and possibly as high as 7 or 8 percent, and per capita income at a rate somewhat lower because of population increase. The gross value of industrial production increased at an average annual rate of approximately 12 percent during the 1962–65 period, with rates of 15 percent and 14 percent being achieved in 1964 and 1965, respectively. By the end of 1965 total industrial production probably surpassed the 1958 level and was about 50 percent greater than the volume achieved in 1957.[59]

The Chinese Communists claim that industrial output grew by 20 percent in 1966 over 1965.[60] If this figure is accurate, this would mean an average growth rate of about 14 percent during the 1963–66 period. It is conceivable that a 20 percent increase in industrial production could have been achieved in 1966, since the Red Guards, the army, or the people's militia had not yet been sent to factories—or the farms—and the Cultural Revolution did not break out into violence or serious civil strife until the end of December of that year. Many of the industrial enterprises surveyed in 1966 claimed substantial increases in production targets over 1965, and their managers told me that the 1966 quarterly targets to date were being met in most cases. (Data on 1966 enterprise targets will be presented in a later chapter.) On the other hand, the Chinese industrial growth figure of 20 percent for 1966 could be an exaggeration for propaganda, ideological, and motivational purposes. In any event, it is likely that sizable gains—quite possibly 15 percent—were made in industrial growth in 1966 and that the 1963–66 period was one of steady overall growth and relative economic stability. Moreover, industrial growth has been much more real and meaningful than the statistical growth reported during the Great Leap. In general, and if the pendulum swings in the direction of ideological moderation, Red China is likely to reach the pre-Great Leap peak in aggregate industrial output within the next few years.

Heavy industry probably recovered from the economic depression by the end of 1965, with aggregate output being about double the 1957 level. Recovery and growth have probably been slower in light industry and handicrafts, largely because of the persistent shortage of raw materials from the agricultural sector.[61] Chinese Communist pronouncements claim bumper crops and record harvests for 1966.[62] The agricultural sector has made steady, though still inadequate, gains since about 1962, and 1957 per capita levels of farm output or caloric intake have probably not yet been achieved. When China's imported artificial-fiber and fertilizer plants are put into full use, this could lead to substantial increases in light industry and handicrafts production, as well as farm output.

Although industrial employment increased somewhat during the 1962–65 period, it stood at approximately 14 million at the end of 1965, still some 40 percent below the 1958 peak. In 1966 industrial employment may have reached 15 million. However, industrial labor productivity is undoubtedly significantly higher and more meaningful than it was during the Great Leap. At the end of 1964 total nonagricultural employment stood at 45.8 million, still over 20 percent below the 1958 peak level of about 56.9 million.

When I was in Red China in 1966, the country seemed to be experiencing relative economic stability, progress, and prosperity. It is still too early to tell what the phase of ideological extremism—in the form of the Great Proletarian Cultural Revolution—has cost China in economic stability, managerial effectiveness, or industrial progress. The losses are likely to be large if ideological extremism persists.

A *Comment on Economic Stability in India*

While Red China has done significantly better than India in terms of aggregate and per capita measures of economic growth and industrial progress since 1949, economic instability per se has probably not been as serious a constraint on managerial effectiveness and industrial progress in the Indian economy in the past seventeen years.[63] Nothing nearly as severe or damaging as the Chinese Great Leap and subsequent depression has occurred in India.

During the 1949–66 period India achieved an average annual growth rate in GNP of roughly 3.5 percent, compared with about 6 percent for China. Per capita income grew at an average annual rate of roughly 1.4 percent, compared with approximately 4 percent for China. India's aggregate and per capita growth have by no means been steady or sustained. There have even been no growth or actual declines in GNP and per capita income from the previous year in 1952–53, 1954–55, 1960–62, and 1965–66, all of which have led to economic instability and related industrial and managerial problems. However, fluctuations—either upward or downward—in GNP and per capita income have never been greater than 10 percent from year to year, and in most cases they have been significantly less. Hence, general economic instability has not been as extreme or damaging in India as in Red China.

Fluctuations in agricultural production have contributed greatly to general economic instability in India. While India's aggregate agricultural production has increased modestly since 1949, this growth has been erratic, barely keeping up with population growth in many years, and falling below it in some. Abnormal droughts during 1965–66 caused a severe agricultural crisis, which, in turn, led to serious stability problems and actual declines in both GNP and per capita income of roughly 6 percent and 4 percent, respectively.

During the 1949–66 period India's industrial output grew at an average annual rate of about 6.5 percent, compared with 11 percent for China. However, India's industrial growth was substantially more stable and sustained than China's over this period, in spite of brief periods of quite serious instability. Indian industrial production fell off in 1965 and stagnated through most of 1966. Industrial employment has grown at an annual average rate of about 2 to 2.5 percent since 1949. This growth has been quite steady and sustained, although industrial employment has stagnated in the last few years, probably declining in 1965 and possibly in the first half of 1966 as well. There are some indications and preliminary estimates suggesting that industrial growth, as well as GNP and per capita income, had begun to increase modestly by late 1966, and modest growth probably continued in 1967. However, such growth is probably not as substantial as that achieved by Red China annually during the 1963–66 period.

Organization of Capital Markets

Republican China

In Republican China the banks, business profits, individuals with wealth and, of course, supplier credit were the only potential sources of capital—both investment and working capital—available to industrial enterprises. Formal or organized capital markets were highly underdeveloped, and personal relationships—in politics, family, close friendships, favoritism—played the dominant role in the granting of funds to productive firms. Apart from the commercial banks, private lending institutions, such as those found in the United States and elsewhere—for example, savings and loan companies, life insurance firms, pension plans, finance companies—were practically nonexistent. Those that did exist had negligible amounts of funds available for industrial firms, as did the few existing governmental financial institutions.

As inflation became rampant, the cost of available capital soared, capital scarcity and credit squeeze became severe, the value of money capital declined sharply, and enterprise profits approached zero levels, with numerous firms experiencing large losses, shutdowns, and bankruptcy. Those relatively few firms that had, or could get, capital for investment, expansion, diversification, or similar purposes typically preferred not to take the precarious risks involved. Instead they channeled their efforts into inventory speculation and hoarding. More often than not, those few firms that were willing to use available capital to increase production could not obtain the necessary equipment, components, or materials to do so.

If it were not for severe inflation and economic collapse, the informal capital markets—which operated on a personal and individual level, in conjunction with the potential entrepreneurship that existed among businessmen in Republican China—could have contributed more significantly to economic development. There tended to be a bond of trust among businessmen in pre-1949 China, as there is today in Hong Kong, Singapore, and other places where there are large communities of Chinese businessmen. They were often willing to make loans, even sizable ones, and extend credits to one another without even signing formal contracts. Not to meet financial commitments would have meant great loss of face, disgrace, and loss of reputation; and these were generally adequate penalties or pressures to induce businessmen to try to meet their financial obligations.

However, funds available through such informal capital markets also grew increasingly scarce and costly as inflation mounted. But even if it were not for inflation, existing capital markets by themselves could not have really done a great deal to achieve really substantial economic development or industrial progress. In both the informal as well as formal capital markets, personal and subjective factors, rather than an analysis of productive efficiency or economic contribution to society, were more often than not the key criteria in making capital available. Furthermore, business entrepreneurs typically preferred to invest in commercial, rather than industrial, ventures, and when they did invest in industry, this usually entailed relatively small-scale operations. In fact, there was little indigenous capital available for financing large-scale industrial enterprises, and few were willing to take the risks entailed in embarking on such a venture. This would have probably been the case—but, of course, to a substantially lesser degree—even if inflation had not been as severe, given the other negative environmental constraints that existed.

Communist China

Under China's Communist regime the state plays the omniscient and omnipotent role in the organization and operation of capital markets. The great bulk of both fixed- and working-capital funds of industrial enterprises is allocated through the state budget and banking system, both of which, in turn, distribute funds on the basis of the planners' priorities expressed in physical terms in the national economic plan.

The way that capital markets operate in Red China and the financial constraints on industrial enterprises and their managers have already been discussed in the sections on monetary and fiscal policy. We have also noted previously that the absence of interest or rent charges on funds allocated to enterprises deters efficient resource allocation and utilization in many instances. However, in spite of many problems and in spite of the Great Leap era when financial planning and control were grossly ineffective, Red China has done much better on the whole—and specifically in terms of industrial progress and managerial effectiveness—in providing funds to productive enterprises than Republican China did through its various capital markets.

Since the state in Communist China controls the nation's financial resources, the state, rather than individuals or enterprises, also plays the key and omniscient entrepreneurial role in industry through the overall state plan. Such major entrepreneurial decisions as expansion to achieve economies of scale and/or to serve potential markets that exist, as well as entry into new markets, diversification, and the like, are made by state planners rather than by enterprise managers. In fact, firms or their managements usually do not even have the right to introduce new technology or a new cost-saving device involving a fairly modest expenditure of, say, $2,000 or to develop a new product or market of much importance unless such an action is sanctioned by the formally approved plan.

This places great constraints on independent entrepreneurship and innovation of a major nature at the enterprise level, although the state does encourage enterprise personnel of all types to initiate and introduce innovations and improvements of a relatively minor nature involving small amounts of funds. In a relatively backward economy, such as China's, substantial gains in productive efficiency and industrial progress can, and do, result from modest innovations and grass-roots entrepreneurship. But as Chinese industry continues to develop and becomes more complex, it will become increasingly more difficult for the state to play effectively the role of omniscient entrepreneur and distributor of funds. There is a limit to the number of new capital projects and ventures that can be effectively initiated, planned, implemented, and controlled in a comprehensively planned economy. Hence, a growing number of lost opportunities of a major nature are likely to evolve in time because of rigid constraints on financial and entrepreneurial freedom at the individual and enterprise levels in Chinese industry—that is, unless Red China's system of state planning and capital markets undergoes major basic changes.

A Comment on India

India's system of capital markets allows for considerably more entrepreneurial freedom of a major nature at the individual and enterprise levels than does Red China's. Various sociological-cultural, political-legal, and other economic factors dealt with in this study tend to be substantially greater negative constraints on managerial effectiveness and industrial progress in India than the nature or general effectiveness of her capital markets. For example, high taxes which bite greatly into profits and dominant attitudes among individual investor potential and firms alike tend to constrain large-scale private investment in industry—often even where quite lucrative potential-market opportunities might exist.

It is true that favoritism, subjectivism, excessive bureaucratic procedures, politics, and personal factors (as opposed to economic criteria), long delays in securing funds, and particularly in most recent years the rising cost of capital and serious credit squeezes all hinder the availability as well as the efficient allocation and use of money capital in Indian industry. It is also true that the public sector has been increasingly favored in the allocation of funds, often to the detriment of private industry, and that there has been much waste in the use of funds in the public sector in particular, and to a lesser degree in the private sector. Various major credit institutions that have been set up by the government have given the politicians and the state a considerable amount of direct control over the public sector and indirect control over the private sector. Frequently such control hinders managerial effectiveness and productive efficiency in both sectors.

In spite of many problems—some of them quite serious—India has a relatively well-organized and well-functioning system of capital markets, as compared with those in most poor or developing mixed and capitalistic economies. There is also a great deal of "black-market" money in the Indian economy, and many firms obtain funds of this type through various channels. The availability of funds—apart from foreign exchange—is not generally as critical a problem for firms as obtaining desired equipment, components, spare parts, or materials of various kinds.

India's commercial banks are a major supplier of short-term credits to industrial firms. Most of the financial resources in the banking sector are greatly concentrated in a small number of large banks with branches in many parts of the country. Most of the other banks are very limited in financial resources. Commercial banks are usually unwilling to advance long-term loans against fixed assets, and they typically make only medium-term loans provided for in India's five-year plans.

India's stock exchanges in seven major cities comprise one source of long-term capital for industrial enterprises. There are more than two thousand security issues—nearly two thirds common stock, over 25 percent preferred stock, and less than 10 percent debentures—listed on these exchanges. However, purchases and shares are concentrated in a small number of listed securities—usually those which promise substantial quick gains and those of a small number of progressive and prestigious firms with managements that are highly regarded and trusted by the public. In general, only a very limited number of Indian companies can successfully and efficiently raise money through public issues.

The bulk of outside long- and medium-term capital, and some of the short-term capital available to industrial enterprises is provided by a variety of financial institutions—the large majority being governmental organizations—which have been established since India gained her independence in 1947. There are some general financial institutions serving a wide range of sectors and types of firms; but the majority concentrate on public- or private-sector financing, specific branches of industry, or large, medium, or small enterprises. Among India's major financial institutions which provide capital to industry are the Industrial Finance Corporation of India, Refinance Corporation of India, National Industrial Development Corporation, Industrial Credit and Investment Corporation, Industrial Credit and Investment Corporation, National Small Industries Corporation, Life Insurance Corporation of India, and the Industrial Development Bank set up in 1964. Each of India's states also has its own financial corporation.

Factor Endowment

The term "factor endowment," as used in this study, is well known to economists and has already been defined, in general, and with regard to its key components, in Chapter 2. The factors of production of greatest interest here are land—with the emphasis on agricultural land, climate, natural mineral resources, and derived materials for industry—and labor, with the emphasis on population problems and the general health and energy of the labor force. We have already considered the qualitative dimension of labor, in terms of skill and knowledge, in our education chapter. Management (including entrepreneurship) as a factor of production is the central focus of the entire analysis in this book, and there is no need to treat it as a separate variable in this section. Not a great deal of additional space needs to be devoted to capital as a factor of production since it has been a major subject of discussion in the sections on fiscal policy, view toward wealth, and elsewhere.

Mineral Resources

We shall deal with China's mineral resources first and then proceed to a discussion of her agricultural sector.

The availability of different kinds of minerals in any country has a major bearing on managerial effectiveness, productive efficiency, and general progress in the industrial sector. If the country is endowed with an abundant and diversified mineral-resource base which is exploited, and where the minerals are accessible and relatively inexpensive to exploit, the industrial-management task tends to be substantially easier. More efficient choices in factor inputs can be made at industrial enterprises, a wider change of products can be produced more cheaply and economically, and planning the supply of required mineral inputs can be carried out with greater certainty in a richly endowed country, other things being equal, than in a country with poor resources. A nation's mineral-resource base tends to have a significant impact also on various other critical elements of the management process in industry, such as organization structures, staffing requirements, research and development, and so forth. It also tends to affect patterns of imports and exports in the industrial sector, as well as the country's foreign-exchange reserves and balance-of-payments position over a period of time.

China has always been favorably endowed with a wide range of mineral resources. However, until the Communists came to power, relatively little was done to effectively exploit and develop these resources. The types of educational, sociological-cultural, political, legal, and economic constraints, most of which retarded industrial progress in Old China, also retarded the development of mineral resources.

Since the Communist regime came to power in China and embarked on comprehensive development planning, high priority has been given to the exploitation and utilization of the country's mineral resources.[64] Educational programs have produced large numbers of specialists needed for this purpose, and much manpower has been allocated to the mining sector. Substantial amounts of capital investment and technology have also been allocated to the mining sector. Vast sums of money have been spent on geological surveys and exploration work. Hydroelectric power and transportation facilities, mainly railroads, have been greatly expanded to serve the mining, mineral, and metal-processing sectors. (Power and transportation will be dealt with in the section on social overhead capital.) Soviet aid—in the form of technical assistants and the provision of technology and other strategic supplies—also greatly facilitated the development of Red China's natural resources in the 1950's.

Contrary to the exaggerated claims of peak levels of mineral output achieved during the Great Leap Forward, the Great Leap period actually resulted in a temporary setback in the exploitation and utilization of China's mineral resources. The Soviet pullout in mid-1960 further aggravated the situation. However, during the 1960's China recovered from these setbacks and has continued to make considerable progress in the mining sector, despite a variety of serious problems and constraints which still exist—especially in knowledge, skill, transportation, and technology. China also has geographical and geological idiosyncrasies, so that surpluses and deficiencies exist in both actual mineral production and potential mineral production.

Barring severe ideological extremism, Red China should, however, continue to make impressive progress in the exploitation, development, and utilization of her mineral resources in the future. Moreover, China's mineral-resource base is diversified enough to place her in a relatively favorable position to adjust to the shifting importance of different kinds of basic materials in the development of her overall industrial sector and in her potential export markets. While India, for a poor developing country, is also relatively richly endowed in mineral resources and electric-power potential, Communist China has made substantially more progress in this sphere to date, and will probably continue to maintain her lead over India in the future.

Communist China is now a leading world mineral producer in absolute terms, but not yet in per capita output. Her estimated 1965 mineral-output value (mine output, plus added value derived from smelting and processing) of approximately $4 billion (U.S.) ranked the country just within the top ten mineral-producing nations in the world. Although still substantially behind that of Japan—chiefly because of Japan's large smelting and processing sectors, rather than her mining output—China's mineral-output value exceeded that of the rest of the Far Eastern countries put together. China has been exporting a growing volume of minerals and metals. The mining component of the Chinese mineral industry remained substantially stronger than the metallurgical component in 1965–66.

The map shown on the cover of this book indicates major mining and industrial centers in Communist China by type of product as of the 1965–66 period. China's mineral-output value rose by possibly 5 percent over that of 1964. The 1965 level was higher than in any other year, except for the exaggerated peak figures claimed during the Great Leap. Several major mineral targets were overfulfilled in 1965—including coal, petroleum, iron ore, salt, and various nonferrous metals and chemical raw materials. It is likely that significant gains continued to be made in 1966, and several key mineral targets, notably oil, were again overfulfilled.[65] There is no available evidence regarding the impact of the ideological extremism or the political crisis on mineral production in 1967.

Table 6–4 indicates the estimated degree of Red Chinese self-sufficiency in the production of major minerals and selected strategic metals as of 1965. This table also indicates where China leads the world in estimated mineral reserves and resources.

TABLE 6–4

DEGREE OF SELF-SUFFICIENCY IN THE PRODUCTION OF MAJOR MINERALS IN COMMUNIST CHINA
(Estimates as of 1965)

Big Surplus	*Modest Surplus*	*Adequate Supply*	*Moderate Deficiency*	*Serious Deficiency*
Antimony* ‡	Asbestos †	Anthracite † ‡	Pyrite †	Nickel
Mercury † ‡	Magnesite † ‡	Bituminous coal †	Refined petroleum	Chromite
Tin † ‡	Salt † ‡	Coke †	Copper	Phosphate rock
Tungsten concentrate* ‡	Sulfur †	Iron ore † ‡	Gold (could use more)	
Bismuth † ‡	Talc †	Pig iron †		
Molybdenum †	Borate	Steel ingot		
Fluorspar †	Cement	Graphite †		
	Manganese ore	Gypsum		
	Lead	Aluminum		
	Zinc	Crude petroleum (nearly adequate)		

*** Ranks first in world production.**
† Ranks among top five world producers.
‡ Ranks first in world reserves or resources.

SOURCE: Data in this table have been derived from K. P. Wang, "The Mineral Resource Base of Communist China," ***An Economic Profile of Mainland China*****, Vol. I (Washington: U.S. Government Printing Office, 1967), p. 170, Table 1.**

From Table 6–4 we see that China is the leading world producer of antimony and tungsten concentrate. She is among the top five producers of some sixteen other types of mineral resources. China ranks among the top ten world producers for all items on Table 6–4, except copper, zinc, nickel, gold, chromite, and crude and refined petroleum. However, she has large unexploited petroleum resources. China will probably be faced with domestic deficiencies in copper, lead, zinc, and especially nickel and chromium for some years to come. However, she will undoubtedly be able to import adequate supplies of these commodities as long as she maintains a sound foreign-exchange position. The table also indicates that China has the world's largest reserves in nine minerals. She also has considerable reserves of several others.

With the exception of tin and tungsten concentrate, which are in abundant supply in China, there were no other declines in output from 1961 to 1965 in the minerals indicated in Table 6–4. The output of all the other minerals was at least as great in 1965 as in 1961. In fact, in most cases there were increases, and in many cases the increase in output from 1961 to 1965 was 15 percent or more.[66]

There is little concrete information on Red China's resources of radioactive materials or rare earth metals and alloys used in atomic energy and in optical and metallurgical industries. It is known that uranium rather than plutonium is used chiefly in China's atomic bombs. I was told by a prominent Chinese Communist economist that China has large uranium deposits. In 1966 some newly discovered uranium deposits were being exploited in the Kansu region of northwest China. This economist said that China's uranium resources may turn out to be as big as those of Canada.

According to other sources three uranium mines were reported to have started production in recent years. These are Maoshau and Chushau in Kiangsi Province, and Hailachuang in Kwangtung Province. Their combined daily output was said to be 2,500 metric tons of uranium ore. This was partly processed at the Chuchou plant in Hunan Province, and from there sent to Czechoslovakia for further treatment. China has also been exploiting and producing various kinds of rare earth metals and alloys for use in the atomic-energy, optical, and metallurgical industries. Probably the most important producing center has been Chinchow in Liaoning Province.

Table 6–5 compares Chinese and Indian output for selected basic minerals. The comparisons are based on information for available years and commodities.[67]

This table reveals that China has a big lead over India in the production of coal, iron ore, lead, salt, crude petroleum, and magnesite. China also probably has a substantial lead in the production of those items listed in Table 6–4 but not in Table 6–5. India has a big edge over China in copper, gypsum, and gold. India is also a major world producer of mica, ilmenite, and manganite, which are not indicated on Table 6–5. China's output of these commodities is probably relatively small. Both countries probably have adequate hydroelectric power potential to develop their mineral-resource bases, although China may have an edge. India produces a large amount of refined petroleum products in relation to its indigenous crude-petroleum output. This is due in substantial part to the relatively large number of motor vehicles in operation in India. India still relies heavily on imported crude petroleum, but she has begun to exploit what will probably turn out to be sizable—but not easily accessible—oil reserves in the western part of the country.

TABLE 6–5

COMMUNIST CHINESE VERSUS INDIAN OUTPUT FOR SELECTED BASIC MINERALS

(Ores, Concentrates, and Fuels in Millions of Tons except Gold)

	India—1963	*Communist China (Estimates)*		
		1961	*1963*	*1965*
Coal	66.9 (fiscal 1964–65: 64.4; expected 1965–66: 70)	250	270	300
Iron ore	14.8 (1964–65: 15.1; expected 1965–66: 23)	35	35	39
Manganese ore	1.1	.8	1.0	1
Copper	.474	.08	.090	.090
Lead	.056	.09	.100	.100
Bauxite	.556	.50–.60	.50–.60	.50–.60
Gypsum	1.178	.400	.500	.600
Gold (ounces)	150,000	60,000	60,000	60,000
Salt	.0045	11.0	10.5	13.0
Crude Petroleum	1.648	6.2	7.5	10.0
Petroleum Products (refined)	7.650 (1964–65: 8.4; expected 1965–66: 9.9)	5.5	7.0	9.0
Magnesite	.239	7	.9	1.0

SOURCES:

Communist Chinese estimates derived from K. P. Wang, "The Mineral Resource Base of Communist China," ***An Economic Profile of Mainland China*****, Vol. I (Washington: U.S. Government Printing Office, 1967), p. 174, Table 2.**

Indian figures derived from ***India's Draft Fourth Plan, 1966–70*** **(New Delhi: National Planning Commission, Government of India, 1967);** ***India: Pocket Book of Economic Information*****, (New Delhi: Ministry of Finance, Government of India, 1964);** ***Statistical Outline of India*****, (Bombay: Tata Industries Private Ltd., published by Popular Prakashan, 1964).**

India's most critical mineral shortages are sulfur, copper, and various other nonferrous metals. However, during India's current foreign-exchange crisis industrial enterprises have suffered because they have not been able to import various other types of basic and processed minerals and metals of required or desired qualities and specifications. Chinese industrial enterprises that I surveyed in 1966 did not seem to be adversely affected in a serious way by shortages of basic mineral inputs, with the possible exception of nickel and copper in a few cases. There did, however, appear to be significant shortages of processed metals and minerals in several cases. But this was probably due chiefly to planning errors, production bottlenecks, and/or lack of production know-how rather than the unavailability of basic ores or concentrates.

In spite of the fact that India has had much more foreign assistance—especially since 1960—in the exploitation of her mineral resources than China, China has made more progress. While India is also a relatively favorably endowed nation in mineral resources, China appears to be substantially better endowed. Moreover, there are signs that China may now be moving in the direction of greater foreign collaboration in the exploitation of her minerals. With the Soviet withdrawal in 1960 the Chinese regime made it clear that it intended to ban foreign assistance in future activity that might reveal China's mineral resources. However, in 1967 an unprecedented contract for geological prospecting was said to be under discussion between Communist China and a West German company.[68]

In conclusion, I concur with the following recent summary statement regarding Red China that was made by a leading Western authority on Red China's mineral resources: "China's mineral industry is being built up to a new plateau of 50 to 100 percent greater than present size. This will be accompanied by more diversity and sophistication. Achievements will be notable by developing the country's standards, but the gap with industrialized countries will not necessarily be reduced." [69]

The Agricultural Sector

Having dealt with China's mineral resources, we will proceed to a discussion of her agricultural sector. Agricultural performance tends to have a substantial bearing on managerial effectiveness, productive efficiency, and general progress in the industrial sector in a number of major ways. Critical food shortages have a negative impact on the industrial labor force because they tend to adversely affect human energy, stamina, health, absenteeism, turnover, motivation, morale, and productivity in the industrial sector. The agricultural sector also provides many of the basic raw materials required by industry, particularly light industry, and poor farm output which leads to critical shortages of such materials sharply constrains balanced industrial growth and development.

In a country such as China where the bulk of her exports (and hence foreign exchange earnings) are derived from the agricultural sector, poor agricultural performance tends to reduce sharply the amount of imports available to the overall industrial sector. This in turn tends to lead to less efficient combination of factor inputs and higher costs in the production process, less product diversification, and frequently a significant increase in idle resources, production bottlenecks, and waste. Poor or highly erratic agricultural performance also typically contributes greatly to the types of economic instability and inflationary problems discussed earlier.

For all of the above reasons—as well as others of lesser importance—

poor agricultural performance in China's (and India's) economy tends to make the managerial job substantially more difficult throughout much, if not virtually all, of the overall industrial sector because of constraints which are largely or wholly beyond the control of the individual industrial enterprise. It will become evident in this section that agricultural performance in Red Chinese has correlated quite closely with industrial performance since 1949.

During China's Republican era of 1911–49, with the probable exception of the 1931–37 period, poor performance in the agricultural sector did substantially constrain industrial development for the reasons noted above. However, various other environmental constraints undoubtedly had a much more negative effect throughout the 1911–49 period as a whole. During much of the 1931–37 period, farm results were relatively good for China, per capita food-consumption levels were probably equal to peak levels achieved so far under Communist rule, although income distribution and food consumption were much more inequitable—and China's very modest and narrow industrial sector was provided with substantial amounts of agricultural raw materials. The fact that the industrial sector did not grow or develop more substantially or broadly during this period of relative prosperity cannot be blamed in any truly significant degree on performance in the farm sector. Other environmental constraints were probably substantially more important than land or farm output per se in this connection.

Let us now turn to the agricultural sector's performance in Communist China.[70] Communist China is the second largest agricultural nation in the world, after the United States. China can produce virtually every type of farm crop and breed all types of farm animals, and in this connection she is more diversified than India. But when one views Red Chinese agriculture in per capita terms, we can see why this sector is so precarious—substantially more so than in Russia—and why it does little better than stagnate even in relatively good periods. In fact, Red China's volume of farm output in relation to her huge population is perhaps her most basic and critical general and social economic problem. The same is true for India. When ideological extremism is pushed too far in China's highly sensitive farm sector, the problem tends to become one of disaster.

Since 1950, farm output has comprised from one-third to one-half of China's GNP annually. In 1957 it reached a peak comprising about 50 percent of GNP, and since then it has been less. Farm output in India has been comprising from 40 to about 60 percent of that nation's annual GNP since 1950.[71] Roughly 60 to 70 percent of China's total exports have been dependent on the agricultural sector, and in India the percentage has been even greater. In both China and India agriculture provides a livelihood for more than 80 percent of the working population.

Red China is one of the world's most densely populated nations, with roughly 75 people per square kilometer. But India is even much more densely populated, with approximately 155 people per square kilometer. China contains 25 percent of the world's population, but only 7.8 percent of the world's cultivated land. China's land surface exceeds that of the continental United States by 4.2 percent, but the United States has roughly 35 percent more cultivated land, and more than five times as much per capita. In the United States there are about 1.9 acres of cultivated land per person, as opposed to .35 acres in Red China. Moreover, the cultivated land in the United States is, on the average, much more productive than in China because of technology, climate, terrain, geography, knowledge, skill, and various other reasons. In the late 1950's, 31 percent of Red China's cultivated farmland was reported to be fertile, 40 percent ordinary, and 29 percent low-yielding.[72] This situation probably is roughly the same today.

While Red China's population is estimated to be roughly 50 percent greater than India's, total sown acreage in China's agricultural sector is only about 15 percent more than in India, and total acreage for food-grain crops only approximately 10 percent more than in India. (See Tables 6–4 and 6–5.) However, agricultural productivity is generally substantially greater in China than in India.

Agricultural development in the western two-thirds of Communist China is greatly hindered by climate, terrain, and isolation. China is also faced with a serious problem of unbalanced water distribution, with critical shortages in the north and overabundance in the south. About half of the farmland in the hilly and mountainous regions of the nation is not suitable for significant improvement by means of conventional irrigation programs. Serious monsoons, floods, and droughts arise from time to time in various parts of the country, causing considerable damage to farm output. However, China tends to fare somewhat better in terms of these hazards and general climatic conditions than India.

When the Communists came to power in 1949, agricultural output was at a very low level in China. Under Communist rule, considerable—though erratic—progress has been made in China's agricultural sector through irrigation, water conservation, capital investment, flood and pest control, much greater use of chemical fertilizers, modest increases in mechanization, rural electrification, better seed selection and development, improvement in farm-plant and animal-breeding techniques, and various educational and training programs. In virtually all of these spheres China has done more than India to date. However, the ill effects of ideological extremism, further aggravated by adverse weather conditions during and following the Great Leap, caused tremendous damage to China's agricultural sector from which it has probably not fully recovered.

For the 1949–65 period, as a whole, Red China's agricultural growth may have lagged slightly behind that of India. India has also experienced considerable instability and period declines in output in her agricultural sector, but they have not been quite as severe as those experienced during the 1958–62 period in Red China. However, since about mid-1965 India has been experiencing a very serious agricultural, and hence general economic and social, crisis. The United States alone has supplied India with some 15 million tons of food-grain from June 1965 to June 1967, more than twice as much as China's total grain imports during this period.

In spite of China's erratic but significant progress in her agricultural sector since 1949, only between 11 and 13 percent of the entire country is cultivated, and the amount of cultivated land per person has been declining through much of the Communist era.[73] In other words, population growth has been outstripping increases in cultivated land. The same is true for India. Both countries are sharply handicapped by limited potential acreage expansion for crops and other farm products.

Both interpersonal and regional income inequalities are much greater in India than in China, so that poor agricultural performance and food shortages have many more negative implications for vast numbers of the population in India than in China. Moreover, China has a much more effective system of food distribution and rationing than India. Therefore, per capita consumption figures are a better indication of how the average Chinese citizen is faring than they would be for India and Indian citizens. Hence, a subsistence-level per capita caloric intake of food for both India and China would imply that a substantially larger segment of the population in India is not being provided with subsistence-level food requirements than in China. In turn, this is likely to mean that a larger proportion of India's population is likely to be more susceptible to malnutrition, disease, loss of energy, and so forth.

Table 6–6 presents some key statistical estimates pertaining to Chinese Communist agriculture.[74] It should be noted that even many estimates for the 1950's, when official data were published regularly by the regime, are quite crude because of Red China's deficient statistical system in the agricultural sector. Table 6–7 contains some similar types of agricultural statistics for India.

During the 1952–57 period virtually all aspects of Red China's agricultural performance improved quite significantly. One exception was per capita grain output, which was probably slightly higher in 1952 than 1957. Total agricultural production increased by about 20 percent, or an average annual rate of roughly 4 percent. Population increased by about 11 percent during this period. Hence, per capita growth in agricultural output was 9 percent, providing for an average annual rate of roughly 1.5 percent. Total food-grain production increased by 10 percent, or at an annual average rate of roughly 2 percent. There was also gains in the farm-animal pop-

TABLE 6–6

SOME KEY AGRICULTURAL ESTIMATES FOR COMMUNIST CHINA

	1952	*1957*	*1961*	*1965*
ACREAGE (*million hectares*)[a]				
Cultivated farmland	109.9	111.8	106.7	109.0
Sown acreage	147.3	157.2	142.2	156.0
Multiple crop index[b]	134.0	140.6	133.0	143.1
Total food-grain crops	116.3	120.9	120.0	125.0
Rice	30.0	32.2	30.0	33.0
Wheat	25.0	27.5	22.0	24.0
Cotton	5.6	5.8	3.5	4.8
OUTPUT (*million tons*)				
Total food-grain output[c]	170.0	185.0	162.0	200.0
Rice	78.6	86.8	75.0	97.8
Wheat	20.0	23.7	15.4	20.4
Cotton	1.3	1.64	.9	1.4
YIELDS (*tons per hectare*)				
Rice	2.62	2.692	2.5	2.96
Wheat	.8	.855	.7	.850
Cotton	.234	.284	.257	.292
Total availability of chemical fertilizers[d] (*thousands of tons*)	433	1,800	2,283 (1960—3,320)	7,000 (1966—8,500)
NUMBER OF TRACTORS (*average unit, 15 horsepower*)	probably less than 1,000	25,000 (perhaps only 12,500 in use on farms)	95,000–99,000 (about 20% not in use)	135,000 (in use)
PER CAPITA GRAIN OUTPUT[e] (*kilograms per year*)	296	287	250	265–275
PER CAPITA FOOD CONSUMPTION				
Caloric intake per person per day[f]	not available	2,200 (1958)	1,790 (1959–61)	2,000–2,100 (1964 and 1966 may have been as high as 2,200)

	1952	1957	1961	1965
Food grains available for consumption per person, per day[g] (*grams*)	not available	278–281	247	275–279

[a] One hectare = 2.471 acres. Cultivated farmland in 1949 was about 108 million hectares.

[b] Obtained by dividing sown acreage by cultivated farmland.

[c] Peak year was 1958, with estimated 204 million tons; low year was 1960, with estimated 160 million tons. Pre-1949 peak estimated at 170 million tons.

[d] For indigenous fertilizer production nitrogenous fertilizer output has averaged about three times more than all other types combined. Imports have comprised an increasing amount of China's available fertilizers. In 1966 imported chemical fertilizers accounted for about 70% of the total tons available.

[e] Peak year was 1958, with estimated 310 kilograms; low year was 1960, with estimated 237 kilograms. Pre-1949 peak estimated at 320 kilograms.

[f] It is estimated that the 2,200 peak caloric intake per capita level was achieved through much of the 1931–37 period. The low point under Communist rule was probably the spring of 1961.

[g] Includes adjustments made for imports minus exports.

SOURCES: Most of the estimates in this table are from E. Jones, "The Emerging Pattern of China's Economic Revolution," *An Economic Profile of Mainland China*, Vol. I (Washington: U.S. Government Printing Office, 1967), especially his Tables II and III on pp. 93–94. Figures pertaining to chemical fertilizers and tractors are from M. Larsen, "China's Agriculture under Communism," *op. cit.*, p. 246, Table 2, and pp. 247–50. The 1961 tractor estimate is also based in part on tractor-production data provided to me by managers of the Loyang No. 1 Tractor Plant. Per capita caloric-intake estimates are from Larsen, *op. cit.*, p. 265, Table 3, and the other sources cited therein; and comments by E. Jones, in *Mainland China in the World Economy* (Washington: U.S. Government Printing Office, 1967), p. 236. The per capita food-grain-consumption estimates are probably the crudest of all; they are based on O. L. Dawson's food-grain-output figures as presented by T. C. Liu, *op. cit.*, p. 41, Table 1.

ulation and its productivity. Per capita farm output in both the state and small private sectors showed general increases during this period. Even during the poor crop weather years of 1954 and 1956 significant setbacks in overall agricultural performance did not occur.[75] Per capita output declined in these two years, but not very severely. Consumption of chemical fertilizers in the agricultural sector increased greatly during 1952–57.[76] The number of tractors in operation on farms also increased sharply, but the number was still very small compared with that of the United States or even Russia.

At the outset of the Great Leap Forward, per capita caloric intake was probably just about as high as the pre-1949 Chinese peak of about 2,200 calories achieved during the 1931–37 period. This 2,200 figure is substantially below the 3,000, or more, per capita caloric intake common in ad-

TABLE 6–7

SOME KEY AGRICULTURAL STATISTICS FOR INDIA
(All Fiscal Year Ranges)

	1955–56	1960–61	1963–64
ACREAGE (*in million hectares*)			
Sown acreage (estimates)	129	133	135
Total Food-grain crops:	110.6	113.2	115.8
Rice	31.5	33.6	35.5
Wheat	12.4	13.0	13.3
Cotton	8.1	7.6	7.9
OUTPUT (*in million tons*)			
Total food grains*:	66.8	81.0	79.4 (89.0 for 1964–65; 72.3 for 1965–66)
Rice	27.6	34.2	36.5
Wheat	8.8	11.0	9.7
Cotton	3.95	5.3	5.4
YIELDS (*in tons per hectare*)			
Rice	.9	1.0	1.0
Wheat	.7	.9	.7
Cotton	.5	.7	.6
TOTAL AVAILABILITY OF CHEMICAL FERTILIZERS (*in thousands of tons*)	360–400	900–950	2,800–3,100 (1964–65)
NUMBER OF TRACTORS	negligible	probably less than 1,000	5,600 (1965–66)
PER CAPITA GRAIN OUTPUT (*estimated kilograms per year*)	167	185	170
PER CAPITA FOOD CONSUMPTION			
Caloric intake per person, per day †	1,950	2,100	1,900–2,000
Food grains available for consumption per person, per day (grams) ‡	416	461	434 (431 for 1964–65; 347 for 1965–66)

* Mid–1964 to mid–1965—89 million tons, India's peak year; 1965–66 dropped to 72.3 million tons.

† Mid–1965 to mid–1966—probably under 2,000 and maybe even below 1,900. 1950–51 per capita caloric intake was 1,800.

‡ 1964–65 dropped to 431 grams in spite of relatively good crops; 1965–66 dropped to 347 grams with poor crops.

SOURCES: *India's Draft Fourth Plan, 1966–70* (New Delhi: National Planning Commission, Government of India, 1967); *India: Pocket Book of Economic Information* (New Delhi: Ministry of Finance, Government of India, 1964); *Statistical Outline of India* (Bombay: Tata Industries Private Ltd., published by Popular Prakashan, 1964); and *United Nations Statistical Yearbooks* for 1964 and 1965.

vanced industrial nations. However, it is adequate for the Red Chinese population which is accustomed to a relatively low level of food consumption, and which can maintain reasonably good physical condition and work quite effectively at the 2,200 per capital level.[77] Of course, the Chinese are substantially smaller than, say, Americans, and are not on the average as physically powerful. This frequently is likely to result in lower labor productivity and possibly less mental alertness since it typically takes more man-hours to do similar types of physical work in China, other things being equal, than in the United States or even Russia. When per capita caloric intake in China, or elsewhere, approaches the 2,000 level, and especially if it falls below 2,000, there are likely to be significant drops in labor productivity, substantial losses of body weight, serious retarded growth among children over a prolonged period, and an increasing number of nutritional diseases and other health problems.

There is some question as to whether the quality or nutritional makeup of per capita caloric intake in Red China has ever been as high as that of the 1931–37 period.[78] Even if food-quality levels have not reached the per capita levels of the 1930's, such per capita averages are somewhat misleading. In Republican China the privileged classes consumed as much or more food of just as good variety and quality as in advanced countries, while a vast number of Chinese citizens consumed substantially less than 2,200 calories per day consisting of a very narrow range of foods. Food distribution and consumption have been much more equable under China's Communist regime. When necessary, rationing has been quite effective. In fact, food rations have been based on energy requirements for different degrees of physical work in an effort to maintain desired levels of industrial labor productivity.[79] For example, the grain-rationing system introduced for urban areas in August 1956 placed the daily rice ration in rice areas of the nation for a worker engaged in heavy physical work at 833 grams, moderate physical work at 667 grams, light physical work at 433 grams; for white-collar workers it is 467 grams, university and high school students 533 grams, and so forth.[80] There is a similar wheat-rationing system for wheat-consumption areas of the country.

Let us make some suggestive comparisons of agricultural output and consumption between India for fiscal 1955–56 (1957 data are not readily available for India) and China for 1957 on the eve of her Great Leap. India's total food-grain output increased from 53 million tons in 1950–51 to 66.8 million in 1955–56. This represented an annual average increase of roughly 5 percent, compared with 2 percent during the 1952–57 period in China. However, China's total food-grain output was more than 250 percent greater than India's for 1955–56; her wheat and rice output were both about three times greater than India's. Both China's rice and wheat yields were more than double India's. However, India's cotton output was about three times greater than China's, and her cotton yields about double China's. While jute is an unimportant commodity in China, India has long been a major world jute producer, and she earns a substantial proportion of foreign exchange through jute exports. In 1957 Red China was using much more chemical fertilizer—roughly five times more—than India around that time.

India's 1955–56 estimated per capita grain output of 167 kilograms was much less than China's 296 kilograms in 1957. On the other hand, India had 416 grams of available food grains per person per day compared with about 280 grams in China in 1957. However, because of much hoarding, black-marketing activity, and corruption in India, a substantial amount of the available grain does not reach the common man. Moreover, because of Hindu religious bans on cow slaughter and widespread taboos on the eating of meat, dairy products, and certain other foods, grains make up a substantially bigger share of the average Indian's diet than the typical Chinese citizen's diet. In general, the average Red Chinese citizen has a more balanced diet than his Indian counterpart. In India in 1955–56 the per capita food intake of 1,950 calories was also significantly below China's 1957–58 level of about 2,200.

With the onslaught of the Great Leap in 1958 a severe setback was inevitable, even though agricultural performance continued to advance through 1958, chiefly because of very good weather conditions and short-lived enthusiasm and motivation. Total farm output, per capita grain production, consumption, and caloric intake all probably reached peak levels in 1958. In fact, 1958 was probably the best single year for Chinese agriculture. China continued to be a net exporter of farm products until 1960.

However, highly irrational and ineffective agricultural policies, programs, and techniques introduced with the Great Leap, and which were intensified and in full swing by 1959, began to take their toll in 1959. Among the chief ideologically inspired reasons for the collapse of China's agriculture were the confiscation of private plots and farm animals in conjunction with extreme emphasis on altruism and moral stimuli at the expense of self-interest and material incentives; the breakdown of the family through rigid communal living; the transfer of millions of farm workers to industry; the employment of Reds and ill-suited peasants rather than Experts or relatively competent personnel in charge of farm operations; and the widespread use of a variety of illogical techniques in plowing, in plant and seed development, and in animal breeding, as well as in irrigation, water conservation, and so forth. Adverse weather conditions in 1960 and 1961, along with the Great Leap ideological extremism, spelled disaster for the farm sector and the economy at large. This happened despite large increases in the availability of chemical fertilizers, tractors, and other types of mechanization and farm implements during the 1958–60 period.

For example, the amount of chemical fertilizer available increased to

2.7 million tons in 1958, a 50 percent rise over 1957. It increased further in 1959 to 2.96 million tons and still further in 1960 to 3.32 million tons. The total amount of available fertilizer has always been more than the amount actually consumed in Communist China. There are always significant losses and waste because of low-quality indigenous fertilizer output which deteriorates rapidly, ineffective distribution, improper usage, inadequate storage and transportation facilities, and so forth. However, these problems became much more serious and pervasive during the Great Leap period.

The number of tractors in the country more than doubled between 1957 and 1959, when there were about 59,000. Red China started producing her own tractors in 1958 at the large Loyang Tractor Factory setup with Russian help. By 1961 there were probably roughly 95,000 tractors in China, but 20 percent or more were not working because of lack of repair and spare parts. There were also large increases in the number of diesel engines, pumps, and other farm implements during the 1958–60 period, but here too, many were not functioning in 1960–61. In fact, many of them were of poor, even unusable quality and durability because of hasty production by the grossly inefficient small-scale plants that sprang up on the communes.

Table 6–6 indicates significant declines in all reflected aspects of aggregate and per capita agricultural performance and food consumption in 1961, as compared with 1957. For most performance indicators the drops were very sharp, particularly for a bare subsistence-level agrarian type of economy. For a majority of performance indicators 1961 was even substantially worse than 1952, and the population was more than 100 million greater in 1961. While the amount of chemical fertilizer was greater in 1961 than in 1957, there was a 50 percent drop from 1960 to 1961. Tractors had reached a peak number in 1961, but all the tractors in the world could not have prevented China's agricultural crisis. The drop in total food-grain output from the peak level achieved in 1958, as compared with 1961, was about 20 percent per capita food-grain output, and food consumption dropped pitifully. The Great Leap also resulted in serious losses of farm animals.

Although the 1959–61 food crisis hit the rural areas of the nation the hardest, it also had a significantly adverse impact on the industrial work force in the cities, in spite of rationing. Sharp declines in labor productivity, substantial increases in absenteeism (due largely to low resistance, nutritional deficiencies, and disease), and rest periods ordered by the government attest to the tight food situation even in urban areas.[81] The sharp drop in raw materials provided by the agricultural sector to industry had a stifling impact on industrial development. The extremely critical food situation in the countryside contributed greatly to low labor productivity on the farms, and probably placed lower ceilings on the productivity gains achieved once the agricultural sector began to recover.

Table 6–7 shows that while Chinese agriculture hung on the brink of devastating famine during the 1958–61 period, India's agricultural sector made quite substantial gains during the 1956–61 period. Indian total food-grain output increased by about 20 percent during this period, and per capita caloric intake rose significantly to 2,100. The only performance indicator that shows a decline from 1955–56 to 1960–61 on Table 6–7 was cotton acreage, although this decline was small and cotton output actually rose substantially. Because of India's relatively good agricultural performance during this period there were gains in managerial effectiveness, productive efficiency, and general progress in the overall industrial sector. The reverse was true for China.

Red China has experienced a substantial recovery in her farm sector since 1961 as the pendulum has swung from ideological extremism to managerial, technical, economic, and motivational rationality in agriculture.

Major efforts have been underway to modernize and mechanize the farm sector, although this is still in the embryonic stage in most of the countryside. In the 1960's there have been sharp rises in the use of chemical fertilizers, tractors, and other farm machinery and implements.

The system of private plots and farm animals was revived toward the end of 1961. Although the private farm sector contains only about 5 percent of the country's cultivated land, it may produce as much as 20 percent of the nation's daily food requirements. It produces an estimated 80 percent of Red China's hogs, 95 percent of her poultry, and a large proportion of her fruits and vegetables.[82] In general, the private agricultural sector provides a high percentage of the quality foods in the Chinese diet and is a big foreign-exchange earner. Both aggregate and per capita outputs have increased sharply in the private farm sector.

While there has also been a substantial recovery in the state and overall agricultural sector since 1961, per capita performance has been stagnant or declining in some spheres, and in many spheres the 1957–58 aggregate or per capita peak levels had not been achieved by 1965. The gross value of total agricultural output grew by only an estimated 8 percent from 1957 through 1965; or at an annual average rate of about 1 percent, substantially less than population growth.[83] If we use 1958 as the base year for this period, agricultural growth is even less than 8 percent. Food-grain output increased by about 25 percent from 1961 through 1965, or at an annual average rate of roughly 5 percent. By 1964 food-grain output was at the 1957 level—but not the 1958 peak—but population was up by about 12 percent. Total food-grain output nearly reached the 1958 peak level in 1965 and may have exceeded it in 1966. However, per capita total farm and food-grain outputs have not yet achieved earlier peak per capita levels.

The regime officially intends to regain 1957 per capita levels of farm output by 1970, suggesting an annual growth target of 3 percent. But it is likely that the Chinese planners are really only hoping for a 2 percent annual growth rate in agriculture until 1970, and this may be attainable, barring ideological extremism on the farms.[84] This would mean stagnant per capita agricultural performance but at adequate levels for gains in industrial productive efficiency and general progress.

In spite of large net imports of grain since the early 1960's, per capita food-grain consumption and caloric intake have not achieved 1957–58 peak levels. It is likely to take several years—even without ideological extremism—before peak per capita consumption levels are again achieved; but here too, if current consumption levels are maintained, they should be adequate for sustained industrial progress. In spite of the agricultural recovery since 1961, Red China was a net importer of farm products, chiefly grains through 1964. In 1965, and probably in 1966, China's agricultural exports exceeded imports, in spite of her large grain imports. Undoubtedly a sizable amount of food is being stockpiled in the event of poor crops in the future. I observed many large grain elevators and other food-storage facilities in much of the Chinese countryside through which I traveled. The same is not true for India.

An official Chinese Communist spokesman claimed in a 1966 interview with the Chinese authoress Han Suyin that China had at present about 120 million hectares of cultivated farmland, comprising 13 percent of her total land area.[85] This 120 million figure is about 10 percent higher than the 1965 estimates made by Western experts of Red China's cultivated land. It is conceivable that the 1966 Chinese Communist figure is reasonably accurate, but it seems more likely that it is exaggerated, unless perhaps it includes Taiwan's arable farmland as being part of Red China's—which is highly improbable.

According to Western estimates (see also Table 6–6), by the end of 1965 available arable acreage for most crops—and all major ones—had not yet regained their earlier peak levels.[86] Rice yields (per hectare) reached their highest levels in 1965; white wheat, most other grains, and potatoes remained below earlier peak-yield levels.

Cotton yields attained a new peak level in 1965, but total raw-cotton output was still less than in 1957. However, Peking's *People's Daily* claims a big gain in cotton production in the industrial sector for 1966 and, in fact, states that 1966 was a record peak year in this regard.[87] If this is true, a fairly sizable amount of imported cotton was probably provided to China's cotton-textile industry. The cotton mills that I visited seemed to be humming along at close to full capacity. Lagging domestic-cotton output has constrained growth in the textile and clothing industries in earlier years following the Great Leap.

The farm-animal population has increased fairly substantially since 1961, but it still probably remains significantly below earlier peak levels. This, too, has constrained growth in those industries requiring animal by-products as material inputs.

India's agricultural performance during the period from mid-1960 to mid-1964 has not been as good as China's for the 1961–65 period, but India was not recovering from a severe agricultural crisis. Total food-grain and wheat production, per capita grain output, per capita food consumption, and wheat and cotton yields all showed declines in India in 1960–61 as compared with 1963–64. Other farm sectors showed only slight gains. Sizable gains over 1963–64 were achieved in 1964–65 in Indian agriculture. However, from mid-1965 until mid-1967 India was faced with a serious agricultural crisis. The 1965–66 period was nearly as bad as the 1959–61 period in China. And if it had not been for vast sums of foreign aid and huge food imports it may well have been even more severe than China's food crisis or general economic depression.

India lags far behind China in the availability and use of chemical fertilizers, tractors, and other farm machinery and implements. Even if India achieves her targets in these spheres in her 1966–70 Fourth Five-Year Plan, she will still lag quite far behind China's levels of farm modernization and mechanization in 1965.

After traveling through a fair extent of the Red Chinese countryside—mostly by train—and spending a day or so in each of the five Chinese communes that I visited in different parts of the country, and after traveling through much of India and visiting many agricultural villages, I am convinced that, as of the mid-1960's, Red China has a significant edge over India in agricultural productivity and, more important, in agricultural potential. I arrived at this firm conviction before I had a chance to study agricultural statistics for either of these countries. Available statistics and estimates seem to clearly support my conclusion. Similarly, after spending time and eating at a fairly sizable number of factories in both Red China and India, and after visiting the homes of industrial workers in both countries, I have the strong impression that the average Chinese worker is better fed, healthier, in better physical condition, and stronger than his Indian counterpart. (On the other hand, enterprise executives in India may eat more on the average than their Chinese counterparts.) If my subjective appraisal is actually true, the complications in terms of labor productivity—particularly in such relatively high labor-intensive economies—are obvious.

The ideological pendulum and population growth are probably the most crucial factors facing Chinese agriculture in the future. In spite of the Cultural Revolution, Red Chinese leaders declared a hands-off policy in the farm sector in 1966. Apparently ideological extremism and Red Guard activity were pretty much isolated from this sector through 1966. However, this may not have been the case in 1967 or 1968, although there is little available clear-cut evidence that major or pervasive damage has been done to Chinese agriculture. It is possible, however, that Red Guards, the army, people's militia, and/or various new revolutionary groups have been seriously disrupting farm production and operations in some areas.

Labor and Population

Because of China's tremendous overpopulation problem the great bulk of available manpower must work on the farms in order to provide the nation with at least a subsistence-level food supply from its backward agricultural sector. The Great Leap suggests what can happen to the Chinese agricultural sector when large numbers—that is, millions—of farm workers, including many of the relatively skilled and better-educated ones, are suddenly and abruptly transferred to the industrial sector and the cities.

Not only must Red China's farm workers feed themselves and the urban work force, they must also feed hundreds of millions of dependent people who are not employed in any directly productive capacity: the young, those in school, the old and retired, the sick, and the disabled. And the proportion, as well as the absolute size, of China's dependent population is much greater than in advanced economies. During the 1949–66 period, about 35 to 40 percent of Communist China's population was under fifteen, roughly another 8 percent was over fifty-nine, and several more percent in the fifteen to fifty-nine age group were not in suitable physical condition for productive labor.[88] Moreover, where the average American farmer produces the equivalent of enough food to feed himself and his family, plus a sizable number of urban workers and their dependents, each year, many peasants in Red China are required to produce enough food for themselves and their dependents *plus one* urban worker and *his* dependents.

In spite of tremendous educational and training achievements in Red China, the bulk of the nation's available manpower is still relatively unskilled and untrained. This means a considerable amount of surplus labor in the sense that much of the available manpower cannot be used very effectively or efficiently with existing levels of arable land, readily available natural resources, capital equipment, and managerial skill. The result is much unemployment and underemployment (especially concealed unemployment in the countryside) and, to a lesser degree, underemployment of industrial manpower, all of which lower labor productivity substantially.

Tens of millions of unskilled peasants in the communes work for a few months at harvest time and remain idle for a considerable part of the rest of the year, even though substantial progress has been made in expanding "side occupations" such as fishing, silkworm breeding, and flower growing in China's farm sector. In the industrial sector numerous enterprises maintain substantially more manpower than they require for the same volume of work. The negative effect of such disguised unemployment and underemployment on overall efficiency of the system is large, particularly if one looks at output performance in per capita terms.

Furthermore, in a vastly overpopulated country, such as Red China, where the leaders are highly welfare-conscious, much of the country's limited wealth is expended on public health, medicine, sanitation, schools, and even housing. Even though the amounts spent in these areas are small in per capita terms, they are very sizable in absolute terms. Such expenditures, though certainly justified from an ethical or moral standpoint, nonetheless mean that substantially less of the nation's wealth is directly available for the development and expansion of the industrial sector. On the other hand, such expenditures do a great deal in providing industry (and agriculture) with a better-educated, healthier, more energetic, and more productive labor force.

Even before the Communist state was established, China had long been faced with a critical overpopulation problem. It is true that the rate of population growth was significantly lower in pre-1949 China—well under 2 percent and in many years under 1 percent—chiefly because of much higher mortality rates and substantially shorter life spans. In fact, during the 1937–49 period population growth was quite stagnant because of abnormally low fertility rates and high mortality rates caused by wars, famine, severe inflation, depression, and the like. However, there was still a large amount of surplus labor which could not be efficiently or effectively utilized in the nation's overall productive system. Moreover, the proportion of the labor force in Republican China that was unskilled, untrained, unhealthy, and physically weak was substantially greater than that of Red China because of the tremendous expansion of welfare, health, and educational programs under the Communist regime.

When the Communists came to power in 1949, China had a population of roughly 540 million. Red China's population at the end of 1965 was probably in the range of 725 to 750 million. Experts generally agree that it was more than 700 million but no more than 775 million. Red China's leaders are not sure themselves of their country's population because of statistical and census deficiencies, which are further magnified by a tendency for many rural families to conceal deaths in order to augment their rations.[89]

Since 1949 Red China's population has grown at an annual average rate of at least 2 percent, and possibly by as much as 2.2 percent. India's population-growth rate has been roughly the same as China's since 1949—possibly a bit higher—although India has probably had a lower birth rate and higher mortality rate.[90] In both countries, life expectancy at birth increased from the low thirties to over forty since 1949, with China possibly having an edge of a few years. In general, Red China's rate of population growth has been somewhat more uneven from year to year than India's.

Assuming an annual rate of population increase of at least 2 percent for Red China, this means that with China's existing population of, say, 750 million, there will be some 15 million new mouths to feed this year with the number increasing in future years if the 2 percent rate is maintained. This is fantastic when one realizes that of the approximately one hundred and forty nations in the world only thirty-five, or 26 percent of the total, have populations of 15 million or more.[91] There can be little doubt that birth control is one of Communist China's most critical general problems now, and one that will become increasingly critical in the future.

In the early 1950's Red China's leadership felt that birth control was unnecessary, a device of decadent capitalism, and "a means of killing the Chinese people without shedding blood." [92] However, as the rate of population increase began to rise quite sharply with better general economic, food, and health conditions, the regime had second thoughts. A birth-control campaign was introduced during the 1954–58 period, but it apparently lost much of its momentum before 1958. This campaign had some effect in the cities but little in the countryside. During the 1950–58 period the average annual rate of population growth was probably about 2.1 to 2.2 percent, with the actual rate approaching 2.4 or 2.5 percent during one or two years. Where life expectancy in China before 1949 was in the early thirties, it increased to around the early forties in the 1950's.

By the time of the Great Leap, Red China's leaders were once again viewing the nation's huge population as an asset rather than a liability. However, with the severe economic depression and famine that emerged during the 1959–62 period there was obviously little need for a birth-control campaign. Fertility and marriage rates dropped substantially, while the mortality rate rose. Probably relatively few deaths were attributable directly to starvation, but severe malnutrition, low resistance, and disease were primary reasons for the rising mortality rate. Annual population growth fell below 2 percent during this period. It is estimated that China's population was set back between 40 and 60 million during the 1959–62 period through reduced fertility and life expectancy.[93]

Since around 1963, when Red China's general economic recovery and improved food situation began, the annual rate of population increase has again been exceeding 2 percent. In 1964 Chou En-lai stated that population growth had approached the earlier 2.5 percent peak level again.[94] During the 1963–66 period China's annual population growth probably averaged about 2.2 and possibly 2.3 percent. A Chinese doctor in Wuhan told me that he thought average life expectancy in Red China as of 1966 was in the mid-forties, and possibly even in the late forties.

Since late 1962 or early 1963 Red China's leadership has become very concerned about population growth and birth control. A vigorous birth-control campaign has been waged in the cities in particular, apparently with significant success. The campaign has been extended to the rural areas, but as yet is still substantially more limited in scope and less effective than in urban areas. Educational, public-health, advertising, and family-planning programs, and the dissemination of information on contraceptives and birth-control literature, buttressed by stringent social pressures—including coercion at times—and a variety of outright rewards and penalties constitute Red China's overall birth-control campaign.

Although Red China's 1950 marriage law set the minimum age for marriage at twenty for men and eighteen for women, in recent years doctors, counselors, and party cadres have been advising ages of twenty-two to twenty-six for women (preferably not before twenty-five) and twenty-eight to thirty-two or a little later for men. At a number of Chinese factories that I visited I was told that the party holds regular family-planning and marriage-counseling meetings. At most, if not all, enterprises which provide employee housing, single employees get rent-free quarters, while married couples must pay rent. Moreover, single employees are generally entitled to longer vacations than married personnel. There have even been some reports that urban couples who have married "too young" have been split up by having one of the spouses transferred to another city, at times very far away.

Information from various areas, both urban and rural, in China indicate that the authorities have devised various other methods of influencing the size of families including the limitation or denial of maternity supplies and denial of food rations for new family members beyond a prescribed number, typically two to four children. In some areas peasants have been informed that the size of private plots could no longer be enlarged to accommodate more than the stipulated family size.

In the Chinese cities visited I noticed that contraceptives of various types were on prominent display in many stores. I also saw contraceptives on display in the stores of a few communes that I visited. These communes were near major cities, but I was told by one of my interpreters that contraceptives are available at all communes. Some of the farming officials whom I met said that at their communes there are family-planning and marriage-counseling sessions, films, lectures, and educational programs and that there are even medical teams sent to their communes with the aim of "supporting" the country's birth-control program.

During the 1949–66 period China's population growth was centered in the dependent age groups because of increased life spans and reductions in infant mortality. Experts estimate that the working-age population grew by no more than 1 percent from 1948 to mid-1963, but will grow by about 2.25 percent annually through 1978, with growth concentrated in the fifteen- to twenty-nine-year age group. This projected pattern of growth places a particular urgency on population-control measures. The twenty- to twenty-nine-year age group is the most fertile of all age groups, and its impending rapid increase raises the prospect of an accelerating birth rate in the absence of a reduction in fertility. On the other hand, the growing fifteen- to twenty-nine-year age group will probably be comprised of persons more vigorous, mobile, and better-educated than the rest of the labor force. Its employment is likely to provide the Red Chinese regime with both opportunities and problems, with the severity of the problems depending in large part on the effectiveness of birth control and agricultural performance.

Chou En-lai told the American writer Edgar Snow that the regime's birth-control goal is to reduce the annual natural increase to 2 percent by 1970, 1.5 percent (roughly the current U.S. rate) by 1980, and 1 percent (approximately the present Japanese rate) by the year 2000.[95] These goals are very ambitious. However, in view of the present official determination and apparent successes (though still modest), the new effective birth-control techniques available, and the prospective revolutionary change in Chinese society, these goals are not impossible.

The Indian government (aided and encouraged by foreign assistance and experts) has also been striving to check population increase through a variety of birth-control programs. In my opinion, Red China is likely to have significantly greater success with her birth-control campaigns and programs than India. India has nothing equivalent to China's pervasive party organization which can do a great deal to help implement birth-control programs and break down cultural traditions at the grass-roots level of society that favor large families. Moreover, the Indian government is not as inclined to use coercion and penalties or to curtail individual freedom to the same degree or extent as the Red Chinese leadership in order to enforce birth-control programs. On the other hand, Red China's population is presently some 250 million, or 50 percent, greater than that of India. Therefore, population increase in absolute terms will continue to be substantially greater in China for many years to come.

Before concluding our discussion of labor, a word about the general health of the labor force is in order because this tends to have a significant bearing on labor productivity and turnover. Both Red China and India have made impressive progress in improving the general health of their vast populations since the late 1940's. This is reflected in an aggregate way by increases in average life expectancy of more than ten years in both countries in the last generation. However, China has probably made even more progress than India. I am not the only observer to hold this opinion. (Incidentally, I actually received treatment for an ear infection and a cold at the hospital and health clinics of two Chinese enterprises and one commune, and in all cases the treatment was effective.) It is also the opinion of some Western doctors and diplomats who have spent time in both India and China and whom I have met. And it is also borne out by some fragmentary aggregate statistics.

In the mid-1950's Red China had about 2.6 graduate or professional physicians (including dentists) per 10,000 population, as against 1.5 for India.[96] (The figures for the United States, the Soviet Union, and Japan at that time were 18, 16.7, and 13.5, respectively.[97] In 1963 the Indian figure was around 2 per 10,000, but China's proportion probably exceeded 3 per 10,000, given the sizable number of graduates from her medical colleges during 1957–63.[98] As of 1967, China still maintained a substantial lead over India. In 1949 there were fewer than 1,400 medical doctors graduated in China. By the mid-1950's the number of new graduate doctors reached 7,000 annually, and during the 1962–66 period an average of 20,000 were graduated annually. During the 1949–66 period about 10 percent of all Red China's higher graduates were in medicine, a significantly greater proportion than in India. Increases in the numbers of hospital beds, nurses, and semiprofessional medical personnel and technicians in Red China have been much greater than in India in the past eighteen years.[99]

The quality of medical practice in both China and India is relatively high for poor countries. Experts point out that Chinese medical training and practice equal the standards of advanced countries, such as Canada, in many areas, although physical medical facilities still lag far behind on the average.[100] However, China has a distinct edge over India in the effectiveness of her medical and health programs because they are buttressed much more intensively and effectively by radio propaganda, dissemination of information, counseling, party meetings, and group talks aimed at enlightening and directing the entire population in a mass program of health and sanitation consciousness. This was much in evidence during my stay in China and my visits to factories and communes.

There is general agreement among Western doctors, medical school professors, and other visitors to China, as well as U.S. medical and public health experts, that Red China has achieved very impressive overall improvements in the practice of personal hygiene and general environmental sanitation in both the urban and rural areas.[101] Cholera, smallpox, venereal disease, typhus, and typhoid have been almost eliminated in Communist China. Major parasitic infections, hookworm, dysentery, tuberculosis, and malaria have been brought under control. Germ-carrying insects and rats are noticeably less common than in many relatively affluent economies.

Industrial personnel seemed to me to be on the average healthier and in better physical condition in China than in India. (This is also true for Chinese, as against Indian, farmers.) Medical facilities are generally better at Chinese enterprises, when firms of roughly the same size and in the same industry are compared. All of the Chinese factories visited provide free medical care to their employees. Most Indian industrial workers are covered by medical and health insurance, but the extent of their coverage and quality of medical treatment do not seem to be generally as good as in China. All but a few of the smallest of the Chinese factories visited have their own clinics, doctors, nurses, and sickbeds, and those that do not can make use of nearby facilities. Many Indian firms employing upward of five hundred employees do not have their own doctors or nurses, although other medical facilities available locally are usually no better, and quite frequently worse, than in China. (There are of course notable exceptions. Many Indian companies do have very good medical facilities.)

A number of the large Chinese industrial enterprises even have their own hospitals; and in some cases they have more than one hospital. For example, Wuhan Iron and Steel has two hospitals with several hundred beds. These hospitals employ over 500 personnel. About 5,000 of this firm's 35,000 employees are engaged in welfare and service activities, including medical and health work, housing, education, and so on. Shanghai Steel Mill No. 3 had no medical facilities in 1949, when it employed 302 people. In 1966, with an employment of 13,000, it had its own hospital with about 100 beds, five clinics located in major workshops, 170 doctors and nurses, and over 100 other supporting medical workers. Nanking Chemical Fertilizer, which employs 10,000 people, has its own large hospital, and approximately 800 or 900 of its personnel are engaged in medical, welfare, and other service activities. Shanghai Sung Sing (Joint) Cotton Textile Mill No. 9 had a maximum of two sickbeds, one part-time doctor, and one nurse prior to 1950, even during years when employment was over 2,000. In 1966 this firm had 6,000 employees, seven full-time doctors, over a dozen nurses, and 40 hospital beds, even though there is a large public hospital very close by.

The sizable staffs of medical, welfare, and other service personnel found at Chinese industrial enterprises—at most enterprises visited this type of personnel constituted from 4 to 7 percent and, in some cases, more than 10 percent of total employment—tend to make the overall managerial job broader and more complex. However, because of the critical shortages of external (external to individual enterprise) medical, housing, educational, and other welfare facilities in China, as compared with facilities in advanced Western nations, the gains in productivity undoubtedly outweigh the losses which may occur from the increased managerial burden.

Red China has many more rest homes and workers' sanitariums for the treatment of mental ailments and nervous disorders than does India. All major industrial centers in China apparently have such facilities. Industrial employees are sent upon recommendations by their enterprises and receive free care. The enterprise trade-union committee usually decides who should be sent and handles all of the paper work and procedures. I visited three sanitariums of this type. One was the Tai Lake Workers' Sanitarium on the outskirts of Wusih on a lovely lake and set among the rolling hills. It is a very modern, well-equipped and well-staffed hospital. About half of the three hundred patients were suffering from insomnia, hypertension, high blood pressure, and other stress and strain ailments of a nervous disorder or mental nature. Many of the patients suffering from arthritis or rheumatism are treated through traditional Chinese medicine, particularly acupuncture, rather than Western medicine.[102] Acupuncture involves treatment by the application of needles to strategic parts of the body.

In general, Red China's apparent edge over India in the general health and physical condition of her industrial—and agricultural—labor force probably contributes to greater labor productivity. As was noted in Chapter 5, absenteeism and labor turnover appear to be less in Chinese industry than in Indian industry. While there are a variety of reasons for this (some of the major ones have been discussed in earlier chapters), differences in the general health level and condition of the labor forces in the two countries are probably a significant contributing factor. Daily physical exercise is compulsory for all able industrial personnel in China. This undoubtedly also contributes to better health and physical condition, and hence greater labor productivity. China also seems to have an edge over India in public sanitation, including sewer systems, water supplies, and worker-housing conditions. This edge implies less rapid spreading of diseases, debilitating maladies, and respiratory infections and, in turn, greater labor productivity and less absenteeism and turnover.

Some experts and many laymen contend that climate has a significant impact on labor productivity. This is not a definitively proven contention. Moreover, the development of internal climate-control technology—such as fans, ventilation, air conditioning, heating—has done much to reduce the impact of adverse climatic conditions in enterprises, even in poorer countries, such as China and India. Somewhat greater progress seems to have been made in Chinese industry, on the average, than in Indian industry in reducing the impact of adverse climatic conditions in factories. If it is true that climate does have a significant impact on the labor force and its productivity, it must be admitted that China as a whole is endowed with a somewhat more moderate climate than India as a whole, although both countries have both moderate and extreme climatic regions. But in the final analysis, even granting a significant relationship between climate and labor productivity, climate per se, in my opinion, is of secondary importance compared with most, if not all, of the other environmental constraints under study in this book. Japan, Hong Kong, and Israel are not endowed with very favorable climates for a good part of the year, but look at the quality and performance of their labor forces, and their economic progress. Similarly, one can point to other countries in Africa, Latin America, Asia, and elsewhere which have relatively good climates but poor economic progress.

Capital

The meaning of capital here is real capital in the form of physical goods used in future production, and not money capital. Real capital is derived from savings which are then invested, and it must be manufactured laboriously by previously existing capital, natural resources, and labor and management. We have already discussed savings and investment as well as the buildup of real capital in the Chinese economy in earlier sections, but some additional comments seem in order here.

Both Communist China and India have done impressive jobs in building up their industrial real capital since the beginning of the 1950's, but both still lag far behind advanced nations like the United States and even Russia and Japan in real capital in per capita terms. China's progress has been even greater than India's, and China's capital stock is substantially larger than India's in absolute terms (this is evident from the industrial performance data to be presented in Chapter 8) and probably in per capita terms as well. Chinese industry also has a significant lead over Indian industry in the breadth and diversity of its real capital stock, though not necessarily in quality or complexity in some sectors.

In spite of impressive accumulations of real capital, both countries, being relatively poor, are still faced with capital scarcity in relation to what they would like to achieve industrially, economically, politically, and, in the case of China in particular, militarily. Moreover, neither country can afford to seriously misuse or waste its real capital on a significant scale.

Both China and India have followed a pattern, common in developing nations that are in a big hurry, of generating large savings which are used chiefly for the rapid buildup of heavy industry—particularly the machinery, equipment, and metal-producing areas—at the great expense of other sectors of the economy. The excessively rapid development of heavy industry greatly outstripped the available supply of essential inputs of raw materials and other commodities, skilled and high-talent manpower, and managerial know-how. The result has been a large and wasteful pile-up of idle real capital and other resources, as well as serious imbalances, mismatches of factors, and bottlenecks which have developed throughout the economy. As has been noted earlier, both countries have now apparently realized their past mistakes regarding a too rapid buildup of real capital in heavy industry. In recent years they have been moving in the direction of more balanced capital investment and economic development, with China evidently following this course even more effectively and vigorously than India.

Although many economic sectors in China and India have suffered substantially because they have not been provided with adequate amounts of real capital, relatively high degrees of labor-intensive methods make much more sense in many areas than would be the case in advanced economies, given the severe overpopulation problems and the large amounts of surplus labor which exist in India and China. Handicrafts or cottage industries, such as those producing arts and crafts, embroidery, pottery and porcelain, some types of clothing, and jewelry, can operate in a reasonably efficient manner with relatively little real capital. The same is true for various other types of factories such as those involved with certain types of furniture, food processing, machinery repairing and remodeling, toys, radio and TV assembly, and so forth.

Given the relatively low wage rates in China and India, the gains from substantially reducing labor and in raising labor productivity by substantially increasing the capital intensity of operations would frequently be more than offset by the additional costs—including opportunity costs—involved in various industries and operations. Moreover, by maintaining highly labor-intensive production techniques much productive use can be made of otherwise surplus labor. This typically has economic benefits as well as good psychological effects on society at large.

On the other hand, there is a distinct tendency in Indian industry, and probably in China as well, to assume automatically that highly labor-intensive techniques are the most beneficial in certain areas, without adequate analysis of true costs versus benefits. It is automatically assumed that labor is cheap because of low wages, and indirect costs related to labor—such as turnover, absenteeism, waste and spoilage in production, recruitment, training, and supervision—which may be very substantial are, for the most part, ignored.

In Chinese (and Indian) industry as a whole, material-handling operations, warehousing, and transportation tend to be highly labor-intensive, even where very bulky commodities are involved. Such activities provide employment for many people—at many of the Chinese industrial enterprises surveyed, 10 to 20 percent and in a few cases even more of their personnel were engaged in such activities—but in many cases more use of capital-intensive techniques would undoubtedly be substantially more beneficial, certainly from an economic standpoint. Serious diseconomies of scale, much interference with direct production workers and the production process, considerable confusion, great damage, spoilage, and waste of goods, as well as very low labor productivity, were all very much in evidence at a number of Chinese (and Indian) factories largely because of extremely labor-intensive methods of material handling, warehousing, and transportation. One truly wonders whether opportunity costs really support the use of so little real capital in such activities in many instances, even for poor overpopulated countries like China and India. The same is true for the production process itself at various types of industrial enterprises. In Chinese industry in 1966 there seemed to be a fairly common tendency particularly among Reds to shun additions of real capital and to prefer striving for self-sufficiency, innovation, and improvisation through highly labor-intensive and frequently highly efficient methods.

Some of the Chinese factories surveyed which were sadly deficient in real capital even in the production process and which seemed to be very inefficient for this and other reasons were Hangchow Machine Tool, Wuhan Diesel Engine, Peking Steel Wire, Canton Electrical Appliance, and Tientsin Shoe. On the other hand, I visited well-equipped plants, such as Tientsin Watch, which appeared to be operating inefficiently, and substantially undercapitalized factories, such as Shanghai Wei Ming Battery, which appeared to be operating quite well with available technology. More will be said in a later chapter about technology and performance of Chinese enterprises surveyed, but a few additional comments are in order here.

Tientsin Shoe employed only 200 workers before 1950, and employment had increased to 1,000 employees as of 1966. This growth in employment was achieved primarily through the absorption of individual shoemakers and shoemaker cooperatives by the Tientsin firm during the 1950's. In spite of this sharp growth in employment, the factory still remained highly labor-intensive in 1966. The majority of its sparse equipment—much of it idle—was made by the factory itself. Although the quality of the shoes produced seemed quite good—perhaps because much of the output is for export—labor productivity was very low. But then, leather shoes are still a luxury in Red China, and cloth shoes are still the norm.

I was surprised by the amounts of modern real capital at the two Chinese clothing factories and the cotton-textile and woolen plants run by the state. A substantial proportion of the output of these enterprises is exported, and this may have something to do with their relatively good technology. They were more capital-intensive and better equipped, in general, than most of the Indian firms in these industries which I managed to visit. Both the Peking and Hangchow clothing firms have evolved through amalgamations of individual handicraftsmen, handicrafts cooperatives, and small handicrafts workshops. Peking Clothing had only 400 employees in 1952, but subsequently employment increased sharply—it was 1,700 in 1966—with the consolidation and integration of ten small handicrafts workshops. Hangchow Clothing was established in 1954 through a consolidation of cooperatives, small workshops, and individual craftsmen. Employment in 1966 stood at 400. As these firms have grown in size, a substantial amount of real capital has been added.

Tientsin North Lake Instrument and Wusih Red Flag Machinery, both highly labor-intensive and small-scale, also reached their existing levels of employment—165 and 300, respectively—largely through amalgamations of individual craftsmen, handicraft cooperatives, and small labor-intensive workshops. However, unlike the two clothing factories, relatively little real capital was added with their growth in employment. Wusih Machinery seemed to be performing more efficiently than Tientsin Instrument, but both seemed to be worthwhile operations in spite of their highly labor-intensive nature. The former repairs and rebuilds machines for other enterprises and engages in various other subcontracting wo:k. Its profits, as a percent of sales, amounted to 30 percent in 1965. The latter makes and assembles a variety of instruments, tools, components, and small machines. Its profits, as a percent of sales, in 1965 were 28 percent. Perhaps one of the most important contributions of enterprises like these two to Chinese industry is that they evidently serve as a training ground for the development of skilled personnel who are often transferred to larger and more important firms. This provides for relatively low-cost human-resource development, with little investment in real capital.

Between my wife—who was in Red China with me during the early part of my stay—and myself we visited seven factories based on pure handicraft in Canton, Fushan (near Canton), Tientsin, Wusih, and Soochow. Actually four of them were not factories, although they all produced handicraft items: one was a handicraft cooperative, another a workshop, the third an "institute," and the fourth a "studio." The largest of these handicraft organizations—the Tahsin Ivory-Carving Factory in Canton—employed several hundred people; the smallest, the Fushan Arts and Crafts Studio, employed about thirty people. (I do not include purely handicraft establishments as part of my Chinese sample of industrial enterprises or factories surveyed in this book.) The types of products manufactured and processed by these seven handicraft establishments included porcelain, pottery, toys, embroidery work, jewelry, paper products, leather goods, clay statuettes, ivory carvings, and silk, cotton, and woolen clothing, and other articles.

All of these establishments were wholly labor-intensive, with the exception of a few small power drills and a very small lathe at one or two of them. At most of the handicrafts establishments visited, the workers seemed to work very hard, productivity appeared to be quite high, and product quality good for this type of work. The bulk of the items and virtually all of the "traditional" articles produced and processed at most of these organizations were for export and foreign consumption. I mention foreign consumption since they are available in larger Chinese cities chiefly for the tourist trade and for diplomats.

In general, the highly labor-intensive handicrafts sector of Red China's industry has been an important source of state accumulation—through profits and taxes—used for investment and the buildup of real capital in other sectors. It has also been an important source of exports and hence foreign-exchange earnings, which have been and are used in large part for the buildup of real capital in other sectors. And it has also provided employment for a significant part of the employed labor force.[103]

Handicrafts production, considered as part of the industrial sector, grew at an estimated average annual rate of 8 percent during 1950–52, 7 percent from 1953 through 1957, and 10 percent in 1958–59. During the 1952–62 period urban handicraft output contributed to Red China's net national product at an annual average rate of roughly 6 percent. During the 1952–57 period industrial and other urban handicrafts averaged more than 15 percent of the total gross value of combined industrial and agricultural production, while subsistence handicrafts in rural areas contributed an additional 8 to 9 percent. As the modern industrial sector expanded sharply in the 1950's, however, the total proportion of total value added in industry derived from handicraft output declined from an estimated 32 percent in 1949, to 20 percent in 1962, 14 percent in 1957, and 10 percent in 1959. Reliable estimates for more recent years are not available, but handicrafts contribution to value added in the overall industrial sector is probably not substantially less than 10 percent and may be more than 10 percent.

Handicrafts employment in nonagricultural or urban sectors grew steadily from about 5.86 million in 1949 to a high of 8.91 million in 1954. In 1955 it declined to 8.2 million, declining further to 5.8 million in 1956, but rising to 6.6 million in 1957, the last year for which reasonably accurate handicrafts-employment data were available. It should be noted that millions of workers in China's rural economy also engage in handicrafts production on both a full-time and part-time basis.

There was a dramatic shift in the structure of employment in the overall handicrafts sector beginning around 1954. Individual or self-employed handicraftsmen—labeled as such where no more than the craftsman's immediate family and three hired helpers are involved—comprised over 90 percent of employment in this sector in 1949 and the early fifties; by the end of 1956 they comprised only about 10 percent. In Indian industry, employment is still larger in the handicrafts sector than all other sectors, and the great majority of handicraftsmen are still self-employed. The great majority of the Chinese handicraft workers transferred to handicraft cooperatives, workshops, factories, and stores as the regime stepped up and climaxed its efforts to socialize and communize the private sector. During 1954–56—before all private firms were turned into joint state and private enterprises—private handicraft workshops and factories, as well as other types of private plants, that were the most capital-intensive were transferred to joint ownership first, typically through coercion or because of bankruptcy, and the least mechanized ones were transferred last. After 1957 a great many handicraft cooperatives and workshops were consolidated and converted into factories, thus giving most of them the classification status of "modern" industrial enterprises.[104] This was the case with some of the enterprises discussed above. At the same time greater emphasis was given to the production of producer goods in the handicraft sector but still largely through highly labor-intensive methods.

There are still some individual self-employed handicraftsmen in scattered parts of some of Red China's major cities. They are typically confined to certain sections of town, such as one old section of Wuhan which I visited, and which, I was told, contains "several thousand" self-employed handicraftsmen operating in an entirely labor-intensive manner. These mini-private entrepreneurs set their own prices, keep most of their profits, and sell to both individual consumers and organizations, including factories. In fact, they provide some beneficial flexibility in procurement and supply for industrial enterprises, but only for minor commodities. They work in their homes and on the streets near their homes. Some of the items which I saw them making and processing included wire, rope, brooms, cans, crates, and containers, baskets, shoes, pots and pans, dishes, simple chemical mixtures, rather primitive small tools, paper products, imitation jewelry, fasteners, nails, various wooden items, and clothing. They use scrap materials for most of their work, and in some cases they repair simple machines and appliances.

With the formation of large numbers of handicraft cooperatives, and particularly with the formation of handicraft factories, a major aim of the state was to increase productivity, lower costs, and derive more revenues in substantial part through additions of real capital and improved technology in the handicrafts sector. There are indications that real capital did increase, especially in the factory part of the handicrafts sector, and possibly modestly in the cooperative sphere, but the extent of capital investment in the overall handicrafts is not known. There have also probably been substantial improvements in technology particularly in the factory sphere. Labor productivity in the overall handicrafts sector may have increased substantially, although this is not verified. It is also possible that labor productivity has not increased very significantly because of a decline in the motivation of many previously self-employed handicraftsmen who have been forced to work for state establishments.

Market Size

Ideally, from an economic standpoint, the markets for all of the types of products manufactured and processed by the overall industrial sector in a given country would be large enough to have each branch of industry characterized by optimum-sized firms. Such optimum-sized firms would enable maximum economies of scale to be derived in production, marketing, and procurement, as well as various other critical functions of the enterprise and management. In virtually all cases, commodity markets—which consist of existing and/or potential uses of the items in question—would be large enough for industrial enterprises to make reasonably full use of their equipment and other productive resources. For producer goods, the size of consuming industrial sectors would be the critical factor. And for many types of enterprises the number of potential users for their products might be affected by obtainable export markets and/or competitive (including substitutable) imports allowed into the country. It would tend to facilitate managerial effectiveness and productive efficiency in the overall productive sector, however, if a major portion of each firm's customers—and suppliers, assuming they are relatively efficient and the law of comparative advantage in foreign trade is not seriously abused—were not located very far away from its production operations.

Of course, such optimum conditions regarding market size and location would not by themselves provide for a high degree of managerial effectiveness, productive efficiency, or general industrial progress. All of the other environmental constraints under study in this book are also critical in this regard, but optimum or even relatively favorable market structures would mean that industrial firms and their managements would have one less negative environmental constraint to contend with. An important separate but related problem is that individual firms must base their plans and operations on reasonable accurate predictions of the size of the markets for their products in order for them to perform at a high degree of effectiveness and efficiency. Here, too, a variety of educational, sociological-cultural, political, legal, and economic environmental factors are critical because they determine the accuracy of such predictions. If market size is overestimated, the result is likely to be idle resources and waste. If it is underestimated, productive opportunities will be lost if the firm cannot adjust operations in time to meet the unanticipated demand for its products.

In general, the wealthier a country is in both absolute and per capita terms—reflected effective purchasing power, and income distribution—the larger the markets are likely to be for a wider range of products. However, in the real world even the most advanced, affluent, and largest industrial economies fall substantially short of the ideal or optimum situation regarding market size and location discussed above, because of the existence of a variety of environmental constraints. But they are generally much closer to the optimum situation than relatively poor countries, including poorer and smaller nations that are struggling to develop, and particularly those countries, both large and small, that have not progressed to the developing stage. China before 1949 fell into the category of a very large, very poor country that had not really entered the developing stage in a substantial way.

Republican China

In Republican China, particularly during 1937–49, extreme economic and political instability, price inflation, and war made it impossible for even the best-managed firms to predict with confidence the sizes of markets or the number of potential users for their products. This great market uncertainty sharply constrained the size of firms, and most branches of industry were dominated by relatively small and inefficient enterprises typically operating under considerable diseconomies of scale by modern standards. The small number of relatively large industrial enterprises that did exist were also typically constrained from deriving potential economies of scale during much of the Republican era because of extreme market fluctuations and uncertainty as well as other unfavorable environmental conditions. The relatively large firms consisted primarily of textile producers, many of which produced substantially for export when they could get sufficient raw materials and other supplies, and a few heavy industry plants, mostly in Manchuria, largely producing commodities for war.

It is true that China had a population of roughly 400 to 540 million during the Republican era, but even industrial firms producing products that were consumed by a substantial portion of the population were typically small because of market uncertainty and a wide variety of other environmental constraints. When adequate materials and other supplies could be obtained, even the small inefficient firms could make adequate profits, but critical supplies became increasingly difficult to get particularly during the 1937–49 period. Grossly deficient and primitive social-overhead-capital facilities, particularly transportation and warehousing, fostered the industrial make-up of small firms serving only local markets.

In order to move manufactured goods to, and raw materials from, the millions of small farming villages that comprised the great bulk of the nation's huge population, or to get manufactured items to the greatly scattered inland nonindustrial cities, numerous middlemen were required. This was not as inefficient as it may sound, however, since such middlemen could earn an adequate living—the equivalent of a few dollars a week—by taking small percentages on a very limited number of commodities. Nevertheless, the distribution of the population, in conjunction with severe social-overhead-capital constraints, greatly retarded the formation of relatively large-scale or technologically efficient industrial enterprises.

Prior to 1949 over 75 percent of the value of China's industrial output came from the eastern coastal areas—and mostly from Shanghai, Tientsin, and a few major cities in Manchuria—which constituted less than 10 percent of the country as a whole, while the other 90 percent of the nation produced less than 25 percent. In 1947 Shanghai was reported to have over half of the industrial enterprises and workers employed in industry, while Tientsin had 9 percent and 8 percent, respectively.[105] The great bulk, probably well over 90 percent, of the producer goods were manufactured in a few eastern industrial centers which were under foreign domination during most of the Republican era. Inland manufacturing was confined almost entirely to the production of consumer goods and other light-industry commodities.

Although Republican China was an extremely poor country, it had enough relatively affluent people who were potential users of virtually any type of consumer goods. (Even a potential market of merely one-tenth of 1 percent of the population would have comprised four or five million people.) But even the very small portion of the population that was relatively wealthy was quite scattered in different parts of the country; many of the affluent were wealthy landlords, war lords, officials, and their chief aides who lived in rural areas.

Most types of consumer goods, with the exception of various foodstuffs, textiles, clothing, and a few other products bought by the wealthier classes, were imported. To have produced most of the imported type of consumer goods and producer goods in China in a profitable or reasonably efficient way would have frequently required fairly large-scale operations, sizable amounts of money and real capital, relatively high degrees of managerial and technical know-how and considerable skilled labor, much greater dependability of critical supplies, and much better access to, and much greater certainty of, markets.

In Republican China, environmental conditions especially retarded the creation of relatively large-scale producer-goods factories in all but a handful of major coastal industrial centers, such as Dairen, Shanghai, Shenyang, Tientsin, and Harbin. Domestic markets for almost all types of producer goods were negligible, and the quality specifications and costs of such products if produced indigenously could not have withstood competition in world export markets. Moreover, essential feeder industries and most types of domestic materials were virtually nonexistent in connection with all but a few types of producer goods in a handful of cities. Hence, in the eyes of the typical potential private investor or entrepreneur in Republican China it would have taken many years, if ever, for a newly created plant of substantial size in the producer-goods sector to become a profitable venture. Market size would have been one of the most crucial constraints.

For the creation of new, relatively large-scale producer-goods enterprises to have been economically feasible—even within a period of several years—the simultaneous development of critical feeder and consuming plants would have been required in most instances. But the development of such integrated industrial complexes would have required such large sums of money, including large amounts of foreign exchange in most cases, that even the wealthiest citizens were not willing to undertake the risks, given the various negative environmental conditions that existed. And even if they were, the foreign exchange and imports required for such projects would probably not have been obtainable, especially during the 1937–49 period. Prior to this period, foreign interests had established most of the large-scale producer-goods firms in China. The Republican government did not have the resources, a real opportunity, or an urgent desire to create the types of large, integrated industrial complexes required for economic development and sustained industrial progress; moreover, the Kuomintang was almost entirely preoccupied with problems of war and political control throughout much of its rule.

Communist China

The earlier sections of this book have shown that since the early 1950's Communist China—and, to a lesser degree, India—has made great progress in creating many new industries and numerous large-scale firms—including large integrated industrial complexes, in greatly broadening the scope of traditional industries and in developing domestic and, in many cases, export markets for manufactured products. This has been accomplished through state planning, resource allocation and investment. In India, the state has also played a vital role in the development of particularly the heavy-industrial sector. Both countries have been motivated largely by their desires for long-run self-sufficiency, prestige, pride, better living standards, and in Red China in particular, national security. But in both countries gross errors have been made in estimating and balancing market requirements and needs with productive capacity and resources, and great waste and inefficiency have resulted in the industrial sector, most notably during the 1958–62 period in China.

Although Red China's seven coastal provinces still contribute a substantial majority of the nation's industrial output, great strides have been made in developing important inland industrial and mining centers. (See the map presented on the book cover.)[106] China's Communist leadership, for reasons of economics, national security, sentiment, and strategy, was determined from the outset to effect a much more widespread distribution of industry and the creation of new markets throughout the country. A majority of the large new industrial projects of the First Five-Year Plan were located in the interior. Wuhan, Paotow, Chungking, Lanchow, Taiyuan, Loyang, and Chengchow are some of the important heavy-industry centers that have been created in the interior. Many new mines and other sources of raw materials have also been developed inland. There has also been considerable light-industry development in the interior, chiefly to gain new sources of essential raw materials and markets for finished goods.

By 1958 Red China's inland areas—excluding the seven coastal provinces—were producing over one-third of the nation's gross industrial output by value, compared with less than 25 percent prior to 1950.[107] This is a remarkable achievement, considering that China's total industrial production increased several-fold during the 1950's.

India has also made considerable progress in opening up new industrial areas and creating essential new markets, but China's progress in this regard has been more extensive and effective in spite of many serious problems that still persist. In both countries, but especially in China, inadequate social-overhead-capital facilities have been a major constraint in the development of new industrial areas and new markets.

While continued industrial development and economic self-sufficiency in China's interior areas are still regarded as highly desirable aims, some of the Red Chinese planners, industrial officials, and economists whom I met acknowledged that these are still essentially long-term propositions. It seems that the aim is to attain a high degree of economic self-sufficiency at the provincial, and even the municipal, levels where possible, and where provincial conditions are not adequate, some form of regional self-sufficiency appears to be the goal. Perhaps Red China's six major regions—each containing a number of provinces, special municipalities and/or so-called autonomous regions—where special party bureaus were reestablished in 1961 will form the bases of self-sufficient regional economic development.[108]

It appears from my research in China that relatively self-sufficient provinces and municipalities, where most of their sources of supply and customers are in the vicinity, have substantially more authority and independence over their industrial affairs than relatively dependent areas. Hence, a great industrial city like Shanghai, or even industrial Wusih with a population of only 750,000, probably has much greater industrial decision-making powers than provinces and cities which have relatively sparse industrial facilities. The latter are no doubt subject to relatively high degrees of central planning, resource allocation, and control.

Red China's industrial base is now broad and diverse enough to support at least several large-scale or optimum-sized firms in almost all producer-goods sectors, with the exception of a few highly complex and unique items, such as certain types of nuclear, radar, and advanced electronic equipment. In this regard China has a lead over India.

Because of the vast populations of China and India, there are adequate potential markets to support at least some large-scale or optimum-sized consumer-goods plants for most types of products. In addition, both countries have sizable export markets for various consumer products. In general, textile, clothing, and various other types of consumer-goods plants seem to be larger, on the average, in China than in India.

Both China and India have achieved greater equable income distribution in the last fifteen years or so, thus sharply increasing the number of potential uses for many consumer goods—especially essential and relatively cheap items. But China has gone even further than India in achieving equable income distribution and more widespread purchasing power. On the other hand, India still has a sizable number, in absolute terms, of relatively affluent people who can afford luxury items and other expensive consumer goods, including cars. Hence, the Indian economy can, and does, support relatively large-scale firms which produce a variety of expensive consumer products. (Since India does not have any television networks, there are no plants producing TV sets.)

In Communist China all affluent classes—with the exception of the very small class of wealthy capitalists, which will be discussed in a later chapter—have been abolished. However, there still are relatively large-scale, or otherwise near-optimum-sized, factories producing such expensive items as TV sets, musical instruments, refrigerators, and washing machines in sizable quantities.

China has produced a negligible number of its own automobiles beginning around the late 1950's at two truck factories: one in Changchun, the other in Shanghai.[109] Chinese car production is apparently carried out on a very small scale in a highly inefficient manner. Many imported parts and components are evidently used, and, in speaking of the Chinese automobile industry, car assembly rather than production may be the more accurate term. The regime seems to follow an on-again-off-again policy with regard to automobile production. When the Changchun Truck Plant has produced cars, they have been the Red Flag model. The Shanghai Three-Wheeled Truck Factory produces the Phoenix model, which appears to be based on Mercedes Benz designs, in negligible quantities from time to time. I don't think I saw more than one Red Flag car on the streets in Red China, and saw only a few Phoenix models, mostly in parades. Most cars in use in China seem to be Polish models. There are also Russian, Czech, British, French, and U.S. cars in use. Most of the American autos are vintage pre-1950 models, although I did come across some fairly new U.S. models—probably imported from Hong Kong or purchased by the Chinese government from foreign residents—in Shanghai, Peking, and Canton.

As of 1966 there were only an estimated 40,000 to 50,000 cars in use in Red China.[110] In general, there are adequate domestic markets justifying optimum-sized plants which permit economies of scale in the production of a fairly wide range of expensive consumer goods in Red China. But these markets are comprised of institutional buyers for the most part, rather than individuals. It is common for Chinese factories, communes, schools, hospitals, large offices and stores, and various other types of organizations to have TV sets, refrigerators, washing machines, and the like. This very fact will permit the establishment of many more large-scale and optimum-sized consumer-goods plants on economic grounds.

At present, because of capital scarcity, the dearth of high-talent manpower (particularly managerial and technical know-how), large pools of surplus labor, population distribution, and the inaccessibility of large quantities of diverse supplies and substantial markets, many branches of Red Chinese industry are still characterized in substantial part by numerous small and highly labor-intensive factories. The same is true in India for similar reasons. Given these and various other environmental conditions, however, such factories—and individual handicraftsmen as well—probably, much more often than not, play a useful and desirable role in the economy, for reasons discussed in the earlier section on factor endowment. This is not doubt true in spite of their production methods, limited output, and the smallness of the markets they serve. However, from what I saw I feel that excessive vertical integration and the lack of specialization at many types of Chinese factories are leading to a considerable amount of avoidable economic waste and inefficiency. In many cases—for example, at Tientsin Shoe, Hangchow Machine Tool, Wuhan Diesel Engine, and Canton Electrical Appliance which produce much of their own equipment, spares, and components—there now seem to be adequate and readily accessible markets, as well as potential resources, to warrant the creation of more specialized types of plants, rather than having so many existing factories produce such large amounts of their own machinery, equipment, components, spare parts, materials, and so on.

Even though there are at least several enterprises in virtually all branches of Chinese industry, numerous firms in many branches, and frequently many firms producing the same types of products in the same locality, Chinese industrial enterprises are typically monopolists because they have protected markets prescribed by the plan for the great bulk of their output. Their customers, and the amounts and types of products they are to supply to each, are spelled out in the plan in the great majority of instances. Customer enterprises typically do not have alternative sources of supply available if their supplier lets them down. Hence, firms in their roles as producers and suppliers generally function in a sellers' market and need not be overly concerned about the wishes, needs, or requirements of their customers. The same situation exists in the Soviet

Union. In India, firms in various branches of industry—particularly heavy industry—also function as monopolists in sellers' markets.

This means that the typical Chinese industrial enterprises—as well as Soviet firms and, in many cases, Indian enterprises—need not bother much with the hard sell, sales promotion, advertising, and other marketing techniques so common in the United States and other advanced Western economies. However, the Chinese seem to have a greater flair for, and interest in, the marketing function than the Russians; China has traditionally had a sizable population of merchants, traders, and shopkeepers. As a result, one tends to find greater attention paid to marketing and to serving the customer at Chinese industrial enterprises—particularly in Chinese retail stores—than in comparable organizations in the Soviet Union, at least in the early 1960's when I was last in Russia. This also seems to be true for Chinese firms, as compared with many Indian firms, in highly monopolistic positions.

Moreover, it is likely that the typical Chinese industrial enterprise and its management are more concerned about, and try harder at improving, efficiency and overall performance than the typical Indian firm functioning in protected markets largely free from competitive forces. If this is true, achievement motivation, attitudes toward risk taking and change, basic economic system, and legal rules of the game are probably among the most important environmental factors accounting for this difference.

China has gone much further than India in shortening distribution channels from producers to end users, and in eliminating vast numbers of small middlemen in the supply and marketing of a great many commodities. China's central and local governments have taken over the larger wholesale and distribution organizations moving goods within and between all basic sectors—that is, industry, agriculture, and domestic trade. More will be said about such organizations in later chapters. It will suffice to say here that the overall distribution of goods appears to be more economical and effective in China than in India from an organizational standpoint, but not necessarily from a customer-service standpoint.

The creation of communes throughout China's rural areas has also made the marketing job of getting commodities to and from these areas a simpler and more efficient task.[111] Formerly, distribution in China's countryside typically involved business dealings with millions of tiny villages, and tens of millions of households. With the Great Leap some 26,500 communes were set up, comprising virtually all of the rural population. Major business transactions were conducted through the managements of these communes. Fairly large stores, depots, and warehouses were set up in the communes. In 1960, the three million production teams comprising the communes obtained substantially greater authority in business negotiations and transactions, and this probably made the job of distributing industrial supplies and consumer goods to the rural areas and procuring raw materials from them more complex. In 1964 the number of communes was apparently increased to 74,000—with an average of about 7,000 to 8,000 people per commune—and the several million production teams have continued to be an important business-transacting, financial, profit-and-loss, and accounting unit.[112]

Nevertheless, the functions of distribution, procurement, and marketing of goods in rural areas are still simpler and probably more economical in China than in India. Most of the Chinese communes that I visited had sizable general stores, depots, and storage facilities. Marketing and procurement in India's countryside involves some 566,000 small villages which contain millions of tiny shops and tens of millions of households. The individual household in India is still the basic business unit for many goods that are bought and sold in India's rural areas, and village shops, depots, and storage facilities seem to be smaller and more numerous in India than in the Chinese communes.

Social-Overhead Capital

The term "social-overhead capital," as used in this study, has already been defined in Chapter 3. There it was also pointed out that industrial enterprises in countries which have poorly developed social-overhead-capital facilities tend to be more difficult to manage and operate efficiently than those in countries with good facilities. Where social-overhead-capital facilities and their management external to the industrial firm are relatively good, external economies are derived by the firm; where the reverse is true the industrial enterprise is typically confronted with serious external diseconomies. (An external economy is defined here as a favorable effect on a given industrial enterprise that emanates from the service, action, and/or performance of an external organization or facility.)

Earlier we have discussed housing, schooling, public health, sanitation, and medical facilities bearing on the industrial sector in Communist China, chiefly in the section on factor endowment, but also in a few other sections in earlier chapters. In this connection it was pointed out that Chinese industrial enterprises, particularly larger ones, typically have quite extensive facilities of their own of these types, as well as sizable numbers of personnel to operate and maintain them, thus broadening the scope and complexity of the management job. Critical shortages of warehousing facilities and resulting adverse consequences at the level of the enterprise in Chinese industry have been pointed out in our discussion of contracts in the section dealing with relevant legal rules of the game in Chapter 5. In the present section we focus on China's transportation, communications, telephones, telegraph, postal, and electric-power systems, and the way they tend to affect managerial performance, productive efficiency, and general progress at the industrial-enterprise level of the economy.

Dimensions of China's Transportation System

Transportation has historically been a very serious problem in China and it still is, but to a substantially lesser degree, as we shall see, because of her huge population, its distribution, and the immense distances from east to west and north to south in the country. The close relationship between transportation and industrial development is self-evident, since raw materials of relatively low unit value must be obtained from the source, and products delivered to customers and other consuming markets. The extremely backward and sparse nature of transportation facilities in pre-1950 China was one of the most crucial factors hindering the development of the interior and general industrial progress. Lack of transportation made most of the nation's rich reserves of mineral resources inaccessible; it greatly limited sources of raw materials required by industry, and confined markets for most products to very limited local areas.

By 1949 most of what there was of China's very underdeveloped and sparse transportation system—particularly the railroads—had been cut, recut, seriously damaged, and destroyed by contending armies in both the Japanese and civil wars. The Chinese Communists disrupted, immobilized, and strove to take over railways, roads, docks, and waterways, and communications during periods of civil war and political strife because these were strategic for political and economic control. Such was their strategy before they gained power in 1949; more recently they have used the same tactics in handling strikes and civil unrest in Hong Kong and Macao. And during the Cultural Revolution in Red China Mao's supporters have moved very swiftly to mobilize and maintain control over transportation and communications. Both these sectors have played highly strategic roles in this later "revolution."

China's existing social-overhead capital in general was largely a shambles by 1949. Railroads have always been the backbone of China's transportation system. In 1949 freight and passenger turnover on China's railways was well under half that of the pre-1949 peak year. The same was true for motor and water transportation. Before the 1950's, civil aviation had been virtually nonexistent in China. Even in the pre-1949 peak years, China's transportation system was very backward in absolute, as well as per capita, terms. For example, her railways and roads were less extensive than relatively tiny Italy's during similar periods, and substantially less extensive than those of India which is some three to four times smaller than China in area.

Under China's Communist regime considerable progress has been made in the development of her transportation system, and without such progress overall industrial progress and the development of the interior would have been very much less substantial.[113] The army has played an important role in restoring, maintaining, and building China's transportation networks. However, Red China is still very backward in transportation, as well as in communications and electric power, when compared with industrialized nations, and transportation is still a serious constraint on managerial effectiveness and productive efficiency in the industrial sector. In spite of its relatively backward nature, India's overall transportation system is probably better in terms of industrial development than Red China's system.

During the 1950's the transportation sector—and also the communications sector—were somewhat grudging recipients of state investment, and this has remained more or less true in the 1960's. The construction, development, and operation of Red China's transportation networks have been carried out through highly labor-intensive methods. A major reason for this is to provide employment for millions of unskilled laborers who otherwise would be unemployed, or at best grossly underemployed. Rugged terrain and great capital scarcity—both money and real capital—have also been major constraints with regard to the development of the transportation sector.

During the 1950's the percentage of gross fixed investment provided to transportation and communications averaged only about 11.5 percent, with the high for a single year (1956) being 13.8 percent, and the low (1953) 9.4 percent. Railways received over 60 percent of this investment, and in some years the railroad sector received over 70 percent. In 1958, at the outset of the Great Leap Forward, only 10 percent of gross fixed investment went to transportation and communications.[114]

During the Great Leap the transportation system experienced severe breakdowns because it could not adequately cope with the great upsurge in industrial production, which consisted in substantial part of unplanned output. The transportation system did not have the capacity to deal with the great demands placed on it; nor could it effectively plan or schedule its activities to mesh with the supply and delivery requirements of the industrial sector. In turn, transportation bottlenecks and breakdown sharply reduced managerial effectiveness and productive efficiency in industry. The transportation system improved considerably in the 1960's, but it still places serious constraints on industrial management and enterprise performance, as will be discussed in the folowing section.

When the Communists took over power in China in 1949, there were only about 19,000 kilometers of usable railroad track (one kilometer equals five-eighths of a mile). By 1957, about 32,000 kilometers of track were in use. Much of this increase came from the restoration of old tracks, but over 10,000 kilometers of new track were laid. Since the Great Leap, only a few thousand miles of additional track have been added, and as of 1967 there were approximately 35,000 to 38,000 kilometers of railway track in Communist China, of which no more than a few hundred miles, mostly on the Peking-Chungking line, were electrified.[115] As of 1963 India had over 57,000 kilometers of railway track, of which 1,614 kilometers were electrified.[116] In 1959 the U.S. had over 400,000 kilometers of track, about 1 percent of which was electrified, with virtually all of the rest being dieselized.

Some of the biggest railroad development projects in China have been in the interior, for both economic and political reasons. Some of the major inland projects have connected Peking with Outer Mongolia, Lanchow, to Lhasa in Tibet, and Lanchow to Urumchi in the remote northwest province of Sinkiang, with the original ultimate objective of establishing a connection with Soviet railroads leading to Alma Ata and/or Novosibirsk in the USSR.[117]

Outstanding developments of the last decade were the completion of railroad all the way from Shanghai to Urumchi, some building of double tracks in north and northeast China, and construction of a few new lines to southwest China.[118] That so much freight and passenger traffic has been carried on such a limited mileage of tracks reflects relatively good railroad management in Red China, probably better than in India. One American expert of Chinese descent estimates that for China to achieve an industrial growth of 50 percent over the present GNP would probably require that railroad mileage be expanded to more than 50,000 kilometers, mainly in the western parts of the country.[119]

In 1949 total freight turnover on China's railroads amounted to only 18 billion ton-kilometers, as compared with a pre-1949 peak of about 40 billion. Railway freight turnover increased steadily during the 1950's, reaching 134 billion ton-kilometers in 1957, and sharply increasing to 184,500 billion in 1958 with the onslaught of the Great Leap. In both 1957 and 1958 the railroads accounted for nearly 80 percent of all Red China's freight turnover by modern means of transportation—motor vehicles on roads, ships and barges, and airplanes. In 1957 passenger traffic on Red China's railroads amounted to 36 billion passenger-kilometers, or nearly 80 percent of the total for all means of modern transportation.

In India during the 1962–63 fiscal year, railroad-freight turnover amounted to 100,800 million ton-kilometers, and passenger turnover was 84,500 million passenger-kilometers. Although China's 1958 freight turnover was nearly 85 percent higher than that of India in 1962–63, it should be remembered that China is more than 300 percent greater in area than India. India's big lead in passenger turnover probably reflects much greater individual freedom to travel when and where one likes in India.

Even poor Indians can frequently scrape up enough funds to travel by train for special occasions.

There are no recent figures available on freight or passenger turnover for Red China's railroads. It is possible that with better planning and meshing of activities with the industrial sector, improvements in operating efficiency in the railway sector, and no major disruptions because of the Cultural Revolution, the present turnover would be around the peak levels achieved during the late 1950's—and perhaps even greater. From data available, it is clear that there were significant and steady efficiency increases in the utilization of locomotives and railway wagons from 1950 until the Great Leap.[120] During most of the 1950's most of China's locomotives and many of her wagons were imported mainly from Russia. Now China is manufacturing most, if not all, of her own locomotives and apparently virtually all of her own wagons as well as special grades and shapes of steel for the railway sector.[121]

As a passenger myself, I found the Chinese railways to be substantially more efficient—particularly in terms of departure and arrival times—pleasanter, cleaner, more sanitary, and offering better customer services than Indian railways on the average. The equipment also seemed to be generally newer and superior in China. The food and wines were superb, as were the sleeping accommodations, on all of the Chinese trains on which I traveled, even on the nontourist inland routes, such as Wuhan-Chengchow-Loyang. The only disturbing thing that I found was the blaring and continuous propaganda, in Chinese, that comes over the loudspeaker system. There is a switch in each compartment to turn it off, but it is difficult to find.

Red China's road system still remains highly underdeveloped and grossly inefficient in terms of serving the industrial sector. And there is no such thing as motoring through Red China, or "seeing China by car." While the streets in major cities are generally usable and very good in many cases, there is little motor vehicle traffic to make use of them. Surfaced or paved roads are extremely rare when one goes beyond forty to eighty miles from even the largest cities. In the countryside, roads consist of unpaved routes, mud tracks, and paths, which are in large part inaccessible to trucks or cars; even jeeps cannot travel over them in numerous cases. Heavy rain and snow further reduce the usability of China's roads. On several occasions we had to travel ten or twenty miles and more by car (and in some cases by jeep) on barely usable roads, even in good weather, to visit factories on the outskirts of Wuhan, Shanghai, Tientsin, Canton, Nanking, Wusih, and elsewhere. In general, India has a significantly better nationwide road system—including bridges—especially in nonurban areas, than China. This has been in large part inherited from British rule.

It is estimated that in 1949 only 77,000 to 81,000 kilometers of roads existed in China.[122] By the end of the 1950's, Red China had about 400,-000 kilometers of roads, but probably much, if not most, of this was unusable by motor vehicles, and as of 1966 there were probably, at most, 500,000 kilometers of roads, which is a figure well under 10 percent of the immensely superior U.S. road system. As of 1966 India had about 709,000 kilometers of roads, of which some 500,000 were motorable, and 236,000 surfaced. It is estimated that as of 1966 there was a total of roughly 300,000 to 360,000 motor vehicles of all types in use in Communist China. About 250,000 to 300,000 of these were trucks (jeeps were probably included in the category, but, in any case, their number was not very great), 10,000 buses, and 40,000 to 50,000 cars.[123]

In India there was a total of 675,000 motor vehicles in use, and this probably increased to roughly 900,000 by 1966. (In the 1964–65 fiscal year alone, India produced about 70,000 motor vehicles of all types, and in 1962, she produced 23,300 cars.) Of the total number of motor vehicles in use in India in 1961 nearly half were trucks and buses—mostly the former. As of 1966 India probably had well over 400,000 trucks in use. Although the trucks and buses in use in China seem to be, on the average, newer and more efficient than in India, India has many more, thus enabling better and more effective service for the industrial sector (as will be discussed in the following section).

A good deal of the road building under the Chinese Communists has been for political, military, and national-security purposes, rather than for economical reasons. For example, Chinese road construction has been quite extensive from Tibet to the Indian frontier and to Bhutan and Nepal, and near the North Vietnam frontier.

Red China imports many of her trucks and buses, and almost all of her cars. There are, however, large truck and bus factories in Changchun, Nanking, and Shanghai. As has been mentioned elsewhere, I visited a fairly small truck plant in Shanghai. Other Westerners have also visited truck and bus factories, including the largest ones, in China.[124] Most of the trucks and buses produced in China are of Russian and, to a lesser extent, Czech design. The regime has been negotiating with Berliet of France to build a new truck plant in China.

In 1949 motor-vehicle freight turnover in China was slightly less than 250 million ton-kilometers, compared with 460 million in the pre-1949 peak year. Freight turnover of this type increased steadily, and was substantial in the 1950's, reaching 3,900 million ton-kilometers in 1957, and increasing sharply to 6,920 million in 1958. But in 1957 motor vehicles still accounted for no more than only 2.5 percent of all the freight turnover handled by modern modes of transportation. In 1958 motor vehicles were reported responsible for 28 percent of the freight handled by all forms of modern transportation, but in terms of ton-kilometers they still accounted for only about 3 percent. This clearly indicates that motor trucking in China was confined to very short hauls. I could not locate any data on freight turnover for India's motor trucking sector, but it is no doubt considerably greater than in China.

There are also no recent figures available on motor trucking in Red China. But it probably increased quite substantially in the 1960's, given the much greater availability of petroleum and new trucks produced in China. However, freight and passenger travel by motor vehicles are still no doubt substantially less in both absolute and per capita terms in China than India.

In spite of the progress that has been made in road building and motor transportation in Communist China, pure footpower, handcarts, bicycles, and rickshaws (hand-pulled rickshaws have been replaced by bike-propelled models for passenger service to preserve dignity and to eliminate class distinctions and human exploitation, I was told) all relying on human power, still provide the great bulk of freight and passenger turnover (in tons and miles) on China's roads. A fantastic variety of goods are transported by such purely labor-intensive modes of transport. The same is true in India—where hand-pulled rickshaws are still predominant in Calcutta and some other areas—although to a noticeably lesser degree.

China has always had great potential for the development of modern water transportation—that is, ships and barges—particularly inland. Nearly every province has a good river system, suitable for year-round navigation.[125] Although mainland China also has some 14,000 kilometers of coastline, coastal shipping is confined to the east coast, thus making it difficult, time-consuming, and relatively costly to use coastal-water transportation for many commodities obtained from the deep interior, since they must first be transported over long distances cross-country.

Historically junks and sampans have played a vital role in China's inland water transportation and also in India's, but to a lesser extent. In spite of the progress in modern water transportation under Communist rule, junks and sampans still play an important role, especially for short hauls. I saw large numbers of them transporting goods to and from factories and communes particularly along the Wuhan-Nanking-Wusih-Soochow-Shanghai inland waterways. Managers of several factories that I visited indicated that they receive sizable amounts of their supplies and deliver some of their output via junk and sampan, as well as by modern means of water transportation. In the major coastal cities of Shanghai, Canton, and Tientsin (which is the seaport for Peking), many factories depend in substantial part on coastal shipping for the supply and delivery of commodities. In general, I was amazed to see the overwhelming variety of goods transported by both traditional and modern modes of water transport in China. They include machinery, steel beams, components, cement, coal, radios, foodstuffs, live farm animals and fowl, clothing, textiles, wheelbarrows, light bulbs, wire, and metals and alloys.

In 1949, when China's Communist regime was established, there were only about 75,000 kilometers of inland waterways, most of which were not accessible to steamships or larger diesel-driven vessels. Through dredging and other major improvements about 150,000 kilometers of inland waterways were in use by 1958, of which 40,000 were accessible to modern large vessels. As of 1966 there were more than 55,000 kilometers of navigable inland water routes, of which roughly 19,000 kilometers were accessible to steamers and modern diesel-driven vessels.

During the 1950's inland water shipping grew more rapidly than coastal shipping, which was limited by military harassment by the combined forces of Taiwan and the United States. In the 1960's coastal shipping was expanded considerably. As of March 1964, shipping capacity of coastal shipping lines north of Shanghai increased by more than 100 percent over 1957.[126] By September 1964 Red Chinese ships had traveled to some thirty countries in Asia, Africa, and Europe. Several new giant seagoing steamers were under construction, and some of them are now in use.[127]

In 1949 China's freight turnover via modern water transportation amounted to a mere 4,280 million ton-kilometers, nearly two and one half times less than the 12,750 million achieved during the pre-1949 peak year. Turnover by this mode of transportation increased steadily and considerably in the 1950's, reaching 34,200 million ton-kilometers in 1957, and increasing sharply to 43,655 million in 1958. In the pre-1949 peak period modern water transportation accounted for about 23 percent of all freight turnover by modern means in China. In 1949 it accounted for 18 percent of total turnover, in 1957 about 20 percent, and in 1958 nearly 19 percent.

There are no recent figures on freight turnover by modern means of water transportation for Red China. It is likely, however, that it has increased considerably in absolute terms during the last four or five years. It may now account for 20 to 25 percent of turnover by all forms of modern transportation, in view of the increases achieved in navigable inland water routes and China's stepped-up foreign trade with noncommunist nations.

I could not find any comparable water-transportation freight-turnover figures in ton-kilometers or ton-miles for India. Red China has a distinct advantage and much more potential regarding the use of modern inland water transportation than India, but the latter has an advantage in coastal shipping. However, coastal shipping in India is typically not feasible for transporting goods from industrial centers, such as Bombay, on the west coast, to those like Calcutta on the east coast. Much of India's—like China's—coastal shipping involves foreign trade. In the absence of an extensive system of inland water routes in India, the great bulk of goods going cross-country—east-west or north-south—must go by rail or road.

Before the early 1950's China had no civil aviation system to speak of. In 1958 civil aviation handled a mere 113 million ton-kilometers of freight, or less than one-hundredth of 1 percent of that handled by the railways. Red China's commercial air transportation in 1958 accounted for only 109 million passenger miles, a mere three-tenths of 1 percent of the volume handled by the railways.[128] Before the 1960's the lack of petroleum was a key constraint on the development of air transportation in China. With the great progress made in the 1960's air transportation has no doubt increased substantially, although no aggregate statistics are available.

Red China's civil airlines increased both their freight and passenger turnover by a reported 31 percent during the first nine months of 1964 over the same period for 1963. Eleven new civil air routes were opened up in 1964, and by the end of that year China's internal air routes were reported to be 39,000 kilometers, linking seventy cities served by over fifty carriers.[129] When I visited China in 1966, I was surprised by the number of cities—many of them entirely unfamiliar to me and in remote areas—and routes indicated on the official airline timetable given to me. I was told that more than seventy-five cities were served by commercial air service; although I did not bother to count those listed on the timetable, the figure given to me was probably accurate.

The only way to reach many of China's more remote areas in a reasonable period of time, if at all, is by air. Air transportation is also apparently used quite frequently to provide urgent shipments of components, spare parts, and other commodities to factories, particularly when considerable distances are involved. (The same is true in the Soviet Union.) The cargo that I saw on some of the airplanes that I traveled on appeared to consist mostly of industrial supplies, as well as much mail. No doubt, freight accounts for most of the volume on many flights to remote areas of the country. Some of the flights that I traveled on left several hours late, and in general, air schedules seemed to be violated much more frequently and with much longer delays than railway schedules. This is largely due to the very tight scheduling that is required by the limited number of airplanes. In many instances it is probably also due to decisions to wait for special or highly important passengers and/or commodities to be shipped by air at the last minute.

Red China's commercial airplane fleet is made up almost entirely of fairly old Soviet Illyutions which seem to be kept in good working condition. There are a few British Viscounts that travel the Canton-Peking-Shanghai routes, but I do not think Red China has any modern commercial jets, even on its very limited international routes. In 1966 there seemed to be quite a bit of airport-construction activity in some of the Chinese cities visited.

India has more commercial airplanes, including a number of jet Boeings and Caravelles, and new non-jet Friendship Fokkers, than Communist China. Air service is also used to connect remote parts of India. However, India's airlines have even considerably less freight turnover than China's small volume. In 1963 civil aviation within India had a freight turnover of only 17.5 million ton-kilometers. India's freight turnover is much lower than that of China chiefly because of greater railroad capacity and the much greater amount of freight that can be handled by truck transportation because of a more extensive and superior system of roads. On the other hand, passenger turnover is much greater on Indian airlines; for example, it amounted to 760 million domestic passenger-miles in 1963. The reasons for India's substantial lead over China in domestic air-passenger miles are: greater individual freedom in India to travel domestically (as well as abroad), the existence of a sizable number of affluent Indians who have the means to travel by air, and the substantially greater numbers of foreigners traveling by air in India than in China.

I encountered significantly worse air passenger service and much longer delays in India during 1965–66 than in China in 1966. However, much of this period was abnormally bad for commercial air travel even for India. Not only was there the Indo-Pakistani war, but there was also the loss of three commercial aircraft through crashes—one Boeing, one Caravelle, and one Friendship. But even in normal times, personnel problems, strikes, and poor management frequently result in poor passenger service and serious delays in India's domestic airline, the Indian Airline Corporation. Delays in China's commercial-airline sector are not usually for these reasons. India's international airline, Air India—for which no statistics have been provided above—has worldwide routes and a good international reputation.

Transportation Constraints at Industrial Enterprises

Thus far, we have been considering Communist China's transportation sector largely in general and aggregate terms. Let us now examine it from the standpoint of constraints on industrial enterprises and their managements. Before proceeding, it should be noted that my information, observations, and impressions of transportation constraints at Chinese industrial enterprises have been derived from investigations in relatively developed and self-sufficient parts of the country. The transportation problems to be discussed would tend to be substantially greater in more remote and less developed areas of the country.

Transportation deficiencies frequently result in supply and delivery failures in China's industrial sector. This, in turn, results in a kind of chain reaction of production bottlenecks and idle resources among independent factories. I was told by officials at a number of enterprises surveyed that inadequate capacity and bottlenecks in the transportation sector, rather than failure of a given plant to produce according to plan, are often the major causes of late supply shipments and deliveries. It is not uncommon for factory supplies to be damaged or misplaced in transit, and it is common for products to be picked up late at enterprises. Because of inadequate storage facilities they are often damaged while they lie idle in the factory's shops and yards, and in nearby streets. Transportation deficiencies also frequently cause instability in production processes and prevent economical production runs from being achieved.

It was apparent at a number of firms visited that they were located near their suppliers and customers because of transportation constraints. Similarly, the types of raw materials and equipment used in production are often restricted to those available locally, largely for reasons of inadequate transportation. For example, the Han Yang Paper Mill, located on a barely accessible dirt road about twenty or thirty miles from Wuhan, uses wood reeds and "dragon beard" grass in its paper production. I was told by the enterprise's director that these raw materials were readily available in abundant quantities from nearby communes and that they were transported to the plant chiefly by hand, handcarts, bikes, and animal-pulled carts. He admitted that production would be more efficient and product quality higher if wood pulp, timber, and other more conventional materials were used. But he said that due to transportation difficulties, as well as various other problems, most of which were of lesser importance, the use of such unconventional raw materials was best from the standpoint of the economy and the state. I could cite many other examples of this type.

Because of transportation uncertainties and difficulties, Chinese enterprise managers are probably inclined to maintain large—as compared to similar U.S. firms—inventories of materials, components, spare parts, and equipment when they are not prevented from doing so by the plan, or higher authorities, or overzealous party cadres. Many of the plants visited did have large stocks of various types of commodities; but at the same time many also had critical shortages of key items which caused stoppages in the production process.

At Chinese factories the great emphasis on self-sufficiency, vertical integration, and making rather than buying numerous items stems substantially from transportation deficiencies in numerous cases. In turn, the quest for self-sufficiency in supply and production leads to large numbers of auxiliary personnel at numerous enterprises—which does much to explain the very low ratios of auxiliary to direct-production personnel which I found at a number of the enterprises surveyed. For example, some of the firms that had direct-production workers to auxiliary personnel ratios of 1.5 to 1 or less were Shanghai No. 3 Machine Tool, Wuhan Paper, Canton Electrical Appliance, Wusih Diesel Engine, Wuhan Diesel Engine, and Canton and Nanking Chemical Fertilizer. The latter three enterprises had ratios of less than 1 to 1. Although the Wuhan and Shanghai steel firms had ratios of more than 1.5 to 1, the former had some 6,000 auxiliary plant workers—this is in addition to the 5,000 welfare and service employees—and the latter had over 2,000.

A sizable proportion of employees at most of the enterprises surveyed were engaged directly in transportation activities, including road building and maintenance around their factories. This is generally the case because of serious external transportation deficiencies and the resulting need for many industrial firms to be relatively self-sufficient in transportation. This also contributes greatly to low ratios of auxiliary to direct-production personnel.

At several of the enterprises visited, more than 10 percent of their personnel were employed directly in transportation work and related activities of supply, delivery, and maintenance, and at probably a majority of firms 5 percent or more were thus employed. Many of them are employed in in-plant transportation because of the highly labor-intensive methods used. The need for their own extensive transportation operations has a substantial impact on the sizes, organization structures, grouping of activities, degree of work specialization, division of labor, and staffing requirements of Chinese industrial enterprises. It also tends to make the overall managerial task substantially broader and more complex than in similar types of industrial enterprises.

For example, Nanking Chemical Fertilizer employs over 1,000 workers exclusively involved in transportation, the great majority of whom carry goods by handcarts, bikes, and by hand both within the vicinity of this enterprise and to and from customers and suppliers. This firm has its own railway tracks, some of which connect with its own docks on the Yangtze River. It also has a few of its own locomotives and many railway wagons, four fairly big boats and several barges, about a dozen jeeps, a few trucks, and five or six old automobiles, which are frequently used for hauling goods. When Nanking Chemical delivers and obtains commodities via its boats, its workers usually transport the goods on and off the boats and barges using only their arms, backs, heads, handcarts, and rickshaws.

A few of the large firms visited in Shanghai and Wuhan also had their own large boats and barges. It is quite common for enterprises—even relatively small ones—located near waterways in the Wuhan-Nanking-Wusih-Soochow-Shanghai area to have their own junks and small barges which they use for transporting commodities. Like Nanking Chemical Fertilizer, a few of the larger plants surveyed, including the two steel firms and Peking Coke Chemical, had their own locomotives, goods wagons, sidings, and tracks. While probably a majority of enterprises visited had at least one automobile—Wuhan Steel had the most, about ten—not as many firms had their own trucks or jeeps. Factory roads, while generally kept tidy, are frequently not paved. They are frequently built and usually maintained by factory personnel.

Transportation is also frequently a serious problem for Chinese enterprise officials who must travel or desire to travel to other cities for business purposes. It is typically impossible for an industrial executive to get an airline reservation without requesting it at least several weeks in advance, unless he is a very high-level official or has been authorized to go on urgent business by influential higher authorities. Even when he holds a reservation, there is a pretty good chance that he will not take off because a higher-level official, someone on even more urgent business, or a foreigner is allocated his seat at the last moment. It also tends to require considerable lead time for an enterprise manager to obtain a seat on an express train on major routes, and here, too, he may find that his reservation is no longer valid at the last moment. This frequently leads to significant delays in decision making which hinder managerial effectiveness and productive efficiency at industrial enterprises because much slower means of transportation and/or less effective forms of communication must be resorted to. (More will be said about communication facilities in the next section.) While it is often not easy for an Indian businessman to get a seat on a plane or express train, this type of problem seems to be substantially more serious in China.

The number of operating shifts, and the number of personnel working on each, did not generally seem to be seriously restricted because of inadequate municipal or local transportation to get people to and from work at the Chinese enterprises visited. Many of the enterprises housed most or all of their employees in nearby housing which they either control or obtain for their employees. In a few cases, large enterprises had their own means of transportation for getting personnel who live some distance away to and from work. In larger cities, municipal bus services seem to be fairly well coordinated with the hours of work in major industrial areas. However, probably the majority of people who must make their own way to their enterprises do so on foot or by bike.

In general, the availability of local transportation, particularly very late at night, in Indian cities seems to be more of a restraint at factories on shifts operated and the number of night-shift personnel than in China. One reason for this is that more employees live greater distances from their factories in India because factory housing is less common and less extensive—with the notable exception of firms located in remote parts of the country. Moreover, there is probably not as much effort on the part of Indian transit authorities, as compared with their Chinese counterparts, to coordinate schedules with hours of work at plants.

A few other comments about transportation constraints in Indian industry seem to be in order here.[130] In general, Indian industrial enterprises tend to be confronted with transportation problems similar to those of Chinese firms—but with some being greater and others lesser. While India has an edge in existing capacity over China with regard to railway, air, and particularly road transportation, China reduces this edge in reality because more effective utilization is probably made of her more limited transportation capacities. Better management, less labor unrest and featherbedding, the absence of strikes during normal times, less congestion, and greater interorganizational cooperation in China all seem to contribute to more effective utilization of transport equipment and facilities. Moreover, there has been more comprehensive planning and greater coordination between and within China's overall transportation and industrial sectors—probably during the Great Leap period—than in India. This, too, facilitates more effective use of transportation networks and better service to enterprises in many instances. On the other hand, Indian firms frequently have greater flexibility in dealing with unforeseen problems requiring transportation services. Such desirable flexibility emanates in large part from the availability of private trucking services and India's relatively good (for such a poor country) system of roads.

While Indian enterprises tend to make, rather than buy, many items in their quest for self-sufficiency, transportation deficiencies probably do not generally foster such behavior to as high a degree as in China. Similarly, although many Indian enterprises operate a considerable amount of their own transportation services and employ many workers who use highly labor-intensive methods, they seem to have less, on the average, than those services found at similar types of Chinese firms. Again, one major reason for this is that there are many private trucking firms, mostly small ones, that Indian industrial enterprises can utilize at reasonable costs. Of course, in isolated areas, Indian industrial firms are often required to operate transportation services and maintain related facilities and personnel at least to the same extent as in China.

It is likely that loss of goods in transit and pilferage are considerably more common in India's overall transportation sector than in China's. Managerial deficiencies, ineffective control, more extreme poverty, and various sociological-cultural factors account for this difference. On several occasions Indian managers told me that their firms were faced with crucial shortages of various items because they had been lost or stolen in transit. Chinese managers would probably not be as candid about such matters, but such problems are nevertheless probably more pervasive and serious in India.

It is not possible to even estimate the extent or degree to which Red China's Cultural Revolution has led to even greater transportation constraints at industrial enterprises. Mass movements of Red Guards by rail and, to a lesser extent, by water to different parts of the country during the last several months of 1966 and in early 1967 undoubtedly disrupted the flow of goods within the industrial sector and among all economic sectors. Moreover, they no doubt made it even much more difficult for industrial officials to travel, even on pressing business.

There were Chinese press and radio reports that the army, people's militia, and newly formed revolutionary bodies were instructed to take over control of transportation networks, particularly railways in different parts of the country; and apparently they did so, at least in a number of areas. These Super-Reds were ordered to wipe out self-interest and material gain (also referred to now as "economism") as well as class distinctions in the transport sector.[131]

There were some reports of serious disruptions in transportation in late 1966 and 1967 which had adverse consequences for industrial enterprises. For example, with the onslaught of Red Guards on the factories, raw materials and products piled up on railway sidings in some areas, causing damage to the track as well as to the customers. Large pile-ups near the railroad tracks around the inland industrial center of Taiyuan were also reported. There were also widely reported delays of shiploading and unloading in Shanghai.[132]

On the other hand, there were a few scattered reports of gains in efficiency in the transportation sector arising from takeovers by Super-Reds and new revolutionary groups. For example, in February 1967 the newly formed Shanghai Revolutionary Railway Headquarters "decisively grabbed power from the capitalistic-minded (Shanghai) railway authorities who stress economism." As a result, it was claimed that a "new five-month record for punctuality of train departures was established from February 7th through the 9th when virtually all trains departed on time from Shanghai." In many instances even trains arriving late were reported to have left on time. The report goes on to say that the Shanghai railway station was "nearly paralyzed" during the civil unrest and strikes that took place before the Super-Red group "grabbed power." [133]

In general, there can be little doubt that the Cultural Revolution has done, so far, considerably more damage than good in China's overall transportation sector. And the resulting impacts on managerial effectiveness and productive efficiency in industry have probably been, on the whole, substantially more negative than positive. However, the transportation difficulties and constraints (as of mid-1967), in themselves, are not likely to have truly serious lasting effects unless involvement of the Cultural Revolution in transportation—and the economy as a whole—persists and/or once again becomes greatly intensified.

Communications

I have not been able to find any statistics, or even estimates, on the telephone system, telegraph networks, or postal facilities in Communist China. Therefore, the little that I have to say about this subject is based on my observations, impressions, experiences, and a bit of factual information derived during my stay in China. Again, I caution the reader that communications facilities—like transportation—are no doubt less adequate in many parts of the country that I did not visit.

I did observe telephones at even some of the smallest enterprises that I visited. It is probable that all of the firms that I surveyed had telephones. On those occasions where I used the telephone in China, I experienced no difficulty whatsoever. When I observed other people, including my interpreter and some enterprise officials, using the phone at enterprises and elsewhere, there were no apparent significant problems or delays. This was also true for one or two long-distance calls that I observed being placed. No doubt, telephone service is much less extensive and efficient in cities farther inland than I was, as well as in the rural areas, although all of China's communes are apparently hooked up with telephone service.

It is likely that India has more telephones than China per capita, and possibly in absolute terms as well; as of 1966 there were about 870,000 telephones in use in India. A substantially greater number of urban Indian households have phones than in China. However, it appears to me that telephone service, in general, is more efficient in China. This is also the opinion of a number of other people who have spent some time in both countries in recent years.

This may be the case largely because the Chinese seem to be noticeably less inclined to use the telephone when one is available, than Indians—and, for that matter, than people in most of the other countries that I have visited. This is probably due to a variety of cultural and psychological phenomena which I cannot explain. I was struck by the little use made of the telephone particularly at Chinese enterprises. For some reason Chinese executives, and other types of industrial personnel, seem typically to much prefer face-to-face communications within the enterprise, and even with personnel of other organizations who are located in the same city, to communication by telephone. Meetings are common at all levels in Chinese industry. Perhaps nonverbal communications that manifest themselves only in face-to-face encounters are much more important in China than in most other countries.

When messages have to be sent quickly to other cities in Chinese business and industry, the telegraph system is often used. For messages to be sent in the same city enterprise messengers are frequently sent on foot or by bike to deliver them, and they often wait for an answer. This is also true in India. For less urgent written communications the postal service is used.

Telegraph service seems to be quite extensive and efficient in the areas of China that I visited. Although China may not have as many telegraph offices as India, which had about 8,600 as of 1966, telegraph service in

India may be less efficient, on the average. However, it is fairly common for large Indian companies which have scattered plants and/or branches to have their own telegraph ("Telex") networks, extending even to offices and plants within the same city. In this way they need not rely as much on the often erratic and inefficient external telephone or telegraph systems. I know of no similar Telex-type system in use at any level of Chinese industry.

Postal service seems to be quite adequate in China, and is probably as good as in India, and some of the enterprises surveyed seemed to receive and send out a fair amount of mail, although not typically as much as at comparable Indian firms. Perhaps the antibureaucracy emphasis—letters and memos are viewed as bureaucratic methods of communication—in China accounts in part for this difference. The Indians tend to be much more bureaucratic and seem to thrive on written communications. India had about 97,000 post offices as of 1966, and it is conceivable that China had less, because the commune setup makes it less necessary for China to have as many postal stations in rural areas.

In general, telephone and telegraph facilities are much less adequate, even in major industrial cities, in China (and India) than in an advanced country, such as the United States or even Japan and the Soviet Union. No doubt, in a substantially greater proportion of instances where the Chinese industrial manager attempts to contact suppliers, customers, higher authorities, or other parties in other parts of the country by telephone or telegraph, he is faced with significant difficulties and delays. As a result, it is likely that quite often critical information cannot be obtained on time, and important decisions are delayed, with adverse consequences for managerial performance and productive efficiency. In cases where the Chinese manager chooses to, or must rely on, fairly prompt face-to-face communication with people in other cities or rural areas the transportation system tends to be, as noted earlier, a serious constraint.

There is little evidence available regarding the effects that China's Cultural Revolution is having on telephone, telegraph, or postal services. From the standpoint of managerial effectiveness and productive efficiency in the industrial sector the effects are no doubt, on the whole, more damaging than favorable. The Maoists have apparently maintained control over Red China communication networks, including the radio, TV, official publications, and other mass media. The opposition has to rely chiefly on large wall posters for their propaganda efforts and the dissemination of information.

Power and Water Supply

China has always been one of the most highly endowed countries of the world in terms of potential energy resources for the development of electric power generation, which is essential for industrial development and expansion. China's potential hydroelectric and coal resources compare favorably with those in the United States and the U.S.S.R.[134] However, the development of this potential was neglected and was very slow before 1949, thus greatly hindering industrial development in all but a handful of major industrial centers.

During the early part of the twentieth century the large majority of China's relatively few electric power stations were built along the eastern seacoast in her largest trading and manufacturing cities. Most of the power plants were built by Western countries until the 1930's, when Japan started building power stations in Manchuria (now comprising north China). By 1944, installed capacity of power plants was 3.1 million kilowatts. Of this capacity the Japanese had constructed 55 percent in Manchuria and 20 percent elsewhere in China, 10 percent was in coastal city power plants built and owned by Western countries, and only 15 percent was owned by small inefficient Chinese power firms scattered in different parts of the country.[135] During the 1944–49 period foreign and civil wars put many power facilities out of commission, and following the Japanese defeat the Soviets removed over 1 million kilowatts of generating equipment in Manchuria. So, by the time the Communists came to power in 1949 only 1.8 million kilowatts of generating capacity were in operating condition.[136]

The Communist regime has made much progress in developing and expanding China's electricity-generating capacity, but it was not until the mid-1950's that the pre-1949 peak level of over 3 million kilowatts was achieved. The irregular flows of China's extensive river systems, containing many waterfalls and rapids which are good for power generation, present many problems in their utilization for generating power. However, the Chinese Communists have made considerable progress, mainly through highly labor-intensive methods, in flood control, water conservation, dam and reservoir construction, and in overcoming severe silting problems in various riverbeds. But coal still furnishes by far the greatest proportion of energy utilized in Red China. It is reported to comprise 66 percent of the fuel and power base of the country, and supplies some 90 percent of the nation's commercial primary energy. In the last several years hydroelectricity has averaged about 20 percent of the total electric energy generated in China, while the rest has been thermal electricity. In the earlier years of Communist rule hydroelectricity accounted for less than 15 percent of total output.[137]

At the end of 1952 China's electric-energy capacity was 2 million kilowatts, and generation of electric energy amounted to 7.3 billion kilowatt hours.[138] During the 1953–57 period capacity more than doubled to 4.5 million kilowatts at a cost of 3 billion yuan. Gross output increased during this period by some 166 percent to 19.3 billion kilowatt hours. During the 1958–60 Great Leap Period capacity of installed equipment in power plants more than doubled to 9.5 million kilowatts, by the end of 1959, and the projects started during the Leap brought it to 10.9 million by the end of 1960. Total investment in the 6.4 million kilowatts of new capacity (and associated transmission lines) during 1958–60 was nearly 5 billion yuan. But a substantial amount of this investment was wasted at that time because much wasteful industrial output occurred, and much idle generating capacity began to emerge at the end of the Leap and persisted for some time in the 1960's. The annual utilization factor plummeted sharply below 30 percent, as compared with 42 percent in earlier years.

The problem of electric power was not a serious constraint in the industrial sector during the Great Leap Period and its aftermath; the problem was actually one of too much generating capacity for existing levels of industrial production. From 1957 to 1958 electric-energy output increased by nearly 50 percent to 27.5 billion kilowatt hours. It increased by another 50 percent to 41.5 billion in 1959, and by nearly an additional 20 percent to a peak of 47 billion in 1960. Then it dropped dramatically to 31 billion in 1961, and fell further to 30 billion in 1962, bringing it down to the level of the mid-1950's. In the early 1960's little new generating capacity was added; and what was added was in a few strategic parts of the nation and in a few strategic industries, such as defense, including nuclear development, petroleum, and chemicals.

While different experts and sources agree that China's electric-power capacity and output both increased in 1963, and continued to increase after 1963, there is significant disagreement as to the magnitude of the increases. John Ashton estimates that total investment in Red China's electric-power sector during 1961–64 did not exceed 2 billion yuan, reaching a low of about 200 million yuan in 1964. He estimates electric-power capacity at 12.7 million kilowatts in 1963, 12.9 million in 1964, and 13.5 million in 1965. He estimates electric-power output for these years as 33, 36, and 40 billion kilowatts hours, respectively.[139] R. M. Field agrees with Ashton's estimates, as does the U. S. State Department for the 1965 output figure, the only recent year for which they give an estimate.[140] *Current Scene*, a Hong Kong publication, estimates output during the 1963–64 period to be a bit lower than the estimates given by Ashton or Field.[141]

Soviet sources estimate output at 37 billion kilowatts for 1963, and 55 billion for 1964 and 1965.[142] A Japanese source estimated Red China's electric-power output at 75 billion kilowatt hours in 1964, but this figure seems implausibly high.[143] Kong Chao prefers the Soviet estimates and presents some fairly convincing arguments, information, and estimates of his own to support his position.[144] Chao also estimates 1964 electric-power capacity in China at 14.16 million kilowatts—compared with 12.9 million by Ashton—for 1964 and, by implication, at least that much in 1965.

Chao prefers the Soviet estimates and, of course, his own, for a number of reasons. He feels that because of past intimate Sino-Soviet relations, and Soviet knowledge (much of it firsthand) of Chinese defense and nuclear programs which are major electric-power consumers, the Soviet Union is in the best position of any foreign country to assess Chinese electric-power output. Moreover, the Soviets designed and set up most of China's modern civilian, as well as defense, capital-intensive industries, which are big power users. I should also add that it appears that there would be no good reason why the Soviets would exaggerate Communist China's electric-power capacity or production.

Chao has collected data, as yet unpublished, on the progress of construction and completion of individual power plants in Red China during 1960–64. From these data he is confident that approximately 4.16 million kilowatts of capacity were added in this period, bringing 1964 capacity to 14.16 million kilowatts. According to recent Chinese Communist reports, the electric-power sector is officially listed as one which has witnessed rapid increases in output and capacity in the past few years.[145] Chao goes on to point out that Ashton's distribution of hydro versus thermal power in his capacity estimates for recent years contradicts Peking's announced policy in favor of hydropower over thermal power and the reduction of coal production in the early 1960's.[146]

Chao also shows that Ashton's estimates give an average utilization factor of generating equipment in 1964 of only 32 percent, substantially less than the 40 percent and higher levels achieved through much of the 1950's. If Chao's 14.16 million kilowatt capacity figure is accepted, the utilization factor would be only 29 percent for 1964. However, with the Soviet electric-power output figure of 55 billion kilowatt hours achieved with a capacity of 14.16 million kilowatts, the utilization factor becomes 44 percent, which is much more acceptable to Chao than Ashton's implied figure of 34 percent. To Chao, the 34-percent figure implies a tremendous amount of idle capacity and is implausible in view of reportedly accelerated construction of new generating plants in 1965, and sizable annual-output gains since 1963 or 1964.

In my opinion, Chao is inclined to paint a rosier picture than what probably exists in some important aspects of Red China's industrial and economic performance. However, in the case of the electric-power sector I am inclined to accept the Soviets' and Chao's estimates as being closer to the real situation than those of Ashton, Field, the Japanese source, the U. S. State Department, or *Current Scene*. It is conceivable that China's electric-power output in 1965, and certainly by the end of 1966, had surpassed the Great Leap peak level of 47 billion kilowatt hours.

According to some experts on the Chinese economy, in 1953 the percent distribution of electric power to the overall industrial sector as a proportion of total net domestic-power supply in China was about 83 percent. This increased to 88.2 percent in 1957, and an estimated 92 percent in 1960, falling to an estimated 88.8 percent in 1962.[147] According to Ashton's estimates, industry and construction in China—apparently the above figures do not include the construction sector which, compared with the industrial sector, consumes only a small fraction of electric power—consumed 82 percent of the nation's electric-power output by end use. (End-use figures are generally a bit higher than net production figures because they include transmission losses and adjustments for imports and exports.) In 1956 the proportion of power consumed by industry and construction in end-use terms had risen to 87 percent, rising further to 90 percent in 1959, and reaching a peak of slightly more than 90 percent in 1960. In 1964 Ashton estimates that it was down to 83 percent, rising slightly to about 84 percent in 1965.[148]

There are clearly some significant differences implied in the above two sets of estimates, particularly if one set includes the construction sector—as small a consumer as it is—and the other does not. In my opinion, in view of China's industrial recovery and substantial rises in production after 1962, and given the structural changes in industry in favor of more electricity-consuming branches, it is possible that the overall industrial sector is now once again consuming close to 90 percent of the country's electric-power output in terms of end use, and perhaps even in terms of net domestic production.

India's electric-power capacity in 1965 was about 9 million kilowatts, and it was expected to increase to over 10 million in 1966, although this target may not have been achieved.[149] About 29 billion kilowatt hours of power were generated in India in 1965, and the 1966 target, which may not have been achieved, was 36.4 billion. By all available estimates China has a lead over India in both total electric power capacity and output, and this lead is greater if Chao's estimates are accepted. If Chao's estimates are accepted there is little difference in per capita capacity and output between China and India, but if the lower figures are accepted, India has an edge over China. Per capita power consumption in India in 1964 was about 54 kilowatt hours, compared with roughly 40 to 52 kilowatt hours in China. India's per capita lead is probably due primarily to the power consumed in the urban household sector, and not the industrial sector, which is substantially greater in both absolute and per capita terms in China. India's industrial sector consumed only 70 percent of the country's electric power output in 1963. A significantly larger share of India's electric-power capacity and output is hydroelectric power—about 45 percent in recent years—than in China, where it is in the range of 20 to 25 percent.

Substantial overall generation efficiencies have been achieved in China's electric-power sector under Communist rule. Red China now makes its own large generators, the maximum being about 100,000 kilowatts in capacity. Capital scarcity, rather than know-how, is the key constraint in the further development of China's electric-power sector.

In spite of the progress that Red China has made in the electric-power sector, she still lags immensely behind advanced industrial nations in this sphere. The state of Alabama alone generated nearly 37 billion kilowatt hours of net power output in 1965, or more than all of China's output until 1959. The general level of technology in China's electric-power sector at present was achieved in the United States in the 1920's. The average heat rate—a good technical efficiency measure—for Chinese thermal power plants in 1964 was only about 17,360 B.T.U. kilowatt hours; this rate was achieved in the United States by the late 1930's. In 1956 China's power industry employed thirty-five people per megawatt of installed capacity, as compared with three in the United States, thus reflecting the highly labor-intensive nature of China's power industry. The present consumption of electric energy per worker in China is still around the same level reached by the United States before World War I.[150]

Before discussing some of the impacts of electric power on the industrial sector, let me comment briefly on the organization of Communist China's electric-power sector.[151] The central government controls almost all of the generation of electric energy and the construction of major electric-power facilities in China. The larger and more important power stations as well as the power-transmission networks are directly under the Ministry of Water Conservation and Electric Power. Smaller electric-power stations at industrial enterprises are under the operational control of the enterprises' direct superiors—that is, industrial ministries, provincial industrial departments, and municipal industrial bureaus. Most of the local facilities used for rural electrification are under the administration of county, municipal, and provincial power agencies.

Each municipality has a utilities commission which distributes electricity, purchased from the electric-power industry, for general urban uses, such as street lights, households, and various types of organizations and enterprises not supplied by other sources. These commissions also distribute heat and water, and handle customer billing, other paper work, maintenance, and so on. But they are not considered part of the electric-utility industry as they are in the United States. The Chinese electric-power industry sells at wholesale prices to larger industrial firms, municipal governments, rural communes, and other types of large consumers who have their own substations.

Power failures or shortages did not generally seem to be serious constraints on productive efficiency at the enterprises in the Chinese cities that I visited. Power failures and shortages are no doubt much more serious problems in various remote industrial areas and in many rural areas throughout the country. Where there are power shortages in China which prevent production from continuing at factories, they are much more likely to be anticipated in the enterprise plan than in Indian industry—that is, the Chinese enterprise's plan takes into account work stoppages resulting from power shortages. This reduces the likelihood of undesirable effects on customer enterprises, and it also enables management to plan alternate uses of shutdown time in advance. (Chinese firms are also allocated electricity, as well as heat and water, in their plans.) At Indian industrial enterprises there typically seems to be considerably more uncertainty regarding the future availability of power and the likely occurrence of sudden acute shortages or power failures. Chinese authorities are also more likely to cut off household and other uses of electricity when necessary in order to keep industry operating than their Indian counterparts.

In general, work stoppages, productivity declines, idle resources, higher costs, disruptions in production, sales and delivery schedules, and financial difficulties arising from power shortages or failures seem to be more frequent and extensive at the Indian firms than at the Chinese enterprises that I visited.[152] It is true that electric-power constraints tend to be much more serious in relatively isolated or nonindustrialized areas in India—as in China—such as the states of Kerala, Assam, and Uttar Pradesh, but power failures and acute shortages are also fairly common and adversely affect the operations of firms in major Indian industrial cities, such as Bombay and Calcutta, because of the relatively large amounts of power that are consumed there. I know of a number of cases where the expansion programs of Indian firms in major cities have had to be curtailed because of the unavailability of power supplies, and in some cases the construction of plants and commencement of operations have also been delayed for this reason. Similarly, power shortages quite often prevent Indian firms from operating as many shifts at capacity levels as they would like.

Although I saw, and was told about, only a few cases of power shortages in Chinese industry, they no doubt exist even in the cities that I visited, although probably not to the same degree or extent as in Indian industry. No doubt, on many occasions the unavailability of adequate electric power has actually deterred large-scale plants and refineries from being located in various areas of China even though such locations were otherwise suitable or even desirable.

Several of the larger Chinese industrial enterprises that I surveyed had their own electric-power stations, heating, water, and other types of public-utility facilities, as well as sizable numbers of personnel to operate and maintain them. These included both of the steel firms and both of the chemical-fertilizer enterprises visited, Wuhan Heavy Machinery, and a few others. No doubt in more remote, less self-sufficient inland areas the proportion of enterprises that have their own public-utility facilities and the proportion of personnel employed in public utility work are greater than in the parts of the country that I visited. This would tend to make the overall managerial task substantially more diverse, and probably more complex. It is likely that in India's major industrial cities the extent of public-utility facilities and the size of related staffs at industrial enterprises are, on the average, less than in China's industrial cities. But in more remote and less self-sufficient areas of India, as in China, much more extensive public-utility facilities and greater numbers of related personnel are found at industrial enterprises.

Water supply, in general, seems to be a greater industrial constraint in India than in China, particularly at plants producing chemicals, chemical fertilizer, and certain types of drug plants. All of the plants of these types that I surveyed in China seemed to have adequate power resources, but this was not true of some of the Indian firms. In fact, one large chemical-fertilizer complex in India had delayed the commencement of operations for many months chiefly because of an acute water shortage. In this case the municipal authorities could not supply the firm's daily requirement of five million gallons of water.[153]

I have not been able to locate any information in Chinese or Western publications regarding the impact of the Cultural Revolution on electric power and water supply in the industrial sector. But I can say with confidence that it is very unlikely that the unrest has had a net positive effect on power or water supply.

PART III

STRUCTURE, OPERATIONS, and PERFORMANCE

CHAPTER 7

Quantitative Dimensions of Communist China's Aggregate Economic and Industrial Performance

THUS FAR, we have been primarily concerned with discussing, analyzing, and explaining trends in management, industrial performance, and economic development in China; we have not devoted much attention to measurement of the quantitative results in the industrial sector or the economy as a whole. In this chapter a number of tables will be presented which depict key quantitative dimensions of China's industrial and overall economic performance. This involves some repetition of data presented earlier—particularly in the section on economic stability in Chapter 6. But this is justified by the intent of presenting a comprehensive summary analysis in this chapter. There is no need, however, to repeat the capital-investment or agricultural data presented in Chapter 6.

We shall briefly examine peak levels of industrial and economic performance in pre-1949 China, before the Communists came to power, and see when these peaks were surpassed under the Communists. We shall also examine key trends for the entire 1949–67 period as well as for different segments of this period. And we shall compare critical aspects of China's performance with that of India, in particular, but also, to some extent, with those of the Soviet Union, Japan, and the United States. Finally, a suggestive quantitative rating of the environmental constraints under study in this book will be undertaken in terms of their impact on managerial effectiveness and industrial progress in Red China and the other four countries.

As can be seen on several of the tables to be presented, I have used ranges—some of them relatively large—in estimating various aspects of China's performance. This is necessary because the available data to work with are quite speculative and sparse in many instances, and there are frequently significant variations in the estimates made by experts and secondary sources which I must draw on for my own analysis. However, I strongly believe that suggestive estimates and comparisons based on a careful analysis of available information, sound reasoning, interpretation, and plausible assumptions are better than bypassing the entire problem—particularly for as large, important, and unique a country as Red China. Moreover, in spite of differences in the precise magnitudes of the estimates available in various reputable sources, there is almost universal consensus with regard to broad performance trends during the 1949–66 period.

In general, statistics and estimates involving Communist China's performance tend to be most reliable for the 1952–58 period, particularly the 1953–57 portion. For the other periods the reader will see that the estimates of performance tend to be in even broader ranges. In my opinion, the low points of most ranges understate China's performance, but I have presented them anyway since they have some basis in information, reasoning, and assumptions. The low-point estimates are in large part from the same studies written by experts who, in my opinion, tend to significantly underestimate China's industrial progress and economic growth.[1] At the same time, some of the upper limits of the estimate ranges in the following tables are, in my opinion, too high, but here again, I present them anyway for the same reasons that I include those that I personally feel are too low. However, I have ignored available estimates involving China's performance which seem to be unrealistically high or low, and are inadequately supported.

Aggregate Growth Trends: 1949–66

If we look at key quantitative indicators of Communist China's aggregate performance for the 1949–66 period as a whole (see Tables 7–1 and 7–2), it is evident that China has achieved substantial economic growth, industrial progress and, by implication, sizable gains in managerial effectiveness. As we shall see shortly, Red China's growth and development record appears to be substantially better than India's to date, better than the Soviet Union's from 1918–1935, and roughly as good as Soviet performance during the 1928–40 period, after Russia embarked on a vigorous development campaign through her five-year plans beginning in 1927–28. But Red China's performance is not nearly as impressive as Japan's "economic miracle" since the late 1940's.

China's impressive growth record, so far, has been achieved in spite of erratic industrial performance and extreme periods of economic instability, most notably during the superficial and short-lived boom of the Great Leap and the severe economic depression which followed. The Great Leap and subsequent depression cost Red China at least several years, and perhaps as many as six or seven, in overall economic growth and industrial production.

Had it not been for the Leap and the depression, Red China's GNP, per capita income, and industrial production would have probably been at least 40 or 50 percent greater than what they were as of 1966–67 and, conceivably, even double that.

Poor weather caused poor agricultural performance, and the Soviet pullout of mid-1960 contributed greatly to China's general economic and industrial crisis, but I am strongly convinced that ideological extremism was, by far, the most important basic cause of the crisis. Ideological extremism did great direct damage not only to managerial effectiveness, productive efficiency, and general progress in the overall industrial sector, but it also contributed greatly to the agricultural crisis, and probably to the Soviet pullout as well.

Growth in GNP and Per Capita Income

Table 7–1 indicates that gross national product in Communist China grew at an average annual rate of 5.5 to 7.2 percent during the 1950–66 period, and per capita GNP at 3.4 to 5.2 percent, and only slightly less if one wishes to ignore 1966 because of the uncertainty caused by the Cultural Revolution. In my opinion, GNP probably grew at a rate of 6 percent or slightly more, and per capita GNP at about 4 percent. Even if we take the low point of these ranges, China's GNP and per capita growth are significantly higher than India's for this period. Table 7–3 indicates that India's GNP grew at a maximum average annual rate of 3.7 percent, and per capita GNP at a maximum rate of 1.4 percent. Some experts may claim that I am making an unfair comparison between China and India for the 1950–66 period, and there is some justification for the criticism. It is true that China achieved abnormally high growth rates during the 1949–52 period of economic rehabilitation in large part by putting a vast amount of existing, but idle, productive capacity and skilled human resources back into operation; while India, which was not so seriously torn by war or civil strife, had to rely much more on the creation of new capacity and critical resources for growth during this period. But the point still remains that when the Chinese Communists came to power they did bring about, create, and put into effect an overall environment much more conducive to managerial effectiveness, industrial progress, and economic growth than had ever previously existed in China.

If we compare Red China's economic growth for only the 1953–66 pe-

TABLE 7–1

SOME KEY GROWTH RATE ESTIMATES FOR COMMUNIST CHINA'S ECONOMY AND INDUSTRIAL SECTOR, 1949–66
(Estimates are annual average compounded growth rates in percent)[a]

Period	*Gross National Product*[b]	*Per Capita*[b] *GNP*	*Industrial Production* (Including manufacturing and mining and public utilities)	*Industrial Employment*	*Industrial Labor Productivity*[c] (Output per man-year, all industrial employees)
1950–66	5.5–7.2	3.4–5.2	11.5–12.0	9.7–10.0	1.7–2.0
1950–65	5.3–7.0	3.2–5.0	11.0–11.6	9.5–9.8	1.4–1.7
1950–52	21.0–26.0	19.2–24.0	25.0–29.0	19.0–21.0	6.0–8.0
1953–66	3.5–4.7	1.4–2.6	9.7–10.7	6.4–6.8	1.1–1.5
1953–65	3.3–4.5	1.2–2.4	8.8–9.4	7.0–8.0	1.2–1.4
1953–57	6.2–8.8	3.9–6.6	15.0–16.0	8.4–8.6	6.0–6.2
1958 to mid–1960[d]	7.0–15.0	4.5–12.6	20.0–30.0	80.0–90.0 (nearly tripled in 1958)	– 33.0 to – 40.0
1960–62[e] (low point from 1958–60 peak)	– 20.0 to – 35.0	–22.0 to – 37.0	– 40.0 to – 45.0	– 45.0 to – 50.0	1.0 to 2.0 (for period)
1957–65	1.6–2.6	(– 0.5) to + 0.6	4.6–5.3	7.1–7.2	– 2.0 to – 2.5
1957–66	1.8–2.9	(– .02) to 1.0	5.5–6.5	7.3–7.4	– 1.5 to 0
1963–65	5.7–8.0	3.3–5.7	10.0–11.3	5.1–5.6	4.7–5.7
1963–66	6.0–8.3	3.6–6.0	10.5–12.0	5.5–6.0	5.0–6.0

[a] The estimates are based on a careful study of many available studies and sources, the most important of which are cited below. I have used ranges for all of my estimates, eliminating figures and estimates from other sources which seem to be unrealistically high or low. The most reliable estimates in this table are for the 1952–57 period. The least reliable are probably for the 1958–60 and 1961–62 periods.

[b] My GNP estimates are based on a variety of national-income-type data including figures for gross and net national product, gross and net national income per se, gross and net domestic product, net material product, etc. For definitions of these terms with particular reference to the case of Communist China, see T. C. Liu and K. C. Yeh, *The Economy of the Chinese Mainland* (Princeton: Princeton University Press, 1965), especially p. 119 and pp. 214 ff.

[c] I have computed labor-productivity growth rates from a labor-produc-

tivity index which I have constructed from industrial production and employment data.

[d] Peak-level GNP during 1958–60 was probably reached in 1959, although some experts place it in 1960, and one (T. C. Liu) at the end of 1958. The different estimates regarding the GNP peak level and the subsequent low point account in part for the sizable ranges in GNP and per capita growth rates after 1957. Industrial production probably roughly doubled during the 1958–60 period, although some official Red Chinese pronouncements claimed that it tripled. The highest rate of industrial growth probably came in 1958, with somewhat lower growth in 1959, and a rate of probably well under 10 percent in 1960. It is likely that industrial production actually declined in the second half of 1960. Industrial employment nearly tripled in 1958 and may have begun to decline somewhat by the end of 1959.

[e] For the 1960–62 period the figures indicate total percentage declines from the peak levels reached during 1958–60, except for labor productivity which is an average-growth-rate estimate.

SOURCES:

[1] For data on total GNP and per capita GNP: Liu and Yeh, *op. cit.;* T. C. Liu, "The Tempo of Economic Development of the Chinese Mainland," *An Economic Profile of Mainland China*, Vol. I (Washington: U.S. Government Printing Office, 1967), pp. 45–75; E. Jones, "The Emerging Pattern of China's Economic Revolution," *Economic Profile*, Vol. I, pp. 77–95. Statements, comments, and papers by A. Eckstein, J. Gurley, K. Chao, T. C. Liu, E. Jones, and W. Proxmire, *Mainland China in the World Economy* (Washington: U.S. Government Printing Office, 1967), pp. 108, 159; W. Hollister, *China's Gross National Product and Social Accounts, 1950–57* (Glencoe, Ill.: Free Press, 1958); Y. L. Wu, F. Hoeber, M. Rockwell, *The Economic Potential of Communist China* (Menlo Park, Calif.: Stanford Research Institute, 1964); Y. L. Wu, *The Economy of Communist China* (New York: Praeger, 1965); A. Eckstein, *The National Income of Communist China* (Glencoe, Ill.: Free Press, 1961); A. Eckstein, *Communist China's Economic Growth and Foreign Trade* (New York: McGraw-Hill, 1966); C. M. Li, *Economic Development of Communist China* (Berkeley and Los Angeles: University of California Press, 1959); *Ten Great Years* (Peking: Foreign Languages Press, 1960); *Current Scene*, Vol. IV, No. 3 (February 1, 1966); *World Bank Atlas of Per Capita Product and Population* (published by the International Bank for Reconstruction and Development, 1966); "Economic Indicators for the Soviet Bloc," *Annual Economic Indicators for the USSR* (Washington: U.S. Government Printing Office, 1964); D. Perkins, "Economic Growth in China and the Cultural Revolution," *The China Quarterly*, No. 30 (1967). See also my comments in Note 53 in Chapter 6 of this book. An important new book published in 1968 (a few parts of which I have seen in manuscript) is W. Galenson, A. Eckstein, and T. C. Liu, eds., *Economic Trends in Communist China* (Chicago: Aldine Publishing Co. 1968).

[2] For population estimates used in estimating per capita GNP: J. Aird, "Population Growth and Distribution in Mainland China," *An Economic Profile of Mainland China*, Vol. II (Washington: U.S. Government Printing Office, 1967), pp. 341–400; and E. Jones in *Economic Profile*, Vol. I, pp. 80–82, 93, Table II.

[3] For data on industrial production: R. Field, "Chinese Communist Industrial Production," *Economic Profile*, Vol. I, pp. 269–95; Jones, *Economic Profile*, Vol. I, pp. 85–88, p. 95, Table V; K. Chao, *The Rate and Pattern of Industrial Growth in Communist China* (Ann Arbor: University of Michigan Press, 1965), especially pp. 88 and 96; Liu and Yeh, *op. cit.*, especially pp. 66, 146, 573, and 585; Perkins, *op. cit.; Far Eastern Economic Review*, September 29, 1966; *Peking Review*, Nos. 1, 2 (1967). *New China News Agency, International Broadcast*, September 30, 1966; Ta Kung Po (Peking), September 10, 1965; *Peking People's Daily* (in Chinese), January 1, 1967.

[4] For data on industrial employment: J. Emerson, "Employment in Mainland China," *Economic Profile*, Vol. II, pp. 403–69; L. Orleans, *Professional Manpower and Education in Communist China* (Washington: National Science Foundation, 1961), Chap. VIII.

TABLE 7–2

ESTIMATES FOR CHINA OF SOME KEY ASPECTS OF PERFORMANCE: PRE-1949 AND UNDER COMMUNIST RULE

Period	*Gross National Product*[a]	*Per Capita GNP*[a]	*Index of Industrial Production*	*Industrial Employment*
(Year-end estimates)	(Figures through 1952 are in 1952 yuan; after 1952, they are in current U.S. dollars.)	(Figures through 1952 are in 1952 yuan; after 1952 they are in current U.S. dollars.)	(1952 = 100)	(Millions of people)
Pre–1949 peak level	58–62 billion yuan	117–121 yuan (under $60)	66–69[b]	Probably well under 3 million
Year of pre–1949 peak	(1933)	(1933)	(1933)[b]	(Possibly 1936 or 1942–44; in 1933 about 2 million)
1949	40–45 billion yuan	70–80 yuan (under $50)	48–50	3.059 (at year's end)
Year pre–1949 peak was surpassed	(1951)	(1952)	(1951)	(1949)
1952	68–73 billion yuan	121–126 yuan	100	5.26
1957	(a) $40–$50 billion (official exchange rate)	(a) $63–$80	195–205	7.9
	(b) $60–$70 billion (internal purchasing power rate)	(b) $95–$108		
1958–60 peak year	(a) $50–$65 billion (official exchange rate)	(a) $73–100	390–400	23–24
	(b) $70–$88 billion (internal purchasing power rate)	(b) $110–$132		
1961–62 low year	(a) $35–$45 billion (official exchange rate)	(a) $50–$67	200–240	11.5–12.0

	(b) \$50–\$65 billion (internal purchasing power rate)	(b) \$75–\$90		
1965	(a) \$47–\$72 billion (official exchange rate)	(a) \$65–\$93 [c]	265–300	13.7–14.0
	(b) \$70–\$95 billion (internal purchasing power rate)	(b) \$95–\$125		
1966	(a) \$50–\$75 billion (official exchange rate)	(a) \$69–\$105 [c]	292–360	14.6–15.0 [d]
	(b) \$75–\$100 billion (internal purchasing power rate)	(b) \$100–\$137		

[a] I have not attempted to convert yuan to U.S. dollars for 1952 or previous years since I do not consider myself an expert on yuan-dollar conversion rates. For the conversions for 1957 and later years I have estimated GNP and GNP per capita in current U.S. dollars at both the official exchange rate prevailing in 1965 (roughly 2.5 yuan to the dollar) and the internal purchasing power rate estimated by people more knowledgeable in this area than myself. It is possible that the official exchange rate undervalues China's output of the producer-goods industries and undervalues agricultural output and various other types of goods and services.

At the hearings on Communist China's economy conducted by the Joint Economic Committee of the U.S. Congress in April 1967, there seemed to be general agreement—with only a few minority dissenters, on the high and low side, among experts that Red China's GNP in the 1965–66 period was in the range of \$70 to \$100 billion in terms of internal purchasing power or in comparison to the United States' GNP; the majority opinion placed it around \$90 billion.

These hearings were based, in large part, on an analysis of the two-volume study prepared for the Joint Economic Committee in early 1967 and published under the title *An Economic Profile of Mainland China* by the U.S. Government Printing Office. The hearings themselves were published under the title *Mainland China in the World Economy.* See pages 108 and 159 of this volume for the majority position among the participants regarding the dollar value of China's GNP.

For other estimates of China's GNP and per capita GNP in U.S. dollar values, see E. Jones, in *Economic Profile of Mainland China*, Vol. I, p. 96, Table 6; "Economic Indicators for the Soviet Bloc," *Annual Economic Indicators for the U.S.S.R.* (Washington: U.S. Government Printing Office, 1964), p. 131; especially Table xl–1; *Current Scene*, Vol. IV, No. 3 (February 1, 1966), p. 1; *World Bank Atlas of Per Capita Product and Population;* H. Kahn, "Uncertain Road to the 21st Century," *Think*, Vol. 33, No. 1 (January–February 1967), p. 5; Eckstein, *op. cit.*, p. 249, Table 7–1; *Indicators of Economic Strength of Western Europe, Canada, United States, and Soviet Bloc, 1959–62* (Washington: Department of State Intelligence Reports, 1963).

[b] It is possible that industrial production was somewhat higher during 1936 and/or sometime during the 1942–44 period under Japanese occupation.

[c] I was told by a Chinese Communist central-planning official in Peking in May 1966 that he thought that per capita income in Communist China "might currently be around 225 to 250 yuan." He made it clear that this was a personal opinion rather than an official estimate—although he no

TABLE 7–2 (*continued*)

doubt has access to key economics statistics. He would not elaborate as to what definition of national income or GNP he was referring to or whether the yuan were in 1966 or earlier prices. He would not say whether all services were included in his figures. He also would not say whether his figures were for 1965 or expected 1966 performance. In any event, his per capita income range, when worked out, approximates the upper limits of my GNP and per capita income estimates for 1965 and 1966 in U.S. dollars at the official exchange rate.

[d] I was told by a Chinese Ministry of Labor official in Peking in May 1966 that the industrial labor force was expected to grow by roughly 5 percent to 7 percent in 1966 over 1965. He would not give me an absolute employment figure, however. Industrial employment was around 14 million in 1965 (as estimated by Emerson, *op. cit.*, p. 445), and an increase of 5 percent to 7 percent in 1966 would place it around 14.6 to 15 million in 1966.

SOURCES: The estimates in this table are based on a careful study of the sources cited in Table 7–1 of this chapter. The 1933 and 1949 figures are from Liu and Yeh, *op. cit.*, pp. 69 and 181; Chao, *op. cit.*, Table C–1; Field, *op. cit.*, appendix D, p. 295, Table 10; Eckstein, *op. cit.*, pp. 20 ff. and Table 2–1, and A. Eckstein, *The Economic Heritage* (mimeographed), prepared for the Conference on Economic Trends in Communist China sponsored by the Social Science Research Council's Committee on the Economy of China held in Chicago, October 21–24, 1965.

riod—after economic rehabilitation—with the 1950–66 period in India, China would still probably come out ahead. China's GNP growth averaged 3.5 to 4.7 percent annually, and, in my opinion, it was probably at least 4 percent, while India's was in the range of 3.5 to 3.7 percent. (See Tables 7–1 and 7–3.) Even if we take the low point of the range for China—which I feel would be a mistake—China did about as well as India. China's per capita GNP grew at an average annual rate of 1.4 to 2.6 percent (I would place it around 2 percent), during the 1953–66 period—while India's rate was 1.2 to 1.4 percent during 1950–66. Here again, China's low-point estimate is as good as India's maximum rate estimate.

Red China has done roughly as well in GNP growth as the Soviet Union during its first two five-year-plan periods, 1928–38, when its growth rate was about 6 percent, and during the 1950–66 period in Russia when GNP growth averaged 6 percent to 7 percent. However, the Soviet Union may have had a somewhat higher per capita income-growth rate—about 4.5 percent—because of her lower rate of population growth. Since the early 1960's the Soviet Union's GNP average growth rate has fallen slightly below 5.5 percent, and in per capita terms to about 3.5 percent. (See Table 7–14.) The United States has had a long-term historical GNP growth rate of only about 4 percent, and in per capita terms about 2.5 percent, although in the 1960's it has averaged about 5.5 percent and 4.0 percent, respectively. (See Table 7–14 in a later section of this chapter.) But China has not done as well as Japan since 1950. Japan's GNP has grown at an average annual rate of 7 percent to 8 percent, and in per capita terms at 6 to 7 since 1950, with rates exceeding 10 percent during some periods and in the 1960's. (See Table 7–14.)

Growth in Industrial Production

Table 7–1 indicates that industrial production grew at an average annual rate of 11.5 to 12 percent during the 1950–66 period, and only slightly less if we ignore 1966. This is substantially higher than India's rate of about 6.5 percent noted on Table 7–3. Even for the 1953–66 period China's industrial production grew at an annual average rate of around 10 percent. China's rate of industrial growth is roughly equal to the Soviet Union's during the 1928–38 period, when it was 10 percent to 14 percent (depending on whose production index is used), and a bit higher than the 1950–66 Soviet rate of about 9.5 percent. In the United States, industrial production has grown at a somewhat lower rate than in Russia since 1960. Red China has not done as well as Japan, which has had a fantastic average annual rate of growth in industrial production of more than 14 percent since 1950.

TABLE 7–3

STATISTICS ON SOME KEY ASPECTS OF INDIA'S ECONOMIC AND INDUSTRIAL PERFORMANCE, 1949–66

Part I: Critical Growth Rates[a]

(Average annual compounded rates of growth in percent)

	GNP	*GNP Per Capita*	*Industrial Production* (Including manufacturing, mining and public utilities)	*Industrial Employment*[b]	*Industrial Labor Production*[b] (Output per man-year)
1950–1966 period	3.5–3.7%	1.2–1.4%	6.4–6.7%	2.2–2.4%	3.6–4.3%

Part II: Absolute Levels of Performance[a]

	1950	*1966*
Gross national product		
In current U.S. dollars at 1965 official exchange rate of 4.75 rupees = $1 (U.S.)	$20–$22 billion	$34–$38 billion
In current U.S. dollars at internal purchasing power rate estimated by expert sources	$25–$27 billion	$47–$51 billion
Per capita GNP		
In current U.S. dollars at official exchange rate	$55–$60 billion	$68–$75 billion
In current U.S. dollars at internal purchasing power rate	$75–$80 billion	$75–$104 billion
Industrial employment[b] (*in millions*) (Includes manufacturing, mining, utilities)	5.9–6.2	9.5–9.8

[a] Ranges are used—although much smaller than those for China—since there is some disagreement among basic sources as to India's precise level of economic and industrial performance during various periods. This is due to several factors. Different concepts and measurements of GNP, national income, etc., as well as industrial production and employment indexes, are used. Some sources report results for calendar years, others for fiscal years (April 1–March 31 in India), and some do not indicate which of the two they are reporting for. Similarly, some sources do not indicate whether constant prices for a base period or current prices are used in computing national-income figures. There are also deviations in the internal purchasing power rates used in converting rupees to U.S. dollars.

[b] Industrial employment does not include the roughly 8 to 10 million persons engaged in "household industry," which is essentially like handicrafts where a portion of the output is consumed by the producers and their families. However, much of the output of this sector goes through regular marketing channels and is probably included in industrial-output statistics. Whereas the large majority of handicraftsmen making factory-type consumer or producer goods have been absorbed in the "modern" or factory industrial sector in China, this is not true for India. Moreover, there is apparently much more seasonal and contract labor in Indian industry than in Chinese industry which is not reported in official employment statistics. This also means that industrial-labor productivity tends to be overstated in India in relation to China.

SOURCES:

India's Draft Fourth Plan (New Delhi: National Planning Commission, Government of India, 1966).

Gross National Product, Growth Rates and Trend Data by Region and Country (Washington: Agency for International Development, Statistics and Reports Division, March 31, 1967). *World Bank Atlas on Per Capita Product and Population* (International Bank for Reconstruction and Development, 1966). *Eastern Economist*, 1965 and 1966 (New Delhi). *United Nations Statistical Yearbook* (various years during 1950–65 period). *Monthly Commentary on Indian Economic Conditions*, September, October, and December 1966, January and February 1967 (New Delhi Indian Institute of Public Opinion). *India: Pocket Book of Economic Information*, 1964 and 1965 (New Delhi Ministry of Finance, Government of India). *Statistical Outline of India*, 1964 and 1965 (Bombay: Prepared by Tata Industries Private Limited, published by Popular Prakashan).

Growth in Industrial Employment and Labor Productivity

Table 7–1 reveals that industrial employment in China grew at an average annual rate of 9.7 to 10 percent during the 1950–66 period, and by about 6.5 to 7 percent from 1953. However, industrial labor productivity has grown at the modest rate of 1.7 to 2 percent during 1950–66, and by no more than 1.5 percent from 1953. Lack of skill and experience, highly labor-intensive techniques at tens of thousands of enterprises and in certain sectors, and the regime's desire to substantially increase industrial employment for its own sake (particularly where relatively well-educated people have been involved), with productivity given lower priority in many instances, are probably among the major reasons for this modest rate of productivity growth. Moreover, industrial employment tripled during the Great Leap Forward, and the regime was probably reluctant to dismiss all of the unneeded manpower—again, particularly the better-educated and relatively skilled—during the depression of the early 1960's. Hence, excess labor has probably persisted for several years. Now that the Red Chinese are rapidly developing new and sophisticated branches of industry—for example, chemicals, electronics, more complex machine tools and types of steel—a great deal of manpower is needed in these relatively new sectors to make up for the lack of know-how and real capital.

Finally, there is some possibility that the employment estimates for the 1960's (in Tables 7–1 and 7–2) are significantly overstated since they are based on fragmentary data. If this is true, labor-productivity performance is understated. (More about industrial employment in China shortly.) From Table 7–3 we can see that industrial employment grew at a very modest average annual rate of 2.2 to 2.4 percent in India during the 1950–66 period, but industrial-labor productivity grew at the rate of 3.6 percent to 4.3 percent, or significantly higher than in China. However, industrial labor-productivity growth in India is probably substantially overstated—by how much I do not know.

There are roughly eleven to thirteen million workers in the household-industry sector who are not included in Indian industrial-employment statistics. This sector produces handicrafts, a sizable proportion of which are consumed by the producers and their families. However, much of those goods that enter regular marketing channels shows up in industrial-output statistics, and since many (probably most of the people producing these goods) are not included in industrial employment, this leads to an overstatement of industrial-labor productivity. Whereas the large majority of handicraftsmen in China who make factory-type products were absorbed in the "modern" or factory sector in the mid- and late-1950's, this is still not true for India.

There is also probably much more seasonal and contract labor in Indian industry than in China which is not reported in official employment statistics. It was common for firms in India that I surveyed to have 25 to 50 percent of their factory employment comprise contract and/or seasonal labor, even though many of these workers were employed over periods of several or many years. This, too, leads to an overstatement of labor productivity in India in relation to China.

On the other hand, it is likely that there are significantly higher proportions of welfare, service, and auxiliary personnel in Chinese industry than in India, and this reduces labor productivity in China in relation to that in India. Very high degrees of vertical integration, extremely high labor-intensive methods (particularly in transportation and material-handling methods), and extensive educational, housing, medical, and other welfare and service activities at Chinese enterprises are major reasons for the relatively high proportions of auxiliary, service, and welfare personnel in Chinese industry. In my opinion, the availability of real capital or technology with regard to direct-production processes is not a critical factor in explaining differences in labor productivity in the Chinese and Indian industrial sectors as a whole. As for motivational or sociological-cultural factors, I feel they are much more conducive to higher industrial-labor productivity in China than in India.

Aggregate Performance in Real Terms: 1933–66

Absolute Levels of GNP and Per Capita Income

Table 7–2 indicates that in absolute terms, Red China's GNP as of 1966 (year-end) was probably in the range of $75 to $100 billion if we convert yuan into U.S. dollars at an internal purchasing power (IPP) rate, and $50 to $75 billion at the official exchange (OE) rate. The latter rate probably leads to a significant understatement of China's GNP in terms of living standards—which are still very low with either rate—and economic and industrial strength, not to mention military power. Using the IPP rate, China's per capita GNP was probably in the range of $100 to $137 as of 1966, and at the OE rate $69 to $105. The majority of experts place Red China's 1966 population at around 750 million and her real GNP in 1966 at about $90 billion. (See the sources and notes in Tables 7–1 and 7–2. It should be pointed out that Note *c* in Table 7–2 comments on a per capita income estimate given to me by a central Chinese Communist official in May 1966.) At this population level, and with a GNP of $90 billion, per capita income would be $120. This seems to be a pretty realistic figure to me. I do not feel that China's per capita GNP at the IPP rate was significantly lower than $120 in 1966, and it could conceivably have been higher.

In pre-1949 China, before the Communists came to power, the peak GNP for a single year was probably around $36 billion (in present U.S. dollars) at the IPP rate, and $24 billion at the OE rate. (See Table 7–2.) Peak per capita income was probably never higher than $60 at the IPP rate in pre-1949 China. In 1949, when the Communists took over, GNP at the IPP rate was only about $27 billion, and at the OE rate $18 billion, while per capita income at the former, and higher, rate was probably significantly less than $50. Hence, during China's Communist era until 1966, GNP and per capita GNP probably more than doubled. The pre-1949 peak levels of GNP and per capita income were surpassed in 1951 and 1952, respectively.

I am sure that in 1966 the average citizen in China was living substantially better—and could expect to live twelve to sixteen years longer—than the average citizen did at any time before the Communist takeover. I know that some veteran Sinologists will disagree with this statement, but I am convinced they are wrong.

Table 7–3 indicates that India's GNP as of 1966 was approximately $48 or $49 billion at the IPP rate of conversion, and about $36 billion at the OE rate, or substantially less, perhaps as much as 50 percent, than in Red China—at either rate. Per capita income in India in 1966 was in the range of $90 to $104 at the IPP rate, and $68–$75 at the OE rate. The high points of the ranges for India's 1966 per capita GNP are approximately equal to the low points of China's ranges. It is quite likely that China's real per capita GNP was at least 20 percent higher than India's as of 1966. Moreover, India's GNP increased by no more than 70 to 80 percent during the 1950–66 period, while China's probably increased by more than 100 percent. Similarly, India's per capita income—which was about $58 (current U.S. dollars) at the OE rate and $78 at the IPP rate in 1950—increased by roughly 20 percent during the 1950–66 period, while China's increased by approximately 75 to 100 percent. Even if we compare the 1952 or 1953–66 period for Red China with the 1950–66 period for India, China comes out ahead. In general, very few poor or developing countries have done as well as China in terms of growth and development since 1950.

However, as will be discussed later, and as can be seen from Table 7–14, Red China has a long, long way to go—several generations— before she achieves the present level of total GNP in the United States, several decades before she reaches Russia's present GNP, and quite possibly a decade —even barring severe ideological extremism—before she achieves Japan's 1966 total GNP. As for per capita income, China is likely to take well over a century before she achieves the present level of per capita income in the United States, and at least several generations before she achieves current levels of per capita income in the Soviet Union and Japan. But one must also judge Red China in absolute terms to gauge her existing and potential industrial, economic, and military power.

Absolute Levels of Industrial Production

Table 7–2 indicates that Chinese industrial production in real terms at the end of 1949 was only about 70 percent of the pre-1949 peak level. It is likely that industrial production at the end of 1948—before the Communists gained control over major industrial centers—was less than 50 percent of the pre-1949 peak level. As the Communists seized control of major industrial areas during the spring and summer of 1949, they immediately began putting idle productive capacity back into operation.

During the 1950–52 period industrial production doubled. At the end of 1965 real industrial output was about five or six times greater than in 1949, and two and a half to three times greater than at the end of 1952, in spite of the great damage done to industry during the 1959–62 period. It is likely that industrial output by the end of 1966 was at least three times greater than at the end of 1952, and six times that of 1949. While industrial performance has been substantially less erratic and more sustained in India during the 1950–66 period, real industrial output was only about two and a half times greater in 1966 than in 1950.

Absolute Levels of Industrial Employment

As indicated on Table 7–2, before the Communists came to power in China, peak industrial employment was probably well under 3 million. Although there are no statistics available, industrial employment at the end of 1948 was probably less than 2 million. At the end of 1949 it was a bit over 3 million, and by the end of 1952 it increased by more than 70 percent to 5.26 million.

The best available estimate places industrial employment in Red China in 1965 at around 14 million. This estimate—by John Emerson—is based on two pieces of information and one assumption.[2] A Chinese Communist source stated that in 1965 the number of women workers in industry was more than double what it was in 1957. In 1957 there were about 1.37 million female personnel in Chinese industry, and this figure is probably quite accurate. Thus in 1965 there were probably about 2.8 million female industrial personnel. In 1963 Chinese sources reported that females comprised 20 percent of the industrial-labor force in 1963. If it is assumed that they comprised about the same proportion in 1965, there would have been about 14 million personnel employed in the Red Chinese industrial sector.

If this 14 million estimate is reasonably accurate, this means that industrial employment nearly tripled from 1952 through 1965. I was told by a Chinese Ministry of Labor official in Peking in May 1966 that industrial employment was expected to grow by roughly 5 to 7 percent in 1966, but he did not give me an absolute employment figure. If it did grow by this much, it is quite likely that industrial employment toward the end of 1966 was around 15 million.

Whereas it is quite likely that Chinese industrial enterprise employment was roughly five times greater in 1966 than in 1949, and about three times greater in 1966 than in 1952, it did not even double in India between 1950 and 1966.

Growth and Environmental Trends during Selected Critical Periods

Because of the erratic nature of Communist China's economic growth and industrial development it may be useful to briefly summarize performance and key environmental changes during critical periods since 1949.

1950–52: *Economic Rehabilitation*

As mentioned earlier, the 1950–52 period was essentially one of economic rehabilitation, as was the portion of 1949 when the Communists gained control over key industrial areas and economic sectors. Economic and political stability were the most crucial environmental constraints that underwent vast improvement during 1950–52. The Communist regime also achieved great improvements in monetary and fiscal policy, central banking, and the utilization of available transportation, electric power, and other social-overhead-capital facilities, as well as agricultural land. It also made a start in vigorously tapping the nation's rich mineral resources. Sharp improvements began to emerge in the health and energy of the labor force. The motivation and performance of the work force also increased sharply because latent favorable sociological-cultural forces were released, and new changes for the better in most of the sociological-cultural factors discussed in this book were created and implemented.

Available high-talent and skilled manpower resources were quickly drawn on and used quite effectively in putting existing productive facilities back into use. On-the-job educational and training programs became extensive and intensive because the regime did not wish to rely on the slow process of the formal educational system to produce urgently required types of skilled human resources. Little in the way of new capital was needed to put existing productive resources back into operation. The outbreak of the Korean War did not seriously constrain economic rehabilitation since the Russians footed most of the bill in terms of nonhuman resources. In fact, this was Russia's major type of aid to the Red Chinese during this period.

In general, the Chinese Communists developed and brought into play an overall environment tremendously more conducive to managerial effectiveness, productive efficiency, and industrial progress than that which existed before they came to power. As a result, during 1950–52 GNP grew at an annual average rate of 21 percent to 26 percent (my estimate would be about 24 percent), per capita income by 19 percent to 24 percent (I would say about 22 percent), industrial production by 25 percent to 29 percent (I would say about 27 percent), industrial employment by about 20 percent, and industrial labor productivity around 7 percent. (See Table 7-1.)

1953–57: *The First Five-Year Plan*

During this period big gains were made in education and training, and sizable numbers of new graduates from the formal educational system began to enter the industrial sector. Further improvements were probably achieved in most areas of the sociological-cultural environment of management and industry, thus raising further human motivation and performance. Although the system of state planning and resource allocation that emerged with the First Five-Year Plan was crude and very imprecise in many respects, it was adequate for impressive industrial progress. Soviet aid reached a high point, and this contributed immensely to greater managerial effectiveness and industrial development. New investment and real capital were required for sustained progress since the large backlogs and windfalls derived from putting idle productive facilities into use were pretty much absorbed. The regime responded effectively with high rates of capital formation and investment. Considerable progress was made in exploiting and utilizing the nation's mineral resources, and big gains were also made in the social-overhead-capital sphere. Good weather and a wide variety of other favorable factors led to relatively good agricultural performance, although population growth became a more serious problem.

Although growth rates were not as great during 1953–57 as they were during 1950–52, they were nevertheless still impressive. GNP grew by at least 6.2 percent and possible by more than 8.5 percent (I would say at least 7.5 percent), per capita GNP by about 4 to 6.5 percent (I would say at least 5.4 percent), industrial production by around 16 percent, industrial employment by 8.5 percent, and labor productivity by at least 6 percent.

One expert, W. Hollister, has computed incremental capital-output ratio (ICOR) for Red China during the 1950's.[3] This ratio was calculated by dividing the average rate of gross fixed investment in relation to

GNP for a given period by the average rate of growth in gross national product. The lower the ICOR the higher the return on investment, or the lower the capital investment per unit of output. In effect, this ratio provides an answer to the question, How much does output grow in proportion to the increase in capital? For the 1950–57 period Red China's ICOR is estimated to have been 1.8, 2.3 for 1952–57, .8 for 1950–53, and 1.3 for 1958–60. The 1952–57 period is the most normal one, and the ICOR estimate for this period is the most meaningful one for comparing China's performance with that of other countries in the 1950's. China's ICOR for 1952–57 of 2.3 is substantially lower than that for India during 1950–59, which was 4.8, and about the same as Japan's which was 2.4 during 1950–59.[4] Russia's ICOR during 1950–58 was a bit over 3.5, and in the United States it was a bit higher.[5]

Another expert, T. C. Liu, has made a combined estimate for fixed capital and labor-productivity growth in the Chinese economy as a whole for the 1952–57 period.[6] He assigned arbitrary weights of seven and three to labor and capital, respectively, so that he could compare China's performance with computations made on a similar basis for ten industrial nations in another study—that of S. Kuznets.[7] This formula provides a productivity growth of 3.9 percent for the period based on official reconstructed Chinese Communist data, and 2.9 percent based on Liu's own estimates. I feel that Liu's 2.9 percent rate is too low and that a rate of about 3.3 to 3.5 percent would be more accurate. But even the 2.9 percent rate would mean that Red China did better during this period than seven of the ten relatively advanced countries in the Kuznets study—including the U.S.S.R. At the 3.9 percent rate China would have done better than all ten. The productivity-growth rates for some of these other countries in the 1950's were U.S.S.R. (2.5 percent), Japan (3.1 percent), France (3.3 percent), West Germany (3.8 percent), and the Netherlands (2.6 percent).

1958–60: The Great Leap Forward

There is no need to rehash the damage done to the environment of management and industry during the Great Leap. It will suffice to say here that virtually all of the environmental factors under study were adversely affected as the Leap became intensified. It is probably true that gains in industrial performance were real during the first half of this period. There was some lead time required before the Great Leap policies, programs, and objectives could do serious damage to the environment of management and industry, and hence managerial effectiveness and industrial performance. In 1959 the Leap was probably beginning to take its toll, and by mid-1960 a severe crisis had emerged which was recognized by the leadership, who called off the Leap and scrapped the related Second Five-Year Plan of 1958–62.

From 1958 to mid-1960, GNP grew at a rate of 7 to 15 percent (I would say about 10 to 12 percent), per capita income by 4.5 percent to over 12 percent (I would say roughly 7.5 to 9.5 percent), industrial production by at least 20 percent; industrial employment approximately tripled, and labor productivity fell by 33 to 40 percent. Peak levels of total and per capita GNP were probably achieved in 1959, although some reputable sources place the year at 1960, and one at year-end 1958. Industrial production probably achieved its highest rate of growth in 1958, declining somewhat in 1959, and dropping well below 10 percent in 1960. In fact, it is likely that industrial production actually declined during the second half of 1960.

The Great Leap was actually a superficial boom. Even without the fanatical ideologically inspired Leap, industrial progress and growth would have undoubtedly been quite impressive—although probably not as high statistically—since much of the essential groundwork and productive capacity had been created anyway. Certainly industrial and productivity growth, managerial effectiveness, and general economic progress would have been much more sustained, and would have achieved substantially higher levels as of the mid-1960's without the Great Leap Forward.

1960–62: Economic Crisis and Consolidation

At the low point of Red China's economic depression during 1960–62, GNP dropped by 20 to 35 percent from the high point reached during the Great Leap (I would say close to 30 percent), per capita income by roughly 32 percent in my estimation, industrial production by about 40 or 45 percent, industrial employment was approximately cut in half, while labor productivity increased by about 1 or 2 percent during 1961–62 because of the huge cutbacks in employment.

By mid- or late-1961 the regime began making environmental changes conducive to greater managerial effectiveness, industrial productive efficiency, and general economic growth. However, here too, lead time of one or two years was required before these changes reaped desired results, including industrial and general economic recovery. It has taken even longer—several more years—for new industrial progress and earlier peak levels of overall industrial performance to be achieved.

1963–65: Recovery and New Growth

During the 1963–65 period the overall environment of management and industry was immensely better than during the 1958–62 period, and in many spheres better even than during the 1950–52 or 1953–57 periods. There were probably significant improvements in the precision of state planning and resource allocation, as compared with 1953–57. Industry is now more complex and requires greater precision than before in planning, resource allocation, and control in order to achieve sustained and substantial growth. Monetary and fiscal policy and central banking have probably been better than ever before in China, but here too, greater precision is required as the economy develops and grows more complex. New gains have been made in social-overhead capital, and particularly in the exploration and exploitation of mineral resources. Performance in agriculture has improved sharply, but in per capita terms it may have not yet achieved earlier peak levels as of mid-1967. At the same time population growth remains a serious problem, although the regime seems to be taking vigorous steps in birth control.

The regime seems to have overcome the problems resulting from Soviet pullout and the sharp decline in Sino-Soviet trade by vigorously stepping up trade with the West and Japan, including the purchase of a sizable number of complete plants. Red China apparently can import most of the critical materials, equipment, and other supplies of a nonmilitary nature that it requires to carry out her industrial plans and objectives. While the regime's defense and military policies, particularly in the nuclear field, do drain critical resources from the civilian industrial sector, this does not constrain industrial growth or progress too seriously. On the other hand, various legal rules of the game and the nature of Red Chinese law, in general, seem to seriously constrain managerial effectiveness and industrial performance.

During 1963–66 substantial gains were made in education and training, and hence in the supply of high-talent and skilled manpower in the overall industrial sector.

In recent years the main educational problem with regard to industry has not been so much the lack of adequate numbers of higher semiprofessional or secondary school graduates; rather, it has been that of finding employment for new graduates in industrial enterprises without extensively displacing existing personnel who are less qualified. In spite of impressive industrial growth, the industrial sector has not been expanding fast enough to take full advantage of the potential supply of new graduates. But this should be no means imply that Chinese firms now have all of the higher-talented or skilled manpower they need for efficient performance. This is still far from the case.

While the sociological-cultural environment has been generally conducive to gains in managerial effectiveness, productive efficiency, and industrial progress during 1963–65, it is likely that a few factors of this environment have not been quite as favorable as they were during the 1950–57 period. Specifically, I question whether the achievement drive or motivation of managers, engineers, the intelligentsia, and other experts in general have regained pre-Great Leap levels. This may even be true for numerous workers and party cadres who were greatly disillusioned by the Great Leap experience. In any event, during the 1963–65 period, the achievement drive and motivation of personnel and, in fact, the overall sociological-cultural environment were still higher and better in Red Chinese industry than in most other countries of the world, and clearly favorable enough for fairly impressive performance to be achieved.

During 1963–65, GNP grew at an average annual rate of about 6 to 8 percent (I would estimate at least 7 percent), per capita and GNP by around 3.5 to 5.5 percent (I would say at least 4.5 percent), industrial production by approximately 11 percent, industrial employment by a bit over 7 percent, and labor productivity probably about 5.5 percent. As will be discussed later, substantial progress in the development of new products and the introduction of more complex and productive technology was also achieved during this period.

The Cultural Revolution—1966–?

In my opinion, 1966 was a relatively good year for industrial and general economic performance in Communist China in spite of the emergence of the Cultural Revolution—but indications are that 1967 was certainly poor; 1968 is still in question. The secondary schools and higher educational institutions were closed down at the end of the 1966 academic year, and although they were officially declared open in 1967, they have generally not been functioning very well, if at all. But this had a negligible impact on the industrial scene in 1966, although it is likely to have adverse effects in later years, particularly if ideological extremism prevails in Chinese education.

It is also true that I found that the ideological pendulum was beginning to swing in the direction of extremism at a sizable number of the industrial enterprises that I visited, as discussed in an earlier chapter. But at least several months' lead time was probably required for serious damage to be done to industrial performance on a national scale. If ideological extremism in industry persisted and/or became intensified through 1967, substantial damage is likely to have resulted. But we cannot say for certain whether this has happened or whether a compromise between ideology and managerial, technical, and economic rationality has been worked out in the industrial sector in general.

While the Red Guards briefly swept down on many factories, presumably disrupting operations and efficiency in most cases, the onslaught did not occur until late December of 1966. The other types of Super-Reds—the army, people's militia, new revolutionary groups—did not take charge of any industrial enterprises until 1967.

The Chinese Communists claim that industrial output increased by 20 percent in 1966 over 1965.[8] It is quite possible that this claim was made for ideological, propaganda, and motivational purposes in support of the Cultural Revolution, and that it is exaggerated. However, I am convinced that industrial production grew by at least 10 percent in 1966, and quite possibly by 15 percent or more. I was told by fairly high-level Communist Chinese officials that the planned rate of new capital investment in 1966 was at least 20 percent of national income and that industrial employment was expected to grow by 5 to 7 percent. I found at several of the industrial enterprises surveyed that they had recently expanded operations quite substantially through the acquisition of real capital, and that their employment had increased in 1966 by 5 to 10 percent. Virtually all of the firms surveyed claimed that their production plans called for increases in output over 1965, in many cases by at least 10 percent, in most cases by 5 percent or more, and in several cases by 15 to 20 percent or more. I shall present some concrete figures in this connection in Chapter 9.

Official Red Chinese sources also report large increases in production and, in some cases, record-level performance for various specific industrial and mining sectors in 1966. These include chemicals, a particularly large amount of chemical fertilizer, crude and refined petroleum, light-industry products (including textiles, especially cotton textiles), various types of machinery and equipment, coal, uranium, and various types of minerals. There have also been reports that new and expensive products, such as big steel items, were produced for the first time in 1966.[9]

In the agricultural sector, the Chinese claimed record harvests for 1966.[10] Even if this is exaggeration, agricultural progress was probably relatively good in 1966. I was certainly surprised by the amounts and varieties of foods available to, and consumed by, the population in those parts—admittedly the more affluent parts—of China that I visited.

Hence, it seems quite likely that GNP grew by 7 or 8 percent, and by at least 6 percent in Red China in 1966, while per capita GNP probably grew in the range of 4.5 to 6 percent, and by at least 3.6 percent. It is unlikely that such growth rates were achieved in 1967.

Industry's Contribution to China's National Income: 1933–65

Part A of Table 7–4 indicates that the industrial sector (including manufacturing, mining, and public utilities, but excluding handicrafts) contributed only about 6.6 percent to China's net domestic product in 1933, 11.5 percent by 1952, 20.7 percent in 1957, and about 25 percent in 1959 during the height of the Great Leap. If handicrafts are included, the figures would be 14 percent for 1933, 18.1 percent for 1952, 26.3 percent for 1957, and nearly 30 percent for 1959. If the manufacturing portion of the industrial sector is considered alone, contribution to gross domestic product during the 1933–59 period increased from 5.6 percent, at the beginning of the period, to 9 percent in 1952, 16.8 percent in 1957, and by roughly 20 percent in 1959. In general, it is evident that industrial output has comprised a much greater share of China's gross domestic product under Communist rule than in the past and that it increased substantially and steadily during the 1950's.

Part B of Table 7-4 shows the same trends for the industrial sector in the 1950's. Modern industry (including manufacturing, mining, and utilities) contributed 11 percent of Red China's net national product in 1952, almost doubling to 20 percent by the end of 1957, and increasing to 30 percent or more during the Great Leap. However, it is estimated that only about 15 percent of China's net national product in 1962 came from the industrial sector. This sharp drop was due to the great cutbacks in production and tremendous idle capacity that evolved during 1960-62.

TABLE 7-4

ESTIMATED SECTORAL CONTRIBUTIONS TO CHINA'S NATIONAL INCOME
(In Percent)

A: *Liu-Yeh Estimates for Net Domestic Product* [a]
(Based on 1952 yuan prices)

	1933	*1952*	*1957*	*1959*
Industry (factory, manufacturing only)	5.6	9.0	16.8	25.0 (Industry, Mining, Utilities combined)
Mining	0.8	2.1	3.2	
Utilities	0.2	0.4	0.7	
Handicrafts	7.4	6.6	5.6	4.8
Transportation and communications	1.8	2.9	4.0	Not available—included in other sectors
Construction	1.7	2.6	4.8	6.5
Agriculture	56.9	47.9	39.0	33.9
Retail stores and restaurants	10.3	10.7	10.5	Not available—included in other sectors (Retail stores, Finance, Government administration)
Finance	0.6	1.8	1.9	
Government administration	2.4	4.6	5.3	
Other sectors[b]	12.2	13.4	9.2	29.8

[a] Domestic product is obtained from national product by excluding factor income received from abroad and adding factor income remitted abroad. Net domestic product, like net national product, excludes depreciation on capital goods.

[b] Includes old-fashioned transportation, peddlers, rent, and personal services.

SOURCE:
T. C. Liu and K. C. Yeh, *The Economy of the Chinese Mainland* (Princeton: Princeton University Press, 1965), p. 88, Tables 19 and 20. Their 1959 figures are from a Rand Corporation memorandum, F No. RM-3519-PR, of the same title, prepared in two volumes in 1963. They do not cite the 1959 estimates in their book, and this may mean they now consider them too inaccurate. Their 1959 figures have also been cited in C. M. Li, ed., *Industrial Development in Communist China* (New York: Praeger, 1964), p. 18, Table 5.

TABLE 7–4 (*continued*)

B: *Wu–Hoeber–Rockwell Estimates for Net National Product*
(Based on 1952 yuan prices)

	1952	*1957*	*1959*	*1960*	*1962*
Modern industry (includes manufacturing, mining, and public utilities)	11	20	30	35	15
Handicrafts	7	6	5	4	6
Agriculture	49	39	32	24	47
Other sectors	33	35	33	37	32

SOURCE:
Y. L. Wu, F. Hoeber, M. Rockwell, *The Economic Potential of Communist China* (Menlo Park, California: Stanford Research Institute, 1963), p. 241, also cited in part in Liu, *op. cit.*, p. 18. It should be noted that in a later study Wu has revised his gross (and net) domestic and national product figures for 1962 downward by over 20 percent. (See his book *The Economy of Communist China* [New York: Praeger, 1965], p. 91, Table V–1.) This revision could have implications for the 1962 breakdown cited in my above table.

C: *Jones Estimates for Gross National Product*
(Based on current U.S. dollar estimates)

	1957	*1965*
Industry, transportation, and construction	27	30
Agriculture	48	46
Trade, services, etc.	25	24

SOURCE:
E. Jones, "The Emerging Pattern of China's Economic Revolution," *An Economic Profile of Mainland China* (Washington: U.S. Government Printing Office, 1967), p. 96, Table VI. Jones does not specify, but industry may be the modern sector only, with handicrafts being placed in the other categories. He does not indicate whether industry includes public utilities and/or mining.

The estimates in Part C of Table 7–4 lump together industry, transportation, and construction and indicate that the contribution of these sectors to GNP increased modestly from 27 percent in 1957 to 30 percent in 1965. On the basis of these figures I would estimate industry's contribution alone to GNP to have been in the range of 24 percent to 27 percent in 1965. It is likely that the proportionate contributions made by the construction and transportation sectors were not as great in 1965 as 1957.

Table 7–5 indicates the contribution made by India's industrial sector (including manufacturing, mining, and public utilities) to that country's national income during the 1950/51–1965/66 period. During this entire period industry's share of India's national income only increased from 16.1 percent in 1950/51 to an expected 20.8 percent in 1965/66. Hence,

TABLE 7–5

SECTORAL CONTRIBUTIONS TO INDIA'S NATIONAL INCOME
1950/51–1965/66
(Percent Distribution Based on 1960–61 Prices*)

	1950/51	*1960/61*	*1964/65*	*1965/66* (expected)
Industry (manufacturing, mining, public uitilities)	16.1	18.3	19.0	20.8
Agriculture (including forestry and fishery)	51.3	48.3	44.7	39.6
Transport, communications, trade and commerce (railway figures in parentheses)	17.7 (1.9)	16.6 (2.6)	17.3 (2.8)	18.2 (3.0)
Other services	14.9	16.8	19.0	21.4

*** All periods relate to fiscal years beginning April 1.**

SOURCES:
This table is based on data presented in the sources cited in Table 7–3 in this chapter.

Red China's industrial sector did better than India's in growth and proportionate terms, and substantially better in absolute and per capita terms with regard to its contribution to GNP or national income.

BRANCH OF INDUSTRY PERFORMANCE: 1933–66

Value Added by Basic Industrial Sector, 1933–65

Table 7–6 presents estimates on the value-added contributions of the producer-goods and consumer-goods branches of industry, mining, and handicrafts within the overall industrial sector. We see from the estimates in this table that the producer-goods sector comprised a mere 10 percent of total value added in Chinese industry as a whole in 1933, and by 1952 its value-added contribution was 25 percent, or two and a half times greater, even though total industrial production was substantially greater. This sector's value-added proportionate contribution nearly doubled again by the end of 1957, when it was 44 percent. The 1965 estimates are less reliable, but producer-goods share of value added is estimated at 57–63 percent, and it was probably more than 50 percent.

On the other hand, proportionate value-added contribution of the consumer goods and handicrafts sectors declined in 1952 as compared with 1933—the proportionate decline in handicrafts was very sharp—but their absolute volumes of output (particularly factory-produced consumer goods) were substantially greater in 1952. These two sectors continued to decline in terms of their shares of proportionate value added in the 1950's

TABLE 7–6

ESTIMATED PERCENT CONTRIBUTION TO TOTAL VALUE ADDED IN INDUSTRY AND MINING IN CHINA, 1933–65
(In Percent Based on 1952 Prices in Yuan)

	1933	1952	1957	1965
Total	100	100	100	100
Producer-goods sector	10	25	44	57–63
Consumer-goods sector	30	26	20	24–29 (consumer-goods and handicrafts combined)
Handicrafts sector	53.4	37.5	23.5	
Mining sector	.60	11.4	12.5	13–14

SOURCES:
The 1933, 1952, and 1957 figures were computed from the data in T. C. Liu and K. C. Yeh, *The Economy of the Chinese Mainland* (Princeton: Princeton University Press, 1965), p. 66, Table 8. The 1965 estimates are from D. Perkins, "Economic Growth in China and the Cultural Revolution," *The China Quarterly*, No. 30 (1967), Table II. Perkins indicates the methodologies, assumptions, and sources utilized in arriving at his estimates, and they seem to be quite plausible.

For a more detailed breakdown of value added by specific branches of industry in the 1950's, see R. Field, "Chinese Communist Industrial Production," *An Economic Profile of Mainland China*, Vol. 1 (Washington: U.S. Government Printing Office, 1967), p. 274, Table 3.

and until 1965. It is likely that consumer goods have gained in value-added contribution in 1966 over 1965 and that volume of output was significantly higher, particularly because of gains made in cotton textiles.

Table 7–6 indicates that value added in the mining sector increased very sharply in both proportionate and absolute terms in 1952 as compared with 1933. Value-added contributions of the mining sector increased modestly in proportionate terms during the 1952–65 period, but very substantially in absolute terms.

Output of Various Major Commodities, 1933–52

Table 7–7 indicates the production of eight major commodities for 1933, the pre-1949 peak year, 1949, and 1952. For all of the commodities in the table output was substantially less—in most cases at least several times less—in 1949, when the Communists took over than during the pre-1949 peak year. The volume of output of pig iron, cement, cotton yarn, and possible crude oil was significantly greater as far back as 1933 than in 1949, while the production of coal was only slightly greater in 1949. Only the output of electric power, crude steel (ingots), and paper was significantly greater in 1949 than 1933. If we had 1948 output statistics for these commodities, it is conceivable that they would reveal lower output for these commodities than in 1933. By 1952 the production of the

TABLE 7–7

SELECTED INDUSTRIAL PRODUCTION INDICATORS FOR CHINA, 1933–52

Product	*Unit of Measurement*	*1933*	*Pre–1949 Peak Output*	*Pre–1949 Peak Year*	*1949*	*1952*
Pig iron	Thousand M.T.	609.00	1,889.00	(1943)	252.00	1,929.00
Steel ingots	" "	negligible	923.00	(1943)	158.00	1,349.00
Coal	" "	283,800.00	64,860.00	(1942)	32,430.00	66,490.00
Crude oil	" "	89.00	842.00	(1942)	(not available but probably less than 1942)	871.00
Cement	" "	784.00	2,300.00	(1942)	660.00	2,860.00
Machine-made paper	" "	45.00	165.00	(1943)	108.00	372.00
Cotton yarn	Million bales	2.45	2.45	(1933)	1.80	3.62
Electric power	Billion K.W.H.	2.07	5.95	(not available; probably 1942–44 period under Japanese occupation)	4.31	7.26

SOURCES:
K. Chao, *The Rate and Pattern of Industrial Growth in Communist China* (Ann Arbor: University of Michigan Press, 1965), pp. 122 ff., Table C–1. *Ten Great Years* (Peking: Foreign Languages Press, 1960). *Report on National Economic Development and Fulfillment of the State Plan*, State Statistics Bureau (Peking: Foreign Languages Press, 1956). A. Eckstein, "The Economic Heritage" (mimeographed), prepared for a Conference on Economic Trends in Communist China (cited in Table 7–2 of this chapter), p. 73, Table II; Eckstein cites a number of Chinese sources from which some of the pre–1949 figures were derived.

eight major commodities was greater than in the pre-1949 peak years, in most cases substantially greater.

Output of Thirteen Major Commodities, 1953–59

Table 7–8 presents Chinese Communist production figures in two parts for thirteen commodities—six heavy-industry commodities, three consumer durables, cotton cloth, two basic chemical products, and railway wagons—for the 1953–59 period. In Part I of this table Chinese output for five major heavy-industry products during 1953–57 and 1953–59 is compared with Indian output during the 1952–58 period, and Soviet production during the 1928/29–1935 period, which covers the First Soviet Five-Year Plan and about half of the second. Although exaggerated Chinese production claims for the 1958–59 period have been substantially discounted, the Chinese figures for 1953–57 are still probably more reliable than for the 1953–59 period.

Part II of Table 7–8 compares Chinese production for eight products during 1953–57 and 1953–59 with Indian production during her First Five-Year Plan (1950/51–1955/56), and during her first and second five-year plans combined (1950/51–1960/61). While Part I of this table is based largely on computations done by Kong Chao, I have added Part II in order to make some Sino-Indian comparisons for a number of consumer products and other goods not covered in Chao's study.

For the five major heavy-industry goods in Part I of Table 7–8, China achieved much higher average annual-growth rates during both 1953–57 and 1953–59 than India did during 1952–58. This was the case even though India had higher absolute levels of production of steel, pig iron, and cement at the outset of the periods compared. By the end of 1957 China was substantially ahead of India at the end of 1958 with regard to total output of all five commodities, even though we are comparing a five-year period for China with a seven-year period for India. Red China also achieved higher growth rates for all five commodities during 1953–59 than Russia did during 1928/29–35; the Soviet Union achieved slightly higher growth rates for electric power and coal than China in the 1953–57 period; but China still did substantially better on the other three commodities. The Soviets had higher absolute levels of production of steel ingots and pig iron than China at the outset of the periods compared, while China was ahead on the other three goods. China exceeded Soviet output for all five commodities—in most cases very substantially—in 1959 as compared with Russia in 1935. If we look at China's five-year performance only, ending in 1957, Russia was ahead in the absolute output of electric power, and steel ingots and pig iron in 1935, but here we are comparing a five-year period for China with a period of nearly 7.5 years for Russia.

Part II of Table 7–8 compares Chinese and Indian performance for eight products—four of them consumer goods—during the 1950's. In comparing Red China's First Five-Year Plan period (1953–57) with India's (1950/51–1955/56), we see that China achieved substantially higher average-annual growth rates for crude petroleum, sulfuric acid, radios, and bicycles, while India has a substantial edge in railway wagons and cotton cloth. The difference in growth rates for caustic soda and sewing machines in the two countries was not significant. By the end of 1957 China had achieved substantially greater absolute levels of production of crude petroleum, sulfuric acid, and caustic soda, and slightly greater volume of radios than India did by the end of her Second Five-Year Plan in 1961.

In comparing the 1953–59 period for China with the 1950/51–1960/61 period for India, we see that China achieved much higher average annual rates of growth in railway wagon, crude petroleum, sulfuric acid, cotton cloth, and bicycle production, and slightly higher growth rates for caustic soda and sewing machines. There are no data available for China's radio production in 1958–59 to enable a comparison for this product. China had achieved substantially greater absolute levels of production in 1959 for the seven products for which we have data—in some cases several times greater—than India had achieved in 1960–61. This was the case even though we are comparing a seven-year period for China with a ten-year period for India. Even if we were to further discount Chinese production figures for 1958–59 quite substantially, the results would still be the same.

In terms of overall industrial growth, Red China achieved an average annual rate of over 20 percent during 1953–59, and about 15 or 16 percent during 1953–57. India's annual average rate of industrial growth in the 1950's was no more than 6 percent; for Russia it was roughly 9.5 percent, for the United States less than 4 percent, but for Japan it was over 13 percent. The Soviet Union achieved a rate of roughly 12 percent—some industrial-production indexes place it as low as 9.9 percent and as high as 14.2 percent—during the 1927/28–1937/38 period—that is, during her first two five-year plans.[11] Hence, Communist China clearly did very well in terms of industrial growth during the 1950's, even if we ignore the 1950–52 period of economic rehabilitation and substantially discount exaggerated official Chinese claims for 1958 and particularly 1959.

Aggregate Branch of Industry Performance: The 1950's[12]

The most spectacular and sustained gains were made in producer goods in Red China in the 1950's. For example, the ferrous-metals industry achieved an annual average rate of growth of over 100 percent during 1950–52, about 31 percent during 1953–57, and roughly 40 percent in 1958–59. The average annual rates of growth for nonferrous metals during these three periods were roughly 47 percent, 30 percent, and 39 percent, respectively. The machine-building and metal-processing sector achieved

TABLE 7–8

Comparison of Output of Major Commodities in Communist China, India, and the Soviet Union during Their First and Second Five-Year Plans

Part I

Commodity	COMMUNIST CHINA 1953–57	COMMUNIST CHINA 1953–59	INDIA 1952–58	SOVIET UNION 1928/29–35
ELECTRIC POWER (Billion K.W.H.)				
Output at beginning of period (Jan. 1)	7.26	7.26	5.856	5.007
At end of period (Dec. 31)	19.34	41.50	12.37	26.294
Average annual rate of increase	22.3%	28.3%	11.3%	25.79%
COAL (Million M.T.)				
At beginning of period	66.49	66.49	34.98	35.51
At end of period	130.0	347.8	46.01	108.9
Average annual rate of increase	14.2%	26.7%	4.0%	16.7%
STEEL INGOTS (factory-produced only) (Million M.T.)				
At beginning of period	1.35	1.35	1.524	4.25
At end of period	5.35	13.35	1.85	12.59
Average annual rate of increase	31.9%	38.7%	2.8%	16.1%
PIG IRON (factory-produced only) (Million M.T.)				
At beginning of period	1.93	1.93	1.85	3.28
At end of period	9.53	20.52	2.15	12.49
Average annual rate of increase	37.3%	40.2%	2.2%	20.2%

(Million M.T.)				
At beginning of period	2.86	2.86	3.25	1.85
At end of period	6.86	12.27	6.17	4.49
Average annual rate of increase	19.0%	23.1%	9.6%	13.0%

SOURCES:
K. Chao, *The Rate and Pattern of Industrial Growth in Communist China* (Ann Arbor: University of Michigan Press, 1965), Tables 28 and C–1. *Ten Great Years* (Peking: Foreign Languages Press, 1960). *United Nations Monthly Bulletin of Statistics*, July 1957, pp. 27–62, and June 1960, pp. 28–65 (for India). D. Hodgman, *Soviet Industrial Production, 1928–51* (Cambridge, Mass.: Harvard University Press, 1954), pp. 194–204 (for the Soviet Union). Chao's 1953–57 statistics for China are much more reliable than those for the 1953–59 period because of possible intentional exaggeration on the part of the Chinese Communists and considerable waste in production in 1958, and probably even more so in 1959. Chao has discounted the Chinese claims somewhat by not including the indigenous method of production, or small-scale, highly labor-intensive pig-iron and crude-steel output, for 1959.

Part II

Commodity	COMMUNIST CHINA *1953–57*	COMMUNIST CHINA *1953–59*	INDIA *1950/51–1955/56* (Fiscal Years)	INDIA *1950/51–1960/61* (Fiscal Years)
RAILWAY WAGONS (Thousands of units)				
At beginning of period	5792	5792	2900	2900
At end of period	7300	30,000	15,300	8200
Average annual rate of increase	5%	26%	30%	11%
CRUDE PETROLEUM (Thousand M.T.)				
At beginning of period	436	436	269	269
At end of period	1458	3658	347	514
Average annual rate of increase	26%	36%	6%	6.5%

TABLE 7–8 (*continued*)

Part II (*continued*)

Commodity	COMMUNIST CHINA		INDIA	
	1953–57	*1953–59*	*1950/51–1955/56* (Fiscal Years)	*1950/51–1960/61* (Fiscal Years)
SULFURIC ACID (Thousand M.T.)				
At beginning of period	190	190	101	101
At end of period	632	1056	167	368
Average annual rate of increase	26%	28%	11%	14%
CAUSTIC SODA (Thousand M.T.)				
At beginning of period	79	79	12	12
At end of period	198	360	36	101
Average annual rate of increase	20%	25%	25%	24%
COTTON CLOTH (Millions of meters)				
At beginning of period	4158	4158	4215	4215
At end of period	5050	7500	6260	6738
Average annual rate of increase	4.5%	9.0%	8.0%	5.0%

SEWING MACHINES (Thousands of units)				
At beginning of period	84	84	33	33
At end of period	267	563	111	303
Average annual rate of increase	26%	31%	27%	25%
RADIOS (Thousands of units)				
At beginning of period	17	17	54	54
At end of period	295	not available	201	282
Average annual rate of increase	85%	not available	30%	18%
BICYCLES (Thousands of units)				
At beginning of period	80	80	99	99
At end of period	806	1498	513	1071
Average annual rate of increase	59%	53%	38%	27%

SOURCES:
Ten Great Years and *U.N. Monthly Statistics* (both cited under Part I). Other Indian data have been obtained from *India's Draft Fourth Plan* (New Delhi: National Planning Commission, Government of India, 1966); *Eastern Economist, 1965* (December 24, 1964), especially pp. 1337 and 1354; *India: Pocket Book of Economic Statistics* (New Delhi: Ministry of Finance, Government of India, 1964); *Statistical Outline of India, 1964* (Bombay: Popular Prakashan, 1964).

rates of approximately 42 percent, 22 percent, and 40 percent during these three periods respectively, while the growth rates for chemical processing were about 60 percent, 26 percent, and 40 percent, respectively.

While light-industry and consumer-goods branches expanded substantially in the 1950's, their growth rates were not as impressive. For example, overall textile production grew at an average annual rate of 36 percent during 1950–52, dropping sharply to 9 percent during 1953–57, and rising to 26 percent in 1958–59. The processed-foods industry achieved rates of 22 percent, 12 percent, and 15 percent during these three periods respectively. The output of daily-use commodities grew at an annual average rate of about 15 percent duirng 1950–52, and 12 percent during 1953–57.

Industrial Employment and Labor Productivity in Major Sectors in the 1950's

Table 7–9 indicates employment trends in different branches of Chinese Communist industry during the 1949–58 period. In 1952 industrial employment was about equally divided between producer- and consumer-goods sectors. By 1957 the ratio was 60 to 40 in favor of producer goods. All branches of industry had continual increases in employment during 1949–58 but at widely varying rates. Although we do not have figures for total employment in producer- or consumer-goods sectors as a whole for 1958, it is evident that employment jumped greatly in most producer-goods sectors in 1958, while it increased only modestly in light-industry or consumer-goods branches.

In terms of share of total industrial employment, the iron and steel sector maintained a steady proportion in the range of 4 to 4.5 percent during 1949–57, but increased sharply to 14.4 percent in 1958 as actual employment in this sector increased more than four-fold. The metal processing and machine building, chemical processing, coal, and timber sectors increased their percentage shares of total industrial employment modestly in 1958, but their actual employment rose sharply. The nonferrous metals, building materials, petroleum, electric power, and paper manufacturing branches had declines in the percentage shares of total employment in 1958 as compared to 1957, even though the actual number of personnel in these sectors increased substantially. The textile- and food-processing sectors experienced sharp drops in their proportionate shares of total industrial employment in 1959, although their actual employment increased modestly.

Table 7–10 presents some crude but suggestive labor-productivity computations and trends for a limited number of branches of industry in Red China during 1949–58. It should be noted that the employment figures used in computing labor productivity are for an entire sector, whereas the related output of the sector is only a limited portion of the total production of the sector in most cases. For example, the same employment figures have been used to compute labor productivity for pig iron, crude steel, and rolled (finished) steel separately and combined. Similarly, in the case of coal, timber, and paper only the end products have been used in computing productivity, although the total employment for each of this sectors was used. The productivity computations for electric power and textiles are probably more accurate and meaningful than for the other sectors.

In spite of such crude methodology and significant limitations, Table 7–10 does depict some interesting and suggestive trends. In a later chapter we shall present labor-productivity data for Chinese industrial enterprises surveyed in 1966. At that time reference will be made to some of the labor-productivity figures for the 1950's contained in Table 7–8.

Table 7–10 indicates that impressive and sustained labor-productivity gains were achieved during 1949–57 in the production of electric power, pig iron, crude steel, and rolled steel, coal, paper, and timber. Labor productivity for crude petroleum doubled during 1949–52, but it only increased by a modest 10 percent during 1953–57. Productivity for textiles and cotton fabrics increased quite substantially between 1949 and 1953, but fell off slightly during the 1953–57 period. The relatively small amount of investment funds allocated to most consumer-goods sectors, including textiles, during China's First Five-Year Plan probably accounts in large part for the relatively poor labor-productivity performance regarding textile products during this period. The nationalization of private textile firms, which constituted a large portion of this sector, during 1954–56 in particular, may have led to a substantial drop in the motivation of former owner-managers who stayed on at these firms, and even in the motivation of many long-time employees loyal to the original managements. This, too, could have contributed to the relatively poor labor productivity showing.

In 1958, with the exception of textiles and cotton cloth, paper, electric power, and crude petroleum, labor productivity for all of the other sectors in Table 7–10 dropped by at least 50 percent. In the case of the iron and steel branches, labor productivity in 1958 was only in the range of 15 to 25 percent of 1957 performance. In 1958 productivity fell by over 20 percent in the electric-power sector, and more than 10 percent in the petroleum industry. The drop was only slight in the textile and cotton-cloth industries, since employment did not increase very much in 1958. The paper industry shows the only increase in labor productivity in 1958 over 1957, and this branch added only a mere 2,000 additional personnel in 1958.

Table 7–11 compares labor productivity in a number of industries in Red China in 1957 with that in India and the Soviet Union in the late 1950's. These comparisons are even cruder than the internal-period com-

TABLE 7–9

INDUSTRIAL EMPLOYMENT BY SECTOR, COMMUNIST CHINA, 1949–58
(In Thousands)

	1949	1952	1953	1957	1958
Total employment	3,060	5,260	6,120	7,910	22,980
Percent of total	100%	100%	100%	100%	100%
Producer foods sectors	n.a.	2.68	3.24	4.74	n.a.
Percent of total	"	51%	52.9%	60%	"
Consumer goods sectors	n.a.	2.58	2.88	3.16	n.a.
Percent of total	"	49%	47.1%	40%	"
Iron & steel	121	233	258	347	3,304
Percent of total	4%	4.4%	4.2%	4.4%	14.4%
Nonferrous metals (processing & mining)	87	158	183	346	731
Percent of total	2.8%	3.0%	3.0%	4.4%	3.2%
Metal processing (includes machine building)	337	846	934	1,403	3,304
Percent of total	12.3%	16.1%	15.3%	17.7%	18.3%
Electric power	54	64	70	143	251
Percent of total	1.8%	1.2%	1.1%	1.8%	1.1%

Coal	432	494	517	669	2,500
Percent of total	14.1%	9.4%	8.4%	8.5%	10.9%
Chemical processing	63	113	129	253	800
Percent of total	2.1%	2.1%	2.1%	3.2%	3.5%
Building materials	150	421	453	600	1,320
Percent of total	4.9%	8.0%	7.4%	7.6%	5.7%
Timber	160	292	290	333	1,126
Percent of total	5.2%	5.5%	4.7%	4.2%	4.9%
Petroleum	12	22	31	67	124
Percent of total	.4%	.4%	.5%	.8%	.6%
Paper manufacturing	51	84	90	94	96
Percent of total	1.7%	1.6%	1.5%	1.2%	.4%
Textiles	770	1,022	1,080	1,282	1,500
Percent of total	25.2%	19.4%	17.6%	16.2%	6.5%
Food processing	533	1,021	n.a.	1,200	1,410
Percent of total	18.1%	19.4%	"	15.2%	6.1%

SOURCE: Emerson, *op. cit.* (in Table 7–1 above), pp. 466–67, Table A-6.

TABLE 7–10

LABOR PRODUCTIVITY TRENDS IN SELECTED BRANCHES OF COMMUNIST CHINESE INDUSTRY, 1949–58
(Output per Employee-Year)

Commodity	*1949*	*1952*	*1957*	*1958*
Electric power (million K.W.H.)	80	114	135	110
Pig iron, crude and rolled, steel (tons)	4.6	20	45	9–11
Pig iron (tons)	2.1	8.3	17.1	4.1–4.4
Crude and rolled steel (tons)	2.5	13.5	28	4–4.5
Crude steel (tons)	1.3	5.8	15.5	2.4–2.8
Rolled steel (tons)	1.2	5.6	13.0	2.2–2.6
Pig iron and crude steel (tons)	3.4	14	33	6–8
Coal (tons)	75	150	197	80–108
Crude petroleum (tons)	10	20	22	19
Paper (tons)	4.5	6.4	13	17
Timber (cubic meters)	35	39	84	31
Textiles* (sq. meters)	2,870	4,133	4,070	3,950
Cotton cloth only (sq. meters)	4,000–4,700	5,800–6,800	5,600–6,650	5,500–6,500

* Consists almost entirely of cotton, woolen, and silk fabrics.

METHODOLOGY AND SOURCES: It should be stressed that the labor-productivity figures are crude and meant to be only suggestive. The employment figures used in computing productivity are for an entire sector, whereas the related output presents only a limited portion of the total output of the sector in most cases. See the additional comments and notes in Table 7–11.

The labor-productivity figures have been computed on the basis of industrial-production and employment data presented in the sources cited in Tables 7–1 and 7–8 of this chapter. However, the employment figure used in computing labor productivity in the cotton-textile industry is my own estimate based on an assumption that 60 to 70 percent of total employment in China's overall textile sector has been in the cotton-textile industry. This assumption is based on information contained in Emerson, *op. cit.* (in Table 7–1 above), p. 466; Jones, *Mainland China in the World Economy* (cited in Table 7–1 above), p. 238; K. Chao, *Mainland China in the World Economy* (cited in Table 7–1 above), p. 238; Chao, *Mainland*, p. 140; and Liu and Yeh, *op. cit.* (in Table 7–1 above), p. 427, Table F–1.

parisons for Red China alone because of probably substantial differences in the product mixes and employment classifications of the three countries. But in the absence of better data, I still think that Table 7–11 presents some interesting and suggestive comparisons.

The Soviet Union achieved much better labor-productivity performance than both China and India in the latter part of the 1950's for all of the sectors on Table 7–11 with the exception of textiles and cotton cloth. Russia's superior performance for seven of the nine commodity groups compared was due, in substantial part, to superior managerial and technical skill, and technology, and larger amounts of real capital. However, many of the other environmental factors under study in this book have also been more favorable in the Soviet Union, and they, too, must be considered if one wants to explain adequately Russia's superior labor-productivity performance.

The textile and cotton industries in the Soviet Union have been seriously neglected in terms of resource allocation—in relative terms perhaps even more so than in China or India—until most recent times, and this may explain in large part why labor productivity in these branches may have been somewhat higher in India and Communist China in the latter part of the 1950's. Actually the difference in productivity in these sectors in Russia and China was not very large according to Table 7–11. The differences between China and India are also not very substantial. A computation of labor productivity in the textile and cotton sectors of China and India earlier in the 1950's than the periods indicated in the table would reveal that China's performance was as good as, or better than, India's during several years.

According to Table 7–11, labor productivity in the production of pig iron, crude steel, and rolled steel in China and India was not significantly different. China had a substantial edge with regard to coal, timber, and paper, while India had a sizable edge in electric-power productivity. The fact that hydroelectricity has been responsible for a much larger share of total electric-power output in India than in China—where much greater use is made of thermal power—may partly explain India's superior labor-productivity performance in this sector. Labor productivity is generally substantially higher in the production of hydropower than in thermal power.

Physical Output Trends for Twenty Major Products, 1952–65

Table 7–12 presents production-trend data for twenty major commodities produced in Communist China during the 1952–65 period. The figures for 1952 and 1957 are quite reliable, but for the 1958–65 period ranges of estimates are used for the majority of the products for various specific years. For all of the estimate ranges, I feel that their lower limits understate commodity output. For 1965 I think that the level of production of the commodities stated in ranges was at least as high as the mid-points of their ranges. In my opinion, it is quite likely that 1965 production of crude steel, coal, crude oil, chemical fertilizers, and electric power approached the upper limits of their range estimates for that year.

TABLE 7–11

SOME SUGGESTIVE LABOR-PRODUCTIVITY COMPARISONS [a] FOR SELECTED INDUSTRIAL SECTORS, CHINA, INDIA, AND THE SOVIET UNION, LATE 1950'S
(Output per Man-Year)

Commodity	*COMMUNIST CHINA* (1957)	*INDIA* [b] (Late 1950's)	*SOVIET UNION* (Late 1950's)
Electric power (million K.W.H.)	135	225–250	400
Pig iron, crude and rolled steel (tons)	45	40–50	140
Pig iron (tons)	17	15–20	45
Crude and rolled steel (tons)	28	30–35	100
Crude steel—ingots (tons)	15	15–20	55
Rolled steel (tons)	13	10–15	50
Coal (tons)	197	130–140	390
Paper (tons)	13	6–8	21
Timber (cubic meters)	84	25–30 (1960–61)	140
Textiles—all types of fabrics produced (sq. meters)	4,070	4,500–5,000	3,900
Cotton cloth (sq. meters)	5,600–6,650	5,800–6,200	5,600

[a] These are very crude and purely suggestive estimates because the employment figures used in computing labor productivity are for an entire sector whereas the related output of the sector represents only a limited portion of the total production of the sector in most cases. For example, I have used the same employment figures to compute labor productivity for pig iron, crude steel, and rolled steel for each country. In the case of coal, timber, and paper, only the end products have been used in computing productivity, but total employment for each sector was used. In spite of such limitations, however, the estimates do indicate the relative positions of the three countries with regard to labor productivity in the various sectors toward the end of the 1950's.

[b] Indian estimates have been made in ranges since available sources differ in their employment and industrial-output figures even for the same year in several cases. Moreover, some of the figures themselves are estimates or are based on incomplete samples.

As noted in the table the Indian labor-productivity figures tend to be somewhat overstated since seasonal and contract labor comprises a considerable part of the labor force, but much of it is not included in official employment reports or statistics. The same is true in China, but probably to a substantially lesser degree. Moreover, Indian employment statistics for the overall textile, cotton-cloth, and paper industries probably do not include many workers who are classified separately under "household industry" or handicrafts.

SOURCES:
Communist China estimates are based on industrial production and employment data presented in the sources cited in Table 7–1.

Indian estimates are based on the data presented in the sources cited in Table 7–3.

Soviet figures are based on data presented in *Narodnoe Khoziastvo SSSR*, 1958, 1959, 1960, and 1961 (National Economy of the U.S.S.R., Statistical Yearbook), published in Moscow annually by the Central Statistical Administration; *Promishlenost SSSR*, 1958, 1959, and 1960 (Industry U.S.S.R.) published annually in Moscow by the Central

Statistical Administration; A. Katz, *Proizvoditelnost Truda V SSSR i Glavnice Kapitalisticheskich Stran* (Productivity in the U.S.S.R. and Major Capitalist Countries), Moscow: Economica, 1964; G. Schroeder, "Soviet Industrial Labor Productivity," *Dimensions of Soviet Economic Power* (Washington: U.S. Government Printing Office, 1962), pp. 141–62; *Current Economic Indicators for the USSR* (Washington: U.S. Government Printing Office, 1965), p. 82, Table VI–7.

For fifteen of the sixteen products for which production statistics are available in 1952 and 1957, output increased by roughly 100 percent or more in 1957 as compared with 1952. The production of several of these products increased by more than 200 percent during 1953–57—these included pig iron, crude and rolled steel, coke, crude oil, refined petroleum products, chemical fertilizers, and trucks which were not produced at all in 1952 while 7,500 were produced in 1957. Cotton-cloth output increased by only twenty percent in 1957 over 1952.

For the seventeen products for which output figures are available during the Great Leap Period, the output of all but three or four of them at least doubled during 1958–60. Only timber, cotton cloth, sugar, and possibly paper production—depending on which point of the output range is used—did not increase by at least 100 percent during this period. However, as has been mentioned at several points in earlier chapters, such statistical output growth is not very meaningful because of the severe waste and imbalances in the productive system which resulted in the huge stocks of idle commodity inventories.

During the 1960–62 depression the output of about half of the commodities on Table 7–12 dropped by at least one-third in the low year as compared with Great Leap peak performance. The production of cement, crude steel, coal, coke, cotton cloth, and probably trucks dropped by 50 percent or more. Only crude oil and refined-petroleum products may not have been adversely affected during 1960–62 as their output was likely to have increased somewhat during this period.

If we compare levels of production in 1965 with 1957 and 1957 with 1952 for the commodities in Table 7–12, we find that most products achieved substantially higher total percentage increases during 1953–57 than during 1958–65, even though the latter period is three years longer. Only crude oil, refined-petroleum products, and chemical fertilizers clearly achieved higher total percentage increases from 1957 (year-end) to 1965 (year-end) than during the 1953–57 period. Cotton textiles, sugar, and electric-power production achieved larger total percentage increases during 1958–65 as compared with 1953–57 only if we take the upper limits of their 1965 output ranges. In absolute terms the output of trucks, tractors, and aluminum ingots was substantially greater during the 1957–65 period than during 1953–57, since these products were not produced at all until after 1952.

TABLE 7–12

SELECTED INDUSTRIAL PRODUCTION INDICATORS FOR COMMUNIST CHINA, 1952–65[a]

Product	Unit of Measurement	1952	1957	1958	1959	1960	1961	1962	1963	1964	1965
Cement	Million M.T.	2.86	6.86	9.3	12.3	13.5	6.0–8.0	6.0–8.0	7.0–10.0	8.0–11.5	9.0–11.5
Pig iron	" "	1.9	5.9	13.7	20.5	n.a.	15.0	15.0	17.0	18.0	19.0
Crude steel (ingots)	" "	1.35	5.35	8.0	11.0–13.35	15.22–18.45	9.5–12.0	7.0–10.0	7.0–12.0	8.0–14.0	10.0–15.0
Rolled steel	" "	1.31	4.48	7.21	n.a.	n.a.	8.0	9.0	10.0	11.0	12.0
Coal	" "	66.5	130.0	226.4–270.0	292.4–347.8	325.0–425.0	180.0–250.0	180.0–250.0	190.0–270.0	200.0–290.0	210.0–300.0
Coke	" "	2.86	8.0	23.0	n.a.	n.a.	15.0	15.0	15.0	15.0	16.0
Crude oil	" "	.436	1.48	2.26	3.70	4.5–5.5	4.5–6.2	5.3–6.8	5.9–7.8	7.0–8.5	8.0–10.0
Refined petroleum products	" "	negligible	.55 (1956)	n.a.	n.a.	n.a.	5.5	6.5	7.0	8.0	9.0
Aluminum metal	" "	0	.03	.05	.07	n.a.	.1	.1	.1	.1	.1
Paper	" "	.54	1.22	1.63	2.13	2.13–2.8	1.0–2.6	1.0–2.7	1.0–2.85	1.5–2.85	1.5–2.85
Chemical fertilizer[b]	" "	.134	.764–.871	.984–1.35	1.33–2.0	1.68–2.48	1.43–1.45	2.05–2.17	2.6–3.0	3.4–[b] 4.6	4.5–[b] (1966[b]–5.0–8.0)
Refined copper metal	" "	n.a.	n.a.	n.a.	n.a.	n.a.	.1	.1	.1	.1	.1
Refined zinc metal	" "	n.a.	n.a.	n.a.	n.a.	n.a.	.09	.09	.09	.09	.09
Refined lead metal	" "	n.a.	n.a.	n.a.	n.a.	n.a.	.085	.085	.09	.1	.1
Trucks	Thousand units	0	7.5	16.0	15.5	29.0[c] (Chinese Great Leap claim)	n.a.	3.0–[c] 5.0	10.0–[c] 15.0	20.0–[c] 25.0	25.0–[c] 30.0

Tractors	Thousand units	0	0	.957	5.6	15.0	n.a.	n.a.	12.0–[d] 15.0	15.0–[d] 18.0	15.0–[d] 20.0
Timber	Million cu. meters	11.2	28.0	35.0	41.0	33.0– 39.0	27.0– 34.0	29.0	32.0	34.0	36.0
Cotton cloth	Billion (linear) meters	4.16	5.0– 5.05	5.7	7.5	6.0– 7.6	3.0	3.0– 3.3	3.3– 3.6	3.6–[d] 6.0	3.9–[d] 7.8
Sugar	Million M.T.	.451	.864	.964	1.13– 1.26	.92– 1.26	.70– 1.20	.48– 1.30	.54– 1.30	1.05– 1.84	1.5– 1.9
Electric power	Billion K.W.H.	7.26	19.34	27.5	41.5	47.0	31.0	30.0	33.0– 37.5	36.0–[e] 55.0	40.0–[e] 60.0

[a] 1952–57 figures are less subject to error than 1958–65 data. Figures not available are noted in the table as n.a.

[b] Chemical-fertilizer production is in terms of total final output rather than in nutrient. Output in terms of nutrient in 1965 was probably in the range of 800,000 to 1,100,000 tons. In the late 1960's nitrogenous fertilizer has comprised roughly 75 percent of China's total production, while the rest has been mostly phosphatic. See *Fertilizers: An Annual Review of World Production, Consumption and Trade, 1965* (Rome: Food and Agricultural Organization of the United Nations, 1966) and M. Larsen, "China's Agriculture Under Communism," *An Economic Profile of Mainland China*, Vol. I (Washington: U.S. Government Printing Office, 1967), p. 246, Table 2. The 1966 chemical-fertilizer output estimate of 5 million metric tons is from M. Larsen, "China's Agriculture Under Communism," *Profile*, Vol. I, Table 2, p. 246. K. Chao, in his statement to the Joint Economic Committee of U.S. Congress published in *Mainland China in the World Economy* (U.S. Government Printing Office, 1967), pp. 134–42, points out that reconstructed Chinese estimates place 1964 chemical-fertilizer production at 5.57 million tons and 1965 output at 9 million tons, both figures being higher than those presented above in my table. Chao gives reasons in favor of the reconstructed Chinese figures, or at least for figures higher than those cited by other experts. E. Jones refutes Chao's arguments and presents some additional data in *Mainland China*, pp. 237–38, but implies that estimates made by other sources may prove to be on the low side. I have used as my upper limit for chemical-fertilizer output for 1964 and 1965 the midpoint between the other experts' estimates and those of Chao. My 1966 upper limit has been arbitrarily assigned.

[c] Truck-production estimates for 1960–64 are from *Current Scene*, Vol. III, No. 17 (April 15, 1965), p. 10. This source notes that the 1960 figure is probably a grossly exaggerated "Great Leap" claim. I have estimated 1965 truck output about 20 percent higher than in 1964, as I was told by a manager at a Shanghai truck factor that total truck production in Red China "increased by 15 percent to 25 percent over 1964 in 1965."

[d] Tractor-output estimates for 1960–65 are based on information given to me by executives of the Loyang Tractor Factory and data contained in E. Snow, *The Other Side of the River* (New York: Random House, 1962), pp. 516–17; C. Lynch, *China: One Fourth of the World* (Toronto: McClelland and Stewart Ltd., 1965), pp. 35–36; and Larsen, *op. cit.*, pp. 247–50. On the basis of the data and arguments presented in K. Chao, in *op. cit.*, pp. 134–42, I have placed an upper limit on cotton-cloth output in 1965 at 7.8 billion meters. This is substantially higher than other available estimates, and double one. I have also set a higher upper limit on 1964 cotton output than available estimates indicate because of Chao's statements. Jones, *op. cit.*, p. 238, finds Chao's arguments convincing with regard to cotton production and states that he would be inclined to accept higher estimates than those given by other experts, specifically Field, but not necessarily as high as Chao's.

TABLE 7–12 (*continued*)

[e] Chao, *op. cit.*, again supports the 55 billion K.W.H. electric output figure for 1964, which is from a Soviet source, over the 40 billion figure of other experts. For reasons which I have discussed in the electric-power section of Chapter 6 of this book I agree with Chao that the 40 billion figure is probably an understatement. For 1965 I have placed the upper limit at 60 billion K.W.H., assuming about a 10-percent increase over 1964.

SOURCES: R. Field, "Chinese Communist Industrial Production," *An Economic Profile of Mainland China*, Vol. I (Washington: U.S. Government Printing Office, 1967), pp. 293–94, Table 9. This source contains estimates made by Field as well as a variety of reputable U.S. and foreign (including Soviet) experts and sources for crude steel, coal, cement, crude oil, electric power, chemical fertilizer, timber, paper, sugar and cotton cloth for the 1957–65 period. K. P. Wong, "The Mineral Resource Base of Communist China," in *Profile*, Vol. I, p. 175, Table 2, presents output data for pig iron, rolled steel, coke, refined petroleum products, refined copper, lead and zinc metals, aluminum for the 1961–65 period. Steel output estimates can also be found in T. C. Liu, *Profile*, Vol. I, p. 71, Table 10. Other data for the 1952–59 period are from K. Chao, *The Rate and Pattern of Industrial Growth in Communist China* (Ann Arbor: University of Michigan Press, 1965), pp. 122–32, Table C–1, and *Ten Great Years* (Peking: Foreign Languages Press, 1960).

According to the estimates in Table 7–12 the production of the following commodities was at a peak level in 1965: rolled steel and coke (for which there are no 1959–60 figures), crude oil and refined-petroleum products, aluminum metal, chemical fertilizer, refined copper, lead, and zinc (for which there are no figures prior to 1961), tractors, and probably trucks and sugar. If we take the upper limits of range estimates, paper, electric power, and cotton cloth would be added to this list. The other four commodities on the table had definitely not yet achieved Great Leap peak levels of output as of the end of 1965. These include pig iron, crude steel, coal, and coke.

Product Development and Technology

Although it is not possible to measure product development or technological progress in any precise quantitative way, a brief overview of a qualitative nature is warranted with regard to Red China's achievements in these spheres. More will be said about product development and technology at specific enterprises visited in 1966 in a later chapter.[13]

Before the Communist regime was established, China had produced nothing or virtually nothing in the way of chemicals; drugs; complex industrial or agricultural machinery, equipment, or components; scientific instruments; motor vehicles, locomotives, ships, or planes; petroleum products, refined metals, or alloys; synthetic materials; watches, radios, TV sets, refrigerators, washing machines, or most other consumer durables —and I could go on and on.[14] Even in sectors where pre-1949 China had many and/or relatively large factories engaged in producing such commodities as iron and steel, mining, textiles, clothing, processed foods, paper products, and various other light-industry goods, product lines and varieties were typically very limited and technology utilized in production very backward and sparse.

Since the early 1950's thousands of new classes of products and tens of thousands of new varieties have been produced in Communist China. Many of them have been developed with foreign aid—chiefly Soviet aid in the 1950's, and help from Western countries and Japan in more recent times—but the Chinese have also developed numerous products basically on their own, albeit often with considerable struggle and inefficiency and at relatively great cost. Each year hundreds of new products are developed and produced in Communist China, and at this point the Chinese are capable of producing almost anything found in more advanced countries, as can be seen by their current achievements in the nuclear field.

I do not mean to imply that Red China is nearly as advanced in terms of product development or know-how—or technology—as countries such as the United States, West Germany, Great Britain, or even the Soviet Union or Japan. China is probably still a few generations behind current U.S. performance in terms of know-how and overall capability, and probably ten to twenty years behind Japan and Russia in most product fields, with the likely exception of textiles, clothing, processed foods, and perhaps a few other types of goods. But the point is that the Chinese can produce practically anything they wish to, though in limited numbers and at great costs in many cases. I feel that Red China has a significant lead—perhaps five to ten years—over India in overall product development and know-how in spite of the considerable amount of foreign collaboration and assistance in India's industrial sector. China certainly produces a substantially wider range of products than India, particularly producer goods and other heavy-industry commodities, and is relatively self-sufficient in significantly more fields.

Before 1949 China's chemical (including drugs) industry was very insignificant. By 1957 more than 2,000 types of chemical products were being manufactured in Red China, and in 1960 this had increased to over 8,000.[15] In 1966 I was told by a manager of a Shanghai pharmaceutical firm that the range of chemicals and drugs of all types produced in Red China in the last five years had more than doubled, and may have almost tripled. If true—and it conceivably is—Red China currently produces roughly 16,000 to 24,000 chemical and drug products. In the pharmaceutical field she produces antibiotics, penicillin, and most of the sophisticated drugs manufactured in the West. In the chemical industry China is vigorously expanding its product lines in fertilizers, plastics, and synthetic products, in particular, in substantial part with foreign assistance.

The number, variety, and complexity of machines, equipment, instruments, components, agricultural implements, and transportation vehicles produced in Red China since 1949 have increased manifold. The same is true for petroleum, minerals, refined metals, alloys, the sizes, shapes, and quality of steel (including stainless steel), as well as most types of durable and nondurable consumer products. Red China is now relatively self-sufficient in such complex spheres as metallurgy, scientific instrumentation, radar machinery and instruments, and nuclear fields.[16] She produces TV sets, radios, refrigerators, and most other types of modern consumer goods in sizable quantities, with the notable exception of automobiles, which are produced in negligible numbers and with crude technology.

In order for Communist China to have made such impressive overall gains in product development, she has also had to achieve impressive technological progress.[17] Capital scarcity is probably now a bigger constraint with regard to future technological progress—and hence new product development as well—than technical know-how or motivation. Considerable technological progress has been made in mining, oil exploitation and refining, and in the chemical sector as a whole. In the metallurgical sector the introduction of fuel injection in blast furnaces at a number of major plants has resulted in reduced coke ratios. Greater use is being made of oxygen and magnesia-alumina bricks in open-hearth furnaces. The first locally made top-blown oxygen converter has been put into operation at a Peking steel mill. New electric furnaces and steel-production mills have been under negotiation with Japan and various West European companies. Substantial technological improvements have also been introduced in the production of industrial, agricultural, and transportation machinery, equipment, and components. Even in traditional sectors such as textiles, clothing, and food processing much more productive and effective technology is being used at many factories.

Unfortunately, I am not an engineer by training and could not therefore analyze in much depth the technology and production processes that I observed at Chinese industrial enterprises. However, from a layman's standpoint, I would say that Red China is still one or two generations behind average current U.S. levels of technology in most branches of industry. The gap may be even larger when one takes into account material handling, in-plant transportation and conveyer equipment, and packaging technology where applicable. Even the best Chinese plants producing machinery, steel, agricultural implements, and chemicals that I visited do not seem to be significantly better than even average U.S. factories in these industries.

China is also substantially behind—probably at least one and perhaps two or more decades—Russia and Japan in these fields in terms of technology. But some of the best Chinese consumer-goods plants—for example, textiles, clothing, and watches—are probably not too far behind the better ones in Russia, and possibly Japan.

A senior official at Japan's Ministry of International Trade and Industry, Genko Uchida, who is an engineer by formal training, visited a number of Chinese industrial enterprises in 1966.[18] He has been heading a major study dealing with technology in China. He has also studied and done first-hand research in England and undertaken a first-hand study of automation in U.S. industry. Uchida feels that industrial-labor productivity in Red China averages only about 20 percent of that in Japan in general and that superior Japanese technology is one of the most critical reasons for this gap. For industry as a whole he feels that Japan has a technological lead of ten to fifteen years.

He estimates that China is about fifteen years behind Japan in steel industry technology and that technological deficiencies prevent China from producing various types of high-grade steel. However, he also estimates that China may surpass Japan's steel output by 1973, thus becoming the number-three steel producer in the world—behind the United States and Russia.

As for technology in the chemical sector, he also estimates that Red

China is about fifteen years behind Japan. However, he presents some data on product development and technological improvements in China's chemical industry which indicate that substantial progress is likely to continue in the future.

As for China's machinery and equipment industries Uchida perceived a mixed picture, estimating some branches to be about fifteen years behind Japan in technology, and others roughly twenty years behind. However, he feels that China can catch up to Japan in machine-tool and heavy-electrical-machinery technology in a decade if China imports technical know-how—presumably by having foreign technicians set up new plants—and some key commodities. He feels that China has achieved considerable technological progress to date in the manufacture of various types of heavy electrical equipment, boilers, turbines, conventional grinding tools, various types of agricultural machinery, locomotives and, to a more limited degree, ships. On the other hand, he feels that China is further behind technologically in most types of giant lathes, boring, hobbing, roll grinding, and planing equipment.

With regard to China's motor vehicle industry he estimates that it is a good twenty years behind that of Japan and the West, including Russia, in terms of technology. The same is true for China's aircraft industry in relation to the West. As for technology in the electronics industry, he points out that China is just getting out of the laboratory in many areas where Japan and the West have achieved much experience. While China has made substantial progress in some sophisticated transistor fields and in analogue computers, she is far behind in digital computers and probably in most other advanced electronic spheres.

It is difficult to compare levels of technology in Red China's industrial sector with those in India. In branches such as steel, chemicals, drugs, batteries, and various types of machinery, equipment, electronics, and motor-transportation vehicles where India has benefited by a considerable amount of foreign collaboration and technical assistance—chiefly from the U.S., Russia, Western Europe, and Canada—the best Indian plants in terms of technology are probably better than the best Chinese factories in the same sectors in many cases. The better or best essentially indigenous Indian firms in these sectors are quite possibly not as good as comparable superior Chinese enterprises in terms of technology, while the average basically indigenous Indian plant is probably not as good as the average Chinese factory.

In other fields, Red China probably has a fairly significant technological lead over India in the general sectors of basic-clothing fabrics (excluding varieties not produced in either or both countries), food processing, agricultural machinery and implements, cameras, radios, and TV sets (India produces no TV sets), as well as the manufacture of many types of components and parts for producer and consumer goods. India probably has a general technological lead in the production of various types of consumer durables, such as fans, and certain other types of electrical and home appliances.

In general, Red China appears to be substantially more self-sufficient in technology and product development and much less dependent on foreign assistance or imports than India. These are critical factors to be considered in assessing future technological and product-development prospects in the two countries, and in predicting their industrial and economic growth potential.

Production of Twenty Major Commodities in Red China, India, Russia, Japan, and the United States, Mid-1960's

Table 7–13 presents estimated production figures for China of twenty major commodity groups for China, India, the U.S.S.R., Japan, and the United States for 1964 or 1965. Before proceeding, it should be noted that for some commodity groups the true production gap between relatively more and less advanced industrial countries is likely to be somewhat understated because the more advanced nations typically produce a wider variety of higher-quality, more complex, and more effective products. In particular, this is probably true for such items as steel, chemical fertilizers, refined-petroleum products, tractors, trucks, and perhaps paper. China probably has an edge over India for a majority of the commodity groups in the table in terms of product mix and quality. But both China and India no doubt lag significantly behind the other three countries, in varying degrees, with the possible exception of cotton-cloth production in the Soviet Union. China may also have a qualitative edge over India in cotton cloth.

From Table 7–13 Red China clearly leads India in the production of sixteen of the twenty commodities, and in most cases China's lead is big in both absolute and per capita terms. If the upper-limit estimates for China's output of cement, trucks, and cotton cloth are taken, China leads India in the production of nineteen commodities. India has a definite lead only in sugar production.

China is clearly ahead of Japan only in the production of coal, crude oil, and cotton cloth. China leads Japan in tractors if the maximum output estimate for China is used, while China's sugar output is about the same as Japan's, and her pig-iron production is not far behind that of Japan. Japan's relatively low performance in these sectors is a reflection of low levels of factor endowment with regard to minerals and agricultural land.

TABLE 7–13

PRODUCTION OF TWENTY COMMODITIES IN COMMUNIST CHINA, INDIA, JAPAN, THE SOVIET UNION, AND THE U.S. IN THE MID–1960'S

Commodity[a]	*China* (1965)	*India* (1964 or 1965 unless otherwise noted)	*Japan* (1964 or 1965)	*Soviet Union* (1965)	*United States* (1965)
Cement (million tons)	9.0–11.5	9.6	33.0	72.4	65.4
Coal " "	210.0–300.0	64.4	51.0	378.0	475.0
Coke " "	16.0	4.8 (1961)	17.9	64.0 (1962)	66.5
Pig iron " "	19.0	6.6 (1963)	23.8	62.4	88.2
Crude steel, ingots (million tons)	10.0–15.0	6.1	39.8	91.0	121.0
Rolled (finished) steel (million tons)	12.0	4.4	31.9	57.4	99.3
Crude oil, petroleum (million tons)	8.0–10.0	1.65	.66	243.0	385.0
Refined petroleum products (million tons)	9.0	8.4	58.4	not available	407.0 (1964)
Aluminum ingots (million tons)	.10	.054	.266	.91	2.75
Refined copper metal (million tons)	.10	.006	.392 (copper wire)	.60	1.71
Refined zinc metal " "	.09	negligible	.007 (zinc plates and sheets)	.42 (zinc concentrates)	1.01 (zinc concentrates)
Refined lead metal " "	.10	not available	.68 (lead products)	.36 (lead products)	.418 (lead concentrates)
Chemical-fertilizer " "					
(a) Total output (in terms of end products)	4.5–6.8	1.7–1.98	14.64	31.3	50.0
(b) In terms of nutrient	.8–1.0	.36–.42	3.0	7.4	11.0

Paper (million tons)	1.5–2.85	.50	7.34	3.4	18.0
Timber (million cu. meters)	36.0	1.7 (1960–61)	53.3	258.0	190.0
Agricultural tractors (thousands of units)	15.0–20.0	5.6 (expected 1965–66)	20.9	355.0	not available
Trucks (thousands of units)	25.0–30.0	29.5 (includes buses 1963/64 fiscal yr.)	1,160.0	418.0	1,777 units sold (includes buses)
Sugar (million tons)	1.5–1.9	2.6 (1963) 3.6 (expected in 1965/66 fiscal yr.)	1.7	11.1	8.0
Cotton cloth (billion sq. meters)	3.9–7.8	4.43 [b] (expected, in linear meters, 1965/66 fiscal year)	2.97	5.5	8.3 [c]
Electric power (billion K.W.H.)	40.0–60.0	29.3	179.6	507.0	1,221.0

[a] Some output figures for some countries are in metric tons and in a few cases in short tons. However, since the maximum margin of error is only about 10 percent, I use conventional U.S. tons (2,000 pounds) as the unit of measure for all commodities stated in tons.

[b] This figure is for the industrial cotton-textile sector only. The household industry or handicrafts sector produced roughly 2,900 million linear meters of cotton cloth in the 1963/64 fiscal year, much of it being consumed by the producers and their families. It is likely that total cotton-cloth ouput (including this household sector) in India in 1965 was over 7 million meters.

[c] In basic sources, U.S. cotton-cloth output is given in linear yards, which I have converted to linear meters. Cotton-textile output in the United States typically varies from a minimum width of 12 inches to a maximum of more than 60 inches, with the average being 24 to 48 inches at most factories.

SOURCES:

Communist Chinese estimates are from the sources cited in Table 7–12 of this chapter.

Indian figures have been derived from the sources cited in Table 7–3 of this chapter.

Japanese and U.S. figures have been obtained from the sources on these countries cited in Table 7–14 which follows in this chapter.

Soviet output statistics are from *Narodnoe Choziaistvo SSSR, and Promishlenost SSSR*, 1965 yearbooks, both cited in Table 7–14 in this chapter; and *New Directions in the Soviet Economy* (Washington: U.S. Government Printing Office, 1966), Appendixes I and II, pp. 1029–31.

For pig iron it is also due, in part, to the advanced technical processes used in the manufacture of Japanese steel. However, Japan has a big lead over China in the production of the other commodities in absolute terms, and even more so in per capita terms.

If we take the maximum cotton-cloth estimate for China, China leads the Soviet Union in the production of this commodity, and is not far behind the United States. But for all of the other commodities China is very far behind the United States in absolute terms, and even further behind in per capita terms. China is also far behind the Soviet Union in the production of nearly all of the twenty commodity groups on the table. In fact, the gap between Russia and China is greater than that between the United States and China for cement, coal, timber, sugar, and possibly even coke if we had a more recent Soviet output figure for this commodity.

Suggestive Comparisons of Some Key Aspects of Aggregate Performance for China, India, Russia, Japan, and the United States, 1963–66

Table 7–14 indicates that in 1966 Communist China had a total GNP at least 50 percent greater than that of India, and possibly nearly 100 percent greater or double that of India. I would estimate that China's GNP was at least 80 percent greater than India's in 1966. However, China's GNP was only about 10 to 15 percent as large as that of the United States, about 25 to 40 percent as large as the Soviet Union, and roughly 60 to 75 percent as big as Japan's. China will probably surpass Japan's level of GNP in the early 1970's, barring severe ideological extremism.

The IPP conversion rates in Table 7–14 probably give a more realistic picture of GNP and per capita income in China and India than the official exchange (OE) rates. However, it is likely that the OE rates give a more accurate picture of the value of industrial production in India and China. The reason for this is that the prices of numerous producer goods —and probably various consumer goods as well—tend to be unrealistically high in terms of price levels in advanced countries. It is possible that even the official exchange rates somewhat overstate the value of industrial production in China and India. On the other hand, it is likely that the official exchange rate significantly undervalues agricultural commodities in these countries. A major portion of China's and India's national product—particularly agricultural output—never enters marketing channels, and this is another reason for evaluating GNP and per capita income at the higher IPP conversion rate. As for Japan and Russia the IPP rate probably also gives a more realistic picture of their GNP and per capita income than the OE rate. The same is true for Japan's industrial output. While there are some experts who may feel that the IPP rate used in Table 7–14 for the Soviet Union somewhat overvalues that country's industrial output, probably only few, if any, would want to apply a rate as low as the official exchange rate.

Table 7–15, in the following section, to which we shall turn shortly, indicates the approximate year when China will achieve existing levels of GNP per capita income, and total and per capita industrial output in Japan, Russia, and the United States at various rates of growth. Table 7–16 indicates levels of Chinese performance as of the year 2000, assuming various rates of growth.

Table 7–14 indicates that during the 1963–66 period China achieved the highest average annual GNP growth rate of all five countries, with the exception of Japan, which may have achieved a rate as high as double that of China. China's GNP growth rate during this period was substantially higher than that of India.

As for per capita GNP, India led China slightly in 1966 only if we take the lower-limit estimate for China and the maximum figure for India. In my opinion, Red China's per capita income was about $120 to $125 in 1966, while India's was about $100 (both in terms of internal purchasing power, or IPP, conversion rates). However, China's 1966 per capita income was probably only around 10 percent of Japan's, not more than 9 percent of the Soviet Union's, and less than 4 percent of that in the United States.

During the 1963–66 period China achieved a substantially greater average annual per capita GNP growth rate than India, regardless of which figures we take for either country. In my opinion China achieved a rate closer to 6 percent than to 3.3 percent, the low point of the estimate range. It is likely that China's per capita growth rate was surpassed only by Japan during this period.

As for value of industrial output, in my opinion, China's was about double that of India at the end of 1965 (at the OE rate; and even more if the IPP rate is used). Japan's industrial output was probably about two-thirds greater than that of China in 1965, but China should surpass Japan's 1965 level by the mid-1970's at the latest, assuming relative ideological moderation. However, it will take China much longer to surpass the present value of industrial production in the United States, or even the Soviet Union. The former leads China by more than ten to one by any calculation, while the latter probably leads China by at least five to one.

China achieved a much greater average annual rate of industrial growth than India during 1963–66 and, in fact, substantially greater than the Soviet Union and the United States as well. Only Japan achieved a higher rate of industrial growth, but not by much.

TABLE 7–14

SUGGESTIVE COMPARISONS OF KEY ASPECTS OF ECONOMIC AND INDUSTRIAL PERFORMANCE FOR COMMUNIST CHINA, INDIA, SOVIET UNION, JAPAN, AND U.S., 1963–66 PERIOD (Estimates)[a]

	COMMUNIST CHINA	INDIA (April–March fiscal years in most cases)	U.S.S.R.	JAPAN	U.S.
GROSS NATIONAL PRODUCT					
1966—In current U.S. dollars (billion) converted at 1965 OE rates	\$52–\$73	\$34–\$38	\$250	\$94.5	\$739.5
1964—In current U.S. dollars based on IPP conversion rates arrived at by experts (billion)	\$65–\$89	\$45–\$49	\$293	\$101	\$631.7
1966—Projection of 1964 GNP in current U.S. dollars (billion) based on experts' IPP conversions	\$75–\$100	\$47–\$51	\$325	\$130	\$739.5
AVERAGE ANNUAL RATE OF GROWTH IN REAL GNP, 1963–66 (%)	6.0–8.3%	2.4–2.8%	5.2%	11.0%	5.5%
PER CAPITA GNP					
1966—In current U.S. dollars converted at 1965 OE rates	\$70–\$100	\$68–\$75	\$1,060	\$875	\$3,700
1964—In current U.S. dollars based on IPP rates	\$88–\$117	\$88–\$107	\$1,289	\$1,040	\$3,272
1966—Projection of 1964 per capita GNP based on experts' conversions	\$100–\$137	\$90–\$104	\$1,400	\$1,220	\$3,700
AVERAGE ANNUAL RATE OF GROWTH IN REAL PER CAPITA GNP, 1963–66	3.3%–6.0%	0–1.0%	3.4%	10.0%	3.9%
Converted at official exchange rates (billion) prevailing in 1965 to current U.S. dollars	\$13–\$18[c]	\$7–\$8	\$80	\$21	\$225

Converted to current U.S. dollars (billion) by using estimated IPP rates	\$19–\$25[c]	\$8.05–\$10	\$105	\$29	\$225
TOTAL VALUE OF INDUSTRIAL OUTPUT (total value added in manufacturing, mining, utilities), 1965					
Average annual rate of real industrial growth, 1963–66 (includes manufacturing, mining, and public utilities)	10.5–12.0%	6.0–7.0%	7.5%	12.5%	6.5%
INDUSTRIAL EMPLOYMENT					
Total industrial employment, year-end 1965,[b] all workers, employees, owner managers, manufacturing, mining, utilities (million)	13.7–14	8.9–9.5 (excludes household industry)	27	12.6	19.6
Industrial employment as a percentage of total population, year-end 1965	1.8–2.0%	1.8–2.0%	11.2%	12.0%	10%
Industrial employment as percentage of total employment in the whole country, year-end, 1965	4.5%	4.2–4.5%	24%	27%	27.8%
Average annual rate of increase in industrial employment, 1963–65	5.1–5.6%	2.3–2.4%	2.0%	2.0%	2.3%
Average annual rate of increase in industrial-labor productivity (in terms of output per man year), 1963–65	4.3–5.7%	1.9–2.4%	3.0%	8.5%	3.4%
Value-added contribution of overall industrial sector to gross domestic product, 1965 (manufacturing, mining, utilities estimated at factor cost)	22.0–28.0%	19.0–22.0%	34.0%	33.5%	34.5%
Value of industrial output per industrial employee, 1965					
At OE rates in current U.S. dollars	\$950–\$1,300	\$750–\$900	\$3,000	\$1,670	\$11,500
At IPP rates in current U.S. dollars	\$1,350–\$1,800	\$925–\$1,100	\$3,850	\$2,300	\$11,500

TABLE 7–14 (*continued*)

	COMMUNIST CHINA	INDIA (April–March fiscal years in most cases)	U.S.S.R	JAPAN	U.S.
Value of industrial output per employee in the entire economy (that is, in all sectors including agriculture), 1965					
At OE rates in current U.S. dollars	\$38–\$65	\$32–\$41	\$720	\$450	\$3,200
At IPP rates in current U.S. dollars	\$54–\$90	\$39–\$50	\$850	\$520	\$3,200
Industrial output per capita (total population), 1965					
At OE rates in current U.S. dollars	\$18–\$25	\$15–\$17	\$345	\$192	\$1,150
At IPP rates in current U.S. dollars	\$26–\$35	\$18–\$21	\$445	\$240	\$1,150

[a] Estimates for the 1963–65 period take the end of 1962 as the point of departure and include all of 1965. Year-end estimates are used for 1966. All growth rates have been compounded.

As noted earlier, the estimates for China are based on a careful study of a variety of studies and sources. I have used ranges for all Chinese estimates, eliminating the estimates from secondary sources which seem clearly to be unrealistically low or high. The estimates for India are also in ranges since there are some significant differences in the figures, concepts used in measurement, and methods of reporting in the various sources from which I have derived my Indian data. The Soviet figures are more reliable but even these should be taken with some reserve. This is also true for the conversion of foreign currencies into current U.S. dollars at internal purchasing power rates. Some of the 1965 and 1966 statistics are referred to as "preliminary" or "provisional" in the sources from which I have obtained them.

[b] As rated in earlier tables, the Indian industrial employment figure excludes "household" industry which probably amounted to 11 to 13.5 million people. I have no idea what proportion of household-industry employment corresponds to industrial employment in the other countries. It is likely that industrial-output-per-employee figures for India are significantly too high. It is also possible that growth of industrial-labor productivity in India is somewhat distorted by ignoring household-industry employment. The industrial-output figures for India do apparently include handicrafts and other products from the household-industry sector.

It should also be noted that there is a considerable amount of seasonal and contract labor in Indian industry which is not reported as part of industrial employment. At many Indian firms I have surveyed, from 25 percent to 50 percent of their factory employment consisted of seasonal or contract labor. There is also a fair amount of seasonal and contract labor in Japanese and, probably to a lesser extent, in Chinese industry which is not included in their employment statistics. However, in both these countries it is substantially less than in India. But in all cases it leads to overstatements in industrial-labor-productivity computations.

[c] The official exchange rate dollar estimate is probably a more accurate measure of China's industrial output. The internal purchasing power rate may overrate its value in U.S. dollars quite significantly. This is probably not true for other sectors of China's economy however.

SOURCES:

Estimates for Communist China and India are based on the sources cited in Tables 7–1, 7–2, 7–3, and 7–12 above.

Conversions of foreign currencies to current U.S. dollars in terms of internal purchasing power and at official exchange rates for Japan, the U.S.S.R., and India are based on the following sources: S. Cohn, "Soviet Growth Retardation: Trends in Resource Availability and Efficiency," *New Directions in the Soviet Economy*, Part II–A (Washington: U.S. Government Printing Office, 1966), pp. 108–16, Tables 7, 8, 15, 19; "National Income Accounts," *Annual Economic Indicators for the USSR* (Washington: U.S. Government Printing Office, 1964), pp. 96–98, Tables VIII–5, VIII–6, VIII–7. These two sources list the original sources upon which many of their own statistics are based: *Growth Rates and Trend Data by Region and Country* (Washington: Agency for Economic Development, Statistics and Reports Division, March 31, 1967); *World Bank Atlas of Per Capita Product and Population* (International Bank for Reconstruction and Development, 1966).

It should be noted that the Indian currency was devalued from 4.76 to 7.50 rupees to the U.S. dollar in mid–1966. However, I used the 4.76 rate in this table.

Soviet figures are based on Cohn, "National Income Accounts"; J. Noren, "Soviet Industry Trends in Output, Inputs, and Productivity," *New Directions in the Soviet Economy*, pp. 271–325, especially Tables 1–4, 7, 9; M. Feshback, "Manpower in the U.S.S.R.," *New Directions in the Soviet Economy*, pp. 703–85, especially appendix tables; "Trends in Soviet Gross National Product," *Current Economic Indicators for the USSR* (Washington: U.S. Government Printing Office, 1965), pp. 11–21; *Narodnoe Choziaistvo SSSR* (Statistical Yearbooks on the National Economy of the USSR), published in Moscow in Russian; *Promishlenost SSSR* (Industry, USSR), Statistical abstract for 1964 and 1965, published in Moscow in Russian. Reports on 1966 Soviet performance have appeared in *Pravda*, January 26, 28, 29 and February 15, 1967; *Izvestia*, January 27, 28 and March 2, 1967; *Los Angeles Times*, January 29, 1967, Section I, p. 2.

Japanese figures are based on *Japan Statistical Yearbook*, 1964 and 1965 (Tokyo: Bureau of Statistics, Office of the Prime Minister, 1965 and 1966); *Japanese Economic Statistics*, 1965 (Tokyo: Economic Planning Agency, 1966); *Yomiuri Yearbook 1966*, in Japanese (Tokyo: published by Yomiuri Newspaper Company, 1967); *Mainichi Yearbook* 1967, in Japanese (Tokyo: published by Mainichi Newspaper Co., 1967); *Monthly Statistics of Japan*, various 1966–67 issues (Tokyo: Office of the Prime Minister, Bureau of Statistics); *Asia Scene*, Tokyo, February 1967.

U.S. statistics are derived from *Statistical Abstract of the U.S.*, 1964, 1965, 1966 (Washington: Dept. of Commerce, Office of Business Economics); *President's Economic Report, January 1967* (Washington: 1967); *Manpower Report of the President* (Washington: March 1966), 87th Edition (Washington: 1967); *Annual and Supplemental Reports*, 1965 and 1966 (Washington: Bureau of Labor Statistics, Department of Labor).

The proportion of value added to gross domestic product by the overall industrial sector in 1965 was probably significantly greater in China than in India. I would estimate the proportion in China in the range of 25 to 27 percent, and that for India at 20 to 21 percent. However, the proportions for Japan, Russia, and the United States were in the range of 33 to 35 percent, or significantly higher than in China.

Industrial output per industrial employee—in value terms at the OE rate—was probably significantly higher in China than in India in 1965. I would estimate that it was at least $1,150 or $1,200 in China, and around $850 in India. This suggests higher levels of absolute labor productivity and general industrial efficiency in China, but significant differences in price structures, employment classifications, product mixes, and other factors make this contention at most only a conjectural conclusion or a tentative hypothesis warranting further verification. However, I do feel that labor productivity and efficiency are probably generally higher in absolute terms in China's overall industrial sector than in India's. Industrial output per industrial employee was probably about double in Japan as compared with China, roughly three times greater in Russia, and nearly ten times greater in the United States.

In Table 7–14 I have also estimated value of industrial output per employee in all sectors of the economy—that is, for the entire working population. The estimates for China and, to a lesser degree, for India, are very precarious since there are millions of youths, housewives, and other dependents who work part time or only a small portion of the year in the agricultural sector. The question of how many of them are included in official national employment statistics or estimates, or in what way they are accounted for, is in substantial part a matter of conjecture. That is why the estimate range for China in this case is even longer than usual. On the bases of available data, I would estimate that the value of industrial output per employee in the economy at large was at least 25 percent greater in China than India in 1965. Japan probably led China in this regard by roughly ten to one, Russia by perhaps fifteen to one or more, and the United States by possibly as much as sixty to one.

Industrial output per capita, in terms of total population, was probably at least 50 percent greater in China than India in 1965. However, Japan probably led China by roughly seven or eight to one, Russia by perhaps as much as fifteen to one, and the United States by at least thirty-three to one.

Industrial employment was approximately 40 to 50 percent greater in China than India, and perhaps 10 to 15 percent greater than in Japan in 1965. However, as already noted, Japan's industrial output was at least 50 percent greater than that of China. Industrial employment in 1965 was about 40 percent greater in the United States than China, and nearly 100 percent greater in the Soviet Union. Of the five countries, China may have had the biggest annual average increase in industrial employment during the 1963–65 period, but this may well not continue in the future.

As for industrial employment as a proportion of total employment in the country as a whole, there was not a great difference between China and India as of the end of 1965—it is possible that the proportion was about 10 percent higher in China. However, the proportions for the three advanced industrial nations ranged from 24 to nearly 28 percent, while China's proportion was only 4 to 5 percent.

As for industrial employment as a percentage of total population, it was probably approximately the same in China and India in 1965. However, Japan, Russia, and the United States all had at least a five-to-one edge over both China and India in this sphere.

China achieved the highest annual average rate of increase in industrial-labor productivity of all five countries during 1963–65, with the exception of Japan, which may have achieved a rate almost double that of China. China's rate of 4.3 to 5.7 percent (I would estimate at least 5 percent) was probably at least double that of India.

From Table 7–14 it seems evident that Communist China has done substantially better than India in general economic and industrial performance during the 1963–66 period. As of the mid-1960's it was likely that China had a big lead over India in absolute levels of economic and industrial performance, and a fairly significant lead in per capita terms. An analysis of the environmental constraints bearing significantly on managerial effectiveness, productive efficiency, and general economic progress, which have been the focal points of this book, hopefully will shed much light as to why China is ahead of India. In the following section a suggestive quantitative rating of the critical environmental factors under study is undertaken for Red China and India, as well as for the Soviet Union, Japan, and the United States.

While Communist China is ahead of India in economic development and industrial progress, she is still far behind Russia and the United States in absolute terms, and very far behind Japan, as well as these other two countries, in per capita performance. The gap between China and these three countries in per capita terms in particular is tremendously greater than that between China and India. However, I feel that China has a better chance than India of narrowing the gap between her and the advanced countries in the long run, or at least in widening the gap which presently exists between her and India. For China to make substantial gains, however, managerial, technical, and economic rationality will have to prevail over ideological extremism.

China and the Future

Table 7–15 indicates the approximate years in which China would achieve the 1966–67 levels of total GNP and industrial output in Japan, the Soviet Union, and the United States, assuming average annual growth rates of 5, 7.5, and 10 percent. In the table we have assumed a GNP for China of $100 billion as of 1967 and an industrial-output figure of $18 billion. These figures may be somewhat on the high side. If lower figures were used, a few or several years would have to be added to the projected years in the table. But even at a GNP figure of $80 to $90 billion and an industrial output of $15 billion not more than about three to five years would have to be added.

Table 7–15 indicates that even at an annual average GNP growth rate of 5 percent China would achieve Japan's present level of GNP in the

TABLE 7–15

Approximate Year in which China would Achieve 1967 Levels of GNP and Industrial Output in Japan, the Soviet Union, and the United States at Various Rates of Growth

Part I: GNP
(Assuming China's GNP as of 1967 is equal to $100 billion)

At Annual Average GNP Growth Rate of:	*Approximate Year When China Would Achieve 1967 Levels in:* Japan	U.S.S.R.	U.S.A.
5%	1972	1990	2007
7.5%	1970	1982	1994
10%	1969	1978	1987

Part II: Industrial Output in Terms of Value
(Assuming China's output as of 1967 is equal to $18 billion)

At Annual Average Industrial Growth Rate of:	*Approximate Year in Which China Would Achieve 1967 Levels in:* Japan	U.S.S.R. (Assuming current level of $10 billion)	U.S.S.R. (Assuming current level of $80 billion)	U.S.A.
5%	1976	2002	1996	2017
7.5%	1973	1991	1987	2002
10%	1971	1986	1982	1993

early 1970's. But at this rate she would not reach the current Soviet level until 1990, and the U.S. level would be reached only in 2007. At a 7.5 percent rate the current Soviet GNP would be reached by China in the early 1980's, and that of the United States by the mid-1990's. At a 10 percent rate China would reach the current Soviet level in about a decade, and that of the United States in two decades.

As for industrial output, Table 7–15 indicates that China will achieve the present level in Japan by the mid-1970's, or in less than a decade, even at an annual rate of industrial growth of 5 percent. However, at this rate she will not achieve the present level of Soviet output until the 1996–2002 period (depending on what conversion rate is used for Russia) and that of the United States until the year 2017. At a 7.5 percent rate China will achieve the Soviet's current level of performance in the late 1980's or early 1990's and that of the United States at the beginning of the twenty-first century. If China's industrial production grows at an average annual rate of 10 percent, she will not achieve the present Soviet level until the early or mid-1980's and that of the United States until 1993.

It should be pointed out that these projections do not necessarily mean that China will narrow the GNP or industrial-output gaps between herself and the advanced countries. Moreover, it is likely that China will never really catch up with, or surpass, the absolute levels of performance in Russia and the United States in particular; and in per capita terms she is even less likely to ever catch up with Japan, as well as Russia and the United States—assuming, of course, that these countries (and the world at large) survive in the long run, and that they maintain viable and reasonably dynamic economies. This will become evident when we examine Table 7–16 and present some projections for the United States.

It seems likely that China's GNP would have to grow at an average annual rate of at least 10 percent over the next several decades if China is to have any chance of substantially narrowing the gap between herself and Japan. For China to make possibly big dents in the GNP gap between herself and Russia and the United States a growth rate of at least around 7.5 percent would seem to be required—a 5-percent rate is unlikely to suffice.

As for industrial output, it would appear that China would have to achieve an annual average growth rate of more than 10 percent over the next several decades to close substantially the gap between herself and Japan. A rate of close to 10 percent, and probably more than 7 percent, would seem to be called for if China is to make sizable inroads into the output lead now commanded by the Soviets and the United States.

What seem to be Communist China's chances of significantly narrowing these gaps during the remainder of this century? Assuming that relative ideological moderation prevails, China's leaders may well be inclined to accept a fairly modest, but still quite substantial, annual GNP growth rate of about 4 to 6 percent, and an annual industrial growth rate of 6 to 8 percent in the short run—that is, during the next four or five years. An annual growth rate of about 2 percent or 3 percent in agricultural output would probably be acceptable to a relatively rational leadership during this period.[19] Growth rates around these levels are likely to be acceptable to a rational leadership since they would provide for the necessary groundwork for significantly higher rates of sustained growth in the future.

Industry has now reached a stage of development in Red China where extremely high degrees of vertical integration of production in thousands of plants have become obsolete, and grossly inefficient. Increasing plant specialization and interchange of products involving greater standardization and precision, as well as more sophisticated and high-quality output, now appear to be required for marked increases in productivity and general industrial efficiency. Moreover, the Chinese have relatively little experience in some of the new and complex industries—such as chemicals, electronics, sophisticated industrial and agricultural machinery and equipment, and motor vehicles—which they are expanding rapidly, and which are integral to future industrial progress and agricultural productivity. If they move too fast in these fields, considerable waste and inefficiency sharply detrimental to future growth are likely to occur. It will also take time to get modern agricultural supplies and technology in large quantities to the thousands of communes and tens of thousands of farm-work brigades throughout the nation and to get the peasants to effectively utilize them on an extensive scale.

To effectively promote such a development program, it would probably be necessary to permit a fair amount of industrial slack over the next several years and to maintain adequate inventories. If this is not done, industrial-enterprise managers are likely to resort to inventory hoarding, subsidiary plant-production operations, skimping on quality and/or disregard for costs, as well as various other disfunctional practices, in an attempt to assure fulfillment of top-priority aggregate enterprise targets—typically total output, and perhaps sales, profits, and/or labor productivity.

Hence, an annual average rate of industrial growth of roughly 7 percent, a GNP rate of about 5 percent, and a rate of around 3 percent for agricultural output would seem to be rational and feasible during the next five years or so. At these growth rates China could still make progress in her ambitious military and defense programs. How well she does in per capita terms, or in terms of improvements in living standards, depends on the effectiveness of her birth-control program. If annual population growth can be contained at a level not significantly higher than 2 percent, modest increases in living standards can be achieved even at these growth rates.

If Red China does pursue and effectively implement a development strategy resembling the one outlined above, she is likely to be in a position to achieve significantly higher and sustained growth rates by the early 1970's. A sustained annual average GNP growth rate of 7 or 8 percent over a period of several decades would appear to be definitely in the realm of possibility, but a sustained rate as high as 10 percent would not seem to be too likely in a country such as China. However, in industrial growth a sustained average annual rate of around 10 percent would seem to be quite conceivable.

At a sustained average annual GNP growth rate of 7.5 percent, and a rate of 10 percent for industrial growth, China would become a leading world economic, industrial, and military power before the end of this century. Substantial gains would also be made in per capita terms and in living standards. These gains would be that much larger if China can get population growth down to an average annual rate of less than 2 percent, say 1.5 percent. The 2 percent rate seems to be a definite possibility in the foreseeable future, while a 1.5 percent rate seems conceivable in not less than a generation. I would be very surprised if the regime does achieve its stated goal of 1 percent annual population growth by the year 2000.

Table 7–16 projects where China will be in terms of total and per capita GNP and industrial output as of the year 2000 at various rates of growth. We see from this table that China would have a GNP approaching $500 billion at an average annual growth rate of 5 percent, $1,100 billion at a rate of 7.5 percent, and $2,325 billion at a 10 percent rate. However, even at a rate of 3 percent the United States would have a GNP of around $2,000 billion in the year 2000, or larger than that of China's at the 5 percent and 7.5 percent Chinese growth rates. At a 4 percent rate, GNP in the United States would be close to $2,800 billion, at 7.5 percent it would be $7,600 billion, and at 10 percent a fantastic $15,800 billion.

If China succeeds in keeping the average annual rate of population increase down to 2 percent, her population would be 1.6 billion in the year 2000; at a rate of 1.5 percent it would still be 1.23 billion. At a 2 percent population-growth rate and a GNP rate of 5 percent, China's per capita GNP in 2000 would be only $310, and at a 1.5 percent population-growth rate it would be $405. At the 2 percent population-increase rate and a GNP growth rate of 10 percent her per capita income would be about $1,450; and at a 1.5 percent population rate $1,800. Hence, even at the highest GNP growth rate and lowest population-increase rate in the table, China's per capita income in the year 2000 would still be less than that of the United States in 1966. At a 10 percent GNP rate and 2 percent population-increase rate, China's per capita GNP in 2000 would be only about what it was in the Soviet Union in 1966, and not much larger than that of Japan in 1966. (See Table 7–14.)

TABLE 7–16

PROJECTIONS OF CHINA'S ECONOMIC AND INDUSTRIAL PERFORMANCE AS OF THE YEAR 2000 AT VARIOUS RATES OF GROWTH

Total GNP (in current U.S. dollars), *assuming $100 billion as of 1967*		
At average annual growth rate of 5%	$500 billion	
At rate of 7.5%	$1,100 billion	
At rate of 10%	$2,325 billion	
Total Population in year 2000		
At average annual rate of increase of 1.5%	$1,230 million	
At 2% rate of increase	$1,600 million	
Per Capita GNP (in current U.S. dollars)	*At Population of 1,600 Million*	*At Population of 1,230 Million*
At 5% GNP growth rate	$310	$405
At 7.5% GNP growth rate	$700	$900
At 10% GNP growth rate	$1,450	$1,800
Total Industrial Output (in current U.S. dollars) *assuming $18 billion as of 1967*		
At average annual growth rate of 5%	$92 billion	
At rate of 7.5%	$196 billion	
At rate of 10%	$418 billion	
Per Capita Industrial Output (in current U.S. dollars)	*Assuming a Population of 1,600 Million*	*Assuming a Population of 1,230 Million*
At annual average industrial growth rate of 5%	$58	$75
At rate of 7.5%	$123	$160
At rate of 10%	$260	$340

The United States would have a population of around 325 million in 2000 at an annual average rate of population increase of 1.5 percent, which is roughly the present rate. At this population and a GNP growth rate of only 3 percent her per capita income would be over $6,100 at the turn of the century. At a GNP growth rate of 5 percent it would be $11,000, and at 10 percent an unbelievable $50,000.

As for China's industrial production in 2000, at an annual average growth rate of 5 percent it would be $92 billion, at 7.5 percent $196 billion, and at 10 percent $418 billion. At the 5 percent rate China's industrial output in 2000 would be several times greater than that of Japan today, not far from the present Soviet level, but still less than half of the present U.S. level. At the 7.5 percent rate it would be nearly double Russia's 1966 level, but still less than present industrial production in the

United States. Only at the 10 percent rate in the table would China surpass U.S. industrial output in 1966. But even at an annual average growth rate of 5 percent, U.S. industrial output in the year 2000 would be $1,930 million, or nearly four times greater than China's—assuming a 10 percent rate for China.

Assuming an average annual population growth for China of 2 percent, and an industrial output rate of 7.5 percent, per capita industrial output in 2000 would be only $123; at a 1.5 percent population growth rate it would be $160. Even a per capita output of $160 for China would be about one-third less than Japan's 1966 level, several times less than that of Russia, and only about 12 percent of that of the United States. If China achieves an industrial output growth rate of 10 percent, at a population of 1.6 billion in the year 2000 her per capita output would be $260; at a population of 1.23 billion it would be $340. But, even at $340, China's per capita output in 2000 would still be substantially less than that of Russia in 1966, about 50 percent greater than the 1966 level in Japan, and still less than one-third of the present U.S. level.

Suggestive Quantitative Ratings of Environmental Constraints for China, India, U.S.S.R., Japan, and the United States

Table 7–17 is essentially a matrix which contains suggestive quantitative ratings of the critical environmental factors under study in this book in terms of their impact on managerial effectiveness, productive efficiency, and general industrial progress in Communist China, India, U.S.S.R., Japan, and the United States. Before we proceed with the rating, some words of caution are in order about the limitations and deficiencies of such a quantitative analysis. Additional comments to this effect can be found in a book I coauthored with Professor Richard Farmer.[20]

I feel that an attempt to quantify the environmental constraints in spite of many limitations, including serious data deficiencies and knowledge gaps, is justified on the grounds that it contributes to a better and more precise understanding, explanation, evaluation, and prediction of China's critical strengths, weaknesses, and potential in the industrial sphere in relation to other countries—in this case the countries mentioned above.

I am convinced that the effort is worthwhile in spite of the sizable margins of error in quantification—in terms of reality—that will inevitably result. I chose India as one of the other countries to be used in the analysis for reasons already discussed in some detail in the preface and introductory chapter. The Soviet Union was selected since it is the leading Communist industrial, economic, and military power and also because I have had the opportunity to do firsthand research there, besides having done a considerable amount of work on that country over a period of several years.

Japan was selected, even though I have been there only very briefly in a research capacity, because it is by far the most advanced industrial nation in Asia, a close neighbor of China, and has experienced a very impressive rate of industrial growth. The fact that I have had an exceptionally able Japanese research assistant in the person of Akira Arakawa, who has been on leave as a Fulbright scholar from his important executive position in Japan's second largest company, Nippon Telegraph and Telephone Corporation, was an important factor in selecting Japan. I have also had the opportunity to talk at length about management and industry with many Japanese industrial managers and professors who have visited the United States. And, of course, I have read fairly extensively about the country. Hence, although I have not discussed Japan very much in this study, there is nevertheless a reasonably sound empirical and objective basis in my ratings for Japan. The reasons for selecting the United States as one of the countries are quite obvious and need no explanation.

In my earlier book, referred to above, we quantitatively rated the environments of all of the countries to be rated here—plus six others—with the exception of Communist China. However, the rating system used at that time was different in several respects from the one to be used here. For the earlier ratings we made limited and basically experimental use of the "Delphi Technique" developed previously by Olaf Helmer and others at the Rand Corporation.[21]

This technique is a method for obtaining a consensus—usually among experts—about a matter or problem not subject to precise quantification. It was developed to handle problems of the sort presented here (as well as others), where interactions of variables, difficult aggregations, difficulties of quantification, and/or uncertainty in predictions make it impossible to apply more common—or scientific—methodologies. The Delphi Technique was used in our earlier study to help assign weights to each category of environmental constraints, and to each specific constraint. It was then used to rate each country considered on each constraint.

Over a hundred experts—consisting of U.S. and foreign professors, researchers and doctoral students in various fields (chiefly the social sciences), managers, bankers, government officials, and officials of international organizations such as the United Nations—participated in the weighting of factors and the rating of countries. This was conducted in large part through independent weightings and ratings involving a series of rounds with controlled information feedback. A basic aim of the Delphi Technique is to achieve a convergence of expert opinion based on an objective and independent analysis of facts and available data, additional information which is generated in the process, sound assumptions, estimates, and reasoning, clarification, and interpretation.

We found that in the time available a clear-cut convergence of expert opinion regarding the total weightings for each broad category of constraints—that is, those that are educational, economic, political-legal, and sociological-cultural—did not emerge. So we arbitrarily assigned weights of 250 to each category. However, there was a fairly high degree of convergence with regard to the weighting of the specific constraints within the four broad categories that were each assigned a weight of 250. However, since a fairly high degree of convergence has not yet been obtained for the weighting of the broad environmental categories, in this study I am arbitrarily assigning a weight of 100 to each of the twenty-nine specific constraints.

In reality, I realize that some factors are more important than others. For example, I feel that literacy level and several of the sociological-cultural variables are probably more important than any of the other constraints.

As for the specific country ratings in our earlier study, there were fairly high degrees of convergence for several of those on which we spent the most time, and for which we typically had several rounds of controlled information feedback. The degree of convergence for the U.S. environment as a whole was quite high, for India and Japan somewhat lower, and for the Soviet Union, for which only very limited use was made of the Delphi Technique, the results were more mixed. In almost all cases the experts had considerable firsthand knowledge about at least two countries, and in several cases as many as four or five countries. Practically all of the experts rated more than one country in total or for certain portions of the environment. Their ratings were done primarily on a relative, rather than on an absolute basis, but there were major conceptual problems.

Although maximum scores were set for each constraint, the ratings were done in a basically open-ended way, with the maximum possible score implying an optimum or ideal situation with virtually no negative constraint impact on managerial effectiveness and industrial progress. In general, the higher the score for a given environmental factor, the lower the negative impact or constraint on managerial effectiveness and industrial progress. We realized then, as now, that this type of procedure is in significant ways tantamount to a mathematical abortion and is far from being a sophisticated scientific method. But at the time we thought it was the best method to use under the circumstances.

In the present study I have chosen to deviate from the above procedure. Here I shall use no open-ended type ratings which imply optimum situations with maximum scores. Instead, I shall rate the countries in a strictly relative, rank-order type of manner. Where a given country—or countries

—is judged to lead the others being rated with regard to a specific environmental factor, it will automatically be given a score of 100 for that factor. The other countries will be given scores reflecting their estimated relative positions in relation to the leader in each case. Hence, a score of 100 on a given factor for a given country does not imply that a country is perfect with regard to this factor and cannot achieve any improvements; it only means that this country is better on this factor than the other countries being rated.

I draw quite heavily on the relative rating results for the United States, India, Japan, and Russia in my earlier study. But some deviations from earlier results have been made to reflect changing conditions, and also where more recent research has shed more, or a different, light on various environmental factors in some of the countries. Because of time and various other limitations, I have made no systematic attempt to make further use of the Delphi Technique in this study, although I have discussed Red China in particular at considerable length with a variety of experts and Sinologists.

All of the environmental constraints for any country are subject to change, either positive or negative, over time, and some—such as legal rules of the game, political stability, defense policy, or even fiscal level—can change drastically in a relatively short period of time. This is evident from Red China's sharp and oscillating environmental changes on a wide front in the short run, particularly since 1949.

It generally tends to be much more difficult for relatively advanced countries to improve their environmental conditions substantially than relatively poor nations. For example, very big gains in managerial effectiveness, productivity, and general industrial progress have been achieved in China by bringing about more favorable environmental conditions in a very short period of time. In such a country relatively small or simple environmental improvements can yield big gains in the industrial sector. The situation is different in the United States, where much more delicate and complex improvements would typically have to be achieved in educational or sociological-cultural factors, fiscal or monetary policy, price stability, social-overhead capital, and so on before it could derive large improvements in the overall industrial sector at the present stage of development.

Since many of the environmental factors are so intimately interrelated in reality, it is not possible to avoid at least some double counting and various types of distortion in quantification. Moreover, we add the factor scores to get a total score for each country, but in reality the relationships tend to be multiplicative rather than additive. In fact a zero score on a critical factor—such as literacy, legal rules, political or economic stability—for a given country could well mean that industry cannot function at all. Therefore, no zero scores are assigned in the matrix.

All of the constraint variables to be rated are highly aggregative, and hence subject to considerable loss of detail when applied to specific countries or situations. For example, achievement motivation was probably much higher for workers and party cadres than it was for experts or professional managers during China's Great Leap Forward, but the aggregate score for this factor does not tell us this. India has an edge over China in certain aspects of social-overhead capital, but lags in others; but here too the scores for this factor do not spell this out. China is favorably endowed in mineral resources but is greatly overpopulated, and not well endowed in agricultural land in terms of her population. A relatively high degree of price stability has prevailed in Red China even during periods of severe general economic instability.

Similarly, various aspects of interorganizational cooperation may be quite favorable in a particular country, while they may be poor in others. Or attitudes toward change or risk taking may be relatively favorable at the firm-management level but not at the national level, or vice versa, in a given country. Or one country, such as India, may have a big quantitative edge in secondary or higher education over another, such as China, but the latter may have a substantial qualitative edge. Moreover, although one chief interest with regard to education is with the educational level of industrial personnel, the educational backgrounds of parties external to the industrial enterprise, who nonetheless significantly influence industrial activity, also must be given some weight since this tends to have a significant bearing on managerial effectiveness and industrial progress. For some factors, such as fiscal and monetary policy, comparisons between communist and market economies are very difficult, and hence even cruder and more suggestive than for most other factors.

In my rating of factors I try to weigh and consider all of the important disaggregative issues and details. The reader is referred to earlier chapters to get a fuller picture of my reasons for assigning the scores that I do in the matrix, particularly with regard to China and India. I could have perhaps broken down the matrix into more subfactors, totaling even hundreds, but this, I feel, would not warrant the additional effort or space involved.

Ideally, if precise and complete data were available, an accurate rating of environmental constraints for each country would result in a total constraint score that would correlate closely with a variety of managerial and industrial performance indicators that would be combined and weighted in some meaningful formula. The most important performance indicators that would be used for this purpose would include: (a) average annual growth rates—over a period of, say, five to ten years—for total and per capita GNP and industrial output, and labor productivity; (b) absolute levels of performance in these areas at the end of the period, with perhaps a higher weight assigned to per capita than total performance; (c) an index based on the physical output of major commodities, as well as absolute figures for at least the most strategic ones; (d) trends in the incremental capital output ratio; (e) trends in material consumption in the production of major commodities; (f) indexes for product development and technological progress.

We are clearly very far from this ideal situation. However, as mentioned earlier, I still think it is worthwhile to undertake a quantitative rating of the environmental constraints. So let us proceed now with the matrix, keeping in mind the limitations noted above, and remembering that the higher the score on a given factor the less of a negative impact it has on management, efficiency, and industrial progress.

In the Table 7–17 matrix I rate all of the countries except China during the 1963–66 period. For China I use the mid-1962 to mid-1966 period because of the greater-than-usual uncertainty about the impact of the Cultural Revolution on the environment during the second half of 1966 and because my visit to China has given me a fairly good firsthand feel for conditions during the first half of that year. It may be somewhat unfair to use the 1963–66 period for India since some environmental conditions were probably below normal through much of 1965–66 because of the war with Pakistan and the agricultural performance that was even worse than usual. I shall try to compensate for this by mentally giving more weight to 1963–64 in my ratings for India than 1965–66, for the 1963–66 period as a whole. If we used, say, the 1961–64 period for India, the total environmental rating score would be about 5 percent higher than India's 1963–66 score. For the period ratings for all of the countries—with the exception of India, as noted above—I have used a hypothetical period average for each environmental factor because there may have been some fairly significant environmental changes in some instances even during the four-year periods.

From Table 7–17 we see that China's total score is significantly higher than that of India. Even assuming that India has been underrated by as much as 10 percent, China would still lead India by more than 10 percent. But this is not true for Japan and Russia. On this rating scale Japan and Russia lead China by roughly 50 percent, and the United States leads China by about 85 percent.

With a rating system of this type, and with the United States as one of the countries rated, the United States would always come out on top, no matter which countries are rated. Assuming that all countries in the world were rated, the type of scores that they would get, in general, would be as follows: Tribal and primitive countries—typically with per capita incomes under $60—would get environmental-constraint scores under 500. Relatively stagnant underdeveloped countries with some industrial base would get scores in the range of 500–750. Developing countries making some

TABLE 7–17

SUGGESTIVE COUNTRY ENVIRONMENTAL RATING MATRIX

(Each factor has maximum score of 100)*

Constraints	*U.S.A.* (1963–66)	*Japan* (1963–66)	*Soviet Union* (1963–66)	*Communist China* (Mid–1962 to mid–1966)	*India* (1963–66)
Educational					
C1.1	100	100	95	55	40
1.2	90	80	100	25	25
1.3	100	75	80	30	40
1.4	100	75	50	15	55
1.5	90	85	100	90	50
1.6	100	80	75	50	25
Total C1 600	580	495	500	265	235
Sociological					
C2.1	85	100	95	75	55
2.2	100	90	95	75	30
2.3	90	100	75	85	30
2.4	90	100	90	75	40
2.5	100	75	100	55	25
2.6	90	80	100	60	35
2.7	100	70	75	45	30
2.8	100	75	70	60	35
2.9	100	85	70	75	30
Total C2 900	855	775	770	605	310
Legal-political					
C3.1	100	80	65	25	70
3.2	80	100	70	30	45
3.3	80	100	75	50	50
3.4	100	75	85	70	55
3.5	100	90	65	65	35
3.6	100	85	70	35	60
Total C3 600	560	530	430	275	315
Economic					
C4.1	100	75	60	35	25
4.2	100	90	80	65	70
4.3	100	90	80	60	40
4.4	100	80	80	75	50
4.5	100	75	55	35	50
4.6	100	15	80	35	20
4.7	100	80	75	50	50
4.8	100	65	65	25	30
Total C4 800	800	570	575	380	335
Grand Total 2,900	2,795	2,370	2,275	1,525	1,195

* Each factor is weighted in terms of its constraint on managerial effectiveness, productive efficiency, and industrial progress.

progress in their industrialization efforts, but still having modest aggregate levels of industrial production, would score in the range of 750–1,000.

The 1,000-to-1,500 range would be characterized by developing countries making fair progress but which still have not achieved semiadvanced status. Relatively poor, but larger, countries, such as India, which have achieved fairly sizable aggregate levels of industrial output—typically ranking among the top 20 percent or so of the world's industrial producers—would also be in this range.

The 1,500–2,000 bracket would be characterized by semiadvanced nations having relatively diverse industrial structures and producing a pretty wide range of products. Larger, but poor, countries which have substantial aggregate levels of production—ranking in the top 10 or 15 percent of the world's industrial producers—would also be in this bracket. Such countries would be well on the path to laying the groundwork—that is creating environmental conditions—conducive to a breakthrough to a fairly advanced industrial economy within a decade or two. According to Table 7–18, Red China is on the verge of being a country of this type, while India has not yet made it. As said before, China's destiny and degree of capitalizing on her potential depend chiefly on which force wins out—managerial, technical, and economic rationality or ideological extremism.

Countries in the 2,000-to-2,500 score range, such as Japan and the Soviet Union, would be relatively advanced industrially. However, they would not yet be extensively affluent and highly advanced countries unless they had scores over 2,500. Only the United States, Sweden, Canada, probably West Germany, and a handful of others would presently fall into this category.

In general, a substantial majority of the countries of the world would receive scores of less than 1,000, and less than 15 percent would receive scores of over 2,000. I perceive the most critical breakthrough points to be the 500, 1,500, and 2,500 levels.

With the rating system used, as countries progress up the rating scale it would become increasingly difficult to achieve further environmental and performance improvements. For example, it would be substantially easier for a hypothetical country to go from a 600 to a 700 total constraint score, than from a 1,600 to 1,700 score. Similarly, it would be significantly easier to go from 1,600 to 1,700 than from 2,600 to 2,700. Moreover, larger potential relative gains in managerial effectiveness and industrial progress would be likely when there is a rise from a 600 environmental level to a 700 one, than from 1,600 to 1,700. Take the case of literacy, for instance: a country which increases its literacy rate from 10 to 20 percent in, say, five years, would stand potentially to benefit much more industrially and economically than a country which increases its literacy level from 70 to 80 percent.

TABLE 7–18

SUGGESTIVE ENVIRONMENTAL RATINGS FOR CHINA FOR SELECTED PERIODS: 1933 TO MID–1966

(Each factor has maximum score of 100)

Constraints		*Mid–1962 to Mid–1966*	*1959 to Mid–1962*	*1953–57*	*Mid–1949 to 1953*	*1945– Mid–1949*	*Peak Republican* Period (probably 1933–37)*
Educational							
C1.1		55	40	30	20	15	15
1.2		25	20	15	10	5	5
1.3		30	25	20	15	10	10
1.4		15	15	15	10	5	5
1.5		90	70	95	80	45	40
1.6		50	20	30	15	10	5
Total C1	600	265	190	205	150	90	80
Sociological							
C2.1		75	20	85	65	45	65
2.2		75	25	70	65	50	60
2.3		85	60	75	70	15	50
2.4		75	45	85	75	25	50
2.5		55	15	75	70	40	50
2.6		60	15	75	55	30	45
2.7		45	5	30	20	10	15
2.8		60	15	45	35	10	40
2.9		75	20	70	75	20	35
Total C2	900	605	220	610	525	245	410

TABLE 7–18 (*continued*)

Constraints		*Mid–1962 to Mid–1966*	*1959 to Mid–1962*	*1953–57*	*Mid–1949 to 1953*	*1945–Mid–1949*	*Peak Republican* Period (probably 1933–37)*
Legal-political							
$C_{3.1}$		25	10	20	15	5	35
3.2		30	40	60	20	5	30
3.3		50	15	70	30	10	50
3.4		70	35	80	60	5	60
3.5		65	20	60	50	5	35
3.6		35	15	25	10	5	25
Total C_3	600	275	135	315	185	35	235
Economic							
$C_{4.1}$		35	20	30	20	10	30
4.2		65	40	50	35	5	15
4.3		60	30	45	35	5	15
4.4		75	15	70	50	5	55
4.5		35	20	25	15	5	10
4.6		35	20	25	20	10	15
4.7		50	25	30	15	10	20
4.8		25	15	20	10	5	5
Total C_4	800	380	185	295	200	55	165
Grand Total	2,900	1,525	730	1,425	1,045	425	890

*Although there may have been higher levels of industrial production during the 1942–44 period, this would have been achieved under Japanese occupation. Therefore, that period is not considered in the matrix.

Hence, from Table 7–17 it appears that China has a significant lead over India in creating a potential environment conducive to sustained and impressive industrial progress and general economic development in the long run. As of mid-1966, China clearly had a commanding lead in the overall sociological-cultural sphere, coordination of educational background and employment, political organization (this factor may have changed sharply for the worse in China in 1967), economic stability, factor endowment (particularly mineral resources). China also led on several other factors. India led China on only eight of the twenty-nine variables rated, and had big leads only in management-development programs, legal rules of the game, flexibility of law and legal changes, and organization of capital markets.

In Table 7–18 China is rated for five additional periods; the pre-1949 ratings are even more speculative, especially those for 1933–37.

The period scores in Table 7–18 reflect the dramatic way in which environmental conditions have periodically shifted upward and downward in China since 1930. Few, if any, other major countries in the world have had an overall environment that has oscillated so dramatically since 1930.

Figure 7–1 plots the environmental scores for China since 1930. It also contains a suggestive trend line for India's environment since 1930. This figure vividly portrays China's highly erratic environment in contrast to the relatively stable pattern of evolution for India's environment.

Red China's significant lead over India as of mid-1966 is reflected in

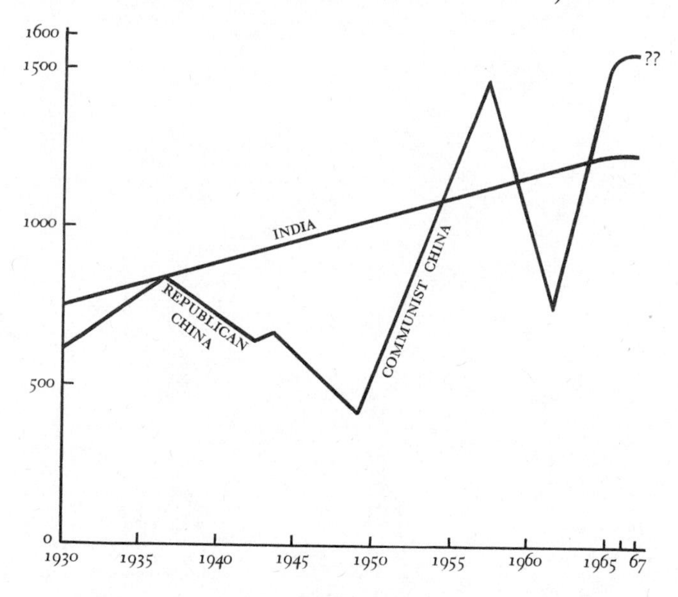

FIGURE 7–1
LONG-RUN ENVIRONMENTAL TRENDS FOR CHINA AND INDIA, 1930–1966

Figure 7–1. Whether China can maintain this lead in the long run will, in my opinion, be determined primarily by whether ideological extremism or managerial, technical, and economic rationality triumphs in China. If the former wins and persists, the chances are very good that India will not only narrow the gap between China and herself but she will in time actually surpass China. However, if rationality wins out, China's lead over India is likely to increase over time, probably substantially.

CHAPTER 8

Chinese Industrial Organization and Planning

VARIOUS ASPECTS OF industrial organization and planning in Communist China have already been discussed and analyzed (in the chapters on political-legal and economic constraints). The aim in this chapter is to describe in greater detail the nature of China's system of industrial organization and planning, particularly those aspects having a significant bearing on the functioning of industrial enterprises. Our focus here will be on pertinent relationships between macromanagement, involving higher levels of the industrial hierarchy, and micromanagement at the enterprise level. The following two chapters focus on micromanagement only and the structure, operations, and performance of Chinese industrial enterprises surveyed in 1966.

This chapter deals with the Chinese system of industrial organization and planning as it existed at the time of my trip to China in 1966. It is based mainly on the firsthand information that I obtained at that time. For those readers who desire additional information, there are other published works[1] on the subject dealt with here. As of late 1967 there was no available concrete evidence which indicated that there have been basic changes in the hierarchical structure of Chinese industry or in the planning process since mid-1966. However, there have undoubtedly been some drastic changes in interpersonal relationships, the roles of Reds—and Super-Reds—and Experts, and in personnel in important jobs. Hopefully, my firsthand findings in 1966 will serve as a useful historical backdrop for analyzing and interpreting future structural changes in the Chinese economy.

Organization of Government and Party

Before proceeding with a discussion of the Chinese industrial structure per se, a brief general discussion about the overall political structure, which is comprised of governmental and Communist Party organizations, is warranted. Chinese Communist state administration is concerned basically with two major problems: first, the organization of what may be called the "traditional" governmental or state functions common to any type of country; and second, the organization of the economically productive sphere of the economy which is basically communistic or socialistic in nature.

The traditional problems on the national level involve such critical matters as national defense and military affairs; foreign affairs; health, education, and welfare; monetary and fiscal policy and the state budget; and other domestic affairs of national importance. On the local level, state administration is concerned with such traditional matters as sanitation, police and fire protection, parks and recreational facilities, roads and zoning, medical care, culture, and education. In the overall economically productive sector the state deals directly and pervasively with industrial, commercial, and agricultural matters in Communist China.

Chinese government organization extends from the central or national level to China's twenty-one provinces, five autonomous regions, and Peking and Shanghai (China's two special municipalities with basically provincial status), then down to the municipal, county, and district levels of governmental administration. As shown on a formal organization chart the Chinese industrial hierarchy functions, at least on a day-to-day basis, within the governmental hierarchy. There are individual industrial enterprises operationally under central industrial ministries, provincial industrial departments, and municipal industrial bureaus, either directly or through industrial corporations at these levels. Table 9–2 in the following chapter indicates the higher authority directly above each of the thirty-eight Chinese industrial enterprises that were surveyed in 1966.

Underlying the elaborate Chinese governmental structure at all levels—as well as at a few additional levels—is the Communist Party of the People's Republic of China, the engine actually driving the Chinese state. The party stands in alter-ego fashion alongside every organized unit of state, government, and society. The pervasive Chinese Communist Party organization extends from the center, or national level, down through regional party organizations (which have no governmental counterparts) to the provinces, autonomous regions, and the two special municipalities, then to the other cities, counties, and local districts, and finally to the basic or primary level comprised of individual enterprises and other types of micro-organization. Party organs at all levels are, at least theoretically, wholly subordinate to the central leadership in Peking.

This party-government parallelism results in direct party domination and control in those spheres it wishes to exercise such prerogatives.

The Chinese government at all levels exists to carry out the basic objectives and policies set forth by the party, while the party itself also guides and controls governmental activity. When the ideological pendulum has swung in the direction of extremism, party cadres—and more recently, various kinds of Super-Reds—have come to play the dominant role in operational administration and implementation, including detailed decision making and control.

Let us examine the basic levels of echelons of the Chinese Communist state, focusing chiefly on those organs that have a direct bearing on industrial organization and management.

The Center or National Level

Central Party Organization

Chart 8–1 presents an outline of China's central Communist Party organization. The National Party Congress theoretically represents the ultimate source of authority and legitimation of the operative central party organs. The Chinese Communist Party Constitution provides that Congress be "elected" every five years and hold annual sessions. However, the present Eighth Congress was elected in 1956, and a full National Party Congress last met in 1958. This congress is responsible for developing long-term national policy and the overall party line. It legitimates appointments to the party's Central Committee and other key central party organs which are headed by top leaders. The Politburo and its standing committee exercise the authority of the Central Committee when the full committee is not in session. The Chairman, Mao Tse-tung, and deputy chairmen of the Central Committee are simultaneously chairman and deputy chairmen of the Politburo.

The Central Secretariat of the Politburo handles the day-to-day business of the Central Committee, and is in charge of various central party bureaus and departments. The Industrial Work Department under the Secretariat is normally the main central party organ that concerns itself directly with industrial matters. However, an Industry and Communications Political Department was created to deal chiefly with political and ideological aspects of organization and management. No doubt this department has come to play a more active and important role in the functioning of industry than the Industrial Work Department during the Cultural Revolution.

CHART 8–1

CHINESE COMMUNIST PARTY ORGANIZATION, AUGUST 1966

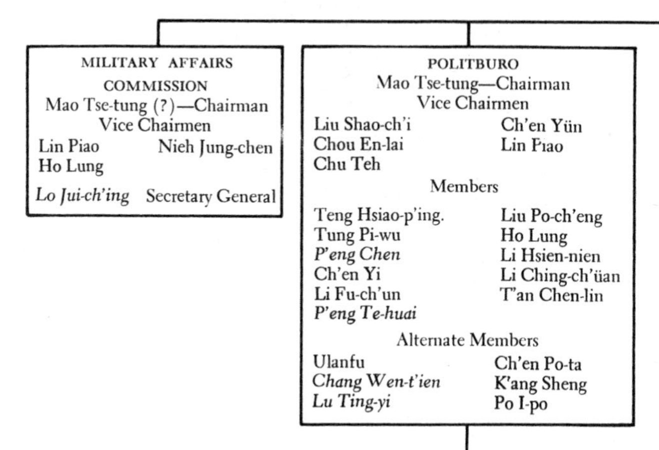

CENTRAL COMMITTEE

Mao Tse-tung—Chairman

Vice Chairmen

Liu Shao-ch'i — Ch'en Yün
Chou En-lai — Lin Piao
Chu Teh

Teng Hsiao-p'ing—General Secretary

Members

An Tzu-wen	Hsieh Fu-chih	Liu Lan-t'ao	Teng Tzu-hui
Chang Chi-ch'un	Hsü Hai-tung	Liu Ning-yi	Teng Ying-ch'ao (f)
Chang Ting-ch'eng	Hsü Hsiang-ch'ien	Liu Po-ch'eng	Ts'ai Ch'ang (f)
Chang Wen-t'ien	Hsü Kuang-ta	Liu Shao-ch'i	*Tseng Hsi-sheng*
Chang Yün-yi	Hsü T'e-li	*Lo Jui-ch'ing*	Tseng Shan
Chao Erh-lu	Hu Ch'iao-mu	Lü Cheng-ts'ao	Tung Pi-wu
Ch'en Yi	Hu Yao-pang	*Lu Ting-yi*	Ulanfu
Ch'en Po-ta	*Huang K'o-ch'eng*	Ma Ming-fang	Wang Chen
Ch'en Shao-min (f)	K'ang Sheng	Mao Tse-tung	Wang Chia-hsiang
Ch'en Shao-yü	Li Ching-ch'üan	Nieh Jung-chen	Wang En-mao
Ch'en Yü	Li Fu-ch'un	*Ouyang Ch'in*	Wang Shou-tao
Ch'en Yün	Li Hsien-nien	*P'eng Chen*	Wang Shu-sheng
Ch'eng Tzu-hua	Li Hsüeh-feng	*P'eng Te-huai*	Wang Ts'ung-wu
Cheng Wei-san	*Li Li-san*	Po I-po	Wang Wei-chou
Chia T'o-fu	Li Pao-hua	Shu T'ung	Wu Chih-pu
Ch'ien Ying (f)	*Li Wei-han*	Su Yü	Wu Hsiu-ch'üan
Chou En-lai	Liao Ch'eng-chih	Sung Jen-ch'iung	Wu Yü-chang
Chu Teh	Lin Feng	T'an Chen-lin	*Yang Hsien-chen*
Ho Lung	Lin Piao	*T'an Cheng*	Yang Hsiu-feng
Hsi Chung-hsün	Lin T'ieh	T'ao Chu	Yang Shang-k'un
Hsiao Ching-kuang	Liu Ch'ang-sheng	Teng Hsiao-p'ing	Yeh Chi-chuang
Hsiao Hua	Liu Hsiao	*Teng Hua*	Yeh Chien-ying
Hsiao K'o	*Liu Ko-p'ing*	T'eng Tai-yüan	

89 Alternate Members

NATIONAL PARTY CONGRESS

Party Constitution provides that Congress be elected every five years and hold annual sessions. The present Eighth Congress was elected in 1956; last met in May 1958.

SOURCE: *Current Scene*, Vol. IV, No. 15 (August 8, 1966), p. 10.

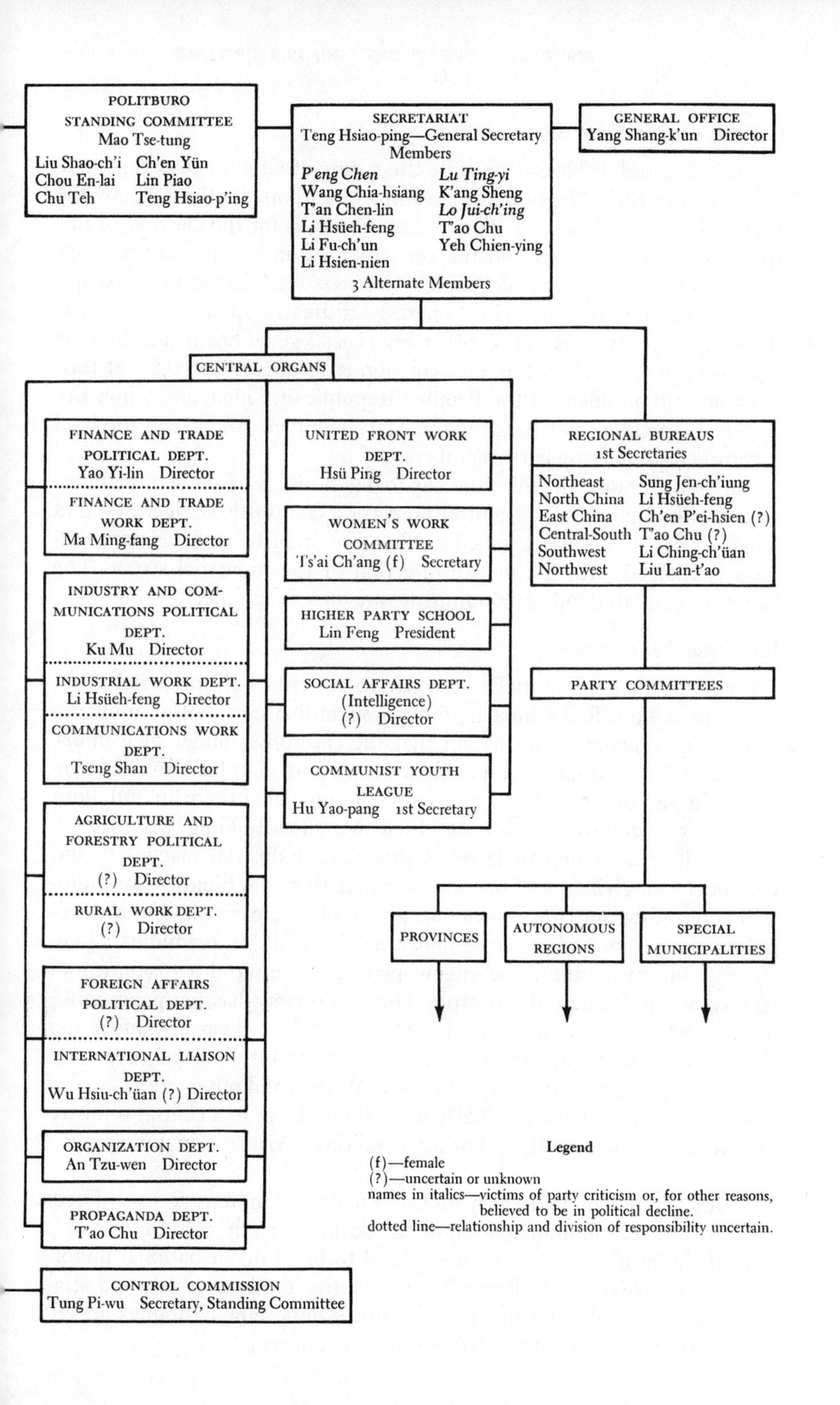

POLITBURO STANDING COMMITTEE
Mao Tse-tung
Liu Shao-ch'i
Ch'en Yün
Chou En-lai
Lin Piao
Chu Teh
Teng Hsiao-p'ing
SECRETARIAT
Teng Hsiao-ping—General Secretary
Members
P'eng Chen
Lu Ting-yi
Wang Chia-hsiang
K'ang Sheng
T'an Chen-lin
Lo Jui-ch'ing
Li Hsüeh-feng
T'ao Chu
Li Fu-ch'un
Yeh Chien-ying
Li Hsien-nien
3 Alternate Members
GENERAL OFFICE
Yang Shang-k'un Director
CENTRAL ORGANS
FINANCE AND TRADE POLITICAL DEPT.
Yao Yi-lin Director
FINANCE AND TRADE WORK DEPT.
Ma Ming-fang Director
INDUSTRY AND COMMUNICATIONS POLITICAL DEPT.
Ku Mu Director
INDUSTRIAL WORK DEPT.
Li Hsüeh-feng Director
COMMUNICATIONS WORK DEPT.
Tseng Shan Director
AGRICULTURE AND FORESTRY POLITICAL DEPT.
(?) Director
RURAL WORK DEPT.
(?) Director
FOREIGN AFFAIRS POLITICAL DEPT.
(?) Director
INTERNATIONAL LIAISON DEPT.
Wu Hsiu-ch'üan (?) Director
ORGANIZATION DEPT.
An Tzu-wen Director
PROPAGANDA DEPT.
T'ao Chu Director
UNITED FRONT WORK DEPT.
Hsü Ping Director
WOMEN'S WORK COMMITTEE
Ts'ai Ch'ang (f) Secretary
HIGHER PARTY SCHOOL
Lin Feng President
SOCIAL AFFAIRS DEPT.
(Intelligence)
(?) Director
COMMUNIST YOUTH LEAGUE
Hu Yao-pang 1st Secretary
REGIONAL BUREAUS
1st Secretaries
Northeast
Sung Jen-ch'iung
North China
Li Hsüeh-feng
East China
Ch'en P'ei-hsien (?)
Central-South
T'ao Chu (?)
Southwest
Li Ching-ch'üan
Northwest
Liu Lan-t'ao
PARTY COMMITTEES
PROVINCES
AUTONOMOUS REGIONS
SPECIAL MUNICIPALITIES
CONTROL COMMISSION
Tung Pi-wu Secretary, Standing Committee
Legend
(f)—female
(?)—uncertain or unknown
names in italics—victims of party criticism or, for other reasons, believed to be in political decline.
dotted line—relationship and division of responsibility uncertain.

Central Government Organization

Chart 8–2 and Table 8–1 indicate the nature of China's central government organization. The supreme government authority is theoretically the National People's Congress. The constitution calls for the election of this congress every four years and the convening of annual plenary sessions. The present Third National People's Congress was elected in 1964, and last met in January 1965. This congress legitimates appointments to its standing committee, as well as other key central government jobs held by top level leaders, such as Liu Shao-chi who is, as of October 1967, at least in name, still president of the People's Republic of China, and Chou Enlai who is premier and head of the State Council. All of the top-level government leaders are party members.

The State Council handles the day-to-day business of the national government through its many central ministries, commissions, agencies, and other organs. The State Council's Office For Industry and Communications is charged with the overall direction of the industrial sector. The twenty or so central industrial ministries are under this office.

Industrial Ministries

I was told that substantially less than 10 percent of all industrial enterprises throughout Red China are directly subordinate to central ministries or their administrative organs but that the enterprises under such ministries probably account for more than 10 percent of total industrial employment and output value. For example, in Shanghai there are only four machinery enterprises under the First Machine-Building Ministry although there are scores of factories producing industrial machinery and equipment for civilian use. In Canton, where there are hundreds of industrial enterprises, only three—one machine tool, one paper, and one chemical fertilizer—are under central ministries. Of Wusih's 417 industrial enterprises only two, the diesel-engine plant surveyed and a machine-tool factory, are under central ministries. Hupeh Province has ten paper mills, none of which are under central control. Three of them are under the Provincial First Light-Industry Department, and the other seven are under municipal light-industry bureaus in Wuhan and other cities.

In general, an enterprise is likely to be subordinate to a central ministry only if one or more of the following conditions exist to a high degree:

1. If it is producing primarily for the defense and military sector. (There are five central industrial ministries dealing directly with this sector.)
2. If the firm's products are considered to be of major national importance. These would typically be expensive producer goods and strategic materials, and many of the firm's important customers are located in other provinces (or in foreign countries).

3. If a large proportion of the firm's important suppliers are in other provinces—or in foreign countries—and the commodities which they supply are considered to be of major national importance.
4. If the firm is utilizing new and expensive techniques and/or technology on a substantial scale—for example, a Peking steel mill using a new oxidizing process which is much smaller than the Shanghai No. 3 Steel Mill discussed below.
5. If the firm is, or has recently been, set up with foreign assistance and/or makes extensive use of recently introduced foreign techniques. (In 1966 there were a number of enterprises involved in foreign collaborations with Western European and Japanese companies, especially in the chemical industry.)

TABLE 8–1

SPECIAL AGENCIES UNDER THE STATE COUNCIL
(August 1966)

Administrative Bureau for Travel and Tourism	Director	?
Agricultural Bank of China	Director	Hu Ching-yün
Broadcasting Administrative Bureau	Director	Mei Yi
Bureau of Government Offices Administration	Director	Kao Teng-pang
Bureau of Religious Affairs	Director	Hsiao Hsien-fa
Central Administration of Industry and Commerce	Director	Hsü Ti-hsin
Central Bureau of Meteorology	Director	Jao Hsing
China Civil Aviation General Administration	Director	K'uang Jen-nung
Committee for Reforming the Chinese Written Language	Chairman	Wu Yü-chang
Counsellors' Office	Director	Tseng Yi-fan
Bureau of Foreign Experts Administration	Director	Mi Yung
Bureau of Foreign Language Publication and Distribution	Director	Lo Chün
Hsinhua News Agency	Director	Wu Leng-hsi
National Commodity Price Committee	Chairman	Hsüeh Mu-ch'iao
People's Bank of China	Director-General	Hu Li-chiao (acting)
Bureau of Scientific and Technological Cadres Administration	Director	Yüeh Chih-chien
State Housing Administration	Director	Chao P'eng-fei
State Archives Bureau	Director	Tseng San
State Bureau of Surveying and Cartography	Director	Ch'en Wai-ou
State Oceanography Bureau	Director	Ch'i Yung
State Organization Committee	Chairman	Chou Jung-hsin
State Statistical Bureau	Director	Wang Szu-hua

SOURCE: *Current Scene*, Vol. IV, No. 15 (August 8, 1966), p. 15.

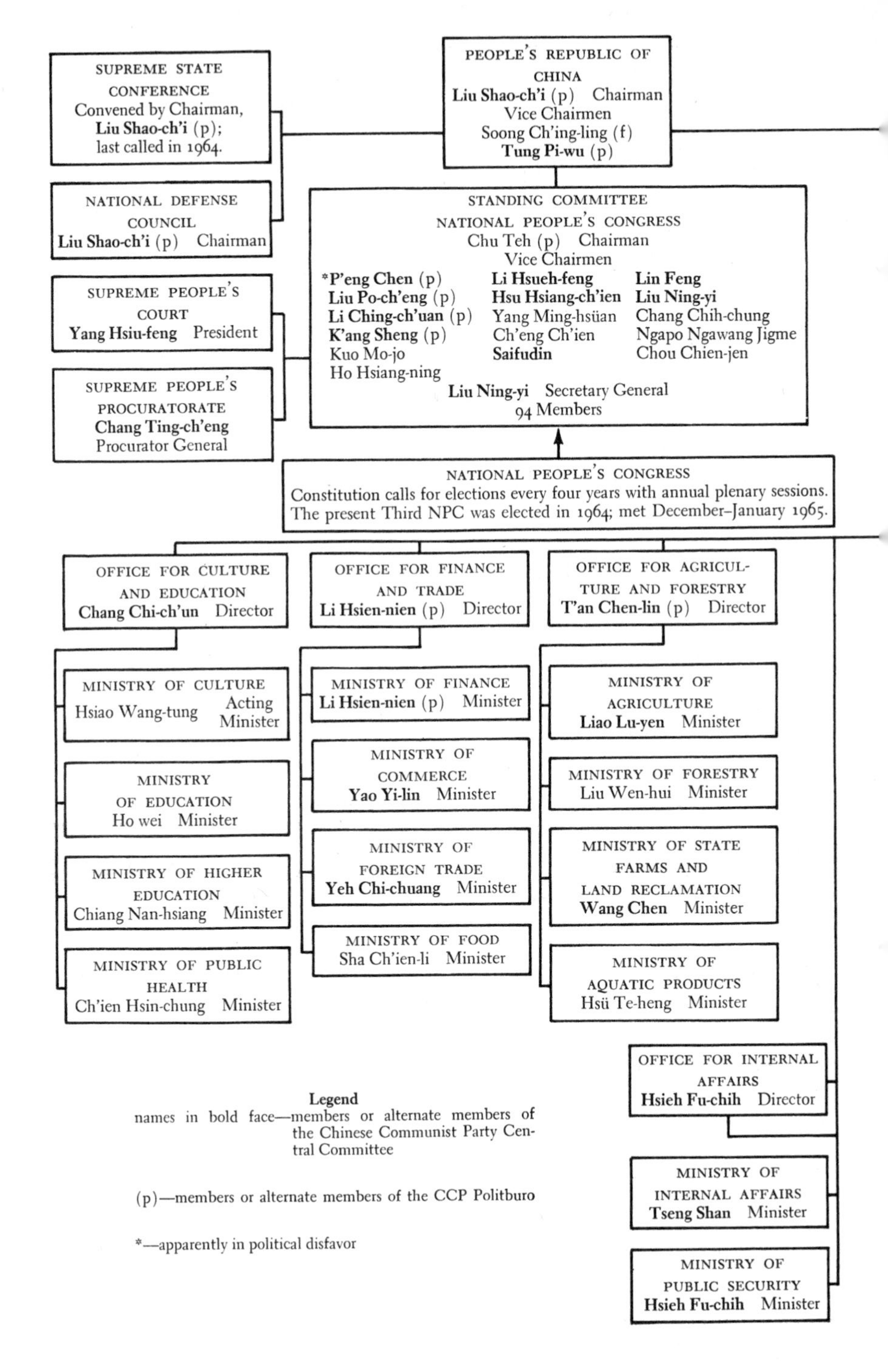

SOURCE: *Current Scene,* Vol. IV, No. 15 (August 8, 1966), p. 11.

CHART 8–2

CHINESE COMMUNIST GOVERNMENT ORGANIZATION

(August 8, 1966)

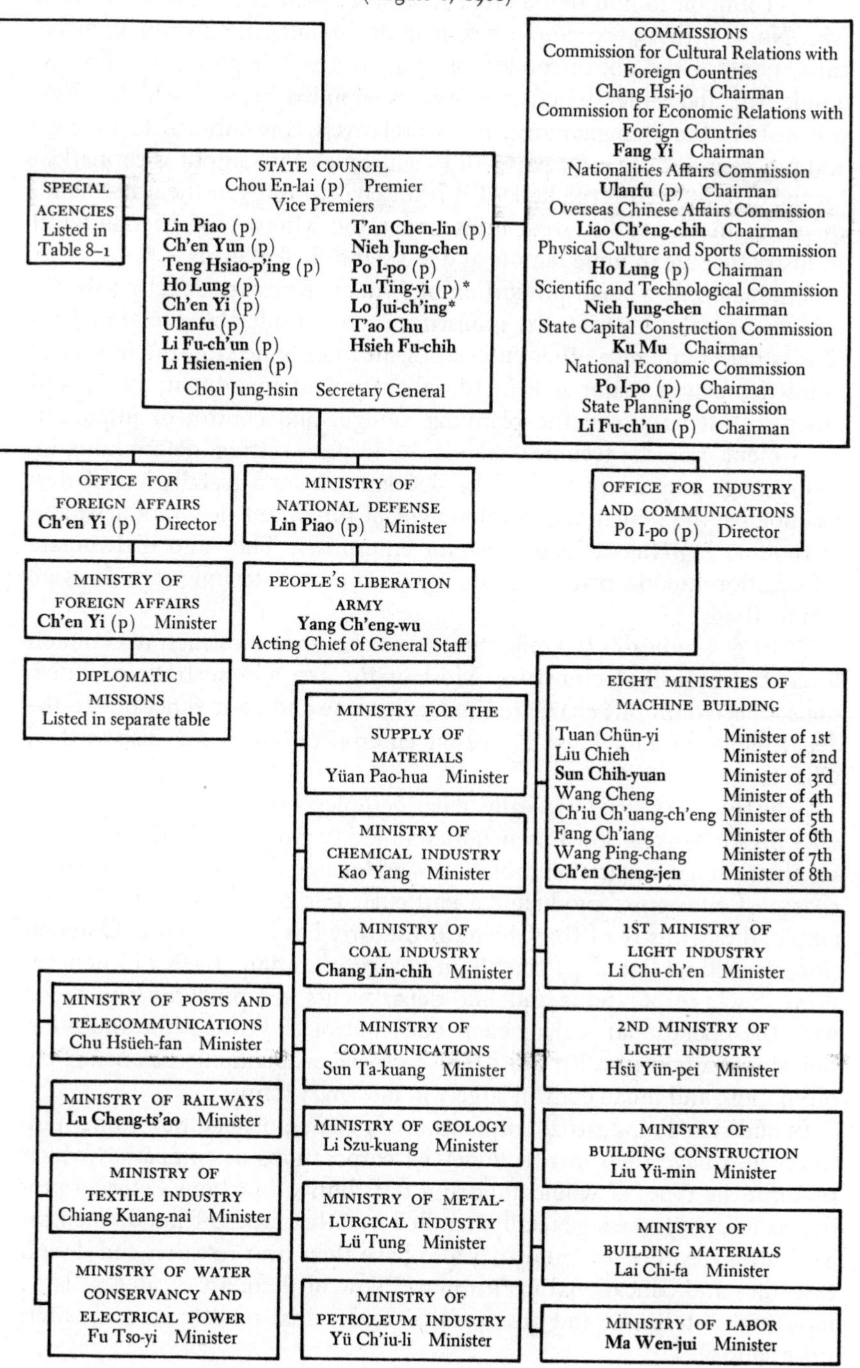

It is common to find that a large enterprise, such as the Shanghai Steel Mill No. 3 with 13,000 employees, is under municipal subordination because none of the above conditions exist to a very high degree. For example, the above-mentioned steel firm is supplied by, and sells to, firms primarily in the Shanghai area. It uses relatively conventional technology and processes for the most part. Although some of its output is earmarked for the defense sector, the bulk of it is for civilian use. On the other hand, there are much smaller steel mills under the Ministry of Metallurgical Industry that are in more remote and less self-sufficient areas.

Although only a small proportion of Chinese firms are directly subordinate to central ministries, the ministries exert considerable functional authority over numerous other enterprises. In this connection the industrial ministries play a major role in the allocation of investment funds and other critical resources; the planning, design, and control of important investment projects; technical standard and price setting; determining industry wage and salary grades; the development and installation of new technology; the design and development of important new products; and in training high-talent manpower for enterprises. They also disseminate information among plants pertaining to improved techniques processes, and methods.

Chart 8–3 indicates the minimum basic organization structure common to central industrial ministries. Most of the key administrative subdivisions reflected on this chart are similar in name and basic functions to the departments of individual industrial enterprises which are discussed in Chapter 9.

Industrial ministries typically have complex networks of supply and sales organs broken down by major commodity groups. It is also common for them to have special corporations and/or line departments directly in charge of enterprises producing a particular line of commodities. For example, the Ministry of the Chemical Industry has its own Drug Corporation, as well as line departments in charge of various types of chemical firms. Such corporations and line departments are primarily concerned with the operational management and control of firms, while the other ministerial administrative units tend to focus on planning, balancing, coordination, and broad control largely in monetary terms.

In addition to industrial corporations in charge of factories, some ministries also have their own commercial corporations or companies which perform the types of wholesaling and distributive functions between producers and customers generally handled by other types of middlemen organizations. Moreover, ministries also have their own research and design institutes and educational institutions. Many of them are located at large industrial enterprises and are operated under dual ministerial and enterprise control.

CHART 8–3
Basic Organization of a Central Industrial Ministry
(Indicates Minimum Structure Common to Most Industrial Ministries in 1966)

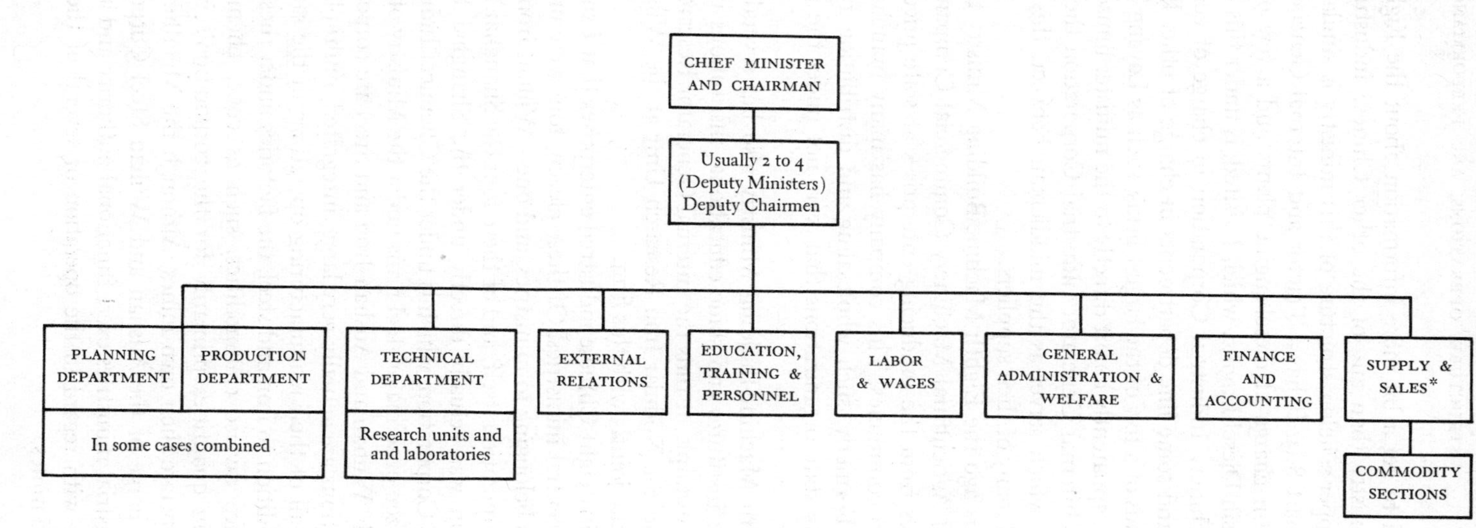

* Typically includes transportation.

I managed to get a bit more information about the Eighth Machine-Building Ministry than any of the other Chinese industrial ministries. The basic upper-echelon structure of this ministry is similar to that presented in Chart 8–3. It has a Tractor and Internal Generator Industrial Corporation in charge of diesel-engine plants and a few other kinds of plants—Wusih Diesel Engine, which I visited, is under this corporation—a Farm Machinery Industrial Corporation in charge of certain types of enterprises, and some line departments in charge of other kinds of factories. The heads of a few of the largest firms, such as Loyang Tractor under this ministry, apparently report directly to the minister himself. Under the Tractor and Internal Generator Industrial Corporation there is a supply subcompany which serves as the middleman between this corporation's factories and many of their suppliers.

A few years ago the Eighth Machine-Building Ministry took charge of the National Agricultural Machinery Commercial Company which buys diesel engines from the producing enterprises at state prices and distributes them to communes. This company has many branches throughout the nation. Formerly, such wholesaling and distribution functions were performed by state organizations that were not under the jurisdiction of this ministry.

The Eighth Machine-Building Ministry also has several research and development institutes and some educational institutions under its jurisdiction. For example, it runs the Internal Generator Research Institute in Shanghai and the Nodular Iron Research Unit at the Wusih Diesel Engine Enterprise jointly with this firm.

Of the thirty-eight Chinese industrial enterprises that I surveyed, eleven were under central ministries. Of these eleven, four were under industrial corporations belonging to ministries, and one—Wuhan Iron and Steel—is actually a corporation itself, and of these four the Shanghai No. 3 Pharmaceutical Firm was actually directly under the Shanghai branch of the China Drug Corporation, which is under the Chemical Industry Ministry.

Of the dozen or so major steel firms under the Ministry of Metallurgical Industry only Wuhan and Anshan Iron and Steel are corporations. These two corporations are actually very large, integrated, multi-plant complexes with nearly all of their manufacturing operations in the same general vicinity. In addition to iron and steel, the factories under these two corporations produce diverse commodities, such as coke, chemicals, cement, machinery in quantities primarily for the corporation's internal needs. They also operate their own mines. Although the Metallurgy Ministry is directly in charge of the Anshan and Wuhan Steel Corporations, other central industrial ministries exert functional authority and act in an advisory capacity with regard to the operation of several of the corporation's factories and mines.

Chart 8–6 presents the organization structure of the Wuhan Iron and Steel Corporation. More will be said about the organization of this corporation in a later section.

Other Key Central Organizations Involved in Industrial Administration

The central industrial ministries comprise the top echelon of the industrial hierarchy in terms of operational management. However, there are several types of other central organs that play key roles in industrial administration and general economic management through their various functions—planning, policy making, advisory, coordinating, informational, implementational, and control.

The national economic plan, as well as five-year and longer-term plans when they exist, are formally approved by the State Council with at least the tacit approval of the highest party and governmental bodies in the country. The State Planning Commission (SPC) actually prepares China's annual and five-year plans, and its proposed plan in final form is generally ratified as "law" by the central government. I was told in April 1966 that the State Planning Commission had recently taken over the responsibility of annual planning from the National Economic Commission, (NEC), also called the State Economic Commission.

The SPC compiles, coordinates, consolidates, and approves the sectoral and territorial plans passed up by the industrial ministries and other economic sectors, including those in the provinces and other geographic entities. This balancing job is carried out in both physical (real) and monetary terms through the use of input-output, intersectoral, and interterritorial matrixes. The State Statistical Bureau collects and processes much of the information used by the SPC, as well as other central agencies.

The SPC employs hundreds of people and has balancing departments for major commodity groups, such as coal and coke, iron and steel, timber, machine tools, equipment, petroleum, chemical fertilizer, and basic drugs. This agency decides on the allocation and the prices of a number of strategic commodities. It also plays a major role in determining the allocation of investment funds. The price-fixing powers of the SPC have apparently been expanded in recent years as it has assumed some of the authority in this sphere formerly held by the National Commodity Price Committee, which is directly under the State Council, and the National Economic Commission. However, these latter two agencies still are responsible for the pricing of various commodities.

The Ministry of Commerce plays a major role in the pricing, allocation, and distribution of various basic consumer goods, such as cotton and wool commodities. The ministry is chiefly concerned with domestic trade and the retail sector (which is the subject of Chapter 12). Many of this central agency's powers and functions were decentralized down to the provincial and municipal bureaus of commerce several years ago.

I could not obtain any concrete statistics regarding the proportion of commodities in China that are subject to centrally fixed state prices—that is, rationally set factory selling prices. One Chinese central administrator said that his "guess" was that the prices of less than 10 percent of all types of manufactured goods are fixed centrally but that, in terms of total value of output, such commodities account for "much more" than 10 percent. Some of the major commodities that have their prices set centrally are coal, iron, and various other basic minerals and alloys, chemical fertilizers, various other types of chemicals and drugs, petroleum, raw cotton and wool, cotton cloth, newsprint, timber, leather, and many standardized types of steel, machine tools, and equipment.

I also could not obtain much concrete information regarding the manner in which the central price-fixing powers are divided among the SPC, the NEC, the National Commodity Price Committee, the Ministry of Commerce, or various other central agencies. (I am not even sure whether prices for various commodities set by the industrial ministries are considered to be centrally fixed state prices.) The following examples show the complexity of the system. The prices of coke and coal are fixed by the SPC; some of the drugs produced by the Peking Pharmaceutical Firm have their prices fixed by the National Economic Commission after consultation with the Ministry of the Chemical Industry and Ministry of Health. Some of the standardized and small series products of Wuhan Heavy Machinery enterprise are fixed by the National Price Committee, while the prices of most of its custom-built output are formally approved and set by its direct superior agency, the First Machine-Building Ministry; the same ministry sets the prices of various standardized products produced by the Peking First Machine-Tool Plant. The director of Wuhan's Han Yang Paper Mill said that the price of his newsprint output was fixed centrally, but he wasn't sure by what agency since such price-fixing powers may have shifted recently.

From what I could learn, it seems that not all commodities having centrally fixed prices are centrally planned and allocated. For example, the factory sales price of ammonium sulfate is fixed centrally, but within the city of Peking this commodity is planned and allocated locally because the area is self-sufficient in ammonium sulfate and also consumes most of the local output. Similarly, in Shanghai, raw cotton, as well as cotton cloth are, for the most part, planned and allocated locally—on the basis of centrally approved prices—because the surrounding district and neighboring province is a major cotton-growing area and supplies nearly all of Shanghai's needs. Hence, it seems that when a given geographical area is self-sufficient in a given commodity, it is much more likely that this commodity will be subject to local, rather than central, planning and allocation.

I could not obtain any specific figures on the proportion of commodities or product groups that are subject to central planning and allocation on a substantial scale. I was told that the proportion was less in recent years than during China's First-Five-Year-Plan period of 1953–57, substantially less than the proportion in the Soviet Union in the 1950's and probably less than in the Soviet Union in recent years. According to secondary sources, the number of basic types or groups of commodities actually centrally planned, allocated, and/or distributed in Communist China was only 28 in 1952, and 235 in 1956. In 1957 central authorities dealt with 729 types of commodities, but the nature or extent of such dealings is not spelled out.[2] In the 1950's, on the average, about 1,500 basic types or groups of commodities were centrally planned and allocated annually in the Soviet Union, and in the early 1960's the number was well over 1,000 according to information that I obtained in Moscow.

While price fixing, as well as supply planning and allocation, has not been so highly centralized in the Chinese economy—considering that it is a communist state—the planning and allocation of investment have been, and undoubtedly still are, at present. For example, in 1960 only about 15 percent of all state investment was not centrally planned in China.[3]

The National Economic Commission is involved in perspective long-term planning—for such periods as ten to twenty years, or more—and determines China's general economic and industrial development objectives, strategies, and policies. It deals with such strategic issues as the relationships between light and heavy industry and agricultural development, automation and technical progress, the types, locations, and construction of new industries and factories, priorities for product development, optimum plant size in a given sector, and so forth.

Here are a few examples of specific problems that the NEC was concerned with in 1966:

(1) What new types of chemical fibers should be developed and produced in China, when, and in what order.
(2) The optimum size and technical processes of iron and steel plants.
(3) Areas of technical collaboration with foreign countries.

The NEC also plays a major role in the allocation of investment funds to industrial ministries and in coordinating the ministries in terms of national-development priorities and strategies. It was mentioned earlier that the State Council's Office for Industry and Communications is the highest government agency directly in charge of the general direction of China's overall industrial sector. It was not surprising that the director of this office, Po I-po, was also chairman of the National Economic Commission. By wearing these two hats he was in a strategic position to interpret and enforce the industrial aims, priorities, and policies of the regime. The status of Po I-po in 1967 was uncertain. There were rumors that he had been dismissed, that he had tried to commit suicide, and even that he succeeded in killing himself or had been killed because of his opposition to Mao and the Cultural Revolution.

The Ministry for the Supply of Materials was set up in 1965. It was initially called the Ministry for the Allocation of Materials. With related sub-organs throughout the country, the Ministry handles the details of supply planning and allocation; controls the implementation of centrally approved supply, sales and distribution agreements and schedules prescribed in the state plan; and coordinates supply allocations among the industrial ministries and the Ministry of Commerce, which is concerned with domestic trade and retailing. It apparently plays a key role in ironing out conflicts and revising supply allocations, when necessary, through its interpretation of national interests and policies. This agency also handles the details of contractual agreements involving major centrally planned and allocated commodities. Along with the SPC, the Ministry for the Supply of Materials organizes national supply and sales order meetings (also referred to as material allocation conferences). Such meetings have the purpose of arriving at contractual agreements. Industrial ministries, provincial and municipal agencies, large factories, and other organizations send representatives. The meetings are organized along branch-of-industry lines, with organizations having supply and sales relationships participating. (More will be said about such meetings in a later section.)

At the national level there is a vast maze of supply and marketing organs. There are such organs under the SPC, the Ministry for the Supply of Materials, the ministries of Commerce, Food, Agricultural, and Foreign Trade, directly under the State Council itself, as well as under the industrial ministries.

The Ministry of Labor sets basic wage and salary scales in close consultation with the industrial ministries, as well as provincial and municipal authorities. The details of implementing wage and salary scales are worked out locally in large part. The average basic industrial wage varies somewhat in different parts of the country and in major cities because of the cost of living, types of industries in the area, and the qualifications of industrial personnel. Shanghai has the highest average industrial wage in the nation—about 75 yuan per month. The average basic monthly-pay figures for industrial personnel given to me by officials in other cities were 71 yuan in Canton, 63 to 65 in Peking, about 60 to 62 in Tientsin, 60 in Nanking and Wuhan, 58 in Soochow, and 50 to 55 in Wusih and Hangchow.

Table 9–3 in the next chapter presents wage and salary data for the thirty-eight enterprises surveyed in 1966.

The Ministry of Labor also plays a key role in interprovincial labor transfers; recruitment of personnel for important new factories; planning and allocation of high-talent manpower (often in consultation with the education ministries, the central Bureau of Scientific and Technological Cadres Administration, and the Bureau of Foreign Experts); training, particularly where new skills are involved; safety, labor insurance, and other personnel-welfare matters.

The Scientific and Technological Commission, set up in 1958, establishes state technical standards for products considered of major national importance and promotes technical standardization. The SPC also sets technical standards for some commodities. However, for the large majority of goods their technical standards are determined by the central industrial ministries, local authorities, and even enterprises themselves for products not considered of major importance and for various unstandardized items.

The Scientific and Technological Commission also plays an important role in giving general direction to, and coordinating, the scientific and technical work of the Academy of Sciences, educational institutions, and the research organizations under the central ministries. Some of this agency's other major functions include long-run technical development planning, the dissemination and application of technical knowledge, conducting basic experiments for new products and processes, and the promotion of international technical cooperation.

Other central agencies, such as the Ministry of Finance, the State Bank, the Ministry of Foreign Trade, and the National Export-Import corporations, which play important roles with regard to the industrial sector have already been discussed in Chapters 5 and 6.

Central Decision Making and Control

Even with the recentralization of many powers and the strengthening of the central industrial ministries at the end of the Great Leap period, provincial and municipal authorities have maintained considerable powers and independence. This is especially true in the more self-sufficient areas of the country. In relatively self-sufficient provinces and cities the local authorities seemed to have a good deal of autonomy in 1966 in production planning, target setting, establishing commodity prices, allocating resources among enterprises, and in generally determining many of the "rules of the game" for enterprises under their jurisdiction.

Central decision making and control at the provincial and autonomous-region level dealt chiefly with the following major spheres of activity at the time of my visit to China:

(1) Total investment funds allocated; major capital projects and new productive capacity; scale of capital investment, and a few strategic investment ratios.

(2) Output and transfer balances to and from provinces for strategic

commodities. Where the province is relatively self-sufficient the number of commodities subject to central planning, allocation, and control would typically be substantially less than if the reverse were true.

(3) The development and experimental manufacture of a limited number of new products considered to be of crucial national importance.
(4) Price fixing for major goods deemed of national importance, as discussed earlier.
(5) Volume of exports and imports to and from the province.
(6) Total profits and taxes remitted to the center or national level.
(7) Total wages and salaries; average numbers of workers, cadres, administrators, and technical personnel.
(8) Enrollment in higher educational institutions; allocation of higher graduates and certain other types of key personnel.
(9) Total of key personnel. Volume of rail freight, other forms of transportation, and other utility services under central control.

In general, in 1966 the regime seemed to be relying quite heavily on fairly broad financial controls at the provincial and municipal levels. It seemed that as long as external commitments were being met by individual provinces and cities they were being allowed considerable autonomy in industrial administration. Of course, a relatively sufficient area would typically have many fewer external commitments than a dependent one, in terms of resource and product needs, and the former would typically have much more autonomy than the latter.

The Provincial Level

China's provinces, and apparently her autonomous regions as well, are organized along lines similar to the national level. The ultimate source of provincial authority rests in reality with the Provincial Party Congress. On the government side, it rests with the Provincial People's Congress and, on a day-to-day basis, with the Provincial People's Council.

Instead of ministries involved in industrial administration at the provincial level, there are departments (or bureaus) directly in charge of industrial enterprises.

Of the thirty-eight industrial enterprises surveyed only three were under provincial departments: these were the Hangchow and Nanking machine-tool enterprises and Wuhan Paper. In those provinces, such as Hupeh and Hopeh, where a majority of industrial enterprises are located in one or more relatively self-sufficient industrial cities, there is typically a substantially smaller proportion of the province's factories under provincial industrial departments than municipal industrial bureaus. The number and types of provincial industrial departments depend primarily on the representation and locations of industrial firms within the province.

For example, Chekiang, with a population of roughly 30 million, is not a very industrialized province. It has two industrial departments in charge of enterprises: one for light industry and one for heavy industry. Even though there are only two provincial industrial departments, a sizable proportion of the factories in the province are under such departments because there are no major relatively self-sufficient urban industrial centers. Hangchow is one of the few important industrial cities in Chekiang Province, and it has several hundred factories under its municipal industrial bureaus. Of the twenty or so machine-tool and equipment plants in Hangchow, two are under the Provincial Heavy-Industry Department—including the Hangchow Machine Tool enterprise which I visited—one is under a central ministry, and the rest are under the Hangchow Machinery Industry Bureau.

Kiangsu, with a population of over 55 million, is a more industrialized province than Chekiang, and it has four industrial departments—Light and Chemical Industry; Machinery; Heavy Industry; and Textiles. In addition, there are some factories under the Hydraulics, Construction, and Communications departments of Kiangsu Province. There are also some important industrial cities in Kiangsu—including Wusih and Nanking, both of which I visited—which have hundreds of industrial enterprises under their jurisdiction.

Hupeh Province, with a population of about 35 million, is a major industrial region and has six provincial industrial departments: First Light Industry; Second Light Industry; Electrical Industry; Fuel; Chemical; and Heavy Industry and Machinery. However, because there are several major industrial centers in Hupeh, a substantially larger proportion of factories are under the direct control of municipal, rather than provincial, authorities. As noted earlier, this province has ten paper mills, only three of which are under provincial control, with the other seven being under municipal authorities. Only the three largest paper mills are under provincial control, and all three of them produce large quantities of newsprint, which is a centrally priced and allocated commodity. Wuhan, Kiangsu's leading industrial center, has six municipal industrial bureaus, and a large majority of Wuhan's enterprises are under municipal control.

Tientsin, the leading industrial center in Hopeh Province (population over 50 million), has more industrial enterprises under its jurisdiction than the industrial departments at the provincial level. The great majority of industrial enterprises in Hopeh Province that are not in Tientsin, with the exception of those under central ministries, are under provincial industrial departments. I was told by high-level municipal authorities in Tientsin that roughly 40 percent of the value of Tientsin's industrial output is subject to local planning, allocation, and price setting, that about the same proportion is centrally determined, and that only about 20 percent is under the direct control of provincial authorities.

In Kwangtung Province (population roughly 40 to 45 million) most factories employing over 1,000 people which are not under central ministries are under provincial industrial departments. However, most plants in Canton, the province's largest city, are under municipal control. Only three enterprises are under central ministries. Kwangtung's steel mill is under provincial control.

Some provincial industrial departments apparently have corporations under them which are directly in charge of factories, although I personally did not come across any corporations at this level. I was told by officials in Nanking that there were provincial-level corporations in Kiangsu for drugs, timber, textiles, and motor vehicles and accessories. There are also a few similar types of corporations, plus a few more, under Nanking's municipal industrial bureaus.

Where a given provincial industrial department has a fairly wide range of diverse factories under its control, there are typically operating line departments, or corporations, in charge of enterprises of a certain type in terms of products produced, technology, production processes, and so on. Provincial industrial departments generally have the same basic type of administrative organization as central industrial ministries, municipal industrial bureaus, industrial corporations, and individual enterprises. There are subdepartments or sections for planning, production, technical affairs, supply and sales, finance and accounting, labor and wages, and so forth.

It is common for central industrial ministries to exert functional authority in various spheres over industrial enterprises which are subordinate to provincial industrial departments. This was the case at the Hangchow and Nanking machine-tool firms, as well as Wuhan's Han Yang Paper Mill. However, it is apparently less common for provincial industrial departments to exert direct authority or control over enterprises under the jurisdiction of municipal authorities, although they do so in certain spheres in some cases.

In addition to departments in charge of factories at the provincial level, there is also a wide variety of other departments, bureaus, commissions, and committees similar to those at the national level which are involved in industrial and general economic affairs. For example, Kiangsu Province has about forty departments, bureaus, and other agencies, about half of which are concerned with the industrial sector in a direct and significant way. Each province typically has a planning commission, a price committee, and bureaus or departments of labor, statistics, finance, the supply of materials, commerce, foreign trade, agriculture, construction, transportation and communications, and so forth. Some also have an economic commission. In addition, provinces have such traditional-type agencies as education, health, culture, and the like.

Provincial-level agencies generally perform the same basic functions and have similar types of relationships with industrial organizations, chiefly under provincial jurisdiction, as the central agencies having similar names. The central agencies exert functional authority and control in various spheres over their provincial counterparts, which, in turn, also extend functional authority and control over their municipal counterparts.

There is also a network of commodity supply and sales organs at the provincial level, some of which have a direct relationship with similar kinds of central organs, others with municipal organs, and still others which are relatively self-contained. Some of these organs are corporations or companies, others are departments or bureaus, and still others are merely offices or depots. In general, I did not learn much about this sphere of Chinese economic organization, but it does seem like a very complex and rather confusing setup. For example, the Han Yang Paper Mill in Wuhan obtains its basic raw materials, dragon-beard grass and wood reeds, from the Hupeh Provincial Supply and Marketing Agricultural Organization which, in turn, gets these materials directly from communes. While this organization has no central relationship with regard to the supply or distribution of wood reeds or dragon-beard grass, it does have such a relationship for various other commodities which it deals with.

The Kwangtung Provincial Marketing and Supply Department arranges the shipment of various supplies as well as sales and transportation details for the Canton Chemical Fertilizer enterprise which is directly under the Chemical Industry Ministry in Peking. This department is related in some way to a central marketing and supply organization under the state council, as well as with some municipal and county level organizations. It has a number of sub-departments which handle different types of commodities.

The Municipal Level

China's cities are organized along similar lines as her provinces. The ultimate source of municipal authority in reality rests with the Municipal Party Congress. On the government side, it rests with the Municipal People's Congress and, on a day-to-day basis, with the Municipal People's Council.

Under the Municipal People's Council are industrial bureaus and corporations directly in charge of factories, plus the other types of bureaus,

CHART 8–4
INDUSTRIAL ORGANIZATION IN THE CITY OF WUSIH
(Mid-1966)

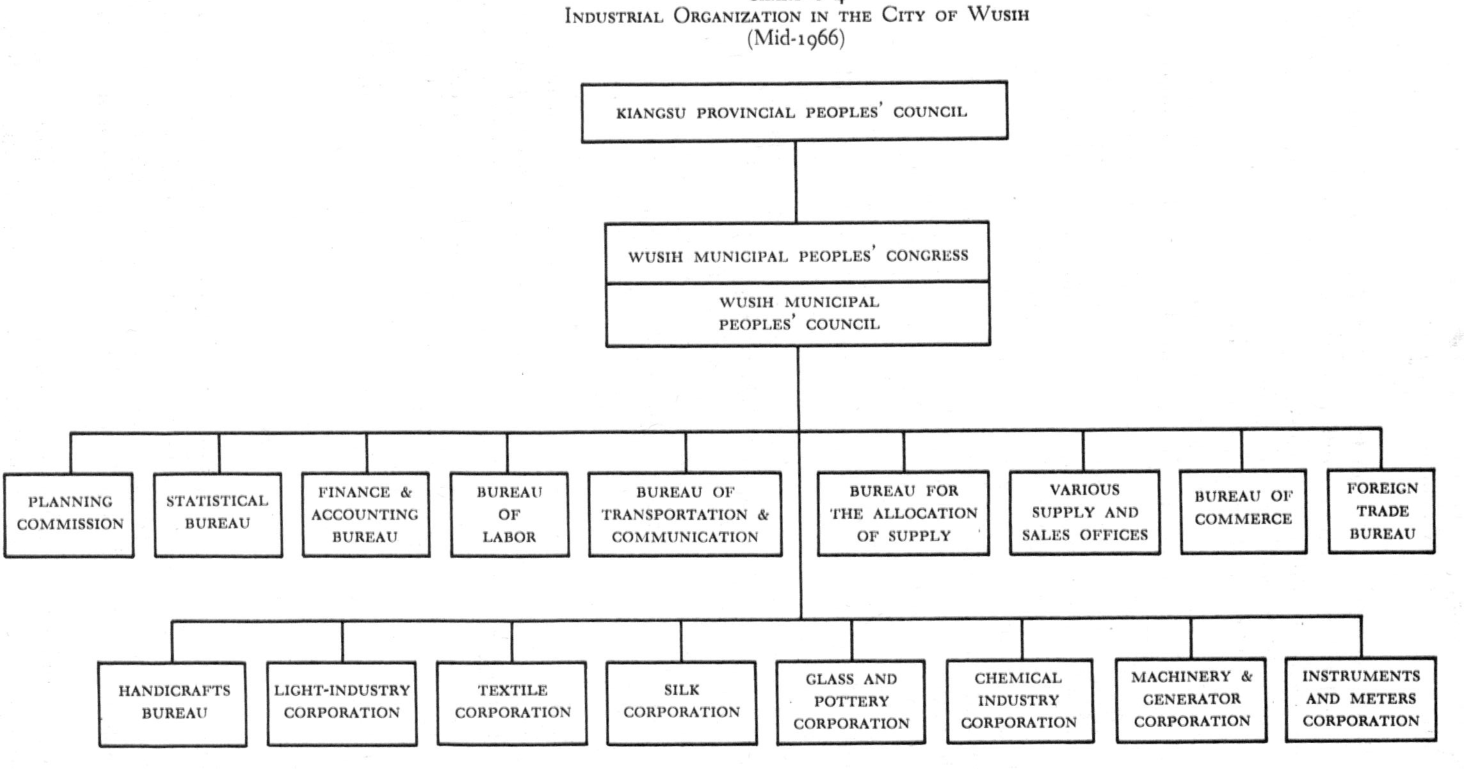

organs, and agencies involved in industrial and general economic affairs found at the provincial and national levels. Chart 8–4, which outlines the industrial setup in the city of Wusih, indicates the general nature of these other types of municipal-level administrative units. The industrial hierarchy per se is somewhat unusual in Wusih, as compared with other Chinese cities that I visited. Wusih underwent an industrial reorganization a few years ago (more will be said about this shortly). Wusih's Municipal Planning Commission performs basic functions similar to those performed by provincial planning commissions, the State Planning Commission at the national level, as well as other municipal planning commissions. Wusih's Planning Commission was employing about fifteen people in 1966, and Tientsin's more than forty.

Peking and Shanghai are classified as "special municipalities" and have provincial status. Top-level party and government organs in these two cities are directly subordinate to the center, or national level. These two cities enjoy special status because they are the largest and most important in the nation. In the 1950's Tientsin, as well as a number of other cities, enjoyed similar status, but they were all placed under provincial jurisdiction by the late 1950's.

Industrial enterprises under municipal jurisdiction come under municipal industrial bureaus or municipal industrial corporations which are usually under the bureaus. These bureaus report directly to the Municipal People's Council. In some instances—most notably in Wusih, which recently embarked on an experimental industrial reorganization—municipal-level industrial corporations are directly under the Municipal People's Council, rather than industrial bureaus.

Of the thirty-eight industrial enterprises that I surveyed, twenty were under the jurisdiction of municipal authorities. Of these twenty, only six were directly under municipal industrial bureaus, while the other fourteen were under municipal-level industrial corporations, most of which were, in turn, under municipal bureaus. In a few cases, industrial corporations that are familiar to me reported directly to a municipal people's council.

It seems that it is more common for factories under municipal handicrafts-industry bureaus to report directly to the bureau, rather than to a corporation which, in turn, is under the bureau, than for factories under other types of industrial bureaus. Handicrafts-industry bureaus are typically in charge of a wide variety of labor-intensive and mostly relatively small enterprises which function quite autonomously once the key sections of their plans are approved. Municipal industrial corporations are generally in charge of relatively homogeneous enterprises. Moreover, corporations are involved in operating concrete management and control with regard to their subordinate factories, whereas industrial bureaus typically deal primarily with broad planning, particularly resources and output balancing, and general coordination. Industrial corporations are considered to be managerial agencies in China, while industrial bureaus are seen as balancing and general administrative organs.

Wusih's Handicrafts Bureau was directly in charge of eighty-two labor-intensive factories, the great majority of which employed less than 400 people. There was great diversity in the products produced by these factories—clothing, screws, tubes, locks, arts-and-crafts products, leather goods, containers, pipes, certain types of furniture and appliances, and other items. The Wusih Red Flag Machinery Plant, which I visited, was the only machinery or equipment enterprise under this bureau, because of its highly labor-intensive operations. The other thirty or so machinery plants under municipal jurisdiction in Wusih were under the Wusih Machinery Corporation.

Peking's Handicrafts Industry Bureau had several hundred enterprises producing a wide range of products directly under it. One of the largest was Peking Clothing—which I visited—with an employment of 1,700. This clothing firm was not really that highly labor-intensive. Fu Chang Clothing enterprise in Hangchow was under that city's handicrafts bureau.

Tientsin's North Lake Instrument enterprise—a highly labor-intensive plant—was directly under the city's Second Light Industry Bureau. Tientsin did not have a handicrafts industry bureau, however. The other two enterprises surveyed that were directly subordinate to municipal bureaus were Shanghai Truck and Soochow Cement Products. The former was under the Shanghai Bureau of Transportation and Communications, and the latter was under the Soochow Construction Bureau. Neither of these two types of bureaus are industrial bureaus in the conventional sense, although it is quite common for them to have a small number of factories under their jurisdiction.

The types of industrial bureaus and corporations found in a given city is generally determined largely by the number, types, and diversity of industrial enterprises under municipal control. Shanghai, with a population of more than ten million, is China's leading industrial center with over 3,000 factories and 1.2 million industrial employees. In this city there are about twenty industrial bureaus corresponding to the twenty or so central industrial ministries in Peking. There are several dozen industrial corporations under Shanghai's industrial bureaus. The great majority of Shanghai's factories are directly subordinate to these corporations; relatively few report directly to the industrial bureaus. An exception which I came across was the Shanghai Bureau of Metallurgy which had seven large plants directly under it, plus an industrial corporation which was directly in charge of several dozen—mostly quite small—factories.

In Peking there are a dozen or so industrial bureaus, and a greater number of industrial corporations.

Wuhan, which is really three adjoining cities and related districts with a combined population of roughly 8 million—is one of China's leading inland industrial centers with an industrial labor force of nearly 300,000. This municipality had eight industrial bureaus in 1966: (1) First Light Industry; (2) Second Light Industry; (3) Textile; (4) Chemical; (5) Electrical; (6) Machinery and Mechanical; (7) Heavy Industry; and (8) Handicrafts. There was a larger number of industrial corporations directly in charge of factories under these municipal bureaus. Some of these corporations were (a) Drugs; (b) Metallurgical Materials; (c) Equipment and Tools; (d) Chemical Raw Materials; and (e) Chemical and Electrical Instruments.

Nanking, with a population of 1.6 million, has approximately 300 industrial enterprises and an industrial labor force of about 235,000. In 1966 this city had industrial bureaus for heavy industry, light industry and chemicals, textiles, and handicrafts. Under these bureaus there were the following corporations, plus a few more: (a) Drugs; (b) Textiles; (c) Telecommunications and Instruments; (d) local processed food products; (e) Motor Vehicle Parts and Accessories; (f) cultural goods. In total, Nanking has about 37 municipal bureaus and agencies of all types.

Tientsin had the following seven industrial bureaus: (1) First Light Industry; (2) Second Light Industry; (3) Machinery; (4) Iron and Steel; (5) Nonferrous Metallurgy; (6) Chemical; (7) Textiles. There were well over a dozen industrial corporations under these bureaus. None of Tientsin's industrial corporations were directly under the Municipal People's Council; they all reported to industrial bureaus.

Wusih, with a population of roughly 650,000, is often referred to as "little Shanghai" in China because it is so industrialized for a city of its size. It had 417 factories in 1966, with 50 of them employing over 500 people, and all of them employing at least around 100. In total, about 130,000 people—or about 20 percent of the city's population—were employed in Wusih's industrial sector.

Wusih is a particularly interesting city since it undertook an experimental industrial reorganization in the latter half of 1965. Prior to this reorganization, the formal chain of command in Wusih's overall industrial sector ran from the Municipal People's Council to the industrial bureaus, to industrial corporations, and finally to individual enterprises. There were two industrial corporations—textiles and silk—reporting directly to the Municipal People's Council and an organizational level would be eliminated. It was felt that this would substantially reduce bureaucracy, provide for better and faster decisions in light of local conditions, improve communication and control, release a sizable number of high-talent people employed in the industrial bureaus for employment in key jobs at the enterprise level, and lead to various other improvements.

This proposed reorganization was formally approved by top level provincial government and party authorities in Kiangsu province in 1965, and it was complemented shortly thereafter. Appropriate central authorities in Peking were informed about this decision, and have apparently been highly interested in the results of the reorganization. If they turn out to be favorable the Wusih experiment may be extended not only to other cities in Kiangsu province, but to municipalities in other provinces as well. In fact, I was told in Peking—before I went to Wusih—that the Peking Chemical Industry Bureau had been transformed into a corporation in early 1966. Whether this had anything to do with the Wusih experiment, I do not know.

Chart 8–4 indicates the industrial organization of Wusih as of mid-1966, after the reorganization had been implemented. The functions of the former Heavy Industry Bureau were taken over by two industrial corporations; Machinery and Generator and Instruments and Meters. The functions of the former Light Industry Bureau were taken over by three corporations; Chemical, Light Industry, and Glass and Pottery. The Textile and Silk Industry corporations remained basically intact, and continued to report directly to the Municipal People's Council.

The Handicrafts Industry Bureau was not abolished. I was told that this was the case since a wide variety of highly labor-intensive, mostly small factories, have been under this bureau, and they function quite autonomously. Given the diversity and range of enterprises under the Wusih Handicrafts Bureau, as well as the fact that most of them operate with a relatively high degree of autonomy once their plans and resource allocations are approved by this bureau, it was decided not to abolish this bureau in Wusih.

Wusih officials whom I interviewed seemed to be sincere in their claim that industry is generally functioning more efficiently under the new organizational setup. In addition, several dozen high-talent personnel—including university and semiprofessional graduates—have been transferred from the defunct bureaus to important jobs at industrial enterprises.

The city of Soochow, which is also in Kiangsu province, was considering a reorganization of industry along the lines of the Wusih experiment when I visited there. Soochow industrial officials admitted that their organizational setup was too bureaucratic and complex. Though this city is not nearly as industrialized as nearby Wusih, it had the following seven industrial bureaus in 1966: (1) Chemical; (2) Light Industry; (3) Heavy Industry; (4) Machinery; (5) Textiles; (6) Handicrafts; (7) Crafts and Fine Arts. There were also a number of factories under the Municipal Construction Bureau. Under the industrial bureaus there were about six or seven industrial corporations.

The basic administrative organization of municipal industrial bureaus resembles that of provincial industrial departments, central industrial ministries, industrial corporations, and individual industrial enterprises. A typical municipal industrial bureau is headed by a director who has a number of vice directors reporting to him. The heads of the industrial corporations and/or individual factories directly under the bureau report to the bureau's director or his key line deputies. It seems that light industry bureaus are likely to have more industrial corporations under them than other types of bureaus, because of the wide range of products typically produced by plants under their overall jurisdiction. The bureau also has departments or sections for planning, production, technical affairs, capital construction, supply and sales, finance and accounting, labor and wages, and so forth.

Chart 8–5 presents the basic organization structure of the Tientsin First Light Industry Bureau. In 1966 there were 8 industrial corporations, 140 industrial enterprises, and 56,000 people under the overall jurisdiction of this bureau. The bureau itself employed about 115 people. All of the 140 enterprises were directly under industrial corporations. The largest enterprise employed several thousand people, and the smallest slightly less than 100. The largest corporation employed about 70 people in its offices and the smallest about 40. Most of the corporations employed 50 to 60 people. I met with officials of the Daily Usage Industrial Corporation which is under this bureau, and which was in charge of the Tientsin Watch factory which I visited. The products that fall under the direct jurisdiction of this corporation are almost entirely all planned, allocated, and distributed locally in Tientsin. The Daily Usage Corporation was organized basically like the bureau itself, as were apparently all of the bureau's corporations.

I was told that the largest number of industrial corporations in Tientsin were under the First Light-Industry Bureau. (This was also true of Shanghai's First Light-Industry Bureau which had about fifteen corporations under it.) This is not surprising, considering the wide range of products produced by the factories under its overall control. The products include watches, perfume, cosmetics, decorations, films, chemical powders, glass, paper and cellophane, bicycles, small tools, enamelware, pots and pans, pens and pencils, stationery, office supplies, sugar products, wines, books, and musical instruments. I was told that about 1,400 new products—not counting sizes or patterns—were produced for the first time in 1965 by the plants under this bureau.

The technical department, which had fifteen people, was the largest administrative department at Tientsin's First Light-Industry Bureau. This department deals with such matters as research, technical improvement, quality control, standards and measures, and the dissemination of information. The supply and sales department employed about seven or eight people, the planning department about the same number, and finance and accounting a few more.

CHART 8–5
ORGANIZATION OF THE TIENTSIN FIRST LIGHT-INDUSTRY BUREAU
(May 1966)

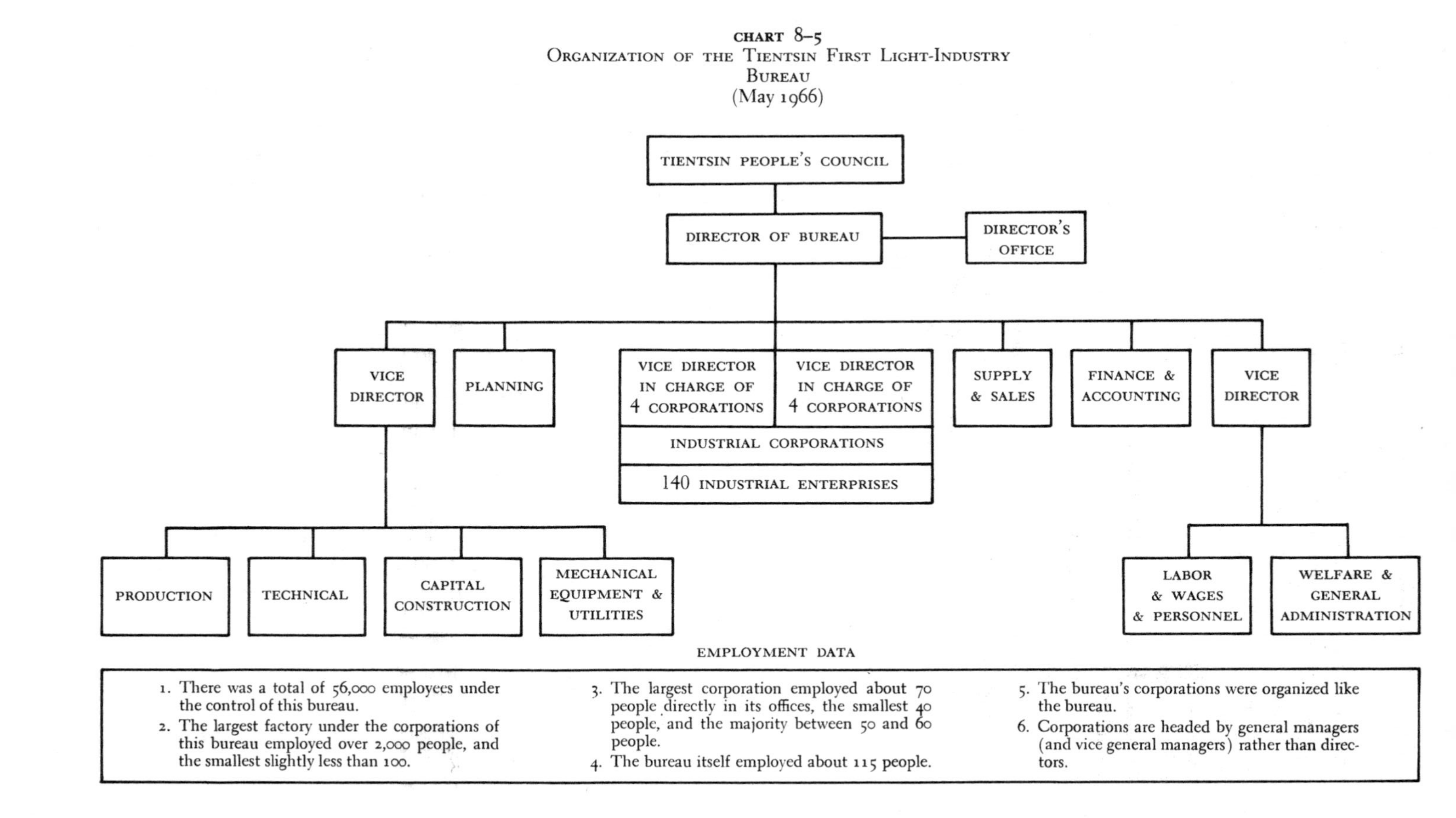

EMPLOYMENT DATA

1. There was a total of 56,000 employees under the control of this bureau.
2. The largest factory under the corporations of this bureau employed over 2,000 people, and the smallest slightly less than 100.
3. The largest corporation employed about 70 people directly in its offices, the smallest 40 people, and the majority between 50 and 60 people.
4. The bureau itself employed about 115 people.
5. The bureau's corporations were organized like the bureau.
6. Corporations are headed by general managers (and vice general managers) rather than directors.

I was told by officials of the Tientsin First Light-Industry Bureau that the bureau has five basic tasks:

(1) Politics (that is, running industry along the lines of Mao's Thought)
(2) Organizing, compiling, and balancing annual plans
(3) Technical revolution and scientific research
(4) General coordination including investigation, inspection, and control work
(5) Researching and improving the management of its industrial corporations and enterprises.

Concrete management—that is, day-to-day operations and control—is the responsibility of the industrial corporations and the individual enterprises.

The Tientsin Municipal Planning Commission, acting for the Tientsin People's Council, approves the key targets and resource limits annually for this bureau, as well as the other industrial bureaus in Tientsin. More than half of the commodities produced and consumed by the factories of the First Light-Industry Bureau in 1965–66 fell within the jurisdiction of municipal-level planning, allocation, and price setting. About 30 to 40 percent of such commodities were under the direct control of the bureau itself and its corporations and factories. The balance was subject to central or provincial-level approval, mainly the former.

The bureau also required higher approval—primarily from the Municipal Planning Commission—for the following parts of its annual plan: total capital-investment allocation and various major capital projects; total employment and payroll, and the allocation of certain types of high-talent manpower; a number of technical quality standards; total costs and operating expenses; total profits; and a small number of targets pertaining to public utility and transportation services, as well as new product development.

In turn, similar types of annual resource-allocation limits and operating targets were approved by the First Light-Industry Bureau for its industrial corporations. The targets and resource allocations approved for the corporations are substantially more aggregate, less detailed, and smaller in number than those approved by the corporations for individual enterprises. Moreover, it is common for the corporations to require formal approval of the quarterly—and in some cases the monthly—plans of their industrial enterprises. This is usually not true for the plans of the corporations or those of the bureau; they are typically subject to higher formal approval only on an annual basis.

The director and vice directors of the Tientsin First Light-Industry Bureau are appointed by the Municipal People's Council—no doubt with the approval of top-level municipal party authorities. The First Light-Industry Ministry in Peking, as well as top-level provincial authorities, are consulted on such appointments, but apparently they act essentially in an advisory capacity. The top managers of this bureau's corporations are nominated by the bureau, but formal approval for their appointment comes from the Municipal People's Council. In turn, the directors and vice directors of the individual enterprises under the corporations are nominated by the corporations, but formal approval comes from the bureau itself.

Industrial Corporations

Chinese planners and industrial officials whom I interviewed admitted that there are no uniform criteria applied on a widespread scale with regard to the formation of industrial or commercial corporations, or whether a given enterprise or group of factories should be placed under a corporation. It seems that this sphere of Chinese industrial organization is still in a general state of experimentation. Many of Red China's present-day corporations—particularly those in charge of textile and other light-industry plants, as well as commercial corporations—have their origins in corporate structures (mostly involving private enterprise) which existed prior to the Communist takeover and nationalization of business and industry.

Chinese corporations are judicial entities. They can enter into contractual agreements, sue and be sued, have their own bank accounts, and work on a profit-and-loss basis—though profits are not necessarily essential to survival. Generally industrial corporations are in charge of a number of relatively similar types (in terms of branch of industry and products produced) of enterprises or factories. However, there are a few integrated corporations, such as Wuhan and Anshan Iron and Steel, which are in charge of a pretty wide variety of factories contributing to the production of some end product such as steel.

As noted earlier, industrial corporations have the same type of basic departmentalization as ministries, industrial bureaus, and industrial enterprises. The corporation is, however, usually headed by a general manager, rather than a director, who typically has one or more vice general managers reporting to him. The directors of industrial enterprises under corporations typically report to the top management of the corporation.

The number of people employed within the dozen or so industrial corporations for which I obtained such data—excluding Wuhan Iron and Steel (to be discussed shortly)—ranged from a minimum of about 25 to a maximum of nearly 200. The smallest number of industrial enterprises or factories under a corporation that I know about was 7, and the largest number was more than 30. The number of factories under each of the eight corporations under Tientsin First Light-Industry Bureau ranged from a minimum of 9 to a maximum of 26. The number of industrial enterprises under some of the other corporations for which I obtained such information was as follows in 1966. The Peking Chemical Industry Corporation was in charge of 9 factories—the 6 Peking chemical enterprises, Peking Coke and Chemical, an oil refinery, and a rubber plant. The Peking Metallurgical Corporation was in charge of 20 factories. Under the Shanghai Daily Usage Industrial Corporation there were about 40 enterprises, including 3 battery plants, and others producing such commodities as soap, toiletries, cosmetics, and decorations. The Shanghai Machine-Tool Corporation had 30 plants under it. The Shanghai branch of the All China Drug Corporation had about 50 plants under it, and this corporation had several hundred factories under its overall jurisdiction throughout the country. The Wusih Machinery Corporation was in charge of about 30 factories, Wusih Textile Corporation 30, and Wusih Silk Industry Corporation 7. There were 30 enterprises under the Shanghai Cotton Textile Industry Corporation.

The Peking Textile Industry Corporation was in charge of 3 woolen mills, two of which I visited, and dozens of cotton mills, one of which I visited. This textile corporation is unique, although its actual place in the industrial hierarchy was never made very clear to me. Toward the end of the 1950's China's textile industry underwent a major decentralization. At the time apparently all textile corporations and factories under the central textile ministry were placed under provincial and municipal jurisdiction. The Peking Textile Industry Corporation was placed under Peking municipal authorities. However, a few years ago this corporation was once again placed under the Ministry of Textile Industry, but also remained under municipal control for various matters. It seems that the ministry plays the major and direct role with regard to the formulation of this corporation's production plan, supply and capital allocations, technical and new product development, broad control, allocation and appointment of key personnel, and certain other matters. The ministry has a department or division under a deputy minister which deals with the wool sector and has another for the cotton sector. The Peking Textile Corporation is under municipal jurisdiction for labor transfers within the city, most recruitment, welfare, certain types of supply and sales contracts, and a wide range of mostly relatively routine matters.

I am not sure why this textile corporation has a more direct and closer relationship with the textile ministry than other Chinese industrial corporations or enterprises. One reason may be that the ministry may want to maintain a direct relationship with at least some portion of the nation's textile firms so that it can be in a better position to formulate policies and decisions, and exert functional authority more effectively throughout this sector. Since the ministry and this corporation are both located in Peking, and since Peking is a major textile center, the Peking Textile Corporation would be a logical choice for central control. In addition, several of the factories under this corporation—including those that I surveyed—have become involved in the development and production of new products (for example, rayon, nylon, vinyl), as well as the introduction of new technology and processes on a substantial scale. Furthermore, much of the output of many of this corporation's factories is exported, and several of the mills use sizable quantities of imported materials and equipment.

Chart 8–6 outlines the organization structure of the Wuhan Iron and Steel Corporation. The corporation is headed by a general manager with three vice or deputy general managers reporting to him, There is a deputy general manager in charge of technical matters and operations (which includes the eighteen factories), mines, and welfare and general administration, respectively. It is likely that the staff assistants under the vice general manager, who is in charge of the factories, actually function in a line capacity in certain areas. If not, this manager's span of control is likely to be seriously overburdened, given the large number of factories and departments under him.

The head office of this corporation was reorganized in 1964. Prior to this reorganization there were ten vice general managers, and about twice as many departments, sections, and offices. At that time about 20 percent of the corporation's employees were employed in corporate-level administration and related clerical work. At the time of my visit in 1966 this proportion had been cut to 13 or 14 percent. However, the ratio of direct to indirect production personnel was still only around one to one in 1966.

In 1966, total employment of the entire Wuhan Iron and Steel Corporation stood at 35,000. About 5,000 employees were engaged in welfare and service work, and another 5,000 were employed in the six mines. There were 2,300 technicians and engineers, of which 800 were engineers, and approximately 7,000 administrative cadres at all levels. Before the 1964 reorganization there were over 8,000 administrative cadres.

Under the corporation's eighteen industrial enterprises or factories there was a total of 101 workshops. Each enterprise was headed by a director who had two to four vice directors under him. Most of the factories also had their own chief engineer and, in several cases, deputy chief engineers as well. The number of administrative sections or departments at the enterprise level ranged from four to ten. They were basically similar in nature to the departments found at other enterprises, as well as the head office of this corporation.

The Ministry of Metallurgical Industry approves the annual output targets, supply allocations of all key commodities, as well as aggregate capital

CHART 8–6
WUHAN IRON AND STEEL CORPORATION
(Mid-1966)

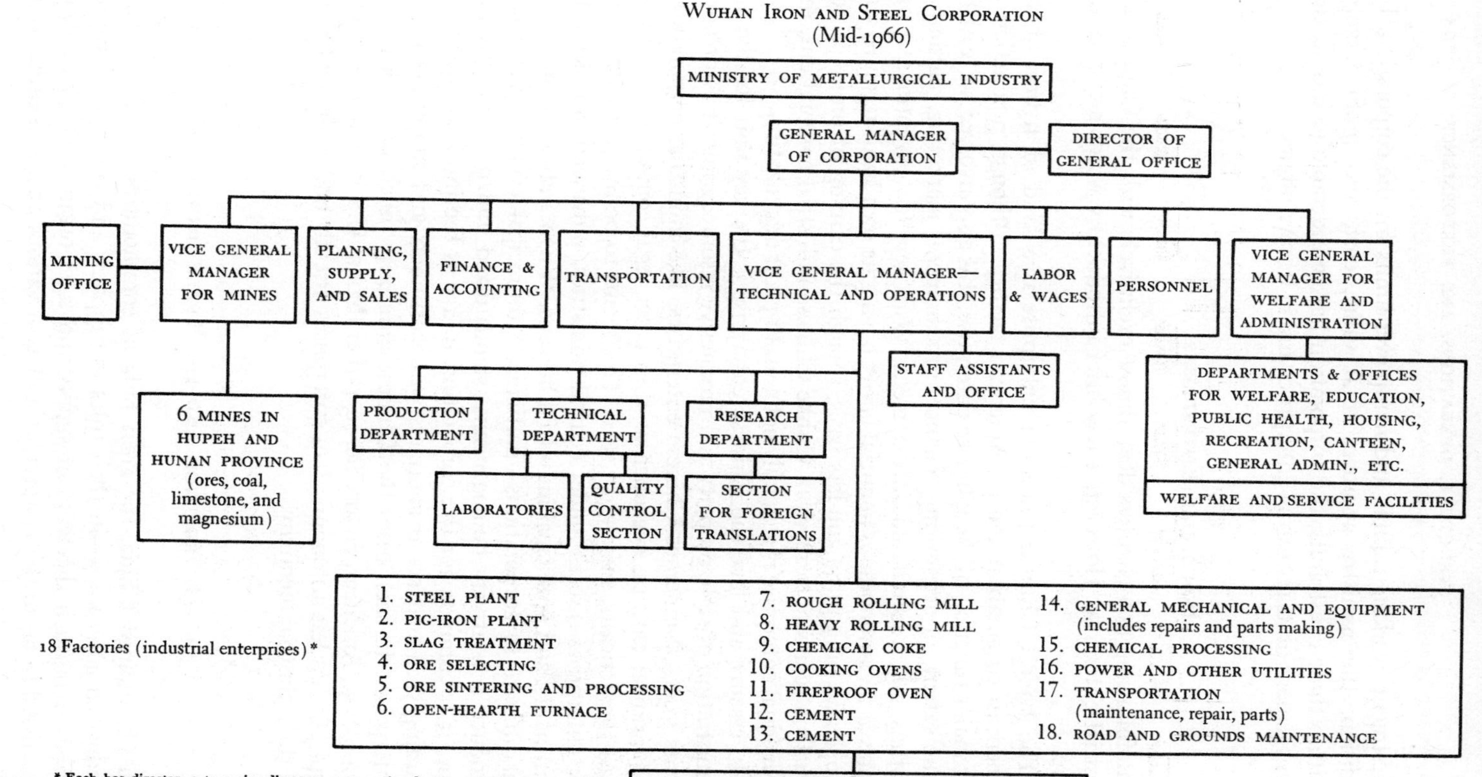

* Each has director, 2 to 4 vice directors, 4–10 major depts. or sections, 3–9 workshops.

investment, working capital, and manpower limits for the corporation. In addition, the ministry approves total value, cost, and profit targets. Within these constraints, the corporation has considerable leeway in the management of its industrial enterprises and in its own affairs.

Industrial Enterprises

The following two chapters deal almost exclusively with the Chinese industrial enterprise. However, a few brief introductory words are in order here.

The typical Chinese industrial enterprise is a kind of hybrid of an American corporation and an American factory. Although production is the major function of the Chinese enterprise, it is also involved, at least to some extent, in accounting, finance, procurement, marketing, personnel matters, and research and development. With very few exceptions, it operates as an autonomous financial entity having its own bank account; and it operates on a profit-and-loss basis, though the earning of profits is not usually a requisite to survival. Unlike Chinese industrial corporations, the individual enterprise is generally not a multi-plant organization.

In essence and law, the Chinese enterprise is the key unit for the administration of state property and productive resources, and it owns none of its assets. Numerous Chinese enterprises, like industrial corporations, are juridical entities, inasmuch as they enter legal contracts and can, at least theoretically, sue and be sued. This seems to be the case most often for enterprises directly under central ministries, provincial industrial departments, and municipal industrial bureaus. Where industrial enterprises subordinate to corporations—particularly municipal-level corporations—produce a relatively homogeneous, standardized and/or stable product line, it is common for the corporation to act as the juridical entity—regarding such matters as contracts with customers and suppliers—for its enterprises. In such cases the Chinese enterprise much more closely resembles an American factory per se, rather than a U.S. corporation, and it typically has less autonomy than enterprises directly under different levels of the industrial hierarchy.

Distribution and the Trade Sector

In Communist China, the great bulk of commodities that flow among industrial enterprises—in their roles as suppliers and customers—are distributed through the types of supply and sales organs and relationships discussed so far in this chapter, as well as at various points in earlier chapters. The distribution setup for supplying factories is sometimes referred to as the "material- and technical-supply" network in China, and also in the Soviet Union. Within this network, there are supply and sales organs under the State Planning Commission, the Ministry for the Supply of Materials, and at each level of the industrial hierarchy. In many cases, industrial enterprises negotiate directly with each other in their roles as suppliers and buyers.

There are a number of other distribution networks which have relationships with the industrial sector in China. The distribution, and allocation, of some types of commodities flowing between industrial enterprises and agricultural communes are handled by agricultural supply and marketing organs at various levels of the agricultural hierarchy, that is, the Ministry of Agriculture at the center, the provincial and local agricultural organizations, and the communes themselves. Mention has been made of a few specific agricultural supply and marketing organizations earlier in this chapter.

In many cases where factories use imported commodities and/or produce goods which are exported, foreign-trade organizations are involved in their supply and distribution. At the central level there is the Ministry of Foreign Trade and about a dozen national export-import corporations, as discussed in Chapter 5. At the provincial and municipal levels there are foreign-trade bureaus and branches of these state export and import corporations.

In addition to the above distribution networks, there is the domestic-trade network which encompasses both intermediary wholesale organizations and retail stores. The great bulk of manufactured and processed consumer goods are distributed to end users and the public through this network. The Ministry of Food and its related organs are involved in the distribution of food products. Chapter 11 deals with domestic trade and the retail sector in China, but a few brief comments are in order here.

The domestic-trade distribution network extends from the Ministry of Commerce at the center, down through the provincial, municipal, and district bureaus of commerce. Under each level there are commercial corporations, wholesaling stations, and various other types of wholesaling and marketing organs. Most of these organizations handle a specific product line or group of commodities. In fact, it is very common for commercial corporations to have similar names and to deal with the same product lines as the industrial corporations in the same geographic area. Commercial organizations are often under the control of more than one level with regard to their plans and operations. For example, a municipal commercial corporation may be under the control of the municipal bureau of commerce for various matters, and under the Ministry of Commerce or one of its sub-organs for other affairs—for instance, the planning and allocation of commodities. Retail outlets are generally under municipal jurisdiction, although some big department stores are subject to central and/or provincial control in connection with such things as the allocation of certain major commodities—cotton cloth, for example.

Wholesale trade organizations serve as the link between producer enterprises and retail outlets, and perform distributive and warehousing functions. They are also responsible for analyzing and transmitting consumer demand—regarding types, varieties, styles, designs, colors, and sizes of products—to producers. Retail outlets are also involved in such activities, and in some cases they work out sales orders directly with the factories.

In general, the relationship between the domestic-trade sector and the industrial sector primarily involves product-mix decisions. The trade sector plays a major role in determining the detailed product mixes of industrial enterprises producing consumer goods, but it usually has little, if anything, to do with the setting of aggregate output targets or with the allocation of resources to industrial enterprises. While the trade sector is primarily concerned with the distribution of goods from the factories to the retail outlets and the public, it does also supply factories (mainly small ones) with various kinds of commodities, such as lubricants, small tools and hardware items, cloth and paper materials, paint, brooms, rope, and minor chemicals. For more important commodities the factory may be specifically allocated the goods supplied by the trade sector in its plan. In other cases, the factory may independently procure the needed items.

Industrial Planning

Industrial and general economic planning in Communist China has been discussed at earlier points in this book. However, some additional details may be of interest to many readers.

The annual national plan is the basic operational document for China's overall industrial sector and the economy in general. It is the basis for actual central resource allocations, related output-supply relationships, and the major contracts which express them. This plan is related to longer-range plans—when they exist—only in the sense of being a practical expression of the same basic economic objectives and policies. But even economic goals and policies may be amended during the course of a given five-year or other long-term plan.

Planning Methodology

The starting point for all Chinese state planning is the formulation of essentially political directives by top party and government authorities indicating their key priorities and preferences with respect to national economic activity—for example, the relative emphasis on the development of heavy and light industry, defense, agriculture. These directives are translated into concrete operating terms by the State Planning Commission and other appropriate central organs. The planning process takes as its starting point an achievement balanced for the entire economy and each of its major sectors, as well as tentative growth rate goals.

The decisions on "what to produce" are essentially political decisions. Capital formation, through the expansion of heavy industry, and defense production have typically been pushed hard under the Communist regime. In recent years, however, greater deference has been given to consumer goods and the agricultural sector. The decisions on what is to be produced, and how much of each item, are worked out according to the aims of the plan, available resources, and the need for feasible balance and integration of interdependent production processes.

With regard to decisions on "for whom to produce" the Chinese economy still works to a considerable degree for the state and the future. The Chinese leaders can, and do, push economic growth by enforcing a restriction in consumption, which is no doubt contrary to the wishes of a large portion of the consuming public.

The question "how to produce" in the industrial sector is answered almost entirely by resource allocations rather than by market possibilities. To date it seems that the problem of how to produce most economically cannot be fully or properly answered without a competitive price system. Prices set by the Chinese planners typically have little or no guiding function in terms of economic efficiency. Since factors of production are substitutable within limits, the National Production Program must be drawn up, if it is to be workable, with reference to the given technical possibilities. By trial and error a modicum of technical integration evolves. However, gradual achievement of a workable technical integration is not sufficient if one wants to make the "best" economic use of the factors of production. At best, technological integration may guarantee that the system will function without breakdown and that resources will be fully utilized, but it does not provide for the best combination of factors in an economic sense.

The whole process of Chinese—and Soviet—economic planning relies heavily on "planning by material balances." It involves a simplified and rather crude form of input-output procedure, carried on largely in physical terms. A "balance" in physical terms presents the current, or intended, relations between certain supplies and their allocation for specific commodities or groups of commodities. The total bill of goods to be produced during a given planned year is determined centrally, although the breadth and detail prescribed for different classes of commodities vary at this level, and much of the planning work and details are performed at lower levels.

To secure this bill of goods the central planners allocate major supplies primarily in physical terms by establishing product requirements on the basis of technical coefficients (production functions), and by using physical balances to equate sources and uses of intermediate and final products. Because of the great multiplicity of products produced even in the Chinese economy, goods are grouped into certain conventional classifications by using technical conversion factors, such as steel content, horsepower, square meters of cotton cloth, and other physical common denominators. The entire plan is built around national output targets and the expansion of capacity needed for major industrial sectors.

Fixing physical-output targets for major commodities may be crude. but it does have substantial validity because the most common combinations are reducible, as in chemistry, to a relatively small group of elements (such as iron, coal, steel, rolled metals, fuels, electricity, various fabrics, rubber, timber, leather, basic chemicals, and the principal nonferrous metals). The physical balancing process is based on technical coefficients linking various factor inputs to various commodity outputs (for example, W tons of coal to produce X tons of steel; Y tons of steel to produce Z number of lathes). These coefficients are derived by crudely aggregating and averaging past input-output relationships at producer enterprises, with adjustments often made for anticipated improvements. The central allocation of supplies depends on the input schedules for each industry, given its output targets. Resource allocations must also necessarily be subdivided and further elaborated by industrial ministries, geographic entities, and individual enterprises themselves.

The national plan, as well as lower-level plans, also includes as basic components a manpower balance and a balance for capital construction. The latter balance indicates sectoral production capacities, and it details volume, location, and structure of capital installations. It also specifies in itemized lists the main capital projects and the timetable for their completion. Monetary balances, which supplement physical balances, are needed as a common denominator because of physical dissimilarities among materials, equipment, output, and labor. In reality, the planning and balancing process is a never-ending one, constantly attempting to make the balances balance in order to provide for technical consistency in the light of national economic objectives.

As noted earlier, Chinese planning at the top level deals primarily in aggregates, expressed, for example, as so many tons of steel or so many X-type lathes. But as the plan works down to the operating level, increasingly complex details must be included: Precisely what kinds of steel or machines? To be produced where, when and for whom? With what specific resources? These and a myriad other detailed questions become relevant for administrators further down the industrial hierarchy. The process is far from being one-sided. If the national plan is to be realistic and reasonably consistent, enterprise managers must tell the planners above them what can realistically be expected from each plant in terms of production, and what amounts and kinds of resources are necessary to meet the output targets. In order to tie the myriad component parts of the national plan into a workable unified whole, a common classification of planning indexes (discussed in detail in the next chapter) is utilized at all levels.

The Planning Process

The actual process, sequence, and timing entailed in constructing China's annual national plan and all of its derivative plans—including those of individual enterprises—vary at least somewhat from year to year. In general, the planning process in Chinese industry seems to be significantly less monolithic or standardized than it has typically been in Soviet industry.[4] This section focuses chiefly on what I learned about the planning process in Chinese industry in 1966.

The planning process in China comprises stages of proposals, counterproposals, and reconciliations in conjunction with extensive negotiations —and undoubtedly much hard bargaining—at each level of the industrial hierarchy. The actual process generally begins each year with the issuance of preliminary directives—also referred to as control figures—by the State Planning Commission at the center. These directives flow down the industrial hierarchy, where they are disaggregated, elaborated on, added to, and generally worked out in increasingly greater detail, right to the level of individual factories and their shops. This stage is referred to as the "first down" stage in the planning process. Apparently in some years the planning process in Chinese industry has started from the bottom up, but apparently not in 1966. A few enterprises surveyed did state that they began preparing their 1966 and/or 1967 plans before any planning directives had been issued by the center or other higher authorities, but the great majority of firms visited indicated that they began annual planning in earnest only after they received preliminary directives from higher authorities.

The "first down" stage is followed by the first, and frequently the last "up" stage. During this stage, the draft plans, which take into account earlier higher directives, of the subordinate levels (the individual enterprises and their workshops at the bottom of the hierarchy) are discussed, aggregated, and channeled upward until they reach the center. Then comes the "second down" stage. During this stage most parts of the plan are finalized and formalized at each level through negotiations, hard bargaining, and compromises. Where necessary, there may be another up-and-down sequence involving those details of the plan that are not resolved during the "second down" stage. Most of the enterprises surveyed claimed that most, if not all, parts of their operating plans are usually finalized during the second "down" stage, but some firms indicated that another up-and-down series of negotiations is often needed before their plans are formally approved. However, the State Planning Commission—or State Council—is usually not involved in this additional up-down sequence.

The above down-up-down description of Chinese industrial planning is, of course, oversimplified. In reality, various directives, proposals, and counterproposals continuously flow up and down the industrial hierarchy until the plans for each level and each individual organization are formally approved. In fact, interactions of this type continue—albeit on a much more limited scale—even after the national plan is put into operation and revisions are undertaken.

All of the enterprises surveyed prepared some form of annual plan and required formal higher approval for at least a few targets and/or resource limits on an annual basis. However, at many of those enterprises where their quarterly, monthly, or weekly plans were their real operating plans, usually only one or a few broad targets, such as total quantity and/or value of output, total costs, and total profits, are formally approved on an annual basis by higher authorities. Those firms that have relatively operational and detailed annual plans typically begin fairly detailed planning for the next year sometime between June and early September of the current year. Those that have only very general annual plans typically begin planning for the next year only during the last quarter of the current year.

Most of the large machinery and equipment enterprises surveyed—particularly those under central ministries—had relatively operational annual plans. At these enterprises their annual plans were typically approved along with a general quarterly breakdown, but higher approval was not required each quarter unless major revisions were involved. These firms also worked out their monthly plans independently. The Hangchow Machine Tool Enterprise did, however, require higher approval for its quarterly plans each quarter. The provincial industrial department, which was the direct superior of this Hangchow firm, approved its quarterly plans, while the First Machine-Building Industry approved a number of key output targets and resource allocations in its annual plans.

It is more difficult to generalize about the planning process at the small machinery, tool, instrument, and component plants visited. In some cases their annual plan was quite operational, in others the quarterly or monthly plan was the true operating document. Similarly, some of them needed higher approval for their quarterly, as well as annual, plans, and others did not. However, all firms of this kind worked out their monthly plans independently.

The Wuhan Iron and Steel Corporation needed higher approval only for its annual plan, and it had much autonomy in formulating and carrying out its quarterly and monthly plans. The corporation formally approved the quarterly plans each quarter for nearly all of its factories, and for several of their monthly plans as well. The annual plan of Shanghai's No. 3 Steel Mill was quite operational. The Ministry of Metallurgy Industry played a major and direct role in the approval of this firm's annual plan, while its direct superior, the Shanghai Bureau of Metallurgy, approved its quarterly plans.

Wusih Diesel Engine required only formal higher approval for its annual plan, which reflects quarterly subdivisions. Wuhan Diesel Engine had a very vague and nonoperational annual plan. Its quarterly plans required higher approval each quarter.

Nanking Chemical Fertilizer required only formal higher approval for its annual plan. It worked out its own shorter-term plans. In theory the annual plan is supposed to be the operational one for Canton Chemical Fertilizer, but its 1966 plan was apparently not finalized until the middle of that year. It was working on the basis of quarterly plans which required higher approval. Peking Coke and Chemical does not usually require higher approval for its quarterly or monthly plans; in fact, it frequently does not prepare a detailed quarterly plan even for its own use. It does, however, prepare detailed monthly plans which become the key operating document for most of the firm's workshops.

Shanghai Pharmaceutical's annual plan, showing quarterly breakdowns, required higher formal approval. The plan is approved by the China National Drug Corporation, and for 1966 it was not approved until the spring of 1966. The Shanghai branch of the above corporation approves and controls the fulfillment of this firm's monthly plans. The same corporation—not a branch of it—approved the annual plans of the Peking Pharmaceutical Enterprise, but this firm works out its own monthly plan quite independently. I was told by the chief of planning at Peking Pharmaceutical that their quarterly plan is not really very important. The annual plan is the important one in terms of aggregate targets and resource limits, and the monthly plan is the key operating document in terms of detailed product mix.

Only the annual plan of Wuhan's Han Yang Paper Mill requires formal higher approval; the firm works out only its quarterly plan, and some of its shops also work out monthly plans. The First Light-Industry Ministry actually approves, on an annual basis, the quantity of output (in tons) for the main products produced by Han Yang. However, this enterprise's direct superior, the Hupeh Province First Light-Industry Department, communicates to the firm the centrally approved targets (and resource limits), as well as those it decides on.

The quarterly as well as the annual plans of both Tientsin Watch and

Shanghai Wei Ming Battery required formal higher approval. For the Canton Electrical Appliance firm the monthly and annual plans required higher approval, but not its quarterly plan.

The quarterly plan, which required higher approval, was the key operating document for the cotton- and woolen-textile firms surveyed, although in a few cases certain key output targets and supply allocations also required higher monthly approval. At these enterprises, planning for the next quarter started in the middle of the current quarter. For example, the Peking Woolen Enterprise began working on its July-September plan for 1966 in May of that year. Their annual plans were stated only in very broad terms, and they are not usually prepared until late in the year. This was also true for the two clothing firms and the shoe factory surveyed. A main reason for this may be that these kinds of enterprises are dependent on the agricultural sector for their raw materials, and agricultural results are not generally known with much certainty until quite late in a given year.

Peking Clothing does not usually get its preliminary annual targets and resource-allocation indicators—during the "first down" stage—for the next year until November or December. Its broad annual plan, which is not really operational, is not typically approved until the planned year is well underway. The key operating plan for this enterprise is the monthly one, and it has a good deal of autonomy in designing and carrying it out. The basic operating plan for Hangchow Clothing is also the monthly one, but it also prepares weekly plans which often call for revisions in the monthly plan. Tientsin Shoe's annual plan is also not operational, and its 1966 plan had not yet been approved by May of that year. This firm required formal higher approval for the aggregate targets and resource limits of its quarterly plan and, at times, its monthly plan as well. However, Tientsin Shoe had considerable autonomy with regard to its product mix and various other operations.

Supply and Sales Order Conferences

Several years ago Communist China introduced a new phase in its industrial planning process on a widespread scale. This phase involves supply and sales order conferences or meetings—also known as material-allocation conferences—and, as far as I know, it is highly unusual even among communist countries.

The major purpose of these order conferences is to bring related industrial buyers and sellers together in one place so that they can negotiate face-to-face and sign detailed supply and sales contracts. They are usually held after the parties involved have received their aggregate output targets and resource-allocation limits for a given year or for a shorter period in some cases. At the conferences, detailed commodity supply and sales relationships, specifications, and delivery dates are worked out. Such order meetings are organized along branch-of-industry lines, with key representatives from directly interdependent branches in attendance.

National order conferences are the most important—since they deal with commodities deemed of major and strategic importance which are usually centrally allocated—and are generally the most common. They are sponsored, called, organized, and coordinated by the State Planning Commission and the Ministry for the Supply of Materials in all cases. The former agency deals chiefly with general coordination, ironing out major conflicts and compromises, the formalization of contracts, and the issuance of special allocation certificates which give industrial organizations the legal right to receive stipulated types and quantities of centrally allocated goods. The latter agency handles various details involved in working out contractual agreements and controls the implementation of these contracts.

Each national order meeting is also sponsored by at least a third party—that is, the central ministry or one of the specialized ministries having overall control over the commodities under consideration. For example, if it is steel or pig iron, the third party would be the Ministry of Metallurgy Industry, for machine tools and equipment it would be one of the machine-building ministries, for chemical fertilizer or coke it would be the Chemical Industry Ministry, and so forth.

These national conferences are attended by representatives from the same branch of industry as the sponsoring ministry, as well as representatives of those industrial sectors that are the major users or buyers of the commodities involved. It is also quite common for representatives from those industrial sectors which supply critical commodities to the sponsoring branch of industry to attend as well, although a separate order meeting may be called for this purpose. In addition to participants sent by the central organizations, representatives to the national order conferences are also sent by counterpart agencies, departments, and bureaus at the provincial and municipal levels, as well as by corporations and enterprises—generally major ones.

Apparently all of the industrial ministries involved in the production of important producer goods are sponsors of national order conferences at least once a year. Larger and/or more important industrial enterprises manufacturing producer goods frequently send their own representatives, especially where they have the right to negotiate and conclude their own supply and sales contracts. Other enterprises are likely to be represented by officials from their superior organizations—that is, corporations, municipal bureaus, and so on.

Supply and sales order conferences are also quite common on the provincial level and, in large industrial cities like Shanghai, on the municipal level. They are sponsored and run by the planning commission, bureau for the supply of material, and appropriate industrial bureaus or departments at this level. Usually representatives are sent only by organizations in the related geographic area, but at times participants do come from other areas as well. In some cases, regional order conferences are called which involve a number of provinces, autonomous regions, and/or major cities, such as Shanghai or Peking. They are sponsored jointly by the appropriate agencies and industrial organizations of the geographical areas involved.

In many cases, order conferences serve useful purposes in addition to the main purpose of working out sales and supply contracts. They are often used to disseminate information of common interest, to demonstrate new products, and to consider future trends and needs in the industries represented.

In order to shed a bit more light on China's supply and sales order conferences, I shall present some of the information on this topic given to me by some of the specific enterprises surveyed.

Peking Coke and Chemical sends representatives to a national meeting dealing with the allocation and distribution of coke and benzine at least once a year. This conference is held at the end of the current operating year, or early in the planned year. It is usually called after the aggregate output targets and supply-allocation limits involving coke have been determined for the producing and major consuming sectors, including important specific factories.

The last supply order meeting that this firm had taken part in was held for about a thirty-day period between mid-December 1965 and mid-January 1966. The key sponsoring industrial ministry of this meeting was the Ministry of Metallurgy, with the chemical and coal-industry ministries also playing important roles. Hundreds of people, representing all levels of the industrial hierarchy in these sectors, attended. Delegations were selected and organized in various provinces and some major industrial cities by the local planning commissions, bureaus for the supply of materials, and appropriate industrial bureaus and departments.

The Peking Coke and Chemical Firm sent the head of its supply and sales department with the Peking city delegation. He attended almost the entire conference, and the firm also sent other executives for shorter periods, usually for a few days. Some of these other executives included the chief engineer, the heads of the technical, planning, and production departments, and the director went for about one day. Peking Coke and Chemical's representatives negotiated and signed detailed annual contracts for 1966—with monthly breakdowns in many cases—with its chief coke and benzine customers, as well as its coal supplier. These contracts indicated the suppliers and customers, the quantities and precise specifications of commodities involved, delivery dates, prices, modes of shipment, and various other terms and conditions. At this conference, contracts were worked out for virtually all of the 1966 planned coke production in the nation that was subject to central allocation.

The Shanghai Heavy Machine Tool Enterprise generally sends people to at least two national order conferences for each planned year, one involving its supply allocations and the other its products' sales. The head of the firm's supply and sales department is its key representative at these conferences. The supply meeting is usually held in October or November, before the sales order conference, which is generally held in January of the planned year. In both cases the meetings are typically called to work out the details—such as how much of what commodity is to be supplied by what supplier, and in what specifications—based on aggregate allocations and output targets already approved. And both supply and sales order conferences typically last from two to four weeks.

At the supply conferences attended by this enterprise it negotiates supply contracts for such goods as pig iron, steel, coke, oil, and standardized electrical equipment. Shanghai Heavy Machine Tool's direct superior, the First Machine-Building Ministry, is the key sponsoring ministry of the national sales order conferences attended by the firm. Most of the sales and supply contracts worked out at these meetings are on an annual basis with quarterly breakdowns. When more than one conference of each type is called involving the same annual plan, contracts are often worked out for shorter periods. However, it is common for some of this enterprise's major suppliers and customers to negotiate further and agree on revisions after the conferences are over. From time to time this enterprise participates in special-purpose national supply or sales order conferences, which may be called at any time when serious unforeseen problems arise.

The role of the Wuhan Heavy Machinery Enterprise in national order conferences was basically similar to that of the above Shanghai firm. This was also true for the Peking First Machine Tool, Hangchow Machine Tool, and Shanghai No. 3 Machine Tool enterprises. However, the Hangchow enterprise also sometimes attends provincial-level supply and sales order conferences where various aggregate supply allocations and output targets may be worked out, as well as the details. Shanghai No. 3 Machine Tool sometimes takes part in local order conferences organized by its direct superior, the Shanghai Machine Tool Corporation. Most of the representatives at the local meetings are from Shanghai organizations, but at times some come from other cities.

The Wuhan Iron and Steel Corporation sends representatives to national sales order meetings involving steel at least once a year. It only attends supply conferences when its own factories cannot provide major centrally allocated commodities it requires. Usually the corporation's plants and mines can satisfy its own internal needs for coal, coke, cement, iron ore, pig iron, various chemicals, and certain kinds of equipment, parts, and components. Where the corporation's plants are scheduled to produce substantial quantities of the above types of commodities in excess of the corporation's own needs, it often sends representatives to sales conferences to negotiate contracts for their sale. Although the corporation signs both the supply and sales contracts for all of its factories and mines, the plants and mines frequently send their own representatives to take part in the negotiations as well. Frequently the individual enterprises under this corporation actually work out the contractual details with their suppliers and customers, and then the corporation signs them on behalf of the enterprise.

The Shanghai No. 3 Steel Mill also attends national supply and sales order conferences each year. At the supply meetings it signs contracts with suppliers for such goods as coke, standardized equipment, scrap metals, and pig iron. However, it does not usually go to supply conferences dealing with coal allocations; its direct superior, the Shanghai Metallurgy Industry Bureau, handles this for the firm. From time to time, this enterprise also attends local supply or sales conferences sponsored by Shanghai's Planning Commission, Bureau for the Supply of Materials, Metallurgy Industry Bureau, and various other municipal industrial bureaus.

The Han Yang Paper Mill in Wuhan sends representatives to national supply and sales order conferences at least a few times a year, and in some years they have sent executives to as many as four supply order meetings. These meetings typically last about one or two weeks. The First Light-Industry Ministry is the key sponsoring industrial ministry for the national sales conferences attended by this firm, and the mill's customers, mostly publishing houses, are also represented. Han Yang also attends provincial order conferences from time to time, when the Hupeh Province Light-Industry Department is a major sponsor. In many instances this enterprise signs quarterly and, at times, even shorter-term contracts rather than annual contracts with suppliers and customers at the conferences it attends. The last national order conference that Han Yang had participated in, at the time of my visit there, was a sales meeting held in the spring of 1966. Shortly after this meeting it participated in a provincial sales meeting to arrange for the conclusion of detailed contracts for the rest of the year with some customers, and for the next quarter with others.

Nanking Chemical Fertilizer also goes to national supply conferences to work out contracts with suppliers of major raw materials and equipment. It also attends national sales meetings. Most of the contracts it signs at national order conferences are annual ones.

Wusih Diesel Engine usually attends one national sales order conference and one national supply conference each year. The firm's contractual negotiations at the supply conferences are involved mainly with major parts and components, which are centrally allocated. Supply contracts involving raw materials and equipment are typically worked out and signed by this enterprise's direct superior, the Tractor and Internal Generator Industrial Corporation, which belongs to the Eighth Machine-Building Ministry. For all of the centrally allocated commodities that the firm obtains it receives special certificates stipulating quantities allotted. These certificates are issued by the State Planning Commission and given to the firm by its superior industrial authorities. In some cases decisions involving aggregate supply allocations and output targets are made at the order conferences attended by Wusih Diesel Engine. The Eighth Machine-Building Ministry is the key sponsoring ministry at the national sales conferences attended by this firm. The Ministry of Agriculture often sends representatives to the national order meetings in which Wusih Diesel Engine participates.

The Wusih enterprise also attends regional sales and supply conferences, which are often held several times in the same year. These regional conferences deal with supply and sales agreements that are not worked out at the national meetings or those which require further elaboration or revision. The Agricultural Commercial Machinery Corporation, which is also under the Eighth Machine-Building Ministry, plays an important coordinating role at the national, and particularly the regional, sales order conferences attended by Wusih Diesel Engine. The regional conferences are typically attended by representatives from organizations situated in two or three neighboring provinces, such as Kiangsu, Anhwei, and Chekiang, and often from the city of Shanghai as well. In general, Wusih Diesel Engine sends a variety of executives to the order conferences in which it participates. These include, at various times, the heads of the supply and sales, planning, and technical departments, engineers, and even the director or workshop directors.

To the best of my knowledge the types of national order conferences in which producer-goods industries take part in are not nearly as common for consumer-goods industries. However, for various types of consumer goods—particularly final, or end, products produced in many varieties which change substantially from year to year, such as clothing and shoes—there are national and local exhibitions. At these exhibitions, usually organized along the lines of branch of industry or commodity group, regular products and samples of new products are put on display, and sales orders and contracts are frequently negotiated on the spot by representatives from industry and the commercial sector.

The Ministry of Commerce or its local counterparts plays a major role in organizing and coordinating consumer goods exhibitions. Representatives are sent from different levels of the branch of industry whose products are on display, as well as from appropriate wholesale and retail organizations. Where substantial export orders and promotion are involved—as at the Canton Trade Fair—the Ministry of Foreign Trade, its local counterparts, and the national export-import corporations play key roles in organizing and running the exhibitions.

Both the Peking and Hangchow Clothing firms generally send representatives to national exhibitions at least twice a year, and sometimes as many as four times (once each season). The exhibitions are usually held in Shanghai, Canton, Peking, or Tientsin. At these exhibitions they display their products—giving special attention to new ones—exchange ideas, and get opinions and suggestions from customers and potential customers. They also take sales orders directly from customers located in the same city and work out detailed contracts. Where customers are in other cities (or countries) the firms' higher authorities typically must approve the sales orders and formalize the contractual agreements. Detailed sales contracts are usually signed on a quarterly or monthly basis.

The two clothing enterprises also participate in local branch-of-industry exhibitions from time to time. They also hold their own exhibits, panels, and meetings at least a few times each year which are attended by customers and, at times, even representatives of the consumer public. These two firms, as well as various other consumer-goods producers surveyed, engage in other kinds of product planning, marketing research, and sales-promotion activities (which will be discussed in the next chapter).

As far as I know, none of the consumer-goods factories surveyed send representatives to national supply conferences. Where consumer-goods industries do participate in conferences of this type, higher authorities above the enterprise level generally send representatives and act for their subordinate firms. For example, in late 1965 there was a national supply conference dealing with the allocation and distribution of leather for 1966. The Tientsin Shoe Factory did not send any representatives, but its direct superior, the Tientsin Second Light-Industry Bureau, did, along with the Tientsin Planning Commission, the Tientsin Bureau for the Supply of Materials, and the local bureau of commerce. The key sponsoring ministry of this conference was the Second Light-Industry Ministry, and the agricultural sector was represented as well.

The cotton- and woolen-textile firms surveyed—as well as various other consumer-goods plants visited—rarely, if ever, send representatives to national supply or sales order meetings. They also do not generally attend provincial or municipal-level conferences of these types. Higher authorities usually work out most of the supply and sales agreements for them.

Flexibility in Planning

One way that the Chinese provide for flexibility in industrial planning is by allowing for revisions once the plans are implemented. As noted in earlier chapters (see especially the section "Basic Economic System" in Chapter 6), the Chinese have apparently been less reluctant than the Soviets to allow for revisions, including changes in aggregate targets and resource allocations, in the operating plans of industrial enterprises. In fact, there frequently seems to be too much flexibility in Chinese industry in this regard, since interdependent plans are often not properly brought into balance when changes are made in the plan of a given firm or sector.

The Chinese also provide for some planning flexibility by not spelling out the production plans of numerous enterprises in complete detail, thus allowing for reserves to produce items that may suddenly be required. Where enterprises overfulfill their plans—and produce immediately needed products in doing so—this too provides for some flexibility in China's system of economic planning.

Some flexibility is also achieved by providing for "reserve stocks" of commodities—mostly major materials, and standardized equipment, tools, components, and parts—in plans at each level of the industrial hierarchy. In an attempt to hedge against planning errors and failures in the supply system, such reserve stocks are maintained at the center, mostly by the industrial ministries, and at the provincial and municipal levels, as well as industrial corporations in many cases. Similar types of "reserves" for flexibility are frequently supposed to be built into the plans of individual enterprises. It seems that planned reserves—that is, commodities in excess of planned and anticipated needs—typically range from roughly 2 to a maximum of 7 or 8 percent of total planned output value in different sectors and at different levels of the hierarchy. While such reserve stocks undoubtedly play an important, highly useful role in Chinese industry in many instances, probably more often than not they do not expeditiously provide an enterprise facing a supply failure with the precise goods that it requires; only a limited number of commodities make up such reserve stocks, and even for those items in stock it is likely that they are not typically provided to needy enterprises immediately, or even shortly, after they apply for them. Higher approval and/or rather time-consuming negotiations may frequently be entailed.

In recent years a relatively continuous type of exhibition has been set up in China with the purpose of providing a market for commodities that are unneeded by various organizations which possess them but are needed by others. The sellers of such commodities can get cash, credits, or exchanges of other commodities that they may require. Purchasers can buy the items they need on the spot. Apparently the first exhibition of this type was set up in Peking in April 1964. It was organized by the Central Commodities Control Department, which may be under the Ministry for the Supply of Materials, and a Peking municipal department of the same name. Different industries and areas of the country participated. During the April-November period of 1965 about 35 million yuan's worth of goods were sold through this exhibition.[5] I was told that since 1965 many other cities were holding similar types of exhibitions. It is likely that they provide for an important, though limited, supplementary channel of planning flexibility and procurement.

Another recent innovation which probably facilitates planning flexibility and supply, at least somewhat, in Chinese industry is the "commodity banks" that have been set up in some cities for such goods as metal equipment and minor machinery, components and parts, wood, cardboard and paper, and certain types of scrap metals and chemicals. Individual enterprises can deposit or withdraw commodities from these banks. When they deposit items, they can immediately obtain others of similar value in exchange or maintain a credit with the "bank." In some cases, they can apparently be paid off in cash if they wish, and buyers can procure goods for cash. A "wood bank" was founded in 1966 in Tientsin by the Municipal Supply and Sales Department. In an economy drive Tientsin factories "saved" and deposited 110,000 cubic meters of wood in this bank in 1966. A total of 120 local industrial firms made use of the wood bank by buying and selling "tens of thousands cubic meters of wood."[6] Apparently commodity banks have been catching on and have been set up in a number of other cities.

Let us now focus our attention on the Chinese industrial enterprise, examining in some depth its structure, operations, personnel, and performance.

CHAPTER 9

Survey of Chinese Industrial Enterprises: Structure and Operations

IN THIS CHAPTER the discussion and analysis pertain mainly to my first-hand findings, observations, and impressions with regard to the Red Chinese industrial enterprises that I surveyed in 1966. There is a small number of significant published works dealing with Chinese enterprises which the reader may wish to refer to in order to gain a better historical perspective of the subject, or to obtain certain types of information not presented here.[1] The chief topics to be covered in this chapter include a brief historical sketch of the enterprises I visited; the product lines and number of shifts operated at the enterprises, objectives, content of plans, and nature of success indicators; wages, salaries, and material incentives; personnel and organization structure; roles and behavior of key executives and groups; and decision making, authority, and independence at the enterprise level. The following chapter deals with quantitative dimensions of Chinese enterprise performance with some suggestive comparisons with other countries.

BASIC OBJECTIVES OF THE CHINESE INDUSTRIAL ENTERPRISE

The state prescribes the ultimate objectives to be pursued by all Chinese industrial enterprises. With regard to basic economic objectives, the enterprise is supposed to achieve as great a quantity of production as possible with given resources; or, given certain production targets, they should be achieved with minimum practical resources and costs. The production program is supposed to be carried out in accordance with predetermined time, sales, and delivery schedules. Within the overall output targets and resource limits prescribed by the plan, the detailed product mix, including the quality of output, is supposed to conform to the requirements of customers as agreed upon in the plan. The enterprise is supposed to introduce its own innovations and improvements in operations within the resource limits and targets set in the plan. A balance between short-run and long-run consideration is also called for so that current decisions and activities should not endanger future operations, but rather, should enhance them and further the future needs of society.

In addition to these basic economic objectives the state prescribes certain policies to be followed for their achievement—for example, the use of the most progressive factor input, working capital, and inventory norms in planning and operations, the constant improvement of technical processes, product quality, and employee skills, and so forth.

The Chinese do not generally seem as concerned as the Soviets about short-term economic inefficiency at the enterprise level which results from state-planning and resource-allocation problems. During periods of ideological extremism—such as the Great Leap Forward, and probably at many enterprises during the height of the 1966–67 Cultural Revolution—economics becomes subservient to politics and ideology. Even during periods of relative ideological moderation, however, the Chinese enterprise is not viewed as a purely economic entity, although economic efficiency, in general, is a priority desideratum of performance. There are still other objectives pursued pertaining to education, training, politics, ideology, and welfare, and these are often compatible with improving longer-term economic results.

Moreover, in their overpopulated country with huge surpluses of unskilled labor and very low wages, the regime is not as concerned about underemployment or disguised unemployment of industrial manpower—which lowers per capita productivity—as the Soviet Union, where there is a shortage of labor, and where the cost of labor has become quite expensive. But under relatively normal conditions the Chinese regime does not seem to want excess manpower at the enterprise level to the point where the law of diminishing returns sharply upsets productivity. There have been reports in recent years in the Chinese press of substantial retrenchments and layoffs of personnel at enterprises, sometimes involving as much as one-third or more of their employees. And, as already noted in Chapter 7 and elsewhere, at the end of the Great Leap Forward, industrial employment was cut by roughly 50 percent on a national scale. I was also told of cutbacks—though not very sizable—in excess personnel in the last few years at some of the Chinese enterprises that I visited in 1966.

While there were signs that the pendulum was swinging from economic, managerial, and technical rationality in the direction of greater emphasis on ideology and politics at a number of enterprises surveyed in 1966, economic results generally still seemed then to be of major importance. This situation may well have changed in numerous instances with the late 1966 and 1967 onslaught of Red Guards, followed by the military, people's militia and new "revolutionary" committees, at Chinese factories with the aim of "revolutionizing" industrial management.

In the spring of 1966 the Chinese industrial enterprise seemed to be a place where much ideological indoctrination and political education occurred—though still largely after working hours—at both the group and individual levels, with the twofold aim of developing the pure communist man, as conceived by Mao, and motivating personnel to work harder and more efficiently. It was a place where illiterate workers learned how to read and write, and where all types of employees could, and did, improve their work skills and develop new ones through part-time schools and self-education, and through formal and informal training on and off the job. It was a place where housing, schools, recreational and welfare facilities, roads, shops, and offices were often being constructed or remodeled by enterprise employees. It was also a place from which employees sometimes went out into the fields and helped the peasants with their harvesting when there was not much to do at the factory, typically because of breakdowns in the plan. In general, Chinese enterprise employees spent considerably more time than Soviet employees at activities not directly related to the firm's economic plan or performance.

Hence, if, for example, supplies did not arrive according to the plan or because serious unforeseen production bottlenecks arose, Chinese enterprise employees generally did not remain idle or unproductive—at least, by the regime's standards. At enterprises I visited where this type of situation arose, workers undertook some functional education or training during the period of delay in order to improve their skills; or they studied and discussed Chairman Mao's works; or, as was the case at the Tientsin Shoe and Wuhan Diesel plants, they undertook various construction and modernization activities; or they worked on developing new or improved processes and products often not stipulated in the plan.

This type of activity makes more sense than meets the eye in a nation where illiteracy has been widespread, the level of industrial skills generally low, and enterprise shops, offices, housing, and other welfare facilities are inadequate and sparse. The benefits of political indoctrination seem more questionable, but even this activity, when not carried too far, seems to have a favorable, motivating impact, which is often difficult for my capitalistic Western mind to grasp fully.

One clue as to the regime's priorities with regard to basic enterprise objectives on a national scale in the first half of 1966 may be contained in a 1966 issue of the Peking *Worker's Daily* which I came across after I had left Red China.[2] In this issue the seventy most "progressive" and best industrial enterprises in Communist China were named and honored. These seventy firms were selected—under party direction, I am sure—at a series of national worker and political conferences. Some 20 percent of them were in Manchuria, and nearly 20 percent in the Shanghai area.

I visited four of the seventy enterprises selected when I was in China; from this experience some insight into the regime's priorities may perhaps be derived. If the four enterprises I surveyed do, in fact, represent an approximate cross section of the seventy firms in terms of why they were chosen, I would conclude that in the first half of 1966 the Red Chinese leadership had not made up its mind as to whether economic or political-ideological objectives should receive top priority at the industrial-enterprise level throughout the country.

The Shanghai Heavy Machine Tool Firm was among the seventy leading enterprises selected and one which I visited. This firm was clearly one of the best managed, best equipped and most economically efficient of all those that I visited. Its director was the top-paid person that I encountered at any of the enterprises surveyed. He was also an Expert, being one of the very few directors with a university education. I was told by the management of this firm that some of the products that the plant produces rank with the best in the world. There may well have been a good deal of Redness and ideologically correct behavior at this enterprise, but economic, technical, and managerial performance was probably of major importance in its selection as one of the nation's seventy most progressive and best enterprises.

The same was probably true for the Peking No. 3 Cotton Textile Enterprise which I surveyed, and which was also selected. This firm went into rayon production in the mid-1960's, and was embarking on nylon and vinyl production when I was there. The considerable amount of time it was spending on product development and experimentation may have also been a critical factor in its selection.

The Shanghai No. 3 Steel Enterprise, which I visited, was probably selected, in large part, for ideological reasons, although it seemed to be doing adequately in the sphere of managerial, technical, and economic performance. This firm had a relatively young work force which acquired much of its experience on the job and through trial and error, "struggle," "innovational" activity and persistence. Its personnel had designed many new products and had also done a considerable amount of work in the renovation, design, and construction of the enterprise's facilities, shops, and equipment in the name of self-sufficiency. I was told by its management that the enterprise constantly compared itself with, followed, and tried to catch up to, and surpass, the performance of the leading steel firms in the nation, while assisting those that lagged behind. In this connection, this enterprise was apparently sending personnel to leading steel centers like Anshan, while receiving and training people from newer and less advanced steel mills. The three top-paid people at Shanghai No. 3 Steel were the director, party secretary, and a leading skilled worker—an ideologically excellent situation. Of all of the enterprises visited it also had one of the largest proportions (15 percent) of party members among its employees. Moreover, there were two workers on the enterprise party committee of nineteen—an unusually high number of workers among the enterprises visited. The welfare, educational, and cultural facilities of this enterprise also seemed to be very extensive and above average.

By all indications the Wuhan Diesel-Engine Enterprise which I surveyed was not selected as one of the country's most progressive firms for managerial, economic, or technical performance. In fact, its management readily admitted that the firm was operating at a substantial loss. When I visited it, this enterprise was in a state of great inefficiency bordering on chaos and suspended animation. It was apparently selected because of its ideological purity with regard to self-sufficiency, innovation, the three-in-one method, experimentation, struggle, and persistence. It had worked for long periods, first in the development of a new tractor, then in the design, development, and production of a diesel engine, which it was manufacturing erratically, very inefficiently, and in limited numbers when I visited the plant. The enterprise had also built or rebuilt most of its own shops, equipment, warehouses, roads, and buildings. No doubt its relatively inexperienced and low-paid work force deserved an A for effort, guts, persistence, and, of course, politics and ideology, but certainly not for economic results. The Reds were clearly in control here. The director had come up from the workers' ranks and had also been in the Red Army. When I was at this enterprise, it had recently abolished all bonus payments and extra-reward programs.

Hence, in 1965 or early 1966 it was likely that for a Red Chinese industrial enterprise to have been judged by the regime as outstanding, it would have had to have been at least one of the following: (a) outstanding in economic and managerial performance and technical achievements, but at the same time adequately Red and ideologically correct; (b) successful in achieving adequate economic results, making substantial gains in managerial and technical know-how, and displaying a relatively high degree of Redness and ideologically correct behavior; (c) extremely Red and ideologically pure, with little or no concern for economics, technical rationality, or managerial know-how along a broad front.

Before proceeding with a discussion of the content of the economic plan of Chinese industrial enterprises, I shall briefly present some general background information on the thirty-eight enterprises which I surveyed.

General Historical Information, Product Lines, and Number of Shifts at Thirty-Eight Enterprises Surveyed in 1966

Iron and Steel Enterprises

(1) Shanghai Steel Mill No. 13 This firm was originally founded in 1914, when it began producing liquid iron. It began steel production in the late 1940's, utilizing all imported equipment obtained in 1946–47. Peak pre-1949 annual output was 1,500 tons achieved in 1948 with two very small open furnaces, one casting machine, and 302 employees. In 1966, 1,500 tons of steel was being produced in one day with two shifts. The plant area in 1966 was twenty-one times greater than in 1949 and employment was forty-three times greater. In recent years each of the plant's large Martin furnaces had been renovated to produce about 70 tons of steel daily, as compared with 10 in the past.

In 1966 the mill expected to produce 250 varieties of rolled steel and 650 varieties of castings. Management claimed that 70 percent of total output was considered to be high quality by Chinese standards. The firm's products are used in part for wheels, boilers, enamel plates, ships and chassis. The mill and its shops were operating three shifts.

(2) Wuhan Iron and Steel Corporation This industrial complex may have been the largest of the basic projects set up with direct Soviet aid. Construction began in 1955, and the corporation's first of eighteen factories was completed in 1957. The first blast furnace was put into operation in 1958. Open-hearth steel production began in 1959, and the rolling mill was put into operation in July 1960, one month before the Soviet technicians departed. The maximum number of Soviet technicians on the job at one time was twenty-two. During 1956–57 the corporation employed 100,000 people, mostly in construction work.

A new blast furnace was added in 1962. In 1966 the iron plant was, of course, producing pig iron, and the steel mill was producing chiefly rough steel bars, referred to as I-shaped steel. While the giant steel roller in use had an annual capacity of about 3 million tons, it was operating only at roughly 50 percent of capacity in 1966. Management expected full roller capacity to be achieved by 1970 at the latest, when the new large workshop which was being constructed was expected to be completed and put into operation. This shop will produce more complex sizes and shapes of steel, mostly of high quality. When I visited this partially completed shop, very litle construction work was being done. Most of the other shops in the iron and steel plants were operating three shifts.

(3) Peking Steel Wire Before 1958 this firm produced only straw ropes. During 1958–60 it produced copper wire. In the late 1950's Soviet

experts arrived to help set up steel wire production, but they pulled out, taking all of their drawings and designs with them, before this type of production commenced. The plant began producing steel wire on its own on a limited basis at the end of 1960. This firm was Red China's first steel-wire producer. Several new shops, offices, and buildings have been added since early 1963.

By 1965 the firm had an annual capacity of 2,000 tons of steel wire, but 1965 output was only 1,000 tons and the 1966 plan called for 1,600. Management felt that this target may be revised downward. In 1966 the plant was producing basic types of stainless, high-speed, electrical-resistant, and carbonized steel wire in seventy to eighty varieties. A majority of its customers were electrical-appliance and gauge producers. Because of serious equipment imbalances and production bottlenecks some shops were operating only one shift, others two, and a few three shifts. For example, the stretching shop was working one shift, forging and pressing two shifts, and smelting, as well as the parts and repair shops, three shifts.

Large and Medium-Sized Industrial Machine-Tool and Equipment Enterprises

(1) Wuhan Heavy Machinery Construction began on this enterprise in 1956. It was completed in July 1958, and the plant started operations that year. A large Leningrad machinery firm (Sverdlovsk) sent experts to help set up this enterprise. The plant area in 1966 was 500,000 square meters.

During the 1958–64 period forty varieties of large lathes, planers, cutters, turners, and boring and drilling tools were produced. Most products are custom-built according to customer specifications. In 1965 twenty types of products were produced, nearly half of them for the first time by this firm. In 1966, twenty types were also being produced, eight of them for the first time. In 1960, 670 giant machine sets were produced. In 1965 the number was 650, but they were, on the average, much more complex and of substantially greater tonnage than in 1960. The 1966 plan called for 650 sets, but a significant proportion of them were to be more complex and heavier than those produced in 1965. The smallest planer produced was 1.5 meters wide and 8 meters long, while the biggest was 5 meters wide and 40 meters long. The smallest lathe to be produced in 1966 was 10 tons, and the largest 430 tons.

(2) Shanghai Heavy Machine Tool During the 1946–49 period this enterprise was under the control of Kuomintang and U.S. interests. At that time it produced mainly agricultural implements. In 1958 the firm diversified and expanded greatly, producing complex and large machine tools for the first time. In 1966 the total area of the enterprise was 400,000 square meters, 100,000 of which was factory floor space.

During the 1958–66 period the firm produced 130 varieties of conventional and high-precision machine tools and equipment. Management claimed that four of its precision machines—cylindrical, crankshaft, surface, and ball-bearing grinders—ranked with the best in the world. Its major product line consisted of seven large types of grinders. In recent years plant output was about 2,000 machines annually. Most of the production and auxiliary workshops were working three shifts in 1966.

(3) PEKING FIRST MACHINE TOOL In 1949 this firm was engaged primarily in repair, equipment renovation, and the manufacture of simple tools. It had a hundred old machines and a few hundred employees. It began producing relatively simple lathes on another site in 1952. By 1957 the firm had several hundred machines and 500 employees. The present factory was established and began operating in late 1958.

In 1966 the factory extended over 30 hectares in area and had 1,000 machines and 4,000 employees. The major product was a universal milling machine, and it made about twenty types. In 1965 the factory produced 2,400 machines, and the 1966 plan called for a slight increase. Each of the workshops was operating either two or three shifts.

(4) CANTON MACHINE TOOL The plant was built in the latter half of the 1950's. It produces over a dozen varieties of lathes and other types of machine tools. Most workshops were operating three shifts in 1966, although a few were working only two.

(5) NANKING MACHINE TOOL This firm was set up during the First Five-Year Plan. In 1957 it employed 600 people. In 1966 employment was about 1,300, and it was producing seven or eight basic types of conventional lathes and milling and boring machines. The plant was operating three shifts.

(6) HANGCHOW MACHINE TOOL Prior to 1949 this enterprise was a blacksmith shop. In 1949 it started taking minor repair jobs, and in 1951 it became a foundry shop, employing 24 workers. In 1952 it began manufacturing machine tools, mostly small lathes. The plant's employees made the original heating furnaces and castings used in machinery production. In 1957 the firm employed 500 people and made 53 machine tools.

In 1966 the enterprise became the Hangchow Machine Tool Factory and was placed under provincial control; it had previously been under municipal control. In 1966 the plant had 1,000 employees, was equipped with 240 of its own machines—many built by the plant itself—and factory buildings extended over an area of 30,000 square meters. The firm's basic product line in 1966 consisted of seven types of milling machines and several kinds of grinding machines. In 1965 it produced 560 machines, the bulk of which were horizontal grinding machines, most of them being of one type. Because of serious equipment imbalances and bottlenecks some shops were operating only one shift, others two, and still others three. For example, the assembly shop was working one shift, forging operations and the foundry two shifts, and the parts-manufacturing and equipment-repair, maintenance and reconstruction shops three shifts.

(7) SHANGHAI NO. 3 MACHINE TOOL Until 1958 this was a cigarette factory employing many of the same personnel as in 1966. It became a machine-tool plant in 1958, and its employees built much of the equipment used in manufacturing machine tools. It now makes five or six types of precision machinery which the Soviet Union will no longer sell to Red China. Its major products include an optical-jack boring machine and a high precision semiautomatic cylindrical grinder. I was told that all workshops operate at least two shifts.

Enterprises Making Small-Scale Machinery, Instruments, and Components

(1) SHANGHAI NO. 3 FORGING AND PRESSING MACHINE TOOL This factory was established in early 1960 through an amalgamation of eight essentially handicrafts workshops and small plants. In 1966 the enterprise had three production shops located in different parts of Shanghai. It began by producing only hammers for forging and pressing machine tools. Its 1966 product line consisted of pliers, cutting tools, wrenches, tongs, and hammers, with about twenty different specifications. These tools are used primarily for repairing motor vehicles, tractors, and other types of agricultural equipment. The tongs and plier processing shops were working one shift, and the shaping and molding plier, wrench, and hammer shop was working two shifts.

(2) WUSIH RED FLAG MACHINERY This factory was established in August 1958. It produces simple types of lathes, planing, and punching machines. Much of its output involves the rebuilding, overhauling, and repair of machines of the above types, as well as other kinds of equipment, on a subcontracting basis for other enterprises. The plant has eighty pieces of its own equipment, much of it built or rebuilt by its own employees. In general, it is a highly labor-intensive factory. The two metallurgical shops work at least two shifts and, at times, three, often with temporary workers. The overhauling shop works one or two shifts depending on the work load, while the assembly shop generally works only one shift.

(3) TIENTSIN NORTH LAKE INSTRUMENT This factory was built almost entirely by its own employees and went into operation in 1958. It was formed from a handicrafts cooperative employing mainly housewives. In 1966 about half of the employees were still housewives. The plant had little in the way of fixed capital in 1966. It had only about seven small lathes, five of which were very old, one planer, a few drills, and an electric saw. The factory comprised an area of 800 square meters.

The enterprise produced about forty kinds of products, with tin being the major material input of many of them. Some of its products included electrical transformers and converters, small electrical meters, connections and circuits, small and simple instruments and tools, and cigarette cases. In 1965 it began to produce—actually, to assemble—a type of chemical-analyzing equipment having 6,050 parts and components. At that time it also began producing a type of equipment used for balancing and washing delicate parts for watches and other products. Three of the factories' four workshops worked two shifts, and the other worked one.

Enterprises Making Agricultural and Transportation Machinery and Equipment

(1) LOYANG NO. 1 TRACTOR This large and highly vertically integrated enterprise was set up with Soviet help in the late 1950's. Its basic product is the 54-horsepower multipurpose diesel tractor called the East Wind. It started producing tractors for sale in 1959, when output was claimed to have been 15,000 tractors. An American author who visited this firm in 1960 was told that the production target for that year was 30,000 tractors, or capacity. Charles Lynch, a Canadian journalist, visited this enterprise in 1965, and was told that annual output was about 15,000 tractors, and this was also given as the firm's capacity. I was given the same figures as those given to Lynch. I was told that most of the workshops were operating two shifts, while a few (including parts manufacture) operated three shifts.

(2) WUSIH DIESEL ENGINE Prior to 1949 this firm employed a maximum of 160 people, had 60 pieces of machinery, and achieved a peak annual production of only 48 diesel engines with a total-output tonnage being less than 5 tons. The maximum horsepower per unit was 25.

In 1965, 2,015 diesel engines were produced, and total-output tonnage was over 2,000 tons. Unit horsepower ranged from 25 to 60, with the average being 30 to 35. Three- and four-cylinder engines were produced. The average engine weighed 960 kilograms and was four cylinders. In 1966 the enterprise employed 2,700 people, and the production target was 2,715 engines. The engines are used chiefly for irrigation, drainage, navigation, geological surveying, agricultural processing, and as generators. Each of the workshops was operating either two or three shifts.

(3) WUHAN DIESEL ENGINE This enterprise was originally an agricultural-implement repair shop. In 1958 it designed a small-armed tractor. It produced this tractor and various parts from 1958 until 1964 and began working on the design of a one-cylinder, eight-horse-power, 185-kilogram diesel engine in 1963. It took the factory eighteen months to produce its first diesel engine. Diesel-engine production began on a limited "experimental" scale in 1965. Management claimed that 1966 production capacity was 30 engines per day, or about 10,500 per year, but "trial" production

was still being carried out. Maximum production achieved during any one day up to early June 1966 had been 20 engines, and production had been zero on many days. The number of shifts operating in different workshops in 1966 was erratic. The assembly shop rarely worked more than two shifts; the shops for tools and molding, cold forging, foundry, and repair usually worked no more than two shifts; and the big- and small-parts shops operated two or three shifts depending on their work loads.

(4) SOOCHOW CEMENT PRODUCTS This enterprise was established in 1962. Its chief product line is cement boats held together by steel wire, and it is China's first cement-boat producer. They developed a cement boat to conserve on timber, because it is claimed to be cheaper, and I was told it has a bigger carrying capacity (7 tons) than wooden boats of comparable size. The boats are produced in five varieties, ranging in weight from 3 to 5 tons. They are used chiefly to transport commodities to and from agricultural communes, with chemical fertilizer being the major commodity transported to the farms. The factory also produces cement telephone poles, pipes, and other tubular cement products which are used primarily in communes and in rural areas in general. The number of shifts worked was not reported.

(5) SHANGHAI TRUCK Before 1949 this enterprise was first a depot run by a British merchant and later a godown. It began repairing motor vehicles and various types of equipment in 1949 for the local Transportation and Communications Bureau. It began producing trucks in 1958, and output for that year was one truck. Nearly half of the equipment used in the plant was built by its own employees, and many of the machines do indeed have the firm's name plate on them. About 80 percent of the parts and components for their trucks are made by this enterprise, and it also supplies parts to other factories.

In 1959 the firm produced fifty trucks, in 1960 three hundred, and in 1964 and 1965 six hundred each year. In 1965 the plant also rebuilt one hundred old trucks. The 1966 plan called for six hundred trucks, plus substantially more parts for other factories than in 1965. Virtually all of the firm's trucks were used by its directly superior organization, the Shanghai Bureau of Transportation and Communications. The brand name for these trucks is Communication. The trucks weigh 4 tons, are 92-horsepower, have a maximum speed of 80 kilometers per hour, and consume an average 24 litres of gas per 100 kilometers. The enterprise stopped producing its dump-truck model in 1965. In 1966 the assembly and engine shops were operating one shift, while the shops for parts, foundry, forging, maintenance and repair, and body and chassis were working three shifts. None of the workshops was working two shifts.

Chemical, Pharmaceutical, and Paper Enterprises

(1) NANKING NATIONAL CHEMICAL FERTILIZER A small part of the enterprise's production facilities were built by "bureaucratic" capitalists during the 1934–37 period. Peak annual production prior to 1949 was 18,000 tons of nitrogenous fertilizer. The firm was expanded during 1953–57, but most of the expansion has taken place since 1958. Sizable sums of capital investment were also allocated to this enterprise during the 1960's. The 1966 plan called for one million tons of chemical fertilizer, a substantial increase over 1965 output, as I was told by the director. Some forty varieties of fertilizer were produced by this enterprise. Basic commodities included sulfuric acid (which averaged about 13 percent of annual production), nitric acid, and nitrogenous and phosphatic fertilizers. About seventeen of the firm's twenty workshops operated three shifts, while the others worked two.

(2) CANTON CHEMICAL FERTILIZER Construction of this enterprise began in 1959, and the first phase was completed in 1963, when production commenced. The second phase or project was completed in 1965. I was told that the design, equipment, and materials used by this enterprise were 100 percent Red Chinese. Annual production capacity since 1965 has been 200,000 tons of chemical fertilizer, but 1965 actual production was 280,000 tons. The 1966 plan tentatively called for a 5-percent increase in production, but the 1966 output target had not been officially finalized by mid-June 1966. About 60 percent of the factory's production was comprised of ammonium sulfate, 30 percent of sulfuric acid and link ammonia; and 10 percent of potassium. The factory as a whole operated three shifts.

(3) PEKING COKE AND CHEMICAL This enterprise was established in 1959. Its major product is coke, used in the metallurgical and machinery industries, but it also produces coal gas, as well as a variety of chemicals and by-products. I was told by the director that the factory was completely Red Chinese in design, construction, and equipment. Construction and expansion activity was still going on when I visited the enterprise in May 1966. A large third coke furnace was being built, and it was expected to go into operation at the end of 1966.

In recent years annual coke production has been one million tons, and the 1966 plan called for the same amount. With the new coke furnace, coke production was expected to be substantially greater, beginning in 1967. The 1966 plan called for about 1.3 million tons of coal to be consumed by this enterprise in its production operations. According to the director, coal input per ton of end-product output has gone down in recent years.

Annual coal-gas output in recent years has been 500 million cubic meters. This firm provides coal gas to Peking residences and serves about 400,000 people. As of 1966 it was the only source of coal gas in Peking. The enterprise also supplies coal gas to about twenty other local factories. Other products produced by this firm include coal oil used chiefly for dyes at textile factories (about 50,000 tons per year), benzene (about 12,000 tons annually), ammonium sulfate (15,000 tons per year), sulfur (500 tons annually), and photographic hypo (about 100 tons per year). All of the factory's six workshops operate three shifts.

(4) PEKING PHARMACEUTICAL This enterprise was built during 1953–54, and production commenced in 1955. The factory is capable of producing 400 product varieties, and it produces an average of 100 varieties each month. Among its main products are vitamins, pills, tablets, cough syrup, eye and nose drops, TB drugs, sulfanilamide, and a variety of injectable serums. Most workshops were running three shifts in 1966, while a few, such as bottling and packaging, were working only two.

(5) SHANGHAI PHARMACEUTICAL NO. 3 This enterprise emerged from a research institute that was established in 1950 to develop penicillin. The enterprise itself was actually formed in 1953. It became the first plant in China to produce penicillin and other more advanced antibiotics. It now produces six different basic types of antibiotics, plus one formulation. In 1966 I was told that factory capacity and output were five times greater (in physical volume) than in 1953. New workshops and/or sections and new equipment have been added almost every year since 1953. All of the enterprise's six workshops were running three shifts in 1966, except the packaging unit, which was working two shifts.

(6) WUHAN HAN YANG PAPER Construction began on this enterprise in 1950, and the plant started producing in 1953. The plant's annual capacity was expanded by nearly 50 percent during 1956–57, when it reached 25,000 tons. Capacity was expected to increase to 40,000 tons in August 1966, when a huge machine and supporting equipment were operative, after being in a partially assembled and nonproductive state for nearly ten years. The enterprise manufactures mainly thin copypaper—both ordinary and superfine—not of very high quality, in six or seven varieties. Its output is used primarily for publishing purposes. Dragon-beard grass, which is a local type of grass, and wood reeds are the basic material inputs used. It takes 2 tons of the former and 2.2 tons of the latter to produce 1 ton of paper. In 1966 the factory was working three shifts.

Light-Engineering Enterprises

(1) TIENTSIN WATCH This enterprise was originally established in 1957. In 1959 three Soviet experts came as technical advisers from the large Kirov Watch Firm in Moscow; Swiss companies which provided much of the factory's equipment have also provided some on-the-spot

technical assistance. Watch production began in 1957 on a very limited scale, and in 1963 the enterprise moved into a new and much larger building and plant. Watch production increased from less than 100 per day in 1962 to 500 per day in 1965. The 1966 plan called for an average of 600 watches per day, or nearly 250,000 for the year. Production consisted of a limited line of steel and semisteel watches sold under the brand name of Wuyi. The cheapest watch sold retail at 70 yuan, and the most expensive at 115 yuan. In 1966 the enterprise was operating on only one shift.

(2) CANTON LAN YONG ELECTRICAL APPLIANCE Prior to 1949 this enterprise was an electrical-fan workshop occupying a production area of 400 square meters, containing 14 units of equipment, and employing only 18 workers. In 1966 it had 840 employees, 350 units of equipment—about half of them made by the factory—and a production area of 15,000 square meters. It began producing motor starters in 1958. Since then, a number of new items had been added to its product line, which still had table fans as its major product. In 1966 it was producing over 100 varieties of low-voltage parts and components for electrical appliances, distribution boxes, motor starters, and fans. The assembly shop was working one shift, the machinery-processing and repair shops two shifts, and the electric-fan shop three shifts because export orders were up.

(3) SHANGHAI WEI MING BATTERY This enterprise was established in 1925. During the 1925–48 period it was controlled by British and U.S. interests. Its major product is the R20 internationally standard flashlight battery. Over 60 percent of the batteries produced are of this type. It also produces two smaller-sized dry-cell batteries, the R10 and R14. The batteries are used in transistor radios, toys, and a variety of other products in addition to flashlights. The brand name of its export output is White Elephant, and for its domestic output it is Dawuwei. Total production in 1965 was about two and one-half times greater than in 1956, the pre-1957 peak year under Communist rule. The 1966 plan called for an increase of 15 to 20 percent in total number of batteries to be produced over 1965. One of the production shops was operating two shifts in 1966, while the other two were working only one shift.

Textile Enterprises

(1) SHANGHAI SUNG SING NO. 9 (JOINT) COTTON TEXTILE This mill was purchased in 1934 by the Sung Sing Corporation, which, according to the regime, was headed by "nationalistic capitalists." Even at that time it was an old plant with much of its equipment dating back to the 1890's. A substantial amount of new equipment was added during 1935–40. This enterprise was nationalized by the Communist regime in December 1965, when it became a joint state and private enterprise. (More details about this will be presented in the chapter on Red China's capitalists.)

Much of the factory's nineteenth-century equipment was still in use in 1966, as well as that added in the 1930's. New capital investment under the Communist regime has been very limited, although some new combing machines have been added in recent years. In 1966 the plant had 110,000 spindles and 1,000 looms. I was told that the 1965 output, in square meters of cotton cloth and bales of yarn, was 65 percent greater than that achieved in the pre-1949 peak year. In 1966 this firm was producing ten varieties of cotton cloth and thirty varieties of yarn. Top-quality cloth was 80 counts, minimum quality was 60 counts, and the bulk of the cloth output was 70 counts or higher.

(2) PEKING NO. 3 COTTON TEXTILE MILL This enterprise started production in 1957. In 1966 the enterprise extended over an area of 420,000 square meters, about half of which was production space. It had 87,000 spindles and 3,200 looms. It was producing about thirty varieties of cotton cloth in 1966. Quality ranged from 40 to 70 counts, with most output being in the range of 55 to 65 counts. The enterprise began producing rayon a few years ago. Rayon production was to consist of 25 to 30 percent of total fabric production in 1966 according to the plan. The firm began producing vinyl and nylon on a limited experimental basis in 1966. In the future six varieties of nylon are to be produced. In 1966 the factory's workshops were working two and three shifts.

(3) SHANGHAI COTTON TEXTILE NO. 19 This enterprise was set up in 1921 by the Japanese. Physical output in 1965 was 3.5 times greater than in 1949, the value of production (in comparable prices) was 2.5 times higher. New combing machines and other types of fixed capital have been added at this factory in recent years. In 1966, 83,000 yarn and cotton spindles and 2,100 looms were in use. The factory was producing nine varieties of plain cotton cloth and poplin (for men's shirts). Maximum quality was about 65 counts, minimum about 45 counts, and most of the cotton-cloth output was 50 to 60 counts. In 1963 this firm began producing vinyl on an experimental basis. In 1966 vinyl was expected to amount to 10 to 15 percent of total fabric output. At the time of my visit all of the workshops were operating three shifts.

(4) PEKING WOOLEN FABRIC This enterprise was originally built in 1908. Prior to 1949 it had a maximum of only a few thousand spindles and produced only a few dozen varieties of fabrics. Spinning operations and weaving capacity were greatly expanded in 1956 and again in 1958. In the 1950's this plant along with the next-door Peking Wool Carpet Factory (discussed below), and a third nearby woolen mill were all part of one enterprise. In July 1962 they were split into three separate enterprises because of the inefficiencies and diseconomies of scale under the former organizational setup. I was told that this reorganization has led to much better specialization, productivity, general efficiency, and more effective

control. In 1966 the Peking Woolen Fabric Enterprise had over 10,000 spindles and was producing several hundred varieties of woolen fabrics. Its three production shops were running three shifts.

(5) PEKING WOOL CARPET In 1966 this enterprise had about 20,000 spindles and was producing several hundred varieties of wool carpets. Five of this factory's six workshops were operating three shifts, while the other was working two shifts.

(6) TIENTSIN JEN-YI (JOINT) WOOLEN FABRIC This enterprise was originally established in 1930 as a fairly small-scale operation producing only carpet yarn. It started weaving and trimming operations in the 1950's. In 1954 it was nationalized and became a joint state and private enterprise, with the former owners staying on in key jobs. (More about this in a later chapter.) After 1954 a substantial amount of real capital was added, and operations were expanded greatly. However, in 1966 this plant was not as well equipped as the Peking Woolen Fabric Firm. The Tientsin firm's 1965 wool-fabric output of 1.2 million square meters was claimed to be 5.5 times greater than the physical volume achieved in the pre-1949 peak year. In 1966 the enterprise was producing eight basic kinds of clothing materials in about a dozen varieties. It had 6,000 spindles, 100 looms, and 50 dyeing machines. Its three major workshops and their work sections were all operating three shifts.

(7) HANGCHOW SILK REELING, DYEING, AND WEAVING This enterprise had its beginnings in the 1930's. In the 1950's it became a large vertically integrated factory involved in all of the basic stages of silk processing and manufacturing. In 1966 the firm employed some 6,000 people, several times more than the late forties or early fifties. It was operating on a two-shift basis, using much of the original equipment from the 1930's.

(8) WUSIH NO. 2 SILK REELING This enterprise was originally set up in 1927. With the Communist victory it was confiscated from its "bureaucratic" capitalist owners. It produces raw white silk with average quality being 3A grade, as compared with D grade prior to 1949. It receives a processing fee of 750 yuan for every .1 ton of silk that it processes. In 1966 the factory was working two shifts.

Clothing and Shoe Enterprises

(1) PEKING CLOTHING This enterprise was created in 1952 through a merger of ten small factories, workshops, and handicrafts cooperatives. Total employment in 1952 was 400, as compared with 1,700 in 1966. In recent years the enterprise has been producing 300 to 400 varieties of men's and women's suits, slacks and shirts, as well as a limited line of dancing costumes. Most of its products are made of cotton or wool. From 100 to 200 new product designs and styles have been introduced each year. One of the plant's shops makes custom-made clothing for department

stores which provide the raw materials. All of the firm's eight workshops were working one shift in 1966.

(2) HANGCHOW FU CHONG CLOTHING This enterprise was originally established in 1954, when it employed about 100 people. In 1965 the firm moved into a new, modern, and well-equipped building with an elevator, which is quite rare for Red Chinese consumer-goods enterprises. Employment in 1966 was 400. The factory was producing men's and women's shirts, pants (for women too), and regular coats made of cotton, wool, and silk. It produced about thirty-six product varieties, and shirts comprised its major product line. About a dozen new product varieties were produced in 1965, and about fifteen new ones were to be produced in 1966. All of its work was done on a cost-plus processing fee basis with the raw materials provided by its customers, mostly retail stores. The enterprise had no workshops per se—only work sections for cutting, sewing, attaching fasteners and buttons, pressing, and packing. The sewing and pressing sections were running two shifts, and the other three sections one shift.

(3) TIENTSIN SHOE Prior to 1949 this enterprise employed a maximum of 200 people and produced only a few simple kinds of shoes made of leather or cloth fabric. At that time the plant had virtually no equipment to speak of, and all production operations were manual. In the 1950's the enterprise expanded considerably as many individual craftsmen and shoemakers who had their own small shops and stores or worked for them joined the plant. Most of the enterprise's 366 units of machinery and equipment which it had in 1966 were produced by its own employees. In total the enterprise had made 47 different kinds of machinery and equipment since 1957, but production operations were still highly labor-intensive in 1966. In 1965 the firm produced 350,000 pairs of leather shoes, as compared with only 50,000 to 60,000 annually in the early 1950's. About 28 different styles were produced in 1965, and in 1966 the enterprise expected to produce about 30 varieties of men's, women's, and children's shoes. The production of cloth shoes has been negligible or nil in recent years. Employment in 1966 was 1,000. Two of the enterprise's four workshops were working two shifts, and the others one shift.

THE ENTERPRISE PLAN

Since the ultimate economic objectives or desiderata to be pursued by Chinese enterprises represent a high level of abstraction—like the profit-maximization goal in an American firm—they must be translated into concrete operational terms. The plan is reduced, for the most part, to quantitative terms stated in physical, monetary, and time units of measure.

A system of interconnected plan indexes which constitutes the enterprise annual plan with its quarterly, monthly and, at times, weekly subdivisions, and which is directly linked to higher-level state plans, is the device used for this purpose. As was mentioned in Chapter 8, for some enterprises the annual plan is the basic operating document, for many, if not most, it is the quarterly plan, for others it is the monthly plan, and in some cases—typically where product mixes cannot be planned very far ahead—it is the weekly plan. At a number of the firms surveyed their annual plans were not approved until well into the operating year, if at all, and they had to operate entirely on the basis of shorter-term plans. As noted in earlier chapters, none of the enterprises surveyed had long-term plans, or plans extending beyond one year, although in a few cases they had some projections involving a few years for specific capital-investment projects. The Chinese enterprise's economic plan is referrred to as the industrial-production plan, or at times simply the industrial-enterprise plan. It is basically similar in structure and concepts to the enterprise plan in Soviet industry which is called the technical-industrial-financial plan or *tekhpromfinplan.*[3]

The Chinese enterprise plan is supposed to indicate the best overall projected course of action for achieving economic objectives. An implicit condition is that the indexes be mutually consistent in terms of resources and factor inputs, costs, output targets and product mixes. If the enterprise receives a substantially deficient approved plan in terms of true productive capabilities and resource needs, the mere fulfillment of such a plan would not yield a high degree of attainment of overall economic objective or desiderata. If the overall plan is sound and is adhered to during the related operating period, a favorable degree of attainment of desiderata would result—as long as the enterprise is in timely possession of required resources stipulated in the plan. Shortages or excess amounts of certain resources imply excesses or shortages of others, thus preventing the efficient or reasonably full utilization of the entire production-input-factor mix. For example, if the enterprise finds itself short of certain raw materials, some equipment and labor are likely to stand idle, at least in the directly productive sense; or if it has substantially excess machine capacity some equipment will remain unproductively idle, even though manpower and materials are fully utilized.

The planning process within a Chinese enterprise probably resembles that in an American firm, particularly a factory, in many ways. No doubt similar problems of intraorganizational budgeting and bargaining for resources emerge, and interdepartmental shop conflicts or contradictions are likely to arise, particularly when the enterprise as a whole is confronted with significant resource scarcities in relation to output targets.

While the trend has been in the direction of greater employee or lower-level participation in planning and decision making in American industry for some time, there is probably even more in Red Chinese industry with more people getting involved. At the Chinese enterprise, meetings at all levels are organized to discuss various aspects of the plan and to make suggestions and recommendations. Much of this is organized and directed by party cadres and, to a lesser extent, trade-union officials. Worker representative councils with elected members—typically comprised of roughly 5 to 15 percent of the enterprise work force—usually discuss the overall enterprise plan directly with top management and the enterprise party committee. One area where there is a big difference between employee participation at Chinese, as compared with American, enterprises is that at the former a great deal more time is spent in after-hours meetings and discussion groups.

Let us now briefly examine the major sections of the enterprise plan. Each sectional plan contains a number of sub-indexes (building blocks) which culminate in aggregate indexes or targets. The overall plan is summarized by a cluster of basic aggregate targets and resource limits.

Production Plan

The production plan is the keystone of the enterprise plan. Total planned production is determined by taking into account estimated available productive capacity and the numbers of shifts to be worked. Aggregate planned output is summarized by two indexes expressed in money (yuan)—these are referred to as gross output and marketable or sales output. Where appropriate, the total ouput is also expressed in a physical unit of measure such as tons, square meters, or number of units. This is typically done only when the firm's product mix permits such a physical aggregation.

The index of gross output expresses the entire planned production program in constant factory prices. It includes completed production, net changes in the value of goods in process, the manufacture of auxiliary items used in the production of basic commodities, subcontracting services performed for other organizations (if any), major repairs, and direct enterprise costs involved in installing its own new equipment. Constant prices do not exist for every specific item or service; rather, they are based on representative or standard items or units of measure corresponding to a given class of commodities or services. For example, a square meter of cloth, a ton of steel or a given class of machinery, leather shoes, wool suits, regardless of their actual specifications, are likely to have one representative constant price. The use of constant prices may permit time comparisons of the growth of output. However, such comparisons may not be very meaningful if the enterprise's product mix does not remain quite stable over time.

The index of marketable output represents only finished production and completed services performed for customers. The index is expressed in current factory prices. This is the price the producer receives from customers. The firm's costs, expenses, and profits are also measured in current prices. Constant and current prices are typically quite similar, if not identical, for given commodities at the beginning of a given base period, but tend to diverge over time. However, my limited information seems to show that differences between constant and current commodity prices tend to be greater in Soviet industry than in Chinese industry. As will be discussed shortly, gross output does not generally seem to be as important a success indicator at Chinese enterprises as it has been—at least until very recently—at Soviet enterprises.

Factory wholesale prices and retail prices are rarely, if ever, the same in either country because of profit and distributor margins, turnover taxes, and the like. Retail prices are generally of no concern to the producer. They are fixed with the aim of clearing the market as the retail level in aggregate and for each type of product.

Both aggregate gross and marketable output are expressed in both value terms and as a percentage relationship to performance in the preceding period or expected performance during the current period if actual results are not yet known.

The physical assortment or product mix of the enterprise is supposed to conform to customer needs. The production plan contains a set of subtargets indicating the quantity of different types of goods to be produced. The principal items or major product groups are typically expressed in both physical and value terms. Other output may be expressed only in yuan.

In general, the overall production plan is broken down into assortment or product-mix classifications. The degree of detail in the product-mix plan varies with the nature of the firm's product line. Certain major types of producer goods, such as standardized machine tools, types of steel, components, or chemicals, are likely to be specified in detail as to type, grade, or size. Nonstandardized commodities and those of lesser importance are typically indicated in weight and/or value. For consumer-goods enterprises—particularly where it is difficult to anticipate demand for their produce a year in advance—their annual plans would not contain a detailed breakdown of product mix in terms of varieties, styles, designs, colors, and so on. The assortment indexes in the annual plan are usually stated in broad terms, such as square meters, number of items, and value. Only their quarterly, monthly or, in some cases, their weekly plans would spell out their product mix in detail. This is also true for various types of producer-goods firms.

Most types of output in Chinese industry are supposed to conform to prescribed quality standards and technical specifications. Depending on the product, its standards and specifications may be established centrally, at the provincial, municipal, or corporation level, or, in some cases, even by the enterprise itself. Products are supposed to meet the minimum standards and specifications in order to gain the approval of quality-control inspectors both within and outside of the producing enterprise. Many firms producing consumer goods in particular have quality indexes representing grades of output. Here the production program is divided into allowable proportions of different grade, such as first, second, third, with first grade being the highest. Quality gradings take into account such factors as texture, flaws, durability, and design.

Product Development and Research Plans

New products to be produced and sold for the first time by a given firm are assimilated into the production plan. They are typically indicated by value indexes as well as some physical unit of measure. If they are considered to be relatively important, time schedules regarding their development and production would be spelled out in the plan. The factory sales price for a new product is initially established on a temporary basis, and this price becomes the constant price. Eventually a current price is likely to be set, and it would tend to be lower than the constant price since unit costs tend to decrease in time.

If the enterprise engages quite extensively in product development and/or technical research it is likely to have a separate sectional plan for these activities. It would indicate special projects, experiments, dates for the pilot production of new items, and similar tasks.

Sales and Delivery Plan

The enterprise production (or services) to be sold during the planned period is tied to a series of delivery schedules indicating dates, quantities, and types of products, prices, and customers. The delivery schedules comprise the crux of the sale plan. Total sales revenues are also projected in this plan. At some of the firms surveyed—a few of the textile enterprises, Shanghai Truck, Shanghai Pharmaceutical—most of the sales and delivery planning is handled by their direct superior organizations.

Plan for the Utilization of Plant and Equipment

This sectional plan determines total estimated plant capacity, taking into account anticipated condition of existing fixed assets and capacity of new ones scheduled to be installed for use during the planned period. The plan is closely related to this plan.

Total output is typically related to plant capacity by using representative physical units of output. Historical equipment-utilization norms, revised through time, are generally used to estimate the capacity of existing fixed assets. For new machinery and equipment, their utilization norms are typically prescribed by higher authorities on the basis of information provided by the producers. Some Chinese enterprises may have a capital construction plan in addition to this plant utilization plan. Apparently none of those surveyed had a formal or comprehensive plan of this type, although a few, such as Peking Coke and Chemical, had some projections pertaining to new capital projects under construction at their plants. Where Chinese firms do have a sectional basic-construction plan it would be similar to a capital budget at U.S. firms. It deals with the introduction of new machinery and equipment, long-term projects, major improvements and enlargements in capacity of existing fixed assets, rebuilding and/or the rehabilitation of equipment, and so forth. Such activities are different from normal capital repairs since they increase productive capacity.

Maintenance and Repair Plan

This plan contains schedules and broad expense estimates pertaining to the preventative maintenance, repair, and overhaul of plant machinery and equipment. In some cases, similar programs involving other types of enterprise facilities are indicated in this plan. Funds for capital repairs and basic maintenance are generally derived from earmarked depreciation funds.

Plan of Labor and Wages

This plan indicates total manpower needs required to carry out the production plan. Manpower requirements are estimated by taking the tentatively (and typically broadly) planned production program as given and then applying labor-utilization norms (standards) to all of the functions necessary to fulfill the plan. The total enterprise work force is divided into a number of different classifications according to occupations or activities performed.

At nearly all of the enterprises surveyed there were at least a few hundred and, in some cases, thousands of specific labor-utilization norms used in preparing this sectional plan. However, there seemed to be more types of jobs, processes, and activities than in Soviet industrial enterprises for which no labor norms were established. Moreover, at the Chinese factories, historically based statistical labor-utilization norms—often with improvement factors applied—seemed to be used in virtually all cases. No use was being made of time and motion or empirical studies, and little if any use was being made of other types of technically calculated labor standards. While rather heavy reliance is placed on historical norms—with correction factors applied over time—in Soviet industry, there is also quite extensive use made of the other techniques and methods in labor norm-setting.

At Soviet firms the methods used to determine the number of administrative, technical, and auxiliary personnel required to fulfill the plan are rather crude. For example, past relationships between the numbers of direct and indirect production workers, administrative staffs, technicians, engineers, and other personnel are one of the chief bases used. In some cases general branch-of-industry averages or averages for groups of roughly comparable firms are used for estimating purposes. At the Chinese enterprises surveyed where a detailed analysis was undertaken to determine requirements of administrative, technical, and/or auxiliary personnel, equally crude methods were being used. However, it seems that in most cases less attention is paid to estimating such requirements or relationships at Chinese industries than in Soviet enterprises.

The wage and salary (payroll) plan is arrived at by applying wage rates and salary schedules or by determining the physical breakdown of planned manpower. If the enterprise is permitted to have a bonus fund, the total value of this fund is reflected in this plan.

Labor-Productivity Plan

This is basically not a plan, but rather a target or set of targets often included in the plan of labor and wages. Labor productivity is determined by dividing total gross output or total marketable output, and, at many enterprises, both by total number of enterprise personnel (apparently excluding some types of welfare and service personnel, such as teachers, doctors, nurses, and housing custodians). Output is also usually divided by direct-production workers as well, giving another measure of labor productivity. At all of the enterprises visited, output figures used in computing labor productivity are expressed in value, and at most in broad physical terms as well. At some firms labor-productivity targets are also expressed in terms of cost production per employee. At a number of firms labor productivity is calculated for major products or product groups, as well as total output. Output per man-year, man-quarter, and man-worth is computed at all of the enterprises which provided information on this subject. While most of them also compute labor productivity in terms of manhours, apparently some of them do not. All labor-productivity targets are typically also expressed as a percentage relationship to actual or expected performance in the preceding period.

At some of the enterprises surveyed, the plan of labor and wages, the labor-productivity plan or the plan of organizational and technical measures (discussed later) spells out special training programs to be conducted with the aim of increasing productivity.

Supply Plan

This plan is sometimes also referred to as the plan of material and technical supply. It is typically drafted by taking the tentative production plan as given, with changes made as plans become more refined and eventually finalized. Quantities of basic and auxiliary materials—fuel, electricity, as well as other supplies required to fulfill the overall enterprise plan—are determined on the basis of input-utilization norms. There are typically hundreds and frequently thousands of individual material and supply-input norms used in preparing this plan. These norms are generally based on a given set of technical conditions. At the Chinese enterprises surveyed, even greater reliance seems to be placed on historical material-utilization patterns in calculating such norms than at Soviet firms. Soviet enterprises apparently make greater use of norms based on drawings, normative technical calculations, and pilot projects. In both countries it is quite common for material-input norms for new products to be analogously derived from basically similar types of products produced in the past.

The supply plan contains a material-balance schedule indicating material and supply needs by major individual items and commodity groups in both physical and value terms. The sources of supply are also indicated—for example, other factories, the firm's own output, industrial wholesale organizations, commercial organizations or retail outlets (this usually applies only to purchases by smaller enterprises), independent procurement of nonallocated items, and so on. For allocated commodities, the higher-level and state organizations making the allocations to and/or supplying the enterprise are also usually stated.

This plan not only indicates the supply inputs needed to fulfill the production plan but also the planned inventory for flexibility purposes. Inventory norms are prepared for basic and auxiliary supplies, spare parts, goods in process, and finished production. They are expressed in value terms and, for major items or product groups, usually in physical terms as well. At the enterprises surveyed, no precise formula or techniques seem to be used in computing inventory (or working-capital) norms. Much use is made of past percentage relationships. Use is also made of a variety of qualitative factors based primarily on judgment. These include locations of suppliers, frequency of deliveries, amount of material consumed per unit of output or time, and operating conditions of the plant.

The enterprise may have a separate transportation plan, or the plan may be integrated into its supply and sales plans.

Cost Plan

This plan contains an aggregate index reflecting all enterprise costs and expenses which is subtracted from sales revenues to arrive at a profit target in the finance plan to be discussed shortly. There is also a cost-of-production target broken down further into direct and indirect costs and expenses. Some of the enterprises surveyed also have a cost target expressed in terms of cost per one yuan of marketable output expressed in Chinese cents; but this target is not nearly as common as it has been in Soviet industry. At most of the enterprises average unit-cost targets are established for major types of products, product groups, and/or the total product line if it is homogeneous enough. The more important cost targets are commonly stated as a percentage relationship—frequently reflecting reductions in unit costs—to expected or actual results in the preceding period, as well as in absolute value terms.

Overhead, general, and various miscellaneous expense estimates are typically based, in large part, on past relationships between these expenses and production costs. Past relationships are also typically weighed quite heavily in allocating such expenses among individual types of products or product groups. Some adjustments may, of course, be made in view of anticipated conditions during the planned period. It is also quite common for various types of general and administrative expenses to be estimated and allocated as a proportion of total direct-labor costs involved in the production of given commodities or product groups.

Plan of Organizational and Technical Measures

This plan indicates measures, tasks, programs, and projects aimed at achieving improvements in operations and performance during the related planned period or in future periods. It may include major capital additions, as well as relatively minor technical improvements; reorganizations in production processes, shops, departments, and/or general administration; better quality-control measures and higher product quality; better equipment utilization and maintenance and repair methods; improved storage and shipping operations; programs to reduce material wastage; new cost-saving innovations; and special training programs.

This sectional plan is supposed to estimate the impact that all such measures will have on the basic indexes and targets of the overall enterprise plan. For major measures and projects, cost-benefit estimates in value terms are often prepared along with time schedules. Those measures requiring sizable expenditures or substantial changes in existing operations are classified as major or large-scale innovations or improvements. Worker suggestions planned for implementation relate, for the most part, to improvements in existing operations and do not usually entail very large outlays; they are therefore typically classified as minor innovations.

Short-Run versus Long-Run

Measures and tasks incorporated into the plan of organizational and technical measures, or the product-development and technical-research plan, may have both short-term and long-run implications. Some of them may improve enterprise economic results and directly benefit society during the planned year, whereas others may not lead to significant internal or external benefits until future years. A basic desideratum of enterprise performance advocates that a balance between short-term and longer-run considerations be achieved during a given planned period. Therefore, innovation and improvement measures should be undertaken, even when there may not be any related short-run gains, if they are likely to yield substantial gains in the future. It is, of course, frequently very difficult to translate such a general objective into concrete operating terms, except perhaps by stipulating time schedules and/or budget estimates or carrying out specific measures, tasks, or projects.

Financial Plan

This sectional plan translates all other sections of the enterprise plan into money values. It consists of a comprehensive categorized breakdown of revenues and expenses, and also presents a breakdown of sources and uses of funds. The financial plan indicates fixed and working capital funds forthcoming from the state budget and other external sources, as well as the enterprise's own funds which it is allowed to maintain and use during the planned period. It also indicates payments to be made to the state —in the form of remitted profits and taxes—during the planned period and, where applicable, interest to be paid for bank loans. The financial plan contains a number of summary indexes.

There are aggregate working-capital indexes for the planned period, and, at many enterprises, working capital at the end of the period is also projected. At any point in time, enterprise working capital is likely to be held in several forms—for example, bank deposits, inventories, work in process. The various working-capital requirements are projected and aggregated in money terms. The financial plan also projects the pattern of planned sales revenues.

There is a total profit target which is determined by deducting total planned costs and expenses from total planned revenues. The profit target is really a passive residual derived only after the other plan indexes are established, rather than a dynamic or starting-point objective, as is commonly the case in American industry. This target is usually expressed as a percentage relationship to profit performance in the preceding period or expected performance for the current period if actual profit results are not yet known. Enterprises operating at a planned loss would, of course, have loss rather than profit indexes.

The financial plan typically contains one or more profitability indexes, that is, profits in relation to some other area of performance. Most of the enterprises surveyed compute profitability targets by dividing total profits by total sales, total costs, and/or cost of production. At some they have profitability targets based on all three computations, and at many they have at least two such types of profitability targets. Apparently only a limited number of the firms visited also compute profitability in relation to total fixed capital and/or total fixed and working capital combined.

A few of the enterprises surveyed had no formal profit or profitability targets at all. For example, at Shanghai Truck and Peking Pharmaceutical I was told that their directly superior authorities handle all profit calculations involving their enterprises entirely.

Targets and Indexes Considered as Maxima or Minima

The key targets and indexes which summarize the enterprise plan are supposed to be considered as maxima and minima results to be achieved. The firm and its management should try to better operating targets with given resources. For example, quantity of production, labor productivity, sales, and profit targets should be exceeded where possible; similarly, costs and resource inputs should be below planned levels if possible. The plan is supposed to represent the minimum degree of desideratum attainment expected, based on an honest estimate of enterprise capabilities and resource requirements. The state utilizes the device of maxima and minima indexes since perfect planning is not possible. Unforeseen reserves, opportunities, and/or conditions may evolve during the course of plan fulfillment enabling the enterprise to perform better (or worse) than planned.

Enterprise Plan Indexes Requiring Higher Approval

The Chinese enterprise generally sends a complete copy of its overall draft plan, reflecting a myriad sub-indexes, norms, calculations, estimates, and so on, to superior authorities for finalization and formal approval. Higher authorities can, in principle, veto virtually any detail of the plan, or bargain with enterprise management about minute details. In reality, superior authorities typically focus their attention on, and need formally approve, only a limited number of targets and a sizable number of resource allocations reflected by resource-limit indexes. At nearly all of the firms surveyed, higher authorities approved the major targets and resource limits of their annual plans; at a substantial majority, of their quarterly plans as well; and in a limited number of cases, their monthly plans. In the few cases where the enterprise's real operating plan was the weekly one, higher approval was not needed for the plan.

At the firms surveyed, superior authorities typically formally approved the following aspects of the enterprise plan.

(1) TOTAL VALUE OF OUTPUT In all cases the marketable output target and in a sizable number of cases the gross-output target in value were not considered of major importance for operating purposes. Gross output seemed to be more important in general for statistical purposes. It seemed to be most important for operating, control, and evaluating purposes at producer-goods firms with relatively long production cycles, where there were continually sizable amounts of goods in process—such as at Wuhan Heavy Machinery. A number of the enterprises, particularly consumer-goods firms, apparently did not even obtain formal higher approval for gross value of output.

(2) PHYSICAL OUTPUT AND PRODUCT-MIX TARGETS At enterprises having an overall product line that could be meaningfully summarized by one homogeneous type of physical measure (such as weight square meters, number of standardized units), they generally required formal higher approval for a gross or total output target in physical terms. At all of the firms surveyed, superior agencies formally approved physical and/or value targets for at least some specific major products and/or product groups making up the overall product mix. The degree of specificity and units of measures applied by higher authorities varied with the types of commodities involved, as discussed in the earlier section on the production plan. Greater use is typically made of physical targets for relatively standardized and important goods. Value targets are frequently used for other products and product lines.

For numerous goods their detailed specifications are not subject to higher approval—they are worked out directly between suppliers and customers. However, most enterprise sales and supply contracts are subject to higher approval in aggregate terms, that is, the total quantities, prices, and usually basic-quality standards of goods appearing in such contracts. Some of the enterprises required higher approval for rate-of-production indexes, which indicate the pattern of output in physical terms to be achieved during a given quarter, month, week, and, in one or two cases, daily.

(3) SALES TARGETS Many of the enterprises surveyed required formal higher approval for their total-sales targets. However, where this was not the case the firm's sales program was still largely subject to implicit higher approval since superior agencies do sanction most sales (and supply) contracts at least in aggregate terms. I was told by several managers that the difference between value of the firm's marketable output and actual sales during a given year is not very substantial—rarely more than 20 percent, and typically less than 10 percent.

(4) PRODUCT QUALITY Most of the enterprises surveyed receive formal higher approval on the quality of a sizable proportion, if not all, of their product mix. It is common for consumer-goods producers to receive targets indicating the proportion of goods to be produced within each of various grades, namely first, second, third.

(5) COST TARGETS All but a few of the enterprises had at least one type of cost target approved by higher authorities. More of them seemed to require higher approval for cost of production than for total enterprise costs and expenses, but a majority received both types of targets. Only about 20 or 25 percent of the enterprises required formal approval for the unit costs of major products or product groups. And less than 20 percent of them required formal higher approval for a target expressed in terms of costs per one yuan of marketable output.

(6) LABOR PRODUCTIVITY More than half of the enterprises required formal approval for their labor-productivity targets. In most cases where labor-productivity targets were approved by superior authorities they were based on total employment rather than number of direct-production workers. Labor-productivity targets expressed in terms of output value and physical production were about equally common, and at a number of enterprises higher authorities approved both types of targets. In some cases the labor-productivity target requiring higher approval was expressed in terms of cost of production per employee rather than output.

(7) PROFIT AND PROFITABILITY TARGETS All but three of thirty-four enterprises reporting on the subject of total profit targets received formal higher approval for such a target. Only a limited number of the firms visited required higher approval for profitability targets of any type—in terms of sales, cost of production, fixed and/or working capital—although many of them did compute such targets in their plan.

(8) PRODUCT AND TECHNICAL DEVELOPMENT, RESEARCH, AND ORGANIZATIONAL MEASURES, TASKS, OR PROJECTS About 25 percent of the enterprises surveyed regularly require higher approval for indexes of these types. They are typically firms involved quite extensively in the development of relatively complex and/or important new products, the introduction of new technology and production processes, and/or technical research. Most of them are major heavy-industry enterprises, such as Wuhan Heavy Machinery, Shanghai Heavy Machine Tool, Peking No. 1 Machine Tool, and Peking Steel Wire. It is also quite common for the chemical and pharmaceutical firms to require higher approval for such measures, projects, and tasks. In general, virtually all of the enterprises surveyed have required higher approval when they have received sizable amounts of new capital investment, increased their productive capacity or expanded facilities substantially, developed major new products or produced important new products for the first time, and/or undertook major organizational changes. A few of the enterprises required higher approval for some of their equipment maintenance and overhaul schedules in 1966.

(9) PRODUCT YIELDS AND MATERIAL-CONSUMPTION NORMS Roughly 20 percent of the enterprises regularly received higher approval for product yields and/or material-consumption norms involving some of their basic and usually standardized products. Product-yield targets are generally ex-

pressed in percentage terms which represent production efficiency in avoiding material wastage. Material-consumption norms are typically expressed in real terms indicating the amount of a given type of material consumed in producing a given product. Some of the firms which regularly required formal higher approval for certain product-yield and/or material-consumption targets were Peking and Shanghai Pharmaceutical, Peking Coke and Chemical, Wuhan Paper, both of the steel firms for some basic types of steel, and Soochow Cement Products.

(10) RESOURCE LIMITS At all of the enterprises their total wage funds and total employment for the planned period required formal higher approval. In a number of cases such approval was also needed for certain broad categories of personnel such as production workers, auxiliary employees, managerial personnel, white-collar staffs, technicians, engineers, and/or party cadres. As noted in the chapter on education, there is very tight state control regarding the assignment of high-talent manpower, college graduates especially, to industrial enterprises.

At most enterprises the great majority of their materials and supplies were allocated and approved by higher authorities. However, this was typically done in fairly aggregate terms for most commodities with the firm playing a major role in working out and negotiating detailed commodity specifications, delivery dates, and so on. Higher authorities also generally approved at least some inventory and working-capital norms or limits for all of the enterprises surveyed. Capital-investment expenditures of any significant magnitude also usually required formal higher approval.

From the above discussion it may seem to some readers that Chinese enterprise managers have little authority, independence, or influence with regard to their plans or operations. This is far from the case in reality, as will be discussed in a later section.

KEY ENTERPRISE-SUCCESS INDICATORS

In the section dealing with China's basic economic system in Chapter 6 we discussed the inherent problems involved in measuring and evaluating economic performance at the enterprise level. In that section, as well as in the discussion of legal rules of the game in Chapter 5 and at other points in earlier chapters, we also discussed and analyzed the nature of enterprise-success indicators, along with problems pertaining to enterprise and managerial behavior. There is no need to go over this ground again in any detail, but a few more comments about success indicators at the enterprises surveyed are warranted here.

In the discussion that follows I use the term "key enterprise-success indicators" in reference only to those major enterprise targets which were utilized as the key or top-priority measures for evaluating overall enterprise and managerial performance. All such success indicators required formal higher approval, but not all enterprise targets or tasks requiring higher approval can be considered as key success indicators.

I have used several criteria in determining what appear to have been the key success indicators at the various Chinese enterprises that I surveyed in 1966. One approach was simply to ask the enterprise executives—and in some cases higher-level industrial officials—what the key success indicators were at their enterprises or at those under their jurisdiction. In this connection I also asked which targets generally receive the most attention by the enterprise's top management and higher-level agencies in planning and control, and particularly in the measurement and evaluation of economic performance, and why. This approach yielded a considerable amount of pertinent information since the Red Chinese do not tend to treat such information as confidential or secret.

A second approach was to find out which, if any, enterprise targets had to be fulfilled in order for bonuses (extra rewards) to be paid to personnel who were allowed to receive them. It is true that top-level executives could not receive bonuses at any of the firms surveyed, that no personnel could receive bonuses at some enterprises, and that even at a number of enterprises where personnel could receive bonuses their payment did not depend on the fulfillment of any overall enterprise targets. However, there still were a sizable number of firms in my limited sample—as will be discussed in a later section—that had to fulfill certain enterprise targets for bonuses to be paid out to eligible personnel. Such targets were clearly key enterprise-success indicators.

The third approach was to find out which targets had to be fulfilled for the firm to establish an "enterprise fund," if it was allowed to have one at all. More will be said about this fund later, but a few words of explanation are in order here. Most of the enterprises surveyed were allowed to have an enterprise fund which was created annually or quarterly, and in a few cases monthly, by a small proportion of its earned profits. This fund is essentially a reward or award fund which the enterprise and its management can use for a variety of purposes, such as welfare, recreation, special bonus payments, expanding or improving operations, and so on. It could only be formed when certain enterprise targets determined by higher authorities were fulfilled. Hence such targets were clearly key enterprise-success indicators. At most of the firms that had enterprise funds and also paid out individual bonuses only when certain enterprise targets were fulfilled, there was considerable overlap in the targets that had to be fulfilled for bonus payments and those that had to be fulfilled to establish an enterprise fund.

It was mentioned in the section on the basic economic system in Chapter 6 that the number of key or top-priority success indicators ranged between three and six at most of the enterprises surveyed. I would estimate the median number to be about four.

Total profit was one of the key success indicators at the great majority of enterprises, but it was the clear-cut top-priority indicator at only a few. Profitability computed in relation to total costs or sales had become a key success indicator in recent years at about 20 percent of the enterprises. Profit in relation to sales as a key success indicator was more common at consumer-goods firms than at producer-goods enterprises, and it had apparently been adopted to encourage the enterprises to be more concerned about the requirements and desires of their customers.

Apparently only a few of the enterprises—all heavy-industry firms—had gross output in constant-price or physical terms as a key success indicator. More than half of the enterprises had marketable output in current prices as a key success indicator, but at only about 25 to 30 percent of the firms having enterprise funds did this target have to be fulfilled to establish such a fund. Total sales was a key success indicator at quite a few enterprises, and in some cases this was also true for sales volume for major product groups. Virtually all of the enterprises surveyed had, as key success indicators, some measure of physical output for total output, and in most cases for at least some major products or product groups as well. In most cases such physical indicators were stated in broad terms such as tons, square meters, kilograms, or number of units. Many of the firms also had value-success indicators, in current prices, for various products and product groups making up their total product mix.

A large majority of the enterprises had some measure of product quality as a key success indicator. Officially, items produced are not supposed to be reflected in output, sales, or profit results unless they conform to prescribed minimum technical standards. In reality, this tends to be difficult to enforce in a detailed way, thus reducing the potency or effectiveness of product quality as a key success indicator.

Some type of cost target was a key success indicator at roughly half of the enterprises, but it was a required condition for forming an enterprise fund at only about 25 percent of the firms that were allowed to have such a fund. Total costs and cost of production were the most common cost-success indicators. Costs in relation to sales or marketable output and unit costs were key success indicators at only a small number of firms. Labor productivity in either value or physical terms was a key success indicator at about 20 to 25 percent of the enterprises and only in a few cases for establishing an enterprise fund. In all cases where labor productivity was a key success indicator it was expressed in terms of total number of employees rather than production workers. (It is likely, however, that certain types of welfare, educational, medical, and housing personnel were not included in the labor-productivity computation at various enterprises.)

Only a small number of firms had major innovation tasks pertaining to technical or product development or organizational improvements as key success indicators in 1965 or 1966, and in only one case was this an obligatory criterion for forming an enterprise fund. Where enterprises did have key success indicators of this type, they were typically stipulated in terms of time schedules and, in a few cases, expense budgets as well. About five or six of the enterprises—roughly 15 percent of the total—had product yields and/or material-consumption norms, mostly the former, as key success indicators.

Given the fact that Chinese enterprises typically have a number of key success indicators and do not have as clear-cut or precise a system of success-indicator and related rewards as in Soviet industry, how are unclear priority choices made by management? Generally stated state policies as interpreted by Chinese enterprise party cadres appear to be one common way that this type of situation is resolved. If the party cadres are not too extreme in interpreting such policies in one direction, more balanced overall enterprise performance can frequently be achieved than has typically been the case at Soviet enterprises. On the other hand, the Chinese firm is less likely to maximize results to the same degree in one or two clearly top-priority areas, such as total output, cost reduction, profit, or labor productivity.

Broad Breakdown of Enterprise Personnel and Employment

Table 9–1 below contains employment and personnel data for thirty-three Chinese industrial enterprises surveyed in 1966. It indicates total employment, percentage of female employees, and proportions of administrative and technical personnel (combined and separately) for each firm. Female employment has already been discussed in the class-structure section of Chapter 4, and there is no need to elaborate further on this topic here.

The classification of administrative cadres in Chinese industry defies precise definition. At all enterprises it apparently includes managerial personnel of all types (including group leaders or floor foremen), as well as party cadres and trade-union officials who do managerial, organizational, and administrative work. It also includes those personnel considered as key staff specialists and/or those who spend most of their working time doing creative or nonroutine mental, as opposed to physical or manual, work—and this is where the problem of definition becomes most cloudy. Accountants, statisticians, planning and financial specialists, economists, and experts on personnel, labor and wage, procurement, and sales are usually all considered part of the system of administrative cadres. However, at some firms various bookkeepers, office machine operatives,

TABLE 9–1

EMPLOYMENT AND PERSONNEL DATA FOR THIRTY-THREE CHINESE ENTERPRISES SURVEYED[a]

Enterprise	Total Employment	Percent of Female Employees	Admin. and Tech. Personnel		Admin. Cadres		Tech. and Engrs. Only[b]		Engrs. Only[c]
			Number	Percent of Total Employ.	Number	Percent of Total Employ.	Number	Percent of Total Employ.	Number
STEEL AND IRON									
Wuhan Iron and Steel (Corporation)	35,000	10%	9,300	27%	7,000	20%	2,300	7%	800
Shanghai Steel Mill No. 3	13,000	8	2,730	21	2,210	17	520	4	175
Peking Steel Wire	800	30	235	30	150	18	85	12	15
Totals	48,800		12,265	25%	9,360	19%	2,905	6%	
LARGE AND MEDIUM-SIZED MACHINERY AND EQUIPMENT									
Wuhan Heavy Machinery	7,000	21%	2,550	36.5%	1,750	25%	800	11.5%	80
Shanghai Heavy Machine Tool	6,000	15	1,200	20	750	12.5	450	7.5	140
Peking First Machine Tool	4,000	20	1,100	27.5	700	17.5	400	10	40
Hangchow Machine Tool	1,000	12	200		140	14	60	6	9
Shanghai No. 3 Machine Tool	1,000	40	200		100	10	100	100	5
Totals	19,000		5,250	27.5%	3,440	18%	1,810	9.5%	
SMALL-SCALE MACHINERY, INSTRUMENTS, COMPONENTS									
Shanghai No. 3 Forging & Pressing Machine Tool	405	15%	49	3%	37	9%	12	3%	0
Wusih Red Flag Machinery	300	22	40	13	36	12	4	1.3	0
Tientsin North Lake Instrument	165	50	10	6	10	6	0	0	0
Totals	870		99	11.5%	83	9.5%	16	2.0%	

DIESEL ENGINES AND TRUCKS									
Wusih Diesel-Engine	2,700	18%	540	20%	256	9.5%	284	10.5%	22
Wuhan Diesel-Engine	992	40	138	14	108	11	30	3	4
Shanghai Truck	1,050	20	105	10	63	6	42	4	6
Totals	4,742		783	16.5%	427	9%	356	7.5%	
CEMENT									
Soochow Cement Prod.	680	12%	60	9%	51	7.5%	9	1.5%	0
PAPER									
Wuhan Han Yang Paper	2,000	33%	420	21%	360	18%	60	3%	3
CHEMICALS AND DRUGS									
Nanking National Chemical Fertilizer	10,000	25%	2,700	27%	2,000	20%	700	7%	70
Canton Chemical Fertilizer	2,400	20	552	23	360	15	192	8	10
Peking Coke & Chem.	2,100	20	420	20	211	10	200	10	not reported
Peking Pharmaceutical	3,000	50	540	18	240	8	300	10	not reported
Shanghai Pharmaceutical No. 3	1,200	42	306	25.5	156	13	150	12.5	35
Totals	18,700		4,518	24%	2,967	16%	1,542	8%	
LIGHT DURABLE GOODS									
Tientsin Watch	1,400	50%	218	15.5%	120	8.5	98	7%	not reported
Canton Lan Yang Elec. Appliance	840	33	134	16	84	10	50	6	3
Shanghai Wei Ming Battery	563	45	73	13	56	10	17	3	1
Totals	2,803		425	15%	260	9%	165	6%	
TEXTILES									
Shanghai No. 9 Sung Sing (Joint) Cotton Textile	6,000	70%	450	7.5%	300	5%	150	2.5%	(but at least 2) not reported

TABLE 9–1 (*continued*)

Enterprise	*Total Employment*	*Percent of Female Employees*	*Admin. and Tech. Personnel* *Number*	*Admin. and Tech. Personnel* *Percent of Total Employ.*	*Admin. Cadres* *Number*	*Admin. Cadres* *Percent of Total Employ.*	*Tech. and Engrs. Only*[b] *Number*	*Tech. and Engrs. Only*[b] *Percent of Total Employ.*	*Engrs. Only*[c] *Number*
Peking Cotton Tex. No. 3	5,000	70	500	10	400	8	100	2	not reported
Shanghai Cotton Tex. No. 19	4,800	70	374	8	240	5	134	3	16
Peking Woolen Fabric	1,800	60	234	13	162	9	72	4	5
Tientsin Jen Yi (Joint) Woolen Fabric	1,800	60	187	10.5	126	7	61	3.5	not reported
Wusih Silk Reeling No. 2	1,500	90	188	12.5	150	10	38	2.5	1
Totals	20,900		1,933	9%	1,378	6.5%	555	2.5%	
CLOTHING									
Peking Clothing	1,700	50%	85	5%	83	5%	2	negligible	0
Hangchow Fu Chong Clothing	400	60	16	4	13	3	3	1	0
Totals	2,100		101	5%	96	4.5%	5	0.5%	
SHOES									
Tientsin Shoe	1,000	33%	225	22.5%	75	7.5%	150	15%	3
GRAND TOTALS	121,986		26,079	21.5%	18,497	15%	7,582	6.2%	

[a] Some figures are not exact because of rounding. In a few cases small ranges (not varying by more than 1 percent) were given to me by enterprise executives. Where this is the case I have arbitrarily used the midpoint of the ranges in the above computations.

[b] Technical personnel includes only those employed as engineers or technicians, not those employed in managerial jobs. Administrative personnel or cadres includes some types of white-collar employees not considered as part of management in U.S. (or Soviet) industry. Roughly 17,500 to 21,500 of the 26,079 Chinese administrative-technical personnel would correspond to the Soviet classification of Engineering-Managerial-Technical Personnel (ETMP), roughly 9,500 to 13,500.

[c] Excludes engineers classified as part of management or administrative personnel; includes only those working as engineers.

cashiers, and other white-collar employees are considered to be administrative cadres; at other firms this is not so with seemingly similar types of personnel. But at none of the firms surveyed did administrative cadres include all white-collar employees. For example, the administrative-cadres group typically excludes file clerk and others doing similarly routine types of clerical jobs, typists and routine secretaries, timekeepers, receptionists, telephone operators, guards and custodians, and various types of sales, procurement, storeroom, warehousing, shipping and receiving personnel doing routine jobs requiring little or no creative effort.

I would estimate that about 35 to 50 percent of the administrative cadres at Chinese industrial enterprises would correspond to managerial personnel (including all foremen) in U.S., Soviet, and Indian industry. (Indian firms frequently do not include low-level foremen as part of management.)

In Table 9–1 technical personnel refers to employees with the title of engineer or technician, regardless of their formal education. This category also includes chemists and other natural scientists, pharmacologists, medical doctors and technicians doing chiefly technical or research work as opposed to managerial or administrative jobs, designers, and draftsmen who are considered to be doing creative mental work rather than purely routine manual tasks. Various engineers and technicians also do such jobs as setting utilization norms and quality standards, directing maintenance and repair work, and so forth. Usually technically competent people, including engineers, who hold managerial positions and/or who spend much of their time doing administrative work are classified as administrative cadres rather than as engineers or technicians. For example, this would be true of a chief engineer.

The combined classification of administrative and technical personnel at the Chinese enterprises corresponds approximately to the Soviet classification of leading enterprise personnel, also referred to as leading managerial, administrative, technical, and specialized personnel.[4] It also corresponds roughly to the classification of managers, officials and proprietors, and professional, technical, and kindred employees in U.S. manufacturing industries. About 65 to 80 percent of the administrative and technical personnel at most of the Chinese enterprises surveyed would correspond to the engineering-managerial-technical personnel (EMTP) classification in Soviet industry.[5] At the sixteen or so Chinese enterprises where I obtained specific data on their managerial personnel per se, their managerial staffs comprised from 35 to 52 percent of all administrative and technical personnel, and from about 52 to 73 percent of their administrative cadres.

Table 9–1 indicates that for the thirty-three Chinese firms their combined administrative and technical personnel constituted 21.5 percent of their combined total employment in 1966. Administrative cadres alone comprised 15.3 percent of total employment, and technicians and engineers 6.2 percent. A fairly substantial proportion of the enterprises did not have any engineers. At those enterprises reporting on their employment of engineers, at only six of them did engineers account for 1 percent or more of total employment. These six were the two steel firms, the Wuhan and Shanghai Heavy Machine Tool enterprises, Peking First Machine Tool, and Shanghai No. 3 Pharmaceutical.

This table does not include specific data on auxiliary workers or welfare and service personnel since these personnel have already been discussed in the sections on factor endowment and social-overhead capital in Chapter 6. To summarize briefly: many Chinese enterprises surveyed had ratios of 1.5 to 1 or less, with regard to the relationship between direct-production workers and auxiliary employees. In some cases the ratio was less than 1 to 1—that is, the enterprises had a greater proportion of auxiliary workers. As for welfare and service personnel, at most firms they ranged between 4 and 7 percent of total employment, and at a few the proportion was 10 percent or more.

Before analyzing the Chinese figures in Table 9–1 in detail, it may be illuminating to make some broad, suggestive comparisons with Russia, the United States, and India. In January 1957 leading personnel at the enterprise level in Soviet industry comprised about 10 percent of total employment, and by 1960 about 11 percent.[6] From more recent available Soviet data, I would estimate that in recent years roughly 13 to 15 percent of all enterprise personnel in Soviet industry have corresponded to the Chinese classification of administrative and technical personnel in Table 9–1.[7] If this estimate is reasonably accurate this means that the proportion of administrative and technical personnel for my sample of thirty-three Chinese enterprises is significantly larger than the proportion of similar types of personnel in Soviet industry as a whole.

This may well be true since Chinese enterprises typically have significantly larger proportions of administrative personnel (including managers per se) than roughly comparable—in terms of size and branch of industry—Soviet enterprises. Differences in the proportion of technical personnel at roughly comparable types of firms in the two countries do not seem to be very great on the average. But technicians and engineers as a group have more formal education in Russia, and Soviet enterprises typically have a significantly greater proportion of engineers.

In 1963 ETMP comprised 9.2 percent of total employment at Soviet industrial enterprises.[8] For my sample of Chinese firms I would estimate that ETMP comprised 14.4 to 17.6 percent of total employment. In 1962 engineers and technicians comprised 6.5 percent of total enterprise employment in Soviet industry compared with 6.2 percent in my sample of Chinese firms.[9] Engineers alone accounted for nearly 2 percent of Soviet enterprise employment in 1962,[10] while the overall proportion of engineers for the Chinese firms reporting this type of information was well under 1 percent in 1966.

Hence, it is likely that, on the average, Chinese industrial enterprises have significantly larger proportions of both nonmanagerial and managerial administrative cadres, including party cadres, than do similar types of Soviet firms. Chinese enterprises are also likely to have larger proportions of routine types of white-collar workers and welfare and service personnel, and substantially larger proportions of auxiliary workers than Soviet firms.

In U.S. industry in 1960 the total proportion of managers, officials and proprietors, and professional, technical, and kindred employees was about 17.2 percent of total employment at manufacturing enterprises.[11] This was 4.3 percent less than the proportion of administrative and technical personnel in my sample of Chinese enterprises. The proportion of managerial and technical personnel—the ETMP equivalent—at U.S. manufacturing enterprises in 1960 was about 15.1 percent, compared with an estimated 14.4 to 17.6 percent for my Chinese sample. The U.S. figure of 15.1 percent is made up of 9.5 percent for managers (including foremen), officials and proprietors, and 5.6 percent for engineering-technical types of personnel. Engineers comprised about 2.7 percent of total enterprise employment in U.S. manufacturing industries in 1960. U.S. firms, of course, typically have much larger sales staffs than similar kinds of Chinese (or Soviet) industrial enterprises but much smaller proportions of auxiliary workers and welfare and service personnel.

From my firsthand research in India, I would estimate that Indian industrial enterprises tend to have smaller proportions of managers, auxiliary workers, and welfare and service personnel than Chinese firms, but larger overall white-collar staffs (particularly clerks) than Chinese enterprises in similar industries and of roughly comparable sizes. There does not seem to be any clear pattern with regard to technical personnel in the two countries, except that a significantly greater proportion of them at Indian firms seem to be bachelor of science graduates (and at times arts or commerce graduates), while in Chinese industry there are substantially more semi-professionals and professionals—particularly the former—trained in technical and engineering fields per se. U.S. subsidiaries and joint ventures in India, as well as a limited number of highly progressive indigenous Indian firms, employ significantly greater proportions of managers, staff specialists, engineers, and engineering-type technicians than do typical indigenous Indian enterprises, and their patterns of employment in these areas tend to be closer to those found at Chinese industrial enterprises.

Let us now look at some of the branch-of-industry figures in Table 9–1. As a group the large and medium-sized Chinese machinery and equipment enterprises had the largest proportion (27.5 percent) of administrative and technical personnel. Other sectors or firms with proportions greater than 20 percent were iron and steel, chemicals and drugs, and the Wuhan Paper and Tientsin Shoe enterprises. With the exception of Tientsin Shoe, all of these enterprises are characterized by relatively highly capital-intensive plants, and they each employ at least 1,000 people. It is common for such types of firms to require relatively high proportions of administrative and technical personnel. The Tientsin Shoe enterprise is a different story. Its large proportion is due chiefly to the fact that technicians comprised nearly 15 percent of its employment in 1966. It is likely that a sizable number of the firm's older skilled craftsmen and veteran workers having long experience were given the title of technician for status, psychological, and ideological reasons.

The Chinese clothing enterprises as a group have the smallest proportion of administrative and technical personnel; these are followed by the textile group and Soochow Cement Products. The firms producing small-scale machinery, instruments, and components, the diesel-engine and truck group, and the light-durables group rank in the middle of all the sectors in Table 9–1.

If we compare the rank ordering of administrative and technical personnel by sectors in Table 9–1 with that for administrative cadres only, a few significant differences emerge. The category iron and steel replaces the large and medium-sized machinery firms in first place; Tientsin Shoe drops down three rungs; Wuhan Paper moves up three places: small-scale machinery, etc., and Diesel Engines and Trucks move up two rungs; Soochow Cement Products and the light-durables group move up one place; the chemical and pharmaceutical, textile, and clothing groups remain the same.

Comparing the rank ordering for administrative cadres with technicians and engineers we see that Tientsin Shoe jumps to first place, followed by the large and medium-sized machinery group. Iron and steel drops from first to fourth place, and the chemical and drug group from second to third place. The small machinery group drops three places, while the diesel-engine and truck and light-durables groups go up one position. Soochow Cement Products drops a bit, while the chemical and drug, textile, and clothing groups remain about as they were.

From available Soviet branch-of-industry employment statistics and my first-hand knowledge of specific Soviet, Indian, and U.S. industrial enterprises, it appears that the rank orders in my Chinese sample with regard to proportions of overall administrative and technical personnel, administrative cadres, and engineers and technicians are not too different in general from the patterns in these three other countries.

The Party at the Industrial Enterprise

The nature, roles, and activities of the party at Chinese industrial enterprises have been discussed at several points in earlier chapters.[12] However, some additional comments and data are in order here.

The enterprise as a whole, and the top director as an individual, are officially and formally under the authority of the enterprise party committee which is headed by the party secretary. There was no clear pattern at the enterprises visited as to how often the party committee meets. In most cases it met regularly at least once a month, and only in rare cases did it meet regularly more than once a week, typically for not more than a few hours. While the size of the enterprise—in terms of employment—does seem to be a factor regarding the number of members on the enterprise party committee, the total number as well as the proportion of employees who are party members seem to be the key factors in this connection. The number of party committee members at several of the enterprises surveyed in 1966 is indicated in the organization charts presented in the section on enterprise-organization structure. At firms that do not have a fairly sizable number of party members—at least several dozen—they have a party branch, rather than a committee, to which all of the party members belong. It is common for such party branches to be broken down into subgroups, each handling certain party functions. About five of the enterprises surveyed, all employing less than 1,000 people, had a party branch, which was headed by the party secretary, rather than a party committee.

The Shanghai Battery and Tientsin Shoe enterprises had the smallest party committees, with seven members on each. Wuhan Iron and Steel had a corporation party committee of over thirty members. Several of the factory directors of the corporation were not on this committee, but apparently most of the factory party secretaries were. This corporation actually had a number of party committees at different levels with interlocking members. Most of the factory workshops had shop party committees, headed by a shop party secretary, and this setup is common at all types of enterprises where their workshops have fairly sizable numbers of party members. The enterprises per se, as opposed to corporations, that I surveyed which had the largest party committees were Wuhan Heavy Machinery and Shanghai Steel with twenty and nineteen members respectively.

The firms having by far the largest proportions of employees who were party members were Wuhan Paper and Shanghai No. 3 Machine Tool with 30 percent and 20 percent respectively. Those having the smallest proportions were Hangchow Cothing and Nanking Chemical Fertilizer with 6 percent and 7 percent respectively. The proportions at most of the enterprises surveyed ranged from 10 to 15 percent.

A majority of the enterprises did not have any workers on their party committees. With the exception of three firms the rest had only one or two workers on their committees. The three exceptions were Wuhan Heavy Machinery, Canton Electrical Appliance, and Shanghai Truck with seven-, and four- and three-worker committee members, respectively. At almost all of the enterprises there were vice directors not on the party committee, but the vice director in charge of welfare virtually always was. It was also common for sizable proportions of department heads, workshop directors, engineers, and technicians not to be on the enterprise party committee.

Under the enterprise party committee there is typically a political-work department—or some similar type of administrative unit—usually headed by the firm's vice party secretary. Where the enterprise has a relatively sizable number of party members there are generally several subdepartments or sections under this political-work department. These are typically the publicity, cadres, and organizational departments or sections. This party organizational setup is reflected in Chart 9–1 for the Shanghai Pharmaceutical enterprise. But it was similar at many of the other firms surveyed.

The publicity department handles such matters as special study groups, special campaigns, slogans and wall posters, and the dissemination of information and propaganda. The organizational department deals with applications for party membership, the appraisal of party members and potential members in particular, as well as contacts with external party organizations and, at times, other types of organizations as well. The cadres department handles ideological and political education, and also apparently plays a key role in appraising, promoting, grading, and possibly determining the pay of personnel in important nonparty jobs. The employees of the publicity and organizational department, as well as the central political-work department, had to be party members at all of the firms where I obtained data on this subject. Some of the enterprises did not officially require all jobs in the cadres department to be filled by party members, but they all were anyway. Where the enterprise did not have an adequate number of party members to warrant such an elaborate party structure, the political-work department alone handled all of the affairs handled by subdepartments at other firms.

At a number of the enterprises visited, the party committee set up special subcommittees from time to time to deal with special problems or projects. Subcommittee members were selected from different parts of the enterprise. Some of the party subcommittees functioning at various enterprises dealt with such matters as special ideological-training programs, campaigns to raise quality and/or to reduce material wastage, product development, innovation and experimentation, serving the customer better, and learning from more advanced work groups and/or enterprises.

In general, party functionaries seem to comprise a larger proportion of administrative cadres and managerial staff at Chinese firms than at Soviet industrial enterprises. Where data of this type were obtained from Chinese enterprises, party functionaries comprised a minimum of about 7 percent to a maximum of nearly 25 percent of their administrative cadres. However, it is common for various types of party cadres, such as party secretaries in smaller shops, to spend a good part of their time on nonparty work.

The Trade Union at the Enterprise

We have dealt at some length with trade-union activities at Chinese industrial enterprises in earlier chapters,[13] and only a few brief additional comments will be presented here. The number of members on the enterprise trade-union committee is determined primarily by the number of union members employed by the firm. At the enterprises surveyed, the vast majority of employees were union members, and hence the size of the union committee was in effect determined by their total employment. At the seven or eight firms where I obtained data of this type their trade union committees ranged in size from six to twenty-two members. Shanghai Truck represented the average in this sample with a thirteen-member trade-union committee, headed by a chairman and having three vice chairmen. Six of the seven workshops at this factory had shop union committees, headed by a shop chairman, ranging in number from five to eleven. It was even more common for a shop trade-union chairman to be a regular worker than a shop party secretary.

At several of the enterprises the trade-union committee carried out orders initiated by the party's political-work department or one of its subunits. In this connection, the union committee dealt with such things as worker mobilization and motivation, dissemination of information, slogans, wall posters, and, in a few cases, after-hour study sessions. In most instances, however, trade-union officials received their assignments directly from the party leaders at the enterprise.

It seemed to be much more common for union officials to spend most of their time in nonunion work than for party cadres to spend theirs in nonparty work. In fact, most shop union officials were assigned to regular jobs in the shop. Even most of the enterprise trade-union committee chairmen and vice chairmen whom I met spent at least three days a week in some form of physical labor, compared with an average of one to two days for enterprise party secretaries and vice secretaries. The factory trade-union committees typically played very active roles in encouraging workers to put forth "innovational" and technical-improvement suggestions, and in spreading the word about worthwhile new methods, techniques, and processes that have potential application in different parts of the enterprise.

Time Spent in Political Education and Ideological Indoctrination

I am sure that at the time of my visit to Red China the amount of on-the-job time spent in political education and ideological indoctrination sessions was much less at the enterprise level than during the Great Leap period. Formal on-the-job political sessions were not very much in evidence at most of the firms surveyed. However, in many instances there did seem to be quite a bit of informal on-the-job activity revolving around ideology and politics.

Managerial, technical, and party meetings dealing with business affairs were held during working hours (more will be said about this in the next section). I was told that most meeting and discussion sessions relating to worker participation in management were held after working hours. However, in both on- and off-the-job meetings it was likely that a fairly substantial amount of time was often taken up by ideology and politics. If this practice is not carried to extremes it can and probably does have some positive motivational effects and other beneficial impacts on economic, managerial, and technical performance. But when employees must frequently spend long hours after work in ideological sessions their productivity is likely to suffer on the job.

Higher-level executives—both Reds and Experts—and often key technical personnel at many of the enterprises surveyed were required to spend about a half day, or a maximum of one full day on the job each week, usually a half day, at meetings and study sessions dealing chiefly with politics and ideology. (More about this later.) As noted in earlier chapters, at the enterprises surveyed the most common Maoist works studied by both managers and workers were "On Contradictions," "On Practice," "In Memory of Norman Bethune" (which extolls selflessness, dedication, and moral stimuli), and "The Foolish Old Man Who Removed Mountains" (which stresses persistence and self-confidence in overcoming obstacles).

By June of 1966, with the intensification of the Cultural Revolution, it became increasingly difficult for me to get appointments with key enterprise executives and, for that matter, with higher-level industrial officials as well. The reason usually given was that they were tied up in political and ideological meetings because of the Cultural Revolution. This was no doubt true in many if not most cases. On an increasing number of occasions during my stay in China, enterprise executives were called out of my sessions with them to attend special meetings or conferences. At some of the enterprises I was told that the director, party secretary, or some other high-level manager had just been to, was in, or was going to Peking to attend a special conference on the Cultural Revolution.

With the onslaught of the Red Guards, followed by the military and people's militia at industrial enterprises, and with the formation of new "revolutionary" committees composed of Super-Reds, no doubt a great deal of time has been—and may still be—spent on intensive ideological sessions and political meetings at numerous enterprises. There have been a sizable number of reports in official Red Chinese sources indicating that this was the case in 1967. Managerial effectiveness, productive efficiency, and general industrial progress are clearly the losers when a substantial part of the working day is taken up by politics and ideological indoctrination.

How Key Managers and Officials Typically Spend Their Time at Chinese Enterprises

It is, of course, difficult for me to draw a clear-cut picture of how a typical Chinese enterprise director, vice director, or party secretary spends his time. There was a considerable amount of variation at different enterprises visited, and I did not spend enough time in Chinese industry to find out in depth how key executives spend their time. I came away with the feeling, however, that there is greater diversity regarding the ways in which a given type of manager spends his time at Chinese firms as compared with the activity of his Soviet counterpart. This may be the case because of the less monolithic and more decentralized nature of Chinese industry, compared with the Soviet industry of the early 1960's, when I was last in Russia.

This does not mean that Chinese executives do not schedule or organize their activities in advance or have no programmed work patterns. They did, in fact, seem to have fairly clear-cut, but varying, work patterns in spite of the antibureaucratic emphasis in industry. For bureaucracy and programmed work schedules up to a point are not necessarily synonymous.

There were some clear similarities in managerial work patterns at Chinese enterprises which generally accounted for one-third to one-half of the time of high-level executives. As was discussed in the previous section, key managers and officials typically spent about a half day each week in studying and discussing Mao's works and ideology in general. At a few enterprises they were spending the equivalent of a full day each week in this type of activity. The enterprise party committee—probably often on orders from higher party agencies—usually determined the amount of time to be spent on required political study each week. It is interesting to note the findings of Rosemary Stewart, a British industrial sociologist from Oxford University's center for Management Studies, who visited eight Chinese industrial enterprises in the fall of 1966—after I had left China. Some of these eight factories were ones which I had also visited. She found that managers were spending a minimum of a half day and in several cases as much as a day and a half each week studying politics and ideology on the job. Hence, it is likely that the amount of time devoted to such study had been increased at the enterprise level as a whole and at numerous individual firms between June and October of 1966.

As I have noted in Chapter 4, higher-level managers and party executives typically were spending one or one and a half days a week in compulsory physical labor at the enterprises that I visited. Only in a few rare cases were they spending as much as two days a week in such activity. Department managers and workshop managers were spending about the same amount of time in physical labor at various enterprises, but at some firms it was less or apparently not even required of these types of managers. Rosemary Stewart found at the enterprises she visited that workshop managers typically were spending three days a week doing manual work, while directors, vice directors, department managers, and, in fact, all other managers were spending two days each week in compulsory physical labor. Hence, it is likely that the amount of time managers (and party cadres) had to spend in physical labor at enterprises was increased in numerous cases after I left China.

Most types of managers and key officials apparently spent at least a half day each week at regular business meetings at the enterprises that I surveyed. Directors, vice directors, and key technical people typically spent more time in such meetings than lower-level managers. At some of the enterprises, such as Shanghai Pharmaceutical, Wuhan Paper, and Wusih Diesel Engine, senior executives held regular business meetings four or five times a week, with each meeting lasting an average of about two hours. In general, directors and vice directors spent more time in business meetings at enterprises than party cadres. But this was clearly not the case at some firms, most typically those that seemed to be run by Reds, even in terms of operational management.

It was very common for the enterprises surveyed to send one of its directors, the party secretary, and/or a small delegation of other key executives to their directly superior organization once a week (in some cases more often) to attend a regularly scheduled meeting or give a report. Written reports seemed to be prepared and used significantly more often at such higher-level meetings than at meetings within the enterprise.

Fairly often enterprises also sent representatives to a higher organization two or three levels above the firm. For example, enterprises under municipal corporations sent people to the municipal industrial bureaus and, at times, the provincial industrial departments; firms directly under municipal bureaus sent people to the Municipal People's Council, provincial-level organizations, or even the related central industrial ministry. In fact, even most of the smaller enterprises, particularly those manufacturing producer goods, under direct municipal control sent representatives at least once or twice a year to Peking to attend meetings held by the related industrial ministry and/or various other central organizations.

Again at enterprises where the Reds seemed to be in control of operational management, it was more common for the party secretary, or vice secretary, to attend higher-level business meetings. In general, the types of managers who most regularly attended higher-level meetings at the enterprises surveyed seemed to be the directors and vice directors, the chief engineer and vice chief engineer, and the heads of the planning, technical, and finance and accounting departments. It was much less common for other managers or personnel to attend meetings at levels above the firm, and workshop chiefs rarely did.

Within the Chinese enterprise, top management typically spent the rest of its time on broad planning and control, major problems involving resources, informal communication, and other managerial and administrative activities common in many aspects to management in U.S. firms, particularly U.S. factories. While higher-level Chinese executives often get involved with departmental and workshop problems, they apparently were not generally inclined to seriously undermine or usurp the authority of lower-level managers who were typically permitted to direct their operations within the limits set by the plan and the firm's basic organizational structure.

Enterprise-Organization Structure

Chinese industrial enterprises are organized on a rather highly standardized basis, patterned in substantial part after organizational structures at Soviet enterprises.[14] However, the Soviets have traditionally had a distinctly more monolithic form of organization at the enterprise level than the Red Chinese. This difference has probably been due largely to the greater decentralization of authority that has been permitted in Chinese industry—at least until very recently—as well as more favorable attitudes toward flexibility, diversity, and organizational improvisation at the enterprise level.

But even so, the degree of standardization or uniformity in organizational structures among enterprises in Chinese industry is still significantly more pronounced than in U.S. industry, although similarities in structure do exist between the two countries. The Red Chinese, like the Soviets, employ relatively monolithic forms of enterprise organization in order to support their systems of state planning, control, and direction of economic activity. Greater standardization of plans, policies, procedures, methods, and information feedback is made possible by employing a system of uniform and parallel departmentalization at each level in the industrial hierarchy. This basic form of industrial organization greatly facilitates uniformity of plans, operations, and information reporting at each level, frequently through the exertion of functional authority emanating from successively higher organizational levels. The Chinese enterprise is subject to functional authority exerted by a variety of higher-level organizations. Such a relatively monolithic organizational setup also facilitates the coordination of educational and manpower planning with industrial and general economic planning.

Within the Chinese industrial enterprise there are several strata of managerial personnel, with directors and vice directors at the top and department heads and workshop directors under them. In larger departments and shops there are often deputy heads, section chiefs, and even subsection chiefs, with front-line supervisors and group leaders at the lowest rungs. The same basic concepts—and many of the problems—of line and staff, functional authority (that is, higher authority exerted over specific policies, procedures, methods, and so on of lower administrative units), service departments, and chain of command exist in Chinese industrial organizations as in U.S. firms.

Charts 9–1A to 9–11 present organization charts for eleven of the Chinese enterprises that I surveyed. I have chosen to present charts for enterprises of varying sizes and in a fairly broad cross section of industries. In most cases I had to draw the organization charts of Chinese firms from scratch, on the basis of data obtained from my interviews because the managers claimed not to have any detailed formal charts of this type. At virtually all of the Soviet enterprises that I surveyed several years ago, they had very detailed charts typically indicating even the lowliest floor cleaner on the night shift. In most cases Soviet managers were even willing to provide me with copies of their enterprise-organization charts.

Why this difference between Chinese and Soviet enterprises? I am quite sure that secrecy on this subject in China was usually not the reason. Rather, it is likely that a formal organization chart tends to be viewed, at least officially, as a rather bureaucratic, nonhuman and inflexible device by the Red Chinese. The informal organization is viewed as being at least as important, if not more so, than the formal organization at Chinese firms. Moreover, people are frequently shifted around at Chinese enterprises,

CHART 9–1A

SHANGHAI NO. 3 PHARMACEUTICAL ENTERPRISE
(Figures in brackets indicate approximate number of personnel in each unit)

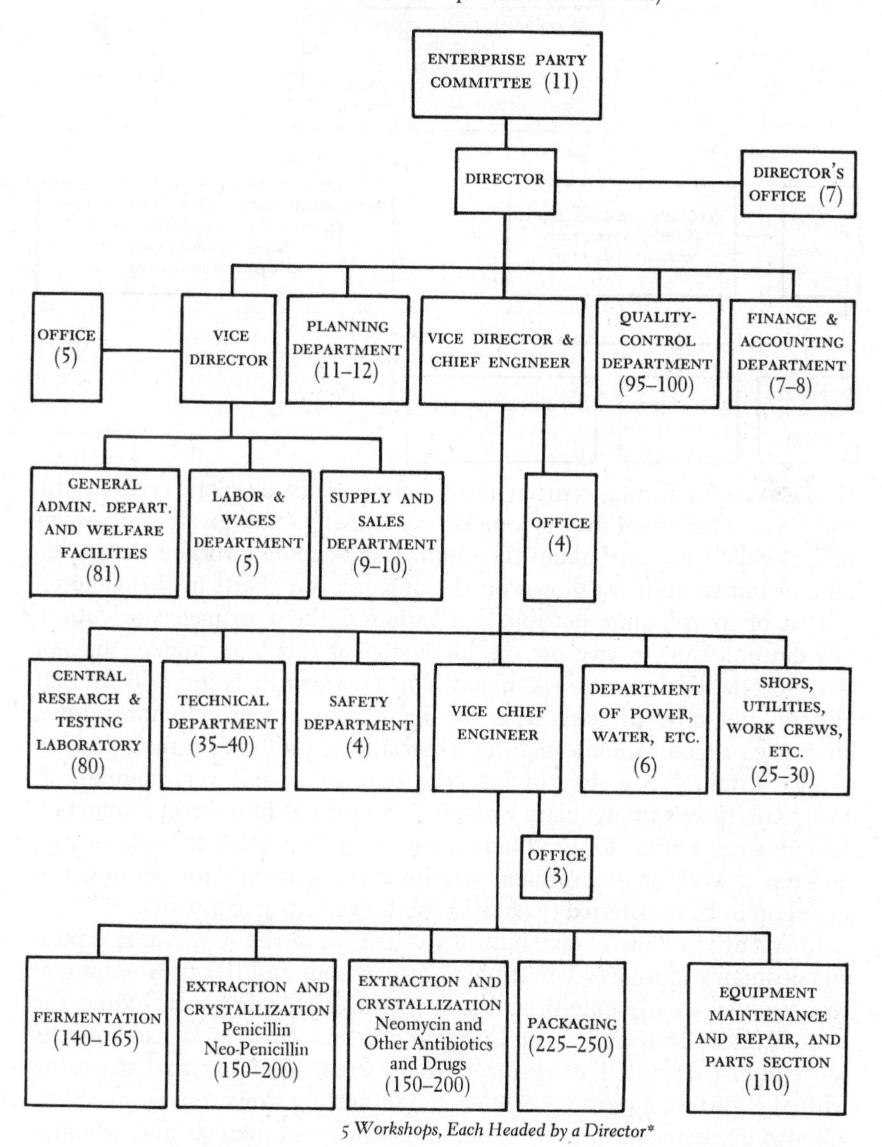

*5 Workshops, Each Headed by a Director**

* Each workshop also has one or more deputy directors, section heads, and group leaders. Shops also have labor and material norm setters, quality-control personnel, and in some cases planners and accountants working in them.

CHART 9–1B
ENTERPRISE PARTY ORGANIZATION
SHANGHAI NO. 3 PHARMACEUTICAL ENTERPRISE

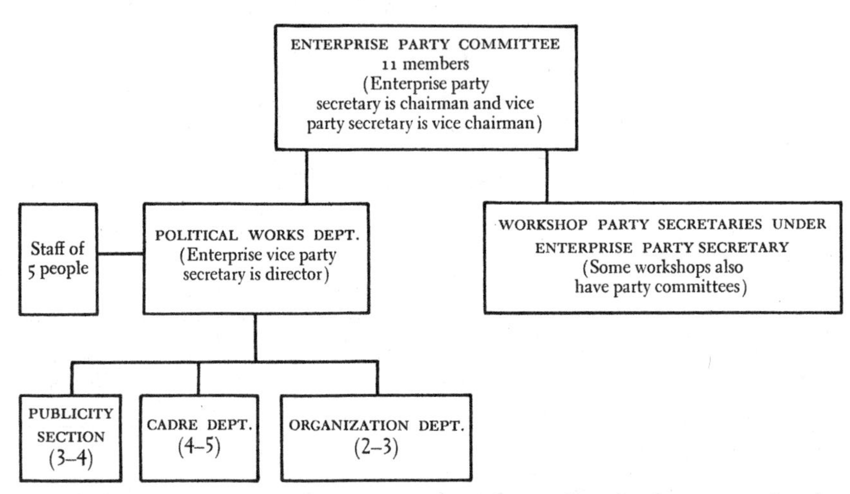

thus making a formal written chart substantially obsolete even in the short run. This factor may be one key reason why I was given fairly broad ranges when I inquired about the number of personnel working in specific administrative units, as shown on the organization charts in this chapter.

It is, of course, quite possible that various Chinese managers intentionally did not want to give me specific figures of this type, and/or did not wish to take the time to assemble them. However, it is more likely that they did not know precisely what the figures were at a given point in time, since their organization structures, especially at the bottom rungs, are almost constantly in a state of flux. For example, it was very common at many enterprises for auxiliary workers to be shifted into direct-production jobs on short notice, for production workers to be shifted to maintenance and repair work or innovational activities, and generally for personnel of one shop to be transferred to another job for various assignments.

In recent years there have been many articles in the Red Chinese press and economic journals advocating reorganizations and the streamlining of management at the enterprise level. Several of the firms, including the huge Wuhan Iron and Steel Corporation, that I surveyed had recently introduced substantial reorganizations in their administrative structures with the aim of increasing efficiency and cutting down on bureaucracy. Various departments and units were abolished and merged, and administrative staffs cut down, with most of the members being assigned to other types of jobs. Managers of a number of other enterprises—among them Wusih Diesel Engine, Wuhan Paper, Canton Electrical Appliance, and Tientsin Shoe—indicated that they felt that their organizational structures could be improved considerably, but they candidly admitted that they were not sure how best to attack the problem.

CHART 9–2

PEKING FIRST MACHINE-TOOL ENTERPRISE

(Figures in brackets indicate approximate number of personnel in each unit where such data was obtained)

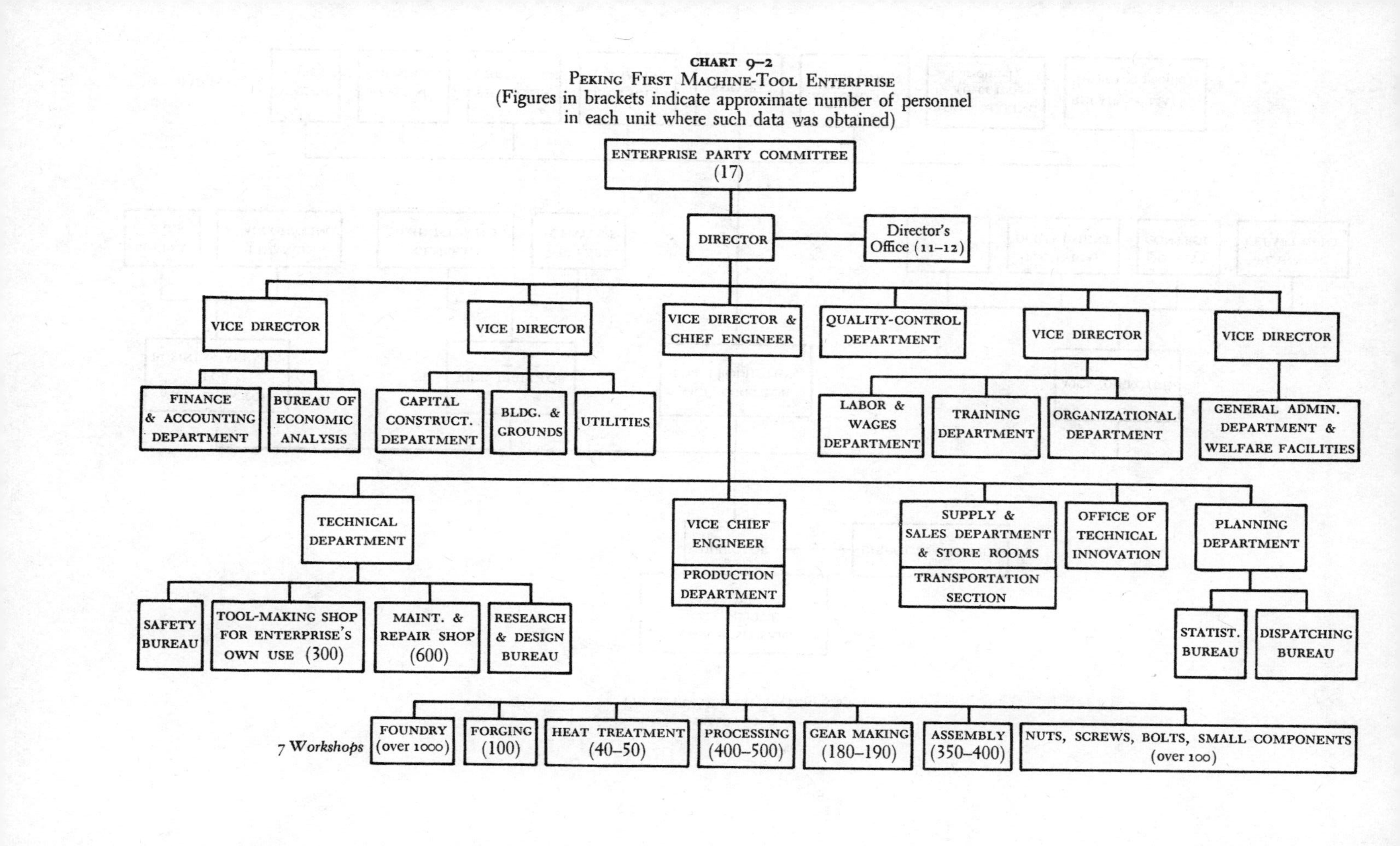

CHART 9–3
TIENTSIN WATCH ENTERPRISE

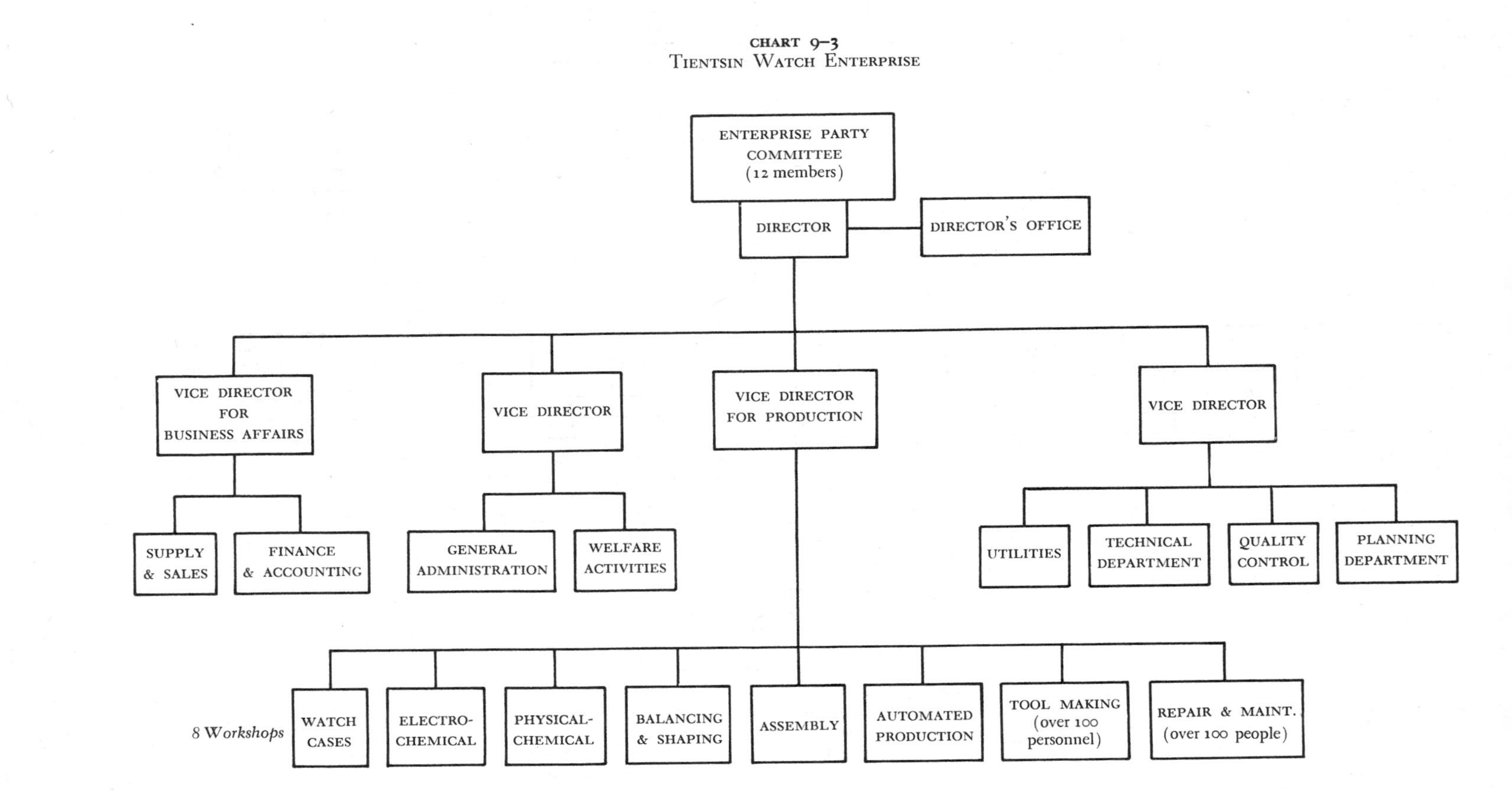

With the intensification of the Cultural Revolution, official attacks against bureaucracy have also been intensified. There were reports that various enterprises under the control of new Super-Red revolutionary committees or groups had been reorganized with the aim of eliminating bureaucracy and of streamlining and revolutionizing management. For example, in February 1967, in a matter of days, 60 percent of the administrative and nonproduction personnel were transferred to production jobs at the Tsingtao Red Guard Metal-Product Factory by the newly formed revolutionary group in command. Many administrative units were merged and abolished, twenty-nine of forty-four administrators and technicians were transferred to the production line, and several managerial levels were eliminated.[15] Such drastic and hasty organizational changes undertaken by inexperienced Super-Reds with the chief or sole purpose of blindly fighting bureaucracy undoubtedly tend to hinder rather than increase efficiency.

I shall now describe some of the basic features of the organization structures of the enterprises surveyed.

Vice Directors

Most of even the smallest enterprises had several vice directors, while some of the largest had as many as nine or ten. Where the firm had a chief engineer he was usually also a vice director. Workshops were generally under the chief engineer, vice chief engineer, or a production department which was under one of these two executives. In a few cases workshop heads reported right to the director. It seems to be much more common for workshops to be under a production department at Soviet enterprises than at Chinese firms. Perhaps the Chinese dichotomous conception of planning and operations is one major reason accounting for this apparent difference. Most of the enterprises had a vice director, usually a Red, in charge of welfare and general administration, and one in charge of commercial matters, such as supply and sales, and finance and accounting. It was also common to have a vice director in charge of the technical department and other technical activities, in addition to the chief engineer, who was also usually a vice director. Generally, the heads of white-collar departments reported to a vice director or the director, but in a few cases a vice director was himself in charge of such a department. At many enterprises various white-collar administrative units were referred to as sections, bureaus, or offices, rather than departments.

Planning and Production Departments

At some firms these were two separate units, but at most they were combined into one. The planning unit or department usually deals with the compilation of the overall plan for the enterprise, starting with, and

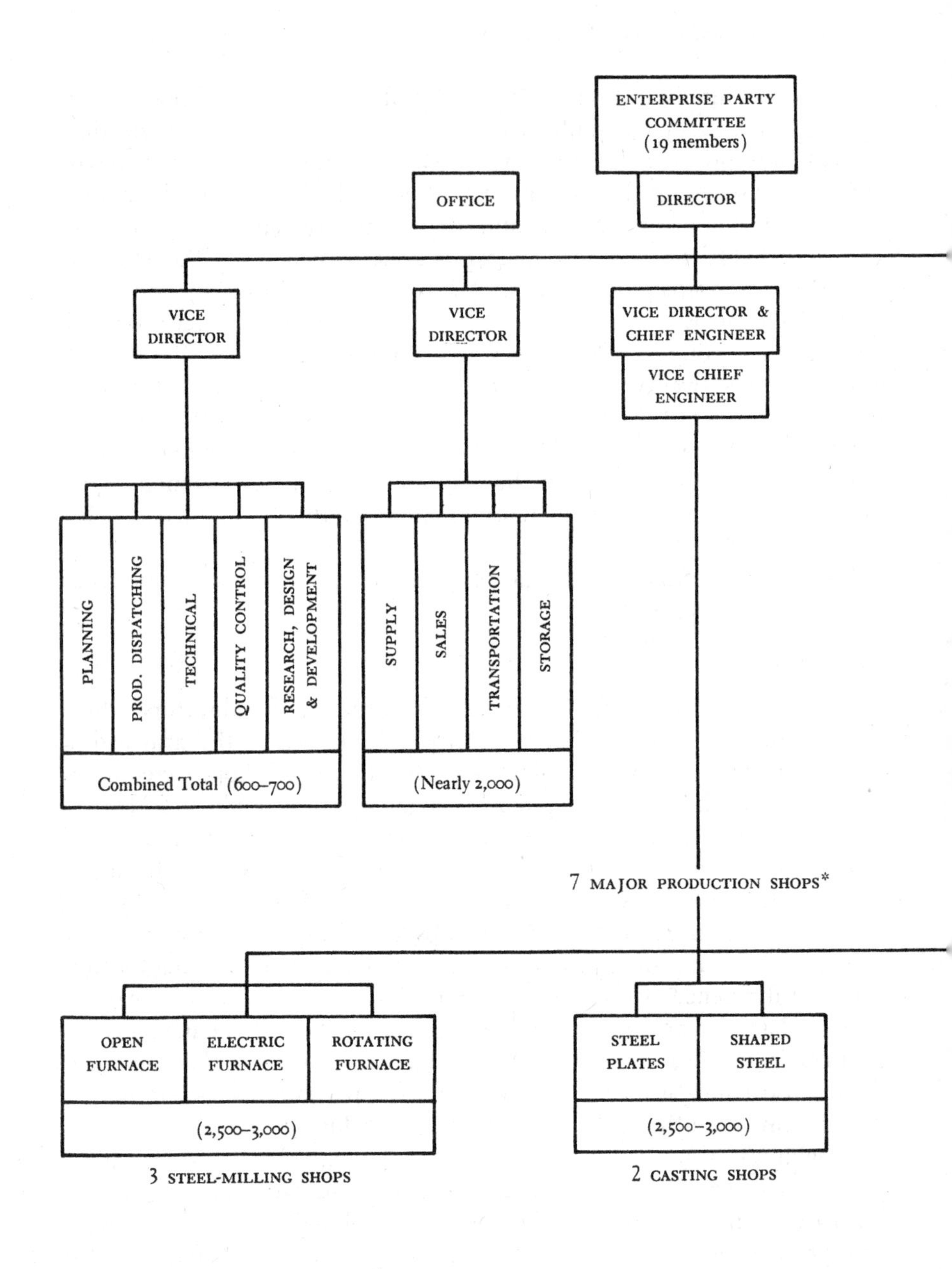

ADMINISTRATIVE ORGANIZATION OF A TYPICAL MAJOR PRODUCTION SHOP

SHOP DIRECTOR
DEPUTY SHOP DIRECTORS
SECTION CHIEFS
DEPUTY SECTION CHIEFS
GROUP LEADERS
WORKERS

CHART 9–4
SHANGHAI NO. 3 STEEL ENTERPRISE
(Figures in brackets indicate approximate number of personnel in each unit where such information was obtained)

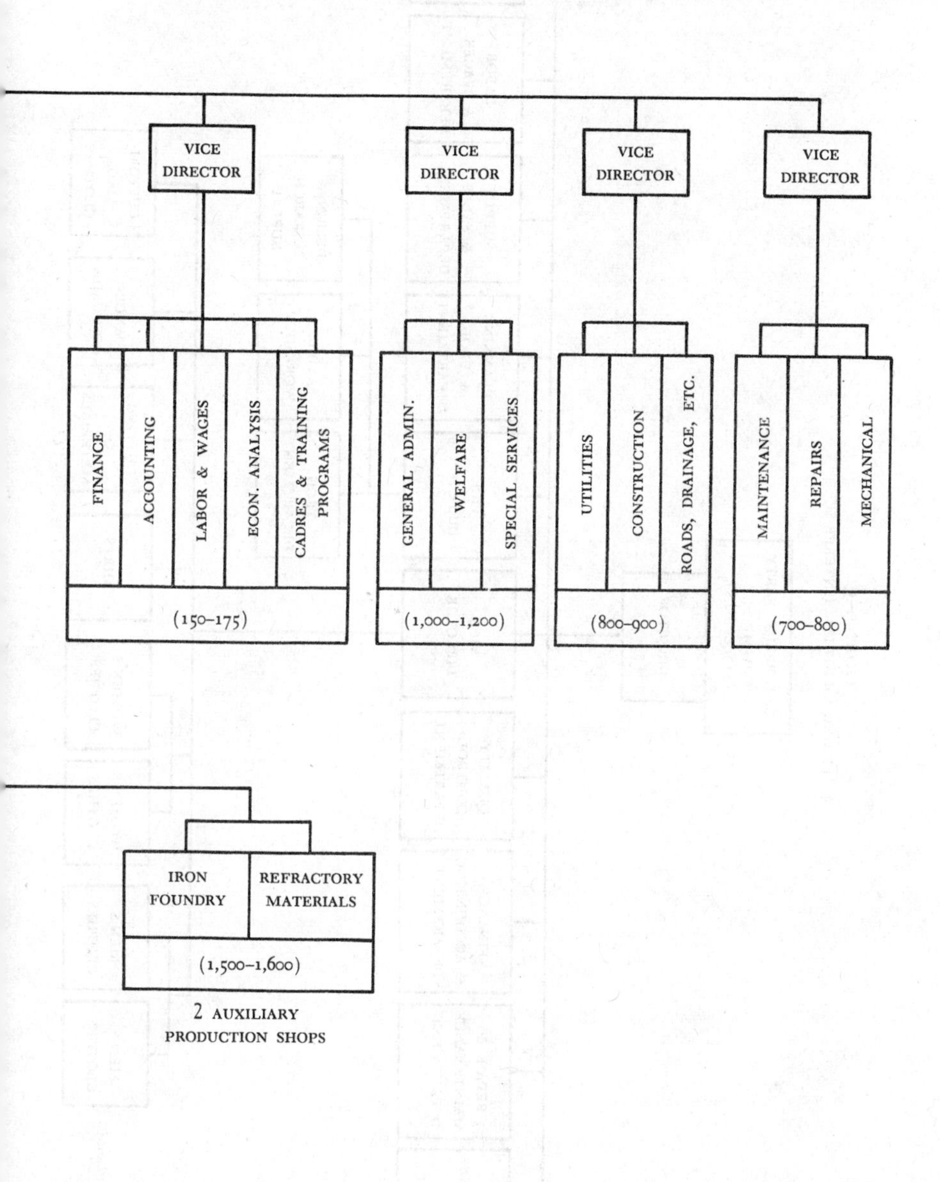

* Shops have their own planners, statisticians, accountants, norm setters, quality-control staffs, technicians, designers, engineers, and maintenance and repair crews, most of whom are under the direct or functional control of the appropriate central departments.

CHART 9–5
PEKING CLOTHING ENTERPRISE

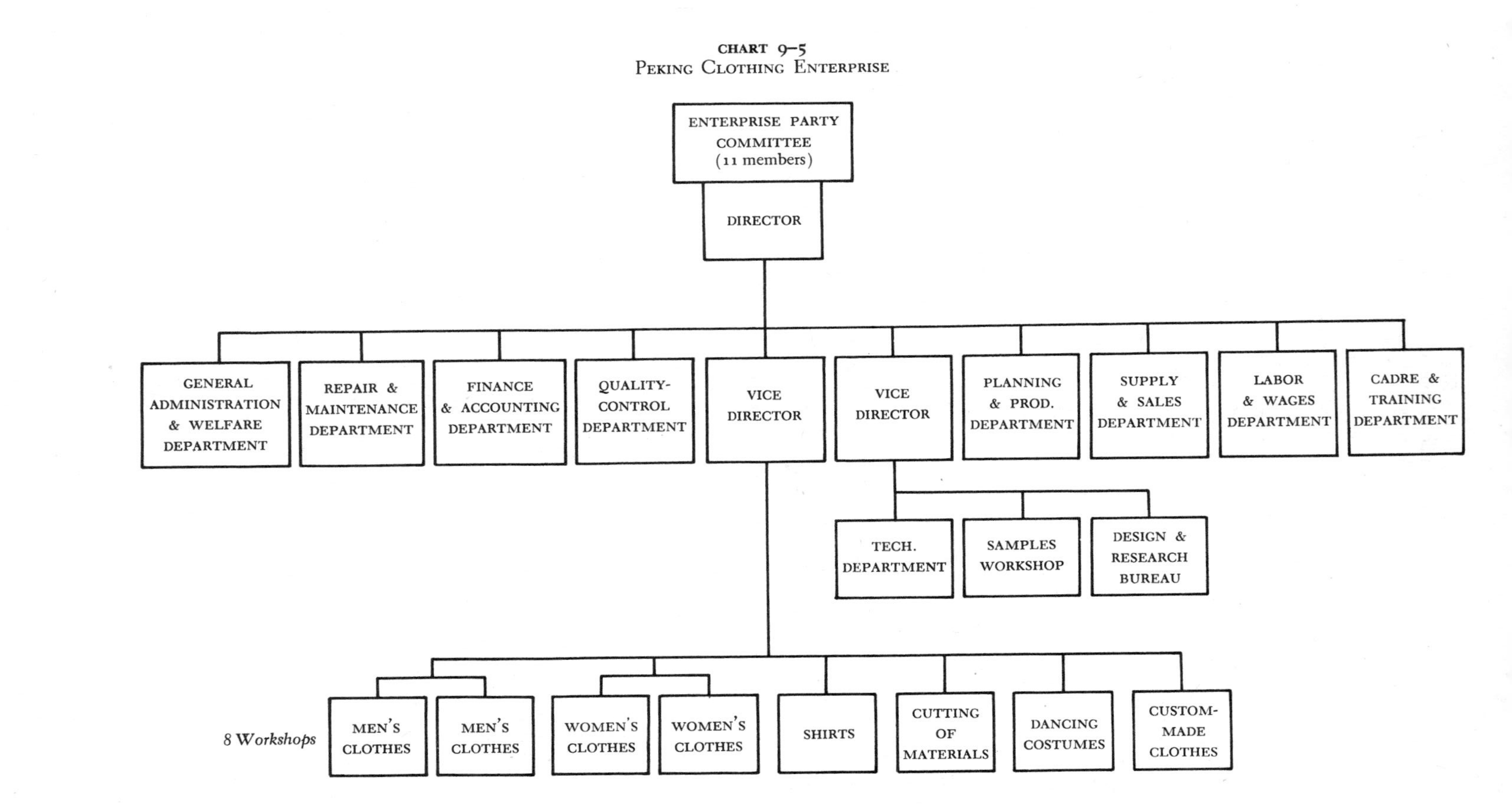

CHART 9–6

Shanghai No. 19 Cotton Textile Enterprise

(Figures in brackets indicate approximate number of personnel in each unit where such data was obtained)

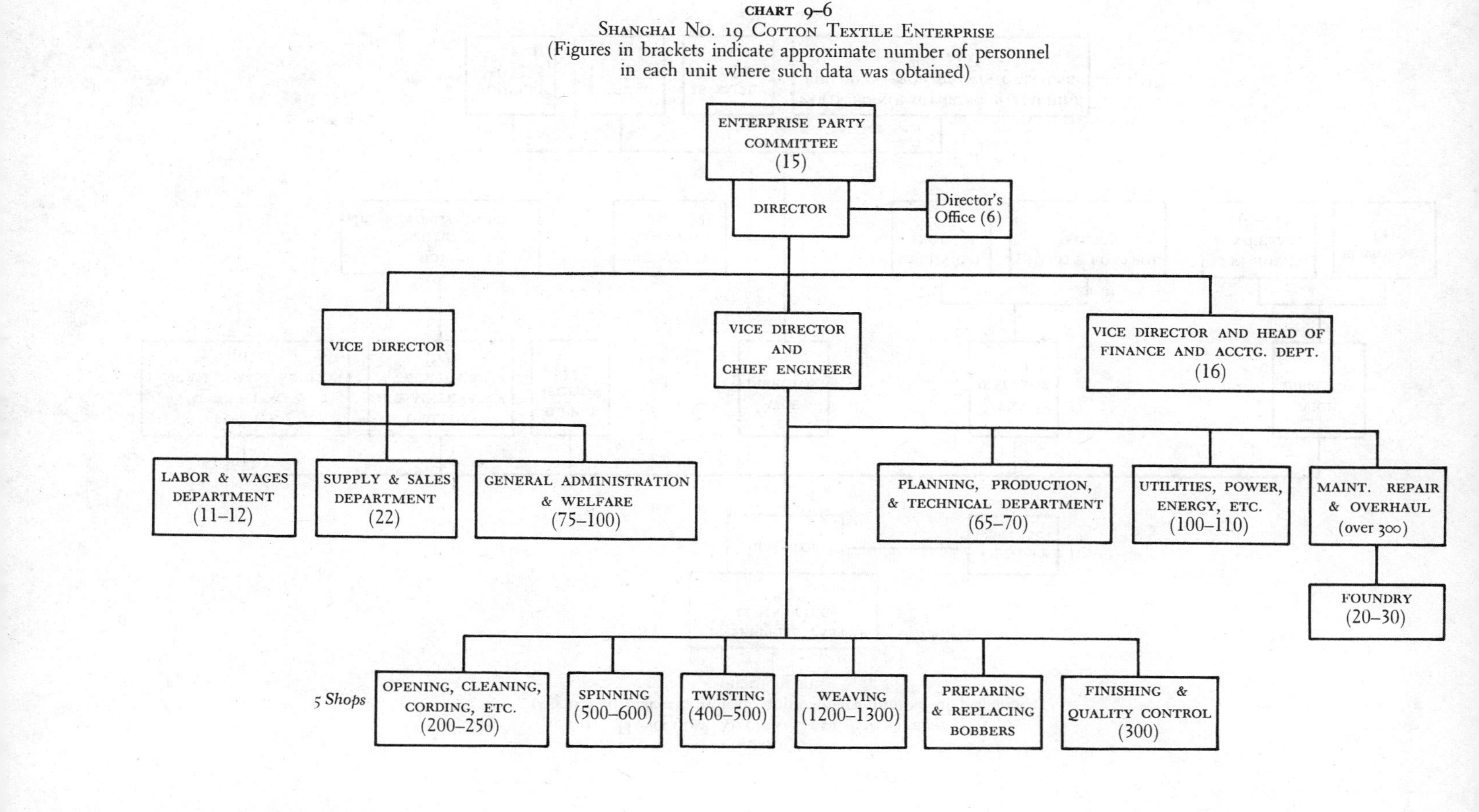

CHART 9–7
HANGCHOW MACHINE-TOOL ENTERPRISE
(Figures in brackets indicate approximate number of personnel in each unit)

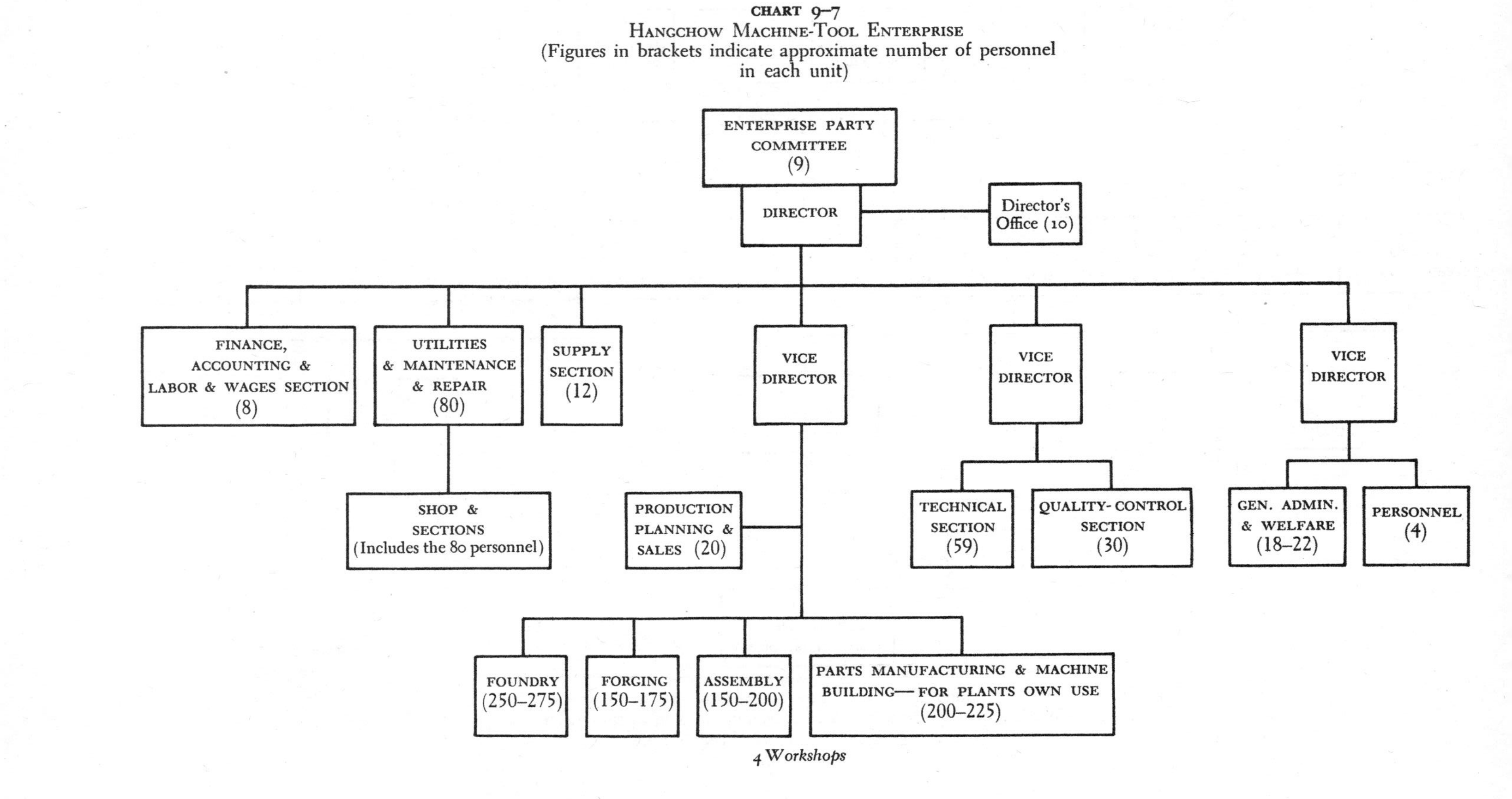

CHART 9–8A

CANTON CHEMICAL-FERTILIZER ENTERPRISE

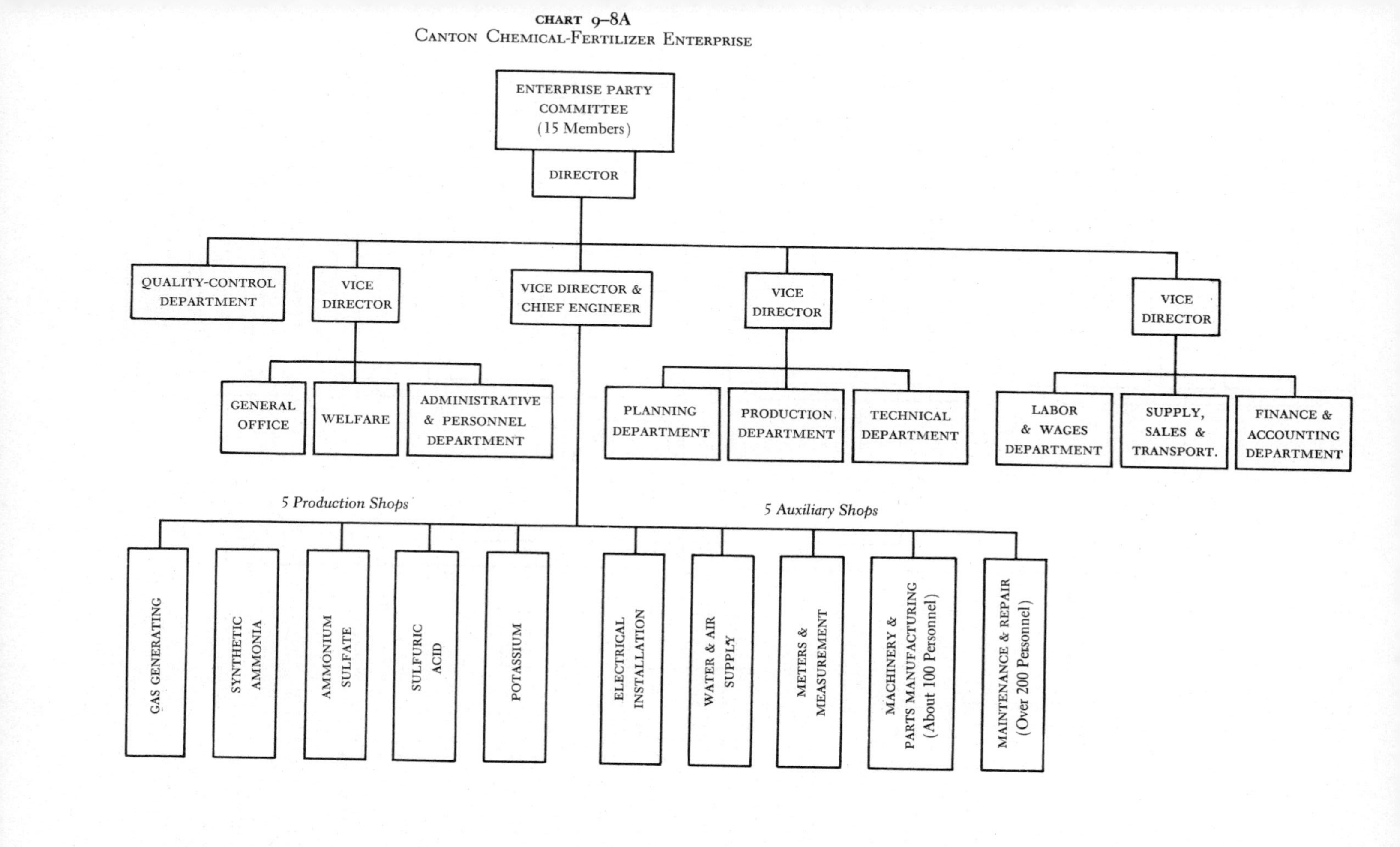

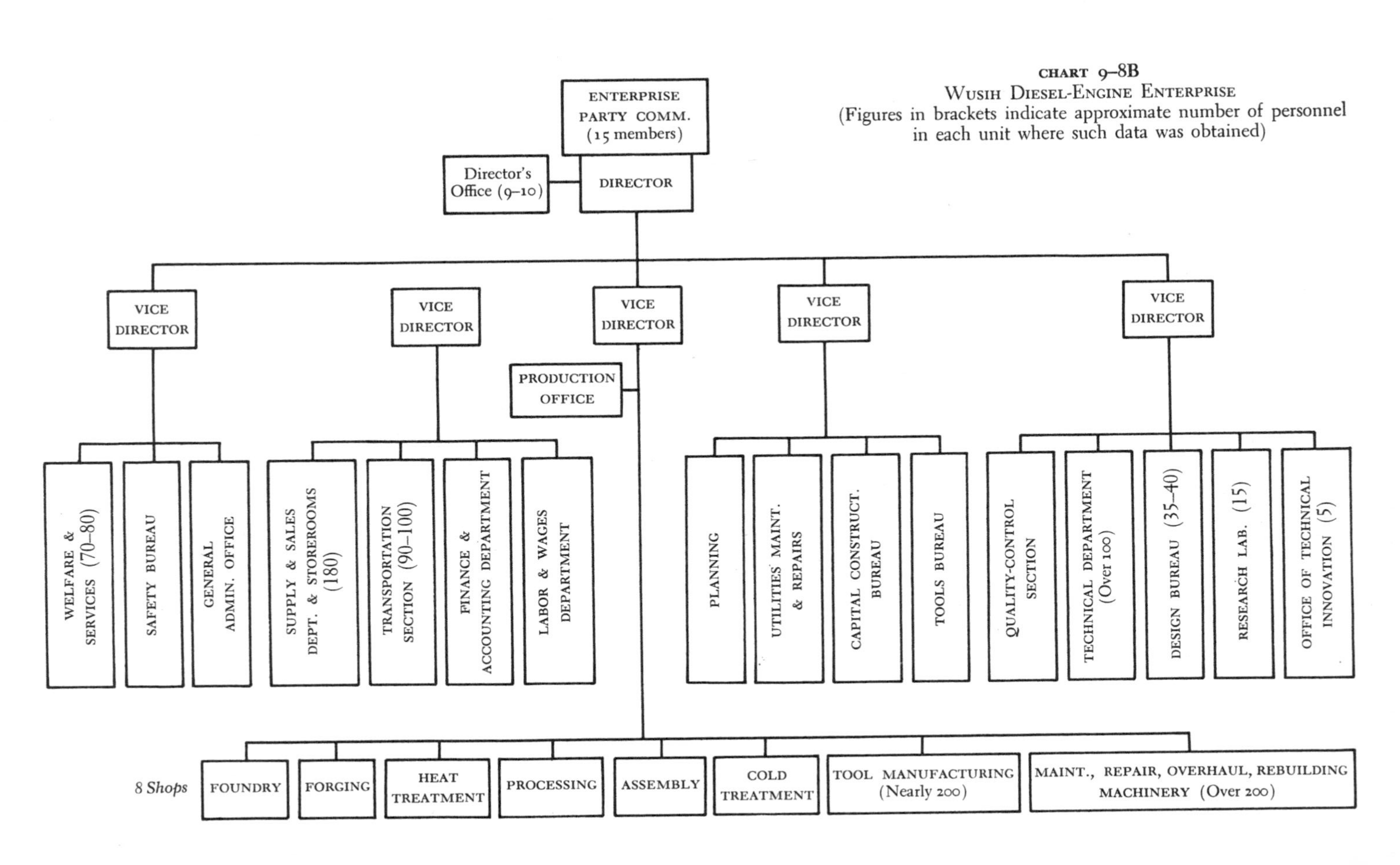

CHART 9–8B
WUSIH DIESEL-ENGINE ENTERPRISE
(Figures in brackets indicate approximate number of personnel in each unit where such data was obtained)

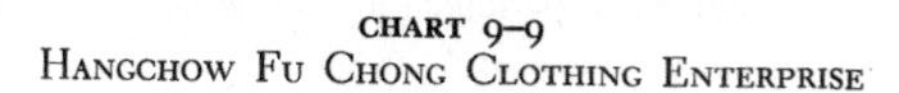

CHART 9–9
HANGCHOW FU CHONG CLOTHING ENTERPRISE

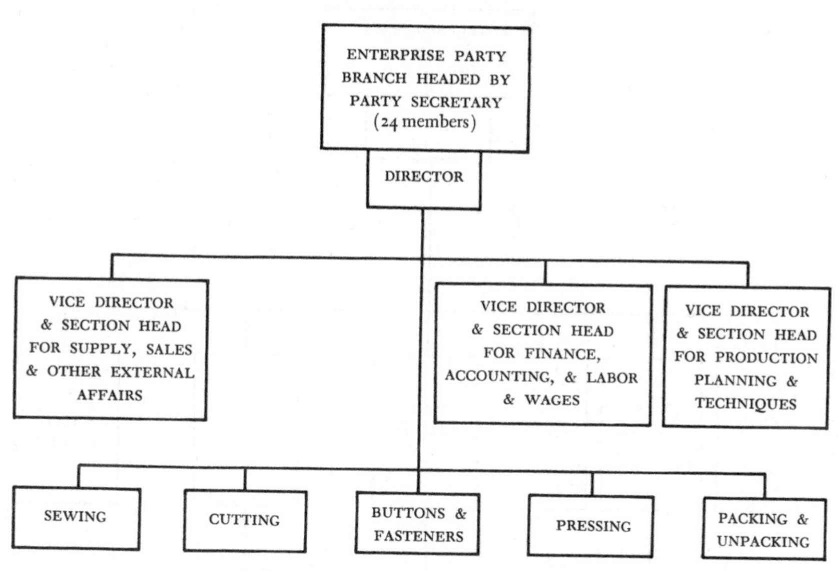

5 Work Groups, Each Headed by a Group Leader

focusing on, the production plan. The production department or unit deals chiefly with detailed production-scheduling coordination and control, dispatching and distribution of resources to shops, the preparation of graphs, and similar activities. The planning department deals more with general economic planning and control, while the production unit engages in more detailed and operational production plans which follow from the general plan, and which have shorter time perspectives—they are typically monthly, weekly, and/or daily plans. The planning unit typically has a staff of statisticians which prepares reports for use by top management as well as superior organizations. In some cases material and/or labor-utilization norms are worked out by the planning or production unit, but generally they are worked out elsewhere, as will be indicated below.

Technical Department and Design, Development, and Research Activities

The technical department typically deals with technical-feasibility studies, cost estimates, quality standards, the setting of material- and equipment-utilization norms, and in some cases labor norms as well. Such information and calculations are passed on to other departments and shops for planning, coordination, and control purposes. This department usually has under it a design unit and often also a special product-development section and the central research laboratory (where the enterprise has

CHART 9–10
TIENTSIN SHOE ENTERPRISE
(Figures in brackets indicate approximate number of personnel in each unit)

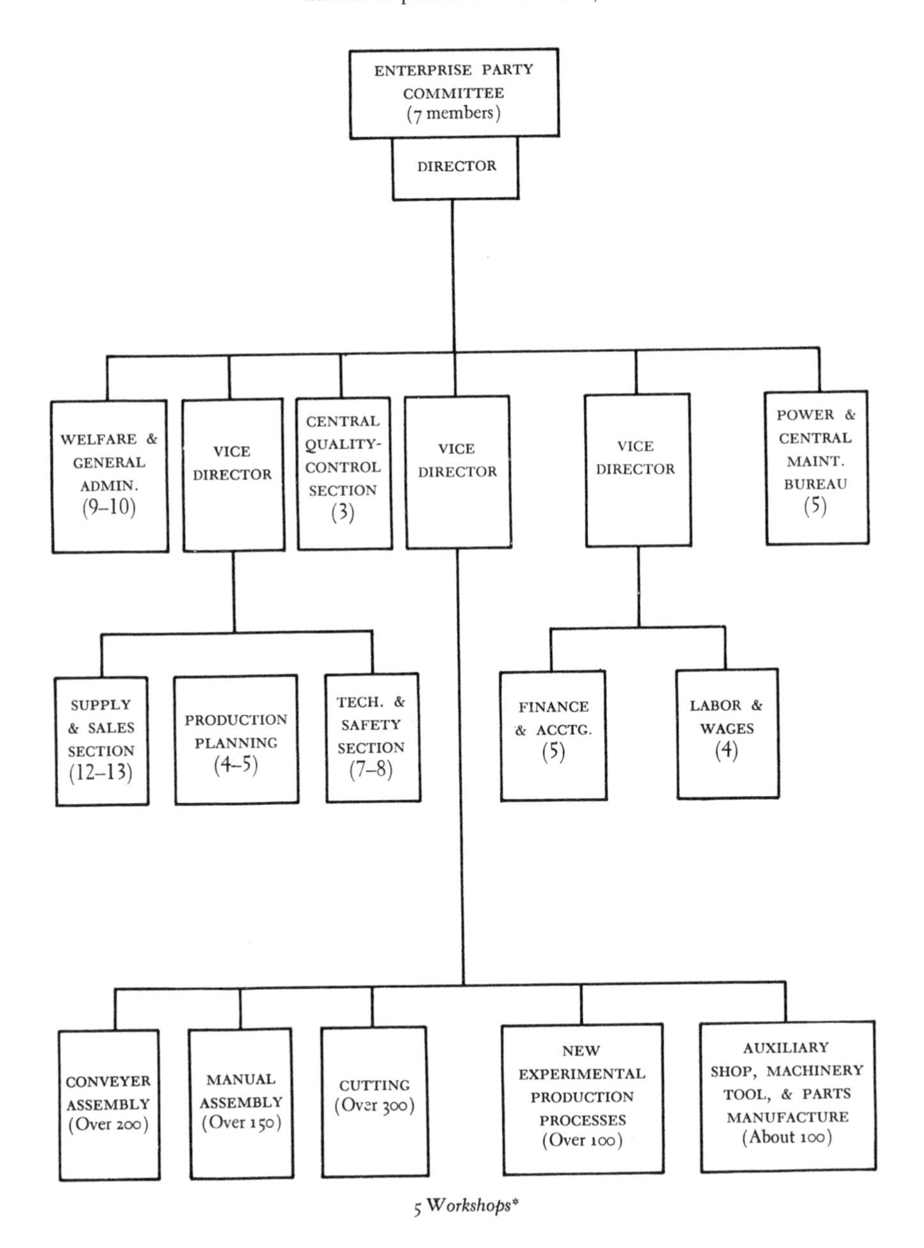

* Each production shop has its own quality-control inspectors (about 3 on the average) and technicians who are under the leadership of their central depts.

CHART 9–11
SHANGHAI NO. 3 MACHINE-TOOL ENTERPRISE
(Figures in brackets indicate approximate number of personnel in each unit)

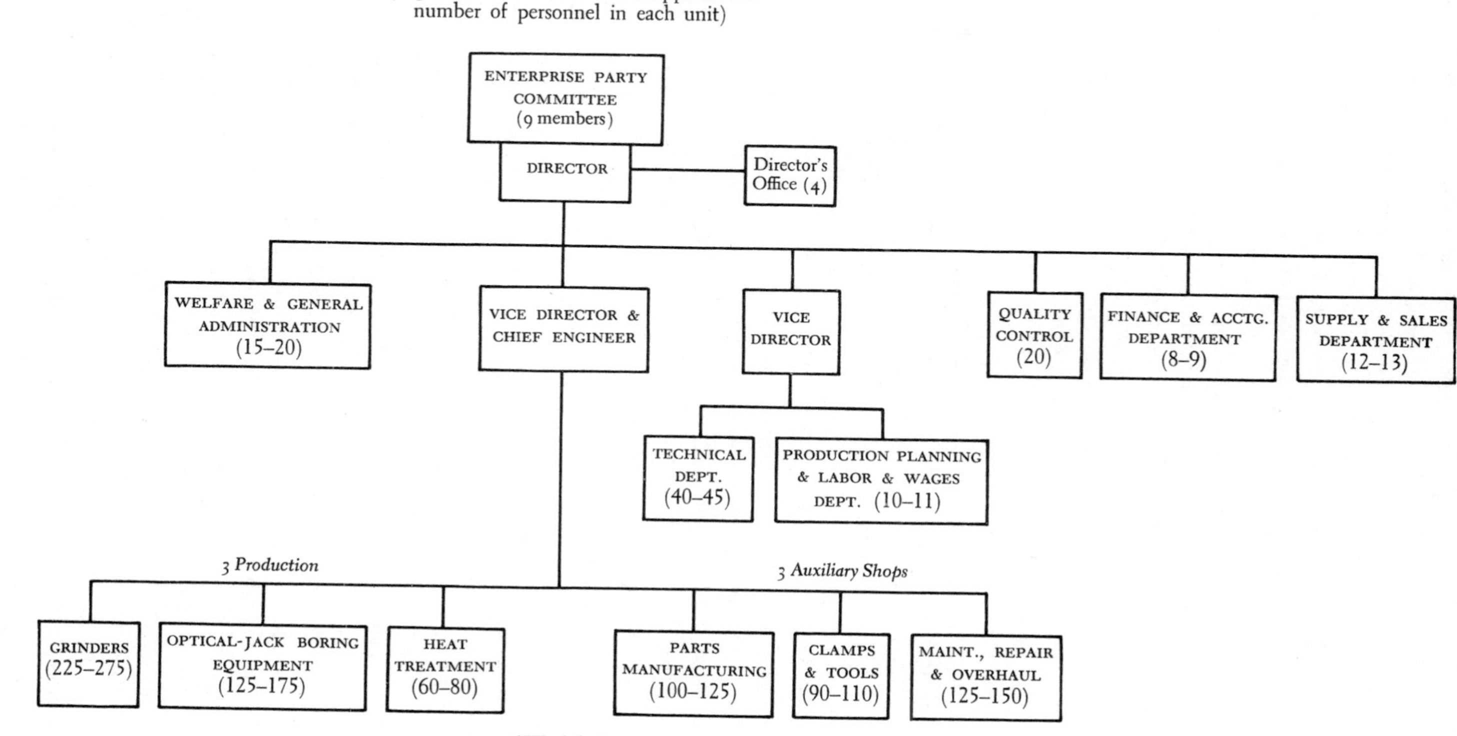

such units). In other cases, the product-development unit and/or the central laboratory are under a vice director (typically the chief engineer) and, in a few cases, the director. The technical department or one of its sections prepares drawings for new products, changes in plant layout, the installation of new production processes and technology, and analyzes technical operations in general. It also frequently plays a major role in determining equipment maintenance and overhaul requirements. In addition, this department or one of its subdivisions generally deals with the external research and development organizations with which the firm has a relationship. At a number of enterprises that I visited the technical department had its own development or experimental workshop, where it manufactures prototypes or samples of new products and/or new production processes, and undertakes various pilot projects.

At several of the enterprises—mainly consumer-goods producers—the technical department or one of its subdivisions undertook fairly extensive marketing-research activities. In this connection, designers, stylists, artists, and/or technicians went to customer organizations, including retail stores, to learn about the tastes, desires, and demands of their customers. In fact, Peking Clothing, Peking No. 3 Cotton Textile, Tientsin Shoe, and some of the other firms surveyed even sent personnel, including higher-level executives at times, to work incognito as salesmen in the stores that sell their products as regular employees scheduled for one day each week, fortnightly, or monthly. The aim was for them to get to know the ultimate consumer firsthand, and to improve existing products and develop new products and varieties that would serve the customer better. For example, I learned that on a Sunday a few days before I visited the Peking Clothing Firm, twenty of its employees—most of them from the design room and sample workshop, but also a few high-level managers—went to work as salesmen in several department stores and other larger retail outlets in the area. This enterprise had a design and product-development unit (under its technical department) employing forty designers, stylists, artists and technicians, as well as a new-products and samples workshop employing several dozen workers. Peking No. 3 Cotton Textile also sent some of its people to work regularly in the stores.

It also seems quite common for consumer-goods producers in particular—but not exclusively—to organize consumer or customer panels at their enterprises two to four times each year in order to display samples of new products and to get feedback and reactions on them, as well as on their regular product lines. In the case of consumer goods, not only retail and wholesale representatives come, but also ultimate consumers sent by various social, educational, and cultural organizations. Several of the enterprises surveyed send technical-department representatives to local, provincial, and national exhibitions, where their products are displayed and ordered. Where enterprises export significant portions of their output they frequently send representatives from their technical department or its subdivisions along with a high-level executive to take part in negotiation at the import-export corporations and trade fairs, such as the Canton International Fair.

Hence, at Chinese industrial enterprises the technical department or one of its sections typically plays the major role in marketing research and product development rather than the sales unit, which is usually part of the supply and sales department. The sales unit does often provide sales and inventory data to the technical department, but apparently it rarely does much if anything in the way of marketing research or product development per se.

Technical Innovation Unit

To the best of my knowledge most of the enterprises visited had a bureau, office, section, and/or committee to deal with technical innovation and improvement measures. This type of unit or committee is usually under the technical department, the chief or vice chief engineer, or a vice director in charge of various technical operations. For example, Wuhan Heavy Machinery had a technical-innovation committee with members—mainly engineers and technicians—from different parts of the enterprise. The committee was headed by the vice chief engineer of the factory, and it had an office of technical innovation with several permanent employees. Wusih Diesel Engine had an office of technical innovation under the head of the technical department.

The technical-innovation committee, where there is one, discusses and analyzes a wide range of technical problems. The office or section of technical innovation works out feasibility studies, prepares reports, keeps records, and handles the general paperwork pertaining to innovational and improvement measures. It also analyzes employee suggestions as to their feasibility, handles the payment of rewards to innovators (where such a system is used), and disseminates information about worthwhile measures to appropriate parts of the enterprise. In addition, it maintains contact and exchanges information with other firms in the same industry.

As noted in earlier chapters, when I was in China, there seemed to be a tendency to de-emphasize, and even abolish, the payment of cast awards to individuals based on the economies derived from their implemented suggestions. However, employee suggestions were still highly encouraged and publicized with much use being made of nonmaterial incentives. The suggestion systems at most of the Chinese firms where I obtained this type of information were very informal and unsystematized, as compared with those in Soviet industry. Typically cost-benefit studies were not undertaken for most suggestions, even major ones, that were implemented, and few, if any, related records were kept. For example, I was told by the chief engineer at the Peking First Machine Tool Firm that roughly three thousand employee suggestions were implemented in 1965, but cost effectiveness calculations were made for only a small number of them. In fact relatively few of the suggestions were even prepared in writing at any stage. At Wusih Diesel Engine I was told that in 1965 the workers made over a thousand proposals, few of which were presented in written form. Of the thousand or so suggestions, 274 were judged important, 120 were introduced, and experiments and studies were being, or would be, undertaken on another 50 or so. At Shanghai Truck workers take their suggestions either to their superiors, who pass them on to the technical department, or to the technical department directly. I was told that in 1965 over three hundred suggestions were put into writing and adopted, and that on the average about 75 percent of the suggestions had been implemented. Apparently none of the above-mentioned firms were paying out cash rewards for implemented suggestions at the time of my visit. However, Wuhan Heavy Machinery, which had a formalized suggestion-reward system introduced by Soviet experts in the 1950's, was still paying out a limited number of modest cash rewards to worker-innovators, even though it had recently abolished its other bonus-payment systems.

Quality-Control Department

At most of the enterprises visited, this was a separate department with its head typically reporting to the director, but at some it was part of the technical department or directly under the chief engineer. It deals with the quality control of raw materials in process production, finished goods, and often plant machinery and equipment. It carries out its control activities on the basis of prescribed technical standards and specifications. At many enterprises all quality-control inspectors are under the direct jurisdiction of this department; at most enterprises at least those responsible for finished products are; and at others it extends functional authority over the quality-control bureaus and staffs located in the workshops.

Supply-and-Sales Department

At nearly all of the enterprises, supply and sales functions were combined in one department. Where this was not the case, sales was part of the planning or finance department. At Soviet enterprises it is much more common for sales to be either a separate department or part of the finance department. I was told by several Chinese managers that supply and sales are usually in the same department, along with transportation, warehousing and storerooms, because this enables better coordination between these intimately related functions in preparing the enterprise plan, and especially in revising it expeditiously and consistently when, for instance, supplies do not arrive on time. There is probably more to be said in favor of such an organizational setup than for the traditional Soviet arrangement. However, in recent years a trend has emerged in Soviet industry to combine supply, sales, and often transportation and warehousing functions as well, in one large administrative unit under one head, particularly at larger firms.

The supply section at Chinese firms prepares the supply (purchasing) plan and, in many cases, calculates material-consumption norms for some, if not most, types of supplies. The preparation of the supply plan is a critical activity since failure to adequately anticipate needs for materials and components may involve the enterprise in serious difficulties. Just as important as supply planning is the task of seeing that needed items are actually received on time, and in the proper quantities, qualities, and specifications.

The sales section works out detailed delivery schedules and projects the pattern of enterprise sales revenues. It also deals with inventory levels of finished goods, controls deliveries to customers, and handles customer complaints. At consumer-goods enterprises it is quite common for the sales section to receive detailed sales and inventory reports from wholesaling organizations and the larger retail outlets which distribute and sell the firm's products. If the firm engages in any advertising or sales promotion activity, it is usually handled by the sales unit.

Senior officials of the supply-and-sales department engage in contract negotiations with the enterprise's suppliers and customers as well as higher agencies. In many cases they attend local and/or national material-allocation and sales order conferences as well as various types of product fairs and exhibitions. If the firm engages in barter deals and/or unofficial or illegal procurement or marketing activities, members of this department are typically directly involved.

Department of Labor and Wages

This unit works out in detail job grades and classifications, wage and salary rates, standard hours, and at some enterprises labor-utilization norms, upon which the overall plan of labor and wages is based. It often works out the detailed collective agreements with the plant trade-union committee. This department also sometimes handles the firm's actual payroll, but under the close scrutiny of the finance department.

Finance and Accounting Department

At nearly all of the Chinese enterprises surveyed, the accounting section is part of the finance department, while at most Soviet enterprises there is a separate accounting department. Perhaps the greater emphasis on independent checks and balances in the Soviet Union is a major reason for this difference. The finance department works out the overall plan of costs, expenses, and revenues, and the firm's profit and monetary working-capital plans. It also works out the liquid-capital plan, determines sources and uses of funds, handles bank relations, as well as financial allocations and payments to and from the state budget. In addition, it controls all types of costs and expenses during the operating period.

In general, the Chinese financial manager's job tends to be relatively simple compared with that of his American counterpart. The former need worry little, or not at all, about long-term financing, sources of capital, stock options, market prices for company shares, dividend payments, meeting interest payments and other obligations on debt capital, and many of the other financial problems of major concern in U.S. firms.

The accounting section deals chiefly with historical data pertaining to enterprise accounts and balances. It also controls expenditures and calculates enterprise depreciation charges using prescribed rates. This section prepares certain critical annual, quarterly, and monthly accounting reports upon which the evaluation of the enterprise and its management is likely to depend in significant measure.

In recent years there has been much discussion in Chinese sources about replacing the conventional double-entry, debit-credit accounting system at enterprises with an increase-decrease single-entry system involving only direct addition and subtraction.[16] The advocates of the latter system feel that it would be simpler for less-educated and less-experienced personnel to comprehend, thus making it possible to draw more people into the accounting field and related control process. To the best of my knowledge, none of the industrial enterprises visited were using the single-entry accounting system, though I was told that it is being used in the retail sector—apparently at relatively small stores in particular.

Department of Personnel, Cadres, or Manpower

This unit handles employee recruiting, coordinated training programs, and often plays a part in personnel appraisal. It sometimes organizes work teams for carrying out the plan, and handles the transfer of personnel among different parts of the enterprise, and to and from other enterprises.

Other Departments and Administrative Units

Among the other types of administrative units found at several or many of the enterprises surveyed, especially the larger ones, were maintenance and repair; safety and/or working conditions; welfare facilities and housing; general administration; capital construction (investment); equipment utilization; utilities; fuel, water, and electricity supply; mechanical; buildings and grounds; organizational or economic analysis, the director's office; and a few others. The functions of these departments, bureaus, sections, and offices are apparent in most cases from their names.

Organization of Workshops

Larger workshops typically have one or more deputy directors and are divided into sections, subsections, and work teams under group leaders and shift supervisors. The typical organization structure of a relatively large workshop is indicated on Chart 9–4 which deals with the Shanghai No. 3 Steel Enterprise. Small shops, of course, have fewer managerial levels.

The organization structure of a relatively large shop, or even a large section, is often like a microcosm of the enterprise itself in many respects, with its head functioning somewhat like the enterprise director. The shop or section head is likely to have under him a staff of planners, dispatchers and expeditors, accountants, statisticians, labor- and material-norm setters, engineers, technicians, quality-control personnel, and maintenance and repair crews. There does not seem to be any extensive clear-cut pattern regarding the official to whom such personnel must report. It is quite common for them to report directly to higher-level administrative units involved in similar functions. But even when they report directly to shop or section managers, they are typically supposed to carry out various shop activities in accordance with procedures, policies, and methods prescribed by the appropriate higher-level functional or service administrative unit within the enterprise.

At a number of enterprises surveyed—mainly consumer-goods plants producing relatively simple products and not using very complex technology, such as Tientsin Shoe, the two clothing firms, Shanghai Battery, Canton Electrical Appliance, and some of the textile factories—the workers themselves perform various functions in addition to their production assignments. For example, work teams elect or appoint fellow members to be responsible for in-process quality-control, safety, seeing that equipment is properly maintained and repaired, ordering and collecting required supplies, recording production results, and so forth. This is compatible with the Red Chinese stress on informal organization, the creation of generalists, and grass-roots social control and coordination.

Managerial Autonomy at the Enterprise Level

By managerial autonomy I mean the authority, independence, and influence that the Chinese industrial enterprise has in formulating its overall plan and in carrying it out. The term managerial autonomy is used here to mean autonomy of the enterprise in a system which places the Chinese enterprise formally under the collective leadership of the party committee.

Patterns and Degrees of Autonomy at Enterprises Surveyed

The degree and extent of autonomy varied quite substantially at the thirty-eight Chinese enterprises surveyed in 1966, although all of them played important roles in the planning process and in the execution of their plans. Table 9–2 presents my subjective rating of the degrees of autonomy existing at the thirty-eight enterprises. This table also contains a subjective grading for each firm in terms of managerial know-how and general operating efficiency with available physical technology (more will be said about this in the following chapter).

Those enterprises having the greatest managerial autonomy in decision making typically produce a wide and heterogeneous product mix which changes quite substantially from year to year. The firms in this category include Wuhan and Shanghai Heavy Machinery which produce much custom-built output, the two clothing manufacturers, Wusih Machinery, which does a considerable amount of subcontracting and job-order work independently, and the Wuhan Iron and Steel Corporation (but not its factories).

Enterprises directly under corporations, particularly municipal-level corporations, generally seem to have less authority than firms in the same level under municipal bureaus, provincial departments, and particularly central ministries. Among the firms surveyed that seem to have the least autonomy were most of the textile enterprises, Shanghai Truck (which has most of its financial and accounting affairs handled by its direct superior municipal bureau), Shanghai No. 3 Pharmaceutical, and Canton Electrical Appliance.

Some Sino-American Comparisons

Those Chinese enterprises with the least autonomy and influence on their plans and operations may be roughly compared with factories per se of U.S. companies where the plant managers have a low degree of authority or independence. However, the management of such Chinese firms would typically be at least somewhat more involved in functions other than production, such as finance, accounting, and possibly marketing. Many of the Chinese enterprises surveyed have roughly the same amount of autonomy as U.S. plant managers who have a moderate or fairly high degree of authority and independence, with the possible exception of freedom in procurement and in deciding on the prices to pay for various factors of production. Those Chinese enterprises having the greatest autonomy with regard to their plans and operations are roughly analogous to product divisions of U.S. corporations where management has a fairly low degree of autonomy. Industrial corporations in China are generally more comparable to U.S. product divisions than to U.S. factories.

Production, Product-Mix, and Resource Planning

Chinese managers can, and do, influence in varying degrees the aggregate targets and factor resource limits—for example, materials, equipment, inventories, finances, manpower—stipulated in the formally approved enterprise plan through their proposals, calculations, and estimates during the planning process. Such proposals, calculations, and estimates pertain to enterprise capabilities, productive capacity, and resource requirements. The plan is based on a multitude of detailed technical calculations, and most enterprises independently establish the great majority of their labor, material, and equipment-utilization norms. Higher authorities typically tend to prescribe factor-utilization norms for only a limited number of strategic commodities and new equipment, and in some cases where highly standardized and stable methods or processes are used. Enterprise management also prepares estimates of fixed and working capital and general overhead requirements on the basis of many computations and estimates.

Hence, through their important roles in the planning process, Chinese enterprise managers do generally significantly influence, but in varying degrees, the types and quantities of outputs, resource allocations, and aggregate resource limits and operating targets approved by higher authorities. In addition, at most of the enterprises surveyed, the quantities and varieties of products approved by superior organs do not add up to the approved aggregate-production targets, and the firms' managers can determine independently from about 5 percent to as much as 30 percent or more (in a few cases) of their planned outputs. This production capacity is typically utilized for by-products, subcontracting activities, independently negotiated orders, and the production of relatively minor items. The amount of detailed product-mix planning and control undertaken by higher authorities depends chiefly on the nature and extent of the enterprise's product line. Firms producing a wide range of heterogeneous goods tend to have substantially more authority, independence, and influence over their detailed product mixes than those producing a narrow line of homogeneous output. For example, as indicated in the section on organization structure, the clothing firms surveyed—as well as Tientsin Shoe—play major roles in their product-mix planning and control, and even in marketing-research activities. About 35 to 40 percent of the Wuhan Paper Mill's production each period consists of local orders which its management independently negotiates. Close to half of Wusih Machinery's actual production is not subject to higher approval during some periods, and usually at least 30 percent of it is not.

TABLE 9–2

GRADING OF THIRTY-EIGHT CHINESE INDUSTRIAL ENTERPRISES IN TERMS OF MANAGERIAL KNOW-HOW AND GENERAL EFFICIENCY WITH PHYSICAL TECHNOLOGY AVAILABLE, DIRECT SUPERIOR ORGANIZATION, AND ESTIMATED DEGREE OF ENTERPRISE AUTONOMY

*Grade**	*Total Employment*	*Higher Authority Directly Above the Enterprise*	*Estimate of Relative Degree of Enterprise Autonomy* (rated on a 1–to–5 scale with 5 being the highest degree among firms surveyed)
BEST			
Peking Coke and Chemical	2,100	Peking Chemical Industry Corp.	3
Peking Cotton Textile No. 3	5,000	Peking Textile Corp. (under Textile Ministry)	1
Shanghai Cotton Textile No. 19	4,800	Shanghai Textile Corp. (under local bureau)	2
Shanghai (Joint) Sung Sing Cotton Textile No. 9	6,000	Shanghai Textile Corp.	1
Shanghai Machine Tool	6,000	First Machine-Building Ministry	5
Wuhan Heavy Machinery	7,000	First Machine-Building Ministry	5
Hangchow Clothing	400	Hangchow Handicrafts Industry Bureau	5
ABOVE AVERAGE			
Peking Wool	1,800	Peking Textile Corp.	1
Peking Woolen Carpet	2,700	Peking Textile Corp.	1
Tientsin (Joint) Jen Yi Wool	1,800	Tientsin Wool Corp.	1
Wusih Silk Reeling	1,500	Wusih Silk Industry Corp.	2
Peking Clothing	1,700	Peking Handicrafts Bureau	5
Peking First Machine Tool	4,000	First Machine-Building Ministry	4

Shanghai Machine Tool No. 3	1,000	Shanghai Machine-Tool Corp. (under local Electrical Machinery Bureau)	2
Shanghai Wei Ming Battery	563	Shanghai Daily Usage Chemical Indust. Corp.	3
AVERAGE			
Peking Pharmaceutical	3,000	China Drug Corp. (under Chemical Ministry)	3
Nanking Chemical Fertilizer	10,000	Ministry of Chemical Industry	3
Canton Chemical Fertilizer	2,400	Ministry of Chemical Industry	2
Canton Machine Tool	3,100	First Machine-Building Ministry	2
Wusih Machinery	300	Wusih Handicrafts Industry Bureau	5
Shanghai Steel No. 3	13,000	Shanghai Bureau of Metallurgy	3
Shanghai Forging & Pressing Machine Tool	405	Shanghai Machine-Tool Corp.	3
Soochow Cement Products	680	Soochow Bureau of Construction	3
Hangchow Silk Reeling, Dyeing & Weaving	6,200	Hangchow Silk Textile Corp.	1
BELOW AVERAGE			
Shanghai Pharmaceutical No. 3	1,200	Shanghai Branch of China Drug Corp.	2
Shanghai Truck	1,050	Shanghai Transportation and Communication Bureau	1
Loyang Tractor	20,500	Eighth Machine-Building Ministry	3
Wusih Diesel-Engine	2,700	Tractor and Internal Generator Corp. (under Eighth Machine-Building Ministry)	2
Wuhan Iron and Steel Corp. and its factories	35,000	Ministry of Metallurgy	Corporation 5 (Factories of this corp. 1 & 2)
Wuhan Paper	2,000	Provincial First Light-Industry Bureau	4
Nanking Machinery	1,300	Provincial Machinery Dept.	4
Tientsin North Lake Instrument	165	Tientsin Second Light Industry	4

TABLE 9–2 (*continued*)

*Grade**	*Total Employment*	*Higher Authority Directly Above the Enterprise*	*Estimate of Relative Degree of Enterprise Autonomy* (rated on a 1--to–5 scale with 5 being the highest degree among firms surveyed)
WORST			
Peking Steel Wire	800	Peking Metallurgical Industry Corp.	3
Tientsin Shoe	1,000	Tientsin Second Light Industry	4
Tientsin Watch	1,400	Tientsin Daily Usage Industrial Corp. (under Tientsin First Light Industry Bureau)	2
Canton Electrical Appliance	840	Canton Electrical Industry Corp. (under local Electrical Machinery Bureau)	1
Hangchow Machine-Tool	1,000	Provincial Heavy Industry Dept.	3
Suhan Diesel-Engine	992	Wuhan Mechanical Electrical Industry Bureau	3

* No attempt is made to rank enterprises within each category.

Product Pricing

While most commodity prices are set by superior state organs—and are typically revised only at infrequent intervals—enterprise management plays a key role in price setting under certain conditions. It can usually initiate price proposals for new, custom-built, and other unstandardized products, and in many instances where changes in product specifications and designs are undertaken. It can also often independently establish cost-plus prices for subcontracting services of a relatively minor nature. The prices of new and significantly modified products are also proposed on a cost-plus basis. At many enterprises visited, such cost-plus product pricing provides for planned profit margins in the range of 10 to 20 percent in order to encourage product development and innovation. The lowest allowable planned profit margin on new products that I was informed about at the firms surveyed was about 5 percent. This was the case at Peking Clothing and a few of the textile enterprises where I obtained this type of information. In general, however, planned profit margins allowed on new products in Chinese industry are usually higher than those that have been allowed in Soviet industry, where they have typically ranged from 3 to 6 percent on most items.

Although an appropriate superior authority usually must formally approve product and subcontracting prices proposed by enterprises—the most common exceptions being prices for minor new products and product-specification changes—it seems that the price proposed by the firm is generally adopted.

Technical-Quality Standards and Specifications of Factor Inputs

Many enterprises independently determine the technical-quality standards for various minor and unstandardized products that they produce. All of the enterprises surveyed have an important voice, often a quite big one, in proposing the types and specifications of factor inputs to be utilized in production. For a limited number of commodities of relatively minor importance, most of the firms have complete discretion over both the specifications and types of inputs to be used. In some such cases they are even free to search out supplies and procure needed items without higher approval. A sizable majority of the enterprises also engage in direct negotiations with many, and in several cases all, of their suppliers and customers. In this connection they determine the detailed specifications of materials, equipment, components, and other products to be bought and sold within the aggregate limits set by their approved plans. They also sign supply and sales contracts which stipulate detailed product mixes, prices, delivery dates, modes and terms of deliveries, and the like. There seem to be substantially more direct contractual relations and negotiations among enterprises in Chinese industry than in the Soviet Union in the early 1960's.

Make or Buy Decisions

One important way by which a Chinese enterprise can influence the types and costs of factor inputs utilized in production is through make versus buy decisions. A number of enterprise executives indicated that higher authorities frequently go along with their desire to make or process rather than buy various materials, machines, and components. This was certainly reflected in the high proportion of auxiliary personnel in relation to direct-production workers at many of the plants visited.

Wages, Salaries, Monetary Incentives, and Staffing Decisions

Basic wage and salary scales for all industrial occupations—including general categories such as unskilled and semiskilled labor in different industries—are established by central authorities, with the Ministry of Labor and industrial ministries playing the major roles. Allowances are made for regional differences in the cost of living. For each occupation or type of job there are grade scales which provide for substantial differences in pay between their maxima and minima. The enterprise has considerable authority and independence in determining the basic pay of its workers and most other types of personnel by assigning them grades. Skill, productivity, experience, and general performance are the major criteria applied in grading personnel. Hence, management can do much to spur productivity through its authority to appraise, grade, and determine the wages and salaries of individual employees—but within the limits of the approved total payroll figure.

Where there were bonuses and/or other monetary incentive schemes in use at the enterprises surveyed, there was considerable local autonomy in determining how the incentive pay was to be divided up among employees. As we shall discuss shortly, ideology and politics—and not only productivity and job skill—play an important role here. However, there was more independence in the sphere of monetary incentives at Chinese enterprises than at the Soviet enterprises I visited in the early 1960's.

But this is not true with regard to the classification of many types of personnel by occupation or profession, the recruiting and hiring of new employees of any kind, or the transferring or retrenching of existing personnel. Soviet enterprises tend to have more autonomy in these areas than their Chinese counterparts, and higher-level constraints on labor mobility in general are substantially more rigid in Chinese industry. There is also a higher degree of centralization in Chinese industry in connection with the assignment of high-talent manpower and new graduates from higher educational institutions to enterprises, but their numbers are much smaller in

China than the Soviet Union. Such assignments are frequently made by central agencies in China.

Enterprise management typically has considerable autonomy with regard to the training, appraisal, direction, and motivation of personnel—with party cadres playing key roles in these spheres. At virtually all of the enterprises surveyed, decisions regarding the promotion or appointment of managers up to the level of department heads and shop chiefs could be made independently within the enterprise. While the promotion or appointment of personnel as department heads and shop chiefs could be decided on internally at a majority of the enterprises, higher-level formal approval was required in several cases. The same was true for shop party secretaries who had to be approved by higher party organs at some firms. At virtually all of the firms their directors and all their vice directors—even where the enterprise had "elections" to choose their high-level managers—had to be approved by superior authorities. In a number of cases they had to be approved by higher bodies two or three levels above the enterprise, and at a few large firms final approval came from as high up as the state council. The same was true for party secretaries and vice secretaries at some of the enterprises. Their appointments had to be approved by higher party committees, and in a few cases formal approval came from as high up as the Central Party Committee in Peking.

Financial Planning and Operations

Management can influence the cost, inventory, financial, and profit indexes of the approved enterprise plan through its decisions, calculations, and proposals during the planning process. In the financial sphere, many enterprises have the right to independently negotiate and obtain modest short-term bank loans for seasonal needs, the introduction of techniques and various other improvements or expansions in operations. Management also usually has considerable leeway in establishing internal enterprise-control systems of various types.

Within the limits of their financial plans, enterprise managers typically have at least some official leeway to shuffle funds among various accounts in order to carry out the plan. The directors of all the enterprises surveyed had discretionary funds, ranging from 250 to 1,000 yuan which they could use as they saw fit, and which were generally replenished if necessary at least quarterly, and in some cases more frequently. At firms having enterprise funds set up from retained profits, management has considerable discretion in using this fund within broadly defined events.

Revisions in the Enterprise Plan

In executing the plan, enterprise management can, and often does, initiate changes in its product-mix plan as well as other parts of the firm's plan. However, substantial revisions in the plan would typically only be considered official or "legal" if the proper procedures for ratification and formal approval are adhered to. This would normally entail the sanction of the superior body originally responsible for approving the element of the plan involved. Often, where changes relate to product specifications rather than the total number of products of a given type, the enterprise can undertake them independently with the consent of the customer. In cases where the items, tasks, standards, targets, or activities are not subject to higher approval, enterprise management has virtually complete independence in making changes in its plan. Most of the enterprises visited also seemed to have considerable independence in choosing the types of above-plan output to produce when they overfulfill their plans.

Organizational Changes and Other Forms of Autonomy

Where enterprise management wishes to undertake major reorganizations of departments, shops, and sections it must usually acquire higher approval, although they are free to propose such changes at any time. A few of the firms surveyed had recently initiated and obtained approval for substantial reorganizations involving administrative units, personnel, activities, and facilities. Most of the enterprises had considerable autonomy in connection with relatively minor organizational changes of these types.

Product and Technical Innovation

The state, rather than individuals or enterprises, plays the key and omniscient entrepreneurial role in Chinese industry through the state plan. For example, no manager or firm has the right to introduce fairly expensive new technology or a new cost-saving device—involving an expenditure of a few thousand yuan or more—or develop and market a new product of much importance unless such an action is sanctioned by the formally approved plan. But in spite of great constraints on enterprise-level innovation of a major nature, enterprises and their personnel are encouraged by the regime to initiate and independently introduce relatively minor innovations and improvements in processes, products, procedures, methods, and techniques. In this respect Chinese enterprises have a great deal of autonomy.

Wages and Salaries

Table 9–3 indicates the average, maximum, and minimum basic monthly pay, and the personnel receiving maximum pay at the thirty-eight enterprises surveyed in 1966. It also indicates the maximum allowable bonus fund as a percent of total basic wages and salaries for the enterprise having such a bonus fund. Bonuses and other incentives are the subject of the following section. Before proceeding with an analysis of Table 9–3 a few general comments about wages and salaries in China are in order.

Administrative cadres and various types of professional and technical personnel at Chinese enterprises receive salaries usually quarterly, but in some cases monthly. All other types of enterprise employees receive wages which are usually paid monthly—and sometimes more frequently—although they may be based on hourly, daily, or weekly rates in specific cases. As noted in earlier chapters, in China there are basic wages and salary scales broken down into grades for different major industrial sectors which provide for some regional differences based on cost-of-living indexes. There is no personal-income tax in Red China.

Salaries paid to administrative cadres, professionals, and leading technical personnel, regardless of what sector they work in are based on a nationwide point system, consisting of several dozen grades. The lowest basic monthly salary according to this national point system is less than 40 yuan. The highest I was told is about 400 yuan received only by some top-level party, government, and military leaders (such as Mao, Liu Shao-chi, Chou En-lai, and Lin Piao), a small number of top-level administrators, such as those heading certain ministries and other central agencies, and a few of the most prominent scientific, educational, professional, and artistic people in the country. However, this 400-yuan maximum salary figure does not apply to many of Communist China's capitalists (who are the topic of Chapter 12). It also does not include other sources of income such as royalties paid to authors, or special monetary rewards received by artists or scientists.

At the enterprises surveyed, few of the managers, engineers, technicians or other salaried personnel were receiving the theoretical maximum for their jobs as indicated in the official salary scales. The basic salary of the top-paid employee at all of the enterprises in my sample was 210 yuan per month. This salary fell roughly one-third of the way from the top of the nationwide salary point system, and was more than 30 percent below the theoretical maximum allowed for the position involved. This highest-paid employee was the director of the Shanghai Heavy Machinery Firm. At the Peking Coke and Chemical Firm the highest-paid employee was the director who was receiving a thirteenth-grade basic monthly salary of 150 yuan, which was nearly 50 percent less than the official maximum allowed for his job. At this plant a fourteenth-grade engineer and a vice director of the same grade were receiving salaries of 138 yuan, while the sixteenth-grade vice directors, department heads, party cadres, and key technical personnel were receiving salaries of 122 yuan. At most of the enterprises the average pay for administrative cadres was a bit higher than that for workers, but there were exceptions.

There was a minimum of eight grades with regard to basic wage scales applying to workers and other types of personnel at the enterprises sur-

TABLE 9–3

WAGE, SALARY, AND BONUS DATA FOR THIRTY-EIGHT CHINESE ENTERPRISES SURVEYED IN 1966

Enterprise	*Average Basic Monthly Pay* (In yuan)	*Minimum Basic Monthly Pay* (In yuan)	*Maximum Basic Monthly Pay* (In yuan)	*Personnel Receiving Maximum Pay*	*Maximum Allowable Bonus Fund*[a] *as a Percent of the Enterprise's Total Wage (and Salary) Fund*
Shanghai Cotton Textile No. 19	78	39	200	Vice director and chief engineer	6
Shanghai Sung Sing No. 9 (Joint) Cotton Textile[b]	78	50	100	2 vice directors, party secretary	7–8
Shanghai Wei Ming Battery	78	37	120	Director, party secretary, vice director	15
Shanghai No. 3 Machine-Tool	75	42	126	Vice director, engineer	15
Shanghai Forging and Pressing Machine-Tool No. 3	75	38	115	Skilled worker	10
Shanghai Truck	72	41	140	Engineer, workshop director	13–14
Shanghai Steel No. 3	71	50	120	Director, party secretary, skilled worker	6
Wuhan Iron and Steel (Corporation)	70	38	180	Vice chief engineer	None (stopped in 1965)
Shanghai Heavy Machine-Tool	70	42	210	Director	10
Tientsin Jen Yi (Joint) Woolen[b]	67	30	122	Skilled worker	6
Canton Machine-Tool	67	not reported	140	Chief engineer	None (stopped in 1966)
Wuhan Heavy Machinery	66	37	150	Director, chief engineer	None (as of 1966)

Shanghai Pharmaceutical No. 3	66	40	174	Party secretary, vice director, chief engineer	5
Canton Chemical Fertilizer	65	46	200	Vice director and chief engineer	7
Peking Clothing	65	36	110	Skilled worker	7
Tientsin Shoe	62.5	37	84	Skilled craftsman	None
Nanking National Chemical Fertilizer	62	34	170	Engineer	None
Peking Coke and Chemical	61	34	150	Director, party secretary	6
Hangchow Machine Tool	61	33	108	Party secretary	8
Canton Lan Yang Electrical Appliance	60	40	135	Skilled worker	None (stopped May 1966)
Nanking Machinery	60	not reported	120	Party secretary	None (stopped late 1965)
Peking Pharmaceutical	60	30	138	Director, party secretary	7
Peking Cotton Textile No. 3	60	not reported	150	Director, party secretary, chief engineer	7
Peking Wool Fabric	60	36	130	Director, party secretary	7
Peking Wool Carpet	60	38	135	Director, party secretary	7
Wuhan Paper	54	35	170	Director	8
Wuhan Diesel-Engine	52.5	37	110	Director	None (stopped March 1966)
Wusih Diesel-Engine	52	38	190	Chief engineer	8
Peking Steel Wire	52	34	98	Director, party secretary	3–5 (% of market value[c] of output)
Peking First Machine-Tool	52	34	180	Vice director and chief engineer	8–9
Wusih Silk Reeling No. 2	52	41	100	Director, party secretary	5
Hangchow Silk Reeling, Dyeing, and Weaving	50	not reported	110	Skilled worker	7
Soochow Cement Products	50	40	100	Engineer, department head	3

TABLE 9–3 (*continued*)

Enterprise	*Average Basic Monthly Pay* (In yuan)	*Minimum Basic Monthly Pay* (In yuan)	*Maximum Basic Monthly Pay* (In yuan)	*Personnel Receiving Maximum Pay*	*Maximum Allowable Bonus Fund*[a] *as a Percent of the Enterprise's Total Wage (and Salary) Fund*
Tientsin Watch	50	34	150	Technician, department head	7
Loyang Tractor	49	30	205	Engineers	15 (planned to stop July 1966)
Wusih Red Flag Machinery	48	39	87	Skilled worker	7
Hangchow Clothing	48	30	69	Director, vice director, skilled worker	7
Tientsin North Lake Instrument	47.5	32	96	Skilled worker	4

[a] Actual criteria used for paying out bonuses to individuals vary at different enterprises.

[b] Pay figures for these two joint state-and-private enterprises exclude data pertaining to the former owners (capitalists) who are still employed by these firms. Their compensation will be discussed in a later chapter.

[c] Peking Steel Wire had a unique bonus system, which is discussed in the section on incentives in the text. Only a small portion of the 3 to 5 percent of the value of output was used for paying individual cash bonuses.

veyed. A number of firms in various industries were paying workers according to twelfth-grade, and in some cases higher-grades, wage scales. While there were many more workers receiving maximum allowable wages, as indicated in the grade system, than administrative cadres receiving maximum allowable salaries for their jobs, still only a very limited number of workers at most of the enterprises surveyed—with the notable exception of some of the consumer-goods plants, especially in Shanghai —were in the maximum allowable wage grade. At Peking Coke and Chemical actual wage grades applied ranged from one to twelve, with the top-grade basic monthly wages being 109 yuan and the lowest 34 yuan. At the Tientsin Instrument Factory seven wage grades were in use, with the top wage being 96 yuan (received by two workers), and the lowest 32 yuan. The average or mean wage grade at this enterprise was 2.5.

In general, the lowest-paid people at Chinese industrial enterprises are unskilled workers—both blue and white collar—junior apprentices, and new graduates from primary and/or junior middle schools. Typically a new graduate from any level of the educational system must spend two or three years working before he is entitled to more pay. Apprentices are usually paid special under-scale starting rates. After two or three years they receive grade-one wages, and after another three or four years they are generally moved up to grade two. After this there is typically no set pattern for basic wage increases, which are then based chiefly on skill, experience, productivity, and general performance, with politics playing a minor role, at least in relatively normal times.

Wage and salary scales allow for more basic pay in most heavy-industry sectors than in most branches of light- or consumer-goods industries, although the size of the enterprise is also often an important factor in determining the salaries of key executives. However, one could not infer this from the data presented in Table 9–3. This table indicates that of the seven enterprises having the highest average pay (wages and salaries combined) in 1966, four of them were not heavy-industry firms, and all of them were in Shanghai. The last point is simpler to explain than the first. Industrial wages and salaries are, on the average, higher in Shanghai than anywhere else in China because of the higher cost of living, and also because there is a much higher porportion of skilled, very experienced, older, and high-talent industrial personnel in Shanghai than anywhere else in the country, with the possible exception of Manchuria. The average basic industrial wage (including salaries) was 75 yuan per month in Shanghai in 1966. Average industrial-wage figures given to me by authorities in some other cities that I visited were 71 yuan for Canton, 62 to 65 yuan for Wuhan, 60 to 65 yuan for Peking, about 60 to 62 yuan for Tientsin, 60 yuan for Nanking, and 50 to 55 yuan for Hangchow and Wusih.

Now to the first point raised above. It is common for sizable numbers of personnel employed in China's traditional industrial sectors—most notably textiles, clothing, and various other branches of light industry—as well as other types of individual firms which have been in existence for a relatively long time to be graded at the top or near the top of the applicable wage and salary scales. This is generally not true for newer enterprises or entire relatively new sectors, such as chemicals and drugs, petroleum, machine building and equipment, components, and nonferrous metallurgy. There are frequently significantly large proportions of personnel in the former types of firms and industries who have a great deal of skill, know-how, experience, and seniority than in the latter.

The Red Chinese regime has followed a general policy from the outset of not reducing the basic salaries or wages paid to industrial personnel before 1949 where such personnel have continued to work. As a result, many of them had been placed in top or nearly top allowable pay grades. There have undoubtedly been some deviations from this policy—for example, possibly where the salaries of some relatively highly paid people have been cut during periods of ideological extremism—but in general it has apparently been adhered to quite closely.

Hence, it is likely to take at least several more years, and possibly a decade or longer, before actual average-pay levels and theoretical pay scales in different sectors correlate closely throughout Red Chinese industry. Back in 1955 average-wage grade levels were highest in the coal and textile industries, followed by light industry, food processing, and iron and steel.[17] These have historically been the oldest and most developed industrial sectors in China, with iron and steel less so than the other four. Average-wage grade levels at that time for relatively new industries, such as chemicals, petroleum, building materials, metal processing (including machine building) and nonferrous metals, lagged behind these five sectors. This pattern may still exist today in Chinese industry.

Income and Ideology

The Chinese Communist regime fully realizes that one sure way to create class distinctions and privileged elites is to allow big income and living-standard differentials in society. For ideological reasons income differentials in Chinese Communist industry, and in other sectors as well, are probably significantly smaller than in any other country in the world.

At a majority of the enterprises surveyed, the ratio between the top pay and average enterprise pay was less than 2.5 to 1; the highest ratio—and this was a very unusual case—was about 4 to 1. The highest-paid employee in my entire sample of thirty-eight firms received only seven times more than the lowest-paid employee in this sample—210 yuan, as against 30 yuan. This is an amazingly small differential compared with what would probably be found in a roughly similar sample of firms in virtually any other country.

At least equally unusual was that workers were the top-paid employees at eight Chinese enterprises and shared this slot at two others. The director alone was the top-paid employee at only three of the thirty-eight firms visited, although he shared the top slot with the party secretary, workers and/or other personnel at twelve other enterprises. At most enterprises the ratio between the director's salary and the average enterprise-pay figure was less than 2 to 1, and the highest was only 3 to 1. At the great majority of Chinese firms, directors and party secretaries received identical or nearly identical salaries, while at Soviet enterprises it is common for directors to get more—quite often, considerably more. At two of the Chinese enterprises the party secretary alone was the highest-paid employee, and at twelve others he shared this distinction with other personnel. Vice directors, department heads, workshop chiefs, engineers and/or other technical personnel were the highest paid at twelve firms, and shared this position at seven others. The salaries of the capitalist managers at the two joint state-and-private enterprises surveyed are excluded from the above discussion.

At twelve Soviet industrial enterprises that I visited several years ago, the directors and various other top-paid employees received from about four to nine times more than the average enterprise wage, and in a majority of cases they received around five times more. This is not significantly different from the pay differentials—after taxes—found at numerous U.S. industrial firms. Even the top-level managers of U.S. factories commonly receive four or five times more, after taxes, than the average wages of their plants. In Indian firms, even at the factory level, the income gap between management and labor is typically much greater—even after taxes—than in Russia or the United States. High-level Indian company and plant managers often receive net incomes twenty to thirty times greater, and even more, than the average worker wage including worker fringe benefits and special income payments. In addition, Indian managers typically get very substantial perquisites as compared with those that may be received by the workers. In no case was, or is, a worker the highest-paid person in any of the Indian, Soviet or U.S. firms or factories that I know about. And in virtually all cases the top-level enterprise executives in these countries are the highest-paid employees.

Living Standards, Welfare and Fringe Benefits

At Chinese enterprises there also generally does not seem to be very substantial difference in the housing or living standards of managers, Reds, technicians, or workers. At Nanking Chemical, Wuhan Iron and Steel,

Peking Cotton Textile and a few other enterprises visited, I spent much time inspecting their employee housing. Top executives, lower-level managers, technical and staff personnel, party cadres, trade-union leaders, and workers were all integrated in the apartment houses. However, some of the relatively highly paid employees did live in somewhat better-furnished flats.

All Chinese enterprise personnel eat together in the same canteen. Even though many of the factories, mainly the larger ones, had cars (some of which were old U.S. models), top managers, key experts and party officials claimed that they walked, rode bikes or took the bus to work. I was told that cars are only for official use or emergencies and are available to all personnel for such purposes. One can usually tell very little about an employee's status from his dress or personal appearance. Most employees, even the women, at all levels generally wear the conventional blue workday suits, often with caps. It is often difficult to tell the women from the men!

Soviet and Indian top-level enterprise executives—including factory managers in India—are commonly provided with chauffeur-driven cars and superior housing. They also typically dress better and generally live substantially better than the average worker. It is likely that the gap in living standards between industrial executives and workers is lower in the United States than in Russia, India, or, for that matter, most other countries. A substantial majority of American workers have cars, TV sets, a wide range of consumer durables, and live in houses or apartments that are superior to those occupied by Soviet workers, and unbelievably superior to those lived in by most Indian workers. Numerous U.S. workers own their own homes. It is rather paradoxical that, apart from Red China, the average gap in living conditions and class distinctions between industrial managers and workers is probably smaller in the United States than in most countries of the world.

One good way to get a sense of the living conditions and purchasing power in Red China is to note the prices for a variety of goods and services. The cost of basic foods and clothing, living accommodations, medicine, education, and entertainment is very low in China and are well within the economic means of industrial workers. Moreover, it is common for both husbands and wives to work, particularly in the cities.

Rent for factory housing is usually limited to a maximum of 4 or 5 percent of the employee's basic monthly pay. Actual monthly rent averaged roughly .1 yuan per square meter and ranged from 1 to 7 yuan (including utilities) for married couples and families at those enterprises where I investigated the housing situation. Apartments at enterprises typically contain one or two bedrooms, sometimes a small den or sitting room, and a small kitchen, rooms with a toilet and shower or a room containing both which are often shared by two or three apartments. They are small and very austere by Western standards, but nevertheless adequate. Meals for enterprise employees—three a day, plus much tea and minor snacks in many cases—cost 10 to 13 yuan per month at the enterprises visited. In general, rice, bread, sugar, and various fruits and vegetables are very cheap in Chinese stores and markets. But chicken usually costs from .7 to 1.7 yuan per pound, pork around 1 yuan, and fish .5 to 1 yuan, depending on the type and quality. Hence, it would usually cost an average worker the equivalent of at least a few hours' pay to buy a pound of fowl, meat, or fish.

Depending on the child's age, it generally costs a factory employee about 4 to 7 yuan per month to keep one of his children in the enterprise nursery. This includes meals during the nursery's working hours. Medical care is usually provided free to employees at the enterprises surveyed, and typically at a discount of roughly 50 percent for their dependents. Most forms of entertainment and recreation charging admission or fees cost only a small fraction of the industrial employee's pay; movies, plays, operas, and sports events typically cost the equivalent of only a few hours' pay or less. The great bulk of most educational expenses are borne by the state. Educational, welfare, medical, and recreational facilities at Chinese industrial enterprises have already been discussed in earlier chapters. A brief comment on how they are financed seems in order at this point. There are apparently two types of special funds for this purpose at most Chinese firms. One welfare fund consists of the equivalent of from 1.5 to 3 percent of the enterprise's total wage-and-salary fund. At those firms where information on this welfare fund was obtained, employees apparently did not contribute to it from their pay, although in some cases they had done so in the past. This welfare fund was typically used for certain types of social insurance, pensions, trade-union activities, and minor medical expenses, and various other minor fringe benefits.

A number of the enterprises surveyed also had a major welfare fund equivalent to about 12 to 13.5 percent of the firm's total basic wage-and-salary fund. This fund was typically used for relatively large expenditures, such as building and expanding welfare facilities, paying the salaries of doctors, teachers, and various other social-welfare personnel, and paying the cost of major medical, trade-union, and social-security services. For example, the Canton Chemical Fertilizer Enterprise had a major welfare fund equal to 13 percent of its wage-and-salary fund; about 42 percent of this fund was used for medical purposes, 15 percent for trade-union operations, and the rest for a variety of welfare, educational, recreational, cultural, insurance and social-security purposes.

Let us see approximately how many days' pay it would require for a Chinese enterprise employee earning a basic monthly wage or salary of 60 yuan to buy some specific products. The interested reader can readily figure out the cost of the products presented in the table below in terms of the number of working days required to purchase them by employees earning different rates of pay.

TABLE 9–4

NUMBER OF DAYS' PAY REQUIRED FOR A CHINESE WORKER EARNING A BASIC MONTHLY WAGE OF 60 YUAN TO BUY VARIOUS PRODUCTS

Product	*Approximate Number of Days' Pay*
Man's cap	1½–2
Child's cotton suit or dress	1–2½
Cotton socks	⅜–⅝
Wool socks	2–2¾
Man's or woman's conventional 2-piece cotton suit	5–7
Man's 2-piece wool suit, military-cut	30–50
Man's or Woman's wool (cashmere) sweater	7–15
Man's Wstern-style suit, cheaper material	35–50
Man's Western-style suit, good material	60–90
Man's light overcoat	70–80
Woman's cloth overcoat	90–120
Man's or woman's shirt or pajamas western-style	4–6
Meal at a fairly good restaurant	2–7
Chocolate bar	⅛–¼
Pack of cigarettes	⅕–⅖
Large bar of soap	½–1
Bottle of wine or alcoholic beverage (gin, vodka, brandy, whisky)	3–15
Sunglasses (without case)	⅓–¼
Flashlight	1½–3
2 standard flashlight batteries	¼–⅓
Box of matches	negligible
Cheap clock	5–6
Watch	30–60
Radio (including transistor radios)	25–50
T.V. set (14″ to 17″ screen)	165–425
Camera	25–50
Film (roll of black and white)	½–1½
Child's cloth shoes	⅓
Child's leather shoes	1–1½
Men's or women's cloth shoes	2–3
Men's or women's leather shoes	5–10

Product	*Approximate Number of Days' Pay*
Adult's leather sandals	3–6
Lady's simple leather handbag	2½–4
Suitcase (leather or similar material)	15–25
Sewing machine	75–100
Bicycle	60–90
12-piece set of home furniture (cheap wood)	at least 350
Single bureau with mirror	40–50
Car (if allowed to purchase)	More than 12,000

The above discussion and Table 9–4 suggest that out hypothetical average Chinese industrial employee can clearly afford the basic necessities of life for himself and a family of modest size. If his wife also works, they can probably afford a number of (by Chinese standards) luxury items, such as a radio, sewing machine, camera, watch, bicycle, and a few articles of good and relatively stylish clothing for special occasions. But he clearly lives very simply, austerely, and in a starkly utilitarian manner, when compared with the average living standards in advanced countries.

Once a Chinese industrial employee has the types of luxury goods noted above, there is usually little he can buy with his excess cash.

Luxury items common in advanced countries such as cars, modern private homes, TV sets, washers and dryers, air conditioners, fine jewelry, works of art, and rare antiques are either not available or beyond the financial means of even the highest-paid industrial personnel. Such items are typically purchased only by organizations or allocated to individuals; they are rarely bought by individuals. Hence, it is likely that for at least some of the higher-paid Chinese industrial personnel the identification with the country's goals and progress, a deep sense of commitment, pride, and purpose all undoubtedly play vital roles in motivating them. But the marginal utility of money begins to diminish at a certain level of income; in turn, this is likely to mean that monetary incentives and material gain lose some of their potency as potential motivating forces.

Incentives: What Makes Wong Run?

Top-level Enterprise Executives and Experts

What motivates the director, vice directors, party leaders, and leading technical and other experts to perform well and to improve their performance at Chinese industrial enterprises? Income and material gain do not generally seem to play the key role, particularly for top-level executives who are not allowed to earn any bonuses or extra pay. As was mentioned above, the marginal utility of money may diminish for top-paid personnel since there often is little they can buy with their excess savings when they reach a certain point on the pay scale. This type of situation has posed a serious problem for the Soviet regime in recent years. The current Soviet response involves a substantial expansion in the production of more stylish and luxury-type consumer goods—including private cars, many of which are to be produced by a large new plant set up by Fiat of Italy—more good and expensive restaurants and relatively plush resorts, even some night clubs, as well as somewhat greater opportunities for the elites to build their own dachas (villas or homes).

The Red Chinese may well be faced with a similar situation in the not-too-distant future. And it is also very likely that greater emphasis will have to be placed on material incentives in general in order to achieve sustained and substantial industrial progress and economic development.

At present, dedication, loyalty, and zeal are shown by key enterprise managers and officials (particularly the Reds, but probably many of the Experts as well), and the achievement drive of such personnel probably tends to be quite high, although on the average it may well be lower than during the 1950–57 period because of the Cultural Revolution.

Individual power is quite restricted, even for top-level enterprise officials. However, there seems to be considerable status and prestige attached to being a key enterprise official—with the exception of various Experts during very intense periods of ideological extremism—and this is likely to be a significant motivating force. Although a Red Chinese citizen with the correct political attitude is not supposed to be interested in personal prestige or status, I came across a number of obvious indications that differences in status and deference to those of higher standing still exist, and that such attitudes are clearly far from being eliminated in Communist China.

As noted elsewhere, there are typically relatively large numbers of vice directors at Chinese firms. Why appoint so many if the title, and the status and prestige that go with it, do not mean much? As for the Reds or party leaders at Chinese enterprises, they are clearly a type of elite or class, although very different from the old Chinese elites or ruling classes. The title of engineer or even technician seems to be highly respected in Red China, even though such title holders may be somewhat self-conscious or defensive at times about being part of the intelligentsia. When technicians and engineers have been promoted from the ranks of the workers, they tend to be more openly proud of their titles than those who achieved such positions largely because of formal education.

Key enterprise personnel may also be motivated by their opportunities to do more interesting work, to be creative, to share in greater responsibilities, and to make or at least influence relatively important decisions. At

Chinese enterprises the general absence of very significant penalties and the de-emphasis of individual responsibility, both of which are often potent negative motivating forces in Russia and the West, for unintentional managerial errors or economic inefficiency (but not for serious ideological deficiencies) may have a positive motivational effect.

Bonuses and Extra Material Rewards

References have been made to monetary incentive schemes in use at Chinese enterprises in the section on the attitude toward wealth, material gain, and self-interest in Chapter 4, and at various other earlier points in this book. A brief summary and some additional information seem to be in order here. However, there is no need to discuss again the rewards for innovational and technical-improvement measures since they have already been discussed adequately in the section on organization structure in the present chapter and elsewhere.

I found that at all of the firms surveyed there were no individual piece-rates payment systems in use, and where there were in the past they had been abolished. There was also apparently very little use being made of collective piece-rate wages of any type at the enterprises visited.

At about 80 percent of the thirty-eight enterprises there were bonus payment systems in effect for workers, middle- and lower-level managers, technical employees, and various other personnel apart from top management. Bonuses were being paid monthly or quarterly, and in a few cases only annually. The vast majority of the bonus payments came from a special bonus fund—also called the extra reward fund—based on a specified percentage of the enterprise's total basic wage-and-salary fund.

The actual bonus fund was financed from the enterprise's profits. Table 9–3 indicates the maximum allowable bonus fund at those enterprises that had such a fund. We see from this table that eight of the thirty-eight enterprises—or slightly over 20 percent—did not have a bonus fund in 1966, that Loyang Tractor planned to abolish its fund in July 1966. I was also told by executives at several other enterprises—about eight or nine of them—that they were seriously considering the abolishment of their bonus funds, though no specific dates were given as to when this would be done. At a few of the enterprises having bonus funds none of the administrative cadres or certain types of cadres—apart from high-level executives—were entitled to any bonuses. For example, no cadres at all were eligible for bonuses at Tientsin Instrument, and workshop directors were not allowed any bonuses at Peking First Machine Tool.

In many cases where bonuses were paid to workers they were for group or collective performance rather than individual contributions. Furthermore, worker bonuses were frequently not based solely on economic results or productivity; political attitude, ideologically correct behavior, and/or helping co-workers were also key criteria. Peking Coke, which had based workers' bonuses entirely on job performance, began awarding them only for attendance and safety in January 1966. Only at relatively few enterprises were workers' bonuses contingent on the fulfillment of certain key success indicators by the enterprise as a whole; and even here, bonuses could still be awarded in most cases where superior authorities judged the nonfulfillment of success indicators to have been due to factors largely beyond the enterprise's control.

At about 20 or 25 percent of the enterprises, administrative cadres and certain types of technical personnel could not receive bonuses if specified enterprise success indicators were not fulfilled. At a number of enterprises bonuses were paid to them when key departmental, shop or section targets and/or tasks were fulfilled. At other firms they were based on individual contributions and performance, which often involved evaluation criteria similar to those applied in worker-bonus payments.

A few of the enterprise-success-indicator bonus systems in my sample were quite unusual, and may be worth mentioning. The Tientsin Jen Yi Wool Factory had a maximum allowable bonus fund equal to 6 percent of its wage fund. To achieve this maximum the firm had to fulfill six success indicators (more than at most enterprises). For each success indicator not fulfilled the enterprise lost 1 percent of its wage fund for bonus payments. This firm paid out a total of 40,000 yuan in bonuses in 1965. Tientsin Instrument had a system similar to that of Tientsin Wool. But at the instrument firm only 4 percent of the wage fund and four success indicators were involved. Peking Steel Wire was still using basically the same success-indicator reward system that had been set up by Soviet experts some years ago. If the aggregate marketable-output target expressed in yuan was fulfilled, the enterprise kept the equivalent of 3 percent of total marketable output. It could keep up to an additional 2 percent by overfulfilling this target. However, only a minor portion of the reward fund earned by the enterprise under this system could be used for individual bonuses. The rest was used for collective welfare, improving operations, and financing relatively minor expansion programs. In 1965 extra rewards amounted to about 100,000 yuan at Peking Steel Wire. The only difference in this firm's extra reward system in 1966 and the one originally set up by the Soviets was that gross output was the success indicator used under the Soviet system and individual bonuses comprised a greater share of the reward fund.

At the enterprises surveyed, there were typically three grades, maximum, middle, and minimum, of bonuses awarded each period. At most of the firms, administrative and technical staffs were entitled to smaller absolute bonuses—usually 10 to 15 percent less, but in some cases even less—than workers. At Shanghai Truck, where bonus payments were about the largest of any of the enterprises surveyed, quarterly bonus grades for workers were 18, 24, and 36 yuan; for administrative cadres they were 13, 18, and 24 yuan. At Shanghai No. 3 Machine Tool, where bonus grades were also among the highest at firms visited, quarterly worker-bonus grades were 15, 20, and 25 yuan, and for cadres and various technical personnel 13, 18, and 23 yuan.

In general, a worker receiving average basic pay at the above two enterprises, as well as a few others with relatively high bonus grade systems, could earn additional seven or eight weeks' pay annually if he received maximum bonuses each quarter under the bonus systems in effect in the spring of 1966. An administrative cadre who maximized his bonuses could earn an amount about one week's less pay than a worker who did so.

Where bonuses were being paid monthly, Shanghai Battery had the largest bonus grades. They were 3.5, 6, and 9 yuan for workers, and 7, 9, and 12 yuan for cadres. This was one of the few firms where cadres were entitled to larger bonuses than workers. An average-paid administrator or manager who received maximum bonuses each month for a year under Shanghai Battery's system would earn about the equivalent of an additional six- or seven-weeks' pay. An average-paid worker would earn about five-weeks additional pay.

Tientsin Instrument had one of the smallest levels of quarterly bonus grades—5, 10, and 15 yuan—of all the firms surveyed that had such a system. However, wages at this factory were well below the average for my sample. An average-paid worker at Tientsin Instrument who maximized his bonuses under the system in use would earn the equivalent of nearly six-weeks' additional pay. As noted above, administrative cadres of all types could not receive bonuses at this enterprise. Hangchow Clothing and Wusih Silk had the smallest levels of monthly bonus grades, which applied to both workers and cadres. They were 3, 4, and 5 yuan, and 2.5, 3 and 4 yuan respectively. An employee receiving average basic pay at these two enterprises who maximized his bonuses over the year would earn the equivalent of three- to four-weeks' additional pay.

At the enterprises having bonus funds, the proportion of eligible personnel who received maximum bonuses averaged about 20 percent during 1965 and in the first quarter of 1966. The lowest actual proportion was 3 percent, and the highest 35 percent. It was common for smaller proportions of eligible administrative cadres and technical personnel to receive maximum bonuses than workers at the firms surveyed. The proportion of eligible personnel who received no bonuses during the period mentioned above averaged about 10 to 15 percent. The highest actual proportion of this type was 30 percent, and the lowest 5 percent.

The Enterprise Fund

Reference was made earlier in this chapter to the enterprise fund. A majority of the firms surveyed in 1966 were allowed to have such a fund which was formed annually, quarterly, or monthly. At some of the firms the enterprise fund had recently been abolished, and at a number of others abolishment was being contemplated.

A majority of the firms not having a bonus fund were also among those not having an enterprise fund. The enterprise fund was formed from a small proportion of earned profits when certain key enterprise-success indicators were fulfilled. The fund typically ranged in size from 2.5 to 10 percent of the firm's total earned profits, the average being 5 percent at the firms surveyed having such a fund. Some of the textile firms visited had the smallest funds (about 2.5 percent of profits), while Wuhan Heavy Machinery and Wuhan Steel and its factories could keep 10 percent of their profits if key success indicators were fulfilled. In some cases the actual size of the enterprise fund was based on a certain percent of the wage fund—say, 6 or 7 percent—rather than earned profits, but it still came from the firm's profits.

At a number of enterprises, including a few that had no bonus fund of the kind discussed above, management could use a small portion of the enterprise fund to pay special bonuses to deserving personnel for a variety of reasons. However, a number of firms had recently stopped this practice. In general, individual bonuses from the enterprise fund were typically smaller than those paid out of the regular bonus fund, where there was one. It was fairly common for individual rewards paid for by the enterprise fund to take the form of various prizes, books, plaques, medals, special trips, and various special fringe benefits, rather than cash.

The great bulk of the enterprise funds at firms visited was used for welfare and recreational purposes, such as housing, clinics, education, library acquisitions, canteens, athletics, clinics, and employee clubs, to improve and expand enterprise operations, and to buy small tools, used equipment, and various other supplies. At some firms fairly sizable projects were undertaken through the enterprise fund. For example, Wuhan Iron and Steel used part of its enterprise fund one year to build an ice plant, and during another year it installed air conditioning in its small hotel for foreign visitors.

At a sizable proportion of the firms surveyed, the enterprise fund was based solely on profit performance, although some enterprises had recently de-emphasized profit as a key success indicator for forming their enterprise fund. In a majority of cases, however, two to four success indicators had to be fulfilled for an enterprise fund to be formed, and in a few cases as many as five or six. In addition to profit, the other common key success indicators pertaining to the formation of enterprise funds at the firms surveyed were quantity of output, sometimes in total, but more often for major products or product groups, total marketable output in yuan, output quality, some measure of cost performance, labor productivity, product yields, and in rare cases other indicators such as major product- or technical-development measures.

A few of the enterprises had unique criteria for forming their enterprise fund. In such cases, conditions for forming an enterprise fund were similar to those that have been used quite extensively in Soviet industry. At Peking Steel Wire 2 percent of earned profits formed its enterprise fund if the profit target was fulfilled. However, the enterprise fund would receive an additional 1 percent of profits for each 2 or 3 percent of overfulfillment of the profit target, up to a maximum of 10 percent of total earned profits.

At Canton Chemical Fertilizer 5 percent of profits formed the enterprise fund when the total quantity of production target (in tons) was fulfilled. However, the firm could receive progressively more profits for the enterprise fund by overfulfilling the quantity of production target according to a fixed formula. In theory there was apparently no limit to the size of the firm's enterprise fund, but the largest that it had ever been to date was 10 percent of monthly profits. I was also told that during some months the output target had not been fulfilled and no enterprise fund was established.

Wuhan Paper's enterprise fund had been solely based on profit performance until the latter part of 1965. In 1966, 7 percent of earned profits were allocated to the enterprise fund each quarter if three success indicators were fulfilled—total marketable output in tons, quality of output (by goods), and the average cost target for a ton of paper. If only two of these success indicators were fulfilled, 5 percent of profits would be allocated to the enterprise fund, and if only one was fulfilled only 2 percent of profits would be allocated.

Nonmaterial Incentives

Probably much greater use is made of nonmaterial incentives to motivate industrial personnel in Communist China than in any other country in the world. Extensive and constant use is made of socialist emulation drives, mass participation in special campaigns, slogans, wall posters, motivational sessions and discussion groups, and the awarding of titles such as "model worker," "leading worker," and "five-good worker," as well as similar titles for leading work groups and, at times, enterprises.

Special conferences are frequently held at the municipal, provincial, and national levels to choose award-winning workers, work teams and enterprises. The winners receive considerable publicity at all levels where they are victorious, often get their names and even their pictures in the papers, and are sometimes received and honored by top-level local and national leaders. Red banners, certificates, plaques, medals, flowers, specially bound copies of Mao's works, and sometimes membership in various honorary societies are also among the most common nonmaterial incentives used. In some cases, awards or rewards (apart from bonuses) to outstanding workers or other enterprise employees are not entirely nonmaterial. Special privileges in welfare benefits, educational opportunities, improved chances of promotion and more pay, and a better chance of getting into the Communist Party, where various additional privileges may be gained, are often won by those employees judged to be outstanding for various reasons.

From what I learned at the Chinese enterprises that I visited, the greatest official honor or recognition that can be received by a worker is to be elected or otherwise chosen as a five-good worker. The five basic criteria here are (1) competence in his job and in performing his tasks; (2) attitude of cooperation; (3) political study and overall correct ideological attitudes; (4) regular study and self improvement; (5) and observance of regulations pertaining to attendance, safety, use of state property, and so on. There are five-good-worker competitions at least annually at the enterprise on municipal, provincial, and national levels—typically along branch-of-industry lines above the enterprise. There are also similar competitions to choose five-good work groups or teams. In addition to public praise, honor, and recognition, the winners usually receive some of Mao's works, a medal or plaque, and a certificate.

At a majority of the enterprises surveyed, the proportion of workers selected as five-good workers each period usually ranged from about 7 to 15 percent. The Peking Woolen Mill had the highest proportion, nearly 50 percent, in the last quarter of 1965. Peking Pharmaceutical and a few other firms had the lowest proportions, 1 or 2 percent, in recent competitions. At some of the enterprises one or more of their workers had recently won municipal, provincial, and in a few cases national five-good-worker competitions. It is not uncommon for the same worker to be so honored quite often, even quite regularly in some cases.

It is also quite common for five-good workers to receive below-average pay at their enterprises and to earn less than maximum bonuses or even no bonuses (where the firm has a bonus system) because their tasks are not adequately fulfilled and/or overfulfilled, although they may excel in the other four achievements that made them five-good workers.

Mrs. Chiang, who puts caps on batteries at the Shanghai Wei Ming Battery Factory, was a fairly representative five-good worker among those whom I met. I was told she is the daughter of poor peasants, who died of starvation when she was quite young. Her husband works in the same factory and was earning a basic monthly wage of 93 yuan, and had not been chosen as a five-good worker. At the time I met Mrs. Chiang she had been employed at the factory for eight years, and had been selected as a five-good worker quite regularly during the last three. Her basic monthly wage was 66 yuan, compared with an enterprise average of 78 yuan and an average of 70 yuan for her work group of fifteen. The highest-paid worker in her group was receiving 96 yuan. In the preceding month Mrs. Chiang had earned a 6-yuan or second-grade bonus, and not the maximum bonus of 9 yuan. In 1965 she earned no bonus in some months and the maximum bonus in some.

In general, nonmaterial incentives have undoubtedly been highly effective in motivating enterprise personnel in Chinese Communist industry. However, when they are pushed too far for the sake of ideology, they lose much of their potency, and, in fact, at a certain point they become ineffective and lead to indifference, boredom, and eventually outright opposition and hostility.

The force of nonmaterial disincentives in Chinese industry should not be overlooked. Public criticism and obligatory self-criticism at meetings or on wall posters can be a severe penalty for incorrect attitudes or behavior, slackness, carelessness, and other misdemeanors, especially in a society like China's that is so traditionally devoted to external appearances and concern over loss of face. However, penalties of this type are much more likely to be applied for ideological deficiencies than for unintentionally poor job performance.

CHAPTER 10

Survey of Chinese Industrial Enterprises: Performance

THIS CHAPTER DEALS WITH a qualitative and quantitative analysis of key aspects of performance at the Chinese enterprises surveyed in 1966. Pertinent statistical data and other figures will be presented, and some suggestive comparisons will be made with industrial performance in India, the Soviet Union, and the United States.

Because of my limited sample of Chinese enterprises and the very limited time I spent at each of them, much of what I have to say in this chapter is necessarily more subjective than conclusive. Moreover, it would be wrong to generalize about whole branches of Chinese industry on the basis of the findings derived from a study of such a small sample of firms. Nevertheless, it is hoped that the data, evaluations, and analyses to be presented will shed useful light on Chinese industrial performance and potential.

The reader is justified in asking "How representative were the enterprises surveyed of their branches of industry as a whole?" Or "How much did the Chinese really let the visitor see and find out?" In answer I should say that apparently I was not "managed" very strictly since most of my requests regarding types and sizes of firms, new versus older firms, and so on were met with little or no hesitation. Moreover, I visited enterprises which I perceived as good, average, and poor in terms of technology, managerial know-how, productivity, and general operating efficiency.

The reader may also justifiably question the accuracy of statistics and other quantitative performance data given to me by Red Chinese officials. With very few exceptions I do not believe that they gave me intentionally distorted figures, although there may have been some unintentional errors in data provided because of faulty recording or analysis. When Chinese officials whom I interviewed did not want to give me a figure, they usually said so. For example, I could obtain very little in the way of concrete capital-investment data—and very few macro statistics. At several enterprises I could not get very concrete data on physical production, value of output, profit and/or cost. In general, I was more successful in getting desired statistics from light-industry enterprises, particularly consumer-goods producers, than from larger heavy-industry firms, which the authorities probably feel have more strategic importance.

It was common for enterprise executives to state statistics that I requested in ranges, rather than providing a single figure. In most cases, and often through good-natured bargaining, I was able to get such ranges down to quite narrow limits so that they were meaningful for computational and analytical purposes. In several cases I have had to compute my own estimates of performance from averages (in time, units, etc.) given to me; but here, too, the likely margins of error do not tend to be very significant.

With the above precautions and limitations in mind, let us proceed.

Managerial Know-How

Thus far, Red China has achieved substantial industrial progress, more through sheer managerial motivation and zeal than through managerial or technical know-how. In some critical ways the Chinese manager typically seems to resemble the commonly accepted image of the American manager in that they both appear to have a relatively high achievement drive.

A great many more Indian managers whom I have met know more about managerial techniques than do most of the Chinese managers, and the former have substantially more potential managerial know-how. Indian managers frequently read Western literature on management, and many have attended formal management-education programs. Chinese managers, on the other hand, may read a good deal of purely technical literature and undergo technical training, but they are not generally exposed to much management literature or formal management training. However, perhaps because of a relatively low achievement drive—as well as various other environmental constraints—the Indian manager frequently does not apply much of his potential know-how effectively in practice. The Chinese manager is typically more pragmatic, inventive, flexible, action-oriented, and interested in improving performance and results. He learns much through trial and error and persistence.

Chinese industry has also made significant progress because of the motivation, dedication, resourcefulness, and hard work on the part of its labor force. Here greater credit must be given to the Reds than to the Experts or career managers. The Communist Party has organized and motivated workers on a national scale to identify with, and strive for, national economic progress and power. This has been a macro type of motivation, organization and leadership rather than micro. Hence, enterprise management has a good part of its job done at the outset in terms of motivating personnel. In fact, there is a sharp dichotomy in the managerial job. The Reds typically play the key role in personnel matters, direction, leadership, selection, and, to a lesser extent, training and appraisal. The managers and Experts are primarily involved in planning, technical decision making, control, organizing activities, technical training, and some personnel-appraisal work. In these latter areas Chinese managers do not, in general, seem to have as much know-how as Soviet industrial managers, and much less than their U.S. counterparts.

At a majority of the Chinese enterprises surveyed, there was an apparent lack of integrated, in-depth planning throughout the organization. A systems approach, which is essential to well-balanced and coordinated plans, is clearly lacking. In designing the plans almost complete reliance is placed on historical norms of labor and material input, historical inventory norms and other relationships based on past performance. Virtually no use is made of time-and-motion studies, and little use is made of designs, drawings, or analytical computations for determining other factor-input standards. At most enterprises there seems to be considerable difficulty in integrating technical and economic factors in decision making. There is also little use made of contingent or alternate plans. If the plan breaks down because of supply failures, for example, a completely new plan must often be drafted.

Control systems found at many enterprises are also far from efficient. Apart from after-the-fact control and information feedback related to aggregate targets, managerial control typically seems to be quite weak and results in much inefficiency and waste. Perhaps the Chinese factory is not bureaucratic enough, since more formal reports, procedures, and policies would probably improve efficiency in most cases. Chinese managers do not seem to make much use of written control reports or written communications in general. In-process cost control, or controls over material and labor usage, is practically nonexistent at many factories. There is much stress placed on finished-product quality control—and this generally seems to be done quite well—but in-process quality control frequently tends to be quite ineffective. Hence, many rejects are sent back through the production process.

There appears to be a great deal of stress on preventative maintenance in order to preserve and conserve equipment. However, this type of work seems to be frequently carried out in an inefficient manner because of the lack of a clear-cut division of labor. Production workers often do maintenance and repair work, rather than personnel from the repair and maintenance department. Even managers often are involved in this type of work.

Most of the Chinese managers clearly lack experience in organizing work efficiently. Poor organization, particularly in larger firms, is also due in part to the overly flexible nature of the informal organization and the constraints placed on reorganizing departments and shops by higher authorities. Work flows suffer greatly in many cases because of the lack of specialization or efficient integration of activities. This ties in with poor planning and norm setting. At many plants there are large auxiliary work forces—in some cases they exceed the number of production workers—and this is frequently due, at least in part, to inefficient planning and organization of activities. As noted in the previous chapter, several Chinese managers expressed concern that, although they felt their firm's organization structure could be substantially improved, they did not know how to go about making an appropriate analysis.

Most of the Chinese managers also lack experience in training subordinates in technical and managerial skills. And many are also not very clear on how to appraise their subordinates' performance. Noneconomic factors seem to make appraisal of work performance a rather nebulous process.

In general, Soviet industrial managers seem to have more know-how than the Chinese in the functions of production, procurement, finance, accounting, and research and development, although they often do not make effective use of this ability because of the incentive system they work under. The Chinese manager, however, seems to have a greater flair for, and interest in, the techniques of marketing. More attention is typically given to product planning, marketing research, product development and improvement, customer satisfaction, and even to analysis of finished inventory levels at Chinese industrial enterprises. This was particularly true at several of the consumer-goods firms, but even in the case of industrial goods Chinese managers generally seemed to have more marketing know-how than their Soviet counterparts.

It would seem that without considerably more basic and more extensive managerial know-how, Chinese industry will undoubtedly run into serious trouble as it develops and grows more complex. It is not too difficult to achieve substantial industrial progress in an industrially backward country even with rather sloppy management if people have the basic drive, motivation, and resourcefulness to improve their economic performance and productivity. However, at a certain point along the development spectrum, managerial talent and knowledgeableness become just as important as motivation and attitudes. If such motivation and attitudes lose some of their effectiveness, managerial know-how will become more important that much sooner.

In any event, the Chinese will have to face up to the problem of managerial know-how in the foreseeable future, as the Soviets are now doing. If they do not, they certainly will not evolve from a merely effective to an efficient industrial system; indeed, they probably will not be able to maintain even an effective system.

Technology

Table 10–1 contains my subjective evaluation of the nine best-equipped and nine worst-equipped Chinese factories visited in terms of plants in similar industries in the United States and Canada; the other plants surveyed fall somewhere in between. In some cases key personnel at Chinese enterprises surveyed were willing to give me an opinion as to where their factory stood in terms of technology as compared with others in the same industry in China.

Officials at a majority of the Chinese enterprises in the best-equipped category in Table 10–1 admitted that they were above average in their industry. Several of the heavy-industry plants surveyed, including both of the steel firms, that are not in the best-equipped group claimed that they were average or below average. Some of them said that the best factories in their industries were in north China (Manchuria), an area I was not permitted to visit. Some of the worst-equipped enterprises, such as the shoe and battery factories, claimed to be about average in their industries. Both of the joint state-private textile firms (Tientsin Jen Yi Wool and Shanghai Sung Sing No. 9 Cotton) said they were below average in terms of technology; they were certainly not nearly as well equipped as the other woolen- and cotton-textile factories I visited. (The Sung Sing Mill had recently undergone extensive capital repairs and overhaul work.)

Grading of Enterprises in Terms of Managerial Know-How and General Operating Efficiency with Available Technology

In Table 9–2 of Chapter 9 I have subjectively graded the thirty-eight Chinese industrial enterprises surveyed in terms of managerial know-how and general operating efficiency with physical technology available. It is often difficult to determine whether a specific Chinese enterprise is managed well and performing well or poorly largely because of internal reasons or external factors. For example, there might be much unproductive time, idle resources, and/or waste because the external resource-allocation and supply system has failed the enterprise, or because there is internal mana-

TABLE 10–1

ESTIMATE OF NINE BEST-EQUIPPED AND NINE WORST-EQUIPPED CHINESE FACTORIES OF THOSE VISITED*

(In terms of firms in similar industries in the U.S. and Canada)

Best equipped †

Peking Pharmaceutical (mostly Chinese equipment, some Japanese; only real technological weakness was lack of packaging machinery)

Peking Chemical Coke (mostly Chinese equipment)

Peking Cotton Textile No. 3 (mostly Chinese equipment)

Shanghai Machine-Tool (mostly Chinese equipment, some machines from Eastern Europe)

Wuhan Heavy Machinery (Chinese, Russian, Czech, German, British equipment)

Canton Chemical Fertilizer (nearly all Chinese equipment)

Tientsin Watch (mostly Swiss, some Russian and British machinery)

Hangchow Clothing (nearly all Chinese equipment)

Wusih Diesel-Engine (much Chinese, Swiss, and Japanese equipment for research and development and quality control)

Nanking Machinery (almost all Chinese equipment)

Worst equipped ‡

Shanghai Battery (mostly Chinese machines, some British, U.S., and Japanese)

Tientsin Shoe (more than 50% of the equipment made or rebuilt by this factory)

Tientsin North Lake Instrument (not much equipment; most made or rebuilt by factory)

Wusih Machinery (most machines rebuilt by this factory)

Shanghai (Joint) Sung Sing Cotton Textile (mostly very old imported equipment—much from Britain, some from United States)

Hangchow Machine Tool (mostly second-rate Chinese equipment, some from Eastern Europe, some rebuilt by factory)

Wuhan Diesel-Engine (much equipment rebuilt by this factory)

Canton Electrical Appliance (about 50% of equipment made or rebuilt by this factory)

Wuhan Paper (mostly Chinese equipment; a few machines from East and West Europe)

* No attempt is made to rank enterprises within the best or worst category.

† Those Chinese enterprises in the best category typically seem to be as well equipped as average or slightly above average U.S. or Canadian factories in similar industries, with the exception of material-handling equipment at the Chinese chemical and machinery plants. Few if any of the Chinese firms have plants equivalent to the first-rate factories in the U.S. or Canada.

‡ Few firms in the United States or Canada are probably as poorly equipped as these Chinese plants.

gerial incompetence. In addition, in a brief visit one may be biased in viewing a firm as being well managed or efficient because it is modern and well equipped, or vice versa. In my grading of Chinese enterprises I have tried to isolate the technological factor and focus on managerial know-how, productivity, and general level of efficiency in operating with available physical factors of production.

Tables 9–2 (in Chapter 9) and 10–1 show that enterprises rated as well equipped are not necessarily rated as being well managed in the framework of available technology, and vice versa. For example, Tientsin Watch and Wusih Diesel Engine are in the best-equipped category but are in the worst and below-average groups, respectively, in terms of managerial know-how and operating efficiency. Shanghai Sung Sing Cotton and Shanghai Battery are in the worst-equipped group but are rated best and above average, respectively, in terms of managerial know-how and general efficiency.

It may prove interesting to make some comparisons of the best and worst firms in Table 9–2 with the data on wages and bonus funds for these firms presented in Table 9–3 of Chapter 9. Of the seven best firms in Table 9–2 the director was the top paid or among the few top-paid personnel at five of them. At Shanghai Cotton Textile No. 9 the vice director and chief engineer, an expert with a good education, was the top-paid employee. At Shanghai Sung Sing Cotton a vice director and the party secretary were the top-paid people, but this firm had a number of capitalists receiving much higher pay who were in key positions. Hangchow Clothing was the only firm in the best category having a skilled worker as one of the top-paid employees.

Of the six enterprises in the worst category in Table 9–2, the director was the top-paid employee only at Wuhan Diesel, and shared this slot with the party secretary at Peking Steel Wire. At Hangchow Machine Tool the party secretary alone was the top-paid employee; at Tientsin Shoe and Canton Electrical Appliance it was a skilled worker; and at Tientsin Watch a technician.

There is no clear-cut correlation between the firms rated in the best-managed and most efficient category with average wages and salaries. However, the two cotton-textile enterprises in this group ranked one and two among the thirty-eight firms surveyed in average pay, and Shanghai Heavy Machine Tool ranked ninth. Hangchow Clothing ranked next to last in pay, while the other three firms in the best category ranked around the middle range of the thirty-eight enterprises in terms of average pay.

There is not much more of a correlation between the worst firms in Table 9–2 and levels of average pay. Two of the six firms in the worst category also ranked among the bottom ten of thirty-eight firms in average pay; these were Tientsin Watch, thirty-fourth; and Peking Steel Wire, twenty-ninth. The average-pay rankings of the other four firms in this worst category were Wuhan Diesel, twenty-sixth; Canton Electrical Appliance, twentieth; Hangchow Machine tool, nineteenth; and Tientsin Shoe, sixteenth.

There is a rather close correlation between the best and worst firms in Table 9–2 and whether or not they had bonus funds (see Table 9–3 of Chapter 9). Six of the seven enterprises in the best category had bonus funds at the time of my visit in 1966. Only Wuhan Heavy Machinery did not have a bonus fund, but it had just been abolished. Of the eight firms in the entire sample that had no bonus funds three of them are in the worst category in Table 9–2. The fact that a given enterprise had or did not have a bonus fund may not by itself have been a very critical determinant as to whether it was well or poorly managed, or operating relatively efficiently or inefficiently in many cases. However, where bonus funds had been abolished, this suggests that the Reds may well have been in charge of operational management as well as general policy, and this is likely to have been contributing substantially to serious managerial and efficiency problems in several cases.

There is no clear-cut correlation between the best and worst firms in Table 9–2 with their proportions of administrative and/or technical personnel or engineers (see Table 9–1 of Chapter 9). There is also no significant correlation between the best and worst firms with levels of higher and semiprofessional education among their total employment or administrative and technical personnel (see Tables 3–13 and 3–14 of Chapter 3). Although the textile and clothing firms rank relatively low in educational level as a total group and in most individual cases, they typically have significantly larger proportions of personnel (managers, technicians and workers) with long experience than firms in China's relatively new industrial sectors.

Table 9–2 indicates no clear relationship between the best and worst groups of firms and the types of superior agencies to which these enterprises are directly subordinate, although two of the firms in the best group are under central ministries while none in the worst group are under ministries. Table 9–2 also does not reveal a close correlation between best- and worst-group enterprises and relative degrees of autonomy. However, three of the seven firms in the best group have the highest degree of autonomy on the scale, while none in the worst group do.

As for the sizes of the firms in the best and worst category, they are on the average substantially larger in the best group. In this group all but one firm, Hangchow Clothing, have more than 2,000 employees, and five of them have 4,800 or more. However, the four largest enterprises in the entire sample are rated either average or below average. In the worst group, half of the firms have 1,000 or more employees, and all of the enterprises here fall in the 800 to 1,400 employment range.

We shall consider the grading of firms on Table 9–2 in terms of branch-of-industry representation when an analysis of productivity is undertaken later in this chapter.

Quantitative Performance Trends in the 1960's

In this section I shall present trend data on physical production, value of output, profits, capital investment, employment, and other aspects of performance in the 1960's for the various firms that provided me with significant information of this type. In most cases such data are expressed in percentage increases or decreases from year to year. The interested reader can convert many of the percentage figures into absolute figures by utilizing the data presented in Tables 10–2 and 10–3.

Textile Enterprises

Peking Cotton Textile No. 3 reported that its 1965 total output target in square meters was overfulfilled by 4 percent and its profit target by 3 percent. Its 1966 plan called for an increase of 6 to 7 percent in physical output, 10 percent in value of output, and 13 to 15 percent in profits over 1965 actual performance. About 7,000 new spindles were added to the existing 80,000 in 1966, while employment was reduced by roughly 10 percent as compared with 1965.

Shanghai No. 19 Cotton Textile fulfilled its physical output target by more than 5 percent in 1965, and its 1966 plan called for a 10 percent increase over 1965 production. This plant has been fully re-equipped with new combing machines since 1964. The Shanghai No. 9 Sung Sing Firm had a 1966 plan calling for "more than a 5 percent increase" in physical production, output value, and profits over 1965. The firm was provided with some new combing machines in 1965–66, and major capital repairs and equipment overhauls have been undertaken in its plant in recent years.

Tientsin Jen Yi Wool reported that its 1965 physical-output target was fulfilled by 5 percent, profit by nearly 10 percent, and labor productivity by 6 or 7 percent. Its 1966 plan called for further increases ranging from 5 to 10 percent in the above-mentioned targets over the 1965 performance. The 1966 plan of Wusih Silk Reeling No. 2 called for a 20 percent increase in tons of silk to be processed, 15 percent in profits, and a 20 percent increase in total revenues from processing fees over the figures for 1965.

Clothing Firms

Peking Clothing reported that its 1965 plan was overfulfilled by 10 percent in physical output (square meters and number of articles), output

TABLE 10–2

QUANTITATIVE DIMENSIONS OF PERFORMANCE FOR THIRTY-THREE CHINESE ENTERPRISES SURVEYED[a]

(All figures are for 1965 calendar year unless otherwise indicated; where no figures are given they were not available)

Enterprises	*Physical Production*[b]	*Total Value of Marketable Output*[c] (In yuan)	*All Material*[d] *and Supplies as % of Total Value of Output*	*Wages*[e] *and Salaries as % of Total Value of Output*	*Other*[f] *Costs and Expenses as % of Total Value of Output*	*Profit as*[g] *a % of Total Value of Output*	*Total*[h] *Value Added (2–3)* (In yuan)
TEXTILES							
Peking No. 3 Cotton Textile	93 million sq. meters of fabrics (of which 50 million cotton, 35 to 40 million rayon, and the rest nylon and vinyl); the mill also processed cotton yarn for its own use.	70 million	61%	5.5%	7.5%	26%	27.3 million
Shanghai No. 19 Cotton Textile	50 million sq. meters of cotton, including poplin cloth. (Actually a small portion of this consisted of vinyl, but apparently less	60 million	63	7	5	25	22.2 million

TABLE 10–2 (*continued*)

Enterprises	*Physical Production*[b]	*Total Value of Marketable Output*[c] (In yuan)	*All Material*[d] *and Supplies as % of Total Value of Output*	*Wages*[e] *and Salaries as % of Total Value of Output*	*Other*[f] *Costs and Expenses as % of Total Value of Output*	*Profit as*[g] *a % of Total Value of Output*	*Total*[h] *Value Added (2–3)* (In yuan)
	than 10%. This firm also processed 20 million lbs. of cotton yarn for its own use.)						
Shanghai No. 9 (Joint) Sung Sing Cotton	25 million sq. meters of cotton cloth; 40 million lbs. of cotton yarn, about 10 million of which it consumed and the other 30 million lbs. were sold to other factories.	75 million	60	8.5	6.5	25	28.5 million
Peking Woolen Fabric	1.8 million sq. meters of woolen cloth	15.5 million	58	8.5	8	25.5	6.5 million
Peking Wool Carpet	1.8 million sq. meters of woolen carpets	—	—	—	—	—	—

Tientsin Jen Yai (Joint) Woolen Fabric	1.2 million sq. meters of woolen cloth	11 million	52	12.5	6.5	29	5.3 million
Wusih No. 2 Silk Reeling	Processed 166 tons of white silk (Cocoons were provided to factory)	1.5 million (processing fee)	Basic raw material provided free for processing. Other materials and supplies were about 110,000 yuan.	6.6	1.2	15	1.39 million
CLOTHING AND SHOES							
Peking Clothing	1.25 million garments	20 million (includes million yuan in sales tax)	75.5	7	7	10	4.65 million
Hangchow Fu Chang Clothing	550,000 garments	Works on a cost-plus job order basis	Basic materials provided by customers. Other material and supply costs were roughly 90,000 yuan.	250,000 yuan	200,000 yuan	400,000 yuan net processing fee (average profit margin was cost plus 6%) or 6%	760,000
Tientsin Shoe	350,000 prs. of shoes	8 million	81	10	4	5	1.52 million
CHEMICALS AND PAPER							
Nanking Chemical Fertilizer (1966 plan)	1 million tons of chemical fertilizer	—	—	—	—	—	—

TABLE 10–2 (*continued*)

Enterprises	*Physical Production*[b]	*Total Value of Marketable Output*[c] (In yuan)	*All Material*[d] *and Supplies as % of Total Value of Output*	*Wages*[e] *and Salaries as % of Total Value of Output*	*Other*[f] *Costs and Expenses as % of Total Value of Output*	*Profit as*[g] *a % of Total Value of Output*	*Total*[h] *Value Added (2–3)* (In yuan)
Canton Chemical Fertilizer	280,000 tons of chemical fertilizer	110 million	71%	2%	9%	18%	31.9 million
Peking Coke & Chemical	1 million tons of coke; 500 million cu. meters coal gas; 77,000 tons chemical by-products	60 million	70	2.7	6.3	21	18 million
Wuhan Han Yang Paper	25,000 tons of paper	52.5 million	62.5	3	8	26.5	19.6 million
LIGHT DURABLE GOODS							
Tientsin Watch	153,500 watches	7.75 million	67	12	8	13	2.56 million
Shanghai Wei Ming Battery	48.5 million	8.5 million	65.5	7.5	5	22	2.93
Canton Lan Yang Elec. Appliance	35,000 fans plus other products	—	—	—	—	—	—

DIESEL ENGINES, TRACTORS, TRUCKS, AND CEMENT PRODUCTS							
Loyang Tractor	15,000 tractors	300–325 million	—	—	—	—	—
Wusih Diesel-Engine	20.5 diesel engines	21 million	69	9	8	14	6.5 million
Wuhan Diesel-Engine	Planned to produce 9,000–10,000 engines but was falling way short of plan in first half of 1966	—	—	—	—	—	—
Shanghai Truck	600 trucks (plus 100 rebuilt)	—	—	—	—	—	—
Soochow cement products (1966 plan)	4,000 cement boats (also cement telephone poles and pipes). Total weight of boats 16,000 tons, plus 3–4 tons of other products	2.4 million	64	18	4	14	864,000
IRON AND STEEL							
Wuhan Iron & Steel Corp.	1.225 million tons of steel; 1.35 million tons of pig iron	over 1 billion	—	—	—	—	—

TABLE 10–2 (*continued*)

Enterprises	*Physical Production*[b]	*Total Value of Marketable Output*[c] (In yuan)	*All Material*[d] *and Supplies as % of Total Value of Output*	*Wages*[e] *and Salaries as % of Total Value of Output*	*Other*[f] *Costs and Expenses as % of Total Value of Output*	*Profit as*[g] *a % of Total Value of Output*	*Total*[h] *Value Added (2–3)* (In yuan)
Shanghai No. 3 Steel	700,000 tons of steel ingots; 600,000 tons rolled finished steel	400 million	68	3	6.5	22.5	128 million
Peking Steel Wire	1,000 tons of steel wire	—	—	—	—	—	—
LARGE AND MEDIUM-SIZED MACHINERY EQUIPMENT							
Wuhan Heavy Machinery	650 sets of equipment (100,000 tons total weight)	227.5 million	64.8	2.8	7.4	25	79.5 million
Shanghai Heavy Machine Tool	2,000 completed units of machinery and equipment	—	—	—	—	—	—
Peking First Machine Tool	2,400 completed units of machinery & equip.	—	—	—	—	—	—
Hangchow Machine Tool	560 completed units (of which 475 standard horizontal grinders)	—	—	—	—	—	—

Shanghai No. 3 Machine Tool	350 automatic precision grinders, 150 optical jack-boring machines	—	—	—	—	—	—
SMALL-SCALE MACHINERY, TOOLS, INSTRUMENTS, AND COMPONENTS							
Shanghai No. 3 Forging & Pressing Machine-Tool	3.12 million items (small tools)	8.4 million	72	5	8	15	2.35 million
Wusih Red Flag Machinery	216 machines (manufactured or rebuilt)	1.04 million	45	18	7	30	572,000
Tientsin North Lake Instrument	not reported	509,000	49	19.5	3.5	29	260,000

[a] Only about half of the above enterprises gave me precise figures for the categories in this table. In other cases they gave me ranges—in most cases less than 10% ranges—from which I have arbitrarily used the midpoints for my estimates; or I have computed estimates from other data they gave me such as daily production, average unit value, or weight, average enterprise wage times, total number of employees, etc.

[b] More details on the enterprise's product mixes are presented in the second section of Chapter 9.

[c] Value of marketable output is expressed in current factory selling prices.

[d] Includes raw and subsidiary materials, fuel, electricity, sundry supplies, and services purchased from other organizations. This category is deducted from total value of output to arrive at value-added estimates. However, there are probably some expenses for supplies, and/or services consumed in the "other costs and expenses" category, although they are probably not very substantial in most cases.

[e] Includes bonuses and other cash incentive payments to employees. However, the category for wages and salaries does not include the major welfare or social security fund (typically 12 to 13.5 percent of total wage fund) or other welfare benefits. Such expenses are in the "other" category, and this may lead to a small understatement of wage and salary expenses, especially when comparisons with industries in various other countries (including the Soviet Union) are made.

[f] Includes items noted in Note e above, as well as depreciation, interest (if any), rent (if any), fines or damages (if any), certain types of capital repairs, and miscellaneous general and overhead expenses not clearly specified (perhaps travel expenses are included here, thus reducing the accuracy of value-added estimates slightly in some cases).

[g] At most enterprises, profit as a percent of sales would not differ by more than 10 or 15 percent from profit as a percent of value of output.

[h] Value-added estimates have been derived by subtracting material and supply costs from total value of marketable output.

value by about the same, and profit by 2 or 3 percent. Its 1966 plan called for an increase in number of articles of 20 percent, in output value of 20 percent, and in profits 10 percent. All of the firm's key targets were overfulfilled—by 3 to 6 percent—in the first quarter of 1966. Since 1964 Peking Clothing's plant capacity and machines have been expanded by about 20 percent. It received several dozen new sewing machines in 1965, and a few more in the first quarter of 1966.

Hangchow Clothing's physical output (number of garments) increased by about 65 percent in 1964 over 1963, more than doubled in 1965 over 1964, and a further increase of 22.5 percent was planned for 1966. Its processing-fee revenues increased nearly threefold from 1963 through 1965, and a further increase of about 30 percent was planned for 1966. Hangchow Clothing's employment increased by only 33 percent during 1963–66—from 300 to 400 personnel. In 1966 there were only about ten more employees than in 1965. However, the firm moved into a new and well-equipped plant in 1964; an elevator and several dozen new machines were added in 1965; and a few more new sewing machines were added in 1966.

Chemical and Drug Enterprises

Peking Coke and Chemical's 1966 output plan called for the same levels of performance achieved in 1965. Its 1965 output target for coke was overfulfilled by 6 or 7 percent, and for most of its chemical by-products by 5 to 8 percent. Since 1963 there has been quite a bit of new capital investment, construction, and plant expansion at this firm. At the time of my visit in 1966 a third coke furnace was being built. The director expected to have two new production shops—one for coke oil, the other for benzine—built and put into operation before 1970, but he was uncertain as to exactly when the additions would be made.

The director of Nanking Chemical Fertilizer claimed that output had increased every year since 1958, and since the early 1960's it had increased by 20 to 25 percent in most years, and in some years even more. He said that the 1966 physical-output target was more than 20 percent greater than the 1965 performance. Sizable amounts of real capital were added in recent years, along with several thousand new employees since the early sixties.

Canton Chemical Fertilizer claimed that it produced about 35 to 40 percent more tons of fertilizers and related commodities in 1965 than in 1964, even though its key quarterly targets were not always fulfilled in 1965. Since 1965 this plant had sharply increased its output of sulfuric acid and link ammonia, and had begun to produce potassium in addition to ammonium sulfate and the above two products. Its 1966 total-output target had tenatively been set at 5 percent above 1965 production. The production capacity of Canton Chemical Fertilizer had increased by 40 to

50 percent since 1964. Employment increased from 2,000 in late 1964 to 2,400 in mid-1966. However, ten of its original twenty engineers had recently been transferred to other firms and projects immediately after the enterprise's expansion projects had been completed and put into operation.

Shanghai No. 3 Pharmaceutical reported that physical output was about 50 percent greater in 1965 than 1964, with antibiotics accounting for most of the increase. Output in 1964 was 32 percent greater than in 1963. I was told that the 1966 plan called for "a further significant increase" in output. Since 1964 real capital at this plant had increased "by roughly 25 to 30 percent," while employment had increased by 10 to 15 percent.

Large and Medium-Sized Machine-Tool and Equipment Enterprises

Wuhan Heavy Machinery reported that total machinery output in tons increased by 3 to 5 percent in 1964 over 1963, 5 to 10 percent in 1965 over 1964, and the 1966 plan called for a 10 to 15 percent increase over the 1965 performance. Value of production increased by 5 to 10 percent in 1964 over 1963, 10 to 15 percent in 1965 over 1964, and the 1966 plan called for more than a 20 percent increase over 1965. I was told that enterprise employment had increased by several hundred since 1965, but it was still below the 1959–60 level of 7,500. Management claimed that only modest amounts of real capital had been added in the last few years.

Shanghai Heavy Machine Tool reported that quantity of production, in both tons and number of units, had increased by more than 40 percent since 1963. Physical output, value of production, labor productivity, and profit targets were overfulfilled in the range of 4.5 to 8 percent in 1965, and the 1966 plan called for further, but unspecified, increases over 1965 results. Apparently a fair amount of new capital investment had been provided to this firm in the last several years, but no new workshops had been added in the 1960's. I was told that only negligible numbers of new managers, technicians, engineers, or skilled workers had been added since 1964, although total employment had increased by "a few hundred" people.

Hangchow Machine Tool reported that total output in tonnage was 300 percent greater in 1965 than 1957, and that more than ten times as many machines were produced in more than twice as many varieties. The 1966 output plan called for a tonnage increase of about 10 percent, and an increase in number of machines of about 7 percent over the 1965 performance. Management claimed that value of production increased by 25 percent in 1965 over 1964, and the 1966 plan called for a 10 percent further increase. Profits increased by over 20 percent in 1965 and 1964, and the 1966 plan called for a further increase of 6 or 7 percent. Although Hangchow Machine Tool was provided with new capital investment in recent years, the plant still seemed to be in bad shape when I was there. Since 1964, employment had increased nearly 70 percent, from 600 to 1,000 in mid-1966, with actual increases of about 100 in 1964, 200 in 1965, and 100 in 1966.

Shanghai No. 3 Machine Tool reported that the 1966 plan called for increases of 8 to 10 percent in the number of grinders and boring machines to be produced in 1966 as compared with 1965 results. Physical output in 1965 was more than 10 percent greater than in 1964. Employment had been about 1,000 since 1960 or 1961, and only negligible amounts of real capital had been added in recent years.

Small-Scale Machinery, Tool, Component, and Instrument Enterprises

Shanghai Forging and Pressing Machine Tool reported that its 1966 plan called for a 17 or 18 percent increase in number of items to be produced, 9.5 percent in output value, and 8 to 12 percent in profits over 1965 results. These targets had been overfulfilled in the range of 1.5 to 5 percent in 1965. There had been no new capital investment or employees at this firm in recent years.

Wusih Red Flag Machinery's 1966 plan called for an increase of 15 to 20 percent in the number of machines to be produced or rebuilt, 36 percent in output value, and 6 to 7 percent in profits over 1965.

At Tientsin Instrument, output value increased by about 8 percent in 1965 over 1964, and the 1966 plan tentatively called for an increase of 100 to 160 percent over 1965. This sharp increase was to come from two new and relatively expensive types of delicate pieces of equipment that the firm began to assemble in 1965. Profits had increased by around 155 percent in 1965 over 1964, and the 1966 plan tentatively called for an increase roughly 70 to 100 percent over 1965. These broad value and profit ranges for 1966 were due to the fact that sales and selling prices with regard to the two new products were not yet formally approved at the time of my visit. The firm had very little in the way of fixed capital, and its work force had increased by an average of 10 percent annually during the last four or five years.

Iron and Steel Firms

Apparently Wuhan Iron and Steel experienced a modest drop in pig-iron and steel output in 1965 because major overhaul and repair work was done on its blast furnaces. Output in 1966 was expected to be "somewhat" above 1965. A new workshop in the steel plant with a planned capacity of 600,000 to 700,000 tons of rolled steel in special shapes and sizes stood uncompleted, with little or no work being done on it at the time of my visit.

Peking Steel Wire claimed to have an annual production capacity of

2,000 tons of steel wire, although it produced only 1,000 tons in 1965. The 1966 plan called for an output of 1,600 tons—with little addition of real capital or manpower—but management felt that this target might be revised downward.

Agricultural Machinery and Cement Products

Wusih Diesel Engine reported that it overfulfilled its 1965 output plan, in terms of number of engines, by about 1 percent, and that the 1966 target called for a 3.5 percent increase over 1965. Some new equipment had been added in recent years, but total employment remained around the same level. (We have already discussed the dilemmas of Wuhan Diesel Engine in Chapter 9.)

Soochow Cement Products reported that the number of cement boats and the approximate total tonnage of output increased by 16 or 17 percent between 1963 and 1965 and that the 1966 plan called for an 11.5 percent increase over 1965.

Loyang Tractor claimed to have been producing about 15,000 tractors a year during the last five or six years. I was told that employment had increased slightly since 1965 but that it was still a few hundred less than six or seven years ago.

Light Durable-Goods Enterprises

Tientsin Watch's 1966 production plan called for about a 20 percent increase in the number of watches to be produced over 1965. The firm moved to a new and well-equipped building and plant in 1963. There had been a considerable amount of new real capital added since 1964, but employment increased only slightly.

Shanghai Battery's 1966 output plan called for about 15 percent more batteries to be produced than in 1965. Very little real capital had been added in recent years, and employment had been stable.

Other Enterprises

Shanghai Truck reported that the 1964 truck output was double that of 1959. Production of new trucks was the same in 1965 as in 1964, though 100 trucks were rebuilt in 1965. The 1966 plan called for no increase in new trucks over 1965, no trucks to be rebuilt, but substantially more parts and components to be produced for other enterprises.

Wuhan Paper's 1966 plan called for an increase in tonnage output of 10 to 12 percent over 1965, 15 to 20 percent in output value, and about 15 percent in profit. Management expected these targets to be raised substantially if the 15,000 tons of additional plant capacity were to be brought into operation as planned in August 1966.

The other firms surveyed but not discussed above either indicated that there had been no significant changes in performance in recent years or planned for 1966, or they did not provide me with any information on the subject.

Labor Productivity

Red China: 1957 versus 1965

Table 7–11 of Chapter 7 presented some crude labor-productivity estimates for various branches of Chinese industry in 1957—as well as similar data for India and Russia in the late fifties. These were rough estimates because the employment figures used in computing productivity were for an entire sector, while the related output did not include total sectoral production.

Among the commodity groups for which productivity was computed in Table 7–11 were pig iron, crude steel, rolled steel, paper, and cotton textiles. Table 10–3 of the present chapter contains labor-productivity figures for these commodities in 1965 at various Chinese firms that I surveyed in 1966. Even allowing for a 50 percent margin of error for overestimation in Table 7–11, labor productivity for the above-mentioned commodities in Table 10–3 is still higher in all cases except for paper, which is nearly the same in the two tables.

Limitations of Inter-Country Productivity Comparisons

Table 10–4 contains some suggestive labor-productivity comparisons involving various Chinese enterprises surveyed, branch-of-industry averages for similar commodity groups in India, the Soviet Union, Japan, and the United States, as well as some individual enterprises in India and the Soviet Union. There is undoubtedly a substantially large margin of error in many of these comparisons because of significant differences in product mix and quality, employment classifications, the sample of enterprises, and various other factors and measurement problems. In spite of such margins of error, however, I am quite confident that the relative rankings and relationships of sectoral-productivity performance in the countries considered still provide a reasonably accurate and meaningful reflection of reality. Even allowing for substantial margins of error, the relative rankings would not be changed in most cases, especially with regard to Chinese performance in relation to the other countries.

I have tried to base the productivity comparisons on as similar classifications of employment as possible.[1] One generally finds a much smaller proportion of sales personnel at Chinese enterprises as compared with American or even many Japanese and Indian firms. On the other hand, Chinese enterprises typically have substantially more welfare and service personnel than American companies and, to a lesser extent, firms in India, Japan, and even the Soviet Union in numerous cases. These differences in

TABLE 10–3

LABOR PRODUCTIVITY AND VALUE OF MARKETABLE OUTPUT, VALUE ADDED AND PROFIT PER EMPLOYEE FOR THIRTY-THREE CHINESE ENTERPRISES SURVEYED

(Figures are for 1965 calendar year unless otherwise noted; where no figures were given they were not available)

Enterprises	*Labor Productivity* (Physical output per employee year)	*Value of Marketable Output per Employee* (In yuan)	*Value Added per Employee* (In yuan)	*Profit per Employee* (In yuan)
COTTON TEXTILES				
Peking No. 3 Cotton Textile[a]	14,700 sq. meters of cotton cloth	14,000 (total)	5,460 (total)	3,600 (total)
	28,700 sq. meters of rayon (include small amounts of nylon and vinyl)			
Shanghai No. 19 Cotton Textile	10,400 sq. meters of cotton cloth	11,460	4,625	2,925
Shanghai No. 9 (Joint) Sung Sing Cotton Textile[b]	8,300 sq. meters of cotton cloth	12,500 (total)	4,750 (total)	3,125 (total)
	10,000 lbs. of cotton yarn produced for other factories			
Average Cotton-cloth output per[c] employee for above 3 enterprises	11,000 sq. meters			
WOOLEN MILLS				
Peking Woolen Fabric	1,000 sq. meters of woolen cloth	8,611	3,500	2,080
Tientsin Jen Yi (Joint) Woolen Fabric	666 sq. meters of woolen cloth	6,100	2,945	1,778
Average woolen-cloth output per employee for above 2 enterprises[d]	833 sq. meters			
Peking Wool Carpet	670 sq. meters of wool carpets	—	—	—

TABLE 10–3 (*continued*)

Enterprises	*Labor Productivity* (Physical output per employee year)	*Value of Marketable Output per Employee* (In yuan)	*Value Added per Employee* (In yuan)	*Profit per Employee* (In yuan)
Wusih No. 2 Silk Reeling	11 tons of silk	revenue—1,000 (raw material provided by customers)	927	164
CLOTHING AND SHOES				
Peking Clothing	735 garments	11,175	2,735	1,175
Hangchow Fu Chang Clothing	1,250 garments	works on cost-plus fee	1,900	1,000
Average garments for above 2 enterprises	945 garments			
Tientsin Shoe	350 pairs of shoes	8,000	1,520	400
CHEMICALS AND PAPER				
Nanking Chemical Fertilizer (1966 plan)	100 tons of chemical fertilizer	—	—	—
Canton Chemical Fertilizer	117 tons of chemical fertilizer	45,815	13,300	8,330
Average chemical-fertilizer output per employee for above 2 enterprises[e]	103 tons			
Peking Coke and Chemical	About 500 tons of coke and related chemical by-products (coke only, 477 tons; above productivity figures exclude output of 500 million cu. meters of coal gas)	28,570	8,570	5,950
Wuhan Han Yang Paper	12.5 tons of paper	26,250	9,800	7,200

LIGHT DURABLE GOODS				
Tientsin Watch	110 watches	5,540	1,830	715
Shanghai Wei Ming Battery	86,000 batteries	15,200	5,200	3,320
Canton Lan Yang Electrical Appliance[f]	117 fans	—	—	—
DIESEL ENGINES, TRACTORS, TRUCKS, AND CEMENT PRODUCTS				
Loyang Tractor	0.75 tractors	14,600–17,000	—	—
Wusih Diesel-Engine	0.75 diesel engines	7,777	2,410	1,110
Wuhan Diesel-Engine	(planned 9–10 engines per employee, but was falling way short of target in first half of 1966)	—	—	—
Shanghai Truck	0.6–0.7 trucks	—	—	—
Soochow Cement Products (1966 plan)	5.6 cement boats (total weight of boats 16,000 tons, plus 3–4 tons of other cement products; total tons of output per employee about 300)	3,520	1,270	440
IRON AND STEEL				
Wuhan Iron and Steel Corporation[g]				
1. Using total corporation employment figure	74 tons of pig iron and rolled (bar) steel combined	over 30,000 (includes all marketable output of the corporation)	—	—
	39 tons of pig iron only	—	—	—
	35 tons of steel only	—	—	—
2. Excluding 8,000 mine workers	95 tons of combined pig iron and steel	—	—	—
	50 tons of pig iron only	—	—	—
	45 tons of steel only	—	—	—

TABLE 10–3 (*continued*)

Enterprises	*Labor Productivity* (Physical output per employee year)	*Value of Marketable Output per Employee* (In yuan)	*Value added per Employee* (In yuan)	*Profit per Employee* (In yuan)
3. Excluding 8,000 mine workers and 5,000 nonindustrial welfare and service personnel	116 tons of combined pig iron and steel	—	—	—
	61 tons of pig iron only	—	—	—
	55 tons of steel only	—	—	—
4. Excluding above mine and welfare employees and 4,900 employees of corporation's head-office staff	145 tons pig iron and steel combined	—	—	—
	78 tons of pig iron only	—	—	—
	67 tons of steel only	—	—	—
Shanghai No. 3 Steel [h]	100 tons of steel ingots and rolled steel combined	30,800	9,850	6,880
	54 tons of steel ingots only	—	—	—
	46 tons of rolled steel only	—	—	—
Average for above two enterprises	Using total pig-iron and steel output and total employment—81 tons			
Peking Steel Wire	1.25 tons of steel wire	—	—	—

LARGE AND MEDIUM-SIZED MACHINERY AND EQUIPMENT				
Wuhan Heavy Machinery	0.1 sets of equipment; 14.3 tons of equipment	32,500	11,360	8,145
Shanghai Heavy Machine Tool	0.33 units of machinery & equipment	—	—	—
Peking First Machine Tool	0.6 units of machinery & equipment	—	—	—
Hangchow Machine Tool	0.56 units of machinery & equipment	—	—	—
Shanghai No. 3 Machine Tool	0.45 units of machinery & equipment	—	—	—
SMALL-SCALE MACHINERY, TOOLS, INSTRUMENTS, AND COMPONENTS				
Shanghai No. 3 Forging and Pressing Machine Tool	7,800 items	20,740	5,800	3,090
Wusih Red Flag Machinery	0.7 machines (manufactured and rebuilt)	3,470	1,900	1,027
Tientsin North Lake Instrument	—	3,100	1,575	847

[a] In computing labor productivity this firm allocated approximately 70 percent of its employees to cotton-fabric production and the rest to rayon and its other products.

[b] In computing labor productivity this firm divided its employment about equally between cotton-cloth output and yarn output produced for other factories.

[c] This average has been obtained by dividing total cotton-cloth output of the three firms by the total number of employees used in computing labor productivity for this type of output.

[d] This average has been obtained by dividing the combined woolen-fabric output of the two firms by combined employment.

[e] This average has been obtained by applying the same method as in Note d above. Chemical-fertilizer output is expressed in end-product weight, not in terms of nutrient.

[f] About 300 of this enterprise's employees were engaged directly or indirectly with fan production, which amounted to 35,000 units in 1965.

[g] The separate productivity figures for pig iron and steel are based on the total employment figures specified in each category.

[h] The separate productivity figures for steel ingots and rolled steel are based on the firm's total employment figure.

TABLE 10–4

How Labor Productivity[a] at Chinese Enterprises Surveyed Compares with Productivity in India, U.S.S.R., Japan, and the U.S.

(Physical output per man-year except for antibiotic drugs)

Industry and Product Line	*Unit of Measure*	*Chinese Enterprises* (From table 10–3)	*Indian Industry Averages and Selected Enterprises* (1963 unless otherwise noted)	*Soviet Industry Averages and Selected Enterprises* (1963 or 1964 unless otherwise noted)	*Japanese Industry Averages* (1964 or 1965)	*U.S. Industry Averages* (1964 or 1965 unless otherwise noted)
COTTON TEXTILES	sq. meters of cotton cloth	Avg. for 3 enterprises —11,000 Maximum for 1 enterprise—14,700 Minimum for 1 enterprise—8,300	Industry avg.—8,604 Avg. for 3 enterprises—8,120 Maximum 9,000 (firm employ. 4,765) Minimum 3,780 (firm employ. 1,430) Other firms—8,650 (employ. 4,780)	Industry avg.—6,400	Industry avg. for cotton and rayon —20,300; Cotton only—14,000 to 16,000 (est.)	1965 industry avg. —20,600 linear yards (Most U.S. factories produce cotton cloth varying from about 24 to 48 inch. in width.)
RAYON AND OTHER SYNTHETIC FABRICS	sq. meters of fabric	Peking No. 3 Cotton Textile—28,700	Not available	Industry avg.—30,000 (est.) 1960 Moscow Sverdlov Textile Enterprise—47,000 (produces silk & rayon fabrics)	See cotton and rayon above. Industry avg. for rayon—33,000–36,000 (est.)	1963 industry avg. —40,000 sq. meters (approx.)

WOOL TEXTILES	sq. meters of woolen cloth	Avg. for 2 enterprises —833; maximum 1,000; minimum 666	Industry avg.—855	Industry avg.—1,860	Industry avg.—5,500	1966 industry avg. —6,070 linear yards; 1963 ind. avg. 5,000 sq. meters (approx.)
	sq. meters wool carpets	Peking Wool Carpet —670	Kashmir Enterprise —185 (in 1965), employment 890; very labor-intensive operations	Not available	Not available	Industry avg.—8,000 yards
CLOTHING	No. of garments	Avg. for 2 enterprises —857; maximum 1,250; minimum 735	Not available	Industry avg.—1,080 Kharkov Tinakov Clothing enterprise produced 620 garments per employee in 1960	Industry avg.—1,129	1962 industry avg. for men's and boy's clothing—7,024
SHOES (leather)	No. of pairs	Tientsin Shoe—350	Industry avg.—886	Industry avg. 974 The Leningrad Skorokhod Shoe Enterprise produced 1,750 prs. per employee in 1960	Industry avg.—928	Industry avg.—2,704 (includes leather slippers)
CHEMICAL FERTILIZER (in terms of completed and mixed output that is not pure nutrient)	tons	Avg. for 2 enterprises —103; maximum 117; minimum 100 (planned for 1966)	Industry avg.—34	1962 industry avg. —492	Industry avg.—403	Industry avg.—1,100 (approx.) computed from nutrient units

TABLE 10–4 (*continued*)

Industry and Product Line	*Unit of Measure*	*Chinese Enterprises*	*Indian Industry Averages and Selected Enterprises*	*Soviet Industry Averages and Selected Enterprises*	*Japanese Industry Averages*	*U.S. Industry Averages*
COKE	tons	Peking Coke and Chemical—500 (includes a small proportion of chemical by-products)	Not available	1962 industry avg. —1,200	Not available	Industry avg.— 2,400 (est.)
ANTIBIOTIC DRUGS (Represents efficiency in avoiding material wastage)	avg. product yields in percent	Shanghai No. 3 Pharmaceutical—80%–82%	Indigenous Indian firm (1965–66)— 80% U.S. subsidiary in India, 1965–66— 86%	Not available	Typically over 90% at Japanese factories	Typically over 94% at U.S. factories
PAPER	tons	Wuhan Han Yang Paper—12.5	Industry avg.—8.3 (includes paper boards and cartons) National Newsprint and Paper Mills Ltd., (1965–66 fiscal year) 21 tons of newsprint (This firm employed 1,440 people in that period.)	Industry avg. paper only—36; including paper board and other paper products— 173	Industry avg.— 157 (includes paper boards and other paper prod.)	Industry avg.— paper only—143; all paper products—595

WATCHES	No. of units	Tientsin Watch—110	Watch factory of Hindustan Machine Tool Corp. in 1964 had a factory labor productivity of 181 watches.	Moscow Kirov Watch enterprise (1960)—317	Industry avg.—166	Not available
PRIMARY BATTERIES	No. of units	Shanghai Wei Ming Battery—86,000	Indigenous Indian firm 1964–65—42,300 [b] Old factory of U.S. subsidiary (1965–66)—84,000 New factory of U.S. subsidiary (1965–66) slightly over 100,000 (Above dates are in fiscal years.)	Not available	Industry avg.—200,000 (approx.)	It is common for labor productivity at U.S. battery factories to exceed 200,000 units per employee.
ELECTRIC FANS	No. of units	Canton Electrical Appliance—117	Industry avg.—135	" "	Not available	Not available
DIESEL ENGINES	No. of units	Wusih Diesel Engine—0.75 Wuhan Diesel Engine—1966 plan, 9–10, but was falling way short of plan in first half of 1966	Industry avg. (1961)—4.5 (Avg. diesel engine produced has been substantially smaller and less powerful than those produced by Wusih plant and a bit bigger than those produced by Wuhan factory.)	" "	" "	1962 industry avg. for engines and turbines—133 (includes gas, gasoline, and diesel units).

TABLE 10–4 (*continued*)

Industry and Product Line	*Unit of Measure*	*Chinese Enterprises*	*Indian Industry Averages and Selected Enterprises*	*Soviet Industry Averages and Selected Enterprises*	*Japanese Industry Averages*	*U.S. Industry Averages*
TRACTORS	No. of units	Loyang Tractor—.75	Not available	" "	" "	1962 industry avg. for industrial trucks and tractors—2 (Average unit is much larger and more powerful than tractors produced by Loyang firm. U.S. output includes huge pieces of road-building and construction equipment.)
TRUCKS	No. of units	Shanghai Truck—0.6 (including rebuilt trucks—0.7)	Industry avg.—about 1 (includes cars and trucks)	1959 Industry avg.—1.5	" "	Industry avg. for truck and bus bodies—45 (see also comments above on tractors).
STEEL AND PIG IRON						
Combined pig iron, steel (rolled and finished)	tons	Avg. of two firms for total pig-iron and steel output using total employment—81 Avg. of two firms for total output using	Industry avg.—70	Industry Avg.—240	Industry avg.—206	Industry avg.—466

		27,000 employees for Wuhan—95 Avg. of two firms using 22,000 employees for Wuhan—111				
Pig iron and rolled steel	tons	Wuhan using 35,000 employees—74 Wuhan using 27,000 employees—95 Wuhan using 22,000 employees—116	Industry avg.—55	Industry avg.—144	Industry avg.—120	Industry avg.—283
Pig iron only	tons	Wuhan using 35,000 employees—39 Wuhan using 27,000 employees—50 Wuhan using 22,000 employees—61	Industry avg.—28	Industry avg.—70	Industry avg.—52	Industry avg.—133
Rolled steel only	tons	Wuhan using 35,000 employees—35 Wuhan using 27,000 employees—45 Wuhan using 22,000 employees—55 Shanghai firm—46	Industry avg.—17 Tata Iron and Steel Corp.[c] (1965–66 fiscal yr.)—25.5 Hindustan Steel Ltd.[c]—25 tons in 1965	Industry avg.—74	Industry avg.—68	Industry avg.—150
Steel ingots only	tons	Shanghai firm—54	Industry avg.—25; Tata Corp.—32; Hindustan Steel—33.8	Industry avg.—96	Industry avg.—86	Industry avg.—183

TABLE 10–4 (*continued*)

Industry and Product Line	*Unit of Measure*	*Chinese Enterprises*	*Indian Industry Averages and Selected Enterprises*	*Soviet Industry Averages and Selected Enterprises*	*Japanese Industry Averages*	*U.S. Industry Averages*
Steel ingots and rolled steel combined	tons	Shanghai firm—100	Industry avg.—42 Tata Corp.—57.5 Hindustan Steel—58.8	Industry avg.—170	Industry avg.—154	Industry avg.—333
STEEL WIRE	tons	Peking Steel Wire—1.25	1961 industry avg. for steel wire rope—9.1 (Steel-wire rope is bulkier and easier to produce than the steel wire produced by the Peking plant.)	Not available	Industry avg.—8	Industry avg. for all types of wire—65
HEAVY MACHINERY	tons	Wuhan Heavy Machinery—14.3	Not available	Leningrad Enterprise—about 20 in 1960 (produces similar products as Wuhan plant)	Not available	Not available

[a] Unless otherwise noted, total branch-of-industry or enterprise employment figures have been used in computing labor productivity. It should be noted that Chinese industrial enterprise employees work about 15 to 20 percent more hours per year than personnel in U.S. or Soviet industry, and probably roughly 5 to 10 percent more hours than in Indian industry because of the greater number of holidays and longer vacations in India. On the other hand, some of the Indian productivity figures are likely to be overstated because seasonal and contract labor, of which there is often much, is usually not fully reported in official employment reports or statistics.

[b] For the indigenous Indian battery firm total employment was used in computing productivity. Its total employment was 1,300. For plans of the U.S. subsidiary, factory employment was used since this is a diversified multi-plant firm. The old U.S. subsidiary plant was employing about 2,500 people and the new one about 1,500.

[c] Tata Iron and Steel Corporation had a total employment of 61,700

during the 1965–66 fiscal year. It produced 1.979 million tons of steel ingots and 1,568 tons of finished steel during that period. Hindustan Steel had an employment of about 92,000 in 1965 (excluding construction personnel), and it produced 2.325 million tons of finished steel and 3.1 million tons of steel ingots. Statistics for this firm's 3 steel units are given in the text for the 1964–65 fiscal year.

SOURCES:

For India:
India: Pocket Book of Economic Information, 1964 and 1965 (New Delhi: Ministry of Finance, Government of India); *Statistical Outline of India*, 1964 and 1965 (Bombay: prepared by Tata Industries Ltd., published by Popular Prakashan); *India's Draft Fourth Plan* (New Delhi: National Planning Commission, Government of India); *Monthly Commentary on Indian Economic Conditions*, selected issues 1965 and 1966 (New Delhi: Indian Institute of Public Opinion); *Eastern Economist*, annual numbers 1965 and 1966 (New Delhi); *Annual Survey of Industries*, 1961 and 1962 (Calcutta: Central Statistical Organization of the Indian Government); *Programmes of Industrial Development 1961–66* (New Delhi: Government of India Planning Commission, 1962; Calcutta: 1966); *Journal of Industry and Trade*, April 1966 (New Delhi: Government of India); *Monthly Labour Review*, selected 1965 and 1966 issues (New Delhi: Government of India); *United Nations Statistical Yearbooks* (for selected years during 1961–65 period).

For Soviet Union:
Narodnoe Khoziaistvo SSSR V Godu 1960 through 1965 (National Economy of the USSR Statistical Yearbooks, for 1960–65 period; published annually in Moscow in Russian by the Central Statistical Administration); *Promishlenost SSSR*, 1962–65 volume (Industry USSR, published annually in Moscow in Russian by the Central Statistical Administration); A. Katz, *Proizvoditelnost Trudav SSSR i Glavniki Kapitalisticheskikh Stran*, Labor Productivity in the USSR and in the Main Capitalist Countries (Moscow: Econoruca, 1964); *Current Economic Indicators for the USSR* (Washington: U.S. Government Printing Office, 1965), Chap. II, and pp. 74–82, Tables VI–5 and VI–7; M. Feshback, "Manpower in the USSR," *New Directions in the Soviet Economy*, Part III (Washington: U.S. Government Printing Office, 1966) Table A–2, pp. 774–78; *New Directions*, Part IV, Appendix I; *Annual Economic Indicators for the USSR* (Washington: U.S. Government Printing Office, 1964), Appendix I.

For Japan:
Japan Statistical Yearbook 1964 and 1965 (Tokyo: Bureau of Statistics, Office of the Prime Minister, 1965 and 1966); *Monthly Statistics of Japan*, various 1966–67 issues (Tokyo: Bureau of Statistics, Office of the Prime Minister); *Japanese Economic Statistics*, 1965 (Tokyo: Economic Planning Agency, 1966); *Asia Scene*, Tokyo, February 1967; *Yomiuri Yearbook 1966*, in Japanese (Tokyo: published by Yomiuri Newspaper Co., 1967); *Mainichi Yearbook 1967*, in Japanese (Tokyo: published by Mainichi Newspaper Co., 1967).

For the United States:
Statistical Abstract for the U.S., 1962–66 volumes (Washington: U.S. Department of Commerce, Census Bureau); *U.S. Bureau of Census: Annual Survey of Manufactures*, 1962–65 volumes (Washington: General Statistics for Industry Groups and Industries); *Survey of Current Business* and *Statistical Supplements*, 1963–65 volumes (Washington: U.S. Department of Commerce); *Monthly Bulletin of Employment and Earnings*, various 1962–66 issues (Washington: Bureau of Labor Statistics, Dept. of Commerce); *Employment and Earnings 1909–1966* (Washington: Bureau of Labor Statistics, Dept. of Commerce). U.S. output of textile fabrics in square meters for 1963 can be found in *Current Economic Indicators*, Table 111–13; U.S. output of chemical fertilizer in conventional (completed and mixed) units for 1965 can be found in *New Directions*, Part IV, Appendix I. Labor productivity for the U.S. coke industry has been estimated from data contained in *Narodnoe Khoziaistvo*, 1963–65 volumes, Katz, *op. cit.*, and *Current Economic Indicators*, p. 82, Table VI–7.

enterprise and branch-of-industry employment between China and the other countries probably offset each other in large part in terms of the comparability of total employment figures used. Chinese and Soviet industries and enterprises are the most comparable of all among the above-named countries in terms of employment figures used in calculating labor productivity.

In Table 7–4 total enterprise and appropriate sectoral-employment figures have been used in computing productivity unless otherwise noted. The productivity figures are calculated as output per man-year. Since there are differences in the average man-hours worked per year in the different countries, there is also a margin of error here. Chinese industrial employees typically work a 48-hour week and have fewer holidays than their counterparts in the other countries, particularly India. Soviet industrial personnel were working about a 41-hour week, Indians around 45 to 48, and Americans and Japanese approximately 40 during the years used in calculating productivity. At many Indian enterprises in particular, there is a good deal of contract and temporary labor, much of which is often not reflected in official employment reports or statistics. Where this is the case in Table 10–4, Indian productivity figures would have an upward bias.

The problem of productivity comparability is also significant in connection with physical production used in calculating productivity because of the product-mix and quality problem. For most if not all commodities, product quality, diversity, and complexity tend to be greater in the United States than in China. The same is generally true for Japan as compared with China, but to a lesser degree. Soviet heavy-industry goods tend to be of better quality and of greater diversity and complexity than those in China, but the same has probably not been true for many types of consumer goods. Physical production and product mixes are probably generally the most comparable in Chinese and Indian industries. Using productivity comparisons computed in value terms are not generally very meaningful because of big basic differences in the price structures in the various countries and difficulties in foreign-exchange conversions. Finally, one should bear in mind the noneconomic objectives of Chinese industrial enterprises when analyzing labor-productivity figures.

In spite of limitations and problems of comparability, the productivity data presented in Table 10–4 are suggestive, possibly interesting, but certainly not conclusive.

Textiles

It appears that the Chinese cotton-textile enterprises (a traditional Chinese industry) are relatively well managed and productive. This is also true of the joint state-private Shanghai Sung Sing cotton firm, which still had its old capitalist managers and whose equipment was relatively old.

Table 10–4 indicates that the three Chinese cotton-textile firms, as a group, are substantially more productive than the Indian and Soviet cotton-textile industries as a whole, and also than the sample of three Indian firms. However, the Chinese firms lag behind the average branch-of-industry labor productivity in the United States, and to a lesser degree that of Japan. The Peking Cotton Firm was the most productive Chinese plant, producing 14,700 square meters per year, but with a fairly narrow product line. I was told by the chief engineer of Peking Cotton Textile that in the early 1950's it was considered good if one worker could handle 600 spindles or 20 looms. In 1965 one worker operated about 1,200 spindles and 32 looms on the average, and a further improvement of nearly 10 percent was planned for 1966. None of the Indian textile mills that I visited had workers who handled as many spindles or looms as at the Peking plant in 1965. The Shanghai Joint Sung Sing Mill has the lowest productivity of the three Chinese cotton firms—8,300 square meters, which is a bit more than the average for three Indian firms. However, this Shanghai firm has the oldest equipment and produces a fairly wide line of relatively high-quality (up to 80 counts) cotton cloth.

Labor productivity for rayon at the Peking Cotton Textile Firm is not far behind average industry performance for rayon and other synthetic fabrics in Russia, further behind that of Japan, and well behind that of the United States. The Peking mill's rayon productivity is far behind the level achieved for rayon and silk by the Moscow Sverdlov Textile Enterprise in 1960. The Moscow firm is reputed to be one of the world's leading rayon and silk producers; in 1960 it produced nearly 95 million square meters of fabrics.

Labor productivity is higher at the Peking Woolen Mill than at the Tientsin Joint Jen Yi Firm, which has a much older plant. The Tientsin firm seemed to be operating quite well, although it appeared to be running into some noticeable managerial and technical problems. This may have been due at least in part to the fact that the general manager, a seventy-four-year-old capitalist and former major owner of the firm, had been ill for the last year and was not coming to work very much. In his absence perhaps the Reds were playing an increasing role in running the firm.

The two Chinese woolen fabric firms were about as productive in 1965 as the Indian woolen textile industry was in 1963, about half as productive as firms in the Soviet Union, and far behind those of the United States and Japan. However, the quality and variety of wool produced by the Chinese mills are probably significantly better than those of the average wool produced in India and possibly Russia.

Labor productivity at the Peking Wool Carpet Enterprise in 1965 was several times greater than that of the typical Indian wool-carpet producer. Indian firms produce a wider range of custom-made carpets through highly labor-intensive techniques. Labor productivity for the U.S. wool-carpet industry in 1962 was much higher than that of the Peking carpet firm.

Clothing

It is more difficult to assess productivity in the clothing industry than in the cotton or woolen textile industry. Both of the Chinese clothing factories seemed to be significantly better managed and more efficient than Kharkov's Tenakov Clothing Enterprise, which I visited in the U.S.S.R. in 1961. The Kharkov plant was producing a product line similar to, but with more heavier articles, than the Peking factory. Hangchow Clothing's product line was less diversified or complex. Both of the Peking clothing firms produced more garments per employee in 1965 than the Kharkov plant did in 1960, but the average for the two Chinese firms was a bit less than the Soviet branch-of-industry average of a few years ago. The figure for garments produced per employee in Japan's clothing industry, which is still quite labor-intensive, is only a bit higher than the average for the two Chinese enterprises, and less than that of Hangchow Clothing. Labor productivity in the men's and boys' clothing industry in the United States is much higher than that of the Chinese factories.

Shoes

China's Tientsin Shoe firm seemed to be poorly managed, inefficient, and relatively unproductive. Traditionally most shoes in China were made of cloth and other non-leather materials, and therefore the manufacturing of leather shoes is a relatively new industry in China. Labor productivity at Tientsin Shoe is less than half that of the leather-footwear industries in India, the Soviet Union, and Japan—which have quite similar levels of performance—and is only a small fraction of the productivity achieved in the United States. In 1960 Leningrad's Skorokhod Shoe Enterprise, Russia's leading shoe producer, had a labor productivity five times greater than that achieved by Tientsin Shoe in 1965. However, the Chinese plant was producing a broader line of higher-quality and more stylish shoes than the Soviet factory.

Chemicals and Drugs

Chemical-fertilizer output per man-year at the two Chinese fertilizer enterprises was much higher than that of the Indian fertilizer industry as a whole in 1963, but about four to five times less than that in Japan and the Soviet Union in the 1960's, and more than ten times less than in the United States.

Peking Coke and Chemical seemed to be one of the best-managed and most efficient Chinese enterprises that I visited. However, labor productivity for coke was only about half that in the Soviet coke industry in 1962 and an estimated 25 percent of that in the U.S. coke industry.

The two Chinese pharmaceutical firms surveyed appeared to be well below typical U.S. drug firms in terms of know-how or productivity. I was told at Shanghai No. 3 Pharmaceutical that its product yields for antibiotics averaged 80 to 82 percent. At a roughly comparable indigenous Indian firm that I surveyed in 1966 the average yield was about the same; and at a U.S. subsidiary firm in India the average yield was about 86 percent. Antibiotic producers in Japan typically achieve an average product yield of over 90 percent, and in the U.S. over 94 percent.

Paper

The Wuhan Paper Mill was not functioning very well, and productivity was well below that of the Soviet and Japanese paper industries, and less than 10 percent of that of the U.S. paper industry. The Wuhan firm's labor productivity was also significantly lower than that of a leading Indian newsprint producer in 1965–66, but significantly greater than that of the Indian paper industry as a whole in 1963–64.

Watches

The Tientsin Watch Firm seemed to be one of the worst managed and least efficient of the Chinese firms surveyed, even though it was relatively well equipped in large part by modern Swiss and British technology. In general, firms in the newer indigenous Chinese consumer-goods industries, such as those for watches, leather shoes, and electrical appliances, do not appear to be well managed or productive.

Productivity at Tientsin Watch was lower than that of the Hindustan Machine Tool Corporation's watch factory (in India) in 1964, and only about one-third of that of Moscow's Kirov Watch Enterprise in 1960. The Soviet firm sent some experts to help set up the Tientsin plant several years ago. The Tientsin watch factory produces a narrower product line and is better equipped than the Moscow plant. Labor productivity in Japan's watch industry is also greater than that of Tientsin Watch.

Batteries and Electric Fans

The Shanghai Wei Ming Battery Firm, which has an old pre-1949 plant and an experienced work force, seemed to be relatively well managed and productive. The productivity of this battery enterprise was substantially higher than that of an indigenous Indian firm I visited in 1966 which is quite comparable in terms of technology—the latter's is somewhat better—and product mix. The Chinese firm has a slightly higher output per man-year than one of the battery factories of a U.S. subsidiary firm in India, but the latter has a product line that is much broader and more complex. A second battery factory of this U.S. subsidiary in India—which has a more comparable product line but better technology—is somewhat more productive than the Shanghai plant. Battery producers in the United States and Japan are typically much more productive than the Chinese enterprise because their technology is far superior.

Labor productivity for electric fans at Canton Electrical Appliance is less than the industry average in India. Moreover, India's fan industry produces a wider line of more complex products than the Canton plant.

Diesel Engines, Tractors, and Trucks

Labor productivity at Wusih Diesel Engine was only a minute fraction of that for the U.S. diesel-engine and turbine industry in 1962, and significantly less than that of India's diesel-engine industry in 1961. However, the average diesel engine produced in India is substantially smaller and less powerful but a bit bigger than those produced by the Wuhan Diesel Engine Plant, which was barely functioning at the time of my visit.

Productivity at the giant Loyang Tractor Firm, which was set up in the 1950's with Soviet aid, was significantly less than in the Soviet tractor industry, according to officials at the plant. Productivity in the American industrial truck and tractor industry, which produces giant pieces of road-building and construction equipment, large trucks, and tractors that are much bigger than those produced by Loyang Tractor, in 1962 was nearly three times greater than that of the Chinese enterprise. At Canadian and U.S firms producing roughly comparable types of tractors as the Loyang plant the labor productivity is four to six times greater.

Shanghai Truck's labor productivity is about the same as that of India's truck and car industry, since the Indian figure also includes small cars which are somewhat more easily produced than trucks. In both countries very extensive vertical integration in motor-vehicle production contributes greatly to the relatively low levels of labor productivity. Productivity at Shanghai Truck was less than that of the Soviet truck industry in 1959—moreover, since 1959 Russia's truck industry has undergone major improvements—and obviously much lower than that of the United States in recent years even though the U.S. productivity figures are for truck and bus bodies and industrial trucks and tractors.

Output per man-year in 1965 at China's No. 1 Motor-Vehicle Factory in Changchun (which I did not visit) was about 1.3 trucks, or about double that of Shanghai Truck, according to figures given to Charles Lynch, a Canadian journalist.[2] The Changchun plant was also visited by the American author Edgar Snow in 1960, when he was given the same figures as Lynch.[3] The figures given to Snow may have been exaggerated Great-Leap production claims, but if they were not, this would mean that labor productivity did not increase at all during the 1960–65 period. According to the firm's management, it has been producing 30,000 six-cylinder, 95-horsepower, 4-ton trucks per year with a stable employment of 23,000 personnel.

Steel and Pig Iron

The Wuhan Iron and Steel Corporation did not seem to be operating as well as the Shanghai Steel firm that I surveyed. The Wuhan enterprise was set up with Soviet aid, and apparently had not yet fully recovered in 1966 from the abrupt Soviet withdrawal. The Wuhan firm is much larger and more vertically integrated, and hence more difficult to manage than the Shanghai steel enterprise.

The labor productivity of both of these firms is better than the average levels achieved in India's iron and steel industry in 1963. The productivity in 1965 is also better than that of both the Tata Iron and Steel Corporation and Hindustan Steel Limited. Tata is reputed to India's most efficient steel producer, and it produces a more diverse and sophisticated product line of finished steel than either of the two Chinese firms, especially Wuhan. Hindustan Steel, a public-sector firm with three large steel mills, is India's largest steel producer, and it employed about 92,000 people in 1965 (excluding construction personnel, who are included in the Tata and Chinese figures). The 35,000 employment figure for Wuhan Steel is the most meaningful one to use in comparing its productivity with Tata and Hindustan Steel since all of them employ sizable numbers of welfare, service, and other auxiliary personnel.

I have computed labor-productivity figures for each of Hindustan Steel's three mills in 1964–1965, and they may be of interest to some readers. The Bhilia plant employed over 35,000 people, and labor productivity for steel ingots and finished steel combined was 57.5 tons, for ingots only 25.7 tons, and for finished steel only 31.8 tons. The Durgapur Mill employed about 24,000 people, and its productivity was 71.7 tons for ingots and finished steel combined, 41.7 tons for ingots only, and 30 tons for finished steel. The Raurkela plant had an employment of nearly 26,000, and labor productivity for ingots and finished steel combined was 64.2 tons, ingots only 37.5 tons, and finished steel only 26.7 tons. In all three cases labor productivity was lower than the corresponding figures for the two Chinese firms.

The two Chinese steel firms lag behind average industry productivity in Japan, further behind the Soviet Union, and way behind the United States.

Peking Steel Wire seemed to be on the brink of chaos when I was there. Top executives of the enterprise seemed to be the most upset and were the most outspoken about the sudden Soviet pullout of all the Red Chinese officials whom I met. Its labor productivity was much lower than that of Japan's steel-wire industry in 1965, and lower than that of India's steel-wire rope industry in 1961. For the United States I could obtain a productivity figure only for all types of wire produced, but even this figure suggests that Peking Steel Wire's productivity is very low compared with U.S. performance in this sphere.

Machinery and Equipment

It is very difficult to make labor-productivity comparisons in the machinery and equipment sector because of the varying and greatly heterogeneous nature of goods produced. Only one comparison of this type has been attempted in Table 10–4. This involves a comparison of tons of equipment and machinery output for the Wuhan Heavy Machinery Firm and a Leningrad enterprise which produces a basically similar line of products. Productivity at the Soviet firm in 1960 was about 50 percent greater than that of the Wuhan enterprise in 1965.

Some experts were sent by the Leningrad plant, as well as various other Soviet organizations, to help set up the Wuhan plant in the 1950's. Even though the Wuhan firm's labor productivity lags behind that of the Leningrad enterprise, it seems to have successfully recovered from the sudden Soviet pullout. Wuhan Heavy Machinery seemed to be one of the best-managed and most efficient Chinese enterprises that I surveyed.

In general, the management, productivity, and general performance of Chinese machinery, equipment, tool, instrument, and component firms that I surveyed varied widely. Soviet enterprises of these types typically seem to be better managed, more efficient, and produce better-quality and more sophisticated products. The same is probably true for Japanese firms in general. U.S. enterprises are typically far superior. Indigenous Indian firms of these types typically seem to be no better, and often worse, than roughly comparable Chinese enterprises.

The largest and most important Chinese machinery and equipment enterprises surveyed seemed to be functioning relatively well. They also had relatively large proportions of university and semiprofessional graduates, engineers, technicians, and managers in most cases. But there are clearly not enough experts or skilled workers around, and some of the medium-sized firms in particular in this sector did not seem to be very well managed, productive, or efficient. The smaller machinery, tool, component, and instrument plants—typically following a policy of intensive self-sufficiency, and probably viewed as a training ground for manpower—were functioning at best on an average level, as judged from my entire sample of Chinese enterprises, and in other cases below average or poorly.

Value of Output Per Employee

Table 10–3 presents the value of marketable output (in current factory selling prices) per employee for twenty-two Chinese enterprises from which enough data were obtained to make such a computation. Because of the nature of China's pervasive system of state-controlled—and in many instances somewhat illogical or arbitrary—commodity prices, value of output in total or per employee is generally not a very meaningful measure of efficiency. However, I have presented value of output data for Chinese firms since it may shed more light on the price structure and pricing policy in China. In addition, it may prove interesting to compare the ranking of value of output per employee by branch of industry for my Chinese sample of firms, and also in relation to firms in the Soviet Union, India, and the United States.

Table 10–3 indicates that the average figure for Canton Fertilizer and Peking Coke and Chemical ranks first in value of output per employee, and Wuhan Heavy Machinery is second. This machinery firm is far from representative of China's machine-tool and equipment sector. It probably uses substantially more costly and complex material inputs, produces much more sophisticated and expensive products, and is significantly more capital-intensive than the average Chinese firm in this sector. Continuing with the ranking of firms in terms of value of output per employee: the two steel firms rank third; Wuhan paper is fourth; Shanghai Forging and Pressing Machine Tool is fifth; Shanghai Battery and Loyang Tractor are sixth and seventh (the precise order depending on which point in Loyang's range is used; the average for the three cotton-textile enterprises places eighth (but if they were treated individually they would rank eighth, ninth, and tenth); Peking Clothing places ninth; Peking Wool ranks tenth, but the average for Peking and Tientsin Wool places eleventh with Tientsin Shoe in tenth place; Wusih Diesel Engine is twelfth; Tientsin Watch is thirteenth; Soochow Cement Products ranks fourteenth, followed by Wusih Machinery and Tientsin Instrument. Wusih Silk Reeling is a special case since it works on a processing-fee basis with raw materials provided by its customers.

Table 10–5 compares the ranking order of value of output per employee for some of the Chinese firms with seven related branch-of-industry averages in the Soviet Union; one might expect a somewhat higher degree of correlation in such Sino-Soviet comparisons than in Sino-Indian or Sino-U.S. comparisons because the pricing philosophies and systems may be assumed to be more similar in China and Russia. I could only obtain value of output per employee data for seven corresponding branches of Soviet industry for recent years.

Table 10–5 indicates that there is a fairly low degree of correlation in the ranking order between the sample of Chinese firms and the seven corresponding branches of Soviet industry. The biggest difference is in the machine-building sector, but, as noted above, the Wuhan firm is a poor representative of this sector in China. Only clothing and iron and steel correlate fairly closely in this table in terms of value of output per em-

TABLE 10–5

Value of Output and Profit per Employee: Suggestive Rank Order for Selected Chinese Enterprises and Soviet Industries

	VALUE OF PRODUCTION PER EMPLOYEE			PROFIT PER EMPLOYEE		
		1963 Soviet Industry Average[a]			1960 Soviet Industry Average[b]	
Industry	*Chinese Enterprises' Rank Order* (Based on data in Table 10–3)	Rank Order	In Rubles	*Chinese Enterprises' Rank Order* (from Table 10–3	Rank	In Rubles
Chemicals	1. (based on average for Canton Chemical Fertilizer and Peking Coke and Chemical)	3	8,625	2 (average for 2 firms)	1	1,067
Machine building	2. (Wuhan Heavy Machinery)	7	5,485	1 (Wuhan firm)	5	514
Iron and steel	3. (based on average for 2 steel firms)	2	9,800	3 (Shanghai Steel)	3	700
Paper	4. (Wuhan Paper)	6	7,880	4 (Wuhan firms)	4	520
Textiles	5. (5 cotton and woolen mills)	1	12,540	5 (5 firms)	2	835
Clothing	6. (Peking Clothing)	5	8,180	6 (2 firms)	6	384
Leather products	7. (Tientsin Shoe)	4	8,230	7 (1 firm)	7	381

[a] Value of production for Soviet industries is for gross output in constant factory-wholesale prices. However, the rank order would probably be the same if marketable output in current prices were used. Rank orders and approximate 1960 figures in rubles based on marketable output prices for 5 Soviet enterprises surveyed by this author in 1961 are: Moscow Watch (17,500); Moscow Textile (17,200); Average for Leningrad and Kiev Machine Building (10,400); Leningrad Shoe (8,500); Kharkov Clothing (7,800).

[b] 1960 rank orders and approximate figures for 4 Soviet enterprises surveyed by this author are: Moscow Textile (3,250); Leningrad Machine Building (1,950); Leningrad Shoe (1,700); Kharkov Clothing (300).

SOURCES:
Soviet figures have been derived from *Narodnoe Khoziaistvo V 1963; Gody, op. cit.* in Table 10–4, and J. Thornton, "Estimation of Value Added in Soviet Industry from Cross-Section Data," *Journal of Political Economy*, Vol. LXXIII, No. 6 (December 1965), pp. 625 ff.

ployee. The difference in the textile-sector rankings for the two countries is so great that even with such a small sample of Chinese enterprises it is likely that the price structure and philosophy with regard to the textile industry differ significantly in the two countries. There is also a fairly low degree of correlation in the ranking orders of five Soviet enterprises referred to in Table 10–4 and corresponding Chinese firms in terms of value of output per employee.

Table 10–6 presents data on value of output per employee for twelve branches of Indian industry for 1961–62, the latest period for which such data could be obtained. The only sectors where there is a fairly close correlation in ranking order between the sample of Chinese firms and the corresponding Indian industries are iron and steel, textiles (particularly cotton), and watches.

Table 10–7 presents value of output per employee figures for fourteen Indian companies for the 1964–66 period. The Indian firms are in most

TABLE 10–6

VALUE OF OUTPUT PER EMPLOYEE AND PROFITABILITY DATA FOR SELECTED BRANCHES OF INDIAN INDUSTRIES

(Figures are for 1961 or 1962)

Industry	*Value of Output per Employee* (In Rupees)	*Profit per Employee** (In Rupees)	*Total Profits as a Percent of Total Value of Production**
Paper and paper products	22,750	2,790	12.8%
Iron and steel	20,100	2,160	10.8
Primary batteries	20,000	2,667	13.7
Chemical fertilizer	16,000	2,150	13.4
Leather footwear	13,500	1,377	10.1
Diesel and internal-combustion engines	12,800	2,400	18.7
Woolen textiles	11,900	1,810	18.3
Cotton textiles	8,500	1,010	12.0
Machine tools	7,750	1,200	15.4
Forgings and castings	6,600	333	5.2
Watches and clocks	6,333	171	2.7
Clothing	5,500	675	12.7

* Profits before taxes, dividends, or special adjustments for reserves.

SOURCES:
Annual Survey of Industries, 1961 and 1962; Indian Engineering Association, *Handbook of Statistics* 1965. (These sources are cited in full in Table 10–4 of this chapter.)

TABLE 10–7

VALUE OF OUTPUT, VALUE ADDED AND PROFITABILITY DATA FOR FOURTEEN INDIAN ENTERPRISES
(1965–66 Fiscal Year)

Enterprise	*Employment*	*Value of Output per Employee* (In Rupees)	*Value Added per Employee* (In Rupees)	*Profit per* Employee* (In Rupees)	*Total Profits as a Percent of Total Value of Production*
TEXTILE FIRMS					
Coimbator Cotton	1,431	17,000	6,550	negligible	negligible
Ahmedabad Cotton	2,986	14,300	7,750	1,000	6.4
Swadeshi Cotton	4,778	14,000	8,400	900	1
Tata Cotton	4,765	13,000	6,500	75	5.2
Central Suda Cotton	8,093	10,000	4,800	190	2
Average for above 5 firms		12,700	6,455	490	4.8
Raymond Woolen	2,037	19,000			
CHEMICAL FERTILIZER AND PAPER					
Fact Fertilizers	2,912	22,500	5,300	2,420	11
National Newsprint and Paper	1,440	22,000	7,840	3,900	17.9

PRIMARY BATTERIES						
Union Carbide of India †	6,000	35,000	12,000	5,000	16.7	(batteries only about 20%)
ESTRELLA	1,300	14,000	7,846	1,231	8.8	
Average for above 2 firms		25,800	9,740	4,325	16.0	
MACHINE TOOLS AND EQUIPMENT						
Indian Tool	1,341	20,900	11,500	3,500	16.8	
Hindustan Machine Tool	10,993	13,000	6,650	3,600	26.6	
Praga Tools	1,354	11,000	6,500	950	8.7	
Average for above 3 firms		13,600	7,250	3,225	23.5	
STEEL						
Tata Iron and Steel	61,700	20,000	5,859	2,700	13.6	
Hindustan Steel	91,927	22,270	7,924	1,855	8.5	
Average for above 2 firms		21,500	7,100	2,225	10.5	

*** Profits before taxes, dividends, or special adjustments for reserves.**

† While batteries comprise the major output of this firm in value it also produces various chemicals, flashlights, and a few other products.

cases more comparable to the sample of corresponding types of Chinese enterprises than Indian branch-of-industry averages. There is a significantly higher degree of correlation in the ranking order of the Chinese and Indian enterprises in terms of value of output per employee, but the degree of correlation is still far from perfect. Chemical fertilizer, paper, steel, and textiles correlate quite closely, athough the ranking order of wool and cotton textiles is reversed in the two samples; if we used value of output per employee for the indigenous Indian battery firm (Estrella) only, this sector would also correlate fairly closely.

Table 10–8 presents data on value of output per employee for eleven branches of American industry for 1962, the most recent year for which I was able to obtain such data. Perhaps surprisingly, there is a higher degree of ranking-order correlation between Chinese firms and corresponding branches of U.S. industry than in Sino-Soviet or Sino-Indian comparisons. In fact, if we ignore the machinery and forging sectors, there is a perfect ranking-order correlation for chemical fertilizers, iron and steel, paper, and batteries, with only minor differences in most of the other sectors. Could it be that the price structure in U.S. industry has had a greater influence on enterprise-level selling prices than the Soviet price structure? This may be a hypothesis warranting further study in the future.

Value Added per Employee

Value added for a given firm or industry consists of total wages, salaries, and other forms of material compensation; profits; depreciation charges; interest; rent; and at times certain types of expenses for capital repairs. It is a measure of contribution to a given country's gross national product, since GNP is comprised of value added by each firm and entire sector in the country. Value added can also be derived by subtracting all material, supply, fuel, energy, and the cost of services (such as subcontracting) perchased from other enterprises from the total value of output (or revenues) of a given enterprise or branch of industry.

Table 10–3 presents value added per employee figures (in yuan) for twenty-one Chinese enterprises. Table 10–9 presents similar data for corresponding branches of industry in the Soviet Union, India, and the United States, as well as ranking order comparisons. Table 10–6 contains data on value added per employee for fourteen Indian firms for the 1965–66 period.

Table 10–9 indicates a significantly higher degree of ranking-order correlation in value added per employee for seven branches of Soviet industry and corresponding Chinese enterprises than in the value of output per employee; however, this ranking-order correlation is far from a perfect fit.

TABLE 10–8

VALUE OF OUTPUT AND PROFITABILITY DATA FOR SELECTED BRANCHES OF U.S. INDUSTRY
(Figures for 1962)

Industry	*Value of Output per Employee* (In Dollars)	*Profit per* Employee* (In Dollars)	*Total Profits as a Percent of Sales**
Chemical fertilizer	50,500	1,758	3.6
Iron and steel	36,200	2,800	8.0
Paper and allied products	32,500	2,040	7.7
Primary batteries	26,000	not available	not available
Machine tools and industrial machinery	23,600	910	5.3
Woolen textiles	22,500	790	3.4
Watches and clocks	22,000	595	3.7
Cotton textiles	17,300	800	5.2
Forging and foundries	15,850	505	4.1
Clothing (Men's and boys')	14,350	108	2.9
Shoes and slippers (leather)	12,500	418	3.8

* Profit before taxes and dividend payments.

SOURCES:
Annual Survey of Manufactures, 1962, also cited in Table 10–4 of this chapter; *Survey of Current Business and Statistical Supplements*, 1962 and 1963, cited in Table 10–4; *Statistics of Income 1961–62* and *Corporation Income Tax Returns* (Washington: U.S. Treasury Dept., Internal Revenue Service).

There is an identical value added per employee ranking correlation for paper, and for textiles—if we average the figures of the five Chinese cotton and woolen mills. There is a one-rank difference in all other sectors except steel, where there is a two-rank difference.

If we compare value added per employee rankings for the eleven branches of Indian industry with corresponding Chinese enterprises, we get a fairly low degree of rank correlation. In no case is there an identical ranking. There is a one-rank difference for steel, watches, and cotton textiles, and a two-rank difference for chemical fertilizer, paper, and clothing. The rank differences in the five other sectors are greater, with a maximum spread of seven for leather footwear.

If we compare the value added per employee rankings for the Indian companies in Table 10–6 with corresponding Chinese enterprises, the degree of correlation is very low when the averages for the Indian cotton, machinery, and battery firms are used. If we use the figures for Estrella Battery—which is much more comparable to Shanghai Battery than

TABLE 10–9

Value Added per Employee for Selected Chinese Enterprises and Industries in India, U.S.S.R., and U.S.

	Chinese Enterprises		*1961 or 1962 Indian Industry Averages*		*1960 Soviet Industry Averages*		*1965 U.S. Industry Averages*	
	In Yuan[a]	Rank Order	In Rupees[b]	Rank Order	Rubles[c]	Rank Order	Dollars	Rank Order
Chemical fertilizer	13,300 (Canton firm), 8,570 (Peking Coke and Chemical)	1	4,005	3	2,700 (all chemicals)	2	16,265	2
Heavy machinery	11,360 (Wuhan firm)	2	3,454 (machine tools)	7	2,630 (machine building and metal processing)	3	13,534	5
Steel	9,850 (Shanghai firm)	3	5,201	2	300 (ferrous metallurgy)	1	16,460	1
Paper	9,800	4	3,522	6	2,300	4	15,477	3
Forging & pressing	5,800	5	1,710	10	not available	—	13,085 (forgings)	6
Primary batteries	5,200	6	5,300	1	not available	—	15,667	4
Cotton fabrics	4,625–5,460 (3 firms)	7	2,951	8	2,000 (all textiles)	5	8,061	9
Wool fabrics	2,945–3,500 (2 firms)	8	3,680	5	2,000	5	9,295	8
Clothing	1,900–2,735 (2 firms)	9	1,400	11	1,300	7	6,423	11
Watches	1,830	10	1,833	9	not available	—	11,724	7
Shoes	1,520	11	3,750 (leather footwear)	4	1,545 (all leather prod.)	6	6,548 (leather footwear)	10

[a] 1 yuan approximately equals 40 U.S. cents.

[b] There were about 4.75 rupees to the U.S. dollar until June 1966, when the devalued rate became 7.50 rupees = $1 (U.S.).

[c] A ruble equals $1.11 (U.S.) at the official exchange rate.

SOURCES: Indian and U.S. figures have been derived from the sources cited in Table 10–4. Soviet figures are from J. Thornton, "Estimation of Value Added in Soviet Industry from Cross-Section Data," *Journal of Political Economy*, Vol. LXXIII, No. 6 (December 1965), pp. 625 ff.

Union Carbide—and Hindustan Machine Tool—which is much more comparable to Wuhan Heavy Machinery than the other two Indian firms in this sector—instead of averages for these two sectors the degree of rank-order correlation increases significantly. However, there is still not a very high degree of overall rank correlation between the Indian and Chinese firms.

The degree of rank-order correlation between eleven branches of U.S. about one-third of that of Moscow's Kerov Watch Enterprise in 1960. industry (see Table 10–8) and corresponding Chinese enterprises in terms of value added per employee is higher than the Indian branch-of-industry comparison with China, but not quite as high as the Sino-Soviet correlation. However, the Sino-U.S. degree of overall rank correlation is certainly not very high. There is an identical rank correlation only for woolen textiles, chemical fertilizer, paper, forgings, and leather footwear, which differ by one rank, while steel, batteries, cotton textiles, and clothing differ by two ranks. There is a three-rank difference for watches and machinery.

PROFITABILITY

Table 7–3 gives profit-per-employee figures for twenty-one Chinese enterprises. Table 10–5 presents similar data for seven branches of Soviet industry (for 1960), as well as the ranking order for these industries and clothing, and leather products in terms of profit per employee. It also contains profit data for four Soviet enterprises in Note *b*.

Table 10–4 reveals an identical ranking order for iron and steel, paper, clothing, and leather products in terms of profit per employee for the seven Soviet industries and the corresponding Chinese enterprises. There is a one-rank difference for chemicals. However, there is a four-rank difference for machine building, and this is probably due in large part to the nonrepresentative nature of Wuhan Heavy Machinery in terms of China's machine-building sector. There is also a three-rank difference for textiles. A chief reason for this relatively large difference may be due to smaller profit margins in the Soviet textile industry in conjunction with the price structure.

In the section on fiscal policy in Chapter 6 it was noted that in Russia sales (turnover) taxes provide for greater state revenues than enterprise profits in the textile industry and various other consumer-goods sectors. The reverse seems to be true in China. In the fiscal policy section, profit-margin data in relation to output value and costs were presented for several Chinese and Soviet industries and individual enterprises. (See Tables 6–1, 6–2, and 6–3.) In no case were the Chinese profit margins lower than those of the Soviet Union.

Table 10–6 presents data on profit per employee and profits as a percent of total value of production for twelve branches of Indian industry. (Figures for 1961–62 are used since more recent data of this type could not be found.) If we compute the ranking order for these eleven Indian industries and corresponding Chinese firms (from Table 10–3) in terms of profit per employee, there turns out to be a fairly low degree of correlation. There is only an identical rank order for watches; a one-rank difference for clothing and a two-rank difference for iron and steel, chemicals, wool, and cotton textiles. The differences in rank order for the other six industries are greater, with as much as six to eight differences in ranks in three cases. The greatest rank difference is for diesel engines.

The degree of rank-order correlation with regard to profit as a percent of output value for the twelve Indian industries and corresponding Chinese enterprises is also quite low. There is an identical rank order only for woolen textiles. Machinery differs by one rank, while batteries, chemical fertilizer, leather footwear differ by two. The rank differences in the other seven sectors range from three to eight, with diesel engines again differing the most.

Table 10–7 contains data on profit per employee and profits as a percent of total value of production for fourteen Indian enterprises. The degree of rank-order correlation with Chinese firms is also relatively low; but a bit higher than for entire Indian industries. There is a one-rank difference for woolen textiles and cotton textiles, two-rank differences for paper, machinery, steel and chemical fertilizer, and a five-rank difference for batteries. By eliminating Union Carbide from the Indian sample, the degree of rank-order correlation increases significantly with only a one-rank difference in all sectors except paper, which has a three-rank difference. There is also a low degree of rank correlation with regard to the profit margins (in relation to output value) of Indian and corresponding Chinese enterprises. There is a one-rank difference for paper and steel, a two-rank difference for chemical fertilizer, and a difference of three ranks for machinery and batteries and four ranks for woolen and cotton textiles. Even if we eliminate Union Carbide from the Indian sample, the degree of overall rank-order correlation would still be low.

Table 10–8 presents data on profit per employee and profits as a percent of sales for ten branches of American industry. Using profit margins in relation to sales rather than value of production probably does not upset the rank order of U.S. industries in this area. The degree of rank correlation for the ten U.S. industries and corresponding Chinese firms in terms of profit per employee is fairly low, but higher than the Sino-Indian correlations. There is an identical rank order for chemical fertilizer and shoes, a one-rank difference for steel, cotton textiles and woolen textiles, two-rank differences for paper and clothing, and three-rank differences for the other three sectors. If we eliminated the machinery and forging sectors, the degree of overall rank correlation would increase significantly.

The degree of rank correlation for the U.S. industries and corresponding Chinese firms in terms of profit margins is somewhat lower than for profit per employee. There are no identical rank orders. There is a one-rank difference for paper, machinery, cotton textiles, watches, and clothing, two-rank differences for forgings and chemical fertilizer. The biggest difference (seven ranks) is in the woolen-textile sector. If the machinery and forging sectors were eliminated, there would be no significant change in the degree of overall rank correlation.

Cost Structure

Table 10–10 contains cost-structure data for twenty Chinese enterprises surveyed. This table indicates that material costs in relation to total enterprise costs and expenses are relatively high for all of the firms. They are over 80 percent of total costs at the chemical and drug, steel, heavy machinery, forging and pressing, machine-tool, cotton-textile, clothing, shoe, and battery firms. They are less than 70 percent only at Wusih Red Flag Machinery and Tientsin Instrument, both very labor-intensive plants. Wages and salaries as a percent of total cost are also highest at these two enterprises, as well as Soochow Cement Products, because of the highly labor-intensive nature of operations.

Payroll costs tend to be proportionately the lowest at firms which are highly capital-intensive and/or which use very expensive material inputs, such as special shapes, grades and sizes of steel. Wage and salary expenses are as high as they are at several of the textile firms, Peking Clothing, and Shanghai Battery because they employ large proportions of veteran workers and other personnel with long experience who receive significantly above-average pay.

I have no explanation for the proportions of "other costs and expenses" at many of the enterprises surveyed. At relatively capital-intensive plants, such as those in the chemical and drug sector, and at factories having sizable amounts of recently imported equipment, such as Tientsin Watch and Wusih Diesel Engine, depreciation charges are probably relatively high. Where firms, such as the Shanghai Sung Sing Cotton mill, undertook major capital repairs in 1965 other costs tended to rise quite substantially. Various welfare expenses, social security benefits, and interest payments on bank loans are some of the other major items reflected in "other" costs.

Table 10–11 contains cost-structure data for seven branches of Soviet industry, thirteen branches of Indian industry and sixteen individual Indian firms, and twelve branches of U.S. industry.

Part I of this table deals with Soviet industry. Material costs as a percent of total costs are slightly higher in the Soviet cotton-textile, clothing, and leather-products industries than at similar types of Chinese enter-

TABLE 10–10

Cost Structures for Twenty Chinese Industrial Enterprises Surveyed

(Figures are expressed as a percentage of total enterprise costs and expenses for 1965)

Enterprise	*Total Costs and Expenses (100%)* (In Millions of Yuan)	*All Materials*[a] (% of Total)	*Total Wages and Salaries*[b] (% of Total)	*Other Costs and Expenses*[c] (% of Total)
TEXTILES				
Peking Woolen	11.55	78%	11.2%	10.8%
Tientsin Joint State and Private Woolen	7.8	73	18.0	9.0
Peking Cotton Textile No. 3	52.0	82	7.5	11.5
Shanghai Cotton Textile No. 19	45.0	84	10.0	6.0
Shanghai Sung Sing No. 9 Joint State of Private Mill	56.25	80	11.5	8.5
CLOTHING				
Peking Clothing	17.0	84	8.0	8.0
SHOES				
Tientsin Shoe	7.6	83.3	10.5	4.2
CHEMICALS, DRUGS				
Peking Coke and Chemical	47.5	88.5	4.0	8.5
Canton Chemical Fertilizer	90.0	86.5	2.5	11.0
Shanghai No. 3 Pharmaceutical	not given	80–85	6.0–7.0	10.0–13.0
PAPER				
Wuhan Hau Yang Paper	38.5	85.0	4.0	11.0

LIGHT DURABLES				
Tientsin Watch	6.75	77.5	13.5	9.0
Shanghai Wei Ming Battery	6.63	84.0	9.5	6.5
STEEL				
Shanghai No. 3 Steel	310.0	87.5	4.0	8.5
HEAVY MACHINERY				
Wuhan Heavy Machinery	170.5	86.8	3.3	9.9
AND COMPONENTS				
SMALL-SCALE MACHINERY TOOLS, INSTRUMENTS,				
Shanghai No. 3 Forging and Pressing Machine Tool	7.15	84.5	6.0	9.5
Wusih Red Flag Machinery	0.73	64.0	26.0	10.0
Tientsin Instrument	0.37	68.0	27.0	5.0
Wusih Diesel-Engine	18.0	80.5	10.3	9.2
Soochow Cement Products	2.1	75.5	20.0	4.5

[a] Includes raw and subsidiary materials, fuel, electricity, sundry supplies, subcontracting value-added computations. However, there are likely to be some expenses for material, supplies, or services consumed (e.g., travel) in the "other" category, although they probably are not very substantial.

[b] Includes bonuses and other cash incentive payments to employees. The administrative staff and important technicians are generally paid "salaries," and other personnel "wages."

[c] Includes welfare and social security fund (typically 12–13.5 percent of total basic wages and salaries), other welfare expenses, depreciation, interest (if any), fines and damages (if any) paid to other parties (typically customers), certain types of capital repairs and miscellaneous overhead expenses not clearly specified (perhaps travel expenses are included here).

Only about half of the above enterprises gave me precise figures. In other cases they gave me small ranges from which I arbitrarily took the midpoint as my estimate; or I computed the figures from other data they gave me (e.g., average enterprise wage, total number of employees plus extra monetary incentive payment) to arrive at a total wages and salaries estimate. No range given was bigger than those for Shanghai Pharmaceutical. It is likely that the margins of error in most, if not all, cases are not more than about 5 percent.

TABLE 10–11

COST STRUCTURES FOR SELECTED BRANCHES OF INDUSTRY IN THE SOVIET UNION, INDIA, AND THE UNITED STATES

Part I: SOVIET UNION (1964 figures in percent)[a]

Industry	*Total Costs and Expenses* (%)	*All Materials* (% of Total)	*Total Wages and*[b] *Salaries* (including social insurance) (% of Total)	*Other*[c] (% of Total)
Ferrous metallurgy	100	69.9	18.8	11.3
Machine building	100	61.5	30.1	8.4
Chemicals	100	75.4	15.1	8.5
Paper	100	70.1	19.9	9.0
Cotton textiles	100	85.2	12.3	2.5
Leather products	100	85.4	13.3	1.3
Clothing and sewn articles	100	86.6	12.2	2.2
Moscow Sverdlov Textile Enterprise[d] (1966)	100	90.5	7.0	2.5

[a] I have organized the cost categories so that they are probably roughly comparable to the categories used for the Chinese enterprises. The accounting and statistical systems at the enterprise level in both countries seem to be quite similar.

[b] Unlike the Chinese enterprise figures, social insurance is included in wages rather than in the "other" category for the Soviet Union.

[c] This category for the Soviet industries is less likely to contain expenses for any material, supplies, or services consumed than the Chinese figures given to me.

[d] Rayon- and silk-manufacturing enterprise surveyed by this author in 1961.

SOURCE: *Narodnoe Khoziaistvo-SSSR v 1964 Gody* (Moscow, 1965), pp. 153 ff.

prises. Chinese proportionate material costs are significantly greater for chemicals, paper, ferrous metallurgy (iron and steel), and machine building (if the Wuhan Heavy Machinery figure is used). Wage and salary expenses in relation to total costs are higher in Soviet industries than at corresponding Chinese firms, and with the exception of clothing, cotton textiles, and leather goods the Soviet figures are several times greater. This is not surprising, given the much higher wage rates and salary scales in Soviet industry, particularly the newer, modern sectors.

China ranks higher than Russia on other costs and expenses for all sectors compared except iron and steel. I have no conclusive reasons as to why this is so. Higher depreciation charges at Chinese firms, where there is much new equipment, than average Soviet branch-of-industry depreciation charges and major capital repairs at some Chinese plants might account for part of this difference. Proportionately larger welfare expenses

Part II–A: INDIAN INDUSTRIES (1961 figures in percent)[a]

Industry	*Total Costs and Expenses* (%)	*All Materials* (% of Total)	*Total Wages and Salaries* (% of Total)	*Other* (% of Total)
Iron and steel	100	55	17	28
Machine tools and equipment	100	49.5	30.5	20
Chemical fertilizer	100	52	16	32
Pharmaceuticals	100	73	14	13
Paper and paper products	100	69	11.5	19.5
Cotton textiles	100	62	26	12
Woolen textiles	100	74	15.5	10.5
Clothing	100	78.5	14	7.5
Footwear	100	77	19	4
Forgings and castings	100	62.5	22	15.5
Diesel and other combustion engines	100	65.5	20	14.5
Primary batteries	100	74	19	7
Watches	100	57	27	16

[a] Here too, cost categories have been organized to make them roughly comparable to those for the Chinese enterprises. Commissions paid to personnel, as well as social security and fringe-benefit income payments, have been placed in the wages and salaries category. Careful effort has been made to get all of the costs pertaining to materials, supplies, fuel, services, etc., in the material category. However, there is undoubtedly some margin of error since some of the accounts were not detailed enough for the computations and allocations desired.

SOURCES:
Annual Survey of Industries 1961 **(Calcutta: Central Statistical Organization, Industrial Statistical Wing, 1962);** ***Indian Engineering Associations: Handbook of Statistics*** **(Calcutta: 1966);** ***Journal of Industry and Trade*****, April 1966 (New Delhi: Government of India).**

and social security benefits at various Chinese enterprises than the average costs for corresponding branches of Soviet industry might be another important factor.

Part II-A of Table 10–11 presents cost-structure figures for thirteen Indian industries. The figures are for 1961, the latest year for which I could obtain comprehensive data of this type, and more recent statistics might perhaps reflect some significant differences. Material expenses as a percent of total costs are lower for all of the Indian industries than at corresponding Chinese enterprises. (The material costs for woolen textiles are higher in India, only if we use the figure for the Tientsin woolen mill).

For all sectors wage and salary expenses as a percent of total costs are higher in India, and in most cases they are several times greater. (Proportionate wage and salary expenses would be lower for woolen textiles in

TABLE 10–11 (*continued*)

Part II–B: SIXTEEN SELECTED INDIAN ENTERPRISES[a] (1965–66 period)

Enterprise	*Employment*	*Total Costs and Expenses* (%)	*All Materials* (% of Total)	*Wages and Salaries* (% of Total)	*Other*
IRON AND STEEL					
Tata Iron and Steel	61,700	100	63	21	16
Hindustan Steel	not reported	100	45	12	43
MACHINE TOOLS AND HEAVY EQUIPMENT					
Hindustan Machine Tool	10,993	100	55	29	16
Praga Tools	1,354	100	36	32	32
Indian Tool Mfg.	1,341	100	43	33	24
CHEMICAL FERTILIZER, PHARMACEUTICALS AND PAPER					
Fact Fertilizers	2,919	100	61	16	23
Alembic Chemicals (main line is drugs, including antibiotics)	2,406	100	64	14	22
Merck, Sharp and Dohme of India (drugs)	540	100	50	20.5	29.5
National Newsprint and Paper	1,440	100	69	17	14
PRIMARY BATTERIES					
Estrella	1,300	100	47	27	26
Union Carbide of India[b]	6,000–6,500 (approx.) 5,000 (permanent only)	100	70	17.5	12.5
WOOLEN TEXTILES					
Raymond Woolen	2,037	100	50	25	25
COTTON TEXTILES					
Central Suda Cotton	8,093	100	49	30	21

Enterprise	*Employment*	*Total Costs and Expenses (%)*	*All Materials (% of Total)*	*Wages and Salaries (% of Total)*	*Other*
Swadeshi Cotton	4,778	100	43	27	30
Tata Cotton	4,765	100	50	28	22
Ahmedabad Advance Cotton	2,986	100	43	27	30

[a] See Note a above for Indian industries in Part II–A.

[b] Batteries are the major product line of this firm, but it also produces some inorganic chemicals, flashlights, electrodes, and a few other types of products. At its two battery plants, which comprise more than two-thirds of total enterprise employment, the average cost structure in 1965–66 was roughly as follows: all materials, 75–80 percent; total labor and salaries (including all forms of remuneration and allocations of overhead payroll), 9–12 percent; other, 8–16 percent.

Part III: U.S. INDUSTRIES (1962)[a]

Industry	*Total Costs and Expenses (%)*	*All Materials (% of Total)*	*Total Wages and Salaries (% of Total)*	*Other (% of Total)*
Steel rolling & finishing	100	62.5	24.0	13.5
Iron and steel foundries	100	41	41	18
Machine tools and heavy equip.	100	34	44	22
Diesel and other combustion engines and turbines	100	52.5	31.5	16
Chemical fertilizer	100	74	12	16
Pharmaceuticals	100	32	23.5	44.5
Paper	100	60	23	17
Watches and clocks	100	47	32	21
Woolen textiles	100	64	21.5	14.5
Cotton textiles	100	63	26	11.0
Men's and boys' clothing	100	58	28.5	13.5
Footwear (leather)	100	49.5	33.5	17

[a] Cost calculations have been done in the same way as in the other parts of this table and for Chinese enterprises.

SOURCES: *Annual Survey of Manufactures 1962* (Washington: Bureau of Census, U.S. Dept. of Commerce); *Statistics of Income 1961–62* (Washington: U.S. Dept. of the Treasury), *Statistical Abstract for the U.S.*, 1962 and 1963 (Washington: U.S. Dept. of Commerce).

India only if we used the figure for the Tientsin woolen textile firm.) The much higher pay received by Indian managerial and leading technical personnel—but not the average worker—is the major reason for this overall difference. Of course, higher material costs in Chinese industry in general, as well as more capital-intensive operations at various newer Chinese plants, as compared with the average level in corresponding Indian industries, also contribute to this difference.

The Indian industries and the corresponding sample of Chinese firms are not nearly as far apart in terms of other costs as a percent of total costs and expenses as they are for wage and salary costs. With regard to other costs, there is very little difference for the pharmaceutical, battery, woolen-textile or shoe sectors, and only a modest difference for cotton textiles. In the other sectors India's proportionate "other" costs are clearly greater—in a few cases considerably greater—than those of the corresponding Chinese firms. There are probably many reasons for these differences, and it is not worth the time to speculate on them in this study.

Part II-B of Table 10–11 presents 1965–66 cost-structure data for sixteen Indian enterprises representing eight distinct industrial sectors. Material costs as a percent of total costs and expenses are less at all of the Indian firms than at corresponding Chinese enterprises, while proportionate wage and salary costs are higher at all of the Indian companies—in most cases much higher. Other costs in relation to total costs and expenses are also higher—in most cases considerably so—at all of the Indian firms. Sizable interest payments, rent (actual or imputed) for housing (typically expensive), and other substantial perquisites granted to managerial personnel, as well as a wide variety of miscellaneous, selling, and general expenses, largely account for the proportionately high "other" costs at most of the Indian firms.

Part III of Table 10–11 contains cost-structure data for twelve branches of U.S. industry: here too, material costs as a percent of total costs and expenses are lower—in most cases considerably lower—for all of the U.S. industries than at corresponding Chinese enterprises, while proportionate wages and salary expenses are much higher for the U.S. industries. As for other costs, there is not a very significant difference for the woolen- or cotton-textile sectors, but in all other sectors they are proportionately higher for the U.S. industries—in some cases several times higher.

Concluding Remarks

In spite of the obviously serious managerial, technical, productivity and other efficiency problems at many of the Chinese industrial enterprises surveyed, I was surprised and impressed by the wide range of goods that Red China, for such a relatively poor and newly developing country, is capable of producing. Communist China seems to be able to produce nearly any type of product it wants to produce, but often very inefficiently and at great expense.

CHAPTER 11

China's Domestic Trade and the Retail Sector

THUS FAR, we have examined the Chinese Communist economy chiefly in terms of what goes on at industrial enterprises in response to environmental forces. China's domestic trade, including the retail sector, has been dealt with only peripherally and, even then, mainly from the standpoint of the industrial sector. In order to round out this study of the Chinese economy, a short journey through the trade sector—and particularly China's major retail department stores—seems to be in order. We shall look at what goes on within the trade sector, and also at the relationship between this sector and the industrial sector as seen from the standpoint of the trade sector.

Relatively little has been written about Red China's domestic trade and retail sector, as compared with the other sectors, such as industry, agriculture, or even finance and banking.[1] The discussion which follows is based almost entirely on information, observations, and impressions derived during my research trip to Communist China in 1966.

ORGANIZATION OF DOMESTIC TRADE

China's domestic trade sector is essentially comprised of the country's myriad retail establishments and the thousands of wholesaling organizations which serve as intermediary links in the distribution of consumer goods from the industrial sector to the retail sector.

The top-level Communist Party organs concerned directly with domestic trade are the Finance and Trade Work Department and the more recently established Finance and Trade Political Department, which are both under the Secretariat of the Party's Central Committee and Politburo. The latter organ was created to deal with ideological education in the trade and finance sectors with the aim of merging Redness and Expertness along the lines desired by the regime. These two organs are indicated on Chart 8–1 of Chapter 8.

The top-level government organ directly concerned with China's domestic trade is the Office for Finance and Trade under the State Council. There are four ministries under this office: Commerce, Foreign Trade, Finance, and Food. The director of this office, Li Hsien-nien, is also Minister of Finance, as well as a member of the State Council and the party's Politburo. (See Chart 8–2 of Chapter 8.)

The Ministry of Commerce is the central ministry in charge of the domestic-trade sector on a national scale. This ministry is concerned with general supply, sales, and inventory-level planning primarily in financial terms, although it also deals with the physical balancing and pricing of a limited number of commodities on a national scale. It also approves and broadly controls the inflow and outflow of major consumer goods among different provinces and major cities, and tries to assure proper financial and critical commodity balancing among local bureaus of commerce.

There are, in addition, specialized national trading corporations under this ministry, most of which have branches in different cities and, in some cases, at the provincial level as well. Most of these corporations are organized along product lines—for example, drugs, chemicals, textiles, leather products—and each performs wholesaling and distribution functions. There is also the China General Department Store Corporation under the Ministry of Commerce, and it is involved in the management and operations of a limited number of key retail department stores. This national department store corporation allocates a number of major commodities for retail trade through its branches in different parts of the country.

National commercial corporations also allocate and distribute various major commodities, such as cotton, textiles, sports equipment, and drugs, for retail trade among the different provinces and cities. The branches of these corporations, as well as other local wholesaling organizations, deal with products not under central control—for instance, glassware, cosmetics, various synthetic leather items, sweets, and handicrafts.

The local bureaus of commerce balance commodity flaws and finances within their locality. There are wholesaling "stations," organized along product lines, under local bureaus of commerce which balance the inflows and outflows of goods to and from the district or province. Local commerce bureaus also deal with such matters as personnel, wages, welfare, and product prices not subject to higher-level control. In some larger cities and provinces there are two bureaus of commerce. One deals with manufactured consumer goods, and the other with food, hotels and restaurants.

There are bureaus of commerce and pricing commissions at the provincial, municipal, and district (within cities) levels, as well as branches of national trading corporations, local commercial corporations, and other wholesaling organizations at these levels. The vast majority of China's retail stores are under municipal and district control, although, as indicated above, a few are under the China General Department Store Corporation—usually one of its branches—for certain matters. I am not sure whether any retail stores are directly under provincial control, but I did not learn of any that were.

The bulk of consumer goods distributed from factories to retail outlets pass through commercial wholesaling organizations, although it is not uncommon for retail stores to negotiate product orders directly with industrial organizations. National consumer-goods exhibitions organized along product lines are usually held several times a year for each major consumer-product group. In many instances similar exhibitions are held at the local levels as well. One set of exhibitions involves industrial organizations and commercial wholesaling organizations (chiefly corporations and wholesaling stations) with only limited direct participation by retail stores (mainly large ones). (This type of exhibition was mentioned in Chapter 8.) The other type of exhibition involves commercial wholesaling organizations and retail stores, with only minor participation by the industrial sector. The primary purpose of these consumer-product exhibitions is to negotiate detailed supply and sales orders and finalize contractual agreements. Wholesaling organizations play major roles in both kinds of exhibitions since they are the key link in the distribution of consumer goods from industry to retail trade.

In general, China's domestic trade sector is characterized by complex networks of dual subordination. For example, municipal-level commerce bureaus are typically subordinate to the municipal people's council for various matters—particularly those involving personnel, welfare, and the pricing of various products—and under provincial commerce bureaus, and even the Ministry of Commerce, in such areas as broad planning and control, the allocation of various commodities, the pricing of major products, and key financial matters. Municipal branches of national commercial corporations are commonly subordinate to the municipal bureau of commerce for such things as personnel, while they are under central corporate control for other matters involving planning, supply allocation, and financial control. At the same time there are also commercial organizations entirely under the control of local bureaus of commerce. For instance, the Tientsin First Light Industry Commercial Corporation is largely under the control of the municipal commerce bureau, but also is subordinate to one of the central trading corporations in certain spheres. The same is true of the leather and chemical commercial corporations in Tientsin, but the Tientsin Daily Usage Commercial Corporation is wholly subordinate to the Tientsin Bureau of Commerce.

In general, where a municipal-level commercial corporation, including branches of national corporations, is located in a city which is quite self-sufficient in the products that it handles, it is likely to be subject to significantly less central control than if the reverse were true. The same seems to hold true with regard to the degree of control exerted over a municipal—or district or provincial—bureau of commerce by higher-level commerce bureaus and/or the Ministry of Commerce.

It is also common for retail stores to be subject to dual control. For example, department stores are often subordinate to the municipal commerce bureau in personnel and welfare matters, as well as the retail prices charged for various products, but at the same time they are under the control of commercial corporations for other business affairs. The same is true for smaller retail stores which are under the dual control of district-level commerce bureaus and local commercial organizations.

All in all, it seems that China's domestic trade sector is indeed organizationally very complex. I must admit that even after interviewing several Chinese commercial and retail executives I am still quite hazy about the general organization of this sector. This is the chief reason why I have not even attempted to draw organization charts for this sector. Those executives interviewed were quite candid about the organizational and other problems in the trade sector. They admitted that there is too much overlapping and duplication of activities, as well as too many links, unclear relationships, and outdated procedures and regulations.[2] They pointed out that much "experimentation" and many organizational changes have been, and were still being, undertaken in the trade sector in order to constantly improve the organizational setup and operations.

Trade Organization in China's Leading Cities

In Shanghai the first Bureau of Commerce—under the Municipal People's Council—is in charge of trade involving manufactured consumer goods. Under this bureau in 1966 there were about ten commercial corporations, each concerned with the wholesaling and distribution of a specific commodity. They operate networks of warehouses. There were also about ten wholesale stations corresponding to the commercial corporations. In fact, on a formal organization chart the corporations are likely to be reflected in a directly subordinate position to the wholesale stations, with these stations coming directly under the commerce bureau. These wholesale stations are concerned with balancing the inflow and outflow of commodities to and from Shanghai. They deal with corresponding wholesale stations in other cities and provinces. The commercial wholesaling corporations balance, distribute, and control the flow of goods and serve the market within Shanghai. They have their own product-group departments and sections.

Under Shanghai's First Bureau of Commerce there is also a corporation in charge of a number of larger retail stores. Most of the smaller stores in Shanghai are under the control of district bureaus of commerce, which are, in turn, subordinate to the Shanghai Municipal Bureau. There are also smaller and specialized district-level commercial corporations and wholesaling organizations.

Shanghai's twelve largest department stores, including Wing On, China's largest joint state-private store, are under the dual control of the Municipal First Bureau of Commerce and the Shanghai Branch of the China General Department Store Corporations, which is under the Ministry of Commerce. The Shanghai branch of this corporation deals with products that come under the local bureau of commerce for balancing purposes. This branch employs around three thousand people, with over one hundred in its head office. It has seven departments, basically similar to those found in large retail department stores, five major product-group wholesale-balancing sections, and over a dozen warehouses.

The trade setup in Peking and Tientsin was basically similar to that in Shanghai in 1966. Mention has already been made of some of Tientsin's commercial organizations in an earlier section. Under Peking's Bureau of Commerce in 1966 there were the following six major wholesale stations:

(1) Textiles
(2) Clothing, shoes, and other daily-life products (e.g., soap)
(3) Groceries
(4) Stationery and sports equipment
(5) Metals, appliances, chemicals, and telecommunications
(6) Local products (including handicrafts, porcelain, toys, brooms, bamboo and straw items, glassware, etc.)

As in Shanghai, the Peking wholesale stations are concerned with intercity procurement and sales. For example, the Peking Textile Wholesale Station deals directly with textile wholesale stations and, in some cases, textile commercial corporations in other cities and provinces. This station, like most of the others, does not employ a large number of people because its main job is commodity balancing rather than operational management. There were no more than a dozen people working for the Peking Textile Wholesale Station in 1966.

There was a commercial corporation under each of Peking's wholesale stations, each one dealing with product lines similar to those of its organizationally superior station. The Peking Textile Commercial Corporation employed well over a hundred people and had several large warehouses in Peking. This corporation had cotton cloth, woolen goods, and silk commodity sections, as well as a few others. It also had departments for supply and sales, planning, finance and accounting, general administration, and one or two other functions.

There were five major retail department stores directly under Peking's Bureau of Commerce. I am not sure whether, or to what extent, these stores were also subordinate to the China General Department Store Corporation or its local branch. In Peking there were seven district bureaus of commerce under the municipal bureau. Most of the small stores in the city—including smaller joint state-private retail outlets, private shops, and cooperatives—were under district commerce bureaus. At the district level there were also branches of municipal commercial corporations, some district-level corporations, as well as various other district-level wholesaling organizations.

Some Sino-Soviet Comparisons[3]

It appears that domestic trade is substantially more decentralized down to the municipal and district levels in China than has been the case in the Soviet Union. In both countries considerably greater powers were pushed down to trade authorities of the provincial level (the republic level in the Soviet Union) some years ago, but the Chinese have apparently carried this decentralization down to the municipal level to a greater degree than the Soviets.

In China's domestic-trade sector there are clearly serious and widespread deficiencies in marketing research, consumer-demand analysis, consumer satisfaction, product planning, sales promotion, available statistics, (particularly involving rural areas), and information gathering and processing in general. However, the Chinese began paying serious attention to these problems before the Soviets did, and the Chinese, so far, may well have made more effective progress in some of these areas. It seems that Red China has better commercial instincts, as well as a greater flair for, and interest in, marketing and consumer satisfaction, than the Soviet Union. There certainly seems to be substantially greater direct contact in China between the trade and industrial sectors—including contact between factories and retail stores. There also seems to be much greater concern for consumer satisfaction and customer service at the retail level in China. The Red Chinese have also been involved with advertising and sales promotion longer and more extensively than the Soviets, although advertising in China is still basically informative rather than persuasive. There have been special advertising organizations in Red China for some years, while they have only recently been created in Russia. The press, magazines, billboards, telephone directories, and the cinema are the major advertising media in China. Greatest use is made of them in major cities, such as Shanghai, Canton, Tientsin, and, to a lesser extent, Peking and Wuhan. While much of the advertising, carrying the producer's names, is aimed at wholesale and retail organizations, there is also a fair amount aimed at the ultimate consumer. Shanghai is China's leading and best-run commercial and retailing center, and it is held up by the regime as a model for other parts of the country to emulate.

From the very sparse data that I obtained from the handful of Chinese retail stores surveyed, it appears that pay differentials between industrial and retail personnel may be substantially smaller in China than in the Soviet Union, where industrial employees receive considerably more pay on the average.[4] It also seems likely that, on the average, large Chinese stores, at least, have a somewhat larger proportion of employees who have had higher education than similar stores in the U.S.S.R.[5] It is quite possible that the Chinese regime has been allocating a larger proportion of higher-education graduates to the trade sector than the Soviet Union. Pay scales and education statistics for three of China's leading department stores will be presented shortly.

Ideology in China's Trade Sector

China's trade sector has been subject to the same swings in the ideological pendulum and the same forms of ideological extremism as the industrial sector. In fact, when the pendulum has swung in the direction of extremism, domestic trade, commerce, and finance have tended to be the first spheres to come under attack. The reason is that these sectors have been regarded as being politically very sensitive because of the large number of bourgeois personnel—capitalists and former private merchants, employees of former private local and foreign firms in China—they have employed and still employ. Moreover, trade and commerce are viewed in traditional Marxist terms as rather parasitic and relatively unproductive spheres of activity. This may explain why trade and finance were chosen as the first spheres in 1964 in which special party political departments were established at all levels, in addition to the regular party works departments, committees, and branches in the trade and finance organizational hierarchies (see Chart 8–1 of Chapter 8). The party political departments in industry and communications were not established until later.

The most recent pervasive ideological campaign involving the domestic-trade sector began really picking up steam around September 1965 and continued through 1966.[6] It apparently began to peter out in 1967. It began some six or seven months before the Cultural Revolution burst into the open and also before the ideological pendulum began shifting significantly in the direction of extremism in the industrial sector.

During the period between September 1965 and April 1966, in particular, the Communist Chinese press was filled with articles calling for "ideological revolution" and much greater adherence to Mao's Thought in trade and commerce. The major themes of these articles involved the merging of Redness and Expertness; self-interest versus serving the customer wholeheartedly; profit versus service; materialism versus altruism; attacks against localism (especially the reluctance to sell goods in short supply to other cities and provinces); improper business hours; poor product planning, stocking the wrong goods, and poor-quality repair work because of inadequate concern for customers and their needs, and so on. Socialist educational campaigns and ideological sessions were frequently organized by party political departments at all levels of the trade hierarchy. Model trade workers, such as Yang Chen-yu, a sales clerk at the Fong Chi-cheng Department Store, were exalted in the press.[7] Yang, and others, were praised for "serving the people with [their] whole being" under Mao's guidance, and for putting customer and state interests above their own.

By the time I surveyed three of China's largest retail department stores and a number of smaller shops, the ideological campaign in the trade sector may have already passed its peak. The stores that I surveyed seemed to be functioning quite well. I was much more impressed with them than the Soviet stores that I visited in the early 1960's—and there were no obvious symptoms of very serious inefficiencies resulting from ideological extremism. However, the Tientsin State Department Store had abolished its system of extra rewards (bonus payments) at the end of 1965, and I was told by the manager of the Peking Department Store in April 1966 that they were considering a similar move. I did not learn enough about the Tientsin store to determine whether the end of its bonus system was having any negative impacts on productive efficiency and customer service.

The rest of this chapter will deal in more detail with what I learned about the three leading Chinese department stores that I surveyed, particularly the ones in Shanghai and Peking where I spent the most time.

Survey of Chinese Retail Department Stores

Shanghai General Department Store No. 1

Red China's largest retail department store, it was founded in October 1949. During its first year of operations it had a total area of 1,100 square meters, employed 100 people, and handled 3,000 varieties of products (not counting sizes, colors, or patterns). In 1966 it had selling space totaling 17,100 square meters, employment stood at 2,014, and the store was carrying nearly 50,000 varieties of products annually. Some 2,000 new varieties were introduced in the preceding twelve months. About 1 percent of the goods in stock was imported—the items included cameras, film, and watches—although domestic brands were also available.

The Shanghai General Department Store is housed in a large and quite modern five-story building on Nanking Road. It has several elevators—for which peasants from the countryside excitingly form long lines to take a ride on their days off—is very clean, and has many artistic and effective merchandising displays. The store serves an average of 90,000 to 100,000 customers daily, and on Sundays and holidays the figure often reaches 200,000.

In 1965 total sales amounted to 74.5 million yuan (nearly 30 million U.S. dollars at an exchange rate of 2.5 yuan = $1), and profits were 9 million yuan. The 1966 plan tentatively called for sales of 80 million yuan, and profits of about 10 million yuan. In May 1966 the store's inventory amounted to about 7.5 million yuan, and I was told that in slack periods it sometimes goes as high as 8.5 million yuan. The manager claimed that the shortages of goods are more common than gluts but that there had been very few serious shortages in the store for several years.

Of the store's 2,014 employees, 135 (6 percent) were administrative cadres, 1,388 were sales people, and 596 (27 percent) were women. The store employs many older people. The average basic monthly store wage was 67 yuan; the minimum wage was 40 yuan, and the maximum, which was paid to the party secretary, was 145 yuan. The director who had left just prior to my visit was also receiving 145 yuan. The acting director received 130 yuan, and the two vice directors 116 yuan each. The top wage paid to a nonmanager, who was a salesman, was 92 yuan. The basic monthly pay of sales section chiefs and department heads ranged from 74 to 116 yuan.

All employees, except the director, vice directors, party secretary and vice secretaries, could earn extra rewards each quarter. The bonus fund amounted to 7 percent of the store's total wage fund. There were three bonus grades, 25, 20, and 15 yuan. Generally about 20 percent of the employees earn the maximum bonus, 60 to 65 percent the second grade, 15 percent the minimum bonus, and 7 percent nothing. The payment of bonuses does not depend on the fulfillment of key targets of the store's plan. It is based on individual productive contribution, customer service, and ideological purity, as assessed by one's fellow employees. In the cases where personnel do not receive any bonus, the major reasons are typically absenteeism and ideological deficiencies.

Of the 2,014 employees 20 had higher educations. None of the higher graduates studied technical fields; most of them majored in accounting, finance, economics or trade, and a few in other social-science fields or the humanities. None of the top executives were higher graduates. Most of the higher graduates were employed as managers or staff specialists in various departments and sales sections. About 250 of the employees were senior-middle-school graduates, and 60 percent of the personnel had completed junior-middle school. The party secretary, who was forty-one, was a junior-middle-school graduate. The acting director, who was forty-two, was completing his senior-middle-school studies part time, and the two vice directors, aged thirty-four and thirty-nine, were senior-middle-school graduates. Both of the vice directors began their business careers as salesmen in fairly small stores.

As is the case at industrial enterprises, the store is officially under the leadership of the store party committee. This committee consisted of eleven members, all of whom were party executives and managers. Approximately 9 or 10 percent of the store's employees were party members.

The store was under the dual control of the Shanghai branch of the China General Department Store Corporation and Shanghai's First Bureau of Commerce. The former organization was primarily concerned with supply, sales, and financial matters, and the latter with personnel matters.

The general manager of the Shanghai Branch Corporation had a monthly salary of 150 yuan, the vice managers' salaries ranged from 106 to 140 yuan, and the average pay for this organization was 75 yuan. The director and vice directors of the store were appointed by the Municipal People's Council, and the department heads and sales section chiefs by the commerce bureau. Only the sales group leaders were appointed within the store. The party secretary and vice secretaries were "elected" by the store's party members and formally approved by the party committee of the commerce bureau.

The store had the following six major administrative departments:

(1) Planning, which deals with supply, sales, commodity circulation, inventory levels, pricing, merchandising, and sales promotion. This department was employing thirteen people.
(2) Labor and Wages, which had seven people.
(3) Finance and Accounting, with thirty-three people.
(4) General Administration and Welfare, with eleven people.
(5) Publicity and Education, which employed about six full-time people and ran a spare-time school setup in 1953.
(6) Organizational Techniques, with six people. This department deals with inventory handling, warehousing and storage, reordering stocks, counter displays, high-speed calculating abacuses, packing

methods, sales techniques, introduction of new products, ways to improve customer service, and the dissemination of advanced experiences and methods throughout the store. The idea for a department of this type was originated by the Shanghai Bureau of Commerce in 1953. In 1966 there was a department of this kind at the commerce bureau and at the Shanghai branch of the China General Department Store Corporation, as well as at this store.

The Shanghai No. 1 Department Store had seven major sales sections and fifty-four sales groups each headed by a group leader. The seven major sales sections were textiles; clothing; underwear, socks, and pajamas; cosmetics; hardware and electrical items, and furniture; "cultural" goods, such as watches, clocks, musical instruments, sporting goods, stationery, and books; handicrafts and local products, including enamelware, arts and crafts, toys, hats, and shoes.

Each sales section was broken down into a number of sales groups. For example, there were five sales groups just for shoes, including those for children, and other footwear of leather, plastic, rubber, and cloth. The store also had four auxiliary shops employing a total of 400 people. These shops were tailoring, sewing of children's clothing, watch repair, and one for making socks, pajamas, underwear, kerchiefs, and hats.

The store has only a very general and tentative annual plan. Its key operating plan is the semiannual plan, and particularly the quarterly subdivisions of this plan which may be revised each quarter. The semiannual plan is essentially a circulating plan mainly in financial terms indicating sales, supply, working-capital, and inventory levels. The quarterly plan spells out values for each product group and detailed varieties. In general, considerably less emphasis seems to be placed on physical-commodity planning at Chinese retail stores than at industrial enterprises, and the stores appear to have substantially more independence in working out and executing their plans. The Shanghai Department Store's plan is approved by the Shanghai branch of the China Department Store Corporation, with certain items, such as employment and wages, requiring the approval of the Shanghai Bureau of Commerce. In 1966 the store's plan for the second quarter was approved in early April. It was working on its third-quarter plan when I visited there, and it was expected to be approved at the beginning of July.

I was told that the following data and major criteria were used in preparing the store's overall sales and product-mix plans.

(a) Information on general-market and sales analysis provided by the Shanghai branch corporation and the Shanghai Bureau of Commerce.

(b) Projected levels of Shanghai purchasing power, taking into account levels of industrial and agricultural production in the vicinity.
(c) Projected market share of the store in Shanghai's retail trade.
(d) Post-annual, semiannual, and quarterly sales of the store, and for Shanghai's retail sector as a whole. Data provided by several agencies, including the store's direct superiors, and Shanghai's Municipal Planning Commission, Finance Bureau, and Statistics Bureau.
(e) Data and forecasts generated within the store. Each sales section and group arrives at proposed aggregate-sales figures and then details product-mix forecasts for each planned period.

The store also engages in a number of other marketing-research and product-planning activities. It sends out questionnaires periodically to customers asking them about products they have bought, suggestions for improvements, and ideas for new products. Salesmen and even managers frequently obtain opinions and suggestions orally from customers regarding products and service. There are also customer suggestion books readily available on the sales counters. I saw several such books and examined a few of them. In the textile section's book seven suggestion forms had been filled out on the previous day, and about an average of two to eight forms had been filled out each day during the first half of May 1966. Some recorded suggestions had recently been implemented. For instance, one customer suggested that rubber be placed on the bottom of hot serving dishes so that they wouldn't ruin furniture that they were placed on. The store discussed this with the local manufacturer who has since been putting rubber on the bottom of some of its products. One sales section that I spent some time in—this happened to be for cultural goods—had received over a dozen unsolicited postcards and letters from customers that week. Some were critical, while others praised the store and its products or offered suggestions.

The store also organizes meetings two or three times a year with its suppliers, customers, and representatives from industry to discuss product improvements and new product ideas. There are special new-product counters in the store where new items are demonstrated, often by personnel. Since the beginning of 1966 the store had been sending representatives to the homes of customers, to nearby rural areas, and to local factories to give suggestions and information regarding product improvements and new products. In February 1966 a vice director, a party official, and a group of sales people from the store joined a group of employees from nearby enamel- and aluminum-ware factories and went to a local county with the aim of serving the product needs of the peasants better. An average of twenty cadres were being sent from Shanghai factories each week to work as salesmen in the store so that they could get to know better the needs of the ultimate consumers of their products.

The store does not do much advertising because as the acting director stated, "we are usually very busy anyway." Attractive window displays and counter merchandising are the main sales-promotion appeals utilized. Customer delivery service is contracted out to local cartage firms.

I was given the following information about the store's sources of supply. About 75 percent of its merchandise is negotiated with, and comes directly from, the wholesale departments of Shanghai's ten commercial wholesaling corporations. For example, batteries are supplied by the Shanghai Electrical Equipment Commercial Corporation. Approximately 15 percent comes directly from local factories. This 15 percent includes in part such products as leather and cloth shoes, sweets, pots and pans, arts and craft items, and various kinds of furniture. Another 7 percent comes from wholesale stations in other cities, and detailed supply contracts for these goods are usualy negotiated at national order meetings. The store obtains about 2 percent of its merchandise by sending representatives to producers in other cities and towns to buy such relatively minor items as Peking vases, Fukien lacquerware, porcelain, embroidery, and other local native products. The remaining 3 percent or so comes from the store's own production and processing shops.

The store usually participates in national order meetings twice a year and in local meetings of this type from time to time as well. The national meetings are attended by representatives from all levels of China's overall domestic trade sector, but few, if any, industrial people attend. The meetings are organized by the China General Department Store Corporation and are usually held in Shanghai, Tientsin, Peking, or Canton. Over a thousand people attend, and the meetings generally last from seven to ten days. There are many product exhibits, with samples of new products put on display and demonstrated. The store negotiates supply orders involving various key commodities with representatives of the wholesale stations in other cities. Supply orders involving products considered to be of lesser importance are negotiated directly with the commercial corporations of other cities. For example, for Canton's products the store deals with a Canton wholesale station for soap and toothpaste and with Canton commercial corporations for such relatively minor items as hardware and belts. The store usually signs semiannual contracts with its suppliers at the national order meetings, while most of its other contracts are signed quarterly, and in some cases more often.

The retail prices of the majority of the products carried by the store are set by the Shanghai branch of the China Department Store Corporation. Central authorities—the Ministry of Commerce and the Price Commission under the State Council—set national retail prices for a few key items, such as cotton and certain foods. The Shanghai Municipal Price Commission is consulted on the prices charged for some of the store's products and sets a few of them itself. The prices of some types of new products require the approval of the Shanghai Bureau of Commerce. The store determines the prices of some items, such as the clothes it tailors and various other products it makes. Charges for watch repairs are standard throughout Shanghai.

The store can recommend retail-price changes. It does recommend price cuts quite often, which must be approved by the appropriate higher agency, but it rarely proposes price increases. I was told that price cuts are undertaken fairly often, usually when significant inventory gluts arise or when products become obsolete. The store can independently discount expensive damaged or substandard products up to a maximum of 500 yuan. For less expensive items the limits are lower.

Ideology dictates that the store must adhere to three basic "taking part-ins."

(1) Participation of salesmen and other workers in management through elected representative meetings, convened at least quarterly, and special meetings whenever the need arises.
(2) Participation of cadres in sales and physical labor. (Store managers and party officials were spending a half day each week as salesmen and another half day in office clerical work or other forms of essentially manual labor. Cadres were also being sent to the store every Thursday from the Shanghai Bureau of Commerce and the Shanghai branch of the China Department Store Corporation to engage in sales work and manual labor.)
(3) Participation of the store's customers in product planning and service improvement through the devices indicated above.

Peking Department Store

Peking Department Store, which I visited for a day in connection with my research, is the largest retail store in Peking. Many of the things that I learned about the Shanghai Department Store No. 1 apply to this store, as well as to the Tientsin Department Store, and there is no need to repeat identical data.

The Peking Department Store, a five-story modern building with elevators, was established in 1955. In 1966 it had a total area of 22,000 square meters, half of which was selling space. The store sold about 22,000 varieties of products. In 1965, sales totaled 60 million yuan, and profits 7.2 million. No significant difference in sales or profits was planned for in 1966. In 1965 year-end inventories on hand totaled 8 million yuan.

During the fall and spring months the store was open from 9 A.M. to 9 P.M. weekdays, thirty minutes more on Saturdays and thirty minutes less on Sundays. In the summer the store remained open until 9:30 P.M. on weekdays, and in the winter only until 8:30 P.M. There were two shifts, and employees were working a six-day, forty-eight-hour week.

In 1966 the store was employing 1,600 people, of whom 1,000 were sales personnel, 40 were managers, and 200 were tailors, sewers, and workers in the store's own workshops. The average basic monthy wage was 60 yuan, the minimum was 30, and the director and party secretary received the top pay of 100 yuan. The top pay for salesmen, sales chiefs, and department heads was 80 yuan. The minimum pay for cadres was 50 yuan. The store had a bonus fund amounting to 7 percent of its total wage funds, and bonuses were paid monthly on three grades—10, 5, and 2 yuan. I was told that "most" of the employees were not very happy about the extra-reward system since it tended to stress selfish interests, and hence they were seriously considering putting an end to it.

Ten of the store's 1,600 employees were university graduates, none in technical or scientific fields. None of the top executives had a higher education. There were a few semiprofessional graduates who had majored in finance, accounting, economics, or trade.

About 15 percent of the store's employees were party members. There were ten members, including one salesman, on the store's party committee.

The store was under the Peking Bureau of Commerce, and I am not sure if it had a relationship with the China General Department Store Corporation or its local branch. There were four major administrative departments in the store:

(1) Finance and accounting, which also handled labor and wages.
(2) Vocational, which dealt with planning, buying, selling, inventories, and pricing.
(3) General administration.
(4) Trade union, whose functions I am not sure of. All of the store's salesmen were union members.

There were the following ten sales sections in the store, each one containing a number of sales groups:

(1) Groceries and toiletries
(2) School supplies
(3)–(6) Clothing of all types
(9)–(10) Higher-value goods, such as TV sets, radios, sewing machines, furniture, art work, cameras, watches, and bicycles

There were twenty people in the average sales group. In each group salesmen were responsible for six basic tasks: (a) supply ordering and sales; (b) property care; (c) statistics regarding sales, commodities, and inventories; (d) prices; (e) displays and cleanliness; (f) customer service and correct attitudes.

The store's annual and quarterly plans were approved by the Peking Commerce Bureau, while its monthly plan was made independently at the store itself. The few general financial targets which summarize its annual plan were usually approved in January each year. The following targets required higher approval annually with a formal review each quarter:

(1) Total sales in yuan
(2) Total commodity supply in yuan
(3) Total value of inventories
(4) Total profits
(5) Total expenses
(6) Total working capital
(7) Capital investment
(8) Total payroll and number of employees

Sales and product planning, marketing research, and sales promotion were handled in pretty much the same way as at the Shanghai Department Store, although the latter seemed to have more know-how in these areas.

Peking Department Store obtained about 60 percent of its merchandise from local commercial corporations under the Peking Commerce Bureau. It bought such merchandise from the corporations directly or through their warehouses on the basis of predetermined factory orders in many cases, but for a number of products sales from warehouses did not require prearranged factory orders. About 20 percent of the store's merchandise was purchased directly from local factories in many, but far from all, cases, with the required approval of the commerce bureau. Such merchandise included such items as clothing, arts and crafts, toys, furniture, and groceries. The store undertook product-quality control checks at its factory suppliers from time to time. The detailed varieties of direct factory purchases were negotiated on the basis of aggregate commodity allocations approved by appropriate higher commercial and industrial authorities. For various minor items such higher approval was not necessary.

The remaining 20 percent of the store's supply came from other cities and was negotiated at national, and in some cases regional, order meetings and related exhibitions. These order meetings were said to be generally held in February and May each year. The store negotiated and signed its own contracts with wholesale stations and commercial corporations of other cities at the order meetings, and sent copies of the contracts to the Peking Bureau of Commerce. The top manager of the Peking Department Store was quite candid about the problems of localism and obtaining needed products from other cities when they are not in abundant supply. He admitted that central trade authorities, including the Ministry of Commerce, were by no means always effective in coping with such problems.

Price setting of this store's products was handled in more or less the same way as at the Shanghai store that I surveyed. I was told that price changes are quite common at the Peking store. Often when the retail prices of certain items were reduced, the prices of fast-moving or better-quality goods were increased in order to keep the financial plan in balance. The store manager could reduce the price of substandard and damaged products up to a maximum of 500 yuan per purchase for expensive items. Sales section heads could make such reductions up to a maximum of 50 yuan. When price cuts of this type were made, the store got an adjustment from the factory or the wholesaler, who in turn received a credit from the factory.

Even when the store bought directly from the factory it generally paid the wholesale rather than the factory price. Then appropriate debits and credits were made with the commercial corporation that handled the types of products involved. However, for some varieties, such as toys and minor hardware items, the store paid the factory selling price.

Tientsin Department Store

I did not learn as much about this store as I did about the Peking and Shanghai department stores. Hence, my comments will be very brief, focusing on a few statistics.

The Tientsin Department Store, Tientsin's largest retail outlet, had about 23,000 product varieties in stock in 1966. It was employing 1,000 people, of whom 40 were managers and 870 were salesmen. Sales totaled 25 million yuan in 1965. The store had six floors devoted to sales, each one being supplied chiefly by a different municipal commercial corporation. The store was directly under the Tientsin Bureau of Commerce.

Over 70 percent of the store's merchandise was produced in Tientsin or neighboring counties in the same province. Central organizations were involved in the allocation of the other 30 percent or so.

The average monthly wage at the store was 50 yuan, the minimum was 30 yuan, and the maximum, received by a vice director and a veteran salesman, was 100 yuan. As mentioned earlier, extra monetary rewards were abolished at this store in late 1965.

All in all, I was surprised and impressed by the merchandise and activities at the Chinese department stores that I visited, especially in view of the fact China is both poor and communist.

CHAPTER 12

Communist China's Red Capitalists

ON MY VISIT to Shanghai in May 1966 it was indeed disconcerting for me to be picked up by a native Chinese capitalist in a new Jaguar, taken to his large factory for a day of discussions, and later to his sumptuous home, where he still lives as a wealthy industrialist does in a capitalistic nation. Mr. Wu Tsung-i, my Chinese Communist capitalist acquaintance, not only lives like a capitalist but also looks like a capitalist and, at times, still thinks and acts like a capitalist. Wu, who went to college in England, admits that he has not yet been completely remolded into a good Maoist Socialist man. However, he does not talk like a capitalist. In fact, he is verbally enthusiastic about the joys of communism—the Maoist brand, of course—and has much to say about the evils of capitalism (not to mention Soviet revisionism).

Mr. Wu is one of the four native capitalists I met in Red China, a land where some 300,000 capitalists still receive interest—also referred to as dividends—on their former business investments, and where many of them still hold managerial positions at their nationalized firms which are called joint state-private enterprises.[1] Most of China's capitalists are small businessmen or shopkeepers, but there are also many industrial capitalists, a sizable number of whom are wealthy managers of their large-scale nationalized firms.

In spite of the Great Proletarian Cultural Revolution—which became greatly intensified after I left China in June 1966—it is likely that Wu and his fellow Red capitalists (particularly the industrial capitalists) will continue to live and work in about the same way that they have under the Communist regime. Perhaps they will continue in this way until they die.

For these capitalists have served, and are likely to continue to serve, useful purposes for the Red Chinese regime.

It is true that during the fanatical Red-Guard and other Super-Red rampages angry wall posters and official party publications on occasion attacked the existing Chinese capitalists as being evil remnants of feudalism and bureaucratic monopoly capitalism. They demanded, among other measures, an end to the capitalists' high salaries, dividends on investments, and officially sanctioned political party (the Democratic Party). It is also true that youthful mobs paraded men in dunce caps hung with placards reading "Dirty Capitalists." In some instances the men thus paraded actually were capitalists—most were party deviants and intellectuals—and one was a leading commercial capitalist, the president of the Wing On Retail Department Store in Shanghai, China's largest joint state-private retail organization. However, there were only a few concrete reports that actual capitalists were overtly abused during the recent upheavals, and as far as I know, no industrial capitalists were so abused.

Before returning to the world of Mr. Wu and other individual Red Chinese capitalists, it may be well to consider briefly the general topic of Chinese capitalists and joint private-state enterprises in historical perspective.[2]

The Rise and Fall of Private Enterprise in Communist China

When the Communists came to power in 1949, the regime differentiated between two types of capitalists: (a) "bureaucratic" and (b) "national," or "nationalistic." The bureaucratic (monopoly) capitalists were typified by the very rich "big four" Kuomintang families, the Soongs, Kungs, Chiangs and Chens, and their close associates in industry, commerce, banking, and politics who formed an interlocking directorate of government and business. They controlled large business monopolies and had great powers in Chiang Kai-shek's corrupt regime. Most of the bureaucratic capitalists fled China; those few who remained behind were typically killed or imprisoned. All of the assets of this type of capitalist were expropriated outright by the Communists without compensation.

The national capitalists may or may not have had big businesses, but they did not actively or strongly support the Chiang Kai-shek regime or play a very significant role in politics. At the outset of the Communist takeover, the Red regime encouraged the national capitalists to stay on and run their businesses, and even to expand their enterprises and establish new ones. The regime also did much to persuade those who fled China to return home and run their companies. These capitalists were assured good treatment, their old incomes and assets, and an important role in building a socialist economy with the help of "state capitalism." Although tens of thousands of respectable businessmen did flee China because of the Communist takeover, many did return, and by far the majority stayed in Red China.

During the 1949–52 period large numbers of private firms—mostly small ones—were established and expanded not only in traditional sectors, but also in such enterprises as iron foundries, coal mines, machinery plants, and so on. However, under the type of state capitalism that emerged in the private sector the government and party exerted more and more control. Private industrial firms became increasingly dependent on the state for the allocation of resources and customer orders. Private retail and wholesale enterprises also had to rely on state allocations for their merchandise. The state also played a growing role in price fixing, determining wage rates and working conditions, and various other managerial activities. Worker councils were set up at private factories under trade-union and party direction, and they played a major role in enterprise management. The capitalist owners had to negotiate and gain approval from these worker councils on numerous matters. Although private enterprises and their owners could still keep much of their profits, the amount of profit realized was, in effect, largely under the state control. In reality, private industrial enterprises became essentially processing plants for the state, and commercial organizations became state distribution channels. Nevertheless, with the end of the civil war resulting in political and economic stability, and various other environmental improvements, private-sector output and economic performance increased and improved substantially in the early 1950's.

But in early 1952 the Chinese capitalists were confronted with their first really serious disillusionment. At that time the "Five-Anti's" campaign, or the "Wuhan Movement," was launched primarily against the bourgeoisie and private enterprise, and this campaign provided the first hint that the transition from state capitalism to state ownership would be much briefer than the more optimistic capitalists had supposed. This campaign was officially proclaimed as a movement to wipe out bribery of officials, tax evasion, fraud in fulfilling state contracts, theft of state assets, and theft of official secrets, but one of its real chief aims was to speed up the transformation of private enterprises into joint private-state and pure state ownership.

The charges during the Five-Anti's Campaign were framed so that relatively few private firms—including the innocent—escaped prosecution and sanctions. More than 450,000 private businesses were investigated in China's nine biggest cities. Capitalist offenders found guilty were heavily fined, had to pay back taxes, lost more, if not all, of their managerial powers and influence, and in many cases were imprisoned—a few even apparently "disappeared." [3] This forced many of them out of private business entirely or at least depleted their resources enough to force them to accept capital from the state, thus becoming participants in joint private-state enterprises. During this campaign the state also used many other coercive tactics to speed up the "voluntary" decline of private enterprise. They included labor agitation, withholding of supplies, boycotts of the firm's products, and humiliation of capitalists. Here was an onslaught against a class as a whole, but, in contrast to what happened to the gentry on the land, the bourgeoisie was not obliterated as a class.

In October 1953, after the Five-Anti's Campaign subsided, having taken its toll, Peking summoned a national congress of representatives of private industry and commerce and announced that the private sector was to be completely absorbed by the state without compensation—a process envisaged then as spreading over about fifteen years. From 1954 the party press continuously attacked capitalist incompetence, mismanagement, and exploitation, and this campaign was greatly intensified during 1955.

In 1956 the regime made it clear that all remaining private industrial enterprises that could be labeled as factories, and virtually all private commercial organizations would be transformed to joint status by the end of that year. (This did not, however, include a million or so individual operators engaged in "petty private enterprise" to be discussed shortly.) In June 1956 the regime adopted legislation providing for annual dividend (interest) payments to the capitalists amounting to 5 percent of the value of their invested capital as assessed by appointed committees under state and party control. These dividends were to be paid quarterly for seven years, until the end of the Second Five-Year Plan in 1962.

The regime did stick to its interest-payment commitments to the capitalists with few exceptions. (Apparently in some cases the interest rate was cut, typically "voluntarily," to 4½ percent, private investment upon which such payments were computed were reassessed downward, and/or capitalists were paid off in part with nonredeemable government bonds.) In fact, although the interest payments to capitalists were supposed to terminate at the end of 1962, they were renewed in 1962 for three more years—until 1965. After that time the situation was to be further considered. At the time that I was in Red China, the capitalists were still receiving interest on their capital, and some of those whom I met expected this to continue in the future. To date there are no available indications that such payments have been terminated.

While the regime has, by and large, more than stuck to its end of the bargain with regard to interest payments to capitalists, the initial valuations of their capital assets—upon which actual interest payments have been based—were no doubt greatly understated in many cases. About 80 percent of Shanghai's private firms received an assessed capital value of 2,000 yuan ($800) or less, providing their owners with annual dividends of 100 yuan ($40) or less.[4] A Chinese capitalist who escaped from Red China in 1957 claims that the three mills that he managed were actually worth 18 million yuan, but the state valued them at only 4 million yuan. Subtracted from this 4 million was 600,000 yuan in fines levied for embezzlements "confessed" by the owners during the Five-Anti's Campaign. Hence, the owners of these mills received less than 20 percent of the interest that they were really entitled to—but still this came to 170,000 yuan ($68,000) per annum, an immense sum in Communist China.[5]

Under the joint state-private enterprise setup numerous capitalists were urged to stay on as managers at their nationalized firms (usually at their former salaries), but they were to do so under state direction and party leadership. In addition to a party secretary, directors and vice directors were appointed by the state to run these firms.

During 1956 virtually all of the remaining private enterprises applied for joint ownership. Prior to 1956 the switch to joint ownership was made enterprise by enterprise, but in 1956 whole trades and branches of industry, locality by locality, were changed in large batches from private to joint ownership. By September 1956 Chou En-lai stated that 99 percent of former private firms had been nationalized. By the end of 1956 virtually no enterprise larger than a small shop remained private. The transformation from state capitalism to state ownership had in effect been completed. During this process tens of thousands of private firms had been merged, broken up, or transformed directly into joint state-private firms.

Table 12–1 indicates the short-lived rise and plummeting decline—to virtual extinction—of China's private sector under the Communist regime, and the rise of the joint state-private sector. This table shows that the number of private industrial enterprises and total employment therein rose during the 1949–53 period, started declining in 1954, fell very sharply during 1956, and virtually disappeared by the end of 1957. Larger private firms were initially the prime target for nationalization. In 1954 two-thirds of China's 134,000 private factories were small handicrafts workshops—in most cases with no modern power equipment at all—employing less than ten people, and only about 12 percent of all private firms were classified as "large scale"(these probably employed at least a hundred people and/or used some power equipment).

Private industry's share of China's total industrial production by value fell steadily from 39 percent in 1952 to 16 percent in 1956, then to almost zero in 1956. The same patterns emerged in the private wholesale and retail trade sectors during this period, although the private retail sector was still accounting for 3 percent of China's total retail trade as of the end of 1957. Many tiny owner-managed retail shops employing only one or a

TABLE 12–1

Statistics on Red China's Private and State and Private Enterprises

(All figures are as of year's end)

	1949	1950	1951	1952	1953	1954	1955	1956	1957
Private enterprise's share of total value of industrial output[a] (%)	n.a.	n.a.	n.a.	39.0	36.8	24.9	16.2	.1	—
Private enterprise's share of total value of wholesale trade[a] (%)	n.a.	n.a.	n.a.	36.3	30.3	10.2	4.4	—	—
Private enterprise's share of total value of retail trade[a] (%)	n.a.	n.a.	n.a.	57.8	50.3	26.4	17.5	3.0	3.0
Number of private industrial establishments[b] (thousands)	123	133	148	150	150	134	117	89	1
Employment in private industry[b] (thousands)	1644	1816	2023	2057	2231	1796	1310	14	—
Individual (self-employed) handicraftsmen[b] (thousands)	5766	6969	7118	7136	7488	7697	5996	597	670
Number of joint state-private industrial establishments[b] (thousands)	.193	.294	.706	.997	1.04	1.74	3.19	32.17	n.a.
Employment in joint state-private industry[b] (thousands)	105	131	166	248	270	533	785	2386	n.a.

n.a. = data not available
— = negligible or 0

[a] T. C. Liu and K. C. Yeh, *The Economy of the Chinese Mainland* (Princeton: Princeton University Press, 1965), p. 15, Table 1. Private industrial production excludes output of handicrafts cooperatives and individual handicraftsmen.

[b] J. Emerson, "Employment in Mainland China: Problems and Prospects," *An Economic Profile of Mainland China*, Vol. II (Washington: prepared by the Joint Economic Committee of U.S. Congress; published by U.S. Government Printing Office, 1967), pp. 427–28, Tables 3 and 4.

few people—usually members of the same family—were permitted to stay in business. I came across some shops of this type in Red China. They typically sold such things as candy, cigarettes, pots and pans, brooms, minor utensils, small handicrafts, glassware, furniture (often used), decorations, and minor clothing articles.

As for joint state-private enterprises, Table 12–1 indicates that their number and total employment increased steadily during the 1949–55 period, and then jumped greatly in 1956. Such growth was achieved primarily through the creation of relatively large-scale joint firms. For example, in 1952, of the 997 joint firms in existence 820 were classified as large-scale, and by 1954, 1,603 of the existing 1,744 joint enterprises were large-scale. Joint state-private industry's share of China's total industrial production by value was negligible in 1949 and the early 1950's, but it accounted for about 30 percent in 1956.[6]

During my trip to China in 1966 I was told that roughly 30 to 35 percent of all textile mills in Shanghai were still joint state-private enterprises, while in Tientsin and Peking their proportion approximated 25 to 30 percent. In these three cities, as well as a few others, such as Canton and Wuhan, sizable numbers of various other kinds of factories and many retail establishments were still joint state-private organizations. In Shanghai alone there are some 90,000 capitalists today.

Table 12–1 shows that the number of self-employed handicraftsmen increased quite substantially during the 1949–54 period, declined in 1955, and fell off dramatically by more than 90 percent in 1956. In the mid-1950's most of China's self-employed handicraftsmen were sent to work in handicrafts cooperatives and factories.

Table 12–1 does not take into account many of China's individual private entrepreneurs—if they can be so labeled—engaged in what the regime calls "petty private enterprise." In August 1960 Yao I-lin, Red China's Minister of Commerce, told Edgar Snow, the American writer, that there were still about a million people engaged in petty private enterprise but they contributed only a fraction of 1 percent of the nation's output. This group, or class, consisted of carters, carriers, peddlers, tradesmen, and various kinds of artisans and craftsmen, who make and sell minor items at their homes. I have already discussed these mini-capitalists in the sections on market size and factor endowment in Chapter 6.

The Strange World of China's Capitalists

Since the time that the Communists took over China, the regime has continually sought to remold the national capitalists into socialist men of correct thought and action through intensive and persistent thought reform, ideological education, and "persuasion." This remolding process has continued until the present day, and is discussed in vivid, chilling detail in a book by Robert Loh, the capitalist who escaped from Red China in 1957. A Chinese capitalist friend of mine who fled to Hong Kong in 1949 and now has a successful industrial firm there told me that although the Chinese Communists have not been inclined to kill their national capitalists physically they tend to kill them mentally and internally through the remolding process.

The Chinese Communists are almost always prepared to forgive and welcome the converted sinners into their midst—big cruel landlords and bureaucratic capitalists are among the few exceptions—but the conversion must be genuine and complete, at least in the eyes and minds of the party judges. Several of Red China's top leaders are of capitalist or otherwise bourgeois origin, and ex-Kuomintang leaders, direct spiritual descendants of the Manchu Dynasty, and quite a few capitalists occupy leadership position near the top. About a hundred and ten capitalists have been members of the National People's Congress in recent years, and twelve of them have been members of the standing committee of this congress. Hundreds more have been members of top-level municipal government bodies in those cities where there are sizable numbers of capitalists. Some specific examples of Red Chinese capitalists holding major government, but not party, posts will be presented later.

In general, the process of remolding capitalists is aimed chiefly at "transforming them from exploiters into working people living by their own labor." This remolding is conducted through intensive short-term and spare-time formal study programs conducted at special educational indoctrination centers, periodic formal and informal meeting and group therapy sessions both on and off the job at the capitalists' place of work, and through various other devices.[7] In the special formal programs, the topics covered include the evils of imperialism and bureaucratic capitalism, modern (Soviet) revisionism, speculation, self-interest, exploitation, and personal gain; the Constitution of the People's Republic of China; the party line; and the five-year plans.

"Progressive" capitalists who zealously support the party, at least outwardly, play key roles as lecturers and discussion leaders in the programs. They try to arouse patriotism and instill a law-abiding socialist spirit in the capitalist participants. Robert Loh was a progressive capitalist of this type before he fled from Red China. The All-China Federation of Industry and Commerce—which evolved from a type of national chamber of commerce during the Republican era—and its branches is in a number of major Red Chinese cities where there are sizable numbers of capitalists who have played a major role in conducting remolding programs for the capitalists. This federation is comprised of Chinese capitalists, plus a small number of party and government officials.

At their places of employment the capitalists must take part in intensive sessions of group or individual therapy and self-criticism—typically quite frequently. In committee meetings and other on-the-job activities the capitalists have often been made to criticize their own decisions, opinions, and advice by party cadres, state-appointed managers, and even workers when it has been felt that they (the capitalists) are thinking or behaving in an ideologically incorrect manner.

No doubt, among those capitalists labeled as "progressive"—and hence well along the socialist road—there are many whose reformation is expedient rather than genuine, and they must exercise great self-control. Among their comrades are self-appointed, as well as official, guardians of the faith, watching for deviation or regression with puritanical fervor. Furthermore, it is not easy to disguise one's inner thoughts when one meets with the same group of people regularly for purposes of political discussion and self-criticism. Silence at these discussion group sessions is usually not allowed. Everyone must put his thoughts and attitudes into words.

There are a sizable number of "progressive" large-scale Red capitalists who play prominent and important roles in the present life of their country. Those "elected" to government bodies are usually members of the Democratic Party, a party formed especially for capitalists because they cannot be Communist Party members. There have been indications in the Chinese and Western press that under the Cultural Revolution so-called "opposition" parties may be banned in China. This could include the capitalists' Democratic Party, although it has never really been an opposition party but rather merely an advisory body. There have not been any indications that the All-China Federation of Industry and Commerce—a more influential capitalist organization with regard to the regime's policies and economic plans—is to be liquidated.

Among the leading Red Chinese capitalists whom I know something about—in addition to Wu Tsung-i (who will be discussed shortly)—are the Yung brothers (H. J. and I. J. Yung) in Shanghai, T. K. Liu, another Mr. Liu, a second Mr. Wu, and one whose name I do not know whom James Duncan, a leading Canadian industrialist, met on one of his trips to China. Before their enterprises were nationalized, the Yung brothers were close business associates of the Mr. Wu who was my host, and they are still associated with the same joint state-private firms.[8] Yung I-jen has been vice mayor of Shanghai (in 1966 Shanghai had eleven vice mayors) and a vice member of the Ministry of Textile Industry for some time. He has also been general manager of the Sung Sing Textile Corporation in Shanghai. Yung Hung-jen, I.J.'s American-educated younger brother, is a member of the Shanghai Municipal Committee of the Chinese People's Consultative Conference as well as an industrial manager. The Mr. Wu whom I did not meet is a vice mayor of Shanghai and chairman of the Shanghai Federation of Industry and Commerce.[9] The capitalist whom James Duncan met is a scion of a great Chinese industrial family who, like his other brothers, was educated at Cambridge.[10] Under the Communist regime he has been responsible for the operation of more than fifty factories, and has been a member of the National People's Congress. One of his brothers, who lived in England for six years, has been a manager in many Shanghai industrial enterprises and organized a new watch industry several years ago which has been turning out some 850,000 watches a year.

Liu Tsing-Kee, a member of both the Shanghai Congress and the National People's Congress, is a leading textile tycoon, whose assets have included five major cotton mills (now jointly owned with the state), employing some 11,000 people, personal interest payments amounting to $400,000 annually, and a monthly salary of $300.[11] His family's total assets, including broad real-estate holdings, have been valued at $16 million. (In all the above cases 1 U.S. dollar = 2.5 yuan.) Mr. Liu did inherit much of his father's wealth several years ago, and since he was already a capitalist, there was apparently no social stigma involved. However, it is very likely that his own nine children will "refuse" to inherit his wealth when he dies. All of his children are college graduates, two are party members, and none are capitalists. He fled to Hong Kong in the late 1940's but returned home shortly after the Reds took over. He sent most of his capital out of China but brought it all back by 1954. His sumptuous home is filled with many three-hundred-year-old antiques—some as old as six hundred years. He employs four servants and has a chauffeur-driven Humber sedan. Another Mr. Liu, who is in the match business, gets $320,000 in interest annually and has also held various key state positions.[12]

In general, important progressive capitalists are, at times, allowed to travel abroad—usually to other socialist countries and without their families—and some of them even have foreign investments abroad (including factories, mostly in Hong Kong) from which they derive foreign exchange to buy imported goods, such as cars, appliances, clothing, jewelry, and works of art. In recent years the regime has apparently been exerting pressure on capitalists to give their foreign-exchange earnings to the state and to "donate" their more valuable art treasures and antiques to state museums. While the children of Red China's capitalists are legally entitled to inherit their family's wealth, there are strong social pressures applied, so that most of them renounce such an inheritance. The children of capitalists can become party members if they prove themselves to be ardent believers, but there are many strikes against them which they must overcome.

Let us now turn to the specific world of Mr. Wu Tsung-i.

The Case of My Cautious Capitalist Friend Mr. Wu

It is quite common for Westerners who go to Communist China—especially the city of Shanghai—to ask for, and be assigned, a Red capitalist to interview. You can usually get a choice of sizes ranging from tiny to giant-size capitalist. Since I had already read about a number of giant-size "progressive" Chinese capitalists, I requested a "fairly" big one, two medium-sized ones, and a fairly small one. Wu Tsung-i was assigned to me as the fairly large one, and my encounters and experiences with him were the most involved and by far the most interesting.

Before proceeding with an account of my encounters with Mr. Wu, I should make a few general comments about the Chinese capitalists whom foreigners are allowed to interview. There is no way of telling how sincere the capitalists, like Mr. Wu, who are interviewed by Westerners are about their dedication to the Red regime or how happy—or miserable—they are with their way of life under it. Mr. Wu seemed to be very sincere and convincing about his dedication and contentment, although he was apparently a bit more candid in some areas than other Red capitalists interviewed by Westerners. It is only because Mr Wu appeared to be a loyal supporter of Chairman Mao and the regime, as well as a remolded capitalist who said nothing ideologically out of order, that I do not hesitate to use his real name without fear of endangering his personal well-being.

However, I still have a strange intuitive feeling that Wu, as well as many, if not most, of the other Chinese capitalists interviewed by foreigners, do not express many of the key deep-down feelings that they have in their hearts and minds. I had this strange feeling even before I had read Robert Loh's book and article in the *Atlantic Monthly* which, in spite of evident biases, gave me a much deeper insight into what really goes on behind the façade of the world of China's progressive and remolded capitalists.[13] With very few exceptions, it was only with the Chinese capitalists, among all of the Red Chinese citizens interviewed, that I sensed that their answers and comments were in substantial part far from truthful or genuinely sincere. In his published works Lah describes in detail the process of selecting and intensively rehearsing the Red capitalists who meet with foreigners in such a way that the precise image desired by the regime is effectively put across. Given the experiences that China's national capitalists have gone through since the early 1950's, it is likely that in numerous cases—also involving "progressive" capitalists—their hearts and minds are filled with disillusionment, insecurity, fear, loss of dignity and self-respect, and much ambivalence.

Wu and many other Chinese capitalists are probably caught between two worlds, and I sincerely sympathize with them. On the one hand, I believe that they tend to feel that in numerous respects the present regime is much better for the country and for its people than the former highly inept one. Being basically patriotic, proud, and nationalistic, as most Chinese tend to be, they feel they should contribute what they can to their country, regardless of who is in power. Moreover, numerous Red Chinese capitalists still maintain their formal standards of living and collect dividends. This is certainly more than can be said for the fate of the capitalist class under the ruthless and murderous regime created by the Soviet revolution. Or, for that matter, of the "thought remolding" of the Bourbonists as carried out by the French guillotine. On the other hand, with very few exceptions China's capitalists are now mere cogs in a giant machine, with very little real freedom, prestige, or influence as compared with what they enjoyed in the past. In fact, they are, in a sense, freaks put on display for the local population as well as for visiting foreigners, such as myself. They are perpetually surrounded by party cadres and other people who tell them what they can and cannot do, what to say, whom to see, and even what to think. If they do not toe the line they will immediately be put through more thought remolding or otherwise be subject to harassment.

Let me now retell Mr. Wu's personal story and that of his firm. Mr. Wu is a distinguished and handsome gentleman in his early fifties; he is married and has four children. In the early 1930's he studied at Bolton Technical College in Manchester, England. He is quite representative of Red China's bigger industrial capitalists, but he is far from being the wealthiest, and he is not among the few most important or influential ones.

Before the Communist takeover, Wu and his family owned 30 percent of the Sung Sing Textile Corporation which controlled nine textile mills in Shanghai. They were the major owners of Mill No. 9, which I visited, and Wu was its general manager. He was also a vice general manager of the Sung Sing Textile Corporation, one of the largest textile mills in China, with 6,000 employees, 110,000 spindles, and over 1,000 looms, and the largest joint state-private one. The Yung family, referred to in the previous section, were the major owners of this corporation, which was founded with its first mill in 1915. During the 1915–35 period the corporation expanded to nine mills, and by 1935 it was the largest Chinese-owned national textile corporation with ten major shareholders, all in the Yung and Wu families, and several minor shareholders.

In 1936, shortly before the Japanese attack, Sung Sing's assets were 85 million old yuan, but the corporation had an outstanding bank debt of 82.6 million yuan. During the Japanese occupation Mr. Wu spent two months in jail. He was a strong nationalist, and this made him feel very insecure about himself and his country.

During 1946–49, after the Japanese defeat and before the Red Chinese victory, U.S. and Chinese bureaucratic capitalists controlled about 90 percent of China's cotton industry. The Sung Sing Corporation was virtually a mere processing plant for the monopolists, and virtually all of its profits went to them. During this period of skyrocketing inflation the monopolists and the Kuomintang demanded all of the corporation's output at a fixed price. In 1948 the general manager of the corporation was put in jail by the Kuomintang with no clear reason given for the action. The corporation paid a $150,000 bribe to the U.S. consulate in Shanghai to get him out after forty days.

After Japan was defeated, Wu felt he could not trust the corrupt and inept Kuomintang regime, but he also feared the Chinese Communists—he was not sure what the party's policies or aims were, and he believed that they were murderers, believed in free love, and were generally evil. In 1947 he began to send capital abroad—chiefly to Hong Kong—and in 1948 he took his whole family to Hong Kong. His business agent, a less successful capitalist, was left in charge of his factory as vice director and acting director.

In 1949, after the Communists took control of Shanghai, they did not confiscate his enterprise, and his business agent went to Hong Kong to see him. Wu came to Shanghai alone in late 1949. He then learned for the first time about the new regime's policy toward national capitalists and was encouraged to return to run his firm. He told me that he was classified as a national capitalist because he had bravely resisted the Japanese and was even jailed by them, and also because his business had suffered at the hands of the Kuomintang, bureaucratic capitalists, and foreign imperialists. In addition, he had a reputation as being relatively fair and humane with his workers.

In 1950 Wu returned permanently to Shanghai with his wife. They were joined by their children in 1951, but his father and some other relatives chose to stay behind. During the 1949–50 period his factory was still operating, but barely. The U.S. cotton embargo, and poor domestic cotton crops greatly depressed China's textile industry. Cotton was strictly rationed by the new regime, and the plant was allocated raw materials by the state. Management had to negotiate with the factory trade-union representatives in order to get government cotton contracts. Initially the plant was under the "armed" control of the workers, but subsequently a union-management committee, under party surveillance, was set up to run it.

In the early 1950's all of Red China's cotton industry was completely dependent on the state for raw material allocations, and textile firms were, in effect, merely processing plants for the state. In 1953, with the First Five-Year Plan, capitalist industry officially started its socialist transforma-

tion, and the first stage involved "state capitalism." Under state capitalism the government controlled all critical physical resources, prices, and distribution channels. In the same year the question of nationalization and joint state-private ownership was officially raised for the first time. It then became evident to Wu and his business associates that it would not be too long before state capitalism evolved into state ownership.

In 1954, because of pressure, and seeing the writing on the wall, the board of directors of the Sung Sing Textile Corporation applied for joint ownership. According to Wu, there were several reasons why the directors decided to apply rapidly for joint ownership. The chief ones were the following:

(a) To avoid worker and union-management conflicts, which they were sure would become serious if they did not soon take such action.

(b) All indications were that the state would hold back material allocations, restrict customers, organize boycotts, and exert other pressures against those private firms—particularly larger ones—that delayed in applying for joint ownership. Joint firms, on the other hand, could be expected to receive equal treatment with pure state enterprises. The directors took note that Sung Sing was prohibited in 1954 from supplying commodities to Shanghai's largest private retail department store, Wing On, or to other suppliers of this store, and the store itself was being subject to much mass picketing and boycotts.

(c) Party and government officials, using a variety of arguments and a proaches, persuaded the directors that to apply for joint owner as soon as possible was in their own and their corporation's interests.

(d) The directors felt that joint ownership was inevitable any by showing acceptance and even active support of th aims early they could expect to be much better off in t

In September 1955 Sung Sing's application for joint ow proved, and at the end of that year the state appointed tv and a new permanent party secretary to Wu's industri Sing Mill No. 9. Wu stayed on with the title of dire state-appointed vice directors was to be his counter Wu's business agent and seven other minor capi tively small number of shares in the corporation a jobs at their old salaries.

Here is what Wu told me about the valuati ration's and his own factory's assets in 1956 appointed managers, and worker represe

place a value on the assets for each of the corporation's enterprises, including Wu's, and for the corporation as a whole. The proposed values were then discussed with the Shanghai Textile Guild. Until the end of 1956 each industry where there were private firms had its own guild under the Federation of Industry and Commerce. These guilds were abolished and the federation was reorganized after the massive nationalization campaign of 1956. After discussing the asset-value figures with this guild, each plant and the corporation as a whole gave their value proposals to the Shanghai Bureau of Industry and Commerce, where they were compared with the current value of assets at state-owned factories. The final assessed values were formally approved by the Shanghai People's Council and the Shanghai Party Committee.

An approved value of roughly 50 million yuan ($20 million) was placed on the assets of the Sung Sing Corporation, and Mill No. 9 was valued at about 16 million yuan ($6.4 million). Wu's personal share in the corporation and this mill was placed at 1.6 million yuan ($640,000). Although members of his family—chiefly his father—owned about 30 percent of the corporation, they were not entitled to any compensation if they did not live in Communist China. Wu's father, who was about eighty years old in 1966, chose to remain in Hong Kong and give up his fortune entirely on the Chinese mainland. Apparently in such cases, family members and heirs living in Red China had no claim to such wealth, and the state wrote it off its books.

On his appraised capital, Mr. Wu was receiving 80,000 yuan ($32,000) annually—paid quarterly—since 1956. Wu told me that a major reason for the state's dividends payments to capitalists was so that "they could accept remolding with greater ease and security." I asked him whether his business assets were evaluated fairly, and he answered that "under the circumstances" his compensation was "reasonably just and adequate." He would not comment further on this subject. H. I. and J. I. Yung, who chose to stay in Communist China, were receiving much larger interest payments, as principal shareholders of Sung Sing, than Wu. The Yung family owned about 70 percent of this corporation.

Wu vividly described to me the big parade and two days of celebrations hat took place in late 1956 after virtually all remaining private firms of ny size had applied for joint ownership. The festivities were organized by e Shanghai Federation of Industry and Commerce, and similar events re held in other major cities. The capitalists and workers rejoiced toher since they all felt that they would enter a new era of harmonious ions and comradeship under the joint-enterprise setup.

ith the notable exception of the presence of former capitalist owners g as managers, joint state-private industrial firms are organized and e like state enterprises. At Wu's enterprise there were four vice di-

rectors when I visited there. One was a state appointee in charge of the whole plant; the other state-appointed vice director was in charge of welfare and general administration. The other two vice directors were capitalists: one was Wu's agent who was in charge of production and was also vice chief engineer; the other was in charge of supply and sales, and various other commercial activities. There were also six other relatively minor capitalists employed in this enterprise. Three of them were department heads or deputy heads, two were more minor white-collar cadres, and one was a workshop chief. None of those eight other capitalists were members of Wu's family.

All of these capitalists received their former salaries, which in each individual case came to substantially more than any of the other employees received. Mr. Wu received 380 yuan per month, the two capitalist vice directors about 350, and the other six capitalists from 220 to 350 yuan. However, the dividend payments were modest in all cases. The top-paid state employees were the party secretary and the other two vice directors who received 100 to 110 yuan per month. The average factory monthly pay was 78 yuan.

The capitalist general manager and former chief owner of the Tientsin Jen Yi Woolen firm, the other joint enterprise that I visited, was being paid 460 yuan per month, an even higher monthly salary than Wu's. He was one of the two medium-sized capitalists I met in China. However, his quarterly divident payments were only 1,275 yuan. There were four other capitalist ex-owners working at this Tientsin enterprise, and their quarterly dividends ranged from 91 to 363 yuan per month. Their monthly salaries ranged from about 100 to 160 yuan per month and all of them were employed in managerial jobs. I met the one who was employed as a deputy shop director at a salary of 160 yuan per month, and who received 363 yuan in dividends each quarter.

The "fairly" small Chinese capitalist I met was working as the manager of a rather small retail store which he used to own but which became a joint enterprise in 1956. The store was employing about sixteen people. The general manager was receiving a monthly salary of 90 yuan and quarterly dividends of about 45 yuan. He told me that, on the average, he had been making more money and living better and more securely under the Communist regime but that during some prosperous years before 1949 he had made more money.

The party and state appointees, and particularly the enterprise party committee, were in control at the two joint industrial firms that I visited. I am sure that this was typically the case at other joint enterprises as well. However, Wu and numerous other capitalists, because of their knowledge, experience, and skills, still play important roles in decision making, rendering advice, and generally in the management of their enterprises, although they are, of course, subject to the veto powers of party and state appointees. When the ideological pendulum swings in the direction of extremism, however, there probably tends to be much greater misutilization of the talents and know-how of the capitalists.

Some of the areas in which Wu seemed to play an important managerial, or at least advisory, role were maintenance scheduling and procedures, the introduction of new technology and production process and the reorganization of existing ones, economizing on material usage, and quality control. Even though Wu has been undergoing ideological education and remolding, and studying the works of Chairman Mao since 1951, he admits that he at times still "regresses" and behaves as he used to when his enterprise was privately owned. For example, he sometimes thinks in terms of maximizing profits at the expense of human welfare, or he wants to buy some components rather than make them in accordance with the current state policy of self-sufficiency at all levels of the economy. But fortunately, he points out, the enterprise party committee or the state-appointed director makes him see the errors in his thinking and potential behavior. In general, he seems to have more leeway in making technical decisions and in drawing up plans than in making decisions directly involving personnel matters.

Wu spends about the equivalent of three days each week on the average at his enterprise. The rest of his working time is spent in civic and political activities. As of 1966, he was active in the Democratic Party and was vice chairman of the Shanghai branch of the party. He was also an elected deputy of the National People's Congress and was on the executive committee of the Shanghai Federation of Industry and Commerce.

As of 1966, Wu was still allowed to keep the profits he earns from a textile firm in Hong Kong of which he is part owner. This is how he gets foreign exchange to buy imported goods, including his cars. He told me that the state had recently begun to "persuade" him to turn over all of his foreign-exchange earnings to the government and that he was "seriously considering this proposal." He has been free to travel to Hong Kong —always leaving his wife and children behind—several times a year on business, and to see his aging father. He also visited Russia in 1956 with a delegation of Chinese capitalists, and North Korea on another trip.

Wu lives with his attractive wife, who speaks English quite fluently, and four children in his original sumptuous home in the plush Su Wei district of East Shanghai, an elegant old area where many wealthy Chinese capitalists have lived, and still live. The house has about fourteen rooms, and several of the family's pre-1949 servants still work for them. He spends some of his income on luxury goods, antiques, art, and his coin and stamp collections. However, in recent years he has been "persuaded" to turn over some of his best antiques and works of art to the Shanghai

Museum; for this he gets award certificates from the Ministry of Culture. He admits that he cannot find ways to spend most of his money, so he banks it and earns about 3.3 percent interest on it. This life, he claims, is far better than his decadent life before Communism, when he and his capitalist friends "used to dance vigorously, gamble widely, drink too much and play around with women."

None of his four children wants his wealth when he dies because they want to be good Maoists and perhaps get into the party someday. His charming teenage daughter—then a high school senior—who played "Granada" for me on her Steinway piano, may not yet be fully remolded. He has another daughter who was twenty-two and still single. She was in medical school and a member of the Young Communist League. It seemed that she had a fairly good chance of getting into the party eventually. She was not at home when I visited there. He has a son in his twenties, who was studying physics at the university, and another boy in high school who briefly and reluctantly practiced his English on me. To me, those of Wu's children whom I met seemed to be quite respectful, and affectionate toward their parents. Whether this is really the case or whether this is part of a carefully constructed façade of the Chinese capitalist world, I shall never know for sure.

Why Has the Red Chinese Regime Kept Capitalism—and the Capitalists—Alive?

Many people have asked me why the Chinese Communists have behaved as they have toward the national capitalists while the Soviet Union liquidated or imprisoned most of their business capitalists. There seem to be several key reasons:

(1) The capitalists' experience, knowledge, and skill in running industry and business were seen as, and have proved to be, highly beneficial in Red China. This has been the case in spite of the gross misutilization of the capitalists' talents, especially during periods of ideological extremism and national anticapitalist campaigns. When the Chinese Communists took over, both the educational level of the population and native experience in running industries were substantially below those of the Soviet Union after its revolution. In addition, in general, industry has become much more complex in recent decades than it was in the 1920's and 1930's.

(2) The Red Chinese have probably felt that the numerous capitalists could be trusted because they were basically nationalistic. It is a fact that many of them did suffer at the hands of the old regime, the bureaucratic capitalists, and foreign interests. If given a fair chance, the Communist

regime felt that they could even be remolded into hybrid socialists. If such remolding proved to be effective, it would give the Communists and their supporters even greater confidence in the possibility of a remolded, pure Communist "One World," as conceived by Mao.

(3) The Chinese also felt secure about their revolution in the early stages because Russia was around to give them protection. They were not greatly worried that their capitalists, through contacts in capitalist countries, would be able to spearhead an effective counterrevolution—something that the Soviets had been concerned about in the Bolshevist revolution.

(4) By following the policies that they did, the Chinese regime also hoped to lure back many of the capitalists, professionals, and other talented people who had fled the country. In this respect they have apparently been quite successful.

(5) The regime felt that there could be good general propaganda value in displaying an image of a humane and fair government that allowed capitalists to coexist with Communists, at least in the short run.

(6) A very important reason pertains to the Maoist concepts of contradiction and class struggle. By having the capitalists live as they used to, the regime could keep various aspects of the past alive—for example, the relatively few "haves" living in splendor among masses of poverty-stricken "have nots." Today, as then, the Chinese Communists feel that contradictions or conflicts in society are good in that they keep people on their toes. By having the capitalists around, people can be kept "fighting" to wipe out all elements of bourgeois mentality and behavior. The capitalists give the regime a good, though largely impersonal, target for carrying out the class struggle and moving forward to the pure Maoist communist society.

(7) Finally, it is likely that only very few of the Chinese capitalists' children will lay claim to the inheritances left by their fathers. Therefore, the wealth and remaining assets of the capitalists will be taken over by the state in any case in the not-too-distant future.

As mentioned at the outset of this chapter, Red China's capitalists, especially the industrialists, were apparently subjected to little serious personal abuse during the Cultural Revolution and related purges. The reason is that the capitalists have relatively little real power in setting basic national policy or in influencing political affairs and are therefore no real threat. The purges involved mainly Communist Party and important government officials whose ideology was at variance with that of Mao and his more ardent supporters and who were secure enough and powerful enough to vie for key leadership positions.

Looking ahead, it seems likely that the present generation of Chinese capitalists will continue basically as at present because they will continue to serve the aims of the regime.

CHAPTER 13

Conclusion

Communist China has achieved substantial, if erratic, industrial progress and general economic development since 1949. The nation has done better with regard to industrial development than the Soviet Union did during its first two decades under communism, and substantially better than India to date. Very few poor countries in the world have done as well in economic growth or industrialization as China has since 1950.

There is no doubt in my mind that in 1966 when I was in China the average Chinese citizen was living substantially better—and could expect to live about twelve to sixteen years longer—than the average Chinese citizen did at any time before the Communists came to power. China currently has a significant lead over India in industrial and overall economic performance in both absolute and per capita terms. Moreover, China has gone substantially further than India in creating a *potential* overall environment conducive to sustained and substantial industrial progress and economic growth in the long run. The present development gap between China and advanced nations such as the Soviet Union, and especially the United States, is great in absolute terms, and much greater in per capita terms even when compared with Japan. However, I feel that China's potential in narrowing the gap between her and the advanced countries is substantially greater than that of India. China also is in a potential position to widen, probably substantially, the development gap between herself and India.

But in the final analysis, China's destiny—industrial, economic, and even military—and degree of fulfillment of her potential depend, in my opinion, chiefly on whether ideological extremism prevails or whether managerial, technical, and economic rationality becomes dominant. If ideological extremism is victorious and persists, the chances seem good that India will not only gain on China but will actually surpass her. However, if rationality wins out in China, she is likely to be the undisputed victor in the development race with India.

In general, there seems to be an inherent conflict between the pure ideology and the ultimate power and materialistic objectives that the Chinese Communist regime, as currently represented by the orthodox Maoists, desires to implement and achieve. The regime clearly wants China to be a leading world economic, political, and military power, with its ideology dominating the universe. In order to achieve such national and international power and influence, the Chinese domestic economy, and industry in particular, must develop on a sustained, broad, substantial, and impressive scale. The effectiveness of the industrial-management system is crucial because it is at the enterprise level, particularly on the factory floor, that the economic progress, power, wealth, and influence of a nation are so largely determined. However, key aspects of Red China's brand of Maoist-Marxist-Leninist ideology are in basic conflict with effective management and efficient enterprise performance and, hence, with the attainment of Peking's ultimate national and international objectives.

It is conceptually possible that the Chinese Communist Maoists may have discovered a magic tool which no other country has come upon. They may have a key which will allow ideology not only to create a pure philosophical state in reality but also to develop a leading world productive system at the same time. To date, all evidence indicates that the chances of this being true are very remote.

It is true that various aspects of Maoist-Marxist-Leninist ideology have had a significantly favorable impact to date on productivity and industrial development in Red China. It is also true that the Chinese have learned much from the Soviet Union's experiences and mistakes in industrial and general economic management. Yet, at the same time, the Chinese regime stubbornly tries to implement certain aspects of pure ideology which the Soviets have long abandoned because the ideas were found to be unworkable from a managerial, technical, or economic point of view.

There is the basic question of self-interest and monetary incentives, as opposed to pure altruism and nonmaterial stimuli. Centuries of world history and experience strongly indicate that the Chinese regime will not be able to eliminate self-interest and material gain as major motivating forces for managers, technicians, or workers, and at the same time achieve sustained and impressive industrial progress in the long run. If by some miracle they do succeed, this would have a very great philosophical and cultural impact on the functioning of the rest of the world. But I am betting against such a miracle. I am also betting against the workability of a classless society with no noticeable distinctions between managers and workers, superiors and subordinates, leaders and followers, experts and nonexperts, mental and physical work, and so forth.

There is also the crucial question of Red versus Expert—or ideology and politics versus managerial, technical, and economic rationality. If the Reds, and particularly the Super-Reds—represented by the Red Guards, the military purists, the people's militia, and newly formed "revolutionary" groups and committees—maintain the dominant upper hand in operational management as industry attempts to develop and grow more complex, this would surely lead to serious and pervasive efficiency problems, including stagnation in the economy and probably even regression at a certain point. It may be possible to develop a fairly large and adequate pool of managers and technicians who are both ardent Red ideologists and effective Experts, but this would take decades and may prove extremely difficult. Finally, managerial effectiveness and economic performance are also the chief losers when an excessive amount of time is spent on political education and ideological indoctrination at industrial enterprises or, for that matter, at higher industrial levels or regular educational institutions.

The Chinese Communist regime constantly accuses the Soviets of being "modern revisionists," "ideological heretics," and much worse. Some of my Soviet acquaintances who consider themselves to be good Communists ardently insist that it is the Chinese Maoists who are the real revisionists and heretics. Their rationale or argument runs basically like this.

Marx envisaged the pure communist state emerging gradually in an evolutionary manner after the dictatorship of the proletariat was established and when the state (that is, the government) had "withered away." There is nothing inherently wrong—in this (very long) interim period—with using material incentives; or with paying people according to their productivity, skill, individual contributions, and/or achievements; or having some people living better than others; or putting an expert, or the best man in general, in a managerial, technical, or other type of job requiring certain skills, abilities, or other qualifications; or from isolating political education from productive-work requirements.

If such practices help to build a strong and affluent country, the state will wither away that much sooner, and then the great Marxian concept of "from each according to his ability" and "to each according to his needs" will become a reality. At that time, in a utopia of abundance, with machines doing virtually all of the mundane and physical work, everybody would be well educated, selfless, altruistic, classless, and free from status consciousness, hostility, exploitation and insecurity.

But the Red Chinese fanatics are following a blindly revolutionary, grossly impatient, and irrational course in the implementation of ideology and economic development; theirs is not the evolutionary approach envisaged by Marx. They will never achieve the utopian society in this way because they cannot become sufficiently strong or affluent. This view coincides with the typical Soviet reasoning regarding Red China and her ideology.

In my opinion, you cannot convince any true fanatic or extremely ardent irrational believer that he is wrong about his ideology or theology. I therefore believe that the orthodox Chinese Communist leaders will not readily moderate their inflexibility. I do not think that the Soviets, on the other hand, are, in general, the fanatics, blind believers, or rigid dogmatists that they may have been at one time; and for this reason they have become, and will continue to be, a leading world power.

It remains to be seen if, how, or when the Red Chinese will come to grips with their ideological dilemmas. If they do not resolve this basic difficulty, it is very unlikely that they can achieve their national and international objectives of economic and political power; truly effective international military power in the long run would also require a relatively strong and effective economy. If Communist China does ever evolve into a truly first-rate power, it would appear that some of the more important aspects of pure Maoist-Marxist ideology would have to be abandoned, or at least greatly compromised in the process.

NOTES

Chapter 1

1. The classification scheme used to describe the overall managerial task and Table 1–1 of this chapter are for the most part taken from R. Farmer and B. Richman, *Comparative Management and Economic Progress* (Homewood, Illinois: Richard D. Irwin, Inc., 1965), Chap. 2. This book contains extensive documentation of other sources from which the categorization of the critical elements of the management process has evolved. See also R. Farmer and B. Richman, *International Business: An Operational Theory* (Homewood, Ill.: Richard D. Irwin, Inc., 1966).
2. This concept of micromanagement and macromanagement was first presented in B. Richman, *Soviet Management: With Significant American Comparisons* (Englewood Cliffs, New Jersey: Prentice-Hall, 1965), Chap. 1; and B. Richman and R. Farmer, "Ownership and Management: The Real Issues," *Management International,* Vol. V, No. 1, 1965.
3. Market corrections depend in part on the degree of market concentration in the industry. Monopolies and oligopolies can often resist adjustments more successfully than firms in more competitive markets. See J. F. Due and R. W. Clower, *Intermediate Economic Analysis,* 3d ed. (Homewood, Ill.: Richard D. Irwin, Inc., 1961), pp. 185–294, for an extended discussion of enterprise behavior under various competitive conditions.

   Union pressure, government regulations, and technical constraints may also tend to make rapid adjustment difficult.
4. Hence, the notion of satisficing rather than maximizing in managerial decision making has evolved in recent years. H. Simon, *Administrative Behavior,* 2d ed. (New York: Macmillan, 1961), p. xxv and Chaps. IV and V.
5. A. Berle and G. Means, *The Modern Corporation and Private Property* (New York: Macmillan, 1932); A. Berle, *Power Without Property* New York: Harcourt, Brace and World, 1959), esp. Chap. XI.
6. This concept of contributions and inducements evolves from Chester Barnard's concept of organizational equilibrium; see his *Functions of the Executive* (Cambridge: Harvard University Press, 1938, 1962). See also H. Simon, *op. cit.,* Chap. IV.
7. Such conflicts of economic and noneconomic issues are debated at great length by economists and others. See P. A. Samuelson, *Economics,* 6th ed. (New York: McGraw-Hill, 1964), particularly Chaps. III, IV, VII, and VIII.
8. For an intriguing discussion on hypothetical capitalist economic system with absolutely free competition see L. Von Meses, *Human Action: A Treatise on Economics* (New Haven: Yale University Press, 1949).
9. For an interesting discussion on Walrus see Due and Clower, *op. cit.* W. Leontief's major study is *The Structure of the American Economy,* 1919–1939 (New York: Oxford University Press, 1951).
10. In 1953 there were some 175,000 industrial firms in China, of which about 83 percent were small-scale. In 1955, after many consolidations, there were still

about 125,000 industrial enterprises, and the percent of small-scale ones declined somewhat. See D. Perkins, *Market Control and Planning in Communist China* (Cambridge: Harvard University Press, 1966), p. 109, Table 9.

11. This is the central theme of Farmer and Richman, *op. cit.*
12. The discussion on Chinese Communist ideology is based in large portion on Franz Schurmann's excellent and comprehensive book *Ideology and Organization in Communist China* (Berkeley and Los Angeles: University of California Press, 1966), especially Chap. 1.
13. To understand why, see B. Richman, *Soviet Management*, especially Chaps. 7 and 12; and B. Richman, *Management Development and Education in the USSR* (East Lansing, Michigan: Institute for International Business and Economic Development Studies, Michigan State University, 1966), especially Chaps. 5, 9, and 10.
14. For a comprehensive listing of the various types of contradictions within Chinese society as perceived in the Thought of Mao Tse-tung and the statements of other top Chinese leaders, see Schurmann, *op. cit.*, pp. 102–3.

    Contradictions pertaining directly to industrial and business management are discussed in Jen Yung-chiang, "On the Question of Certain Relationships in the Management of Industrial Enterprise," *Economic Research*, No. 1 (Peking, 1966), pp. 12 ff., translated in Joint Publications Research Service (JPRS), *China and Asia Series*, No. 34568 (Washington, D.C.: March 15, 1966). See also Hsinhua News Agency, *Daily News Release*, Hong Kong, August 4, 1966, pp. 19 ff., and August 23, 1966, pp. 20 ff.
15. *People's Daily*, Peking, December 4, 1965, p. 1; translated in *JPRS*, No. 33603, January 3, 1966.

Chapter 2

1. *Training of National Technical Personnel for Accelerated Industrialization of Developing Countries* (United Nations Economic and Social Council, New York, 1961), Report No. E/3901, Part I, Add. 1, p. 85.
2. R. Farmer and B. Richman, *Comparative Management and Economic Progress* (Homewood, Illinois: Richard D. Irwin Inc., 1965). This chapter, including the two tables and two figures, is based in large part on this book and the numerous sources cited therein.
3. Cf. Farmer and Richman, *op. cit.*, Chap. 5 and the many sources cited therein.
4. This analysis is based on Farmer and Richman, *op. cit.*, and the numerous sources cited therein. While I have spent some time in such developing countries as India and China, my colleague Professor Richard Farmer spent more than two years actually managing a locally owned firm in Saudi Arabia. Saudi Arabia is a backward underdeveloped country in the true sense, although this might be deceptive if one looks at its per capita gross national product which is larger than China's or India's because of the huge oil royalties paid to a few of its citizens. In terms of average Saudi living standards, however, they are very low.
5. For major studies which shed light on the environment of industry, business, and management in pre-1949 China, see A. Feuerwerker: *China's Early Industrialization* (Cambridge, Mass.: Harvard University Press, 1958); P. Ho, *The Ladder of Social Success in Imperial China* (New York: Columbia University Press, 1962) and *Studies on the Population of China 1368–1953* (Cambridge, Mass.: Harvard University Press, 1959); A. Wright, "Struggle vs. Harmony–Symbols of Competing Values in Modern China," *World Politics*, Vol. VI, No. 1 (October 1953),

pp. 31–44; M. Levy, and Shih, *The Rise of the Modern Chinese Business Class* (New York: International Secretariat, Institute of Pacific Relations, 1949); the essays in the two volumes *Republican China* and *Imperial China* by F. Schurmann and O. Schell (New York: Random House, 1967); E. Snow, *Red Star Over China* (New York: Modern Library, 1944); and E. Snow, *The Other Side of the River* (New York: Random House, 1962); C. King, *The Ethics of the Profession and of Business: Modern China and her Present Day Problems* (Philadelphia: American Academy of Political and Social Sciences, 1922); D. Bodde, *China's Cultural Tradition* (New York: Holt, Rinehart and Winston, 1957) Y. L. Fung, *A History of Chinese Philosophy*, translated by D. Bodde (Princeton: Princeton University Press, 1952); J. Fairbank, *The United States and China* (Cambridge, Mass.: Harvard University Press, 1958); *The Essays in China's Cultural Heritage and the Communist Political System* (Chicago: University of Chicago Press, 1967); *Ten Great Years* (Peking: Foreign Languages Press, 1960); *Ten Glorious Years* (Peking: Foreign Languages Press, 1960); D. McClelland, "Motivational Patterns in Southeast Asia with Special Reference to China," *Journal of Social Issues*, No. 1, 1963, pp. 6–19.

For major works in the economics sphere see A. Young, *China's Wartime Finance and Inflation, 1937–1945* (Cambridge, Mass.: Harvard University Press, 1965); S. H. Chau, *The Chinese Inflation*, 1937–49 (New York: Columbia University Press, 1963); K. N. Chang, *The Inflationary Spiral: The Experience in China* (New York: Wiley, 1958); T. C. Liu and K. C. Yeh, *The Economy of the Chinese Mainland* (Princeton: Princeton University Press, 1965); C. M. Hou, *Foreign Investment and Economic Development in China*, 1840–1937 (Cambridge, Mass.: Harvard University Press, 1965); A. Eckstein, *The Economic Heritage* (mimeographed), presented at the Conference on Economic Trends in Communist China, Chicago, October 21–24, 1965, sponsored by the Social Science Research Council, Committee on the Economy of China.

6. D. McClelland, *The Achieving Society* (New York: D. Van Nostrand, 1961), p. 105.
7. For studies and extensive documentation on the behavior patterns of managers who have a high achievement drive, see the sources cited in Farmer and Richman, *op. cit.*, p. 155, and McClelland, *op. cit.*
8. R. Heilbroner, *The Great Ascent* (New York: Harper and Row, 1963), p. 62.
9. H. Maslow, "A Theory of Human Motivation," *Psychological Review*, Vol. L, 1943, pp. 370–96; and *Motivation and Personality* (New York: Harper and Row, 1954).
10. Cf. B. Berelson and G. Steiner, *Human Behavior: An Inventory of Scientific Findings* (New York: Harcourt, Brace and World, 1964), pp. 613 ff.
11. M. Nash, "Applied and Action Anthropology in the Understanding of Man," *Anthropological Quarterly*, Vol. XXXII, 1959, p. 79.
12. Cf. A. Waterston, *Planning in Yugoslavia* (Baltimore: John Hopkins Press, 1962); and B. Richman, *Soviet Management: With Significant American Comparisons* (Englewood Cliffs, N.J.: Prentice-Hall, 1965), especially pp. 238 ff.

Chapter 3

1. Two excellent comprehensive sources on Chinese education are L. Orleans, *Professional Manpower and Education in Communist China* (Washington, D.C.: National Science Foundation, 1960); and C. Cheng, *Scientific and Engineering Manpower in Communist China, 1949–1963* (Washington, D.C.: National Science Foundation, 1965). See also the essays on Chinese education by T. Chen

and C. Oldham in R. Adams, ed., *Contemporary China* (New York: Vintage Books, 1966); and I. Hsu in F. Harbison and C. Myers, *Manpower and Education* (New York: McGraw-Hill, 1965). For an outstanding study of Soviet education see N. DeWitt, *Education and Professional Employment in the USSR* (Washington, D.C.: National Science Foundation, 1961).

2. Figure 3–1 is from Orleans, *op. cit.*, p. 11.
3. Table 3–1 is based on C. Cheng, *op. cit.*, p. 81, Table 8.
4. These figures are based on Cheng, *op. cit.*, and the national income figures presented in C. Liu and K. Yeh, *The Economy of the Chinese Mainland* (Princeton, N.J.: Princeton University Press, 1965), and C. Liu, ed., *Industrial Development in Communist China*, p. 68, Table 10; (New York: Praeger, 1964), pp. 15–19.
5. F. Harbison and C. Myers, *Education, Manpower, and Economic Growth* (New York: McGraw-Hill, 1964), pp. 46–48. These authors point out that there is the problem of margin of error in these figures, and they are not precisely comparable.

   One American author suggests that in 1960 actual expenditures on education and scientific research of all types and at all levels in China may have been as high as 15% to 20% of national income, but this seems rather high. See E. Snow, *The Other Side of the River* (New York: Random House, 1961), p. 224.
6. For a good historical perspective of Chinese education see Cheng, *op. cit.*, and Orleans, *op. cit.*
7. See for example the account by C. Lynch, *China: One Fourth of the World* (Toronto and Montreal: McClelland and Stewart Ltd., 1965), pp. 164–67.
8. *Red Flag* (Peking), No. 13, December 6, 1965, pp. 34–40.
9. For some translated articles see *Selected Hsinhua News Items* (published by Hsinhua News Agency, Hong Kong branch), No. 26, August 15, 1966; and *Hsinhua Daily News Release*, August 4, 1966. See also D. Munrow, *Dissent in Communist China*, Vol. IV, No. 11 (June 1, 1966).
10. Chinese literacy figures have been derived from the *Peking Daily Worker* (Gongren Ribao), January 26, 1964, p. 1; Snow, *op. cit.*, pp. 223–27; Orleans, *op. cit.*, pp. 49 ff.
11. From official Government of India statistics.
12. See Snow, *op. cit.* Chap. 31, and Oldham, *op. cit.*, p. 286.
13. From Orleans, *op. cit.*, p. 49, Table 9.
14. My comments in this book on Indian industrial management and its environment are based on my own as yet unpublished empirical research as well as two recent doctoral dissertations based on extensive field research in India. These dissertations are by A. Phatak, *External Environmental Constraints and Their Impact on the Internal Operations of Firms in the Pharmaceutical and Engineering Industries in India* (University of California at Los Angeles, 1966); and M. Copen, *Manufacturing Management in Developing Nations: a Comparative Study of Problems and Practices of U.S. and Indigenous Companies in India* (Harvard University, 1967).
15. Harbison and Myers, *op. cit.*, pp. 46–47, Tables 6 and 7.
16. Indian figures are from official Government of India sources.
17. Table 3–3 is based on data presented in Orleans, *op. cit.*, p. 32, Table 2, and p. 49, Table 9. The 1964–65 figure is from Lynch, *op. cit.*, p. 167, and the 1965–66 figure was given to me as a rough estimate by a Chinese education official in Peking. The 1958–62 figure is from Oldham, *op. cit.*, p. 286.
18. Orleans, *op. cit.*, p. 35. The 1959–60 figures are from Snow, *op. cit.*, p. 227; and the 1964–65 figures from Lynch, *op. cit.*, p. 167.
19. Harbison and Myers, *op. cit.*, pp. 46–47.
20. Indian figures and the related analyses in this section are derived from *India:*

Pocket Book of Economic Information (New Delhi: Ministry of Finance, Government of India, 1965); L. Chandrakant, *Fourth Five-Year Plan of Technical Education,* A Draft Report (New Delhi: Ministry of Education, November 1965); and various published reports prepared by the Institute of Applied Manpower Research, New Delhi.

21. Harbison and Myers, *op. cit.*, p. 112.
22. From Orleans, *op. cit.*, p. 97.
23. J. Duncan, *A Businessman Looks at Red China* (Princeton: D. Van Nostrand, 1965), pp. 82–85.
24. From Orleans, *op. cit.*, p. 49, Table 9. The 1958–62 figure is from Oldham, *op. cit.*, p. 286.
25. Snow, *op. cit.*, p. 237.
26. For a comprehensive study of Russia's system of semiprofessional education see DeWitt, *op. cit.*, Chap. 111. See also B. Rediman, *Management Development and Education in the Soviet Union* (East Lansing, Michigan: Institute for International Business and Economic Development Studies, Michigan State University, 1967), Chap. 6. For more background on the Chinese system see Orleans, *op. cit.*, Chap. 3.
27. Table 3–7 is derived from Orleans, *op. cit.*, p. 42, Table 5.
28. Cited in Orleans, *op. cit.*, p. 48.
29. Derived from Orleans, p. 49, Table 9.
30. Table 3–11 is derived from Orleans, p. 47, Table 8.
31. It should be stressed that Table 3–12 presents estimates only of Chinese semiprofessional technicians, and they are probably maximum estimates. Chinese sources are not clear in indicating the proportion of technicians and engineers who are professionals, semiprofessionals or practicals (promoted from the ranks as workers). It does appear from the data presented in Cheng, *op. cit.*, pp. 108–16, and especially Tables 15, 16, and 18, that our estimates in Table 3–12 are reasonably accurate.
32. Soviet figures in this section regarding semiprofessional education, employment, and graduates are derived from Dewitt, *op. cit.*, Chaps. 2 and 6; Richman, *op. cit.*, Chaps. 3–6; and *Naradnoe Khoziaistvo SSSR V, 1963, 1964 and 1965 Goda* (National Economy of the USSR for the years 1963, 1964, and 1965; published in Moscow).
33. Cf. H. David, ed., *Education and Manpower* (New York: Columbia University Press, 1960), especially Chaps. VII and VIII; J. Conant, *The American High School Today* (New York: McGraw-Hill Book Company, 1969), pp. 127 ff.; G. Henning, *The Technical Institute in American Education* (New York: McGraw-Hill Book Company, 1959), especially pp. 139 ff.; Harbison and Myers, *op. cit.*, p. 145, pp. 160 ff.; *Business Week*, October 3, 1964, p. 19. A close look at the want ads of the 1966 newspapers of large American cities also suggests that this is true.
34. A vice director of the Peking Machine-Tool Factory whom I interviewed studied engineering and worked in the Soviet Union in the 1950's. He was familiar with the Soviet ETMP category and estimated that about two-thirds of the administrative cadres and technical personnel at the Peking enterprise would correspond to the ETMP category. An engineer at the Peking Steel Wire Enterprise who also studied and worked in Russia, estimated that about 75 percent of the administrative and technical personnel at his enterprise approximates the Soviet ETMP category. Both of these Chinese enterprise employees said that virtually all of the engineers and technicians at their firms would fit into the ETMP category, and they thought this was probably generally true for other enterprises as

well. Employment data from several other Chinese enterprises suggest that about 60 to 80 percent of their administrative and technical personnel correspond to the Soviet ETMP category. For a precise definition of ETMP in the U.S.S.R. see Dewitt, *op. cit.*, pp. 496–97.

35. For more detailed information of Chinese higher education including the names of schools, types and contents of programs, etc., see Cheng, *op. cit.*, Orleans, *op. cit.*, Oldham, *op. cit.*, Chen, *op. cit.*, and Hsu, *op. cit.* A deeper insight into Chinese higher education can be obtained by studying the Soviet system; see Dewitt, *op. cit.*, and Richman, *op. cit.*
36. Table 3–15 is derived from data presented in Hsu, *op. cit.*, pp. 219–21; Cheng, *op. cit.*, pp. 74–80. The 1964–65 figures are from Lynch, *op. cit.*, p. 167. The 1965–66 figures are from Oldham, *op. cit.*, p. 283. The 1960 figure is from Snow, *op. cit.*, p. 226.
37. Unless otherwise noted, Indian figures regarding higher education are derived from the sources cited in Note 20 above.
38. Harbison and Myers, *op. cit.*, pp. 45–48.
39. Unless otherwise noted, Soviet figures and other information pertaining to higher education are derived from the sources cited in Note 26 above.
40. Unless otherwise noted, U.S. figures and other data regarding higher education are derived from the publications (and sources cited therein) referred to in Note 33 above.
41. Table 3–16 is based on Orleans, *op. cit.*, p. 49, Table 9. The 1960 figure is from Snow, *op. cit.*, p. 237.
42. Oldham, *op. cit.*, p. 286.
43. For figures and more information on graduate education in China see Cheng, *op. cit.*, pp. 53–56; Orleans, *op. cit.*, Appendix D; Oldham, *op. cit.*, pp. 283 ff.
44. Orleans, *op. cit.*, pp. 125–28.
45. *Ibid.*, Chap. VIII.
46. Cheng, *op. cit.*, p. 128, Table 24.
47. Table 3–17 is based on Cheng, p. 78, Table 7; the 1964–65 figure is from Lynch *op. cit.*, p. 166.
48. Harbison and Myers, *op. cit.*, pp. 45–48.
49. *Ibid.*
50. Cheng, *op. cit.*, p. 77.
51. *Ibid.*, p. 116, Table 18.
52. Table 3–18 is derived from Cheng, p. 134, Table 28.
53. Much of the Chinese information in this section is based on interviews I had with faculty members of Tsinghua Polytechnic University and to a lesser extent with engineers and managers working in industry and some of my interpreters. The following sources also proved helpful to me: Cheng, *op. cit.*, Orleans, *op. cit.*, and Hsu, *op. cit.*
54. Hsu, *op. cit.*, Cheng, *op. cit.*, and Orleans, *op. cit.*, provide early data on Tsinghua Polytechnic University.
55. James Duncan, a Canadian industrialist, was told the same thing by the chancellor of Chungking Polytechnic University in 1964. The university planned to cut the number of graduates from 1,800 to 1,300 in future years. See Duncan, *op. cit.*, p. 82.
56. The *Peking People's Daily*, in a February 1957 article, indicated that specialized courses dealt with factory organization and management, planning of enterprises, economics, etc. See Orleans, *op. cit.*, p. 133, Table 4. This table also compares the 1955 actual and 1957 planned curricula of Tsinghua with Soviet programs and the California Institute of Technology.

57. Table 3–19 is derived from Cheng, *op. cit.*, p. 78, Table 7. The 1964–65 figures are from Lynch, *op. cit.*, p. 166.
58. This section is based largely on information obtained from faculty members I interviewed at China People's University and to a lesser extent on information provided by one of my interpreters who was a graduate of the Peking Institute of Foreign Trade, a central planning official, and some enterprise managers. Helpful published sources in this sphere are Cheng, *op. cit.*, and Orleans, *op. cit.*
59. See Cheng, *op. cit.*, p. 115, Table 17. This table also indicates that only 3 percent of the industrial leaders were graduates of specialized secondary schools in 1955. It presents some rather confusing figures regarding engineers and technicians. For engineers and technicians the proportion of higher graduates was 35 percent, and 22 percent were semiprofessional graduates; but for the category "engineering and technical personnel" the figures were 16 and 22 percent respectively.
60. Figures on educational background of U.S. managers and other personnel are derived from the surveys cited in Richman, *op. cit.*, Chap. 2.
61. See *Staffing Procedures and Problems in Communist China*, prepared by the Committee on Government Operations of the United States Senate (Washington, D.C.: U.S. Government Printing Office, 1963), pp. 18–19.
62. For a discussion of Soviet programs of this type see Richman, *op. cit.*, Chap. 6.
63. *Ibid.*, Chap. 9.
64. See Harbison and Myers, *op. cit.*, pp. 178–81, and C. Kerr, J. Dunlop, F. Harbison, and C. Myers, *Industrialism and Industrial Man* (Cambridge, Mass.: Harvard University Press, 1961), pp. 47–76 and 118–19.
65. See the essays by Suyin, Oldham, and Chen in *Contemporary China.*
66. Wen Yu, "The New Generation of Skilled Workers," *China Reconstructs,* August 1960, p. 24.
67. Cf. *Peking People's Daily*, March 10, 1957, p. 1; Orleans, *op. cit.*, p. 90.
68. Cf. Chen, *op. cit.*, p. 267; and T. Chen, "Education and Economic Failures in Communist China," *The Educational Record,* October 1963, pp. 348–53.
69. Unemployment statistics for India have been derived from "Nature and Dimension of Unemployment Among Educated Persons in India, 1953 to 1964" (New Delhi: Institute of Applied Manpower Research, September 1965); and *Stock Taking of Engineering Personnel* (New Delhi: Institute of Applied Manpower Research, December, 1963).
70. Delhi University statistics are from V. Rao, *University Education and Employment: A Case Study of Delhi Graduates* (Bombay: Asia Publishing House, 1961).
71. For an excellent historical perspective on the utilization of high-talent manpower in Red China see Cheng, *op. cit.*, Chaps. 5 and 6.
72. For an enumeration of Chinese holders of doctoral degress from the United States and Canada by field from 1905 to 1960, see Cheng, *op. cit.*, Table 20.
73. Cf. *Peking People's Daily* (Jen-min Jih-pao), editorial, December 28, 1961.
74. K. Shih, "Fully Tap the Strength of Technical Staff," *Red Flag* (Hongoi), Nos. 8–9 (April 25, 1962), p. 44.
75. The plight of Red China's social scientists is examined in Cheng, *op. cit.*, Chap. 9.
76. For an indication of the range of jobs held by important people in China, including higher intellectuals, see *Who's Who in Communist China* (Hong Kong: Union Research Institute, 1966).
77. Cf. D. Munrow, "Dissent in Communist China," *Current Scene*, Vol. IV, No. 11 (June 1, 1966); F. Yu, "With Banners and Drums," *Current Scene*, Vol. IV, No. 9 (May 1, 1966); *JPRS*, No. 34659, March 22, 1966 (translation of article titled "Let Politics Command Scientific Work").
78. Cf. *Peking People's Daily* (article titled "Ideological Reform for Leading

Cadres"), October 17, 1966; *People's Daily* (article titled "Let Us Address Ourselves to the Masses and Serve Production"), September 24, 1965; *JPRS*, Vol. IV, No. 7; *Daily News Release*, Hsinhua News Agency (Hong Kong), August 23, 1966.

79. Excerpts from *Peking People's Daily*, December 27, 1966, regarding the Red Guards onslaught into factories, are presented in R. Elegant, "Red China Turmoil Seen in New Edict," *Los Angeles Times*, December 28, 1966, p. 1.
80. R. Elegant, "China Purge Widened to All Aspects of Life," *Los Angeles Times*, January 3, 1967, p. 5.

Chapter 4

1. E. Ayal, "Value Systems and Economic Development in Japan and Thailand," *Journal of Social Issues*, IX (1963).
2. Cf. R. Elegant, "China Has Only One Thought," *Los Angeles Times*, October 23, 1966, Section B, pp. 2–3.
3. Cf. J. Duncan, A *Businessman Looks at Red China* (New York: D. Van Nostrand, 1965); C. Lynch, *China: One Fourth of the World* (Toronto: McClelland and Stewart Ltd., 1966); H. Suyin, "Social Transformation in China," in R. Adams, ed., *Contemporary China* (New York: Vintage Books, 1966); J. Myrdal, "The Reshaping of Chinese Society," also in *Contemporary China*; E. Snow, *The Other Side of the River* (New York: Random House, 1961); J. Levenson, *Confucian China and its Modern Fate*, Vols. I, II (Berkeley and Los Angeles: University of California Press, 1958 and 1964).
4. Some sources dealing with management and industry in China prior to 1949 are F. Schurmann, *Ideology and Organization in Communist China* (Berkeley and Los Angeles: University of California Press, 1966), especially Chap. IV and the references cited therein; A. Feuerwerker, *China's Early Industrialization* (Cambridge, Mass.: Harvard University Press, 1958); M. Levy and K. Shih, *The Rise of the Modern Chinese Business Class* (New York: Institute of Pacific Relations, 1949); K. Shih, *China Enters the Machine Age* (Cambridge, Mass.: Harvard University Press, 1944); A. Eckstein, *The Economic Heritage*, a paper presented at the Conference on Economic Trends in Communist China, October 21–25, 1965, sponsored by the Social Science Research Council (this paper contains copious documentation and footnotes).
5. The Red vs. Expert syndrome is dealt with at length in Schurmann, *op. cit.*, especially Chaps. I and IV.
6. For related sources on the Soviet Union see B. Richman, *Management Development and Education in the Soviet Union* (East Lansing: Bureau of Business and Economic Research, Michigan State University, 1967); P. Rossi and A. Inkeles, "Multi-dimensional Ratings of Occupations," *Sociometry* (September 1957), pp. 241 ff; J. Azrael, *Managerial Power and Soviet Politics* (Cambridge, Mass.: Harvard University Press, 1966).
7. The oscillation between Reds and Experts and regarding favorable vs. unfavorable attitudes toward industrial managers from 1949 to about 1965 in China is well documented in Schurmann, *op. cit.*, A. Donnithorne, *China's Economic System* (London: Allen and Unwin, 1967); D. Perkins, *Market Control and Planning in Communist China* (Cambridge: Harvard University Press, 1966); the articles by C. Li and F. Schurmann in C. Li, ed., *Industrial Development in Communist China* (New York: Praeger, 1964).
8. This wage reform is discussed in C. Cheng, *Scientific and Engineering Manpower*

in Communist China: 1949–1963 (Washington, D.C.: National Science Foundation, 1965), pp. 150–51.

9. Perkins, *op. cit.*, p. 121.
10. *Red Flag* (Hung-chi), Nos. 8–9 (1962), pp. 42–45; cited in Cheng, *op. cit.*, p. 182.
11. *Daily Worker*, August 5, 1962, p. 2 (cited in Donnithorne, *op. cit.*, Chap. VII).
12. See Donnithorne, *op. cit.*, Chap. VII.
13. *Ibid.*
14. "Running Enterprises in Line With Mao Tse-tung's Thinking," *Peking Review*, April 15, 1965, translated from the editorial in *People's Daily*, April 3, 1966.
15. S. Meng, "Do Not Forget Party Work," *People's Daily*, April 6, 1966, p. 5; cited in Donnithorne, *op. cit.*
16. *People's Daily*, February 25, 1965; *Southern Daily*, November 2, 1964 (both cited in Donnithorne, *op. cit.*). J. Ashdown, "China's Proletarian Problems," *Far Eastern Economic Review*, March 12, 1965, p. 440.
17. Donnithorne, *op. cit.*, Chap. VII.
18. Cf. *People's Daily*, October 17, 1965; *Economic Research*, No. 1 (1966); *Red Flag*, No. 1 (1966); these sources are translated by *Joint Publication Research Service* (JPRS), Washington, D.C.
19. *People's Daily*, September 24, 1965 (translated by *JPRS*).
20. An article about him can be found in *Chinese Agricultural Machinery*, Peking, May 1965, pp. 21–26. The article is entitled "The Success in Technical Reform at the Wuhan Diesel Engine Manufacturing Plant," and is partially translated in *JPRS*, No. 33603, January 3, 1966.
21. The Taching oil fields are discussed in "Taching Oil Fields Developed Under the Direction of the Thought of Mao Tse-tung," *Red Flag*, No. 13 (December 6, 1965).
22. Duncan, *op. cit.*, p. 94.
23. Lynch, *op. cit.*, p. 80.
24. Snow, *op. cit.*, p. 576.
25. Most of the enterprises that Snow visited were in north China (Manchuria). It is possible that incomes for managers and experts have been and are above average in this region since it is a relatively old and advanced industrial area in China.
26. Article entitled "The Younger Generation in Anshan Iron and Steel Works," translated in *Hsinhua Daily News Release*, Hong Kong, July 30, 1966, pp. 21 ff.
27. Articles of this type have appeared frequently in the second half of 1966 in leading American newspapers, such as the New York and Los Angeles *Times*, and magazines, such as *Time* and *Newsweek*. The British *Economist* has also presented a good running account. *JPRS* and *Hsinhua News Agency* in Hong Kong have also translated numerous articles of this type.
28. See the late December 1966 issues of the *Los Angeles Times* or *New York Times*.
29. See daily coverage in January 1967 copies of the above or other leading newspapers. See also *Time* magazine, January 13, 1967.
30. See the quantitative scientifically derived evidence presented in D. McClelland, *The Achieving Society* (Princeton: D. Van Nostrand, 1961), pp. 241 ff., especially in Tables 6.5 and 6.6.
31. See sources cited in Note 6 above.
32. See David McClelland, "Motivational Patterns in Southeast Asia with Special Reference to the Chinese Case," *Journal of Social Issues*, Vol. XIX, No. 1 (1963), pp. 6–19. See also his book *The Achieving Society* cited above.
33. For sources pertaining to old China see Note 4 above.
34. Relevant comprehensive sources dealing with Red China up until about 1966

include Schurmann, *op. cit.*, Donnithorne, *op. cit.*; Li, *op. cit.*; *Peking Review*, February 26, 1965.

35. Quoted in W. K. Ma, "Industrial Management in China," *Peking Review*, February 26, 1965, p. 20.
36. From *Electric Motor Industry* (Dianji Gongye), No. 10 (May 25, 1959), p. 2; (cited in Donnithorne, *op. cit.*, Chap. VII). Donnithorne presents considerable documentation of this type.
37. Cf. the sources cited in Notes 16 through 21.
38. Cf. the sources cited in Notes 26 through 29.
39. This section is based on my own research in India, the two doctoral dissertations cited in Note 14 of Chap. 3, and the sources on India cited in R. Farmer, and B. Richman, *Comparative Management and Economic Progress* (Homewood, Illinois: Richard D. Irwin, Inc., 1965), p. 130.
40. For a comprehensive general discussion on the Chinese Communist Party, see Schurmann, *op. cit.*, Chap. 11.
41. For an analysis of the effectiveness of the party in the Soviet Union see B. Richman, *Soviet Management: With Significant American Comparisons* (Englewood Cliffs, N.J.: Prentice-Hall, Inc., 1965), especially pp. 220–24 and the references cited therein.
42. For sources dealing with trade unions in Communist China see Donnithorne, *op. cit.*, Chap. VII; Snow, *op. cit.*, Chap. 31; *Peking Review*, April 30, 1965, pp. 22 ff.; *China Reconstructs*, May 1963, pp. 27 ff. It should be noted that figures on union membership cited in Snow and Donnithorne are not compatible with each other.

    For an examination of the role of trade unions in Soviet industry see E. Brown, "The Local Union in Soviet Industry," *Industrial and Labor Relations Review* (January 1960) and "Interests and Rights of Soviet Industrial Workers and the Resolution of Conflicts" in the same journal, January 1963 issue; *Current Digest of the Soviet Press*, Vol. XIV, No. 28 (1962), pp. 24 ff.; *Pravda*, July 14 and August 15, 1962; Richman, *Soviet Management*, pp. 225–26.
43. Snow, *op. cit.*
44. Cf. Richman, *Soviet Management*, especially Chaps. 6, 8, and 11, and the sources cited therein.
45. For a discussion of research organizations and institutes in China see C. Cheng, *Scientific and Engineering Manpower in Communist China*, 1949–63 (Washington, D.C.: National Science Foundation, 1965), especially Chap. 2.
46. Cf. Richman, *op. cit.*, Chap. 10; B. Richman, "Managerial Opposition to Product Innovation in Soviet Union Industry," *California Management Review*, Winter 1963, pp. 11–26; Richman, "Innovation Problems in Soviet Industry," *Management International*, Vol. 3, No. 6 (1963), pp. 67–96.
47. Richman, *op. cit.*, Chaps. 8 and 9.
48. *Ibid.*, especially Chap. 6.
49. There is some scientifically derived evidence which suggests that Indians tend to prefer individual rather than cooperative group activities. See McClelland, *The Achieving Society*, pp. 197–201.
50. See the evidence presented in McClelland, *Achieving Society*, especially Chaps. 1–7. Richman and Farmer, *op. cit.*, pp. 153–65, and the references cited therein.
51. McClelland, *Journal of Social Issues*. The standard n-achievement scores derived from children's stories for Republican China of the 1920's, and Communist China and Taiwan for the 1950's repectively are —.90, +.32, and —.25.
52. J. Lewis, "Education and the Chinese Party: Themes in Development," in J.

Coleman, *Education and Political Development* (Princeton: Princeton University Press, 1963).

53. R. Bauer, "The Psychology of the Soviet Middle Elite: Two Case Histories," in H. Kluckhohn, H. Murray, and D. Schneider, *Personality in Nature, Society and Culture* (New York: Knopf, 1955), pp. 633–50.
54. The standard n-achievement score for the U.S.S.R. in 1925 was −.78, and for 1950 +.13.
55. The standard n-achievement score derived from Indian Children's readers in the 1950's is +.95, compared to +.32 for Red China. In addition to my own observations and findings about achievement motivation in Indian industry, the analysis in this chapter also draws on Phatak's doctoral dissertation cited in Chap. 3 above.
56. The standard n-achievement score for the Soviet Union for 1925 and 1950 are given in Note 54 above. It is likely that a standard n-achievement score, if it is taken, and particularly the actual achievement drive of Soviet industrial personnel, are higher in the 1960's than in 1950. The standared n-achievement score for the United States in 1925 was +.52 significantly higher than most other countries at that time. The 1950 U.S. score was +.32 for the population in general, and an amazing + 2.16 for Catholics. See McClelland, *op. cit.*, Appendix II. The reasons for such a high n-achievement among American Catholics is discussed in McClelland, *op. cit.*, Chap. 9.
57. Cf. P. T. Ho, *The Ladder of Social Success in Imperial China* (New York: Columbia University Press, 1962); W. Lockwood, "Japan's Response to the West, the Contrast with China," *World Politics*, Vol. IX, No. 1 (October 1956), pp. 37–54; Eckstein, *op. cit.*
58. From Cheng, *op. cit.*, p. 88, Table 12.
59. *Ibid.*, p. 87.
60. Figures on female employment and student enrollment in China, apart from those I obtained in China, have been derived from Cheng, *op. cit.*, pp. 144 ff.

    The Soviet figures, apart from those I obtained firsthand, are derived from the sources cited in N. Dewitt, *Education and Professional Employment in the USSR* (Washington, D.C., 1961), Chap. IV and VI; Richman, *Management Development, op. cit.*, Chap. 5; and, *Staffing Procedures and Problems in Soviet Union* (Washington, D.C.: U.S. Government Printing Office, 1962), pp. 4–5.
61. For pertinent studies dealing with India see R. Lambert, *Workers, Factories and Social Change in India* (Princeton: Princeton University Press, 1963) especially Chap. V; G. Ghuyre, *Caste and Class in India* (Bombay: Popular Book Depot, 1957); W. Knapp, *Hindu Economic Development and Economic Planning* (New York: Asia Publishing House, 1963); S. Jain, "The Man in the Grey Flannel Achkan," *Columbia Journal of World Business*, Vol. 1, No. 4 (Fall 1966), pp. 123–35; Farmer and Richman, *op. cit.*, pp. 168–69; E. Driver, "Caste and Occupational Structure in Central India," *Journal of Social Forces* (October 1962) pp. 26 ff.; C. Vokil, "Business Leadership in Underdeveloped Countries," *Industrialization and Productivity*, No. 2 (1959) pp. 46–51; A. Agarwala, "Management of Big Business in India," *The Indian Journal of Public Administration* (April-June 1962), pp. 178 ff.
62. Knapp, *op. cit.*, p. 47.
63. Agarwala, *op. cit.*, p. 178.
64. Cf. B. Schwartz, *In Search of Wealth and Power, Yen Fu and the West* (Cambridge: Harvard University Press, 1964); Eckstein, *op. cit.*
65. Cf. Schurmann, *op. cit.*, pp. 227–31. I have also obtained pertinent background

information on the Republican period in China from a mimeographed manuscript on industrial management written by Franz Schurmann around 1965.
66. *Ibid.* See also Eckstein, *op. cit.*; B. Higgins, *Economic Development* (New York: W. W. Norton, 1959), pp. 256–57, 276.
67. Cf. R. Dernberger, "Economic Realities," *Contemporary China*, pp. 125 ff.
68. Cf. the article by Suyin, in *Contemporary China*, pp. 99 ff.
69. See Donnithorne, *op. cit.*, Chap. XV.
70. *Ibid.*
71. *Ibid.* Donnithorne reports that about 4.8% annual interest (.4% per month) was paid on one-year-period (fixed) deposits in 1959. The monthly interest paid on six-month-period deposits was .3%, and on current accounts .18%. She reports on 1966 interest rate as being equivalent to 3% on one-year fixed deposits—.33% per month—but I was told by a number of people around mid-1966 that the annual interest rate on personal savings was 3.3%.
72. Important sources dealing with the use of material incentives and wages in Chinese industry since 1949 include C. Hoffman, "Work Incentive Policy in Communist China," and F. Schurmann, "China's New Economic Policy—Transition or Beginning," C. Ti, "China's Industrial Development, 1958–63"; these are in Ti, ed., *Industrial Development in Communist China*. Other sources are Schurmann, *op. cit.*, Chaps. I and IV, Donnithorne, Chap. VII; P. Schran, "Unity and Diversity of Chinese Industrial Wage Policies," *Journal of Asian Studies*, Vol. XXIII (February 1964), pp. 245–51; Perkins, *op. cit.*
73. For a comprehensive discussion of managerial and worker incentives in Soviet industry see Richman, *Soviet Management*, Chaps. 6 and 10.
74. Donnithorne, *op. cit.*, Chap. VII; Li, *op. cit.*, pp. 28–29.
75. *Ibid.* See also other sources cited in Note 72 above.
76. Donnithorne, *op. cit.*
77. Schurmann, *op. cit.*, pp. 101–3.
78. Cf. Donnithorne, *op. cit.*, Chap. VII; Hoffman, *op. cit.*, pp. 106 ff., Y. Wong, "Attend to the Livelihood of Workers," *People's Daily*, May 19, 1961; *Economic Research* (in Chinese), No. 4 (April 1959), p. 20.
79. Donnithorne, *op. cit.*, Hoffman, *op. cit.*, Wong, *op. cit.*, Schurmann, *op. cit.*, Schran, *op. cit.*, H. Chen, "Strengthening of the Piece Work System, *Ta Kung Pao*, August 23, 1961, translated in *JPRS*, No. 10720; F. Lin, "A Discussion on the Forms of Wages," *People's Daily*, October 28, 1961, translated in *JPRS*, No. 11969.
80. Hoffman and Lin, *op. cit.*
81. *Peking Review*, December 6, 1963, p. 7.
82. Reported in Donnithorne, *op. cit.*, Chap. VII.
83. *Labor* (*Laodoug*), No. 8, August 1964, p. 30. *Chinese Textiles* (*Zhunggui Fangzhi*), No. 1, January 10, 1965; also cited in Donnithorne, *op. cit.*
84. Donnithorne, *op. cit.*, *People's Daily* (*Renmin Ribao*), December 2, 1963.
85. Daily Worker (*Gongren Ribao*), July 14, 1965, p. 1.
86. See *Far Eastern Economic Review*, January 1961, p. 80.
87. Cf. "High Standard Quality Comes From High Standard Thinking," editorial, *Red Flag*, No. 1 (1966), translated in *JPRS*, No. 33889; "Let Politics Command Scientific Work," *Kuang-ming Jih-pao*, February 18, 1966, pp. 1–2, translated in *JPRS*, No. 34658; Donnithorne, *op. cit.*
88. Numerous articles to this effect have appeared in the Western press and magazines during late 1966 and 1967. Many translations of articles of this type from Red Chinese sources can be found in the *JPRS Series*, *The Daily News Releases* from

Hsinhua News Agency, Hong Kong, and *Selected Hsinhua News Items* from the same agency.

89. *Ibid.*
90. Cf. Suyin, *op. cit.*, pp. 97 ff.
91. Cf. Oldham, *op. cit.*, pp. 281 ff, Chen, *op. cit.*, pp. 269 ff., Orleans, *op. cit.*, especially Chap. VII; Cheng, *op. cit.*, especially Chap. 2.
92. See "Theories Form on Contradictions Applied in Cement Kilns," *Red Flag*, No. 2, February 11, 1966, pp. 28–30, translated in *JPRS*, No. 34405. For another report on how Mao's "On Contradictions" and "On Practice" helped a worker to apply scientific methodology and experimentation, see "Chinese Worker Scientists on Making Lamps," translated in *Hsinhua Daily News Release*, Hong Kong, August 23, 1966, pp. 20–22.
93. Other Western visitors to Red China have come away with impressions and observations similar to my own with regard to scientific method and experimentation in industry. One such is C. H. Oldham, a Canadian scientist, who is a geologist by profession. See Oldham, *op. cit.*, pp. 308–10.
94. Cheng, *op. cit.*, pp. 263–65.
95. *Ibid.*
96. Cf. Richman, *Management Development*, Chaps. VI and IX; Farmer and Richman, *op. cit.*, pp. 193–94; R. Bauer, "Our Big Advantage: The Social Sciences," *Harvard Business Review*, May-June 1958, pp. 125 ff., A. Broderson, "Soviet Social Sciences and Our Own," *Social Research* (Autumn 1957), pp. 253 ff, R. Meek, "The Teaching of Economics in the USSR and Poland," *Soviet Studies* (April 1959), pp. 343 ff.
97. See Richman, *op. cit.*, Chap. 9; D. Bell, "Erosion of Ideology," *Survey* (April 1963), pp. 64 ff.; *Stroitelstva Kommunisma i Obshestuennie Naukii* (*The Building of Communism and the Social Sciences*) (Moscow: Publishing House of the USSR Academy of Sciences, 1962).
98. For discussions of scientific method and the social sciences in Communist China, see Cheng, *op. cit.*, Chap. 9; Chen, *op. cit.*, pp. 270 ff., Oldham, *op. cit.*, pp. 295–96.
99. See Schurmann, *op. cit.*, pp. 222–31; Levy and Shih, *op. cit.*; Feuerwerker, *op. cit.*
100. Cf. B. Higgins, *Economic Development* (New York: W. W. Norton, 1959), pp. 256–57, 276, 281.
101. Schurmann, *op. cit.*, pp. 229–31.
102. D. Perkins, "Centralization versus Decentralization in Mainland China and the Soviet Union," *The Annals of the American Academy of Political and Social Science*, Vol. 349 (September 1963), p. 73. For a comprehensive analysis of China's statistical system see C. Li, *The Statistical System of Communist China* (Berkeley and Los Angeles: University of California Press, 1962).
103. G. Uchida, "Technology in China," *Scientific American*, Vol. 215, No. 5 (November 1966), p. 41.
104. For a discussion of risk taking in Indian industry see Farmer and Richman, *op. cit.*, p. 214 and the sources cited therein; Vakil, *op. cit.*, pp. 46–51; K. Sundram, "Social and Human Problems in Introducing Technological Change," *CIOS Proceedings*, 1963, pp. 495 ff. See also the doctoral dissertations by Phatak and Copen cited in Chapter 3 of this study.
105. For an analysis on risk taking in Soviet industry see Farmer and Richman, *op. cit.*, pp. 211–12; Richman, *Soviet Management*, *op. cit.*, Chap. 9, and the two articles by Richman cited in Note 46 above.
106. Our discussion and analysis of the Yenan period of Communism and the "mass line" is based in large part on Chalmers Johnson's excellent, thoroughly docu-

mented, mimeographed paper *Chinese Communist Leadership and Mass Response: The Yenan Period and the Socialist Education Campaign Period.* This paper was prepared for the University of Chicago Center for Policy Study's Conference on "China's Heritage and the Communist Political System," January 30 to February 4, 1967. It was also discussed by members of the Communist Countries Study Group, to which I belong, at the University of California, Berkeley, March 7, 1967. The prominent American journalist and author, Edgar Snow, visited Yenan and interviewed at length Mao and other Chinese Communist leaders in the early part of the Yenan period of Communism. For his very interesting and prophetic story, first published in 1937, see *Red Star Over China* (New York: Modern Library, 1944). It is important to note that of the 158 articles and essays contained in the four volumes of *The Selected Works of Mao Tse-tung,* 93 of them were written while Mao was in Yenan. See "Mao Tse-tung's Thought on the Common Treasure of the World's Revolutionary People, An Account of the Visits of Foreign Friends to Yenan," *Peking Review,* September 30, 1966, p. 18.

107. Johnson, *op. cit.*, p. 14; and Mao Tse-tung, "A Single Spark Can Start a Prairie Fire," *Selected Works of Mao Tse-tung,* Vol. I (Peking: Foreign Languages Press, 1965), pp. 117–28.
108. For concrete statistics see Johnson, *op. cit.*, pp. 26–27.
109. See A. Wright, "Struggle vs. Harmony—Symbols of Competing Values in Modern China," *World Politics,* Vol. VI (October 1953), pp. 31–44.
110. Johnson, *op. cit.*, p. 35.
111. *Ibid.*, pp. 36 ff.
112. For a discussion and analysis of the Great Production Movement see Johnson, *op. cit.*, pp. 29–33; Chiang Chen-yu, "On Self Reliance—Notes on the Study of Chairman Mao's Works," *Survey of China Mainland Magazines,* 1965, No. 460 (translated by the U.S. Consulate General, Hong Kong; *Peking Review,* September 30, 1966, p. 19).
113. Johnson, *op. cit.*, pp. 34–35.
114. Text prepared by Harvard University East Asian Center, *Communist China, 1955–59* (Cambridge: Harvard University Press, 1962), pp. 275–76.
115. For a discussion and analysis of the Socialist Education Campaign and the Cultural Revolution, see Johnson, *op. cit.*, pp. 33 ff.; H. Chung, "Revolutionization and Modernization of Socialist Industrial Enterprises," *Ching-chi yen-chiu,* No. 12 (December 20, 1964), pp. 21–29; Schurmann, *op. cit.*, pp. 90, 354, 464, 493; J. C. Chen, "A *Nation in Agony, Problems of Communism,* November-December 1966.
116. Johnson, *op. cit.*, p. 6; H. Yu, *Ch'un chung lu-hsien shin-ti* (*Ten Topics of the Mass Line*), Peking: Chung-kuo ching-nien chu-pan-she, 1965, p. 3.
117. C. Soong, "Sixteen Years of Liberation," *China Reconstructs,* Vol. XV, No. 1 (January 1966), p. 5.
118. Cf. Schurmann, *op. cit.*, pp. 12, 144, 150, 176, 303–305; Donnithorne, 1967, *op. cit.*, Chap. VI.
119. See also Johnson, *op. cit.*, p. 47.
120. *Ibid.*
121. Sundaram, *op. cit.*, p. 497.
122. *Ibid.*
123. Our analysis of leadership styles is based in large part on Schurmann, *op. cit.*, especially pp. 166–67 and 235–39; see also P. Selznick, *Leadership in Administration* (Evanston, Illinois: Row, Peterson and Co., 1957; A. Etizioni, *A Comparative Analysis of Complex Organizations* (Glencoe, Ill.: The Free Press, 1961);

M. Weber, *The Theory of Social and Economic Organization* (Glencoe, Ill.: The Free Press, 1947).

124. The notion of "Theory X" or traditional-type managers preoccupied with the formal organization and "Theory Y" types who focus on human organization, true democracy, and participative management was a major contribution of Douglas McGregor; see his book *The Human Side of Enterprise* (New York: McGraw-Hill, 1960). In reality, the typical modern Chinese manager—like his American counterpart and probably even more so—is quite a way along the continuum from the pure Theory X type, although he still probably tends to lean much closer to Theory X than the party cadre.
125. See Schurmann, *op. cit.*, Chaps. I, III, and IV.
126. M. Janowitz, "Hierarchy and Authority in Military Establishments," in Etzioni, *op. cit.*, pp. 210–11.
127. For an analysis of the conception of policy and plan in China, see Schurmann, *op. cit.*, especially pp. 28, and 238–39.
128. Cf. W. K. Ma, "Industrial Management in China," *Peking Review* (February 26, 1965), pp. 20 ff.; "Let Us Address Ourselves to the Shift Team and Masses and Serve Production," *People's Daily*, September 24, 1965, translated in *JPRS*, Vol. IV, No. 7 (on microfilm); "Discuss Post Plan Budgetary Weaknesses," *People's Daily*, August 3, 1965, translated in same *JPRS* source as above.
129. These two examples are presented in *People's Daily*, August 3, 1965, *op. cit.*

Chapter 5

1. Three good papers on the Chinese legal system are G. Hsiao, "Legal Institutions in Communist China," *Problems of Communism* (March-April 1965), pp. 112–21; J. Caber, *The Criminal Process in China*, unpublished paper, Harvard Law School, Cambridge, Mass., February, 1965. This chapter draws mainly on the Hsiao article. See also T. T. Hsia, "Justice in Peking: China's Legal System on Show," *Current Scene*, Vol. V, No. 1, January 16, 1967. Glimpses of the Chinese legal system are also presented in E. Snow, *The Other Side of the River* (New York: Random House, 1961), especially Chap. 74.

   Numerous laws and regulations introduced in Red China since 1949 which have a bearing on industrial enterprises are contained in A. Donnithorne, *China's Economic System* (London: Allen and Unwin, 1967).
2. Hsiao, *op. cit.*
3. F. Schurmann, *Ideology and Organization in Communist China* (Berkeley and Los Angeles: University of California Press, 1966), p. 188.
4. Snow, *op. cit.*, Chap. 74.
5. This situation is acknowledged in leading Chinese sources such as Peking's *People's Daily* and *Red Flag*. Cf. the editorials in *People's Daily*, January 25 and 26, February 15 and 23, March 7 and 13, 1967. For a U.S. commentary see R. Elegant, "Army's Bayonets, Guns Sustain Power of Mao," *Los Angeles Times*, March 17, 1967, Part I, p. 4; *Los Angeles Times*, March 19, Part I; R. Elegant, "Maoists Order Militia into Fight for Control," *Los Angeles Times*, March 21, 1967, Part I, p. 22.
6. Snow, *op. cit.*, p. 240.
7. As cited in Snow, p. 241.
8. See the penetrating discussion of wage determination in China in D. Perkins, *Market Control and Planning in Communist China* (Cambridge, Mass.: Harvard University Press, 1966), Chap. VII.
9. *Ibid.*

10. See B. Richman, *Soviet Management: With Significant American Comparisons* (Englewood Cliffs, N.J.: Prentice-Hall, 1965), pp. 79–81; M. Weitzman, et al., *Employment in the U.S.S.R., Dimensions of Soviet Economic Power* (Washington, D.C.: U.S. Government Printing Office, 1962), p. 635.
11. *Jen-min Jih-pao*, July 7, 1965 (article entitled "Retrenchment Improves Labor Productivity,") translated in *JPRS*, Vol. IV, No. 8 (July 1965–June 1966), on microfilm, Reel No. 52.
12. Snow, *op. cit.*, p. 235.
13. *Ibid.*, p. 236.
14. *Ibid.*
15. For comprehensive discussions and analyses of Red China's price system and price controls see Perkins, *op. cit.*, and N. R. Chen, "The Theory of Prize Formation in Communist China," *The China Quarterly*, No. 27 (July–September 1966), pp. 33–53.
16. For discussions of the pricing problems common to all communist economies see Richman, *op. cit.*, especially pp. 235 ff., and A. Nave, *The Soviet Economy* (New York: Praeger, 1961), especially Chaps. 4, 7, 8, and 9.
17. For a comprehensive presentation and Chinese sources dealing with taxation in Communist China see Donnithorne, *op. cit.*, Chap. XIV.
18. Cf. Donnithorne, *op. cit.*, Chaps. XIV and XV, and the many sources cited therein.
19. *Ibid.*, Chap. XV.
20. *People's Daily*, August 3, 1965 (article titled "Discuss Post Plan Budgetary Weaknesses"), translated in *JPRS*, Vol. IV, No. 7 (July 1965–June 1966), on microfilm, Reel No. 50. See also *Red Flag* (Hongoi), No. 1, January 4, 1964, p. 27.
21. See C. Y. Chen, *Scientific and Engineering Manpower in Communist China* (Washington, D.C.: National Science Foundation, 1965), pp. 149 ff.
22. For a general discussion of Chinese contract law see Hsiao, *op. cit.*, and Donnithorne, *op. cit.*, Chap. VII. See also a Chinese article by C. Sung, "A Brief Discussion of the Nature and Function of Contracts in Our National Economy," *Economic Research*, No. 2 (February 1965).
23. Cf. Richman, *op. cit.*, Chaps. 6, 7, 8; E. Johnson, "Planning and Contract Law," *Soviet Studies* (January 1961); *Ekonomicheskaya Gazeta*, October 26, 1963, pp. 24 ff.
24. Cf. C. Weng, "The Problem of Developing Fixed Cooperation and Fixed Point Supply in Local Industry," *Economic Research*, No. 4 (April 1965); see also Donnithorne, *op. cit.*, Chap. VII.
25. See the related discussions and sources cited in Donnithorne, *op. cit.*, Chaps. VII, XI. W. L. Yuan, *The Economy of Communist China* (New York: Praeger, 1965), pp. 69 ff.; H. T. Wong, "The New Five-Anti Campaign of Communist China," *Studies on Mainland China*, Vol. VII, No. 1 (Taiwan, January 1964), pp. 52–58.
26. See Richman, *op. cit.*, Chaps. 6, 7, 8.
27. Donnithorne, *op. cit.*, Chap. XI; *Southern Daily* (Nanfang Ribao), January 14, 1966.
28. See Yuan, *op. cit.*, and Wong, *op. cit.*
29. See especially Donnithorne, *op. cit.* Throughout much of Donnithorne's comprehensive book numerous laws, regulations, resolutions, decrees, policies, and other rules of the game pertaining to industrial management are cited. It is clear that there have been frequent and often major changes in rules of the game since 1949, many of them quite difficult to interpret and inconsistent. There have

been many published volumes of *Collected Laws and Regulations.* There have also been numerous other official Communist Chinese documents spelling out rules of the game for firms and managers and including in part *Reports on Party Congresses, People's Handbooks, State Plans,* and the *Constitution of the People's Republic of China.*

30. A. Eckstein, *Communist China's Economic Growth and Foreign Trade* (New York: McGraw-Hill, 1966), pp. 42 and 314, Table 3–1.
31. *Ibid.* See also A. Bergson, *The Real National Income of Soviet Russia Since 1928* (Cambridge: Harvard University Press, 1961), p. 46, Table 3. The Soviet Union allocated only 3 percent of GNP to defense in 1928 and reached a level of only 7 percent in 1937.
32. Eckstein, *op. cit.*, pp. 262, 331, 332.
33. *Ibid.*

33a. *Kung-tso Tung-hsun*, August 4, 1961.

34. This is my own speculative estimate based on what I have read and on pure intuition.
35. Defense spending figures for these other countries have been derived from their official government publications.
36. D. Perkins, *The Economics of Chinese Communist Foreign Policy* (mimeographed, July 1964), p. 18.
37. *Ibid.*; Eckstein, *op. cit.*, pp. 262–63, 332.
38. C. Y. Cheng, "Peking's Minds of Tomorrow," *Current Scene*, Vol. IV, No. 6 (March 15, 1966), p. 4. About 150,000 engineers and technicians were employed in China's defense industries in 1959.
39. M. Halperin, *China and the Bomb* (London: Pall Mall Press, 1965), p. 74.
40. Cf. Eckstein, *op. cit.*; Perkins, *op. cit.*; the articles by C. Fitzgerald and A. Halpern in R. Davis, (ed.), *Contemporary China* (New York: Vintage Books, 1966); Snow, *op. cit.*; A. Dallin, *Diversity in International Communism* (New York: Columbia University Press, 1963); W. Griffith, *The Sino-Soviet Rift* (Cambridge: Massachusetts Institute of Technology Press, 1964); D. Zagoria, *The Sino-Soviet Rift* (Princeton: Princeton University Press, 1961); essays by R. Price and M. Kovner and the Appendix in *An Economic Profile of Mainland China* (prepared for the Joint Economic Committee of the U. S. Congress), Vol. 2, (Washington: U.S. Government Printing Office, 1967).
41. For an excellent historical perspective on China's foreign trade, see Eckstein, *op. cit.*
42. Cf. J. Duncan, "Red China's Economic Development Since 1949," *Contemporary China*, pp. 139–50. See also Duncan's book, *A Businessman Looks at Red China* (New York: D. Van Nostrand, 1965).
43. Cf. Snow, *op. cit.*, especially Chap. 25; see also Chaps. 14, 56, 82, 83.
44. Cf. Eckstein, *op. cit.*; *The Sino-Soviet Conflict*, Hearings of the House Subcommittee on the Far East (Washington: Government Printing Office, 1965); R. Price, "International Trade of Communist China, 1950–65," *An Economic Profile of Mainland China*, II, 579–608.
45. Price, *op. cit.*, p. 591.
46. Duncan, *op. cit.*, p. 144.
47. Eckstein, *op. cit.*, Chap. 5.
48. In the October 6, 1959 issue of Peking's *People's Daily*, Chou En-lai gave an official figure of 10,800 Soviet technicians and experts and 1,500 from other East European countries during the 1950's.
49. At a diplomatic dinner attended by Edgar Snow in Peking in 1960 a Western diplomat stated that there had been 22,000 Soviet technicians and advisers in

China during the 1950's. A Russian diplomat who was present and heard this figure did not disclaim it. See Snow, *op. cit.*, pp. 217–18.

50. *Ibid.*, p. 218.
51. Price, *op. cit.*
52. See Donnithorne, *op. cit.*, Chap. VII. Donnithorne's source is *New Hunan Daily*, February 13, 1960, a copy of which I could not obtain to check this figure.
53. Cheng, *op. cit.*, Chap. 4, pp. 93 ff.
54. *Ibid.*, and Snow, *op. cit.*, p. 226.
55. Snow, *op. cit.*, p. 226.
56. Soviet assistance and aid to China is discussed and analyzed by Eckstein, *op. cit.*, Price, *op. cit.*, Duncan, *op. cit.*, and R. Dernberger, "Economic Realities," *Contemporary China*, pp. 125–37.
57. D. Davies, "Interview with Han Suyin," *Far Eastern Economic Review* (November 24, 1966), p. 431. Miss Suyin was told this in Peking by Mr. Yung, vice chairman of the China Council for the Promotion of International Trade. I too was also told this by Mr. Yung in May 1966.
58. These figures are from Snow, *op. cit.* See also C.M. Li, "The First Decade: Economic Development," *China Quarterly*, No. 1 (January-March 1960).
59. "Communist China's Balance of Payments," *An Economic Profile of Mainland China*, II, 625.
60. Cf. C. Lynch, *China: One Fourth of the World* (Toronto: McClelland and Stewart Ltd., 1965), Chap. 4; Duncan, *op. cit.*, especially Chaps. 4 and 10; Snow, *op. cit.*, especially Chap. 27.
61. Productivity figures for these plants in the 1959–60 period are given in Snow, *op. cit.*, pp. 516 and 575–76. I discuss 1965 in a later chapter.
62. See the sources cited in Notes 40 and 44 above and G. Hudson, R. Lowenthal, and MacFarquhar, *The Sino-Soviet Dispute* (New York: Praeger, 1961).
63. Her findings were presented in her article "Managers Under Mao," *Management Today*, April 1967, pp. 67–71.
64. Eckstein, *op. cit.*, p. 94.
65. *Ibid.*, pp. 120–21, Table 4–9.
66. "China in World Trade," *Current Scene*, Vol. IV, No. 3 (February 1, 1966), Part I.
67. Soviet exports rose by about 50 percent between 1960 and 1966. See "The Foreign Trade of the Soviet Union," *The Financial Post*, Report on the U.S.S.R. (April 15, 1967), p. R–5; this is a Canadian publication. The actual 1966 foreign trade figure given is 15 billion rubles.
68. China's balance-of-payments position and foreign-exchange reserves are analyzed in "Communist China's Balance of Payments, 1950–65," *An Economic Profile of Communist China*, pp. 621 ff.
69. Cf. H. Lu, "On China's Guidelines of Self-Reliance in Socialist Construction," *Ching-chi Yen-chiu*, No. 7 (July 20, 1965).
70. This section is based largely on data presented in Eckstein, *op. cit.*, especially Tables 4–5 and 4–7; Price, *op. cit.*, and "China in World Trade," *Current Scene*, Parts I and II, February 1 and 15, 1966. The 1965 figures are from Price and *Current Scene*.
71. This section is based in large part on data presented in the sources cited in Notes 68 and 69 above.
72. For detailed data on these complete plants see Price, *op. cit.*, especially Table 16, and pp. 602–4.
73. Cf. R. Thompson, "Selling to Communist China," *Foreign Trade* (published by the Canadian Department of Trade and Commerce, Ottawa), April 18,

1964; R. Thompson, "How to Travel in Communist China," *Foreign Trade*, January 23, 1965; R. Thompson and P. Roberts, "Communist China," and N. Gish, "Why Not Visit the Canton Fair," *Foreign Trade*, April 17, 1965; I. Litvock, "Canadian-Chinese Trade," *Business Quarterly*, Vol. XXVII, No. 2 (Summer 1962), pp. 49–54; *China's Foreign Trade* (published in Peking in English), No. 2, April 1966.

74. Data on the Canton Trade Fair has been obtained from *China's Foreign Trade*, pp. 12–13.
75. Cf. Price, *op. cit.*, p. 606; and the report by P. Braestrup in the *New York Times*, February 19, 1967. See also D. Perkins, "Economic Growth in China and the Cultural Revolution," *The China Quarterly* (1967).
76. Braestrup and Perkins, *op. cit.*
77. An analysis and related data pertaining to China's foreign trade during 1967 and 1968 can be found in the following articles: B. Richman, "China Organizes Foreign Trade to Accelerate Development," and R. Dernberger, "The China Trade," in *Columbia Journal of World Business*, November 1968.
78. Cf. *Import Trade Control Policy—For the Year April 1965 to March 1966*, (New Delhi: Ministry of Commerce, Government of India, 1965). In 1965 the Office of the Controller of Imports and Exports in New Delhi alone processed 324,000 formal import and export applications submitted by Indian enterprises. This figure is given in *The Statesman* (Calcutta), February 14, 1966, p. 1. Numerous government ministries, commissions, committees, offices, directorates, bureaus, departments, and sections are involved in import and export decisions pertaining directly to Indian firms.
79. For a more detailed discussion see Schurman, *op. cit.*, pp. 109 ff.
80. See C. Johnson, "Chinese Communist Leadership and Mass Response: The Yenan Period and the Socialist Education Campaign Period," *China's Heritage and the Communist Political System* (Chicago: University of Chicago Press, 1967).
81. See also B. Richman, "Capitalists and Managers in Communist China," *Harvard Business Review*, January-February 1967, pp. 57 ff.
82. For a discussion and analysis of purges in Red China during the 1949–65 period see Schurmann, *op. cit.*, pp. 56, 71, 174, 205, 215 ff., 238 ff., 267 ff., 318, 333 ff., and 353 ff.
83. The Soviet industrial reorganization of 1957 is analyzed in Richman, *Soviet Management*, especially Chap. 2. The Chinese reorganization of industry during the Great Leap is dealt with in some depth in Schurmann, *op. cit.*, Chaps. I–IV; C. M. Li, *Economic Development of Communist China* (Berkeley and Los Angeles: University of California Press, 1959).
84. For an analysis of the role of the party at Soviet enterprises see Richman, *Soviet Management*, pp. 220 ff. See also J. Hough, *The Role of the Local Party Organs in Soviet Industrial Decision Making* (Cambridge: Harvard University, unpublished doctoral dissertation, 1961).
85. This opinion is also expressed in Perkins, *op. cit.*
86. See the sources cited in Note 5 above. See also Perkins, *op. cit.*, Braestrup, *op. cit.*, New China News Agency's English release of February 27, 1967, and a Peking broadcast of March 7, 1967.
87. Elegant, *op. cit.*
88. Elegant, *op. cit.*
89. Editorials in Peking *People's Daily*, January 26 and 27, 1967.
90. "Cultural Revolution Spurs New All-Round Leap in China's Economy," *Peking Review*, No. 2 (1967), p. 15.

91. Cf. Y.L. Wu, *op. cit.*, Chap. 1.
92. See F. Schurmann and O. Schell, *Republican China* (New York: Random House, 1967), especially pp. 133–34. See also the essay entitled "The Rise of the Kuomintang" by T. H. White in this book, pp. 135 ff.
93. Wu, *op. cit.*, p. 5.
94. Detailed organization charts of the central government and the central party apparatus in Red China are contained in "Who's Who in Peking," *Current Scene*, Vol. IV, No. 15 (August 8, 1966).
95. Cf. Y. Wu, "Planning, Management and Economic Development in Communist China," *An Economic Profile of Mainland China*, Vol. 1 (Washington, D.C.: U.S. Government Printing Office, 1967), pp. 97–118; R. Diao, *Communist China's Financial Planning in National Economy and Industry*, in Chinese (Hong Kong: Union Research Institute, 1966); a report by F.C. Li (chairman of Red China's State Planning Commission) in *People's Daily*, Peking, September 25, 1956; "Post Plan Budgeting Weaknesses," *People's Daily*, Peking, August 3, 1965; *Ta Kung Pao*, Peking, September 10 and 13, 1965; *JPRS*, No. 33893, January 26, 1966.
96. See the sources cited in Note 25 above.
97. For sources dealing with the Soviet Union see Note 26 above.
98. For related discussions see Donnithorne, *op. cit.*, especially Chap. VI; Schurmann, *op. cit.*, Chaps. I–IV; C.M. Li, *op. cit.*, D. Perkins, *Industrial Planning and Management in Communist China* (mimeographed), to be published by Aldine Press, probably in 1967; F. Schurmann, "Party and Government," *Communist China*, pp. 112–32.
99. There are currently the following six regional party bureaus in China: North China, Northeast, East China, Central-South, Southwest, and Northwest; see "Who's Who in Peking," *Current Scene*, p. 10.
100. For an examination of Soviet enterprises see Richman, *Soviet Management*, especially Chaps. 3, 5, 7, and 10.
101. For discussions and analyses of current Soviet reforms and dilemmas see Richman, *op. cit.*, J. Felker, *Soviet Economic Controversies* (Cambridge: The M.I.T. Press, 1966); "Ivan Looks to the West: Russia's Next 50 Years," *Business Week*, April 29, 1957, pp. 86 ff.
102. This very brief and general discussion of the impact of India's political organization on industrial firms and their managements is based on my as yet unpublished firsthand research in India. See also the following firsthand studies: A. Phatak, *External Environmental Constraints and Their Impact on the Internal Operations of Firms in the Pharmaceutical and Engineering Industries in India* (Los Angeles; University of California, unpublished doctoral dissertation, 1966); A. Negandhi, *Private Foreign Investment Climate in India* (East Lansing, Michigan: Institute for International Business Management Studies, Michigan State University, 1965). Numerous concrete examples of the negative constraints on managerial effectiveness and productive efficiency in Indian industry arising from problems within the government bureaucracy are presented in the *Annual Reports of the Indian Engineering Association*, Calcutta, and in the monthly news bulletins of this association.

Chapter 6

1. By the early 1950's a great deal had already been published in these areas. Cf. J. Bell, *A History of Economic Thought* (New York: The Ronald Press, 1953),

particularly the numerous references which show how extensive this economic work has been.

2. A large proportion of these studies are cited and discussed in the two volumes of *An Economic Profile of Mainland China* (Washington, D.C.: U.S. Government Printing Office, 1967). See particularly the survey article by W. Galenson, "The Current State of Chinese Economic Studies," in Volume I, pp. 1–13. A comprehensive economic study not cited in the above two-volume study because it was not yet published is A. Donnithorne, *China's Economic System* (London: Allen and Unwin, 1967). See also the very detailed bibliography in N. R. Chen, *The Economy of Mainland China, 1949–63, A Bibliography of Materials in English* (Berkeley: Committee on the Economy of China, Social Science Research Council, 1963).
3. The following sources have been particularly helpful to me in my analyses throughout this section of economic system constraints in Red China: Y. L. Wu, "Planning, Management, and Economic Development in Communist China," *An Economic Profile*, Vol. 1, pp. 97–119; Donnithorne, *op. cit.*, R. Diao, *Communist China's Financial Planning in National Economy and Industry* (in Chinese) (Hong Kong: Union Research Institute, 1966); *Jen-min Jih-pao*, (*People's Daily*, Peking), September 25, 1956, report by Li Fu-ch'un, chairman of China's State Planning Commission; *People's Daily*, Peking, August 3, 1965, article titled "Past Plan and Budgeting Weaknesses," *Ta Kung Pao*, Peking, September 10, 1965; *Joint Publications Research Service* (JPRS), Washington, D.C., No. 33893, January 26, 1966.
4. For pertinent studies dealing with the Soviet economic system and management see A. Nave, *The Soviet Economy* (New York: Praeger, 1961); J. Felker, *Soviet Economic Controversies* (Cambridge: M.I.T. Press, 1966); B. Richman, *Soviet Management: With Significant American Comparisons* (Englewood Cliffs, N.J.: Prentice-Hall, 1965); B. Richman, *Management Development and Education in the Soviet Union* (East Lansing, Mich.: Institute for International Business and Economic Development Studies, Michigan State University, 1967); R. Campbell, *Soviet Economic Power* (Boston: Houghton Mifflin, 1960)—see 148 ff. of Campbell for an excellent discussion of Soviet financial control and fiscal policy. These sources contain extensive documentation.
5. For a comprehensive study on China's statistical system see C. M. Li, *The Statistical System of Communist China* (Berkeley and Los Angeles: University of California Press, 1962). Two pertinent sources on China's economic accounting system are: C. W. Kwang, "The Economic Accounting System of State Enterprises in Mainland China," *The International Journal of Accounting*, Vol. 1, No. 2 (Spring 1966), pp. 61–99; and P. Kircher, "Accounting Revolution in Red China," *Financial Executive*, February 1967, pp. 39 ff.
6. Wu, *op. cit.*, p. 110.
7. *Ibid.*, p. 109.
8. See B. Richman, "Managerial Decision Making and Performance of the Enterprise Level in Communist Chinese Industry," a paper prepared for the Hearings on the Economy of Mainland China, April 10, 1967, conducted in Washington by the Joint Economic Committee of the U.S. Congress; published in *Mainland China in the World Economy* (Washington, D.C.: U.S. Government Printing Office, 1967), pp. 50 ff. See also *Socialist Industrialization and Agricultural Collectivization in China* (Peking: Foreign Languages Press, 1965.)
9. Cf. D. Audette, "Computer Technology in Communist China," *Communications of the ACM*, Vol. 9, No. 9 (September 1966), pp. 655–61. For sources on computers and sophisticated mathematical-planning techniques in the Soviet

economy see Richman, *Management Development*, *op. cit.*, especially pp. 130–31, 148–49, 222–23, and 242–43; Richman, *Soviet Management*, 1965, pp. 241–46; V. Glushkov, "Apply Computer Technology to the Administration of the National Economy," translated in *Current Digest of the Soviet Press* (*CDSP*), Vol. XVI, No. 28 (1964), pp. 23–25; V. Glushkov and N. Federenko, "On Certain Problems of Cybernetics," *CDSP*, Vol. XVI, No. 36 (1964), pp. 37–39; L. Kantenavich, "Mathematics and Economics," *CDSP*, Vol. XVII, No. 34 (1965), pp. 7–9; C. Nardov, "On Systems Network Planning and Control," *CDSP*, Vol. XVII, No. 9 (1965), pp. 26 ff.

10. The discussion of monetary policies and banking in Republican China is based in large part on the following sources: A. Young, *China's Wartime Finance and Inflation* 1937–1945 (Cambridge: Harvard University Press, 1965); S. H. Chou, *The Chinese Inflation* 1937–49 (New York: Columbia University Press, 1963); K. N. Chang, *The Inflationary Spiral: The Experience in China* (New York: Wiley, 1958); T. C. Tsiang, "Money and Banking in Communist China," *An Economic Profile of Mainland China*, Vol. I (Washington, D.C.: U.S. Government Printing Office, 1967), pp. 325–28; J. Gurley, Book Reviews, *American Economic Review*, Vol. LVI, No. 5 (December 1966), pp. 1266–69, 1276–77.
11. These figures are summarized in Gurley, *op. cit.*, p. 1267.
12. Tsiang, *op. cit.*, p. 325.
13. I have made considerable use of the following sources in my discussion and analyses of money and banking in Communist China: Tsiang, *op. cit.*, pp. 323–39; Donnithorne, *op. cit.*, Chap. XV; Gurley, *op. cit.*, pp. 1268–77; T. Miyoshita, *The Currency and Financial System of Mainland China* (Tokyo: The Institute of Asian Economic Affairs, 1966); Perkins, *op. cit.*, Chaps. VIII and IX; C. K. Liu, "How the Law of Money Circulation Operates Under the Socialist System," *Ching-chi Yeu-chiu* (*Economic Research*), No. 2 (February 17, 1963); D. Davies, "Interview with Han Suyin," *Far Eastern Economic Review*, November 24, 1966, pp. 430–34.
14. For an excellent discussion of money and banking in the Soviet Union and East Europe see Nave, *op. cit.*, Chap. 3; G. Garvey, *Money, Banking and Credit in Eastern Europe* (New York: Federal Reserve Bank, 1966); *Ekonomicheskaya Gazeta*, November 30, 1963, pp. 13–15.
15. Cf. Y. Po, "New China's Price Policy," *Peking Review*, No. 47 (November 20, 1964); Perkins, *op. cit.*, Chaps. VIII and IX; Davies, *op. cit.*; N. R. Chen, "The Theory of Price Formation in Communist China," *The China Quarterly*, No. 27 (July-September 1966), pp. 33–53.
16. Tsiang, *op. cit.*, pp. 333–34.
17. Cf. Donnithorne, *op. cit.*, Chap. XV.
18. Cf. *People's Daily*, August 3, 1965 and the sources cited in Note 20 of Chap. 6 in this book.
19. Cf. editorials, *People's Daily*, September 26 and December 30, 1965. See also the translations of Chinese articles on banking and finance in *Joint Publications Research Service* (JPRS), Vol. IV, No. 8 (February 4, 1966), microfilm reel No. 52.
20. See the sources cited in Note 40 in Chapter 5. See also Richman, *Soviet Management*, *op. cit.*, pp. 226–27; J. Berliner, *Factory and Manager in the USSR* (Cambridge: Harvard University Press, 1957), Chap. XVI.
21. The discussion of fiscal policies in Republican China is based largely on the sources cited in Note 10 above.
22. T. C. Liu, and K. C. Yeh, *The Economy of the Chinese Mainland: National*

Income and Economic Development, 1933–59 (Princeton, N.J.: Princeton University Press, 1965).

23. These figures are summarized in Gurley, *op. cit.*, p. 1267.

23a. I have made considerable use of the following sources in my discussion and analyses of fiscal policies and the state budget in Communist China: W. Hollister, "Trends in Capital Formation in Communist China," *An Economic Profile of Mainland China*, pp. 121–53; *Ten Glorious Years* (Peking: Foreign Languages Press, 1960); E. Jones, "The Emerging Pattern of China's Economic Revolution," *An Economic Profile*, pp. 77–95; C. M. Li, "China's Industrial Development, 1958–63," *Industrial Development in Communist China* (New York: Praeger, 1964), pp. 3–38; L. K. Yung, "Self-Reliance Has Proved Itself," *China Reconstructs*, Vol. XV, No. 4 (April 1966), pp. 6–11; Miyoshita, *op. cit.*, Davies, *op. cit.*, Donnithorne, *op. cit.*, especially Chaps. VI and XIV; Perkins, *op. cit.*, Po, *op. cit.*, Chen, *op. cit.*, Diao, *op. cit.*, and R. Diao, *Communist China's Finance in* 1964 (mimeographed paper reproduced by Union Research Institute, Hong Kong, 1965).

24. See Tsiang, *op. cit.*, p. 332.

25. For outline and discussion of the financial plan of the Chinese firm see C. W. Kwang, "The Economic Accounting System of State Enterprises in Mainland China," *The International Journal of Accounting*, Vol. 1, No. 2 (Spring 1966) especially pp. 71 ff. More will be said about the overall enterprise plan in Chapter 8 of this book.

26. Davies, *op. cit.*, p. 430; and Perkins, *op. cit.*

27. Davies, *op. cit.*, p. 430.

28. Li, *op. cit.*, p. 20.

29. Perkins, *op. cit.*, p. 103, Table 7.

30. Gurley, *op. cit.*, p. 1269.

31. These gross domestic investment and GNP figures have been derived from Hallister, *op. cit.*, p. 125, Table 1; Li, *op. cit.*, p. 21; Y. L. Wu, *The Economy of Communist China* (New York: Praeger, 1965); T. C. Liu, p. 91, Table V-1; "The Tempo of Economic Development of the Chinese Mainland, 1949–65," *An Economic Profile of Mainland China*, Vol. I, p. 50, Table 1. T. C. Liu estimates only a 15 percent drop in GNP and 19 percent in per capita income but most experts disagree and place their estimates significantly higher.

32. Davies, *op. cit.*, p. 430; see also Yung, *op. cit.*, pp. 6 ff.; Jones, *op. cit.*, p. 85.

33. The gross fixed investment data used in this section are derived from Hollister, *op. cit.*, pp. 124 ff.

34. The data for other Asian countries can be found in Hollister, *op. cit.*, p. 126, Table 3, and *Economic Survey for Asia and the Far East*, 1961 (New York and Geneva: United Nations, 1962).

35. Figures on industrial investment for the 1950's have been derived from Hollister, *op. cit.*, pp. 128 ff. The qualitative analysis is based in part on Hollister's study and Jones, *op. cit.*, pp. 85 ff.

36. Jones, *op. cit.*, p. 85; R. Field, "Chinese Communist Industrial Production," in *An Economic Profile*, I, pp. 269 ff.

37. Donnithorne, *op. cit.*, Chap. VI.

38. Jones, *op. cit.*, p. 87.

39. Cf. Davies, *op. cit.*, and Yung, *op. cit.*

40. Hollister, *op. cit.*, Table 4, and pp. 128–29.

41. Gurley, 1966, *op. cit.*, p. 1271.

42. Revenue figures for the 1960–64 period are from Donnithorne, *op. cit.*; *Peking Review*, January 3, 1964 and January 1 and July 30, 1965.

43. Davies, *op. cit.*, p. 430. Other tax data in this section are derived from Perkins, *op. cit.*; Donnithorne, *op. cit.*, Chaps. VI and XIV; Chen, *op. cit.*; Po, *op. cit.*
44. Unless otherwise specified, Chinese profit data in this section are also derived from the sources cited in Note 43 above, and Yung, *op. cit.*, F. Schurmann, *Ideology and Organization in Communist China* (Berkeley and Los Angeles: University of California Press, 1966), especially Chaps. I and IV.
45. Donnithorne, *op. cit.*, Chap. XIV.
46. The figures presented in Table 6–1 are from Perkins, *op. cit.*, p. 111, Table 10.
47. Cf. Donnithorne, *op. cit.*, Chaps. VI and XIV; Perkins, *op. cit.*, especially Chap. VI.
48. Cf. the sources cited in Note 19 above.
49. In addition to my own firsthand research in India, the discussion of Indian fiscal policy is also based on the sources cited here. The Indian figures presented in this section—with the exception of the 14.9% rate of gross fixed investment—have been derived from the following sources which contain a great amount of figures and detailed information:

    A series of four articles by N. Palkhivala, "Most Taxed Nation," *The Times of India*, February 6, 7, 8, 9, 1965; *Report on Currency and Finance, 1964–65* (Bombay: Reserve Bank of India, 1965); United Nations Conference on Trade and Development, Geneva, March 23–June 15, 1964 (New York: United Nations, 1964, report E/Conf. 46/76); V. Phatak, *External Environmental Constraints and Their Impact upon the Internal Operations of Firms in the Pharmaceutical and Engineering Industries in India*, unpublished doctoral dissertation (Los Angeles: University of California, 1966), especially Chap. III; A. Negandhi, *Private Foreign Investment Climate in India* (East Lansing, Mich.: Institute for International Business Management Studies, Michigan State University, 1965), also published in a longer version by Vora and Company Private Ltd., Bombay, 1966; *Journal of Industry and Trade* (Government of India), 1965 and 1966 issues; *Monthly Abstract of Statistics* (Government of India), 1965 and 1966 issues; *The Statesman*, Calcutta, November 10, 1965, February 23, March 18, June 28, July 1, 1966; *The Economic Times*, Bombay, December 2, 1965, January 10, March 28, June 30, 1966.
50. For a thorough discussion and analysis of price stability in Red China see Perkins, *op. cit.*, especially Chaps. VII, VIII, IX. The price figures for Communist China are derived from this source.
51. For a list of these prices see J. Duncan, *A Businessman Looks at Red China* (New York: D. Van Nostrand, 1965), pp. 96–97.
52. Price data for India have been derived from *India, Pocketbook of Economic Information* (Delhi, Government of India Press, 1964 and 1965 editions); *Statistical Outline of India*, 1964 and 1965 editions, prepared by Tata Industries Private Limited (Bombay: Popular Prakashan, 1964 and 1965); *Report on Currency and Finance*, 1964–65, *The Times of India*, February 25 and July 3, 1966; *The Statesman*, Calcutta, December 18, 1965, July 2, 1966.
53. I agree, with the aggregate GNP and per capita average annual growth rates for 1949–66 cited by J. Gurley, in *Mainland China in The World Economy*, Hearings of the Joint Economic Committee, Congress of the United States, April 5, 10, 11 and 12, 1967 (Washington, D.C.: U.S. Government Printing Office, 1967), p. 188. Gurley, who is editor of the *American Economic Review* and professor of economics at Stanford University, has very recently made a comprehensive analysis, as I have tried to do, of available GNP, per capita income, and other growth estimates for Red China. Of the estimates made by leading and respected Sinologists, T. C. Liu's growth estimates appear to be the lowest,

and most experts disagree with him on the basis of available data, objective analyses, interpretation of information, and sheer intuition. See Liu's estimates, analysis, and statements in *An Economic Profile, op. cit.*, pp. 45–75; and in *Mainland China in the World Economy*, pp. 36 ff.

Criticisms of Liu's estimates and alternative estimates can be found in a letter, comments, and a statement by W. Macomber, Jr., E. Jones, and K. Chao, respectively (as well as Gurley) in *Mainland China in the World Economy*. See also Wu, 1965, *op. cit.*, Table V-1 and pp. 90 ff; and D. Perkins, "Economic Growth in China and the Cultural Revolution (1960-April 1967)," *The China Quarterly*, 1967.

Unless otherwise noted GNP and per capita income figures cited throughout this section are based on a careful analysis of the above sources.

54. R. Field, "Chinese Communist Industrial Production," *An Economic Profile*, p. 273, Table 1. Most of the industrial growth data in this section have been derived from this source. Unless otherwise noted, the figures to be presented here are derived from this source.
55. These employment growth-rate estimates are based on data presented in J. Emerson, "Employment in Mainland China: Problems and Prospects," *An Economic Profile*, pp. 403–469; and L. Orleans, *Professional Manpower and Education in Communist China* (Washington, D.C.: National Science Foundation, 1961), Chap. VIII. Unless otherwise noted, employment figures cited in this section are derived from these sources.
56. See Field, *op. cit.*, pp. 278–80 and Table 4.
57. Cf. Jones in *An Economic Profile*, and *Mainland China in the World Economy*, Perkins, *op. cit.*, Field, *op. cit.*
58. Pertinent sources dealing with Red China's agricultural performance since 1949 include M. Larsen, "China's Agriculture Under Communism," *An Economic Profile*, pp. 197–267; statements and papers by Jones and Liu in *Profile* and *Mainland China in the World Economy*; Perkins, *op. cit.*; L. Kuo, "Agricultural Mechanization in Communist China," in Li, ed., *Industrial Development in Communist China*.

    For those readers interested in Chinese Communist agriculture the above sources contain comprehensive documentation and cite many other works in this field.
59. Field, *op. cit.*, places the 1965 level of industrial output somewhat lower than 50 percent above the 1957 level. However, I agree with the arguments supporting the 50 percent figure presented by Perkins, *op. cit.*, and Jones, *An Economic Profile*. See also *Far Eastern Economic Review*, September 29, 1966.
60. "Cultural Revolution Spurs New All-Round Leap in China's Economy," *Peking Review*, No. 2 (1967), p. 15.
61. See the analysis in Perkins, *op. cit.*
62. *Ibid.*; "Record Harvest in Red China," *San Francisco Chronicle*, December 28, 1966, p. 1; *Peking Review*, Nos. 1 and 2, 1967.
63. Figures for India cited in this section have been derived from the statistical and economic information sources cited in Note 52 above; *Outline of India's Draft Fourth Five-Year Plan* (New Delhi: National Planning Commission, Government of India, 1967); *United Nation's Statistical Yearbooks; Monthly Commentary on Indian Economic Conditions*, published by the Indian Institute of Public Opinion, New Delhi; *Gross National Product, Growth Rates and Trend Data by Region and Country* (Washington, D.C.: Agency for International Development, Statistics and Reports Division, March 31, 1967); Field, *op. cit.*, pp. 278–80 and p. 295, Table 10; Gurley, *op. cit.*, p. 188.

64. Our discussion and analysis of Red China's mineral resources is based largely on the information and documentation provided by K. P. Wang, "The Mineral Resource Base of Communist China," in *An Economic Profile*, I, 167–95; and Wang's chapter on China in *U.S. Bureau of Mines 1965 Minerals Yearbook*, Vol. IV.
65. *People's Daily*, Peking, January 6, 1967.
66. Wang, *op. cit.*, p. 80; *Far Eastern Economic Review*, December 9, 1965, p. 76.
67. Data on India's mineral resources have been derived from the sources cited in Table 6–5 of this chapter.
68. *London Sunday Times*, May 25, 1967, and *Los Angeles Times*, May 25, 1967, Part I, p. 2.
69. Wang, *op. cit.*, p. 195.
70. Our discussion is based in large part on the sources cited in Note 58 above.
71. Indian agricultural data presented in this section have been derived from the sources cited in Table 6–7 of this chapter.
72. Larsen, *op. cit.*, p. 209.
73. See Larsen, *op. cit.*, p. 199. The 13 percent figure was given by a high-level Chinese Communist official in an interview with Han Suyin; see Davies, *op. cit.*, p. 432.
74. I use the estimates of Jones, Larsen, and O. L. Dawson, the former U.S. agricultural attaché in China, as cited by Jones in *An Economic Profile*, and *Mainland China in the World Economy*; Larsen, *op. cit.*; and T. C. Liu, in *Mainland China in the World Economy*. Liu disagrees with many of these estimates, preferring lower ones in most cases. However, Liu is clearly among a very small minority of leading Sinologists and agricultural experts. I agree with the positions, analyses, reasoning, and supporting evidence of Liu's opponents in this debate. In addition to the Jones and Larsen studies and statements cited above, see also the statements by J. Gurley, R. Dernberger, and A. Eckstein, in *Mainland China in the World Economy*, and Perkins, *op. cit.*
75. See Jones, *An Economic Profile*, p. 93, Table II. Official Communist Chinese statistics actually show increases in total grain output for 1954 and 1956. O. L. Dawson estimates a slight increase in total output for 1954, and a slight decline for 1956, with per capita output declining in both years.
76. For more comprehensive statistics on China's availability of chemical fertilizers since 1941, see Larsen, *op. cit.*, p. 246, Table 2.
77. See W. Kaye, "The State of Nutrition in Communist China," *China Quarterly*, (July-September 1961), pp. 126 ff.
78. Cf., the nutritional breakdown of estimated per capita caloric intake in Larsen, *op. cit.*, p. 265, Table 3.
79. Cf., I. May, *The Ecology of Malnutrition in the Far and Near East* (New York: Hafner, 1961), pp. 20–21.
80. Y. Gluckstein, *Mao's China* (Boston: The Beacon Press, 1957), p. 262.
81. Cf., the information obtained from Red Chinese refugees cited in F. Harper, ed., *Out of China* (Hong Kong: The Green Pagoda Press Ltd., 1964).
82. Larsen, *op. cit.*, p. 260.
83. Jones in *Profile*, p. 96, Table VI.
84. *Ibid.*, p. 84. Chou En-lai told Edgar Snow in an interview that China intends to regain 1957 per capita levels of farm output by 1970.
85. Davies, *op. cit.*, p. 432.
86. For additional information not contained in Table 6–6 see Larsen, *op. cit.*, pp. 259–60.

87. *People's Daily*, January 4, 1967 (article entitled "Production of Cotton Reached Another Height").
88. See J. Aird, "Population Growth and Distribution in Mainland China," *An Economic Profile*, II, 341–401, especially Tables 3–6, pp. 363 ff., and Jones, in *Profile*, pp. 80–82, and p. 93, Table I. Aird's population study of Red China is very comprehensive and extensively documented. Most of the Chinese population figures in this section are derived from these two studies and from S. Chandrasekhar, *China's Population: Census and Vital Statistics* (Hong Kong: Hong Kong University Press, 1960).
89. Cf. E. Snow, "Interview With Mao," *The New Republic*, February 1965, p. 20.
90. Indian population data are derived from the sources cited in Notes 52 and 63 above.
91. Population statistics for 136 countries are presented in *World Bank Atlas of Per Capita Product and Population* (published by the International Bank for Reconstruction and Development, September 1966).
92. For fuller discussions, analyses and documentation of birth-control efforts to date in Communist China see Aird, *op. cit.*, especially pp. 358–59; Jones in *Profile*, pp. 80–82; Larsen, *op. cit.*, pp. 211–13; Chandrasekhar, *op. cit.*; E. Snow, *The Other Side of the River* (New York: Random House, 1962), pp. 413–17, 452, 586, 732.
93. Jones in *Profile*, p. 81.
94. *Washington Post*, February 3, 1964, p. A–12. From an interview granted Edgar Snow by Premier Chou En-lai in Guinea on January 23, 1964.
95. *Washington Post*, February 3, 1964, and Jones in *Profile*, p. 81.
96. F. Harbison and C. Myers, *Education, Manpower, and Economic Growth* (New York: McGraw-Hill, 1964), pp. 46–47, Tables 6 and 7.
97. *Ibid.*, p. 48, Table 8.
98. The Indian figure of two is from *India: Pocket Book of Economic Information*, 1964, p. 144.
99. Chinese data on medical graduates and other aspects of medicine and health are found in L. Orleans, "Communist China's Education: Policies, Problems, and Prospects," *An Economic Profile*, II, 511 ff.; C. Y. Cheng, "Scientific and Engineering Manpower in Communist China," *An Economic Profile*, Vol. II, p. 533, Chart 4; Snow, *op. cit.*, Chaps. 37, 38, 41, 42. Indian data can be found in the sources cited in Note 52 and 63 above.
100. Cf. G. Wilcox, "Contemporary Chinese Health, Medical Practice, and Philosophy," in Ruth Adams, ed., *Contemporary China* (New York: Vintage Books, 1966), pp. 105–20; G. Wilcox, "Observations on Medical Practices," *Bulletin of the Atomic Scientists*, June 1966, pp. 52 ff. (Dr. Wilcox is a Canadian physician and clinical professor of surgery at the University of Alberta); K. Elliott, "Observations on Medical Science and Education for the People's Republic of China," *The Canadian Medical Association Journal*, January 9, 1965, pp. 73 ff. Dr. Elliott is a professor at McGill University in Montreal and was an exchange professor in Red China in 1964.

    See also comments of Western doctors visiting China and other information in Snow, *op. cit.*, pp. 219, 301–8, and Chaps. 37 and 38; W. Chen, "Medicine and Public Health," in L. Gould, ed., *Science in Communist China* (Washington, D.C.: American Association for the Advancement of Science, 1961); Gurley, *Mainland China in the World Economy*, pp. 187–88.
101. See the sources cited above in Note 100.
102. For more information on traditional Chinese medicine including acupuncture, see Snow, *op. cit.*, Chap. 42; and Wilcox in *Contemporary China*, pp. 113–15.

103. Statistical estimates in this section pertaining to China's handicrafts sector have been obtained from Field, *op. cit.*, pp. 273–74, Tables 1, 2, and 3; Emerson, *op. cit.*, pp. 425–33, and p. 427, Table 3; P. Schran, "Handicrafts in Communist China," in C. M. Li, ed., *Industrial Development in Communist China,* pp. 151–73; C. M. Li, "China's Industrial Development: 1958–63," *Industrial Development,* pp. 15 ff.; Y. L. Wu, F. Hoeber, and M. Rockwell, *The Economic Potential of Communist China* (Menlo Park, Califorina: Stanford Research Institute, 1963), pp. 233–41.
104. The distinction between modern industry and handicrafts, or a modern industrial enterprise and a purely handicraft establishment, usually depends on whether mechanical power is used in the main production processes, irrespective of the number of workers employed.
105. See *Ten Great Years: Statistics of the Economic and Cultural Achievements of the People's Republic of China* (Peking: Foreign Languages Press, 1960), p. 49; and W. C. Tseng, *China's Socialist Industrialization,* in Chinese (Peking: People's Publishing House, 1958).
106. Cf. *Ten Great Years;* R. Hsia, "Changes in the Location of China's Steel Industry," in C. Li, ed., *Industrial Development in Communist China,* pp. 125–33; F. Schurmann, "China's New Economic Policy—Transition or Beginning," in Li, ed., *Industrial Development,* pp. 73 ff.; Donnithorne, *op. cit.*, Chap. VI.
107. *Ten Great Years;* Hsia, *op. cit.*; Donnithorne, *op. cit.*
108. For a listing and discussion of these six regional party bureaus, see Schurmann, *op. cit.*, pp. 148 ff.
109. Charles Lynch, a prominent Canadian newspaperman and writer, visited the two Chinese factories that produce automobiles. See his *China: One Fourth of the World* (Toronto: McClelland and Stewart Ltd., 1965), pp. 90–92, 109–11.
110. H. M. Kaas, "Roads and Rails in China," *Far Eastern Economic Review,* February 17, 1966, p. 326.
111. For statistics and other data on Chinese communes see Larsen, *op. cit.*, pp. 218 ff.
112. *Ibid.*
113. I have drawn chiefly on the following sources in my discussion and analysis of China's transportation sector: V. Lippit, "Development of Transportation in Communist China," *The China Quarterly,* No. 27 (July-September 1966), pp. 101–19; Donnithorne, *op. cit.*, Chap. X; Wong, *op. cit.*, pp. 190 ff.; J. Ashton, "Development of Electric Energy Resources in Communist China," in *Profile,* I, 297–316; Hollister, in *Profile,* I, 128–31, and Table 4; Snow, *op. cit.*, pp. 45, 167, 185, 503, 580–81; Duncan, *op. cit.*, pp. 90–91; *Ten Great Years;* H. M. Kaas, "Roads and Rails in China," *Far Eastern Economic Review,* February 17, 1966, pp. 326 ff.; *Far Eastern Economic Review Yearbook,* 1966.
114. Investment figures are from Hollister, *op. cit.*, and Donnithorne, *op. cit.*
115. Chinese railway figures are from the sources cited in Note 113 above with the exception of Ashton, Kaas, and Hollister. Wong, *op. cit.*, p. 191, estimates that Red China had about 33,600 kilometers of railway track in use around 1965. Snow, *op. cit.*, p. 45, states that China had about 38,000 kilometers of track as of 1960. I estimate about 35,000 to 38,000 kilometers of track in use as of 1967.
116. Indian aggregate statistics cited throughout the entire discussion of social-overhead capital have been obtained from *Fourth Draft Plan; Statistical Outline of India; India: Pocket Book of Economic Information;* and recent United Nations statistical yearbooks.
117. Duncan, *op. cit.*, p. 91.
118. Wang, *op. cit.*, pp. 190–91.
119. *Ibid.*

120. For concrete figures see Lippit, *op. cit.*, pp. 108–17.
121. Cf. "Anshan's New Product—25 Meter Railroad Steel," *People's Daily*, Peking, March 6, 1967.
122. Aggregate statistics on Chinese roads and water transportation are from Donnithorne, *op. cit.*; Kaas, *op. cit.*; Lippit, *op. cit.*; *Ten Great Years*, pp. 146 ff.; Wang, *op. cit.*; Duncan, *op. cit.*
123. Kaas, *op. cit.*, p. 326.
124. Cf. Snow. *op. cit.*, pp. 204, 211; and Lynch, *op. cit.*, pp. 91–92 and 109–12.
125. Aggregate statistics and other data on water transportation in China have been derived from Lippit, *op. cit.*, p. 113, Table 5; Donnithorne, *op. cit.*, Chap. X; *Ten Great Years*, pp. 144 ff.; Ashton, *op. cit.*, pp. 299–301; *JPRS*, Nos. 24999 and 27384 (1964).
126. *JPRS*, No. 24999 (1964).
127. *JPRS*, No. 27384 (1964); and Lippit, *op. cit.*, p. 117.
128. Lippit, *op. cit.*, Donnithorne, *op. cit.*, Chap. X.
129. *Far Eastern Economic Yearbook—1966*, p. 137; *JPRS*, No. 28891 (1964); Lippit, *op. cit.*, p. 117.
130. In addition to infoımation, observations, and findings derived through my first-hand study of Indian industry, the following sources support my basic findings and conclusions regarding transportation constraints in Indian industry: Phatak, especially pp. 112 ff.; an address by C. E. Cargin, chairman of the Indian Engineering Association in *Annual Report of the Indian Engineering Association*, Calcutta, 1964, pp. 130 ff.; P. C. Jain, *Problems in Indian Economics*, 7th ed. (Allahabad, India: Chaitanya Publishing House, 1962), pp. 326 ff., 396 ff., 402 ff., 563 ff.
131. Cf. *People's Daily*, Peking, January 25 and 26, February 14 and 16, 1967.
132. Cf. *New China News Agency*, English release of February 27, 1967, and a Peking broadcast of March 7, 1967; Perkins, *op. cit.*; P. Braestrup, in *New York Times*, February 19, 1967.
133. "New Record of Punctuality in Shanghai Railway Station," *People's Daily*, February 14, 1967.
134. Our general discussion and aggregate statistics pertaining to electric power in China are based in large part on Ashton, *op. cit.*, pp. 297–316; Wong, *op. cit.*, pp. 191–92; Donnithorne, *op. cit.*, Chap. V; Field, *op. cit.*, p. 293, Appendix C; Perkins, *op. cit.*; Y. L. Wu, *Economic Development and the Use of Energy Resources in Communist China* (New York: Praeger, 1963); *Current Scene*, Vol. III, No. 17 (April 15, 1965), pp. 10 ff.; *Ten Great Years*; and a statement and paper presented by K. Chao, in *Mainland China in the World Economy*, pp. 134–42.
135. Ashton, *op. cit.*, pp. 306 ff.
136. *Ibid.*
137. Wang, *op. cit.*, pp. 191–92; Ashton, *op. cit.*, pp. 302 ff.
138. Chinese statistics and estimates cited throughout the rest of this section unless otherwise noted are primarily from Ashton, *op. cit.*, especially pp. 306 ff., and Tables 4, 5, and 6; and also from Donnithorne, *op. cit.*, Wu, *op. cit.*, and *Ten Great Years*. Gross electric production estimates, which include energy used by power stations in the production of electric energy, are used in this section unless otherwise noted. Net power production usually averages about 4 to 8 percent less than gross output.
139. Ashton, *op. cit.*
140. Field, *op. cit.*, p. 293, Appendix C. This source also contains the State Department estimate.

141. "Decision for an Upsurge," editorial, *Current Scene*, Vol. III, No. 17 (April 1965).
142. *Yezhegodnik Bolshoy Sovietskoy Entsiklopedii*: 1965 (1965 Yearbook of the Great Soviet Encyclopedia), Moscow, 1965, p. 283; and, *Mirovaya Ekonomika; Kratiy Spravochnik* (World Economy; A Short Handbook), 2nd ed. (Moscow: Academy of Sciences, Institute of World Economics and International Relations, 1965), pp. 28–29. These sources are also cited in Field, *op. cit.*, pp. 293–94.
143. *Shin Chugoku Nenkan* (Tokyo, 1965), p. 210; also cited in Chao, *op. cit.*, p. 138.
144. See Chao, *op. cit.*, pp. 137–40.
145. Cf. *People's Daily*, Peking, June 7 and September 23, 1966.
146. These estimates are compared in Chao, *op. cit.*, p. 139.
147. See Donnithorne, *op. cit.*, Chap. V; and Wu, *op. cit.*
148. Ashton, *op. cit.*, p. 311, Table 6.
149. Indian statistics in this section have been derived from the sources cited on Note 116 above.
150. The Sino-U.S. comparisons are from Ashton, *op. cit.*, pp. 310 ff.
151. See also *ibid.*, pp. 305–6.
152. See also Phatak, *op. cit.*, and Jain, *op. cit.*, as well as the sources cited therein pertaining to electric power and water supply in Indian industry.
153. See also Phatak, *op. cit.*, pp. 98 ff.

Chapter 7

1. In particular I have in mind T. C. Liu. See, for example, his paper "The Tempo of Economic Development of the Chinese Mainland," *An Economic Profile of Mainland China*, Vol. I (Washington: U.S. Government Printing Office, 1967), pp. 45–75.
2. See J. Emerson, "Employment in Mainland China: Problems and Prospects," *Profile*, II, 445, and the sources cited in Note 16 below.
3. W. Hollister, "Trends in Capital Formation in Communist China," *Profile*, I, 124–27, especially Table 3.
4. *Ibid.* See also *Economic Survey for Asia and the Far East* (New York and Geneva: United Nations, 1962).
5. See *Current Economic Indicators for the USSR* (Washington: U.S. Government Printing Office, 1965), p. 16, Table 1–5.
6. Liu, *op. cit.*, pp. 63–65, and Table 6.
7. S. Kuznets, "A Comparative Appraisal," in A. Bergson, and S. Kuznets, eds., *Economic Trends in the Soviet Union* (Cambridge: Harvard University Press, 1963), pp. 333 ff.
8. *Peking Review*, No. 2 (1967), p. 15.
9. Cf. Peking *People's Daily* (*Jen-min Jih-pao*), January 1 and 4, February 15, March 6, and May 1, 1967; Kuang-ming Jih-pao, January 4, 1967.
10. "Record Harvest in Red China," *San Francisco Chronicle*, December 28, 1966, p. 1. *Peking Review*, Nos. 1 and 2, 1967.
11. For industrial growth rates for these other countries see K. Chao, *The Rate and Pattern of Industrial Growth in Communist China* (Ann Arbor: University of Michigan Press, 1965), p. 101, Table 27; R. Field, "Chinese Communist Industrial Production," *Profile*, Vol. I, Appendix D, Table 10, p. 295. See also the sources on India, Russia, and United States cited in Tables 7–3 and 7–14 of this chapter.

12. The data in this section have been derived from Chao, *op. cit.*, p. 97, Table 24, and Field, *op. cit.*, p. 273, Table 2.
13. Some additional information of this nature can be found at various points in the following books written by Westerners who have visited Red Chinese factories in the 1960's: C. Lynch, *China: One Fourth of the World* (Toronto: McClelland and Stewart Ltd., 1965); J. Duncan, *A Businessman Looks at Red China* (Princeton: D. Van Nostrand, 1965); E. Snow, *The Other Side of the River* (New York: Random House, 1962).

    See also the article by a high-level Japanese official and engineer, G. Uchida, "Technology in China," *Scientific American*, Vol. 215, No. 5 (November 1966), pp. 37–45.
14. One can readily determine other products not produced at all, or produced in negligible quantities, in China before 1950 by perusing the statistics in Chao, *Rate and Pattern of Industrial Growth*, pp. 120–32, Table C–1; and *Ten Great Years* (Peking: Foreign Languages Press, 1960).
15. See C. Y. Cheng, "Scientific and Engineering Manpower in Communist China," in *Profile*, Vol. 2, p. 543.
16. Cf. Uchida, *op. cit.;* Duncan, *A Businessman*, Chapter 10; J. Duncan, "Red China's Economic Development Since 1949," in R. Adams, ed., *Contemporary China* (New York: Vintage Books, 1966), pp. 139–49; K. P. Wong, "The Mineral Resource Base of Communist China," in *Profile*, Vol. 1, pp. 176–87; Peking *People's Daily*, December 23, 1965, May 17, 1966, January 1 and March 6, 1967.
17. For more detailed accounts of China's technological progress in various industries see Wong, *op. cit.*, and Uchida, *op. cit.;* the issue of *People's Daily* cited in Note 16 above as well as the following issues, January 1 and 10, April 14, and June 3, 1966, January 19 and March 2, 1962. See also *Ta Kung-pao* (Peking), January 1 and 10, 1966; *China Reconstructs*, September 1965, p. 19, January 1966, pp. 26–30 (most later issues of this magazine in English also contain information on China's technological achievements); "Ta'ching Oil Field" in *Studies on Chinese Communism* (published in Taiwan in Chinese), Vol. 1, No. 2, February 1967.
18. For an account of his trip to Red China see Uchida, *op. cit.*
19. My assessment of feasible growth rates for China during the next four or five years and the major underlying reasons are in large part similar to those presented in Jones, *Profile*, I, especially pp. 79–80, 87–88.
20. *Comparative Management and Economic Progress* (Homewood, Ill.: Richard D. Irwin, Inc., 1965), Chap. 12.
21. See *Comparative Management*, pp. 329–39; O. Helmer and N. Rescher, "On the Epistemology of the Inexact Sciences," *Management Science*, Vol. VI, No. 1 (October 1959); N. Dalkey and O. Helmer, "An Experimental Application of the Delphi Method with the Use of Experts," *Management Science*, Vol. IX, No. 3 (April 1963); and T. Gordon, and O. Helmer, *Report on a Long-Range Forecasting Study* (Santa Monica, Calif.: The Rand Corporation, 1964).

Chapter 8

1. Cf. A. Donnithorne, *China's Economic System* (London: Allen and Unwin, 1967), especially Chapters VI and VII; Y. L. Wu, *The Economy of Communist China* (New York: Praeger, 1965); Y. L. Wu, "Planning, Management, and Economic Development in Communist China," *An Economic Profile of Mainland China*, Vol. 1 (Washington D.C., prepared by the Joint Economic Committee of U.S. Congress, published by the U.S. Government Printing Office,

1967), pp. 97–119. F. Schurmann, *Ideology and Organization in Communist China* (Berkeley and Los Angeles: University of California Press, 1966); C. M. Li, *Economic Development of Communist China* (Berkeley and Los Angeles: University of Califorina Press, 1950); T. Hughes and D. Luard, *The Economic Development of Communist China* (London: Oxford University Press, 1961); D. Perkins, *Industrial Planning and Management in Communist China* (mimeographed, to be published by Aldine Press in 1967 or 1968).
2. See *Extracts From China Mainland Magazines*, No. 97, pp. 21 ff; D. Perkins, *Market Control and Planning in Communist China* (Cambridge: Harvard University Press, 1966), Chap. X.
3. Perkins, *Market Control*, p. 103, Table 7.
4. For a description of the Soviet planning process see B. Richman, *Soviet Management: With Significant American Comparisons* (Englewood Cliffs, N.J.: Prentice-Hall Inc., 1965), especially Chap. 5; and B. Richman, "Formulation of Enterprise Operating Plans in Soviet Industry," *Soviet Studies*, Vol. XV, No. 1 (July 1963), pp. 58–73.
5. *Ta Kung-pao* (*The Impartial Daily*, Peking), December 10, 1965, p. 1.
6. *Jen-min Jih-pao* (*People's Daily*, Peking), January 8, 1967.

Chapter 9

1. See especially A. Donnithorne, *China's Economic System* (London: Allen and Unwin, 1967), Chap. VII; F. Schurmann, *Ideology and Organization in Communist China* (Berkeley and Los Angeles: University of California Press, 1966), particularly Chap. IV; C. W. Kwang, "The Economic Accounting System of State Enterprises in Mainland China," *The International Journal of Accounting*, Vol. 1, No. 2 (Spring 1966); R. Stewart, "Managers Under Mao," *Management Today*, April 1967. Pertinent Red Chinese sources (some of them in English) include: W. K. Ma, "Industrial Management in China," *Peking Review*, February 26, 1965; "Running Enterprises in Line with Mao Tse-tung's Thinking," *Peking Review*, April 15, 1966; editorial in *Rennin Ribao*, April 3, 1966; Y. C. Jen, "On the Question of Certain Relationships in the Management of Industrial Enterprises," *Ching-chi Yen-chiu* (Economic Research), No. 1, 1966; *Joint Publications Research Service* (JPRS), translations of Red Chinese sources (Washington, D.C.), No. 34568, March 15, 1966.
2. "Seventy Progressive Industrial Enterprises Named," *Kung-jen Jih-pao* (*Worker's Daily*, Peking), March 6, 1966, p. 1.
3. For details on the tekhpromfinplan at Soviet enterprises see B. Richman, *Soviet Management: With Significant American Comparisons* (Englewood Cliffs, N.J.: Prentice-Hall Inc., 1965), Chap. 3.
4. For Soviet definitions and a breakdown of types of personnel in this classification see W. Dewitt, *Education and Professional Employment* in the USSR (Washington, D.C.: National Science Foundation, 1961), pp. 486 ff., and Tables VI–42, VI–49 and VI–50.
5. For a detailed definition of ETMP and a breakdown of personnel in the group in Soviet industry see Dewitt, pp. 496 ff.
6. Derived from Dewitt, Table VI–50, p. 498; *Narodnoe Khoziaistvo SSSR* V1960 *Godu*, V1961 *Godu*, *Statisticheskkiy Yezhegodnik* (The National Economy of the USSR in 1960 and in 1961, annual volumes of a Statistical Yearbook), Moscow, 1961 and 1962; *Vestnik Statistiki* (Statistical Herald), No. 12, 1960.
7. *Narodnoe Khoziaistvo* SSSR, for the years 1963, 1964, and 1965. M. Feshbock, "Manpower in the U.S.S.R.: A Survey of Recent Trends and Prospects," *New*

Directions in the Soviet Economy, Part III (Washington: U.S. Government Printing Office, 1966), Table A–2, pp. 774–81. Feshbock presents a breakdown of industrial production personnel and wage workers for Soviet industry as a whole and for individual branches. From my own firsthand research in Russia, and data presented in Dewitt, *op. cit.*, Chap. VI, as well as annual volumes of *Narodnoe Khoziaistvo* for recent years, I estimate that roughly 75 to 80 percent of industrial production personnel at Soviet enterprises correspond to the Chinese classification of administrative and technical personnel used in Table 9–1 of this chapter.

8. *Narodnoe Khoziaistvo*, for the year 1963.
9. *Ibid.*, 1962.
10. *Ibid.*
11. *National Industrial Conference Board* (*NICB*), *Business Record,* March 1963, pp. 17–18.
12. Particularly in Chapter 4 in the sections on attitudes toward managers, view of authority, responsibility and subordination, interorganizational cooperation, and, class structure; and in Chapter 5 in the sections dealing with political stability and political organization.
13. Especially in the interorganizational cooperation section of Chapter 4.
14. Cf. Richman, *Soviet Management*, pp. 58 ff., and B. Richman, *Management Development and Education in the Soviet Union* (East Lansing, Mich.: Institute for International Business and Economic Development Studies, Michigan State University, 1967), pp. 86–94.
15. *Jen-min Jih-Pao* (*People's Daily*, Peking; article entitled "Reduce Nonproduction Personnel to the Production Front"), February 12, 1967.
16. Cf. P. Kircher, "Accounting Revolution in Red China," *Financial Executive,* January 1967, pp. 39 ff., and the sources cited therein, and *Ta Kung-pao* (article entitled "A Great Reform in Accounting"), December 19, 1965, pp. 1–2.
17. See J. Emerson, "Employment in Mainland China: Problems and Prospects," *An Economic Profile of Mainland China,* Vol. 2 (Washington: U.S. Government Printing Office, 1967), p. 453, Table 15.

Chapter 10

1. Readers who have read my earlier published works on Red China may notice that in some cases labor-productivity figures for India, Russia, and the United States differ quite significantly in this study from my earlier works. One reason is that figures for more recent years have been used. However, another reason in a few cases is that different, but seemingly more accurate, employment figures have been used in computing labor productivity in the present study. For comparative purposes see B. Richman, "Capitalists and Managers in Communist China," *Harvard Business Review* (January-February 1967), Exhibit III, pp. 74–75; and Richman, "Managerial Decision Making and Performance at the Enterprise Level in Communist Chinese Industry," *Mainland China in the World Economy* (Washington: U.S. Government Printing Office, 1967), Exhibit IV, pp. 96–97.
2. C. Lynch, *China: One Fourth of the World* (Toronto: McClelland and Stewart, Ltd., 1965), pp. 90–91.
3. E. Snow, *The Other Side of the River* (New York: Random House, 1962), p. 204.

Chapter 11

1. One good piece of work on China's trade sector is contained in A. Donnithorne, *China's Economic System* (London: Allen and Unwin, 1967), Chap. XI. See also Y. M. Choy, "Wholesaling in Communist China," in R. Bartels, ed., *Comparative Marketing* (Homewood, Ill.: Richard D. Irwin, Inc., 1963), pp. 253–70. For employment data see J. Emerson, "Employment in Mainland China: Problems and Prospects," *An Economic Profile of Mainland China*, Vol. II (Washington, D.C., prepared for the Joint Economic Committee of U.S. Congress, published by the U.S. Government Printing Office, 1967); pp. 431, 448–50.
2. See also *Ta Kung-pao* (The Impartial Daily, Peking), September 10 and September 13, 1965; *Joint Publications Research Service* (JPRS), Washington, D.C., No. 33893, January 23, 1966.
3. In my opinion the two best sources on Soviet domestic trade and marketing are M. Goldman, *Soviet Marketing: Distribution in a Controlled Economy* (New York: Free Press of Glencoe, 1963); and J. Felker, *Soviet Economic Controversies: The Emerging Marketing Concept and Changes in Planning 1960–1965* (Cambridge: M.I.T. Press, 1966). These two major works contain extensive bibliographies and documentation.
4. This statement is based on pay data I obtained in Russia in the early 1960's. Soviet wage figures can be found in N. Dewitt, *Education and Professional Employment in the USSR* (Washington, D.C.: National Science Foundation, 1961), pp. 810–13, Appendix VI-w. See also Felker, *op. cit.*, especially Chap. 7.
5. For Soviet figures see Dewitt, *op. cit.*, pp. 474 and 536; B. Richman *Management Development and Education in the Soviet Union* (East Lansing, Mich.: Bureau of Business and Economic Research, Michigan State University, 1967), pp. 61–69, Tables III–15 through III–22.
6. Cf. the sources cited in Note 2 above. *Ta Kung-pao* carried articles on China's trade sector continously through September and October 1965. See also *Jen-min Jih-pao* (*People's Daily*, Peking), September 25 and December 30, 1965; many articles on Chinese trade and commerce have been translated in *JPRS*, Vol. IV, No. 8, February 4, 1966, Reel No. 52 (on microfilm).
7. See *Hung Ch'i* (Red Flag), No. 2, February 11, 1966, pp. 36–41.

Chapter 12

1. I have written about Mr. Wu in my article "Capitalists and Managers in Communist China," *Harvard Business Review*, Vol. 45, No. 1 (January/February 1967) pp. 57 ff. See also the comments on this article and Mr. Wu in *Time* magazine, February 3, 1967, pp. 74–75.
2. For major sources in this sphere see two detailed official Chinese Communist publications: T. T. Kuan, *The Socialist Transformation of Capitalistic Industry and Commerce in China* (Peking: Foreign Languages Press, 1960); M. C. Hsueh, H. Su, and T. L. Lin, *The Socialist Transformation of the National Economy in China* (Peking: Foreign Languages Press, 1960).

   For an intriguing firsthand account by Robert Loh, a Chinese capitalist who escaped from Red China in 1957, read his story as told to Humphry Evans, *Escape From Red China* (New York: Coward-McCann, 1962). See also Loh's article "Setting the Stage for Foreigners," *Atlantic Monthly*, December 1959, pp. 80–84.

   A number of Westerners who have visited Communist China tell of their experiences with China's Red capitalists in their books. See, for example, C. Lynch, *China: One Fourth of the World* (Toronto: McLelland and Stewart Ltd, 1965), pp. 75 ff.; J. Duncan, *A Businessman Looks at Red China* (Princeton and New York: D. Van Nostrand, 1965), pp. 15 ff.; E. Snow, *The Other Side of the River* (New York: Random House, 1962), Chap. 26.

Other sources that might be of interest include A. Donnithorne, *China's Economic System* (London: Allen and Unwin, 1967), Chap. VI; J. Emerson, "Employment in Mainland China: Problems and Prospects," *An Economic Profile of Mainland China*, Vol. 2 (Washington, D.C.: prepared by the Joint Economic Committee of U.S. Congress, published by the U.S. Government Printing Office, 1967), pp. 425–32; P. Schran, *The Structure of Income in Communist China*, unpublished doctoral dissertation (Berkeley: University of California, 1961), especially pp. 78 ff.; *Peking Review*, April 20, 1962, p. 6; *Ta Kung-pao*, imported daily, Hong Kong, June 1, 1961; *Survey of the Chinese Mainland Press*, No. 2552, 1961.

3. See Loh, *Escape*.
4. *Ibid.*, p. 190.
5. *Ibid.*, p. 191.
6. *People's Handbook* (Renmin Shouce, published in Chinese in Peking), 1958, p. 23; Donnithorne, *op. cit.*, Chap. VI.
7. For more details about the remolding of Chinese capitalists see Loh, *Escape*, Hsueh *et al.*, *op. cit.*, pp. 226 ff.
8. Wu Tsung-i gave me some information on the Yung brothers. They are apparently the same brothers for whom Robert Loh worked and whom he describes in his above-cited book under the name Chan. See also the comments on these brothers in Snow, *op. cit.*, p. 198.
9. I was told about him by the Wu whom I did meet.
10. See Duncan, *op. cit.*, p. 15.
11. See Lynch, *op. cit.*, pp. 75–78.
12. I was told about this Mr. Liu by several people during my stay in China.
13. The full titles of Loh's works are cited in Note 2 above.

INDEX

ABOUT THE AUTHOR

BARRY M. RICHMAN is professor of management and international business at the Graduate School of Business Administration at the Univeristy of California, Los Angeles. He holds a bachelor's degree in economics from McGill University and M.S. and Ph.D. degrees in economics and business administration from Columbia University.

Dr. Richman has been a consultant for a variety of business, educational and government organizations in the United States, Canada and overseas, and has published numerous articles in professional journals. His books include *Soviet Management: With Significant American Comparisons*, *Comparative Management and Economic Progress* (with Professor Richard N. Farmer), *Incidents for Applying Management Theory* (with Professor Richard N. Farmer and W. Ryan), *International Business, An Operational Theory* (with Professor Richard N. Farmer) and *Management Development and Education in the Soviet Union.*

The Ford Foundation has given Dr. Richman a research grant for 1966–1969 for work in the area of comparative and international management and economic development with Professor Farmer.

Dr. Richman lives in Malibu, California, is married and the father of two children.

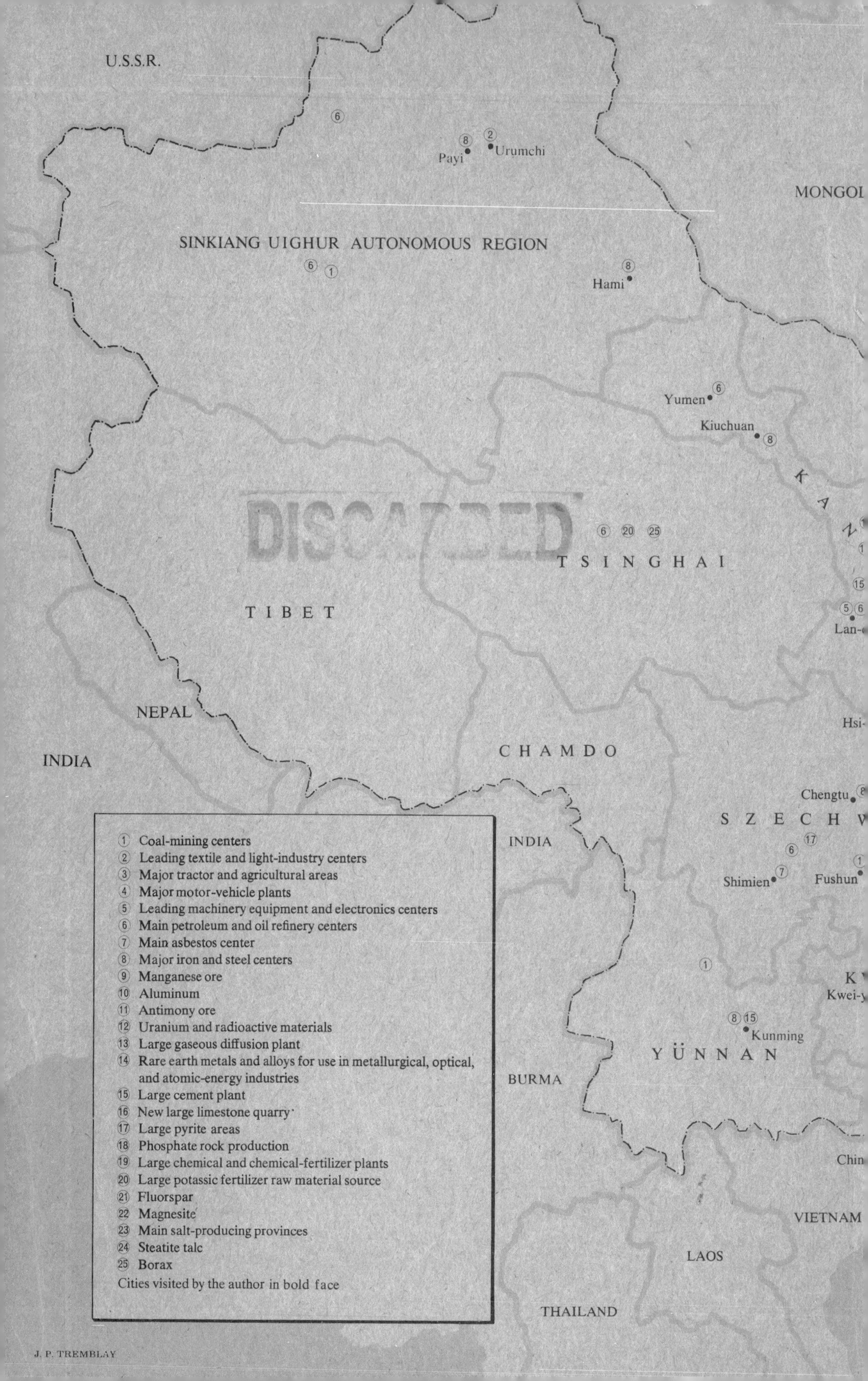
U.S.S.R.
Payi
Urumchi
SINKIANG UIGHUR AUTONOMOUS REGION
Hami
Yumen
Kiuchuan
TSINGHAI
TIBET
NEPAL
INDIA
CHAMDO
Chengtu
Shimien
Fushun
INDIA
BURMA
Kunming
YÜNNAN
VIETNAM
LAOS
THAILAND
1 Coal-mining centers
2 Leading textile and light-industry centers
3 Major tractor and agricultural areas
4 Major motor-vehicle plants
5 Leading machinery equipment and electronics centers
6 Main petroleum and oil refinery centers
7 Main asbestos center
8 Major iron and steel centers
9 Manganese ore
10 Aluminum
11 Antimony ore
12 Uranium and radioactive materials
13 Large gaseous diffusion plant
14 Rare earth metals and alloys for use in metallurgical, optical, and atomic-energy industries
15 Large cement plant
16 New large limestone quarry
17 Large pyrite areas
18 Phosphate rock production
19 Large chemical and chemical-fertilizer plants
20 Large potassic fertilizer raw material source
21 Fluorspar
22 Magnesite
23 Main salt-producing provinces
24 Steatite talc
25 Borax
Cities visited by the author in bold face
J. P. TREMBLAY